HANDBOOK OF

OBJECT TECHNOLOGY

EDITOR-IN-CHIEF

SABA ZAMIR

CRC Press

Boca Raton London New York Washington, D.C.

Acquiring Editor: Jerry Papke
Project Editor: Maggie Mogck
Contact Editor: Dawn Mesa
Marketing Manager: Jane Stark
Cover design: Dawn Boyd

Library of Congress Cataloging-in-Publication Data

Handbook of object technology / [edited by] Saba Zamir.
p. cm.
Includes bibliographical references and index.
ISBN 0-8493-3135-8 (alk. paper)
1. Object oriented methods--Handbooks, manuals, etc. I. Zamir, Saba. 1959- .
QA76.9.035H35 1998
005.1'17--dc21 98-25839
CIP

International Standard Book Number 0-8493-3135-8
Library of Congress Card Number 98-25839
1 2 3 4 5 6 7 8 9

Preface

Almost a year and a half ago, Jerry Papke, my Senior Editor at CRC Press, approached me with the idea of creating a handbook of Object Technology. He had known me when he was an editor at McGraw-Hill and I had authored several books there. "...We do well with mega-projects of this kind," he wrote, and encouraged me to consider this opportunity. I discussed the idea with my ex-editor, ex-co-author and current colleague, Jay Ranade. As expected, he said, "grab the opportunity." He warned me that it would be a difficult task. I would be dealing with some of the most prominent people in the object community. "But if you accomplish this, your contribution to the Object community will be immeasurable." The idea clicked and I decided to go for it.

Eighteen months down the road, this handbook has evolved as a comprehensive and complete reference for the subject areas related to the disciplines that encompass Object Technology. It is a compendium of reference material that allows you to sift through the various options that are available for each discipline. It allows you to evaluate which one of the available options best fits your needs. It helps you further in locating where to obtain additional information for specific topics of interest. However, it is important to understand that the true benefits of object technology are not derived simply by adopting one or more disciplines that are a part of the whole; true value is derived via the *harmonious* interworking of each of these components. Since all of the information is presented within a single volume, the handbook allows you to understand how each of these disciplines can be made to work together to build robust, efficient, and cost-effective software systems using object technology as the main architect.

The chapters in this handbook have been contributed by some of the most prominent and seasoned professionals immersed in the world of Object Technology today. I am proud to say that we have succeeded in assimilating a group of authors which is unprecedented, in terms of their accomplishments and position within the Object community. We have here contributions from the U.S., Canada, Europe (mainly Spain and England), Australia, and India.

Bjarne Stroustrup was one of the first to agree to contribute, and he started the ball rolling. Mr. Booch initially agreed to contribute with the best of intentions, but was unable to do so due to severe time constraints. Mr. Jacobson generously agreed to allow me to "reuse" one of his chapters from a pre-published book, but we were ultimately unable to include this chapter due to unprecedented circumstances. Dr. Henderson-Sellers has kindly contributed three excellent chapters to the handbook. The team of Jackson, Liddle, and Woodfield agreed to write a chapter on UML compared to OSM, and were kind enough to provide an excellent discourse on UML when they discovered that I was unable to include a chapter on this subject from the team of experts that are usually associated with this language. In addition to this, we have excellent contributed material from James Odell, Mary Loomis, David Taylor, Ian Graham, and many, many more. We have the cream of the crop in this handbook.

There are two amazing features about this project which I still find quite hard to believe. First, I never met any of my contributors. I met only three of my advisors, all contacts were made via e-mail from my virtual office. Second, all of the work that my advisors did and all of the contributions that came through were accomplished by virtue of good faith; on the basis of their sense of commitment and commitment *alone.* There was nothing that I could offer them, except request that they give something *back* to the community; that they speak out about whatever they wish to say about their area of interest as an *authority* on the subject! The result is an outstanding collection of chapters that you see in this handbook.

And now, the handbook is complete; all chapters have been submitted. Just a few days ago I received another e-mail from Jerry Papke. He tells me that he is retiring from the business. Could it really have been such a long journey? Jerry, you started this, and now you're leaving before the handbook will be in print! Jerry, thanks for that e-mail you sent me 18 months ago!

Life moves on and not much else changes. But this handbook is complete and I trust you will find it to be the valuable reference we worked so hard to create.

Saba Zamir
Editor-in-Chief
Handbook of Object Technology

Note: I welcome your comments. Please e-mail to: sabazamir@aol.com

Editor-in-Chief

Saba Zamir is a Senior Information Technology professional and management consultant, with specific expertise in database design, wide-scale project management, and technical/nontechnical writing. She is the Editor-in-Chief of the *Handbook of Object Technology*, Series Editor-in-Chief of the *Advanced and Emerging Communications Technologies: A Desk Reference Series* (CRC Press LLC), a regular contributor to *Component Strategies* (formerly called *Object Magazine)*, a freelance writer for other major technical journals (*Unisphere* and *Enterprise Systems Journal*), and an international speaker at object technology conferences.

She has conducted many interviews with prominent personalities in the information technology field and has been the best selling author of technical books for McGraw-Hill. Ms. Zamir has authored/coauthored several books, including *The C Primer*, 3rd ed.; *C++ Primer for C Programmers*, 1st and 2nd eds.; *The Jay Ranade UNIX Primer*, and *The MVS JCL Primer*. Several of these books have been translated into Japanese, Korean, Chinese, and German. Two of the books are currently being used as course books at universities in the U.S. and abroad. She also worked as Consulting Editor to Ventana Press (a subsidiary of International Thomson), and has regularly reviewed/edited technical manuscripts for McGraw-Hill, John Wiley & Sons, and CRC Press LLC. She is currently working on establishing a line of book series based on specific technical subjects in Europe, Japan, and Hong Kong, China.

Advisors

Messaoud Benantar, IBM Corporation, Texas
Section V: Object Technology Standards and Distributed Objects

Frank Budinsky, IBM Canada, North York, Ontario, Canada
Section XIII: Object-Oriented Application Development

Juan Manuel Cueva, Oviedo University, Spain
Section V: Object Technology Standards and Distributed Objects

Ricardo Devis, INFOPLUS SL, Alicante, Spain
Section II: Object-Oriented Methods / Section III: Object-Oriented Programming Languages

Douglas McDavid, IBM Global Services, Elk Grove, California
Section VI: Object-Oriented Databases / Section IX: Object-Oriented Metrics

Dilip Patel, South Bank University, London
Section X: Business Objects / Section XI: Object-Oriented Intranets / Section XII: Object-Oriented Analysis / Design Tools

Luis Joyanes Aguilar (special guest advisor), Universidad Pontificia de Salamanca, Madrid, Spain
(in conjunction with María Luisa Díez Platas and Paloma Centenera)
Appendices A-H: Computer Language Guides

Dan Hanley (special guest advisor), South Bank University, London
Appendices I-N: Glossary, Listings Guides, Who's Who

Paul Schleifer (special guest advisor), South Bank University, London
Appendices I-N: Glossary, Listings Guides, Who's Who

Note: Detailed biographical information for all advisors is available at: *http:/www.arrakis.es/~devis/handbook/toc.htm*

Contributors

Luis Joyanes Aguilar
Universidad Pontificia de Salamanca
Madrid, Spain

Fernando Alvarez-Garcia
Oviedo University
Oviedo, Spain

Dario Alvarez-Gutierrez
Oviedo University
Oviedo, Spain

K. N. Ananthraman
Indian Institute of Technology
Madras, India

Edmund Arranga
Object-Z Systems
Orinda, California

Boumediene Belkhouche
Tulane University
New Orleans, Louisiana

Messaoud Benantar
IBM Corporation
Austin, Texas

Frank Budinsky
IBM Canada
North York, Ontario, Canada

Marco Cantú
Wintech Italia SrL
Piacenza, Italy

Paul Izquierdo Castanedo
Oviedo University
Oviedo, Spain

Paloma Centenera
Universidad Pontificia de Salamanca
Madrid, Spain

Islam Choudhury
South Bank University
London, United Kingdom

Derek Coleman
King's College
London, United Kingdom

Todd Cotton
Hewlett-Packard Laboratories
Palo Alto, California

Ricardo Devis
INFOPLUS SL
Alicante, Spain

Maria de los Angeles Diaz-Fondon
Oviedo University
Oviedo, Spain

Steven R. Dobson
IBM Canada
North York, Ontario, Canada

Thomas Drake
Coastal Research & Technology, Inc.
Ellicott City, Maryland

Desmond D'Souza
ICON Computing, Inc.
Austin, Texas

Richard T. Dué
Thomsen Dué & Assoc., Ltd.
Edmonton, Alberta, Canada

David W. Embley
Brigham Young University
Provo, Utah

Martin Fowler
Independent Consultant
Melrose, Massachusetts

Garry Froehlich
University of Alberta
Edmonton, Alberta, Canada

Julio Garcia-Martin
Polytechnical University of Madrid
Madrid, Spain

Ian Graham
Chase Manhattan Bank
London, United Kingdom

Francisco Gutiérrez
University of Malaga
Malaga, Spain

Dan Hanley
South Bank University
London, United Kingdom

Samuel P. Harbison
Texas Instruments
Monroeville, Pennsylvania

Brian Henderson-Sellers
Swinburne University of Technology
Melbourne, Australia

Ralph Hodgson
IBM Global Services
Boulder, Colorado

James Hoover
University of Alberta
Edmonton, Alberta, Canada

Robert B. Jackson
Brigham Young University
Provo, Utah

Gary Karasiuk
IBM Canada
North York, Ontario, Canada

Setrag Khoshafian
TDI, Inc.
Walnut Creek, California

Graham King
South Bank University
London, United Kingdom

Mohamed Kodeih
IBM Corporation
Austin, Texas

Stephen W. Liddle
Brigham Young University
Provo, Utah

Ling Liu
University of Alberta
Edmonton, Alberta, Canada

Mary E. S. Loomis
Hewlett Packard Laboratories
Palo Alto, California

Ole Lehrmann Madsen
Aarhus University
Aarhus, Denmark

Ruth Malan
Hewlett Packard Laboratories
Palo Alto, California

Robert Marcus
AMS Center for Advanced Technologies
Fairfax, Virginia

Douglas McDavid
IBM Global Services
Elk Grove, California

Simon Moser
Bedag Infomatik
Bern, Switzerland

Farshad Nayeri
Critical Mass, Inc.
Cambridge, Massachusett

James Odell
Ann Arbor, Michigan

Dilip Patel
South Bank University
London, United Kingdom

Shushma Patel
South Bank University
London, United Kingdom

Ernesto Pimentel
Universidad de Malagá
Malagá, Spain

María Luis Díez Platas
Universidad Pontificia de Salamanca
Madrid, Spain

Wilson Price
Object-Z Systems
Orinda, California

D. Janaki Ram
Indian Institute of Technology
Madras, India

Guus Ramackers
Oracle Corporation
Surrey, United Kingdom

Danial A. Rawsthorne
BDM Air Safety Management Co.
Federal Way, Washington

Linda Rising
AG Communication Systems
Phoenix, Arizona

Paul Schleifer
South Bank University
London, United Kingdom

António Rito Silva
Technical University of Lisbon
Lisbon, Portugal

Paul Sorenson
University of Alberta
Edmonton, Alberta, Canada

Jiri Soukup
Code Farms Inc.
Richmond, Ontario, Canada

S. Srinath
Indian Institute of Technology
Madras, India

Bjarne Stroustrup
AT&T Laboratories
Florham Park, New Jersey

Jeff Sutherland
IDX Systems Corporation
Boston, Massachusett

Lourdes Tajes-Martinez
Oviedo University
Oviedo, Spain

David Taylor
Enterprise Engines
San Mateo, California

James Thomann
The Data Warehousing Institute
Gaithersburg, MD

Kresten Krab Thorup
University of Aarhus
Aarhus, Denmark

Bhuvan Unhelkar
Case Digital, Inc.
San Francisco, California

Guido van Rossum
Corporation for National Research Initiatives
Reston, Virginia

Mario Piattini Velthuis
University of Castilla-La Mancha
Madrid, Spain

Kim Waldén
Enea Data AB
Taby, Sweden

Yingxu Wang
South Bank University
London, United Kingdom

Alan Wills
TriReme International Ltd.
Manchester, United Kingdom

Scott N. Woodfield
Brigham Young University
Provo, Utah

Houman Younessi
Swinburne University of Technology
Melbourne, Australia

Note: Detailed biographical information of most contributors is available at:
http://www.arrakis.es/~devis/handbook/toc.htm

Acknowledgments

A project of this magnitude is a success because of the joint efforts of a lot of people, and thanks are owed to each one of them. I am grateful to the authors for their contributions that made this handbook the valuable reference that we intended it to be. Many thanks to Bjarne Stroustrup for the valuable advice which he generously offered throughout the months that the handbook was being created. Many thanks are owed to each of my advisors, Messaoud Benantar, Frank Budinsky, Juan Manuel Cueva, Ricardo Devis, Douglas McDavid, and Dilip Patel; my special Guest Advisors, Luis Joyanes, Dan Hanley, and Paul Schleifer; and my young Webmaster friend, Dani Villar, for generoulsy and selflessly giving of their time and aggressively seeking the best contributors they could find. I wish to thank Nora for her initial help with the project, and Dawn Mesa, for keeping track of the endless flow of Contributor Agreements, Permission forms, and what not! Thanks are owed to Jane Stark, Marketing Manager; Maggie Mogck, Project Editor; Suzanne Lassandro, Production Manager; and of course, Jerry Papke, Senior Editor, for their support and help throughout the evolution and development of this project. Special thanks to Ricardo for introducing me to the wonderful world of tapas in Spain, Rafael Osso for his solid support, and Jay Ranade for giving me the inspiration to go for it!

In conclusion, I must thank David, my husband, for his moral support and encouragement in times of need. And my father, Abjani, for being the "guiding light," always; my mother, Ammi, for her unadulterated love; my Aunt, Khala Jaan, for her love and concern; Fauzi, for his optimism, despite it all; Tazein and Naseem, without whom this summer would not have been complete; and last but not least, Mahboob Sahab, for listening and helping me understand the little secrets of life.

Saba Zamir

Contents

SECTION I The Object-Oriented Paradigm

SECTION II Object-Oriented Methods

SECTION III Object-Oriented Programming Languages

SECTION IV Object-Oriented Frameworks

SECTION V Object Technology Standards and Distributed Objects

SECTION VI Object-Oriented Databases

SECTION VII Patterns

SECTION VIII Application of OO Technology

SECTION IX Object-Oriented Metrics

SECTION X Business Objects

SECTION XI Object-Oriented Intranets

SECTION XII Object-Oriented Analysis/Design Tools

SECTION XIII Object-Oriented Application Development

SECTION XIV Appendices

Dedication

To my son,
Richad Zamir Becker,
and daughter,
Aemin Michele Becker

May your lives be successful,
iridescent, and beautiful

– Your Amma

Introduction

The *Handbook of Object Technology* is intended to be a comprehensive and complete reference for the subject areas related to Object Technology. It contains topics related to object-oriented methodologies, languages, frameworks, standards, distributed objects, databases, applications, metrics, business objects, intranets, analysis/design tools, and application development environments. It also has an elaborate glossary, a rich collection of language guides for most of the major OO languages, and comprehensive listings of existing object-oriented languages, methods, and operating systems in the appendices. Finally, we have here a list of "Who's Who in Object Technology." We asked each of our contributors to list, in his or her opinion, the top five Who's Who in Object Technology, and the result is the tabulation that you see in Appendix N.

The handbook is divided into thirteen sections and fourteen appendices. Each section contains chapters related to a specific discipline related to Object Technology. Each chapter contains information that is current as of the writing of the chapter, which a reader can apply directly to the improvement and/or understanding of his/her job, specific function, or area of interest that is related to the technology. The chapters have been contributed by some of the most prominent individuals in the object community today. You can obtain detailed biographical information of most of the contributors at: http:/www.arrakis.es/~devis/handbook/toc.htm

In order to read the topic of interest to you, you may either go to the appropriate section and browse through the collection of chapters contained therein, or you may go directly to a chapter of your choice. Please refer to the glossary in Appendix I if you need to acquire an understanding of object-oriented terms that you may encounter while reading any of the chapters.

We have tried to make the handbook interesting and enjoyable reading by including technical, non-technical, and informal discourses on various subjects. A wealth of knowledge is presented before you. Enjoy!

I

The Object-Oriented Paradigm

Saba Zamir
Senior Information Technology Consultant

The *object-oriented paradigm* allows applications to be designed in the context of *objects*, as opposed to *processes*. These objects, once designed and created, can be reused partially or wholly to create other objects. Thus, (in a perfect world), a new object may never have to be designed and created from scratch again, since there is probably already an object out there, from which it can be derived. The advantages offered by object technology include improved software quality, economic gains through the use of reusable objects, shorter project development lifecycles, and the creation of truly distributed software across heterogeneous environments.

The object-oriented paradigm has become one of the dominant forces in the computing world today. According to a recent survey conducted by International Data Corporation (IDC), by the year 2000, more than 80% of development organizations are expected to be using object technology as the basis for their distributed development strategies. Another survey conducted by the Gartner and Meta Groups indicates that Objects and Object Technology is currently one of the four most important subject areas in the computer industry, and is expected to become one of the fastest growing areas of interest in this field.

This section provides an introduction to the key concepts in Object Technology.

1

The Keys to Object Technology

David A. Taylor
Enterprise Engines

Object technology is often viewed by potential adopters with a sense of foreboding. There are many new ideas to understand, numerous techniques to master, and countless pitfalls to be avoided in order to achieve success. To some extent, this trepidation is warranted; the physical bulk of this handbook offers compelling testimony to the complexity of the subject. However, the core concepts of object technology are quite straightforward and should not represent a barrier to understanding. This introductory chapter explains these core concepts and provides a foundation for approaching the wide range of topics treated in this handbook.

The organizing theme of this chapter is presenting keys to understanding. The sections of the chapter address, in turn, the key concepts, mechanisms, advantages, innovations, and success factors of object technology. Three keys are presented within each section. Extracting just three key ideas in each of these areas necessarily leaves a great deal unsaid, but providing the wealth of knowledge required by practitioners is the task of the chapters that follow. The purpose of this initial chapter is simply to open the doors to understanding. Three keys should be enough to open any door.

1.1 Key Concepts

The key concepts underlying object technology are objects, messages, and classes.

1. **Objects** are executable software representations of real-world objects and concepts.
2. **Messages** provide a universal communication medium through which objects interact with one another.
3. **Classes** are templates for defining similar objects, providing the basis for abstracting the common characteristics of real-world objects.

0-8493-3135-8/99/$0.00+$.50

1.1.1 Objects

The world around us is made up of physical and conceptual objects. Physical objects include such things as buildings, machines, and products. Conceptual objects include risk, agreement, and profit. There is no sharp boundary between the two, and many objects have both physical and conceptual aspects. A product may be a tangible object, but to be a product also entails the concept of salability. Similarly, an agreement may be an exchange of rights and commitments, but that agreement may lack force unless it is also represented as a signed, physical document.

The most fundamental idea behind object technology is that these real-world objects should be represented in a software system through logical units called objects. Most broadly defined, an *object* is a software package that includes all the necessary data and procedures to represent a real-world object for a specific set of purposes.

There are three broad implications of this definition of an object.

1. **Objects are the new unit of modularity in software.** As such, they replace modules based on functional decomposition, data normalization, and other conventional techniques.
2. **Objects package related data and procedures together** and treat the two kinds of information in a comparable manner. This is in sharp contrast to conventional approaches, which provide different sets of tools and techniques for managing data and procedures.
3. **Modeling is the central activity in designing software.** Objects represent the structure and interactions of real-world objects, and the collective behavior of these representations satisfies the business requirements of a software system.

Understanding the reasons for representing a real-world object within a system is central to designing useful software objects. If the purpose of representing a product is to facilitate the manufacture of that product, then the corresponding *product* object must include sufficient information to represent the physical makeup of that product and the operations necessary to create it. By contrast, if the purpose of representing a product is to support the purchasing of that product, then the *product* object would be more concerned with maintaining pricing information and managing orders.

1.1.2 Messages

Objects interact with each other by sending requests for services known as *messages*. A message is a request to a particular object to execute a specified procedure, typically called a *method* in object parlance. For example, a message of the form

```
product price(quantity)
```

would represent a request for a particular *product* object to apply its *price* method to the indicated *quantity*.

Messages are similar to function calls in conventional programming languages in that they specify an operation to be performed and any parameters required to perform that operation. The specification for a message is typically referred to as the *signature* of that message. The signature of the example message above consists of the method name *price* together with the single parameter *quantity*. Depending on the language, the types of the parameters may also form a part of the signature.

The key difference between a message and a function call is that a function has a single, common implementation, whereas a message can be answered in different ways by different objects depending on how their methods are defined. For example, a conventional language would permit only one *price* function to be defined, whereas an object language would allow each object to implement its own method for responding to the *price* message.

1.1.3 Classes

Classes are generic definitions that apply to sets of similar objects. The primary role of a class is to specify the methods and variables to be used by the objects — typically known as the *instances* of that class — which conform to its definition. All that remains for the instances to do is to contain local values for their variables. For example, a *stock* class might define methods for trading a stock, together with variables for tracking the current trading price and net position for a stock. The instances of the *stock* class would contain the appropriate values for the trading price and position.

Classes represent the primary mechanism for the logical process of *abstraction*, which is the generalization of generic properties that apply to groups of objects. Abstraction is a critical process in both human understanding and in software design. In essence, abstraction defines the different kinds or *types* of objects that can exist in a system. The use of classes to define types represents an extension of the typing mechanisms provided in conventional languages, such as built-in data types (string, integer, real, etc.) and user-definable data structures. The fact that classes define methods as well as data makes them particularly powerful tools for implementing generic types.

Classes are not the only approach to abstracting common properties among similar objects. In some object languages, typically known as *prototype languages*, any object can serve as a template for defining other objects. Although this approach to typing objects can be more flexible and dynamic than class-based typing, it can also lead to confusion between the separate functions of definition and execution. At present, all commercially viable object languages provide explicit support for the concept of a class.

1.2 Key Mechanisms

The key mechanisms of object technology are encapsulation, polymorphism, and inheritance.

1. **Encapsulation** is the mechanism for packaging related data and procedures together within objects.
2. **Polymorphism** is the ability to implement the same message in different ways in different objects.
3. **Inheritance** is the mechanism for disseminating information defined in generic classes to other classes which are declared to be special cases of those generic classes.

There is a natural mapping between these three mechanisms and the key concepts described in the preceding section. Namely, objects support encapsulation, messages support polymorphism, and classes support inheritance. Although this mapping is useful in communicating the basic mechanisms of object technology, the actual implementation of these mechanisms in a particular language usually involves relationships among the concepts. For example, polymorphism is typically achieved by defining methods differently in different classes, in which case polymorphism depends on a relationship between the concepts of a message and a class.

1.2.1 Encapsulation

Encapsulation is the mechanism by which related data and procedures are bound together within an object. In effect, an object is a software capsule that functions as a black box, responding to messages from other objects and dispatching messages of its own in ways that do not reveal its internal structure. In this way, encapsulation supports and extends the proven principle of *information hiding*. Information hiding is valuable because it prevents local changes from having global impact. In the case of objects, it allows the implementations of individual objects to be altered without affecting the way these objects communicate through messages.

Ideally, an object should not only encapsulate data and methods, it should also hide the very distinction between the two. This allows developers to change implementations from data to methods or vice versa without affecting the way the object interacts with other objects. In practice, this is achieved by declaring all variables to be *private*, or hidden from view outside of the object. When another object needs to see or change the value of a variable, it does so by way of an access method. For example, a *customer* object would send a message to a *product* object asking for its price rather than violating encapsulation by accessing a price variable directly.

In most object languages, methods as well as data may be declared to be private. This allows the internal operations of an object to be hidden from view. A well-designed object exposes the smallest feasible portion of its methods as *public* to make them available to messages from other objects. This approach offers the greatest flexibility in terms of future changes to the object. For example, a *product* object might contain several different variables and methods for determining its price, depending on who is asking, the quantity requested, and other factors. All these implementation details would be hidden behind a single public method for requesting a price. So long as the message for asking the price remained the same, any or all of these details could be changed without affecting any other object in the system.

1.2.2 Polymorphism

The fact that different objects can respond to the same message in different ways is known as *polymorphism*, a Greek term meaning "many forms." The power of polymorphism is that it greatly simplifies the logic of programs. A requestor no longer has to use nested IF statements or complex CASE statements to call the appropriate procedure. Instead, the proper procedure is automatically invoked by sending the request to a particular object.

An example should help illustrate this advantage. In a system designed to manage a financial portfolio, different financial instruments would require different procedures for determining their value. In order to calculate the current value of a portfolio, a program would have to iterate through all the financial instruments and then use branching logic to call the appropriate valuation procedures. In pseudocode form, the logic would look something like this:

```
If instrument is
    privateStock then
      value= valuePrivateStock(instrument)
    publicStock then
      value= valuePublicStock(instrument)
    municipalBond then
      value= valueMunicipalBond(instrument)
    corporateBond then
      value= valueCorporateBond(instrument)
    mutualFund then
      value= valueMutualFund(instrument)
    ...
  otherwise
    report error("No such instrument.")
```

In object technology, each type of instrument would be modeled as a separate class, and each would implement its own valuation method. Using polymorphism, the branching logic for determining current value is replaced with a single statement:

```
instrument value
```

If the *instrument* object receiving this message happened to be a private stock, its implementation of the *value* method would be the same as the *valuePrivateStock* function in the case statement above. A public stock would implement *value* using the procedure from the *valuePublicStock* function, etc. So the correct implementation of the *value* method would automatically be resolved by virtue of which kind of object received the message.

Polymorphic messaging has several advantages over conditional execution logic:

1. It is much shorter, reducing the size and complexity of the resulting program code.
2. It executes faster because the program code compiles down to a direct jump to the appropriate procedure rather than passing through a real-time sieve to identify that procedure.
3. It is more flexible in that new financial instruments can be added or old ones removed without having to rewrite the selection logic.

Given that conditional execution logic is known to be the major contributor to the complexity and rigidity of conventional programs, these advantages are substantial. The advantages also increase with the size of a software system, providing object technology with a natural edge in scalability.

Polymorphism is often portrayed as an advanced concept in object technology, but it is really a highly intuitive mechanism. More often than not, it is the technical staff steeped in the tradition of unique functions who have difficulty with the concept. Non-programmers grasp it quite readily because it reflects the natural form of human communication. For example, managers know that they can issue a single request to all their departments, for example — "project your budget for the coming fiscal year" — and each department will use its own methods to generate an appropriate answer. It would never occur to a manager to formulate a unique request for each department just because they had different procedures for putting together their budgets.

1.2.3 Inheritance

Inheritance is the mechanism that allows classes to be defined as special cases, or *subclasses*, of each other. If a *department* class is declared to be a subclass of *organization*, the *department* class automatically incorporates all the methods and variables defined in the *organization* class. Inheritance can cascade down over any number of levels, allowing deeply nested *class hierarchies* to be constructed.

For methods, a class is free to either use the definition of a method inherited from its parent or *superclass*, or to *override* that definition by declaring a new definition within the class. This new definition then becomes the inherited definition for all classes below that class in the hierarchy. Overriding can occur at any number of levels, providing a highly flexible mechanism for capturing both general rules of processing and special cases where processing differs from those rules.

The use of inheritance with overriding allows the declarative capture and implementation of two fundamental cognitive processes — generalization and specialization. In this context, *generalization* is a form of abstraction in which methods are defined at the most general level at which they apply. *Specialization* allows unique cases to be declared simply by overriding the generic methods with more specific methods. For example, it is a reasonable generalization to say that most vehicles have operators, so any methods relating to operators (qualification, authorization, etc.) would be defined in a generic *vehicle* class that spanned subclasses representing automobiles, aircraft, trains, and other types of vehicle; but self-guided trams might not require operators, in which case this special type of train would override the generic methods for dealing with operators to reduce or eliminate their role.

Inheritance represents a further enhancement of the concept of type in object technology. In addition to defining new types that package data and procedures together, developers can define type hierarchies in which the scope and generality of a type is determined by its position within the hierarchy. For example, a *product* class could have subclasses for *serviceProduct* and *physicalProduct* to represent the fundamental differences between these two major types of product. These classes, in turn, could have subclasses to represent the differences among the major categories of services and goods, each of which would be further categorized by its subclasses, etc.

Some languages provide support for *multiple inheritance*, in which a class can have two or more superclasses. Properly used, multiple inheritance can be a real boon to design. In general, its best use is for defining *mix-ins*, in which two or more superclasses are used to define mutually exclusive aspects of a class. For example, a *printingPress* class could inherit its physical characteristics from a *machine* class and its financial characteristics from a *capitalEquipment* class. However, if there is any overlap among the messages handled by the superclasses of a class, resolving conflicts among the inherited definitions can be problematical. Experience to date has shown that, except in the hands of the most skilled object designers, the problems associated with multiple inheritance typically outweigh the benefits.

1.2.4 Defining Object Technology

The three key mechanisms described in this section are generally accepted as the defining characteristics of object technology. That is, a language or environment is considered to be object-oriented if and only if it implements these three mechanisms.

There is considerable confusion about the definition of object technology within the industry, and much of that confusion stems from a failure to understand the difference between the *concepts* explained in the first section of this chapter and the *mechanisms* under discussion in the current section. It is the mechanisms and not the concepts that define object technology. Two examples will illustrate the source of this confusion and help to resolve it:

1. A language can be object-oriented without using all three concepts. The prototype languages described at the end of the preceding section are object-oriented even though they do not use the concept of classes because they implement inheritance among objects without making a distinction between classes and instances.
2. Conversely, a language can fail to be object-oriented even if it does support all three concepts. Version 5.0 of Visual Basic provides support for classes but does not offer inheritance, so it is not fully object-oriented.

Languages that implement encapsulation and polymorphism but do not support inheritance are sometimes called *object-based* languages to distinguish them from object-oriented languages. The term *object technology* is increasingly used as a shorthand reference to object-*oriented* technology and does not include object-based languages. However, usage varies considerably, and the proliferation of similar terms tends to increase the confusion rather than reduce it. Ultimately, getting the "right" definition is less important than getting the right feature set. If there is any question about whether a language or environment delivers the full benefits of object technology, simply check its support for the three key mechanisms of encapsulation, polymorphism and inheritance.

1.3 Key Advantages

Three key advantages of object technology lie in increased productivity, quality and adaptivity.

1. **Productivity** improvements result from the ability to reuse generic logic expressed in previously constructed classes.
2. **Quality** improvements result from the simpler structure of object-oriented programs and a greater opportunity for extensive unit testing.
3. **Adaptivity** improvements result from the ability to alter the structure and behavior of individual objects without affecting other objects in a system.

These advantages are listed in order of the attention they tend to receive in the decision to adopt object technology. The potential value of these benefits to an organization is just the opposite of this order, however. In the long run, adaptivity is far more valuable than productivity.

1.3.1 Productivity

Just about every new generation of software technology has been accompanied by claims of order-of-magnitude productivity improvements, and object technology is no exception. However, the claim has a different basis in the case of objects. The assertion is not that code can be generated ten times faster (it cannot), but that new programs can be assembled from existing components faster than they can be written from scratch.

This is a far more defensible claim, and controlled studies have shown that order-of-magnitude productivity increases can, in fact, be achieved with objects, but some rather special conditions are required to realize such benefits. A company must have constructed or acquired an extensive library of reusable object components that can be combined in new ways to solve new problems. Building up such a library or *framework* of related, reusable components is, at present, an expensive, time-consuming process. It is only after making a substantial investment of time and money that organizations can begin to realize the full productivity benefits of object technology. To date, only a handful of companies have been willing to make the investment necessary to achieve order-of-magnitude improvements.

In assessing productivity improvements using object technology, it is essential to consider the entire lifecycle of software development. Regardless of whether development follows a waterfall, spiral, or iterative development model, there are certain key activities that must take place. Typically, these include analysis, design, coding, testing, and maintenance. Long-term studies indicate that maintenance accounts for at least 80% of the total time and resources devoted to a program. Other studies suggest that the coding process typically consumes no more than about 20% of the premaintenance time and resources. These results suggest that even if the coding process were eliminated altogether, time and cost to first release would be decreased by no more than about 20%, and total time and cost would be reduced by a mere 4 to 5%. Clearly, code reuse in itself is not going to yield order-of-magnitude productivity improvements.

However, *lifecycle reuse* can and has produced the desired productivity benefits. In this larger view of reuse, every step in the development of object components contributes to the acceleration of future development efforts. The analysis and design that goes into each object is directed toward long-term value rather than just immediate benefit. Similarly, each object is designed well and tested thoroughly so that it requires little or no incremental attention in future uses. Finally, objects are designed to be modifiable, greatly reducing the time and resources necessary to modify them during the maintenance phase of the cycle.

1.3.2 Quality

Although productivity benefits have been a major selling point for object technology, the opportunity for quality improvements has the potential for a far greater impact. The quality of contemporary software is abysmally poor and could only be tolerated in an industry which has demonstrated from the outset that it is incapable of doing any better. Eventually, corporate and individual consumers of software will tire of paying the price for defective software and demand the same kind of quality improvements that have taken place in most manufacturing industries. It is at this juncture that the value of object technology as a path to quality will become fully appreciated.

The use of objects does not, in itself, improve the quality of software. If anything, object technology introduces new opportunities to introduce defects. A prime example is the misuse of inheritance. A single change in a badly designed class hierarchy can wreak havoc throughout a software system by producing unintended side effects on numerous subclasses and countless instances in a running system.

In contrast, initiating a quality-first program as part of a migration to object technology can yield remarkable improvements. Objects provide an ideal foundation for unit testing because every object defines a natural unit of work that can and should be able to function properly in any context, including a test jig that traces the accuracy and performance of every possible execution path through the object. Controlled experiments using the zero-defects approach of modern manufacturing have shown that, properly used, object technology can provide a solid foundation for producing defect-free software.

On a larger scale, the key mechanisms of object technology offer many opportunities for quality improvement.

1. **Encapsulation** ensures that related data and procedures are packaged together, improving the ability to isolate and repair problems. This packaging also allows far better control over data access, reducing errors produced by inconsistent storage and access procedures.
2. **Polymorphism** eliminates the need for most of the conditional execution logic in a system, greatly simplifying complex systems and eliminating the major source of errors in program logic.
3. **Inheritance** allows procedures and data to be defined once and reused wherever they apply, reducing the size and complexity of software systems. Moreover, overriding provides a mechanism for handling special cases in a purely declarative manner, again eliminating the need for conditional execution logic.

1.3.3 Adaptivity

The fact that more than 80% of the cost of software development is spent on maintenance is a clear indicator as to where the greatest benefits of object technology can be found. Building systems that can evolve rapidly and gracefully in response to changing needs is arguably the most important challenge facing the software industry today. Achieving this goal cannot only reduce the cost of maintenance, it can eliminate the need to build new applications altogether. If a company's existing systems can be modified to handle new problems as they arise, then the slow, expensive lifecycle of software development can be bypassed entirely in favor of rapid evolution.

Here again, the mechanisms of object technology directly support this goal.

1. **Encapsulation** allows local changes to handle problems that previously required extensive modifications. For example, data structures can be changed without modifying multiple applications because data is encapsulated with the methods that access it.
2. **Polymorphism** allows new kinds of objects to be added to a system without changing existing software because polymorphic messages are unaffected by the number and variety of alternative receivers. To extend a previous example, new financial instruments can be added to a portfolio management system without modifying the system because polymorphic messages such as *instrument value* automatically work with new kinds of instruments.
3. **Inheritance** allows a local modification to a single class to produce large scale changes in a system without requiring individual changes to every affected object. For example, modifying the way an *organization* class responded to a *budget* message would automatically create the appropriate change in all the subclasses of *organization* and all of their instances, changing the way an entire company carried out its budgeting process.

As effective as these mechanisms are in enhancing modifiability, something more is required to create evolutionary software systems. The major obstacle to adaptivity in software is the fact that most systems are designed to solve a specific set of problems, as defined in the requirements-analysis phase of the development lifecycle. This obstacle is embedded in the very definition of application software; namely, the application of software to solve a problem. Truly evolutionary software requires a fundamental shift in how software development is viewed.

Here is where object technology may ultimately have its greatest impact. Recall from the first section of this chapter that, with objects, modeling is the central activity in designing software. Instead of designing a system around a particular set of problems, object-oriented systems are designed to represent and simulate real-world systems. This allows them to address not only the current set of problems but also new problems that arise over time, including problems that cannot even be envisioned at the outset.

Designing software that can evolve to meet future needs may seem like a daunting and expensive undertaking. However, it can actually be easier than conventional application development because a real-world system provides all the necessary structure for its corresponding software system. The goal is simply to build a faithful working model of the real-world system, then use the model to improve the performance of that system.

The biggest obstacle to this approach is not technological but psychological; it requires that managers and developers set aside some of their most ingrained ideas about software development. For example, they must learn to analyze systems rather than analyzing problems, and they must create executable models rather than developing problem-specific solutions. Once this shift in thinking has been made, the development process itself can be greatly streamlined.

1.4 Key Innovations

Object technology has been around for more than 25 years, which is roughly half the life of software development as a discipline. Although all the key concepts and mechanisms described above were part of the original formulation of object technology, significant improvements continue to be made. Three key innovations in the intervening years are interfaces, delegation, and distribution.

1. **Interfaces** provide a systematic way of separating what an object can do from how it carries out its tasks.
2. **Delegation** offers an alternative to inheritance that can simplify a system while increasing flexibility.
3. **Distribution** allows a single set of objects to be deployed across many machines in a network, including the global network known as the Internet.

1.4.1 Interfaces

Experience in building systems with objects has led many experts to conclude that the concept of a class is too broad. In most object languages, the class specifies both *what* an object can do and *how* it carries out its assigned tasks. This double duty represents a potential confounding of two very different concepts: (1) the *what* of a class specifies its *type* and (2) the *how* specifies its *implementation*. There are some significant advantages to be gained in separating these two concepts.

To understand the issues involved, consider two major problems encountered when using commercial classes produced by software vendors.

1. It is nearly impossible to use just one class from a class library. Each class requires other classes to provide it with essential services, and these classes are specified by name. Using any one class from the library typically pulls in half a dozen other classes, each of which may require another half dozen classes, etc. The result is that class libraries must typically be used in an all or nothing manner.
2. It is very hard to mix classes across two or more vendors. Because each vendor's classes specifically reference other classes from their own libraries, there is little opportunity to substitute classes from another vendor or classes developed in-house.

Interfaces offer a solution to these and related problems. In its simplest form, an *interface* is a named set of message signatures. In effect, an interface specifies the type of an object by stipulating the services it offers and the form in which these services are to be requested.

In addition to specifying message signatures, interfaces can also include other interfaces. This feature allows complex interfaces to be built up out of simpler ones. For example, a *product* interface might be defined as the union of the *design*, *production*, *sales*, *pricing*, and *delivery* interfaces. In essence, this interface defines a product as anything that a company can design, produce, sell, price, and deliver to its customers.

If interfaces rather than classes are used to specify the objects required to support a given class, then classes from multiple vendors can more easily be mixed and matched. As long as a class implements the required interface, it can be used to support other classes that call on this interface. The same is true for objects passed as parameters; if they are specified by interfaces rather than classes, it is possible to use any object that implements the interface, regardless of what class it belongs to or who developed that class. In short, interfaces allow instances of unrelated classes to be used interchangeably as receivers or parameters of messages that would otherwise be limited to only a single branch of a specific class hierarchy.

Using interfaces as types offers yet another advantage — interfaces can be used to restrict access to objects based on roles and relationships. For example, giving a *shipping* object access only to the *delivery* interface of a *product* object would guarantee that *shipping* would be unable to affect the design, production, sales, and pricing of the product.

Techniques for separating the definition of type and implementation have been provided in a variety of ways in object-oriented development environments. However, it is only with the introduction of Java that it reached its present level of explicit, systematic support in terms of explicitly defined interfaces. The increased flexibility offered by interfaces should lead to their rapid adoption as the standard mechanism for typing objects. Interfaces should also facilitate the emergence of the long awaited market for reusable objects.

1.4.2 Delegation

Just as the concept of a class may be regarded as too broad, there is concern that the mechanism of inheritance may be too powerful. Inheritance is dangerous because it violates encapsulation by giving subclasses privy access to the private internals of all their parent classes. It is a controlled violation, introduced with forethought and control, but it is a violation nonetheless.

To see some of the effects of this violation, consider once again the problem of mixing classes purchased from different software vendors. Even if interfaces are used to make classes independent of the classes of objects they interact with, this technique does not solve the dependencies created by inheritance, nor should interfaces be expected to resolve this problem. Inheritance is designed to communicate implementation details to subclasses, and interfaces are designed to avoid any involvement with implementation.

The emerging alternative to inheritance is a design technique known as *delegation*. This technique works just like it sounds — rather than performing a task itself, an object will delegate that task to some other object. For example, suppose that a *product* class provides methods for pricing and delivery, and that a more specific *serviceProduct* class adds methods for handling the location and duration of a particular service. There are two ways in which this division of labor can be achieved: (1) *serviceProduct* can inherit the methods of *product* by being a subclass of *product*, or (2) *serviceProduct* can invoke the methods of *product* by delegating activities to an instance of the *product* class.

These two approaches are logically symmetrical, but there is an important difference. With inheritance, all the methods and data necessary to carry out a related set of tasks are combined within a single object. With delegation, these methods and data are separated into two or more objects. If the interactions among these methods and data are minimal, delegation offers an elegant solution. If the methods and data must all be available in a single execution space, delegation becomes more difficult to implement. In the current example, if a *product* can only determine a price by accessing private information within a *serviceProduct*, then it can work using inheritance but not with delegation.

There are techniques in some object languages for giving a delegate object access to the variables of the delegating object, but these techniques tend to recreate the violation of encapsulation that motivated the use of delegation in the first place. Given the trade offs involved, it seems unlikely that delegation will fully replace inheritance. The emerging trend in the industry is to use delegation wherever it is adequate, reserving the use of inheritance for situations that require combining methods and data into a single execution space. The result is a more sophisticated, controlled use of inheritance that preserves its advantages while reducing its liabilities.

1.4.3 Distribution

One of the most important innovations in the last ten years has been the development of standard protocols for deploying objects across distributed systems. The most common protocol in use today is the Common Object Request Broker Architecture (CORBA) promulgated by the Object Management Group. Two other protocols are the Distributed Component Object Model (DCOM) defined by Microsoft for use on its Windows platforms, and the Remote Method Invocation (RMI) technique defined by Sun for communication among remote Java objects.

Of the three protocols, CORBA is the only one that has been defined by an industry standards consortium. This is reflected in the scope of the protocols. DCOM is restricted to the Windows platform, and RMI is restricted to the Java language. By contrast, CORBA is independent of both platform and language. This broad scope makes CORBA the most general purpose protocol. However, CORBA lacks some of the advanced features Sun designed into RMI. At present, it appears likely that CORBA will incorporate most of these features in the near future, leading to a merger between CORBA and RMI. CORBA is also being extended to interoperate with DCOM, which should be a boon to companies that want to support Microsoft's proprietary protocol while also working with an open standard.

The emerging trend is to design object-oriented systems for distribution from the outset. At a minimum, this means supporting remote interactions through one or more of the three communications protocols. A more advanced technique is to provide *location transparency* by using system-wide location services to relieve individual objects from having to track the locations of other objects. The current state of the art is *remoteness transparency*, in which objects can interact with each other as though they were all in the same execution space, regardless of where they are physically located. Remoteness transparency also allows *mobile objects* to move themselves from one machine to another in order to increase communication bandwidth. Mobile objects, in turn, will permit *dynamic load balancing* to optimize the use of network and processing resources in distributed systems.

1.5 Key Success Factors

Three key factors for succeeding with object technology are motivation, education, and determination. Although these factors apply at both the individual and organizational levels, they are more difficult to achieve in organizations and it is here that the greatest effort is required.

1. **Motivation** is a critical concern because adopting object technology for the wrong reasons can often do more harm than good.
2. **Education** is essential because embarking on object-oriented software development with only a partial grasp of the paradigm is a sure way to undermine the success of a project.
3. **Determination** is required in order to survive a period of diminished returns before realizing the full benefits of object technology.

1.5.1 Motivation

Making the move to object technology is a major transition for an organization. For a company to have a reasonable chance of making the move successfully, the company's motivation must be both ample and appropriate. Simple curiosity or a desire to keep abreast of current trends are not sufficient to sustain a company through the challenges of mastering object techniques, nor are they likely to provide the direction necessary to know how best to apply these techniques.

The best motivation for adopting objects is a driving business need that can only be satisfied through the use of an advanced technology. If an organization's existing systems are failing to meet current needs or cannot adapt quickly enough to meet changing needs, the company is a good candidate for object technology. Alternatively, if a company with products that rely on software finds that it cannot develop new products quickly enough to keep up with its market, that company is a good candidate for adopting objects.

Even a full-fledged organizational commitment to adopt object technology can lead to failure if the goals of the initiative are misguided. For example, adopting technology in order to achieve higher productivity can derail an otherwise well-guided effort. The danger is that this goal can lead to rapid development cycles that produce new applications quickly but prevent the organization from making the essential transition to evolutionary business models. Conversely, a single-minded attempt to achieve reuse can lead a company to develop libraries of highly abstract classes that are of little value in enhancing the current operations of the company.

A key to achieving success with objects is to remember that productivity, reuse, and other beneficial aspects of object technology are all means to an end, not ends in themselves. The only end that will provide the right motivation in the long run is a direct, continuing contribution to the profitability of the organization.

1.5.2 Education

A second critical success factor in the adoption of objects is education in the fundamental principles, strategies, and tactics of object technology. Too often, companies simply send programmers out for a week of training on an object-oriented language or development environment, then expect them to return and deliver the promised benefits. These benefits are not the result of a single tool, and training on a tool is no substitute for education in a fundamentally new way of thinking about software. Far better results will be achieved if training is preceded by a thorough grounding in the concepts of object technology and the ways in which it changes the nature of software.

Sooner or later, preferably sooner, this educational process must extend to every level of an organization. Although it is possible to get an object-oriented project off the ground with a few knowledgeable developers, the only way to have a major impact on an organization is to involve all the critical members of that organization.

Here are just a few of the critical shifts that must take place in the thinking of managers. Project managers need to understand and implement new techniques for managing and measuring software development. Line managers need to understand how the use of executable business models can affect their operations and become involved in the process of designing those models. Chief financial officers need to understand the new realities of justifying and amortizing long-term investments in reusable software components and evolutionary business models. Chief information officers need to understand and embrace the profound impact objects will have on the way they manage information, implement business procedures, and deliver rapid solutions to their corporate sponsors.

At present, there are a great many training courses available to programmers, but very few educational offerings for either programmers or managers. Good educational courses are available, however, and seeking them out is critical to succeeding with objects. If none of the commercial offerings is appropriate, a company should set up a small team of educators to build a course specifically for its own needs. This may appear to be an expensive option, but it is far less expensive than spending millions of dollars on object-oriented software only to have it fail because management did not understand how to take advantage of it.

1.5.3 Determination

Motivation and education are necessary but not sufficient conditions for success. The other key ingredient is determination, the organizational commitment to make a sustained investment in a new technology that will only demonstrate its true value after a significant portion of the business is running on object-oriented systems.

All too often, managers insist on "quick hits" with object technology, such as flashy demonstrations of how quickly new applications can be developed. Such demonstrations typically do more harm than good. In the first place, they play to the wrong motivations. Success with object technology requires a deliberate transformation of the organization at every level, which is just the opposite of what the quick hit conveys. In the second place, quick hits set expectations that can never be met. It is relatively easy for a handful of developers to throw together a very compelling solution to a particular business problem. It is another matter entirely to scale that minor victory up to the organizational level. While the original developers are struggling with this larger problem, senior management is becoming disillusioned as they see productivity appearing to decrease rather than increase as the organization gets deeper into its commitment to object technology.

This is not to say that pilot projects are not useful in gaining management buy-in, but the positioning of these projects is critical. They are demonstrations of feasibility, not of achievement. True success in transitioning to object technology requires a systematic, well-managed transformation at every level. Only a company with a real determination to gain strategic advantage from that transformation is likely to make it intact to the other side.

II

Object-Oriented Methods

Ricardo Devis
Infoplus SL

A *methodology* can be considered a combination of a process, a notation, and tools that aid in the construction of the process. A complete methodology can provide additional features, such as measurement and metrics, detailed role descriptions, defined techniques for tailoring methods, procedures, etc. The chapters in this section provide descriptions of the processes, notation, and tools for existing classical and new, emerging object-oriented methodologies.

Object-Oriented Methods

Object-orientation recommends having several approaches (methods) to deal with the heterogeneous nature of reality. Thus, a diversity of options is required in order to capture the complex diversity of reality. In this section you will find chapters on strongly charged OOA methods (as OSM), emerging standards like OPEN, passing by team-capable approaches (Evo-Fusion), semantic derivations (as SOMA), plus many more. In addition to this, we have an excellent chapter that describes UML, and compares it to OSM. This section provides a comprehensive view of the diversity that exists in the OO methods arena, and the differing solutions offered by various schools of thought.

2

OPEN (Object-Oriented Process, Environment, and Notation): The First Full Lifecycle, Third Generation OO Method

B. Henderson-Sellers
Swinburne University of Technology

2.1 What is OPEN?

OPEN is both an acronym (standing for object-oriented process, environment, and notation) as well as an invitation and opportunity to participate in a truly open, worldwide development of a rapidly emerging *full lifecycle* object-oriented (OO) methodological framework which can be loosely termed "third generation." It was initially created by a merger of MOSES, SOMA, and the Firesmith methods commencing at the end of 1994 when it became clear that (1) there were too many first and second generation methods in the marketplace and that their scopes were too limited, and (2) the philosophies underlying these three methods were almost completely compatible.

The OPEN Consortium is a nonprofit organization responsible for developing and maintaining the OPEN method and includes the original authors of the methods cited above together with 29 other members drawn from the OO methodology, research, and training communities worldwide (see Table 2.1). Another early influence and participant in the OPEN development was Jim Odell.

OPEN is essentially a framework for third generation object-oriented software development methods. OPEN provides strong support for process modeling and requirements capture and offers the ability to model intelligent agents. It has an embedded project management and reuse framework. It supports

0-8493-3135-8/99/$0.00+$.50

TABLE 2.1 The Current Members (as of May 1997) of the OPEN Consortium

Colin Atkinson	Jean Bezivin
Ed Colbert	Philippe Desfray
Richard Dué	Daniel Duffy
Roger Duke	Don Firesmith
Yossi Gil	Ian Graham
Brian Henderson-Sellers	Kitty Hung
Graham Low	Jim McKim
Daniela Mehandjiska-Stavrova	Simon Moser
Kinh Nguyen	Alan O'Callaghan
Meilir Page-Jones	Dilip Patel
Rajesh Pradhan	Dan Rawsthorne
Tony Simons	Madhu Singh
Paul Swatman	Bhuvan Unhelkar
Katharine Whitehead	Alan Wills
Russel Winder	Houman Younessi
Ed Yourdon	Hadar Ziv

business process modeling, offers guidelines on migration strategies, and supports links to human relations issues (see Chapter 42). A prime concern of OPEN is software quality and the use of metrics. To that end, close links with quality frameworks including the Software Engineering Institute's Capability Maturity Model are maintained and supported, and links to ISO 9000 and the SPICE software process improvement project are being developed. In addition to being released to the public domain, OPEN can also serve as the publicly available portion of commercial, largely proprietary methods. One such project, with the commercial MeNtOR method, has already begun.

In addition to synthesizing the best ideas and practices from MOSES, SOMA, and Firesmith, OPEN also utilizes concepts from BON, Mainstream Objects, Martin/Odell, OBA, RDD, ROOM, Syntropy, UML, and others. OPEN also offers a set of principles for modeling all aspects of software development across the lifecycle. Individual methods may conform to it by applying its principles and adopting all or part of the OPEN framework specification: management and technical lifecycle processes, techniques, and modeling language (metamodel plus notation). OPEN will continue to evolve as new techniques are developed and enhanced by working methodologists, users, and researchers.

OPEN extends the notion of a methodology by including a process model [8] and guidelines for constructing versions of this model tailored to the needs of industry domains, individual organizations, and problem types. The process model is an object model and, as such, is adaptable. One sample realization of this object model is the contract-driven lifecycle (see Section 2.3) suitable for rapid application development within an MIS context, but other instantiations are not precluded.

2.2 Overview of OPEN

The third generation OO method OPEN encapsulates business issues, quality issues, modeling issues, and reuse issues within its end-to-end lifecycle process support for software development using the object-oriented paradigm. While the technical issues of object model building are relatively well understood, in that OPEN leverages off existing methodological modeling techniques as found in MOSES, SOMA, BON, RDD, and UML (Booch + OMT + OOSE), the larger scale, more important process issues still provide a challenge both to the methodology developer (as described here) and the users of those methodological ideas.

Underpinning any full lifecycle methodology must be a process. However, it is generally believed that, however hard we seek it, a single, generally applicable process will remain an unattainable and illusory Holy Grail of software engineering. Rather, different organizations, different development styles, and different development domains will require their own specialized lifecycle process [1]. The lifecycle process is essentially one part of the methodology, the key elements of which (Figure 2.1) can probably best be grouped into

- Lifecycle process or (meta)model
- Techniques
- Representation

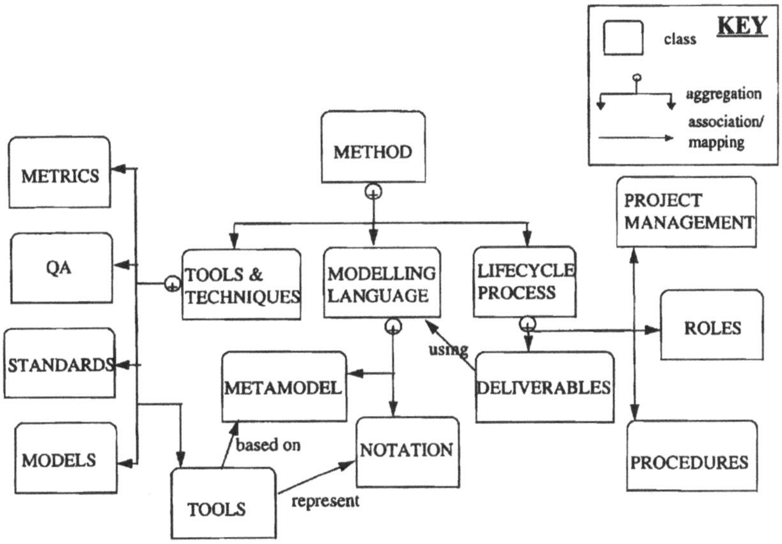

FIGURE 2.1 A Method (or methodology) contains many elements, the three primary ones being lifecycle process, techniques, and modeling language.

Thus, as Younessi and Henderson-Sellers (1997) point out, "methodology" includes (lifecycle) process. However, at a larger granularity, the (software engineering) process must include not only a methodology but also consideration of people/organizational culture and tools/technology available. Each of these software engineering processes (or SEPs) will be highly relevant under specific constraints and as such are fairly widely useful. Generification of these SEPs permits us to seek for an underlying architecture, the software engineering process architecture or SEPA. A SEPA for object-oriented development, which as we shall see is embodied within OPEN, thus provides an integrating framework. No one project will ever use this; rather they will instantiate a particular part of the framework for their own circumstances. This "tailoring of the lifecycle process" is in fact a major Task within the overall OPEN architecture. The SEPA is described by a set of objects. Any type of interaction is possible within these objects in true object-oriented fashion if the messages sent between these OPEN Activities meet the client object's contract. The activities trigger or enable each other by message passing. The messages are guarded by pre- and post-conditions representing tests. The "methods" of an activity are its tasks. Tasks can also be considered the smallest unit of work within OPEN (Figure 2.2). Tasks are carried out by agents (people) using techniques. One example, SEP, the contract-driven lifecycle process architecture, is described briefly below.

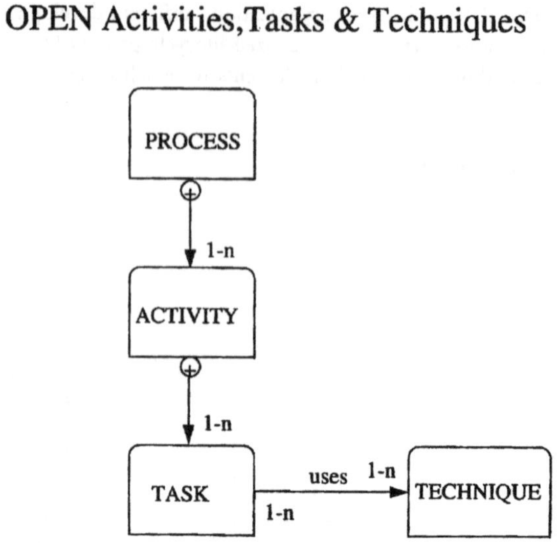

FIGURE 2.2 Activities (with possibly subactivities) have tasks which are realized by the use of one or more techniques.

A two-dimensional matrix then links the Task (which provides the statement of goals i.e., the "what") to the Techniques (which provide the way the goal can be achieved, i.e., the "how"). Techniques range across project management, inspections, etc. through to detailed theories and practices for requirements engineering and system modeling. An example is the SOMA requirements engineering technology which is offered as a superior technique to the primitive use case technique. Others include the ROOM techniques for real-time architectural design, Reenskaug's role modeling, Buhr's time-threads, and the pattern-oriented techniques of catalysis. OPEN provides a large repository of Techniques taken from existing methods.

This approach is not unlike the one recently proposed by Daniels (1997). He clearly distinguishes between the project management/business perspective, which he calls the "lifecycle," and the software developer's viewpoint, the "design process." Daniels argues that much of the failure that has occurred in software development has been the result of force-fitting the lifecycle and the design process together as a single tool for both development and management. Thus progress (in terms of project management) has typically been measured in developers' units (e.g., number of DFDs complete) rather than in business units (e.g., the accounts receivable functionality has been delivered). Thus, any given project has a lifecycle and a design process (which should each be chosen from a suite available at the organizational level); the design process then consisting of Activities, delivering "products" (deliverables in OPEN) by means of Task completion.

A slightly different perspective is offered by Sadr and Dousette (1996) who identify a strategic process and a tactical process as the components of the project. This is more akin to project management (PM) and "project" elements of the OPEN contract-driven lifecycle and the technical lifecycle so it does not fully incorporate the people, tools, and environment issues identified by Younessi and Henderson-Sellers (1997) in their SEP or by Daniels (1997) in his lifecycle.

One of the greatest technical advantages of an OO lifecycle process is that of (almost) seamlessness. "Objects"* are used as the basic concept and unit of consideration during requirements engineering,

*At this stage, we do not want to enter into any arguments regarding the use of the words object, type, class, role, and instance, collectively called CIRT in OPEN, and will just use "object" in a truly generic and undefined sense.

systems analysis and design, and in the OO programming language and future maintenance. Objects are the common language of users as well as technical developers. Of course, the notion of seamlessness causes concern for project managers more used to being able to clearly delineate the end of the analysis phase and the end of the design phase.

In this seamless, iterative lifecycle in which incremental delivery is the norm — and highly advantageous in keeping the user "in the loop" providing immediate feedback, always a currently viable version for use and evaluation and producing higher quality software — the elements which comprise the lifecycle describe the high level Activities which must be undertaken in order to produce the software product(s). The Activities, outlined below, are linked together in an organization's tailoring of the contract-driven lifecycle, which produces their specific SEP. The way in which Activities are linked together depends on the organization and the problem. Case study example SEPs are to be discussed in a future OPEN book, *Tailoring the OPEN Lifecycle — Case Studies* [2].

Finally, OPEN embodies a set of (object-oriented) principles. It permits enhanced semantics for object models based on the contributions of methods such as SOMA, BON, Syntropy, etc. Furthermore, OPEN is fully object-oriented in that encapsulation is a basic principle. To this end, bidirectional associations rarely occur and are strongly discouraged [5]. It is a logical consequence of this that class invariants are not an optional extra in the modeling semantics. Rulesets (which generalize class invariants) can be used to model intelligent agents as objects.

In OPEN, OO principles are basic and should be adhered to. These include:

- Object modeling as a very general technique for knowledge representation
- Encapsulation
- Polymorphism
- Clear, jargon-free and well-founded definitions of all terms
- Extensive use of abstraction techniques, a foundation for semantically cohesive and encapsulated objects

While OPEN's focus has always been full lifecycle, during 1995 the call from the Object Management Group (OMG) for a standardized metamodel and notation led some members of the OPEN Consortium to divert additional effort in these directions. Thus was created the OPEN Modeling Language or OML (Figure 2.3). OML is the name for the combination of metamodel and notation, in parallel to a similar combination created by Rational methodologists, known as UML (Unified Modeling Language). The OML metamodel is derived from the work of the metamodeling COMMA project, which itself has provided valuable input to the OMG metamodeling effort. The notational element of OML also has its own name, Common Object Modeling Notation or COMN (see section below). While it was designed for use in OPEN, COMN is not so restricted and can be used in conjunction with other OO methods. Consequently, we have published the COMN notational standard [3] and the process description [8] in two volumes, thus separating two of the major elements of a methodology noted above—process and its representation. Indeed, we go further and keep the techniques separate again. These will be the topics of other books [6, 13] written by members of the OPEN Consortium.

OPEN supports both the UML notation and the OML notation (COMN) and anticipates endorsing the OMG metamodel when determined.

2.3 OPEN's Contract-Driven Lifecycle

The contract-driven lifecycle, as used in OPEN, is shown in its most up-to-date form in Figure 2.4. The model is, in essence, very simple. In summary, a development program may be decomposed into a network of projects that produce deliverable, working software products. Projects are composed of activities. Each OPEN Activity is shown as a box, either with rounded corners (an unbounded Activity) or with rectangular

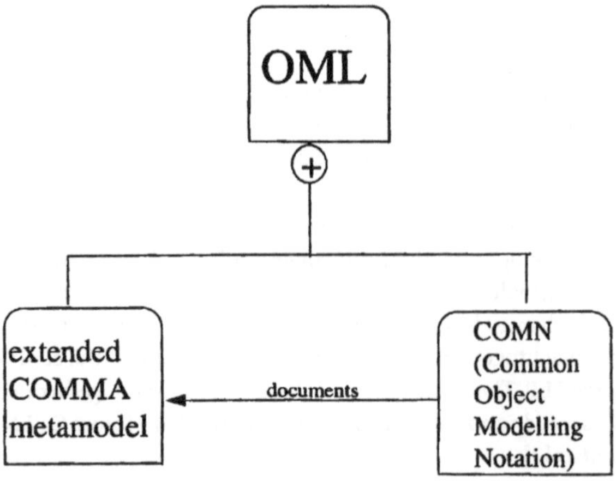

FIGURE 2.3 OPEN Modeling Language (OML) has two parts: the metamodel, derived as an extended version of the COMMA metamodel of Henderson-Sellers and Firesmith (1997) and the notation, COMN (Common Object Modeling Notation). (From [3]. *OPEN Modeling Language (OML) Reference Manual,* 271, SIGS Books, New York. With permission.)

corners (Activity tightly bound in time). Because we are modeling these activities as objects, when we can associate contracts with each Activity object (hence the lifecycle name of "contract-driven"). These are expressed primarily by pre- and post-conditions; in other words, constraints that have to be met before an Activity can be commenced and final conditions that have to be met (and signed off) before another Activity can be initiated (triggered). Testing is an integral part of these exit conditions. Activities include well-specified testing activities and should deliver test results against both task scripts (a higher form of use cases — see Graham, 1997) and a technical test plan of the normal kind, i.e., tests that answer these questions. Does an enhancement leave previous things that worked working? Does the system work well under stress and high volume I/O? These Activities thus provide a largescale structuring in time. Different configurations, chosen to reflect the needs of different problems and different organizations, can be constructed from this flexible framework. Each combination of Activities and interconnecting paths defines a SEP. Once chosen, the lifecycle process is fixed, although still, at least in an OO project, highly iterative, flexible, and with a high degree of seamlessness.

The progression order is neither prescriptive nor deterministic. Rather, the contract-driven lifecycle permits (1) ordering in an iterative and incremental fashion and (2) the tailoring by a given organization to its own internal standards and culture. We indicate in this figure some of the likely routes between Activity objects, but remember, the main governing constraint on the routes are whether you do or do not meet the pre-conditions of the Activity to which you wish to transition.

Interestingly, the OOram lifecycle process (Figure 2.5) is essentially encapsulated within the Evolutionary Development Activity. This rapidly cycles across CIRT* identification, OOAD and OOP followed by test. What is added in this miniature prototyping lifecycle within the contract lifecycle (as exemplified in (Figure 2.5) is the possibility of commencing in one of two alternative positions: either as a full lifecycle OOAD prior to implementation or as a "structured hacking" or exploratory prototyping approach.

*CIRT = class or instance or role or type.

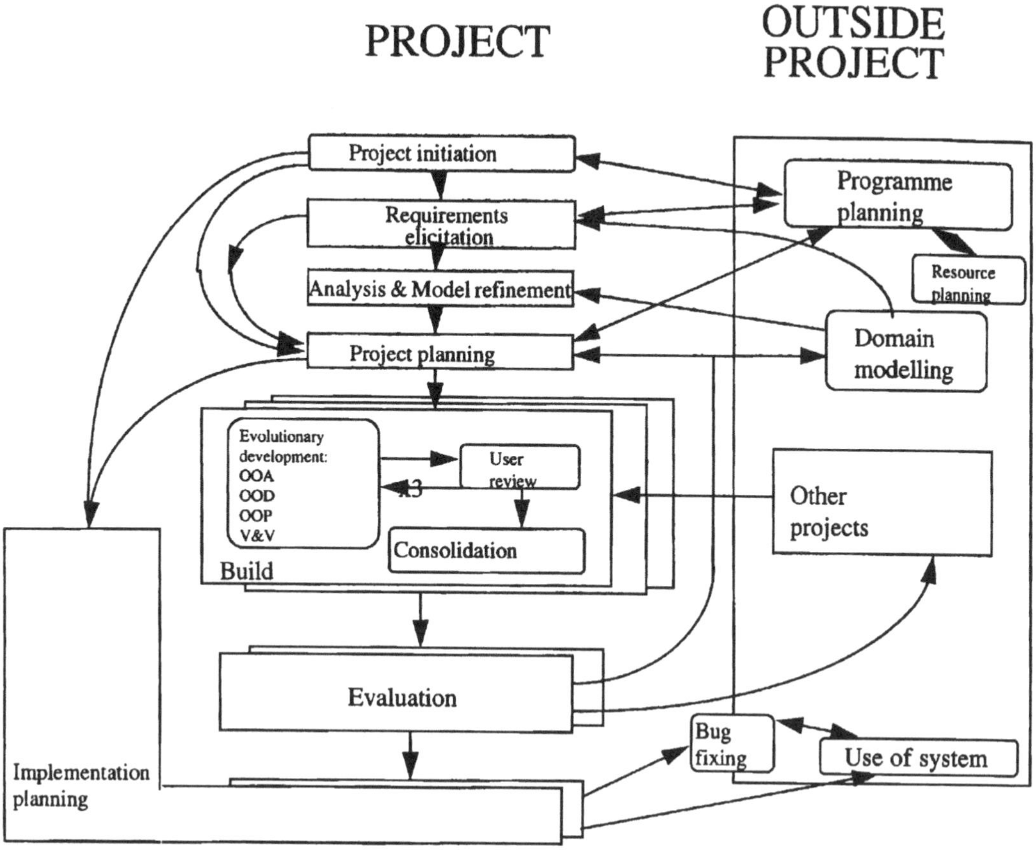

FIGURE 2.4 Contract-driven lifecycle process model (Revised from [9]).

2.4 OPEN's Activities and Tasks

The Activities permit a large scale structuring of the project management for an OO product development. Each Activity represents a set of goals and, in truly object-oriented fashion, has an interface consisting of methods which are the selected Tasks, internal state and external services, and has pre- and post-conditions to satisfy all contractual obligations. The contract-driven lifecycle allows the developer to move from Activity to Activity in any order as long as all the pre- and post-conditions are met. This does not, however, lead to anarchy. Rather it supports flexibility so that different organizations can choose their own tailored lifecycle process model from the OPEN Activities. Secondly, within a single organization, individual projects may have different foci, which require different configurations of this highly flexible lifecycle process. Thus an individually chosen lifecycle can be created for projects and/or organizations while remaining "OPEN-compliant." The developers still speak the same language and can still talk to each other.

What Activities do not do is to identify things that have to be done at a low enough resolution to match with tasks that need to be done in order to meet the goals of each Activity. For example, when the developer is focusing on an Activity such as Evolutionary Development, there are a number of associated Tasks which need to be undertaken successfully (see Chapter 3). One of these is the Task "construct the object model." This is a clearly delineated goal for which someone can take responsibility (the delivery of a well-structured object model for the problem in hand). We should also note that for this particular

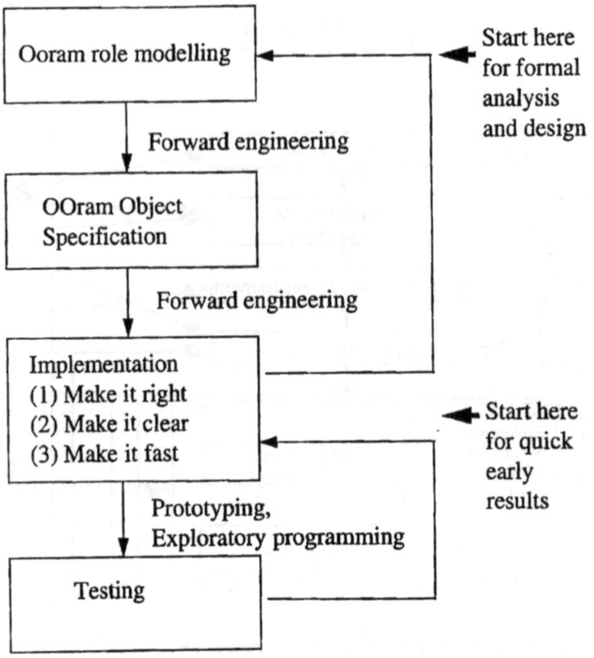

FIGURE 2.5 OOram's "Simple implementation process." (After [11]. *Working with Objects. The OOram Software Engineering Manual,* 366, Manning, Greenwich, CT. With permission.)

Activity, more than one task will be identified; for other Activities there may be predominantly only one Task required. We can think of these links (Tasks to Activities) in one of two ways: in a "probabilistic" manner or in a purer OO fashion by allocating Tasks as methods of the Activity objects (as noted above). At a future time, we assign, in very general terms or in more specific terms for any one, highly specific project, probabilities or, to be more accurate, deontic* certainty factors, for each of these Task/Activity links. As the lifecycle is increasingly tailored to a specific domain, the values of the deontic factors change to a bimodal distribution (0 or 1). This thus allocates with certainty which Tasks are needed for which Activities. These Tasks can now be more usefully modeled as methods of the Activities. Thus the deontic matrix between Activities and Tasks of Henderson-Sellers et al. (1996) turns out to be only an unstable, transient modeling artifact.

OPEN's Tasks are statements of things that need to be done. They are described as the "smallest unit of work on a schedule which contributes to a milestone." Tasks are either completed or not completed and are listed in Table 2.2. From OBA, we can also delineate the information associated with a Task. The figure of merit is between 0 and 1 and is assigned by the project manager. It indicates the importance of the task in meeting the associated milestone. For each individual milestone, the sum of all the associated tasks should be unity.

However, tasks say what is to be done, but not how. The "how" is the role of the Technique.

*Deontic logic is the logic of duty or obligation. It adds extra operators such as MAY, MUST, and OUGHT to ordinary first order predicate calculus.

TABLE 2.2 OPEN Tasks in Alphabetical Order

- Analyze user requirements
- Code
- Create and/or identify reusable components ("for reuse")
  - Construct frameworks
  - Optimize for reuse
- Deliver product to customer
- Design and implement physical database
  - Distribution/replication design
  - Operational and performance design
  - Performance evaluation
- Design user interface
- Develop and implement resource allocation plan
  - Choose hardware
  - Choose project team
  - Choose toolset
  - Decompose programmes into project
  - Develop education and training plan
  - Develop iteration plan
  - Develop timebox plan
  - Identify project roles and responsibilities
  - Manage subsystems
  - Set up metrics collection program
  - Specify individual goals
  - Specify quality goals
  - Use dependencies in the BOM to generate first cut project plan
- Develop business object model (BOM)
- Develop software development context plans and strategies
  - Develop capacity plan
  - Develop contingency plan
  - Develop security plan
  - Establish change management strategy
  - Establish data take-on strategy
  - Integrate with existing, non-OO systems
  - Tailor the lifecycle process
- Evaluate quality
  - Analyze metrics data
  - Evaluate usability
  - Review documentation
- Identify CIRTs
  - Determine initial class list
  - Identify persistent classes
  - Identify roles
  - Refine class list
- Identify context
- Identify source(s) of requirements
- Identify user requirements
  - Define problem and establish mission and objectives
  - Establish user requirements for distributed systems
  - Establish user DB requirements
- Maintain trace between requirements and design
- Manage library of reusable components
- Map logical database schema
- Map roles on to classes
- Model and re-engineer business process(es)
  - Build context (i.e., business process) model
  - Build task object model
  - Convert task object model to business object model
  - Do user training
  - Prepare ITT
- Obtain business approval
- Optimize reuse ("with reuse")
- Optimize the design
- Test
  - Perform acceptance testing
  - Perform class testing
  - Perform cluster testing
  - Perform regression testing
- Undertake architectural design
- Develop layer design
  - Establish distributed systems strategy
  - Select database/storage strategy
- Undertake feasibility study
- Undertake in-process review
- Undertake post-implementation review
- Undertake usability design
- Write manual(s) and prepare other documentation

2.5 OPEN's Techniques

Knowing that the Task "construct the object model" is one (of several) tasks that the developer can undertake in order to complete the Activity does not tell the developer *how* to accomplish the Task(s). The Task is the goal or the what and the how is described by one or more Techniques. Indeed, the developer may have to choose between several possible Techniques, some of which may be always useful and some possibly useful while other techniques should be avoided altogether. The project manager/developer is at liberty to accomplish an OPEN Task with whatever tools and techniques he or she is familiar. OPEN only recommends, it does not mandate. However, in order to aid the developer, OPEN does suggest a large range of techniques which have been found to be appropriate in the OPEN "Techniques Toolbox" (Table 2.3). There is a fuzzy nature to the linkage of Techniques and Tasks represented most successfully by a deontic matrix (Figure 2.6), as discussed earlier. In OPEN we give our overall recommendations in terms of M (mandatory), R (recommended), O (optional), D (discouraged), and F (forbidden). For instance, some tasks are clearly best accomplished with a single, specific technique — a technique applicable to that task and nothing else (for example, implementation of services which support the coding task). Other techniques will be found useful in a range of tasks (for example, contract specification). Finally, for some tasks there may be a choice that the project manager has to make. For example, there are many ways of identifying classes, objects, and types. Which include: interactive techniques such as the use of CRC cards to identify responsibilities; scenarios/task models/scripts/use cases to focus on functionality delivered as a prelude to finding CIRTs within these scripts; textual analysis, in which nouns in the requirements analysis

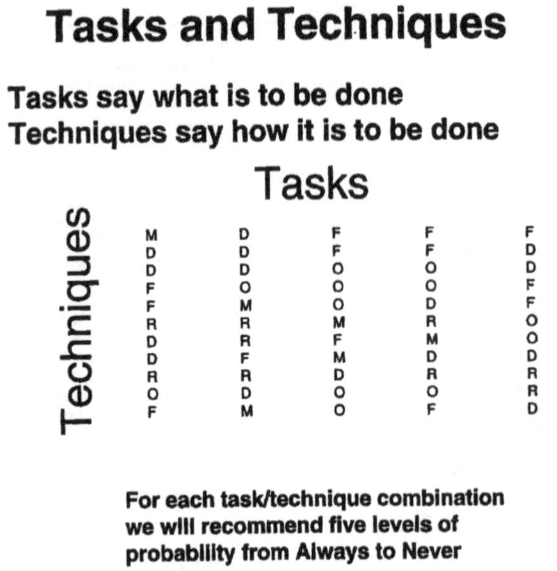
Tasks and Techniques
Tasks say what is to be done
Techniques say how it is to be done
Tasks
Techniques
M D F F F
D D F F D
D D O O D
F O O O F
F M O D F
R R M R O
D R F M O
D F M D D
R R D R R
O D O O R
F M O F D
For each task/technique combination we will recommend five levels of probability from Always to Never

FIGURE 2.6 The core of OPEN is a two-dimensional relationship between Tasks and Techniques. For each task, a number of techniques may be useful. For each combination of Task and Technique, an assessment can be made of the likelihood of the occurrence of that combination. Some combinations can be identified as mandatory (M), others as recommended (R), some as being optional (O), some as unlikely/discouraged (D), and other combinations that are strictly verboten (F = forbidden).

have the potential to be realized as CIRTs; simulation which focuses on the objects within the modeling exercise; and even (for some skilled* people), the use of ER diagrams as a basis for an CIRT structure diagram.

This two-dimensional matrix also offers the project manager significant flexibility. If new tasks and techniques are developed in a particular context, then incorporating them into this framework is extremely easy. It only requires the addition of a single line in the matrix and the identification of the M/R/O/D/F nature of the interaction between this new task and the techniques of the chosen lifecycle process model. This approach is useful at the more generic, almost meta-level of the process description.

In this way, Techniques are intrinsically orthogonal to the notion of Tasks. They can only be grouped together very roughly. They are akin to the tools of the tradesperson like a carpenter's toolbox contains many tools, some of which have superficial resemblances but may have operational affinity to tools of different outward appearance. A full description of the OPEN toolbox of Techniques is a book in itself [5].

2.6 OPEN's Notation

A methodology needs to include a means for representing the generated artifacts — it needs to contain a notational element. While only a small part of a methodology, it is, however, the most obvious part and,

*We say skilled not to disparage ER but rather to stress that it is our experience that good OO designers can make good use of ER since they have the OO mindset, but that novices or poor designers use ER as a crutch to stay within the procedural paradigm while fooling themselves, and probably their managers, that they are doing OO design.

TABLE 2.3 OPEN Techniques in Alphabetical Order

Abstract classes	Fagan's inspections
Abstraction	Formal methods
Acceptance testing	Frameworks
Access analysis	Function points
Access path optimization	Fuzzy logic and fuzzy modeling
Action research	Games
Active listening	Gantt charts
Activity grids	Generalization (see also Classification)
Agents—see Intelligent agents	Generalization for reuse
Aggregation—see Composition	Genericity Specification
structures	GQM
Analysis of judgments	Group problem solving
Approval gaining	Hierarchical Task Analysis
Assertion language	Hypergenericity
Associations	Idioms
Audit requirements	Impact analysis
Beta testing	Impact estimation table
Blackboarding	Implementation inheritance
BNF	Implementation of distributed aspects
Brainstorming	of system
CD-ROM technology	Implementation of rules
CIRT Indexing	Implementation of services
Classification	Implementation of structure
Class internal design	Indexing
Class naming	Information engineering (but take care)
Clustering (DB)	Inspections—see Code/document
Clusters	inspections and Fagan's inspections
Code generation	Integration testing
Code/document inspections	Intelligent agents
Cohesion measures	Interaction modeling
Collaborations	Internet and web technology
Collapsing of classes	Interviewing
Color in UIs	Kelly grids
Completion of abstractions	Law of Demeter
Complexity measures	Lectures
Composition Structures—a.k.a.	Library Class incorporation
Aggregation	Literate programming
Computer-Based Assessment (CBA)	Mapping to RDB
Configuration management	Mechanisms
Connascence	Metrics collection
Containment	Mixins
Context Modeling (BPR)	Multiple inheritance
Contract Specification	MVC analysis
Cost Benefit Analysis (CBA)	Normalization
Cost estimation	Object lifecycle histories
CPM charts	Object replication
CRC cards	Object request brokers (ORBs)
Critical Success Factors (CSFs)	Object retention requirements
Customer (on-site) training	Ownership modeling
Database authorization	Partitions
Dataflow modeling (dangerous)	Password protection
DBMS product selection	Path navigation
DBMS type selection	Pattern recognition
DCS architecture specification	PERT charts
(partitioning and allocation)	Petri nets
DCS optimization	Physical security
Defect detection	PLanguage
Delegation	Polymorphism
Dependency-based testing	Power analysis (political systems analysis)
Descoping	Power types
Dialogue design in UI	Priority setting
Discriminant	Process modeling
Domain analysis	Project planning
Early prototype to exercise DCS	Protocol analysis
Encapsulation/Information hiding	Prototyping
ER modeling (but take care)	PSP
Event charts	Quality templates
Event modeling	Questionnaires
Exception handling	RAD
Expected value analysis	RAD Workshops
Record and playback	Storage of derived properties
Redundant associations	Storyboarding

TABLE 2.3 OPEN Techniques in Alphabetical Order *(continued)*

Refinement	Subsystem coordination
Refinement of inheritance hierarchies	Subsystem identification
Regression testing	Subsystem testing
Relational DBMS interface specification	Task cards
Reliability requirements	Task decomposition
Repeated inheritance	Task points
Responsibilities	Task scripts
Reuse metrics	Team structuring
Reverse engineering	Textual analysis
Rich pictures	Throwaway prototyping
Risk Analysis	Time-threads
Role assignment	TQM
Role modeling	Traceability
Roleplay	Train the trainer
Rule modeling	Traits
Scenario classes	Transformations of the object model
Screen painting and scraping	Tuning of database
Scripting	Unit testing
Security requirements	Usability testing
Self-paced exercises	Usage
Semiotic modeling	Use cases
Service Identification	Variant analysis
Simulation	Versioning
SMART goals	Videotaping
Social systems analysis	Viewpoints
Soft systems analysis	Visibility
Specialization inheritance	Visioning (for BPR)
Specification inheritance	Visualization techniques
Standards compliance	Volume analysis
State machines	Walkthroughs
Static analysis	Workflow analysis
Statistical analysis	Workshops
Stereotypes	Wrappers
	Zachman frameworks

since choosing a methodology also implies choosing a CASE tool, it is a component of the methodology which often surfaces first and, if you do not prevent it, can take over the whole mindset.

For many of us, once we have learned a notation we find no barriers and we can use the notation easily and fluently. It is like learning a programming language or learning a natural language. Some natural languages are harder to learn than others. It is generally appreciated that Chinese and English (for non-native speakers) can present almost insurmountable problems. For a francophone, on the other hand, learning Italian is relatively easy. Even becoming fluent with the basic alphabet (choose from Roman, Japanese, Cyrillic, Arabic, Hebrew and many others) can be a challenge for adults with no previous exposure. So, an interface, here the alphabet, that is unfamiliar or does not include easy to intuit symbols (arguably Chinese is easier here because of its ideographic heredity) makes the syntax and semantics hard to learn. So it is with an OOAD notation.

The OPEN preferred notation* (known as COMN) has been designed with intuition and usability in mind. Granted we cannot find internationally recognizable symbols amenable to all types of novice in every country; however, if we assume we are trying to pictographically describe the main, commonly understood elements of object technology such as encapsulation, interfaces, black box, and white box inheritance, a discrimination between objects, classes, and types, then designing a broadly acceptable notation becomes possible.

Semiotics is the study of signs and symbols. Those semiotic ideas were built into the MOSES notation and into UON, both of which have had influences on the OML notation as well as more recent studies

*OPEN also supports the UML notation as an emerging standard (see Chapter 9).

in interface design and notational design. OPEN has no hereditary biases from an earlier, data modeling history. OPEN's notation has been designed from the bottom up by a small team of methodologists who have over the last decade worked on these issues.

The OPEN recommended notation, COMN, provides support for both the novice and the sophisticate. Here we describe only those elements necessary for beginning and, indeed, which will be found in around 80% of all applications. In a nutshell, we need to have symbols for:

- Class vs. type vs. instance (or object) vs. implementation (Figure 2.7); all icons have optional drop down boxes for information relevant to the particular phase of the lifecycle; drop down boxes may contain information on characteristics, responsibilities, requirements, or stereotypes, for instance; these are all types of traits
- Basic relationships of association, aggregation, containment (Figure 2.8), and inheritance (specialization, specification, and implementation inheritance are clearly differentiated)
- A dynamic model (e.g., a flavor of STD)
- A use case model (or an extension thereof)
- Interconnections between the various models, after all we only have *one* model; different descriptions (static, dynamic, use case) are just different views of aspects of the same entity

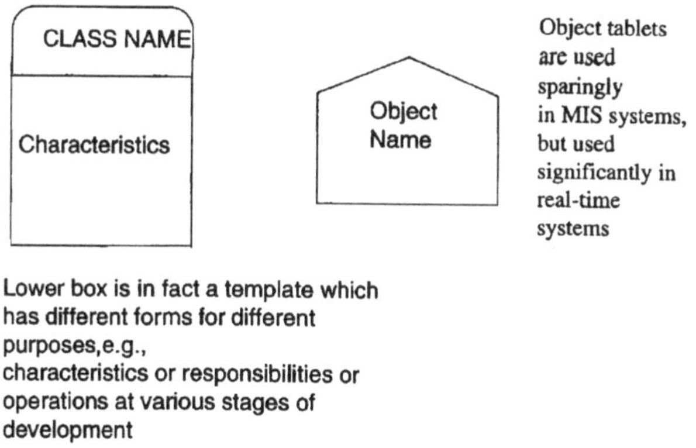

FIGURE 2.7 Classes and drop down boxes.

While OPEN strongly recommends the COMN notation which supports its principles, we realize that many applications will only need a small subset of that published (COMN Light) and that conformant methods will find some of it irrelevant. Equally we understand that other notations will be preferred by some organizations. This is permissible within the OPEN framework. For example, UML can be used to express OPEN models in many cases. However, some things that can be expressed well in COMN cannot be expressed or will not be properly expressible within the semantics of UML (e.g., responsibilities, rulesets, exceptions, cluster encapsulation) and some UML preferences (bidirectional associations) will violate OPEN principles.

2.7 OML's Light Notational Elements

This is OML's "Light Notation": COMN Light. We aim for minimality in semantics while acknowledging that the notation is likely to evolve, especially with niche extensions such as hard real-time, roles and distribution. This will particularly result as more "satellite" methods are merged into the mainstream of

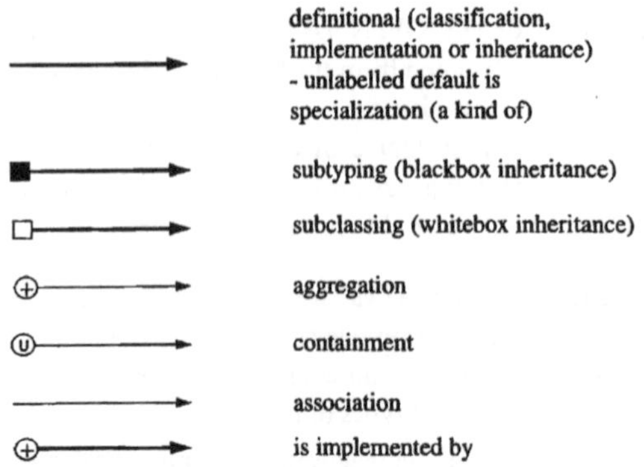

FIGURE 2.8 Relationships are indicated by arrows, some with adornments. The major relationships are illustrated here and form part of the COMN Light notation.

OPEN. Figure 2.7 depicts the basic icons for class and object. Both class and object are similar, however, an object is "more real" than a class so the icon is represented by a sharper icon whereas the class icon is smooth. The class icon itself is also unmistakable and cannot be confused with rectangles as used in structured hierarchy charts, for example. In MIS systems, we usually use class icons and only use object icons for specific message-passing sequences (on collaboration diagrams), whereas in real-time systems it is usually object icons that dominate. Another sign used is that of a dotted line to indicate a more ethereal notion. Abstract/deferred classes are more ethereal than classes so they get a dotted outline.

The other interesting item here is how to design a notation that will "last" throughout the lifecycle. The answer we have come up with is "drop down boxes." These are attached below the icons (for all icons) and can contain information relevant to the particular phase of the lifecycle. They may contain information on characteristics, responsibilities, requirements, or stereotypes, for instance. These are all types of traits.

Figure 2.9 shows how these concepts are related by the core metamodel. Here we introduce for the first time into an OO notation the well-understood notion that a class is composed of an interface plus an implementation. Graphically we "tear apart" the class icon to get the two complementary icons — the type and the class implementation. An object is then an instance of a class which also conforms to a type. Figure 2.9 is an example of a semantic net (a.k.a. class diagram) which uses the OML notation to describe its own metamodel. It can either be read as an example of the OML notation or as a description of a metamodel (actually it is both).

In Figures 2.10–2.13 we see the major relationships illustrated: specialization (Figure 2.10), unidirectional associations (mappings); (Figure 2.11), aggregations (Figure 2.12), and containment (Figure 2.13). Again the icons chosen are self-explanatory. Specializations are very close bindings between sub and super class/type. They have a very thick arrow (a double arrow is chosen as being easier to draw by hand than a thick one and easier to see when different magnifications are used in a drawing tool). A label can be used to indicate the discriminator used for the subclassing. Specialization, the default, is an is-a-kind-of relationship. Other types of "inheritance" can be shown but the basic, encouraged is-a-kind-of gets the easiest-to-draw line. All relationships are unidirectional, as indicated by the arrowhead. Consequently, an association is always, by default, unidirectional. If no decision has yet been made, the arrowhead may be left off until a later decision adds it. This is more reasonable than permitting an unarrowed line to mean bidirectional. Leaving off arrowheads may be carelessness rather than a design decision. Mappings as used here do not break encapsulation, whereas bidirectional associations do. We believe in supporting a true object-oriented paradigm as default.

Aggregation, although not as well-defined as we would all like it to be, represents a fairly permanent binding — an "is-composed-of" or "whole-part" relationship. At the same time, we can see this symbol

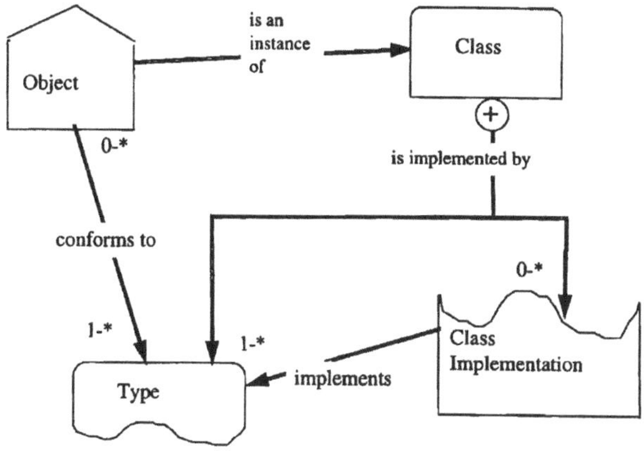

FIGURE 2.9 A metamodel of the relationships between objects, types, and classes which also illustrates the icons for each of these metatypes and also the icon for class implementations.

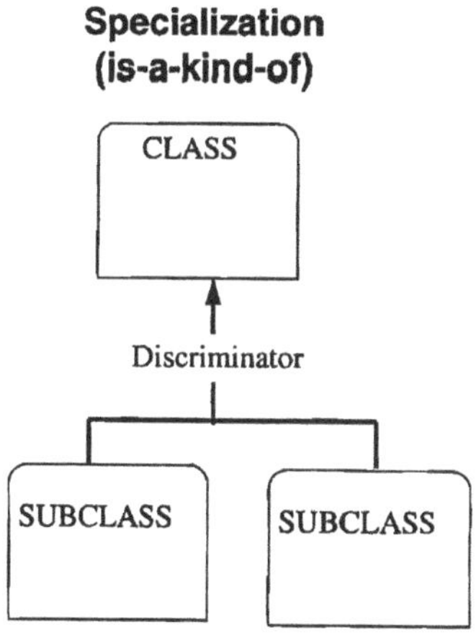

FIGURE 2.10 Example of specialization notation of COMN.

as a plus sign which represents the fact that the aggregate (here the yacht) is (often more than) the sum of its parts.

Often confused with aggregation is the looser collection concept. A good example here is what you store in the trunk of your car. The items are connected with trunk, but that connection may be highly temporary. We replace the plus symbol with a cup symbol to give the visual clue suggested by this icon of a cup and its contents.

One pleasing aspect of the relationship model is its carefully structured metamodel (Figure 2.14). All relationships, as noted above, are binary, unidirectional dependencies or mappings. These can be of two major types (four when we include dynamic models). The two static relationship types are definitional (in which one thing is defined by relationship to another) and referential (in which one thing "knows about" another).

2.7.1 Definitional Relationships

We use a double arrow for the tighter definitional relationship and a single arrow for the less permanent referential. Our default definitional node, the easiest to draw, is the is-a-kind-of which thus gets a double

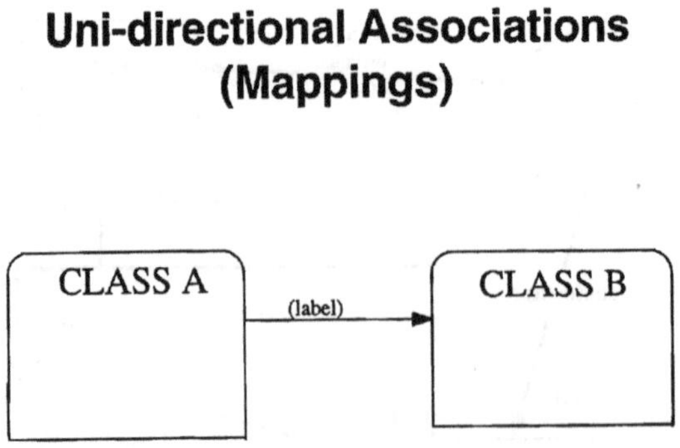

FIGURE 2.11 In OPEN, associations are unidirectional mappings that preserve encapsulation (From [6]). The notation is a simple, directed arrow with optional label.

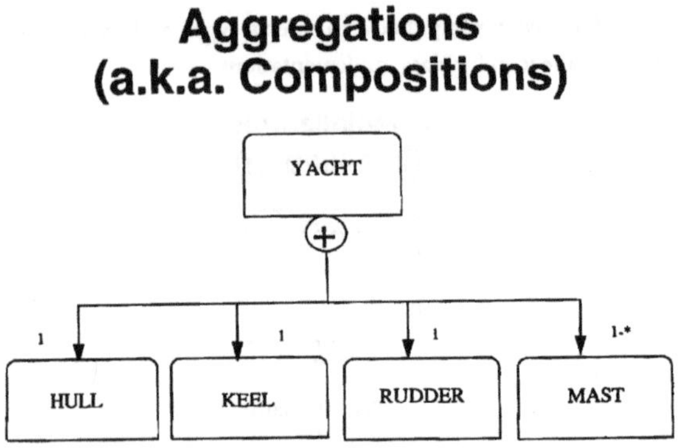

FIGURE 2.12 Example of an aggregation (is-composed-of) relationship showing the appropriate COMN notation.

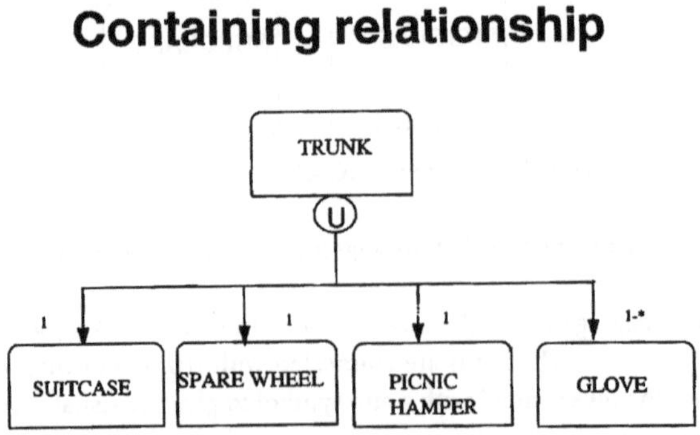

FIGURE 2.13 Example of a containing relationship showing the appropriate COMN notation.

arrow. An is-a-kind-of relationship is good for both knowledge representation (in for example, user requirements/analysis) and in support of polymorphism, through dynamic substitutability. Because we discourage simple subtyping (specification or subtyping inheritance) and implementation inheritance, they are represented as adornments (a black and white box, respectively, at the subclass end of the arrow, to represent black box and white box inheritance).

All other definitional relationships (also with double arrow) carry a textual label. These can be grouped into classification relationships (conforms-to, is-an-instance-of, plays-the-role-of) and implementation relationships (implements, is-implemented-by).

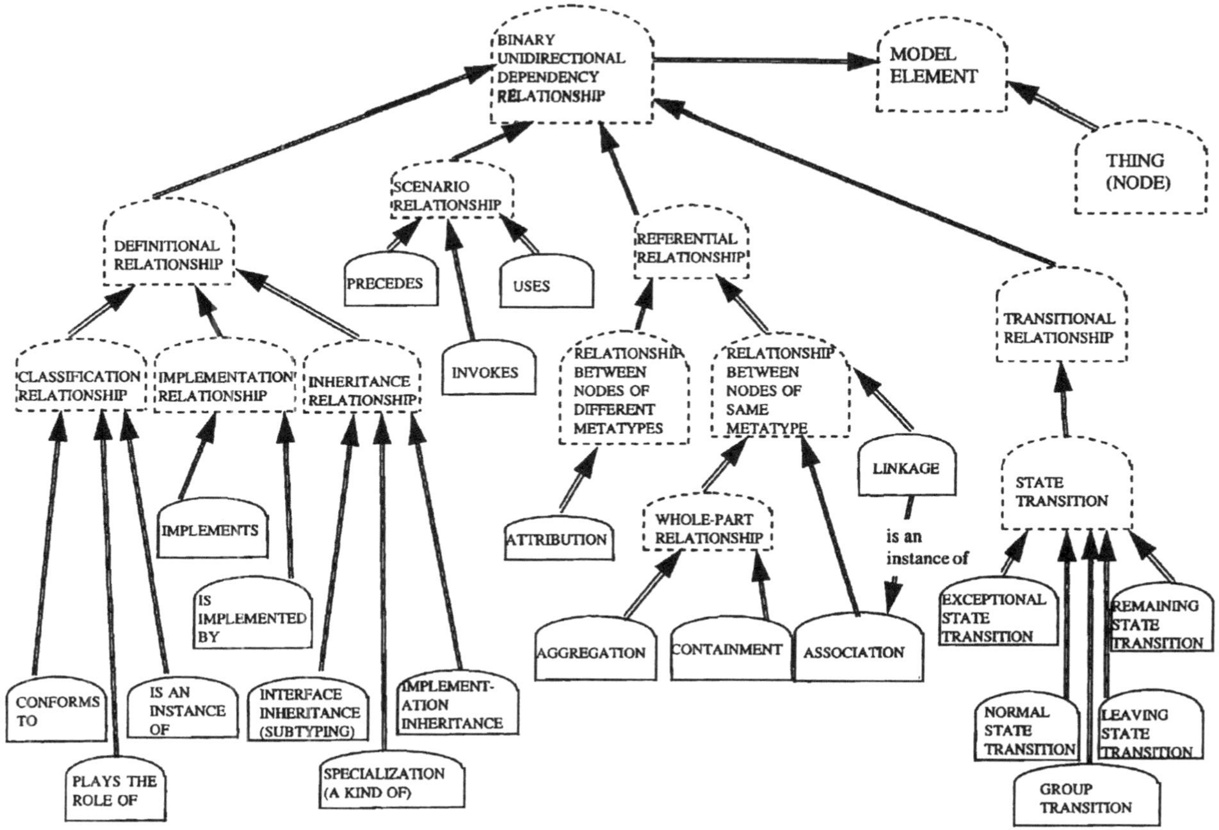

FIGURE 2.14 Metamodel of COMN relationships. These are binary, unidirectional dependency relationships that can be subdivided into definitional relationships, scenario relationships, referential relationships, and transitional relationships.

2.7.2 Referential Relationships

Referential relationships may be between the same or different metatypes. All referential relationships use a single width arrow. A solid arrow is used to indicate relationships between identical metatypes and a dotted arrow to represent connections between different metatypes. This gives us a solid single arrow for associations and linkages (associations for classes, linkages for instances). Similarly, a solid single arrow, but this time with adornment, is used to represent aggregation and containment (see Figure 2.8 above). The referential relationship between nodes of different metatypes is the annotation which is typically to join NOTEs to icons (*viz.* annotations).

2.7.3 Transitional and Scenario Relationships

There are in fact two further types of relationship, transitional and scenario. These are advanced features, not part of OML Light and thus not discussed here [3]. Transitional relationships are not used in the static model (semantic net or class models) but only in the dynamic models and scenario relationships in use case/task script models. Beginners can use any state transition model they choose before investigating the OML dynamic model. Similarly, although we prefer a task script/use case model for large systems, any version of this to help gain understanding of user requirements will be satisfactory for learning the overall OPEN approach. Interconnections between diagrams are similarly reserved for the full notation discussion.

2.8 Summary and Conclusions

The OPEN standardized methodology will facilitate widespread adoption of object technology. It will provide a standard that is flexible enough to be useful to small, medium, and large enterprises — a standard that can be used for different vertical markets — and therefore has a common core with modular extensions. It is *imperative* that this standard is of the highest quality, transcending the vested interests of individuals and individual companies.

OPEN already has users worldwide, consultants and universities teaching it, and CASE vendors supporting its notation. As our name suggests, we are open to further collaboration and all major methodologists have been invited to join and contribute to the work of the OPEN Consortium.

Acknowledgments

Thanks to all members of the OPEN Consortium; in particular Ian Graham for his many contributions to the development of this chapter.

This is Contribution no 97/3 of the Centre for Object Technology Applications and Research (COTAR).

References

[1] Daniels, J., 1997. Object method: Beyond the notations, *Object Expert*, 2(2), 36–40.

[2] Duffy, D., 1997. *Tailoring the OPEN Lifecycle—Case Studies.* In preparation.

[3] Firesmith, D., Henderson-Sellers, B. and Graham, I., 1997. *OPEN Modeling Language (OML) Reference Manual.* SIGS Books, New York, pp. 271.

[4] Graham, I., Some problems with use cases ... and how to avoid them. In *OOIS'96*, Patel, D., Sun, Y., and Patel, S., eds., 18–27. Springer-Verlag, London, 1997.

[5] Graham, I.M., Bischof, J., and Henderson-Sellers, B., Associations considered a bad thing, *J. Object-Oriented Programming*, 9(9), 41–48, 1997.

[6] Graham, I.M., Henderson-Sellers, B., and other members of the OPEN Consortium, *OPEN's Toolbox of Techniques*. Addison-Wesley, Reading, MA, 1997.
[7] Henderson-Sellers, B. and Firesmith, D., COMMA: Proposed core model, *J. Object-Oriented Programming*, 9(8), 48–53, 1997.
[8] Henderson-Sellers, B., Graham, I., and Younessi, H., *Life Cycle Patterns. The OPEN Process Specification*. Addison-Wesley, UK, 1997.
[9] Henderson-Sellers, B., Graham, I.M., Firesmith, D., Reenskaug, T., Swatman, P., and Winder, R. The OPEN heart, *TOOLS 21*, Mingins, C., Duke, R., and Meyer, B. eds., 187–196. TOOLS/ISE, 1996.
[10] Henderson-Sellers, B. and Graham, I.M., with additional input from Atkinson, C. Bézivin, J., Constantine, L.L., Dué, R., Duke, R., Firesmith, D.G., Low, G., McKim, J., Mehandjiska-Stavrova, D., Meyer, B., Odell, J.J., Page-Jones, M., Reenskaug, T., Selic, B., Simons, A.J.H., Swatman, P., and Winder, R. OPEN: toward method convergence?, *IEEE Comp.*, 29(4), 86–89, 1996.
[11] Reenskaug, T., Wold, P., and Lehne, O.A., *Working with Objects. The OOram Software Engineering Manual*, 366, Manning, Greenwich, CT, 1996.
[12] Sadr, B. and Dousette, P.J., An OO project management strategy, *IEEE Comp.*, 29(9), 33–38, 1996.
[13] Swatman, P. and Fowler, D., *Requirements Engineering for High-Quality Information Systems. The FOOM Approach*, 1998. In preparation.
[14] Younessi, H. and Henderson-Sellers, B., *Object-Oriented Processes*, Submitted for publication, 1997.

Further Information

For more information, the OPEN home page is located at URL:
`http://www.csse.swin.edu.au/cotar/OPEN/OPEN.html`
with mirrors at
USA: `http://www.markv.com/OPEN`
UK: `http://www.scism.sbu.ac.uk/cios/mirrors/OPEN/`
Israel: `http://oop.cs.technion.ac.il/OPEN`

3

The OPEN Process (Tasks, Techniques, and Management)

B. Henderson-Sellers
Swinburne University of Technology

H. Younessi
Swinburne University of Technology

I. Graham
Ian Graham and Associates

3.1 OPEN Lifecycle Model

OPEN (Object-oriented Process, Environment and Notation) is a third generation process-focused OO methodology ([16] and see Chapter 2) which is built around a lifecycle metamodel (Figure 3.1) which is its software engineering process architecture or SEPA. Each instantiation of the SEPA is an individual software engineering process (SEP) tailored from and compatible with the overall architecture of OPEN. A single SEP is therefore highly appropriate to a particular problem type and industry domain. It is composed of objects, using the contract-driven, fully objectified lifecycle of OPEN. Each of these objects in the OPEN SEPs is called an Activity. Activities are connected in a flexible fashion by stating pre-conditions that must be satisfied before an Activity can commence as opposed to specifying the previous Activity which must be completed, as would be the case in a waterfall lifecycle metamodel. We indicate in this figure some of the likely routes between Activity objects, although it is important to note that the main governing constraint on the routes are whether you do or do not meet the pre-conditions of the Activity to which you wish to transition. The choice of routes reflects the opportunistic, event-based process modeling approach embodied in OPEN, which in some senses is more realistically described as a meta-process model. Tailoring this lifecycle process framework to any specific organization and project is one of the Tasks of OPEN.

0-8493-3135-8/99/$0.00+$.50

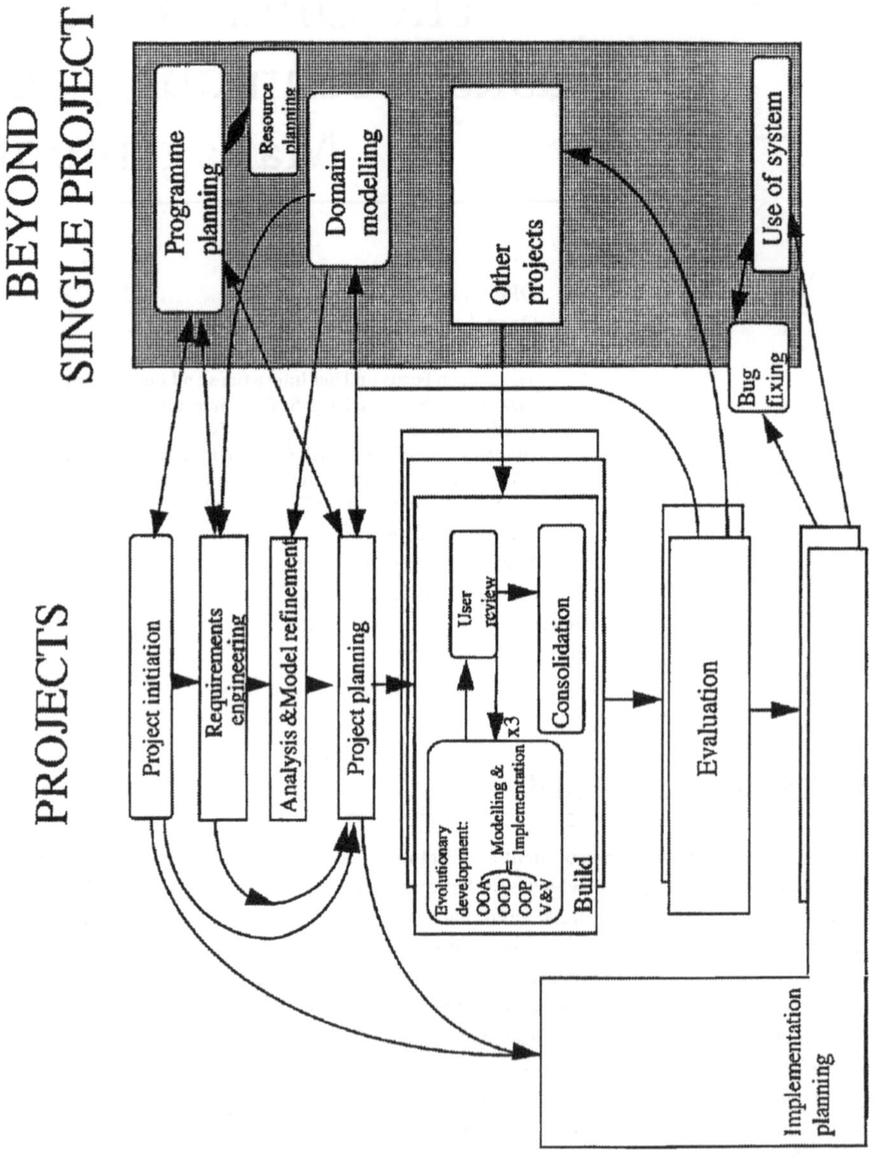

FIGURE 3.1 An OPEN SEP (Adapted from Henderson-Sellers, B., Graham, I.M., et al., *IEEE Comp.*, 29(4), 86–89, 1996. With permission.)

3.2 Open Activities

In visualizing a typical OPEN SEP (Figure 3.1), each Activity is shown as a box, either with rounded corners (an unbounded Activity) or with rectangular corners (Activity tightly bound in time). Because we are modeling these activities as objects, we can associate contracts with each Activity object, (hence, the lifecycle name of "contract-driven"). These are expressed primarily by pre- and post-conditions and by invariants. In other words, there are constraints that have to be met before an Activity can be commenced and final conditions that have to be met (and signed off) before another Activity can be initiated (triggered). Activities include well-specified testing activities as an integral part of the exit conditions and should deliver test results against both task scripts and a technical test plan of the normal kind.

On the left-hand side of Figure 3.1 are Activities which are associated with a single project (discussed here), and on the right-hand side, in the shaded box, are those Activities which transcend a single project and are associated more with strategic planning and implementation concerns, e.g., resources across several projects, reuse strategies, delivery, and maintenance aspects. OPEN includes both projects and organizational software strategies. The relation of the process lifecycle in Figure 3.1 to the business issues is illustrated in Figure 3.2 in which it can be seen that software development can be viewed as a recurring set of enhancements following the first of the iterative cycles (i.e., the growth period).

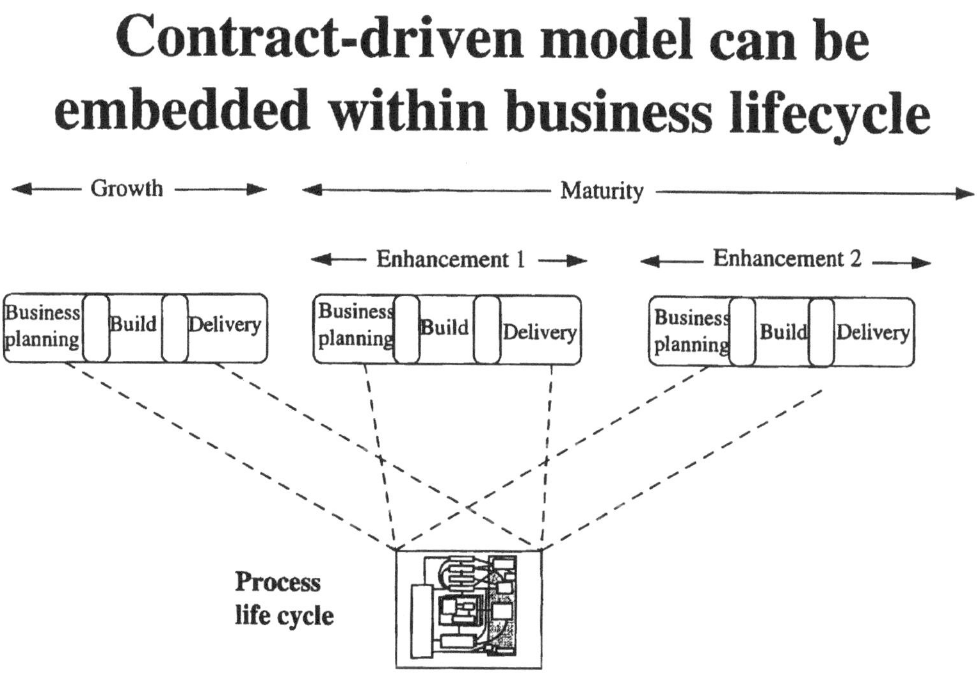

FIGURE 3.2 Contract-driven model can be embedded within business lifecycle.

3.3 Open Tasks

OPEN Tasks can be grouped. Some occur typically earlier in the lifecycle while others group around a particular domain such as distribution or database management. In each of the following subsections we list the Tasks, their Subtasks, and their "star rating" in a table (* means experimental or not well understood, ** means reasonably well validated, and *** means well-tried and tested). We then explore a small number in more detail by selecting the Tasks unique to OPEN or highly relevant to the OPEN foci of process, PM, quality, reuse, etc.

3.3.1 Tasks which Focus on User Interactions and Business Issues

3.3.1.1 Problem Definition and User Requirements (Table 3.1)

TABLE 3.1 Tasks which Focus on User Interactions and Business Issues

(a)	
Identify context	***
Identify source(s) of requirements	***
Identify user requirements	*
Define problem and establish mission and objectives	**
Establish user requirements for distributed systems	*
Establish user DB requirements	***
Analyze user requirements	**
(b)	
Model and re-engineer business process(es)	*
Build context (i.e., business process) model	*
Build task object model	**
Convert task object model to business object model	**
Do customer training	*
Prepare ITT	*
Undertake feasibility study	***
(c)	
Obtain business approval	***
(d)	
Develop business object model	**
Write manuals and prepare other documentation	***
Deliver product to customer	***

The beginning of a project is the identification of a problem within the business domain. It is too easy to see the problem as "automate the accounting system" or "give the customer a faster turnaround." The first statement does nothing to define the problem (which is more likely to be something along the lines of create an efficient means to manage the accounts) and the second leaves us wondering who the customer is: Do we mean ALL customers or just the majority (say 90%), what does faster mean, should it be measured for all customers, should it be relative or percentage change or . . .?

Eliciting user requirements (part of requirements engineering), although undertaken early in the lifecycle initially, should not be seen as a one-off procedure. Indeed, with an iterative lifecycle as commonly advocated in the use of object technology, there are many opportunities to keep the customer/user "in the loop" throughout the whole lifecycle of the development process. This is a significant advantage gained from developing using an object-oriented software development approach (compared to more traditional methods).

Requirements engineering in OPEN derives largely from the techniques advocated in MOSES and in SOMA, although much work remains to be done. Useful SOMA techniques include interviewing techniques, OO RAD workshops, brainstorming, roleplay, user-focused questionnaires, and videotaping. Interviewers should be trained both in interview techniques and in object technology. Interviews should be arranged with the end-users regarding business requirements. However, it is important to note that the user/customer is not interested in the use/non-use of object technology in providing them with their demanded quality product. The final product will be independent of its method of production. Quality and maintainability will be the only manifestations of object technology (OT) which the end-user will ever perceive. Commitment of top executives is particularly needed for the successful adoption of new technologies and OT is no exception. Hence interviews with senior management may also be useful. Information from the interviews and user-workshops is documented using task scripts. Difficult areas may be simulated in a throwaway prototyping environment.

3.3.1.2 Business Process Engineering

Business process engineering has evolved recently often focused upon the notion of business process re-engineering with the well-known acronym of BPR. However, since most business processes have not been engineered in the first place (more a case of slow evolution), the "re-" of BPR may well be inappropriate. Business process engineering, on the other hand, does reflect the need to consider the business from a solid and engineering perspective.

Context modeling is a business process modeling technique in which the business processes and business strategy is analyzed and, it is to be hoped, improved. Hammer and Champy advocate dramatic restructuring and redesign of business processes in order for the desired level of improvement to be achieved. BPR suggests the context for good modeling is no longer the task but the business process. As part of this, technology (such as OT) is quite reasonably seen as an enabler not a prime focus.

Specific example task definitions are listed below.

Task: Model and re-engineer business process(es)—This task focuses on the evaluation and possible restructuring of business process and is usually associated with the OPEN Activities of Program Planning and Resource Planning. Useful supportive Techniques include context modeling, CBA, and visioning.

Business process engineering is all about profit optimization. If the new system is designed using systematic process engineering principles, is customer focused, and targeted toward the real aims of the business, then it has a good chance of contributing to a lowering of costs and to customer satisfaction and, hence, to increased sales. Once these two aims are achieved, higher profits follow.

The essential elements of *doing* business (re-) engineering are as follows:

1. Identify and state the purpose for the business engineering project. This purpose must be *central, real, clear,* and *profit-oriented.* By central, we mean that it must be critical to the business operation. As an example of the importance of this, we can note a major insurance conglomerate that went through a business re-engineering exercise which resulted in a significant and measurable improvement of certain of its processes, yet in six months the company was almost bankrupt. The reason is the areas re-engineered were not central to the business. By real, we mean that the concern must not only be central but also believed by influential stakeholders to be so. Its achievement must be part of the vision of the organization. To be clear, the purpose must be stated in terms of measurable entities, and only then can we be assured of the achievement of our purpose. Profit-oriented means that the purpose when achieved will significantly improve sales, lower costs, or both. To do this, customer orientation is essential.
2. Use the purpose identified to clearly define and model the problem situation. Although related, defining the problem is not the same as stating the purpose for business process engineering. Here, an investigation into possible contributing factors is conducted and individual opportunities for re-design are identified. Sometimes it is useful to create a model of the present situation. This is done for a number of purposes including understanding, communication, and analysis of the way things are. It must be stated that creation of such a model must not be allowed to stifle creativity, ingenuity, or a revolutionary approach to business process design.

This can happen easily if the engineers views become biased toward the existing way of doing things.

In modeling problem situations, object technology, particularly context modeling (subject of a following subtask) will prove beneficial.

3. Commence analysis using the identified opportunities and context models created. Note that this analysis is possible only if a defined and clear model of the process exists. Ishikawa diagrams, root cause, and statistical analysis are among the main tools here. The purpose for this analysis is to identify and separate the common cause from special cause. Once the common and special causes are identified, then a decision may be made whether to go for "gradual process improvement" — that is the removal of special causes — or whether a whole new process is needed. If the latter is the case then we have a design task on our hands: the task of designing a new business process.
4. Design a new business process. This is when principles of process engineering such as maximization of cohesion, minimization of coupling, parallelism, piping, boundary value analysis, flow analysis, and process control may be applied to the design of a new business process. This new process is aimed to be fundamentally different in its internal characteristics (i.e., the structures, transformations, and interactions composing it), yet still fulfill the same purpose as the previous process, only better, and demonstrably so. It is also designed to develop a new process that implements a new purpose, inspired by a new vision.
5. Model the new process. One central issue here is how do we capture and communicate this design. The answer is through creating a model of it. This is where OT (business context modeling, see below) becomes an enabler.
6. Implement the model. Here the business engineer will decide on the performance of various tasks or roles. To do so a number of considerations such as the vision of the organization, best practices, current technology, and funds and human resources available become prominent. Another critical task here is to decide what level of automation and technology to use. In terms of information support technologies, the re-engineered organization is in as enviable a position as there is — through the application of OT — which is a largely seamless path to the design and implementation of software systems.

Subtask: Do user training — It is obvious that competent and effective utilization of a product goes a long way in ensuring the satisfaction of the users needs. Customer training is therefore a most important element of the software lifecycle. Unfortunately, however, this is one step that is often missed or considered to be outside the software process system boundary. This practice must cease if successful product utilization and happy customers are desired.

Customer training has three equally important facets, two have a process and the third a product focus:

1. Educating the customers (stakeholders) in the process and in what is possible — The customer might know best about their requirements as they pertain to the business solution they are seeking. When it comes to how to satisfy these requirements, however — that is how to build the product — "the customer often doesn't know best." Yet they invariably suggest, and often even dictate, a particular course of development action. Faced with this reality the first customer education task of the developer is to sufficiently educate the customer so as to ensure that project goals are attainable given current capabilities.
2. Educating the customer (stakeholders) in how to help you — Despite what most developers may have felt from time to time, customers do want a successful project outcome, and they are willing to help you achieve such success. It is after all to their own benefit. It's just that they often do not know how best to do this. It is again the responsibility of the developer to educate the customer. This educating exercise may take the form of provision of short courses,

workshops, or discussion sessions. It could also be as simple as providing them with relevant literature from appropriately selected magazines, journals, or research paper articles or books. It could be the introduction or provision of a consultant.

3. Educating the customer in how to best use the business solution provided — Among the three, this is the only facet of customer education that is somewhat frequently practiced by developers. This is the kind of customer education we call user training. User training has a very precise aim which is to ensure that those users who interact with the system know how to do their jobs precisely, effectively, and efficiently. As such, training program must be clear and understandable, targeted, precisely defined, and repeatably deliverable. Still there is more. Most training program developers make the mistake of only teaching functionality. Functionality is important, but it has to be taught within context. The customer has to be introduced to what the system will do for him or her, not in terms of the system functions, but in terms of his or her organizational responsibility. As such, training must be provided in terms of *"what the system will do for you,"* and not in terms of *"what the system can do."* To achieve this, it is important to do the following:

    - Identify and put into groups those users whose interaction with the system is identical or very similar (e.g., data entry, claims processing, system administration, etc.).
    - Identify those aspects of the system that impact all users similarly and that all users need to know about. If sufficient material of this nature exists, create an "Introduction to . . ." course that is available to everyone who might come in contact with the system. It is not sufficient to make up an independent course then include these as the starting part of the first round of training courses.
    - Then for each group identified in, develop a training course that describes how their jobs can be done more effectively using the system (their view of the system) and why, that is, what aspects and functionalities in the system ensure this. To contextualize your training, provide examples and exercises from the immediate area of responsibility of the group being trained. Make sure these examples are real, understandable, and of high impact. Also let them get a glimpse of the workings of the product lying just outside their own immediate system view (upstream, downstream, sidestream). This will help them understand how their utilization of the system might impact the effectiveness of their colleagues elsewhere.
    - Pay particular attention to the training of those with systems administration responsibilities. The quality of system administrator training has an inverse relationship with the number of maintenance calls to be received.

In terms of techniques, a wide array of customer education techniques and technologies are available and are included below.

Formal education. University or technical college education — Usually a prerequisite of entry into the organization, this type of training may also be provided as part of a long-term staff development strategy and not for the purpose of acquiring specific skills to use a particular system. This type of education finds importance in relation to the process facets of customer education (points 1 and 2 above). The need for such education is usually determined by the user organizations management and not by the developer, although suggestions from system developers have often been considered. This is particularly the case in customer/developer relationships that span a number of years or relate to large and long projects such as defense contracts.

Short-term traditional training courses — Much more prevalent and a lot more targeted toward teaching system functionality, these training courses may be provided as intense one to five day offerings composed usually of lectures and practice sessions. The alternative is two to three hourly offerings over a period of several weeks. It is customary that during the practice sessions, hands-on interaction with the view of the system being instructed is provided. Written course notes are usually the main source of information in traditional training courses.

In-organization mentor-based training — This approach uses the train the trainer principles. This is when the developer trains one or a handful of individuals in every aspect or various aspects of the system and then the organization uses this individual or individuals to train the rest. It must be mentioned that in-organization mentor-based training must be used with extreme care in that the choice of instructor is critical in the success of this approach.

Interactive multimedia — Under such an approach, multimedia technology is used to enhance or replace the role of the lecturer or provide practice opportunity. CD-ROM, written course notes, and videotaped material may be used as sources of provision of information. CD-ROM or CBA technology may be used for assessment and evaluation purposes. Computer networks may be used to simulate a multiperson work environment and interactivity, which adds to the real world applicability of the training course. The obvious advantage of this approach is that the course may be administered on a self-paced basis or at least reduce reliance on expert instructors. This characteristic makes this technology particularly useful for those situations where the software is installed by numerous customers or the customers are geographically dispersed.

The net — The potential of the Internet, particularly the World Wide Web, as a training provision vehicle must not be ignored. This medium allows virtually all of the technologies mentioned in point 3 above to be made available virtually instantly and worldwide. Considering the fact that your customers are very likely to have access to the Internet, this becomes a real powerful training vehicle.

Other (indirect) training — A lot of organizations forget the importance of what we call indirect training. In this category falls things such as publication of product newsletters, user group meetings, provision of books and other instructional articles, help desks, etc. Finally it is of utmost importance that irrespective of the technology or context of the training course provided, it must be informative, targeted and relevant, precise and error free, and most importantly interesting. Games, roleplays, simulations, and group problem solving have all proven useful.

3.3.1.3 Approval to Proceed

However good a technical case may appear to be, the final arbitration is undertaken on business grounds. Object technology is a supporting technology to help businesses and their information infrastructure to succeed in obtaining the goals that they have set for themselves. Just because a software system can be built, and built very successfully, does not mean that anybody needs it in a business sense either internally to support other business functions or externally as a viable product. Consequently, approval to proceed is necessary before any further investment in resources (time and money) is justifiable.

3.3.1.4 Business Object Modeling

Business object modeling can be best undertaken using task modeling as described in SOMA [11].

Task scripts are primarily used to discover business objects and retained for testing purposes, however, they are objects in their own right, albeit in a different domain. Because of this, task scripts may be organized into composition, classification, and usage structures. The components of a script are arrived at by using hierarchical task analysis and are called *component scripts*. This is where the hierarchical decomposition takes place down to the level of atomic tasks. Atomic tasks permit the identification of the Task Point metric, currently being evaluated empirically by the International OO Metrics Club, and refer directly to objects and their operations. Classifying scripts into more specialized versions gives rise to *subscripts*. When exceptions require the flow of control to be redirected to a script dealing with a special case, the latter is dealt with by a *side-script*. It is important to emphasize that task scripts deal with business processes and not business functions in order to avoid the danger of capturing the requirements in the form of narrow functional specializations which are often present in the existing organization.

One specific task definition is below.

Task: Develop business object model — The focus of this task is modeling the business associated with the Requirements Elicitation, Analysis, and Model Refinement Activities. Useful supportive OPEN techniques are roleplay, use cases, scripting, task scripts, agents, and task decomposition.

The task object model focuses on business processes and is at such a high level that can be best described by tasks, task scripts, task cards, etc. Although tasks can be regarded as objects, they are reified processes and need to be translated (smoothly as it happens) into business objects. Business objects can be considered to be at the same level of abstraction as system objects, but in the business not the technical domain. Business objects thus have a technical flavor while retaining a nomenclature immediately recognizable as belonging to the business domain. Once agreed with management and users, the business object model is the starting point for the technical development and from this can be derived cost estimates and a first cut at the project planning, perhaps using Gantt charts.

3.3.2 Tasks which Focus on Large Scale Architectural Issues

TABLE 3.2 Tasks which Focus on Large Scale Architectural Issues

Undertake architectural design	*
Develop layer design	*
Establish distributed systems strategy	*
Select database/storage strategy	**
Construct frameworks (subtask)	*
Optimize the design	*

Architectural issues (Table 3.2) deal with large scale disposition, style, hardware support, database design strategy, division into subsystems, and extent of distribution [23, 24].

Frameworks offer architectural scope support for reuse. Frameworks thus span reuse concerns and architectural issues. A framework provides a set of predefined subsystems with clearly specified responsibilities which are the skeleton for future applications. Business objects proffer reuse at the Modeling level (ex. OOA/D) where greater benefits can be anticipated compared to design or code reuse. OPEN objects can be represented at all these levels.

A framework is a set of cooperating classes that make up a reusable design for a specific class of software. It also expresses, at the architectural level, a fundamental structural organization for software systems by providing a set of predefined subsystems with specified responsibilities including a set of rules and guidelines for organizing the relationships between them [4]. Typically that means that the CIRT-level elements in the framework will be abstract classes. An application using a framework will then instantiate all the abstract classes in the framework to create the application. It is widely reusable through synthesis and is often available as a packaged product [28, 29]. The framework thus predefines a set of design parameters so that the application developer can concentrate on the specifics of the application itself. Because the framework captures the design decisions common across a whole application domain, it can be considered to be *design reuse* [9, 19].

Using a role modeling approach, a framework has a similar definition as "a reusable component containing a role model describing a general solution, a correlated set of base classes implementing its roles, and possibly descriptions of applicable constraints" [28]. Wills [33] goes further by viewing a framework as, essentially, a role pattern. He defines it to be

- A goal
- A set of typed roles
- A set of (abstract) operations
- A set of trigger rules

This then leads to a more powerful concept than that of subtyping in this context, moving more to the decade-old notion of real pluggable components.

Reenskaug et al. (1996) describe the steps to be taken in creating a framework which is, quite reasonably, similar to those for creating a pattern:

1. Identify consumers and consumer needs
2. Perform a CBA
3. Perform reverse engineering of existing systems to understand all issues and some possible solutions
4. Specify the new framework in general terms
5. Document the framework as a pattern, describing how to use it to solve problems
6. Describe the design and implementation of the framework to aid its usefulness
7. Inform the user community about the existence of this new framework

Investment in frameworks can be substantial such that a quality goal should be dominant [29].

3.3.3 Tasks which Focus on Project Management Issues

TABLE 3.3 Tasks which Focus on Project Management Issues

Develop software development context plans and strategies	**
Tailor the lifecycle process	*
Develop capacity plan	***
Develop security plan	***
Establish change management strategy	***
Develop contingency plan	***
Establish data take-on strategy	*
Integrate with existing, non-OO systems	**
Undertake feasibility study	***
Develop and implement resource allocation plans	**
Choose project team	***
Identify project roles and responsibilities	***
Choose toolset	**
Choose hardware	***
Specify quality goals	*
Specify individual goals	*
Decompose programs into project	*
Use dependencies in the BOM to generate first cut project plan (Gantt chart)	**
Develop timebox plan	**
Develop iteration plan	**
Set up metrics collection program	**
Manage subsystems	***
Develop education and training plan	**

Project management focuses (Table 3.3) on planning, control, and measurement of the allocations of time, money, people, scope, tools and techniques, and quality (see also [14]). The project schedule identifies temporal constraints, possibly temporal orderings (particularly of deliverables), units of work (tasks), and milestones by which to measure progress. A good project manager realizes the knowns and the unknowns of the project environment, what needs to be done to eliminate the uncertainties and unknowns, what needs to be done to ensure milestones are technically and politically feasible, and is able to re-plan as the project unfolds and needs midcourse correction. A winning object-oriented project management strategy delivers results incrementally, building management trust and retaining customer involvement, if possible every 3 months. Time boxes can be usefully deployed in this context.

Large scale software planning must depend upon business decision making. In this task, OPEN focuses on those organizational decisions which define the organizational culture and the software development paradigm. Planning at this level must also take into account the existing culture.

Constantine and Lockwood (1994) describes four stereotypical organizational cultures: closed, random, open, and synchronous. They argue that unless such organizational self-assessment is undertaken, project management — and also change management (from traditional to OO) — will likely be unsuccessful.

Specific task definitions are below.

Task: Develop software development context plans and strategies — In this task, organizational standards and strategies form the focus, associated with the Resource Planning Activity. Useful Techniques are Process modeling, wrappers, database authorization, password protection, and physical security.

Large scale software planning must depend upon business decision making. In this task, OPEN focuses on those organizational (as opposed to project) level decisions which define the organizational culture and the software development paradigm. Planning at this level must also take into account the existing culture [6].

Subtask: Establish change management strategy — Transitioning to OT is not just a simple matter of replacing a structured method and set of tools by an object-oriented one. OO is a way of thinking, a mindset, and not merely the adoption of a language (especially if that language is C++). Some of the organization issues which must be addressed seriously by those transitioning to OT are

- Creating the "new culture" — This includes a focus on quality, reuse, high modularity in both design and coding, more emphasis on requirements engineering and analysis, a cleaner and more frequent dialog between developer and user.
- Evaluating what role reuse has to play in the organization. Initially, focus should *not* be on reuse as a rationale for adopting OT. However, it should be part of the new culture insofar as it should become second nature and should certainly not be an "add-on."
- How to assess and award productivity bonuses — In a software development environment where there is reuse of analysis, design, and code, the best developers are those who *don't* write code. Traditional productivity metrics emphasize personal productivity in terms of output of lines of code per unit time. In good OO projects, that can be a negative value. One manager at the OOPSLA 94 metrics workshop was puzzled about how he reported to his management that the size of his software as it neared completion was shrinking yet proposing that the members of his team were being highly productive and deserved recognition.
- Whether to move to OT wholesale or incrementally and in the selected scenario what is, or should be, the role of retraining — A total commitment is dangerous in the sense of any failure is a company-wide failure; on the other hand, an incremental move brings with it the danger that the move will not be considered as serious by either developers or managers. Indeed, it is more likely that developers will not put in any effort to learn the new paradigm and will continue to code in a non-OO framework despite using an OO language, such as C++ or Java, in which to do it. It is better to invest heavily in retraining at *all* levels and commit to the move. Having done so, then it becomes feasible to move the organization part by part or project by project, as long as the overall lapsed time is not overly long. This way, small glitches can be isolated and treated without disrupting the whole of the organization's day to day business.

Change management is so important and wide in its remit that whole books have been written about the possible pitfalls that may degrade the experience [32].

Subtask: Tailor the lifecycle process — It is clear that no one methodology can satisfy all projects and if it could, then it would be so unwieldy when applied to small projects as to be unusable. OPEN offers the middle ground — a methodology that contains many options from which to choose so that when that choice has been made the resulting method, tailored to your organization and your project, is readily learnable and becomes your organizational standard, yet is completely compatible with the published (and larger, more comprehensive) OPEN methodology, as described in this handbook.

The OPEN lifecycle model, the contract model, offers an overall number of Activities and some likely connection paths. In this Task, you choose which of those paths are appropriate or which Tasks should be used to support those Activities. Which techniques should be used can be left as less prescriptive because the way you accomplish the result (the outcome of the Task) has less impact on project management, as long as the choice is one from several, all being equally efficient and effective techniques, the choice being merely that of personal taste, past experience, etc. In this way, the methodology description can be likened to a salad bar [28] where the chef prepares a number of dishes for your delectation, but it is up to you the customer (read developer) to choose what delights your palate and avoid those items you find unpalatable. (Similar food service outlet analogs are used by Goldberg and Rubin, 1995.) This type of self-selected or tailored methodology approach is advocated by MOSES and OOram, particularly.

Task: Develop and implement resource allocation plan — The focus of this task is Project management (Plan, estimate, control). Relevant OPEN Activities are Project Planning and Resource Planning and supportive OPEN Techniques are PERT charts, priority setting, project planning, risk analysis, time box planning, traceability, cost estimation, Gantt charts, and workflow analysis.

Project management focuses on planning for the allocations of time, money, people, scope, tools and techniques, and quality. In addition, control and measurement, following the project initiation, is part of this overall Task. Here, each of these areas is investigated (see following Subtasks) in order to provide an overarching project management strategic plan and then instantiate it into a tactical project-level resource allocation plan (see also [14]).

The project schedule identifies temporal constraints, possibly temporal orderings (particularly of deliverables), units of work (tasks), and milestones by which to measure progress.

A good project manager realizes what the knowns and unknowns of the project environment are, what needs to be done to eliminate the uncertainties and unknowns, what needs to be done to ensure milestones are technically and politically feasible, and is able to replan as the project unfolds and needs correction midcourse [10]. A winning object-oriented project management strategy delivers results incrementally, building management trust and retaining customer involvement, if possible on a 3 to 6 month time basis. Time boxes can also be usefully deployed here.

Subtask: Choose project team — Selecting both a team structure and members of that team can be critical to the success of the project. A team consists of many individuals, each playing one or more roles. McGibbon (1995) suggests ideally the team should have 7 to 15 members. Project success will be determined both by leadership and by interteam member communication skills.

Team structure can vary from hierarchical (layered) to fully cooperative (flat). Teams may also have different foci from application production to reuse. Roles within the team may also vary, depending upon both organizational culture, type of project, and available resources. All of the participants should be chosen carefully in order to optimize the possibility of success. Various behavioral characteristics (mover, collector, informer, clarifier, philosopher, evaluator, guide, communicator, encourager, mediator, and fixer, McGibbon, 1995) should be noted and roles assigned to take best advantage of contrasting skills. For initial projects, the best team members should be selected from the best and most highly motivated people available. They should be given every opportunity to succeed with access to just-in-time training, time to investigate and understand the new paradigm, protection from unrelated interruptions, and sufficient and timely resources.

Subtask: Manage subsystems — Subsystems (a.k.a. clusters in COMN and BON) need a management plan. The project manager is responsible for identification of the most appropriate subsystems — an architecture decision. Subsystems are needed particularly in large systems as a tool by which to manage technical complexity. It is also necessary to coordinate the development of subsystems. Often, one team is responsible for each subsystem; however, someone needs to be responsible for ensuring compatibility between subsystems. This could be a linchpin person [30] or a member of the Cross-Project Team.

The OPEN contract lifecycle model makes the assumption that subsystems can be developed in parallel. Concurrent development shortens time to market drastically but creates new problems in terms of coordinating multiple, concurrent activities. When the development is distributed too, the complexity may be double that of centralized sequential developments. However, this is the ultimate model for downsizing the development organization and its processes.

To make everything work and maintain consistent levels of quality, everyone involved must speak the same development language and that language must be sufficiently expressive or semantically rich. OPEN is offered as the basis of just such a lingua Franca.

Subtask: Set up metrics collection program — Management of any production process is simplified if some measures of progress toward a quality product are collected and analyzed. In manufacturing, tolerance limits are prescribed and individual components assessed against these "standards." Excessive product rejections suggest that the process producing them is at fault. Costs are tracked during the process and compared with estimates made initially.

It is necessary to know with what precision software development data are obtainable. Clear goals and objectives of the metrics program need to be elucidated early on in the planning process. Are the data to be used to assess, to predict, or to control [10]? Careful planning is required before any collection commences. Those involved and those who feel they are being measured need to be intimately involved with both collection and analysis; in other words, the aims of the metrics collection program need to be widely advertised throughout the organization.

Software development shares with manufacturing industry the need to measure costs, productivity, and quality. The main difference lies in the "one-off" nature of software. Nevertheless, quality can be evaluated against prespecified criteria, progress toward the goal evaluated on a temporal basis, and final costs compared with estimated costs (the differences often called variances by accountants). Specific goals could include the ability: (1) to do cost-estimation from the requirements analysis; (2) to estimate maintenance costs from the code; (3) to evaluate the reusability of designs, frameworks, and code; and (4) to allocate resources most wisely. Such aims require collection of data on the process, effort expended (often measured in time resources × people resources), and objective measures of the code itself.

In introducing a measurement program, an initial question is often "What is to be measured?" A more appropriate question is "What is the goal which we want to attain?" For example, is the goal: to increase programmer productivity; to decrease the number of defects reported per unit of time*; to improve the efficiency of the overall development process; or to attain ISO 9000 accreditation. Until that goal is defined, recommendations on the optimum measurement program cannot be made. This is the Goal–Question–Metric (GQM) paradigm [1] in action.

An OO metrics program can certainly accomplish a number of goals like greater understanding leading to identification of a repeatable, and hence, manageable process for software development. Greater quantification of the process also enhances the organizational process maturity level. At a more technical level, metrics can provide information on which to base standards for assessing maintainability, to evolve best

*Of course this can be easily abused by just not *reporting* any defects.

practice for responding to user change requests and, in the future, to determine "how object-oriented" a particular design or program is [13]. The whole use of metrics is compatible with moving software development toward scientific understanding and engineering practice, i.e., to make software engineering a more mature discipline. Finally, for the people concerned, their involvement in improving the process and the product should not only lead to higher quality systems but also to a sense of ownership and pride.

Still, instigating a metrics program does not bring immediate "magical" answers to all software development. It cannot and should not be used to assess the performance of the developers themselves, nor can it create nonexistent skills in the developers (although it can enhance their awareness of the extent of their skills). A metrics program will not provide a single number for complexity or for quality [7]. Neither will it, overnight and by itself, create a one-off version of a rigid development process which can thereafter be mechanistically (slavishly) followed. Productivity gains are likely but they are a consequence of other factors not a necessary result per se. Finally, almost all managers want a cost-estimation tool. Instigating a metrics program will lead to the ability to create one for your organization, but it cannot provide a "magic formula" applicable in all situations.

A metrics program provides knowledge and understanding, it does not provide quick fixes.

Subtask: Specify individual goals — Management is about getting the best out of people, i.e., out of the members of your team. While software engineering professionals typically get pleasure out of working hard and working well, they also seek some recognition of their skills. Blanchard and Johnson (1983) suggest managers need to clearly set out what is expected of an individual. One technique they suggest is that of SMART goal setting. SMART is an acronym for

Specific: Is it clearly understandable?

Measurable: What would a good (and a bad) job look like?

Attainable: Is it realistic for the individual?

Relevant: Will it make any impact?

Trackable: How will anyone know?

Setting SMART goals requires three stages [21]:

1. Identifying the objective and areas of responsibility
2. Specification of priorities
3. Detailing of at least three ways in which success can be measured.

Another approach to individual goal setting is provided in the Personal Software Process (PSP) of Humphrey (1995). PSP uses a series of interrelated exercises grouped into four levels (PSP0 through to PSP3). These exercises are designed to help the software engineer arrive at a defined and measured PSP. This is done through collecting statistics on a number of metrics relating to planning and management of these personal (individually performed and completed) software projects. This setup develops a framework for a well-defined and statistically managed software engineering approach that is defined, disciplined, measured, and predictable. Once the personal process reaches such level of definition, it will significantly improve the way the software engineer plans, controls, and improves his or her work in the future. The PSP is therefore based on the principles of Plan, Do, Measure, Improve and of statistical quality control.

Given such a basis, the defined and measured personal process of a software engineer, created through the application of PSP, will allow a degree of predictability in terms of how hard and how well the individual works or can work. This can be an excellent guideline for specifying individual goals that are meaningful, attainable, and their achievement measurable.

3.3.4 Tasks which Focus on Quality

TABLE 3.4 Tasks which Focus on Quality Issues

Test	*
Perform class testing	*
Perform cluster testing	*
Perform regression testing	*
Perform acceptance testing	*
Write manuals and prepare other documentation	***
Evaluate quality	**
Analyze metrics data	***
Evaluate usability	*
Review documentation	***
Maintain trace between requirements and design	*
Undertake in-process review	***
Undertake post-implementation review	***

Quality is much more than end-phase testing (Table 3.4). Quality needs to be built in *throughout* the development process, not as a one-off quality assessment test of the final product. Thus, this Task spans the whole lifecycle. Short cycle times have been advocated in a "constant quality management" framework. Metrics provide the tool to accomplish this quality goal.

Testing is part of the post-condition on each Activity in the OPEN process. The basis for testing is closely linked to the task scripts and use cases of the system. Testing is performed at various levels of granularity. The basic unit of OO being the class, much of the "unit testing" is done at that level. As well as class testing, cluster testing is important in OPEN. Regression testing is also advocated and finally, when the product is delivered to the customer, some form of acceptance testing is necessary.

It is also important, in any process, to review the results and compare them to the plan. In this way, and only in this way, can developers and managers learn what works, derive quantitative data about times and costs, and optimize future project plans. Review should, however, not simply be something that is done at the end of the lifecycle (as in a waterfall). Inevitably schedules get squeezed and the review process is dropped. Quality is not something that can be *inspected* in at the end of the lifecycle but has to be built in throughout. One way of facilitating this and encouraging a quality mindset in developers and management is to have repeated reviews throughout the lifecycle (in-process), at the end of the lifecycle, and after the product has been put into service with the customer.

3.3.5 Tasks which Focus on Database Issues

TABLE 3.5 Tasks which Focus on Database Issues

Identify user database requirements (subtask)	***
Select database/storage strategy (subtask)	**
Identify persistent classes (subtask)	**
Map logical database schema	**
Design and implement physical database	***
Distribution/replication design	**
Operational and performance design	***
Performance evaluation	**

Current OOAD methodologies do not, in general, include complete consideration of database issues (Table 3.5). A proposal has recently been made for a generic or metamethodology which extends OOAD concerns into the database arena. Those suggestions provide very general guidelines which were implemented in terms of MOSES [5]. These new findings have now been incorporated into the Tasks and Techniques of OPEN.

Quantitative information on the volume of the objects stored, the ways in which the objects are accessed, the frequency of the accesses, etc., is required from the users when designing a database for an object-oriented system for the same reasons as when designing a traditional system, since one must ensure that the final physical design of the database maximizes all the criteria of the database system being developed, that is, time and storage requirements as well as the functional requirements. Also, performance issues are often important.

Selection of database (i.e., storage strategy) requires the selection of both DBMS style (OB or RDB) and the actual product selection. The first of these can be performed at any point up until the first iteration in which the CIRT model is mapped on to the logical database schema in the Task "Map Logical Database Schema." The second Technique is appropriate at any point until the first iteration of the Task "Design and Implement Physical Database."

3.3.6 Tasks which Focus on Distributed Computing Issues

TABLE 3.6 Tasks which Focus on Distribution Issues

Identify user requirements for DCS (subtask)	*
Establish distributed systems strategy (subtask)	*
Develop security plan (subtask)	***

While it is recognized that a DCS seems to be almost a standard way of building systems in the mid-1990s, better advice would be only to build a distributed system *if it is the only option.* Many industry leaders in OT strongly advise that a distributed environment should only be entered after due consideration. Simply taking a large database and splitting it across several servers does nothing practically to alleviate the size problems of such a data store and, indeed, adds problems which occur as a result of running the application over a network.

Distributed systems development (Table 3.6) may include development work in different cities or even countries. In this case, the development team may need to be split to allow for geographical distribution of its members. Leadership, planning, standards, skills, and support need to be planned in cognizance of this split. DCS issues, hardware, and business requirements [20, 25] are likely to place constraints on the alternative configurations and system designs that may be considered in the feasibility study. Furthermore, hardware, DCS, impact on users, and team planning issues will also have direct impacts on the technical, economic, and operational feasibility of the distributed system alternatives. When considering economic feasibility, the future value of experience with distributed system design and the cost of the extra risk should both be considered.

3.3.7 Tasks which Focus on Modeling Issues

A core task in an object-oriented systems development is the identification of likely or candidate CIRTs (classes, instances, roles, and types) derived from a responsibility-driven viewpoint [34] supplemented by the use of software contracts [22]. Early in the process of deriving a model, the task (Table 3.7) will essentially be one of discovery, whereas later in the process it will be more one of refinement and invention.

TABLE 3.7 Tasks which Focus on Modeling/Building the System

Analyze user requirements	**
Identify CIRTs	**
Determine initial class list	**
Identify persistent classes	**
Identify roles	*
Refine class list	**
Construct the object model	***
Design user interface	*
Map roles on to classes	*
Optimize the design	*
Undertake usability design	*
Code	***
Write manuals and other documentation	***

Refinement will never result in a "perfect" model but will, after a few iterations, lead to a stable model. Newly discovered CIRTs should be documented in the CIRT model (OPEN's semantic nets, primarily) and in the class specification and will be refined as the development proceeds.

Building the object model is the prime *technical* focus of any OO methodology. Based on the stated requirements, an "object model" is built which reflects these requirements and the software solution in increasing detail. In that sense, OPEN is an elaborational methodology. The focus of the activity is adding more and more detail, managing that detail by using abstraction techniques supplied in OPEN. The activity spans the traditional stages of analysis and logical design.

Building the object model thus relies on object modeling techniques. There are a wide variety of these, many of which are well known. These techniques assist in accomplishing Tasks which are then documented by a selected notation set. For OPEN, we recommend the Common Object Modeling Notation, or COMN [8], which is 100% compatible with the concepts and philosophy of OPEN, although the UML notation [26] can also be supported within the OPEN framework.

The object model to be built is best represented by a set of model diagrams which each emphasize different attributes of the whole system. The first model is that of the static architecture, previously known as a class diagram. In OPEN, we classify these as semantic nets of which there are six types. One of these is a class diagram but not so named because it also contains objects, types, and clusters. Semantic nets are used to describe different views and different abstraction levels. Scenario class diagrams (for task scripts and use cases) and two types of interaction diagram (the collaboration diagram and the sequence or fence diagram) are also very useful. Both are relatively standard in the industry, as are STDs.

User interface design is seldom addressed in OO methodologies. SOMA [11] has some guidelines on this topic as does the IBM Visual Modeling Technique method [31] and the GUIDE method [27]. Because this is a crucial component of building an effective system, the full OPEN guidelines also include this critical element.

It is also crucial that the interface designer, like the software engineer, does not stop at merely analyzing and automating existing practices. Computers can, and should, change the tasks they were designed to assist with and this is often their largest contribution. Word processing, for example, has largely changed the nature of document preparation work in offices and groupware and hypermedia systems and the global internet are continuing the trend.

It is only just recognized how often roles occur in an object model. They represent dynamic classification, which is when an object temporarily assumes an additional type. Consider a typical example in an introductory OO text. "Consider an employee who is (of course) a person." Thus, they say, this is a simple example of inheritance since an employee is a type of person and thus CIRT Employee inherits from Person. Wrong.

The Person is only taking on a role temporarily and may indeed take on more than one role contemporaneously. Thus an individual is a Person (permanently), a teacher (Tuesday nights), a researcher (Fridays), an administrator (Wednesday), and an international speaker (occasional). In fact, in the last role we might also be a Teacher and a Traveller and probably a Foreigner (a.k.a. Alien).

How significant roles are in the object paradigm, in contrast to classes and objects and, more recently in OOAD, types, is still open to question. OPEN and OOram [28] support role identification much more strongly than in other approaches (UML does not support them at all). Roles as used in OOram and OPEN are not really supported in OOPLs. Thus, at present, they must be mapped to classes or objects in the language of choice, i.e., of implementation concern.

3.3.8 Tasks which Focus on Reuse Issues

TABLE 3.8 Tasks which Focus on Reuse Issues

Optimize reuse ("with reuse")	**
Create and/or identify reusable components ("for reuse")	*
Construct frameworks	*
Optimize for reuse	*
Manage library of reusable components	**

As an example, let us consider the objective of the Task (Table 3.8): Optimize reuse, which is to maximize the reuse of library components that already exist. OO development emphasizes the importance of reuse in the development process and, as we have already discussed, the successful outcome of this methodology is a software base of reusable components. The fountain model [15] graphically represents this.

Effective reuse involves not only using classes from a library but adding new classes to the library for reuse in later projects. The objective of this task is to improve the quality of the project classes so they can be used outside of the project, and consequently, to maximize the reusability of classes. This task can initially represent a significant investment of time and effort on top of the normal system development process. This task may begin at the end of the basic system development where further work is necessary to guarantee reusability for future projects, although if the goal of reusability is borne in mind throughout the process the task actually should be actioned throughout the whole development lifecycle. This is unlikely in the first few OO projects, but as more OT skills are acquired generalization will become integrated into the overall development process.

The additional work during generalization may be simply a "honing" or refinement of existing classes or it may require the introduction of additional classes (possibly of a deferred or abstract nature *viz.* ones which cannot be instantiated) at intermediate levels in the inheritance hierarchy. Furthermore, overly complex classes may require splitting into a larger number of smaller classes. The underlying guideline here is to consider whether a class developed in the current project really represents a single concept of the domain (an object type) or whether it encompasses two (or more) concepts. This refinement work is needed to ensure classes are really reusable and augments any project-specific refinement of the inheritance hierarchy. Such refinements may, of course, lead to iteration and a reconsideration of the class model describing the system.

3.4 Open Techniques

Tasks are accomplished by Techniques. Techniques are thus ways of doing things. They include the ways that have been tried and tested over the last decade, but they also may include new techniques that are more experimental. Some indication on the level of maturity of the individual technique is thus given as part of its full specification.

One or more techniques is used to accomplish a Task. The developer chooses the appropriate Task(s) from those described in OPEN or from their own experience, sometimes selecting between two competing alternatives. Thus, for example, in order to find objects, the choice may be between, say, using use cases, using noun analysis, identifying concepts and their responsibilities, using CRC cards, etc. In reality, many tasks are best accomplished by a mixture of techniques rather than just one. There are too many cases of the use of a single technique being taken to an extreme. For example, at one conference, a story of noun analysis being used for a 300-page requirements specification rightly created disbelief in the audience at such a gross misapplication of the technique.

In this way, Techniques are intrinsically orthogonal to the notion of Tasks. They cannot readily be grouped in any unique way. They are akin to the tools of the tradesperson — a carpenter's toolbox contains many tools, some of which have superficial resemblances but may have operational affinity to tools of different outward appearance. A full description of the OPEN toolbox of Techniques is a book in itself [12].

3.5 Summary and Conclusions

The major focus of OPEN is its support for the full lifecycle in terms of the (SEP) which is described here in terms of a set of intercommunicating objectified Activities. The Activities are at a coarse granularity. Tasks to support these Activities are finer grained and are the basic unit of work within OPEN and, hence, the focus of the project management. Tasks state what is to be done and Techniques describe *how* these tasks are to be accomplished. In this chapter, we have illustrated these with a few selected examples from the OPEN set of Tasks and Techniques, which itself is described in full length texts by members of the OPEN Consortium who have developed and maintain the OPEN methodological framework.

Acknowledgments

Thanks to all members of the OPEN Consortium for their varied contributions. This is Contribution number 97/18 of the Centre for Object Technology Applications and Research (COTAR).

References

[1] Basili, V.R. and Rombach, H.D., The TAME project: Towards improvement-orientated software environments, *IEEE Trans. Soft. Eng.*, 14(6), 758–773, 1988.

[2] Blanchard, K. and Johnson, S., *The One Minute Manager.* Willow Books, NY, 1983.

[3] Booch, G., *Object Oriented Design with Applications,* pp. 580, Benjamin/Cummings, Menlo Park, CA, 1991.

[4] Buschmann, F., Pattern-oriented software architecture, *Conf. Procs. Object Expo Europe,* 25–29, September, London, England, SIGS Conferences, Ltd., 57–66, 1995.

[5] Case, T., Henderson-Sellers, B., and Low, G.C., Extending the MOSES object-oriented analysis and design methodology to include database applications, *J. Object-Oriented Programming,* 8(7), 28–34, 56, 1995.

[6] Constantine, L.L. and Lockwood, L.A.D., Fitting practices to the people, *Amer. Programmer,* 7(12), 21–27, 1994.

[7] Fenton, N.E., Software measurement: A necessary scientific basis, *IEEE Trans. Soft. Eng.*, 20, 199–206, 1994.

[8] Firesmith, D., Henderson-Sellers, B., and Graham, I., *OPEN Modeling Language (OML) Reference Manual,* pp. 271, SIGS Books, NY, 1997.

[9] Gamma, E., Helm, R., Johnson R., and Vlissides, J., *Design Patterns: Elements of Reusable Object-Oriented Design,* pp. 395, Addison-Wesley, Reading, MA, 1995.

[10] Goldberg, A. and Rubin, K.S., *Succeeding with Objects. Decision Frameworks for Project Management,* pp. 542, Addison-Wesley, Reading, MA, 1995.

[11] Graham, I.M., *Migrating to Object Technology,* Addison–Wesley, Wokingham, U.K., 1995.

[12] Graham, I.M., Henderson-Sellers, B., and other members of the OPEN Consortium., *OPEN's Toolbox of Techniques.* Addison-Wesley, Reading, MA, 1997.

[13] Henderson-Sellers, B., *Object-Oriented Metrics: Measures of Complexity.* Prentice-Hall, Englewood Cliffs, NJ, 1996.

[14] Henderson-Sellers, B. and Dué, R.T., OPEN project management, *Object Expert,* 2(2), 30–35, 1997.

[15] Henderson-Sellers, B. and Edwards, J.M., The object-oriented systems life cycle, *Comms. ACM,* 33(9), 142–159, 1990.

[16] Henderson-Sellers, B., Graham, I., and Younessi, H., *The OPEN Process Specification,* Addison-Wesley, Wokingham, U.K., 1997.

[17] Henderson-Sellers, B., and Graham, I.M., with additional input from Atkinson, C., Bézivin, J., Constantine, L.L., Dué, R., Duke, R., Firesmith, D.G., Low, G., McKim, J., Mehandjiska-Stavrova, D., Meyer, B., Odell, J.J., Page-Jones, M., Reenskaug, T., Selic, B., Simons, A.J.H., Swatman, P., and Winder, R., OPEN: Toward method convergence?, *IEEE Comp.*, 29(4), 86–89, 1996.

[18] Humphrey, W.S., *A Discipline for Software Engineering,* pp. 789, Addison-Wesley, Reading, MA, 1995.

[19] Johnson, R.E. and Foote, B., Designing reusable classes, *J. Object-Oriented Programming,* 1(2), 22–35, 1988.

[20] Low, G., Rasmussen, G., and Henderson-Sellers, B., Incorporation of distributed computing concerns into object-oriented methodologies, *J. Object-Oriented Programming,* 9(3), 12–20, 1996.

[21] McGibbon, B., *Managing Your Move to Object Technology. Guidelines and Strategies for a Smooth Transition,* pp. 268, SIGS Books, NY, 1995.

[22] Meyer, B., *Object-Oriented Software Construction,* pp. 534, Prentice-Hall, Hemel Hempstead, U.K., 1988.

[23] Mowbray, T.J., Essentials of object-oriented architecture, *Object Mag.* 5(5), 28–32, 1995a.

[24] Mowbray, T.J., What OO architecture benefits are you missing? *Object Mag.*, 5(7), 24–28, 85, 1995b.

[25] Rasmussen, G., Henderson-Sellers, B., and Low, G., Extending the MOSES methodology to distributed systems, *J. Object-Oriented Programming,* 9(4), 39–46, 100, 1996.

[26] Rational., *Unified Modeling Language. Notation Guide. 1997. Version 1.0. 13 January 1997,* Available from `http://www.rational.com`.

[27] Redmond-Pyle, D. and Moore, A., *Graphical User Interface Design and Evaluation (GUIDE): A Practical Process.* Prentice-Hall, Englewood Cliffs, NJ, 1995.

[28] Reenskaug, T., Wold, P., and Lehne, O.A., *Working with Objects. The OOram Software Engineering Manual,* pp. 366, Manning, Greenwich, CT, 1996.

[29] Sparks, S., Benner, K., and Faris, C., Managing object-oriented framework reuse, *IEEE Comp.*, 29(9), 52–61, 1996.

[30] Thomsett, R., Management implications of object-oriented development, *ACS Newslet.*, October: 5–7, 10–12, 1990.

[31] Tkach, D. and Puttick, R., *Object Technology in Application Development.* Benjamin/Cummings, pp. 212, Redwood City, CA, 1994.

[32] Webster, B.F., *Pitfalls of Object-Oriented Development,* pp. 256, M&T Books, NY, 1995.

[33] Wills, A., Frameworks and component-based development. In *OOIS'96*, Patel, D., Sun, Y., and Patel, S., eds., pp. 413–430. Springer-Verlag, London, 1997.
[34] Wirfs-Brock, R.J., Wilkerson, B. and Wiener, L., *Designing Object-Oriented Software*, pp. 341, Prentice-Hall, NY, 1990.

Further Information

For more information, the OPEN home page is located at URL:
`http://www.csse.swin.edu.au/cotar/OPEN/OPEN.html`
with mirrors at
USA: `http://www.markv.com/OPEN`
UK: `http://www.scism.sbu.ac.uk/cios/mirrors/OPEN/`
Israel: `http://oop.cs.technion.ac.il/OPEN`

4

Object-Oriented Systems Modeling — Analysis

Robert B. Jackson
Brigham Young University

David W. Embley
Brigham Young University

Stephen W. Liddle
Brigham Young University

Scott N. Woodfield
Brigham Young University

4.1 Overview

This chapter and the next describe Object-oriented Systems Modeling (OSM) — OSM analysis in this chapter and OSM development in the next. Readers who are unfamiliar with OSM should read both chapters. Readers who understand the analysis part of OSM (sometimes referred to as OSA in prior publications; Embley, Kurtz, and Woodfield, 1993) can skip this chapter and learn about the OSM approach to specification, design, and implementation in the development chapter.

In this chapter on OSM analysis we present fundamental OSM model definitions. OSM is rich and expressive with constructs that support the modeling of sophisticated "real-world" entities and their individual and collective behavior. This chapter also presents details about the model-driven approach we advocate for doing analysis, as well as the formal underpinnings of OSM.

0-8493-3135-8/99/$0.00+$.50

4.1.1 Systems Analysis

The objectives of systems analysis are understanding and documenting that understanding. Systems analysis is not solution oriented, rather it is discovery oriented. Because systems analysis is so frequently performed by technical, solution-oriented people, it is not uncommon, especially with small systems, for analysis simply to become a minor subactivity in the design and programming of a solution. In actuality, analysis requires a different mind set. It requires a focused study of the real world at the conceptual level. The real world can be a system that is either extant or proposed or either manual or automated. True analysis, especially in the object-oriented paradigm, entails understanding objects and their behavior without consideration of solution artifacts. As you read this chapter, notice the emphasis on the lifecycle of objects such as *Purchase Order* or *Computer Item* — their lifecycles are expressed in terms of what they do in the real world, not how they "pass messages" or "invoke methods" (which are implementation constructs, not real-world conceptual constructs).

The other objective of analysis is documentation. We document our understanding by building model instances. A "model instance" is defined as a particular configuration of modeling constructs provided by a model, OSM in this chapter. The objective of a model instance for analysis is to capture and document the knowledge obtained during analysis. You will find in this chapter and the next that we provide very little direction on the "method" of doing analysis or development. Our approach to systems analysis is "model driven" rather than "control driven." By this we mean that we are not tied to a particular method or set of controls. Every project is unique. Thus, in one situation "use cases" may be most effective to understand real-world processes, in another a "spiral" approach may be required, etc. In a model-driven approach the fundamental issue is to perform the requisite activities that ensure the model is complete, comprehensive, and accurate. A model-driven approach thus permits tremendous flexibility, is applicable to many different problem domains, and is scalable from small to large systems. Because our approach is model-driven, this chapter consists mainly of descriptions of OSM's modeling constructs. We proceed by first giving a brief overview of OSM followed by a detailed consideration of OSM's modeling constructs.

4.2 Introduction to Object-Oriented Systems Analysis (OSA)

OSA denotes the analysis portion of the OSM model. OSA is a complete, comprehensive object-oriented model consisting of both structural and behavioral components. Because its primary objective is analysis, it has no design or implementation components. As we present OSA, you will see that even though it is expressive for real-world concepts, it does not include constructs for programming or design concepts such as "modules," "functions," "messages," or other computer software constructs (Embley, Jackson, and Woodfield, 1995). This "purity" extends even to the point that OSA includes neither attributes nor types (Liddle, Embley, and Woodfield, 1994). OSM extends OSA to include these additional constructs as appropriate for design and implementation, but we only use OSA constructs during analysis.

OSA has three submodels. Structural information is described in an OSA submodel called the Object-Relationship Model (ORM), which includes two primary types of components: object sets and relationship sets. ORM components also include aggregations, which describe complex objects and their subparts, and generalization/specializations, which describe superset/subset relationships. Several types of constraints capture rules about relationship-set and object-set membership. High-level object sets and high-level relationship sets provide additional levels of abstraction. High-level constructs allow analysts to construct views to enhance understanding or eliminate clutter.

Behavioral information is captured in two submodels, the Object Behavior Model (OBM) and the Object Interaction Model (OIM). The OBM for a model instance consists of a set of state-transition graphs called state nets. Each object set has a state net that describes the possible states and transitions of all objects within the object set. Thus a state net represents the real-world behavior of an object. In addition to "doing things" and "being in states," objects communicate with other objects. The interactions in the OIM capture information about the interactions among objects. Similar in purpose to high-level object sets and high-level relationship sets, high-level states, transitions, and interactions provide additional levels of abstraction for OBM and OIM submodels.

Since the purpose of this book and this chapter on OSA is to serve as a handbook or reference manual for understanding OSA, Side Panels 4.1, 4.2, and 4.3 provide a quick reference of OSA's modeling constructs. These three side panels can be considered the "handbook." The rest of the chapter uses a running example to elaborate and explain the semantics of these components. The objective of the running example is to explain the constructs of the side panels, rather than provide a complete analysis. The examples are based on the requirements of a *Computer Inventory Tracking System*. Text Box 4.1 presents a brief description of this system.

> The Computer Inventory Tracking System has three primary objectives:
>
> 1. Maintain an inventory of all personal computers in use within the university
> 2. Facilitate the timely upgrade of personal computers by ensuring that high-end users are provided with the latest technology
> 3. Coordinate the surplusing of high-end equipment with the acquisition requirements of medium-capability users to control personal equipment costs university wide

Text Box 4.1 Objectives of the Computer Inventory Tracking System.

In the following three sections, we describe the ORM, the OBM, and the OIM. Once we have explained the constructs of OSA, we then present a few guidelines about how to do systems analysis using it. As mentioned, we prefer a model-driven approach, and we discuss the kinds of activities that are normally performed to develop an OSA model instance. The final major concept of this chapter is the formal foundation of OSA. In this brief chapter it is impossible, and probably not of interest, to include the complete formal definition of OSA. However, we show the approach used and the fundamentals of what is necessary to define the syntax and semantics of OSA completely and formally.

Before describing OSA, we wish to clarify our terminology. Because the term model has so many different meanings, we need to be very explicit in its use. We use the term "model" to mean a software engineering model such as OSM. We use the term "model instance" to mean an application model such as an analysis model of a bank's data processing system. When we present the OSM formalisms we use the term "metamodel" to mean a model instance that describes a model.

4.3 Object Relationship Model (ORM)

Side Panel 4.1 provides the components used to develop an ORM instance. Figure 4.1 is an example of a simple ORM model instance for our *Computer Inventory Tracking System*. The purpose of this model instance is to capture information about how computers are acquired, assigned, used, and sold at a university.

4.3.1 Object Sets

An "object set" represents a collection of objects that share some characteristics that cause them to be classified and grouped together. The OSM graphical notation for an object set is a simple rectangle. Rectangles drawn with solid lines represent "nonlexical" object sets, while rectangles with dashed lines represent "lexical" object sets. Lexical objects represent themselves, e.g., strings for names and dates. Nonlexical objects have no direct computer representation other than an object identifier (OID), e.g., person or computer item. A rectangle encloses the name of an object set. Occasionally an object set has more than one name, in which case we separate the names with a bar (|). In Figure 4.1 *Computer User* and *Computer Item* are examples of nonlexical object sets. The only lexical object set in Figure 4.1 is *Date*. One object set has two names — *Computer Support Representative* and *CSR* both name the object set.

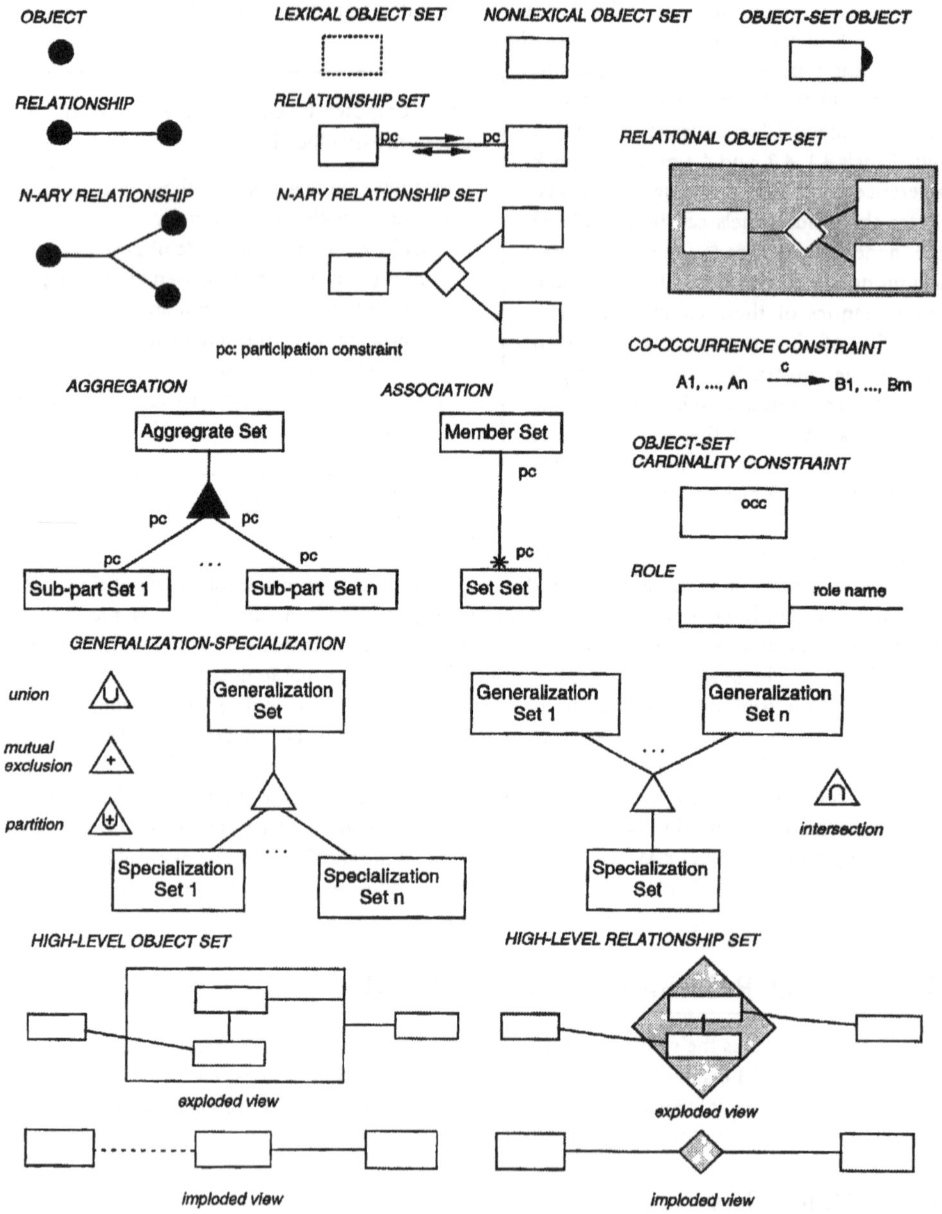

SIDE PANEL 4.1 Object relationship model (ORM) graphical components. (From Embley/Kurtz/Woodfield, *Object-Oriented Systems Analysis: A Model-Driven Approach*, Prentice-Hall, Upper Saddle River, NJ, 1992, pp: Inside Cover. With permission.)

If desired, the number of objects allowed in an object set can be constrained by an "object-set cardinality constraint." Most object sets in the example permit an unlimited number of objects. However, the *VP of Information Technology* object set is constrained to have only one object. The *1* in the upper right corner of the rectangle specifies the constraint. A different example of a single object is the *University* object set. In this case, *University* is a constant singleton object set. A singleton object set has exactly one member,

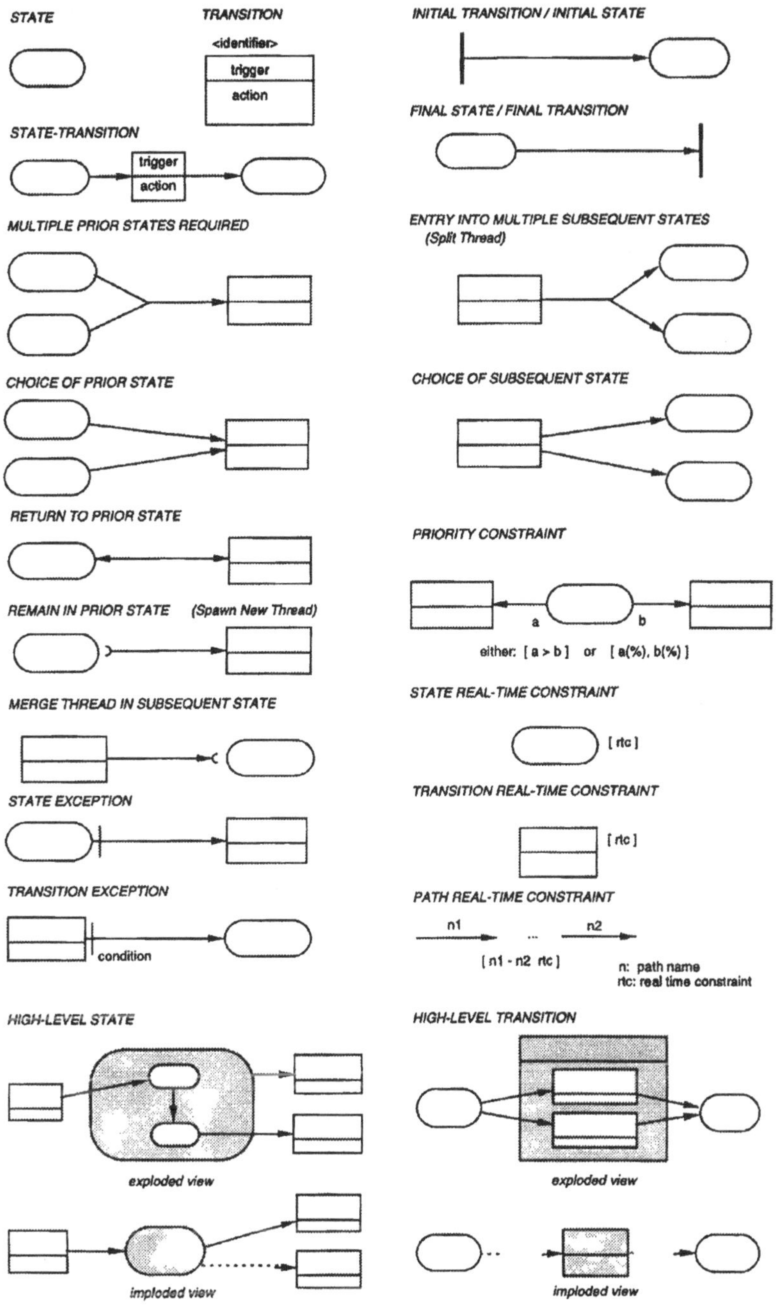

SIDE PANEL 4.2 Object behavior model (OBM) graphical components. (From Embley/Kurtz/Woodfield, *Object-Oriented Systems Analysis: A Model-Driven Approach*, Prentice-Hall, Upper Saddle River, NJ, 1992, pp: Inside Cover. With permission.)

and a constant object set has fixed, unchanging membership. We represent a constant singleton object set with its name written near a black dot. Because constant singleton object sets are one-to-one with objects, we often simply refer to them as "objects." Thus we may say that *University* is an object.

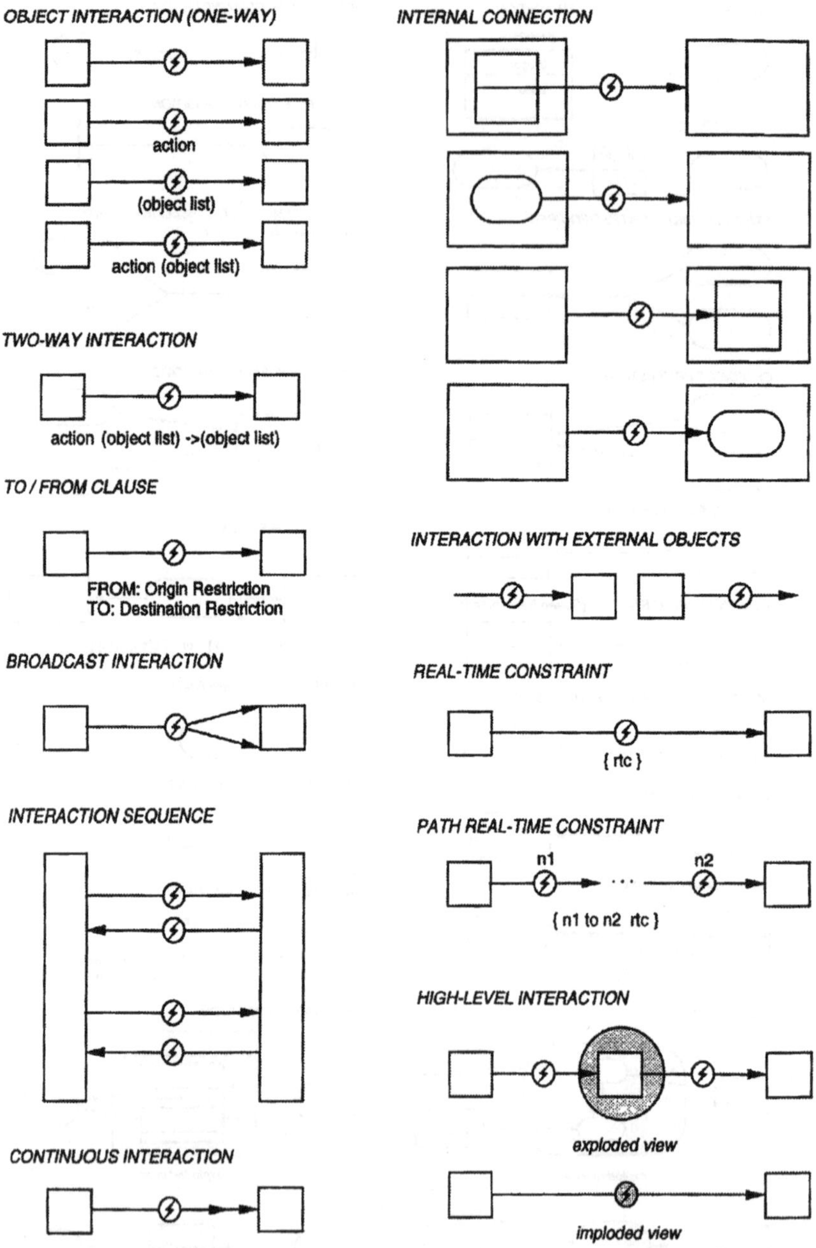

SIDE PANEL 4.3 Object interaction model (OIM) graphical components. (From Embley/Kurtz/Woodfield, *Object-Oriented Systems Analysis: A Model-Driven Approach,* Prentice-Hall, Upper Saddle River, NJ, 1992, pp: Inside Cover. With permission.)

4.3.2 Relationship Sets

Objects in an object set can have relationships with objects in other object sets. A collection of similar relationships is called a "relationship set" and is represented in the graphical notation as a connecting line between object sets. A relationship set can connect two object sets, in which case it is a binary

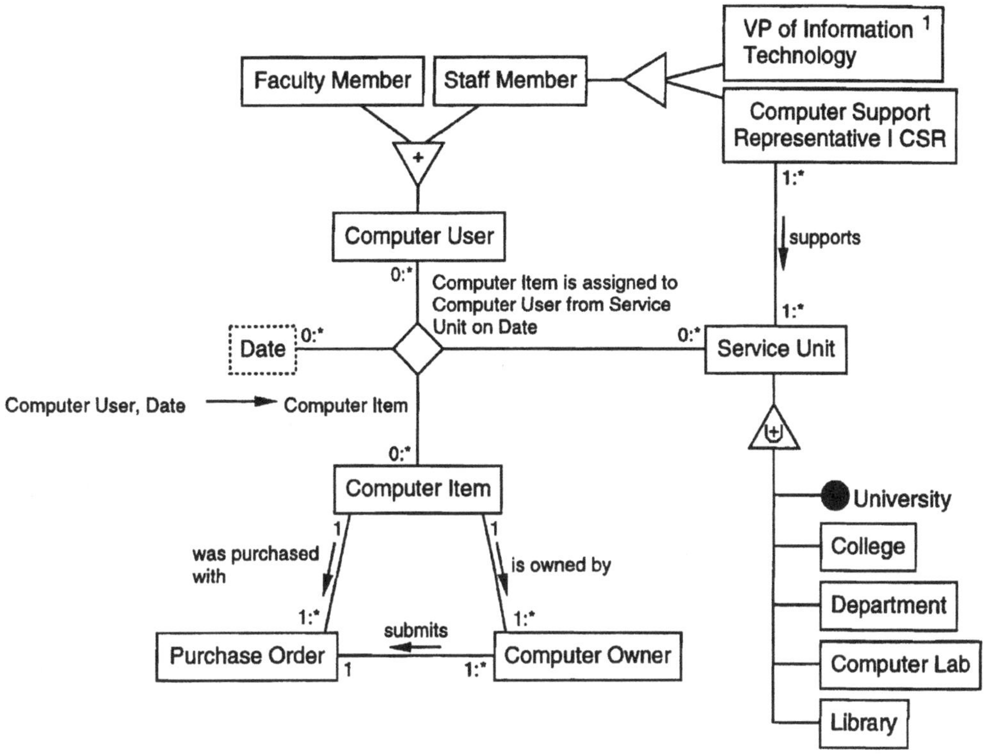

FIGURE 4.1 ORM of Computer Inventory Tracking System — primary view.

relationship set, or more than two object sets, in which case it is *n*-ary. Each relationship set has a name that consists of the names of the connected object sets and some description, usually a verb phrase that describes the relationship between the object sets. In Figure 4.1 *Computer Owner submits Purchase Order* is a binary relationship set. *Computer Item is assigned to Computer User from Service Unit on Date* is an example of an *n*-ary (quaternary) relationship set. Although the complete name of a relationship set always includes the names of all attached object sets, for binary relationship sets we frequently refer to the relationship set with only its relation name, such as *submits*. It should be remembered that this shortened form of the name is for brevity only and is not the formal name.

Each connection of each relationship set to an object set has a "participation constraint" that specifies the number of times an object from the corresponding object set can participate in the relationship set. For example, the *1* participation constraint for the *Computer Item* object set in the relationship set *Computer Item is owned by Computer Owner* specifies that a computer item participates exactly once in the relationship set and that there is exactly one owner. On the other hand, a *Computer Owner* object must participate at least once, and may potentially participate an unlimited number of times, and thus a computer owner owns one or more computers. The * represents "multiple" or "arbitrarily many."

For *n*-ary relationship sets, participation constraints have the same meaning as for binary relationship sets. The *0:** participation constraint in Figure 4.1 on *Computer Item* specifies that a computer participates zero or more times in the relationship set *Computer Item is assigned to Computer User from Service Unit on Date.* For *n*-ary relationship sets, OSA includes another type of constraint called a co-occurrence constraint, which is a generalized functional dependency between various object sets in the relationship set. For example, in Figure 4.1, we have the co-occurrence constraint *Computer User, Date → Computer Item.* In other words, a computer user and date in the relationship set functionally determine a computer item, so that for each *Computer User/Date* pair there is exactly one *Computer Item*. We can add participation constraints on the functional dependency to indicate minimum and maximum participation occurrences. The default is 1:1 or just 1.

OSA does not have "attributes," a common modeling construct found in many conceptual models. During analysis, it is difficult at times to determine what "real-world thing" should be an attribute and what should be an entity. This is particularly true for multivalued attributes. We completely avoid having to make this design-related decision during analysis by identifying all "things" as members of object sets. This approach not only avoids having to make a design decision during analysis, but also permits greater flexibility in developing an efficient and well-structured design (Liddle, Embley, and Woodfield, 1994).

4.3.3 Generalization/Specialization

Object sets provide the facility to group objects together into sets. However, there is frequently the need to further refine the classification of objects in a set. "Generalization/specialization" provides this capability. In OSA generalization/specialization is a true set/subset construct. We represent generalization/specialization in an OSA diagram by an open triangle with generalizations connected to the apex of the triangle and specializations connected to the opposite base of the triangle. An object set may have many generalizations and many specializations.

Figure 4.1 contains several examples of generalization/specialization. We can read the open triangle as *IS-A* from the specialization to the generalization. From the figure we see that *CSR IS-A Staff Member*. This simply says that a *CSR* object is also an object in the *Staff Member* object set, or that a CSR is a staff member. Another example indicates that *Faculty Member IS-A Computer User* and *Staff Member IS-A Computer User*. In this case we have two specializations of a *Computer User* that are also related to each other as indicated by their connection to the open triangle with the enclosed plus sign. The plus sign adds a constraint that *Faculty Member* and *Staff Member* are mutually exclusive object sets. Other constraints on a generalization/specialization are a union constraint, denoted by $\cup$, specifying that the generalization is the union of all the specialization object sets, and a partition constraint, denoted by $\uplus$, specifying that the generalization is a partition (i.e., a combination of union and mutual-exclusion) of all the specializations.

4.3.4 High-Level Constructs

One of the perpetual questions in analysis is the appropriate level of abstractness and granularity to be used to analyze a domain of interest. OSA permits flexibility even within a single model instance in the choice of abstraction. Two constructs, namely high-level object sets and high-level relationship sets, permit abstract ORM structures to be defined during analysis. A "high-level" object set is an object set that contains other object sets and relationship sets; similarly, a "high-level" relationship set is a relationship set that contains other object sets and relationship sets. These two high-level constructs allow analysts to hide detail and work at a higher level of abstraction. Even so, these high-level constructs are still "first class." That is, even though a high-level object set represents a higher level of abstraction, it is still truly a set of real objects. Similarly, high-level relationship sets contain real relationships; however, relationships in high-level relationship sets are derived as a query over contained lower level components. The membership of high-level object sets may or may not be derived.

In Figure 4.2 *Computer Item* is an example of a high-level object set. It is shaded, which is our graphical convention for denoting high-level constructs, and it contains several other object sets and relationship sets. *Computer Item* in Figure 4.2 is the same object set as *Computer Item* in Figure 4.1, but we see additional detail about computer items in Figure 4.2. If we implode the high-level *Computer Item* object set by discarding the detail on the inside, the object set would look like the *Computer Item* object set in Figure 4.1, except we may wish to shade it to indicate that if we explode it (as in Figure 4.2) we can see its details.

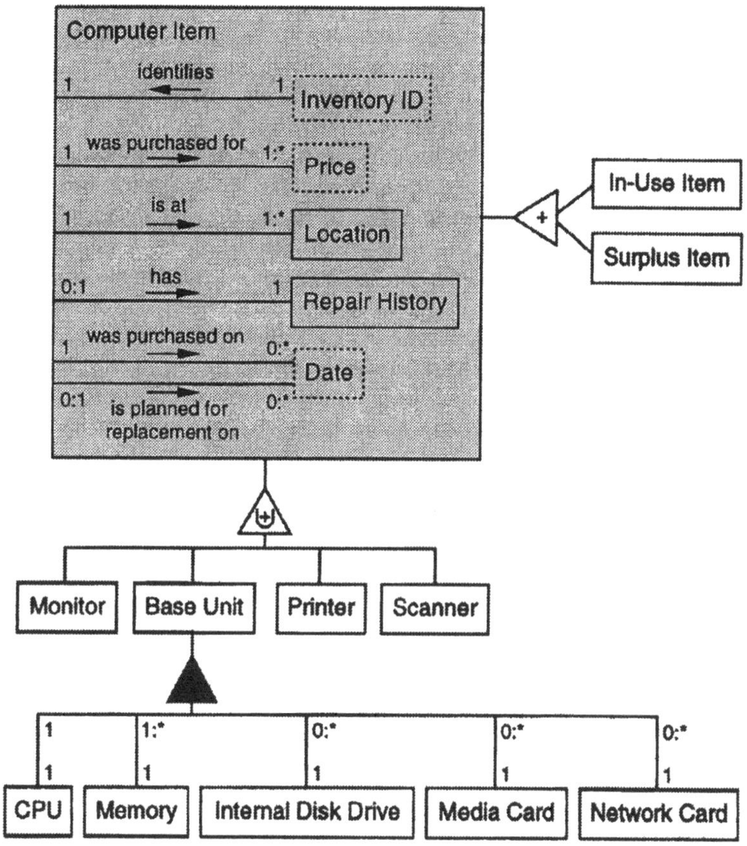

FIGURE 4.2 ORM of Computer Tracking System — detailed view of computer item.

4.3.5 Views and View Integration

Closely related to the concept of high-level constructs in OSA is the idea of a view. One of the primary tenets of OSA modeling is that we should allow maximum flexibility in describing the real world. A "view" is simply an OSA model instance that focuses on object sets and relationship sets of interest for a particular purpose or objective. In Figures 4.1 and 4.2, we see examples of multiple views. Figure 4.1 contains one view of object sets and relationship sets related to *Computer Item*, and Figure 4.2 contains another view. The second view uncovers an internal, lower level view of *Computer Item* and extends the number of object sets and relationship sets related to *Computer Item.*

View integration is the process necessary to combine a set of distinct views into a single model instance. The process of view integration can become important during analysis, especially if a project is large so that several different people have been analyzing different aspects of the project concurrently. To obtain a more complete view of our analysis, we (either actually or mentally) integrate the two ORM views in Figures 4.1 and 4.2.

4.3.6 Templates

OSA consists of a relatively small set of fundamental modeling components. Even though the set of components is small, we have found it to be complete in that it can capture and describe all real-world objects and processes. However, a small set sometimes limits notational expressiveness. We can, however, expand the small set and provide more expressiveness with templates. An OSA "template" is simply a shorthand representation for an interesting and useful combination of fundamental OSA elements. We have defined several templates that we use regularly in model development. Other practitioners may wish to develop other templates particular to their needs as they use OSA.

One common template often used in OSA is an "aggregation," which is a component/part relationship. For example, we think of a computer as an aggregate object with subparts that include a CPU, memory, an internal disk drive, etc. Rather than represent each part of a computer item using relationship sets, we can be more expressive by combining these relationship sets together into a single aggregation. Graphically, we use a shaded triangle to denote an aggregation; the apex of the triangle connects to the object set of the aggregate and the opposite base connects to the subpart object sets. If we wish, we can further decompose aggregate subparts such as the internal disk drive into subparts and form an aggregation hierarchy that gives an assembly for the computer item.

Figure 4.2 shows an aggregation for our example. Individually we say a *CPU IS-PART-OF Base Unit*, *Memory IS-PART-OF Base Unit*, etc. This is a template because it is a shorthand notation for the collection of all of these individual relationship sets. It is more expressive than simple relationship sets, however, because it nicely shows which subparts make up the aggregate object.

One other common example of a template used in OSA is a "role" on a relationship set. Frequently, we may want to identify not only a relationship set, but also the role a particular object set plays in the relationship set. In a university setting, we might have a relationship set *Student is assigned to Faculty Member*. On the *Faculty Member* side we may identify the role as *Advisor*. What this really represents is the generalization/specialization *Advisor IS-A Faculty Member* and a relationship set *Student is assigned to Advisor*. We might use this template because the only interest in the *Advisor* object set is as a role with the *Student*.

4.4 The Object Behavior Model (OBM)

The OBM provides modeling constructs to describe the behavior and life cycle of individual real-world objects. To describe real-world behavior, OSM uses an extended form of state transition diagrams called state nets. A state net is a pattern of states and transitions that describes the potential behavior of each object in an object set for its entire life from creation to destruction. Each object set has a state net. It is important to note that this approach to analyzing the real world maintains the purity of an object-oriented viewpoint. Because in OSA low-level and high-level object sets are all "first class," both types of object sets have state nets. Thus we can model the behavior of a simple object set such as *Purchase Order* or a high-level object set such as *Computer Item*, or even a very high-level object set such as the *Computer Inventory Tracking System* itself.

4.4.1 State Nets

A "state net" is a directed bipartite graph of "states" and "transitions" that describes the behavior of objects within a single object set. States are semi-permanent "states of being" of the objects. An object moves from state to state based on some condition or event as described by a transition. The directed nature of the graph provides a path that describes the possible movement of an object from state to state. As seen in Side Panel 4.2, there are various types of path connections, which provide capability for alternative choices, concurrent paths, exit and return paths, exception conditions, and path real-time constraints. We explain these capabilities in the discussion that follows.

The state net for *Purchase Order*, as seen in Figure 4.3, is fairly simple. Graphically, we represent states by rectangular ovals and transitions by a rectangle split into upper and lower parts. The state net in Figure 4.3 is mostly linear, from the creation of the purchase order until it is discarded three years later. The states represent the states of being of a purchase order, and the transitions specify the "active behavior" of a purchase order.

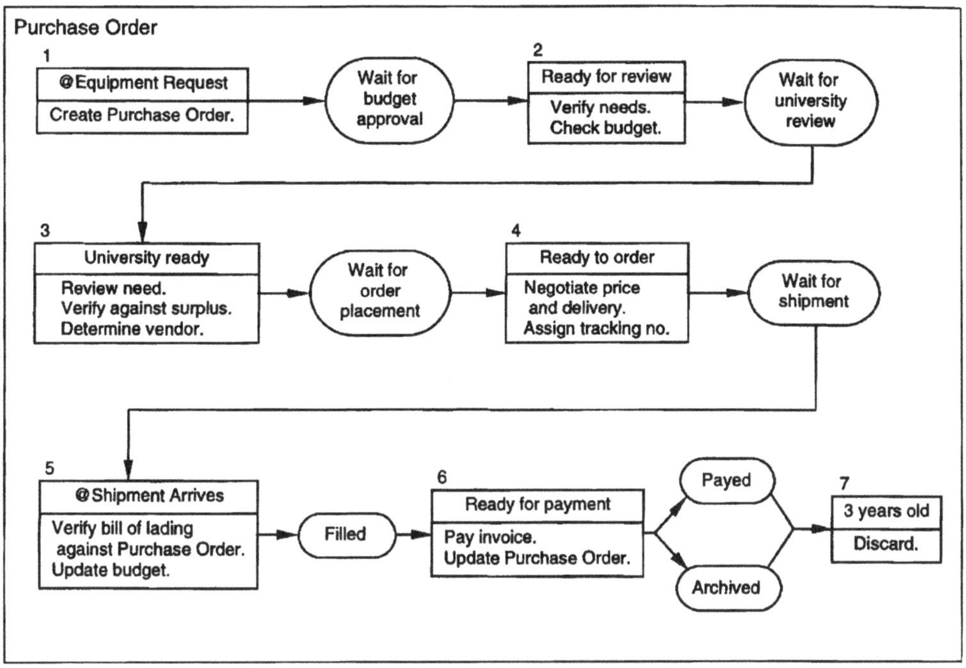

FIGURE 4.3 State net for *Purchase Order* object set.

In Figure 4.3, we see that the state net begins and ends with transitions. Transition *1* is an "initial" transition, and transition *7* is a "final" transition. We can easily recognize these beginning and ending transitions because an initial transition has no prior states and a final transition has no subsequent states. All other transitions have one or more prior states that must be "on" for a particular object x in order for that transition to fire for x. Upon completion of a transition, an object arrives in a subsequent state or states.

4.4.2 Transitions

Looking at a transition more closely, we see that it comprises two parts. A "trigger," written in the upper part of a transition rectangle, specifies a condition that must hold and/or events that must occur before the transition can commence. An "action," written in the lower part of a transition rectangle, describes the behavior or activity of an object as it transitions between states. Triggers fire based on events, conditions, or a Boolean combination of events and conditions. An "event," indicated by an "at" symbol (@), occurs at a specific instant in time. A "condition" is a statement that is true or false. In Figure 4.3, the trigger *@Equipment request arrives* on transition *1* is an event, while *Ready for payment* on transition *6* is a condition.

A transition's action describes steps that must be taken by an object during the transition. When doing analysis, we usually do not try to formalize or constrain too tightly the description of the action. At this point in system description, it is more important to capture knowledge than to worry about syntax, or even a specific algorithm. In transition *5* of Figure 4.3, for example, we have an action that says *Verify bill of lading against Purchase Order and Update budget.* Neither exactly how this is done nor extensive detail about what is involved need be given during analysis.

Even though we permit and often use descriptive, non-algorithmic language statements during analysis, OSA does not preclude the use of these. In the previous example, if there were some pseudo-code or a snippet of a programming algorithm that exactly identified how to do the bill of lading comparison, that

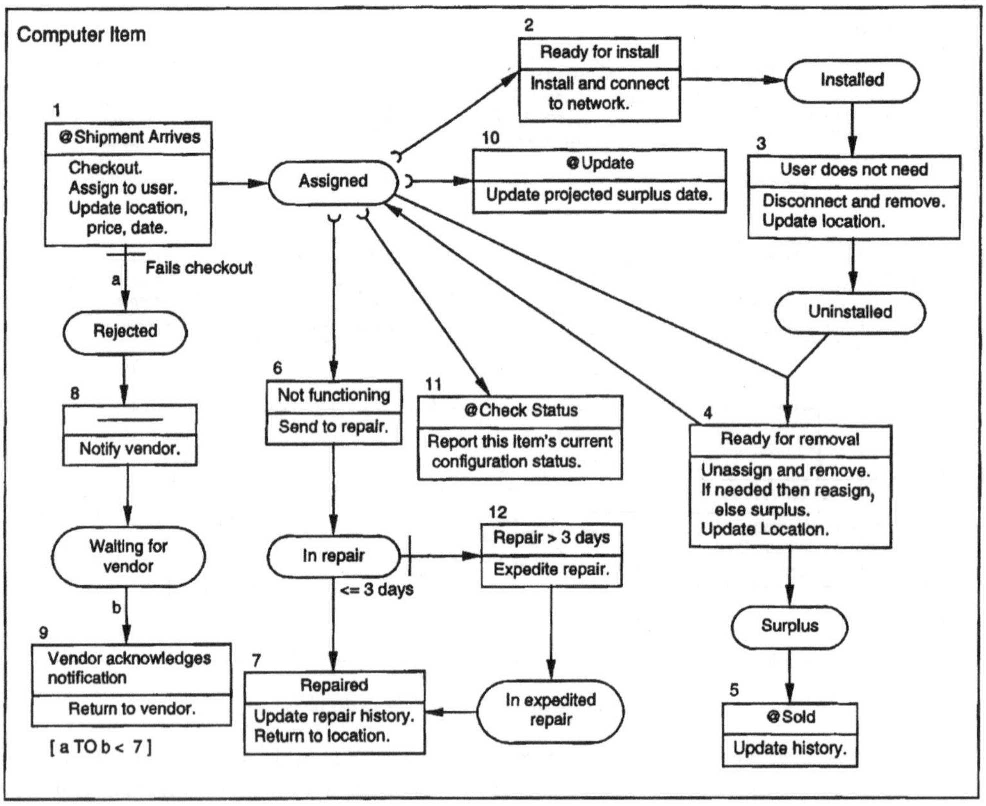

FIGURE 4.4 State net for *Computer Item.*

could be written as the action statement for the transition. As we move from analysis into specification and design, we will change these action statements into more formal language statements.

4.4.3 Exceptions and Real-Time Constraints

In Figure 4.4 we see a more complex state net, one for a *Computer Item* object. On transition *1* we see an exception exit path indicated by an arrow with a cross bar leaving the transition. An "exception" is a path in the state net that is not expected, but it is accommodated by the system. In Figure 4.4, a computer item would normally be assigned out, but there may be some problem that would cause the computer item to be returned to a vendor for repair. Like transitions, exceptions exiting a transition have triggers that specify when the path should be taken. For the exception from transition *1* in Figure 4.4, the condition is *Fails checkout.* We place the exception condition near the bar on the exception as Figure 4.4 shows. An exception condition does not require completion of the action, and in fact, frequently indicates an early exit from the transition caused by some unusual situation occurring in the middle of a transition's action.

States can have exceptions too. State exception exits, however, are just like regular exits from a state — they happen when the trigger in a transition holds. We mark them with a cross bar, however, to specify that the path is an exception path. In Figure 4.4, for example, the path from the *In repair* state marked with a cross bar is an exception. If a non-functioning computer item is in repair for more than three days, there is a notification and the computer item enters the *In expedited repair* state.

Along the exception path exiting from transition *1* in Figure 4.4, we see a "real-time constraint," [*a TO b < 7 days*]. This constraint indicates that a computer item that fails the initial checkout should be returned within seven days (i.e., the object should move from point *a* to point *b* in less than seven days).

Real-time constraints can be placed anywhere on a state net and can constrain the amount of time spent in a state, evaluating a trigger, performing an action, or moving from one point on a path to another. The *In repair* state, for example, has the real-time constraint [<=*3 days*].

Real-time constraints are suggestions rather than constraints unless there is an exception that is triggered when a real-time constraint fails. That is, the computer item sent to the vendor should be returned within seven days, but nothing is said about what to do if the computer item is not returned within seven days. On the other hand, if a non-functioning computer item is in repair for more than three days, the exception on *In repair* is triggered.

4.4.4 Paths and Concurrency

A "path" is a valid sequence of states and transitions that an object can follow. A simple example of a path is the exception path out of transition *1* that was just discussed. A computer item object comes into existence in the initial transition *1*. If it takes the exception path, it proceeds down the path to the final transition *9*. At transition *9* the particular computer item is returned to the vendor and ceases to exist as far as this system is concerned. Thus this path terminates, and in this case so does the object. We refer to the flow of the object through this path as a "thread."

In OSA it is normal and natural for concurrent threads of behavior to exist for a given object. In Figure 4.4, for example, we see several examples of concurrent threads of activity. The *Assigned* state has three transitions that are attached via a "semicircle" connection. This type of connection denotes the creation of a new, concurrent thread. A *Computer Item* object thus remains in the *Assigned* state, i.e., is assigned to a user, while it is scheduled for surplus (path to transition *10*), goes out for repair (path to transition *7*), or is installed and in use (path to transition *3*).

Final transitions on these concurrent paths indicate the completion and destruction of that particular thread of behavior. Although not shown in this diagram, a thread can also be terminated by entering a state with a semicircle connection when there is already a thread of the object in that state. Thus semicircle connections specify the creation or recombination of threads of behavior. Threads of control also recombine when a transition requires an object to be in multiple states simultaneously. In Figure 4.4, for example, transition *4* fires only when a computer item is in both the *Assigned* and *Uninstalled* states. When transition *4* fires, the two threads of control combine as one. Because a transition with multiple prior states requires a thread of an object in every prior state, such a transition can serve as a point of synchronization among multiple threads of control for a single object.

Obviously another type of concurrency exists in that all objects behave independently of each other. A state net is a template for object behavior, and separate objects will exhibit their own behavior separate from and concurrent with the behavior of other objects. Thus, any computer item can be in any state or transition in the *Computer Item* state net in Figure 4.4.

4.4.5 High-Level Components

State nets also support both high-level states and high-level transitions. The only requirement is that the bipartite nature of the state net be preserved. As in an ORM, we indicate high-level constructs by shading and permit views to be nested to arbitrary depths.

A high-level state is one way to model at a higher level of abstraction. In Figure 4.4, for example, we could have created the high-level state in Figure 4.5A. One use for this state would be to implode it, giving us a higher level view in which we do not see the details inside the state. Another use for this state would be to enforce the real-time constraint from *a* to *b*. If we add this high-level state and connect it with a state exception to a transition with the trigger *In Waiting to be Return* >= *7 days*, we could exit the state and do additional actions such as notifying the vendor again that the computer item should be picked up.

Figure 4.5B shows a high-level transition that includes some of the states and transitions of Figure 4.4. Instead of viewing all the details about what happens when an assigned computer item is not functioning,

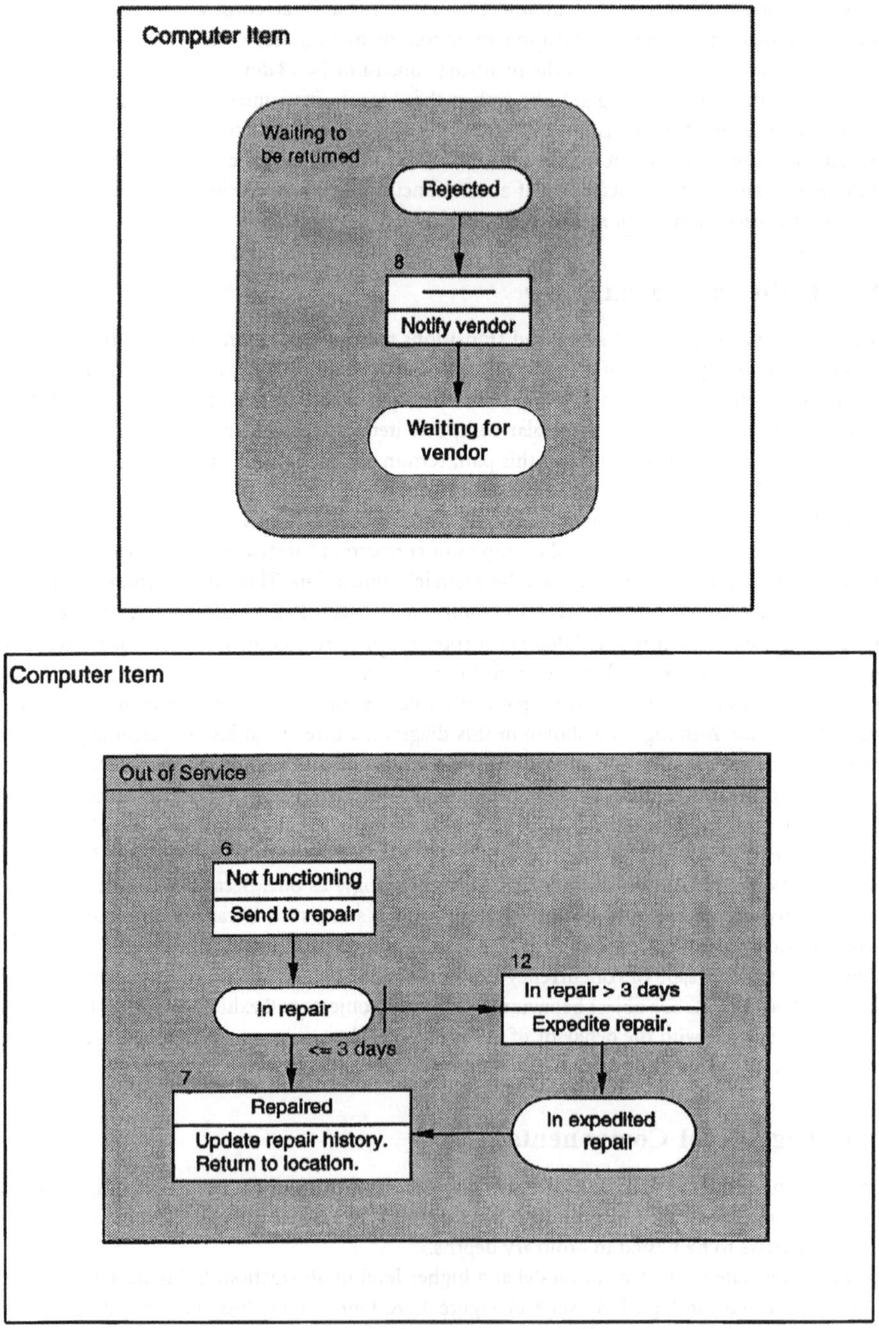

FIGURE 4.5 (A) *Computer Item* state net with high-level state, and (B) *Computer Item* state net with high-level transition.

we can implode this high-level transition and add a comment in the action part of the transition to tell us that a computer item is being repaired. We would leave this imploded transition shaded to indicate that we can explode it to see the details about what is involved in having the computer item repaired.

4.5 Object Interaction Model (OIM)

Analysts can use the OIM to capture information about the interactions and communications between objects. Objects rarely act in pure isolation, they usually interact with other objects. Using "interactions" as the basic form of dynamic interchange between objects more closely models the real world than using constructs such as messages, services, or function calls. These latter constructs are for design and implementation and can be derived from the interaction model instance as the project moves from analysis to design and implementation.

4.5.1 Interactions

As shown in Side Panel 4.3, we represent an interaction in an OSA model instance as a directed arrow with a lightning bolt symbol near the center. Each interaction has a description, an origin, and a destination (either the origin or the destination may be omitted if it is outside the system). An interaction may also pass information in the form of an object list. A "two-way" interaction includes the passing and returning of information via object lists. The TO/FROM clauses associated with an interaction provide the capability to specify a unique object as the receiver or sender of the interaction. Normally, without a TO clause an interaction goes to any object that is in the proper state or transition. A TO clause can also be used to limit receivers to any given subset of the objects in the proper state or transition. A "broadcast" interaction provides a way to have multiple receivers.

4.5.2 Interaction Model Instances

An analyst can specify an interaction model instance as a separate diagram that contains partial views of ORM or OBM components, as Figure 4.6 shows. Frequently, however, we integrate interaction information with other views of object sets and relationship sets or state nets. The amount of detail captured in a given interaction also depends on the level of detail in the rest of the model instance. For example, the origin (or destination) of an interaction may be an object set, or if more detail is known the origin (or destination) may be a particular state or transition within a state net for an object set.

In Figure 4.6, the interaction labeled *Sold* originates with the *CSR* object set and terminates on the *Computer Item* object set. No further detail is provided. Looking at the *Update surplus date* interaction, however, we note that the destination is not only *Computer Item*, but that it is specifically directed to transition *10*. Because we have more information, we can more closely document real-world interactions. This same interaction to transition *10* also illustrates the passing of information (objects and relationships) with an interaction. In this case a member of the object set *Date* is passed to transition *10* when the *Update surplus date* interaction occurs.

Generally an interaction defines an interaction from some unspecified object in an object set to another unspecified object in the same or a different set. We can also put *TO* and *FROM* clauses on an interaction that more narrowly define a particular object or set of objects as the origin or destination. The *Update surplus date* interaction includes a *TO* clause to specify that this interaction is not for just any *Computer Item*, but for a particular one; namely the *Owned computer ready for surplus*. Thus, interactions can be directed to specific objects.

Although not specifically required in the definition of OSM, we see another interesting capability of interactions by the *Update surplus date* interaction and the *@Update surplus date* trigger. By the use of a common name, we indicate that the arrival of an interaction is the event that causes a trigger to be true. Thus this provides a method to model real-time events that cause a transition's trigger to fire.

The *Shipment arrives* interaction in Figure 4.6 demonstrates the usefulness of interactions for synchronizing behavior between two objects. In the *Computer Item* object set, when a shipment arrives along with a bill of lading, an interaction sending the *Bill of Lading* object to the *Purchase Order* object set provides the trigger and the information needed to verify the shipment against the purchase order and to update the budget.

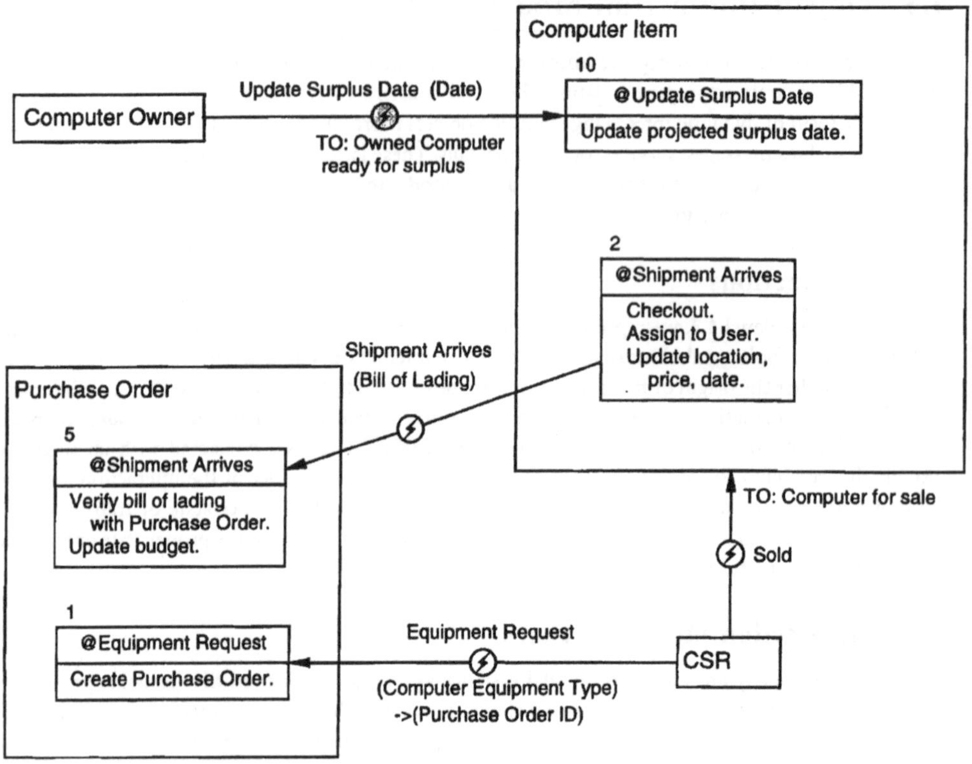

FIGURE 4.6 Partial interaction diagram for Computer Inventory Tracking System.

The *Equipment request* interaction between the *CSR* and the *Purchase Order* is an example of a two-way interaction. Two-way interactions allow sender objects to both send and receive information. Unlike one-way interactions, which we have been discussing, a sender object of a two-way interaction waits for a reply. For the two-way interaction in Figure 4.6, the *CSR* initiates the interaction and sends details of the requested computer items. This interaction triggers the initial transition of a *Purchase Order* object, which creates the *Purchase Order* and returns a *Purchase Order ID* to the *CSR* who sent the request.

4.5.3 High-Level Interactions

High-level interactions are used to hide intermediate information when a higher level of abstraction is desired. We denote high-level interactions with a shaded circle around the lightning bolt. In Figure 4.6, the interaction *Update surplus date* is a high-level interaction. The lower level detail is provided in Figure 4.7. A computer owner does not actually update a surplus date, but he gives it to a CSR to do so. In this case the *Update surplus date* interaction really is two interactions, one from *Computer Owner* to *CSR* and another from *CSR* to *Computer Item*. A single high-level interaction that subsumes the intermediate object set, *CSR*, can hide that detail when it is unimportant at the level of abstraction desired during analysis.

4.6 Guidelines for Model-Driven Analysis

The three common questions with any type of systems analysis are: (1) how and where to begin, (2) how to proceed, and (3) when the analysis is complete? As indicated in the overview, OSA analysis does not demand a specific methodology. Rather, we use a model-driven approach. In a model-driven approach,

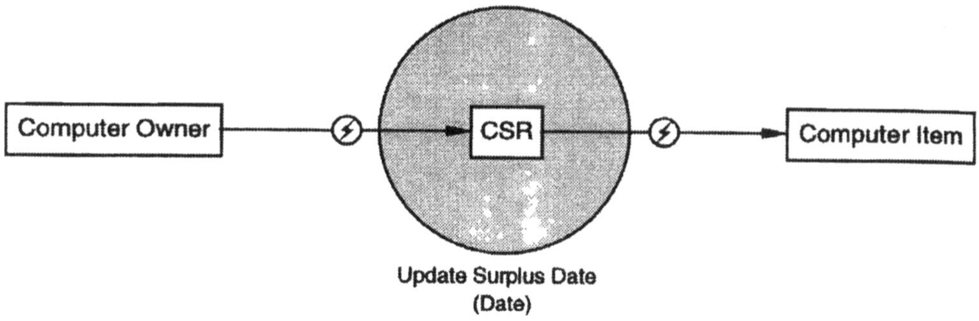

FIGURE 4.7 A high-level interaction showing internal details.

we select any methodology that is appropriate for the problem domain and proceed to elaborate the model instance. Analysis is complete when we deem the model instance to be as detailed, comprehensive, and accurate as we need for our particular application.

The commencement of systems analysis with OSA begins as it does for any development project. The problem domain, business objectives, and system scope are identified to control and direct all subsequent activities. In a model-driven approach we also decide on an appropriate starting point to begin to elaborate the model. For data-oriented systems, it is usually best to begin with the development of an ORM and continue with it until it is close to being complete. For highly interactive systems with substantial user interface, it is frequently useful to begin by developing the OIM. Listings and definition of interactions can then be used to drive the definition of object sets and their required state nets. Use-case analysis is often appropriate for systems with substantial interaction with the outside world. A use-case analysis provides an excellent approach to elaborating the OIM. For control or real-time types of systems, it is frequently best to begin with detailed state nets. Critical object sets are identified, and then the sophisticated behavior and logic of these critical objects is captured in state nets. Thus in this case the OBM controls the analysis process.

Once the decision is made on how to begin, proceeding with the analysis follows quite naturally. Information gathering from use-case analysis, interviews, data requirements, information needs, etc., continues to drive model-instance development. In model-driven analysis the important questions are: "What part of the model can be elaborated next?" and "What information do I need to accomplish this elaboration?" We have found that either a top down or a bottom up approach will work equally well. When we can identify components at an abstract level and understand the overall needs and scope, then a top-down approach works well. High-level components are then identified and are exploded into more detail. When it is difficult to understand the overall picture, we then begin by simply identifying and elaborating pieces: object sets, behaviors, and interactions. This bottom-up approach allows us to collect many individual components and assemble them into a larger system. OSA does not mandate one approach over the other. Again, the important idea is that in a model-driven approach, our objective is to elaborate the model instance.

When is an OSA model instance complete? Generally we can say we have done enough analysis when we understand the problem domain and can demonstrate that understanding to the client. Usually, a completed OSA model instance contains an ORM that identifies all the object sets in the universe of discourse. For each object set of active objects there also should be a complete state net. All interactions should be identified and defined at a level of detail so that their origins and destinations are identified to the transition level. All high-level components should have detailed explosions described. When several views have been created during analysis, all these views should be integrated together to produce a single comprehensive model instance.

Here we have focused exclusively on analysis. This discussion should not be construed to mean that analysis must be complete before specification, design, or even implementation can begin. Generally we find that while the model instance for analysis is being developed, and long before it is complete, we have begun to develop the design model instance. One important thing is that we recognize that OSA is for analysis, and we can use it to faithfully capture real-world information without having to make design decisions or prematurely add design ideas to the analysis model instance.

To facilitate analysis, the OSM research group at Brigham Young University has developed several computer aided tools. The "OSM Composer" is a syntax-directed drawing tool for creating OSM model instances consisting of ORM, OBM, and OIM components. The OSM Composer also serves as a foundation for other tools, such as a component for graphical query specification and a database design assistant. The OSM Composer is research-quality software, and we use it as a platform for experimenting with tool ideas.

4.7 A Formal Foundation

As indicated in the introduction, a formal foundation is required if we hope to introduce rigorous engineering to the task of software development. In this section, we describe how we have formally defined OSM, and we illustrate some of the advantages of our approach. The details of our formalization are quite extensive (Clyde, 1993), so we only give a high-level summary here.

4.7.1 Formal Semantics of OSM

As Figure 4.8 shows, we use a two-step approach to define the formal semantics of OSM. In the first step, we convert an OSM model instance into a set of predicates and formulas expressed in a temporal, first-order predicate logic. In the second step, we instantiate the predicates and verify the set of formulas from step one using standard mathematical model theory. That is, we provide an interpretation by mapping the predicate symbols to objects and points in time. An interpretation is valid if and only if the formulas

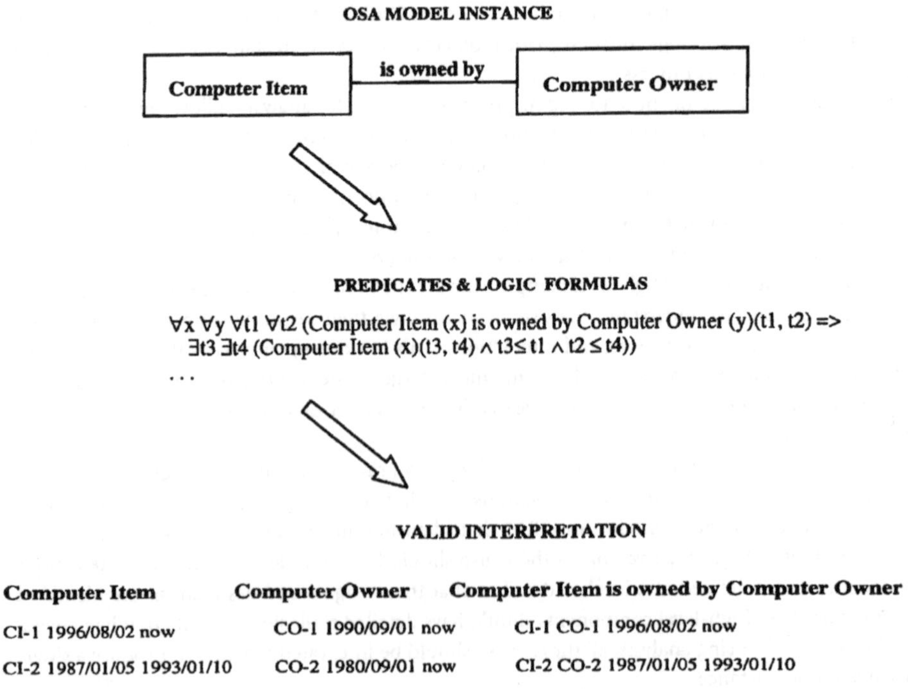

FIGURE 4.8 Creating a formal definition for OSM.

all hold for the instantiated predicates. Given an OSM model instance *M* and the set of predicates and formulas *S* that result from converting *M* to predicate logic, we define the formal semantics of *M* to be the set of all valid interpretations for *S*.

We show how this works with our example system. First, we generate predicates for each object set and relationship set in *M*. Object sets generate one-place predicates, while *n*-ary relationship sets generate *n*-place predicates. For example, some object-set predicates from Figure 4.1 include *Service Unit*(x), *Computer Lab*(x), and *Purchase Order*(x). Relationship-set predicates include *CSR*(x) *supports Service Unit*(y), *Computer Item*(x) *was purchased with Purchase Order*(y), *Computer Owner*(x) *submits Purchase Order*(y), etc. Note that unlike many logic systems, we write our predicates using infix notation. This allows our predicates to have more natural names that better communicate intended meanings. For example, instead of our *Computer Owner*(x) *submits Purchase Order*(y) predicate, a typical logic system would use something like "*submits_order*(*X*, *Y*)." We prefer thorough documentation over brevity in this case.

Next, we generate closed predicate-calculus formulas (or rules) for each of the constraints indicated or implied in *M*. For example, the participation constraint *1:** on *Purchase Order* requires each *Purchase Order* object to be associated with at least one *Computer Item* object and thus generates the formula $\forall\{x(\textit{Purchase Order}(x)) \Rightarrow \exists y(\textit{Computer Item}(y) \textit{ was purchased with Purchase Order}(x))$. The generalization/specialization between *Staff* and *Computer User* requires that objects in *Staff* also be members of *Computer User*, thus we generate the referential-integrity constraint $\forall x(\textit{Staff}(x) \Rightarrow \textit{Computer User}(x))$. We proceed in this fashion for all the components of *M*, until we have generated the set of formulas *S* that captures the full structure *M*.

Thus far we have ignored temporal dynamics. To account for time, our next step is to add zero, one, or two time places to every predicate. For example, instead of *Computer User*(x), we have *Computer User*(x)(t_1, t_2), where t_1 and t_2 indicate the time interval over which x is a member of *Computer User*. We add one time place for events, and zero for time-invariant predicates and rules. Since participation constraints are time-invariant, their corresponding rules have no time places. However, the referential-integrity rule shown before, $\forall x(\textit{Staff}(x) \Rightarrow \textit{Computer User}(x))$, must be modified as follows:

$$\forall x \forall t_1 \forall t_2 \left(\textit{Staff}\left(x\right)\left(t_1, t_2\right) \Rightarrow \exists t_3 \exists t_4 \left(\textit{Computer User}\left(x\right)\left(t_3, t_4\right) \wedge t_3 \le t_1 \wedge t_2 \le t_4 \right)\right) \tag{4.1}$$

This rule asserts that during the time interval for which an object exists as a member of *Staff*, it must also be a member of *Computer User*.

Now that we have temporal predicates, we can also generate predicates and rules for state nets and interactions. For each state, we generate a predicate that lets us assert that an object is in the state for a specific time interval (e.g., *Purchase Order*(x) *in state Filled*(t_1, t_2)). Then for each transition we write several predicates that let us trace the phases (inactive, enabled, committed, executing, finishing) involved in firing a transition. For example, we would write *Purchase Order*(x) *transition 1 enabled*(t_1, t_2). For each trigger of each transition, we write a temporal predicate that lets us determine a time interval when the trigger is true. Then, we generate rules that capture the idea that when the trigger of an enabled transition is true, the transition actually fires. There are other kinds of rules we omit here for the sake of brevity, but suffice it to say that in this fashion we fully describe the model instance as a set of predicates and first-order formulas.

4.7.2 A Metamodel and Formal Syntax

The formalization just discussed provides a precise, formal definition of the semantics of an OSA model instance. This formalization is necessary to ensure a correct definition of OSA model constructs. It is also useful for tool builders to have an accurate and complete definition of OSA. For most practitioners, however, this level of mathematical precision is unnecessary. Even for practitioners, however, there should be a precise definition of the syntax of valid OSA model instances.

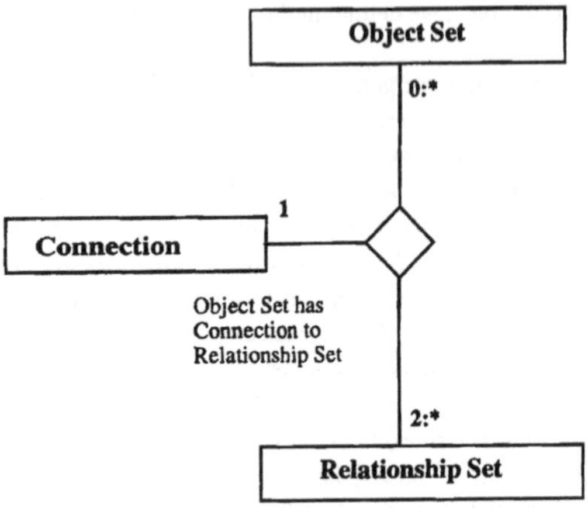

Object Set	Connection	Relationship Set
Computer Item	C1	is owned by
Computer Owner	C2	

Object Set has Connection to Relationship Set

Computer Item	C1	is owned by
Computer Owner	C2	is owned by

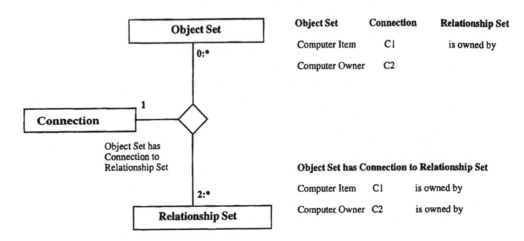

FIGURE 4.9 Partial metamodel and interpretation.

Because an OSA model instance is also a real-world object, we can describe an OSA model instance with another OSA model instance, called the OSA metamodel. The OSA metamodel is an OSA model instance that describes the components of an application model instance. Figure 4.9 gives a very small portion of the OSA metamodel. It shows that an OSA model instance consists of objects in objects sets called *Object Set, Relationship Set,* and *Connection.* Objects in these three object sets are related to each other by relationships in the relationship set *Object Set has Connection to Relationship Set.* The participation constraints guarantee that each connection uniquely determines the object set and relationship set for the connection and that each relationship set connects two or more object sets.

Using the ideas outlined previously, if we develop a set of predicates and formulas from the OSA metamodel, we can use them to test any given OSA model instance to verify that it was developed correctly, i.e., that its syntax is correct. In other words, to test whether a particular model instance M is syntactically correct, we instantiate the predicates of M and test whether they satisfy the set of formulas S from the metamodel. M is syntactically correct if and only if its instantiation satisfies S.

4.8 Concluding Remarks

There are many features that make a model useful for systems analysis. These include such ideas as expressive power, richness, sophistication, ease of use, intuitiveness, accuracy, mathematical correctness, ease of representation, elegance, varying levels of abstractions, views, cohesiveness between submodels, and integration of subcomponents. Other features such as operating efficiency are characteristics that are desirable in design and implementation models, but they are not necessarily helpful in an analysis model. Indeed, the presence of this kind of feature may impede the analysis task, misdirecting the analyst to perform non-analysis activities. In the development of OSA we have attempted to make it truly an analysis model possessing desirable analysis characteristics while avoiding the clutter normally added by design and implementation considerations [URL http://osm7.cs.byu.edu/]. Also, we wanted to do this in a fashion that would support the needs of practitioners and theoreticians, building on a solid, formal foundation that would promote the cause of true software engineering. We believe OSA addresses these stated objectives, and we invite the interested reader to continue exploring the vision of OSM development in the next chapter and other listed references.

References

Clyde, S.W. 1993. An Initial Theoretical Foundation for Object-Oriented Systems Analysis and Design, *Ph.D. Dissertation.* Computer Science Department, Brigham Young University.

Embley, D.W., Kurtz, B.C. and Woodfield, S.N. 1993. *Object-Oriented Systems Analysis: A Model-Driven Approach.* Yourdon Press Series, Prentice-Hall, Englewood Cliffs, New Jersey.

Embley, D.W., Jackson, R.B. and Woodfield, S.N. 1995. OO systems analysis: is it or isn't it?. *IEEE Soft.,* Vol 12 (July) No 4:19-33.

Liddle, S.W., Embley, D.W. and Woodfield, S.N. 1994. Attributes: should we eliminate them from semantic and object-oriented data models?, pp. 340–347. In *Proc. 22nd Annu. ACM Computer Sci. Conf.,* Phoenix, AZ.

OSM Lab Home Page. World-Wide Web URL http://osm7.cs.byu.edu/

Further Information

A good explanation of the basic concepts of Object-oriented Systems Analysis is found in the book *Object-Oriented Systems Analysis: A Model-Driven Approach* by D.W. Embley, B.C. Kurtz, and S.N. Woodfield published by Prentice-Hall (1992). This book includes detailed explanations and examples of OSA, including an expanded version of the metamodel.

Another book which includes information on both OSM analysis and development is *Object Database Development: Concepts and Principles* (Addison-Wesley, 1998) by David W. Embley.

To obtain a more comprehensive list of articles and on-going activities, the official OSM World-Wide Web URL is "http://osm7.cs.byu.edu/." It gives an explanation of the research being done by the OSM research group at Brigham Young University as well as copies of published articles, white papers, and papers in progress.

5

Object-Oriented Systems Modeling — Development

Stephen W. Liddle
Brigham Young University

David W. Embley
Brigham Young University

Robert B. Jackson
Brigham Young University

Scott N. Woodfield
Brigham Young University

5.1 Overview

The description of Object-oriented Systems Modeling (OSM) is provided in this chapter and in Chapter 4. Readers who are unfamiliar with OSM should read both chapters. Readers who understand the analysis portion of OSM (sometimes referred to as OSA in prior publications) can learn about the seamless modeling approach for analysis, design, and implementation in this chapter.

In the analysis chapter we presented fundamental OSM model definitions. OSM is rich and expressive with constructs that support the modeling of sophisticated "real-world" entities and ideas. OSM is also a complete model that supports all phases of the development cycle from analysis to implementation and evolution. The analysis chapter describes the key structural and behavioral modeling ideas of OSM and introduces its formal underpinnings.

In this chapter we present ideas related to the use of OSM for systems development. Integrated throughout this chapter are explanations of extensions to OSM analysis components to support specification,

0-8493-3135-8/99/$0.00+$.50

design, and implementation and concepts related to a model-driven development methodology using OSM. We also present details about the OSM seamless model/metamodel, and we introduce our model-equivalent language, Harmony. The analysis chapter used a Computer Inventory Tracking System as its running example. This chapter builds on that same example, and assumes the reader is familiar with the terminology introduced in the analysis chapter.

5.2 Introduction

The Object-Oriented Systems Modeling Research Group was formed to study and develop object-oriented models, techniques, and tools. The group's mission is to develop a theoretical foundation, professional engineering methods, and research-quality tools for engineering object-oriented software systems, thus helping move software engineering toward the goal of being a true engineering discipline. The first product of our work was Object-oriented Systems Analysis (OSA) (Embley, Kurtz, and Woodfield, 1992), a model designed specifically for systems analysis, not for design or implementation. Later efforts focused on specification, design, and implementation issues. OSM is OSA with several additional modeling constructs needed for specification, design, and implementation.

There are four major tenets that drive our work:

1. Our approach to software development should be model-driven, not process-driven.
2. We can avoid many integration problems that exist in current models, languages, and tools by employing a model-equivalent language within the context of a seamless, ontological model for analysis/design/implementation.
3. Our work must be developed on a rigorous formal foundation if we are to be confident of its properties including repeatability, predictability, reliability, quality, and effectiveness.
4. We advocate the use of synergistic tools that handle tedious development tasks, leaving the human developer more free to perform creative tasks unsuitable for automation.

We now explore these ideas in greater detail.

5.2.1 A Model-Driven Approach

The major difference between OSM and other models/methods is that we advocate a "model-driven approach" to software creation. The essence of the model-driven approach is that we focus primarily on establishing a model, rather than following a finely prescribed set of procedures to develop applications. The difference between the two is like seeking a destination address with either (1) a set of directions (i.e., a set of steps as a method) or (2) a final address and a map (i.e., a model). The set of directions may be easier for the novice, but the map and address provide more options, flexibility, and freedom to pursue better approaches. The model-driven approach is more robust in the face of unusual circumstances. Armed with an explicit conceptual model of the system, we can pursue alternate paths successfully because we understand our environment better. We do not have to rely on an expert to tell us which alternative is best, because we can use our model to generate and judge alternatives ourselves.

5.2.2 A Model-Equivalent Language and Seamless Model

One of the major problems with existing approaches to object-oriented development is poor integration across several spectrums (Liddle, Embley, and Woodfield, 1994), two of which are (1) models, languages, and tools used in various phases of the software development lifecycle are often inconsistent and thus require lossy transformations when moving from one to another and (2) there are "impedance mismatches" between programming paradigms, such as declarative vs. imperative, visual vs. textual, and between the semantics of persistent objects and the behavioral protocols for objects.

This poor integration causes numerous problems. Applications are needlessly complex because developers must devise interoperability interfaces to overcome impedance mismatches (e.g., such as the mismatch between set-oriented semantics of databases vs. scalar semantics of programming languages). Developers must endure difficult and lossy transformations between different languages, models, and tools. Because of the complexity and differing definitions and assumptions that come from this "patchwork quilt" of tools and techniques, it is more difficult to achieve uniform quality of output.

As an example, consider the task of designing a CGI-BIN system that creates a Web interface to a database application. You could start by modeling the database with an ER model. Then, you would need to translate the ER model into a database schema that you could use to initialize your database. Next, you might write a set of C++ programs to process the CGI-BIN requests. These C++ programs would interface to the database either through an embedded SQL mechanism, or a direct API to the database. In either case, you now need to create an interface between C++ processing code and database queries. Because C++ has no set-processing commands, you will be required to process query results in loops, taking into account various possibilities such as no results, one result, or many results. You will also need to establish bindings between elements of your queries with variables in your program, and you may need to convert between data representations (e.g., convert a currency database field to a double C++ variable). Now suppose you want to modify this system. If you go back to the ER model and make changes there, you will need to retranslate the ER model into a database schema, paying special attention to what is different between the previous schema and the new one. Furthermore, you will need to carefully examine your C++ programs to find the places where they are affected by the new schema. This scenario is typical of the complex set of transformations between models, languages, and tools that exists in today's software development environment.

A major thrust of our work has been to develop OSM so that all phases of the software development lifecycle (i.e., analysis, specification, design, implementation, evolution) are supported within one seamless model that eliminates many model/language/tool integration problems. A major component of this integration effort is the development of a model-equivalent language (Liddle, Embley, and Woodfield, 1995) that addresses the poor integration of model and language, which is at the core of the larger problem. The essential idea of a model-equivalent language is that a software-engineering model and a programming language use the same underlying model, so that programs and model instances are really the same thing viewed from two different perspectives. OSM's model-equivalent language is called Harmony. However, whether the model/language pair is OSM/Harmony, UML/Java, or some other combination, the issues and challenges faced are largely the same. What is most important is that the analysis/design model be seamlessly integrated with the implementation language. Given this level of model/language integration, other aspects of the integration problems outlined above are easier to resolve.

5.2.3 A Formal Foundation

We have devoted a significant amount of energy to developing a formal description of our model, because a formal foundation is necessary for thorough understanding and precise communication required by theoreticians. On the other hand, practitioners usually feel that formalisms impede productivity and communication. It takes a great deal of effort to specify and verify a formal definition. Often, formal notations are cryptic and difficult to read, write, and share with others. OSM's approach is to provide tunable formalism (Clyde, Embley, and Woodfield, 1992). That is, OSM is formally defined in a temporal, first-order logic language, and yet model users can choose to work with different levels of formalism from informal natural-language descriptions to mathematically rigorous logic-language expressions. For example, natural-language descriptions constitute a good starting point for the description of many triggers and actions in an analysis model instance, but as we progress toward system implementation, creating specification, design, and implementation model instances, we need to replace these informal descriptions with expressions that can be automatically evaluated by a computer.

If we are to advance software development in the direction of true engineering, we require a formal foundation to answer questions like: "Are two model instances equivalent? and Is a given transformation information preserving?" A formal definition makes unequivocally clear what is syntactically correct in a particular model, and it gives a precise description of a model's semantics. Another benefit of a formal

TABLE 5.1 OSM Software Development Activities.

Deliverable	Content
Analysis model instance	Abstraction of the desired system and possibly the current system
Current system	Structural and behavioral description of the current system (optional)
Desired system	Structural and behavioral description of the desired system
Specification model instance	Document describing a specific system that serves both as a blueprint for the developer and an understandable description for the customer; may be relatively formal or relatively informal.
Design model instance	Architectural and detailed design information organized to have desired software engineering properties
Architectural design	Description of subsystems, interacting active components (object modules), and databases in the system
Detailed design	Data structures and algorithms needed to implement domains and behaviors of components in the architectural design
Implementation model instance	Complete automatically translatable and executable model of the detailed design

definition is that it provides the foundation for executing analysis model instances. We take advantage of this aspect of OSM in our IPOST tool for rapid interactive prototyping of a system specification (Jackson, Embley, and Woodfield, 1995). OSM's formal definition was introduced in the previous chapter.

5.2.4 Software Development Deliverables

Given the major tenets we have just described, we do not prescribe a specific process by which OSM-based software is created, nor do we specify a specific lifecycle such as the "waterfall" or "spiral" lifecycle. We see process and lifecycle issues as largely orthogonal to software modeling. That is, there are many lifecycles that could be appropriately applied to our model, so why prescribe a specific process, thus precluding other valid choices? However, we do recognize that there are various development deliverables, including analysis, specification, design, and implementation documents. So, when we speak of the OSM software development lifecycle, we mean any lifecycle model that produces the documents just mentioned. As long as the various documents are correct, complete, and consistent the order of creation is unimportant. The OSM software development deliverables are summarized in Table 5.1.

We have already described OSM's analysis model in the previous chapter. Next we will introduce Harmony's syntax, then describe OSM's specification model, and then we will explore OSM's design model. We describe how detailed design is different if the target platform is a popular OO language like C++ or Java instead of our own Harmony. Then we describe the key contributions of Harmony, and discuss how implementation in Harmony follows from an OSM design. In this chapter we continue with the running example of the previous chapter, our Computer Inventory Tracking System.

5.3 Harmony Textual Notation

As we move from analysis into specification, design, and implementation, it becomes increasingly more useful to have a textual representation of OSM model instances, since text is often easier than images for developers to create and manipulate. Images are often better for communication and visual conceptualization, but text is often more compact and better suited for expert users. Because Harmony is a model-equivalent language, we can use it to express an OSM model instance in pure text. Also because of this model equivalence, developers can intermingle textual and graphical forms of expression as needed. We find it convenient to represent most of our analysis model instances graphically, but most of our design and implementation model instances textually. Specification diagrams (which serve both developers and customers) often use a mixture of the two forms. We will rely mostly on the textual notation in this chapter, explaining new syntax as we introduce it. A full grammar for Harmony is available from the OSM Web site, http://osm7.cs.byu.edu.

```
Computer Item includes      -- Harmony keywords are in boldface
    Inventory ID: String[1] identifies Computer Item[1];
    Computer Item[1] was purchased for Price: String[1:*];
    Computer Item[1] is at Location[1:*];
    Computer Item[0:1] has Repair History[1];
    Computer Item[1] was purchased on Date: String[0:*];
    Computer Item[0:1] is planned for replacement on Date[0:*];
end;
Monitor, Base Unit, Printer, Scanner is a [partition] Computer Item;
In Use Item, Surplus Item is a [mutex] Computer Item;
Base Unit has subparts      /- denotes aggregation -/
    [1]   CPU                 [1];
    [1:*] Memory              [1];
    [0:*] Internal Disk Drive [1];
    [0:*] Media Card          [1];
    [0:*] Network Card        [1];
end;
```

FIGURE 5.1 Harmony version of OSM model instance.

Figure 5.1 shows a textual version of the model instance from Figure 10.2. Observe the direct correspondence of components in the two figures. For example, *Computer Item* is a high-level object set, which we can tell from the keyword `includes` that introduces the components contained within *Computer Item*. Everything up to the first end statement is included in *Computer Item*. We write relationship sets using their full names, e.g., *Inventory ID identifies Computer Item*, interspersed with participation constraints in square brackets (e.g., [*1*]). Notes or comments may be written in two ways. Any text following a double hyphen (--) up to the end of the line is a comment. Comments may also be bracketed by "/-" and "-/" (this form is useful for multi-line comments). Lexical object sets are distinguished by specializing from other object sets that are known to be lexical. For example, we know that *Price* is lexical because the construct *Price: String* indicates that *Price* is a specialization of the built-in lexical object set *String*. Generalization/specialization may also be written with the keyword `is a`, optionally followed by generalization/specialization constraints in square brackets (e.g., [`mutex`] places a mutual-exclusion constraint on *In Use Item* and *Surplus Item*). Finally, this example illustrates the aggregation template, which is written as the aggregate object-set name, followed by `has subparts`, the subpart components, and the terminating end statement. This template defines binary relationship sets such as *Base Unit* `has subpart` *CPU*. To the left of each subpart object set we write the participation constraint that applies to the aggregate. The subpart's participation constraint is written to the right. Thus, *Base Unit*[*1*] `has subpart` *CPU*[*1*] describes the full relationship set between *Base Unit* and *CPU*. All Harmony statements are terminated by a semicolon (;). "Bulk" constructs, such as high-level components and aggregation, are always bracketed in Harmony by an initial keyword (e.g., `includes`) and a terminating end statement.

5.4 Specification

Analysis is essentially a discovery activity, and hence, the analysis model is oriented toward capturing and documenting the real world. In specification, we turn from discovery to solution. Specification is the transition between analysis and design, and its goal is to document user requirements in terms of a solution system prior to actually designing and creating the solution system.

There are two major uses for a specification. First it provides a technically detailed description of a new system that could be attached to a development contract. As such, it defines the scope of a system and its functions and operations, as well as required interfaces to other systems and its environment. A specification is written in sufficient detail for effective acceptance testing to ensure that individual contractual requirements have been satisfied. Thus, a specification serves as the basis for a client/developer contract.

The second major use of a specification is that it provides a starting point for design, for example, a coarse outline of a system to be designed and implemented. Just as specification is a transformation from an analysis to a high-level solution, design and implementation are essentially transformations of the requirement's specification into well-structured components that efficiently and effectively provide the desired system functions.

To create a specification, we transform an analysis model instance in several ways: we formalize informal elements; we elaborate and refine incomplete elements; and we define a system boundary. We will now discuss each of these in turn.

5.4.1 Formalization

During analysis, many constraints, triggers, actions, and other elements are written using natural language (e.g., "Update location"). Because natural-language sentences cannot usually be processed automatically by a computer, at some point we need to translate these informal statements into a machine-understandable form. Much of this rewriting into formal expression is done as an analysis model instance is transformed into a specification model instance.

There are alternatives for formally representing informal statements. For specification model instances we often write constraints, triggers, and actions in Harmony, OSM's model-equivalent language. The informal statement *Update location* might turn into the Harmony assignment statement, `self`.*Location* := *"Supply Room";* (the particulars depend upon the context, of course). The keyword `self` refers to the object executing this statement. The symbol ":=" indicates assignment. In this case, *"Supply Room"* is added to *Location*, and relationships between the `self` object and *"Supply Room"* are created, replacing any previous relationships between `self` and objects in the *Location* object set.

Another alternative is that we can choose to delay formalization, and yet still make an informal statement compilable in Harmony by surrounding the expression in angle brackets, e.g., << *Update location* >>. If Harmony is not the ultimate target implementation platform, other machine-understandable languages could be used to express triggers, actions, and constraints.

5.4.2 Elaboration and Refinement

Another activity that is similar to the formalization of informal elements is the further elaboration and refinement of components whose level of detail is insufficient for the purposes of requirements specification.

5.4.2.1 State-Net Refinement

Figure 5.2A shows how we might use Harmony to formalize and elaborate some of the transitions in the state net for *Computer Item* (see Figure 10.4). Observe that the trigger of transition *10* now has a parameter, *projected surplus date*, associated with the *@Update* event, indicating that an *Update* event is accompanied by a *projected surplus date*. The parameter is a specialization of the object set *DateTime*, as specified by "*: DateTime*." For transition *10*'s action, rather than "*Update projected surplus date*" (as in Figure 10.4) we now have a Harmony assignment statement to associate the corresponding *Computer Item* with the given *projected surplus date*. Transitions *1* and *11* are also modified during specification to have additional detail. For transition *1* we add parameters necessary to create a new *Computer Item*. For transition *11* we add return parameters to the *@Check Status* interaction and we refine the description of the action to indicate that an asset-management utility will be used to determine the current configuration status. Furthermore, we make the actions of transitions *1* and *11* compilable in Harmony by surrounding the descriptions with << ... >>, indicating that the actions are (still) informal and should be replaced later on with actual code.

5.4.2.2 Harmony Version

Figure 5.2B shows the Harmony textual form of the state net from Figure 5.2A. Transition names (e.g., *1*, *10*, and *11*), if present, are listed on the left. The keyword when introduces the enabling state of a

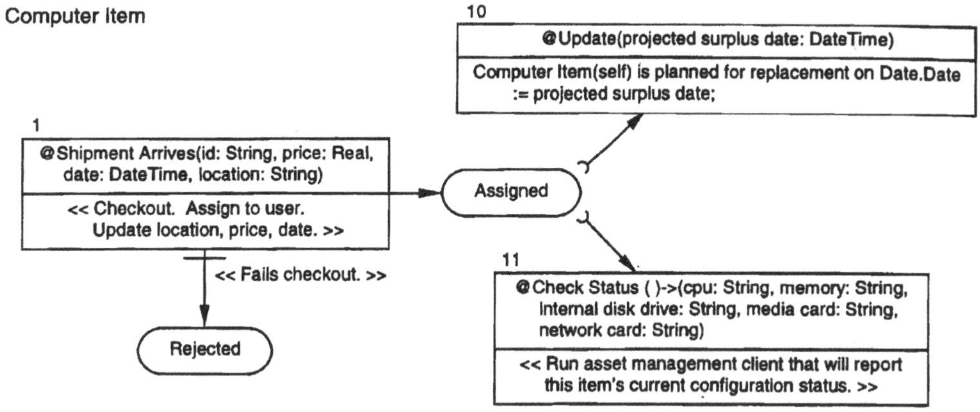

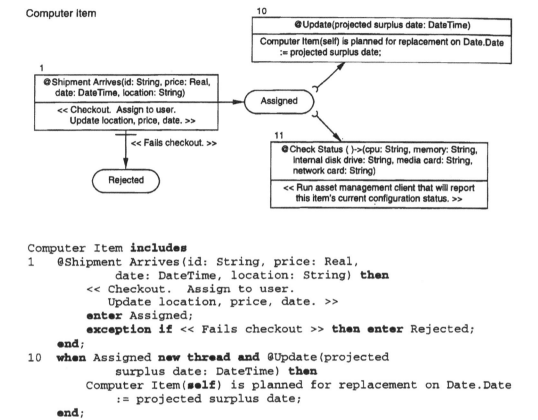

```
Computer Item includes
1   @Shipment Arrives(id: String, price: Real,
          date: DateTime, location: String) then
       << Checkout.  Assign to user.
          Update location, price, date. >>
       enter Assigned;
       exception if << Fails checkout >> then enter Rejected;
    end;
10  when Assigned new thread and @Update(projected
          surplus date: DateTime) then
       Computer Item(self) is planned for replacement on Date.Date
          := projected surplus date;
    end;
11  when Assigned new thread and @Check Status()->(cpu: String,
          memory: String, internal disk drive: String,
          media card: String, network card: String) then
       << Run asset management client that will report this
          item's current configuration status. >>
    end;
end;
```

FIGURE 5.2 (A) Partial view of specification state net for computer item (graphical view) and (B) partial view of specification state net for computer item (textual view).

transition (*Assigned* for transitions *10* and *11*). Because transition *1* has no when clause, we know that it is an "initial" transition that causes the creation of a new *Computer Item* object. The phrase `new thread` indicates that when the transition *10* or *11* fires, it executes in a new thread of control. In this example, all the triggers are event-based, indicated by the "at sign" (@). However, triggers may also consist of Boolean expressions or a combination of events and Boolean conditions. A transition's action follows the keyword `then`. The presence of an `enter` clause (e.g., `enter` *Assigned*) indicates a state that is turned on after the transition finishes firing. Because transitions *10* and *11* have no `enter` clauses, we know that they are "final" transitions that terminate the thread when finished firing. An `exception` clause indicates an abnormal exit path for a transition. A transition is terminated with an `end` statement.

5.4.2.3 OIM Refinement

Observe that as we refined the state net for *Computer Item*, we also refined the OIM (interaction) portion of the analysis model instance. As we refine event-based triggers, we also refine the corresponding

```
Computer Item includes
    Inventory ID: String[1] identifies Computer Item[1];
    Computer Item[1] was purchased for Price: Real[1:*];
    Computer Item[1] is at Location: String[1:*];
    Computer Item[0:1] has /-High Level-/ Repair History[1];
    Computer Item[1] was purchased on Date: DateTime[0:*];
    Computer Item[0:1] is planned for replacement on Date[0:*];
end;
Monitor, Base Unit, Printer, Scanner is a [partition] Computer Item;
In Use Item, Surplus Item is a [mutex] Computer Item;
Base Unit has subparts
    [1]   CPU: String                  [1];
    [1:*] Memory: String               [1];
    [0:*] Internal Disk Drive: String  [1];
    [0:*] Media Card: String           [1];
    [0:*] Network Card: String         [1];
end;
```

FIGURE 5.3 Specification version of detailed ORM for computer item.

interaction that generates the triggering event. For example, our analysis model instance might contain the interaction *Check Status* `from` *CSR* `to` *Computer Item;* (this is the Harmony equivalent of drawing an interaction arrow between *CSR* and *Computer Item* with a label *Check Status*). From the state net in Figure 5.2, we can see that the *Check Status* interaction has been specified more carefully as *Check Status*( )->(*cpu: String, memory: String, internal disk drive: String, media card: String, network card: String*) `from` *CSR* `to` *Computer Item*. Here we have written *Check Status* as a two-way interaction (where the sender waits for the transition to finish firing) instead of a one-way interaction (where the sender generates the interaction event and continues without waiting). We have also added additional detail about information passed between *CSR* and *Computer Item*. It is often the case that interactions are defined at the object-set level in the analysis model instance (as in Figure 10.6) but at the transition level in the specification model instance.

5.4.2.4 ORM Refinement

Figure 5.3 shows how the ORM of Figure 5.1 might evolve during specification. We have chosen to give *Location* and the subparts of *Base Unit* lexical identifiers, presumably because these are strings we want to store (e.g., *"585 TNRB"* for a *Location*, or *"266MHz Pentium® II"* for a *CPU*). Also we marked *Repair History* as a high-level object set (indicated by */-High Level-/*), meaning that its details are described in another view that we have not shown here, but which is necessary to complete the specification model instance. Finally, we refined the lexical descriptions of *Price* and *Date*, making them specializations of the built-in object sets *Real* and *DateTime*, respectively.

5.4.3 Defining a System Boundary

Beyond the constructs of OSA, the OSM specification model includes one additional modeling construct: the "system boundary." A system boundary is merely a high-level object set that separates components that are internal and external to a system. A system boundary has several additional key properties beyond those of ordinary high-level object sets. First, nothing crosses a system boundary except interactions. Relationship sets, object sets, state nets, and constraints are either fully enclosed within a system boundary, or they are fully external to the boundary. Second, no relationship sets or interactions may be connected to a system boundary. Third, a system boundary is neither a generalization nor a specialization of another object set.

The definition of a system boundary marks the beginning of a solution system. Defining a system boundary is a creative process that requires design-oriented decisions in order to achieve the properties

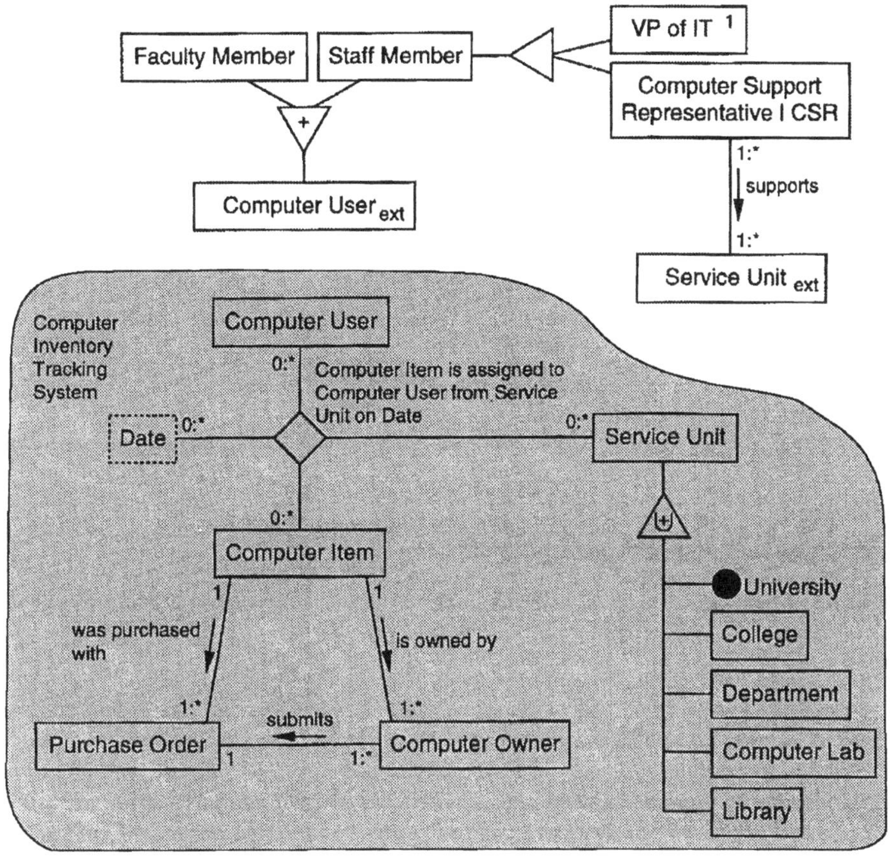

FIGURE 5.4 Computer inventory tracking system automation boundary.

described above. Figure 5.4 shows an OSM model instance for the computer inventory tracking example with a system boundary added.* Notice that the definition of the system boundary required us to modify the model instance so that all elements are either fully included or fully excluded from the automated portion of the system. There are two object sets, *Computer User* and *Service Unit*, that have been split between the automated (internal) and non-automated (external) portions of the system. To distinguish between internal and external versions of an object set, we rename, in this case by adding *ext* subscripts to external object sets. Because interactions are allowed to cross a system boundary, we can synchronize internal and external object sets by inserting appropriate interactions when needed. The full process of splitting object sets is described elsewhere (Clyde, 1993).

Relationship sets that cross a system boundary can be handled in several ways. We might delete the relationship set from the specification view if it has no purpose in the specification, or we could move it entirely outside the system boundary, as we have done with *CSR supports Service Unit* in Figure 5.4. This is done by splitting any connected object sets that are inside the system boundary, as with *Service Unit*. Another possibility, if two or more of the connected object sets are fully enclosed in the system boundary, is that we can reduce the relationship set by removing connections that are not inside the boundary.

*Textually, a system automation boundary is represented like a high-level object set with the prefix `system boundary`. For example: `system boundary` *System Name* `includes` */- contents -/* `end`.

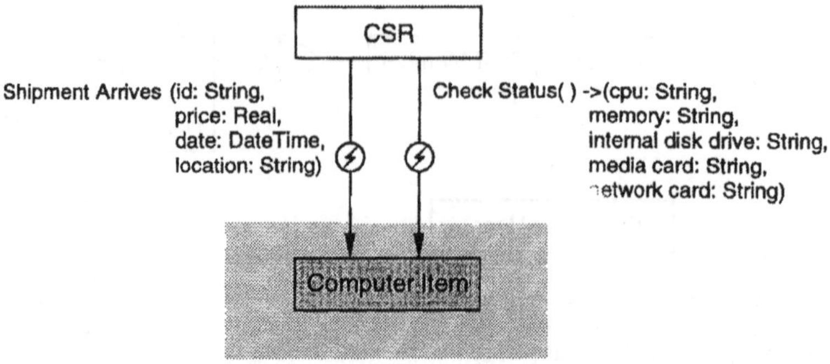


```
Shipment Arrives(id: String, price: Real,
    date: DateTime, location: String) from CSR to Computer Item;

Check Status()->(cpu: String, memory: String, internal disk
    drive: String, media card: String, network card: String)
    from CSR to Computer Item;
```

FIGURE 5.5 (A) Boundary-crossing interactions (graphical view) and (B) boundary-crossing interactions (textual view).

After we have finished describing a system boundary, we are left with interactions that cross the boundary. Figures 5.5A and 5.5B show graphical and textual views, respectively, of two of the interactions that cross the automation boundary of our computer inventory tracking system. Boundary-crossing interactions constitute an interface between the system and its environment. In many cases, such interactions represent a user interface, such as a hierarchy of menus and graphical forms. The *Shipment Arrives* and *Check Status* interactions, for example, could be implemented as dialog boxes that allow a CSR to create or query the status of a *Computer Item* in the inventory tracking system. In other cases, boundary-crossing interactions constitute interfaces to other systems (e.g., we might have two separate automated systems that interact). As mentioned earlier, it is important that an interface specification contain adequate detail to satisfy the needs of specification (i.e., basis for development contract and initial system design). It is the process of refining the interface that brings us to our next idea.

5.4.4 IPOST — A Synergistic Tool

We developed the Interactive Prototyping Object-oriented Specification Tool (IPOST) as a complement to the OSM Composer (the syntax-directed graphical editor for OSM model instances) to help move from analysis to specification. Since analysis models can be executed with the aid of an oracle (i.e., to interpret natural-language and incomplete elements), we have implemented such a system where the IPOST user is the oracle. IPOST executes a model instance created by the OSM Composer. As it executes, IPOST presents questions to the user, allows the user to initiate events, traces the effects of those events, and through an interactive dialog allows the user to refine natural-language constructs dynamically to be written in Harmony. IPOST focuses on the refinement of interactions, triggers, and actions, thus building a prototype of a system directly from its analysis and specification model instances.

IPOST demonstrates many of the advantages of the OSM approach. Our formal foundation provides a path to an executing system directly from analysis and specification artifacts, in the same development paradigm. A more complete description of IPOST is given elsewhere (Jackson, Embley, and Woodfield, 1995).

5.5 Systems Design

Design, like specification, is a synthesis activity, but whereas the specification model is concerned with *what* a system is to do, the design model is concerned with *how* the system is to do this. An OSM design model instance organizes a solution system, producing a set of modules that have good engineering properties and are suitable for implementation on the system's target platform.

OSM design generates both an architectural design (represented by an architectural-design model instance) and a detailed design (represented by a detailed-design model instance). Architectural design covers coarse-grained organization of a system, and detailed design covers fine-grained structure and behavior of individual components.

5.5.1 Architectural Design

An architectural-design model instance describes three aspects of an OSM system: subsystems, object modules, and databases. In this section we describe architectural design for subsystems, object modules, and databases. We also introduce the "object module" modeling construct.

5.5.1.1 Subsystem Design

Smaller projects may not require multiple subsystems, but for large projects it is critical that we divide our system into smaller, manageable pieces. Systems may contain subsystems nested to an arbitrary level, depending on the needs of a particular project. Subsystem design is a variation on the system-boundary specification process. We choose subsystem boundaries in much the same way as we choose an overall system boundary. Again, only interactions may cross subsystem boundaries, and there may not be any relationship or interaction connections directly to a subsystem. If an object set is needed in two subsystems, it must be split using the same kinds of techniques discussed previously. Relationship sets that cross a subsystem boundary may also be transformed or removed as we described in the specification section. The output of subsystem design is a model instance with nested, nonoverlapping system/subsystem boundaries. Interactions between subsystems describe subsystem interfaces, just as interactions that cross the automated system boundary describe the overall system interface.

For the computer inventory tracking system as we have presented it, we chose not to create any subsystems. However, if we were to broaden the project, we might want, for example, to include an interface to an accounting system. In that case, the computer inventory tracking system and the accounting system might well be two subsystems of a larger university information technology infrastructure.

5.5.1.2 Object Modules

Beyond those modeling constructs in the OSM specification model, the OSM design model has one additional construct, the "object module." Like a system boundary, an object module is a high-level object set with some additional properties and constraints. The primary function of an object module is to provide stronger encapsulation than is found in an ordinary high-level object set. Because high-level object sets constitute a view on the underlying system, multiple high-level object sets can include the same low-level details. Thus, the same *Date* object set might be included in both the *Computer Item* and the *Repair History* object sets. Because object sets must flexibly model many distinct views of system structure, two different high-level object sets can overlap in arbitrary ways. However, since object modules are intended to directly support software engineering they may not overlap, and they are better suited for mapping to traditional object-oriented programming languages.

Object modules have three sections: (1) public interface and modifiable structure, (2) visible but read-only structure, and (3) hidden (totally encapsulated) components. Figure 5.6 shows an object module for *Computer Item* with these three sections.

Public interface — A "public interface" defines interactions that may come into and go out of an object module. A public interface may also describe object sets and relationship sets contained within

```
object module Computer Item includes
    -- Incoming interactions
    Check Status()->(cpu: String, memory: String,
        internal disk drive: String, media card: String,
        network card: String) from CSR;
    Shipment Arrives(id: String, price: Real, date: DateTime,
        location: String) from CSR;
    Update(location: String) from CSR + Computer User;
    Update(projected surplus date: DateTime) from CSR;
    ...

    -- Outgoing interactions
    Shipment Arrives(bill of lading: String) to Purchase Order;
    ...

read only:
    Inventory ID: String[1] identifies Computer Item[1];
    Computer Item[1] is at Location: String[1:*];
    Computer Item[0:1] is planned for replacement on Date[0:*];
    Computer Item[1] was purchased for Price: Real[1:*];
    Computer Item[1] was purchased on Date: DateTime[0:*];
    Computer Item[0:1] has /-High Level-/ Repair History[1];

hidden:
1   @Shipment Arrives(id: String, price: Real, date: DateTime,
            location: String) then
        << Checkout.  Assign to user.
           Update location, price, date. >>
        enter Assigned;
        exception if << Fails checkout >> then enter Rejected;
    end;
    ...
```

FIGURE 5.6 Partial view of computer item object module.

an object module but directly accessible to and modifiable by objects outside the object module. We do not require "get/set" interactions for accessing and modifying object and relationship sets in the visible section of a module. We believe that the decision to provide direct or indirect access to object and relationship sets is a style issue that should not be enforced by OSM. In the case of *Computer Item*, only incoming and outgoing interactions are described in the public interface. That is, there are no structures in *Computer Item* that can be directly modified by outside objects. Outgoing and incoming interactions are distinguished from each other by the use of `to` and `from` clauses respectively.

Read-only section — The second part of an object module is its "read-only" section. This section is tagged with the phrase `read only:` and it contains object and relationship sets that are visible to, but not directly modifiable by, objects outside the object module.

Hidden section — The third part of an object module is its "hidden" portion, tagged with the keyword `hidden:`. It contains object and relationship sets that are not visible (neither accessible nor modifiable) to the outside world. It also contains a state net that describes the behavior of an object module. State net components may *only* appear in the hidden portion of an object module. Conversely, the state net of an object set (not an object module) is visible to other objects in the system, and thus, any object can tell whether the *object set Computer Item* is in the *Assigned* state. However, when we transform *Computer Item* from an object set into an object module, we add more encapsulation, and the behavioral state of the *object module Computer Item* cannot be queried directly in the same way. Rather than directly checking the *Assigned* state for a *Computer Item*, we must now use an interaction (such as *Check Status* described in transition *11* of Figure 5.1) to acquire and relay that information.

5.5.1.3 Object-Module Design

The goal of architectural object-module design, also called "high-level design" by some authors, is to organize each subsystem into a collection of loosely coupled and highly cohesive object modules (ideally, these modules are connected to one another only by interactions; Embley and Woodfield, 1987). Another goal is removing unwanted redundancy. There are two aspects of object-module design: (1) we transform each subsystem into a collection of object modules and database components and (2) we apply various design patterns to the object modules to ensure they have desired properties of loose coupling, high cohesion, and minimal redundancy.

Object-module delineation — The essential property of an object-module design is that it reorganizes object sets from a subsystem model instance into object modules. The most common way to create object modules is merely to recast a single high-level object set from the subsystem model instance as a single object module. In our running example, *Computer Item* is a high-level object set that makes sense to designate as an object module in the design model instance. However, it is often the case that a group of object and relationship sets from the subsystem model instance will become a single object module. In either case, what we generate in this initial step of object-module design is a collection of object modules together with a group of OSM components that are not encapsulated within object modules. Those OSM components that remain outside of any object module usually become the database portion of a subsystem model instance (which could itself be modeled as another object module, if this is desired). This initial delineation of object modules is exactly that, an initial step. As we adjust the object-module design to weaken coupling, strengthen cohesion, and remove redundancy, the initial object module organization usually changes.

Coupling and cohesion — After performing the initial reorganization into object modules, we examine our object modules with the intent of minimizing unwanted coupling and maximizing cohesion. There are many ways object modules can be coupled in OSM. For example, behavioral coupling exists when one object refers to a state or transition of another object. This is the strongest (and most undesirable) form of coupling in OSM, and hence, we require object modules to have hidden state nets. Thus transformation from object sets to object modules requires the elimination of all behavioral coupling. Constraint coupling exists when a general constraint refers to object modules that are otherwise unrelated to each other. Global information coupling exists when one object module accesses another object module without receiving knowledge of the other object module through an interaction. Interaction coupling is the weakest form of coupling in OSM and is present when object modules are connected only via interactions.

Suppose we decide that in addition to *Computer Item* becoming an object module, *Purchase Order* also becomes a module. We still have a relationship set, *Computer Item was purchased with Purchase Order*, connecting the two object modules. This relationship-set coupling can be weakened to interaction coupling by creating surrogate identifiers for *Computer Item* (e.g., *Serial Number*) and *Purchase Order* (e.g., *PO Number*), and then letting the *Purchase Order* object module contain a reference to the *Serial Numbers* of associated *Computer Items*. Similarly, the *Computer Item* object module would contain a reference to the *PO Number* of the corresponding *Purchase Order*. As part of this transformation, we should provide interactions to access a particular *Computer Item* given a *Serial Number*, and to access a particular *Purchase Order* given a *PO Number*. Now the relationship-set coupling is gone and only interactions, such as *Shipment Arrives*, connect the two modules.

Behavioral coupling can be removed by replacing a state or transition query with an interaction that determines the same information. For example, rather than ask whether a *Computer Item* is in the *Assigned* state, we could add an interaction *@Is Assigned( )->(assigned: Boolean)* to *Computer Item*. This interaction would put *True* into the return parameter *assigned* if the *Computer Item* is in the *Assigned* state, or *False* otherwise. Now instead of employing behavioral coupling, we can use this interaction to determine whether a computer is assigned.

There are many design patterns we can apply as we seek to reduce coupling or increase cohesion, but perhaps the most common is the simplest: moving components into and out of object modules. We move a component inside an object module when we discover that it is only accessed by objects in that particular module. We move a component out of an object module when we discover that it is being accessed and modified directly by objects in other object modules. This directly aids the cohesion of object modules, but it also provides a good check on object-module coupling (i.e., the presence or absence of coupling gives clues as to the cohesive properties of an object module).

We use a concept called "object-set congruency" to test whether we can improve the cohesion of an object module (recall that an object module is a special kind of object set). An object set is said to be "congruent" when its set of "capabilities" is the same as its set of "common properties." A "common property" is a property that all objects in an object set must possess. For instance, in Figure 5.3 *Location* is a common property of *Computer Item*. That is, every *Computer Item* must have a *Location* (the participation constraint requires it). A "capability" is a property that an object in an object set may or may not possess. All common properties are capabilities but not all capabilities are common properties. For example, since *Computer Item* in Figure 5.3 has a *0:1* participation constraint in the relationship set *Computer Item has Repair History*, we know that having a *Repair History* is not required of every *Computer Item* but it may occur. Thus, *Repair History* is a capability of *Computer Item*.

In the previous example we have an object set (*Computer Item*), in which at least one property (*Repair History*) is a capability but is not a common property. Thus we say that *Computer Item* is "incongruent." We can make *Computer Item* congruent by giving it a specialization, *Repaired Computer Item*, and replacing the relationship set *Computer Item*[*0:1*] *has Repair History*[*1*] in *Computer Item* with the relationship set *Repaired Computer Item*[*1*] *has Repair History*[*1*] in *Repaired Computer Item*.

The previous example is a form of incongruence called "overstatement." That is, we have written down a property of a class that is not a common property. We solve the problem by creating specializations for which the property in question is required. There is another form of incongruence called understatement. An "understatement" exists when the same property appears more than once in a generalization/specialization hierarchy. For example, suppose we evolve our model instance of Figure 5.3 so that *Printer* and *Scanner* both have an associated *Model Number*. Because the same property (*Model Number*) appears in the *Computer Item* generalization/specialization hierarchy twice, *Model Number* is understated. To make this model instance congruent, we make *Model Number* a common property of *Computer Item* and remove the *Model Number* relationship sets from *Printer* and *Scanner*. Removing overstatements and understatements improves object-module cohesion.

As with most aspects of modeling, there is no absolute set of rules that indicates when congruency is most desirable and when it might be best to leave some object sets incongruent. We do not claim that model instances should always be made completely congruent. As always, design is a series of trade offs and compromises, and designers must employ common sense and experience when judging between alternatives.

5.5.1.4 Database Design

The portion of a subsystem model instance that is not contained within object modules is usually construed to be a database with which the object modules interact. Normally, "active" objects (i.e., objects in object sets that have user-defined state nets) either become object modules directly or they are nested within object modules. Thus, it is usually the case that object and relationship sets outside of object modules constitute "passive" objects that represent information of the kind that normally would be stored in a database management system. For this reason, database design becomes an important component of OSM system development.

While OSM database design is a large subject (and is described more fully in a textbook on the subject (Embley, 1998)), we will highlight three of the major activities of database design. These are normalization, denormalization, and lexicalization.

Lexicalization — We have already described lexicalization in the context of specification. In the context of database design, "lexicalization" means replacing a nonlexical object set with a lexical object set instead.

For example, since *Computer Item* is in a one-to-one relationship with *Inventory Id*, we really have no need for the *Computer Item* object set in a database, so we lexicalize *Computer Item*. We do this by eliminating *Inventory Id*[*1*] *identifies Computer Item*[*1*] and replacing *Computer Item* with *Inventory Id*. We preserve the original name of *Computer Item* by renaming *Inventory Id* to be *Inventory Id* (*of Computer Item*). The lexical *Inventory Id* now serves as a surrogate for *Computer Item*. Lexicalization is intended to make information easier to represent and query. It also simplifies the model instance, reducing the number of object sets and relationship sets needed to represent a structure.

Normalization — "Normalization" is the essential activity of database design in most methods (relational and object-oriented). To "normalize" is to reorganize a model instance such that redundancy in the model instance is eliminated or at least minimized (sometimes there are multiple choices for a minimal model instance). Normalization improves update characteristics (i.e., updates need only be done in one place in a fully normalized model instance) and makes certain classes of constraints easier to enforce.

Denormalization — "Denormalization," the process of introducing redundancy into a model instance, can also be useful. As it is with object-set congruency, so it is with normalization, the decision to normalize or denormalize is a compromise that must be evaluated carefully for each particular situation. Sometimes we do not want our data model to be fully normalized because of the performance characteristics of the resulting system. We usually denormalize solely for the purpose of improving efficiency.

5.5.2 Detailed Design

Detailed design is concerned with the choice of data structures and algorithms used to implement the functions of a system. More specifically, detailed design looks at object modules in isolation, and it refines their descriptions individually so that they will exhibit desired characteristics in the resulting implemented system. As with any detailed design method, the goal of OSM detailed design is to optimize a system for various characteristics and resource requirements, depending on the particular needs of a given system. These characteristics and requirements might be the amount of storage space needed to support such a system, the speed with which various functions can be performed, the cost of development, installation, and/or maintenance, ease of maintainability, and ease of extensibility.

Some detailed-design decisions are platform independent. For example, consider that C++ does not have a language mechanism to support concurrency, but Java does. Thus, if we know our system is likely to be implemented in C++ instead of Java, we will probably create the model instance so as to eliminate as much concurrency as possible, but if we know our system will be coded in Java, we will probably not avoid patterns of concurrency that are easy to support in Java. Such considerations cross the line into platform dependence.

Because many detailed design decisions must consider the ultimate target platform, we combine the remaining presentation of detailed design with that of implementation.

5.6 Design and Implementation for a Non-OSM Platform

The end product of design is a set of modules with appropriate components that can guide program development. The form of the final design model instance, and consequently the transformations needed to move from design to implementation, is dependent on the target programming environment. Developers using OSM have two alternatives for design and implementation: (1) stay completely within the OSM/Harmony paradigm or (2) use OSM to model the system, and use another OO programming language such as C++, Ada, or Smalltalk, or a programming language provided by an OO database management system such as O_2 or UniSQL to code the system. For the first option, using Harmony, there are no special transformations needed to prepare for the target implementation language. However, for the second option, it is necessary to make certain language-dependent transformations to prepare the design model instance to be expressed in the target language. Because most systems will be implemented using common languages such as C++ or Java, it is important to understand the issues of translating from OSM to popular environments. For the purposes of this chapter we will assume we are designing for C++.

There are significant (and often subtle) differences between C++ and OSM, but the primary difference is that the main C++ abstraction mechanism (the "class") is based on a standard abstract data type (ADT) with inheritance, while OSM uses the more general idea of "object module." The OSM object module is somewhat different than an ADT, because it is not built on the concept of a record or tuple, but instead is built from an arbitrary object/relationship graph. Thus, the major activity of detailed design when C++ is the target implementation language is to transform object modules from the architectural-design model instance into a form that corresponds more closely to the restrictions of ADT's. We accomplish this by applying structural and behavioral transformations to the object modules.

In this chapter we cannot give a comprehensive description of all the different kinds of OSM-to-C++ transformations. Other transformations include, for example, constraint transformations, speed and space optimizations, and transformations from the static model of OSM into databases. In this chapter we concentrate on structural and behavioral transformations.

5.6.1 Structural Transformations

The structural properties of ADTs are significantly limited when compared with object and relationship sets. The main reason for this difference is that ADTs use attributes which are single-valued. An attribute may be another ADT, so it can be a complex single value, but it is a single value all the same. Essentially, an attribute is like a one-to-many relationship set, as in *ADT[1] has Attribute[1:*]*. Each ADT instance must have exactly one value for the attribute, but a given attribute value may be the same for many different instances of the ADT. However, relationship sets may be *n*-ary, $n \geq 2$, and object sets may have optional participation or multiple participation. To handle these special cases, we apply several OSM-to-C++ design patterns. The goal of these transformations is to rewrite relationship sets included in an object module into the one-to-many form that is easy to implement directly in C++.

```
class Computer_Item {
  private:
    char      inventory_id[12];
    String    location;
    time_t    purchase_date;
    float     purchase_price;
    time_t    replacement_date;
    History   *repair_history;
...
};
```

FIGURE 5.7 Partial C++ representation of computer item object module.

There are many structural-transformation design patterns. In the following paragraphs we describe a subset of those patterns that deals with transforming relationship sets into attributes. Figure 5.7 shows the result of applying some of these transformations to the *Computer Item* object module. As we present these transformations, we assume that *X* is an object module, *Y* is an object set, and *X r Y* is a binary relationship set. Because OSM names allow characters that are invalid in C++ identifiers, we map OSM names *X* and *Y* to corresponding valid C++ names *x* and *y*, respectively. We refer to Figures 5.6 and 5.7 for the following discussion.

5.6.1.1 Representation of Lexical Object Sets

Before we can convert relationship sets into attributes, we must convert participating lexical object sets into their corresponding C++ representation. Normally these lexical object sets are converted directly into C++ strings, integers, floats, or other C++ types as appropriate. If we are mapping a lexical object set to a string, we must decide whether it will be a fixed-length string or an arbitrary length string. For fixed-length strings we can use character arrays. Arbitrary-length strings require dynamic allocation, so we can either manage string allocation directly (using a `char *` for the attribute type) or we can use a string class from a support library. In Figure 5.7 we decided to represent *Inventory ID* as a 12-byte fixed-length string, and we chose to allow *Location* to be arbitrarily large (here we assume the presence of a *String* class that manages this). C++ type annotations for lexical object sets can be attached to an OSM model instance as notes or comments.

5.6.1.2 Mandatory Attributes

If an object module *X* participates in a binary relationship set of the form *X*[*1*] *r Y*[*1:**] or *Y*[*1:**] *r X*[*1*] then we simply make *Y* an attribute of *X*. For instance, in Figure 5.6 we see two relationship sets that satisfy this pattern: *Computer Item*[*1*] *is at Location* [*1:**] and *Computer Item*[*1*] *was purchased for Price*[*1:**]. For these two relationship sets we generate two attributes, *location* and *purchase_price*, respectively.

Creating attributes from relationship sets of the form *X*[*1*] *r Y*[*0:**] is similar, but we must first decide whether the zero minimum participation constraint on *Y* indicates that *Y* really should be an independent C++ class instead of an attribute nested inside *x*. In the case of *Date*, we observe that the reason for *Date*'s participation constraint being *0:** instead of *1:** is that *Date* participates in two relationship sets. By adding a general constraint that each *Date* object must participate in at least one of these two relationship sets, we ensure that there are no stand-alone *Date* objects that might need to be represented through an independent C++ class. Thus, it is proper to implement *Date* as two attributes of the *Computer_Item* class as we have shown.

5.6.1.3 Mandatory Isomorphic Attributes

Some relationship sets are of the form *X*[*1*] *r Y*[*1*]. That is, there is a one-to-one relationship between *X* and *Y*. We translate these relationship sets directly into attributes as we did for mandatory attributes. For instance, the relationship set *Inventory ID*[*1*] *identifies Computer Item*[*1*] becomes the attribute *inventory_id* in Figure 5.7. However, we must ensure that no other *X* (e.g., *Computer_Item*) has the same *Y* (e.g., *inventory_id*) and vice versa. Because there is no way to declare class invariants in C++, we must either guarantee this through proper coding or we must insert additional code to check this constraint as needed.

5.6.1.4 Optional Attributes

If a binary relationship set is of the form *X*[*0:1*] *r Y*[ ] then *Y* can be transformed into an optional attribute *X*. Because attributes in C++ must always have some value, we represent optional attributes either by setting aside a designated null value or by wrapping an optional attribute in another class that flags whether the attribute is currently null. For dynamically allocated attributes, the null pointer (value 0) serves as a good indicator of when an attribute is not present. Thus, for the relationship set *Computer Item*[*0:1*] *has Repair History*[*1*], we use *History** (pointer to *History*) for the corresponding C++ attribute. We do this because *Repair History* is a high-level object set, the C++ type of which we are assuming has already been defined in the *History* class. However, for the relationship set *Computer Item*[*0:1*] *is planned for replacement on Date*[*0:**], we represent the corresponding C++ attribute as `time_t` *replacement_date*. In this case we set aside the value 0 as an indicator that *replacement_date* has not yet been assigned.

Notice that in the pattern *X*[*0:1*] *r Y*[ ] the participation constraint for *Y* is unspecified. If it is *1* then *Y* becomes an optional isomorphic attribute. As with mandatory isomorphic attributes we must ensure through proper programming that no two instances of *X* have the same *Y*.

5.6.1.5 Attribute Sets

Some relationship sets are of the form *X*[*1:**] *r Y*[ ] *or X*[*0:**] *r Y*[ ]. We transform these into attributes by creating attribute sets. That is, associated with *X* is an attribute *y_set* that is an instance of a set of *y* (normally represented using a template, e.g., *Set_of<y>*). For instance, assume that *Computer Item* included the relationship set *Computer Item*[*1:**] *has Peripheral*[*1*]. We would add to the class definition of *Computer_Item* the declaration *Set_of<Peripheral> peripheral_set;*.

5.6.1.6 *N*-ary Attributes

N-ary relationship sets cannot be directly modeled in C++. For a relationship set of the form *X*[ ] r_1 Y_1[ ] r_2 Y_2[ ] ... r_n Y_n[ ] we create a class *Y* that is composed of the attributes $Y_1 \ldots Y_n$. We then make *Y* an attribute of *X*. For example, suppose that the *Computer Item* object module contained the quaternary relationship set *Computer Item*[*0:**] *is assigned to Computer User*[*0:**] *from Service Unit*[*0:**] *on Date*[*0:**].

```
class Assignment {
  public:
    Computer_User   computer_user;
    Service_Unit    service_unit;
    time_t          assignment_date;
};

class Computer_Item {
  private:
    Assignment      *assignment;
...
};
```

FIGURE 5.8 C++ representation of *n*-ary relationship set.

In C++ we could represent this information as shown in Figure 5.8. Notice that we made *assignment* an optional attribute since a *Computer Item* object need not participate in the quaternary relationship (since the minimum participation constraint on *Computer Item* is zero).

5.6.1.7 Behavioral Transformations

Thus far, we have only considered structural transformations. However, interactions and state nets also have concepts that do not directly map to C++. For example, state nets may exhibit intra-object concurrency (an object may be performing multiple actions simultaneously) and inter-object concurrency (multiple objects may be active simultaneously). Because C++ does not support concurrency, it requires a significant amount of additional work to make sure a C++ implementation faithfully (and correctly) represents its corresponding OSM model. To help designers overcome the impedance mismatch between OSM and C++ we provide several behavioral-transformation patterns that reduce concurrency, handle general forms of interaction, and otherwise make state nets easier to implement in C++.

The most common and useful pattern, the "passive object pattern," is an example of our behavioral-transformation patterns. A passive object corresponds nicely to the C++ class. An object set satisfies the "passive object pattern" if its state net consists of a single state *S* together with one or more transitions. Each transition *T* has several properties: (1) *S* is *T*'s single prior state, (2) *T*'s trigger is based on a single, incoming two-way interaction, (3) *T* does not create a new thread when it fires, and (4) *T* re-enters *S* when finished firing. Because each transition is enabled by *S*, this pattern ensures that the object has no intra-object concurrency (i.e., only one transition can fire at a time). Because each transition is triggered by a two-way interaction, the object only "acts" when "invoked" by another object (i.e., much as methods are invoked in a C++ class). We translate a passive object set X into a C++ class by making a public method for each of the transitions in the state net of X. The method signatures conform to the interaction definition in the trigger of the corresponding transition. The transition body is then converted into a method implementation for the appropriate method. To arrive at a passive object pattern, often we must apply concurrency-reduction and condition-to-event transformation patterns, which we do not describe or illustrate here due to lack of space.

5.7 Design and Implementation in Harmony

In the introduction, we defined the idea of a "model-equivalent language" where a software-engineering model and a language are really two views of the same thing. This notion of model-equivalent language helps us overcome some of the major integration problems identified in the introduction and illustrated in the previous section. The primary advantage of a model-equivalent language is that it eliminates the need for many kinds of transformations when moving between different aspects of system development. With a model-equivalent language, transformations are merely shifts in point of view, so model-equivalence leads to faster and smoother application development with correspondingly fewer problems and higher quality results. Accordingly, detailed design in Harmony focuses exclusively on the selection of algorithms and data structures. Unlike the previous section, since impedance mismatches do not exist between OSM and Harmony, we do not spend any extra effort preparing an OSM model instance for implementation in Harmony.

In order to support a model-equivalent language, the model and language must be equally powerful, and each must have all the fundamental features of the other. To support the model/language equivalence of OSM and Harmony: (1) each OSM model construct is directly expressible in the Harmony and (2) each Harmony construct is either part of OSM, or can be mapped directly to model constructs. Thus, for example, Harmony has traditional decision (`if ... then ... else`) and loop statements (`while`, do, and `for each`) that can be written as state nets (the state net constructions are given in Embley, 1998).

Harmony is significantly different from common programming languages, and in the following sections we describe some of the differences.

5.7.1 Variables and Types

Harmony is different from traditional languages in its approach to variables and data types. Rather than use the classical approach of considering variables to be locations in memory that contain scalar values, Harmony instead uses the concept of object set (and relationship set) for holding data. Instead of declaring variables in Harmony, we define object and relationship sets that contain objects and relationships, respectively. Because these sets can hold zero or more members, our language does not have scalar semantics by default. However, Harmony does support scalar semantics because we can attach an object-set cardinality constraint of 1 to an object set, thus forcing the set to hold exactly one object, just like a scalar variable. Also, Harmony automatically converts between scalars and singleton sets when appropriate, so traditional scalar semantics are easy to handle in Harmony. However, our data model is generalized to recognize sets explicitly, and this is extremely important for database applications, where the set/scalar mismatch between databases and languages is painfully prominent.

Harmony contains important constructs and ideas that have evolved in programming language research. However, these constructs manifest themselves in different ways. For instance, a type in Harmony does not immediately appear to be similar to types in other languages. In a traditional language, a variable's type carries a great deal of information, telling us how to interpret the bits stored in that variable and which operations may be applied to the variable. In Harmony, an object set describes the behavior of its members, and generalization/specialization is used to constrain membership, thus giving us many of the effects of traditional data types. Consider what happens when an object set is a specialization of an object set whose membership is fixed. Because a specialization is a subset of each of its generalizations, a fixed-membership generalization restricts the potential members of a specialization. We define such constant object sets for common categories of objects, such as numbers and strings. For example, the set *Integer* contains all integers, and the set *Real* contains all real numbers (obviously, we do not store the full extent of these sets!). Earlier we said that in Harmony we write generalization/specialization either using the key word ***is a*** or the colon (:). Thus, *x* **is a** *Real* and *x: Real* are both statements that define *x* as a specialization of *Real*. Note that *x: Real* looks like traditional code, but it has a generalized meaning in Harmony, since *x* is a set. To force scalar semantics, we apply the cardinality constraint [*1*] *to x* (*i.e., x*[*1*]*: Real*).

To handle set semantics, we provide generalized operators. For example, = and <> test for set equality and inequality, respectively, (formally, given object sets S and T, $S = T$ if and only if $S \subseteq T$ and $T \subseteq S$, and $S <> T$ is the logical negation of $S = T$). Also, the relational comparison operators <, <=, >, >= are defined over sets. If S and T are object sets and ρ is one of {<, <=, >, >=}, we say that $S \rho T$ is true if and only if $\forall s \in S \forall t \in T (s \rho t)$.

5.7.2 Relationship-Set Traversal

Because object sets in OSM do not have attributes, it is also necessary to provide a convenient way to traverse relationships. For example, Figure 5.6 shows a *Computer Item* object module that corresponds to what would be an abstract data type in a traditional programming language, such as the *Computer_Item*

C++ class shown in Figure 5.7. Given a variable *c* of type *Computer_Item*, in a member function of *Computer_Item*, we can access the attributes of *c* with the dot operator: *c.inventory_id*, *c.purchase_date*, etc.

In Harmony we define the dot operator as a relationship-set traversal operator. So when we say *Computer Item.Inventory ID*, the dot represents traversal from *Computer Item* to *Computer Item has Inventory ID*, to *Inventory ID*. In general, given the expression *x.y*, we find a minimal spanning tree from *x* to *y* in our object-relationship graph. If this minimal spanning tree is not unique (i.e., there are two shortest paths from *x* to *y*) then *x.y* is considered invalid and generates a compile-time error, which can be fixed by specifying more of the path.

For query expressions, relationship-set traversal computes a join between object sets and relationship sets along the path. Thus, if *c* is an object set that is a specialization of *Computer Item*, *c.Inventory ID* finds the set of *Inventory ID* objects related to *Computer Item* objects through the *Computer Item has Inventory ID* relationship set. If *c* has only a single member, then there is exactly one object returned by *c.Inventory ID*, and it is the *Inventory ID* of the *Computer Item* object in *c* (this uniqueness is guaranteed not by the dot operator, but by the participation constraints on *Computer Item has Inventory ID*).

This relationship-set traversal operator provides an interesting side benefit of adaptive programming because it abstracts the specific connection path between object sets. Because the path specification is abstract, the object-relationship graph could change without invalidating corresponding code. To see this, suppose *Repair History* contains a count, *Incident Count*, of the number of repair incidents for the corresponding *Computer Item*. In C++, we would access this attribute for *Computer_Item c* as *c->repair_history.incident_count*. If for any reason we decided to move *Incident Count* directly into *Computer Item*, we would need to go to our C++ code, find all uses of *incident_count*, and change, for example, all occurrences of *c->repair_history.incident_count* with *c.incident_count*. However, in Harmony the expression *c.Incident Count* applies equally well whether *Incident Count* is included directly within *Computer Item* or indirectly, in *Repair History*.

5.7.3 Assignment

In traditional programming languages an assignment statement generally takes the form *variable := expression*. The effect of an assignment statement is to replace the contents of a memory cell of fixed size and type with a new value. The left-hand side of an assignment statement evaluates to a storage location (called an *l-value*), and the right-hand side is an expression that returns a value to be stored (called an *r-value*). In Harmony, we do not have fixed-sized cells holding data values, rather, we have object classes as containers holding zero or more objects. Furthermore, these objects may be involved in relationships with other objects. Because Harmony has a generalized concept of data storage, it also has a generalized form of the assignment statement. The full details are extensive, so we only give several examples here.

The general form of Harmony assignment is *path.class := expression*. Suppose we have the following Harmony code fragment:

```
c: Computer Item;
...
c := Inventory ID("126372").Computer Item;
...
c.Date := "15 May 1997";
```

The first assignment statement has the effect of removing any current members of *c* (if any), then selecting and assigning to *c* the *Computer Item* object that is related to the *Inventory ID* object whose value is "*126372*." Note that in general, we cannot guarantee the cardinality of a variable after an assignment statement; it may be empty or it may contain one or more objects. However, in this case we know that the cardinality of *c* after the first assignment statement is either 0 or 1, because the participation constraints on the *Computer Item has Inventory ID* relationship set guarantee that computer-item objects and inventory-ID objects are in a one-to-one correspondence. The second assignment statement is more complex. Because the left-hand side is a path expression, the assignment relates each object in *c* to the

Date object "*15 May 1997*," replacing any existing relationships between *c* objects and *Date* objects. If "*15 May 1997*" is not a member of the *Date* object set, it is added, and any date that is no longer associated with a computer item is deleted.

5.7.4 Integrated Predicate Calculus

An important aspect of Harmony is that it integrates elements of the predicate calculus directly into the modeling and programming paradigm. We pointed out in Chapter 10 that object and relationship sets generate predicates in our formal definition. These predicates are also directly available to the Harmony programmer to query the contents of object sets and relationship sets. Furthermore, existential and universal quantifiers are defined in Harmony. Thus, the expression *Purchase Order*(x) returns the objects in *Purchase Order* if x is empty, or the intersection between x and *Purchase Order* if x is not empty. We can also write the expression $\forall x$ (*Computer Item*(x) $\Rightarrow$ *x.Purchase Date* $\geq$ "*1 January 1997*") directly in Harmony as follows:

```
for all Computer Equipment(x):
                x.Purchase Date >="1 January 1997"
```

5.7.5 Deductive Rule Processing

Another component of Harmony that arises naturally from this integration of predicate calculus with the programming language is the Harmony deductive rule processing mechanism. It is often most convenient to specify a query deductively, especially when recursive traversal of the object-relationship graph is required. Because predicates representing actual (extensional) object and relationship sets are already available in Harmony, it is a small step to think of adding rules to derive intensional object and relationship sets as well. For example, we can define a derived relationship set *CSR supports Computer User* as follows:

```
CSR(x) supports Computer User(y):- CSR(x) supports Service Unit(z),
            Computer Item() is assigned to Computer User(y)
            from Service Unit(z) on Date();
```

5.7.6 Transactions

Harmony uses a nested transaction model that by default corresponds to the nested structure of transitions in a state net. If the developer does not specify otherwise, a transition executes as a transaction, committing upon successful completion of the action. An exception during a transition would cause the corresponding transaction to abort. Developers can control the scope of transactions explicitly with `start`, `commit`, and `abort` statements.

5.7.7 Persistence

Persistence in Harmony is provided automatically. Objects and relationships in the ORM at the global level persist for the duration of the system's execution. However, some objects and relationships need to be transient. We support levels of persistence and transience by allowing nested model instances to be associated with transitions (which themselves can be nested). Structures in a nested model instance exist for the duration of the transition, which may be long or short. The more deeply a transition is nested, the more transient its associated model instance is likely to be.

5.7.8 Summary

When OSM is the model for analysis, specification, and design, then implementation in Harmony is more straightforward than implementation in standard object-oriented languages. Harmony provides a number of advanced features to support the sophisticated needs of modern applications. However, we do not expect the world to drop existing languages and environments in favor of Harmony. Instead, many of the ideas in Harmony should be considered for inclusion in other languages as they are created or as they evolve.

5.8 Conclusions

Virtually everyone agrees that our industry needs better models, tools, and techniques to meet the demands of modern information systems development. We must employ rigorous engineering procedures to inject more quality, repeatability, reusability, maintainability, efficiency, and other desirable characteristics into our development processes. At the same time, we must not attempt to minimize the creative role of humans in these processes. We must recognize the artistic, human element in software and create synergistic tools that "get out of the way" of the imaginative developer, while intelligently performing redundant, uninventive tasks that would otherwise hamper human creativity and productivity. Similarly, our models and languages should reduce excess "cognitive baggage" that impedes clear understanding and straightforward transformations between different aspects of software development.

OSM is an effort to head in this direction. We do not claim that OSM/Harmony is the ultimate environment for object-oriented software development, but it is a powerful model/language that embodies many innovations that contribute to the larger body of object-oriented development. In this chapter we have presented (at a fairly high level) OSM's specification, design, and implementation models, along with the underlying tenets and philosophy of our work. OSM supports a smoother integration of models, languages, and tools than is found in many OO methods.

References

Clyde, S. W. 1993. Object mitosis: a systematic approach to splitting objects across subsystems. *Proc. Int. Workshop on Object Orientation and Operating Systems.* Ashville, NC.

Clyde, S. W., Embley D. W. and Woodfield, S. N. 1992. Tunable formalism in object-oriented systems analysis: meeting the needs of both theoreticians and practitioners, In *Proc. 1992 Conf. on Object-Oriented Programming Systems, Languages, and Applications,* pp. 452-465. Vancouver, Canada.

Embley, D. W. 1998. *Object Database Development: Concepts and Principles.* Addison-Wesley, Reading, MA.

Embley, D. W., Kurtz, B. D. and Woodfield, S. N. 1992. *Object-Oriented Systems Analysis: A Model-Driven Approach.* Yourdon Press Series, Prentice-Hall, Englewood Cliffs, NJ.

Embley, D. W. and Woodfield, S. N. 1987. Cohesion and coupling for abstract data types, *Proc. 1987 Phoenix Conf. on Computers and Communications,* p. 229-234. Scottsdale, AZ.

Jackson, R. B., Embley, D. W. and Woodfield, S. N. 1995. Developing formal object-oriented requirements specifications: A model, tool, and technique, *Inform. Syst.,* 20(4): 273-289.

Liddle, S. W., Embley, D. W. and Woodfield, S. N. 1995. Unifying modeling and programming through an active, object-oriented, model-equivalent programming language, *Lecture Notes in Computer Science,* 1021: 55-64. Springer-Verlag, NY.

Liddle, S. W., Embley, D. W. and Woodfield, S. N. 1994. A seamless model for object-oriented systems development, *Lecture Notes in Computer Science,* 858: 123-131. Springer-Verlag, NY.

Further Information

The most current source of information on OSM is found at the OSM Web site, http://osm7.cs.byu.edu. Here you can find the Harmony grammar, a description of the OSM metamodel, papers related to the OSM project, etc. The original description of OSA is found in the reference Embley, Kurtz, and Woodfield, 1992. The best source of detailed development guidelines for OSM is currently found in Embley, 1998.

6

An Analysis of the Unified Modeling Language: UML Compared with OSM

Robert B. Jackson
Brigham Young University

Stephen W. Liddle
Brigham Young University

Scott N. Woodfield
Brigham Young University

6.1 Overview

Object-oriented (OO) modeling began in earnest during the decade of the 1980s, and OO models and techniques continued to proliferate in the 1990s. During that time there were numerous efforts to come to some kind of common understanding regarding the most important of the major ideas of OO. By the mid-1990s, several methods had become predominant in the marketplace, and a great deal of effort was being expended comparing and debating the relative merits of different approaches. Furthermore, seemingly minor differences (and some major ones) were discouraging more universal acceptance and use of OO models and techniques.

The Unified Modeling Language (UML) was developed in response to this situation, to provide a common language for OO modeling. As such, it was designed to be extensible in order to satisfy a wide variety of needs. It was also intended to be independent of particular programming languages and development methods. While UML draws on a large body of existing OO modeling work, essentially UML is the harmonization of ideas from Booch, OMT, and OOSE.

0-8493-3135-8/99/$0.00+$.50

In this chapter, we describe key ideas of UML, and we discuss its properties from the perspective of experts in the field who are outsiders to the UML creation process. Our experience in OO modeling comes primarily from participation in the research community as we developed the Object-oriented Systems Model (OSM). We are in favor of a standard unified object-oriented modeling language, and we see UML as a positive step in this direction. As we compare UML with OSM, our goal is to describe UML, point out its strengths, and identify ways to improve it. We provide a running example of a simple Computer Inventory Tracking System (CITS) using both UML and OSM in order to illustrate alternative modeling techniques.

Our primary sources for information on UML are the documents written by Rational Software and the other companies in the UML consortium (Rational et al., 1997b and 1997c) which are available at no cost through the World-Wide Web. At the time of this writing, multiple books are planned for publication by the authors of UML (see Booch, Rumbaugh, and Jacobson, 1998, Jacobson, Booch, and Rumbaugh, 1998, and Rumbaugh, Jacobson, and Booch, 1998). These books should be in print by the time you read this, and it is expected that they will be definitive references on UML. Fowler and Scott (1997) and Quatrani (1998) are also helpful as brief introductions to UML.

6.2 Introduction

Because of the perceived advantages of object orientation, OO models quickly became popular among methodologists. Many texts were written proposing variations on the OO theme (see Booch 1996, Embley, Kurtz, and Woodfield, 1992, Coleman et al., 1994, Gamma et al., 1995, Harel, 1987, Jacobson et al., 1992, Martin and Odell, 1992, Meyer, 1997, Rumbaugh et al., 1991, Shlaer and Mellor, 1992, and Wirfs-Brock, 1990). As models and methods proliferated, the sheer number and variety (with their attendant incompatibilities) became a problem for users, tool vendors, and the entire software development community. The UML was developed as an answer to this situation. UML is primarily the integration of Booch, OMT, and OOSE, though it has incorporated ideas from other models as well.

The self-stated goals of UML are to provide an expressive visual modeling language that (1) is formally defined, (2) encourages tool vendors to invest in creating OO tools, (3) allows model interchange, (4) is extensible, (5) is independent of specific programming languages and development processes, and (6) integrates the best practices of the OO modeling community (Rational et al., 1997a).

The semantics of UML are defined around a common metamodel. (A "metamodel" is a model of a model. Think of it as a UML description of UML itself.) Such a metamodel is useful for supporting the first three goals mentioned above. Given a sufficiently formal model of UML, tool vendors can deliver fully UML-compliant tools whose documents can be interchanged because they conform to a common structure. In addition to enabling model interchange, a formal metamodel also improves our ability to verify that a model instance actually conforms to the rules of UML (a deceptively difficult task). It also enhances understanding among methodologists as they work on improvements to UML itself and UML-based methodologies.

The UML metamodel can be segmented into three major categories: structure, behavior, and implementation. Each of these three segments can be considered as a sub-metamodel that provides a formal definition of the components of that sub-metamodel.

Issues of graphical notation are separate from the semantics of the UML metamodel. A graphical notation is a means for presenting concepts described in the metamodel. Thus, a graphical notation represents a "view" into the metamodel. Associated with UML are ten standard types of graphical diagrams that present such notational views of the underlying UML metamodel.

These ten diagrams do not partition the metamodel. In fact there is substantial overlap of the metamodel in these diagrams. For novice UML users, this can be confusing until they realize that, in many cases, the diagrams simply present overlapping views of the same information. Because diagrams constitute end-user syntax for UML, we will take the approach of presenting UML and focusing our discussion in terms of these ten graphical diagrams, pointing out areas of overlap along the way. We organize the presentation of diagrams according to the sub-metamodels they cover.

Structure — Structural diagrams include class, object, and package diagrams. The class diagram supports the specification of object classes and their associations with other classes. The object diagram illustrates specific instances of classes and associations (these instances are called "objects" and "links," respectively). A "package" is an organizing construct. It is used to group and organize other diagrams together into a system or subsystem. All UML structural diagrams are closely related, since all three are built around a common metamodel. Both package and object diagrams are special cases of the class diagram.

Behavior — Behavior diagrams include use case, collaboration, sequence, statechart, and activity diagrams. It is in the behavior diagrams that we see the most conceptual overlap in UML. For example, collaboration and sequence diagrams express mostly the same underlying UML metamodel concepts, emphasizing two different perspectives on those concepts. Also, activity diagrams are a special case of statechart diagrams, again used to emphasize different points of view.

We separate these behavior diagrams into two broad categories: interaction specifications and state machines. The first category (use case, collaboration, and sequence diagrams) describes how entities in a system interact. These interacting entities may be external users, objects, roles that various objects may play, or even threads of control. The most general interaction specification is the use-case diagram, where we describe the processes or activities that external users can perform using the system. Collaboration and sequence diagrams give more detail about how objects play various roles as they interact with (communicate, synchronize, activate) one another inside the system. A collaboration diagram emphasizes associations between objects, while a sequence diagram highlights the temporal relation of one message to another.

The second category includes statechart and activity diagrams, both of which describe process flow using a state machine. A statechart diagram employs a variant of state machines to describe the complete behavior of a single object. An activity diagram uses a restricted form of state machine to specify the behavior associated with a use case or an operation.

UML takes a broad perspective of behavior in that it provides diagrams that are not strictly object-oriented. Because the underlying UML metamodel is object-oriented, all UML systems are also object-oriented, but that does not necessarily imply that all views are entirely object-oriented. For example, a use case describes processes that involve behavior potentially associated with many different objects. Also, an activity diagram is a detailed specification for a process, whether it be a use case or an operation. The behavior described by an activity diagram could be limited to behavior within a single object, but very often it is not. While this may surprise some OO purists, it is actually very useful at times to have process-oriented descriptions that can cut across object boundaries.

Implementation — There are two kinds of diagrams for implementation purposes; namely component and deployment diagrams. A component diagram describes the structure of software components as implemented in actual source code. Component diagrams are used to show dependencies between source code, binary code, and executable software components. A deployment diagram shows the configuration of runtime software elements. A deployment diagram indicates which software components actually execute on which processor nodes, or how software components could migrate from processor to processor at runtime.

6.2.1 Chapter Organization

The previous paragraphs provided a high-level description of UML's different diagrams. In the remainder of the chapter, we examine each diagram in greater detail. As we present each diagram, we describe its features, give examples, and then compare this aspect of UML with OSM.

To illustrate UML, we use as a running example the same CITS developed in the previous chapters on OSM (see Chapters 7 and 8). The primary objectives of this system are

- To maintain an inventory of all personal computers in use within a university
- To facilitate the timely upgrade of personal computers by ensuring that high-end users are provided with the latest technology
- To coordinate the surplusing of high-end equipment with the acquisition requirements of medium-capability users to control personal equipment costs university wide

We do not attempt to develop a complete system specification. Instead, we only develop enough to illustrate the ideas of UML.

In our discussion, we focus primarily on UML modeling concepts and try to avoid methodology issues. However, it is difficult to divorce the development process from the modeling language, and UML is only partially successful at doing so. While UML does not require a particular methodology, appropriate use of all the different diagrams dictates at least part of the development process. The creators of UML advocate a development process that is "use-case driven, architecture centric, and iterative and incremental" (Rational et al., 1997a). We mostly ignore methodology issues, but we assume that the reader will use a process much like the one envisioned by the authors of UML.

In the remainder of this chapter, we present the UML diagrams according to the categories outlined above (structure, behavior, implementation). After presenting the diagrams, we briefly describe the UML extension mechanisms (constraints, stereotypes, and property lists), and then we discuss some ways we have considered to improve UML.

6.3 Structural Diagrams

There are three kinds of structural diagrams in UML all built on the same underlying metamodel that describes objects, classes, associations, and packages. We first present the class diagram and then describe two special cases — object diagrams and package diagrams. Class diagrams are similar to structural diagrams in other OO models. They describe the static aspects of objects and their relationships with other objects. An object diagram emphasizes individual objects and links as opposed to more general classes and associations. Package diagrams are an organizational construct that provide a means to partition a design to facilitate understanding and development.

6.3.1 Class Diagram

Class diagrams describe objects, classes, and the relations between these entities including generalization and aggregation. Class diagrams also represent the attributes and methods of classes.

6.3.1.1 Objects

In UML, "objects" are instances of classes. An object has a well-defined boundary and encapsulates state and behavioral features. An object's state is represented by attributes and relationships ("links" to other objects). Behavior is represented by operations, methods, and state machines. Thus, the attributes, relationships, operations, and methods of an object are all defined by its class. Each object has a unique identity. That is, each object can be distinguished from any other object even if everything but their identities is the same. Significantly, an object may be an instance of more than one class and may dynamically change classes.

As shown in Figure 6.1, an object is represented by a rectangle enclosing an underlined identifier. An identifier may comprise an object's name, its class, or both. For instance, in Figure 6.1 we show an object with the name *Monitor_12255* which is an instance of the class *Computer Item*. Figure 6.1A represents both the object name and the class name. Figure 6.1B shows only the object name, and Figure 6.1C shows only the class name (such an instance is said to be "anonymous"). As Figure 6.1A also shows, the representation of an object may indicate values associated with attributes of that object. In this case we show values for the *Inventory_Id*, *Price*, *Purchase_Date*, and *Replacement_Date* attributes.

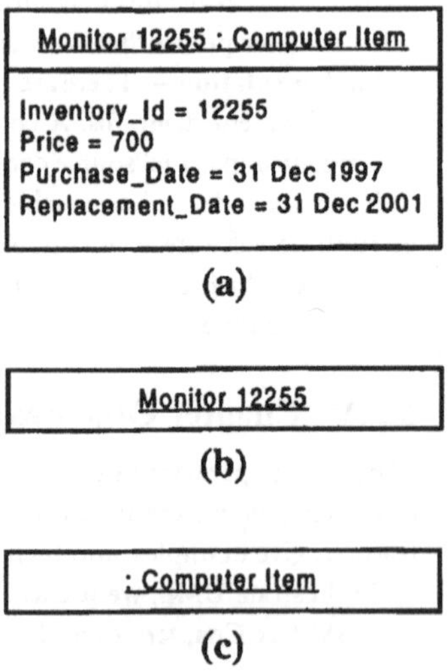

FIGURE 6.1 UML representations of an object.

6.3.1.2 Classes

A "class" is a description of a set of objects that have the same attributes, operations, methods, associations (relationships), and semantics. Thus a class defines a set of properties that all instances of the class will share. If a class has an attribute *Price* then all instances of the class will have a specific *Price*. If there is a method *Print* defined for a class then that method can be applied to any instance of the class. If we show that a class *Computer Item* participates in an association representing the fact that a *Computer Item* has a *Location*, then an instance of *Computer Item* must have a link to an instance of *Location*. When an object is instantiated, it acquires from its class all its attributes, methods, operations, and associations. In this sense a class acts as a template for object creation.

The representation for a class is similar to that of an object, or a rectangle enclosing an identifier. However in this case the identifier is not underlined. As shown in Figure 6.2, a class is often indicated by a rectangle with only a name (e.g., *Computer User, Location, Monitor*), but sometimes it is also desirable to indicate the attributes and methods of a class. In Figure 6.2, *Computer Item* and *Base Unit* are both shown with attributes in the lower section of the class rectangle. Figure 6.3 shows that methods of a class can also be represented in yet another section of the class rectangle. Here, the class name is in the upper section, attributes are in the middle section, and methods are in the lower section.

Attributes are defined using the syntax *name*[*multiplicity*] : *type*, where *multiplicity* and *type* are optional. For instance, in Figure 6.2 the attributes of *Computer Item* include *Inventory Id* which has a type but no multiplicity constraint, and *Repair History* which has a multiplicity constraint but no type.

A multiplicity constraint is a set of integers that constrains the number of values that may be associated with a specific attribute. Thus, the multiplicity *0..1* on *Repair History* indicates that a particular *Computer Item* may either have one repair history or none. The special marker "*" indicates no limit. The multiplicity *3..** indicates three or more. The type attributes in Figure 6.2 include fundamental types such as *string* and types defined in other packages, such as *Currency_Package::Currency*.

Methods of class are usually defined using the syntax of a language chosen by the modelers. It could be C++, Ada, Eiffel, or any other well-defined syntax. In Figure 6.3 we have used C++ syntax to define method signatures (the return type is to the left of the method name, and type names precede formal parameter names).

To indicate class methods and attributes (as opposed to instance methods and attributes) we underline a method or attribute definition. In Figure 6.3, *number_of_items* is a class attribute — a single value associated only with the class *Computer Item*. Also, the method *create()* is a class method. That is, it can only be applied to the class *Computer Item* and not to instances of the class.

In UML we can also represent "parameterized classes" or "templates." A parameterized class is a pattern that can be instantiated to create specific classes. Associated with a parameterized class is a set of one or more formal parameters, typically class names. When specific classes are defined from the parameterized class, an actual parameter is bound to a formal parameter. For instance, in Figure 6.2 we have a parameterized class, *List*, with a formal parameter *Element* from which we can define specific kinds of list classes (the dotted rectangle in the upper-right corner declares the formal parameter). In this case we instantiate the template as *List<Computer Item>* to represent a list of computer items.

In UML, a class is a special kind of "classifier." While classes are the most common form of classifier, there are other kinds, most notably "data types" and "interfaces." The syntax for these classifiers is similar to that of class. The major difference is that the tag "«type»" or "«interface»" appears above the name of such a classifier. In UML, any tag set off in guillemots ("«...»") is a "stereotype." (Stereotypes are discussed later in this chapter.) If a classifier has no stereotype, then it is assumed to be a class. A "data type" specifies a domain of instances together with the operations applicable to its objects. A type may not contain any methods (in UML, a "method" is a particular implementation of an "operation"). An "interface" specifies the external view of a class but provides no specification for the internal implementation. An interface has no attributes, states, or associations. Interfaces only have operations and are similar to abstract classes in many OO languages.

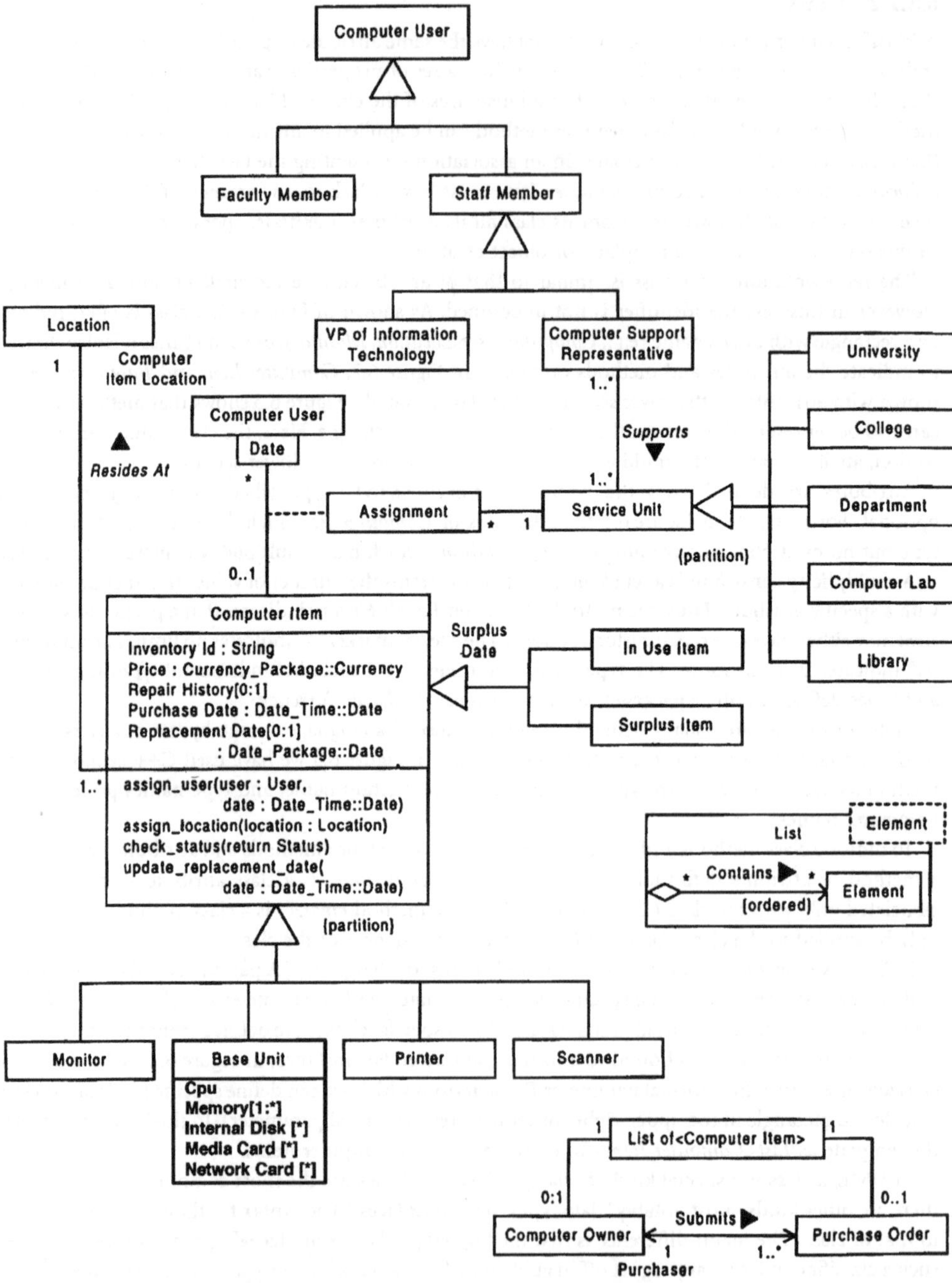

FIGURE 6.2 UML class diagram of the CITS.

6.3.1.3 Associations

Much of the information about objects and classes is described using attributes and associations. An "association" between two or more classifiers defines possible relationships or "links" between instances of the participating classifiers. For our purposes we will describe associations between classes.

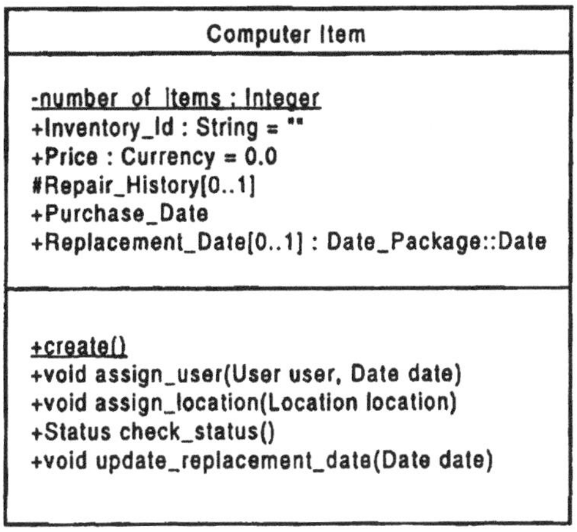

FIGURE 6.3 More details of a class.

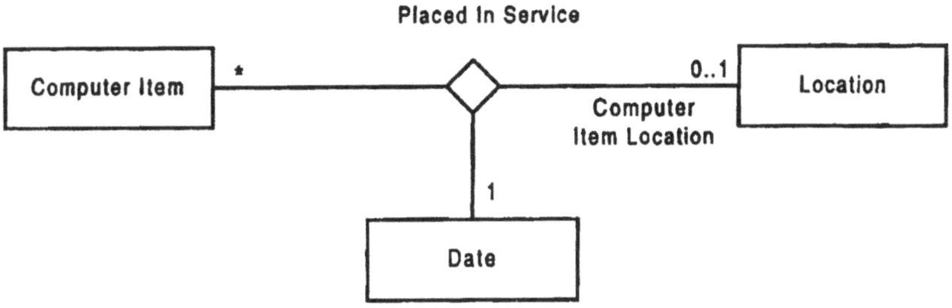

FIGURE 6.4 Ternary association in UML.

An association between exactly two classes is a binary association and is the most common form of relationship found in most conceptual models. A binary association is shown as a line connecting one class to another. An association name, if present, may appear in the middle of the connecting line. For example, in Figure 6.2 there are several binary associations, including the one named *Resides At* drawn between *Computer Item* and *Location*. While not required, association names are written to provide the reader with the intended semantics of an association. In this case it states that the *Location* associated with a *Computer Item* represents the fact that a computer item resides at a given location. The other interesting information about an association appears at an association end, the point at which a line segment attaches to a class rectangle. One of the most useful pieces of information is the multiplicity constraint which describes functional dependencies. In Figure 6.2 the *1* multiplicity constraint on the *Resides At* association indicates that for any *Computer Item* there is one and only one *Location*, while the *1..** multiplicity constraint indicates that for every *Location* there must be at least one *Computer Item* and perhaps many. The phrase *Computer Item Location* next to the class *Location* is called a "role." It classifies any *Location* that is associated with a *Computer Item* as a *Computer Item Location*.

While most associations are binary, there are times when it is desirable to represent *n*-ary associations. Figure 6.4 shows an example of a ternary association. In this case every link (instance of an association) describes the fact that some *Computer Item* was placed in service at some *Location* on a *Date*. Notationally, an association of arity greater than 2 is represented by a diamond with lines connecting it to each of the classes participating in the association. As with binary associations, an *n*-ary association may have a name, and each association end has a multiplicity constraint and possibly a role name. Multiplicity constraints in *n*-ary associations are special forms of *n*-ary functional dependencies. In Figure 6.4 they mean that for any *Computer Item* and *Date* there are zero or one *Locations* where the item was placed into service. For any *Computer Item* and *Location* there is exactly one *Date* on which it was placed into service, and for any *Date* and *Location* there are zero or more *Computer Items* placed into service. The notion of a role in an *n*-ary association is the same as a role in a binary association.

At times it is useful to treat an association as a class. An association that is also a class is called an "association class" and is represented by connecting a class to an association by a dotted line. In Figure 6.2, *Assignment* is an association class. As a class, *Assignment* can have any properties, such as attributes and methods, that can be conferred on other classes. As an association, *Assignment* can also have any properties, such as multiplicity constraints and roles, that can be given to other associations.

6.3.1.4 Links

A "link" is an instance of an association and represents a relationship between objects. A link is drawn as a line between objects (instances of classes). A link name, if present, is underlined, just as object instance names are underlined. Links may have other association-like adornments such as role names, aggregation, and navigation, but links may not have multiplicity constraints.

6.3.1.5 Special Relations

There are three types of special relations that can appear between classifiers. They are aggregation, generalization/specialization, and qualified associations.

An "aggregation" describes the subpart relation and is used to describe aggregate objects and their subparts. As shown in the *Contains* association of Figure 6.2, an aggregation is represented by a diamond at the end of a binary association. In this case, it states that a *List* is an aggregation of zero or more *Elements* and that each *Element* is part of one or more *Lists*. The constraint *{ordered}* states that the *List* is ordered. That is, there is a first element, a second element, etc. The *{ordered}* constraint is optional and can also be applied to ordinary associations.

A special "strong" form of aggregation is called "composition." A composition is an aggregation with an additional constraint. The multiplicity constraint on the aggregate or composite side can only be "0:1" or "1". That is, the subpart of a composition can be a subpart of at most one composition. Conceptually a subpart of a composition is bound tightly to the composite and has a coincident lifetime with respect to the composite. All attributes in UML are formally modeled as compositions. When a class is instantiated, all attributes of the corresponding instance are created at the same time. When the instance is destroyed, so are its attributes. This corresponds with the semantics of composition. Composition is represented as an aggregation with a black diamond instead of an open diamond. Or in the case of attributes, UML uses the previously described attribute notation instead of the usual composition notation.

Another special relation found in UML is "generalization." This is a relation that occurs between a generalization class and a specialization class. The specialization inherits all features of the generalization and may have more. Generalization is represented by drawing a triangle at the generalization end of a line connecting two or more classes. In Figure 6.2 we see, for instance, that *Computer User* is a generalization of *Faculty Member* and *Staff Member*.

Figure 6.2 also shows more advanced forms of generalization. For example, there are two disjoint specializations of *Computer Item*: *In Use Item* and *Surplus Item*. The phrase *Surplus Date* next to the triangle is a "discriminator." It is the information used to determine whether a *Computer Item* is an *In Use Item* or a *Surplus Item*. A discriminator is not required on all generalizations. The other generalization connected to *Computer Item* shows that *Monitor*, *Base Unit*, *Printer*, and *Scanner* are all special types of *Computer Item*. The *{partition}* constraint next to the triangle indicates that these specializations partition the generalization. That is, each *Computer Item* must be an instance of exactly one of these specializations. This constraint is not actually defined in standard UML but is a custom defined constraint whose definition is not shown here. It illustrates our ability to customize UML to contain constraints and other constructs that we may use extensively in our own modeling. The constraints that are defined in UML are "overlapping" (membership in the specializations may overlap), "disjoint" (membership in the specializations may not overlap), "complete" (each generalization must be a member of at least one of the specializations), and "incomplete" (a generalization instance need not be a member of one of the specializations). Our *{partition}* constraint is a combination of "disjoint" and "complete."

The third special relation is "qualified association." An example is shown in Figure 6.2, where we have an association between *Computer Item* and *Computer User* (the qualified class) qualified by a *Date*. It can be thought of as a ternary association between *Computer User*, *Computer Item*, and *Date* such that for every *Computer User* and *Date* there is at most one *Computer Item*. Every *Computer Item* can be associated with zero or more *Computer Users*. In our example there is only one qualifying attribute, *Date*. While this is most often the case, there can be any number of qualifying attributes.

6.3.1.6 Design Features

When doing design, there are some additional features of UML that we can employ. For classes we can describe visibility and define default values for attributes. Figure 6.3 shows an example for the class *Computer Item*. Visibility is declared with "+", "#", and "-" to indicate public, protected, or private, respectively. The specific semantics of these visibility markings ultimately depend on the implementation language chosen for a particular project. Notice also that we can indicate that when an instance of *Computer Item* is created that the *Price* will be initialized to zero and that the *Inventory_Id* will be an empty string.

For associations we can describe such design information as navigability, changeability, and role visibility. For an association between two classes *X* and *Y*, navigability indicates whether in the implementation we will access *X* given *Y*, or access *Y* given *X*, or both. Navigability is indicated by arrow heads on the end of an association. For instance, in Figure 6.2 the *Submits* association has arrow heads on each end. They indicate that given a *Computer Owner* we will want to know the associated *Purchase Orders*, and given a *Purchase Order* we will want to know the associated *Computer Owners*. However, the *Contains* aggregation is unidirectional. We can only look up an *Element* given its *List*, not vice versa (note that attributes are implicitly unidirectional). When navigability is unspecified, as in the *Resides At* association, the user may either assume that the association is bidirectional or that navigability is unknown at this stage.

Changeability is information about an association end, indicating whether links to an object are constant or unchangeable ("*{frozen}*"), can be added to but not deleted from ("*{addOnly}*"), or can be added, deleted, or modified (the default). Role visibility constraints are like attribute and method visibility constraints but apply instead to roles.

6.3.2 Comparison with UML

There are many conceptual similarities between OSM and UML (for example, compare the UML diagrams developed in this chapter with those in Chapters 7 and 8). They can each represent objects, classes, associations (relationship sets), and links (relationships). They both allow role names and require forms of cardinality constraints on associations. They can both treat associations as classes. Generalization/specialization is another feature found in both models.

There are features that UML supports that are not directly supported in OSM. We briefly mention several. UML's navigability and changeability information has no counterpart in OSM. UML also provides template classes. These were recently added to OSM but are not yet as well defined as in UML. UML supports discriminators on generalizations, which OSM does not directly support. UML has qualified associations but OSM does not. However, they can be easily represented by *n*-ary relations and co-occurrence constraints. UML does support the generalization and specialization of associations, but OSM does not.

Likewise, OSM provides features not found in UML. OSM supports high-level object sets and relationship sets. In OSM, high-level constructs provide multiple levels of abstraction to enable information hiding and multiple views of the world during analysis. UML has no such corresponding information. While the cardinality constraints of OSM and UML appear to be similar, those of OSM are more powerful. Multiplicity constraints in UML represent functional dependencies. OSM supports both participation constraints and a more powerful form of generalized functional dependency called co-occurrence

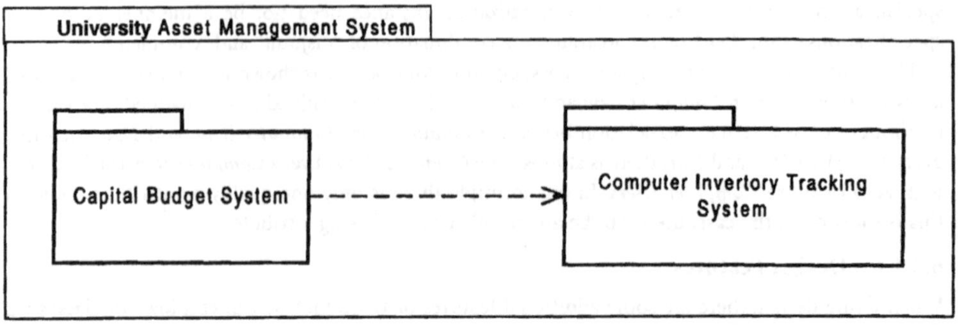

FIGURE 6.5 UML package diagram.

constraints. With participation and co-occurrence constraints, OSM can represent cardinality constraints that are not directly expressible in UML. OSM also supports cardinality constraints on classes restricting the number of objects that can belong to a class. One of the obvious differences between OSM and UML is the name of an association or relationship set. In OSM the name is required, in UML it is optional. Thus, the intended meaning of an association in a UML model may not always be clear.

6.3.3 Package Diagram

A "package" is a mechanism for grouping of model elements. A package may be a subsystem, or it may be a simple grouping of diagrams for the sake of organizational convenience. It should be noted, however, that a package owns all its contained model elements. A model element belongs to only one package, and therefore packages are non-overlapping, though they may be nested in a strict hierarchy. Any kind of model element, including any of the different UML diagrams, may be organized into packages. Probably the most common use of packages is to partition a large system into its component subsystems.

Figure 6.5 shows an example of a UML package diagram. Suppose we were to consider that our CITS example may be a component in a larger enterprise-wide system. Figure 6.5 shows the CITS as a package nested inside a larger *University Asset Management System*. A package is denoted by a folder-like rectangle with a tab optionally labeled with the package name. Contained components are placed in the body of the rectangle. A "dependency" is drawn as a dashed arrow. In this example, a companion package, *Capital Budget System*, depends on the CITS. Because the arrowhead points toward CITS, the *Capital Budget System* references or uses some component in the CITS. The *Capital Budget System* might reference past expenditures on personal computers or anticipated surplus dates and amounts. This diagram shows that whenever any maintenance is done to the CITS, a change to the *Capital Budget System* may also be required. Perhaps the budget system requires methods or data structures defined in the inventory system.

The primary purpose of a package diagram is to show various subsystems and dependencies between them. Both packages and dependencies are elements of a class diagram, so a package diagram is really just a special form of the class diagram. Thus, packages may appear in class and object diagrams as needed.

Because ownership of components within packages must conform to a strict tree hierarchy, one must be careful in the development of packages. Those diagrams that conform strictly to object boundaries, such as class diagrams and statecharts, can be easily developed to ensure strict ownership. However, other diagrams such as use-case diagrams and activity diagrams, which are not sensitive to object boundaries, must be developed carefully to ensure strict ownership within their enclosing packages.

6.3.4 Comparison with OSM

When OSM is used to model large systems, the same need exists to organize the diagrams. In OSM we partition a design by dividing it into high-level object sets. Thus, OSM uses a single, scalable construct — instead of two separate constructs — to represent both classes and packages. Some view this as a benefit while others see it as a vice. OSM does not require that high-level object sets be mutually exclusive, but the developer can enforce this as a policy if desired.

Dependencies in OSM are not specifically identified as a fundamental OSM construct. Dependencies would appear as either relationship sets or interactions between classes contained in the separate high-level object sets. Thus, to show dependencies in OSM, normally we would show the low level information that causes the dependency. If it is beneficial to show only high-level information, a separate high-level relationship set or a high-level interaction can be indicated on the OSM diagram to note the presence of lower level "dependent" information.

6.4 Behavior Diagrams

The behavior diagrams of UML represent dynamic aspects of a system. There are two general kinds of behavior represented in UML: interactions and state machines. Interaction diagrams include use case, collaboration, and sequence diagrams. They are useful for describing how objects within a system interact to accomplish system behavior (sequence and collaboration diagrams), or how external actors interact with a system to perform various tasks (use-case diagrams). State machines, expressed as statechart and activity diagrams, define the details of processes or behavior from the perspective of transitions between states over time. A statechart diagram describes the comprehensive behavior of a single object, while an activity diagram describes a single use case or operation, often involving behavior associated with multiple objects.

In this section, we describe UML's behavior diagrams in the following order. Because the creators of UML advocate a use-case driven development process, we first introduce the use-case diagram. Next, we describe the collaboration and sequence diagrams. Actually, collaboration and sequence diagrams are two views of the same underlying information (as expressed in the UML metamodel). A collaboration diagram emphasizes the roles objects play in a collaboration, whereas a sequence diagram emphasizes the flow of control (which is good for concurrent processes, for example). Next, we describe the statechart diagram, which is used for describing complete object behavior through state machines. Finally, we present the activity diagram, which is useful for describing a use case as a kind of flowchart of actions and transitions between actions. The activity diagram is a special kind of statechart and is based on the same metamodel as statecharts. Its use, however, is similar to that of the use-case diagram in specifying system behavior without consideration for object boundaries.

6.4.1 Use-Case Diagram

In many software development methods, scenarios of typical user/system interaction are defined early in the analysis process. These scenarios are generally developed as analysts interview end users to determine their system requirements. Use cases in UML formalize ideas associated with analysis scenarios. A use case corresponds to such a scenario.

The purpose of a use-case diagram is to define external functional requirements of a system. That is, a use-case diagram shows how users intend to utilize a system to accomplish various tasks. Each "use" of a system is a use case. Thus, a use case represents a typical interaction between a user and a system.

Figure 6.6 shows a use-case diagram for the CITS example. A use-case diagram consists of a system boundary, actors (external entities or users), use cases, and relationships. A system boundary is drawn as a rectangle labeled with the system name (e.g., *Computer Inventory Tracking System*). Actors are represented by named stick figures such as *Owner* and *CSR* (Computer Support Representative). An actor is a role. It may correspond to a particular user, or it may correspond to many users who perform the role. Thus it is important to distinguish between individual users and the roles they play. Also, sometimes the same real user operates in multiple roles. For example, the same real CSR might act in the roles of both *Owner* and *CSR* in our use-case diagram, purchasing a computer at one time, but repairing a computer at another time.

Use cases are drawn as ovals labeled with corresponding use-case names (e.g., *Purchase Computer, Sell Computer, Repair Computer*). Each use case describes one way an actor might use a system. Use cases

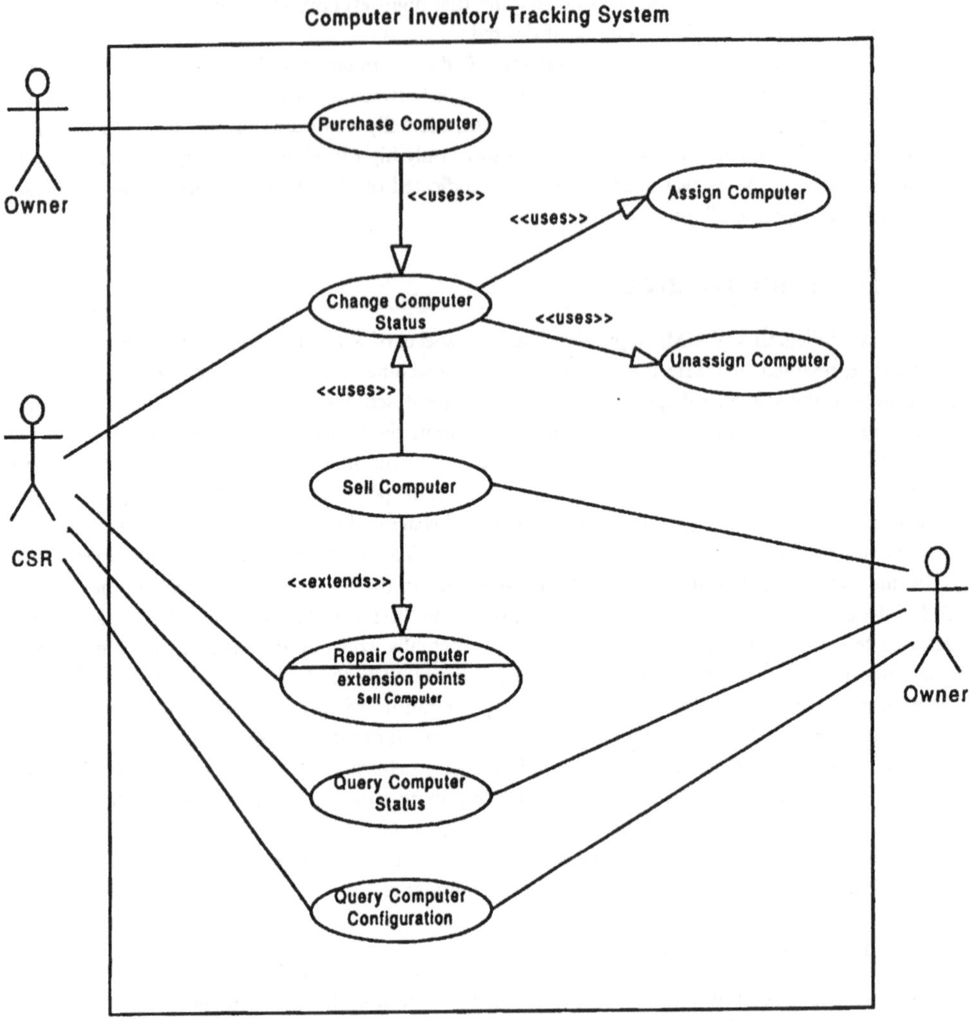

Notes on Extend: A computer in repair may end up being sold. Thus Record Repair Information may in fact need to be extended by Recording Computer Sale.

FIGURE 6.6 UML use-case diagram.

may be simple or complex. For example, an owner might use the CITS system to check a computer's status or its configuration (relatively simple use cases) or to purchase a new machine (a relatively complex use case). A use case is performed by one or more actors, and this relationship is represented as a simple line in a use-case diagram. The line between *Owner* and *Purchase Computer*, for instance, indicates that an owner is the person who purchases a computer.

Relationships between use cases may either be "uses" or "extends" relationships, labeled "«uses»" and "«extends»," respectively, and drawn as a generalization arrow. The «uses» relationship lets one use case utilize another use case like a common subroutine. Indeed, the «uses» relationship is provided primarily to allow common code to be factored out of a use-case model. Since this is a design task, «uses» relationships are generally specified during system design, not necessarily during the initial analysis. Several examples are shown in Figure 6.6. For instance, we can see that both *Purchase Computer* and *Sell Computer* utilize the *Change Computer Status* use case.

The «extends» relationship is intended to support exception handling. In order to keep the description of use cases simple, each exception is generally processed in a separate, extended use case. For example, inside the *Repair Computer* use case, if a computer repair is too costly, we may wish to sell the computer instead of repair it. In that case, which is an exception condition, we invoke the *Sell Computer* use case to extend the functionality of *Repair Computer*. Thus we can describe a normal computer repair without worrying about the details of exception handling, and then later we can extend the original use case to handle exceptions. With an «extends» relationship, we identify those points or conditions that cause the use case to be extended. The direction of the relationship is the reverse of the «uses» relationship in that the use case being extended is the target of the arrow rather than the source. However, it is consistent with the meaning that *Sell Computer* «extends» *Repair Computer*.

As we can infer from Figure 6.6, a use-case diagram does not attempt to capture the internal details of behavior within the system. The purpose of a use-case diagram is to identify external uses of the system, not to specify internal behavior. The only internal information provided is that obtained from the «uses» and the «extends» relationships. UML uses activity, collaboration, and sequence diagrams to further elaborate internal behavior.

6.4.2 Use-Case Analysis Development Process

Even though our emphasis in this chapter is on models rather than methods, at this point some comments on development process are warranted. Use-case analysis provides an effective way to begin the elaboration and definition of a system. Use-case analysis answers questions about what functions need to be provided so that the users can accomplish their objectives with a system. The people who receive value from a system are its users, and as such they are in a unique position to identify important use cases. A use-case model is usually developed by interviewing different users and assessing their needs. One effective way to perform use-case analysis is to identify all external events associated with functions supported by the system.

A prerequisite to defining use cases, then, is that a system boundary must be defined to identify which activities are system activities, i.e., within the system boundary, and which activities originate in the environment and use functions of the system. Since the final system does not exist during the analysis phase, there may be many different interpretations of what the system should do. With OSM, the specification of an initial system boundary is usually postponed until later in the development process.

A use-case diagram is an effective tool to begin the analysis of the system. However, a use-case model in and of itself is not aimed exclusively toward object-oriented development. Use-case analysis can be used to help drive any method of system development. In UML, it functions effectively as the first diagram to be developed. It also functions as a road map to help drive the development of many other diagrams.

OSM models do not require the inclusion of use-case analysis as part of the modeling or development process. However, use cases may be used effectively with almost any type of model of development methodology, including OSM.

OSM does capture the same information that use cases provide through the use of high-level interaction diagrams. High-level interactions that cross the automated system boundary indicate a communication between external objects or object sets and internal object sets. Figure 6.7 illustrates how OSM would capture this same information. Each use case is identified by a high-level interaction. The use case itself is identified as the name of the interaction. Included in a high-level interaction are hidden details about low-level interactions, object sets, and state nets. In this case, OSM does provide additional information by requiring the destination object sets to be identified. Thus the OSM approach to use cases not only identifies specific uses of the system, but it also enables the analyst to begin identifying objects that may be involved in the use case.

The creators of UML advocate a use-case driven approach to software development. Thus, a use-case diagram is usually the starting point in UML development. The creation of a use-case diagram requires careful thought from the beginning concerning what is in the system and what is external. In OSM, the first step is usually to identify object sets and relationships without regard to the automated system or the

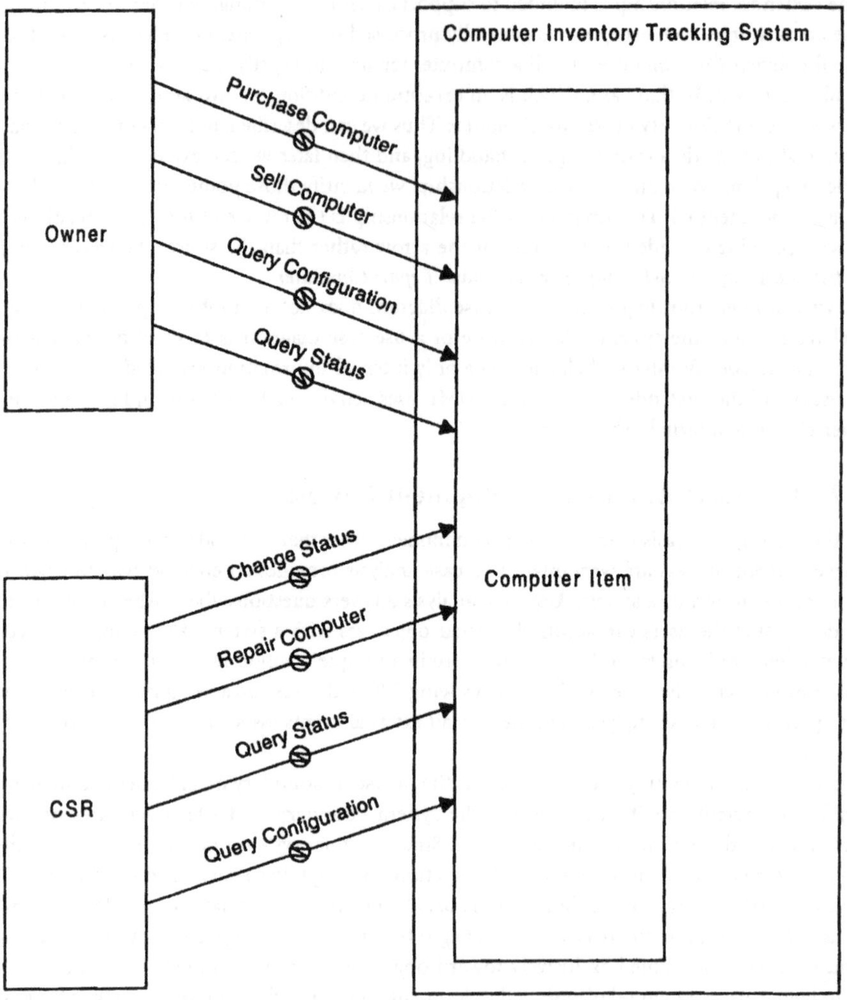

FIGURE 6.7 OSM use case or interaction diagram.

system boundary. The first pass through an OSM model does not require differentiation between object sets that are "real world" and object sets that are part of an automated system. Identification of objects within the system and those outside is done when the system boundary is completed. After the system boundary has been identified, internal and external object sets are identified and interactions between the environment and the system are defined. Thus there is a difference in the use of the models, which may be more pronounced than the actual information captured by each of the two models themselves.

6.4.3 Collaboration Diagram

A collaboration diagram identifies a group of objects that "collaborate" or cooperate to perform an operation or a use case. Thus a use-case diagram can be the starting point for developing a collaboration diagram. The internals of each use case can be elaborated by a collaboration.

A collaboration diagram consists of two types of information. First, the structural information of a collaboration is provided by a set of object roles and links between these objects. These objects and links collaborate to perform the use case or operation being modeled. Second, behavior information is included

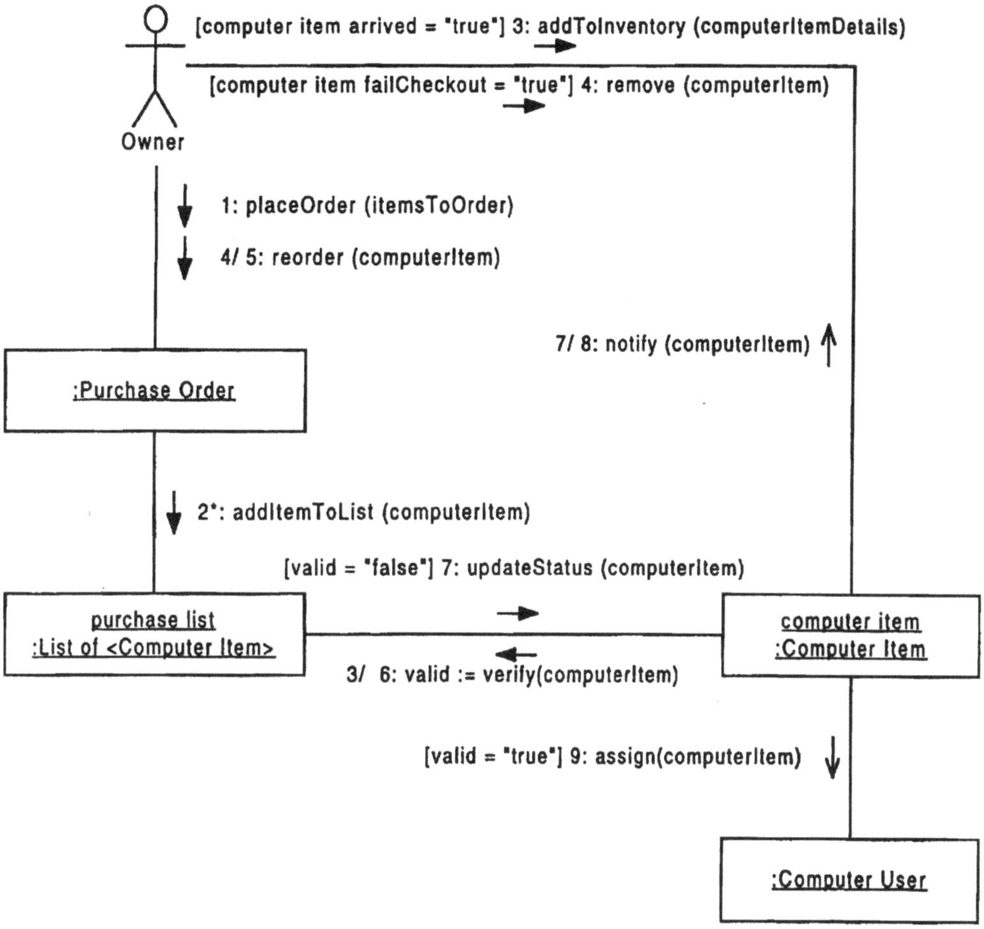

FIGURE 6.8 UML collaboration diagram.

by identifying interactions that occur between collaborating objects. These interactions specify a sequence of messages that are exchanged between the objects in the collaboration. In fact, the same structural information, i.e., the set of objects and their links, may occur for different collaborations, differing only in the set and sequence of interactions. Thus a collaboration diagram is a graph of references to objects and links with messages attached to the links.

Consider the collaboration diagram in Figure 6.8, which describes the *Purchase Computer* use case. Normally a collaboration diagram includes both active and passive roles. Active objects are initiators of interactions, while passive objects respond to messages by return messages or forwarding messages. A role is drawn as a label enclosed in a rectangle. The label specifies a role being played by an instance of a class in this collaboration. (In other words, a role represents an object involved in a particular interaction.) The notation for a role is *RoleName: CassifierName.* If the role name is omitted, an anonymous object is assumed. In UML, underlining distinguishes an instance from a class.

The active role in Figure 6.8 is the *Owner* actor. For this collaboration, all other object roles can be considered passive in that they only respond when messages are sent to them. Observe the different notation of *:Purchase Order* and *purchase list :List of <Computer Item>*. In the first case, the role is played by an unspecified, anonymous purchase order. In the second case, a particular list of computer items is required, specifically the *purchase list* object in the classifier *List of <Computer Item>*.

Links in the diagram show connections between objects in the collaboration. An arrow next to a link indicates a message flowing through the link. The type of message is indicated by the arrow. Standard notation is provided for procedure call (filled solid arrowhead), flat flow of control (stick arrowhead), and asynchronous flow of control (half stick arrowhead). Other notations, which we do not illustrate here, are also allowed.

A message label documents the activation and description of a message with the following syntax:

```
Prerequisite/[Guard] Sequence: Return := Message(ArgumentList)
```

Prerequisite is a list of predecessor messages, each of which must be complete before the current message may be sent. *Guard* identifies a condition that must be satisfied before the message may be sent. *Sequence* is an identifier that indicates the order in which this message should execute within the collaboration. It may be represented as a textual label, or more commonly, as an integer. Usually, message sequences are written in hierarchical, outline form, according to their nesting. For example, suppose message 2.1 results in the execution of two more messages. These would then be numbered 2.1.1 and 2.1.2. The simplest form of numbering is a sequence of integers (e.g., 1, 2, 3, ...), but this form is flat and loses the hierarchical structure inherent in most source code. *Return* is a list of names that contains values returned by the message. *Message* is the message name, and *ArgumentList* describes parameters sent with the message. Only *Sequence* and *Message* are required in a message label. All other parts are optional.

The collaboration in Figure 6.8 includes nine separate messages numbered sequentially in order of execution. Message 1 illustrates the simplest notation. It specifies a procedure call from an owner to a purchase order and passes a set of items to be ordered. Message 2 is an iterated message (indicated by the "*"), meaning that *addItemToList* is called multiple times (once for each item to order in this case). Message 3 has a guard indicating that it only fires after a computer item arrives. When it fires, a message is sent to the computer item so that it can be added to inventory. Later, if the computer item fails its checkout, then it is removed from inventory via message 4. Also, message 5 is initiated by the owner to reorder a replacement. Notice that message 5 has a predecessor of *4/* indicating that 4 must have fired before 5 is eligible.

Messages 6, 7, 8, and 9 also form a kind of series. After message 3 fires, adding the computer item to inventory, then message 6 executes to verify that it was on the original purchase list with a return value to be placed in *valid.* Message 7, and subsequently message 8, fires based on the condition that the computer item validation against the purchase list returns false in the parameter *valid.* If a computer item was not on the original purchase list, its status is updated to reflect that (message 7) and notification is sent to the owner (message 8). If it does pass the validation, then it is assigned to a user. In our definition of the *Purchase Computer* use case, we have included the assignment of the computer item to a user. That is shown by the execution of the guarded message 9.

Note that for messages 1 through 7 we have used solid arrowheads to indicate a procedure call type of message passing. Messages 8 and 9 simply pass along information without requiring a return. This is documented as stick arrows. We could also have used half-stick arrowheads if we needed to emphasize asynchronous message passing. In this case, concurrency is not a major emphasis so we have not included any half-stick arrowheads.

Note also that the objective of a collaboration diagram is to document roles, links between roles, and a sequence of messages. It graphically shows structural information in the roles, links, and messages that travel along links. A collaboration diagram does not emphasize timing or concurrency information, which is better represented in a sequence diagram as explained in the next section.

Since collaboration and sequence diagrams capture essentially the same information, both are represented the same way in OSM. We compare UML and OSM in this regard after the discussion of the sequence diagram.

6.4.4 Sequence Diagram

A sequence diagram has two dimensions: the vertical dimension which represents time, and the horizontal dimension which represents different objects. Figure 6.9 shows a sequence diagram for the *Purchase*

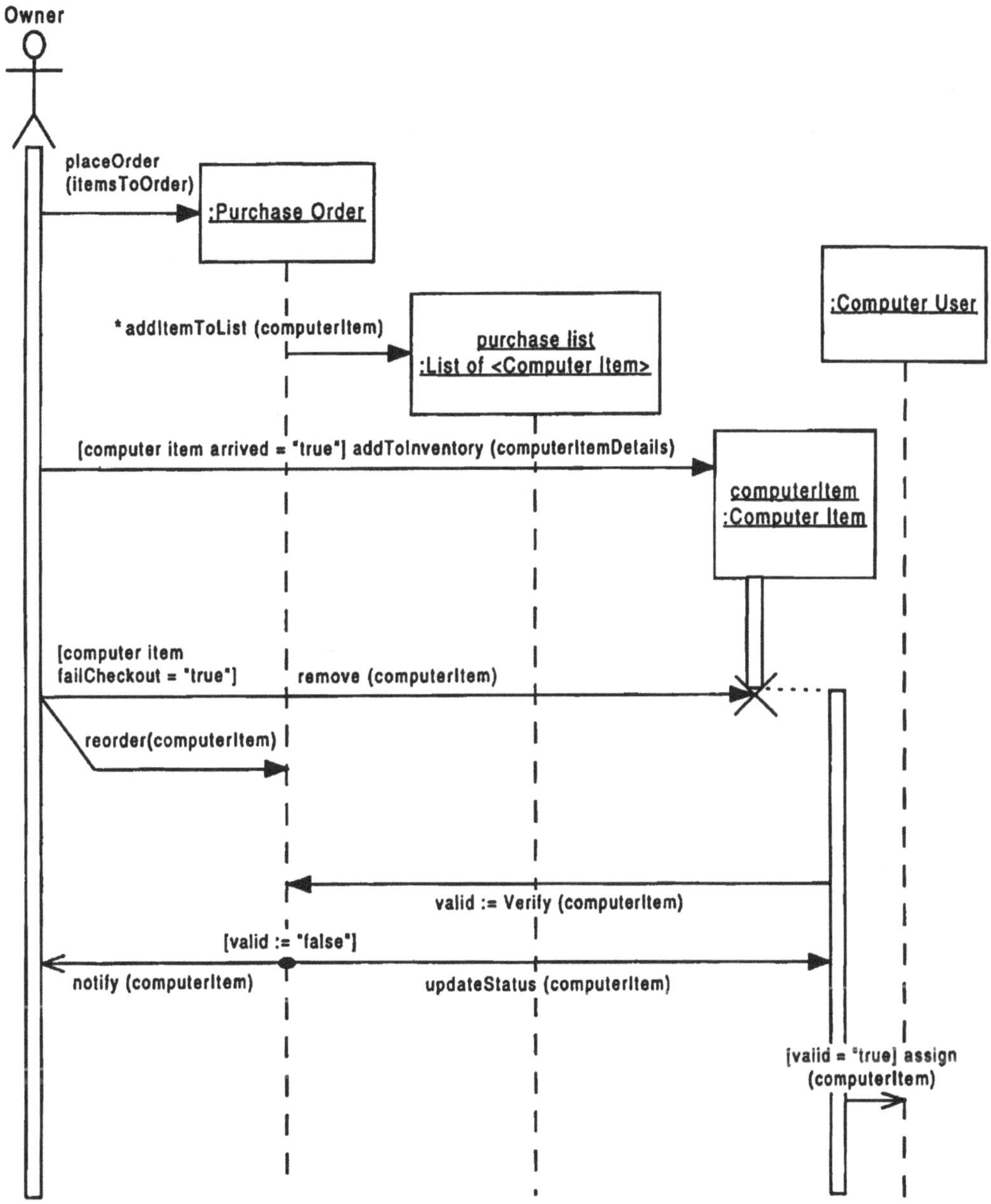

FIGURE 6.9 UML sequence diagram.

Computer use case. Roles are written along the top with associated "lifelines" beneath each role. If the role is primarily a passive object, the lifeline is represented by a dashed vertical line. If the role is an active object, then that is specifically represented by a vertical box, called an "activation," on the lifeline. For example, *Owner* and *computerItem* both have activations along their lifelines. A role object may have multiple activations to indicate concurrent threads of the same role. Activations running parallel and overlapping in time (i.e., along the vertical dimension) indicate concurrency between role objects. In Figure 6.9, *Owner* executes concurrently with the other objects in the scenario. Role objects can come into existence, indicated by a message coming to the role classifier box. Role objects can be destroyed which is indicated by a destroy message coming to a large X at the bottom of the role's lifeline. For example, *computerItem* may be destroyed by a *remove* message if it fails its checkout.

Note that the object roles in Figure 6.9 are the same as the collaboration diagram in Figure 6.8. Also, the sequence of messages as indicated by the progression of time from top to bottom on the page is the same as the numerical sequence in the collaboration. As with collaboration diagrams, messages in a sequence diagram have a type indicated by the associated arrowhead. A solid arrowhead indicates procedure-call semantics, a stick arrowhead indicates flat, sequential flow of control, and a half arrowhead (not shown) indicates an asynchronous call. A major difference between collaboration and sequence diagrams is that sequence numbers are not needed for messages in a sequence diagram. Instead, the sequence of messages is represented by the order from top to bottom in the diagram.

Additional information we can capture in this diagram is that *Owner* is an active object with an activation lifeline whose duration is the entire use case. Message arrows going directly to object role boxes indicate creation of a new object role. In a collaboration diagram, we can specify the same concept with a "{new}" constraint on a message.

In this diagram, we also capture more explicitly the sequence of events when a new computer item fails its checkout. In Figure 6.9 we see that *Owner* initiates two messages if a computer item fails its checkout. One message to the *computerItem* role terminates its lifeline (and removes the computer item from inventory). The other message to the *:Purchase Order* object reorders the needed computer item. This concurrent activity is shown by both messages originating from the same point in time. The lifeline for a computer item either ends at that point or continues if the *failCheckout* condition is false. This is indicated by the continuation of the activation lifeline for *computerItem*. Other information from the messages is identical to that derived from the collaboration diagram.

6.4.5 Comparing OSM and UML

We represent message passing and other communications between object sets with interactions in OSM. An interaction is any kind of communication or synchronization between objects. In OSM the three submodels — the Object-Relationship Model, the Object-Behavior Model (state nets), and the Object Interaction Model — need not be drawn as separate diagrams. Any combination of these models can be used to provide a view that is relevant to the designer's purpose. Thus, the same information captured in UML collaboration and sequence diagrams can be presented in OSM with appropriate views as desired.

One of the primary differences between OSM when used for analysis and UML is that OSM is not oriented toward detail or program implementation. Thus, interactions are of a more fundamental kind of communication that does not attempt to define whether an interaction is a procedure call or some other kind of invocation. It can, however, pass information and receive return information. OSM interactions can also be sent from and to specific objects. Thus when there is the need to identify specific objects which have specified roles, this is identified as the destination object of the interaction.

Figure 6.10 is an example of an OSM sequence of interactions for the *Purchase Computer* use case of the CITS application. The sequence of the interactions is implied by reading the diagram top to bottom. This diagram is a view in OSM that has been drawn to capture the same kind of information that is provided in a UML sequence diagram. Figure 6.11 is an additional unnamed view in OSM that includes not only the object sets, but it also includes some behavior information from the state nets of the involved object sets. In these figures are examples of interactions that pass information and receive information in return. Interactions can also have "to" and "from" clauses that indicate the specific object or set of objects that is the destination or source, respectively, of the interaction. UML's role information is captured in OSM by identifying specific "to" or "from" objects on an interaction.

We make several observations about differences in UML and OSM. First, OSM does not require messages to be attached to links. Link or relationship information is useful for deciding how to implement a procedure call (i.e., a link is necessary in order to find the object reference used to invoke a method), but it is usually not relevant to the conceptual model of interaction. However, if desired, relationship information can be shown in OSM as illustrated in Figure 6.10.

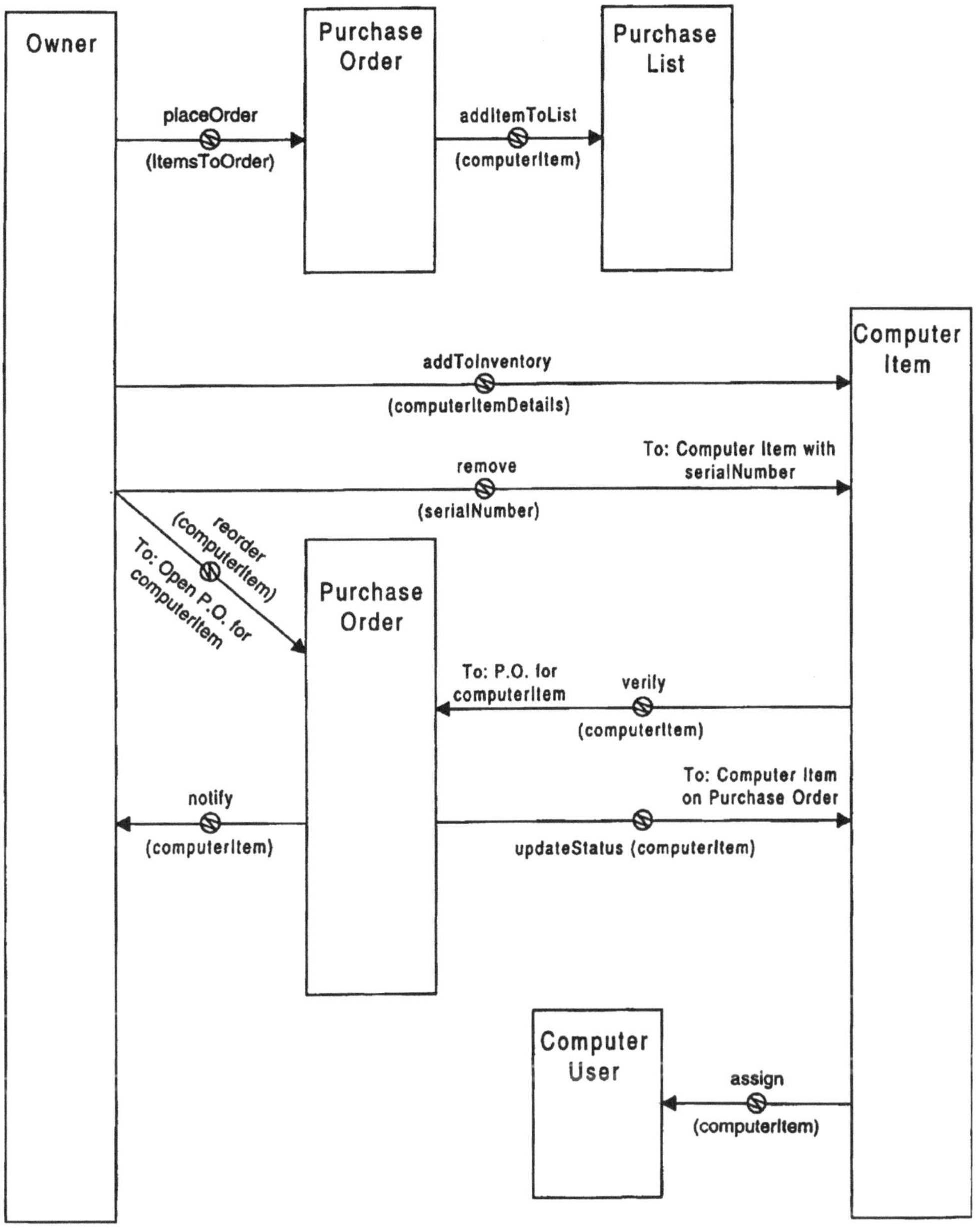

FIGURE 6.10 OSM interaction sequence diagram.

Next, in OSM we do not include guard information on interactions themselves. That level of detail is included in the trigger and action statements of corresponding state nets. In fact, by including partial state nets in a view, detailed information about object behavior — guards, iterations, procedures, sequences, concurrency, timing constraints, and other information associated with the interactions — can be stated explicitly. As we see in Figure 6.11, the sequence of interactions is controlled by the flow of the associated state nets. This sequence can include serial, concurrent, timed, or iterated interactions.

Finally, activation information is also provided in OSM by the inclusion of state net information in a view with interactions. Creation, active lifelines, and termination of objects or roles is described in detail

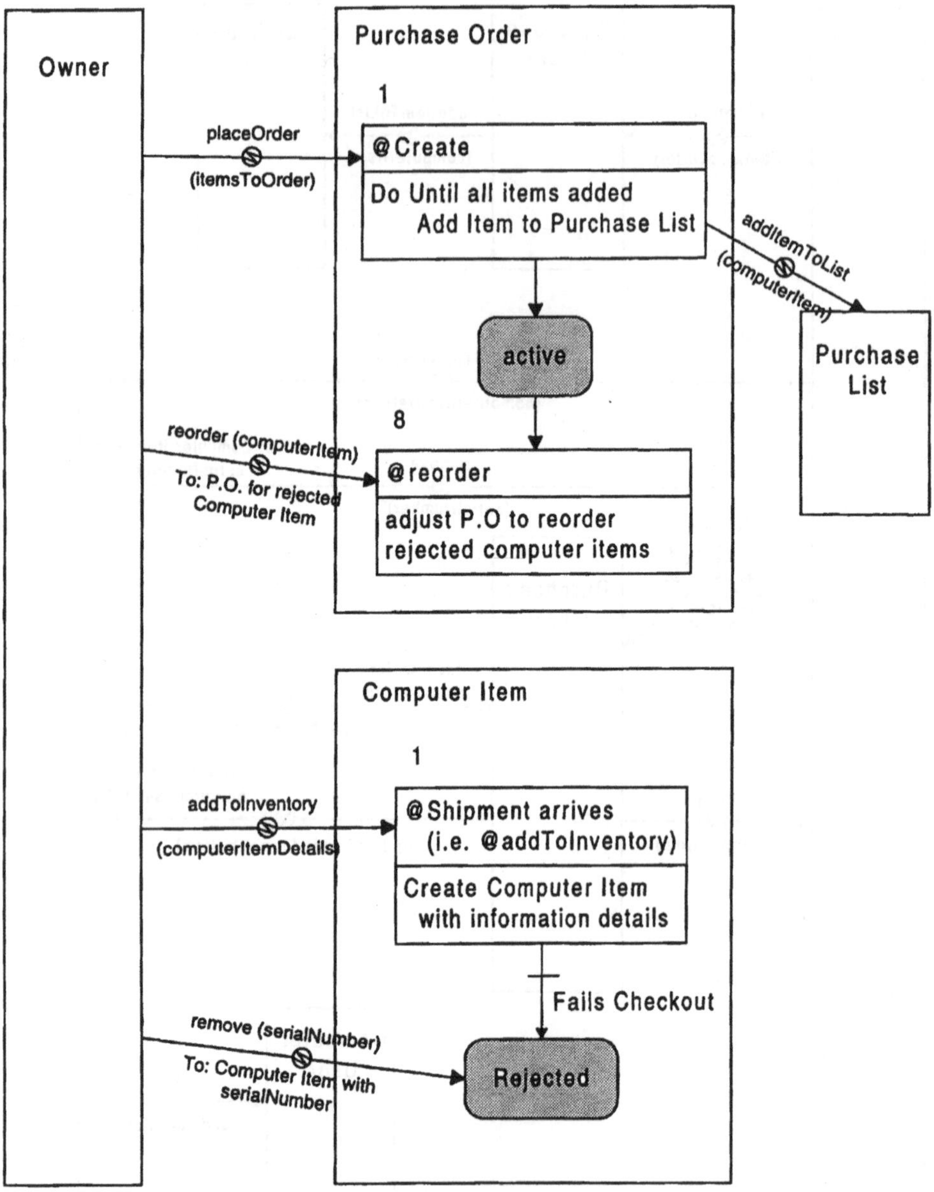

FIGURE 6.11 OSM more detailed interaction sequence diagram.

in the state net. Relevant portions of that information can be shown in a view by the inclusion of appropriate pieces of the state net.

6.4.6 Statechart Diagram

Object behavior in UML is represented by statechart diagrams. The UML statechart model is a variation of Harel's work (Harel, 1987) and is essentially an extension to simple state transition machines. In most OO methods, state diagrams are used to model the behavior of a single object class to describe the behavior of objects in that class throughout their lifetime. In UML, a statechart diagram may be used to describe the behavior of either an entire object or a single method.

In addition to the standard form of statechart, UML provides a special case called an activity diagram. An activity diagram is used to model a method, a procedure, or even a use case. As such, it is not limited to describing the behavior of a single object or method. It can describe behavior that crosses object boundaries. Before discussing activity diagrams, we first explain ordinary statecharts.

A simple example of a statechart for *Computer Item* is shown in Figure 6.12. The large enclosing box represents the *Computer Item* class. When a computer item is created it enters the *Ordered* state. When the physical machine arrives, the corresponding CITS computer item enters the *Inspected* state. If the computer item fails inspection, the vendor is notified. When the vendor acknowledges the notification the computer item is repackaged and returned to the vendor. At this time the computer item ceases to exist as far as the CITS system is concerned. If the computer item passes inspection it enters the composite state *Assigned*. Upon entry, it is assigned to a user, and its price and purchase date are recorded. At this time the computer item begins three concurrent activities which are described later. When the computer item is sold, it exits these three substates, exits the *Assigned* state, and enters the final state which again means that it ceases to exist in the CITS system.

6.4.6.1 States

There are two kinds of "states" in UML: simple or atomic states (such as an idle state) and composite states with nested substates and transitions. A simple state is represented by a rectangle with rounded corners. At the top of Figure 6.12, the *Ordered* and *Inspected* states are examples. A simple state can also have actions associated with it. It can have an entry action, which is performed upon entering the state; an exit action, which is performed when exiting the state; or internal actions performed while in the state. The *Install* state in Figure 6.12 is an example of a state with an entry, an exit, and an internal action. It is assumed that a simple state with actions is like a procedure in that it will perform its associated actions and then terminate. Then the object will either transition immediately to another state or wait for an event to trigger the transition.

There are two special types of simple states found in statecharts. They are initial and final states. An initial state is represented by a small black circle. A final state is represented by a small black circle with another circle around it. An initial state identifies the point at which behavior starts when an instance of the corresponding class is created. A final state identifies the point at which behavior ends. Normally this means the object ceases to exist.

6.4.6.2 Transitions

A transition is a connection between two states indicating that an object in the first state has a path to move to the second state when some event occurs. An event is said to be the trigger for a transition, and a transition is said to "fire" upon the occurrence of the event. A transition is noted in a statechart by a line with a solid arrow, which indicates the direction of the transition. A transition may have an associated descriptor string of the following form:

```
event-signature [guard]/action ^send-clause
```

An "event signature" looks like a procedure signature as found in many programming languages. For example, *arrives* and *Passes Inspection* are both event signatures in Figure 6.12. An event signature defines the event that fires a transition along with any associated parameters or return types. A transition may have a guard. A "guard" is a Boolean condition that must be true for the transition to fire. A transition will not fire, even if the corresponding event has occurred, if the guard is false when the event occurs. An optional "action" expression describes an action that may occur during a transition. A transition may contain more than one action clause to describe an entire activity comprising several actions. Each action itself is considered to be atomic and cannot be interrupted. In Figure 6.12 one action (associated with the transition from *Inspected* to *Waiting for Vendor Acknowledgement*) is *Notify Vendor.* Finally, a "send" clause describes any event or signal that may be sent to another object when the transition is finished. A send clause is really just a special form of action expression that sends a message.

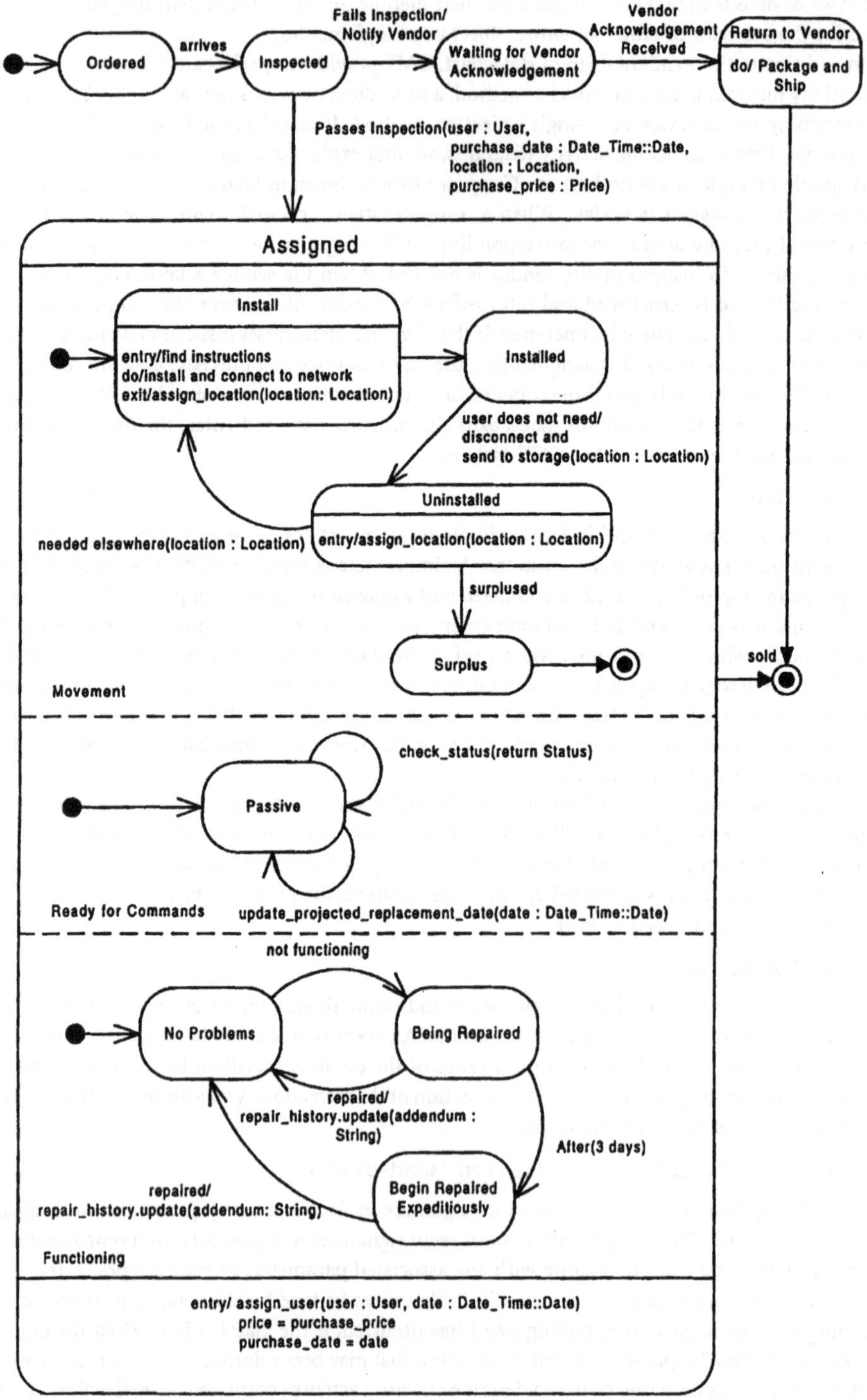

FIGURE 6.12 UML statechart diagram.

All parts of a transition descriptor are optional. In most cases we will have an event signature or a guard, however, it is possible to have nothing but an arrow connecting a source state and destination state. This represents the idea that when an object is finished performing the action associated with the source state it will automatically transition to the destination state.

6.4.6.3 Composite States

Composite states typically represent activities or processes that proceed until interrupted by an event or signal. Behavior of a composite state is represented by another statechart. There are two types of composite states: sequential and concurrent.

As the name implies, a concurrent composite state represents two or more concurrent activities. In Figure 6.12 *Assigned* is a concurrent composite state. Concurrent regions of a composite state are separated by dashed lines. Each of these regions represents a nested statechart, usually with its own initial state and sometimes with its own final state. In our example, when a computer passes inspection and enters the *Assigned* state, it simultaneously enters the *Install*, *Passive*, and *No Problems* states (after executing the *Assigned* state entry action). It continues in these three substates until the computer is sold. It is possible for a computer that is in the *Assigned* state to cease installation/relocation if it ever reaches the *Surplus* state. When a computer is sold, it leaves the three concurrent regions of the *Assigned* state, and if there were an exit action, it would be executed before finishing.

A sequential composite state is like a concurrent composite state with a single subregion. It is worth noting that transitions may cross the composite state boundary. That is, even if a sequential composite state has an initial state, there may be a transition that enters the subregion directly, bypassing the initial state. Similarly, a final state may also be bypassed. All composite states, like simple states, may have entry, exit, and internal actions as desired.

6.4.6.4 Complex Transitions

UML has another construct called a "complex transition" that is similar to a concurrent composite state. Usually a complex transition is used to indicate concurrent paths through a transition. It is represented by a rounded rectangle with two or more disjoint statecharts inside. Each is separated by a dotted line. An abstract example is given in Figure 6.13. A complex transition shows a synchronization bar (a thick black line) for the entry of a complex transition and another synchronization bar for the exit of the transition. They represent the fact that a single thread of control forks into several threads inside the transition and that all the threads are combined upon exiting the transition.

6.4.7 Comparison of OSM and UML

Many behavior modeling concepts in UML are similar to behavior modeling in OSM. Both use state machines with states and transitions. Both have transitions with triggers, guards, associated actions, and signaling of other objects. Forms of high-level states and transitions are also found in each model.

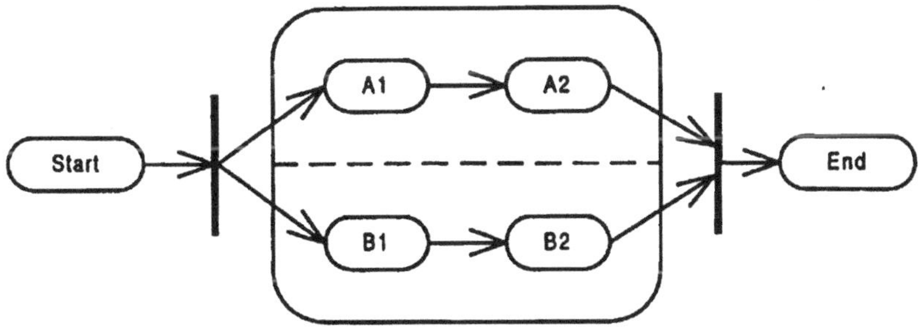

FIGURE 6.13 Abstract UML complex transition.

There are some significant differences, however. In UML, the notion of an action is better developed. A transition without a name means that when the action associated with a state is finished then we transition to another state. This must be represented by an explicitly named transition in OSM. For OSM states there are no explicitly defined entry or exit actions; however, these can be defined easily in OSM state nets.

Concurrency is more naturally expressed in OSM. In UML, intra-object concurrency is generated by entering a concurrent composite state or complex transition. In either case, when exiting the construct the generated threads of control are reunified. Thus, concurrency in UML is a form of synchronized concurrency. In OSM, intra-object concurrency is modeled in a form similar to that of Petri nets. As such, additional threads of control may be created and destroyed at any time. High-level transitions in OSM are also more expressive. In UML we only have complex transitions for representing concurrency within a transition. Transitions with internal statecharts are not allowed. High-level transitions in OSA have state nets describing their possibly concurrent behavior.

6.4.8 Activity Diagram

An activity diagram is a special kind of statechart diagram. It represents the state machine of a procedure without consideration for objects. It is useful in documenting the internals of a use case or some other procedure. An activity diagram is analogous to a traditional flowchart in that it shows the flow of operations within a larger process.

States in an activity diagram represent activities or operations to be performed. Thus, they are called "activities" rather than states. Transitions in an activity diagram are generally triggered by the completion of all preceding activities. Thus, in an activity diagram the states are usually simple states without internal events, actions, or transitions, and the transitions are usually simple orderings that indicate the synchronization and flow of activities within the process being modeled.

Figure 6.14 shows an activity diagram for the *Purchase Computer* use case. Transitions are labeled in the same way as statechart diagrams. However, due to the simple nature of the diagram, transitions normally do not include multiple actions or nested statecharts. Frequently, no description of a transition is required since it is triggered by the completion of its preceding states (activities). Sometimes events and guards are included to describe a transition more precisely.

The completion of an action is the event that "fires" a transition. If there are multiple possible exit paths, these can be controlled by guards on the transitions. If there are complex conditions that determine multiple paths out of an action state then a decision diamond with appropriate guard conditions can be added to denote the various possible paths. For example, in Figure 6.14, the *Check out Computer Items* activity has two possible outcomes: pass or fail. In the event of failure, the item can either be repaired on site or it cannot. Depending on the circumstances, different paths through the activity diagram will be chosen.

As with statecharts, synchronization bars are used in an activity diagram to coordinate and synchronize concurrent behavior. A synchronization bar can be used to fork or combine multiple threads. In Figure 6.14, when an item has failed to check out and it is not repairable on site, the thread of control enters a synchronization bar where it forks into three concurrent activities: *Return Computer Item*, *Reorder Computer Item*, and *Notify Owner of Delay*. When all three of these activities complete, the three concurrent threads merge once more and the use case completes.

Another use of synchronization bars is to handle the effects of "multiple transitions." The transition labeled **For each requested Computer Item* in Figure 6.14 is a multiple transition that occurs once for each item to be placed on the purchase list. The synchronization bar with the guard *[All items added]* is required to synchronize the threads generated by the multiple transition.

Activity charts are meant to document an entire procedure or use case without respect to who performs the actions. However, sometimes it is desirable to identify actors or objects performing the activity, so we may superimpose "swimlanes" on the diagram as shown in Figure 6.14. Swimlanes partition an activity diagram vertically so that every activity is associated with an actor who performs the action. Transitions cross swimlane boundaries as necessary to describe the flow of logic.

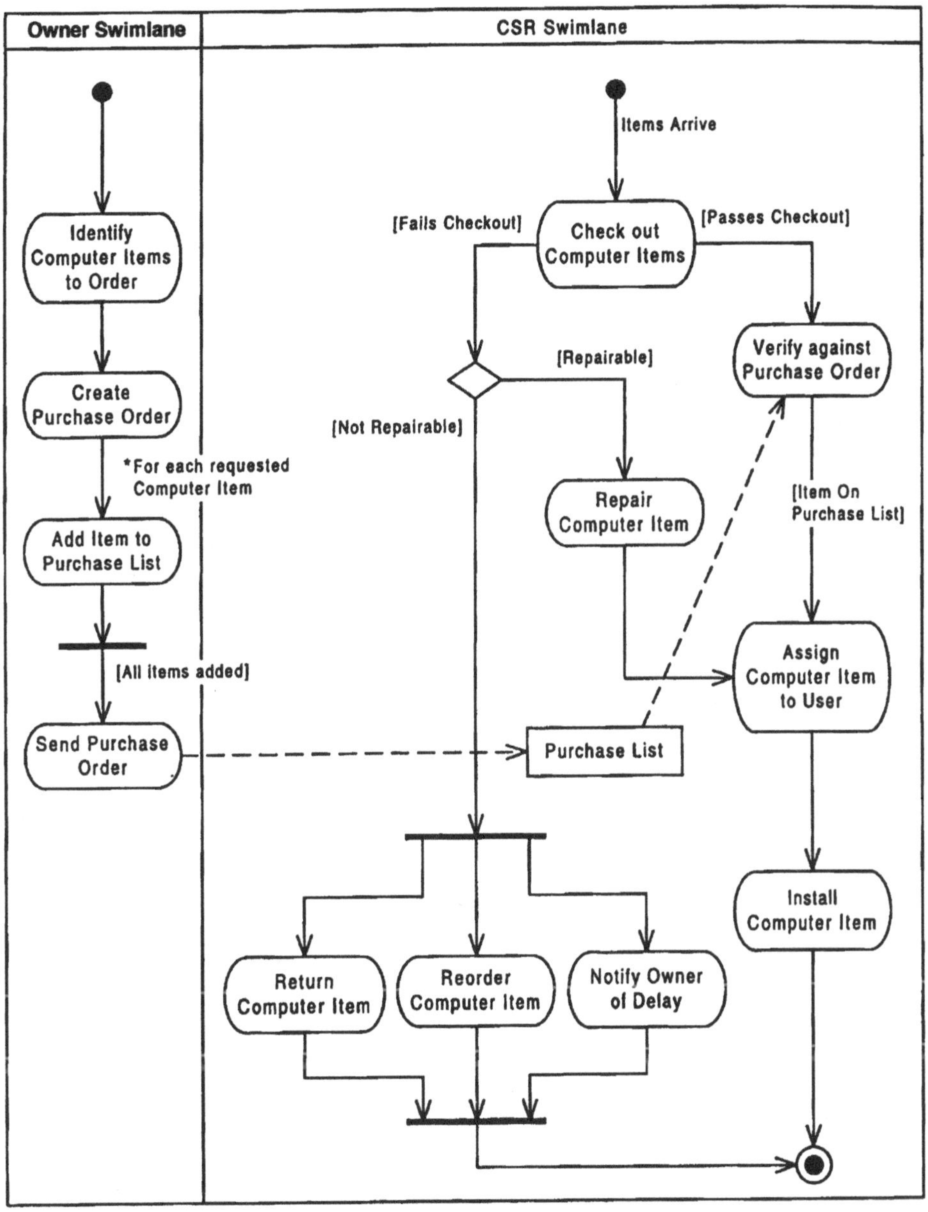

FIGURE 6.14 UML activity diagram.

Messages and objects may be passed between action states. Such messages are identified by dashed arrows. If specific objects are passed, they are placed in boxes that are nested in the middle of the message dashed arrow. In Figure 6.14, the *Send Purchase Order* activity communicates a *Purchase List* to the CSR who needs that list in the *Verify against Purchase Order* activity.

Two things are readily apparent from our sample activity diagram. First, the activity chart is not oriented toward object behavior. There is no identification of behavior particular to the *Purchase Order*, *Purchase List*, *Computer Item*, or any other object. Second, this activity diagram describes activities and transitions from an external, manual viewpoint. Activity diagrams are useful, as are use-case diagrams, to observe behavior that includes both system behavior and manual behavior from the environment. In defining a UML method, it may be helpful to develop the use-case diagram and a set of related activity diagrams early in the analysis stage. This would help define processes even before objects are identified.

Even though the example figure takes a combination environment and internal view, additional activity diagrams could be developed which are constrained to purely internal system behavior.

6.4.9 Comparison with OSM

In OSM, the state net is the underlying model for object behavior, and it is used much like statecharts. Cross-object behavior is captured by interactions between state nets for different object sets.

Both use cases and activity diagrams do provide an additional viewpoint to the system that is not constrained to objects or classes. As such, there may be some benefit in the early stages of analysis to focus only on procedures independently from objects or object classes. However, the disadvantage is that there is not always an obvious or easy mapping for partitioning an activity diagram into object behavior. Swimlanes do provide some direction, but swimlanes are generally used to identify user departments or other user functional areas that may not ever be mapped into system classes.

For this example, OSM would model this behavior in two places. First, as noted earlier, Figure 6.7 describes the purchase process from an external point of view. In OSM we would model the purchase procedure as behavior belonging to the real-world CSR and the real-world owner. From a manual viewpoint, this contains precisely the relevant portions of the state nets for these two external object sets.

The other location where this behavior would be captured in OSM is in the state net for the *User Interface* object set. This state net is usually quite complex and is frequently partitioned into separate state nets based on functional procedures. Thus we would develop a *User Interface* state net for the purchase function. In this state net, we would know the different states of the system as the steps of a purchase were completed. In addition, by adding appropriate interactions, which is normally done, we would know all the other object sets that need to receive messages in order to synchronize their behavior with the interactions between the user interface and external user objects.

6.5 Implementation Diagrams

UML specifies two kinds of implementation diagrams: the component diagram and the deployment diagram. These diagrams capture source-code structure and runtime implementation structure of a software system, respectively.

A "component" in UML is a software module that corresponds to a source, binary, or executable code module. A component provides the physical packaging for UML model elements (e.g., a component called *PurchaseOrder.java* might implement the corresponding UML class in the Java programming language). A "node" represents a runtime processing resource that can carry out system operations. Nodes may correspond to computational devices, humans, or physical machines. Components are "deployed" on nodes. Nodes may communicate with other nodes through associations.

A component diagram indicates the dependencies that exist between software components. Thus, the elements of a component diagram are components and dependency relationships. Components may be nested within other components to show physical containment. We do not illustrate the UML component diagram here, but it is similar to the UML deployment diagram.

A deployment diagram shows the runtime configuration of the software and hardware that constitute a system. Only runtime objects appear on a deployment diagram. A deployment diagram consists of nodes and communication associations. Nodes may contain component instances, which in turn may contain objects. Dependency arrows between components may also be present on a deployment diagram.

Figure 6.15 shows a deployment diagram for a portion of the CITS example. Nodes are drawn as three-dimensional boxes, and components are represented by rectangles with two smaller rectangles along the left edge. Here we see three nodes. First, *aCSRComputer* is a specific computer item that presumably is assigned to a CSR. It runs the client portion (*: Inventory Tracking Client Interface*) of a client/server

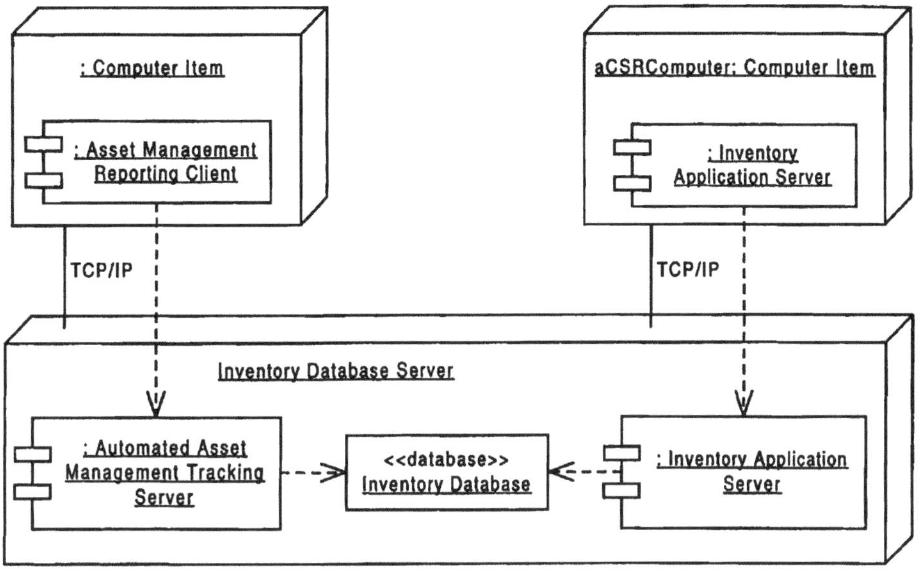

FIGURE 6.15 UML deployment diagram.

inventory database application. The server portion (*: Inventory Application Server*) runs on the *Inventory Database Server* node. The server node also runs an automated asset tracking component (*: Automated Asset Management Tracking Server*) that receives regular inventory reports from computer items in the system. On each computer item in the system, an asset reporting client (*: Asset Management Reporting Client*) executes periodically in the background. Such a component can report information such as amount of RAM, hard drives, operating system version, and other resources on each computer. The dashed arrows are dependencies. We see that the client components depend on corresponding server components, and server components depend on the *Inventory Database.* We know this object represents an actual database because of the *«database»* stereotype above the instance name. Finally, this example shows communication associations among nodes. Both client nodes are connected via *TCP/IP* associations with the server node. Presumably the clients will communicate through TCP/IP sockets or some other similar protocol.

Implementation diagrams are not common in practice, but for large systems they are useful for keeping track of complex dependencies. Component diagrams can be thought of as a graphical extension of the build management systems that are commonplace in the software development industry. No modern software engineer would seriously consider implementing a large system without some kind of source configuration, control, and build system. Similarly, large models need dependency management diagrams. Also, this kind of information is helpful in the design of distributed systems and component-based architectures like Microsoft's ActiveX and Sun's JavaBeans. As OO moves toward distributed object architectures like CORBA, implementation diagrams will likely be used more frequently.

OSM does not explicitly provide for implementation diagrams. OSM has no separate graphical notation for this kind of information. However, components and nodes can be modeled using standard OSM object/relationship diagrams.

6.6 Extension Mechanisms

A key goal of UML is to provide a universal object-oriented modeling language that can be applied to a wide range of specific tasks. To meet this goal, the designers of UML needed to incorporate extension mechanisms so that users faced with new situations could appropriately adapt the existing framework rather than be forced to build an entirely new modeling language. UML has three extension mechanisms: constraints, property lists, and stereotypes.

A "constraint" is just a Boolean condition associated with a model element. Each constraint condition must always be true for every "committed state" of the model. Constraints might not hold for a short time in the middle of a transaction, but when a transaction commits, all constraints must be satisfied. In UML, constraints may be written in any form that is convenient for the task at hand, whether that be natural language, predicate logic, C++ or Java, or any other form. A constraint is represented as a string within curly braces (e.g., "{subset}"). Constraints alter the built-in semantics of model elements by restricting possible instances.

The "property list" (or "tagged value" list) is another way of extending the default semantics of UML. Each model element may have an arbitrary number of associated user-defined "properties." Each property is defined by a keyword/value pair. The "keyword" or "tag" is used to retrieve the value of the property. Generally, a property list has the form "{key_1 = $value_1$, ..., key_n = $value_n$}." For example, "{updated = 01-Jan-1998, creator = "jones", finalized}" is a three-property list, where the first property, *updated*, holds a date, the second property, *creator*, is string-valued, and the third property, *finalized*, is Boolean (its presence indicates the property is true). Property lists can be used to arbitrarily extend the structure of existing models without reworking them or otherwise performing schema evolution. This kind of data structure is popular among LISP-styled languages because it is flexible and general. However, when the inefficiency of large *ad hoc* property lists becomes too burdensome, a particular application model might need to evolve to capture properties instead as classes and associations. But for simple, quick extensions, property lists are quite useful.

A "stereotype" is a cross between a constraint and a template. Defining a stereotype is like subclassing an element in the UML metamodel. However, as with property lists, stereotype extension does not require any change to the existing metamodel, rather, a stereotype is an instance of the class *Stereotype*. This approach to metamodel extensibility is crucial for tool developers and users who want to share application models across tools built by different vendors. Metamodel stability is critical to these goals.

Characteristics of a particular stereotype are defined by attaching constraints and properties (the other two UML extension mechanisms). Additionally, a stereotype refers to a base class (e.g., *Class*, *Attribute*, *Dependency*, *Association*, or other classes from the UML metamodel) and it may have a user-defined icon.

Consider this example. A "dependency" (found on package, deployment, and use-case diagrams, among others) may have many different purposes. Sometimes, a dependency exists because one module "calls" another, or perhaps one package "imports" the name space of another. In these cases, rather than subclass "dependency" in the UML metamodel, we can instead define stereotypes that indicate different kinds of dependency. We mark a dependency with a stereotype such as "«calls»" or "«imports»" to indicate the intent of this particular dependency. For use cases, dependencies may be marked with the stereotypes "«extends»" or "«uses»." In this way, UML captures a great deal of variety with a single metamodel class, *Dependency*. This notion of stereotype keeps the UML metamodel simpler than it otherwise would have been. Rather than add subclasses, we merely define additional stereotypes, which express patterns of use.

As the reader has already observed, stereotypes are represented as a string in guillemots ("«...»") that is used to tag a particular model element. Users may also define graphical symbols to be associated with stereotyped variations. As an example, in the *UML Extension for Business Modeling*, there are class stereotypes for "«worker»," "«case worker»," and "«entity»." Each of these stereotypes is represented using a different graphical notation instead of the ordinary rectangle used for classes in UML (Rational et al., 1997d).

6.6.1 Comparison with OSM

OSM does not have as well-developed an extension capability as UML. OSM does support general constraints like those in UML. OSM also has a template capability that allows shorthand textual and graphical notations to be expressed in terms of underlying metamodel constructs. OSM's metamodel is far simpler than the UML metamodel. Moreover, the OSM metamodel is seamlessly combined with the application model and data instance layers of an OSM-based system. Thus, querying the metamodel from within an OSM application is easy, but model evolution and metamodel evolution are not. We find the stereotype mechanism to be a compelling approach to the problem of developer-friendly metamodel extension.

6.7 Discussion

As we have compared individual features of UML and OSM, in each case we have observed that both models make unique contributions. So asking the question, "Which one is better?" really makes no sense as they play somewhat different roles. UML is useful as an industrial-strength, object-oriented modeling facility for projects that target an implementation using a traditional object-oriented programming language. OSM is more suited to pure conceptual modeling. OSM also provides an excellent facility for conceptual modeling research. However, UML's support infrastructure (tools, texts, development processes, etc.) is much more developed than OSM's.

There are numerous ways to improve UML. Our first suggestion is that the amount of redundancy be decreased. Not only do many of the diagrams present overlapping views into the underlying metamodel concepts, but also the terminology sometimes changes in the different diagrams. For example, a "state" in a statechart diagram and an "activity" in an activity diagram both map to the same metamodel concept of a "state." These sorts of differences and the redundancy of diagrams can be confusing to novices. The initial learning curve for UML could be flattened somewhat by eliminating redundancy and unneeded terminology differences.

There is also conceptual redundancy within the metamodel itself. For example, the metamodel defines a "request" as a communication between instances resulting from an instance performing a request action. Requests are divided into two kinds: "signal" (an asynchronous message with no reply) and "operation" (synchronous or asynchronous, with or without a reply). Thus we see that "signal" could be viewed as a special case of "operation." The corresponding idea in OSM is the "interaction," which serves for all communication and synchronization needs. Another example of conceptual redundancy is the separation of "package" and "class." Both are module concepts that encapsulate features and provide interfaces to other modules in the system. In OSM, high-level object sets serve both purposes. These are just two examples from many we could point out. We recommend that this redundancy and overlap be removed as much as possible.

Sometimes the UML metamodel goes the other direction, using the same term for different concepts. For example, "generalization" works well in relating classes through a traditional "is-a" relationship, but for use cases, generalization is redefined as "uses" and "extends" relationships. Generalization and inheritance are already semantically overburdened terms in the OO community, and in our opinion, this overloading of the term "generalization" detracts from the clarity and elegance of UML.

The UML metamodel is intended to be a logical model, not a physical or implementation model. However, a great deal of implementation-oriented information shows through to the UML user. Prime examples are visibility and navigability specifications. The meaning of UML's private, protected, and public visibilities depends on the particular language being used to implement the model (e.g., "protected" in Java is not the same as "protected" in C++). Some visibility control is desirable in a conceptual model, but it should be a well-defined conceptual form of visibility, not a language-dependent form. Limited navigability is purely an implementation idea. In a conceptual model, navigability should be universal. Only when we move to implementation does the question of efficiency enter into the picture and the consequent desire to limit navigability arise. Thus, for the purposes of conceptual modeling, visibility and navigability could be treated differently.

This also brings up the point that UML makes no attempt to hide the eventual implementation language. In fact the authors of UML went to a great deal of effort to make sure that different languages could easily coexist within the UML framework. This is because UML is intended to be a universal modeling language. However, the result is that a great deal of the user-chosen implementation language will show through. For example, developers can choose to write method descriptions in C++ or any other language that suits their needs. UML also has powerful extension facilities, allowing for end-user customization. Without strong methodological guidance that is adopted industry-wide, it could be difficult for different UML users to communicate even though they both use UML.

Also, the ready availability of implementation-oriented features could encourage the premature use of design concepts during the systems analysis phase of a project. It would be unfortunate, for example, if an analyst started a project by describing details in the analysis model such as visibility, navigability, and changeability. These ideas do not belong in analysis, but rather in design and implementation. As another example, consider the designation of attributes within a class. Attributes could instead be represented through the strong form of aggregation called composition which would define them as classes. However, an entity represented as an attribute is generally considered and used in a much different way than the same entity represented as a class with an association. The choice of making an entity an attribute instead of a stand-alone class is more of a design decision than an analysis decision. Again, an answer to this situation is to provide strong methodological support to help developers decide when to use various features of UML.

The ten different UML diagrams encode a fair amount of methodology information. For example, having a use-case diagram implies something about how we will develop projects in UML. Instead of approaching a system from the perspective of developing objects, we can start by modeling the users of a system and the kinds of functions the system will perform. So there are some process implications in the current UML diagram structure. A truly effective use of UML will require a well-developed methodology. As of this writing Booch, Jacobson, and Rumbaugh are working on their methodology, and their process book should be available by the time you read this (Jacobson, Booch, and Rumbaugh, 1998). They have crafted UML so that other methodologists can also use its framework as the basis for alternative development processes. We anticipate that there will yet be a fair amount of discussion among methodologists about best practices using UML.

The future is bright for UML and the entire object community. UML was approved in November 1997 as a standard by the Object Management Group (OMG) as part of its Object Management Architecture. Status as an OMG standard will enhance UML's ongoing role in the industry. A critical mass of vendors and methodologists are rallying to support UML. It is valuable today in its current form, and it will continue to grow and improve. UML is by no means the only player in this arena, but software developers who want to practice state-of-the-art engineering ought to be aware of the ideas and facilities UML and its supporting technologies have to offer.

References

Booch, G., Rumbaugh, J. and Jacobson, I. 1998. *Unified Modeling Language User Guide.* Addison-Wesley, Reading, MA.

Booch, G. 1996. *Object-Oriented Analysis and Design with Applications, 2nd Edition.* Addison-Wesley, Reading, MA.

Coleman, D., Arnold, P., Bodoff, S., Dollin, C. and Gilchrist, H. 1994. *Object-Oriented Development: The Fusion Method.* Prentice-Hall, Englewood Cliffs, NJ.

Embley, D. W. 1998. *Object Database Development: Concepts and Principles.* Addison-Wesley, Reading, MA.

Embley, D. W., Kurtz, B. D. and Woodfield, S. N. 1992. *Object-Oriented Systems Analysis: A Model-Driven Approach.* Yourdon Press Series, Prentice-Hall, Englewood Cliffs, NJ.

Fowler, M. and Scott, K. 1997. *UML Distilled: Applying the Standard Object Modeling Language.* Addison-Wesley, Reading, MA.

Gamma, E., Helm, R., Johnson, R. and Vlissides, J. 1995. *Design Patterns: Elements of Reusable Object-Oriented Software.* Addison-Wesley, Reading, MA.

Harel, D., 1987. Statecharts: a visual formalism for complex systems, *Sci. Comp. Program.*, 8: 231-274.

Jacobson, I., Booch, G. and Rumbaugh, J. 1998. *The Objectory Software Development Process.* Addison-Wesley, Reading, MA.

Jacobson, I., Christerson, M., Jonsson, P. and Overgaard, G. 1992. *Object-Oriented Software Engineering: A Use Case Driven Approach.* Addison-Wesley, Reading, MA.

Martin, J. and Odell, J. J. 1992. *Object-Oriented Analysis and Design.* Prentice-Hall, Englewood Cliffs, NJ.

Meyer, B. 1997. *Object-Oriented Software Construction, 2nd Edition.* Prentice-Hall, Englewood Cliffs, NJ.

Quatrani, T. 1998. *Visual Modeling With Rational Rose and UML.* Addison-Wesley, Reading, MA.

Rational et al. 1997a. *UML Summary, Version 1.1,* Rational Software Corporation, Cupertino, CA, Document ad/97-08-03, http://www.rational.com/uml, 1 September.

Rational et al. 1997b. *UML Notation Guide, Version 1.1,* Rational Software Corporation, Cupertino, CA, Document ad/97-08-05, http://www.rational.com/uml, 1 September.

Rational et al. 1997c. *UML Semantics, Version 1.1,* Rational Software Corporation, Cupertino, CA, Document ad/97-08-04, http://www.rational.com/uml, 1 September.

Rational et al. 1997d. *UML Extension for Business Modeling, Version 1.1,* Rational Software Corporation, Cupertino, CA, Document ad/97-08-07, http://www.rational.com/uml.

Rumbaugh, J., Jacobson, I. and Booch, G. 1998. *Unified Modeling Language Reference Manual.* Addison-Wesley, Reading, MA.

Rumbaugh, J., Blaha, M., Lorensen, W., Eddy, F. and Premerlani, W. 1991. *Object-Oriented Modeling and Design.* Prentice-Hall, Englewood Cliffs, NJ.

Shlaer, S. and Mellor, S. J. 1992. *Object Life Cycles: Modeling the World In States.* Prentice-Hall, Englewood Cliffs, NJ.

Wirfs-Brock, R. 1990. *Designing Object-Oriented Software.* Prentice-Hall, Englewood Cliffs, NJ.

Further Information

Major texts in the area of object-oriented systems modeling are listed above in the references section. The most current information on UML can be obtained from the Rational Software Corporation web site (http://www.rational.com/uml). Further information on object-oriented software development research can be obtained from the annual OOPSLA Conference proceedings (published by the ACM's SIGPLAN group, see http://www.acm.org for details), and the annual ECOOP Conference proceedings. The premier international research conference for conceptual modeling in general is the annual ER Conference. Proceedings of the more recent ECOOP and ER Conferences are available in the Springer-Verlag *Lecture Notes in Computer Science* series. Our OSM web site is http://osm7.cs.byu.edu.

7

The Semantic Object Modeling Approach (SOMA)

Ian Graham
Chase Manhattan Bank

SOMA is a third generation, full lifecycle method for object-oriented (OO) development. It combines business process modeling and re-engineering techniques, a software engineering process and lifecycle model, an OO notation and metamodel, many specific tasks and techniques, a metrics suite, and a range of modeling heuristics. SOMA's particular strengths are its detailed and clear approach to requirements engineering, its ability to model business rules and intelligent agents, and its completeness and strict adherence to OO principles. In its current version it relies on language specific design techniques from other methods such as Booch, BON, MOSES, etc., and it adopts some of the applicable notation and process from OPEN (Firesmith et al., 1997). The UML notation can also be used but is not preferred due to some violations of the OO principles referred to above.

7.1 The Origins and Goals of SOMA

SOMA has its origins in a business process re-engineering project in 1989 and has been described in various articles and books. Graham (1995) published the definitive version, but the method has evolved considerably since reported by Graham and Jones (1998). It adheres strongly to OO principles but extends the normal object model semantics slightly and applies object modeling to more than just systems and business objects. The founding principles of pure OO are those of abstraction and polymorphism. These

0-8493-3135-8/99/$0.00+$.50

are to be implemented by the modeling techniques of encapsulation and inheritance, which in turn lead to the need to use the metaphors of object identity and message passing to prevent modeling absurdities such as data structure duplication. It is a principle of SOMA that object models should be used wherever possible, so that we minimize the number of modeling languages that must be learned. We apply the KISS principle — keep it small and simple. That is, SOMA projects deliver only what will be really used, avoiding deliverables that only exist to soothe bureaucratic sensibilities or keep the dust off empty shelves. SOMA asserts that system development IS re-engineering. It encourages the use of RAD, workshops, and time boxing. There should be no linearized "phases" in projects. Instead the project consists of parallel, interacting activities. Another important principle is "quality first." Test everything as you produce it and reuse wherever you possibly can. SOMA developers also measure everything that can be measured and rely on software to do as much of this automatically as is feasible. All SOMA product metric collection can be automated as evidenced by the metrics facilities of the *SOMATiK* tool. I believe that users should be given the right solution on time, even if it is incomplete. This is why RAD, workshops, agents, and task modeling are given such focus in SOMA.

Companies that are migrating to object technology must maintain operational integrity during the transition. Therefore SOMA uses its notion of **layer** to describe object wrappers for the legacy. Object request brokers (ORBs) or purpose-written code can be used to implement these wrappers. Because large scale business and process improvement is a key focus, SOMA introduces the **mission grid** to scope and analyze business process re-engineering problems. Shared understanding and partnership result from a workshop-based approach that relies on users and developers manipulating their ideas using a powerful object modeling language that is easy to understand.

7.2 Relationship to OPEN

The SOMA process model and metrics suite are to all intents and purposes identical to their OPEN equivalents. SOMA uses only a part of the OPEN OML notation, however, and diverges from it in some places. Additionally, SOMA adds notation and techniques for problems that OPEN does not pretend to address with agent models of business processes being a good example. It also introduces notation for these models that are not provided by OML or UML. Examples include the important **usage** relationship icons and the "smiley" icon for actors. It is projected that OPEN will include these innovations at some future time. Part of OPEN is described earlier in this book and in Henderson-Sellers et al., 1997. Firesmith et al., 1996 describes OML.

7.3 Basic Object Modeling Technique, Semantics and Notations

I will describe the semantics of the SOMA metamodel as briefly as possible along with the basic modeling concepts and the minimal notation. This can be interpreted in the context of system or business object modeling. Then we shall see how the same language is applied to requirements engineering and business process modeling.

SOMA object models use the concepts of class, instance, type, role, and layer. They also may include five kinds of link between the former: specialization, classification, composition, association mapping, and usage mapping. An **object** is defined as either a class, instance, type, role, or layer. All objects have the following **features**: a unique identifier and zero or more, properties, operations and rulesets. **Properties** are attributes or associations. We distinguish three special kinds of association: superclasses, components, and interfaces. Every feature may have **facets.** A very important facet of an operation, for example, is its **servers** facet, which lists the objects for which it is a usage client (i.e., sends a message to). An object may itself have simple facets such as a stereotype or a simple classification facet such as A/D/I (standing for whether the object is an application, domain or interface object. A small, commonly recurring set of linked objects is known as a **pattern.**

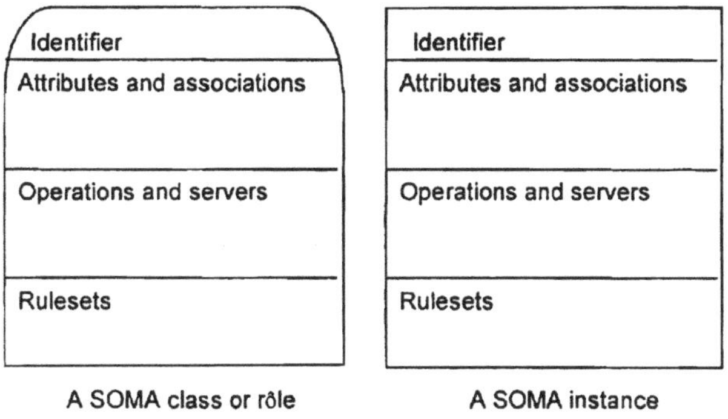

FIGURE 7.1 Object notation.

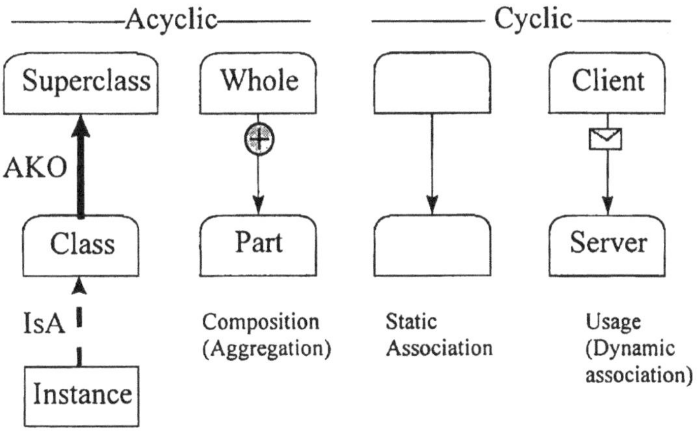

FIGURE 7.2 Link notation.

Figure 7.1 shows the SOMA notation for classes, roles and for types and instances. We adopt the OPEN "index card" metaphor for classes; the rounded corners remind us that classes are insubstantial concepts and not real things with sharp corners that can cut. Instances are rectangles so that we can surround a class icon with a rectangle to denote "a class with instances" when we wish to terminate links at generic instances rather than classes. Classes and roles are named in the plural to indicate multitude and instances and types in the singular. (A type is a single concept and not a collection of its instances.) Figure 7.2 gives the notation for the five basic link types, again following OPEN but adding the envelope icon for usage relationships. We also adopt the OPEN notation of a jagged line through the class icon to designate the separation of interface and implementation, but this is rarely used for business object modeling and thus is not shown here.

This metamodel can be applied everywhere. We will show how it is used to model agent objects representing people and systems in business process models, user task objects, business objects, and system implementation objects. It can even be used to model the software development lifecycle as we will see later. We begin with a discussion of requirements engineering.

7.4 Requirements Engineering with SOMA

In SOMA using the term REQUIREMENTS ENGINEERING seems more appropriate than either REQUIREMENTS CAPTURE or REQUIREMENTS GATHERING, since nothing is captured in the sense of imprisonment and it is wrong to give the impression that the requirements are just there to be gathered from the users. Object-oriented system building is about modeling and, as Bertrand Meyer has so aptly put it, is a process of negotiation (1995). Requirements engineering is no different. Users often only realize the true nature of their requirement when they see the early prototypes. Incidentally, this observation leads us to disagree with Meyer's rather negative views on prototyping as expressed in the work cited above. Requirements engineering is best viewed as a form of knowledge elicitation, because in that discipline it is usually recognized that much knowledge is latent or difficult to verbalize. In discussing object-oriented requirements engineering there is much to write, because of approximately 50 published object-oriented methods, only a handful have anything whatsoever to say about this topic. Arguably, only Objectory (Jacobson et al., 1992) and SOMA (Graham, 1995) have addressed the issue at all, with most methods assuming that a written requirement specification exists at the start of the analysis. In practice, of course, the users of these methods have had to make do and mend in the absence of anything specific in their chosen method. We thus find practitioners like Cook and Daniels (1995) or Odell (Martin and Odell, 1995) using a variant of state and event modeling notations originally included in their methods to model the life histories of individual objects. These notations are, consciously or unconsciously, pressed into service as business process modeling techniques. Of course, this can be made to work, but it may not be as affective as using a technique developed exactly for the purpose. Some academics (e.g., Gilligrand and Liu, 1995) and a few practitioners have proposed using variants of data flow analysis for this purpose, but there are evident dangers of ending up with functionally derived decompositions leading to problems with an object-oriented implementation. Most business process re-engineering (BPR) methods also incorporate process modeling techniques borrowed from old fashioned structured methods. Typically, the process models are arrived at using functional decomposition, flow charting, and data flow techniques. In these methods, processes are viewed as being composed of activities disembodied from the agents responsible for their performance. These activities are linked by so-called "logical flows" that represent information (data actually), materials, or controls. The semantics of such links is sometimes unclear. This approach evades what is actually the key stumbling block in BPR projects — responsibility. Furthermore, much of the semantic content of real business processes is lost by the representation. To solve both problems, we must adopt an object-oriented, responsibility-driven approach to business process modeling based on semiotics of communication (messages).

7.4.1 Requirements for Requirements Engineering

What is needed is a truly object-oriented requirements engineering technique. In our view it should enable developers and users, working together, to build a model of the business processes that a system will support. It should do this while applying the basic principles of object-orientation in a thoroughgoing manner. It must be easy to use and easy to understand. The results should provide a model that is readily accessible and understandable by users as well as developers so that it provides the basis for communication and negotiation between these two groups and their managers. Its models should be small and tractable while capturing all the essential details of a project. In other words, it must capture all the information about the processes and the business objects that they entail. It must allow the processes to be described from both an internal and external viewpoint and its modeling constructs should not multiply beyond manageable proportions, even for complex systems. The requirement engineering and business process modeling techniques of OPEN meet all these objectives.

A key part of the SOMA approach to system development (on which this part of OPEN is based) is the use of rapid application development workshops (RADs) for requirements capture and analysis. The RAD technique, of course, predates object technology and was used long before there were any methods for object-oriented analysis available. Running RAD workshops, it is found that data-centered or static modeling approaches to object modeling are not a good place to start with users. Obtaining an entity model takes quite a long time if attempted at the start of a RAD. Many people with similar experience have observed that users respond better to a process oriented approach. However, if we want to extract an object-oriented model from the activity, constructing data flow diagrams is really worse than useless

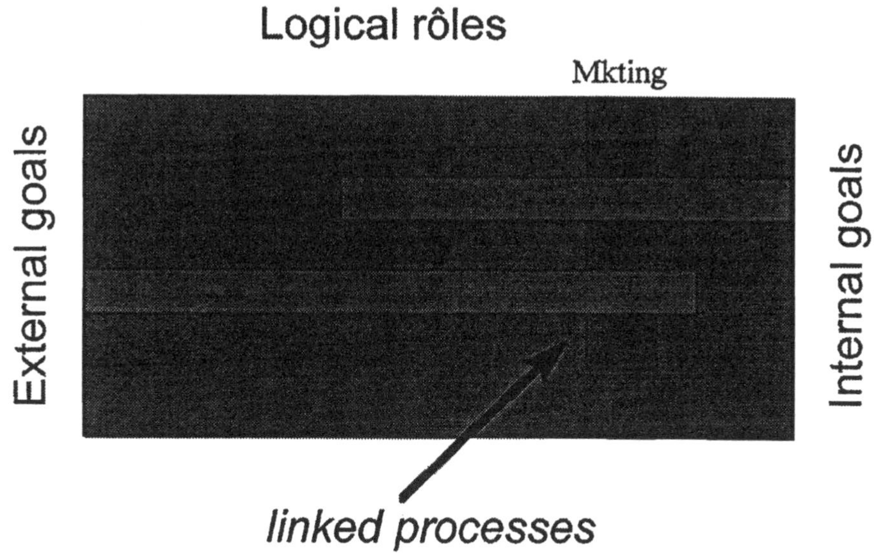

FIGURE 7.3 The mission grid.

and likely to (1) be ignored by real object-oriented programmers and (2) lead to a horrid functional decomposition that poorer programmers can use as an excuse to write functionally oriented code. Our experience has shown that all these problems can be overcome by basing the requirements model on business processes using a modeling technique that is strictly object-oriented and is a generalization of the data flow approach and the use-case approach. As a side effect of the approach, it turns out that if an entity model view is required it can be extracted from the object model and agreed with users in a matter of moments.

Both requirements engineering and BPR must start with a model of the communications and contracts among the participants in the business and the other stakeholders, customers, suppliers, etc. First we need to model the whole organization and decide what business it is or should be in. In conformity with the principles of OPEN we should build an object model of the entire business to address this problem. As it turns out most businesses are far too large and complex to make such an approach viable and we need to apply a simple decomposition technique first. The technique is inspired by the spreadsheet metaphor.

7.4.2 The Mission Grid

We start business process modeling by asking who are its customers and stakeholders. These latter could include regulators, suppliers, shareholders, sister companies, etc. We then work to define the goals that the organization shares with the stakeholders, especially with its customers. These are essentially **external** goals that represent value propositions shared between the organization and the stakeholders, such as "provide reliable product promptly" or "give accurate advice." These shared goals are written along one edge of a grid. In Figure 7.3 the left edge has been chosen. Of course, a company always has goals that it may not share with customers, such as keeping the executives out of jail on charges of false accounting, etc. To represent this we write such **internal** goals on the facing edge of the grid.

For both internal and external goals we now ask: What has to be done to support each goal? In other words, we establish the processes required to support the goals. We can now compare these with the processes currently in place and produce grids representing the situation **before** and **after** re-engineering. At this point we must decide whether to go for a radical restructuring or minor changes. OPEN has little to say on this essentially creative activity but does provide the essential modeling tools to establish which

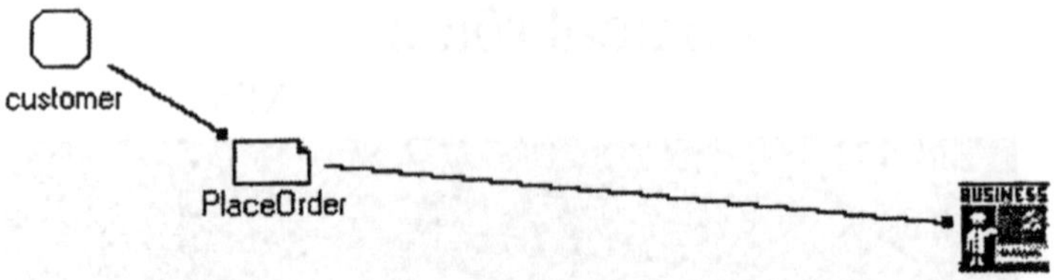

FIGURE 7.4 External context model of placing orders.

processes contribute to the goals so that rational decisions about both the processes and process automation can be made.

The next step is to identify logical roles representing abstract job descriptions for the people who will conduct the processes. The grid is then reorganized iteratively to minimize illogical role and task assignments. Once the processes are assigned to the roles we only need to discover the dependencies between any linked processes to complete the high level business process model represented by the grid. The text of each cell now describes the essential mission of each process area (or business area) along t = with any linkages to related processes and ordering and time constraints.

This technique has decomposed the business into chunks that are small enough to be modeled in detail used an object-oriented style as we now discuss.

7.4.3 Modeling Business Processes with Task Objects

Consider some business process or enterprise area within the grid. It could be an entire company, a division, or department of one such or even a sole trader. It is most likely to be a process-oriented business area and may be represented by one cell in the grid or a few cells representing strongly linked processes. The cells of the grid carry the mission statement for this "business area." Our first task is to refine it into a series of measurable, prioritized objectives as discussed later. The business area is regarded for this purpose as an independent business. This business must communicate with the outside world to exist at all and, if it does so, it must use some convention of signs and signals thereto. These signals are called **semiotic acts** and are *carried* by some material substratum and involve a number of semiotic levels from data flows up to implicit social relationships.* For example, the substrate may consist of filled-in forms in a paper-based office environment and the social context might be that one assumes that no practical jokes are to be played. If the substratum is verbal (or written natural language) communication then we can speak instead of **speech acts** or **conversations**. These are the speech acts of Austin (1962) and Searle (1969). Semiotic acts can be represented by messages, which are directed from the initiator (source) of the communication to its recipient (target). A typical such message is represented in Figure 7.4 where a typical customer places an order with the business. This message includes the definition of the reply: {order accepted|out of stock|etc.}. By *abus de langage* we shall identify semiotic acts with their representation as messages from now on in this paper, although they are strictly different, the same semiotic act may be represented by many different messages. This defines equivalence classes of messages and we can think of our actual message as a representative of its class.

Note particularly that every message should support at least one objective and, contrariwise, every objective must be achieved through the medium of one or more conversations (messages). This is an important check for the modeller to perform.

Of course, in BPR, we are anxious to capture not just the messages that cross the business boundary, such as order placement, but model the communications among our customers, suppliers, competitors,

* Semiotics is the comparative study of sign systems and has been important in such diverse fields as mathematical logic, natural language processing, anthropology, and literary criticism. It holds that signs can be analyzed at at least three levels: those of syntax, semantics, and pragmatics.

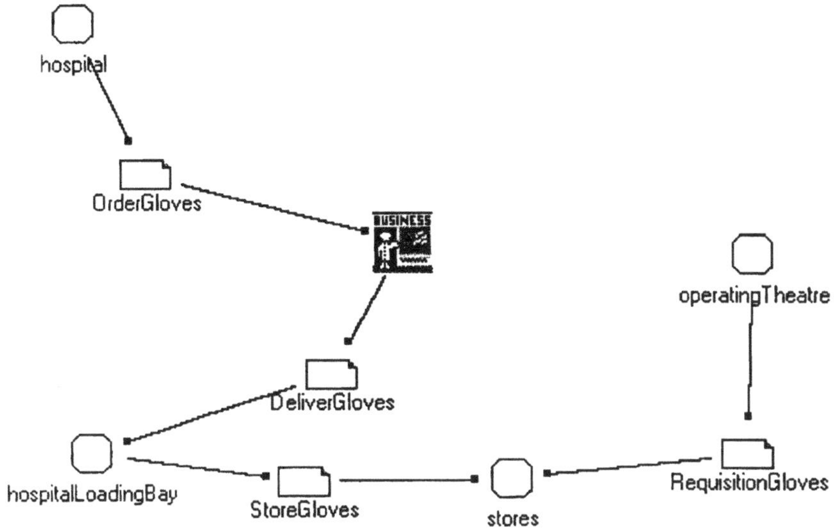

FIGURE 7.5(a) Re-engineering delivery logistics: before.

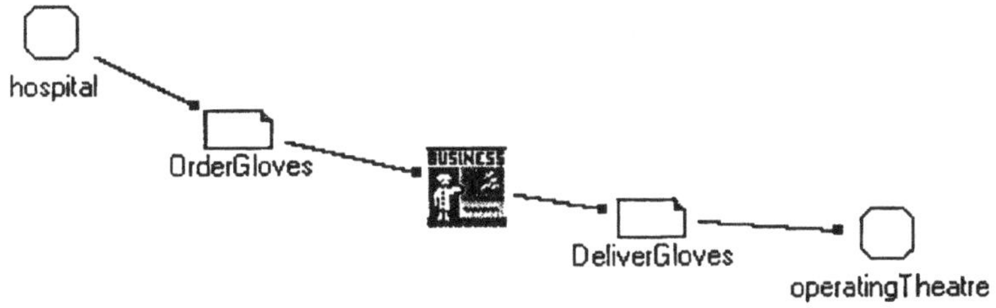

FIGURE 7.5(b) Re-engineering delivery logistics: after.

etc. This provides the opportunity to offer new services to these players, perhaps taking over their internal operations, for a fee of course.

Figures 7.5a and 7.5b shows how this might be applied in the simple case of delivering medical supplies, based on what actually happened at Baxter Healthcare (Short and Venkatramen, 1992). Originally, Baxter took an order from the hospital's procurement department and delivered to its loading bay. Then the hospital was responsible for storing the goods and delivering them to the appropriate operating theater (Figure 7.5a). After re-engineering, goods such as surgical gloves are delivered direct by the supplier to the operating theater where they are required (Figure 7.5b). Of course, the message labeled OrderGloves has been modified. This gives an advantage over other suppliers in terms of service, reduces the hospital's inventory and logistics costs, and means that a higher price can be charged by the supplier while remaining competitive. It also makes the hospital more dependent on the supplier.

A semiotic or speech act is characterized at the semantic and pragmatic levels by a (possibly implicit) contract that both parties understand. The pragmatics of this contract represent a social relation just as a message represents a semiotic act. Many contracts may express the same relationship so we choose one to represent its equivalence class.

A message implies data flow, so that this approach generalizes data flow modeling. However, it also enriches it considerably. For one thing, data flow in both directions along message links. This is why we have chosen to terminate message links at the recipient end with a filled rectangle rather than an arrowhead. The line segment is directed from the *initiator* of the communication not from the origin of the data.

A **business process** is a set of related messages. The relationship between the messages is encoded in a task ruleset.

It is inconceivable in most businesses that the message initiator does not wish to change the state of the world in some way as a result of the communication. This desired state of the world is the **goal** of the message and every message has a goal even if it is often unstated.

A goal is achieved by the performance of a **task**. The tasks we perform can often be reduced to a few stereotypes — typical tasks that act as pattern matching templates against which real tasks can be evaluated and from which real tasks (or use cases) can be generated. This overcomes a possible objection that there could be an explosion in the number of tasks. Our experience indicates that there is no such explosion of tasks. It turns out that tasks can be modeled as objects within a *bona fide* object model in the task domain. It is to these matters that we now turn.

7.4.3.1 Task Scripts

Tasks can be described in several ways but it is most useful to describe a task using a **task script**. A task script represents a *stereotypical* task. This provides a notion of generalized exception handlers that does not seem to be available with use cases, while an exception (extends) path is specific to the use case. As an example, consider a task script that describes the task of going to a restaurant. The idea is that one **always** does the same thing when visiting a restaurant. One **always**:

1. Enters the restaurant
2. Attracts the attention of a waiter
3. Takes one's seat
4. Reads the menu
5. Chooses a meal
6. Eats it
7. Pays
8. Leaves

This is certainly a good stereotype of the situations normally encountered. However, no visit to a restaurant follows this script exactly. One may, for example:

1. Enter the restaurant
2. Attract the attention of a waiter
3. Go to takes one's seat
4. Slip on a banana skin

The script is broken and must be repaired before our culinary cravings can be assuaged. This is accomplished by permitting what we will call **side-scripts** that deal with stereotypical exceptions. In this particular case the sidescript might proceed:

1. Get up
2. Brush oneself down
3. Look around to see who is laughing
4. Abuse them verbally or punch them
5. Return to the interrupted task

The point to note here is that the banana skin script does not just work in the context of the restaurant script. It will work anywhere. The script describes a well-known, stereotypical situation. To process such exceptions, task objects must be able to send messages to each other. It turns out that task scripts can also be classified and (de)composed. In other words they can be regarded as objects within an object model. This object model is not the Business Object Model that we will derive eventually and is known as the Task Object Model.

A sidescript has exactly the same semantics as what Schank and Abelson (1977) called a "subscript." The renaming is necessary to avoid confusion with notions of specialization where the prefix "sub" is commonly used.

The reader may be tempted to confuse sidescripts with Jacobson's "uses" or "extends" relations. This is not exactly the case though there is considerable overlap. Our intention is to utilize a very pure concept of object modeling to model tasks. In this way the developer only has to learn one set of terminology and concepts to model both tasks and business objects. The Objectory "uses" relationship corresponds to task decomposition using the a-part-of relation in SOMA. The difference here is one of interpretation. Objectory does not emphasize the discovery of use-case components of this kind by decomposition. Also the very term "uses" could easily confuse people used to associating this word with some sort of client/server (usage) relationship. Similarly, "extends" in Objectory corresponds to SOMA's "has side script" though the arrows are drawn in the opposite direction in the latter to preserve encapsulation; an extension of a task should not know that it is part of something bigger. To use an example from Jacobson (1992), the Item is stuck use case extends Returning item. It does so in a foreseeable course of events, whereas the restaurant script only uses Banana skin in the most exceptional circumstances, which may not be foreseen. One of the consequences of this in terms of implementation is that EnterRestaurant may have to perform a search for an appropriate script such as Banana skin rather than store a reference to it statically. Once again, for reasons of encapsulation, it is important that side scripts do not know which scripts they "extend," which is why it is important to model this relationship as a message send to the side script, possibly involving a search. We suspect that this different way of thinking about the problem partly reflects differences in the domains within which Objectory and SOMA grew up, especially differences among the typical users that are encountered in these domains. Telecommunication engineers are usually quite happy with detailed specification and will be comfortable with, for example, state machine notations. Bankers do not often respond well to such approaches.

Task scripts *generify* use cases in the sense that a task script is a generic use case. Similarly, a use case is a generic scenario. Thus we have three levels of abstraction: scenarios, use cases, and task scripts. A **use case** is *an equivalence class of scenarios* and a **task script** is *an equivalence class of use cases.* Thus, a use case is equivalent to the set of scenarios that can implement it and a task script is equivalent to the set of use cases that can implement it. The advantage of moving to the task script level is principally that we abstract away from specific exceptions that tend to increase the total number of use cases to an unacceptable extent.

We will now explain how task scripts are used to move from a description of the business process to a description of a supporting computer system based on classes and operations. We must first grasp the concepts of the OPEN external and internal process models and the notion of a business support system.

7.4.3.2 Building the Task Object Model

The external context model is a model of the messages that pass between the business (as defined earlier) and the external objects that represent its customers, suppliers, etc. It also includes messages that pass between external objects that are, as it were, out of context. This permits business process modeling and thus process innovation. The internal context model extends the external context by introducing an object representing the "business support system" within the business that is to be built (usually a computer system). Also, within the business, we define actors in exactly the manner of Objectory as users adopting a role. The internal context model is a model of messages that pass between the support system, actors, and external objects. Note that a message sent by an external object to the business in the external context could, in the internal context, go directly to the support system (implying perhaps an electronic interface) or go to an actor. External objects and actors are bona fide objects with a contractual relationship to other objects in the model.

Messages are triggered by **events**. In the case of messages initiated by actors or objects internal to the support system, we usually know the causes of these events, because they are the direct result of task

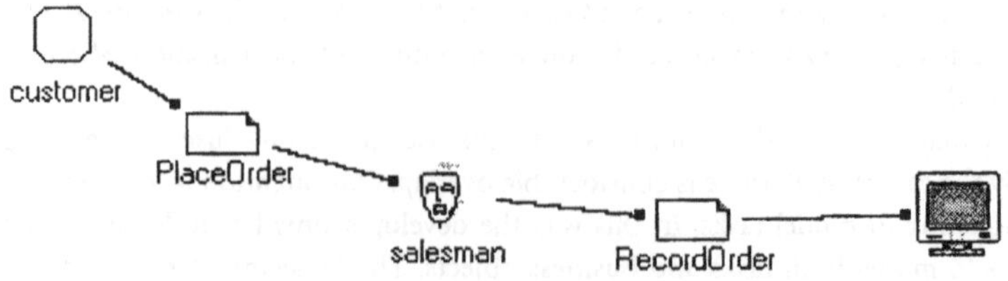

FIGURE 7.6 Internal context model showing an actor.

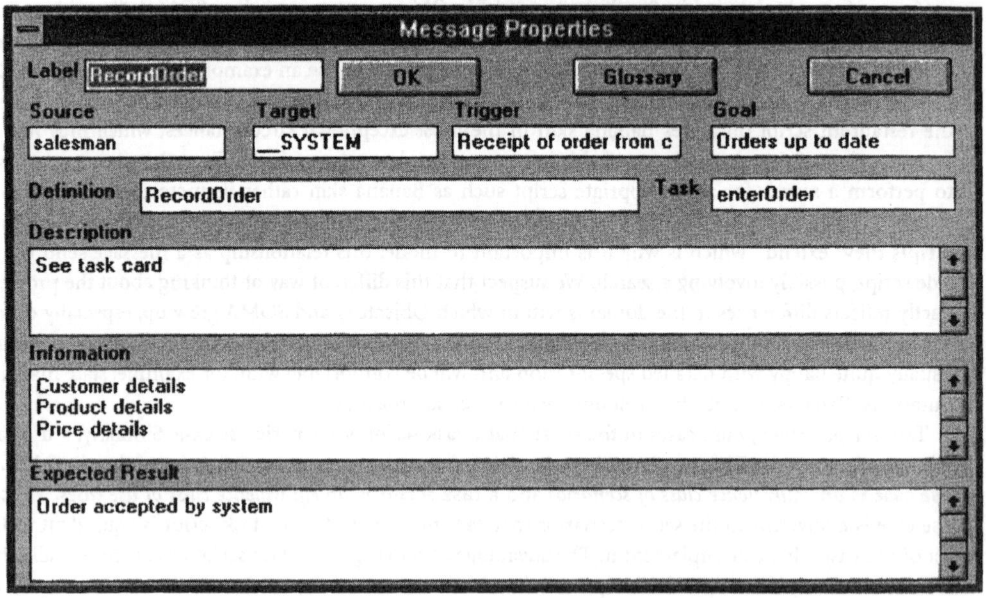

FIGURE 7.7 The structure of the semiotic act: RecordOrder.

execution. When the initiator is an external object we nearly always lack this knowledge and the triggering event appears as a given.

In Figure 7.6 a salesman receives the customer's order and enters it into a business support system. The order is triggered by some unknown condition within the customer. Of course, this business support system is likely to be the computer system that we are trying to construct, but it could just as well be a card index or similar. Let us examine the `RecordOrder` message in more detail. Figure 7.7 shows the detailed description of this message.

This high level task can be decomposed into component tasks that, in *SOMATiK*,* are entered using a structure known as a task card. The decomposition may then be displayed in graphical form automatically as shown in Figure 7.8.

The task card shown in Figure 7.9 emphasizes that tasks are to be regarded as objects (either classes or instances). Tasks may be classified and (de)composed. They may send messages to exception handling tasks and may be associated with other tasks, e.g., this task "reminds one" of that task. Tasks have

---

* Bezant. *SOMATiK User Guide*, (Bezant Object Technologies, 6 St. Mary's St., Wallingford, Oxon OX10 0LE, England, 1995). *SOMATiK* is an MS Windows tool that supports the SOMA method. A free version is supplied with Graham, 1995. The diagrams in this article were all produced using *SOMATiK*.

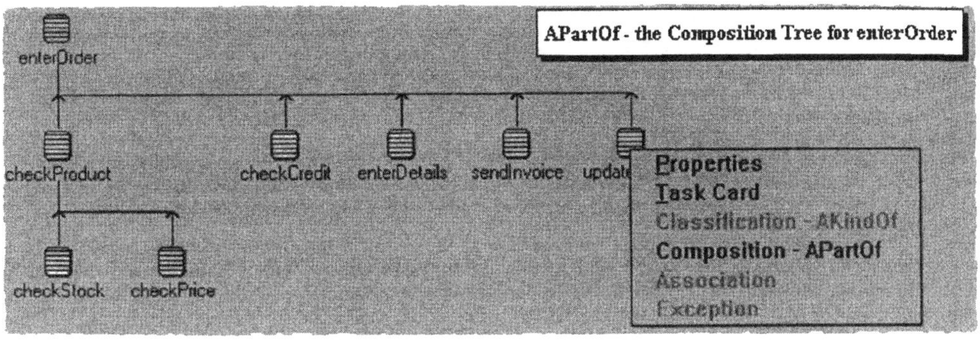

FIGURE 7.8 Task decomposition.

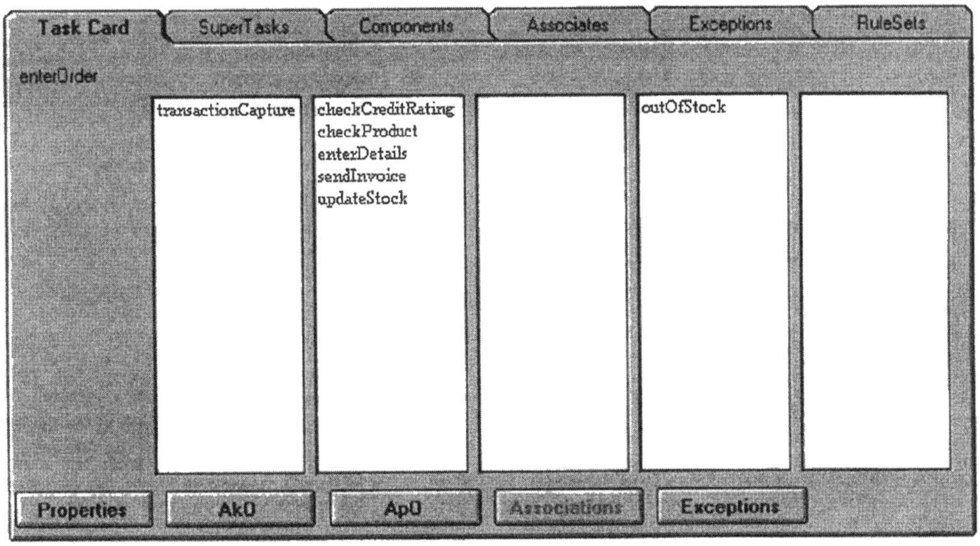

FIGURE 7.9 A task card.

complexity and take time. This is usually only recorded for atomic tasks (defined below) since it can often be inferred for the composite tasks. The time taken is assumed to be the sum of the times for the components at the next level, etc. This of course can be overridden. Complexities are also additive unless otherwise stated. An atomic task is illustrated in Figure 7.10.

External objects differ from actors in two senses: actors work within our business and we know more about the tasks they are carrying out. External objects may conceal tasks of which we have no knowledge that will affect us because they lead to events that trigger messages or **triggering events**. Messages always have triggering events, although for actors and the system we usually know the task that has led to the event. External objects, such as customers, are usually represented in the Business Object Model by objects with few or no operations but typically several attributes. It is important not to confuse these internal representations, which cannot do anything except store static data, with their real-world counterparts that do exhibit, often complex, behavior. Such internal representations of external objects are nearly always persistent objects.

Rulesets in tasks allow the sequencing and coordination of tasks to be described in the high-level SOMA rule language. This effectively describes the way tasks combine to form complete business processes.

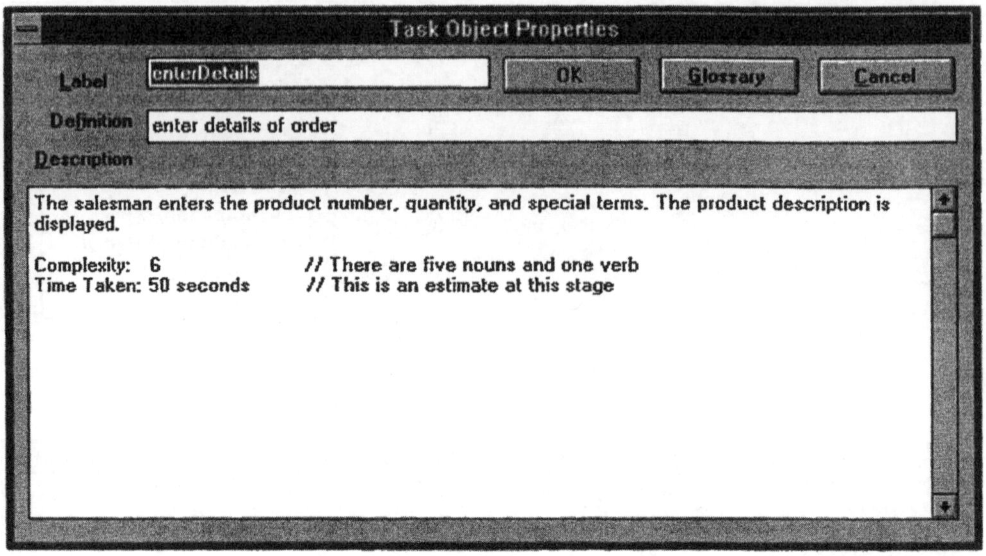

FIGURE 7.10 An atomic task.

7.4.3.3 Converting the Task Object Model (TOM) to the Business Object Model (BOM)

Once the analysis of the context models, business processes, and messages is completed, we end up with a set of task cards representing decomposed tasks. It is assumed the decomposition continues to "atomic" level where an atomic task is one that cannot be further decomposed without introducing terms foreign to the domain. Each atomic task is represented by a sentence in a standard subject/verb/object form where possible. We call this the TOM. The sentences in the TOM are now analyzed (preferably, we find, by users) to discover the true business objects. The technique is basically a textual analysis where nouns indicate objects and verbs operations. The classes thus discovered are represented on class cards in the form shown in Figure 7.11. This process creates the BOM. Note that the class and task cards have exactly the same structure — they are both "objects." Class cards contain the entire model and, as with task cards, structure diagram can be generated from them. These class cards are printed out on paper in a different format (see Table 7.1) for use in CRC style walkthroughs to validate the model and produce event traces.

7.4.3.4 Testing the Requirements Specification

The walkthrough produces a set of event traces or interaction diagrams that effectively describe the way business objects execute operations that support each of the business tasks. If *SOMATiK* is used and the operations have been expressed in the appropriate syntax, these traces take the form of system executions. This provides a test that the two object models are consistent and complete and usually leads to the model being "debugged." The event traces form the basis for system test scripts later in the project.

Because this business object modeling process and the subsequent animation of the specification are not within the main subject matter of this article, they are not discussed any further. Interested readers are referred to Graham's *Migrating to Object Technology* for full details.

The walkthrough tests that the BOM actually supports all the users' tasks. It is instructive to analyze exactly what goes on during such a simulation. The event trace that the walkthrough produces represents a use case, but this use case is generated from the task script and the process is initiated by the workshop facilitator giving a very concrete scenario. For example, for the order capture task, the facilitator might, in acting the role of the order clerk, say: "Boris, my pal down at Ripofmart has just sent in an order asking for 700 chocolate covered widgets for delivery next Wednesday." The movement here is from the

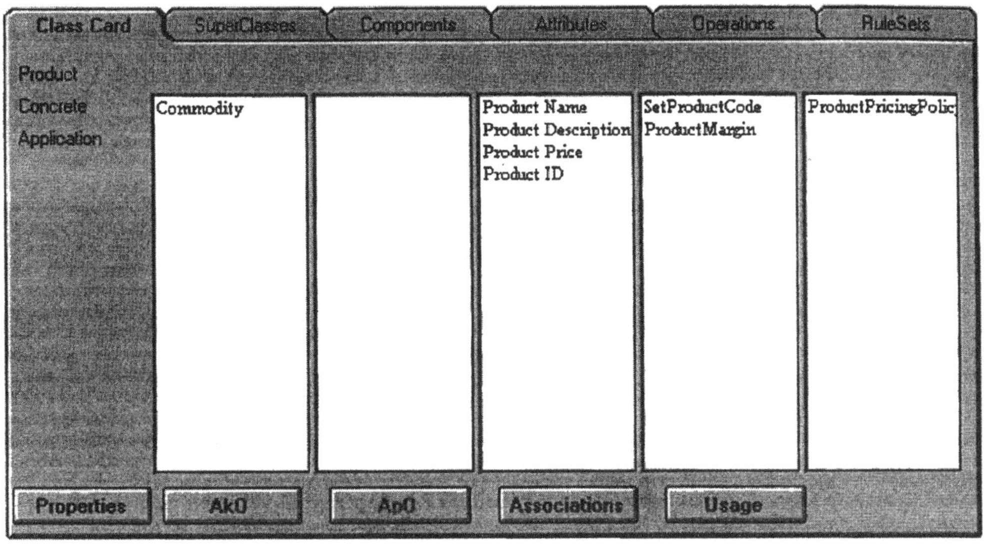

FIGURE 7.11 A class card.

individual to the particular via the general. First start with the (individual) scenario and then use the (universal) task script to generate a corresponding (particular) use case. Our experience has been that this approach is very affective, especially in building an understanding of projects that is shared by both users and developers.

7.5 Seamless Object-Oriented Requirements Engineering and Modeling

We have introduced the reader to two of OPEN's object models: the TOM and the BOM and suggested that they could be linked using CRC style walkthroughs with users and developers. We now show how this linkage can be automated to provide a truly seamless link between a system and its requirements. This link means that if the system changes we can explore the impact on the business objectives and processes. It also offers the possibility of a new notion of provable correctness such as proving that the specification meets the requirements.

7.5.1 Using Object Models in OPEN

OPEN uses a uniform object modeling technique to model several things. The process lifecycle, for example, is a model of a network of activity objects and contracts between them. The TOM is a model of the tasks performed by users as part of their business processes. The BOM is a model of the business objects that constitute a computer system design. In that sense we could call the TOM part a model of the world or *world model.* The BOM could be called a *system object model.* Sometimes there is a more refined system model, built later on, called the Implementation Object Model. The general sequence of these three models is illustrated in Figure 7.12.

7.5.2 Building the TOM

As explained already, task modeling begins with a model of the business processes expressed in terms of messages between actors, external objects, and systems. Each message has a goal as this goal is associated with a unique task that, if performed, will help achieve the goal. This task can be decomposed into atomic tasks, each of which is given a task *script.*

TABLE 7.1 A Printed Class Card

Class Name		Product	Concrete
Description: A product has a code, a name, a description, and a price			Application
SuperClasses:			
Commodity			
Component Classes:			
Attributes and associations:			
Product Name			
Product Description			
Product Price			
Product ID(Product, 1, 1)			
Operations:		**Severs**	
SetProductCode		(Product - Create Product)	
Establishes the product code and other details in the system database			
ProductMargin			
Rulesets:			
ProductPricingPolicy			

The idea of task scripts has its theoretical roots in the AI script theory of Schank and Abelson (1977) and in the hierarchical task analysis popular in HCI work. Also, task scripts can be regarded as generic use cases. Use cases may be one sentence or an essay whereas task scripts should consist of a single sentence. This means that measurement of process models based on task scripts is much easier than with use cases. After building a TOM we use textual analysis to find objects and responsibilities and begin the construction of a BOM. Unfortunately this process is not seamless, violating one of the key benefits claimed for object-oriented methods.

While conventional methods offer different modeling techniques for almost every lifecycle phase, object-oriented methods introduce no such seams between analysis and logical design. There may be a "seam" between logical and physical design when language-dependent features are introduced, but using a language such as Eiffel effectively eliminates this seam too. Thus object-oriented development is claimed to be seamless (Walden and Nerson, 1995). However, leaping from the requirements model to the system

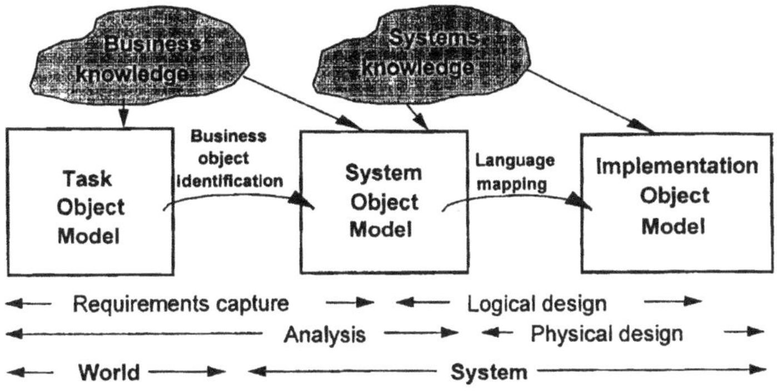

FIGURE 7.12 Object model sequence.

model, there remains more than a seam but a veritable abyss which, once leapt over, cannot be easily retraversed.

SOMA is supported by Bezant's *SOMATiK* software tool (Bezant, 1995). Using *SOMATiK* there is a neat solution to this problem of the World/System seam which we will attempt to explain using a simple example.

7.5.3 An Example

In our approach to object-oriented requirements capture the first thing we do is establish the project mission and then drill down to a number of specific, measurable, prioritized objectives. Next, we build a business process context model showing *external objects* (the stakeholders in our business area), internal *actors*, and support systems. Messages representing semiotic acts between these items are then introduced. Figure 7.13 shows how this might be applied to a system designed to capture foreign exchange trades. In this figure, the external object c/party sends a message to an actor (dealer) inviting him to strike a foreign exchange bargain. The dealer then must negotiate the terms and enter the deal into the system. This is represented by the message `enter_deal`.

We must find a goal for each such message and its associated task. This is called the root task because it is at the root of a composition tree. The tree for `enter deal` is shown in Figure 7.14. We analyze and decompose the tasks for each goal in this way, ending at the atomic tasks, which are the leaf nodes of this tree. Next we write task scripts for the atomic tasks.

Table 7.2 shows the script for the task `Enter Details`. It is easy to see from this script that a number of classes are mentioned, e.g., Instruments, Counterparties, and Deals. Also there are some obvious attributes, such as Buy/Sell. Finally the operation enter is mentioned. After a preliminary analysis of this and all the other scripts and a walkthrough the system design, we realize that the task `enter deal` at the root of the tree corresponds to a responsibility of the class Deals: `captureDeal` in this case.

The Initiating Operation field of the root task object `enter deal` contains the text: "deals -> captureDeal." This makes a permanent link between the process plan represented by the root task and the software that will help the user execute this plan. As a consequence of this link we can animate the specification.

Selecting the Trigger option on the menu shown in Figure 7.13 will display a list of events that are relevant to the dealer actor. Selecting the event `deal done` will trigger the task `enter deal`. This, in turn, triggers its initiating operation: captureDeal. Any operation scripts and windows that the developer has created are executed and displayed for interaction now, and any calculations specified performed. While this is happening *SOMATiK* records a trace of the entire interaction in script form, which can be saved, replayed, and displayed graphically in the form shown in Figure 7.15.

Should the execution crash, some flames appear in this diagram directly underneath the operation that failed. The analyst can click on the operation, emend it, and re-run the trace. The code is written

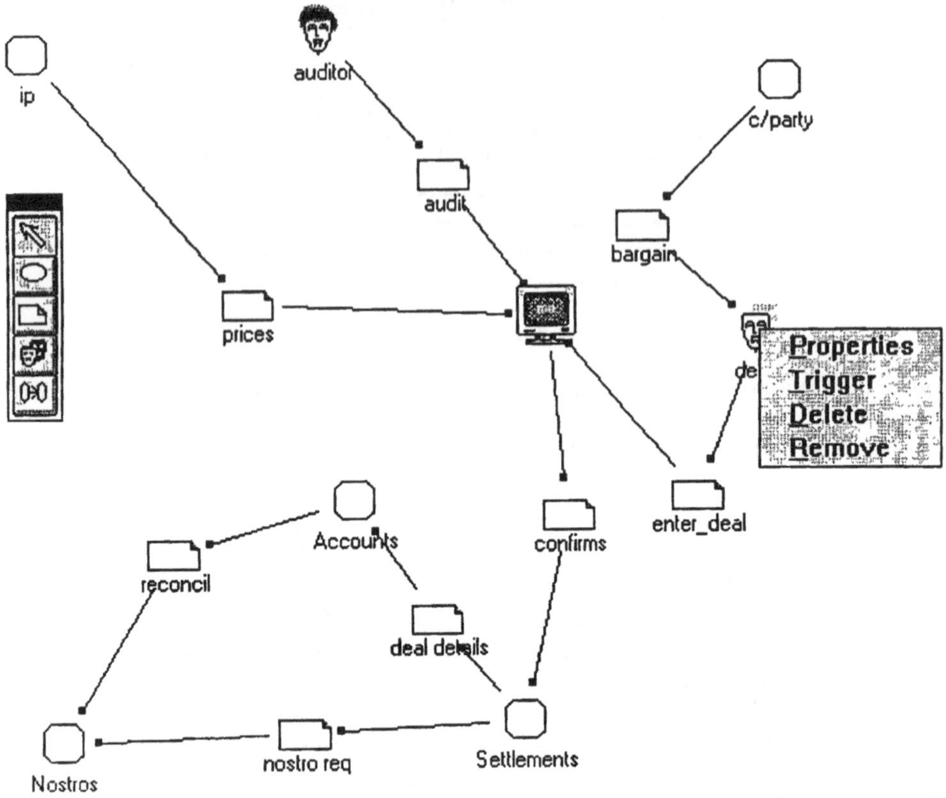

FIGURE 7.13 Business process context model for Forex deal capture.

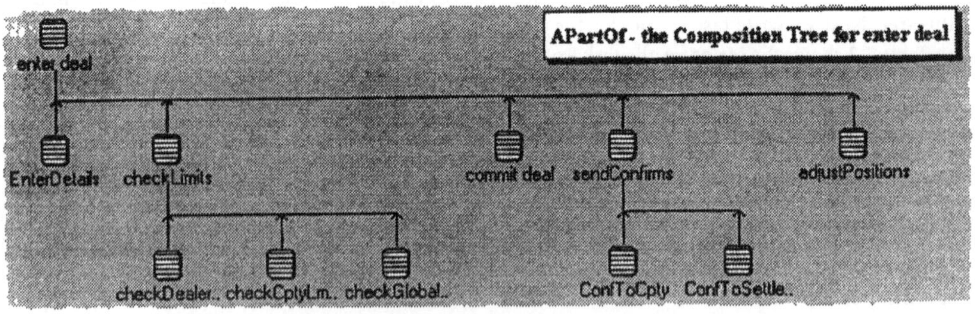

FIGURE 7.14 Task tree for enter deal.

TABLE 7.2 Task Script for EnterDetails

The dealer enters the following data: counterparty, instrument, amount, rate, buy or sell, special settlement conditions

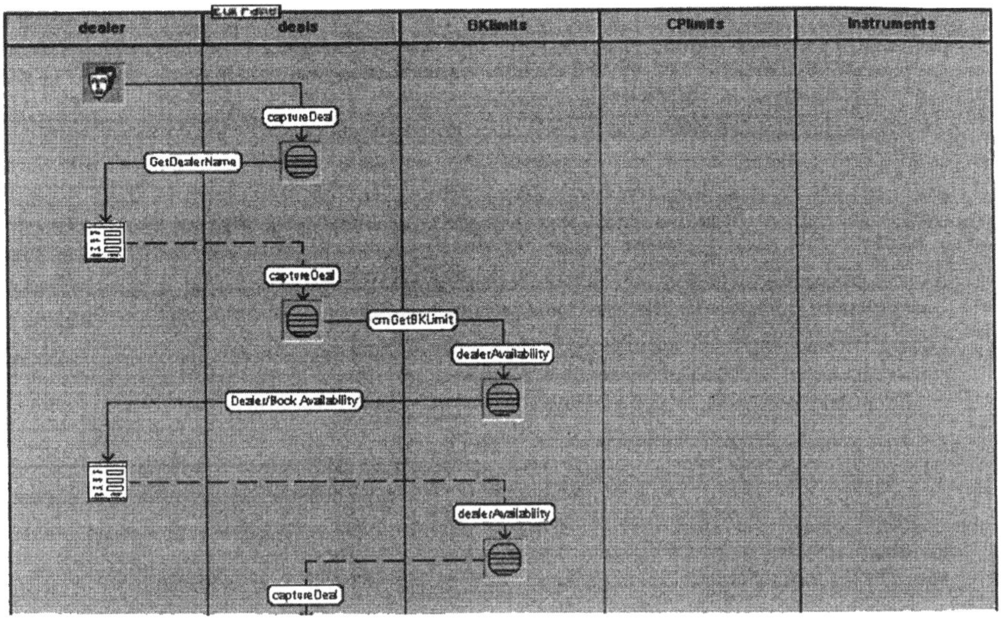

FIGURE 7.15 A small fragment of the active event trace of deal capture produced by *SOMATiK.*

in a high-level scripting language that can be learned in a day or less. *SOMATiK* thus produces a prototype, but this prototype must be thrown away because there are no facilities to develop sophisticated user interfaces. However, code can be generated at this point (currently in C++, Smalltalk, or NeWI).

7.5.4 What is the Trick?

Another way of looking at the seamless nature of the specification process that we have described via this example is illustrated schematically in Figure 7.16. This shows the mission statement of a project

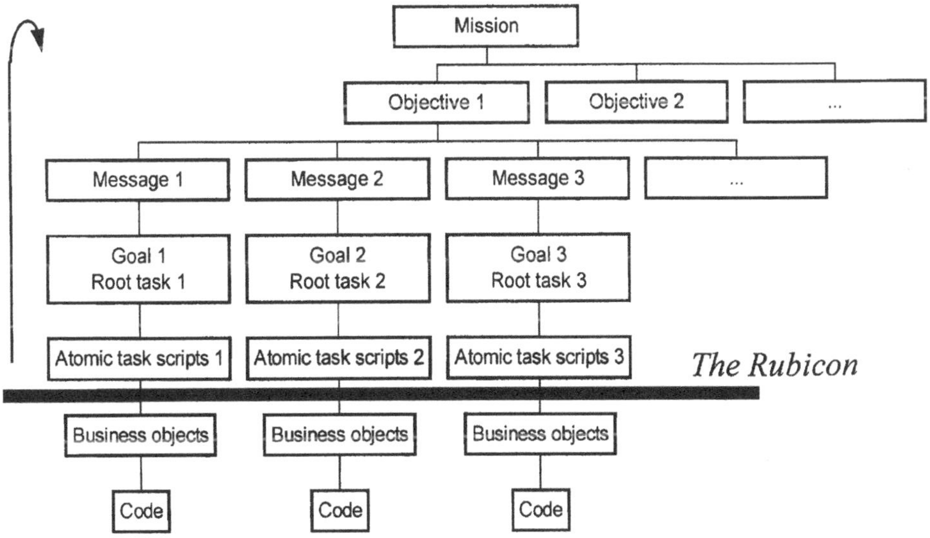

FIGURE 7.16 A seamless process.

fanning out to its various objectives. Each objective relates to a number of communication acts (messages) in the model. Each message has exactly one goal and exactly one root task. The root tasks correspond to one or more atomic tasks. Thus far, all of these links are totally traceable, at least in principle. For that reason, it is easy to arrive at the TOM in an iterative fashion.

Now we take the leap from the world to the system. We identify the business objects partly based on the nouns discovered in the scripts. We define classification, composition, and association structures. For each class we find responsibilities and rules, partly based on the verbs found in the scripts. This is a creative process that cannot be automated. If we have lost traceability we have crossed the Rubicon.

However, we can at least validate the mutual consistency of the two models using a group of users and developers. They walk through with class cards (role playing the classes) to prove that all tasks are correctly supported and that there are no processing or storage absurdities. The automatic linking of the two models described above amounts to finding a means to record and replay this dynamic scenario interaction.

How did we make the leap from world model to the system model seamless? The trick is to notice that the task trees constitute "plans" for interaction during task performance and, thus, for system execution. Each root task corresponds to **exactly one** system operation in the class that initiates the plan. Making this link means that we can generate event traces automatically. Now we have a seamless link from mission down to the code and back. Because we can refine the business object model and generate working code, we can trace changes to the code back to their effects on the task models and even the mission.

The implications of this approach to software engineering for quality and testing are, we hope, obvious.

1. The stored event traces constitute acceptance test scripts for later verification of the system built.
2. The involvement of users in the creation of these traces (during the walkthrough) proves that the BOM supports the TOM accurately and completely.

The second point is that we have a technique for proving the correctness of system specifications against the requirements model. Normally, the notion of provable correctness is only applied to proving that the implementation meets its specification. This suggests an approach that glues the two technologies together, but the demand for a Z code generator for *SOMATiK* is, at present, quite limited we suspect.

7.6 The SOMA Process Model

SOMA advocates the use of object models for most development activities. After scoping a problem using the mission grid and decomposing it into **programs** and further into manageable **projects**, we build an object model of the semiotics of communication within the relevant part of the organization or process area. From this Agent Object Model (AOM) we extract the TOM and use it to make an initial BOM, which is then refined using OO structuring and analysis techniques. We can then generate the Implementation Object Model (IOM). These models are all formally linked.

SOMA takes the principle further and represents the software development lifecycle as an object model too. In this LCOM the objects are activities and their operations are project tasks. This model is precisely the contract-driven model of OPEN which is described in the beginning chapters of this section.

7.7 The SOMA Metrics Suite

SOMA also adopts the metrics suite of OPEN which is as yet unpublished. However, Graham (1995) describes the suite in some detail. If the reader is impatient for the details he is referred to that source and to (Henderson-Sellers, Constantine, and Graham 1996) where some refinements are presented. A book on the OPEN metrics is forthcoming.

7.8 Further Reading

Graham (1995) describes SOMA in detail and Graham and Jones (1998) updates this work with an emphasis on requirements engineering.

References

Austen, J.L. 1962. *How to Do Things with Words.* Harvard University Press, Cambridge MA.

Bezant. 1995. SOMATiK *User Guide.* Bezant Object Technologies, 6 St. Mary's St., Wallingford, Oxon OX10 0LE, U.K.

Cook, S. and Daniels, J. 1995. *Designing Object Systems,* Prentice-Hall, Englewood Cliffs, NJ.

Firestone, D., Henderson-Sellers, B., and Graham, I.M. 1997. *OPEN Modeling Language Reference Manual,* NY: SIGS Books, Cambridge University Press.

Gilligrand, D. and Liu, K.C. 1995. Specification of the Dynamics of Object Behaviour, *ROAD 1(6).*

Graham, I.M. 1995. *Migrating to Object Technology.* Addison-Wesley, Wokingham, U.K.

Graham, I.M., Henderson-Sellers, B. and Yanoussi, H. 1997. *The OPEN Process Specification.* Addison-Wesley, Wokingham, U.K.

Graham, I.M. and Jones, P.L.K. 1998. *Requirements Engineering and Rapid Development.* Addison-Wesley, Wokingham, U.K.

Henderson-Sellers, B., Constantine, L.L., and Graham, I.M. 1996. Coupling and cohesion: toward a valid metrics suite for object-oriented analysis and design, *Obj. Orient. Sys.,* 3(3), 143.

Jacobson, I., Christerson, M., Jonsson, P. and Overgaard, G. 1992. *Object-Oriented Software Engineering: A Use Case Driven Approach.* Addison-Wesley, Wokingham, U.K.

Martin, J. and Odell, J.J. 1995. *Object-Oriented Methods: A Foundation.* Prentice-Hall, Englewood Cliffs, NJ.

Meyer, B. 1995. *Object Success: A Manager's Guide to Object-Orientation, its Impact on the Corporation and its Use for Re-engineering the Software Process.* Prentice-Hall, Englewood Cliffs, NJ.

Schank, R.C. and Abelson, R.P. 1977. *Scripts, Plans, Goals and Understanding.* Lawrence Erlbaum Associates, Boston MA.

Searle, J.R. 1969. *Speech Acts.* University Press, Cambridge, U.K.

Short, J.E. and Venkatramen, N. 1992. Beyond business process redesign: Redefining Baxter's Business Network, *Sloan Manag. Rev.,* Fall, 7-17.

Walden, K. and Nerson, J.-M. 1995. *Seamless Object-Oriented Software Architecture.* Prentice-Hall, Englewood Cliffs, NJ.

8

Responsibility-Driven Design (RDD): The Wirfs-Brock Method and the CRC Cards Mechanism

Ricardo Devis
INFOPLUS, S.L.

8.1 Justification

RDD? Wirfs-Brock? CRC (Class-Responsibility-Collaboration) cards? Aren't these methods and techniques vestiges of an earlier object-oriented state-of-the-art age? In fact we read everywhere: "RDD is not well suited for analysis. No attempt at rigor and formality." However, the very fact is that despite the original contributions from Rebecca Wirfs-Brock ("the concept of stereotypes, her emphasis on responsibilities, and the term *collaboration diagram,*" in OML words) RDD has aged well. RDD and CRC cards are intensely used in most of the current OO methods and modeling approaches, mainly as an exploratory method for discovering classes and dynamic relationships among them. As Reenskaug points out (and A.A.R. Cockburn agrees), "RDD is one of the few published methodologies with a pure object-oriented origin," as OOram undoubtedly is also, and this has led RDD to strongly influence the object thinking in the OO methods arena. While RDD is the heuristic-based method, CRC cards, as the mechanism behind the method, are what have permeated through the OO literature and practice, so CRC and RDD are usually wrongly tied as one only method. But, in practice, and in Fowler's words: "some people find CRC cards to be wonderful; others find the technique leaves them cold." Again, we find contradictory sentiments about the RDD/CRC approach (but notice that an emotional vein is perceived here). Let's see in this chapter how the Wirfs-Brock method and the team-based CRC techniques can contribute to OO software development.

0-8493-3135-8/99/$0.00+$.50

8.2 Short History and Personal Considerations

Are CRC cards indissolubly tied to RDD? No, they aren't. In fact CRC (as the concept behind the cards) was the project and personal leitmotiv, in the late 1980s, of two earlier OO researchers, Kent Beck and Ward Cunningham, in Tektronix Labs, Portland, OR. They tried to create a method for communicating and propagating OO knowledge and collaborative object thinking among human teams. Cards would serve as physical pieces for interchanging information in a very tangible way among partners in analysis and design phases (experts, facilitators, analysts, designers, programmers, consultants, etc.), and, most importantly, for letting people assume object roles, so anthropomorphizing the very abstract, and sometimes abstruse, nature of classes and objects. After having taught OO issues for more than seven years, I have to declare that this kind of personally assumed roles really work. It's like sales meetings, but with software objects. You play some objects behavior and really want to succeed with your cards, so you argue every redirection of responsibilities, every new work load, every attempt for deleting or obviating any of your classes. But, again, we are mixing CRC with RDD. The egg or the chicken? It doesn't seem to matter, anyhow. From now on, we'll consider that the best mechanism for dealing with RDD heuristics is CRC cards, while the best framework for making really effective CRC cards is the RDD behavior-based approach — just the perfect OO symbiosis.

8.3 RDD Dissection

Trying to obtain pseudo-code and essential relationships among classes and objects, RDD is divided into two clear phases:

1. Exploratory
   - *Goals* — Finding classes, determining and assigning responsibilities and identifying collaborations
   - *Models* — CRC cards, hierarchies, collaboration graphs, and Venn diagrams
   - *Suggested Steps* — Read and interpret the specifications, start with tentative classes, walk through possible scenarios, write cards representing candidate classes (extracted from nouns from the SRS), categorize classes, find and assign responsibilities (looking at the classes names, examining classes relationships, etc.), construct rough class hierarchies, and identify collaborations
2. Analysis
   - *Goals* — Refining the classes' behavior found at the exploratory phase, identifying abstract classes, refining class hierarchies, grouping behavior-related responsibilities by means of contracts (although the authors have dropped this part from the latest version of their method), defining subsystems (for helping with the visual representation of the model), and delivering class interfaces (protocols)
   - *Models* — CRC cards, subsystem cards, hierarchies graphs, and collaboration/contract graphs
   - *Suggested Steps* — Heuristics and walkthroughs, iterative spiral development, scenario delimitation, and solution domain analysis

The main goal should be a high-level description of the system to be modeled with graphs organized in comprehensible high-level layers, pseudo-code protocols describing class interfaces, and a well-delimited scenario in which to work.

8.4 Exploratory Phase

Classes — How do you identify the classes populating the system to be modeled in the software domain? RDD relies on Abbott's heuristics*: Just take all the nouns and nominal phrases in the requirements

* In fact, a great amount of the current OOA/OOD methods are based on the well-established Abbott psychological techniques that substitute substantives by classes and verbs and verbal phrases by responsibilities/relationships/methods/messages. It results, in the end, that, as Nietzsche asserted, we are "prisoned by language constructions" and philologists have a great future in the computing field.

specification document, promote them to candidate classes, and then sift through them for evaluating if they have real sense for the proposed scenario. Still, this sounds fuzzy enough to force to consider that it's quite plain that adequate candidate classes come from a good requirements specification, but who and how to redact that document? Despite IEEE recommended practice and guidelines for SRS (System Requirements Specifications), the answer is: You first read the SRS, usually redacted in informal English, and then, assisted by a prudent and experienced OO guru, and as you discuss classes you will gradually become more sensitive about SRS redaction and formalities. It's an involutional process, but you need to start by discussing classes obtained by some heuristic and put into the software domain. While reading the Wirfs-Brock's book you will really facilitate the Zen-like object-thinking awakening. Scenario issues are, anyway, of vital importance in this phase. I always recommend to my alumni to think about if a class behavior, discovered by Abbott's laws, senses the intuitive scenario then they are gradually delimiting and refining. It's, again, an involutive process, where the OO newcomers can learn to establish scenarios and just question themselves about behavior, and, then, when scenarios are well delimited, they can turn to reconsider classes. Consultants and OO gurus serve by transmitting the initial impulse for fueling this gradual implication of the development team in OO issues.

Responsibilities — While class identification is a must, discrimination by means of responsibilities assumption is essential. In Wirfs-Brock words, responsibilities include "the knowledge an object maintains and the actions an object can perform." Following, again, Abbott's heuristics, we will extract verbs and verbal phrases from the SRS and will convert them into candidate responsibilities. We will also look at the name and stated purpose of the earlier found candidate classes and even perform some walkthroughs into the system. The final goal will be to find a set of cohesive responsibilities for every class, helping us, at the same time, to refine and/or drop some of the classes found in the prior phase. At the end, all these responsibilities should be converted into function signatures, but this must not lead us to deal with a great amount of low level responsibilities. Wirfs-Brock practitioners must always take into account that they are dealing with behavior issues, not with the small print. This is the reason this method does not care about attributes and attribute types (so an OOCase tool is even undesirable).

Collaborations — What is a collaboration? In essence, it is a request from a client to a server for fulfilling a client's responsibility. Let's imagine a Mafia-like scenario, where a "Capo" object wants to dispatch another object of type "Person." Let's say that our "Capo" has that responsibility, and for fulfilling it he will perhaps collaborate with an object of type "Murderer" (whose basic responsibility would be "to kill Persons"), and perhaps with an object of type "Traitor friend" and some kind of "Corrupted Cop" objects. That is, fulfilling a given responsibility from a class usually requires that other classes carry out their concordant responsibilities (this is, definitely, about the social anthropomorphization of the classes), etc. If a given class does not need to collaborate with any other to fulfill its responsibilities, it's called a "server". Usually each collaborating class/object assumes the role of either a client or a server.

8.5 Analysis Phase

Brainstorming, not always disjunctive to "stormed brains," is the keyword here. As in the prior phase, RDD does not impose or establish a clear framework for developing and maintaining the software development process, but instead it relies on "object mentation." That is, the capacity of practitioners to anthropomorphize and adjust real models to equivalently modular models in the software domain. This way forces RDD authors to teach by example. You will only understand OO software models when you have read and designed a lot of them. Artifacts, heuristics, and arbitrary mechanisms rule here, trying to imbue newcomers with OO experience in a very practical way. For instance, subsystems did not use to exist in the real world, but they are useful artifacts for dealing with the graph complexity in software development.

8.6 Conclusions

Expressly I have not relied on detailed descriptions of the method heuristics and steps, because the original book is good for this matter. You can even find detailed descriptions of CRC to C++ mapping in the Wilkinson book. But I feel readers will find the real potential of this exploratory method in Bellin's book, where emphasis is directly addressed to the team synergy — team role playing, with psychological techniques for avoiding spaghetti-object bottlenecks, and Java, Smalltalk, and C++ examples (from experts) are the real value of the method, in the very sense proposed by Beck and Cunningham in their original paper and subsequent writings. I have experienced, with both real mission critical development teams and groups of postgraduate students, the strength of working in a higher level than that of X-aided software tools, allowing critical minds to raise questions and answers, seeing how a real team is gradually delimiting human boundaries and, most importantly, experiencing how cohesive team synergy grows where only technology was set up. I feel that the symbiotic Wirfs-Brock/CRC is the only method that brings object orientation to the field of team management and, hence, software productivity, because, as Alan Davis adequately points out, "good management is more important than good technology."

References

Abbott, R.J. 1983. Program design by informal English descriptions. *Commun. ACM,* 26 (11), 882–894.

Beck, K. and Cunningham, W. 1989. A laboratory for teaching object-oriented thinking, pp. 1–6. In *Proc. of OOPSLA 89.* SIGPLAN Notices, Vol. 24, No. 10.

Bellin, D. and Suchman Simone, S. 1997. *The CRC Card Book.* Addison-Wesley, Reading, MA.

Davis, A.M. 1995. *201 Principles of Software Development.* McGraw-Hill, New York.

Firesmith, D., Henderson-Sellers, B., Graham, I. and Page-Jones, M. 1996. *OPEN Modeling Language (OML) Reference Manual, Version 1.0,* 8 Dec.

Fowler, M. and Scott, K. 1997. *UML Distilled: Applying the Standard Object Modeling Language.* Addison-Wesley-Longman, New York.

IEEE P1233/D3 Guide for Developing System Requirements Specifications.

IEEE Std 830-1993. Recommended Practice for Software Requirements Specifications.

Reenskaug, T., World, P. and Lehne, O.-A. 1996. *Working with Objects: The OOram Software Engineering Method.* Manning Publications, Greenwich, CT.

Tkach, D., Fang, W. and So, A. 1996. *Visual Modeling Technique: Object Technology Using Visual Programming.* Addison-Wesley, Reading, MA.

Wilkinson, N.M. 1995. *Using CRC Cards: An Informal Approach to Object-Oriented Development.* SIGS Books, New York.

Wirfs-Brock, R., Wilderson, B. and Wiender, L. 1990. *Designing Object-Oriented Software.* Prentice-Hall, Englewoods Cliffs, NJ.

9

Fusion 2.0: A Process for UML

Derek Coleman
*King's College London**

Ruth Malan
Hewlett-Packard

Todd Cotton
Hewlett-Packard

9.1 Introduction

Fusion 2.0 provides an effective software development process and "just enough" method to manage project risks. By using this team-oriented approach, individual developers can work together effectively, whether as members of small projects or as part of large, geographically dispersed development efforts. The step-by-step process leads a development team from project conception to implementation, providing both management guidance for evolutionary development as well as the engineering models and techniques for requirements, analysis, architecture, and design. In this chapter, we describe the engineering process and provide an overview of the management process. First, we briefly describe the evolution of Fusion and its next generation, namely Fusion 2.0, and summarize the key features of the new method.

9.1.1 History

The Fusion method integrated and extended the best features of the most successful object-oriented development approaches of the early 1990s, including OMT, Booch, CRC, and Objectory. The method authors at Hewlett-Packard Labs in Bristol evolved the Fusion prototype through several iterations as it was used by lead-adopter software development projects within Hewlett-Packard. This culminated in the publication of a reference text on Fusion (Coleman et al., 1994). Since then, use of this systematic but pragmatic approach to software development has spread rapidly within HP (see, for example, Malan et al., 1996 and Malan, 1995, 1996, 1997). It is being used to develop a broad range of products and applications including printers, network management software, telecom applications, and embedded software in the measurement instrument domain. Today, many companies world-wide are employing Fusion in an even wider range of domains including transportation, finance, telecom, and defense systems.

*The work reported here was done while the author was a visiting faculty member at Hewlett-Packard's Software Initiative in July-August, 1997.

0-8493-3135-8/99/$0.00+$.50

The experience-base both highlighted best practices and illuminated deficiencies in the existing methods. This presented the new Fusion method team* with an opportunity to migrate Fusion to the industry-standard notation as defined by the OMG while integrating lessons learned from the use of important software methods, including Fusion, Objectory, OMT, and Booch. The resulting method, Fusion 2.0, is a significant step forward in OOA/D, integrating leading-edge software engineering concepts with best practices from a wide variety of application domains. The key features of this new method are covered in the following section.

9.1.2 Key Features of Fusion 2.0

9.1.2.1 A Process for the Unified Modeling Language (UML)

Fusion 2.0 provides a process for using the UML. UML is an emerging standard OOA/D notation initiated and led by Rational with contributions from Hewlett-Packard, among others. By using UML, Fusion users will be able to communicate with developers using other methodologies and take advantage of industry-standard CASE tools.

However, UML is a set of notations and does not provide guidance on when or how to use the variety of models included in the graphical modeling language. The Fusion 2.0 engineering process guides development teams by providing clear steps indicating which models to use during each phase, and offering techniques and heuristics for using the models, with quality and completeness checks for the phase deliverables. Key innovations in the Fusion 2.0 engineering process are in the areas of requirements and architecture, advancing the state-of-the-art beyond Fusion and the first generation methods, like Booch and OMT, which lacked explicit requirements and architecture phases.

Requirements — Numerous project teams added use cases as extensions to Fusion and in 1996 these were added to the method as documented on the Fusion web site http://www.hpl.hp.com/fusion. These have been retained in Fusion 2.0 as the principal tool for capturing functional requirements. In addition, Fusion 2.0 adds non-functional requirements (constraints and system qualities) ensuring that these are elicited and documented so that they can guide the architects and developers as they evaluate architectural and design tradeoffs.

Architecture-centric — Fusion 2.0 provides a process for architectural design, allowing developers to handle the extra complexities of developing applications for distributed object infrastructures and the internet. It also enables the flexible distribution and partitioning of the system across networks and it enables component interoperability and "plug and play" component reuse. Moreover, architecture is the key to planning and coordinating distributed teams.

9.1.2.2 Evolutionary Lifecycle

Industrial experience has shown that the real benefits of using object-oriented techniques only come in the context of a managed and defined software process at both the individual level and the team or management levels. The engineering process covers the activities of analyzing, designing, and implementing software by individual developers. The management process concerns the way a project is organized to deliver the product or application. Here the alternatives are process structures such as the waterfall and evolutionary development. An increasing number of experts, such as Tom Gilb and Grady Booch, advocate the benefits of an evolutionary or incremental approach to software development. With over ten years of experience in applying the evolutionary development approach in a variety of projects,

---

*The Fusion 2.0 team consists of Derek Coleman, King's College London; Todd Cotton, Hewlett-Packard; Chris Dollin, Hewlett-Packard; Paul Jeremaes, Hewlett-Packard; Matt Johnson, Hewlett-Packard; Ruth Malan, Hewlett-Packard; and David Redmond-Pyle, PostModern Solutions, Inc. Reed Letsinger, also from Hewlett-Packard, played a key role during the early part of the Fusion 2.0 project. Herman Yang, a Stanford University student, contributed during the summer of 1997.

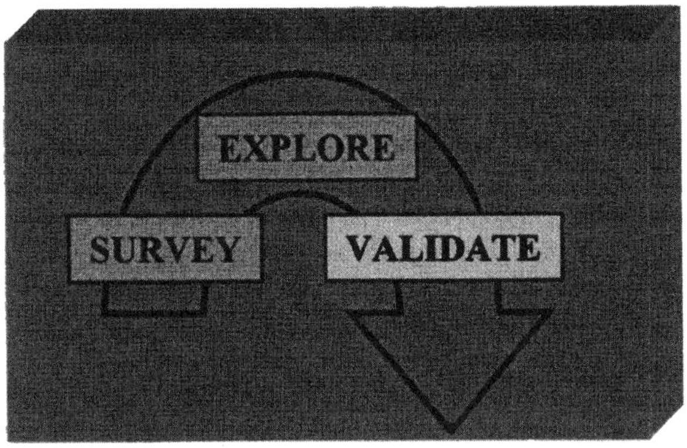

FIGURE 9.1 Development process pattern for Fusion 2.0.

Hewlett-Packard has learned valuable lessons in managing risk and project complexity, and these have been applied in creating the Fusion 2.0 management process.

9.1.2.3 Customizable, "Just Enough" Method

Experience has shown that a one-size-fits-all approach to OOA/D methods does not work. The level of formality, or what Booch calls "ceremony," that a project should employ needs to be determined by the risks facing the project. An individual developer working on an application for his/her personal use may be able to use a much less formal process than a geographically distributed team working on an infrastructure IT system for an international finance house.

Experience with tailoring Fusion to meet the needs of real projects has led us to develop software engineering technology to support highly tailorable methods which can be adapted to meet the needs of a wide range of projects and applications. Such methods we call "*Just enough*." With a Just Enough method an end-user team can adapt the method to make it lightweight, while still being able to overcome their major risks and challenges. In other words, just enough methodology to do what you need to do.

To be tailorable by the end user, a just enough method must be simple and clean. It must be easy to assemble and disassemble the component parts of the method to meet user needs. Fusion 2.0 is an ideal basis for this purpose. It incorporates the simple refinement-based approach of Fusion into a conceptually simple risk-driven management process.

The key enabling technology for just enough methods is to use "*development process patterns*." Development process patterns are similar to the design patterns of Gamma et al., but elevated to the process and methodology domain. By tailoring a Just Enough methodology based on development process patterns a team can architect its development process in much the same way that designers can use design patterns to architect the software they produce.

The principal pattern is "*survey, explore, and validate*" (Figure 9.1), which is used at each phase of the engineering process to make Fusion 2.0 risk driven. The initial *survey* steps are lightweight working at a higher level with less detail, e.g., use-case or architecture diagrams. They produce overview models, which cover the essential features of the deliverables for the phase. The *explore* steps, for example, pre- and post-conditions or collaboration diagrams, refine the information and are generally heavier weight because they model features in detail. It is recommended that the use of explore steps be restricted to situations where their use can be justified, because they produce vital information that reduces key uncertainties. Finally, before exiting from any phase *validation and review* steps provide for quality, completeness, and consistency checks. Projects facing few risks can keep the engineering process lightweight by completing only the initial or survey steps in each phase. Projects dealing with more complexity in the problem to be solved or with larger or distributed teams will still need to start with survey steps and also need to complete more of the explore steps.

9.2 Engineering Process

9.2.1 Overview

This section provides a summary of the engineering activities and models in the Fusion 2.0 process with illustrations to show how some of the models are used.* The description assumes familiarity with UML and focuses on the process steps and guidelines that distinguish the method. Introductory tutorials, case study examples, and more explication of the method will be available through other sources than this chapter.**

This process details the dependencies between models and thus might suggest that a project should adopt a waterfall process when using Fusion. This is not the case and projects are recommended to follow the evolutionary delivery principles outlined in the management process section.

Fusion 2.0 has five separate activities (Figure 9.2) that are summarized below and explained in more detail in the following pages.

- **Requirements** — The requirements phase captures the user's requirements for the system in terms of *use cases, features,* and *non-functional requirements.* The output of the requirements phase includes a *use-case diagram* and several *use-case specifications.*
- **Analysis** — The analysis phase defines what operations and objects will be present in the system to be delivered, without regard to how those operations and objects will be implemented. The output of the analysis phase includes the *system class diagram* and the *system interface* defined in terms of *system operations* and *events.* The system class diagram is developed from the *domain class diagram.*
- **Architecture** — The architecture phase identifies components of the system that handle coherent parts of the system. It defines the approach to concurrency and synchronization issues. The output of the architecture phase is an *architecture diagram* which defines the components, their interactions, and the *component interfaces.* Architecture design is important for team organization and communication, as well as providing a technical framework.
- **Design** — The design phase assigns operations to objects and makes decisions about inheritance, visibility, and the representation of associations. The outputs from the design phase are the *design class diagram, object collaboration diagrams,* and *initial object configuration.*
- **Implementation** — The implementation phase translates the design into code in some target programming language. In addition to method coding, it addresses issues of resource management and performance.

Fusion 2.0 also incorporates two supplementary processes for GUI and Database design. These are not as comprehensive as the other parts of the method; rather they link the ideas and concepts of Fusion 2.0 into best practices in these areas.

In addition to the models of Fusion 2.0, a *data dictionary* is created and utilized throughout the process as a reference for the actors, use cases, classes, associations, system operations, etc., developed from the requirements phase through the beginning of the implementation phase. This forms a common vocabulary that is necessary to facilitate accurate and efficient communication within the team.

Throughout the process, techniques such as JAD workshop sessions and brainstorming may be useful in facilitating communication and creativity. Quality review techniques such as walkthroughs and inspections may also be used as required in the process.

The following sections detail the steps and guidelines of the method.

9.2.2 Requirements

The requirements phase captures the functional and non-functional requirements for the system. The main output of the requirements phase are use cases capturing functional requirements, non-functional

*These examples are taken from a cellular telephone network management application named Cell Keeper.

**The Fusion 2.0 book is due to be completed and published in 1998. The Fusion web site is an excellent source of updates and information on Fusion and Fusion 2.0 evolution and use (http://www.hpl.hp.com/fusion).

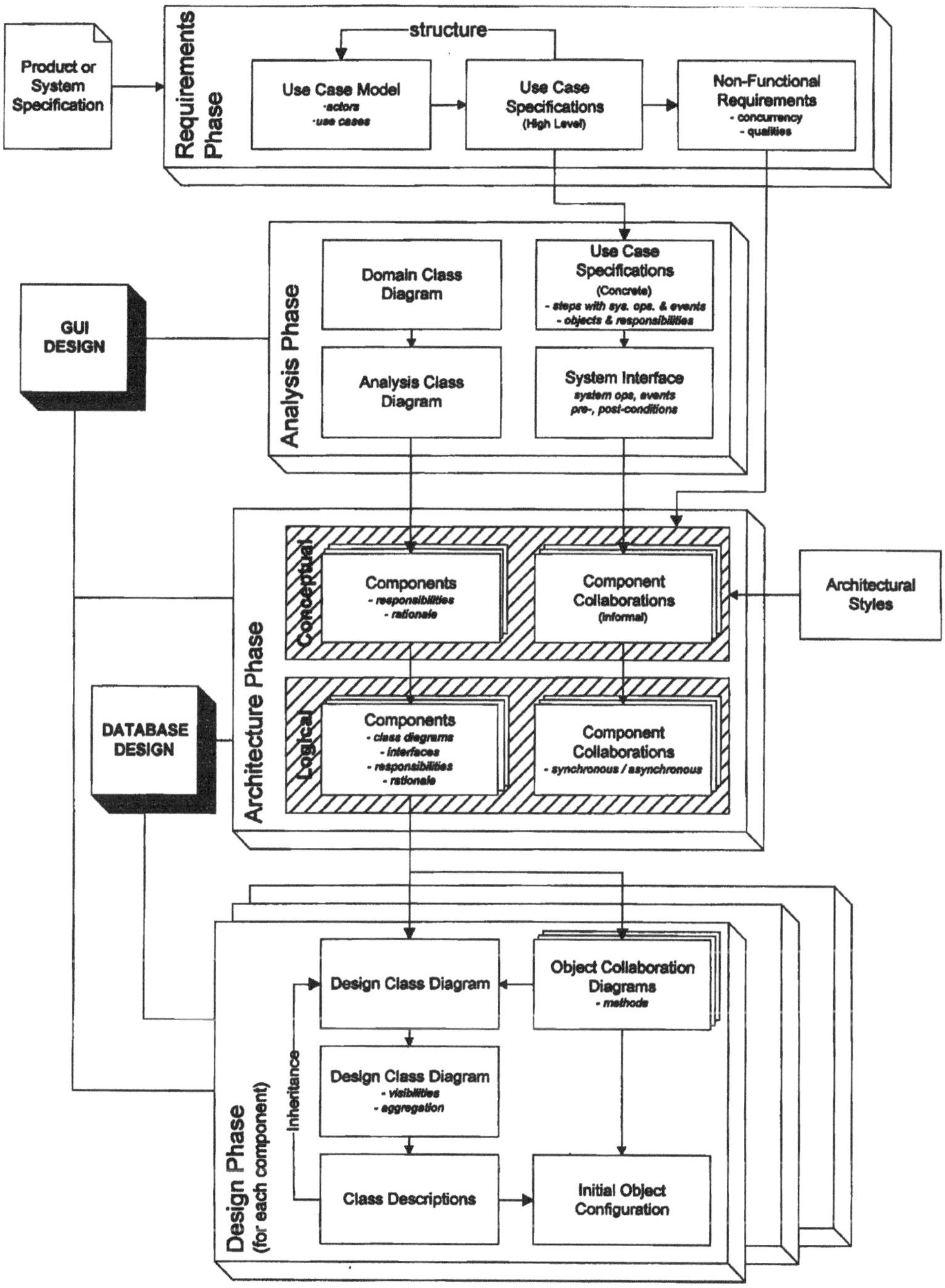

FIGURE 9.2 A diagram of the Fusion 2.0 engineering process.

requirement specifications, and a set of matrices relating the two for each product release. The aim of the requirements phase is to capture the intended behavior of the system in terms that the user can understand.

9.2.2.1 Step 1 — Overview of Requirements

The goal of this step is to provide a high level and complete summary of the functional and non-functional requirements for the system from a business perspective. In order to ensure a complete overview of the requirements consider the entire lifecycle from product conception through system development, deployment, operation, maintenance, enhancement, and obsolescence. For each phase, enumerate the stakeholders and the value proposition of the system to them. A stakeholder is someone with an interest in the success of the system and includes business sponsors, project developers, marketing, sales, and customer and field support, as well as customers and end users.

List the functional and non-functional requirements by considering the core requirements for each stakeholder in each phase of the system lifecycle. Each separate requirement should be given a name and documented in a few natural language sentences. As much as is possible, the description should be related to business need and expected use of the system and avoid details of the internal workings of the system. Also document the source of the information for checking and explanation purposes later.

Functional requirements should be described at a high level of abstraction and in terms of the business process that they support. Capture the desired or necessary features of the system or product. A *feature* is a property of the system that provides some functionality that fulfills a set of customer requirements. Features are often driven by competitive products or the legacy system being replaced.

Capture the non-functional requirements for the system. Non-functional requirements include *constraints* and *qualities*. Constraints are properties that apply to the system as a whole and may apply to the development process, such as time-to-market or the need for interoperability with legacy systems, or use of a particular operating system. Qualities include quality of service (QoS) attributes such as performance, reliability, etc., and concepts such as usability, extensibility, and configurability.

9.2.2.2 Step 2 — Construct a Requirements Matrix

The goal of this step is to produce a set of requirements matrices showing the non-functional requirements for each aspect of system (Figure 9.3). The functional requirements label the rows and the non-functional requirements label the columns. The matrix entries show the minimum and/or planned non-functional measure to be achieved by the corresponding functionality together with an assessment of the technical risk that the measure will not be achieved.

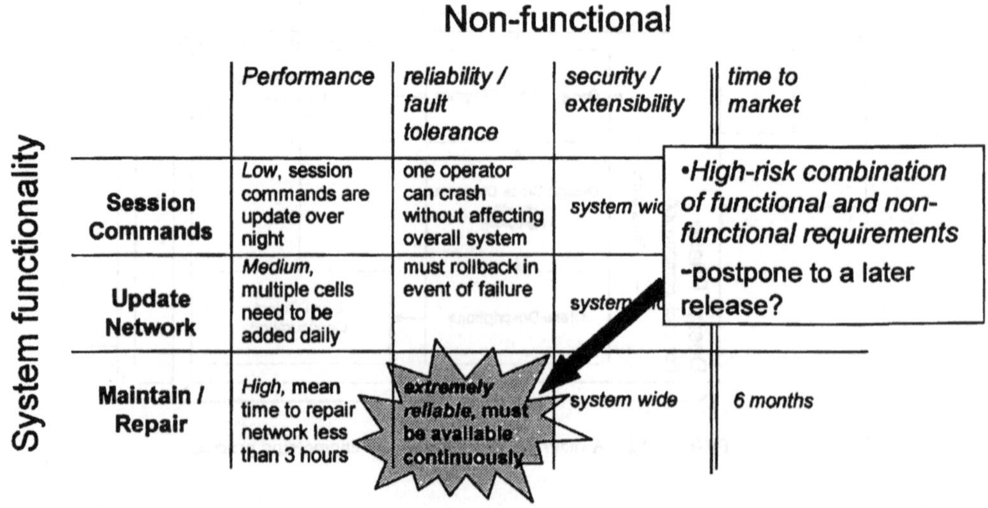
Non-functional
System functionality
Performance
reliability / fault tolerance
security / extensibility
time to market
Session Commands
Low, session commands are update over night
one operator can crash without affecting overall system
system wid
Update Network
Medium, multiple cells need to be added daily
must rollback in event of failure
system
Maintain / Repair
High, mean time to repair network less than 3 hours
extremely reliable, must be available continuously
system wide
6 months
•High-risk combination of functional and non-functional requirements
-postpone to a later release?

FIGURE 9.3 Requirements Matrix showing a high technical risk combination of functional and non-functional requirements (taken from CellKeeper).

In most situations the matrix is sparse as only the high-risk relationships are entered. The level of precision in the table entries will vary. For example, the reliability of a certain functional requirement may be stated simply as "high," or more precisely in terms of mean time to failure and mean time to repair. In a matrix it is useful to indicate the top few priority entries as a requirement conflict resolution guide for use in later phases of the system development.

When precise measures are difficult to determine, develop *scenarios* that can be used to test these qualities. The scenarios should describe specific, expected demands on the system during development or operation and provide clear testable characterizations of the quality requirements. Some non-functional requirements, such as security, are called safety properties because they "forbid bad things from happening." It is not possible to adequately ensure safety properties by test scenarios or use cases alone; they also require reasoned arguments.

The matrices may be used to trade off the technical risk associated with a non-functional goal against the business risk of delaying delivery of the goal until a later product release. Consequently a separate matrix is produced for each release of the system. The requirements matrices are thus also an input into the planning process used in managing Fusion 2.0 projects.

9.2.2.3 Step 3 — Define Use-Case Diagram

A use-case diagram summarizes the functionality of the system in terms of actors and associated use cases. An actor is anything in the environment of the system that the system interacts with, such as a human user or another software system. A use case is a set of interactions between the system and one or more actors that achieves some specific goal. The actors and use cases can be found by considering the stakeholders and functional requirements associated with the operational and the other post-development phases identified in Step 1 in this section.

In general, each functionality from the requirements matrix may give rise to more than one use case. For each, ensure that there are sufficient use cases to fully explore the functionality. This is particularly important for functionality associated with high-risk priority entries.

9.2.2.4 Step 4 — Define Scale of System

The goal of this stage is to define the scale of the system at runtime in terms of the numbers of actors, use-case instances, and amount of concurrent usage that the system will have to handle. This information is appended to the use-case diagram in free form text that documents:

- How the actor instance population changes over time (i.e., time distribution of concurrent users)
- How many use-case instances can be active simultaneously
- Priority ordering between simultaneous use-case instances
- Geographical distribution of actor and use-case instances

9.2.2.5 Step 5 — Define Use-Case Specifications

The role of a use-case specification is to explore and validate the functional requirements in more detail. For each use case identified in Step 3 above, produce a specification (Figure 9.4) which defines the

- Goal of the use case
- Assumptions made regarding the use case
- Actors involved
- Sequence of steps in the interaction between actors and the system
- Source of the information used to construct the use case
- Nonfunctional requirements for the use case

The goal of the use case should be described declaratively. Free form natural language may be used to describe the steps of the use case. If there are important orderings of the interactions, these should be captured in the text. When describing the use-case steps, it may be appropriate to include interactions between actors which do not involve the system, but help clarify the understanding of the system's usage. The granularity of interaction within a use case should be controlled to ensure that it is at a consistent level of abstraction.

USE CASE #0	
Name	Session
Description	Operator session for using system to manage network.
Goal	Manage network as required.
Assumptions	
Actors	Operator (primary) Actual network – comprising base stations, antennae, etc.
Steps	Operator logs into systems. System authenticates operator is valid user. Operator performs any number of splitting a cell use case (#1), adding a cell use case (#2), or tuning a cell use case (#3). After the use cases have been completed, the operator receives the results of their application to the actual network. If the Operator has not logged out, he then does so.

FIGURE 9.4 An example Use Case Specification.

9.2.2.6 Step 6 — Structure Use-Case Specifications

In order to avoid use-case explosion it is necessary to structure the set of use cases. Common behavior that is shared by a number of use cases may be extracted to form a sub use case. A sub use case is a well-formed use case that is documented by a use-case specification. The use-case diagram is modified to show each such *uses* relationship. The uses relationship allows the granularity of interaction to become more detailed as one passes down the hierarchy of use cases.

Use cases variants should be captured using the *extends* relationship. Each variant is described by a change delta use-case specification that documents how the variant differs. The use-case diagram is modified to show each extends relationship.

The uses and extends relationship allow the set of use cases to be structured as a hierarchy. It is good practice to organize the hierarchy around the goals of the use cases (Cockburn, 1997). The goal of top layer use cases in the hierarchy should relate to complex business processes. The goals of lower levels get progressively more detailed. The bottom layer goals correspond to elementary business processes. Extension use cases form variations at each level in the hierarchy that deal with situations in which the use case assumptions may be false.

In practice the structuring must be carried out incrementally as the use cases are produced, rather than as an afterthought. Basing use cases on the summary functional requirements developed in Step 1 helps form well-formed hierarchies.

9.2.2.7 Step 7 — Review and Refine Requirements Models

All the requirements models should be reviewed by the stakeholders and refined. Issues captured during these reviews should be collected and tracked, just as defects are tracked and resolved during implementation. Iteration through review and refinement should continue until an acceptably small number of issues remain that can be deferred to later stages of development.

9.2.3 Analysis

Analysis is about what a system does rather than how it does it. The purpose of the analysis phase is to describe the system in terms of behavior at its interface. The description is in terms of an analysis class diagram and a set of system operation specifications.

9.2.3.1 Step 1 — Develop the Domain Class Diagram

The purpose of the domain class diagram (Figure 9.5) is to capture the concepts that exist in the problem domain by representing them as classes, attributes, and associations between classes. Concentrate on finding high level abstractions, rather than lower level ones.

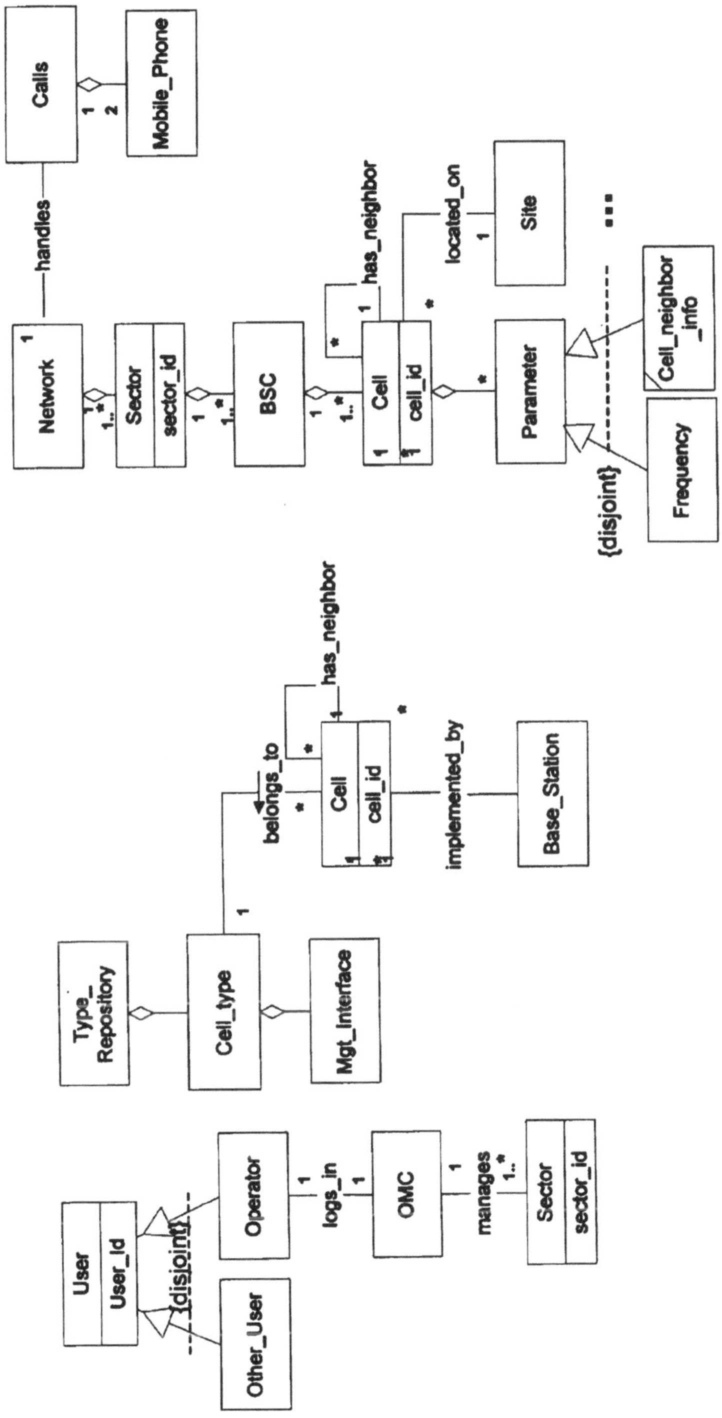

FIGURE 9.5 The Cell Keeper Domain Class Diagram.

Guidelines:

1. If a problem domain class model already exists then use that as a starting point.
2. Examine the use-case specifications to find candidate classes and associations.
3. Brainstorm a list of any further classes and associations that are needed to complete the description of the problem domain. Repeatedly refine the class diagram looking for:
   - Generalizations modeling the kind-of or is-a associations
   - Aggregations modeling part of or has-a associations
   - Attributes of classes
   - Cardinalities of associations

9.2.3.2 Step 2 — Analyze Use Cases to System Operations and Determine the System Interface

Analyze and refine use-case specifications to identify system operations, output events, and objects that are visible at the interface. The steps of each use-case specification are rephrased to make the interactions more precise. Wherever possible the behavior of the system is described in terms of responsibilities (a la CRC). A *responsibility* is a "piece of functionality" that the system has to perform, e.g., a change of state or test on state, or the transfer of data to or from an actor. The refinement process should ensure that:

- Responsibilities that are similar should be clarified and either identified or distinguished.
- Actions on the system (respectively, by the system) are listed as system operations (respectively, output events) and possibly given parameters. The responsibilities associated with each system operation should be recorded.
- The sequential ordering of steps should be made explicit. Where there is concurrency, or potential concurrency, between steps this should also be made explicit. The ordering of interactions within a step may be left unspecified (i.e., potentially concurrent).
- Naming should be consistent across all use cases.

Each use-case specification is amended to list the system operations, objects, and output events that it mentions.

The *system interface* is the set of system operations and output events that pass between the system and actors in its environment. It is formed by collecting the system operations and output events from all the use cases. The parameters of system operations and events are finalized at this stage. System operations and events are entered in the data dictionary, cross-referenced with the use cases from which they are derived.

9.2.3.3 Step 3 — Develop the Analysis Class Diagram

The domain class diagram is refined to produce the analysis class diagram, which shows the classes and associations that are necessary to represent the state of the system. The refinement is constructed by examining the use cases. Each potential object in a use case must belong to some class, association, or attribute type. Furthermore, each parameter of a system operation or output event must be similarly representable on the analysis class diagram.

Classes in the domain class diagram that are "outside the system boundary," are excluded from the analysis class diagram. The analysis class diagram may filter or extend the domain class diagram in various ways (and is equivalent to the System Object Model in Classic Fusion). Classes on the analysis class diagram are often high-level abstractions that later become the basis for architectural components.

9.2.3.4 Step 4 — Develop the System Operation and Event Specifications

The semantics of each system operation is specified by a system operation specification (Figure 9.6). Note that if the system has been architected into components then this step will apply to the (internal) system operations and events of each of the components.

Using the associated responsibilities, specify each system operation and event in terms of its pre- and post-condition, the object types it reads and changes, and the events it sends. During analysis, all

System Operation	*change_implemented(change#, OK?)*
Description	Issued by actual network when changes corresponding to change# have been implemented – OK? reports whether they have been successful
Reads	
Changes	
Sends	
Assumes	
Result	*IF userid was still logged in THEN emails (change#→, ok?→, userid→) has been sent to mailserver ELSE notify user(change#→, ok?→) has been sent to Operator. IF not OK? THEN rollback_to_pre (change#→) has been sent to network*

FIGURE 9.6 System Operation Specification for *change_implemented* (taken from Cell Keeper).

operations are presumed to be atomic, i.e., they happen "instantaneously" and do not interfere one with another. Interference due to concurrency is handled during the architecture and design phases.

9.2.3.5 Step 5 — Review the Analysis Models

These checks provide "just enough" criteria for establishing that the analysis is complete.

- **Consistency between the use cases and the analysis models** — Desk check consistency between use cases and specifications. Choose representative examples of scenarios from each use case. Define expected state change caused by each scenario, then execute the scenarios, using the specifications to define the behavior of each system operation. Ensure that the results are the same.
- **Consistency between system operation specification and the analysis class diagram** — All objects, associations, or parameter values mentioned in an operation specification must be represented in the analysis class diagram. Operation specifications must preserve analysis class diagram invariant constraints. If there is an invariant concerning an association or class, then any operation that can change them must respect the invariant in its specification.

9.2.4 Architecture

An *architecture* is a specification of the system to be built in terms of components and their interconnections. The architecture phase produces architectural descriptions at two different levels of abstraction. A *conceptual architecture* describes the system in terms of component collaborations which are expressed informally and at a high level of abstraction. The primary deliverable of the architecture phase is a *logical* architecture, which specifies collaborations in terms of messaging interfaces.

The logical architectural components are specified in the same way as a system, i.e., an analysis class diagram and an interface consisting of a set of operation specifications and events. Consequently the *architectural phase can be applied recursively* to produce an architectural design at any desired level of granularity.

9.2.4.1 Step 1 — Review and Select Applicable Architectural Styles

An architectural style defines a family of systems in terms of a pattern of structural organization. More specifically, an architectural style determines a vocabulary of components and connectors that can be used in instances of that style, together with a set of constraints on how they can be combined. Standard styles include layers, pipe-and-filter, blackboard, and microkernel. The style of the architecture of a specific system is likely to be a hybrid of standard styles.

Review applicable architectural styles for the domain of concern and create a coherent architectural style by composing and refining pre-existing styles. The architectural style will constrain the decisions made in the subsequent steps of the process. A key criterion for evaluating architectural styles is satisfaction of the non-functional and scale requirements identified in the requirements phase.

9.2.4.2 Step 2 — Informal Design of the Architecture

The goal of this phase is to make a first cut at the architecture. The description should be informal and provide a basis for the more detailed explorations of the later phases of the architectural process. At this stage, the architecture may be described by a:

- List of the components, their responsibilities and the rationale for the choice; enter the information into the data dictionary.
- Description of the behavior of the architecture; use diagrams to show the behavior in terms of dataflows or events passing between components; often box and arrow diagrams are better than using a formal notation.

The description should focus on how the architecture meets the requirements associated with areas of technical difficulty or high risk. It should be at the level of architectural invariants and mechanisms rather than on detailed component collaborations. If no architectural style was chosen in Step 1, then revisit the step to make the architectural style explicit.

Guidelines for identifying components include:

- Candidate components may be invented by subsetting the analysis class diagram. Classes are grouped together so that components are internally cohesive and loosely coupled externally with respect to associations and likely use. An instantiation of the classes will produce a component.
- Specialized components may be needed to support non-functional requirements, e.g., an authentication server to provide security.
- Review existing reusable libraries and existing systems to see if useful components already exist. Such *reusable* or *legacy components* can be used in the design process with their interfaces "as-is" or modified, (e.g., using a wrapper).
- If use cases require the system to interact with human users, then a user interface component will be needed and should be designed according to the GUI design process.
- Candidate components may also be introduced to support clusters of related responsibilities or system operations, for example, those associated with a feature.
- If data needs to be shared between many use cases that are not temporally coincident, then it must be determined if the data must be saved across invocations of the system using a database component or just within a single run of the system using a data structure. The database component should be designed using the database design process.

9.2.4.3 Step 3 — Develop the Conceptual Architecture

The conceptual architecture describes the architecture much more rigorously and precisely. This step details how the components interact in order to satisfy the requirements. Each scenario of use is used to construct a *component collaboration diagram* (Figure 9.7), which documents end-to-end behavior of the architecture. The collaborations between components, for example, the delegation of responsibilities, are indicated by links between components. In a conceptual architecture, the links usually do not show message flows unless they are already known, as for example, with legacy components.

Scenarios may be derived from use cases or, if a more precise understanding of architectural behavior is required, from the pre- and post-conditions for individual system operations. Design alternatives, for example, to meet the non-functional requirements, can be explored and evaluated by developing different collaboration diagrams. Enough scenarios should be explored to ensure that all components and collaborations have been discovered and that the architecture can support the requirements.

An *architecture diagram* (Figure 9.8), which provides a summary description of the system in terms of the components and their interactions, is constructed incrementally from the collaboration diagrams. In UML terms, an architecture diagram is an object collaboration diagram which provides the *context* for the set of collaborations between the components.

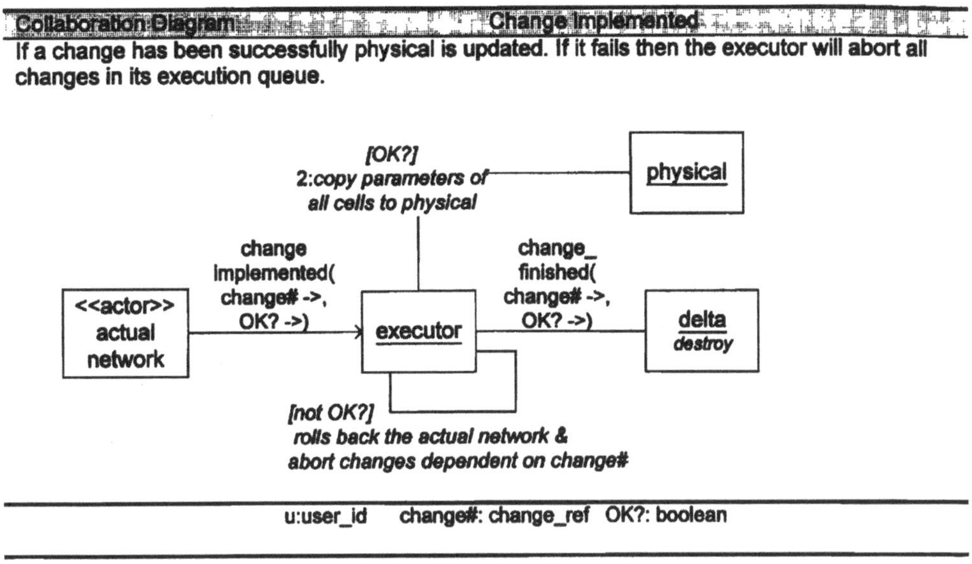

FIGURE 9.7 Component Collaboration Diagram for *change_implemented* (taken from Cell Keeper).

Developing the collaboration diagram for a scenario may refine the architecture by:

- Suggesting new components
- Adding new responsibilities to a component, e.g., designating a component as controller for a system operation
- Introducing new collaborations between components

In a collaboration diagram, links may be annotated with

- *Sequencing information*, i.e., the order in which the collaborations occur
- *Data flows* that occur as part of the collaboration
- *Create* or *delete* which denote component creation and deletion
- *Directionality* of the collaboration, i.e., which component initiates the collaboration

9.2.4.4 Step 4 — Develop the Logical Architecture

In this step the component collaborations of the conceptual architecture are replaced by message flows. Such architectural decisions cannot be finalized by looking at collaborations or components on an individual basis. It is necessary to take a more holistic view and consider how the decisions made for one collaboration can affect all the other collaborations involving the same components. Thus the conceptual architecture should be reviewed in order to establish relevant principles, mechanisms, and/or patterns to guide the logical architecture design.

Using these principles, the logical architecture is developed by examining all the links on all the component collaboration diagrams developed for the conceptual architecture and deciding for each collaboration:

- Whether the collaboration is mapped to a single message or a messaging protocol
- Which component *initiates* the message
- Whether the messaging is *synchronous, asynchronous,* or can be left *unspecified* until the design phase.

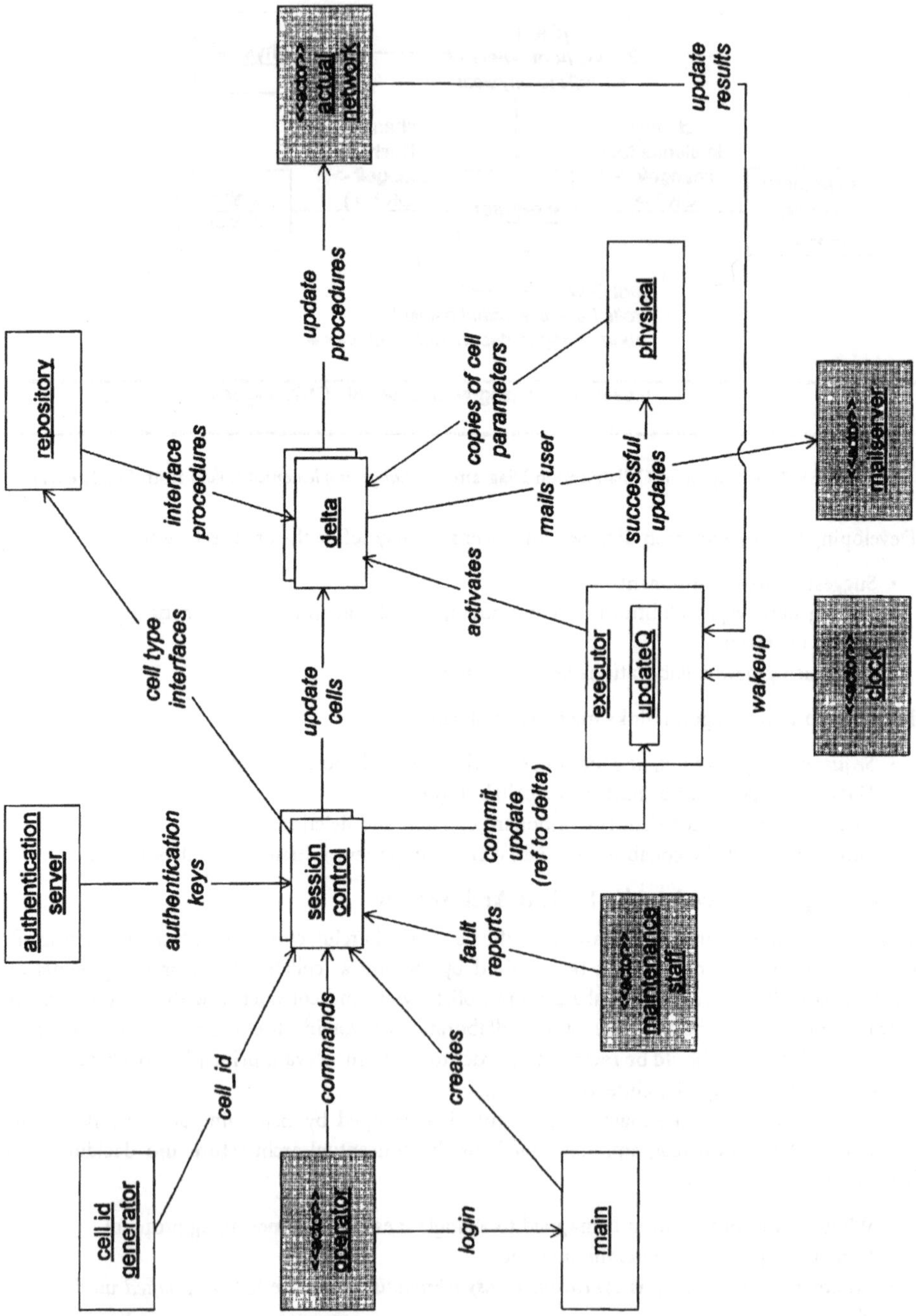

FIGURE 9.8 Conceptual Architecture Diagram for the same Cell Keeper example.

Prioritize the system operations according to real-time, throughput constraints, and all the non-functional requirements. For each system operation make the appropriate decisions for the collaborations involved. If necessary further develop the collaboration diagrams to explore the behavior of the architecture. In order to evaluate how the architecture can meet time-critical system level requirements such as throughput, UML *sequence diagrams* may be used to explore the length and complexity of end-to-end interactions through the architecture.

The pre- and post-conditions and the corresponding collaboration diagrams should be examined to consider whether it is possible for there to be simultaneous read/write access to a component. If so, access to the component may need synchronization and this should be added to the component specification.

As each intercomponent collaboration is refined into a method invocation it should be given a pre- and post-condition specification as in the analysis phase. The objects referred to in the results and assumes clauses must appear in the class diagram for the component.

To summarize, a logical architecture is specified by:

1. An architecture diagram
2. A revised set of collaboration diagrams showing message flows
3. For each component:
   - An interface specification documenting the message interface
   - Each message is specified by a pre- and post-condition, as in the analysis phase
   - An analysis class diagram
   - A list of responsibilities and the underlying rationale
   - Whether it is dynamically created and deleted
   - Whether it may require mutual exclusion

Guidelines:

1. **Asynchronous vs. Synchronous communication** — Asynchronous communication between components should be introduced in order to allow time-consuming computations to be performed "off-line" by another process or thread. Introducing asynchronous communication can also affect interfaces, because in order for a component to receive the results of an asynchronous computation there must be an event to transmit the results back. Further reasons for making interactions asynchronous include:
   - Interaction with a resource component, i.e., a server that can receive requests from multiple clients
   - Handling operations from the environment that are not constrained to appear in any particular order
   - When the client does not care when the required operation gets done
2. **Interfaces** — Decide whether each component needs a *real* interface. A component with a real interface can enforce encapsulation by ensuring that its internal components are only accessed via that interface. Alternatively a component can be treated as a white box that acts solely as an operational grouping of lower level components. In this case its interface is virtual, its internal structure is freely accessible to the environment, and its interface is the union of all its internal component interfaces. Note that a component intended as a unit of implementation or distribution, should have a real interface.
3. Decide whether two components can be merged. It may be desirable to merge two components if they are tightly bound to each other, have little functionality of their own, and collaborate with very few other components.
4. ***Precision*** — The level of precision in describing component interfaces may vary depending on the nature of the project:
   - Leaving some component interfaces only partially specified is appropriate for smaller scale systems developed by small co-located teams. The complete details of the interfaces can be captured bottom-up, during the design of the components themselves. Of course. completing the design

of the architecture in this case relies on good communication and disciplined attention to the component interfaces during design.

- Fuller and more precise interface specifications are more important when:
  1. The components will be developed by teams that are geographically or organizationally distributed (e.g., the development of the component is to be outsourced)
  2. The components are units of distribution, plug-and-play interoperability and/or reuse
  3. Complex forms of concurrency need to be addressed, especially in dealing with real-time constraints

9.2.4.5 Step 5 — Rationalize the Architecture

Assess whether the proposed architecture can satisfy the quality requirements and any other non-functional requirements. Apply the measures and test scenarios that were developed in Step 6 of the requirements phase, and ensure that the architecture meets these requirements. Identify architectural risks, e.g., points where performance is critical. These are candidates for early architectural prototyping.

Consider the architecture against these criteria:

1. Does each component have clearly defined responsibilities? Are there components with a surprisingly large number of interactions? If so, they may need to be merged and re-analyzed. Are there risks of deadlock or races?
2. Are the pre- and post-condition specifications of each system operation satisfied by the architectural collaborations? If not, the architecture does not meet its functional requirements.
3. Check whether the architecture can be mapped to the intended physical architecture. Allocate components to logical processors in the expected execution environment and check interaction path lengths for the scenarios used in constructing the architecture.

9.2.4.6 Step 6 — Form Design Guidelines

Before entering the design phase it is necessary to establish any principles that must be adhered to by the designers. The guidelines provide for consistent design approaches across the system such as preferred communication mechanisms, security policies, and error and exception handling. For example, a design guideline might require all system critical intercomponent messages to return a Boolean value indicating whether the method was successfully invoked.

9.2.5 Design

The outputs from the design phase are a *design class diagram*, *object collaboration diagrams*, and *initial object configurations*. During design, object-oriented structures are introduced to satisfy the abstract definitions produced from analysis and architecture. The design is in terms of *design* objects which are instances of *design classes*. Unlike an analysis class, a design class can have operations associated with it and possibly, additional attributes.

9.2.5.1 Step 1 — Form the Initial Design Class Diagram

The *design class diagram* shows the classes that are used during the design phase of a component. It is formed initially by making a copy of the analysis class diagram for the component.

9.2.5.2 Step 2 — Construct Object Collaboration Diagrams

The purpose of this step is to define object-oriented algorithms that satisfy the analysis specifications for the operations. Before designing the algorithms it is appropriate to review and evaluate whether there are any patterns that are applicable.

The algorithms are represented as *object collaboration diagrams*, one diagram is designed for each operation that the component is responsible. The algorithm may involve *multi-threading* and the messaging model is *procedure call*.

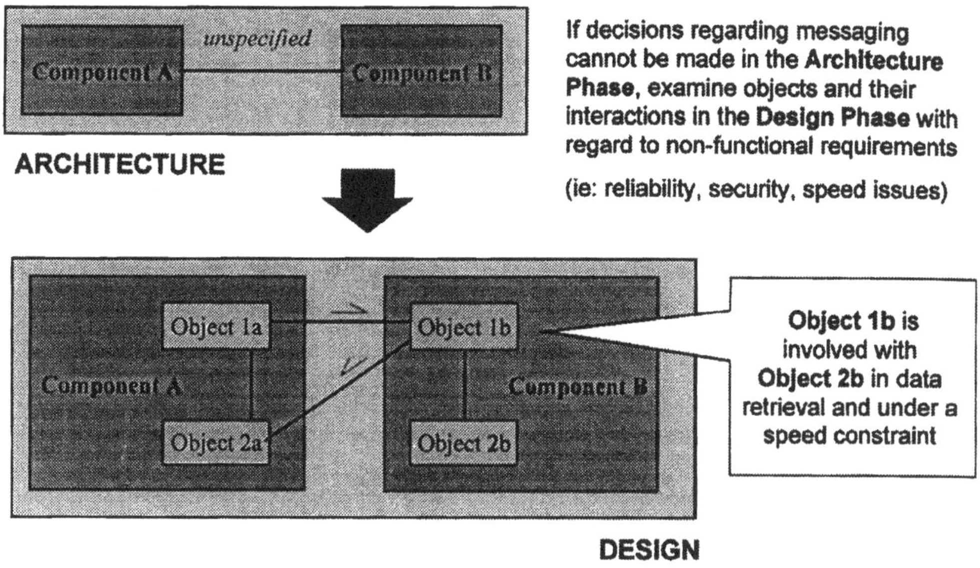

FIGURE 9.9 Schematic illustration showing resolving links left unspecified during the architecture phase.

The objects and associations mentioned in the *reads* and *changes* clauses of the operation specifications help determine the design objects involved in the algorithm. Often analysis objects can be mapped directly to objects of the corresponding design class. However, sometimes they may be mapped to one or more objects from new design classes, making the copied analysis class redundant. Each analysis association may be mapped to an object of a new design class that represents the association, or the association may be represented by attributes of objects involved in the association. Any new classes or attributes are added to the design class diagram.

The object that initially responds to the system operation is called the *controller* and the others are the *collaborators*. The system operation is added to the interface of controller class on the design class diagram. The algorithm determines the messages that flow between objects and the data carried by the messages. When a method is added to a controller object it should also be added to the interface of the corresponding design class.

An object collaboration diagram may be drawn for each method on a collaborator class by treating the method as a system operation. Consequently, the design process can be used recursively to layer the design. The object collaboration step is complete when all methods on objects are sufficiently trivial that they may be safely left to the implementation stage.

The object collaboration diagram for a system operation, or a method, is the design artifact corresponding to the code of the method in some class. Consequently the diagrams must be mapped, or cross-referenced, to the class inheritance structure, in order to provide the design documentation for the virtual methods of superclasses and the inherited methods of subclasses.

Each *unspecified* method that the component is responsible for must be resolved into either a synchronous or asynchronous method (Figure 9.9). The object collaboration diagrams for the alternatives provide a basis for the decision. The decision has to be consistent with the architectural guidelines and the design of all the other components that use this method. Update the architecture to reflect the decisions.

The object collaboration diagrams should be examined to consider whether it is possible for there to be simultaneous read/write access to an object. If so, the object will need to ensure mutual exclusion on the appropriate methods, for example, by using critical regions. If the component is specified as requiring mutual exclusion then each object that appears in more than one object collaboration diagrams should be examined to see if simultaneous access is possible. Simultaneous access can also occur as the result of two threads within a single collaboration diagram passing through the same object.

9.2.5.3 Step 3 — Object Aggregation and Visibility

All the object collaboration diagrams are inspected. Each message on an object collaboration diagram means that a visibility reference is needed from the client class to the server object.

Decide on the kind of visibility reference (bound/unbound, permanent/transient, fixed/changeable, etc.) required, taking into account the lifetime of the reference, the lifetime of the visible object, and whether the reference can change once established. Use this information to decide whether aggregation inherited from the analysis phase should be mapped to aggregation by reference or value. Record these decisions by adding the appropriate object valued and object reference valued attributes to classes on the design class diagram.

Guidelines:

- Check consistency with analysis models. For each association on the analysis class diagram, and that is used in a system operation specification, check that there is a path of visibility for the corresponding classes on the design class diagrams.
- Check mutual consistency. Ensure that exclusive target objects are not referenced by more than one class and that shared targets are referenced by more than one class.

9.2.5.4 Step 4 — Rationalize Design Class Diagram

Search for common objects, common classes, and common behaviors. Consider:

1. If the objects belonging to a class have been given similar methods, can their methods be unified?
2. If objects belonging to different classes have similar behavior, can the classes be unified, e.g., by introducing generalizations/specializations of each other or some new class?
3. Do objects from a class have separable behaviors? If so, should the class:
   - Be split into separate classes
   - Be turned into an aggregate class
   - Or multiply inherit from several parent classes
4. Would plausible changes in the requirements (analysis, architecture) affect several classes? Does this suggest changes to the class structure? Would plausible changes in the class structure make future maintenance easier?

If necessary, revise the design class diagram and object collaboration diagrams.

9.2.5.5 Step 5 — Define Initial Object Configurations

Use the object collaboration diagrams and the known lifecycle of the system to decide which objects must be present when the component starts. The *initial objects* and the *values of their attributes* are the seeds from which the component will grow; they must be allocated either when execution starts or when some agreed entry point of that component is entered.

9.2.5.6 Step 6 — Review Design

Verification of functional effect — Check that the functional effect of each object collaboration diagram satisfies the specification of its system operation given in the operation model.

9.3 Management Process Overview

The engineering process focuses on supporting software development activities in object-oriented requirements, analysis, architecture, and design. The complementary management process is informed both by the Fusion 2.0 engineering models and process as well as industry best practice. For example, Hewlett-Packard has more than ten years experience using an evolutionary lifecycle to manage risk and better address customer needs. This approach to development is a cornerstone of Fusion 2.0's management process, and integrates lessons we have learned applying Evolutionary Development (Evo) Fusion (Cotton, 1996) within Hewlett Packard and elsewhere.

Evo is a software development lifecycle that replaces traditional "waterfall" development with multiple short, time boxed cycles featuring

- Small, incremental product builds
- Frequent delivery of the evolving product to users for feedback
- Dynamic planning allowing response to this feedback

The evolutionary lifecycle suggests the appropriate sequence for the creation of the various UML models, when to refine these models based on greater understanding of the project, and any additional documents or artifacts that will assist in reducing the risk and increasing the chance of success for the project. This lifecycle is flexible enough to support the small co-located development team as well as multiple teams working in parallel, even when geographically distributed.

Classic Fusion (Coleman et al., 1994) provides a thorough and consistent set of models for the software engineer to translate the specification of customer needs into a well-structured software solution. Fusion 2.0 adds a consistent and complete set of models for the manager or technical lead to manage the overall project. Leveraging the best practices of successful managers, Fusion 2.0 provides a structure to lead a project from initiation and initial team building to final release and deployment, offering clear techniques for adapting to change and responding to risk.

The new Fusion evolutionary lifecycle is composed of two nested lifecycles, two phases, and a repeating development cycle or time box. Each of these will be explained in more detail in the following sections.

9.3.1 System Lifecycle

The system lifecycle is the highest level of the Fusion 2.0 evolutionary lifecycle. This lifecycle defines the business context for a product family or system and the major releases or *lineage* of the product or system over time. Through such artifacts as the *Vision, Mission, Business Strategy & Plan,* and *Portfolio and Release Plan,* direction and scope are established for the project. The direction provides the long-term view that all significant decisions can be evaluated against. The scope defines the expected impact of the product family or system over time on the business needs of the organization. Simple systems of limited lifespan may not justify the same level of analysis and architectural investment in extensibility and flexibility necessary for systems that are expected to support a critical business need for many years.

9.3.1.1 Release Lifecycle

A release represents the major versions of a product or system. Each version provides sufficient value to the development organization and the customer to warrant the overhead associated with a release. The release lifecycle defines the two major phases of a release, the *definition phase* and the *development phase.* The definition phase involves establishing the initial development team, establishing the expectations for the team, and understanding the behavior and structure of the system well enough to accurately plan for the development phase. The development phase translates this understanding of the system into reality, using time boxes to take one small step at a time toward that reality. Feedback is solicited after each small step to test against the customer's reality and to revise the plan as appropriate.

9.3.2 Definition Phase

The first step of the definition phase (Figure 9.10) is called *initiate and commit.* The outcome of this step is to establish the initial development team and to gain the appropriate management commitment to move forward. The project *value proposition* is used to gain alignment with and sponsorship from upper levels of management. Establishing *team principles* and defining the team *operating model* are initial steps toward building a highly effective and cohesive development team.

The next step is to begin to elicit and to structure the *requirements* for the system. Through use cases and system qualities, a draft of the functional and non-functional requirements are defined. These important models in the engineering process are also key to project planning.

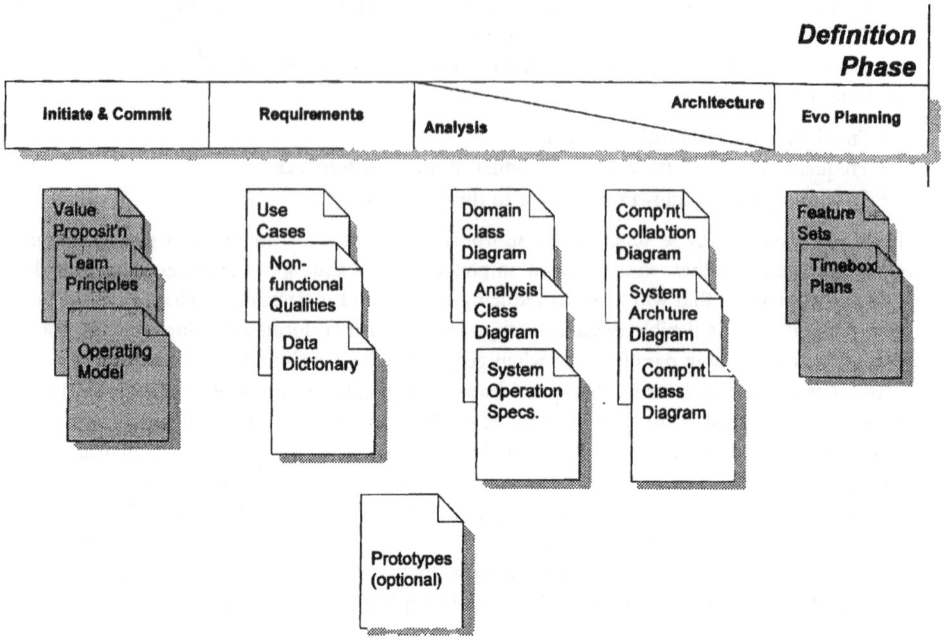

FIGURE 9.10 Fusion 2.0 Definition Phase.

The analysis/architecture steps add the information necessary to complete the last step of the definition phase, the *evo planning* step. For most projects, the development phase represents the biggest portion of the overall investment in a release. For that reason, the quality of the planning for the development phase is critical. Based on an understanding of the key risks faced by the project team, the structured use cases from requirements and system operations from analysis, as well as the component definitions from the architecture step, the team allocates *feature sets* across the small steps of the development phase. The structured use cases also provide a decomposition of the functionality of the system that can be used for effort estimation. The system architecture, by defining coherent parts of the system, plays a key role in allocating development responsibilities across individuals on the team as well as across development teams. The feature sets and the allocation of development responsibilities allow individuals and teams to develop their *time box plans.*

9.3.3 Development Phase

The development phase (Figure 9.11) is the heart of the evolutionary lifecycle. This phase is composed of a sequence of small, incremental product or system builds that are delivered frequently to customers for feedback and of dynamic plans that can be modified in response to this feedback. This phase ends with the final system test and deployment of the release.

The results produced during each time box are given to a customer or surrogate customer for evaluation. This phase is, therefore, characterized by significant amounts of feedback and the need for timely decision making. It is common to establish a decision-making team to address this feedback by weighing each potential change against the value proposition established for the release. Only those changes that strengthen the system's support for the value proposition should be evaluated for inclusion. All other changes and new features are deferred to the next release.*

*They have "missed the elevator" (Khurana and Rosenthal, 1997, p. 110).

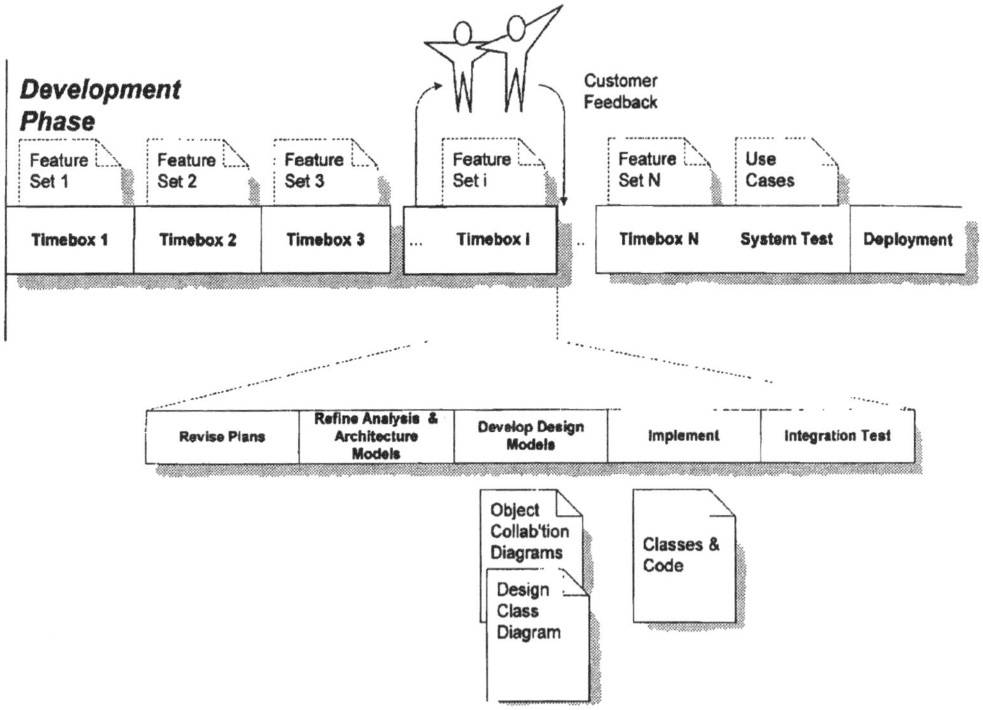

FIGURE 9.11 Fusion 2.0 Development Phase.

The development team can consider revising the plan, product, or process. The plan can be modified to change the content of the feature sets that have yet to be implemented. The product or system can be scheduled for modification if feedback suggests that the current implementation of some feature is not providing value to the customer. The process of development can be modified if it will enhance the development team's ability to deliver greater value to the customer.

Although integration testing is occurring throughout the development phase, there is still the need to conduct a final round of system testing before deploying the release to customers.*

9.3.3.1 Time box

The time box is the repeating implementation cycle that makes up the majority of the development phase. It has a fairly simple structure that defines five steps to be taken for each time box. The first step is to *revise plans.* Based on the decisions made by the management team to address feedback, the plans or feature set content for the current time box as well as future time boxes will need to be changed. The next step is to *refine analysis and architecture models* to accommodate the feature set that will be delivered for the current time box. The next two steps, *develop design models* and *implement,* complete the translation of the feature set into actual code. The final step of the time box is *integration test,* integrating together the work of the development team and validating that the new feature set works correctly with all previously implemented feature sets.

9.3.3.2 Multiple Parallel Teams

The time box structure can be nested to guide the development phase for large projects with multiple teams (Figure 9.12). The highest level time box is driven by a feature set that the collected group of development teams will deliver. The first phase of the high-level time box requires that the technical leads

*We have begun discussions with Shel Siegel (1996) to integrate his approach to quality.

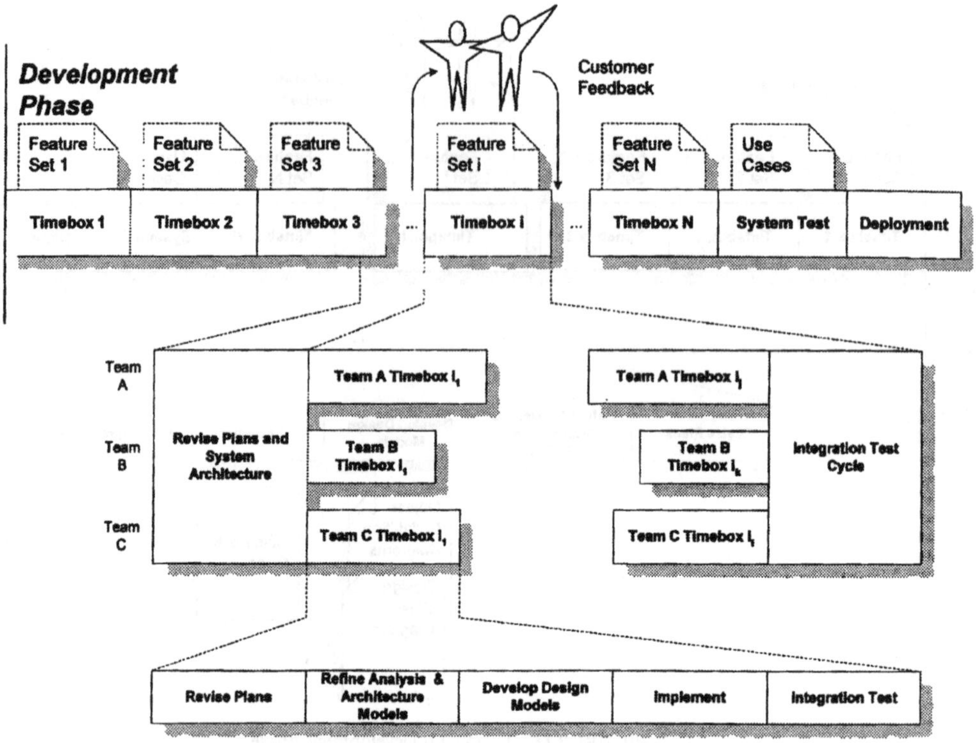

FIGURE 9.12 The Development Phase with Parallel Teams.

and project managers from each team work together to revise their collected plans and the overall system architecture. Once this is completed, each team can apply the time box structure to their portion of the feature set, revise their own plans, refine the analysis and architecture models for their component or components, develop the design models, implement the code, and integrate their work with the work from other members of their team. It may be appropriate for each team to execute multiple time boxes to complete their commitment to the highest level time box. The high-level time box completes with *an integration test cycle* that merges the work of all the teams together.

9.4 Conclusions

The key value proposition of Fusion 2.0 is that it is a highly tailorable method which meets the needs of today's developers, whether they be a small co-located team or a geographically distributed team developing on and for the web. The principal features of the next generation Fusion method are

- Adaptable and pragmatic "just enough" method
- UML notation and techniques
- Full lifecycle process including activities, techniques, deliverables, and team-based project planning models
- Use case and architecture-driven approach
- Time box, risk-, and deliverable-driven evolutionary development
- Support for all types of application development, including *n*-tier system architecture and component definition using OLE/COM and OMG CORBA architectures and internet system design
- Scalable for all sizes of application development projects

Acknowledgments

This chapter reflects the contributions of other members of the Fusion 2.0 team; namely Chris Dollin, Paul Jeremaes, Matt Johnson, and David Redmond-Pyle. We would also like to thank Reed Letsinger and Herman Yang who have contributed at different times to the team. Our colleagues in the Hewlett-Packard Software Initiative, especially Dana Bredemeyer, Mike Ogush, and Steve Rhodes, have also offered many insights and suggestions that have helped shape the Fusion 2.0 method. We have benefited tremendously from the opportunity to work with numerous Fusion and other projects in Hewlett-Packard, as well as outside groups, and we would like to express our gratitude for all the constructive feedback we have had on the new method.

References

Cockburn, A. 1997. Structuring use cases with goals, *J. Object-Oriented Program.* also on the Web at http://members.aol.com/acockburn/papers/usecases.htm.

Coleman, D., Arnold, P., Bodoff, S., Dollin, C., Gilchrist, H., Hayes, F. and Jeremaes, P. 1994. *Object-Oriented Development: The Fusion Method.* Prentice-Hall, Englewood Cliffs, NJ.

Cotton, T. 1996. "Evolutionary Fusion: A customer-oriented incremental life cycle for fusion. In *Object-oriented Development at Work: Fusion in the Real World,* R. Malan, R. Letsinger and D. Coleman, Eds., pp. 179-202. Prentice-Hall, Upper Saddle River, NJ.

Gamma, E., Helm, R., Johnson, R. and Vlissides, J. 1995. *Design Patterns: Elements of Reusable Object-Oriented Software.* Addison-Wesley, Reading, MA.

Khurana, A. and Rosenthal, S. R. 1997. Integrating the fuzzy front end of new product development, *Sloan Manage. Rev.* Winter.

Malan, R., Letsinger, R. and Coleman, D. Eds. 1996. *Object-Oriented Development at Work: Fusion in the Real World.* HP Press/Prentice-Hall, Upper Saddle River, NJ.

Malan, R., ed. 1995. *Fusion Newslet.* URL: http://www.hpl.hp.com/fusion. 3(1).

Malan, R., ed. 1996. *Fusion Newslet.* URL: http://www.hpl.hp.com/fusion. 4(1,2,3,4).

Malan, R., ed. 1997. *Fusion Newslet.* URL: http://www.hpl.hp.com/fusion. 5(1,2,3).

Siegel, S. 1996. *Object-Oriented Software Testing: A Hierarchical Approach.* John Wiley & Sons, New York.

10

Business Object Notation (BON)

Kim Waldén
Enea Data, Sweden

10.1 Introduction

Business Object Notation, commonly known as BON, is a method for analysis and design of object-oriented systems, emphasizing seamlessness, reversibility, and software contracting. Its aim is to narrow the gap between analysis, design, and implementation by using the same semantic and conceptual base for the notation on all three levels. The idea is that if a method is to serve as support for the whole lifecycle of a system, it must be possible to use its models and notations to do both forward and reverse engineering. It must be possible not only to transform an initial problem model into an executable system, but also to reflect source code changes back into design and analysis.

Therefore, in BON you will not find the usual entity-relationship diagrams and statecharts that form the basis of nearly all analysis and design methods on the market today (whether claiming to be object-oriented or not). The reason is that no matter what you think about the expressiveness of these modeling concepts, they are incompatible with what is available at the implementation level and thus effectively prevents reversibility. Instead, BON relies on the power of the pure object-oriented modeling concepts — a system as a set of classes (abstractions) which are related by inheritance and client dependencies. The OO concepts are combined with a clustering mechanism to group related abstractions and with precise component specification based on strong typing and software contracts. The BON method is fully described in the book *Seamless Object-Oriented Software Architecture* (Waldén and Nersson, 1995). It includes concepts and notations for static and dynamic modeling of object-oriented software as well as detailed guidelines for the modeling process.

The short overview in this chapter will concentrate on the general principles underlying the design of BON and the resulting concepts and notations. There will also only be room to touch upon the modeling

0-8493-3135-8/99/$0.00+$.50

process. Readers who want more detail are referred to the book above in which more than 200 pages are devoted to the software process describing the method guidelines and applying them in three extensive case studies drawn from practical usage.

10.2 Basic Principles of BON

10.2.1 Generality

BON targets general software development and does not attempt to cover every conceivable need that may arise for particular applications or with particular programming languages. Only concepts and notations that have proven useful in a wide spectrum of application domains are included in the method. Instead the user is free to complement the BON framework with additional descriptions and conventions that may be useful to a particular project. BON has been used successfully in applications of many different types ranging from embedded technical systems to financial software and MIS applications.

With the growing need for interoperability and information distribution using CORBA techniques, large heterogeneous systems are becoming the norm rather then the exception. This requires a method that captures the essence of OO abstraction without getting bogged down in details of specific language constructs. BON is independent of implementation platform, and has been used in projects targeting languages as different as Eiffel, C++, Smalltalk, and Delphi's Object Pascal. In fact, the strong typing of BON has been appreciated in Smalltalk developments despite the fact that this language is not statically typed. This is because experienced Smalltalk programmers tend to think in terms of typed symbols during design, even if this is not reflected in the program code.

10.2.2 Seamlessness and Reversibility

Using notations based on the same concepts and semantics throughout the development of a software product allows for a smooth transition from the initial analysis and design models down to executable code. However, even more important, it also allows the process to work in reverse. It should be possible to (automatically) extract abstract design views from existing implementations. Since the initial analysis and design is never correct in real projects, and many of the errors and shortcomings are not detected until implementation or testing time, the high-level models need to be continuously updated as the software evolves.

The big challenge is to keep the various models consistent with the code. This is usually not done in practice, because the cost is prohibitive with non-reversible methods. Therefore, as time passes, the design documentation will cease to be a correct description of the implementation and therefore will be of limited or no use to developers trying to understand the system. This in turn makes it much harder to maintain and enhance the software.

If we stick to classes as the main structuring mechanism and use only inheritance and client relationships to describe how the classes are related to each other, reversibility is free, because these concepts are directly supported by the major OO programming languages. On the other hand, if we include concepts that cannot be mapped to and from the eventual code, reversibility is lost. The conclusion drawn for BON is that reversibility is indeed necessary if a method is to play more than a marginal role in supporting software development (Waldén, 1996).

The remaining question is: Is a notation based on class abstractions related through inheritance and client dependencies expressive enough? Can we do without the associations, multiplicities, and statecharts found in nearly all OO analysis and design notations today? The answer is yes. Because BON is a different approach, you gain some and you lose some, but two crucial means of specification can more than compensate for the loss of free associations — strong typing and class contracts.

10.2.3 Typed Interface Descriptions

A class interface consists of the syntax and semantics of its applicable operations. The syntactic part of an operation, often called its *signature*, is the types of its return value and arguments, if any. Strong typing (also known as static typing) means that the class designer must specify the signature of all the services offered by the class. This permits automatic consistency checking already at the specification level. Thus mistakes can be detected early.

However, what is even more important is that typing is an essential conceptual aid in system modeling. Assigning types to names is really classification, which increases the information content in a specification considerably. Instead of relying on more or less vague naming conventions as to what kind of objects will be attached to a certain symbol at runtime, the reader of a typed specification can see this directly with no risk of misinterpretation.

For example, if a class attribute refers to a list of trucks sorted on load capacity in a freight transport system, a typical attribute name in an untyped notation would be:

```
fleetOfSortedTrucks
```

which can be compared with the typed declaration:

```
fleet: SORTED_LIST [TRUCK]
```

The difference in precise information conveyed to the reader is considerable. With the second form we no longer have to guess what entities are described, but we can find out their precise definitions by inspecting the classes *TRUCK* and *SORTED_LIST*.

10.2.4 Software Contracting

Perhaps the most important principle in existence today for constructing correct, reliable software is the theory of Design by Contract (Meyer, 1997). The idea is to treat each subprogram as a subcontractor who undertakes to deliver some service (specified by a postcondition), but only if certain prerequisites are fulfilled (the precondition). Software contracts addresses two issues at once, both essential for understanding large systems. First, the contract specifies formally what each component will do. Second, the responsibilities for taking care of unusual conditions are clearly separated between the supplier of a service and its clients.

This separation of responsibility is crucial. Without it there is no clear strategy that can be used to ensure correctness in a system, leaving developers with *ad hoc* approaches such as the arbitrary, redundant checking known as *defensive programming*. The result is even less understandable software with more errors due to the excessive code in each local component, which increases system complexity and obscures the fundamental logic.

With software contracts this does not happen, and each party can concentrate on its main task without having to worry about irrelevant detail. A contract protects both sides: it protects the client by specifying *how much* must be done and it protects the supplier by specifying *how little* is acceptable. This has much in common with standard practices in human societies, where a network of subcontractors is often employed to carry out a large undertaking.

Class contracts also constitute the precise specification needed by industrial-strength reusable components. No hardware electronics manufacturer would dream of offering standard elements without specifying the exact conditions for their use, and software components are no less critical.

10.2.5 Scalability

An important issue for any method and notation is the possibility to scale up from the small examples presented in textbooks to large, complex real-life systems. To this end we need two things: a facility to recursively group classes into higher-level units, and the possibility to zoom between the various levels of a large structure. The BON notation uses nested clustering and element compression to achieve this.

Classes may be grouped into clusters according to various criteria (part of a subsystem, heirs of a common ancestor, related functionality, etc.). Clusters and classes may in turn be grouped into new clusters on higher levels. Depending on the current focus of interest, many different views of the same underlying system need to be presented. Flat partitioning is not enough in this context, since we need to see different levels of detail in different parts of the system without losing track of how the parts fit into the big picture.

Therefore, most elements in BON may be *compressed*, which means that one or several graphical and textual elements are represented by a simpler element, or its compressed form. Elements containing compressed forms may in turn be compressed. Because the level of compression can be independently selected for each structural element (recursively), the user may freely choose the amount of detail shown for each system part. A few simple changes in the compression levels may yield a dramatically different architectural diagram, making this approach well suited for automatic tools support.

10.2.6 Simplicity

In BON simplicity is a major guiding star. Contrary to many other approaches which try to include everything an analyst/designer might possibly need, BON tries to live by the maxim "small is beautiful." In our experience, if a modeling notation is to be of real use above what is already available in a structured development language such as Eiffel (Meyer, 1992), it needs to be very simple and well-defined. It should be easy for a user to quickly master the whole notation, and its semantics and graphical symbols should be very clear and unambiguous.

For example, special care was taken to have very few different types of relation in BON (in fact only two static and one dynamic), and to craft the relationship symbols in a way that would rule out mistakes regarding the semantics and direction of each relation. Several modeling sessions with industrial users of other notations have shown that this is a real problem. When consulting on object-oriented modeling, we usually begin by translating existing user diagrams into BON notation in order to better understand what they are aiming to do. When asked about details of complex diagrams, users very often become uncertain about the exact meaning of many of the relations, and whether A is related to B or if it was the other way around.

10.2.7 Space Economy

The amount of information that can be conveyed to a reader of an architectural model of some part of a system — a cluster, a group of clusters, a group of related classes — depends strongly on how much can be fitted on one page (where a page is a terminal screen, a paper sheet or whatever can be observed in one glance). Breaking up an integral context into fragments that must be viewed one by one is detrimental to the overall readability.

Therefore, it is important for any notation designed to give global overviews of potentially large and complex structures to avoid wasting space. BON therefore provides compressed forms for all space-consuming graphical layouts. For example, it is too restrictive to have a full interface with operations and attributes as the only way to show a class. In BON the compressed form of a class is simply an ellipse enclosing its name and possibly some additional marker. Similarly, BON provides iconization of clusters and compression of relationships between classes into (fewer) relationships between clusters.

10.3 The Static Model

The static model describes the classes making up the system, their interfaces, how they are related to each other, and how they are grouped into clusters. It shows the system architecture and the contracts between each class component and its clients.

10.3.1 Informal Charts

BON defines three types of informal static charts: the *system chart* listing the topmost clusters of the system, *cluster charts* listing the classes and other clusters contained in each cluster, and *class charts* describing the interface of each class. These are untyped charts meant to be used very early in the modeling process, particularly when communicating with non-technical people such as end users, customers, or

CLASS	*ELEVATOR*	Part: 1/1
TYPE OF OBJECT Models an elevator which is being pulled by a motor.	**INDEXING** **cluster:** *ELEVATOR_CONTROL* **created:** 1997-03-29 kw **revised:** 1997-04-08 kw	
Queries	Current floor, Pending floor requests, Is elevator moving? Are doors open? Is elevator traveling up? Is elevator traveling down? Is elevator idle?	
Commands	Open doors. Close doors. Process floor requests.	
Constraints	Cannot be traveling both up and down. If stopped and no more requests then elevator is idle. Cannot move when doors are open. An idle elevator is not moving.	

FIGURE 10.1 Informal class chart.

domain experts. An example of a class chart is shown in Figure 10.1. The chart contains a standardized header stating the type of chart (class in this case), its name, sequence number, a short description, and an indexing clause. The latter contains a number of keywords defined by the user and one or more value entries for each keyword.

The class interface description is divided into three parts: *queries*, *commands*, and *constraints*. Queries are operations that return information about the system but do not change its state, while commands are operations that do not return information, but may change the system state. A clean separation of operations into queries and commands (which means that functions should not have side effects) makes it much easier to reason about the correctness of classes. Finally, the constraints lists general consistency conditions and business rules to be obeyed.

Class charts are designed to facilitate later translation into typed interface descriptions, but they also resemble formatted memos used to record various aspects of the problem domain. Therefore, it is not uncommon that class charts initially contain operations and constraints, which will later turn out to have no counterpart in a computerized system.

10.3.2 Class Headers

The compressed form of a class is an ellipse containing the class name, possibly adorned by one or more of the graphical annotations shown in Figure 10.2. *Reused* classes are classes from earlier systems or third

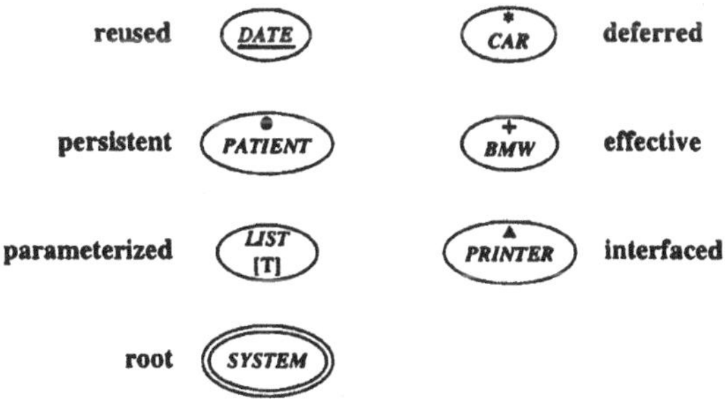

FIGURE 10.2 Class headers with annotations.

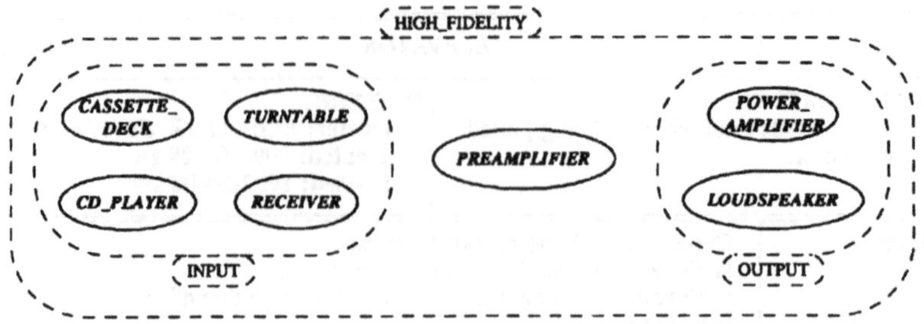

FIGURE 10.3 Nested clusters.

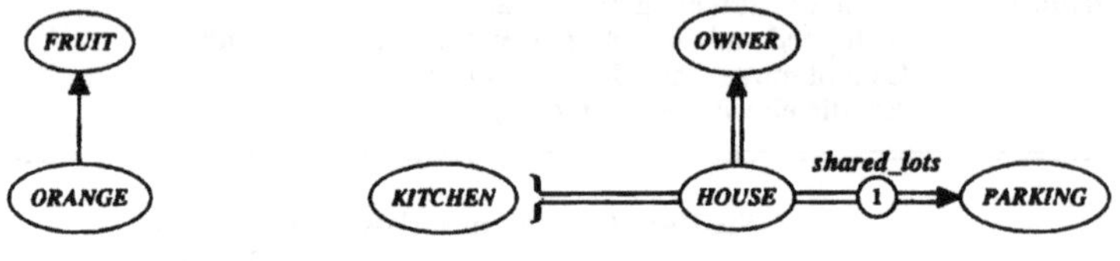

FIGURE 10.4 Inheritance and client relations.

FIGURE 10.5 Generic supplier, expanded form.

parties. *Persistent* classes are classes whose instances need to be stored externally. *Deferred* classes contain at least some operation that will only be implemented through descendant classes, while *effective* classes will be fully implemented. *Interfaced* classes contain external calls to the underlying software platform or to other systems. A *root* class is a class that gets instantiated when a system (or concurrent execution thread) is started.

10.3.3 Clusters

Classes can be recursively structured into clusters, whose graphical representation is rounded rectangles tagged with the cluster name, as shown in Figure 10.3.

10.3.4 Static Relations

There are only two basic types of relation in BON, *client* and *inheritance*. Both are denoted by arrows — single arrows for inheritance and double arrows for client relations. The client relations have three varieties: plain client association, aggregation (part/whole), and shared association. Figure 10.4 show the different types of static relations.

The double arrow ending in an open brace signifies that a kitchen is viewed as an integral part of a house, and the arrow marked by an encircled number states that all houses share one parking lot. The label above the circle is the name of the operation in class *HOUSE* giving rise to the relation.

A common modeling situation is that a class has an indirect client relation to another class through a generic (parameterized) container class, as shown in Figure 10.5. It is then seldom desirable to include the container class (usually a reused library class) at the same level as the classes related to the problem domain.

Therefore, BON provides a compact notation for such relations, as shown in Figure 10.6. Labels of type *LIST [...]* are reminiscent of the semantic labels in entity-relationship diagrams, but instead of

FIGURE 10.6 Generic supplier, compact form.

relying on natural language, the precise semantics of the label can be found in the definition of the corresponding class.

10.3.5 Software Contracts

The contract elements of object-oriented systems are *pre-* and *post-conditions*, which apply to each operation of a class, and *class invariants*, which apply to the whole class. The pre-condition must be satisfied just before the operation is called (responsibility of the client), and the post-condition is then guaranteed to be satisfied when the call returns (responsibility of the supplier). The class invariant must be satisfied both before and after a call to any operation of the class, and it represents general consistency rules defining the valid states for objects of this type.

Since operations may be inherited and redefined in object-oriented systems, a client can never be sure of what exact version will be invoked at runtime. For example, if a client needs to compute the areas of a list of geometric figures referred by an entity of type LIST [FIGURE], all that is available is the specification of the class FIGURE. The contract elements of this class must be enough to guarantee that whatever special figures may be in the list — now or in the future — the client call to compute its area will still be valid; otherwise, the contracting model breaks down.

Polymorphism with dynamic binding is the main key to software flexibility. It has the power to remove most of the discrete case analysis that is so error prone and vulnerable to future changes. However, flexibility is meaningless unless the resulting software is correct. Therefore, the following consistency rules are fundamental.

Laws of subcontracting:

- A descendant class must satisfy the class invariants of all its ancestors.
- A descendant class may never weaken the post-condition of an inherited operation (since this would mean delivering less than specified by the ancestor).
- A descendant class may never strengthen the pre-condition of an inherited operation (since this would mean imposing restrictions on the client not specified by the ancestor).

Note that the above rules must be obeyed for every ancestor in case of multiple inheritance, therefore preventing a combination of incompatible abstractions. This is crucial when building the complicated inheritance lattices needed by, for example, the general data structure libraries of typed language environments.

10.3.6 Typed Class Interfaces

Informal charts, such as in Figure 10.1, may be a good way to start analysis, particularly when non-technical people are involved, but the analyst/designer will soon need something more expressive. This leads us to the structured static diagrams with typing and software contracts. Three class interfaces taken from an elevator control system are shown in Figure 10.7. The interface of class *ELEVATOR* lists seven queries whose names and return types are separated by a colon and three commands with no return types. Lines starting with double dashes signify comments. The query *is_idle* specifies a post-condition, signaled by the framed exclamation point. The post-condition asserts that being idle is the same as being in neither of the states *is_traveling_up* and *is_traveling_down*. The commands *open_doors* and *close_doors* both specify as pre-condition (signaled by the framed question marks) that the elevator must not be moving when these operations are called.

The class invariant specifies a number of consistency conditions for all elevator objects. An elevator cannot be traveling both up and down at the same time. An elevator that does not move and has no pending requests is in an idle state. An elevator cannot move if the doors are open.

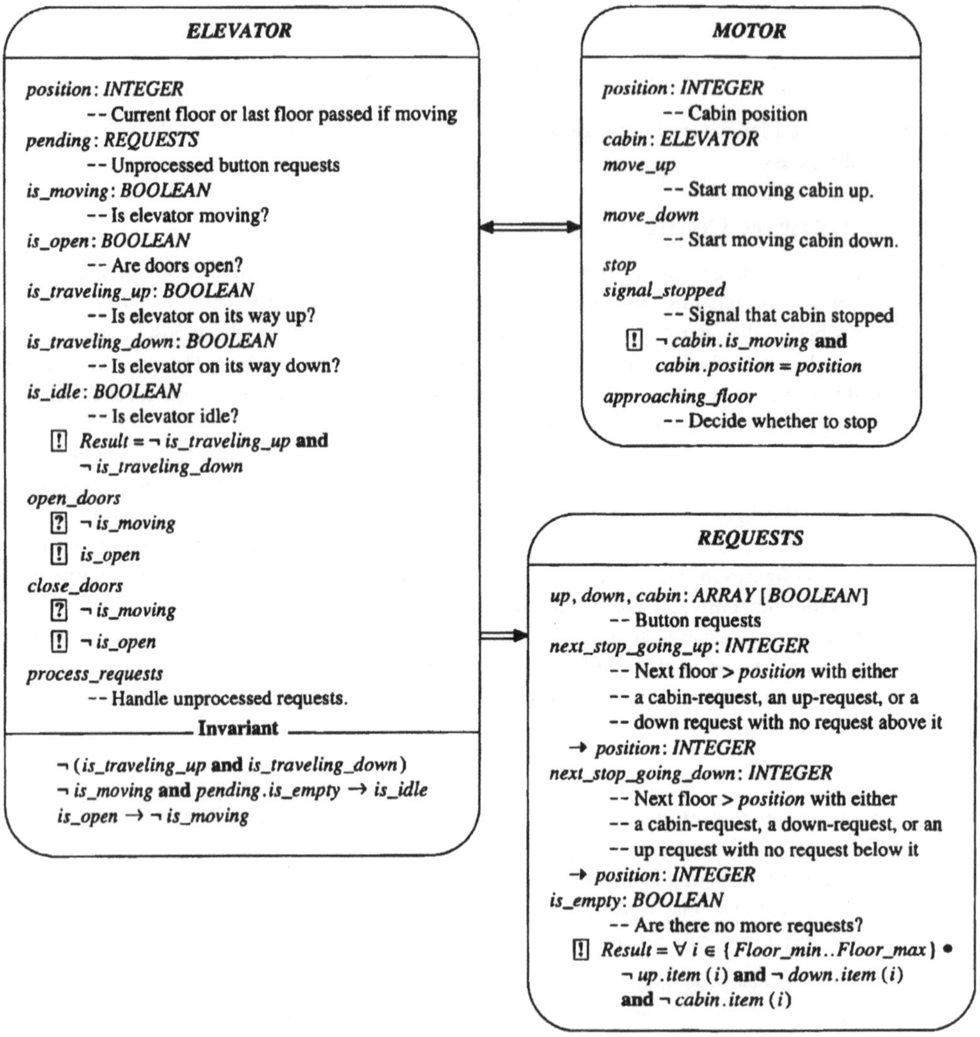

FIGURE 10.7 Interface of ELEVATOR classes.

In class *REQUESTS* the queries *next_stop_going_up* and *next_stop_going_down* each takes an argument signaled by the small horizontal arrow. The query *is_empty* uses the predicate logic notation of BON to specify its semantics. According to the post-condition, being empty means that for each floor number taken from the interval between the lowest and highest floor serviced by the elevators, there is no button request in either of the queues for up requests, down requests, or cabin requests.

10.3.7 Static Architecture

A possible static architecture for the elevator control system is shown in Figure 10.8. Comparing this diagram to the interface specifications in Figure 10.7, shows that we get many of the client relations for free, since they can be derived directly from the return types of the queries defined in the classes *ELEVATOR* and *MOTOR*.

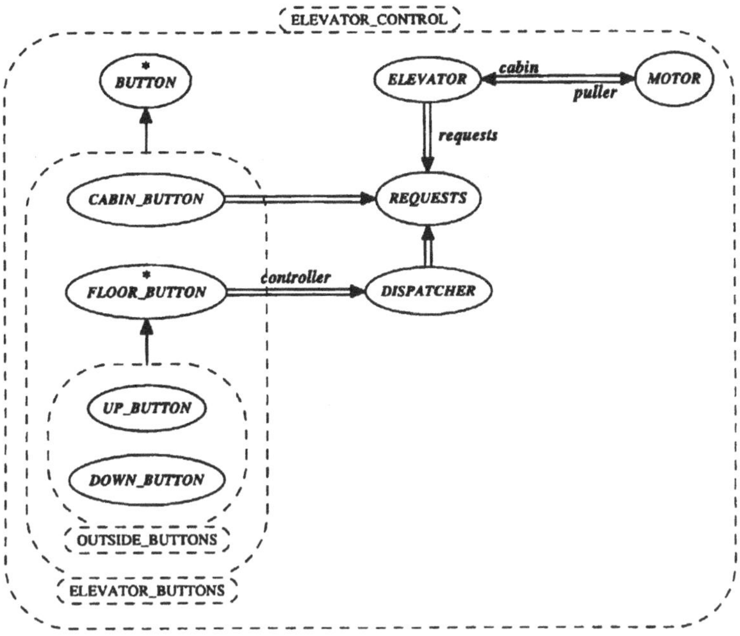

FIGURE 10.8 Elevator system architecture.

10.4 The Dynamic Model

10.4.1 Informal Charts

There are three types of informal charts for dynamic modeling in BON: *event charts* listing incoming external events and outgoing internal events, *scenario charts* listing interesting system usage, and *creation charts* listing the classes responsible for creating instances of problem domain classes in the system. Figure 10.9 shows a scenario chart with three potentially interesting scenarios selected for further investigation. Each scenario has a short phrase for quick reference and a description explaining the scenario a little more.

SCENARIOS	*ELEVATOR CONTROL*	**Part:** 1/1
COMMENT Set of representative scenarios to show important types of system behavior.	**INDEXING** **created:** 1997-04-13 kw	
Visit friend in neighboring apartment: A person leaves her apartment, calls an elevator and goes to see a friend living at another floor level.		
Coming in and going out in parallel: One person enters ground floor, calls elevator, and goes up, while another person enters a floor, calls elevator, and goes down.		
Partly joint ride: One person enters elevator at 5th floor and goes to 2nd, while another person enters at 3rd and goes to basement.		

FIGURE 10.9 Scenario chart.

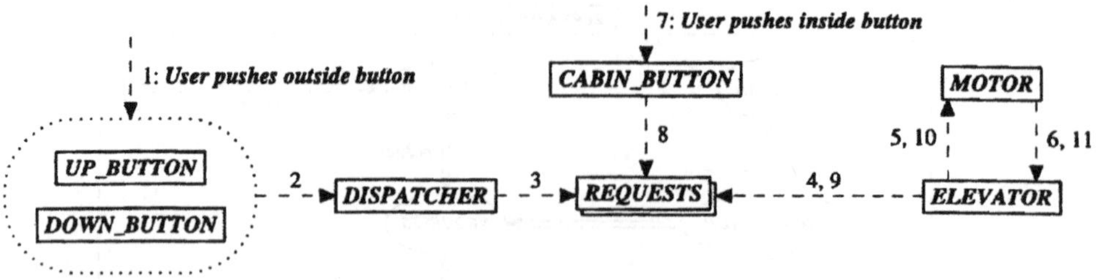

Scenario: Visit friend in neighboring apartment	
1	*User enters floor at own apartment level and pushes floor button.*
2	*Button asks dispatcher to accept request.*
3	*Dispatcher chooses suitable elevator and enters a request in that elevator's queue.*
4, 5	*Chosen elevator takes request from queue and tells motor to move in corresponding direction.*
6	*Motor signals that cabin has stopped at requested floor.*
7	*User enters cabin and pushes button to floor where friend lives.*
8	*Request is entered in elevator's queue.*
9, 10	*Elevator takes request from queue and tells motor to move.*
11	*Motor signals stop and user leaves elevator to visit friend.*

FIGURE 10.10 Dynamic object scenario.

10.4.2 Dynamic Diagrams

The first of these scenarios is illustrated in the dynamic diagram showed in Figure 10.10.

It consists of a number of objects calling each other (sending messages in Smalltalk terminology). Each object is labeled by its type (name of corresponding class) and a parenthesized identifying label if needed. A rectangle signifies a *single object,* while a double rectangle refers to a *set of objects* of the given type.

A dashed arrow represents a message passed from one object to another, and it is called a *message relation.* The arrows are labeled by sequence numbers showing the order in which the messages are sent, and a *scenario box* adds a general free text description of the corresponding actions. Objects may be collected into object groups (dotted rounded rectangles), and messages passed to or from such a group then represent messages to or from one or more of the objects in the group.

A message relation is always potential, since conditional control (such as multiple choice or iteration) is not included in dynamic diagrams, and all data flow resulting from values being returned is also implicit. For reasons of simplicity and abstraction, the diagrams show only passing of control. In case we need to express more, a suitable dynamic modeling notation can be used in the text entries of the scenario boxes.

10.5 The Method

The BON approach contains a set of guidelines regarding what to build such as the BON *deliverables* — informal charts, static architecture, class interfaces, dynamic scenarios—and how and when to do it. Nine standard tasks are defined to be carried out in an approximate order, which represents an ideal process (Parnas and Clements, 1987). Nine standard activities are also defined, some or all of which may be involved in each of the tasks.

The BON process is not meant to be followed to the letter; rather its purpose is to guide managers by providing a bench mark against which progress can be measured and guide the designer when at loss for what to do next. Here we have only room to briefly list the tasks and activities, while a full discussion along with examples of practical usage can be found in Waldén and Nerson, 1995.

10.5.1 BON Process Tasks

The tasks are grouped into three parts: gathering information about the problem, elaborating what has been gathered, and designing a computational model.The first part involves separating what should be modeled from what can be left out, extracting an initial set of candidate classes from the concepts used in the problem domain, and selecting classes from this set, group them into clusters, and sketch principal similarities (inheritance) and collaborations through client dependencies.

The second part involves defining classes in terms of queries, commands, and constraints; sketching system behavior in terms of relevant object scenarios, and defining public features using typed interfaces and formal contracts. Finally, the third part involves refining the problem domain architecture with new design classes and new features, factoring out common behavior into deferred classes, and completing and reviewing the full system architecture.

Gathering analysis information

1. Delineate system borderline
2. List candidate classes
3. Select classes and group into clusters

Describing the gathered structure

4. Define classes
5. Sketch system behavior
6. Define public features

Designing a computational model

7. Refine system
8. Generalize
9. Complete and review system

10.5.2 BON Standard Activities

Of the nine standard activities, the first four are continuously repeated during both analysis and design. The fifth occurs mostly during analysis, but it may also be repeated during design of large systems. The last four are chiefly part of the design task.

Analysis and design

1. Finding classes
2. Classifying
3. Clustering
4. Defining class features
5. Selecting and describing object scenarios

Design

6. Working out contracting conditions
7. Assessing reuse
8. Indexing and documenting
9. Evolving the system architecture

10.6 Conclusions

It is our experience that most developers who use analysis and design methods systematically (already a small minority) use them only as help to produce an initial system design. Whether or not the resulting models turn out to be useful, they usually lose their importance after the first software release (if not before), and the implementation code takes on a life of its own. The BON method has proved that there is a way out of this. By providing a conceptual framework for analysis and design based on pure OO abstraction with software contracts, the necessary reversibility can be achieved at low cost.

Without reversibility it is impossible, in the long run, to ensure consistency between specification and implementation. As long as modeling concepts such as free associations and state diagrams, which are incompatible with implementation languages, continue to be included as essential ingredients in analysis and design methods, reversibility is lost. The goal of BON has been to break this tradition and take the potential of OO modeling to its logical conclusion.

References

Meyer, B. 1992. *Eiffel: The Language*. Prentice-Hall, Englewood Cliffs, NJ.

Meyer, B. 1997. *Object-Oriented Software Construction*, 2nd ed. pp. 331-438. Prentice Hall, Englewood Cliffs, NJ.

Parnas, D.L. and Clements, P.C. 1986. "A rational design process: how and why to fake it," *IEEE Trans. Software Eng.*, **SE-12**(2), 251–257.

Waldén, K. 1996. Reversibility in software engineering, *IEEE Comp.*, Vol. 29, No. 9, 93–95.

Waldén, K. and Nerson, J.-M. 1995. *Seamless Object-Oriented Software Architecture*, pp. 438. Prentice-Hall, Englewood Cliffs, NJ.

11

Martin/Odell Approach: The Philosophy

James Odell

11.1 Introduction

The era of employing a grand monolithic approach to develop data processing systems is coming to an end. Systems developers are now realizing that there are many different ways to specify and program systems. While the traditional IF ... THEN, DO WHILE approach is popular in many situations, it is far from being the best or only way. For instance, a medical diagnosis system might be implemented best with rules and an inference engine. In other situations, conditioning a neural network or genetic algorithm could produce the desired results much more efficiently. Elsewhere, a predicate logic or functional expression would be the best way to specify an application. In other words, if a system can be specified in many ways, why not choose the mix of approaches best for the problem at hand? Why be bound to only one way of doing things, when a combination of approaches might produce a result that is more economical, accurate, understandable, and elegant?

The answer, then, lies in allowing developers to choose those approaches that best solve the problem at hand. However, can such a developers' anarchy be integrated successfully? For instance, can rules, logic, functions, neural nets, structured techniques, SQL, client/server, etc., fit together in any useful way? Without a coordinated and systematic approach, system development would quickly become more of a kluge than it already is. The Martin/Odell approach to object-oriented development is through controlled, flexible methodologies that employ a formal foundation. In this way, systems can be developed using a variety of methods and notation, while at the same time having system specifications based on a sound foundation (Martin, 1995, 1996).

System-Development Philosophy

There are many development approaches, there always will be and always should be. Different tasks can have different characteristics that require different kinds of approaches. The challenge is in the appropriate selection and integration of these approaches.

0-8493-3135-8/99/$0.00+$.50

11.2 Controlled, Flexible Methodologies

> A *methodology* is a body of methods employed by a discipline.
>
> A *method* is a procedure for attaining something.
>
> *Method engineering* is the coordinated and systematic approach to establishing work methods.

Methodologies for information system (IS) development are always of a generic nature. They contain an idealized set of methods, techniques, and guidelines. In reality, methodologies are never followed literally, instead they are tuned to the situation at hand. Steps are sometimes omitted, added, or modified. Guidelines are often modified or ignored to fit special circumstances. Several kinds of factors can affect how a methodology is altered. These factors can include technology, development expertise, the application, and external factors. An example of those technologies that will require specialized treatment in a methodology include client/server architectures, groupware, workflow management, and multimedia.

To complicate things further, numerous methodologies exist for IS development, each with their own set of tools and techniques. As such, comparing and selecting a methodological approach from this methodology "jungle" is confusing and difficult. To facilitate this understanding, various comparison standards have been proposed for object-oriented methodologies, such as (Hutt, 1994). Some approaches attempt to harmonize several methodologies forming yet another methodology (Coleman et al., 1994). Other methodologies provide a choice of options, or *paths*, the user can choose depending on the circumstances. In short, an IS project has three basic choices for a methodology, as depicted in Figure 11.1.

Flexibility without control can hardly be considered a methodology. Rather, it is an absence of any systematic and coordinated approach to establishing work methods. For such an approach to be systematic and coordinated requires method engineering.

11.2.1 Method Engineering

In short, method engineering produces methodologies. For IS, a methodology is a body of methods employed to develop automated systems. A method, then, defines the steps to be carried out to automate a system, along with the techniques to be employed, the tools to be used, and the products to be delivered. To adapt a methodology to the needs of a particular project is called *situational method engineering*. For IS, situational method engineering designs, constructs, and adapts IS development methods.

As indicated in Figure 11.2, method engineering has various degrees of flexibility. These are as follows:

Use of rigid methodology — At one extreme the use of a rigid methodology permits virtually no flexibility. Such methodologies are based on a single development philosophy. They adopt fixed standards, procedures, and techniques. Project managers are typically not permitted to modify the methodology.

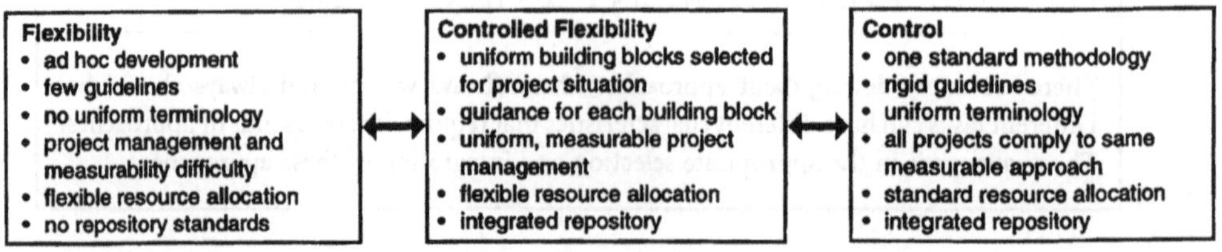

FIGURE 11.1 Adopting a methodological approach falls into three categories (Adapted from Harmsen et al. 1994. *Methods and Associated Tools for the Information Systems Life Cycle.* A.A. Verrijne-Stuart and T. William Olle, eds., pp. 169-194. Elsevier, Amsterdam. With permission.)

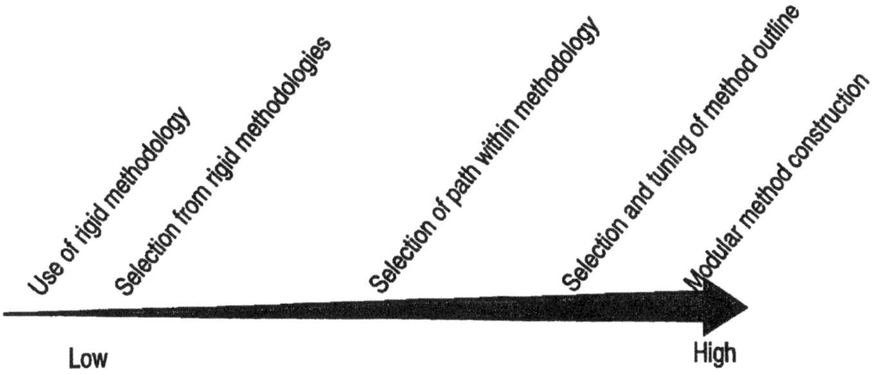

FIGURE 11.2 Degrees of flexibility for IS situational method engineering (Adapted from Harmsen et al. 1994. *Methods and Associated Tools for the Information Systems Life Cycle.* A.A. Verrijne-Stuart and T. William Olle, eds., pp. 169-194. Elsevier, Amsterdam. With permission.)

Selection from rigid methodologies — Instead of permitting only one rigid approach, this option allows each project to choose its methodology from one of several rigid methodologies. In this way, it is possible to choose one approach that might suit the project better than another. However, this is a bit like buying a suit without alteration. Here, you make the best of what is available, because it is unlikely that the chosen methodology will fit the project perfectly. Furthermore, each methodology involves additional purchase and training costs.

Selection of paths within methodology — Many methodologies permit a greater degree of flexibility by providing a choice of pre-defined paths within the methodology. A common selection is to provide *traditional* and *rapid* application development paths. Some methodologies now include paths that support development aspects, such as package selection, pilot projects, client/server, real-time, knowledge-based systems, and object orientation. A common disadvantage, however, is that it may not be possible to combine some options. For instance, real-time, knowledge-based projects may not be supported.

Selection and tuning of a method outline — This option permits each project not only to select methods from different approaches, but to tune a selected method to the needs of the project. Typically, this involves selecting a global method process model and data model. These models, then, are further refined and adapted by the project. This option is best supported by an automated tool, such as that illustrated in Figures 11.3 and 11.4.

Modular method construction — One of the most flexible options is to generate a methodology for a given project from pre-defined building blocks. Each building block is a method fragment that is stored in a method base. Using rules, these building blocks are assembled based on a project's profile. The result is an effective, efficient, complete, and consistent methodology for the project. An automated tool for this option is a requirement. Here, a project's methodology can be generated automatically, and can be refined and adapted further by the project manager. Such an option is illustrated in Figure 11.5.

11.3 The Need for a Foundation

System development should not use an approach that models reality; instead, it should use an approach that models the way *people* understand and process reality. Such an emphasis is placed on people, because people are the ones who build systems. In other words, systems should be constructed from the minds of people to serve people. What better way to begin specifying system requirements, than by documenting the way people think about the system? A basic foundation, illustrated in Figure 11.6, consists of those ideas that are fundamental to human thinking. Such ideas can be used to specify the structure and behavior of the world around us (Martin, 1995).

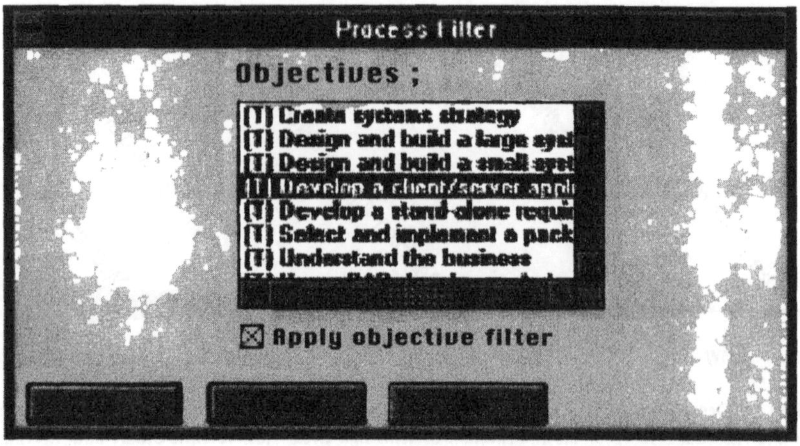

FIGURE 11.3 A screen that offers a choice of project objectives. Based on these objectives, this tool can generate an appropriate methodology (Architect, James Martin & Co.).

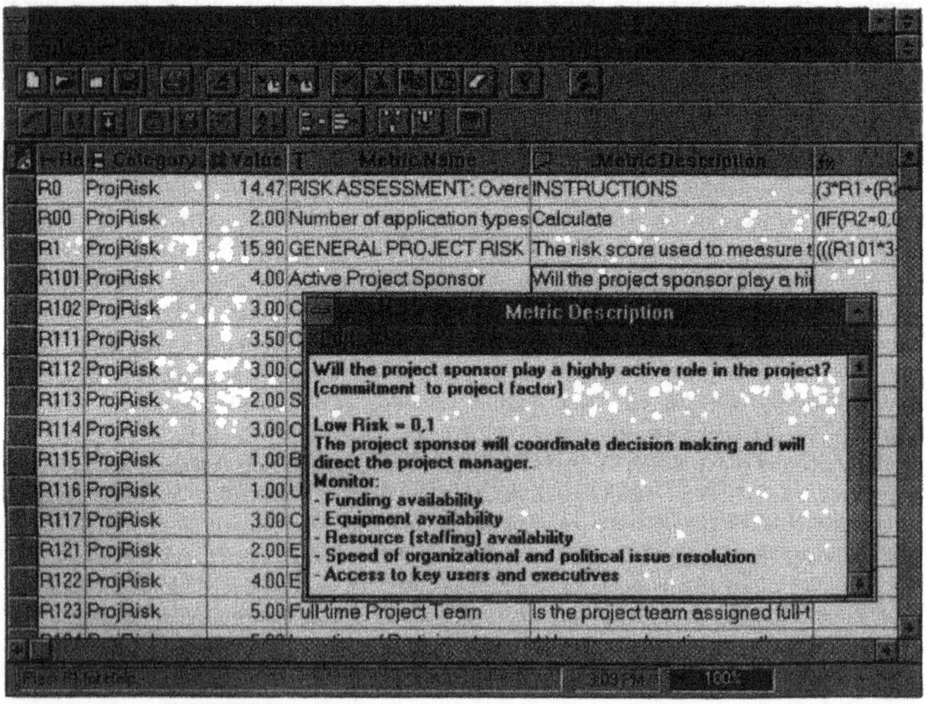

FIGURE 11.4 A screen that maintains and reports on various project metrics, such as duration and risk (Architect, James Martin & Co.).

Furthermore, these basic ideas can be employed to construct new concepts. In other words, the elements in the basic foundation provide building blocks for creating more complex constructs. An extended foundation, illustrated in Figure 11.7, has five ideas contructed from the basic foundation level.

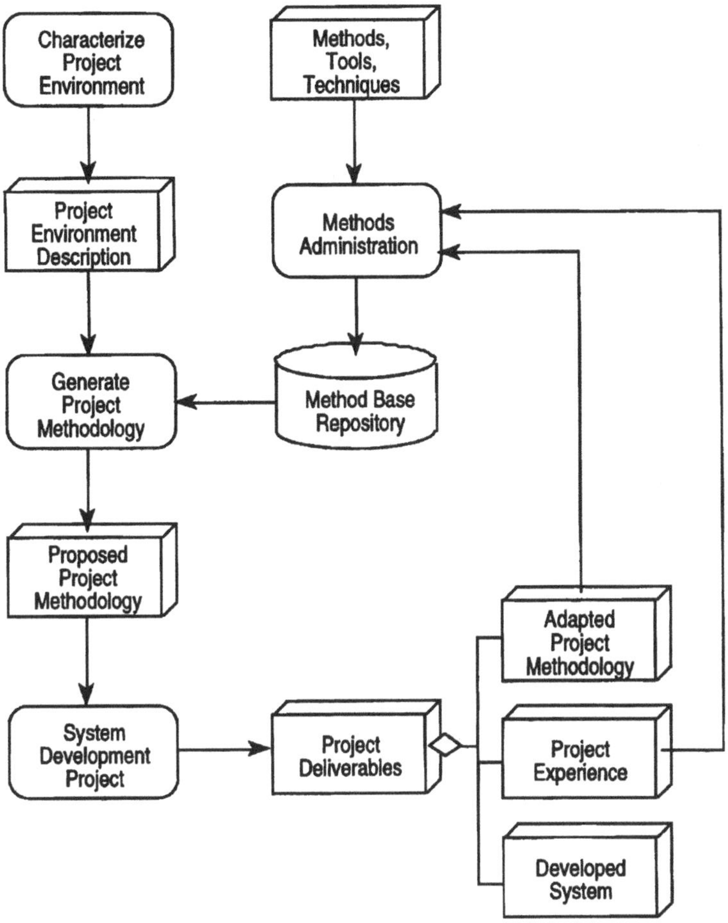

FIGURE 11.5 An object-flow diagram specifying the process of modular method construction.

However, others can be added as they are conceived. You might already have some of your own that you wish to add now. Even more can be added in the future, permitting us to evolve beyond an OO context.

We have many ways of describing our world. Some descriptions are vague and informal, others are precise and unambiguous. If we wish to build systems that perform correctly and consistently, we will want to be clear, concise, and unambiguous in our specifications. Such specifications are made possible only by employing a formally based foundation. These representations can be in graphic or textual form. They can be representations that specify the structure and behavior of a system from a conceptual standpoint or be implementational. They can be implementation expressed as programming languages, database definition languages (DDL), and data manipulation languages (DML). Such implementations could also be extended to include other automated approaches such as control units, robotics, and computer chips.

As illustrated in Figure 11.8, this level is called the *application level* because it is where we make use of our foundation through specification or implementation.

Formally constructing and using this foundation helps us to communicate and to understand our world. Furthermore, since both our specification and implementation representations can be based on the same foundation, we should be able to *generate* one from the other. As Figure 11.9 illustrates, if our conceptual world is represented in terms of our formal foundation, we should be able to use the same foundation to

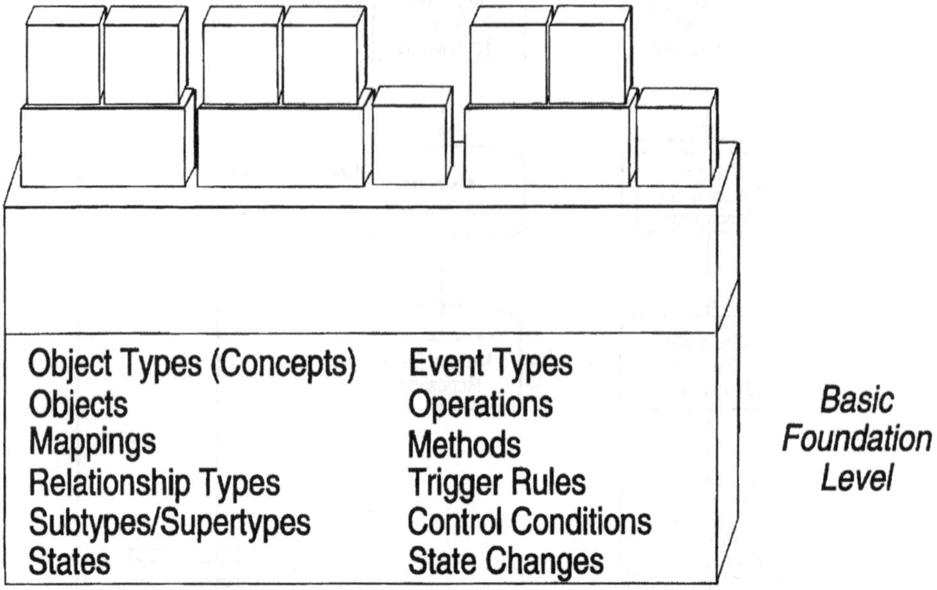

FIGURE 11.6 The basic level of a foundation consists of ideas that are fundamental to thinking about structure and behavior.

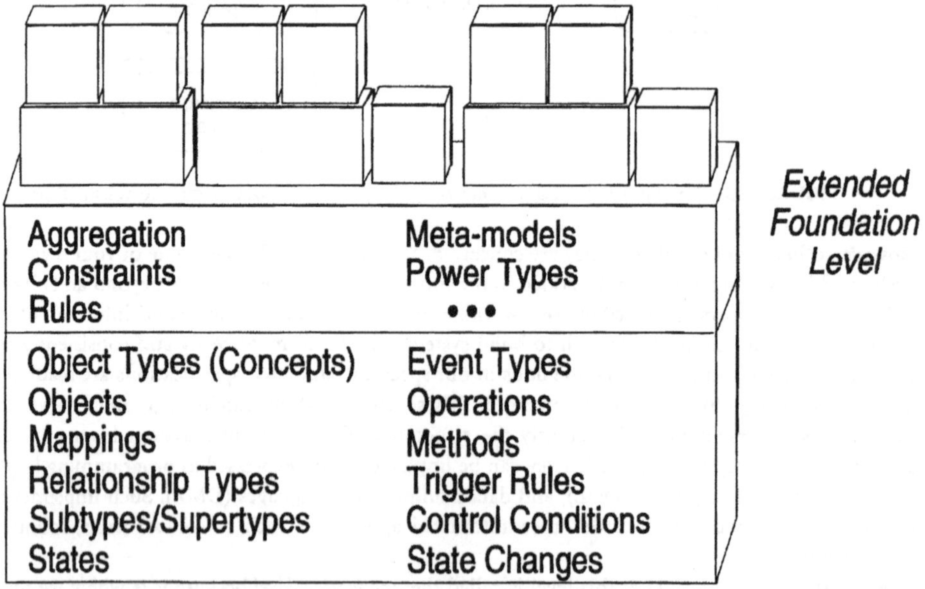

FIGURE 11.7 An extended level of the foundation can be constructed from the building blocks of the basic foundation level.

create an implementation. Some so-called *instant* OO-CASE tools already employ this technique by automatically generating a large portion of the program code *directly* from analysis specifications and design templates. One way to develop such a formal foundation is presented in the next chapter.

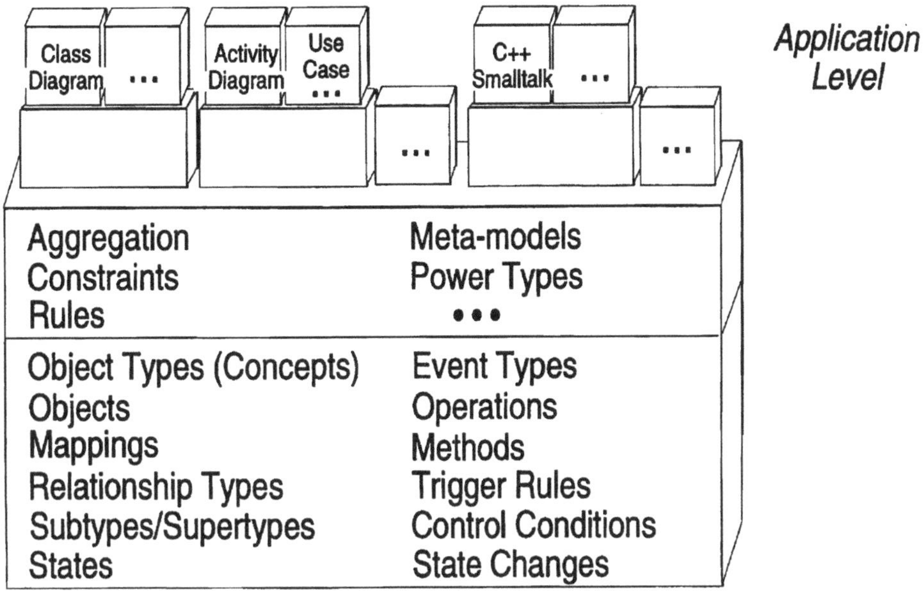

FIGURE 11.8 The application level can be clear, concise, and unambiguous if it is expressed using a formal foundation.

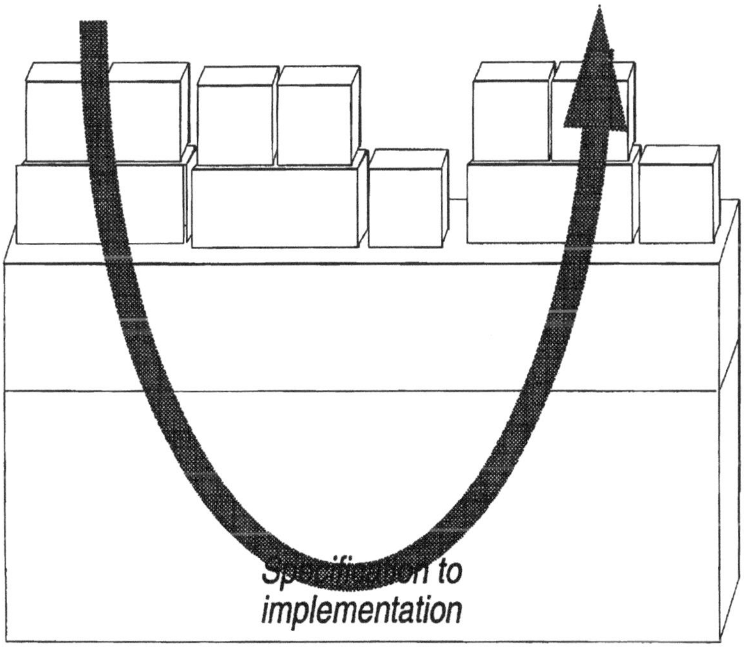

FIGURE 11.9 Clear, concise, and unambiguous analysis specification can generate clear, concise, and unambiguous implementations.

11.4 Notation and Standards

As discussed above, a formal foundation for OO development is necessary for system specification. Without formal underlying semantics, a syntax or notation that expresses a system's specification falls short of expectations. To put it more simply, drawing a diagram without fully understanding its symbols presents problems for the system implementor.

Assuming that there is a formal foundation in place, the next issue is *which* symbols should be used. There are dozens of notations that have been suggested to the industry (Hutt, 1994), but which one is the "right" one? The Martin/Odell approach does not dictate the usage of any particular notation. Instead, it recommends that developers choose a notation that provides the best communication vehicle for the project at hand. However, as a default notation, the Martin/Odell approach uses the OMG standard known as the Unified Modeling Langauge (UML).

References

Brinkkember, S., Lyytinen, K. and Welke, R. J. 1996. *Methods Engineering: Principles of Method Construction and Tool Support.* Chapman and Hall, London.

Coleman, D., Arnold, P., Bodoff, S., Dollin, C., Gilchrist, H., Hayes, F. and Jeremaes, P. 1994. *Object-Oriented Development: The Fusion Method.* Prentice-Hall, Englewood Cliffs, NJ.

Harmsen, F., Brinkkember, S. and Oei, H. 1994. Situational method engineering for information system project approaches, *Methods and Associated Tools for the Information Systems Life Cycle,* A. A. Verrijn-Stuart and T. William Olle, eds., pp. 169-194. Elsevier, Amsterdam.

Hutt, A. T. F., ed. 1994. *Object-Oriented Analysis and Design: Comparison of Methods.* Wiley-QED, New York.

Martin, J. and Odell, J. J. 1995. *Object-Oriented Methods: A Foundation.* Prentice-Hall, Englewood Cliffs, NJ.

Martin, J. and Odell, J. J. 1996. *Object-Oriented Methods: Pragmatic Considerations.* Prentice-Hall, Englewood Cliffs, NJ.

12

Martin/Odell Approach: A Formalization for OO

James Odell

Guus Ramackers

Oracle, UK

12.1 Introduction

While there are many books on OO analysis, few formalize their underlying notions. For most practitioners, this is not a problem. However, building meta-CASE tools, defining repository structures, and comparing OO notations requires an exacting approach. Everything must be clear and unambiguous. One way to ensure clear ideas is through mathematical formalism. This chapter is an initial attempt to produce such a formalism for those notions used to represent the results of OO analysis. Furthermore, it deals with the structural rather than the behavioral notions of objects. (That is, it discusses the "universe of objects" rather than the character of objects as they may change over time.) The basic approach of this chapter is that it presents a basic ontology for expressing our concepts and their relationships using set theory and functions. In short, it defines the essential foundation for metamodeling or repository-building activities.

12.2 Concepts

Due to its conceptual nature, a fundamental notion in analysis is the term *concept*.

> A *concept* is an idea or notion that we apply to classify those things around us.

0-8493-3135-8/99/$0.00+$.50

As Susan Langer puts it, "we are consciously, deliberately abstracting the form from all the things which have it. Such an abstracted form is called a concept" Langer, 1967. For instance, if we list all those things to which the concept "being a mortal" applies, we would form the set of all mortals. Concepts, then, have two important aspects — *intension* and *extension* (Whitehead, 1910; Russell, 1938).

> The *intension* of a concept is its meaning, or its complete definition.
>
> The *extension* of a concept is the collection, or *set*, of things to which the concept applies.

For example, the intension of the concept `Mortal` could be stated as "anything that dies." The extension of the concept `Mortal`, then, would be the collection, or *set*,* of things to which the definition applies. This example could also be expressed in the following manner:

$$\forall x : (x \texttt{ must die}) \Rightarrow (x \in \texttt{Mortal}).$$

This expression says that for any x, if x must die, then x is a member of the set of `Mortal` objects. For example, if "Socrates must die" is true, then Socrates belongs to the set of `Mortal` objects. The set of `Mortal` objects, therefore, is not a fixed collection. It is defined by a propositional form, not by its specific members. In short, if we understand the intension, we are acquainted with the extension, even if we have never seen an individual that belongs to it. (For example, we may possess the concept of `Unicorn` without ever seeing an instance of one.) However, the converse is not necessarily true. If we understand the extension, we do not necessarily know the intension. For example, a set D might contain my pencil, an eraser, and a pad of paper. Here, the intension of D is not clear. Yet, if I define the concept D as all those things currently placed on my office desk, we understand the extension.

As demonstrated above, intensions determine whether or not a given object is a member of an extension. As such, they can be readily expressed as elementary propositions. Every elementary proposition has a truth-value, which is either true or false. In real life, we are not always able to fully formalize our intensions in predicate logic. In these kinds of situations, automated systems would require human intervention to assert whether or not a given object is a `Person`. For those kinds of situations where the intension can be formalized, automating a concept's definition in program code is possible. In contrast, formalizing a concept's extension is much easier. Here, a set-theoretic approach can be used.

In this chapter, concept(C) will refer to the concept of C. The intension of C will be expressed as int(C), and the extension as ext(C). For example, the intension of the concept of `Mortal` could be represented as

$$\texttt{int(Mortal)} = \forall x\text{: } (x \text{ must die}).$$

The extension of the concept of `Mortal` could be represented as

$$\texttt{ext(Mortal)} = \{\text{Socrates, Plato}\}.$$

12.3 Classification Relations

To say that an object o is *classified* as a concept C, then, means that both:

- The intension of C is "true" for the object o
- The object o is a *member* of the extension of C

* Some authors prefer the word *class* instead of *set*. Due to the overloaded usage of the word class, this chapter will use set, instead.

This chapter will represent the *classification* relation with the symbol "∈".* So that $o \in C$ means that the concept *C* *applies* to the thing *o*. Inversely, the thing *o* is an *instance* of the concept *C*.

As discussed above, each concept has two aspects. When considering a concept "in extension," the relation ∈ can also be used to indicate membership when the concept is qualified as such. For example, to express that Socrates is a member of the `Mortal` set could be represented as

Socrates ∈ ext(`Mortal`).

Expressing a classification relation from an intensional perspective, a similar technique can be used. Since this chapter will deal primarily with the extensional nature of concepts, the "ext" qualifier will be removed for ease of readability from this point on. Therefore, an alternate way to represent Socrates ∈ ext(`Mortal`) is

Socrates ∈ `Mortal`.

Finally, to bring the terminology of this chapter in line with accepted usage by the OMG, ANSI, and ISO, a few words must be changed. The term *concept* must be changed to *type*, and the word *thing* to *object*. These terms are expressed formally:

> *Object* is defined as the first element (or left side) of the classification relation.
>
> *Type* is defined as the last element (or right side) of the classification relation.

In other words, an object is defined as an instance of a type. A type is defined as a concept where the membership of the type is a set based on the intension of the type. The terms *instance* and *object*, then, can be used synonymously.

12.3.1 Design Considerations

As defined above, types are free from implementation considerations. Implementing a type could require multiple OO *classes*, or non-OO constructions such as relational tables or business rules. Furthermore, a class may implement more than one type. Since implementations of types are not one for one with classes, types and classes are not the same. *Classes*, then, are defined as OO implementations of concepts, or types.

While OMG, ANSI, and ISO differentiate between type and class as defined above, the term object is used for both conceptual and implementation instances. In analysis, the term object is defined as an instance of a type. In design, object is defined as an instance of a class.

However, the properties of an object will differ between analysis and design usages. For example, in OODB design every object must have a permanent, unique object identifier, or *OID*. Analysis, however, requires no such property. In analysis, permanent unique identity is required only when our perception of the real world requires it. For example, car manufacturers require every vehicle to have a permanent unique vehicle identifier. However, these same manufacturers will *not* require a permanent unique identity for each of its nuts and bolts. In other words, while each nut and bolt is unique, identifiers are not required. In contrast, OO programmers always require a permanent unique identity because OO languages require it.

Similarly, the classification relation requires no specific implementation. It only asserts that a given object is an instance of a given type. To support the classification relation in an OO programming language, every object usually contains a pointer or reference to the class that constructed it.

---

* In this paragraph, ∈ implies both intension and extension. Since ∈ is often thought of solely in terms of set membership, some use the ! symbol as a more general representation. In this situation, *o* ! *C* would mean that the concept *C* applies to the value *o*, implying both intension and extension.

12.4 Generalization/Specialization Relations

> Any type *A*, each of whose objects is also an instance of a given type *S*, is called a specialization (or *subtype*) of *S* and is written as $A \subset S$. *S* is also called the generalization (or *supertype*) of *A*.

As with the classification relation the specialization relation can also be qualified in extensional and intensional terms. For example,

ext(Human) ⊂ ext(Mortal), or simply, Human ⊂ Mortal

means that every member of the Human set is also a member of the Mortal set. In contrast,

int(Human) ⊂ int(Mortal)

means the definition of Human must contain the definition of Mortal. When viewed in extension, the left side of the ⊂ involves fewer than the right, because the left side (by definition) is a subset. When viewed in intension, the left side of the ⊂ involves more than the right, because the definition of the left must also include the definition of the right. In short, when going down a generalization hierarchy, the extension gets smaller while the intension gets bigger. For example, the intension of being Human must involve being Mortal, whereas the intension of being Mortal does *not* involve being Human. In this way, ⊂ really means *inclusion*, that is, the concept of Human is *included in* the concept of Mortal.* Inclusion, therefore, refers to both extension and intension. As with the classification relation, extension and intension can be addressed separately by qualification (as indicated in the examples above).

12.4.1 Design Considerations

With generalization/specialization, the OO analyst would tend to read the expression, Employee ⊂ Human, as "every Employee is also a Human" or that "Employee is a subtype of Human." In other words, being in the Employee set implies being in the Human set, or being an Employee also involves what it takes to be a Human. In contrast, an OO programmer would instead say something like "Employees *inherit* the structure and behavior of Humans." Inheritance, however, is one, of several, *implementations* of generalization. (For other implementations of generalization, see Chapter 12 in Martin/Odell, 1996.) The analyst, who is supposed to think implementation-free, only knows that whatever *applies* to Humans also *applies* to Employees. *How* the properties of a type get applied to its subtypes is an implementation problem, not a conceptual one. In short, generalization expresses *what* and inheritance expresses *how*.

12.5 Relations in General

The *Cartesian product* $S \times T$ of two sets *S* and *T* is the set of all ordered pairs (a,b) with $a \in S$ and $b \in T$.**

> A *relation* $\mathfrak{R}$ on sets *S* and *T* is a subset of the Cartesian product $S \times T$. $\mathfrak{R}$ is said to hold for the ordered pair (a,b) and can be written in the form $\mathfrak{R}(a,b)$.*** The instances of a Cartesian product of *n* sets is called an *n*-tuple.

---

* Since ⊂ is often thought of solely in terms of set membership, some use the < symbol as a more general representation. So that $B < C$ means that the concept *B* is *included* is the concept *C*, implying both intension and extension.

** The instances of a Cartesian product are called *tuples*.

*** A relation on multiple sets can be written $\mathfrak{R}(a,b,\ldots)$.

For example, an employment relation on sets `Person` and `Company` can be written `Employment Contract(Person, Company)` and have the following tuples:

Person	Company
Bob	NASA
Bob	IBM
Betty	IBM
Bernard	NEC
...	...

By definition, each tuple in a relation is an object, because it is an instance of the ordered pair for which the relation holds. In the above example, the tuple (Bob, NASA) is an object because it is an instance of the `Employment Contract` relation. In other words, it can be written, `(Bob, NASA)` ∈ `Employment Contract`, where `Employment Contract` holds for the ordered pair `(Person, Company)`. Furthermore, since the `Employment` relation has instances (albeit tuples), `Employment Contract` is a type, by definition.

Because each relation is also a type, its extension may be a set that participates in another Cartesian product, and, therefore, another relation. For example, every instance of an `Employment Contract` could be assigned to one or more offices for that person's employment (where each office may in turn have one or more employees). Here, such an office-assignment can be defined as a relation on the set of tuples defined by `Employment Contract(Person, Company)` and a set of `Office` objects. This can be written

```
Office Assignment((Employment Contract(Person, Company)), Office)
```

or abbreviated

```
Office Assignment(Employment Contract, Office)
```

and have the following tuples:

Person	Company	Office
(Bob	NASA)	#099
(Bob	IBM)	#123
(Betty	IBM)	#123
(Betty	IBM)	#224
(Bernard	NEC)	#345
...	...	...

The instances of `Office Assignment`, too, may have relationships with other sets. For example, each `Office Assignment` could have an effective date for the office assignment and be expressed as

```
Assignment Effectivity(Office Assignment((Employment Contract(
                        Person, Company)), Office), Date).
```

Any relation, then, can in turn define a set for other relations. In other words, for any relation $\mathfrak{R}$ on sets S and T, S and T can define collections of "simple" objects or "complex" (tuple) objects. Both are instances of sets and therefore may paired using the Cartesian product. A common term used by the OO community for relations is relationship types.

The term *relationship type* is synonymous with *relation.*

12.5.1 Design Considerations

Implementing relations, or relationship types, requires more thought. For example, if you are designing for a relational database, relations like `Employment Contract` would be implemented as a table with its own set of records. If you are designing an OO database, `Employment Contract` might not necessarily be implemented as a class. For instance, if the `Employment Contract` relation was *not* part of any order pair, most OO programmers would not implement the relation as a class. The main reason given for this is that such a class would "break" encapsulation. However, when a relation *is* part of an ordered pair, the relation would be implemented as a class. For example, if `Employment Contract` became a component of the `Office Assignment` relation, `Employment Contract` would become a class, because the `Office Assignment` relation requires instances to pair. In this case, the instances are a Cartesian product of the `Employment Contract` and `Office` classes. However, `Office Assignment` itself would not become a class unless it, too, furnished objects for another relation, such as `Assignment Effectivity`.

12.6 Functions

Thus far we have employed sets and relations as ways of expressing how we think about objects and their associations. In other words, we can formalize — as well as formally manipulate — objects and associations. Therefore, any mathematical function that can be defined on sets and objects may be used, such as union, intersect, difference, compare, and arithmetic operations. To introduce the notion of function, we can start where we left off — with relations.

With mathematics, we can use certain properties of relations to play particular roles (such as reflexive, symmetric, and transitive). In particular, one relational role is quite useful, the *right unique* relation.

> A relation $\mathfrak{R}$ is *right unique* when for all $x, y, z \in S$: if $\mathfrak{R}(x, y)$ and $\mathfrak{R}(x, z)$, then $y = z$.

This right unique relation provides us with a formal way of expressing the mappings of one set of objects to another. Another name for this mechanism is called the *function.*

> A *function* on a set X with values in Y is a *right unique relation* with support (or domain) in X and range in Y.

A function, then, is the set of all ordered pairs (x,y) of a relation $\mathfrak{R}$, with $x \in X$ and $y \in Y$, where there is a many-to-one correspondence between the members of X and the members of Y. In summary, functions are a special case of relation. Relations are useful when we wish to express associations as instances of pairings, or *tuples.* In contrast, when we are given an object of one set and wish to return, or "navigate" to, an associated object in another set, functions are useful.

12.6.1 Functions in Practice

Figure 12.1 depicts an association between two types: `Person` and `Company`. The line associating these two concepts represents the relation `Employment Contract`, which holds for the ordered pair (`Person`, `Company`). As discussed earlier, the instances of relationship types are called tuples. Therefore, any time a user wishes to create an employment relationship between a person and a company, an `Employment Contract` tuple may be created.

However, tuples are not sufficient for every application. Often, a user only knows of objects in one set and wishes to obtain objects in a related set. For example, relationally it could be true that Bob and

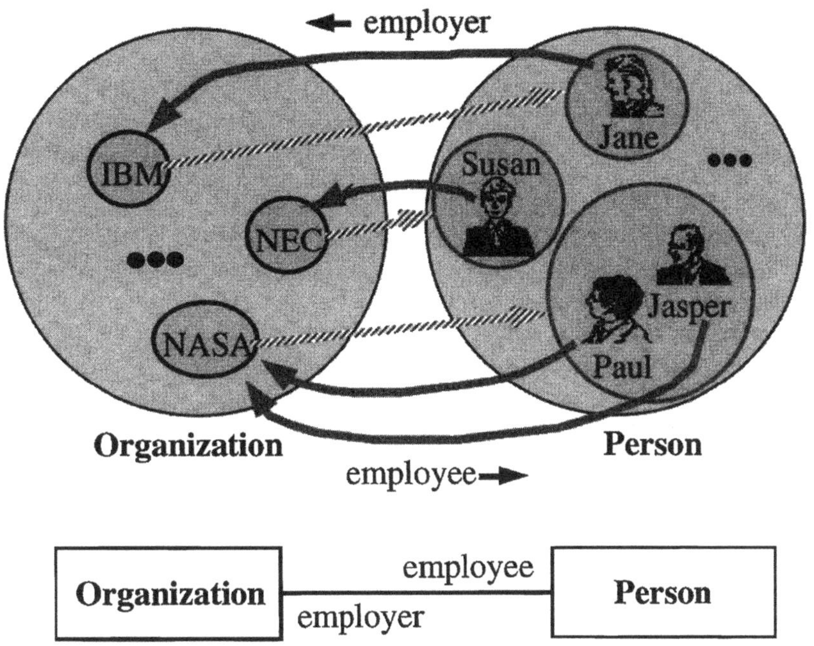

FIGURE 12.1 Association between two types: `Person` and `Company`.

NASA are related as a tuple of `Employment Contract`, so is `(Bob and IBM)`. In other words, `(Bob, NASA)` ∈ `Employment Contract`, and `(Bob, IBM)` ∈ `Employment Contract`. However, what if your application wanted to find out who employed Bob? In other words, you possessed an instance in the `Person` set and wish to determine which object it was related to in the `Company` set. A function (or right unique relation) is used to traverse the Cartesian product `Person` × `Company`, where the domain is `Person` and the range is `Company`. This function is called *employer*. This can be restated in functional terms as, `employer(Person)` = `Company`, yielding `employer`(Betty) = IBM.

This basic approach works fine with Betty but breaks down for Bob who is employed by two companies, NASA and IBM. If the function were evaluated for Bob, two instances would be returned. Since a function, by definition, may return only one instance, such results would be improper. Permitting improper functions can be useful but causes mathematical difficulties. However, multivalued results are highly useful in query operations. In order to preserve the purity of proper functions, yet support multivalued queries, a small adjustment must be made to our foundation. What we must do is permit a function to return multiple instances in the range, yet ensure that the function is proper. One way to achieve this is by using power sets.

> The *power set* of S is the set of all subsets of S, and is written as $\wp(S)$.

Therefore when mapping to a domain, map to the power set of the domain instead of mapping to just the set. A multivalued function assigns to every element x of a set X to a unique element y in the power set on Y. This is written $f\colon X \to \wp(Y)$, where f denotes the function and $\wp(Y)$ the range. It can be stated another way, $f(x) = y$ where $y \in \wp(Y)$. The employer function, above, can be restated as follows:

$$\texttt{employer: Person} \to \wp\,\texttt{(Company)}$$

12.6.2 Function Inverses vs. Reverses

In the example above, the employment association was traversed in one direction using the employer function. Evaluating the employee function in the opposite direction is another situation. For example, given a `Company` object, the employee function returns a single set of `Person` instances. In other words, employee: `Company` $\rightarrow \wp$ (`Person`) or, in its more general form, $f^r: Y \rightarrow \wp(X)$, where $f: X \rightarrow \wp(Y)$. This would be considered the reverse, or adjoint, of the employer function not the inverse.

The inverse function would, in contrast, take the result of the employer function and return the value that the employer function began with. For instance, `f(Bob) = {NASA, IBM}`. The inverse, f^{-1}, would begin with the set `{NASA, IBM}` in its domain and return Bob. Since the range of the inverse may also be multivalued, a more general form for this situation would be where the power type of the domain maps to the power type in the range, or

$$f^{-1}: \wp(Y) \rightarrow \wp(X).$$

In summary, to support a two-place relation in terms of function, a function is paired with another function — either its adjoint or inverse — depending on the user's requirements. The adjoint function provides a function that maps from the set in the range of the original function f; the inverse maps from the power set.

> For each two-place relation, there is an associated function and either its adjoint or inverse function.*

12.7 Attributes, Roles, and Invariants

12.7.1 Attributes and Roles

Most system developers will model functions as attributes or "role" names on relations. Attributes and role names, then, are presentation techniques for expressing a function. Some developers differentiate solely for graphic clarity, using roles for the "more important" functions and attributes for the less important functions. Such a technique reduces the graphic "noise" on a diagram. Some developers define attributes to be those functions that map to data types (for example, Integer, String, and Real Number); where all other kinds of functions are represented as role names on relations. Other developers expand on this to include complex data types such as Name, Address, Time, and Money. In any case, all are based on a deeper notion, the function.

12.7.2 Invariants

Invariants are Boolean functions over one or more object types and relations that must be true at all times. (Invariants are also known as constraints and rules.) For example, the invariant that a person must always have no more than one employer can be expressed as:

$$\forall p \in \texttt{Person}: |\,\texttt{employer}\ (p)\,| \leq 1.$$

In this way, the formalisms that have been presented thus far can be employed to constrain the object types and relations. It provides a richer semantic model that expresses business requirements more accurately. Traditional structural definitions alone cannot support this.

* The *n*-place relations have *n* associated functions and *n* reverse or inverse functions.

12.8 Conclusions

While there are many books on OO analysis, few formalize their underlying notions. For most practitioners, this is not a problem. However, building meta-CASE tools, defining repository structures, and comparing OO notations requires an exacting approach. Everything must be clear and unambiguous. This chapter is an initial attempt to produce such a formalism for those structural notions used to represent the results of OO analysis. It presents a basic ontology for expressing our concepts and their relationships using set theory and functions. In short, it defines the essential foundation for metamodeling or repository-building activities.

References

Gray, P. M. D. 1984. *Logic, Algebra, and Databases.* John Wiley & Sons, New York.

Langer, S. K. 1967. *An Introduction to Symbolic Logic,* (3rd edition). Dover Publications, New York.

Martin, J. and Odell, J. J. 1996. *Object-Oriented Methods: A Foundation.* Prentice-Hall, Englewood Cliffs, NJ.

Martin, J. and Odell, J. J. 1996. *Object-Oriented Methods: Pragmatic Considerations.* Prentice-Hall, Englewood Cliffs, NJ.

Ramackers, G. 1994. *Integrated Object Modeling.* Thesis Publishers, Amsterdam.

Russell, B. 1938. *Principles of Mathematics.* Norton, New York.

Whitehead, A. N. and Russell, B. 1910. *Principia Mathematica.* Cambridge University Press, Cambridge.

13

System Envisioning: An Essential Step in Building Software Systems

Doug McDavid
IBM

Ralph Hodgson
IBM

13.1 Introduction

What is system envisioning? There are many dimensions to this question, and these will be explored in some detail in this chapter. The "elevator answer" (one that might be expressed during a short elevator ride) is: system envisioning is a creative process for imagining and expressing viable system alternatives through a process of understanding problem situations, articulating desired futures, and then nominating specific system structures and technologies. In other words, system envisioning is about creating and communicating a vision of a system that will appropriately address a business need. System development is speculative. Visions and needs can become lost, distorted, and modified as the work of implementing a system proceeds through handovers in the process. It is important that the understanding of what is needed survives the excitement of its discovery and formulation. This understanding must be accurately

0-8493-3135-8/99/$0.00+$.50

communicated to a number of individuals so that it becomes concrete in the systems we end up inhabiting. The use of the word "inhabit" is intentional. Information systems are environments in which organizations and people live. When we create a new system we change an organizational ecosystem. This effort is speculative, because knowing the effect of the new system is a matter of anticipating and envisioning.

Software-based information systems are conceived out of an understanding and conceptualizing of a problem space. System envisioning is about how we create possibilities for what the software system might and should do. How do these possibilities change from abstract thought to system requirements, functional specifications, and system design decisions? What considerations affect the trade offs and the interrelationships between requirements, specification, and design? How are these interrelationships affected by the political, social, and cultural issues within the organization?

The goal of system envisioning is to solve business problems by:

- Formulating relevant problem analogies to achieve a shared understanding of domain concepts that govern work processes of enterprises
- Utilizing key systems thinking ideas to manipulate systematic architectures of businesses
- Leveraging paradigms, such as negotiation, planning, scheduling, and resource management, which represent the essential nature of businesses
- Synthesizing the systems concepts of intended software systems in conceptual architectures
- Realizing opportunities for reuse of conceptual and technical assets at various levels of scale and granularity

System envisioning provides the bridge between problem/situation understanding and the formulation of total system solutions, including software, hardware, communications, people, and information. The general approach to system envisioning involves the following elements:

- Matching business situations to system concepts that comply with viable business architectures
- Shifting from building software to evolving enactable models of business worlds
- Working with the entire picture of the enterprise in its market ecology
- Dealing with the human system in concert with the software system as part of the overall business system
- Creating systems as interacting and evolving components (i.e., objects, at various levels of detail and complexity).

Object-orientation has proven to be an important underpinning to the discipline of system envisioning. Object-orientation provides a way of thinking about and implementing powerful abstractions with rich behaviors. What software objects end up being and doing is governed by early and consistent attention to systems thinking and system envisioning.

13.2 OOPSLA Workshops on System Envisioning

In October of 1996 a series of OOPSLA workshops was launched to explore the subject of system envisioning. A number of experienced object-oriented developers attended. After attending each submitted a position paper on their view of system envisioning.

The participants in the workshop included:

Bruce Anderson	Ralph Hodgson	Petri Pulli
Marilyn Bates	Michael Karchov	Jack Ring
Tom Bridge	Deborah Leishman	Kalev Ruberg
Alistair Cockburn	Charles Matthews	Jim Salmons
Robert Coyne	Doug McDavid	Mark Simos
Martine Devos	Branko Peteh	

The OOPSLA workshop attempted to identify motivational interests and to share experiences on how system envisioning has happened and can happen in system development projects including experiences related to the effectiveness of tools used within the specification and development process. It allowed participants to share stories on the evolution of business and software systems by:

- Re-conceptualizing the possibilities of a software system
- Identifying interventions and techniques that are important for imagining and for sharing the possibilities of moving from a current, or "as-is" system toward a vision or "wanna-be" system via some realizable "could-be" or "to-be" system transitions
- Sharing ideas and experiences on the role of metaphors and analogies in system conceptualization
- Beginning a dialog on the relationships between systems thinking and object thinking
- Defining what system envisioning is.

The workshop proceeded by addressing the following set of questions:

- Why envisioning is important?
- What happens if you do not do it?
- What happens when you are doing it?
- What situations do we know where it has been done?
- What situations do we know where it did not get done?
- What stops it from happening?
- Who needs to be involved in doing it?
- What do the results of envisioning look like?
- How do we, as individuals, get better at envisioning?
- How do we best communicate and share our visions?

This chapter is based on the position papers of the participants in the OOPSLA '96 workshop. It weaves together many of the ideas from a diverse set of viewpoints. Quotes and paraphrases from the various participants in the workshop are noted with the last name of the participant in parentheses.

13.3 System Envisioning and Systems Thinking

System envisioning grows out of the larger discipline of general systems theory, which attempts to deal with systemic phenomena in a holistic rather than a reductionistic manner. System envisioning is based on recognition that information systems are not built in isolation, but rather serve human activity systems — business organizations or enterprises. It is necessary to understand the underlying human activity system — its purpose, its goals, its dynamics, and its context — in order to build effective information systems to serve it.

Systems thinking is a mindset that understands the role of software-based information systems in the context of the purpose and functionality of the organization. It seeks to understand the role of the organization in its larger environment, or marketplace, and it provides a means to assess the impact of information systems development on the enterprise as a whole. The goal of this systemic approach is to assure that the right things are being done on behalf of the business organization. Most information system development methods stress issues of "how to do things right" or how to engineer software systems in the most effective and efficient manner. Systems thinking seeks to raise and answer such questions as:

- What are the goals of the business organization?
- What is its role in some larger enterprise?
- What is its strategic direction?
- What is its marketplace posture?
- What is its level of maturity?
- What business decisions are being made?
- What business problems need to be addressed?

- How will this project affect the working lives of its users when it is complete?
- How will it contribute to the health of the organization as a whole?
- What are upstream and downstream functions that interact with the system to be built?
- What is the existing automation situation of this business?
- What are its existing and proposed technology standards?

This understanding derives from a number of principles of general systems theory, as well as various templates from research and experience. General systems theory recognizes "the existence at certain levels of complexity of properties which are emergent at that level, and which cannot be reduced in explanation to lower levels." This "systems paradigm is concerned with wholes and their properties" (Checkland, 1984). In particular, the concept of soft systems thinking is critical to avoid the trap of treating human systems as equivalent to more deterministic mechanical systems. "'Hard' systems thinking is goal-directed, in the sense that a particular study begins with the definition of the desirable goal to be achieved" (emphasis added). The essence of hard systems is design engineering of a well-known solution to a well-understood problem, where the effort is to choose the best among several alternative approaches. By contrast, soft systems are "management problems … in social systems where the goals are often obscure." The fact is that construction of an information system is an exercise in experimental sociology, modifying the behavior of a business organization. This is not to be entered into lightly, but rather with the best possible conceptual tools that will help understand the current situation, and the expected outcomes of various alternative system architectures and implementations. Thinking systemically helps to avoid solutions that optimize one part of the business at the expense of others. A solution that fixes a bottleneck in one part of the business may actually uncover or exacerbate a bottleneck elsewhere.

13.4 The Mindset of System Envisioning

The activity of envisioning systems, of all sizes and complexity, involves a particular mindset. Aspects of this mindset include:

- Anticipation — seeing the future now, story-telling about future scenarios, imagineering
- Discovery — surfacing of assumptions, deep understanding of need, analogical reasoning
- Creation — construction of shared meaning, invention
- Belief — embracing possibility, suspension of disbelief, detachment from current logic; leap of faith
- Holistic thinking — living in the problem space; seeing the whole system as stimulus/response mechanism
- Dialoguing — suspension of assumptions, tension of opposites, generative listening, disposition to inquiry, ladder of inference
- Acting with conviction — making and keeping to commitments, having the courage to break down barriers, staying with the vision, evangelizing

A program of systematic domain engineering process creates a "cognitive shift" that enables software engineers to view the systems they create and their relationship to the surrounding organizational context in new ways. A major qualitative result is an enhanced capacity to envision new system capabilities, both in terms of innovative features and feature combinations, and in terms of new application contexts for domain functionality. Along with systems thinking and object thinking, domain thinking should be considered as a valuable technique to explore for systematic envisioning (Simos).

13.5 Dynamic Tensions within System Envisioning

The study of system envisioning has uncovered areas of intrinsic dynamic tension for this approach. Natural areas of dynamic tension include the inspired individual envisioner vs. group collaboration, a fresh approach vs. experience, and creativity vs. legacy coexistence.

13.5.1 Inspired Individual Envisioner vs. Group Collaboration

Successful envisioning requires pulling all the spatial and temporal constructs together in a "sketch" of the final system. This typically occurs through one person who, after "living the problem" (requirements gathering), conjures the solution from a personally known solution space (Ruberg).

On the other hand, there is a view that system envisioning is inherently a group, a social (dialectic) process whose outcomes are fundamentally dependent on the quality of the communication and collaboration involved. Even if it were possible for one or two individuals in isolation to brilliantly and comprehensively create and model a vision for a system solution, they are still required to convey their vision — communicate, negotiate, influence, persuade — a large number of stakeholders of diverse perspectives and interests. For the vision to become compelling and useful, that is, accepted and acted on, it must be adopted by a situated community of project participants such that they can each "make it their own" (Coyne).

Envisioning creates a vision, first in the mind of the originator, then, through appropriate communication, in the minds of associates. Having the vision is not enough, it must be shared, nurtured, and allowed to become concrete. Through evangelizing, the vision becomes known and shaped by others. Participation brings endorsement, but none of this will matter if we have not been equally creative in finding the path to implementation and there is enough caring to carry it out.

The ability to communicate a vision is controlled by:

- The degree to which a shared ontology exists between transmitter and receiver
- The learning style of the receiver
- The receptivity of the receiver to both the "facts" of the vision and the "implications" of the vision
- Whether the symbols and notations used in a modeling medium are portable or translatable to a more concrete development medium (Ring)

13.5.2 Fresh Approach vs. Experience

For the envisioner, the ability to detach from the logic of the current situation and to see the possibility of a future world is a critical skill. The envisioner looks at a problem from different perspectives and makes connections between seemingly dissimilar domains. Such an "aha" experience can unconceal the characteristic and governing behavior (paradigms) of the world in which a system is to live (Hodgson). Often envisioning is done by seasoned practitioners who have a portfolio of past systems experience to draw on and are able to communicate this through the use of stories, metaphors, analogies, etc. This envisioning relies on understanding the current problems of the organization in question, formulating those problems so as to be clearly understood by all involved, and then envisioning "possible" solutions (Leishman).

13.5.3 Creativity vs. Legacy Coexistence

Systems being developed today will be deployed tomorrow, and those that are to be deployed the day after tomorrow are being envisioned today so that they can be developed tomorrow. If new systems that we build could be independent from their old (or current) counterparts things would be rather simple. One of the biggest challenges is incorporating existing systems (with all their shortcomings and compromises) into new systems. The challenge lies in the desire to satisfy virtually opposite requirements like people would like new systems to correct all the shortcomings and imperfections of the old systems, but at the same time they would like new systems to be able to just be like the old systems they are supposed to replace. Such contradictory requirements occur quite naturally out of human resistance to change, and they will likely always exist. System envisioning therefore has an important role to try to consolidate such requirements (Peteh).

13.6 Techniques for System Envisioning

There are a number of techniques that have been used successfully in the practice of system envisioning. The following is a summary of a number of these techniques.

13.6.1 Objectifying the Stuff of the Domain

By objectifying the things of interest to the business, we put ourselves squarely in the business problem space. System envisioning frameworks are based on a flexible metamodel which objectifies the building blocks of business people's conceptual models. This metamodel includes (but is not limited to) classes which allow first class expression of business engineering concepts: Business to Process, Goal, Organization, Person, Role, Activity, Task, Actor. Organizations are responsible for Goals. Business Processes fulfill Goals. Organizations own and share with other organizations the processes which address their goals. Organizations may be composed of organizations and relate to each other through shared participation of processes. Persons are Actors of Roles. Staff roles relate persons to organizations. Organizations authorize persons to act of their behalf in the various roles defined by the organization. Business processes do not own consumable resources to achieve their goals. Rather, processes establish collaborations among roles which have the responsibility to perform various Activities. Persons acting in a role are the consumable resources which fuel the ability of an organization to meet its goals. To accomplish an activity, a person performs the component Tasks which make up the activity (Salmons).

13.6.2 Conceptual Architecture

The heart of system envisioning is a conceptual architecture that depicts the system concepts and design objectives. Its aim is to clarify the nature of and intention of the to-be software system. This conceptual architecture needs to be grounded in a model of the enterprise to be served by the software system. There are several useful templates for such human system models, including Miller's living systems model, Beer's viable systems model, Koestler's holonic model, Porter's value chain model, and marketing models such as strategic positioning, customer acquisition, retention strategy. It is also useful to adopt a view of information systems as nervous systems, with reference to Minsky's Society of Mind, Newell's Unified Theories of Cognition, and Trehub's Cognitive Brain.

The need for a conceptual architecture stems from recognition that building an enterprise-class system involves a deep intervention into the social and cognitive fabric of a living system. This is a complex undertaking, and success depends on understanding the nature of the work and the nature of the patient.

System envisioners, equipped with patterns of general systems thinking (living systems, cognitive structures, business strategic patterns, etc.) and knowledge of existing information systems mechanisms (GIS, telephony, brokerage, etc.) can quickly form a preliminary conceptual architecture. This captures the imagination of business people, and it demonstrates that we understand and can deliver an integrated solution that is tailored to their needs and an effective intervention in the living human system that is their business (McDavid).

13.6.3 Pattern Languages

The pattern work of Christopher Alexander, a controversial thinker in the field of architecture and planning for human use of space, has inspired similar thoughts in the field of information systems. Alexander proposes a language that enables envisioning in an inclusive fashion. You do not need to be a professional architect to engage in this kind of discourse. The producer and consumer can jointly discuss what is being proposed. Sketches can be drawn to validate understanding.

There has been significant work on object design patterns, which succeeds as an enabler and allows system architects and designers to engage in a dialog. However, this is implementation-level discussion, and by discussing the Factory pattern with a bank manager you are not going to succeed in facilitating his vision of the thing being proposed for construction.

Object-orientation brings techniques and artifacts that facilitate a degree of common understanding and a form of envisioning. Walkthroughs of an OMT-type object model can help users gain deeper awareness and insights into the system being proposed for development. Building object interaction diagrams in an anthropomorphic fashion has proven very effective at achieving an understanding of requirements. Also, UI prototyping can be an effective means of validating this understanding. However, these techniques do not achieve the same level of common understanding as Alexander's work does. What is needed is a repeatable and executable means of envisioning. Key to this is the development of a shared language which spans both technical implementers and non-technical consumers. We need a pattern language for doing domain analysis (Bridge).

13.6.4 Stories

Stories and metaphors are fundamental thinking blocks. Use cases are part of a technology of stories. They took the OO world by storm for several reasons, one of which was that they tell a story about the life of a user. Other forms of story technology include visualization in sports training and courses on building a future for yourself which have common exercises of picturing a situation and goals. Goal-based use cases provide a very specific form of story. They start from a behavioral goal of one person with respect to the system under design, and then they outline how the person and system interact to achieve or abandon the goal. The use case outlines a concrete set of behaviors, providing many of the details of a story, from which a reader can build an image of the system of use. This allows the readers to put themselves in the place of using the system and critiquing it. The use case also provides an outline of the possible failure and alternative behaviors at even the highest level of description. It therefore gives not just a story, but it gives a configurable set of stories (Cockburn).

13.6.5 Metaphors

The system envisioning method specifically addresses the influence of metaphor in the design process for the domain. System envisioning approaches domain bounding and definition in part through specification of a rich set of types of domain relationships. These include semantic relationships between domains as conceptual entities, not only relations between systems or system components included in the domain. The model of domain relationships is thus quite different from a conventional systems model or a model of assets in an asset base. Analogy domains are an important relationship explored in this process. Analogy domains may influence terminology, design choices, or documented explanations for system behavior provided to users for the domain of focus (Simos).

Metaphors are essentially a loosening of finding maximal similarities, as is done in analogical reasoning, into finding any interesting similarities. Metaphors are about exploring the space of common generalizations (Leishman).

13.6.6 Problem and Control Systems

We envision, design, and build a Problem Control System in an attempt to preclude, mitigate, or nullify the behavior of the Problem System. The first step requires that we understand enough of the Problem System to discern its key aspects and to articulate precisely what problem is to be "solved" for what range of conditions. This is the first form of envisioning. It is followed by envisioning the key aspects of a Problem Control System that would suffice to control the Problem System (Ring).

13.6.7 Boundary Definition

Business Domain Object Model and Business Processes describe activities, entities, and relationships in the business domain as they exist/happen regardless of what can be supported by the computer application. Then business domain experts and software developers make a decision about which parts of the business process could/should be supported by a computer application (system) and capture expectations of the system. These expectations would define the system boundary (the boundary between what system will do and what not). At this point all we should care about is what the system is expected to do for us and we should not care about how it would do it (Karchov).

A central concern of system envisioning is design and/or discovery of optimal boundaries for domains within given business contexts. System envisioning reflects the idea that domains are socially defined agreements about an intended scope of applicability. Domains are always grounded in some organization context, a community of interest that can take many different forms, such as a company or division, a consortium of multiple organizations, or a standards organization. The challenge lies in the fact that, while domains can only be defined and modeled with respect to specific organizations and systems, their boundaries can cut across both organizational and system structural lines. Thus, from the systems engineering point of view, domain engineering may involve incremental, parallel system re-engineering, design recovery, and product-line planning for anticipated systems. While at a business level domain engineering can be complementary to and integrated with areas such as business process re-engineering, redesign, for mass customization, and a shift toward a core competencies-based learning organization ([Seng90]) or knowledge-creating organization [Nona95] paradigm (Simos).

13.6.8 Simulations (Executable Business Models)

An Executable Business Model (EBM) approach is an explicit attempt to leverage object technology by building a collection of Smalltalk frameworks which support the direct execution of analytic business models (the problem space). The goal is to significantly reduce, and eventually eliminate, the need for transformation into design or implementation models of the solution space. An active agent and simulation framework provides a means to exercise a model without requiring piecemeal task-based actions through user-driven interfaces of the desktop. By modeling actor behaviors in agents and capturing system dynamics in scenarios, the same executable model which is used to perform workflow user validation can be exercised as a simulation to perform what-if analyses. These frameworks have been inspired by David Gelernter's Mirror Worlds (Salmons).

13.6.9 Search for Possibility

The envisioning step can provide a picture or feel or story of "what it's all about." It describes the solution-in-domain, i.e., the view of the domain that the proposed (envisioned) solution takes. The envisioning step is also about creating a shared view of the domain. It uses the to-be to illustrate, and re-vision, the as-is. It needs a rationale, both technical and business, so that the stories are discussed and grounded. Envisioning also gives an explicit identification and explanation of how to think in the to-be way (Anderson).

13.6.10 Scenarios

Systems must be envisioned, and modeled, in operational scenarios. This means that system models, whether mental or executable, must represent the dynamics of the entities and relationships as the ensemble interacts with its context. An initial model may be static, but a useful vision must articulate the system in operation including its modes, its states, and its stimulus-response characteristics. When operational scenarios are envisioned, one typically foresees more than one mode of system operation. The intelligent envisioner will consider these as "themes and variations" and envision a system that accommodates all. Fortunately, we have the powers of abstraction and generalization which let us summarize the Stimulus:Response, S:R, of several entities and relationships into a single representor. This, of course, is modeling — to reduce the volume and complexity of the subject by selecting only the minimum, but sufficient, number of key representors (Ring).

13.6.11 Creativity

Envisioning includes creativity or more specifically, innovation. This is sparked by a buildup of tension between the NEED vector and the POSSIBLE vector. When the tension gets great enough, new possibilities are foreseen. Systems envisioning implies a search process in which different patterns of software content, structure, process, and behavior are tried against the needs vector of the problem system to find the better fit to purpose and parsimony. This assumes that systems are not just software. Because software, per se, has no bounds of mass, length or time, a vision about the function, feature, and architecture of software inadequately expresses purpose and parsimony. Software-only visions are often found to be mirages or hallucinations (Ring).

13.6.12 Analogical Reasoning for Reusable Assets and Solutions

A form of envisioning is possible when explicit representations of past problems and solutions are available. This is the notion of developing a system through analogy and making it more concrete through the use of existing reusable solutions and the assets that make up solutions. Assets can be described by various models including architectural descriptions, object models, code, etc. Analogical reasoning is used both to retrieve existing assets that might apply to the problem and to offer new views that may not have been thought of yet. This can be a very powerful mechanism as it provides a context in which to explore both the problems to be solved, as well as possible solutions to those problems.

The ability of reusable assets to both address the known problems and envisioned solutions is made possible through the mechanism of analogical reasoning expressed as a minimal common generalization. Finding the minimal common generalization between a system being developed (the target system) and reusable solutions and assets that could be used, means finding the maximum amount of similarity between the target system and a "possible" vision of the system under development related by the reusable entities. Minimal common generalization means not just indexing into a source solution, but rather that both the target and source descriptions affect each other. A reusable asset affects the way a business problem is described, which in turn affects the choice of reusable asset. In this context, metaphor explores a space of common generalizations between the target problem space and the problem descriptions associated with reusable assets (Leishman).

A key quality of a conceptual architecture has to do with leverage: Are there existing software or model components that can be reused for this project, and, will the key components built by this project create reusable assets for future projects? From this point of view, the problem often becomes less one of system development than one of system integration. For instance, there may be a GIS component in many enterprise systems. This is readily available technology, so there is no need to reinvent it for every project. A relationship management piece may leverage existing assets from telephony vendors or elsewhere (McDavid).

13.6.13 Living Systems

There is a view, based on extensive literature in general systems theory, that organizations are living beings. At a minimum, a living organism can serve as a metaphor, or analogy, for the workings of a human organization. This view forms the foundation for a living systems approach to envisioning the information systems that support business organizations. The living systems view emphasizes the following key points:

- Human activity systems are served by information systems. In order to understand, let alone build, appropriate information systems it is imperative to have a clear understanding, or model, of the human organizations being served.
- Every living system has a required set of subsystems that vary in detail of implementation, but they must be present for the organism or organization to be and remain viable. There are material and energy-related subsystems, such as acquisition, storage, transforming, moving, and structural components. There are information-related subsystems, such as input and output mechanisms, memory, transmission, and transformation. There are also communication mechanisms such as command and control channels, normative functions, future-oriented transformative forces, and control loops that balance today's needs with tomorrow's goals.
- The cognitive processes of organisms and organizations are based upon an agent architecture. Memory is a distributed function. Simple building blocks are combined in increasing complexity that ultimately gives rise to the emergent property of intelligence.

- Intelligence is the ability to optimize across the combination of the system's goals and the system's knowledge.
- Information is the common thread that unites the ability of organs of the body to specialize through inheritance of the genetic code, the ability of species to adapt and thrive within an ecological niche, and the ability of organizations to compete effectively in the ecology of the marketplace.
- Within the constraints of common subsystems, there is astounding variety among the nervous systems required for different types of organisms and organizations. The giraffe's information system is vastly different than the earthworm's system. The telecommunications conglomerate is an enterprise with a vastly different information system than the local hardware store.

For information systems professionals this means that the key to serving the needs of our parent business organizations is clear envisioning of whole systems including the business systems and the information systems. The conceptual architecture of an information system is a high-level model that depicts the system concepts and design objectives. It is composed of a set of basic metaphors and mechanisms that together form a complete understanding of the nature and intention of the software system of the enterprise. It must be grounded in a model of the human organization (the business). The underlying business model must capture the essential nature of the business based on its goals and strategy within its ecological niche in the marketplace. Goals and strategy drive business processes and behavior, which in turn determine the conceptual architecture for the required information systems.

Primitive software mechanisms, analogous to functions of the human brain, include: sensing, novelty detection, object parsing, pattern recognition, multilevel concepts, lexicon, object token to lexical token conversion, semantic processing, logical inference, narrative comprehension, goal setting, resolution of conflicting goals, learning, long-term memory, composing, storing, and recalling of plans of action. Applets and distributed objects enable a cognitive architecture of cooperating agents. These primitive components are combined to form higher level mechanisms within the conceptual architecture, such as geolocators, transactors, traders and exchangers, relationship managers, group work mediators, forecasters, monitors, enforcers, decryptors, broadcasters, simulators, and the like. In this cognitive sense, object-oriented programming might better be thought of as organic programming.

The job of information systems professionals becomes one of matching business patterns with information system mechanisms in order to create viable conceptual architectures. At the highest level this involves the big picture of the enterprise in its market ecology context, enabled by a seamless cognitive structure of standard information system mechanisms. At the most granular level, it involves understanding business concept patterns and language patterns in order to create object and database design patterns (McDavid).

13.6.14 Holonics

Holonics is based on the concept of what John von Neumann called "cellular automata." A system comprised of cellular automata is a dynamical system which derives its attributes of efficiency, flexibility, growth, learning, quality, and survivability from parts which are each functionally complete, self-adaptive, and cooperatively integrated. The term "holon" was coined by Arthur Koestler in his book, *The Ghost in the Machine*, to describe cellular automata. The term, according to Koestler, is intended to describe an entity — sociological, economic, or physical — which is at the same time "a whole unto itself, and a part of other whole(s)." He derived the term holon by combining the prefix "hol," from holistic and the suffix "on," as in proton or neutron. Holons operate purposefully together in what Koestler calls holarchies, temporary assembly of holons which has a specific set of temporal goals and objectives. A holon, according to Arthur Koestler, is "a stable, integrated structure, equipped with self-regulatory devices and enjoying a considerable degree of autonomy or self-government" based on separation, cohesion, self-assertion, and an integrative tendency.

Holonics is in use in several Japanese companies, including Kyocera Corporation, Maekawa Manufacturing, and Honda Motor Company. At Honda, they have concluded that a living body has an information system in which all the components share three characteristics: "They have a common objective; they can work in harmony with each other; and they have flexibility, which comes from independence and freedom. This [living] system is dynamic and flexible, and can respond more quickly to change" (Hodgson).

Holonic thinking is represented in the Group Technology notion of manufacturing. Traditionally, all machines of the same kind would be put into a center and parts would be carried from one center to another. A holonic factory duplicates machines as necessary in order to avoid transporting parts and having to schedule each center (and encounter delays). This trades off increased capital for reduced logistics time, and it yields flexibility from both the process viewpoint and the capital utilization viewpoint.

This kind of thinking is not new to object-oriented software development. OO must now advance to the stage of being able to trade off capital for efficiency (using more memory space by including a method in each of several images rather than doing inter-image messaging) in favor of efficiency and solving the flexibility problem by using traceability and even objects whose role is to remember where all the other methods are located. This requires understanding of traffic patterns in order to organize the holons (a monitor can decide how many methods to duplicate across the images, but it has to know about traffic unless you want it to wait until experience has mounted in which case the unnecessary hardware has already been installed). So the methodology upstream from class design must generate a model of expected traffic and the architect must parse the processes in a way that minimizes the mean square error in fitting traffic to holons (Ring).

13.7 Tools and Methods for System Envisioning

This section addresses the need for better tools and methods to specifially support the incorporation of an envisioning approach into the software development lifecycle.

13.7.1 Appropriate Infrastructure

System envisioning is part of the process of gathering requirements, constructing a design, and implementing a software product. In addition to the necessity of having top quality people following sound, logical development processes, a software project can be aided significantly by an effective suite of project development support tools to assist with tracking the progress and the state of the project. Few vendor tools exist which provide detailed assistance for the management of knowledge about a project. Support tool usefulness appears to be evolving along the line of a "progression of knowledge."

On one end of the progression, there are separate tools which cannot communicate with each other. Even at this level, projects can benefit from having concrete, identifiable objects which represent separate requirements or design change requests. A step up from that level is a flexible framework architecture for accessing disparate databases and providing a single unified view of the data irrespective of its source or database. This architecture allows developers to build support tools which provided a unified method of attaching semantic relationships between data objects programmatically and of reasoning over those relationships. A still higher level is an integrated suite of tools to manage requirements elicitation and construction, functional specification and design, and product implementation. Other specialized tools can be constructed which access the information created as byproducts from these development phases.

Most development projects evolve from an existing design or system rather than a completely new, revolutionary product which springs into existence from the minds of its creators. This evolutionary type of project is critically dependent upon the existence of a project memory of decisions made and reasons why. Effective support tools can provide important assistance for managing a software development project (Matthews).

13.7.2 Improved Semiotics

Envisioning can be done free form or can be done by using pre-defined entities and relationship types. Free form envisioning gives the envisioner more freedom to formulate and give names to notions of system content, structure, process, and behavior, but it makes the subsequent communication to others very difficult and prone to misunderstanding. Envisioning with pre-defined representors seems to offer less freedom, but it makes the communication much easier, especially when the pre-defined constructs are mutually understood. The communication is less error prone to the degree that the constructs are logically complete. For the larger, more complex systems, envisioning with pre-defined representors offers more freedom, in fact, because the use of a bounded vocabulary gives the modeler the freedom to concentrate on the implications of the problem system. In addition, he can highlight any new constructs not represented in the pre-defined vocabulary (Ring).

13.7.3 Envisioning Methodology

Innovation literally falls out of the system envisioning process. Innovative ideas for novel designs, feature combinations, or applications for domain functionality arise almost every time the modeler discovers previously hidden contextual assumptions in exemplars. In effect, the domain modeler "lives out in advance" some of the contextual adaptation process usually deferred until a component is used in a new setting. Such discoveries help to move the process along; they are fun and generate a lot of excitement and energy. Some of the very methodical presentation of system envisioning is in fact designed to discipline or "damp down" innovative discoveries so that they are manageable and do not swamp the process as a whole.

The efficacy of this process depends on several core elements of the method: explicit scoping and clear boundaries established for the domain; thorough descriptive modeling of the commonality and range of variability across a specified set of exemplars; and consideration of specific stakeholder interests and settings for the domain. Yet it also requires a momentary "letting go" of the strict descriptive tether, a free space between empirically driven descriptive modeling and pragmatically driven prescriptive asset base engineering.

The goal of these formal modeling techniques, still an area of active research, is more than just exploration of innovative possibilities for novel features and feature combinations, although this is a valuable side benefit. Their essential role is to achieve "closure" of the domain feature space. Without this step, a domain model would reflect purely accidental descriptive boundaries of the exemplars studied or pragmatic choices of features oriented toward anticipated customers of the asset base. Such a model would not necessarily prove robust and evolvable over time. This is why this is an essential step in the system envisioning process, even for domains where feature innovation per se is not an important motivator for domain engineering. The goal is to discover the "archetypal" domain model which emerges as a coherent matrix of envisioned possibilities — a model only approximated by exemplars examined in descriptive modeling and only partially realized by any set of assets implemented (Simos).

13.8 Improving Envisioning Capability

Systems envisioning is the result of inspired envisioners, supported by collaborative teams, as we have seen above. It is possible that not everyone can be an effective envisioner of systems. However, it is not true that envisioners are strictly born and not made. Envisioning capability can be enhanced by:

- Being sure to operate on all four levels of knowing: what you know, what you do not know, what you do not know you do not know, and what you know — that ain't so
- Building your vocabulary of patterns, especially the behavior pattern of second order, implicit differential equations
- Establishing symbols and notations that are mutually understood and transcendent
- Building abstractions of current technologies, machines, and algorithms (see not what is but the essence of what is)
- Exercising your corpus collosum by practicing the interplay of your right and left lobe
- Diversifying your learning styles (mitigating your tendency to resist cognitive dissonance)

- Learning to recognize your enkaphalons; they tell you when you have found a mutually resonant set of solution concepts that produce sufficient purpose and parsimony
- Learning to help others see the vision — learning to see what they do not see, why they do not see it, and what they have to realize in order to see it

We see holonic thinking in the notion of self-sufficient project teams even if that means having the same skills duplicated across teams. The notion is to make the team skills and capacity equal to the typical process that will be assigned to the team. Thus the extent of a holon is a function of how you parse the processes to be accomplished by all the holons (Ring).

13.9 Examples of System Envisioning

A number of actual instances of systems envisioning are summarized below. In a study of the domain of interactive outline-based textual browser-editors, we found that family genealogy (parents, children, siblings) and trees (branches, leaves, pruning) were two active analogy domains reflected in domain terminology and supported functions. Analogies that remain implicit can limit thinking; conversely, an elicitation process that makes them explicit can reveal gaps and new possibilities in system features (Simos).

For example, a resort property reservation system that consisted of a property-based product pattern, a strong GIS (Geographical Information System) component, directory-based interface metaphor, a brokerage mechanism based on a free market economy of objects, relationship management, etc. (McDavid).

Another example would be an order entry, invoicing, and promotions tracking system. Every customer could be thought of as unique, a case of mass customization. An analogical vision of the situation was like manufacturing, a batch of one processing. Each customer had an arrangement with the supplier and each particular order was a deal-in-progress. Each customer's performance against plan could be managed by the system with feedback and feedforward loops for modifying the behavior of the system. New promotions could be designed using a block diagram editor and, using the analogy of a circuit, wired into the customer's arrangement object. This was envisioned as a smart objects approach that stepped back from the literal statement of the required functionality, created a useful analogy, mapped it to the concepts in the target domain, and postulated a system concept. A conceptual architecture and storyboards developed, and the awe-inspiring executive presentation was created. It was not long before the proposal was won and the project was underway (Hodgson).

Automating telephone directory enquiries by using a distributed system, with the operators working from home is yet another instance of system envisioning. One view of this is as a mapping from enquiry strings to numbers and another would reflect the needs of the operators for social interaction. In this case the envisioning might create a larger and more inclusive picture, and indeed lead to a different technical architecture. In other cases a more abstract technical view might be the key ingredient of the envisioning (Anderson).

A hand-held navigator's assistant for offshore racing for a student final-year project could benefit from system envisioning. Students were asked to write some scenarios to imagine they were in a race, had a task, and were using it. Each was to produce four scenarios, hand-written, and about half to one page long. All the work was useful, and all the work was very different. One of the students had a quite detailed account, including which buttons were pressed, another was much more about what the system could do and what he had to do for himself. Some work focused on tasks and had rather generic commands to the system. This was a great start to the project, and it went pretty well, though some of the functionality had to be removed to get the system running for their project assessment (Anderson).

The envisioning of improvement to the editorial process of a major journal started by recording the path followed by a single paper. This put the paper in context with an issue and a theme and developed a high-level flowchart for the process. Three different roles were discovered: paper editor, issue editor, and theme editor. This led to another visualization, with charts of responsibilities for the different roles.

The flowchart and process charts were reviewed by all of the staff members and their suggestions were incorporated. Occasional conflicts and misunderstandings were clarified and the results added to the charts. This activity brought to light some discrepancies in different views of the process. This led to an implementation-free analysis of the information supported by the current software, followed by an analysis of all the information used to support the current process. Some of the most valuable and detailed feedback came from the editor with the least computer sophistication. This user was able to visualize her part of the process and explain why the OMT charts didn't have it quite right (Bates).

Virtual prototyping of variations of future wrist-held cellular phones relied on a two-phased product development paradigm with a speculative all-digital front-end to develop the product concepts and an agile production capability to manufacture and market the product. Virtual prototyping is the application of advanced modeling and simulation techniques, user interface techniques, and virtual reality techniques to support speculative product design. An object-oriented, virtual reality based development environment for consumer electronics and telecommunication products is described. The aim is to develop all-digital prototypes resembling the physical products as closely as possible in terms of visual 3-D image, behavioral, functional, haptic characteristics, and auditory characteristics. The modeling approach is loosely based on the Selic, Gullekson, and Ward ROOM approach enhanced for software/hardware codesign. Implementation is based on Java, VRML, and Silicon Graphics OpenInventor platforms.

Virtual prototypes and their virtual target environments are able to combine development models of different engineering disciplines, thus enabling the designer to envision and validate product designs before they are actually manufactured. Virtual prototyping provides support for concurrent engineering methodologies. All-digital virtual prototypes will be distributed through the Internet in the future. Envisioning is accomplished by a laboratory environment for virtual prototypes combining a 3-D visual image, hand position tracking, and a haptic interface for virtual keyboard (Pulli).

13.10 Barriers to Implementing the Vision

Even when system envisioning has been done, there are a number of possible barriers that can arise to actually implementing the vision that has been created. A few of these are listed and discussed below.

These include: organizational barriers to breakthrough-thinking; different interests in different parts of the organization, unshared vision, hidden agendas; and denial — we see only what we have cognition of, what fits with our plans, what we have pre-arranged in our minds.

Sometimes the vision of new and re-engineered business processes fails to happen because of problems in realizing new ideas through system development efforts. There is a common situation where an organization wants to move from departmentalized activities to process-centric teams. In one approach business processes, the work of the business, are translated too literally into a system solution. The form and logic of the system follows the form and logic of the business processes. Changing a process means changing the system. Typically this occurs when processes, at their leaf level, are mapped to use cases and use cases are directly mapped to system features. Envisioning, in the form of scenarios, might well have been sufficiently explored, but the system's "effect-in-the-world" and the effect of "changes-in-the-world" might not have been explored. A less than optimal solution is seen to be sufficient (Hodgson).

Customer requirements to deliver business value early can lead to insufficient time allowed for establishing an architecture to support the vision. Insuficient time allowed for building generic structures (Hodgson).

More barriers include: proposal work that happens too quickly to gain a deep understanding, or reflects too literal an interpretation of business needs (Hodgson) and current use cases do not do very well with multi-party and multicast conversations (e.g., modeling a meeting). Even worse, the use case story line is actually the intersection of a number of people's goals, but only the main actor's goals are represented (Cockburn). Envisioning can also be limiting. Many practioners tend to envision only what is deemed "feasible," politically correct, or academically traceable, rather than striving to envision a sufficient design or solution (Ring).

The vision of system envisioning is that there will be breakthrough improvement of the delivery and fit of information systems as the result of taking these key steps in the development process.

- Information systems that are adaptive, or even self-adaptive
- Improved nervous systems and cognition for organizations
- More seamless integration and coexistence among new and existing increments of the overall enterprise system
- Improved competitiveness and evolutionary survival of organizations

Key messages and lessons that have emerged from the brief study of system envisioning include:

- Identify problem analogies that fit with the essential behavior of the problem situation.
- Identify systemic behavior that governs the processes of the enterprise, using systems thinking ideas.
- Model the paradigms that express the behavior of the governing concepts of the domain.
- Hypothesize system concepts that determine the kind of system that should be built.
- Choose viable system concepts, produce storyboards, and do value-propositions.
- Use prototypes to visualize system concepts.
- Do not engage with the customer until you have a prototype.
- Do not mix education and system development.
- Do something of value fast and have a migration plan.
- Symptoms, causes, and underlying systemics need to be clearly separated.

The system envisioning approach is still very much in its infancy. However, a substantial community is forming and using these concepts. The OOPSLA workshop that forms the basis for this chapter has continued and is becoming a regular feature of the conference. Those who are interested in participating in this community may visit and interact with a system envisioning web site at http://www.c2.com:8040.

References

Checkland, P. 1984. *Systems Thinking, Systems Practice,* John Wiley & Sons, Chichester.

14

Models and Code: The Connection in Catalysis

Alan Cameron Wills
TriReme International Ltd.

Desmond D'Souza
ICON Computing Inc.

14.1 The Power of the Big Picture

When you gather around a whiteboard to discuss your design with your colleagues, the last thing you want to write up there is program code. On that whiteboard, you want to show how your piece of the system works (or will work), and how it interacts with things outside it. Whether it's a single procedure or an entire planetwide distributed system, you want to fit it all on that board and convey useful things about it. At the same time, you want the description to be unambiguous enough so that everyone does not go off confidently each with their own different idea of what was said and agreed.

So we draw diagrams: sometimes *ad hoc*, sometimes using a recognized notation (like UML[2], or the others described in this book). The great power of these pictures is their ability to expose the important things you really want to say about the software (or indeed, about hardware or business processes) while setting aside the clutter of fine detail of which you are forced into if you write program code.

Once you leave the whiteboard and everyone is expecting you to write your component as described in the abstract notation, what exactly is acceptable? Do you have to stick exactly to the classes and associations as shown, or is it acceptable to produce something that presents the same behavior to the outside world?

This chapter focuses on this relationship between models and code. It is part of the Catalysis approach to software design (D'Souza and Wills, 1995, 1998), developed by the present authors. Catalysis uses UML notation and provides powerful techniques for builders of component-based and more traditional designs.

0-8493-3135-8/99/$0.00+$.50

14.1.1 Abstract Models

This idea of leaving out the fine detail is called *abstraction*. Although the word sometimes has somewhat esoteric or theoretical connotations, it is actually essential to our capability to think — it is the only way a human-sized brain can grasp the whole thing at once. Natural language (English, etc.) is good at abstraction, but it is notoriously ambiguous, hence, the purpose-built analysis and design notations.

That precision has another benefit, writing down the abstractions often exposes inconsistencies and gaps that would otherwise be glossed over. People sometimes think that it is only when you get to program code that you find these mistakes. This is not so. It is not the detail of programming language that exposes the problems, but its unforgiving precision. Using a design language that is precise and yet abstract gives us a way to assess a design with confidence before getting down to coding. Abstract models can be used to describe requirements or high-level design, or may be not much more than a pictorial presentation of the code.

It is the same with documents. A document written entirely in natural language has more interpretations than readers.* On the other hand, anything written entirely in heiroglyphs is a write-once document. A useful experience for the writer, but no more. In good documentation, the natural language narrative and the more formal descriptions (often supported by a design tool) should complement each other.

This is not to argue that you must always complete the high-level documentation before embarking on coding. There are plenty of times when it is a tactical necessity to do things the other way around. Rapidly Approaching Deadlines is the usual reason; rapid prototyping is another.

Extensive documentation also is not always necessary. A throwaway assemblage from a kit of parts is worth much less effort than a software component that may be used in many contexts.

What I do support is that the project cannot be called complete until the abstract documents (to whatever extent they exist) are true statements about the delivered software; that is, the code should *conform* to the abstractions. The purpose of this article is to examine exactly what is meant by conformance. When you draw a line between a couple of boxes, what are you promising the user or imposing on an implementor? What are you not promising and what can the designer get away with?

The next section discusses the idea of abstract models and how they relate to their implementations. The third section shows an example of how a design can be related to abstract models in terms of a small set of defined conformance relations.

14.2 An Abstract Model

Let's look first at what can be done with a good abstract model. Figure 14.1 shows a model of a spreadsheet together with a dictionary interpreting the meaning of the pieces in the model. A spreadsheet is a matrix of named cells into each of which the user can type either a number or a formula. In this simplified example, a formula can be only the sum of two other chosen cells (themselves either sum or number cells).

The model shows exactly what is expected of a spreadsheet — that it maintains the arithmetic relationships between the cells, no matter how they are altered. In particular, the invariant "{Sum::...}" says that the value of every Sum-cell is always the addition of its two operands.

Notice that this is very much a diagram not of the code, but of what the user may expect. The boxes and lines illustrate the vocabulary of terms used to define the requirement.

The box marked Cell, for example, represents the idea that a spreadsheet has a number of addressable units that can be displayed. It does not say how they get displayed, and it does not say that if you look inside the program code you will necessarily find a class called Cell. If the designer is keen on performance, some other internal structure might be thought more efficient. On the other hand, if the designer is interested in maintainability, using a structure that follows this model would be helpful to whomever will have to do the updates.

* This has kept lawyers and philosophers in work for millenia.

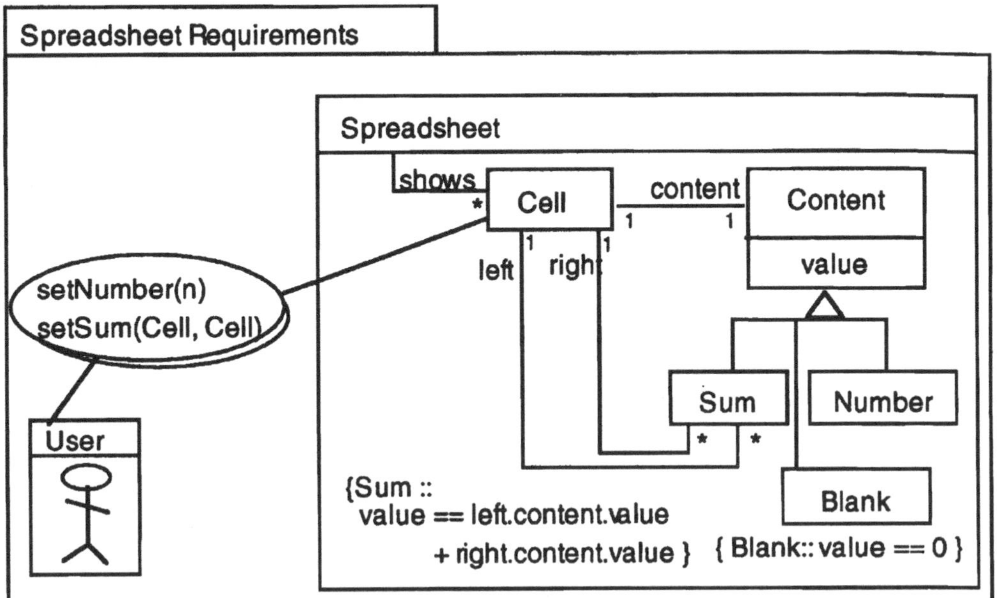

Spreadsheet	Each instance is a collection of interrelated Cells.
shows	Every Spreadsheet contains a collection of Cells. (Often displayed in a 2-dimensional matrix, but other arrangements are possible. We say nothing here about what the user does to see the Cells.)
Cell	Each instanct is a displayable element that can be referred to, by the user (e.g. by name or pointing).
Content	The information displayed in a Cell, which can be set by the user (by some means not defined here).
Number	Each instance represents a number entered into a Cell directly by the user.
Sum	Each instance represents a sum of the content of two other cells determined by the user.
Blank	The initial content of all the Cells of a new Sheet.

User, Cell c ::setNumber(int n)

Represents the ability of the User to set a Cell's content to be a Number.
Postcondition: Cell c's content is a Number, with value == n.

User, Cell c ::setSum(Cell c1, Cell c2)

Represents the ability of the User to set a Cell's content to be the Sum of two other Cells.
Postcondition: Cell c's content is a Sum of the Cells c1 and c2.
Precondition: this is not a descendant of c1 or c2

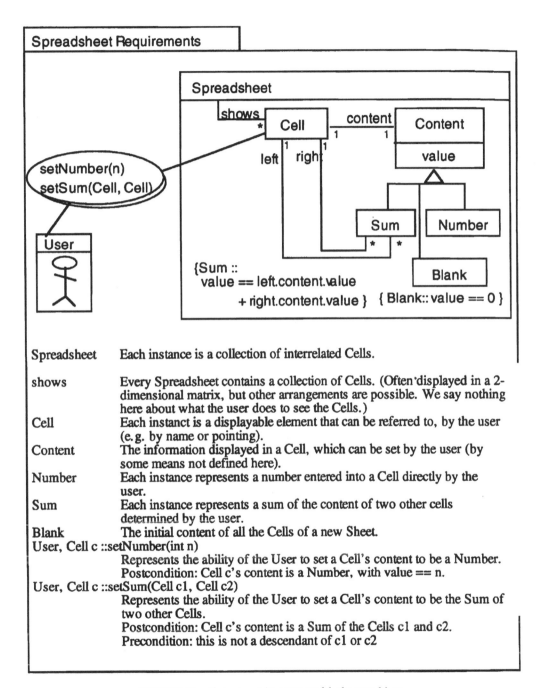

FIGURE 14.1 Abstract requirements model of a spreadsheet.

The model does not even say everything that you could think of to say about the requirements. For example, are the Cells arranged in any given order on the screen? How does the user refer to a Cell when making a Sum? If all the Cells won't fit on the screen at a time, is there a scrolling mechanism?

It is part of the utility of abstract modeling that you can say or not say as many of these things as you like. Also, you can be as precise or ambiguous as you like, we could have put the "{Sum::...}"

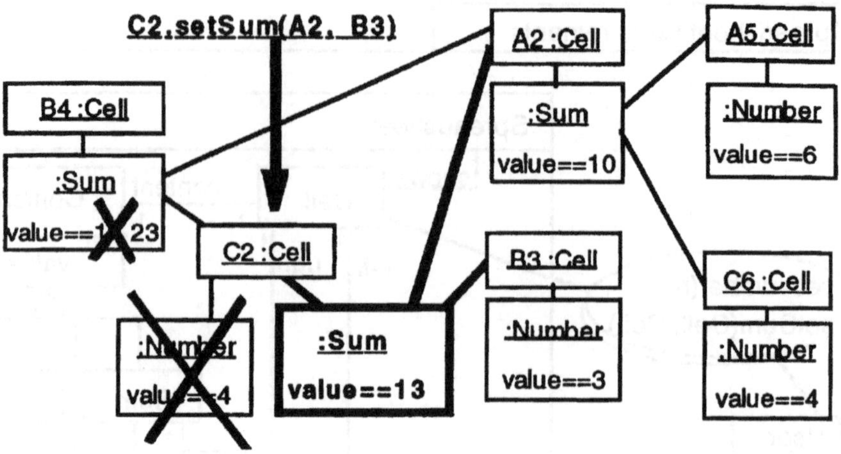

FIGURE 14.2 Spreadsheet snapshots illustrating setSum operation.

invariant as a sentence in English. This facility for abstraction allows us to use modeling notation to focus just on the matters of most interest.

14.2.1 Exercising the Model

Although (or perhaps because) the model omits a lot of the details you would see in the code, you can do some useful things with it. For example, we can draw "snapshots" or instance diagrams that illustrate quite clearly what effect each operation has.

Snapshots illustrate specific example situations. Figure 14.2 shows a snapshot-pair illustrating the state of our spreadsheet before and after an operation. (The thicker lines and bold type represent the state after the operation.)

Notice that because we are dealing with a requirements model here, we show no messages (function calls) between the objects. Those will be decided in the design process. Here we are only concerned with the effects of the operation invoked by the user. This is part of how the layering of decisions works in Catalysis. We start first with the effects of operations, and then we separately work out how they are implemented in terms of collaborations between objects.

14.3 Refinement

Now let's consider an implementation. The first thing to be said is that the program code is very much larger than the model (so we will only see glimpses of it here*). More controversially, the detail of the code does not follow the same structure as the model; for example, there is no class called Blank in the code. For various reasons of performance and design convenience, I have decided to do things differently.

Nevertheless, the program as a whole does exactly what a user would expect by looking at the abstract model. The users cannot see the internal works, and they can only judge from the program's external behavior. I therefore believe I have met the requirements properly. My position is that the model is just there to help explain the effects of the user operations, and it is not a prescription for the design.

Still, suppose I'm asked in a code review to justify the differences between my code and the model. What do I say? The ultimate justification of course is that whatever the program does is at least what you would expect from the model, and testing should bear this out. Some kind of rationale for each difference would give earlier and better confidence. It would convince me, while I'm designing, that I'm on the right track.

* It can be inspected at http://www.trireme.com/trireme/papers/refinement/.

The relationship between a model and a design is called "refinement." A valid refinement does everything you would expect from reading the model. (Some prefer to say that the design "conforms" to the model, and reserve "refinement" to mean the act of making a conformant design or more detailed model.)

In an object-oriented context, we can distinguish a few main kinds of refinement. You can explain most design decisions in terms of combinations of these categories. In a large development, the usual layers of requirements, high-level design, detailed design, and code can be seen as successive combinations of refinements.

Understanding the different kinds of refinement has several advantages:

- It makes clear the difference between a model of requirements (one box on the diagram per user concept) and a diagram more directly representing the code (one box per program class).
- It makes it possible to justify design decisions more clearly.
- It provides a clear trace from design to implementation.

Many of the well-known design patterns are refinements applied in particular ways. The refinements we are about to discuss are, if you like, the most primitive design patterns.

The rest of this chapter illustrates four principal kinds of refinement, using the Spreadsheet as an example. Briefly, the four categories are

1. Model conformance — An abstract model contains much less information than the program code. The class diagram is a lot simpler. Model conformance is the relationship that says "this model represents the same concepts as that, but with more detail."
2. Operation conformance — In a model, we can specify an operation by writing down the effects it achieves (for example, with a pair of pre- and post-conditions). Operation decomposition means writing the program code that meets the spec.
3. Action decomposition — "I got money from my bank" is an abstraction of a sequence of finer grained interactions. A refinement might be "I gave the bank my card; it told me my current balance; I asked it for $50; it gave me back my card; it gave me the cash; it debited my account." Actions involve several participants, each of which is involved in the refinement. An ATM or a customer that understands one protocol will not work with a counterpart that understands another refinement, even of the same "get money" abstraction.
4. Object decomposition — "My bank" is an abstraction referring to a collection of people, buildings, machines, etc. "I [had some interaction with] my bank" means I had some interaction with some part of it. I gave my card to the card-reader forming part of an ATM, which is in turn part of my bank; the screen of the ATM told me my balance; I pressed the keys on the ATM to tell it I wanted $50, etc. (While we are on the subject, "I" is an abstraction for a collection of many pieces as well.)

14.3.1 Model Conformance

Looking at my code for the Spreadsheet, the first thing the reviewer notices is that the classes differ somewhat from those mentioned in the requirements model. "I can see the Spreadsheet class; but what about, say, Sum?," says my reviewer.

I explain that the model's Sum is represented in my class Node; a Node has a list of operands. "So where are its *left* and *right* attributes?" asks the reviewer. "No problem," I reply. "All the information mentioned by the requirements is there, it is just that some of the names have changed. If you really want to get the left and right operands of any Sum, use the first and second items on my Node's list."

14.3.1.1 Documenting Model Conformance

The general rule is that, for each attribute or association in the abstract models, it should be possible to write a read-only function in the implementation code that abstracts (or "retrieves") its value. It does not matter if an abstraction function is hopelessly inefficient; it only needs to demonstrate that the information is in there somewhere. It also does not matter if there is more information in the code than in the model.

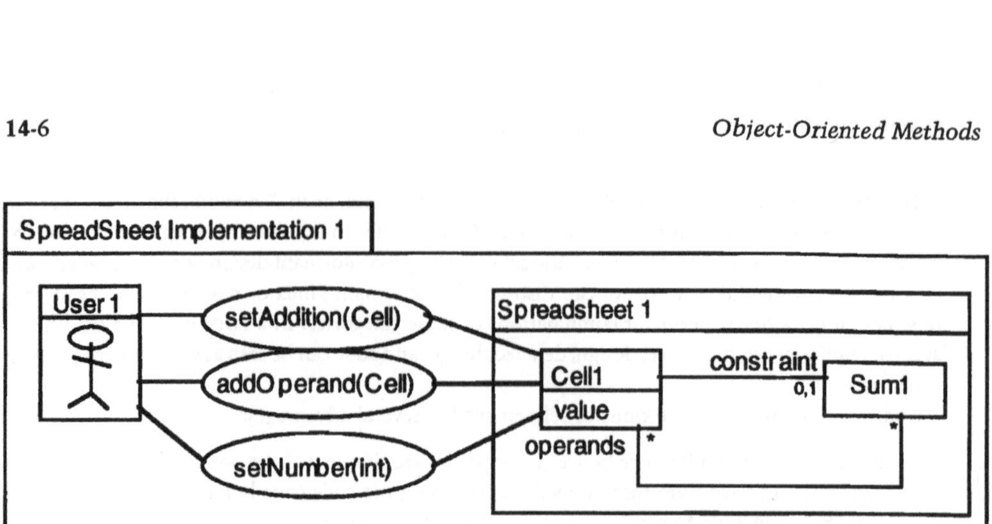

User, Cell c ::setAddition(Cell c1)
    postcondition: c.constraint is a new Sum with c1 as its only operand
User, Cell c :: addOperand(Cell c2)
    postcondition: c2 is appended to c.constraint.operands
User, Cell c :: setNumber(int n)
    postcondition: c.constraint==null && c.value==n

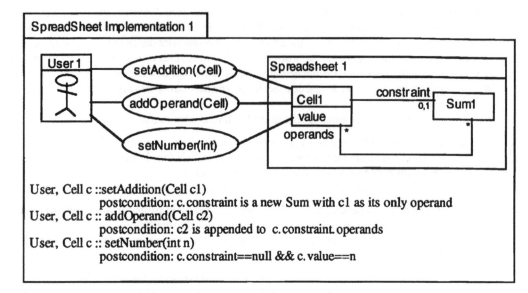

FIGURE 14.3 Spreadsheet implementation.

QA departments may insist that abstraction functions should be written, even though they are not always actually used in the delivered code, because:

- Writing them is a good cross-check, helping to expose inconsistencies that might otherwise have been glossed over.
- They make it clear exactly how the abstract model has been represented in your code.
- For testing purposes, testbeds will be written that test the post-conditions and invariants defined in the requirements models. These talk in terms of the abstract model's attributes, thus the abstraction functions will be needed to get their values.

For example, during testing we could check the invariant after every user operation (Sum:: value == left().content.value + right().content.value). For that to work in my code, we will need my abstraction functions defined for Sums:

```
class Sum1
{
  private Vector operands;              //of Cell
  Cell left () { return (Cell) operands.elementAt(0);}
  Cell right () { return (Cell) operands.elementAt(1);}
...
```

Even worse, my design (shown in Figure 14.3) does not give a content attribute for Cells, and (until I have to include them for the abstraction function) does not have classes Content, Blank, and Number. Still, the information can be abstracted:

```
class Cell1
{ private Sum constraint;         //may be null
  private int value;
  Content content ()
  { if (constraint! = null) return constraint;
    else if (constraint.size() == 0) return new Blank();
    else return new Number (value);
  }
```

Model conformance allows an abstract yet precise picture to be written of the information stored in a system or component. A more detailed model will support a more detailed account of the design, or more features.

14.3.1.2 Model Refinement: A Design Choice

"Now look here, this is ridiculous." My reviewer is getting heated. "The whole point of object-oriented design is that the code reflects the user's way of looking at things, which is what the abstract model is about. But you have a completely different set of classes from the model. That is going to make it difficult to maintain."

Well, yes, that's a good point. On the other hand, if the resulting design performs a lot better than it could have using the original model, then that could be a very practical reason for doing the refinement. We need to balance performance against maintainability — for different projects, the trade off will be indifferent.

For a spreadsheet it is perhaps a less believable excuse, but for some applications, there is no alternative. One of the author's clients is a telecoms company building transmission equipment in which throughput is vital. They did an object-oriented design, but they made many refinements to that 20% of the design that did 80% of the work. By contrast, another client is a financial trading house where the software had to be updated frequently. Maintainability was their big requirement. Their code sticks rigidly to the user models, so that the programmers and traders talk the same language, and change requests can easily be mapped to code updates.

Performance is not the only reason that the abstract and design models may be different. If the design is distributed over many machines, or more than one storage and transmission format is used (objects in store, strings in files, records in databases, ...), there will inevitably be model refinements to do during the design. Another reason for refinement may be that the design is built from pre-existing components designed for more general purposes, and therefore they have their own models. In such cases, the model may have to be turned inside out to write the abstraction function, and the spreadsheet example can look pretty tame.

The most important thing is that whether to refine, or to map the model directly to the design, should be a conscious decision. Where refinement is justified, we have shown a clear way of relating the refined design back to the abstract model.

"Well if you have justified a more efficient design, shouldn't you change the abstract model to reflect the way you have written the code?" No! The point of the model is to represent our understanding of the users' view of the system, uncluttered by design concerns. If we want to draw another set of diagrams to represent the design as opposed to the abstract model, that's fine; but we should keep both of them, and document the relationship between them. In general, the old 80-20 rule tells us that there should not be many areas where two sets of documentation are necessary.

Finally, in case our dubious reviewer still feels we are not following the object oriented relig... sorry, paradigm, very well, there is another point to make. Objects are all about encapsulation, yes? From the external point of view, therefore, we should know nothing about the internal structure of the Spreadsheet; and the same goes for any of the other classes mentioned in the model. A diagram like Figure 14.1 appears to show the internal structure. If you insist that I build my design that way, then you have forced me to expose my internal design to the external clients in contravention of the principle of encapsulation.

Therefore the only way to interpret such a model is as a hypothetical picture that helps explain to a client what the Spreadsheet's operations do, without mandating the designer to build it that way. Yes, it is more maintainable if it is constructed that way when we look inside; but it does not have to be, and when we need to for whatever reason, we know how to relate the abstract model to the internal design.

14.3.1.3 Refinement in Other Methods

Fusion (Coleman et al., 1994) and Syntropy (Cook and Daniels, 1994), are among methods that have a notion of refinement. The idea goes back before object technology, for example, to VDM (Jones, 1986), where it was treated in a degree of formality impractical in most projects.

14.3.2 Action Decomposition

The next thing my code reviewer notices is that nowhere in my code is there a function setSum(Cell, Cell). I explain that I have decided to refine this action (or "use case") to a finer grained series of interactions between the User and the Spreadsheet. A diagram that more closely represents my design is in Figure 14.3.

To set a cell to be the sum of two others as per requirement, the user performs these steps:

1. Select the Cell in question by clicking the mouse
2. Type "=" and click one of the operand Cells (this operation called setAddition)
3. Type "+" and click on the other (this operation called addOperand)

In fact, the requirement is provided by a combination of features in my implementation, which allows for a Cell's contents to be equal to the sum of one or more other cells. My "=" operation turns the Cell into a single-operand sum, and each "+" operation adds another operand. Thus there is no single operation with the signature "setSum(Cell, Cell)," either at the user interface, or anywhere inside the code.

In general, actions shown as ellipses between participants represent some interaction, without going into the details of the dialog. Actions can always be documented with unambiguous post-conditions, stating the overall effect of the process.

Notice that all participants are affected. A user who knows how to use my spreadsheet-implementation will not necessarily know how to use another design. It is the collaboration that has been refined here, not the participants individually.

14.3.2.1 Documenting Action Decomposition

A way of documenting action refinement is as a statechart — the state of the dialog between the participants. The example in Figure 14.4 shows how the initial setAddition operation results in an intermediate state "awaiting next operand"; in that state, an addOperand operation is valid, and results in the completion (marked by the caret ^) of the abstract setSum operation, and the end of this dialog.

More complex relationships between abstract and detailed actions may be represented with more intermediate states. (You may wish to try sketching the statechart relating the abstract action "I get money from bank teller machine" to a more detailed set of actions.)

UML's sequence diagrams can also be used to show detailed operations achieving a higher level goal. They have the benefit that they show distinct participants very clearly, and they help when discussing the participants' separate responsibilities. On the other hand, a sequence diagram only shows one case of an interaction with one set of starting conditions; different cases require separate diagrams. The paths

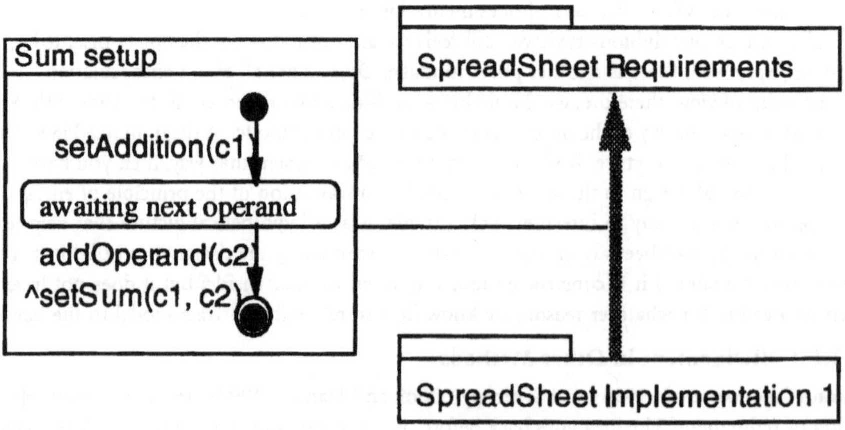

FIGURE 14.4 Action decomposition.

update occurs whenever any operation changes the Cell's value
Cell c, Sum s :: c.value != c.old.value && c in s.operands => update ( )

postcondition: The difference in value is propagated to the Sum.
c.value – c.old.value == s.~constraint.value – s.old.~constraint.value

FIGURE 14.5 Action decomposition in code.

on a statechart can be marked with "guards" or effectively if-clauses that say, you only follow this path if this condition is true. Thus one statechart can show all the possible combinations.

14.3.2.2 Action Decomposition in Code

Action refinement is not just about user interactions. The same principle can be used when describing dialogs between objects in the software. This enables collaborations to be described in terms of the effects achieved by the collaborations before going into the precise nature of the dialog.

For example, in the Spreadsheet implementation, Sums register as observers of their target Cells; so when a Cell's value changes, it must notify all its observers. The local effect is to propagate the change in value. We can document that without deciding whether the Cell sends the new value in the message, or whether the Sum calls back asking for the new value (Figure 14.5).

At the lowest level, the abstract "actions" become individual message-sends or function calls.

14.3.2.3 Using Action Decomposition

Object-oriented programming is very much about focusing on the division of responsibilities between collaborating objects. This is evident from many papers and books (Wirfs-Brock et al., 1990). The idea of treating the collaboration as a unit of design that can be combined with others to make a larger design (rather than composing objects) can be seen in the Helm's (1992) work on "contracts," the OORAM design method (Reenskaug, 1996), and is taken further in the present authors' work on "frameworks" (Wills, 1996 and D'Souza and Wills, 1998).

14.3.3 Object Decomposition

Object decomposition often accompanies action decomposition when it turns out that the detailed dialog is not conducted between the participants as wholes, but between their parts.

For example, the user interface of the spreadsheet should be separated from the core classes. The mouse and keyboard operations are received by different UI objects, depending on mode. By default, mouse clicks are dealt with by a Cell selector that sets the current focus. After an "=" or "+" keystroke, a SumController is created and registered as mouse listener — it interprets mouse clicks as additions to the focus Sum.

14.3.3.1 Documenting Object Decomposition

The refinement relation in object decomposition can best be documented with object interaction graphs or sequence charts. The abstract object can be shown enclosing its refinements (Figure 14.6).

14.3.4 Operation Conformance

The most refined form of action is an ordinary function (or "operation" or "message") defined on a particular receiver class.

Operations can be specified in a model with post-conditions, possibly qualified by pre-conditions. The post-condition tells the designer, "if you achieve this, your design is OK" and the pre-condition

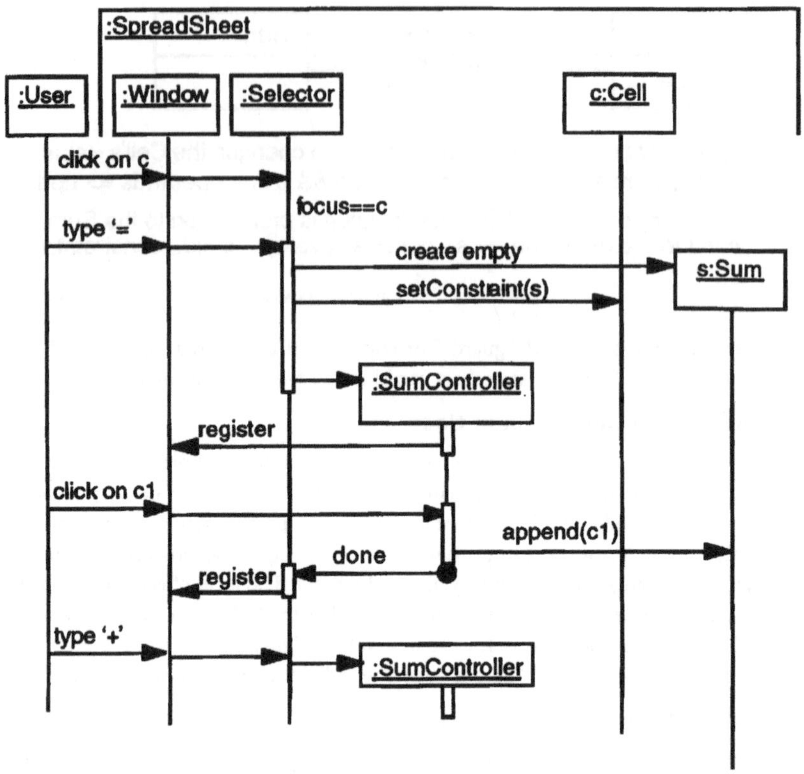

FIGURE 14.6 Documenting object decomposition.

says "but you can assume your design only needs to work if this is true to begin with." There are also invariants, conditions (like the one in Figure 14.1) that apply before and after every operation. As we have seen, this style allows us to say what is required while (in accordance with the principle of encapsulation) leaving the designers to decide how.

(Post-conditions are extremely powerful in abstract classes, where we want to specify an operation that all subclasses must provide, meeting the spec in different ways. The classic example is in a drawing editor, where different subclasses of Shape must all implement operations like "move", but all have different internal representations [Wills, 1992].)

Ultimately, the operation has to be programmed as some block of statements inside the object, which is the refinement called operation conformance. This is the category of refinement that has the longest history, and many old and very formal texts have been written on it. For most purposes, it is sufficient to think of the post-conditions as a testing tool.

The pre-condition can be thought of as a test that, in debug mode, can be applied at the beginning of the operation. If it ever turns out false, there is a problem with the caller. The post-condition has to compare states between the start and end of the operation, and a false indicates a problem with the operation's design. Invariants are ANDed with both pre- and post-conditions.

The syntax of some programming languages, such as Eiffel, provide for pre- and post-conditions as part of an operation's definition, and the compiler provides a debugging mode in which the conditions are tested on entry and exit from every routine. In other languages, it is at least useful to include the conditions in the code; and they can be straightforwardly turned into testbed code for QA purposes.

14.4 Using Refinements

The four kinds of refinement discussed here are used as the basics in the Catalysis approach to software development. We have omitted some complexities associated with callbacks and concurrent threads.

It is possible to construct frameworks of "prefabricated" refinements, which can be used to document the relationship between model and design in the same way as the primitive refinements. Many of the common design patterns can be understood in these terms.

One of the most useful aspects of an abstract model is that it is not the only one. Many useful "views" can be constructed about one piece of program code. Different users' viewpoints and different functional areas are frequently useful parallel abstractions.

It is unfortunate that there is very weak support for refinement among the popular OOA/D tools. In particular, some tool vendors' boasts that their tool can extract diagrams from C++ and vice versa seem to miss the point. Why use diagrams unless they help you get away from the C++? To express your programs in pictures is nice in some ways, but it isn't getting the most out of the notation.

As we have seen, a detailed design can be related to a much more abstract model by using combinations of refinements. This enables the most important design decisions to be separated from the detail and discussed and documented without ambiguity.

References

Coleman, D. et al. 1994. *Fusion.* Discusses abstract models and refinement.

Cook, S. and Daniels, J. 1994. *Designing Object Systems.* PHI. Discusses abstract models, refinement and strong semantics for OOA models, PHI, London.

D'Souza, D. and Wills, A. 1995. Extending fusion: practical rigor and refinement: http://www.trireme.com/papers; also in *Fusion in the Real World,* D. Coleman et al. eds., Prentice-Hall, Englewood Cliffs, NJ.

D'Souza, D. F. and Wills, A. C. 1998. *Software Development with Catalysis.* Addison-Wesley, Reading, MA.

Fowler, M. 1997. *UML Distilled,* Addison Wesley, Reading, MA.

Helm, R., Holland, I. M., and Gangopadhyay, D. 1992. "Contracts: specifying behavioral compositions in object-oriented systems," in proceedings, OOPSLA/ECOOP 1990, 25:10, 169.

Jones, C. 1986. *Software Specification with VDM.* Prentice-Hall, Englewood Cliffs, NJ.

Meyer, B. 1988. *Object Oriented Program Construction.* PHI, New York.

Reenskaug, T. et al., 1996. *Working with Objects.* Manning, Greenwich, CT.

Wills, A. 1991. "Capsules and Types in Fresco," in proceedings, ECOOP 1991, Springer Verlag, London. Also accessible in http://www.trireme.com/papers.

Wills, A. 1996. Frameworks. In *Proc. Object-Oriented Information Systems.* London, December. Also in http://www.trireme.com/papers/.

Wirfs-Brock, R. et al., 1990. *Designing OO Software.* Prentice-Hall, Englewood Cliffs, NJ.

III

Object-Oriented Programming Languages

icardo Devis
foplus SL

Today, with Java and *network-aware* programming issues permeating every zone of the software arena, it would seem that language-based decisions are not essential any more. Users are tempted to envision either an only-Java world or a CORBA-based interoperable scheme where program-ng languages do not matter. But, as in literature, what we say is strongly influenced by the way we press it, so programming languages, encouraged to adopt multi-paradigm characteristics, go beyond eir mere consideration as media and become an essential part of the system modeled through them. ie fact of the matter is that languages distinguish themselves from others by providing facilities for aling with concrete issues associated with the very nature of the modeling process.

So let the authors in this section convince you about what is possible and what is not, what is pretty nple, or just discouragingly complex; and let yourself decide what language best fits into your quirements.

15

An Overview of the C++ Programming Language

Bjarne Stroustrup
AT&T Laboratories

Abstract

This overview of C++ presents the key design, programming, and language-technical concepts using examples to give the reader a feel for the language. C++ is a general-purpose programming language with a bias toward systems programming that supports efficient low-level computation, data abstraction, object-oriented programming, and generic programming.

15.1 Introduction and Overview

The C++ programming language provides a model of memory and computation that closely matches that of most computers. In addition, it provides powerful and flexible mechanisms for abstraction; that is, language constructs that allow the programmer to introduce and use new types of objects that match the concepts of an application. Thus, C++ supports styles of programming that rely on fairly direct manipulation of hardware resources to deliver a high degree of efficiency plus higher level styles of programming that rely on user-defined types to provide a model of data and computation that is closer to a human's view of the task being performed by a computer. These higher level styles of programming are often called data abstraction, object-oriented programming, and generic programming.

0-8493-3135-8/99/$0.00+$.50

This paper is organized around the main programming styles directly supported by C++:

- Section 15.2, The Design and Evolution of C++ describes the aims of C++ and the principles that guided its evolution.
- Section 15.3, The C Programming Model presents the C subset of C++ and other C++ facilities supporting traditional systems-programming styles.
- Section 15.4, The C++ Abstraction Mechanisms introduces C++'s class concept and its use for defining new types that can be used exactly as built-in types, shows how abstract classes can be used to provide interfaces to objects of a variety of types, describes the use of class hierarchies in object-oriented programming, and presents templates in support of generic programming.
- Section 15.5, Large Scale Programming describes namespaces and exception handling provided to ease the composition of programs out of separate parts.
- Section 15.6, The C++ Standard Library presents standard facilities such as I/O streams, strings, containers (e.g., *vector, list,* and *map*), generic algorithms (e.g., *sort* (), *find* (), *for_each* ()), and support for numeric computation.

To round off, a brief overview of some of the tasks that C++ has been used for and some suggestions for further reading are given.

15.2 The Design and Evolution of C++

C++ was designed and implemented by Bjarne Stroustrup (the author of this article) at AT&T Bell Laboratories to combine the organizational and design strengths of Simula with C's facilities for systems programming. The initial version of C++, called "C with Classes" (Stroustrup, 1980), was first used in 1980; it supported traditional system programming techniques (See Section 15.3) and data abstraction (see Section 15.4.1). The basic facilities for object-oriented programming (Sections 15.4.2 and 15.4.3) were added in 1983 and object-oriented design and programming techniques were gradually introduced into the C++ community. The language was first made commercially available in 1985 (Stroustrup 1986a,b). Facilities for generic programming (see Section 15.4.4) were added to the language in the 1987–1989 time frame (Ellis, 1990; Stroustrup, 1991).

As the result of widespread use and the appearance of several independently developed C++ implementations, formal standardization of C++ started in 1990 under the auspices of the American National Standards Institute, ANSI, and later the International Standards Organization, ISO, leading to an international standard in 1998 (C++, 1998). During the period of standardization the standards committee acted as an important focus for the C++ community and its draft standards acted as interim definitions of the language. As an active member of the standards committee, I was a key participant in the further evolution of C++. Standard C++ is a better approximation to my ideals for C++ than were earlier versions. The design and evolution of C++ is documented in (Stroustrup, 1994, 1996) and (Stroustrup, 1997b). The language as it is defined at the end of the standardization process and the key design and programming techniques it directly supports are presented in (Stroustrup, 1997a).

15.2.1 C++ Design Aims

C++ was designed to deliver the flexibility and efficiency of C for systems programming together with Simula's facilities for program organization (usually referred to as object-oriented programming). Great care was taken that the higher level programming techniques from Simula could be applied to the systems programming domain. That is, the abstraction mechanisms provided by C++ were specifically designed to be applicable to programming tasks that demanded the highest degree of efficiency and flexibility.

These aims can be summarized:

- C++ makes programming more enjoyable for serious programmers
- C++ is general-purpose programming language that is a better C, supports data abstraction supports object-oriented programming, and supports generic programming

Support for generic programming emerged late as an explicit goal. During most of the evolution of C++, I presented generic programming styles and the language features that support them (see Section 15.4.4) under the heading of "data abstraction."

15.2.2 Design Principles

In Stroustrup (1994), the design rules for C++ are listed under the headings *General Rules, Design-Support Rules, Language-Technical Rules,* and *Low-Level Programming Support Rules:*

General rules:

- C++'s evolution must be driven by real problems
- C++ is a language, not a complete system
- Don't get involved in a sterile quest for perfection
- C++ must be useful now
- Every feature must have a reasonably obvious implementation
- Always provide a transition path
- Provide comprehensive support for each support style
- Don't try to force people

Note the emphasis on immediate utility in real-world applications and the respect for the skills and preferences of programmers implied by the last three points. From the start, C++ was aimed at programmers engaged in demanding real-world projects. Perfection was considered unattainable because needs, backgrounds, and problems vary too much among C++ users. Also, notions of perfection change significantly over the lifespan of a general-purpose programming language. Thus, feedback from user and implementer experience is essential in the evolution of a language.

Design-support rules:

- Support sound design notions
- Provide facilities for program organization
- Say what you mean
- All features must be affordable
- It is more important to allow a useful feature than to prevent every misuse
- Support composition of software from separately developed parts

The aim of C++ was to improve the quality of programs produced by making better design and programming techniques simpler to use and affordable. Most of these techniques have their root in Simula (Dahl, 1970, 1972 and Birtwistle, 1979) and are usually discussed under the labels of object-oriented programming and object-oriented design. However, the aim was always to support a range of design and programming styles. This contrasts to a view of language design that tries to channel all system building into a single heavily supported and enforced style (paradigm).

Language-technical rules:

- No implicit violations of the static type system
- Provide as good support for user-defined types as for built-in types
- Locality is good
- Avoid order dependencies
- If in doubt, pick the variant of a feature that is easiest to teach
- Syntax matters (often in perverse ways)
- Preprocessor usage should be eliminated

These rules must be considered in the context created of the more general aims. In particular, the desire for a high degree of C compatibility, uncompromising efficiency, and immediate real-world utility counteracts desires for complete type safety, complete generality, and abstract beauty.

From Simula, C++ borrowed the notion of user-defined types (classes, see Section 15.4.1) and hierarchies of classes (see Section 15.4.3). However, in Simula and many similar languages there are fundamental differences in the support provided for user-defined types and for built-in types. For example, Simula does not allow objects of user-defined types to be allocated on the stack and addressed directly. Instead, all class objects must be allocated in dynamic memory and access through pointers (called *references* in Simula). Conversely, built-in types can be genuinely local (stack-frame allocated), cannot be allocated in dynamic memory, and cannot be referred to by pointers. This difference in treatment of built-in types and user-defined types had serious efficiency implications. For example, when represented as a reference to an object allocated in dynamic memory, a user-defined type — such as *complex* (see Section 15.4.1) — incurs overheads in runtime and space that were deemed unacceptable for the kind of applications for which C++ was intended. Also, the difference in style of usage would preclude uniform treatment of semantically similar types in generic programming (see Section 15.4.4).

When maintaining a large program, a programmer must invariably make changes based on incomplete knowledge and looking at only a small part of the code. Consequently, C++ provides classes (see Section 15.4), namespaces (see Section 15.5.2), and access control (see Section 15.4.1) to help localize design decisions.

Some order dependencies are unavoidable in a language designed for one-pass compilation. For example, in C++ a variable or a function cannot be used before it has been declared. However, the rules for class member names and the rules for overload resolution were made independent of declaration order to minimize confusion and error.

Low-level programming support rules:

- Use traditional (dumb) linkers
- No gratuitous incompatibilities with C
- Leave no room for a lower-level language below C++ (except assembler)
- What you don't use, you don't pay for (zero-overhead rule)
- If in doubt, provide means for manual control

C++ was designed to be source-and-link compatible with C wherever this did not seriously interfere with C++'s support for strong type checking. Except for minor details, C++ has C (Kernighan, 1978, 1988) as a subset. Being C-compatible ensured that C++ programmers immediately had a complete language and toolset available. It was also important that high-quality educational materials were available for C, and that C compatibility gave the C++ programmer direct and efficient access to a multitude of libraries. At the time when the decision to base C++ on C was made, C was not as prominent as it later became and language popularity was a minor concern compared to the flexibility and basic efficiency offered by C.

However, C compatibility also leaves C++ with some syntactic and semantic quirks. For example, the C declarator syntax is far from elegant and the rule for implicit conversions among built-in types are chaotic. It is also a problem that many programmers migrate from C to C++ without appreciating that radical improvements in code quality are only achieved by similarly radical changes to programming styles.

15.3 The C Programming Model

A fundamental property of computers in widespread use has remained remarkably constant: memory is a sequence of words or bytes, indexed by integers called addresses. Modern machines say, designed during the last 20 years, have in addition tended to support directly the notion of a function call stack. Furthermore, all popular machines have some important facilities, such as input-output, that do not fit well into the conventional byte- or word-oriented model of memory or computation. These facilities may require special machine instructions or access to "memory" locations with peculiar semantics. Either way, from a higher level language point of view, the use of these facilities is messy and machine-architecture-specific.

C is by far the most successful language providing the programmer with a programming model that closely matches the machine model. C provides language-level and machine-architecture-independent notions that directly map to the key hardware notions: characters for using bytes, integers for using words, pointers for using the addressing mechanisms, functions for program abstraction, and an absence of constraining language features so that the programmer can manipulate the inevitable messy hardware-specific details. The net effect has been that C is relatively easy to learn and use in areas where some knowledge of the real machine is a benefit. Moreover, C is easy enough to implement that it has become almost universally available.

15.3.1 Arrays and Pointers

A C array is simply a sequence of memory locations. For example:

```
int v [10];         // an array of 10 ints
v [3] = 1;          // assign 1 to v[3]
int x = v [3];      // read from v[3]
```

The subscript notation [ ] is used both in declarations to indicate an array and in expressions referring to elements of an array.

A C pointer is a variable that can hold an address of a memory location. For example:

```
int* p;          // p is a pointer to an int
p = &v [7];      // assign the address of v[7] to p
*p = 4;          // write to v[7] through p
int y = *p;      // read from v[7] through p
```

The pointer dereference ("points to") notation * is used both in declarations to indicate a pointer and in expressions referring to the element pointed to.

This is represented graphically in Figure 15.1:

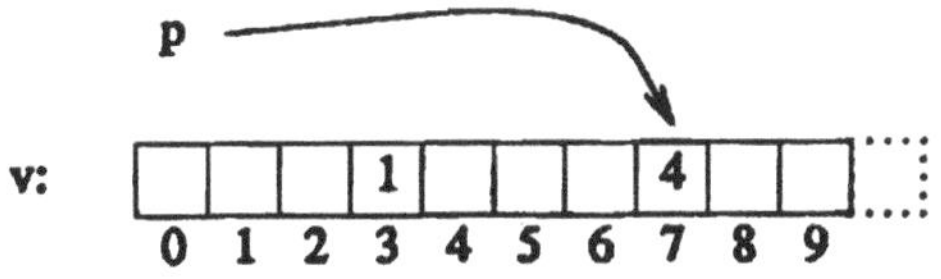

FIGURE 15.1

C++ adopted this inherently simple and close-to-the-machine notion of memory from C. It also adopted C's notion of expressions, control structures, and functions. For example, we can write a function that finds an element in a vector and returns a pointer to the matching element like this:

```
int* find (int v [ ], int vsize, int val)  // find val in v
{
   for (int i = 0; i<vsize; i++)           //loop through 0..vsize-1
      if (v [i] = = val) return &v [i];    // if val is found return pointer
                                                to element
   return &v [vsize];                      // if not found return pointer to
                                                one-beyond-the-end of v
}
```

The ++ operator means increment. Thus, the name C++ can be read as "one more than C," "next C," or "successor to C." It is pronounced "See Plus Plus."

The *find( )* function might be used like this:

```
int count [ ] = { 2, 3, 1, 9, 7, 3, 3, 0, 2 };
int count_size = 9;
```

```
void f()
{
  int* p = find (count, count_size, 7);    // find 7 in count
  int* q = find (count, count_size, 0);    // find 0 in count
  *q = 4;
  // ...
}
```

The C++ standard library provides more general versions of functions such as *find ( );* see Section 15.6.3. A function declared *void,* as f ( ) above doesn't return a value.

15.3.2 Storage

In C and C++, there are three fundamental ways of using memory:

1. **Static Memory,** in which an object is allocated by the linker for the duration of the program. Global variables, *static* class members, and *static* variables in functions are allocated in static memory. An object allocated in static memory is constructed once and persists to the end of the program. Its address does not change while the program is running. Static objects can be a problem in programs using threads (shared-address-space concurrency) because they are shared and require locking for proper access.
2. **Automatic memory,** in which function arguments and local variables are allocated. Each entry into a function or a block gets its own copy. This kind of memory is automatically created and destroyed; hence the name automatic memory. Automatic memory is also said "to be on the stack."
3. **Free store,** from which memory for objects is explicitly requested by the program and where a program can free memory again once it is done with it (using the *new* and *delete* operators). When a program needs more free store, *new* requests it from the operating system. Typically, the free store (also called *dynamic memory* or *the heap*) grows throughout the lifetime of a program because no memory is ever returned to the operating system for use by other programs.

   For example:

```
int g = 7;                    // global variable, statically allocated
void f ( )
{
  int loc = 9;                // local variable, stack allocated
  int* p = new int;           // variable allocated on free store
  // ...
  delete p;                   // return variable pointed to by p for possible
                                 re-use
}
```

As far as the programmer is concerned, automatic and static storage are used in simple, obvious, and implicit ways. The interesting question is how to manage the free store. Allocation (using *new*) is simple, but unless we have a consistent policy for giving memory back to the free store manager, memory will fill up, especially for long-running programs.

The simplest strategy is to use automatic objects to manage corresponding objects in free store. Consequently, many containers are implemented as handles to elements stored in the free store. For example, a *string* (see Section 15.6.1) variable manages a sequence of characters on the free store (Figure 15.2).

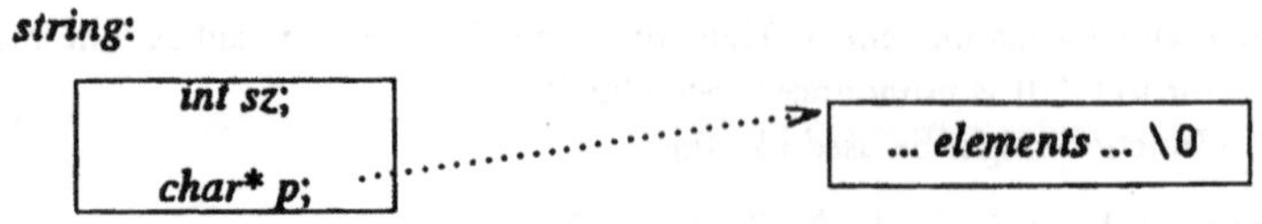

FIGURE 15.2

A *string* automatically allocates and frees the memory needed for its elements. For example:

```
void g ( )
{
    string s = "Time flies when you're having fun";   // string object
                                                          created here
    // ...
}                                           // string object implicitly
                                                  destroyed here
```

The *Stack* example in Section 15.4.2.1 shows how constructors and destructors can be used to manage the lifetime of storage for elements. All the standard containers (see Section 15.6.2), such as *vector, list,* and *map,* can be conveniently implemented in this way.

When this simple, regular, and efficient approach is not sufficient, the programmer might use a memory manager that finds unreferenced objects and reclaims their memory in which to store new objects. This is usually called *automatic garbage collection,* or simply *garbage collection.* Naturally, such a memory manager is called a *garbage collector.* Good commercial and free garbage collectors are available for C++ but a garbage collector is not a standard part of a typical C++ implementation.

15.3.3 Compile, Link, and Execute

Traditionally, a C or a C++ program consists of a number of source files that are individually compiled into object files. These object files are then linked together to produce the executable form of the program.

Each separately compiled program fragment must contain enough information to allow it to be linked together with other program fragments. Most language rules are checked by the compiler as it compiles an individual source file (translation unit). The linker checks to ensure that names are used consistently in different compilation units and that every name used actually refers to something that has been properly defined. The typical C++ runtime environment performs few checks on the executing code. A programmer who wants runtime checking must provide the tests as part of the source code.

C++ interpreters and dynamic linkers modify this picture only slightly by postponing some checks until the first use of a code fragment.

For example, I might write a simple factorial program and represent it as a separate source file *fact.c:*

```
// file fact.c:
    # include "fact.h"
    long fact (long f)      // recursive factorial
    {
        if (f>1)
            return f*fact (f-1);
        else
            return 1;
    }
```

A separately compiled program fragment has an interface consisting of the minimal information needed to use it. For this simple *fact.c* program fragment, the interface consists of the declaration of *fact ( )* stored in a file *fact.h:*

```
// file fact.h:
      long fact (long);
```

The interface is *#included* in each translation unit that uses it. I also tend to *#include* an interface into the translation unit that defines it to give the compiler a chance to diagnose inconsistencies early.

The *fact ( )* function can now be used like this:

```
// file main.c:
#include "fact.h"
#include<iostream>
```

```
int main ( )
{
     std::cout << "factorial (7) is" << fact (7) << '\n';
     return 0;
}
```

The function *main( )* is the starting point for a program, *iostream* is the standard C++ I/O library, and *std::cout* is the standard character output stream (see Section 15.6.1). The operator << ("put") converts values to character strings and outputs those characters. Thus, executing this program will cause

```
factorial (7) is 5040
```

to appear on output followed by a newline (the special character \n).

Graphically, the program fragments can be represented in Figure 15.3.

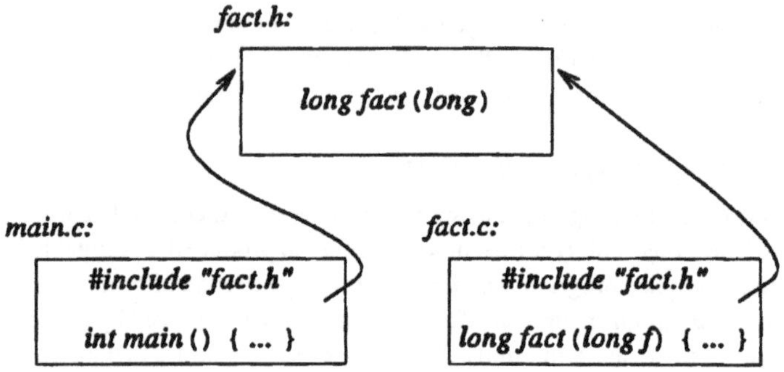

FIGURE 15.3

15.3.4 Type Checking

C++ provides and relies on *static* type checking. That is, most language rules are checked by the compiler before a program starts executing. Each entity in a program has a type and must be used in accordance with its type. For example:

```
int f(double);       // f is a function that takes a double-precision floating
                        point
                     // argument and returns as integer
float x = 2.0;       // x is a single-precision floating point object
string s = "2";      // s is a string of characters
int i = f(x);        // i is an integer
```

The compiler detects inconsistent uses and ensures that conversions defined in the language or by the user are performed. For example:

```
void g ( )
{
   s = "a string literal";     // ok: convert string literal to string
   s = 7;                      // error: can't convert int to string

   x = "a string literal";     // error can't convert string literal to float
   x = 7.0;                    // ok
   x = 7;                      // ok: convert int to float

   f(x);                       // ok: convert float to double
   f(i);                       // ok: convert int to double
   f(s);                       // error: can't convert string to double
```

```
    double d = f+i;             // ok: add int to float
    string s2 = s+i;            // error: can't add int to string
}
```

For user-defined types, the user has great flexibility in defining which operations and conversions are acceptable (see Section 15.6.1). Consequently, the compiler can detect inconsistent use of user-defined types as well as inconsistent use of built-in types.

15.4 The C++ Abstraction Mechanisms

In addition to convenient and efficient mechanisms for expressing computation and allocating objects, we need facilities to manage the complexity of our programs. That is, we need language mechanisms for creating types that are more appropriate to the way we think (to our allocation domains) than are the low-level, built-in features.

15.4.1 Concrete Types

Small heavily used abstractions are common in many applications. Examples are characters, integers, floating point numbers, complex numbers, points, pointers, coordinates, transforms, (*pointer,offset*) pairs, dates, times, ranges, links, association, nodes, (*value,unit*) pairs, disc locations, source code locations, *BCD* characters, currencies, lines, rectangles, scaled fixed point numbers, numbers with fractions, character strings, vectors, and arrays. Every application uses several of these, a few use them heavily. A typical application uses a few directly and many indirectly from libraries.

The designer of a general-purpose programming language cannot foresee the detailed needs of every application. Consequently, such a language must provide mechanisms for the user to define such small concrete types. It was an explicit aim of C++ to support the definition and efficient use of such user-defined data types very well. They were seen as the foundation of elegant programming. The simple and mundane is statistically far more significant than the complicated and sophisticated.

Many concrete types are frequently used and subject to a variety of constraints. Consequently, the language facilities supporting their construction emphasizes flexibility and uncompromising time and space efficiency. Where more convenient, higher level, or safer types are needed, such types can be built on top of simple efficient types. The opposite — building uncompromisingly efficient types on top of more complicated "higher level" types — cannot be done. Consequently, languages that do not provide facilities for efficient user-defined concrete types need to provide more built-in types, such as lists, strings, and vectors supported by special language rules.

A classical example of a concrete type is a complex number:

```
class complex {
public:            // interface:

    // constructors:
    complex (double r, double i) { re=r; im=i; }      // construct a complex
                                                        from two scalars
    complex (double r) { re=r; im=0; }                 // construct a complex
                                                        from one scalar
    complex ( ) { re = im = 0; }                       // default complex:
                                                        complex(0,0)

    // access functions:
    friend complex operator+ (complex, complex);
    friend complex operator- (complex, complex);      // binary minus
    friend complex operator- (complex);               // unary minus
    friend complex operator* (complex, complex);
    friend complex operator / (complex, complex);
    //...
```

```
private:
   double re, im; // representation
};
```

This defines a simple *complex* number type. Following Simula, the C++ term for user-defined type is *class*. This complex class specifies the representation of a complex number and the set of operations on a complex number. The representation is *private;* that is, *re* and *im* are accessible only to the functions specified in the declaration of class *complex*. Restricting the access to the representation to a specific set of functions simplifies understanding, eases debugging and testing, and makes it relatively simple to adopt a different implementation if needed.

A member function with the same name as its class is called a *constructor*. Constructors are essential for most user-defined types. They initialize objects, that is, they establish the basic invariants that other functions accessing the representation can rely on. Class *complex* provides three constructors. One makes a *complex* from a double-precision floating-point number, another takes a pair of *doubles*, and the third makes a *complex* with a default value. For example:

```
complex a = complex (1, 2);
complex b = 3;                // initialized by complex(3,0)
complex c;                    // initialized by complex(0,0)
```

A friend declaration grants a function access the representation. Such access functions are defined just like other functions. For example:

```
complex operator+ (complex a1, complex a2)  // add two complex numbers
{
     return complex (a1.re+a2.re, a1.im+a2.im);
}
```

This simple *complex* type can be used like this:

```
void f( )
{
     complex a = 2.3;
     complex b = 1/a;
     complex c = a+b*complex (1, 2.3);
     //...
     c = - (a/b) +2;
}
```

The declaration *complex* specified a representation. This is not necessary for a user-defined type (see Section 15.4.2). However, for *complex*, efficient and control of data layout are essential. A simple class, such as *complex*, suffers no space overheads from system-provided "housekeeping" information. Because the representation of *complex* is presented in its declaration, true local variables where all data are stack allocated are trivially implemented. Furthermore, inlining of simple operations is easy for even simple compilers even in the presence of separate compilation. When it comes to supplying acceptable low-level types — such as *complex*, *string*, and *vector* — for high-performance systems these language aspects are essential (Stroustrup, 1994).

Often, notation is an important concern for concrete types. Programmers expect to be able to do complex arithmetic using conventional operators such as + and *. Similar programmers expect to be able to concatenate strings using some operator (often +), to subscript vectors and strings using [ ] or ( ), to invoke objects representing functions using ( ), etc. To meet such expectations, C++ provides the ability to define meanings of operators for user-defined types. Interestingly, the most commonly used operators and the most useful, turn out to be [ ] and ( ), rather than + and – as most people seem to expect.

The standard C++ library supplies a *complex* type defined using the techniques demonstrated here (see Section 15.6.4.1).

15.4.2 Abstract Types

Concrete types, as described above, have their representation included in their declaration. This makes it trivial to allocate objects of concrete types on the stack and to inline simple operations on such objects. The resulting efficiency benefits are major. However, the representation of an object cannot be changed without recompiling code taking advantage of such optimizations. This is not always ideal. The obvious alternative is to protect users from any knowledge of and dependency on a representation by excluding it from the class declaration. For example:

```
class Character_device {

public:
    virtual int open (int opt) = 0;         // = 0 means "pure virtual function"
    virtual int close (int opt) = 0;
    virtual int read (char* p, int n) = 0;
    virtual int write (const char* p, int n) = 0;
    virtual int ioctl (int ...) = 0;
    virtual ~Character_device ( ) { }     // destructor
};
```

The word *virtual* means "may be defined later in a class derived from this one" in Simula and C++. A class derived from *Character_device* (see below) provides an implementation of *Character_device* interface. The curious *=0* syntax says that some class derived from *Character_device must* define the function.

The *Character_device* is an abstract class specifying an interface only. This interface can be implemented in a variety of ways without affecting users. For example, a programmer might use this interface to device drivers on some hypothetical system like this:

```
void user (Character_device* d, char* buffer, int size)
{
    char* p = buffer;

    while (size>chunk_size) {
        if (d->write (buffer, chunk_size) = =chunk_size) {// whole chunk
                    written
            size -= chunk_size;       // chunk_size characters written
            p += chunk_size;          // move on to next chunk
        }
        else {// part of chunk written
            // ...
        }
    }
    //...
}
```

The actual drivers would be specified as classes *derived* from the *base Character_device*. For example:

```
class Dev1 : public Character_device {
    // representation of a Dev1
public:
    int open (int opt);             // open a Dev1
    int close (int opt);            // close a Dev1
    int read (char* p, int n);      // read a Dev1
    //...
};

class Dev2 : public Character_device {
    // representation of a Dev2
```

```
public:
    int open (int opt);              // open a Dev2
    int close (int opt);             // close a Dev2
    int read (char* p, int n);       // read a Dev2
    //...
};
```

The relationships among the classes can be represented graphically like this:

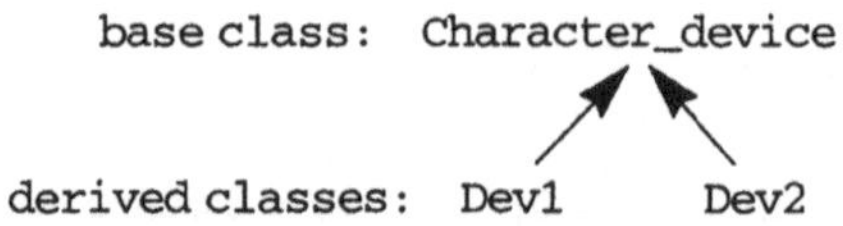

An arrow represents the *derived from* relationship. The *user ( )* does not need to know whether a *Devl*, or a *Dev2*, or some other class implementing the *Character_device* is actually used.

```
void f(Dev1 & d1, Dev2& d2, char* buf, int s)
{
    user (d1, buf, s);      // use a Dev1
    user (d2, buf, s);      // use a Dev2
}
```

A function declared in a derived class is said to *override* a virtual function with the same name and type in a base class. It is the language's job to ensure that calls of *Character_device's* virtual functions, such as *write ( )* invoke the appropriate overriding function for the derived class actually used. The overhead of doing that in C++ is minimal and perfectly predictable. The extra runtime overhead of a *virtual* function is a fraction of the cost of an ordinary function call.

We can represent the object layout of a typical implementation like Figure 15.4.

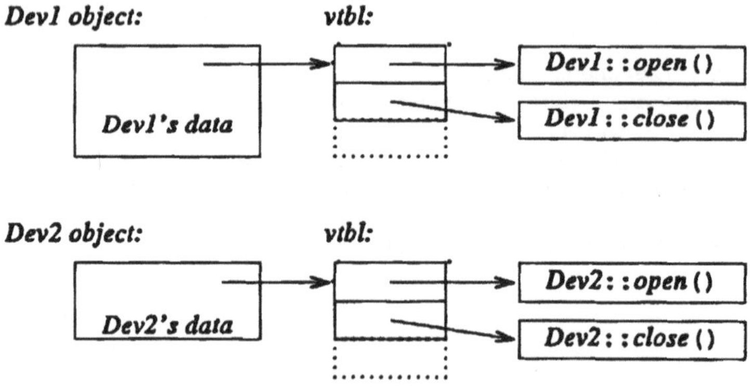

FIGURE 15.4 Object layout of a typical implementation.

Thus, a virtual function call is simply an indirect function call. No runtime searching for the right function to call is needed.

In many contexts, abstract classes are the ideal way of representing the major internal interfaces of a system. They are simple, efficient, strongly typed, enable the simultaneous use of many different implementations of the concept represented by the interface, and completely insulate users from changes in such implementations.

15.4.2.1 Destructors

A constructor establishes a context for the member functions of a class to work in for a given object. Often, establishing that context requires the acquisition of resources such as memory, locks, or files. For a program to work correctly, such resources must typically be released when the object is destroyed. Consequently, it is possible to declare a function dedicated to reversing the effect of a constructor. Naturally, such a function is called a *destructor.* The name of a destructor for a class *X* is *~X ( );* in C++, ~ is the complement operator.

A simple stack of characters can be defined like this:

```
class Stack {
   char* v;
   int max_size;
   int top;
public :
   Stack (int s) { top = v = new T [max_size=s]; } // constructor: acquire
                                                       memory
   ~Stack ( ) { delete [ ] v; }                    // destructor: release
                                                       memory

   void push (T c) { v[top++] = c; }
   T pop ( ) { v[--top]; }
};
```

For simplicity, this *Stack* has been stripped of all error handling. However, it is complete enough to be used like this:

```
void f(int n)
{
   stack s2(n);    // stack of n characters

   push ('a');
   push ('b');
   char c = pop ( );
   //...
}
```

Upon entry into *f( ), s2* is created and the constructor *Stack::Stack ( )* is called. The constructor allocates enough memory for *n* characters. Upon exit from *f( ),* the destructor *Stack::~Stack ( )* is implicitly invoked so that the memory acquired by the constructor is freed.

This kind of resource management is often important. For example, an abstract class, such as *Character_device,* will be manipulated through pointers and references and will typically be deleted by a function that has no idea of the exact type of object used to implement the interface. Consequently, a user of a *Character_device* cannot be expected to know what is required to free a device. Conceivably freeing a device would involve nontrivial interactions with an operating system or other guardians of system resources. Declaring *Character_device's* destructor *virtual* ensures that the removal of the *Character_device* is done using the proper function from the derived class. For example:

```
void some_user (Character_device* pd)
{
   //...
   delete pd; // implicitly invoke object's destructor
}
```

15.4.3 Object-Oriented Programming

Object-oriented programming is a set of techniques that rely on hierarchies of classes to provide extensibility and flexibility. The basic language facilities used are the user-defined types themselves, the ability to derive a class from another, and *virtual* functions (see Section 15.4.2). These features allow a programmer to rely on an interface (a class, often an abstract class) without knowing how its operations are implemented. Conversely, they allow new classes to be built directly on older ones without disturbing users of those older classes. As an example, consider the simple task of getting an integer value from a user to an application through some user-interface system. Assuming that we would like to keep the application independent of the details of the user-interface system we could represent the notion of an interaction needed to get an integer as a class *Ival_box:*

```
class Ival_box {
public :
   virtual int get_value ( ) = 0;        // get value back to application
   virtual void prompt ( ) = 0;          // prompt the user
   //...
};
```

Naturally, there will be a variety of Ival_boxes:

```
class Ival_dial : public Ival_box { /* ... */ };
class Ival_slider : public Ival_box { /* ... */ };
//...
```

This can be represented graphically like Figure 15.5.

This application hierarchy is independent of the details of an actual user-interface system. The application is written independently of I/O implementation details and then later tied into an implementation hierarchy without affecting the users of the application hierarchy (Figure 15.6).

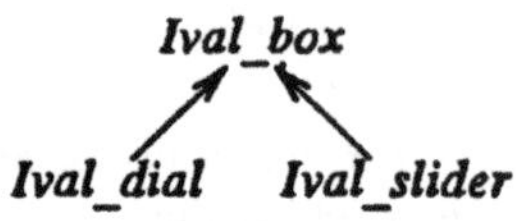

FIGURE 15.5 Variety of Ival-boxes.

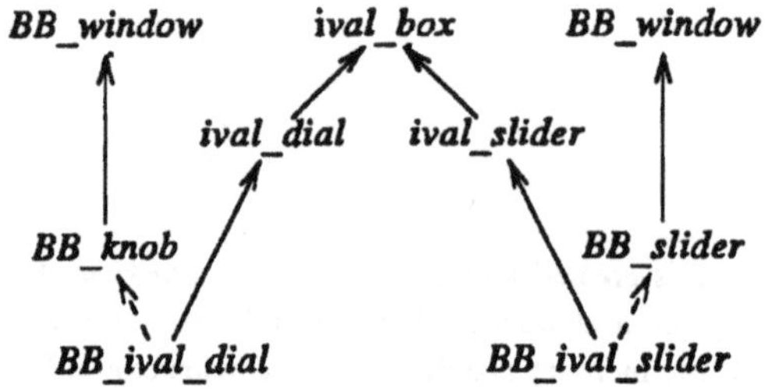

FIGURE 15.6 Application hierarchy.

A dashed arrow represents a protected base class. A protected base class is one that is part of the implementation of its derived class (only) and is inaccessible general user code. This design makes the application code independent of any change in the implementation hierarchy.

I have used the *BB* prefix for realism; suppliers of major libraries traditionally prepend some identifying initials. The superior alternative is to use namespaces (see Section 15.5.2).

The declaration of a class that ties an application class to the implementation hierarchy will look something like this:

```
class BB_ival_slider : public ival_slider, protected BB_slider {
public:
      // functions overriding Ival_slider functions
      // as needed to implement the application concepts
protected:
      // functions overriding BB_slider and BB_window functions
      // as required to conform to user interface standards
private:
      // representation and other implementation details
};
```

This structure assumes that details of what is to be displayed by a user-interface system is expressed by overriding virtual functions in the *BB_windows* hierarchy. This may not be the ideal organization of a user interface system, but it is not uncommon.

A derived class inherits properties from its base classes. Thus, derivation is sometimes called *inheritance.* A language, such as C++, that allows a class to have more than one direct base class is said to support *multiple inheritance.*

15.4.3.1 Runtime Type Identification

A plausible use of the *Ival_boxes* defined in Section 15.4.3 would be to hand them to a system that controlled a screen and have that system hand objects back to the application program whenever some activity had occurred. This is how many user interfaces work. However, just as an application using *Ival_boxes* should not know about the user-interface system, the user-interface system will not know about our *Ival_boxes.* The system's interfaces will be specified in terms of the system's own classes and objects rather than our application's classes. This is necessary and proper. However, it does have the unpleasant effect that we lose information about the type of objects passed to the system and later returned to us.

Recovering the "lost" type of an object requires us to somehow ask the object to reveal its type. Any operation on an object requires us to have a pointer or reference of a suitable type for the object. Consequently, the most obvious and useful operation for inspecting the type of an object at runtime is a type conversion operation that returns a valid pointer if the object is of the expected type and a null pointer if it is not. The *dynamic_cast* operator does exactly that. For example, assume that "the system" invokes *my_event_handler ( )* with a pointer to a *BBwindow,* where an activity has occurred:

```
void my_event_handler (BBwindow* pw)
{
  if (Ival_box* pb = dynamic_cast<Ival_box*> (pw))  { // does pw point to
                                                        an Ival_box?
     int i = pb->get_value ( );
     //...
  }
  else {
     // Oops! unexpected event
  }
}
```

One way of explaining what is going on is that *dynamic_cast* translates from the implementation-oriented language of the user-interface system to the language of the application. It is important to note what is not mentioned in this example: the actual type of the object. The object will be a particular kind of *Ival_box,* say an *Ival_slider,* implemented by a particular kind of *BBwindow,* say a *BBslider.* It is neither necessary nor desirable to make the actual type of the object explicit in this interaction between "the system" and the application. An interface exists to represent the essentials of an interaction. In particular, a well-designed interface hides inessential details.

Casting from a base class to a derived class is often called a *downcast* because of the convention of drawing inheritance trees growing from the root down. Similarly, a cast from a derived class to a base is called an *upcast.* A cast that goes from a base to a sibling class, like the cast from *BBwindow* to *Ival_box,* is called a *crosscast.*

15.4.4 Generic Programming

Given classes and class hierarchies, we can elegantly and efficiently represent individual concepts and also represent concepts that relate to each other in a hierarchical manner. However, some common and important concepts are neither independent of each other nor hierarchically organized. For example, the notions "vector of integer" and "vector of complex number" are related through the common concept of a vector and differ in the type of the vector elements (only). Such abstractions are best represented through parameterization. For example, the *vector* should be parameterized by the element type.

C++ provides parameterization by type through the notion of a template. It was a crucial design criterion that templates should be flexible and efficient enough to be used to define fundamental containers with severe efficiently constraints. In particular, the aim was to be able to provide a *vector* template class that did not impose runtime or space overheads compared to a built-in array.

15.4.5 Containers

We can generalize a stack-of-characters type from Section 15.4.2.1 to a stack-of-anything type by making it a *template* and replacing the specific type *char* with a template parameter. For example:

```
template<class T> class Stack {
   T* v;
   int max_size;
   int top;
public:
   Stack (int s) { top = v = new T [max_size=s];     // constructor
   -Stack ( ) { delete [ ] v; }                      // destructor

   void push (T c) { v[top++] = c; }
   T pop ( ) { v[--top]; }
}
```

The *template<class T>* prefix makes *T* a parameter of the declaration it prefixes. We can now use stacks like this:

```
Stack<char> sc;              // stack of characters
Stack<complex> scplx;        // stack of complex numbers
Stack<list<int> > sli;       // stack of list of integers

void f( )
{
   sc .push ('c');
   if (sc.pop ( ) ! = 'c') error ("impossible");

   scplx.push(complex (1, 2));
   if (scplx.pop ( ) ! = complex (1, 2) error ("can't happen");
}
```

Similarly, we can define lists, vectors, maps (that is, associative arrays), etc., as templates. A class holding a collection of elements of some type is commonly called a *container class*, or simply a *container*.

Templates are a compile-time mechanism so that their use incurs no runtime overhead compared to "hand-written code."

15.4.5.1 Algorithms

Given a variety of semantically similar types, such as a set of containers that all support similar operations for element insertion and access, we can write code that works for all of those types. For example, we might count the occurrences of a value *val* in a sequence of elements delimited by *first* and *last* like this:

```
template<class In, class T> int count (In first, In last, const T& val)
{
   int res = 0;
   while (first ! = last) if (*first++ = = val) ++res;
   return res;
}
```

This code assumes only that values of type *T* can be compared using ==, that an *In* can be used to traverse the sequence by using ++ to get to the next element, and that **p* retrieves the value of the element pointer to by an iterator *p*. For example:

```
void f (vector<complex>& vc, string s, list<int>& li)
{
   int c1 = count (vc.begin ( ), vc.end ( ), complex (0));
   int c2 = count (s.begin ( ), s.end( ), 'x');
   int c3 = count (li.begin ( ), li.end ( ), 42);
   //...
}
```

This counts the occurrences of the *complex 0* in the vector, the occurrences of *x* in the string, and the occurrences of *42* in the list.

A type with the properties specified for *In* is called an *iterator.* The simplest example of an iterator is a built-in pointer. Standard library containers — such as *vector, string,* and *list* — all provide the operations *begin ( )* and *end ( )* that returns iterators for the first element and the one-beyond-the-last element, respectively; thus, *begin ( ) ..end ( )* describes a half-open sequence (see Section 15.6.3). Naturally, the implementations of ++ and * differ for the different containers, but such implementation details do not affect the way we write the code.

15.5 Large Scale Programming

The main part of this paper is organized around the key programming styles supported by C++. However, namespaces and exception handling mechanisms are important language features that do not fit this classification because they support large scale programming in all styles. They are used to ease the construction of programs out of separate parts and they increase in importance as the size of programs increase.

15.5.1 Exceptions and Error Handling

Exceptions are used to transfer control from a place where an error is detected to some caller that has expressed interest in handling those kinds of errors. Clearly, this is a mechanism that should be used only for errors that cannot be handled locally.

One might ask: "How can something that is (eventually) handled correctly so that the program proceeds as intended be considered an error?" Consequently, we often refer to exceptional events, or simply to *exceptions,* and the language mechanisms provided to deal with these events *exception handling.*

Consider how we might report underflow and overflow errors from a *Stack:*

```
template<class T> class Stack {
   T* v;
   int max_size;
   int top;
public :
   class Underflow { };   // type used to report underflow
   class Overflow { };    // type used to report overflow

   Stack (int s);         // constructor
   ~Stack ( );            // destructor

   void push (T c)
   {
      if (top = = max_size) throw Overflow ( );    // check for error
      v[top++] = c;                                // raise top and place c on
                                                        top
   }
```

```
T pop ( )
{
     if (top = = 0) throw Underflow ( );          // check for error
     return v[--top];                             // lower top
  }
};
```

An object thrown can be caught by a caller of the function that threw. For example:

```
void f( )
{
  Stack<string> ss;

  try {
    ss.push ("Quiz");
    string s = ss.pop ( );               // pop "Quiz"
    ss.pop ( )                           // try to pop an empty string: will
                                            throw Underflow
  }
  catch (Stack<string> :: Underflow)  {  // exception handler
    cerr << "error: stack underflow";
    return;
  }
  catch (Stack<string> :: Overflow)  {   // exception handler
    cerr << "error: stack overflow";
    return;
  }
  //...
}
```

Exceptions thrown within a *try { … }* block or in code called from within a try block will be caught by a catch-clause for their type.

Exceptions can be used to make error handling more stylized and regular. In particular, hierarchies of exception classes can be used to group exceptions so that a piece of code need deal only with errors at a suitable level of detail. For example, assume that *open_file_error* is a class derived from *io_error:*

```
void use_file (const char* fn)
{
  File_ptr f(fn, "r");  // open fn for reading; throw open_file_error if
                           that can't be done
  // use f
}

void some_fct ( )
{
  try {
    //...
    use_file ("homedir/magic");
    //...
  }
  catch (io_error) {
    //...
  }
}
```

Here, *some_fct* need not know the details of what went wrong; that is, it need not know about *open_file_error.* Instead, it deals with errors at the *io_error* level of abstraction.

Note that *use_file* did not deal with exceptions at all. It simply opens a file and uses it. Should the file not be there to open, control is immediately transferred to the caller *some_fct*. Similarly, should a read error occur during use, the file will be properly closed by the *File_ptr* destructor before control returns to *some_fct*.

15.5.2 Namespaces

A namespace is a named scope. Namespaces are used to group related declarations and to keep separate items separate. For example, two separately developed libraries may use the same name to refer to different items, but a user can still use both:

```
namespace Mylib {
   template<class T> class Stack { /* ... */ } ;
   //...
}

namespace Yourlib {
   class Stack { /* ... */ } ;
   //...
}

void f ( )
{
   Mylib :: Stack<int> s1;        // use my stack
   Yourlib :: Stack s2;           // use your stack
   //...
}
```

Repeating a namespace name can be a distraction for both readers and writers. Consequently, it is possible to state that names from a particular namespace are available without explicit qualification. For example:

```
void f( )
{
   using namespace Mylib;         // make names from Mylib accessible

   Stack<int> s1;                 // use my stack
   Yourlib :: Stack s2;           // use your stack
   //...
}
```

Namespaces provide a powerful tool for the management of different libraries and of different versions of code. In particular, they offer the programmer alternatives of how explicit to make a reference to a nonlocal name.

15.6 The C++ Standard Library

The standard library provides:

1. Basic runtime language support (e.g., for allocation and runtime type information)
2. The C standard library (with very minor modifications to minimize violations of the type system)
3. Strings and I/O streams (with support for international character sets and localization)
4. A framework of containers (such as *vector*, *list*, and *map*) and algorithms using containers (such as general traversals, sorts, and merges)
5. Support for numerical computation (complex numbers plus vectors with arithmetic operations, BLAS-like and generalized slices, and semantics designed to ease optimization).

The main criterion for including a class in the library was that it would somehow be used by almost every C++ programmer (both novices and experts), that it could be provided in a general form that did not add significant overhead compared to a simpler version of the same facility, and that simple uses should be easy to learn. Essentially, the C++ standard library provides the most common fundamental data structures together with the fundamental algorithms used on them.

The framework of containers, algorithms, and iterators is commonly referred to as the STL. It is primarily the work of Alexander Stepanov (1994).

15.6.1 Strings and I/O

Strings and input/output (I/O) operations are not provided directly by special language constructs in C++. Instead, the standard library provides string and I/O types. For example:

```
#include<string>// make standard strings available
#include<iostream>// make standard I/O available

int main ( )
{
   using namespace std;

   string name;
   cout << "Please enter your name: ";        // prompt the user
   cin >> name;                               // read a name
   cout << "Hello, " << name << '/n';         // output the name followed by a
                                                   newline
   return 0;
}
```

This example uses the standard input and output streams, *cin* and *cout* with their operators >> ("get from") and << ("put to").

The I/O streams support a variety of formatting and buffering facilities, and strings support common string operations such as concatenation, insertion, and extraction of characters and strings. Both streams and strings can be used with characters of any character set.

The standard library facilities can be, and usually are, implemented using only facilities available to all users. Consequently, where the standard facilities happen to be inadequate, a user can provide equally elegant alternatives.

15.6.2 Containers

The standard library provides some of the most general and useful container types to allow the programmer to select a container that best serves the needs of an application:

Standard Container Summary

`vector<T>`	A variable-sized vector
`list<T>`	A doubly-linked list
`queue<T>`	A queue
`stack<T>`	A stack
`deque<T>`	A double-ended queue
`priority_queue<T>`	A queue sorted by value
`set<T>`	A set
`multiset<T>`	A set in which a value can occur many times
`map<key,val>`	An associative array
`multimap<key,val>`	A map in which a key can occur many times

These containers are designed to be efficient yet have interfaces designed to ensure that they can be used interchangeably wherever reasonable. For example, like *list, vector* provides efficient operations for adding elements to its end (back). This allows data that eventually needs to be efficiently accessed by subscripting to be constructed incrementally. For example:

```
vector<Point> cities;

void add_points (Point sentinel)
{
    Point buf;

    while (cin>>buf) {              // read points from input
        if (buf = = sentinel) return;
        // check new point
        cities.push_back (buf);     // add point to (end of) vector
    }
}
```

The containers are nonintrusive; that is, essentially every type can be used as a container element type. In particular, built-in types, such as *int* and *char**, and C-style data structures (*structs*) can be container elements.

15.6.3 Algorithms

The standard library provides dozens of algorithms. The algorithms are defined in namespace *std* and presented in the *<algorithm>* header. Here are a few I have found particularly useful.

Selected Standard Algorithms

`for_each()`	Invoke function for each element
`find()`	Find first occurrence of arguments
`find_if()`	Find first match of predicate
`count()`	Count occurrences of element
`count_if()`	Count matches of predicate
`replace()`	Replace element with new value
`replace_if()`	Replace element that matches predicate with new value
`copy()`	Copy elements
`unique_copy()`	Copy elements that are not adjacent duplicates
`sort()`	Sort elements
`equal_range()`	Find all elements with equivalent values
`merge()`	Merge sorted sequences

These algorithms, and many more, can be applied to standard containers, *strings,* and built-in arrays (Figure 15.7).

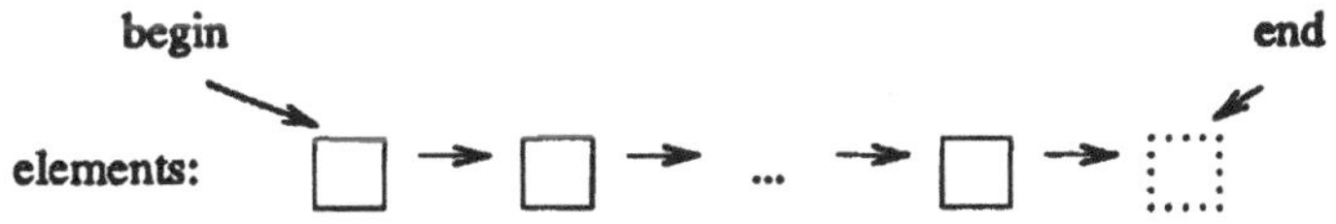

FIGURE 15.7

As mentioned, operator * is used to mean "access an element through an iterator" and operator ++ to mean "make their iterator refer to the next element." For example, we can define a general algorithm that finds the first element of a sequence that matches a predicate like this:

```
template <class In, class Predicate> In find_if(In first, In last, Predicate
          pred)
{
  while (first!=last && !pred(*first)) ++first;
  return first;
}
```

Simple definitions, the ability to choose the right algorithm at compile time based on the type of the input sequence, and the ability to inline simple operations (such as ==, <, and simple user-defined predicates) means that these very generic and general algorithms outperform most conventional alternatives.

15.6.4 Numerics

Like C, C++ was not designed primarily with numerical computation in mind. However, a lot of numerical work is done in C++, and the standard library reflects that.

15.6.4.1 Complex Numbers

The standard library supports a family of complex number types along the lines of the *complex* class described in Section 15.4.1. To support complex numbers where the scalars are single-precision floating-point numbers (*floats*), double precision numbers (*doubles*), etc., the standard library *complex* is a template:

```
template<class scalar> class complex {
public :
  complex (scalar re, scalar im);
  //...
};
```

The usual arithmetic operations and the most common mathematical functions are supported for complex numbers. For example:

```
template<class C> complex <C> pow(const complex<C>&, int);   //
              exponentiation
void f(complex<float> fl, complex<double> db)
{
  complex<long double> ld = fl+sqrt (db);
  db += fl*3;
  fl = pow (1/fl, 2);
  //...
}
```

Thus, complex numbers are supported approximately to the degree that floating-point numbers are.

15.6.4.2 Vector Arithmetic

The standard *vector* from Section 15.6.2 was designed to be a general mechanism for holding values, to be flexible, and to fit into the architecture of containers, iterators, and algorithms. However, it does not support mathematical vector operations. Adding such operations to *vector* would be easy, but its generality and flexibility precludes optimizations that are often considered essential for serious numerical work. Consequently, the standard library provides a vector, called *valarray,* that is less general and more amenable to optimization for numerical computation:

```
template<class T> class valarray {
  //...
  T& operator [ ] (size_t);
  //...
};
```

The type *size_t* is the unsigned integer type that the implementation uses for array indices.

The usual arithmetic operations and the most common mathematical functions are supported for *valarrays*. For example:

```
template<class T> valarray<T> abs (const valarray<T>&); // absolute value
void f(const valarray<double>& a1, const valarray<double>& a2)
{
   valarray<double> a = a1*3.14+a2/a1;
   a += a2*3.14;
   valarray<double> aa = abs (a);
   double d = a2[7];
   //...
}
```

The *valarray* type also supports BLAS-style and generalized slicing. More complicated numeric types, such as *Matrix*, can be constructed from *valarray*.

15.7 Use of C++

C++ is used by hundreds of thousands of programmers in essentially every application domain. This use is supported by about a dozen independent implementations, hundreds of libraries, hundreds of textbooks, several technical journals, many conferences, and innumerable consultants. Training and education at a variety of levels are widely available.

Early applications tended to have a strong systems programming flavor. For example, several major operating systems have been written in C++ (Campbell, 1987; Rozier, 1988; Hamilton, 1993; Berg, 1995; and Parrington, 1995) and many more have key parts done in C++. C++ was designed so that every language feature is usable in code under severe time and space constraints (Stroustrup, 1994). This allows C++ to be used for device drivers and other software that rely on direct manipulation of hardware under real-time constraints. In such code, predictability of performance is at least as important as raw speed. Often, so is compactness of the resulting system.

Most applications have sections of code that are critical for acceptable performance. However, the largest amount of code is not in such sections. For most code, maintainability, ease of extension, and ease of testing is key. C++'s support for these concerns has led to its widespread use where reliability is a must and in areas where requirements change significantly over time. Examples are banking, trading, insurance, telecommunications, and military applications. For years, the central control of the U.S. long distance telephone systems has relied on C++ and every 800 call (that is, a call paid for by the called party) has been routed by a C++ program (Kamath, 1993). Many such applications are large and long-lived. As a result, stability, compatibility, and scalability have been constant concerns in the development of C++. Million-line C++ programs are not uncommon.

Like C, C++ was not specifically designed with numerical computation in mind. However, much numerical, scientific, and engineering computation is done in C++. A major reason for this is that traditional numerical work must often be combined with graphics and with computations relying on data structures that do not fit into the traditional Fortran mold (Budge, 1992 and Barton, 1994). Graphics and user interfaces are areas in which C++ is heavily used.

All of this points to what may be C++'s greatest strength: its ability to be used effectively for applications that require work in a variety of application areas. It is quite common to find an application that involves local and wide-area networking, numerics, graphics, user interaction, and database access. Traditionally, such application areas have been considered distinct, and they have most often been served by distinct technical communities using a variety of programming languages. However, C++ has been widely used in all of those areas. Furthermore, it is able to coexist with code fragments and programs written in other languages.

C++ is widely used for teaching and research. This has surprised some who, correctly, point out that C++ is not the smallest or cleanest language ever designed. However, C++ is:

- Clean enough for successful teaching of basic concepts
- Realistic, efficient, and flexible enough for demanding projects
- Available enough for organizations and collaborations relying on diverse development and execution environments
- Comprehensive enough to be a vehicle for teaching advanced concepts and techniques
- Commercial enough to be a vehicle for putting what is learned into non-academic use

Thanks to the ISO standards process (see Section 15.2), C++ is also well-specified, stable, and supported by a standard library.

15.8 Further Reading

There is an immense amount of literature on C++, object-oriented programming, and object-oriented design. Here is a short list of books that provides information on key aspects of C++ and its use.

Stroustrup (1997a) is a tutorial for experienced programmers and user-level reference for C++ and its standard library. It presents a variety of fundamental and advanced design and programming techniques. Stroustrup (1994) describes the rationale behind the design choices for C++.

Koenig (1997) is a collection of essays discussing ways of using C++ effectively. Barton (1994) focuses on numeric computation and presents some advanced uses of templates. Cline (1995) gives practical answers to many questions that occur to programmers starting to use C++.

Other books discuss C++ primarily in the context of design. Booch (1994) presents the general notion of object-oriented design, and Martin (1995) gives detailed examples of Booch's design method. Gamma (1995) introduces the notion of design patterns. These three books all provide extensive examples of C++ code.

These books are all aimed at experienced programmers and designers. There is also a host of C++ books aimed at people with weak programming experience, but the selection of those varies so rapidly that a specific recommendation would be inappropriate.

Acknowledgments

This paper was written in grateful memory of my *CRC Standard Mathematical Tables*, 17th edition — an essential tool, status symbol, and security blanket for a young math student.

References

Barton, J.J. and Lee, R. 1994. *Scientific and Engineering C++*. Addison-Wesley, Reading, MA.

Berg, W., Cline, M. and Girou, M. 1995. *Lessons from the OS/400 OO Project.* CACM, Vol. 38, No. 10, October.

Birtwistle, G., Dahl, O.J., Myrhaug, B. and Nygaard, K. 1979. *SIMULA BEGIN.* Studenlitteratur, Lund, Sweden.

Booch, G. 1994. *Object-Oriented Analysis and Design.* Benjamin/Cummings, Menlo Park, CA.

Budge, K., Perry, J.S. and Robinson, A.C. 1992. *High-Performance Scientific Computation using C++.* Proc. USENIX C++ Conference, Portland, OR, August.

X3 Secretariat, *Standard — The C Language.* X3J11/90-013. ISO Standard ISO/IEC 9899. Computer and Business Equipment Manufacturers Association, Washington, D.C.

X3 Secretariat, *Standard — The C++ Language.* ISO/IEC:98-14882. Information Technology Council (NSITC), Washington, D.C.

Campbell, R. et al. 1987. *The Design of a Multiprocessor Operating System.* Proc. USENIX C++ Conference, Santa Fe, NM, November.

Cline, M.D. and Lomow, G.A., 1995. *C++ FAQs: Frequently Asked Questions.* Addison-Wesley, Reading, MA.

Dahl, O.J., Myrhaug, B. and Nygaard, K. 1970. *SIMULA Common Base Language.* Norwegian Computing Center S-22, Oslo, Norway.

Dahl, O.J. and Hoare, C.A.R. 1972. *Hierarchical Program Construction in Structured Programming.* Academic Press, New York.

Gamma, E. et al. 1995. *Design Patterns.* Addison-Wesley, Reading, MA.

Ellis, M.A. and Stroustrup, B. 1990. *The Annotated C++ Reference Manual.* Addison-Wesley, Reading, MA.

Hamilton, G. and Kougiouris, P. 1993. *The Spring Nucleus: A Microkernel for Objects.* Proc. 1993 Summer USENIX Conference.

Kamath, Y.H., Smilan, R.E. and Smith, J.G. 1993. Reaping benefits with object-oriented technology, *AT&T Technical Journal,* Vol. 72, No. 5, September/October.

Kernighan, B. and Ritchie, D. 1978. *The C Programming Language.* Prentice-Hall, Englewood Cliffs, NJ.

Kernighan, B. 1981. Why Pascal is not my favorite programming language, AT&T Bell Labs Computer Science Technical Report No. 100, July.

Kernighan, B. and Ritchie, D. 1988. *The C Programming Language (second edition).* Prentice-Hall, Englewood Cliffs, NJ.

Koenig, A. and Moo, B. 1997. *Ruminations on C++.* Addison-Wesley Longman, Reading, MA.

Martin, R.C. 1995. *Designing Object-Oriented C++ Applications Using the Booch Method.* Prentice-Hall, Englewood Cliffs, NJ.

Parrington, G. et al. 1995. *The Design and Implementation of Arjuna.* Computer Systems, Vol. 8, No. 3, Summer.

Stepanov, A. and Lee, M. 1994. The standard template library. HP Labs Technical Report HPL-94-34 (R. 1), August.

Stroustrup, B. 1982. Classes: An abstract data type facility for the C language, Bell Laboratories Computer Science Technical Report CSTR-84, April. Also Sigplan Notices, January, 1982.

Stroustrup, B. 1982. Adding classes to C: An exercise in language evolution. Bell Laboratories Computer Science internal document, April. Software Practice & Experience, Vol. 13, 1983, pp. 139–61.

Stroustrup, B. 1986. *The C++ Programming Language.* Addison-Wesley, Reading, MA.

Stroustrup, B. 1986. What is object-oriented programming? In *Proc. 14th ASU Conf.,* August. Revised version in *Proc. ECOOP'87,* May 1987, Springer-Verlag *Lecture Notes in Computer Science,* Vol. 276. Revised version in *IEEE Software Magazine,* May 1988.

Stroustrup, B. 1991. *The C++ Programming Language (Second Edition).* Addison-Wesley, Reading, MA.

Stroustrup, B. 1994. *The Design and Evolution of C++.* Addison-Wesley, Reading, MA.

Stroustrup, B. A History of C++: 1979–1991. In *The History of Programming Languages,* (Bergin, T.J. and Gibson, R. G., ed., pp. 699–754. Addison-Wesley, Reading, MA. Originally published in *Proc. ACM History of Programming Languages Conference (HOPL-2).* April 1993. ACM SIGPLAN Notices. March 1993.

Stroustrup, B. 1997. *The C++ Programming Language (Third Edition).* Addison-Wesley, Reading, MA.

Stroustrup, B. 1977. A History of C++ in *Handbook of Programming Languages,* Vol. 1, Salus, P.H., ed. MacMillan Technical Publishing, New York.

16

Java

Ricardo Devis
INFOPLUS, S.L.

"Everything should be made
as simple as possible, but no simpler"

Albert Einstein

16.1 Justification

This chapter neither tries to show the Java programming language syntax, nor even to convert readers to Java addicts (C++ methadone is hard to get), nor to serve commercial interests or Internet compulsions. It only tries to introduce to the readers, in a gentle way, a technology platform which is too vast for a few pages, with little technical stuff.

16.2 Introduction

Over the years designers, programmers, and users have been looking forward to some way of providing mobility of code, or software pieces that can be executed on heterogeneous platforms. There is a necessity to provide a solution that allows "writing applications once while running them everywhere, forever...," and the solution may be concerned in several issues: portability, safety, and security (for protecting our system from an individuals stupidity and maliciousness). After too many intelligent efforts, it seems that this solution has been incarnated through the Java language, the Java platform, and the Java way of life.

Java language is both compiled and interpreted. Once it is compiled, instead of generating machine-level code, a set of higher-level set of instructions is generated. This set of instructions, called JCode (formerly Java bytecode), is understood by an abstract machine, the so-called Java Virtual Machine (JVM). Therefore, code composed of these sets of instructions can indeed be executed and run in any platform implementing this virtual machine. So, in the end, it is this abstract machine that is in charge

0-8493-3135-8/99/$0.00+$.50

of translating the bytecodes into native code. As a result, programs written using Java are platform independent.

Java language would not have been so successful as it is, in fact, just on its own. Actually, a question still unanswered is "why did all actual Java industrial partners accept Java bytecode specification without complaining at all?" Nobody knows, even if we point out other facts: the popularization of the Internet, and also the fact that electronic, computer and telecom industries seem to aim at the same finish lane, and the desire for improving technology through simplicity and independence from "monopolist" source codes (this explains why some voices interpreted the Java platform as an anti-Microsoft Holy War).

What happened to the wonderful Smalltalk environments and high productivity tools? They were always based on bytecode, for providing platform independence, and have been stable for more than 20 years. So, what's the point? It's the commercial point, of course. Just ask yourself: Why have all these technologies been applied to a mature language and environment, as Smalltalk undoubtedly is?

16.3 Applets and Servlets

Java popularity also increased due to the fact that it provides a new model of software execution. This way, a program written in Java can be launched from a Web page. But is this really a new model? No it is not. We are only facing mobility in a new more intelligent way. Furthermore, it can be launched in two formats according to their purpose — applets and servlets.

An applet is just a client program that is executed from inside a browser instead of being launched and run from the native operating system downloaded onto your system and executed.

A servlet is a Java program that makes servers extensible. It provides a way to generate dynamic data, replacing the need for CGI scripts. What's more, they can do many things CGI programs cannot.

- They can be uploaded to different servers where they perform the same tasks.
- Due to their ability to run in the background, every new request does not suppose a startup process.
- They allow an interactive communication with a client's applet.

16.4 Security

Nobody of sane mind would allow the execution of foreign software if there is a remote possibility that it comprises its system's existence, that is, what is needed is a condone-like support with quality assurance. In order to make mobility of code really possible, Java must provide answers to two concerns: information confidentiality and vulnerability to corruption or destruction by hackers. Java's security model addresses these two problems. Protective measures applied are of three major types:

1. Language
2. Sandbox
3. Code signing

The **language** itself is more secure than previous languages except for "sociopath" languages like Forth, etc. (no communication, no risk), because all unsafe operations such as pointer arithmetic, explicit pointers, unrestricted casts, unions, unstructured "gotos," operator overloading, and multiple inheritance have been removed. Additionally all accesses to strings and arrays are range checked (but not range validated as catching errors is still a programmer's issue).

The **sandbox** refers to the fact that downloaded applets and servlets are run in a restricted environment that, by default, does not allow access to system resources. When an applet is retrieved, the class loader keeps foreign classes separated from each other and from local classes. The bytecode verifier, implemented as a four-step operation (class file verification, type system verification, bytecode verification, runtime type, and access checking), ensures that the class is formatted correctly, and that it follows JVM restrictions (each operation has the correct number and type of operands and does not leave the stack in an inconsistent state). A class, that is part of the runtime system called SecurityManager, implements the security restrictions applied to the JVM. The SecurityManager has an abstract type that cannot be instantiated by an applet or servlet. It is an extensible class that establishes the namespace for the Java program that can restrict the access to network, local file system, etc. All security-related methods are declared "final," avoiding, in this way, its redefinition. Without this protection, methods could be redefined by malicious applets.

Since the shipping of the JDK 1.1 release, developers can add another security layer, code signing, thanks to the Java Security API. This allows the digital signing of classes using public-key crossed encryption, ensuring that the class has not been modified in the journey from its original server to our computer. This is the same technique that Microsoft uses, as "CaptiveX"* defenders use to claim. Yes, and no, because digital signatures will only become a valuable technology if they are used to support a secure environment such as Java, and this does not happen with the Microsoft secure-way-of-life. For example, with the current Microsoft security model, users can only trust the origin of the software to be installed and run in their machines, but they cannot assure that this piece of software won't damage their local system. As our colleague César Pérez-Chirinos points out, Microsoft digital signing only identifies guilty emissaries, with the additional difficulty of having to count on trusted third parties that cannot ensure local innocuity. That's the reason Sun sympathizers call ActiveX controls "virus factories." But, again, we have no real reasons for not having confidence in the Microsoft ability to generate safe environments for dealing with these issues, despite the fact that they will probably work only in Wintel platforms.

16.5 Java Language Features

Despite its very Internet inception/promotion, Java is currently a general purpose object-oriented programming language with a syntax very similar to a "C++ for dummies" (all those features that make C++ a complex language have been eliminated, loosing at the same time all its flavor and intellectual attraction). This is why many people refer to it as ++C--.

In order to keep the language small and clean, the set of support classes that come with it are grouped in the notion of Java packages. A package is a collection of related classes and interfaces. Unlike other module systems, Java packages are open-ended and can be extended. In this way Java can be expanded easily without increasing language complexity, not only by providing new packages but also by extending existing ones. In fact, packages are, at the same time, physical descriptors and scope identifier namespaces. Java APIs can be divided in two groups:

1. Core APIs bundled with the JDK, like Java language and utilities, Java enterprise, Java commerce, Java security, Javabeans and Javamedia (2D)
2. Optional additions to the JDK like Java Media (3D), Java server, Java management and Java embedded

The following paragraphs describe the most characteristic and atypical features of Java.

16.5.1 Primitive Types

Although Java is an object-oriented language, it is not a pure OO language in the fashion Smalltalk is, where everything (int, char, Boolean) is an object.

This non-pure, object-oriented approach forces the Java platform to implement object wrappers for pre-defined types, because that is the only way to allow pre-built containers to accept those types (do

* As the Javasoft's JavaBeans initiative was immediately next to the Microsoft's ActiveX platform announcement, Microsoft acolytes started to assimilate JavaBeans as "ReActiveX," while Sun's hordes named the revamped OLE/COM object model as "CaptiveX". It seems that very large companies are always kidding and looking for hilarious and stupid language games, and now, what will happen with DNA and COM+?

not forget that Java containers are Smalltalk-copied and inheritance-based, with signatures stating Object arguments, and "int" or "char" are not derived from class "Object," but their wrappers really are).

Java, like C++, has built-in data types that are understood by the compiler itself without any reference to any API. The difference with the C++ data types is that they are uniform across all implementations of Java no matter which hardware we have. This contributes in great manner to portability. These data types can be classified into Numeric, Boolean, and Character.

A special Java feature is that the character type is defined using two bytes to support 16-bit Unicode characters. This means that Java is one of the rare programming languages that really abandons regional software to assist the construction of real international software, allowing programmers to use local identifiers (with accents and all that stuff) in their code, and... wait, wait! Can we code in any human language? Not really! You may code, for instance, in Spanish, but you should not, because you are in fact forced to adopt the conventions established in other parts of the Java platform. So by default JavaBeans will look for Java friends with signatures like "getX" or "setX." But, in fact, is not Java an American-like OOPL? Why not then impose American-like well-n-alive-mannered style?, as Ed Anger would say.

16.5.2 Interfaces

Java only allows single implementation inheritance, so a class can only have one immediate superclass (some voices have claimed that multiple inheritance, MI, is quite dangerous, while others state that MI is more than a necessity). For solving MI problems implementation, Java includes a novel notion on interfaces based on Objective C protocols, which at the same time provides conceptual benefits of MI and solves the diamond problem on method resolution. An interface is a set of constants and abstract methods that can be useful to group classes with common functionality without forcing them into a class hierarchy and to hide the implementation of a class. A class can implement more than one interface and in those cases the class must redefine all the abstract methods of the interfaces it implements.

16.5.3 Automatic Memory Management

Explicit memory management by common programmers is complex and error-prone. In C++, it is the responsibility of the programmers to allocate and free the memory needed, and this drives a lot of errors due to both premature freeing, and forgetting to free the memory at all.* Java solves this problem the same way Smalltalk does by using an embedded garbage collector, and thus similar problems arise. In Java, dynamic memory is allocated as always, but in the background there is a low priority thread whose job is the scanning of memory looking for objects that cannot be reached through the pointers a program has, sweeping the memory space of these objects onto free space for reuse. Garbage collection happens at random intervals, and at those moments there could be an overload of the CPU which might drive to sudden stops. For this reason, Java is not used in embedded or real-time systems. For these cases, Java (as a licensed-based system) offers the programmer the ability to schedule the garbage collection explicitly or turn it off.

Microsoft made an excellent work with its first implementation of the Java platform in Windows, giving nonconservative capabilities to the original GC engine. In JDK 1.2 many performance improvements have to be imposed, so performance and control will undoubtedly grow. Still, most importantly, because of the initially unpredictable and finally undisputed success of the Java platform, garbage collectors are no longer second class citizens, so many GC products are appearing for more "traditional" languages, like C++, and, finally, all of us, prudent programmers, will derive benefits from it.

---

* A common argument has been reproduced here, but the truth is that only error-prone and unskilled C/C++ programmers cause memory errors, and therefore increased divorce ratio. As Viscountess of Vanssey pointed out: "Security is the fool's intelligence."

16.5.4 Multi-Threading

Java is one of the few object-oriented languages that offers a simple and tightly integrated support for threads and related concurrency constructs, without requiring special tools. It supports concurrent programming using only a few basic constructors and classes:

- The class "java.lang.Thread" and the interface "java.lang.Runnable"
- The keywords "synchronized" and "volatile"
- The methods "wait", "notify," and "notifyAll"

As we mentioned before, not only the language has multi-threading support, but also the runtime environment relies on multi-threading to provide multiple services like garbage collection, concurrently. The bad news? Initially (but "things change") Java does not have an independent multi-threading implementation, so every invocation is translated to the subjacent operating system.

Using threads is neither easy nor comfortable, even if they are embedded in the language, as in Java. Readers interested in Java concurrent programming should read the excellent book from Doug Lea, *Concurrent Programming in Java: Design Principles and Patterns.*

16.5.5 GUIs, VUIs, and HUIs*

Since mouse- and icon-driven user interfaces where introduced in the market by Xerox in the 1970s (WIMP: Window, Icon, Mouse, Pointer), we have witnessed the blossoming of several GUI APIs that were mutually incompatible. This was one of the biggest obstacles in the development of cross-platform mobile code. With the AWT (Abstract Window Toolkit) Java provided a platform-independent GUI environment. The AWT drives this into practice, setting an API layer on top of native toolkits. It wraps a native component in each Java component, which JDK refers to as the peer model. In this way it provides a native look-and-feel for each platform. Because the AWT does not provide an exact look-and-feel and therefore the exact pixel dimensions, it ensures that the GUI will look great in all platforms through the introduction of a new notion; the layout managers. These are classes responsible for laying out the visual components without requiring the specification of absolute positions. Due to the fact that each native toolkit has a completely different set of native components and event models, the AWT has restricted itself to the common set. Such an approach is, nowadays and for some developers, too restrictive, but it was enough for the early Java adopters to deliver applets and applications on any Java-enabled platform. Without being frightened to hesitate, we can assure that AWT's biggest error is that it was developed by just one man (well, perhaps from one and a half to two and a half men). Faced with severe time restrictions, JavaSoft adopted a bad architecture for dealing with cross-platform GUI issues, as everybody agrees (so quickly, so bad). The solution? AWT 2.0 (from six and a half men to... the eternity). Let's finish the digression and continue to show the "Diaspora" of graphic notions among the non-Java Gentiles. To address the needs of developers who wanted to create commercial applications that behave and appear identical across all platforms and to provide unbeatable efficiency and extensibility without limits, JavaSoft has created JFC (Java Foundation Classes). JFC is a superset of the AWT based on the Netscape Internet Foundation Classes (coming from ex-NextStep guys), incredibly more mature than its predecessor. The JFC contains a lightweight UI framework that enables components to be peerless, providing a universal look-and-feel. On the other hand, actual investigations are driving us toward a pluggable look-and-feel which will provide the ability to switch from one look-and-feel to a different one at runtime. The JFCs also include a new event model that extends the previous AWT 1.0.X implementation (in fact already extended in JDK 1.1 and JavaBeans component models). In this model, the events are class specific, and can be treated by the object where each event is generated or can be delegated or sent to the object that handles the request, known as listener. JFCs embrace the JavaBeans

* Notice the differences among "Graphical User Interfaces," "Visual User Interfaces," and "Hollywood User Interfaces," in the "GUIs, VUIs, and HUIs" article from Ricardo Devis, RPP, September 97.

component model that will make the developers able to create applets and applications that interoperate with legacy systems.

16.5.6 Serialization

Generally an object does not last longer than the program that created it. This situation can be overridden with persistence, the ability of an object to record its state in a more permanent media than computer's internal memory, so it can be reproduced in the future (or as said in OMG CORBA specs vulgar words: the ability of an object for surviving the process or CPU that created it). Java provides support for object persistence through serialization. Serialization is the process of recording an object by writing out the values that describe its state as an ordered series of bytes. This process is recursive, meaning that if any of the variables is a reference to another object then the referenced object must also be serialized. In order to handle serialization requests, an object must implement either the java.io.Serializable or the java.io.Externalizable interface. In fact the Serializable interface is empty, so it is only a hint for the system to apply default serialization to the chosen class.

Each time an object is serialized there is a potential security problem because data is located outside the Java runtime environment where it can suffer an attack such as the access to sensitive data or the corruption of it. If an object contains certain data values that should be protected against any attack they should not be stored. To accomplish this the transient keyword must be used. If a serialized class comprises the integrity of the system that contains it, that class should not be serialized nor referenced by a serialized one.

Serialization is a proof-of-concept for object persistence. That is, a default behavior is easily guaranteed, but, as pointed in the JavaBeans specs ("do not do the whole thing today"), support can be gradually introduced for more sophisticated storage procedures (from RDBMSs to OODBMSs, passing through POSIX files and INI files). What we have with the Java API is simply an expected well-mannered behavior, but we can augment and refine the naturally given "standard" behavior simply by working. Thus database mappings or data connections can be established without a lot of effort.

16.5.7 Database Integration

Java provides a JDBC (Java DataBase Connectivity? Nobody knows. Java authors deny all knowledge, again) API that allows developers to write client-side applications without concern for the particular database being used. The JDBC API has two levels of interface. First there is the application layer, which defines the Java classes to represent database connections, SQL statements, result sets, database metadata, etc. There is also the driver layer which handles the communication with a specific driver implementation. JDBC, like Microsoft's Open Database Connectivity (ODBC) specification, is based on the X/Open SQL Command Level Interface, but JDBC is written completely in Java getting all the advantages of this language.

JavaSoft and Intersolv also provide a JDBC-ODBC bridge which simply translates JDBC invocations into ODBC calls.

16.5.8 Performance

Java has been accused of having a low performance compared to other OO languages like C++, and because of that JavaSoft is making great effort in this area. In this sense it is noticeable that JDK 1.1 release is much faster than JDK 1.0. And JDK 1.2, and with HotSpots technology, it will be even faster. However, investigations are not only walking this way, but they are also trying to improve both performance when downloading and runtime through the creation of the Java compiler.

In order to minimize applets and servlets loading times, Java's technology provides JAR (Java Archive) files. JAR files are compression archives (as ZIP or TAR ones are), which use a compression scheme based on the one used by the PKZip utility. They additionally provide support for security authentication through digital signing of contained files. Using JAR files, all the ".class" files of an applet can be aggregated into a single archive, so the browser can read it in a single operation, and the extra time needed for opening and closing server connections for each ".class" file is suppressed. The class loader knows how to extract classes from archives so this does not involve extra development. Apart from the ".class" files, JAR files can also include an optional text file, called "manifest" file, that lists information about the files contained in the JAR file. The JAR program is provided as part of the JDK.

In order to improve performance of the JVM, several JIT (just in time) compilers are being developed. The JIT compiler translates bytecode to native code just before execution, but with the advantage of the Java sandbox (bytecode is again verified before being translated).

16.5.9 Javabeans

Almost every human being has the following assertion in mind: *do it and get the best of it!*. But, what does this mean when you apply it to software development?. It means nothing else than the obligation to try to recoup the investment made in software development by reusing it. This can be accomplished through the use of components and frameworks. JavaBeans architecture brings a component model to Java. In conceptual terms, components are self-contained elements of software that can be controlled dynamically and assembled to form an application. As it is said in the JavaBeans specification: *"A bean in JavaBeans is a reusable software component that can be manipulated visually in a builder tool."* The JavaBeans model is made up of an architecture and an API. In order to get a proper participation and interaction in the component structure, beans must provide five major services:

1. Interface Publishing — To enable beans interactions, a bean must provide a mechanism that allows the determination and registration of bean-supported properties and operations both at run and design time. This is accomplished through the Java Reflection API that resembles Self-mirrors.
2. Communication — Beans must provide an event-handling mechanism that implements OO message communication.
3. Persistence — Generally all components have a state, and in some cases it may be interesting to store it. Also in order to be reusable, components must provide a standard mechanism to store its state.
4. Visual Presentation — The component environment allows components to control their visual presentation, layout, and visual relation to other components.
5. Customization — Builder support tools provide some sort of interface for beans attributes customization. The application tool must be able to obtain a catalog of the attributes a bean has, as well as to provide a proper interface to customize them.

One of the principal goals of JavaBeans is its integration with other component models, and as all of you can imagine the first bridge developed has been the one that enables the link between the huge ActiveX component model with the JavaBeans model. This link is carried out wrapping a javabean into an OCX, using a proper tool that generates the types library and the register file in such a way that a javabean can live and understand the ActiveX universe as if it was any other individual of this universe. Javasoft is developing bridges to allow the link to other components model as OpenDoc, LiveConnect, Corba, etc.

16.6 Conclusions

As the reader can see, most of Java's features were present here for a long time in other programming languages, but Java is the first one that presents all of them together. Java's success is a confluence of two main factors: its special features and the opportune time it has been launched into market. Java has a place in the market but the great question nobody answers is: Is Java here to stay?

References

Arnold, K. and Gosling, J. 1996. *The Java Programming Language.* Addison-Wesley, Reading, MA.

Brookshier, D. 1997. *JavaBeans Developer's Reference.* New Riders Publishing, Indianapolis, IN.

Coad, P. and Mayfield, M. 1996. *Java Design: Building Better Apps and Applets.* Prentice-Hall, Englewood Cliffs, NJ.

Chan, P. and Lee, Rosanna. 1997. *The Java Class Libraries: An Annotated Reference.* Addison-Wesley, Reading, MA.

Cornell, G. and Abdali, K. *CGI Programming with Java.* Prentice-Hall, Englewood Cliffs, NJ.

Cornell, G. and Hortsmann, C.S. 1997. *Core Java, 2nd Edition.* Prentice-Hall, Englewood Cliffs, NJ.

Courtois, T. *Java Networking and Communications: Building Communicating Applications with Java.* Sunsoft Press/Prentice-Hall, Englewood Cliffs, NJ.

de Morrison, M., Weems, R., Coffee, P. and Leong, J. 1997. *How to Program Java Beans.* Ziff-Davis Press, New York.

Geary, D.M. and McClellan, A.L. *Graphic Java, 2nd Edition: Mastering the AWT.* Sunsoft, CD-ROM, Prentice-Hall, Englewood Cliffs, NJ.

Gosling, J., Joy, B. and Steele, G. 1996. *The Java Language Specification.* Addision-Wesley, Reading, MA.

Gosling, J., Yellin, F. and The Java Team. 1996. *The Java Application Programming Interface, Volume 1: Core Packages.* Addison-Wesley, Reading, MA.

Harold, E.R. *Java Network Programming.* O'Reilly & Assoc., Sebastopol, CA.

Hughes, M., Hughes, C., Shoffner, M. and Winslow, M. *Java Network Programming.* Manning Publications/Prentice-Hall.

Joshi, D.I. and Vorobiev, P.A. 1997. *The Java 1.1 Programmer's Reference.* Ventana, Research Triangle Park, NC.

Lea, D. 1997. *Concurrent Programming in Java: Design Principles and Patterns.* Addison-Wesley, Reading, MA.

Naughton, P. 1997. *The Java Handbook: The Authoritative Guide to the Java Revolution, 2nd Edition.* Addison-Wesley, Reading, MA.

Sridharan, P. 1997. *Advanced Java Networking.* Prentice-Hall, Englwood Cliffs, NJ.

van Hoff, A., Shaio, S. and Starbuck, O. 1996. *Hooked on Java: Creating Hot Web Applets with Java Applets.* Addison-Wesley, Reading, MA.

Winston, P.H. and Narasimhan, S. 1996. *On To Java.* Addison-Wesley, Reading, MA.

17

Object-Oriented COBOL

Wilson Price
Object-z Systems

Edmund Arranga
Object-z Systems

17.1 Introduction

Since its beginning in the late 1950s, COBOL has seen three major ANSI revisions: COBOL-68, COBOL-74, and COBOL-85. In 1989, the Intrinsic Function Module was added. Work on the next standard began in 1989 when COBOL and object-oriented experts from around the world met to decide how best to "objectify" COBOL. The iterative and incremental approach by ANSI and the ISO ensures that the coming standard, scheduled for completion in 2000, will be completely compatible with earlier standards while introducing more additions to the language than at any other time in its history.

0-8493-3135-8/99/$0.00+$.50

To keep the computing world apprised of progress, the ISO publishes a regularly updated working draft (over 800 pages) that gives a snapshot of the proposed new standard, including its object-oriented features. These drafts have served to drive the efforts of major compiler vendors — including IBM, Micro Focus, Fujitsu, and Hitachi — who have released Object-Oriented COBOL (OOCOBOL) compilers in anticipation of the standard. This chapter focuses on COBOL's OO features as described in the July 1997 ISO Committee Draft 1.1.

OOCOBOL brings its own unique datacentric flavor to object orientation. Strongly influenced by C++ and Smalltalk, the next standard combines aspects of both languages with an eye toward meeting the need of current COBOL users. The result is a hybrid language, capable of supporting procedural methodology of legacy COBOL systems as well as the object methodology so widely accepted today. That is, the next standard is a full superset of COBOL-85/89, providing backward compatibility with previous standards.

If you are a COBOL practitioner unfamiliar with object methodology, you should "lightly" read the following section, then focus on the example beginning with Section 17.3. That should give you sufficient insight to return to this point to appreciate some of the broader implications of OOCOBOL.

17.2 Object-Oriented COBOL Principles

17.2.1 Object-Oriented COBOL and Design/Analysis

Object-oriented analysis and design (OOA&D) serve the function of defining the behavior, attributes, and relationships between classes and between objects. OOCOBOL supports these concepts in a style that facilitates and compliments currently practiced OOA&D techniques. Much of the power of OOA&D results from the common lexicon used throughout the development process. OOCOBOL directly supports these concepts by using the principles of class, object, and inheritance in a manner logically consistent with established terminology. That is, OOCOBOL is consistent at the implementation phase of development with the concepts introduced during the object-oriented analysis phase. Classes, objects, inheritance, methods, attributes, and relationships, all fundamental to object-oriented programming, are conceptually equivalent in OOCOBOL to other object-oriented languages.

17.2.2 COBOL's Class Definition

COBOL programmers are accustomed to the single required entry of the Identification Division — the Program-ID paragraph that designates the name of the program. The next standard adds four additional ID paragraphs including the Class-ID, which indicates that the source unit is a class definition (as opposed to a program definition). The Class-ID identifies the name of the class and optionally may include: (1) an Inherits clause specifying the names of classes that are inherited by this class and (2) a Using phrase specifying that this is a parameterized class.

A conventional COBOL program definition may contain, in addition to the Identification Division, the three divisions Environment, Data, and Procedure. In contrast, a class definition may contain any or all of the following:

- An Environment Division
- A factory (class) definition
- An object (instance object) definition

The general format of a class definition is shown in Figure 17.1.* Both the factory and the instance object definitions designate data and methods that can operate on that data.

* The notation convention used here loosely conforms to that of the standard. Uppercase indicates COBOL key words. Lowercase indicates generic terms representing various COBOL elements, which may be individual items or complete syntactical entries. For instance, in Figure 17.1, `environment division` signifies the ENVIRONMENT DIVISION header and all of its associated entries. Square brackets identify an entry as optional. Ellipses mean that an entry can be repeated.

```
[IDENTIFICATION DIVISION.]
CLASS-ID. class-name Inherits phrase.
[environment division]

[IDENTIFICATION DIVISION.]
factory definition.

[IDENTIFICATION DIVISION.]
object definition

END CLASS class-name.
```

FIGURE 17.1

17.2.3 The Factory Object

The proposed standard designates the factory (or factory object) as the single object of a class that is available at runtime (it does not require instantiation). The factory object is identified as the "creator of objects of the class" by the standard. This can be misleading, as actual creation of instance objects is accomplished by an inherited method from a superclass that is part of a system class library. (Instantiating a class not containing a factory causes a default to the appropriate method of the superclass through inheritance.)

Data of the factory object is thoroughly encapsulated and is accessible only through methods of the factory. As you will see in later examples in this chapter, the programmer is not limited to the actions of creating and destroying instance objects, but he can include methods to provide a variety of generalized control and oversight activities. Data of the factory object is accessible from both within (from instance objects of the class) and without, but only through methods of the factory definition. The general form of the factory definition is shown in Figure 17.2A.

17.2.4 The Instance Object Definition

COBOL's object definition describes the instance object "template." It is, in a sense, an abstract data type comprised of encapsulated data and procedures to operate on that data. Data items listed in the Working-Storage Section (within the Data Division) comprise the object data of an instance. Methods defined under the Procedure Division represent the procedures that provide access to the object data. Instantiation of the class creates an occurrence of the object; a class can be instantiated one or more times during a program run. Referring to Figure 17.2B, you can see that the general form of the object definition is identical to that of the factory definition.

17.2.5 Methods

If you examine a typical COBOL class definition, you will see numerous method definitions, each with the appearance of a "mini-program." That is, each contains its own Identification Division (together

```
[IDENTIFICATION DIVISION.]
FACTORY.
[environment division]
[data division]
[PROCEDURE DIVISION.
  [method-definition...]]
END FACTORY.
```

(a) Factory

```
[IDENTIFICATION DIVISION.]
OBJECT.
[environment division]
[data division]
[PROCEDURE DIVISION.
  [method-definition...]]
END OBJECT.
```

(b) Object

FIGURE 17.2

```
Identification Division.
  Class-id.   SampleClass
     :
  FACTORY.
     :
    Method-id. " do-something".
     :
  OBJECT.
     :
    Method-id. " do-something".
     :
```

FIGURE 17.3

with its Method-ID paragraph), Environment Division, Data Division, and Procedure Division. Experienced COBOL programmers will recognize the procedural code of a method as roughly equivalent to a conventional COBOL paragraph.

17.2.6 Abstraction and Encapsulation

Functional decomposition, breaking a problem down into its primitive functions, is the cornerstone of structured methodology. We strive to decompose a problem such that each leaf module (paragraph) performs a single function and is independent of each other. This is procedural abstraction. However, with global availability of data within a conventional COBOL program, our modules are never as completely independent as we might hope.

OOCOBOL provides for complete independence in that data of the object is accessible only through methods of the class from which the object was created (thereby providing complete encapsulation). Methods are independent of one another because each is effectively a "mini-program" that includes its own working data plus access to the object data. Thus, we have both data and procedural abstraction.

17.2.7 Invoking Methods

You use the `Call` statement to access a subprogram. A method (of either the factory or the object) is called in much the same way, except you use a new verb `Invoke`. The `Invoke` keyword is followed by an object identifier, a method name, and either or both of two keywords identifying the parameters to be operated upon. For instance, consider the class definition skeleton of Figure 17.3 in which the factory and the object both contain the method `do-something`. Note that this apparent duplication is perfectly valid as the factory and the object are completely independent entities of the class definition. For example, by designating the class name (`SampleClass`) after the keyword `Invoke`, the following statement invokes the method of the factory. The parameter list following the keyword `Using` would be in accordance with the definition of the method (the same as calling a subprogram).

```
Invoke SampleClass "do-something" Using...
```

To invoke a method of an object, an instance must first be created (the class must be instantiated) yielding a "handle" that identifies the particular instance. Then, by specifying the handle in the `Invoke` statement, methods of the object can be invoked operating on data of the instance. For example, assume that the class `SampleClass` has been instantiated and that the particular instance is identified by the handle `aSampleObject` (a special data type described in Section 1.3). Then the following statement, using the handle `aSampleObject`, will invoke the method `do-something` of the object.

```
Invoke aSampleObject "do-something" Using...
```

Note that there is no confusion between the two methods (with identical names). One Invoke designates the class name thereby forcing the system to look in the factory object definition. The other designates the handle of an instance, thereby forcing the system to look in the instance object definition.

17.3 A Simple Example

17.3.1 Introduction to the Room Application

The basis for examples of this chapter are components of a room-rental system case study abstracted from a textbook by this author (Price, 1997) in which a company rents conference rooms to its clients. In the interest of removing all extraneous clutter so that you can focus on principles, the first example is a limited conventional program, called a driver program, and a class definition (program). You will first view the class program from the perspective of a class user, a programmer using a prewritten class. As a class user, you need not know how the class performs its operations or the exact nature of the data it owns. You only need to know the programmer interface. In that respect, using prewritten classes of a class library is much the same as using subprograms of a subprogram library.

17.3.1.1 Room Class

File name: ROOM01CL

Purpose: Manage room rental data.

Methods:

get-discounted-room-price

Function: Return a room price using a predefined discount rate. Price is adjusted using the input surcharge amount.
Input: Surcharge amount—PIC 999.
Output: Room price—PIC 999

get-room-price

Function: Return a room price. Price is adjusted using the input surcharge amount.
Input: Surcharge amount—PIC 999.
Output: Room price—PIC 999

17.3.2 The Driver Program

17.3.2.1 Basic Actions of the Driver

For this first illustration, the driver program queries the user, accesses data from the room object, and displays the room price. Specific actions performed are as follows.

1. Create an instance of the room class.
2. Query the user regarding whether or not to apply the discount.
3. Query the user for the room surcharge amount.
4. Invoke the appropriate method of the class to obtain the room price.
5. Display the room price.

The driver of Figure 17.4 looks much like a conventional COBOL program with the exceptions of the following components that identify it as working with an object-oriented class program. (Note: Line numbers are included in this program for easy reference; they are not part of the source code.)

```
1  *>*****************************************************
2  *> Room Rental System
3  *> W. Price 10/7/97                          ROOM01DR.CBL
4  *>
5  *> This creates an instance of room class and
6  *> gains access to room's data by invoking
7  *> instance methods of room.
8  *>*****************************************************
9
10 Identification Division.
11        Program-ID.    Room01Driver.
12
13 Environment Division.
14   Repository.
15     Class RoomClass is "room01cl"
16     .
17 Data Division.
18   Working-Storage Section.
19     01  room-price              pic 9(03).
20     01  surcharge               pic 9(03).
21     01  discounted-price-sw     pic X(01).
22         88  discounted-price      value "Y" "y".
23     01  theRoomHandle           object reference.
24
25 Procedure Division.
26
27   000-process-room-data.
28     *> Create an instance of the room object
29     Invoke RoomClass "New"
30                       Returning   theRoomHandle
31
32     Perform 250-get-user-request
33     If discounted-price
34         Invoke theRoomHandle
35                      "get-discounted-room-price"
36                      Using surcharge
37                      Returning room-price
38     Else
39         Invoke theRoomHandle "get-room-price"
40                      Using surcharge
41                      Returning room-price
42     End-if *>discounted-price
43     Perform 300-display-room-price
44     Stop run
45
46   250-get-user-request.
47     Display " "
48     Display "Do you want discounted price <Y/N>? "
49     Accept discounted-price-sw
50     Display " Enter surcharge amount> "
51     Accept surcharge
52
53   300-display-room-price.
54     Display " "
55     Display "Room price: " room-price
56
```

FIGURE 17.4

- The Repository paragraph at line 14
- The data item at line 23
- The Invoke statements at lines 29, 34, and 39

Free Format

The next standard provides for free format, that is, the programmer is no longer constrained by columns 7, 8, 12, and 72. By designating free format (with a compiler directive) you can position code anywhere. With free format, you indicate a comment with the pair of characters *> (asterisk followed by the greater than symbol). Furthermore, you can include a comment indicator at the end of a statement thereby achieving inline comments. All examples in this chapter use free format.

17.3.2.2 Environment Division Entries

First, look at the repository paragraph of the Environment Division where the single entry of line 15 identifies the class used in this application and relates an internal name (`RoomClass`) to an external file reference (`room01cl`, included within quotes). This need is similar to that of a program that processes a file. That is, you must include a Select clause to relate an internal (COBOL) name to the external file identifier, for instance:

```
Select Room-File assign to disk "room.di"
```

17.3.2.3 The Invoke Statement

As described earlier, where you call a subprogram, you invoke a method of a class; the structure of the Invoke statement is as follows.

1. The keyword `Invoke`
2. The name of the object that is the subject of the `Invoke`; it can be the factory object of a class or it can be an instance object

3. The name, enclosed in quotes, of the object's method to be invoked; there is no equivalent to this in the subprogram Call
4. Optionally, depending upon the nature of the class's method, a `Using` phrase that lists the parameters; its syntax and features are identical to the Using of the subprogram Call
5. Optionally, depending upon the nature of the class's method, a `Returning` phrase listing a single parameter that returns a data item (elementary or group) to the invoking program

17.3.2.4 Creating an Object

Remember, a class is instantiated through the factory of that class. To instantiate a class (create an instance of the class definition object), you must make available three items of information.

1. The name of the class to be instantiated
2. The word New which is the name of a system method (as designated by the next standard) for instantiating the class
3. An object reference name that the system can use to identify the newly created object

The following `Invoke` statement from lines 29 and 30 of Figure 17.4 creates an instance of the room class.

```
Invoke RoomClass "New"
                    Returning theRoomHandle
```

Typical of `Invoke` statements, this one includes the following components.

1. The internal name you have designated (in the Environment Division) represents this class definition (`RoomClass` in this case).
2. The name of the method to be invoked, enclosed in quotes; the method in this case is New. Be aware that New is not a method of RoomClass. It is available to RoomClass through one of the components of the class library furnished with every OOCOBOL compiler. In examples of this chapter, class names use uppercase for the first letter of each word comprising the name; hyphens are not used.
3. A `Returning` parameter required by the method to contain an object handle, the means by which you have access to the newly created object; in this chapter, object handle names follow the same rules as class names except the first word is all lowercase.

17.3.2.5 The Object Handle

As defined in this program, `RoomClass` refers to the general room class. When you create an instance of the class, that instance object is a separate entity from the class itself. You do *not* have access to it through the class name. Your access is through the **object handle** which is designated as a parameter in the `Invoke` statement that creates the instance as illustrated in Figure 17.5. In this example, the name of this identifier is `theRoomHandle`; it is defined in line 20 of Figure 17.4 by the following:

```
01    theRoomHandle          usage is object reference.
```

`Object reference` is a new data type introduced with OOCOBOL specifically to give you access to objects you create.

17.3.2.6 Invoking the Method of the Newly Created Object

Remember from the earlier description of the room class that it includes two methods, both with input and output parameters. With this, the Invoke of lines 39-41 (repeated here from Figure 17.4) should be reasonably straightforward.

```
Invoke theRoomHandle "get-room-prices"
                Using surcharge
                Returning room-price
```

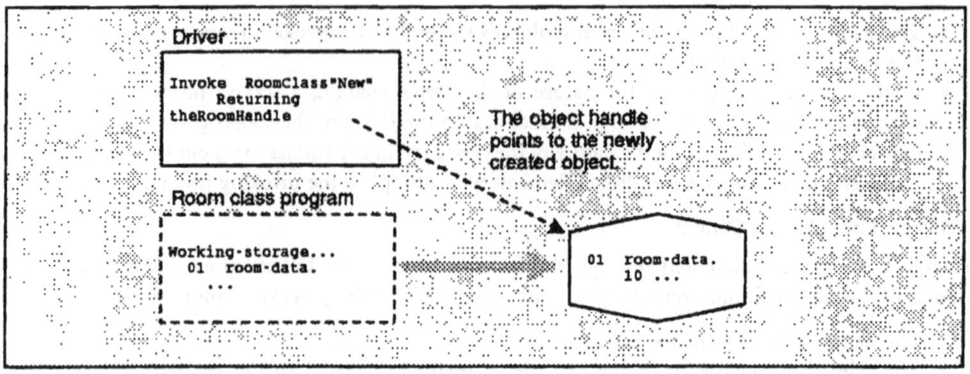

FIGURE 17.5

1. The object handle of the object instance you want, *not* the class name, follows the keyword `Invoke`.
2. Input to the method is designated by the `Using`; you see its data item **`surcharge`** defined in line 20.
3. Output is designated by the `Returning`; you see its data item `room-price` defined in lines 19.

17.3.3 The Class Definition

17.3.3.1 Basic Elements

With this brief introduction, let's look at the Room class definition shown in Figure 17.6 where you see:

- Designation of the class name and an inherits clause
- Association of referenced classes with corresponding physical files on disk
- Definition of the object data
- Methods that allow you to operate on the object's data

17.3.3.2 The Class Base

Recall that Driver created an instance of `Room` by invoking the method New of Room's factory with the following `Invoke`.

```
Invoke RoomClass "New" Returning theRoomHandle
```

Remember that specifying a class name in an Invoke causes COBOL to look for a factory method, rather than an instance method. However, you can see that this program does not include a factory definition. The key is inheritance whereby a class can have complete access to methods of another class from which it inherits. This program, and virtually every class definition you write, requires access to Base. Base includes methods to create and destroy instances of classes, handle errors, and perform other basic functions. You gain this access through the `inherits` clause at line 12. Note that the internal identifier `BaseClass` is related to the external name `Base` in the Repository at line 17.

17.3.4 The Object Definition

17.3.4.1 Defining the Object

At line 21 the keyword `OBJECT` designates the Object paragraph. Under `OBJECT` you see Data and Procedure Divisions. You define data of the object under the Data Division; you define methods of the object under the Procedure Division. The Working-Storage Section of this class definition contains the object's data-items. They are defined in exactly the same way you define data in the Working-Storage Section of a conventional program. As indicated earlier, this example is contrived in that object data is

```
1  *>***********************************************
2  *> Room Rental System
3  *> W. Price  10/7/97                    ROOM01CL.CBL
4  *>
5  *> This class contains room data and the methods:
6  *>     get-room-price
7  *>     get-discounted-room-price
8  *>***********************************************
9
10 Identification Division.
11   Class-id.  RoomClass
12              inherits from   BaseClass.
13
14 Environment Division.
15   Repository.
16     Class RoomClass is "room01cl"
17     Class BaseClass is "Base"
18     .
19 *>______________________________________________
20 Identification Division.
21   OBJECT.
23
24     Data Division.
25       Working-Storage Section.  *>OBJECT DATA
26       01  room-data.
27           10  room-number       pic 9(03)  value 100.
28           10  room-price        pic 9(03)  value 225.
29           10  room-discount     pic v9(02) value .05.
30
31     Procedure Division.  *>OBJECT METHODS
32       *>.........................................
33       Identification Division.
34       Method-id. "get-discounted-room-price".
35       * Input: surcharge      Output: room price
36       *>.........................................
37         Data Division.
38           Working-Storage Section.
39             01  price-factor        pic 9(01)v9(02).
40           Linkage Section.
41             01   ls-surcharge        pic 9(03).
42             01   ls-room-price       pic 9(03).
43
44         Procedure Division Using ls-surcharge
45                            Returning ls-room-price.
46           Move room-price to ls-room-price
47           Add ls-surcharge to ls-room-price
48           Subtract room-discount from 1.0
49                                 giving price-factor
50           Multiply price-factor by   ls-room-price
51           .
52       End Method "get-discounted-room-price".
53
54       *>.........................................
55       Identification Division.
56       Method-id. "get-room-price".
57       * Input: surcharge      Output: room price
58       *>.........................................
59         Data Division.
60           Linkage Section.
61             01   ls-surcharge              pic 9(03).
62             01   ls-room-price             pic 9(03).
63
64         Procedure Division Using ls-surcharge
65                            Returning ls-room-price.
66           Move room-price to ls-room-price
67           Add ls-surcharge to ls-room-price
68           .
69       End Method "get-room-price".
70       *>.........................................
71   END OBJECT.
72 END CLASS RoomClass.
```

FIGURE 17.6

defined with Value clauses. Later in this section you will see how data for an object can be obtained from a conventional indexed file.

17.3.4.2 Methods

Under the Procedure Division of the Object paragraph, you define the object's methods — beginning lines 33 and 55 in Figure 17.6. One aspect of class definitions is the appearance of a complete program structure within the Procedure Division of the object. As is evident here, a method looks much like a subprogram in that it can: (1) include all four divisions and (2) include parameters for interprogram communication. If it uses parameters, then it must include a Linkage Section and a Procedure Division header with parameters. Rules for implementing the Using are identical to those for subprograms. However, the new Standard restricts the Returning parameter to a single 01 entry.

17.3.4.3 End Markers

Within a class definition, you must end all definitions with `End` markers. For instance, the end of each method must be indicated with an `End Method` marker such as the following from line 52 of Figure 17.6.

```
End Method "get-discounted-room-price"
```

Similarly, you end the Object with `END OBJECT` (line 71); notice that no name is associated with the object header (line 21) so none is included in the `END OBJECT` marker. Finally, you end the class definition with `END CLASS` (line 72) which includes the class name.

17.3.4.4 About Surcharge Handling

If you look carefully at this driver/class pair, you will conclude that transmitting the surcharge to Room for inclusion in its calculations is not truly appropriate. That portion of the operation should not reasonably be a responsibility of the class; it should be done in Driver after the price is returned from Room. This contrived example is set up this way to illustrate both Using and Returning parameters and to illustrate handling common code, the next expansion of this example.

```
32  *>..........................................
33  Identification Division.
34  Method-id. "get-discounted-room-price".
35  * Input: surcharge      Output: room price
36  *>..........................................
37    Data Division.
38      Working-Storage Section.
39        01  price-factor          pic 9(01)v9(02).
40      Linkage Section.
41        01   ls-surcharge          pic 9(03).
42        01   ls-room-price         pic 9(03).
43
44    Procedure Division Using ls-surcharge
45                       Returning ls-room-price.
46      Invoke Self " prepare-price
47                       Using ls-surcharge
48                       Returning ls-room-price
49      Subtract room-discount from 1.0
50                             giving price-factor
51      Multiply price-factor by   ls-room-price
52    .
53  End Method "get-discounted-room-price".
54
55  *>..........................................
56  Identification Division.
57  Method-id. "get-room-price".
58  * Input: surcharge      Output: room price
59  *>..........................................
60    Data Division.
61      Linkage Section.
62        01   ls-surcharge               pic 9(03).
63        01   ls-room-price              pic 9(03).
64
65    Procedure Division Using ls-surcharge
66                       Returning ls-room-price.
67      Invoke Self " prepare-price
68                       Using ls-surcharge
69                       Returning ls-room-price
70    .
71  End Method "get-room-price".
72  *>..........................................
73  Identification Division.
74  Method-id. "prepare-price".
75  *> Note: This is a private method for use only
76  *> from within this class.
77  *>..........................................
78    Data Division.
79      Linkage Section.
80        01   ls-the-surcharge           pic 9(03).
81        01   ls-the-price               pic 9(03).
82
83    Procedure Division Using ls-the-surcharge
84                       Returning ls-the-price.
85      Move room-price to ls-the-price
86      Add ls-the-surcharge to ls-the-price
87
88  End Method "prepare-price".
89  *>..........................................
```

FIGURE 17.7

17.3.5 Moving Common Code to Another Method

As COBOL programmers, we strive for code reuse. That is, we place the code for an operation that must be carried out at several points in a program in a separate paragraph or a subprogram. One of the objectives of object methodology is to maximize reuse. To illustrate one of several ways of achieving reuse, look at lines 46/47 and 66/67 of Figure 17.6 and you will see that these pairs are identical. Instead of two code lines, assume that accessing the price and "preparing" it for calculation involves a complicated sequence of 10-15 lines. Furthermore, assume that several other methods of this class required exactly the same operation. Rather than repeat the code in each instance, you would move it to a separate method of this class and invoke it the same as you would invoke any other method. To illustrate the technique, Figure 17.7 shows the subject two code lines moved to a new method named `prepare-price`. It is invoked by specifying `Self` as the object identifier in the Invoke statements — see lines 46 and 67. This forces the system to look for the method in the object's own class definition. In documentation for the room class, it is unlikely that this method would be identified, as it is designed for use only by other methods of the class.

17.4 Inserting Data into an Object

Declaring the data with Value clauses in the previous examples is a good way to get a first look at OOCOBOL. However, that technique has little practical value for most applications. Usually you will create an object and then **populate** it (place data in it). The data to populate an object may be data entered from the keyboard or it may be data from files or a database. Data you often see in an object has the appearance of a single record. However, if you are a COBOL programmer new to object methodology, do not equate object data to record. Classes and their corresponding object data are written to serve a given purpose. Data contained in an object may be data captured from a data-entry program and or from one or more files. In fact, an object may be created as a temporary "data container" required for only a short period of a run and then discarded.

```
Identification Division.
Method-ID. " populate-the-room-object " .
Data Division.
  Linkage Section.
    01 ls-room-data.
       10  ls-room-number       pic X(03).
       10  ls-room-price        pic 9(03).
       10  ls-room-discount     pic v9(02).
Procedure Division Using ls-room-data.
  Move ls-room-data to room-data.
End method " populate-the-room-object " .
```

FIGURE 17.8

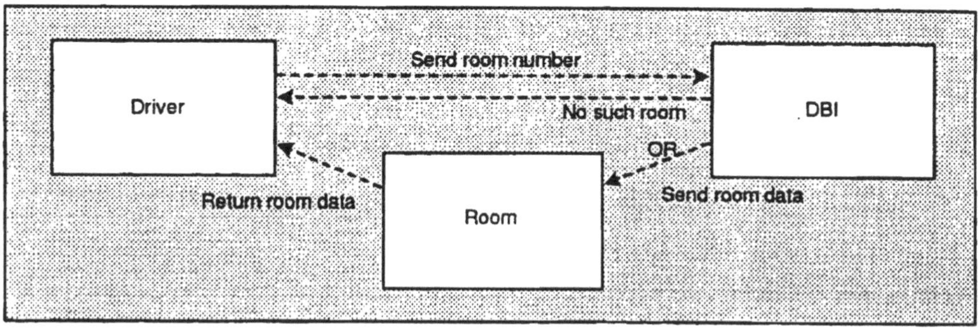

FIGURE 17.9

Remember that the only access you have to an object's data is through methods of the class from which the object was created. Therefore, the OBJECT definition must include a separate method to populate an object. The method of Figure 17.8 would serve this purpose for Room.

17.5 Using a Database Interface

17.5.1 Example Description

The next example expands the room application to include populating the room object with data from an indexed file. Accordingly, this application will consist of three components: Driver, the room class, and a **database interface** (DBI) class as illustrated in Figure 17.9. Driver will still need to communicate with Room to obtain room data. In addition, Driver will need to communicate with DBI to designate the room record to be read. Also, DBI will need to communicate with room to pass it the room data.

Ignoring the creation of objects, you can see that actions of the various components will be something like the following.

17.5.1.1 Driver

- Provide overall program control
- Query user
- Access room data
- Display results

17.5.1.2 Room Class

- Accept room data from DBI
- Calculate the room price
- Return data

17.5.1.3 DBI Class

- Accept room number from driver
- Access the desired record
- Send room data to room

Regarding instantiation of the two classes, perhaps the most obvious approach is to do this in Driver. However, a more versatile technique involves the following sequence.

1. Driver instantiates DBI as part of the initialization process.
2. Driver queries the user for the room number.
3. Driver invokes a method of DBI (sending it the room number) to obtain room data.
4. If the room record is found in the file, DBI instantiates Room, populates it with price data, and returns the room handle to Driver.
5. If the room record is not found in the file, DBI returns a no-record indication to Driver.
6. Driver displays the price or an error message as appropriate.
7. The user is queried about repeating the sequence.

17.5.2 DBI Description

Before looking at Driver, consider the following programmer interface with DBI.

17.5.2.1 Database Interface Class

File name: ROOM02DA

Purpose: Access data from the room file.

Methods:

open-file
- Function: Open the room file.
- Input: None.
- Output: None.

close-file
- Function: Close the room file.
- Input: None.
- Output: None.

read-room-record
- Function: Read a room record, and create and populate a room object.
- Input: Room number—PIC XXX.
- Output: Room handle contains handle to room object if the record was found; set to null if record not found.

For the sake of simplicity in this example, error handling on the file open is ignored.

17.5.3 The Room Class and Driver

The room class is unchanged from ROOM01CL of the first example except the method `populate-the-room-object` of Figure 17.8 has been added. You will see it invoked by the DBI.

Driver requires modification to (1) accommodate entry of a room number by the user and permit repetition and (2) instantiate and communicate with the DBI. You can see by inspecting Figure 17.10

```
 1
*>**************************************************
 2  *> Room Rental System
 3  *> W. Price  10/7/97
ROOM02DR.CBL
 4  *> This driver is an expansion of ROOM01DR. It
 5  *> provides for: (1) acceptance of a user
entered
 6  *> room number, and (2) recovery from a non-
 7  *> existent room number, & (3) program
repetition
 8
*>**************************************************
 9
10  Identification Division.
11         Program-ID.  Room01Driver.
12
13  Environment Division.
14    Repository.
15      Class DatabaseInterface is "room02da"
16    .
17  Data Division.
18    Working-Storage Section.
19      01  room-price                pic 9(03).
20      01  surcharge                 pic 9(03).
21      01  discounted-price-sw       pic X(01).
22          88  discounted-price        value "Y" "y".
23      01  room-number                 pic 9(03).
24          88  terminate-processing      value 0.
25      01  object-handles             object
reference.
26          10  aRoomHandle.
27          10  theDBIHandle.
28
29 Procedure Division.
30
31   000-process-room-data.
32     Invoke DatabaseInterface "New"
33                  Returning theDBIHandle
34     Invoke theDBIHandle " open-file"
35     Perform with test after until room-number = 0
36       Display "Room number <0 to terminate>? "
37       Accept room-number
38       Evaluate room-number
39         When 0
40           Continue
41         When other
42           Perform 200-process-user-request
43       End-Evaluate *>room-number
44     End-Perform *>with test after
45     Invoke theDBIHandle " close-file"
46     Stop run
47     .
48  200-process-user-request.
49    Invoke dBIHandle "read-room-record"
50                              Using room-number
51                              Returning aRoomHandle
52    *> If the record was not found, the room
53    *> object handle is returned as null.
54    If aRoomHandle null = null
55      Display "Invalid room number."
56    Else
57      Perform 250-get-user-request
58      If discounted-price
59        Invoke theRoomHandle
60                 "get-discounted-room-price"
61                 Using surcharge
62                 Returning room-price
63      Else
64        Invoke theRoomHandle "get-room-price"
65                 Using surcharge
66                 Returning room-price
67      End-if *>discounted-price
68      Perform 300-display-room-price
69    End-If *>aRoomHandle null = null
70
 :
```

FIGURE 17.10

that the first of these two needs is served by conventional COBOL code. The inline Perform at line 35 provides loop control using the room number as the key to terminating the loop. The second of these needs involves several items in this program.

1. Driver will need to communicate with both DBI and Room. To that end, it will require handles to both objects; these are defined at lines 25-27.
2. DBI is instantiated at lines 32 and 33. Note that Room is not instantiated by Driver because DBI has been assigned that responsibility.
3. DBI is directed to read the desired record with the Invoke at lines 49-51; the room number is input and the handle of the room object (containing the room price) is the output.
4. The room handle is tested at line 54. A value `null` means the requested room record was not found. The null class is a predefined empty class.
5. The code at lines 57-68 is identical to corresponding code of the first example's driver. The ellipses following line 70 represent the 250 and 300 paragraphs, which are also identical to those of the first example's driver.

17.5.4 The DBI Class

The DBI class definition is shown in Figure 17.11; consider its important elements.

1. The Object paragraph (see line 26) contains Environment and Data Divisions defining the characteristics of the room file. Notice that this is conventional COBOL syntax.
2. Separate methods are included to open and close the file in the usual COBOL manner.
3. In the Procedure Division header of the method `read-room-record` (lines 81 and 82) the method's input is identified `ls-room-number` (defined at line 78) and its output is `ls-theRoomHandle` (defined at line 79).
4. The Read statement beginning line 84 is a conventional COBOL indexed read.

```
1 *>**************************************************
2 *> Room Rental System
3 *> W. Price  10/7/97                      ROOM02DA.CBL
4 *>
5 *> This class definition is the database
6 *> interface for the ROOM system.  It reads a
7 *> requested record from the indexed file ROOM.DI
8 *> Object methods
9 *>   close-file
10 *>   open-file
11 *>   read-room-record
12 *>**************************************************
13
14 Identification Division.
15        Class-ID.  RoomDatabaseInterface
16                   inherits from Base.
17
18 Environment Division.
19   Repository.
20     Class RoomDatabaseInterface is "room02da"
21     Class RoomClass             is "room02cl"
22     Class Base                  is "Base"
23
24 *>________________________________________________
25 Identification Division.
26   OBJECT.
27
28     Environment Division.
29       Input-Output Section.
30       File-Control.
31         Select Room-File assign to disk "room.di"
32                     organization is indexed
33                     access is random
34                     record key is rr-room-number.
35
36     Data Division.
37       File Section.
38       FD  Room-File.
39       01  room-record.
40           10  rr-room-number          pic X(03).
41           10  rr-room-type            pic X(04).
42           10  rr-std-config-price     pic 9(03).
43           10  rr-spec-config-price    pic 9(03).
44           10  rr-room-discount        pic v9(02).
45           10                          pic X(77).
46
47     Procedure Division.
48     *> Object Methods
49       *>..........................................
50       Identification Division.
51       Method-ID. "close-file".
52       *>..........................................
53       Procedure Division.
54         Close Room-File
55
56       End Method "close-file".
57
58       *>..........................................
59       Identification Division.
60       Method-ID. "open-file".
61       *>..........................................
62         Procedure Division.
63         Open input Room-File
64
65       End Method "open-file".
66
67       *>..........................................
68       Identification Division.
69       Method-ID. "read-room-record".
70       *>..........................................
71       Data Division.
72         Working-Storage Section.
73           01  room-data.
74               10  room-number          pic X(03).
75               10  room-price           pic 9(03).
76               10  room-discount        pic v9(02).
77         Linkage Section.
78           01  ls-room-number           pic 9(03).
79           01  ls-theRoomHandle  object reference.
80
81       Procedure Division Using   ls-room-number
82                        Returning ls-theRoomHandle.
83         Move ls-room-number to   rr-room-number
84         Read Room-File
85           Invalid key
86             Set  ls-theRoomHandle to null
87           Not invalid key
88             Invoke RoomClass "New"
89                        Returning ls-theRoomHandle
90             Move rr-room-number to room-number
91             Move rr-std-config-price to room-price
93             Move rr-room-discount to room-discount
94             Invoke ls-theRoomHandle
95                         "populate-the-room-object"
96                         Using room-data
97         End-Read *>Room-File
98         .
99       End Method "read-room-record".
100      *>..........................................
101   END OBJECT.
102 END CLASS RoomDatabaseInterface.
```

FIGURE 17.11

5. If the room record is not found, the `invalid key` phrase results in the room handle being set to null. You use the `Set` to change the value of an object handle data item in exactly the same way you use it to change a condition name value or an index value.
6. An instance of room is created at lines 88 and 89.
7. Needed fields from the room's record are moved to the room data area defined in lines 74-76.
8. The room class' `populate-the-room-object` method is invoked at lines 94-96.

17.5.5 Garbage Collection

One subtle aspect of this example is that for each user request of room data, DBI creates a new instance of Room in memory and leaves the previous one unavailable. To understand that, recognize that creation of an object is a two-step process: the object data is replicated in memory, and the memory address of that data area is returned as a handle. Thus if you have processed, for instance, four user requests, the memory contents would appear as shown in Figure 17.12. You see that the single object handle, `the-RoomHandle`, points to the most recently created object and that the other three have been "cast loose." They are no longer accessible to the program (because they no longer have an object handle), *but* they remain in memory.

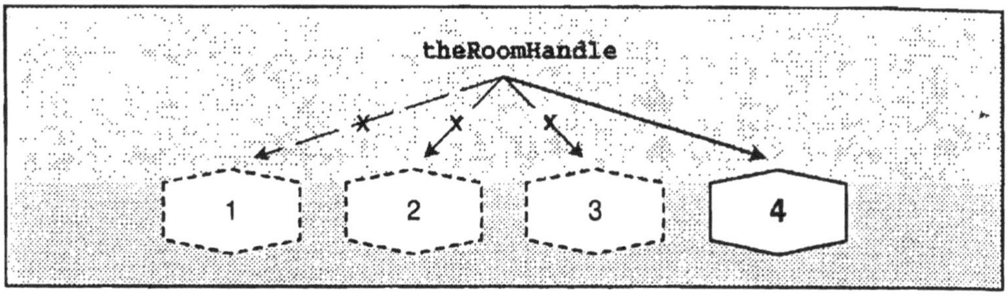

FIGURE 17.12

For this room application in which many inquiries are processed, you might guess that these unaccessible objects would eventually fill memory. Fortunately, that will not occur with COBOL because the next standard requires automatic garbage collection. That is, periodically the system searches for objects that are no longer accessible (no longer have handles pointing to them) and deletes them thereby freeing up their occupied memory.

17.6 The Factory (Class) Object

17.6.1 Inheritance from the Class Base

Remember from earlier in this chapter that the object reference following the keyword Invoke can be:

- A class name, which causes a method of the class' factory to be invoked.
- An object handle, which causes an instance method (method of the Object paragraph) to be invoked

Let's focus on invoking a method of the factory; for instance, consider the following familiar statement.

```
Invoke DataBaseInterface "New" Returning theDBIHandle
```

Although the DBI class does not contain a factory, the above statement is perfectly valid because DBI inherits from the class Base (refer to line 16, Figure 17.11). Thus, Base and DBI represent a **superclass/subclass** pair in which all methods of the superclass are available through the subclass. This is the essence of **inheritance**. Execution is illustrated in Figure 17.13 where the following occurs.

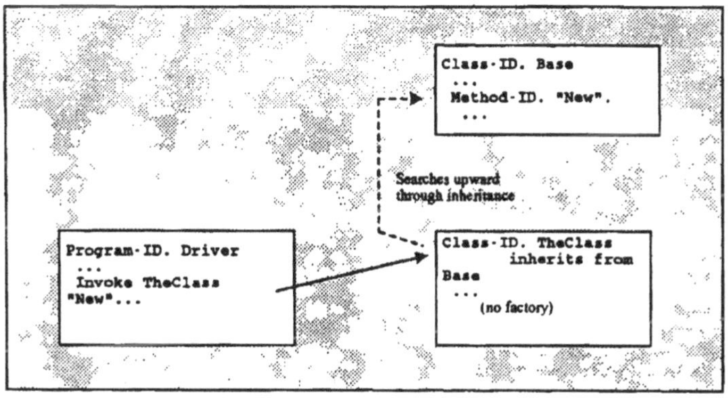

FIGURE 17.13

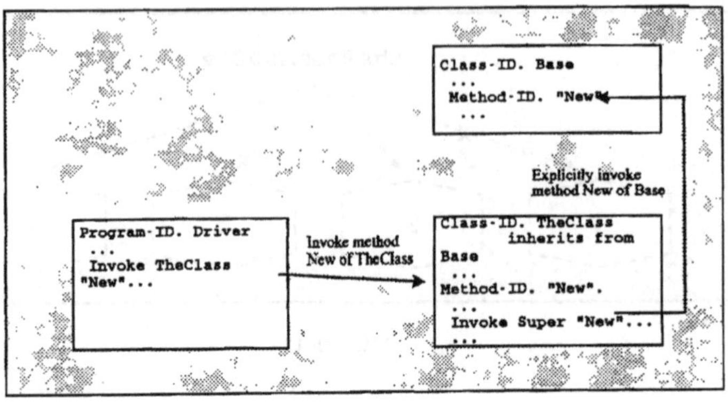

FIGURE 17.14

1. Driver invokes the DBI factory method New.
2. There is no factory method name New (in fact, no factory) in DBI, so the search goes to the next level in the inheritance chain.
3. The method New is found in Base and invoked thereby creating the instance of DBI.

A common practice is to include a method New in a factory definition thereby allowing you to tailor the method to your own particular needs. However, if you do this, then your factory intercepts the message to Base's New thereby thwarting creation of your instance. At some point in your method New, you must issue an Invoke to base for creation of the desired instance. This is illustrated in Figure 17.14; now let's see how it is implemented in a program.

17.6.2 Opening the File in the DBI Factory

In the next example a factory object is included in the DBI to open the room file automatically, thereby eliminating the need for Driver to invoke the open-file method. Appropriate code of this class definition is shown in Figure 17.15; code of the Object paragraph is unchanged from that in Figure 17.11. The first action of this factory method New is to create an instance of the object. Using `Super` as the object identifier forces the system to move up to the next level in the inheritance chain. Notice that it appears the class is instantiating itself. That is not so, as the factory and object definitions are independent of

```
*>***********************************************
*> Room Rental System
*> W. Price  10/7/97                  ROOM03DA.CBL
*>
*> This DBI class definition provides for
*> automatic opening of the room file when
*> the class is instantiated.
*> Factory method
*>   New
*> Object methods
*>   close-file
*>   open-file
*>   read-room-record
*>***********************************************

Identification Division.
       Class-ID.  RoomDatabaseInterface
                  inherits from Base.

Environment Division.
  Repository.
    Class  RoomDatabaseInterface is "room02da"
    Class  RoomClass is "room02cl"
    Class  BaseClass is "Base"

*>-----------------------------------------------
Identification Division.
  FACTORY.

    Procedure Division.
      *>.........................................
      Identification Division.
      Method-ID. "New".
      *>.........................................
        Data Division.
          Linkage Section.
            01 ls-theDBIHandle
                              usage object reference.
        Procedure Division
                          Returning ls-object-counter.
          Invoke Super " N  ew"
                          Returning ls-theDBIHandle
          Invoke  ls-theDBIHandle " open-file"

      End Method "New".
  END FACTORY.

  OBJECT.
:
```

FIGURE 17.15

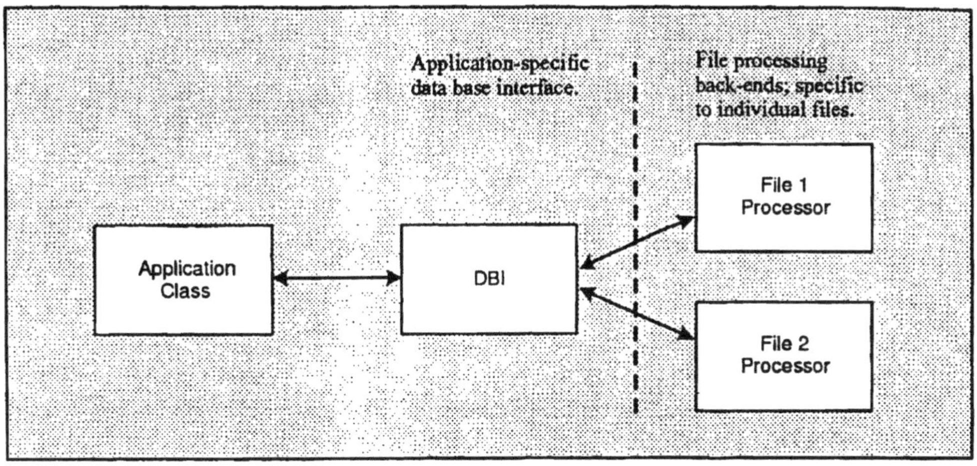

FIGURE 17.16

one another. Once the instance object is created, the `open-file` method of that object is executed thereby opening the room file.

Note that the only change required in Driver is the removal of the Invoke statement to open the file.

17.6.3 A Final Word on File Processing

The preceding file processing examples represent a simplistic approach to handling indexed files. A much more versatile technique is to separate file processing from the DBI and use the DBI as the intermediary between application classes and file processor classes. For each file of a system, this requires an independent file processor class with the following features.

1. Its object data is the file's data record definition.
2. It includes methods to perform all of the standard input and output file operations such as read, write, etc. Each file processor class requires these common methods.
3. For each application in which the file is accessed, the file processor contains a method to access fields from the record required by that application.

The function of the DBI, which is application dependent, is to serve as a front-end between the application classes and the file processor classes as illustrated in Figure 17.16.

17.7 Full Object-Orientation of the Room Example

If you inspect the driver program of Figure 17.10, you see that it contains considerable code in the form of conventional structured techniques. The combination of Driver, Room class, and DBI class is hybrid in nature in that it combines Driver's structured methodology with object methodology which is highly inappropriate. The objective of the object-oriented design phase is to identify classes and their associated responsibilities, which are then ported directly to equivalent OOCOBOL code. In the design phase, a driver is not even a consideration. In action, its sole function is to get things started or, to "prime the pump," then let appropriate classes take over.

Look at Figure 17.10 again and you will see that it serves two basic functions: interface with the user and provide overall program control. In an actual design, you would break these functions out into separate classes yielding the structure shown in Figure 17.17. This form illustrates four basic class stereotypes that are common to most applications.

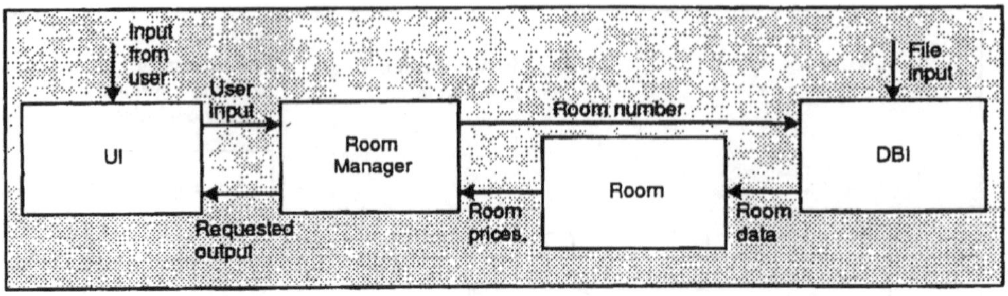

FIGURE 17.17

1. **Presentation/interface** — Responsible for presenting information to and retrieving input from users; these classes/objects are typically responsible for displaying graphical user interfaces or retrieving information.
2. **Control** — Responsible for coordinating the services provided by different classes and objects; this category manages many of the operations in an application, acting as a go-between or middleman in carrying out requests for service.
3. **Application domain** — Perform tasks or contain information specific to an application.
4. **Data management** — Responsible for managing data structures; they hide the details of data structures thereby allowing the structures to change without affecting the other classes and objects in the system.

In this scenario, the functions of Driver would then be limited to (1) instantiating appropriate classes and (2) providing for communication between classes. Because of space limitation of a single chapter, example code for this case is not included.

17.8 Inheritance

17.8.1 Exploiting Commonality

17.8.1.1 Handling Different Room Types

Assume that the room rental system must be expanded to recognize different room types like lecture rooms and laboratory rooms. Unfortunately, data requirements for the two are slightly different. That is, the lecture room data includes a room-capacity field where the lab room includes a number-of-work-stations field and a positions-per-work-station field. The lab room capacity is computed as the product of these two fields. Consequently, you might assume that each will require its own class definition with features shown in Figure 17.18. However, notice the following about these two classes.

- The first three data items of the two classes are identical.
- Other data items are different between the two classes.
- The first two services (corresponding to required methods) are identical.
- Although the service "return room capacity" is the same for both, the procedures for determining the room capacity are different.

Implementing two classes as illustrated in Figure 17.18 produces code redundancy, a bane of good programming practice. The solution to this dilemma is **inheritance.**

17.8.1.2 Classification Hierarchies

As human beings, one of the ways we handle complexity is through proceeding from generalizations to specializations. For instance, in an analysis phase of the room rental system, we might identify room as

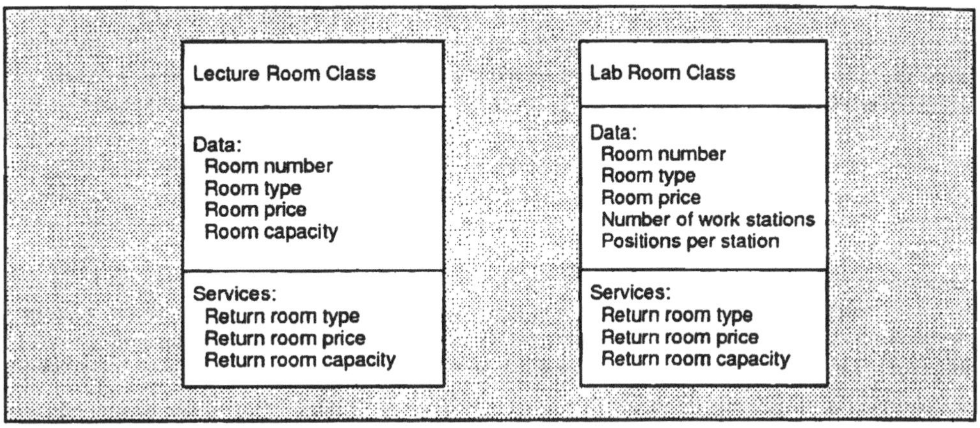

FIGURE 17.18

a potential class. However, as we delve deeper, we become aware of the complexity of room processing, and categories of rooms emerge, for instance, lecture rooms and lab rooms. Although each room type has its own unique characteristics, they all have some common features. The way to handle this is to break those common features out into a separate class that is superior to the unique lecture and lab room classes, as illustrated in Figure 17.19. Notice that a Lecture room is still a room; it includes its own properties *and* those of Room. Figure 17.19 is called a classification hierarchy and is implemented in object methodology through inheritance. That is, Lecture Room and Lab Room inherit the characteristics of their superclass Room. This inheritance is the same inheritance you saw in the earlier examples in which the method New is inherited from the system class Base.

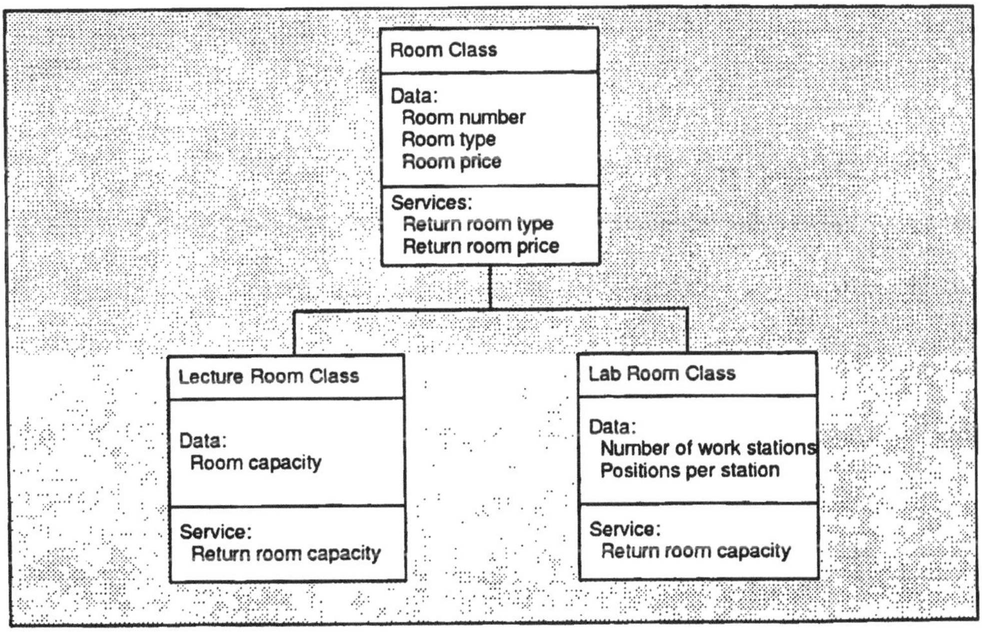

FIGURE 17.19

17.8.1.3 The Classification Hierarchy and OOCOBOL

OOCOBOL implements the classification hierarchy (inheritance) in a way that is completely transparent to the class user. That is, once these classes are written and cataloged in a class library, you see and have access to two *apparently* independent classes: LectureRoom and LabRoom. You instantiate, for instance, LabRoom without any regard to its superclass Room. The resulting object consists of object data from both definitions. Access to the object data is through respective methods of the two class definitions. In other words, you see the lab room class you have instantiated as if it were defined in Figure 17.18.

17.8.2 A Simple Example of Inheritance

As an example of implementing inheritance, the next example employs the structure of Figure 17.19 but omits the room type from the object data. This minimizes the amount of code in the program while preserving the basic concepts to be illustrated.

17.8.2.1 The Room Super Class

First, look at the room class definition in Figure 17.20 and you will see that it looks much like earlier classes of this chapter. You see object data that is accessible through the `get-room-price` method. Although this is a simple move action (line 31), you could imagine in an actual application that this could require extensive calculation, table lookup, or other processing. You also see the method `populate-room-object` (line 37) which is necessary to place data in the object. Notice that there is nothing in this class definition to indicate that it is a superclass to some lower level classes.

17.8.2.2 The LabRoom Subclass

Now look at the LabRoom class definition and notice that it contains only two components that differ from previous examples. First, line 15 denotes that it inherits from RoomClass. Notice that you do not indicate inheritance from Base, as inheritance from RoomClass provides access to all methods of RoomClass and to classes from which RoomClass itself inherits.

The second feature of this class definition is in the method `populate-room-object`, the method DBI invokes to send its data to the object. At lines 51-54 you see Move statements that place data in the LabRoom portion of the object. Because methods of LabRoom do not have direct access to object data from Room, this method must then invoke a method of Room to populate its share of the object data (lines 55 and 56).

Generally, you will never use a superclass such as Room by itself; it is accessible through the inheritance chain. A class such as this for which you do not explicitly create an instance is called an **abstract class.**

17.9 Other Features of Object-Oriented COBOL

17.9.1 Aggregate Structures

Classification hierarchies (the basis of inheritance) allow us to categorize things by proceeding from the general to the specific. Breaking a complex item into component parts is another means of simplifying and understanding. For instance, consider the following breakdown of a personal computer.

- Personal computer system
  - Main unit
    - Disk drive
    - Memory
  - Monitor
  - Keyboard
  - Printer

Such a structure is commonly called a **whole-part hierarchy.** It is also called an **aggregation structure.** You can easily implement an aggregation relationship in COBOL simply by including an object handle

```
*>***********************************************
*> Room Rental System
*> W. Price  11/7/97                  ROOM04RO.CBL
*>
*> This is the room superclass.
*> Object data is:
*>    room number, room price
*> Its methods are:
*>   get-room-price, populate-room-object
*>***********************************************

Identification Division.
   Class-id.  RoomClass
                  inherits from Base.

Environment Division.
   Repository.
     Class RoomClass is "room04ro"
     Class BaseClass is "Base"

*>-----------------------------------------------
Identification Division.
   OBJECT.
     Data Division.
       Working-Storage Section.   *> OBJECT DATA
         01  room-data.
               10  room-number     pic X(03).
               10  room-price      pic 9(03).

     Procedure Division.  *> OBJECT METHODS
       *>-------------------------------------
       Identification Division.
       Method-id. "get-room-price".
       *>-------------------------------------
         Data Division.
           Linkage Section.
             01  ls-room-price  pic 9(03).

         Procedure Division
                          Returning ls-room-price.
           Move room-price to ls-room-price

       End Method "get-room-price".

       *>-------------------------------------
       Identification Division.
       Method-id. "populate-room-object".
       *>-------------------------------------
        Data Division.
          Linkage Section.
            01  ls-room-number        pic X(03).
            01  ls-room-price         pic 9(03).

        Procedure Division Using ls-room-number
                                 ls-room-price.
          Move ls-room-number to room-number
          Move ls-room-price to room-price

       End Method "populate-room-object".
       *>-------------------------------------
  END OBJECT.
END CLASS RoomClass.
```

```
*>***********************************************
*> Room Rental System
*> W. Price  11/7/97                  ROOM04LA.CBL
*>
*> Lecture room class (Inherits from Room)
*> Object data is:
*>    number-of-stations
*>    station-capacity
*> Its methods are:
*>   get-room-capacity, populate-room-object
*>***********************************************

Identification Division.
       Class-id.  LabRoomClass
                     inherits from RoomClass.

Environment Division.
  Repository.
    Class RoomClass    is "room04ro"
    Class LabRoomClass is "room04la"

*>-----------------------------------------------
Identification Division.
  OBJECT.
    Data Division.
      Working-Storage Section.   *> OBJECT DATA
        01 room-data.
           10  number-of-stations   pic 9(02).
           10  station-capacity     pic 9(01).

    Procedure Division.  *> OBJECT METHODS
      *>-------------------------------------
      Identification Division.
      Method-id. "get-room-capacity".
      *>-------------------------------------
       Data Division.
         Linkage Section.
           01  ls-room-capacity         pic 9(02).

       Procedure Division
                       Returning ls-room-capacity.
         Move number-of-stations
                             to ls-room-capacity
         Multiply station-capacity
                             by ls-room-capacity

      End Method "get-room-capacity".
      *>-------------------------------------

      Method-id. "populate-room-object".
      *>-------------------------------------
       Data Division.
         Linkage Section.
           01 ls-room-data.
               10 ls-room-number         pic X(03).
               10 ls-room-price          pic 9(03).
               10 ls-number-of-stations  pic 9(02).
               10 ls-station-capacity    pic 9(01).

       Procedure Division Using ls-room-capacity.
         Move ls-number-of-stations
                           to number-of-stations
         Move ls-station-capacity
                           to station-capacity
         Invoke Super " populate-room-object"
             Using ls-room-number, ls-room-price

      End Method "populate-room-object".
      *>-------------------------------------
 END OBJECT.
END CLASS LabRoomClass.
```

FIGURE 17.20

as an element of an object definition. For instance, assume that the room class has been expanded to include both room data and a reservation calendar. However, as the calendar is used by other applications, you want to maintain it as a separate class. Thus, your aggregate structure could be represented as follows.

Room Master
    Room data
    Calendar data

```
 1 Identification Division.
 2   Class-ID.   RoomMasterClass
 3               inherits from Base.
 4
 5 Environment Division.
 6   Repository.
 7     Class  RoomMasterClass ...
 8     Class  RoomClass ...
 9     Class  CalendarClass ...
10     Class  BaseClass is "Base"
11
12 *>──────────────────────────────────────────
13 Identification Division.
14   FACTORY.
15    Procedure Division.
16       *>.........................................
17       Identification Division.
18       Method-ID. "New".
19       *>.........................................
20         Data Division.
21           Working-Storage Section.
22             01  theRoomHandle object reference.
23             01  theCalendarHandle object reference.
24           Linkage Section.
25             01 ls-theMasterHandle usage object reference.
26
27         Procedure Division Returning ls-object-counter.
28           Invoke Super " New"  Returning ls-theMasterHandle
29           Invoke  RoomClass " New"  Returning theRoomHandle
30           Invoke  CalendarClass " New"  Returning theCalendarHandle
31           Invoke  ls-theMasterHandle " pass-handles"
32                         Using   theRoomHandle,  theCalendarHandle
33
34       End Method "New".
35   END FACTORY.
36
37 Identification Division.
38   OBJECT.
39     Data Division.
30       Working-Storage Section. *> Object data
31         01  theRoomHandle object reference.
32         01  theCalendarHandle object reference.
 :
```

FIGURE 17.21

Figure 17.21 is a code section illustrating this implementation. The following actions take place in its factory.

1. Its own object is instantiated (line 28).
2. The room class is instantiated (line 29).
3. The calendar class is instantiated (line 30).
4. A method of its instance object (`pass-handles`) is invoked to pass the instance the object handles of the two component objects (`room` and `calendar`). This method (not shown in Figure 17.21) moves these handles from the linkage items into the object data items of lines 31 and 32. Thus, the two aggregate objects are available to all other instance methods of this class.

17.9.2 Collection Classes

All COBOL programmers have used tables (arrays) and subscripted data items. An array represents a "collection" of data. The intrinsic functions of the 1989 supplement provide COBOL with functions to perform operations on arrays such as mean, standard deviation, maximum, and minimum. Thus, COBOL's table capability provides us with (1) a data "container" and (2) "procedures" that operate on elements of that container. In a broad sense, we have a primitive *collection* or *container* class that provides means for storing and operating on multiple data entities.

Although we can group objects via their handles using conventional table syntax, we would be using a relatively mundane grouping tool (tables) for a very elegant structure (objects). As you have learned from this chapter, objects denote not only physical entities (data) but also behavior (methods of the class). Therefore, it would seem logical that an object-oriented language would implement a grouping structure that itself has behavior — that structure is called a **collection**. Collections, of which there are several types, are essentially "smart" containers for objects for grouping and managing objects and data. They present a uniform interface to the class-user thereby significantly reducing the amount of code that must be written and maintained. Collection class types in the proposed Standard include:

- Bag (a completely unorganized general collection type)
- Ordered dictionary (the familiar two-entry table, function/argument, in which the function entries are in sequence)
- Queue
- Stack

17.10 Summary and Observations

17.10.1 Chapter Summary

This chapter is a thumbnail sketch of the upcoming object-oriented additions to our venerable COBOL language. As illustrated in this chapter, OOCOBOL supports the basic elements of object-orientation in a style that facilitates and compliments currently practiced object-oriented design and analysis techniques. Examples of the chapter illustrate:

- Classes and objects
- Class instantiation
- Procedural and data encapsulation
- The distinction between the factory object and the instance object
- Classification structures and inheritance
- Aggregate structures

17.10.2 Moving COBOL to Object Orientation

Although as of the publication date of this handbook the next COBOL standard remains a committee item, business and industry cannot take a "wait and see" attitude. The "rules" of software development are undergoing constant and rapid change. Object technology, client/server computing, GUI interfaces, the Internet/Intranet, and a host of other emerging technologies are placing new demands on COBOL developers. The COBOL community must move to transfer established technology from other object-oriented languages (such as Smalltalk, Eiffel, and C++) to the COBOL domain. This technology includes coding practices, modeling techniques, teaching practices, and frameworks/patterns. OOCOBOL arrives a late-comer to the world of objects. The COBOL community stands to benefit by following in the footsteps of its object-oriented contemporaries.

17.10.3 Legacy Code

Many believe that objects working together across system boundaries will define the next generation of computing technology. The COBOL community can play a significant role in this arena. The object-oriented features of the coming standard provide a powerful set of tools to effortlessly integrate into this environment.

However, over 70% of the world's data are locked in mainframe applications where access is via conventional COBOL programs. Must this be rewritten to meld with the world of objects? The answer is "No." It will be possible to expand the scope of many legacy applications to take advantage of this powerful technology without completely rewriting tested code. The technique for making this happen is called **wrapping**.

17.10.4 Wrapping

A **wrapper** is an object that encapsulates code and data in order to act as an intermediary between service providers and clients. Wrapping can be done in either of two ways depending on the structure of the application, its modularity, and its system requirements.

17.10.4.1 The Big Wrapper

The easiest strategy to use is the big wrap, which creates a wrapper object responsible for executing the program in its entirety. This approach surrounds a conventional COBOL program with an object definition and provides one or more methods to execute all or part of the wrapped code. The big wrap strategy is effective when a program's functionality can be viewed as a single service.

17.10.4.2 Wrapping Parts

A more involved strategy involves wrapping individual program components. Although more ambitious, this approach has a higher potential payoff if the individually wrapped components can be used by other applications, and if the program can be partitioned along functional lines. With this approach, each functional component is mapped to individual methods of the wrapper object.

17.10.5 Frameworks and Patterns

Perhaps more than any other programming language COBOL and its practitioners stand to benefit from a maturation of the frameworks and patterns movement. The proliferation of many nearly, but not identical, versions of the same applications, has kept COBOL and the software industry dealing with grains of sand where bricks are needed. Patterns and frameworks applied successfully by 2,000,000 COBOL programmers would certainly produce the scales-of-economy to justify the translation of existing patterns and further research in identification and dissemination of additional business patterns.

17.10.6 COBOL Culture

To quote an esteemed colleague of mine, Edmund Arranga: "On the softer side of technology lie the human issues. And the human issues ultimately determine the degree of acceptance of any technology. As Dijkstra noted more than 25 years ago "... one of the most important aspects of any computing tool is its influence on the thinking habits of those who try to use it." If language is the dress of thoughts, COBOL programmers must learn to wear new clothes, to think new thoughts."

Acknowledgment

I cannot conclude this chapter without acknowledging the significant contributions of Edmund Arranga whose ideas and insights permeate this chapter.

References

Price, W. 1997. *Elements of Object-Oriented Programming*. Object-Z Publishing, Orinda, CA. (For more information, refer to www.objectz.com.)

Further Information

An Introduction to Object COBOL by Doke and Hardgrave, 1998, John Wiley & Sons. An easy-to-read book that provides a basic introduction to what object-orientation is all about and gives you a glimpse at some of the features in OOCOBOL.

Object-Oriented COBOL by Arranga and Coyle, 1996, SIGS Books. An excellent reference for the basic principles of OOCOBOL; includes code for an example library application in an appendix.

Object-Oriented Development in COBOL, Topper, 1995, McGraw-Hill. Read the title on this book. This is a book on object-oriented development (and design) with COBOL in the "background." It will give you an idea of how OOCOBOL can fit into the overall picture.

Standard Object-Oriented COBOL, Chapin, 1997, John Wiley & Sons. The title is a misnomer as there is currently no such "Standard." Examples are thin and many references are outdated.

The COBOL Report, The COBOL Group. A bimonthly newsletter covering a variety of COBOL topics including object-orientation, distributed objects and COBOL, and COBOL and the Web, COBOL, and CORBA. For information, refer to the Web site www.objectz.com.

18
Objective C

Kresten Krab Thorup
University of Aarhus

18.1 Introduction

Objective C is a simple, compiled programming language with most of its concepts and semantics borrowed from Smalltalk (Goldberg and Robson, 1989). It is one of the only languages in the history of programming languages that combines a traditional batch-compilation with a dynamic object-system. The language is a superset of ANSI C (Schildt, 1990) adding basically just objects and messages, and it is easy to learn primarily because it introduces only the most elementary object-oriented concepts. Being a superset of C gives Objective C the advantage that it integrates naturally with much of the existing source code and libraries.

With dominating Smalltalk roots, Objective C uses a programming style much like Smalltalk. Because Objective C is compiled it allows for writing stand-alone applications and libraries, even though this is just an issue of tools, this is still one of the most criticized aspects of Smalltalk. Objective C's combination of support for dynamic loading, runtime dispatch, and introspection provides a framework for writing programs that operate on objects in a generic fashion, as well as allowing features such as remote method invocations to be implemented directly in Objective C; something that is often implemented in the compiler or runtime system of a programming language.

Objective C has evolved significantly since its inception in the mid-1980s, and there is no official standard for Objective C. As a result of this, the language is defined *de facto* by the vendors that provide compilers, and several aspects of the language vary from implementation to implementation. The version which has had the most widespread use is that of NeXT Software, Inc. In NeXT's OPENSTEP operating system Objective C is used to implement all applications and libraries as well as aspects of the operating system. That version of Objective C will also be the application development language used in the "Yellow Box" platform of Apple's Rhapsody operating system.

0-8493-3135-8/99/$0.00+$.50

18.2 The Objective C Programming Language

This section informally describes most of the core of the Objective C programming language syntax and semantics. The next section provides an introduction to some of the library and environment features that are typical in an Objective C programming environment.

18.2.1 What is an Objective C Program?

An Objective C program is a composition of objects and messages being sent to these objects. In response to a message, an object will perform one of its methods; which may in turn send messages to other objects or perform some kind of input/output. Objects are described in classes, which are instantiated at runtime to introduce new objects.

18.2.2 Messages

The only new expression syntax which Objective C adds to ANSI C is for sending messages. To send a message to an object, an expression at the form is used:

```
[receiver message]
```

The *receiver* is a variable or expression evaluating to an object reference, and *message* is a keyword argument list. For example, the following message tells the *myMatrix* object to perform its display method:

```
[myMatrix display]
```

To send a message and pass arguments, these are separated by keywords:

```
cell = [myMatrix getCellAtRow:10 andColumn:15]
```

Objective C message-send syntax is very similar to Smalltalk messaging syntax except for the enclosing square brackets. Like Smalltalk, Objective C also has a special receiver denoted *super.* When messages are sent to *super,* the message will be sent to the current object, but the lookup will start from the parent of the class in which the expression is written. This is, e.g., used for initialization, so that all classes can contribute to the collective initialization of an object.

18.2.3 Typing

A unique feature of objective C, as opposed to many other programming languages, is that entities such as variables, instance variables, arguments, etc., can be either typed or untyped. The special type named *id* is used to specify an untyped object reference. The following declaration introduces a new untyped variable named *anObject,* which can be assigned object references of any kind without generating a warning:

```
id anObject;
```

The type *id* is semantically quite different from typing it with *NSObject,* the parent of all classes in the system. Any message can be sent via an object reference of type *id,* whereas an object reference of type *NSObject* only allows for sending messages declared in class *NSObject.** An untyped reference can refer to any object. Early versions of the Objective C programming language had only an untyped object reference; typed object references were added in NeXT's implementation and later adopted by other vendors.

Alternatively, variables can be declared with a static type as it is customary in other typed programming languages. The following declared a variable *myMatrix* of class type *NSMatrix*:

```
NSMatrix *myMatrix;
```

* The prefix *NS...* is used for all global identifiers in the NEXTSTEP system.

When a variable is declared of a specific static type, it describes the constraint that it is allowed to hold references to instances of the given class, or subclasses thereof; thus Objective C employs simple subtype substitution.

At runtime, the compile time type of entities has no impact on the execution of the program whatsoever. For instance, Objective C does not support overloaded methods, i.e., allowing several methods with the same name, but with different argument types. The static types are only used for error checking, e.g., so that the compiler may warn the programmer if a given object will not be able to respond to a given message.

18.2.4 Classes

Objective C supports single inheritance for classes. Class definitions are separated into two types: an interface declaration and an implementation declaration. These are typically described in separate files, a header file for the interface denoted with .h extension (as in C), and a module file for the implementation, denoted with a .m suffix on the file name. The interface declaration describes the instance variables and the signature for the public methods. Consider for instance the interface for class *Person* described in `Person.h` as follows:

```
#include <objc/NSObject.h>
@interface Person: NSObject
{
    NSString *aName;
    int yearOfBirth;
    Person *mother, *farther
}
- (int)currentAge;
- initName:(NSString*)name;
- initName:(NSString*)name andYearOfBirth:(int)year;
@end
```

Class *Person* is a subclass of *NSObject*, the base class of all classes in an Objective C program. It declares four instance variables: *aName*, *yearOfBirth*, *mother*, and *father*, and the three instance methods: *currentAge*, *initName:*, and *initName:andYearOfBirth:*.

An implementation declaration is very similar to an interface declaration in structure; in the case of the *Person* class it could look like this:

```
#include "Person.h"
@implementation Person
- (int)currentAge { return [Time currentYear] - yearOfBirth; }
- initName:(NSString*)name {
  return [self initName:name andYearOfBirth:[Time currentYear]];
}
- initName:(NSString*)name andYearOfBirth:(int)year
{
    aName = [name retain];
    yearOfBirth = year;
    return [super init];
};
@end
```

As in Smalltalk, classes are singular objects that are managed by the runtime system. These class objects are available as special global variables with the name of the class, which can only be used in receiver context. Class objects are of the special type *Class*, which behaves like a regular type, except there is no corresponding class *Class* in the runtime system. To obtain a reference to the class object for *Person*, one needs to send the message *self* to the special receiver *Person*:

```
Class *p = [Person self]
```

Objective C classes can also define class methods, i.e., methods that are applicable to the corresponding class object. These are identified with a plus "±" instead of a dash in the class declaration. Class methods are typically used to define special instance creation methods or access to global variables.

Class *NSObject* implements a set of standard methods, which can be used, e.g., for programmatically checking if an object is an instance of a particular class or one of its subclasses. This is done by sending the message *isKindOfClass:*, as in the following example:

```
if ([anObject isKindOfClass:[Person self]]) ... else ...
```

As is in C++ (Ellis and Stroustrup, 1990), explicit casts are not checked at runtime, so this style of dynamic queries for type may be necessary to rediscover the type of an object.

Instance allocation is done by sending the message *alloc* to a class object. Alloc is a class method defined on class *NSObject*. The result of sending this message is a reference to a fresh uninitialized object. Initialization of the resulting object is then handled separately, by calling an initialization method which is just an ordinary method that usually starts with *init*... For instance, to create an instance of class Person, one might write:*

```
Person *p = [[Person alloc] initName:@"Madsen"];
```

This two-step initialization (first allocate then initialize) makes writing the initialization code simple, because the programmer only has to worry about initializing the object. In languages with constructors such as in C++, an object is not fully functional until after the initialization process is done.

18.2.5 Protocols

In addition to classes, Objective C has *protocols* which are in many ways similar to interfaces in Java (Gosling, Joy, and Steele, 1996). In fact it is the other way around, the notion of interfaces in Java originates from Objective C. A Protocol is a collection of methods that are collectively given a name, and it can be used for static typing much the same way classes can. In this way, a protocol can be thought of as an abstract class. Protocols can multiply inherit other protocols, and classes can multiply inherit protocols in addition to inheriting from a single class. Consider, for instance, the protocol for archiving (serializing) objects in the NeXT system:

```
@protocol NSArchiving
- encodeUsing:(id <NSCoder>)aCoder;
- decodeUsing:(id <NSCoder>)aCoder;
@end
```

Entities typed with protocols are specified in a special syntax, which allows it to be constrained with both a class type and one or more protocol types. For instance,

```
Person <NSArchiving,NSHashable>* aPerson;
```

Constrain the variable *aPerson* to refer to an instance of *Person*, or any subclass thereof, which also implements the *NSArchiving* and *NSHashable* protocols. To constrain a variable to be pointing to instances of any class which adopts a given protocol, the special type *id* is used, as in the following:

```
id <NSArchiving> anArchivable;
```

which identifies a variable that can refer to any object whose class adopts the *NSArchiving* protocol. For the *Person* class to inherit (or adopt as it is called for protocols) the *NSArchiving* protocol, it has to be specified in the interface declaration for class *Person*, using angle brackets:

```
@interface Person: NSObject <NSArchiving>
...
```

* The syntax `@"..."` creates an instance of class *NSString*.

In interface and protocol declarations, multiple super-protocols can be specified by separating them with commas as when typing a variable. When a protocol is listed in the interface specification for a class, the class is required to also actually implement the methods specified in the protocol.

Just like classes are objects that can be accessed using [*ClassName self*], protocol objects can be accessed using the special expression syntax *@protocol(Name)*. This is useful, for instance, for programmatically checking if a class implements a particular protocol, which is done by sending the message *conformsToProtocol:* to an object:

```
if ([anObject conformsTo:@protocol(NSArchiving)])
     [anObject encodeUsing:aCoder];
else
   ... do something else ...
```

This is similar in notion to how class membership can be tested using the *isKindOfClass:* method described in the previous section.

18.2.6 Categories

As a very unique feature for a statically typed, compiled programming language, Objective C has a feature called *categories* that allows classes to be extended with a new set of methods independently of the original class definition.* In addition to adding methods to a class, a category also allows a class to *post hoc* adopt extra protocols, which are then implemented by the extension category. This is a very useful feature for adapting existing classes, say in a class library, to fit in with a framework of your own, or to otherwise extend classes for which you do not have the source. Categories can also be used to simply separate the definition of a class into manageable units which can then be maintained by different developers.

In the previous section we explicitly added the *NSArchiving* protocol to the definition of class *Person*. Imagine if class *Person* came out of a class library for which you did not have the source. In that case, we could have extended class *Person post hoc* to adopt the *NSArchiving* protocol using a category as illustrated in the following piece of code. The special syntax *Person(Archiving)* in the declaration below identifies that this is an extension of *Person* named *Archiving*, rather than a class definition. The name of the category is not significant.

```
@implementation Person(Archiving) <NSArchiving>
- encodeUsing:(id <NSCoder>)aCoder {
     [aCoder encodeObject:aName];
     [aCoder encodeInt:yearOfBirth];
       ...
}
- decodeUsing:(id <NSCoder>)aCoder {
     aName = [aCoder decodeObject];
     yearOfBirth = [aCoder decodeInt];
     ...
     return self;
}
@end
```

After seeing this definition, the compiler allows object references of type *Person* to be assigned to a variable of protocol type *NSArchiving*. If the compiler had not seen this declaration, then such an assignment would have produced a warning or an error, unless an explicit cast had been inserted. As it is the case for class definitions, category definitions need to have an interface declaration, which is similar

* The name category is rather awkward, *extension* would probably have been more descriptive.

to class interfaces. This is not shown here so see Chapter 3 of NeXT, 1993 for more details. Any compilation unit that includes the definition of a category will have special code generated that makes sure that the category definition is linked into the application.

18.3 Best Practices

A programming language does not "live" in itself, it is put to life by the tools, libraries, and conventions that surround the language technology. In covering Objective C, the most interesting aspects are really how the language is put to use in the OPENSTEP system to provide a very efficient development system for many classes of applications. Several of the following sections have counterparts in other chapters of this book.

18.3.1 Programming with Live Objects

One of the unique features of NeXT's development environment is the use of *InterfaceBuider*™ to develop applications by manipulating live instances of objects, in a way similar to what is being used in JavaBeans (JavaSoft, 1997). Much of this technology was pioneered by Jean-Marie Hüllot at NeXT in the mid-1980s.

As the name suggests, InterfaceBuilder is designed primarily for creating user interfaces. The InterfaceBuilder application is capable of dynamically loading compiled classes and instantiating these presenting visual representations of the objects. In the case of user-interface components, the visual representation is simply the same as the corresponding component in the running program. Saving a set of objects from InterfaceBuilder is performed by serializing the objects along with the external resources (images, etc.) that are required for the objects to recreate themselves. This serialized representation is then used when successively developing an application based on this set of objects, and whenever an application launches it will load, and revive, these serialized objects into the application's memory space.

This style of development with an object-oriented system has the advantage that classes or special code to facilitate a customized set of objects does not need to be created. Conceptually, it is very clean that the same set of objects that "lived" in the InterfaceBuilder application are replicated in the actual program.

One of the drawbacks of this style of software development is that it can be hard to track changes and to manage the process when multiple developers want to work on the same set of objects. For textual source code there are powerful tools for tracking differences, such as the Unix diff program and diverse software revision management systems. Such tools are not as straightforward for developing data that consist of arbitrarily interconnected graphs of objects.

18.3.2 Dynamic Loading

Many applications written using Objective C use dynamic loading of classes, other program code, or different kinds of resources such as serialized objects described above. Objective C's standard library provides an abstraction called a *bundle*, which basically covers a directory containing dynamically loadable code and other resources. A bundle is instantiated from a directory name:

```
NSBundle *b = [NSBundle bundleFor:@"path/to/bundle"]
```

After which the different resources can be accessed via the API for *NSBundle*. Any class can ask for the bundle it came from (the application itself is actually considered a kind of bundle as well) and successively acquire other resources such as images or serialized objects from that bundle.

This approach of using dynamical loading of resources contributes to the software development in several ways:

Generality — Many classes of applications can benefit from a modular structure, where modules or "tools" can be dynamically added. For instance, OPENSTEP's system configuration tool dynamically loads individual configuration panels for different parts of the system. If a new feature is installed in the system, its configuration panel will be installed simultaneously so that it appears nicely integrated with the existing system.

Performance — The application can launch more quickly if auxiliary or seldom-used functionality is not loaded as soon as the application starts. For instance the "about..." panel of an application is only seldomly used, so there is no need for that part of the application to be loaded when the application starts.

Development process — When different aspects of the same application are developed by individual developers, each developer can manage his or her own part of the application, and the "collective" application does not need to be recompiled and linked to be able to test the entire scenario.

Long-lived applications — For applications that have to continue to run for longer periods of time, it can be desirable to dynamically load new functionality, without the need to restart the application. This was, e.g., used in a prototype of a telephone-line monitoring system that had to keep running while new functionality was installed.

Particularly for long-lived applications, it would be nice if updated functionality could be installed without having to shut down the system. This would require support for not only loading, but also unloading classes from a running program. Because the Objective C system is based on ANSI C, which, e.g., makes it impossible to reason about whether a particular piece of code is in use, it turned out to be very hard to implement such features, and it has not been done.

18.3.3 Distribution

The standard Objective C libraries also implement a system for distributed objects. This is surprisingly simple to implement directly in Objective C, because the programming language uses dynamic dispatch that can be intercepted, and it provides good support for introspection. The following sections briefly describe how the remote messaging system is implemented.

The system works by means of proxies, as it is, e.g., used in the Smalltalk distributed object manager described in (Decouchant, 1989). For each remote object, a local proxy (an instance of *NSDistantObject*) is maintained. In principle, the proxy class only implements a single fault-handling method, so any other message sent to it will fail and be redirected to *forwardInvocation:* passing along an *NSInvocation* object as the parameter. The special method *forwardInvocation:* is similar to *doesNotUnderstand:* in a Smalltalk environment. An *NSInvocation* object corresponds to a *Message* object in the Smalltalk system, containing the name of the method that was attempted to be invoked and an array of the parameters that were passed along. After receiving a *forwardInvocation:* message, the proxy object serializes the *NSInvocation* instance passed as an argument and sends the serialized data via some media such as TCP or Mach messaging (Boykin et al., 1993) to a remote application. The remote application revives the *NSInvocation* instance from the serialized data, replacing the target of the invocation with the real remote object in the process, and finally, it re-sends the message to the real object by sending the message *invoke* to the *NSInvocation* object. The result of this invocation is then again serialized and sent back to the originator of the remote method invocation.

While the sending application is waiting for a response to a method, it also accepts incoming calls so that the server can dispatch messages back to the calling client as part of its operation. This way the distinction between server and client is really eliminated, and it is only based on how the system is put to use. The distributed object system actually supports arbitrary n-ary call graphs across many distributed applications at the same time.

A nice property of the system is that nothing special has to be done for an object to be distributable, i.e., remotely accessible. Other distributed object systems, such as CORBA (OMG, 1997) or DCOM (Microsoft, 1997) require generation of stubs that have to be linked into the client application. Generating stubs provides some means to make the system perform better, but on the other hand, it is very useful to have a dynamic system when developing the applications in the first place, because there is much less bookkeeping involved.

In order for the runtime system to generate an instance of the *NSInvocation* object when a message send fails, it needs to know the signature, i.e., the types of arguments, of the method being invoked. The runtime system needs this information to be able to pick the actual arguments off the runtime stack. When invoking any message, a reference to the target object and the selector, i.e., the name of the method, is passed physically on the stack before the ordinary arguments. In NeXT's Objective C system, getting the signature is achieved by sending the message *signatureForSelector:* to the actual target of the message, passing along the selector taken from the stack. In case of a remote message invocation this request would be sent to the proxy object. The proxy object then forwards the request to the remote application and cashes the result for use in future requests. What this means is that a remote method invocation actually sends $n + 1$ remote messages, if the same method is invoked on an object n times. Because sending extra messages can be a performance problem, a proxy object can be given one or more local *protocol* objects, which are then used for retrieving the method signatures locally. In the GNU Objective C runtime system, a method selector includes the signature directly, so the runtime system can create the invocation object without having to request the signature from the target. This improves performance and safety somewhat, but also increases the size of the data segment of the compiled program.

When serializing objects for distribution, e.g., when an object reference is passed as a parameter to a remote method invocation, it is usually desirable to generate a proxy that will be able to redirect messages originating from the remote site, rather than sending a copy of the object itself. To facilitate this, the serialization of objects first gives the object to be serialized a chance to give an alternative representation of itself, by calling *replacementObjectForCoder:*. The default implementation of this method (on *NSObject*) is to answer an instance of *NSDistantObject*, which is then what is actually serialized and sent abroad. Other objects, such as immutable strings, simply return themselves from this method, since they are immutable they can safely be replicated. Objects could also choose to distribute themselves by means of another class that replicates only the immutable aspects of their data, but forwards requests regarding dynamic state to the remote site. This architecture provides an easy and powerful way to control how individual objects are distributed.

18.3.4 Database Integration

Another interesting framework made with Objective C is the *Enterprise Objects Framework* (EOF), a framework for accessing relational databases. This is one of the premiere frameworks developed at NeXT, and it has been successfully used to develop a wide variety of database-backed applications.

The framework uses the meta-programming capabilities of Objective C to map tables directly to arrays of Objective C objects. The translation is data-driven, mapping particular columns of a table directly to instance variables of objects. A separate tool, the *EOModeler*, dynamically loads classes and schemas allowing the developer to interactively define the mapping. At deployment time, when data is retrieved from the database, the classes specified in *EOModeler* are instantiated and initialized from the database data as specified.

EOF also allows lazy loading of data by means of proxies. When lazy loading of a table is requested, it simply returns an array of proxies. The first time such a proxy object is accessed it will itself become the actual objects. Objective C does not implement Smalltalk's *become:* primitive method, so this is achieved by actually allocating the real objects when the lazy array is requested, but delaying the instantiation (and loading of data) until the first time the object is used.

18.4 Perspectives and Summary

Objective C is a simple, compiled programming language with most of its concepts and semantics borrowed from Smalltalk. Objective C is one of the only languages in the history of programming languages that combines a traditional batch-compilation with a dynamic object-system. The unique language-level features of Objective C, seen in a historical perspective, are protocols, which have been included in the Java programming language as interfaces, and categories (*post hoc* class extension) which have yet to be seen in other languages.

Objective C has a very direct approach to introspection and meta programming. The developer can directly intercept message dispatch and request information about such things as byte offsets of particular instance variables, etc. While this is of course unsafe, it still provides a very powerful tool for framework developers to bend the rules of the language a little and easily implement architectures based on proxies and lazy access of data.

With the advent of Apple's new Yellow Box development platform based on OPENSTEP, Objective C is very likely to see a renaissance as an influential programming platform; where the frameworks, tools, and other technologies surrounding it will continue to be role models for other programming environments.

References

Boykin, J. et al. 1993. *Programming Under Mach.* Addison-Wesley, Reading, MA.

Cox, B.J. 1987. *Object-Oriented Programming — An Evolutionary Approach.* Addison-Wesley, Reading, MA.

Decouchant, D. 1989. A distributed object manager for the Smalltalk-80 system. In *Object-Oriented Concepts, Databases, and Application,* W. Kim and F.H. Lochovsky, eds. ACM Press, New York, NY.

Ellis, M.A. and Stroustup, B. 1990. *The Annotated C++ Reference Manual.* Addison-Wesley, Reading, MA.

Goldberg, A. and Robson, D. 1989. *Smalltalk-80 — The Language.* Addison-Wesley, Reading, MA.

Gosling, A., Joy, B. and Steele, G. 1996. *The Java Language Specification.* Addison-Wesley, Reading, MA.

JavaSoft, 1997. *The JavaBeans Specification.* From http://java.sun.com/beans.

Microsoft, 1997. *DCOM Technical Overview.* From Microsoft Developer Library, http://www.microsoft.com.

NeXT Software, Inc. 1993. *Object-Oriented Programming and the Objective-C Language.* Addison-Wesley, Reading, MA.

NeXT Software, Inc. 1996. *Working with Interface Builder.* Addison-Wesley, Reading, MA.

NeXT Software, Inc. 1996. *Enterprise Objects Framework Developer's Guide, 2nd Ed.* Addison-Wesley, Reading, MA.

OMG, 1997. *The Common Object Request Broker: Architecture and Specification.* From http://www.obg.org/corba.

Schildt, H. 1990. *The Annotated ANSI C Standard; American National Standard for Programming Languages — C; ANSI/ISO 9899-1990.* Osborne McGraw-Hill, Berkeley, CA.

Further Information

A thorough introduction to the Objective C programming language is found in *Object-Oriented Programming and the Objective C Language* from NeXT Software. This book presents the language as it is used in the OPENSTEP system. The original reference for Objective C is *Object-Oriented Programming — an Evolutionary Approach,* by Brad J. Cox.

Several of the technologies surrounding Objective C are described in a series of books by NeXT published by Addison-Wesley, particularly *Working with Interface Builder,* and *Enterprise Objects Framework Developer's Guide* are recommendable. Several of these publications are available online from Apple's Technical Publications Department.

There is also a free implementation of Objective C and some tools and libraries that resemble those of the OPENSTEP system available from the GNUSTEP project, see http://www.gnustep.org for current details on this project.

19

Smalltalk

Ernesto Pimentel
University of Málaga

Francisco Gutiérrez
University of Málaga

19.1 Introduction

The definition and development of the Smalltalk language has provided a substantial advance in the field of object-oriented programming. Although it takes ideas from other languages, the original way in which these ideas are incorporated makes Smalltalk especially interesting for the object-oriented community.

In the early 1970s, Smalltalk and its original environment were developed by the Learning Research Group at Xerox's Palo Alto Research Center. The aim was to create a powerful system with mechanisms that would allow simple and flexible information manipulation, with the possibility of increasing the system components depending on the user's requirements. This objective arose out of the original milieu of the research group (i.e., learning), and it explains the main characteristics of Smalltalk: a programming language, connecting conceptual models with computing hardware, and an interaction language (user interface and development environment), which allows flexible communication between user and computer.

The team worked for around ten years on the project to obtain both the language and the environment. The main ideas concerning the language are generally attributed to Alan Kay, who inspired the team to construct a totally uniform object-oriented system, taking ideas from other languages like Simula, LISP, and SketchPad. The first interpreter prototype, Smalltalk-72, introduced the notion of message sending to enable objects to communicate with each other for the first time. Although the concepts of class and instance were already present in Smalltalk-72, the notion of inheritance was not yet provided for. In 1974, a more efficient version of the interpreter was constructed, which was the first one providing overlapping windows, opaque pop-up menus, and graphic control by Bit Block Transfer (BitBlt), based on Dan Engalls' ideas. Inheritance and a first approach to manipulating classes as objects appeared in Smalltalk-76.

The first stable version of the language, Smalltalk-80, was the result of a number of refinements which culminated with the participation of several companies (Apple, DEC, Tektronix, Hewlett Packard) under the direction of Adele Goldberg, and it was licensed by Xerox in April 1983.

Since 1984, a number of implementations have been developed by different companies; in particular, in 1985, Tektronix constructed the Tektronix 4404 computer, a Smalltalk-80 programming environment. The first microprocessor versions appeared in 1985 and were developed by Digitalk and Apple. In 1987, ParcPlace Systems was funded as a spinoff from Xerox to distribute Smalltalk to a wider market. To date a

0-8493-3135-8/99/$0.00+$.50

number of different implementations have been developed. Some of them are freely distributed, such as Smalltalk Express, previously called Smalltalk/V (by ObjectShare, Inc.), GNU Smalltalk (by Free Software Foundation, Inc.), or Squeak (by Apple Computers, Inc.). Other Smalltalk systems are: Dolphin (by Object Arts); IBM Smalltalk, which is complemented with a visual application builder (*VisualAge*); Smalltalk/MT (Object Connect), specially oriented to create Win32 applications; Smalltalk/X (eXept Software AG) for Unix; and VisualWorks, a complete development environment for Smalltalk distributed by ParcPlace. We can also encounter a number of new commercial products based on Smalltalk, focusing on other fields, like databases, visual programming, distributed systems, client-server applications, etc. In 1994, a number of significant companies created the Smalltalk Industry Council (STIC) to cover the needs of the Smalltalk community (`http://www.stic.org`).

Smalltalk can be seen, at one and the same time, as a programming language, an operating system, and a development environment. The influence of Smalltalk on current operating systems and development environments is widely acknowledged. Apple's Lisa and Macintosh are clear examples of this. From the point of view of a programming language we must emphasize the uniform application of very few concepts (object, message, class, inheritance), which have been accorded an unusual terminology. Using these basic notions only, all constructions in the language are obtained. In particular, conditional sentences and control structures are implemented in terms of objects and messages. This makes Smalltalk a pure and homogeneous object-oriented language.

The language itself is very lean and only contains about one hundred primitives. However, as a development environment, Smalltalk includes a profuse class library covering most of a software engineer's needs. The simplicity of the language makes high productivity possible for Smalltalk programmers, once the class library has been thoroughly grasped. In this sense, the environment provides a wide variety of tools (browsers, text editor, inspector, and debugger) specifically adapted to the language's features, thus allowing easy and flexible user-application interaction. All implementations have left the most important classes from Smalltalk-80 unchanged. Only classes concerning graphics, windows, and platform-dependent functions have been adapted in different ways. In this way we can find products running on different platforms.

The basic references which cover the original Smalltalk-80 are four books characterized by their front cover color. The so-called *Blue* book [3] contains an implementation of Smalltalk written in Smalltalk itself for educational purposes. A full definition of the language and a very out of date class library description are also provided by this book. In spite of this, it is still a mandatory reference. The *Purple* book [4] contains an updated version of the blue book, not including the implementation section. The *Green* book [6] is a collection of papers on Smalltalk implementations and on the history of Smalltalk. Finally, the book with an *orange* front cover [2] explains how to use the Smalltalk-80 environment. Due to changes in current graphical interfaces, this book is an interesting but rarely useful reference. One of the most influential publications devoted to Smalltalk was the special issue of *Byte* in August 1981. Other useful references can be found at the end of this chapter.

19.2 Object-Oriented Programming and Smalltalk

Smalltalk is considered a substantial advance in computer languages. This is not only because the main object-oriented concepts were established by this language and were applied in a very homogeneous and elegant way, but also because the special implementation approach allows great code flexibility and portability.

The semantics of the language is highly influenced by its uniformity with respect to the object-oriented philosophy. A first consequence of this is that all Smalltalk entities are objects, including methods and classes. An object includes a *private* memory (variables) and a *public* behavior given by a set of operations (methods) acting on the object's memory, which are activated by sending messages. A message involves a pair of objects—a receiver and a sender. The effect of a message is given by the execution of the corresponding method, where the receiver object is referred to as `self` (a reserved word in the system).

Meanwhile, the sender object waits for an answer. Thus, objects only communicate among themselves by means of sending messages, and this is the only feasible action in a Smalltalk system.

A class encapsulates a group of objects (class instances) sharing a common behavior (*instance methods*) and a similar structure (*instance variables*). All instances of the same class can share references to other objects (*class variables*). As a class it is also considered to be an object, it can include its own instance variables and methods (called *class methods*). This makes classes dynamic entities, which can be manipulated (created, destroyed, modified). Indeed, the only way to create an instance is by sending a message to the corresponding class. This is a specific characteristic of Smalltalk, making it especially convenient for meta-programming.

Smalltalk enables the classes to be organized in an inheritance hierarchy in such a way that every class has only one superclass (simple inheritance*), and perhaps several subclasses. The system provides a large class library having a tree-like arrangement rooted by the `Object` class and covering standard functionality: arithmetic, data structures, control structures, input/output, concurrency issues, graphical user interfaces, etc. The development of applications in Smalltalk is based on the creation of new classes using/specializing the initial class hierarchy.

A Smalltalk variable always represents a reference to a single object, and the variable's name can be used to refer to this object. However, variables are not typed, as happens in other object-oriented languages. This way, a variable might refer to different objects at different instants (unrestricted polymorphism). As a consequence, when a message sending expression involves a variable as the receiver, the compiler is forced to delay method searching associated with the message until the object referred to by the variable is known (dynamic binding).

Abstract classes, i.e., classes with part of their protocol unimplemented, were first introduced in Smalltalk. An abstract class is characterized by fixing a common behavior for all its subclasses. The language does not provide a reserved word to indicate when this behavior cannot be totally defined, due to the high level of abstraction of the class. For this reason, a special method, `subclassResponsibility`, is specified in the `Object` class to deal with this undefined behavior.

As regards information hiding, the language does not provide any possibility for restricting accessing methods of a class. In fact, a method is always considered public. On the other hand, all variables defining the structure of a class are always private, and they can only be accessed through methods. However, variables in a class are always accessible from their subclasses, with no mechanism for restricting this visibility.

From a conceptual point of view, the notions of class and abstract data type are totally equivalent. No distinction is made between an instance of a class and a value of a type. Indeed, all the usual pre-defined types are classes in Smalltalk (e.g., `Integer`, `Boolean`, `Character`, `Array`, `Set`, etc.)

Another important feature of Smalltalk is its implementation. The main part of the system (called the *Virtual Image*) is written in the language itself, usually including (among other things) a compiler, a debugger, editors, and a file management system. The entire virtual image is defined in terms of an abstract machine (called the *Virtual Machine*) consisting of a reduced set of instructions. The compiler translates the method source code into Virtual Machine instructions (called *bytecodes*), thus allowing easy portability among different platforms, since only the abstract machine needs to be redefined (or recompiled) when the system is installed on a target computer.

The implementation of the Smalltalk Virtual Machine is based on an object manager, an interpreter, and a set of primitives. Memory allocation, and consequently, object handling, is carried out by the object manager. Operations such as accessing the instance variables of an object, obtaining the class of an object (e.g., in order to search for an invoked method), or creating new objects, are established by this manager. All entities (as objects) are referred to by a unique identifier, which is an object *pointer*. This allows indirect

*Some Smalltalk systems incorporate multiple inheritance.

access to the object by means of a table, which contains the addresses of the internal structures of all objects. Original Smalltalk implementations coded object identifiers on 16 bits, although current implementations extend the address space to 32 bits. In both cases, the first bit is reserved for indicating whether the object is a small integer in such a way that these integers are directly available, without needing to refer to the object table.

Memory management is directly carried out by the system, and the programmer has no responsibility for managing memory allocation. In fact, explicit operations for memory allocation or deallocation are unnecessary in Smalltalk. These actions are performed by the object manager. Garbage collection is done by assigning a reference counter to each object, which stores the total number of other objects that are pointing to it. A zero count indicates that the space corresponding to the object can be reallocated. Although the advantages of this approach are evident (garbage collection time is uniformly distributed during system processing), it presents some inconveniences in the presence of circular data structures.

The bytecodes generated by the compiler are interpreted by the Virtual Machine, a stack-oriented machine with a set of instructions, which mostly push, pop, and carry out operations on the top elements of the stack. Only message sending behaves slightly differently. After compiling, a message becomes a bytecode referring to the position where the corresponding selector (message name) has been stored. To find the appropriate method to be executed, the interpreter looks up the message selector in a dictionary containing the methods of the class of the receiver object. If the method is not found, the search is extended to the superclass's dictionary, repeating this process until the method is found. If the search fails, a message is sent to the receiver indicating the situation.

Efficiency obliges us to implement certain operations executed by the Virtual Machine as machine-code subroutines [5]. These are called *primitives* and are used to perform basic operations like input/output, arithmetic for integers, screen graphics, etc. Some of the operations described in terms of primitives are difficult or (sometimes) impossible to write directly in Smalltalk. However, certain other operations (e.g., arithmetic for integers) are implemented as primitives because the cost of executing them from bytecodes would be prohibitive from the performance point of view. In both cases, primitives are represented externally as ordinary methods conveniently flagged for recognition by the interpreter.

19.3 Smalltalk—The Language

The main principles of the Smalltalk language have been discussed in the previous section, reviewing the semantics and implementation. Now, we are going to deal in detail with the issues relating to Smalltalk as a programming language, focusing on its features for developing software. The aim of this is to provide a rapid guide of the possibilities of Smalltalk as an object-oriented programming language, and its substantial differences to other languages.

19.3.1 Expressions

As mentioned, programming in Smalltalk is based on describing new classes by defining their (instance and class) variables and methods. Before explaining how to define new classes, we will introduce the legal constructions in the language, i.e., valid expressions.

According to Goldberg and Robson (1983), "an expression is a sequence of characters that describe an object called the value of the expression." In fact, every Smalltalk expression always returns a reference to an object (new or already existing). We can distinguish four kinds of expressions: literals, variables, messages, and blocks.

19.3.1.1 Literals

Literals represent constant objects, like numbers, characters, strings, symbols, and arrays of literals. Examples of numbers are:

Smalltalk Numbers	Decimal Numbers
35	35
−2.7	−2.7
5e−3	0.005
8r100	64
16r0.5Ae2	90

where the decimal point is '.', the scientific notation is introduced by 'e' followed by the exponent, and 'r' is used to represent the radix, such that the prefix includes the digit radix. When necessary the digits greater than 9 are expressed by capital letters starting with 'A.'

In order to represent individual characters the '$' symbol is used as a prefix: **$a**, **$,**, **$$**, **$** , represent the characters 'a', ',', '$,' and the blank space, respectively.

Characters are frequently grouped to form strings. These are delimited with single quotes: `'This is a string.'` Quotes are duplicated inside the string, and every instance of a string is a different literal, even when they have the same content. Symbols are also groups of alphanumeric characters (including the character ':') preceded by the character '`#.`' Two equal symbols are the same object. Symbols are generally used by the Smalltalk system to denote names of classes, variables, and methods: `#new`, `#between:and:`, `#Object`, etc.

An array is a data structure containing other objects. When these objects are literals, the array may be represented by the sequence of literals preceded by '#':

```
#(6 2 -1)
#('Hello' 3 $c)
```

These arrays each have three elements. If an array contains another array or a symbol as an element, then they lose the constructor '#':

```
#(1 ('Hello' 3 $c) Object)
```

is an array with three elements where the second one is another array with another three elements, and the third element is the symbol `#Object`.

19.3.1.2 Variables

A variable maintains a reference to an object. Most variables have a name, which is used in expressions to access the object to which it refers. As usual, the name of a variable is a sequence of letters and digits beginning with a letter.

Variables can be classified into private and shared. Private variables are visible from and accessed by only one object, and their identifier starts with a lowercase. We have two different kinds of private variables — *instances* and *temporaries*. The former are local to an object, whereas the latter have a more reduced scope (a method or a block).

Objects can share two kinds of variables. *Class* variables are shared by all the instances of a class, whereas *global* variables are accessed by the entire system. The name of a shared variable must begin with an uppercase letter.

A variable can point to different objects throughout its existence. The object referred to by a variable can be changed by using an assignment (denoted by '←' or ':='):

```
index ← 1
someDigits ← #(3 2 1 4 6)
newIndex ← index ← 2
```

As an assignment is an expression, and therefore returns an object, it can be used as the right-hand side of another assignment. Thus, the evaluation of the last expression results in variables `newIndex` and `index` referencing the value (object) 2.

Smalltalk provides five *pseudo-variables*, of which three are constants. The pseudo-variable `nil` refers to a special object used to indicate that a variable has no value. The first value referenced by a variable is always `nil`. When logic expressions are evaluated the result is one of the pseudo-variables `true` or `false`. The meaning of the other two pseudo-variables, `self` and `super`, will be explained when the notion of method is introduced.

From now on, we will use the name of the variable to directly denote the object to which it is referred.

19.3.1.3 Messages

A message is a request to an object to perform an operation, and it involves an object receiver, a message selector, and (possibly) arguments. A message expression consists of the object receiver followed (and separated by blank space(s)) by the selector and arguments. Due to the unusual and different ways of constructing a message expression, we will illustrate them with several examples. When messages have no arguments, they are called *unary* messages:

```
someDigits size
5 factorial
Display boundingBox
list removeLast
```

Here, receivers are `someDigits`, `5`, `Display`, and `list`, and selectors are `size`, `factorial`, `boundingBox`, and `removeLast`, respectively. Other kinds of messages are those representing arithmetic and logic operations. These messages use the usual symbols to describe the corresponding operations and are called *binary* messages:

```
counter < upperBound
true & false
index + 1
```

In the first message sending, the receiver is `counter`, the selector is `<`, and the argument is `upperBound`.

The remaining of message expressions (called *keyword* messages) are constructed with a selector composed of as many semicolon finished words as they have arguments. For instance:

```
someDigits at: 2 put: 0
counter min: upperBound
'Small fry' copyReplaceFrom: 6 to: 9 with: 'talk'
```

The last one contains a receiver, the string `'Small fry,'` a selector `copyReplaceFrom:to:with:`, and the arguments 6, 9, and `'talk.'`

Given that the answer to a message is always an object, it can be ignored or used as the receiver or argument in another message expression:

```
newIndex ←  counter min: upperBound
```

where `newIndex` refers to the minimum of `counter` and `upperBound`. When several message expressions are combined they are evaluated following an order of priority: unary, binary, and keyword, and parsing from left to right. Using parentheses this order may be changed. Note that an 'arithmetic' expression like

```
2 + 3 * 4
```

does not return 14, but 20.

Several messages can be sent to the same object by using the ';' separator as in the example

```
stack push: $a ; push: $b ; pop
```

The receiver is always the same object `stack`. This is equivalent to

```
stack push: $a .
stack push: $b .
stack pop
```

where '.' is a message separator. However, the chaining of messages

```
((stack push: $a) push: $b) pop
```

could behave in a different way, depending on the response of the `push:` message.

19.3.1.4 Blocks

A block is a literal denoting a deferred sequence of actions, usually used in Smalltalk to implement control structures. Its syntax is given by a sequence of expressions separated by a full stop and delimited by square brackets:

```
[f ← f*n.   n ← n - 1]
```

A block does not evaluate the messages it contains by itself. Only when requested to do so will they be evaluated, and the final result will be the one produced by the last message expression. Thus, the sequence of actions is only executed when the block receives the `value` message. That is, the evaluation of

```
f ← 1.
n ← 5.
[f ← f*n.  n ← n - 1]  value
```

leaves `f` with the value 5 and `n` with 4, and the final result is 4. When an empty block is evaluated, it returns the pseudo-variable `nil`.

Blocks can also have arguments, which are identifiers of temporary variables appearing at the beginning of the block, preceded by a colon and separated from the rest of the block with a '|'. To evaluate a block with an argument, the keyword message `value:` is used. If it has two arguments, `value:value:` is used instead. For an arbitrary number of arguments the message `valueWithArgs:`, having an array as an argument, can be used. For example,

```
block1  ←  [:p | p * p].
block2  ←  [:a :b | a - b].
block3  ←  [:x1 :y1 :x2 :y2 |
     s1  ←  block1  value: (block2  value: x1  value: x2).
     s2  ←  block1  value: (block2  value: y1  value: y2).
     (s1 + s2) sqrt ]
```

defines three blocks with arguments, such that the expression:

```
block3 valueWithArgs: #(0 0 1 1)
```

returns the distance between the points with the coordinates (0, 0) and (1, 1), i.e., 1.41421356.

As mentioned, Smalltalk uses blocks to describe control structures such as loops, conditional loops, and selection. The following examples show the most frequent constructions, present in traditional programming languages, whose meaning is easily deduced from the expressions themselves. For instance, some loops with a fixed number of iterations are

```
5 timesRepeat: [stack pop].
sum ← 0.  1 to: 10 by: 2 do: [:i | sum ← sum + i].
str ← ''.  #($h $e $l $l $o) do: [:char | str ← str , char asString]
```

where the first expression pops five elements from the object `stack`, the second one leaves `sum` with the sum of odd numbers between 1 and 10, that is 25, and the last one stores a string formed with the characters of the array in `str` (the message `asString` converts a character into a singleton string, and the binary message ',' concatenates two strings).

Conditional loops can also be described in Smalltalk by the messages `whileTrue:` and `whileFalse:` sent to blocks. The following example computes the factorial of a natural number:

```
f ← 1.
[n > 0] whileTrue: [f ← f * n. n ← n - 1]
```

such that `f` will be the factorial of `n`.

Conditional statements are expressed by means of messages sent to the pseudo-variables `true` and `false` (or expressions returning them). Basically, these messages are `ifTrue:`, `ifFalse:`, `ifTrue:ifFalse:`, and `ifFalse:ifTrue:`.

```
(a < b) ifTrue: [max ← b] ifFalse: [max ← a].
(a even) ifTrue: [a ← a // 2].
```

The first expression leaves `max` with the maximum of `a` and `b`, and the second one is equivalent to the following:

```
(a even) ifTrue: [a ← a // 2] ifFalse: [].
```

Note that messages denoting conditional loops are sent to blocks, whereas expressions for conditional statements correspond to messages sent to boolean expressions. The reason for this will be explained later.

19.3.2 Classes and Instances

Every object in Smalltalk is a class instance. A class defines the structure of a group of objects (its instances), and the set of operations that these have to carry out, when receiving messages. Each available operation is described by a *method*. Therefore, the class determines the set of messages that its instances can receive.

Each class is characterized by a name, which is considered a global identifier, and may be used in expressions. Classes are also objects in Smalltalk, which implies they have a structure and can receive messages. For example, the usual way of creating an instance of a class is by sending the `new` message to the class:

```
myDict ← Dictionary new
```

The structure of a class is given by three kinds of entities: *instance variables*, *class variables*, and *pool dictionaries*. Instance variables define the state of an instance of the class, and a private copy is created for each instance. They can have an explicit name to refer them, or they can be indexed. In this case, the messages `at:` and `at:put:` can be used to manipulate them. Class variables are shared by all instances of the class, and only one copy exists for all them. Finally, dictionaries contain a collection of associations between strings and objects.

The behavior exhibited by an object is described in the *instance methods* of the corresponding class. Each method implements the actions to be executed when it is invoked. These actions are sequences of expressions, which can be preceded by a sequence of local and temporary variables delimited by vertical lines. Inside an instance method the following entities can be referred to: global variables, arguments of the method, temporary variables, instance variables, class variables, identifiers from pool dictionaries, and the receiver object (denoted either by the pseudo-variable `self` or `super`). Strings in pool dictionaries define a shared identifier (without quote marks) which can be used to refer to the associated object in the corresponding dictionary.

Actions specified in a method are executed when an instance of the class receives a message with the same selector. We will refer to the method as the *invoked* method, and to the message as the *invoking* message.

The default answer of a message is the receiver object. To specify a different answer the method must include an expression preceded by '↑' or '^.' Once this expression is evaluated, the execution of the method is aborted, and the result object is returned.

On the other hand, a class (as an object) behaves according to another family of methods, called *class methods*, and these correspond to the messages the class can receive itself. The functionality of class methods is the same as that of instance methods, except that instance variables are not visible. In this case, the pseudo-variable `self` denotes the receiver class.

Classes can be viewed in two different ways, the protocol description and the implementation description, depending on the level of abstraction we are interested in. The former only shows the methods (optionally) classified by categories, whereas the latter describes (instance and class) variables, pool dictionaries, and details of the implementation methods.

We have selected a very well-known example, but enriched with several features making it especially useful for understanding all the concepts previously introduced. Thus, the `Point2D` class represents two-dimensional points which can be (optionally) adjusted to a common *grid*. The protocol description for `Point2D` is shown in Figure 19.1. The creation of instances is carried out by the class methods `x:y:` or `origin`. Before creating any instance, the grid size must be initialized, and the *autogrid* option must be enabled or disabled. This is done through the class methods `grid:`, `enableGrid`, and `disableGrid`, respectively. The instances protocol allows standard actions on points to be performed. Thus, for instance, we can calculate the `distance:` between two points, or `mo:ve:` a point.

An example illustrating the creation and manipulation of two-dimensional points is given below:

```
Point2D grid: 0.1 ; enableGrid .
P1 ← Point2D x: 5.76 y: 3.125 .
P2 ← Point2D origin .
P2 mo: 1 ve: 1 .
P1 rotate: (Float pi / 2) wrt:  P2.
```

The first line contains two messages sent to the class `Point2D`, initializing and enabling the grid facility. The next two lines create two points referred to by two global variables, `P1` and `P2`. The next line modifies the coordinates of point P2, and the last one modifies `P1` by applying a clockwise rotation of $\frac{\pi}{2}$ radians with respect to point P2. After evaluating all these expressions, point `P1` becomes the two-dimensional point (3.1, −3.8) and P2 becomes (1, 1).

The implementation description of the `Point2D` class (see Figure 19.2) includes: the instance variables `x` and `y`, representing the coordinates of the point; and the class variables `Grid` and `AutoGrid`, respectively

```
Point2D class protocol
--------------------------------------------------------------------------------
    instance-creation
      x: coordX y: coordY              Answer a two-dimensional point (coordX,coordY)
                                       snapped to grid if necessary
      origin                           Answer the two-dimensional point (0,0)
    accessing
      grid: aGrid                      The grid dimension is changed to aGrid
      enableGrid                       The autogrid facility is enabled
      disableGrid                      The autogrid facility is disabled

Point2D instance protocol
--------------------------------------------------------------------------------
    accessing
      distance: aPoint2D               Answer the distance between self and aPoint2D
      x                                Answer the x-coordinate
      y                                Answer the y-coordinate
      x: coordX                        Change the x-coordinate to coordX,
                                       and snap if necessary
      y: coordY                        Change the y-coordinate to coordY,
                                       and snap if necessary
    transforming
      mo: deltaX ve: deltaY            Move the receiver by (deltaX,deltaY)
      rotate: aNumber                  Move the receiver by applying a
                                       clockwise rotation of aNumber radians
      rotate: aNumber wrt: aCenter     Move the receiver by applying a clockwise
                                       rotation of aNumber radians with respect to
                                       aCenter
      snapToGrid                       Snap the receiver to grid if autogrid
                                       is enabled
    printing
    ◇ printOn: aStream                 Append to aStream a printable representation
                                       of the receiver
    private
      snapToGrid: aNumber              Snap aNumber to the grid if autogrid is enabled
```

FIGURE 19.1 The Point2D protocol.

representing the grid size and a boolean flag to adjust the coordinates to the grid or not. The implementation of all the methods is also described.

19.3.3 Inheritance in Smalltalk

Every class in Smalltalk has a parent class. Thus, when a class is defined, the corresponding superclass must be specified. In fact, the creation of a new class is carried out by sending a message to the parent class. The arguments of this message provide the name of the new class (i.e., the subclass), the instance variable names, the class variable names, the pool dictionaries, and (possibly*) a class category (used to organize the class hierarchy). For instance, to define the subclass Particle, an heir of Point2D, we have to use the following expression:

```
Point2D subclass: #Particle
        instanceVariableNames:  'mass'
        classVariableNames:  ''
        poolDictionaries:  ''
        category:  'Planetary-System'
```

*Some Smalltalk systems do not incorporate this feature.

```
Point2D implementation description

class name                    Point2D
instance variable names       x
                              y
class variable names          Grid
                              AutoGrid

class methods

  instance-creation
    x: coordX y: coordY
      "Answer a two-dimiensional point (coordX,coordY)
       snapped to grid if necessary"
      ↑ (self new) x: coordX ; y: coordY
  accessing
    grid: aGrid
      "The grid dimension is changed to aGrid"
      Grid ← aGrid
    enableGrid
      "The autogrid facility is enabled"
      AutoGrid ← true
    disableGrid
      "The autogrid facility is disabled"
      AutoGrid ← false

instance methods

  accessing
    distance: aPoint2D
      "Answer the distance between the
       receiver and aPoint2D"
      ↑ ((aPoint2D x - x) squared +
         (aPoint2D y - y) squared) sqrt
    x
      "Answer the x-coordinate"
      ↑ x
    y
      "Answer the y-coordinate"
    x: coordX
      "Change the x-coordinate to coordX
       and snap if necessary"
      x ← self snapToGrid: coordX
    y: coordY
      "Change the y-coordinate to coordY
       and snap if necessary"
      y ← self snapToGrid: coordY
  printing
    printOn: aStream
      "Append to aStream a printable
       representation of the receiver"
      aStream nextPut: $(.
      x printOn: aStream.
      aStream nextPut: $,.
      y printOn: aStream.
      aStream nextPut: $)
  private
    snapToGrid: aNumber
      "Snap aNumber to the grid if
       autogrid is enabled"
      ↑ AutoGrid
        ifTrue: [aNumber roundTo: Grid]
        ifFalse: [aNumber]

  transforming
    mo: deltaX ve: deltaY
      "Move the receiver by (deltaX,deltaY)"
      self x: x + deltaX.
      self y: y + deltaY
    rotate: aNumber
      "Move the receiver by applying a clockwise
       rotation of aNumber radians"
      |newX newY aNsin aNcos|
      aNsin ← aNumber sin
      aNcos ← aNumber cos
      newX ← (x * aNcos) + (y * aNsin).
      tempY ← (y * aNcos) - (x * aNsin)).
      self x: newX.
      self y: newY
    rotate: aNumber wrt: aCenter
      "Move the receiver by applying a clockwise
       rotation of aNumber radians
       with respect to aCenter"
      |temp|
      temp ←
          Point2D
            x: (x - aCenter x)
            y: ( y - aCenter y)
      temp rotate: aNumber.
      self x: (aCenter x + temp x).
      self y: (aCenter y + temp y)
    snapToGrid
      "Snap the receiver to grid if
       autogrid is enabled"
      self x: x.
      self y: y
```

FIGURE 19.2 The `Point2D` implementation.

Note the first argument is a symbol, denoting the name of the subclass. After evaluating this expression, the class `Particle` is created in the category `Planetary-System` with an additional instance variable `mass`. Likewise, the class `Point2D` had to be created as a subclass of the `Object` class, which is the root of the class hierarchy. In any case, every Smalltalk system includes a class browser, which facilitates both the creation and modification of classes.

The full protocol of `Particle` class is shown in Figure 19.3. The declaration of `Point2D` as a superclass allows the `Point2D` protocol to be used in the context of the class `Particle`. Thus, for instance, we can move a particle, calculate the distance between two particles, etc. The ◇-tagged methods denote redefined methods. In particular, `printOn:` is a method belonging to the `Object` instance protocol, which is redefined both in the `Point2D` class (see Figure 19.1) and in the `Particle` class. The class method `x:y:` in `Particle` is in the same situation. As can be noted, a particle is considered a two-dimensional point with mass.

Particle class protocol

```
instance-creation
  x: coordX y: coordY mass: aNumber  Answer a particle with mass aNumber
                                     and coordinates (coordX,coordY) snapped to grid if necessary
◇ x: coordX y: coordY                Answer a particle with mass 0 and coordinates
                                     (coordX,coordY) snapped to grid if necessary
```

Particle instance protocol

```
accessing
  attraction: aParticle              Answer the attraction force between aParticle
                                     and the receiver
  mass                               Answer the receiver's mass
  mass: aNumber                      Change the receiver's mass to aNumber
printing
◇ printOn: aStream                   Append to aStream a printable representation
                                     of the receiver
```

FIGURE 19.3 The `Particle` protocol.

The behavior of particles is given by the implementation described in Figure 19.4. A class method `x:y:mass:` is defined to create instances of `Particle` in a similar way to that done in the context of the `Point2D` class. Three arguments are provided to initialize the three instance variables, the two coordinates and the mass. To do this the previously defined class method `x:y:` is invoked through the pseudo-variable `super`. At this point, it is necessary to explain how method selection is solved when `self` and `super` are involved. The appropriate method to be executed when a message is sent to an object is performed by traversing the inheritance tree from the receiver's class to the root of the hierarchy in such a way that the first matching method is selected. Note that the starting point for the search is always the class of the receiver object.

Usually, in a sending expression, the receiver object is explicitly named, but also the pseudo-variables `self` and `super` can be used as receivers inside an invoked method. In both cases, they refer to the receiver of the invoking message. However, they differ in the method selection strategy. When `self` is used the search begins in the class of the invoking message's receiver, whereas `super` forces searching from the superclass of the class containing the invoked method. This situation can be illustrated with an example. Assuming `Prt` represents an instance of the `Particle` class, the following expression

```
Prt snapToGrid
```

is evaluated by executing the instance method `snapToGrid` in `Point2D`. Inside this method, `self` receives the messages `x:` and `y:`, which are initially looked for in the `Particle` class. A more complex situation can be found when the `Particle` class receives the message `origin` to create a particle with

```
Particle implementation description

class name                    Particle
superclass                    Point2D
instance variable names       mass

class methods

  instance-creation
    x: coordX y: coordY mass: aNumber
      "Answer a particle with mass aNumber and coordinates
       (coordX,coordY) snapped to grid if necessary"
      ↑ (super x: coordX y: coordY) mass: aNumber
    x: coordX y: coordY
      "Answer a particle with mass 0 and coordinates
       (coordX,coordY) snapped to grid if necessary"
      ↑ (self x: coordX y: coordY) mass: 0

instance methods

  accessing
    attraction: aParticle
      "Answer the attraction force between aParticle and the receiver"
      | d |
      d ← self distance: aParticle.
      ↑ 6.67e-11 * mass * aParticle mass / d squared
    mass
      "Answer the receiver's mass"
      ↑ mass
    mass: aNumber
      "Change the receiver's mass to aNumber"
      mass ← aNumber
  printing
    printOn: aStream
      "Append to aStream a printable
       representation of the receiver"
      mass printOn: aStream.
      aStream nextPut: $*.
      super printOn: aStream.
```

FIGURE 19.4 The `Particle` implementation.

coordinates and mass zero. Figure 19.5 illustrates the sequence of messages generated in this situation. The `origin` message is initially sent (first arrow) to the `Particle` class (second vertical line), but the appropriate method is not found there and the `Point2D` class is inspected (dotted line). The method is found in the class, and the expression

```
self x: 0 y: 0
```

is evaluated. Now, `self` entity represents the `Particle` class, since it received the invoking message `origin`. Thus, searching for the method `x:y:` begins again in the `Particle` class. As this class contains a method with the same selector, its body is executed:

```
↑ self x: 0 y: 0 mass: 0
```

As before, `x:y:mass:` is found in the `Particle` class defined as

```
↑ (super x: 0 y: 0) mass: 0
```

That is, the message `x:y:` is sent to the pseudo-variable `super`, and therefore the search for a method is directly delegated to the `Point2D` class. At this point, the selected method is defined as:

```
↑ (self new) x: 0; y: 0
```

so that `self` is still the `Particle` class. For this reason, the search for the `new` method begins in that class, although it is found after the `Point2D` class in the hierarchy. The result of the expression `self new` is an instance of `Particle` class. Next, the instance methods `x:` and `y:` have to be looked for in this class (first vertical line). The rest of the generated messages are processed in a similar way.

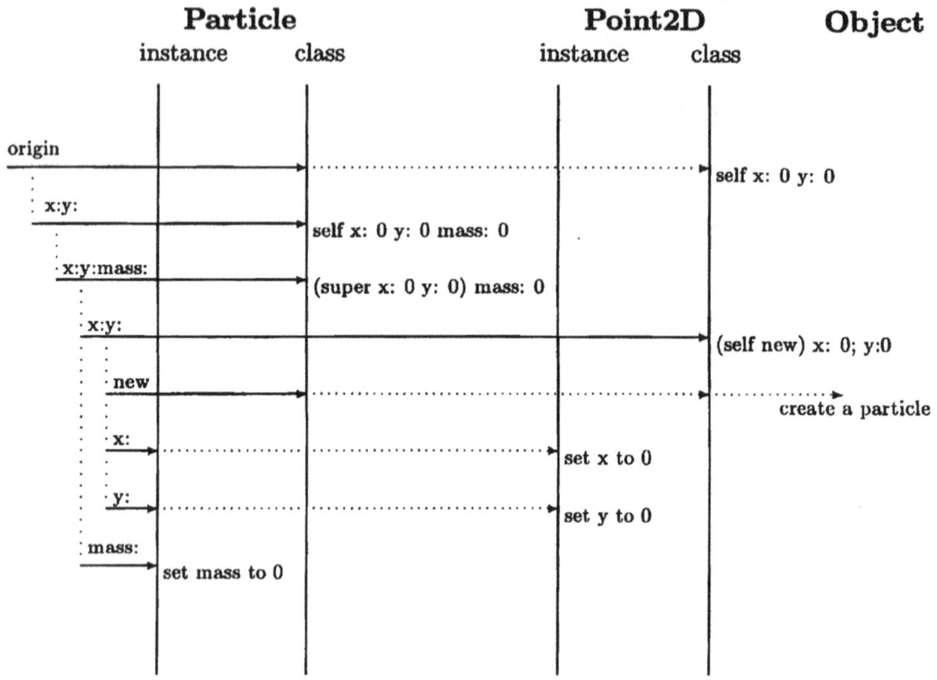

FIGURE 19.5 Sequence of messages initiated by the class method `origin` in `Particle`.

19.3.4 The Metaclass Class

The inheritance hierarchy in Smalltalk is very clear. Every class has exactly one superclass, except the `Object` class, which has no superclass. In this hierarchy we find a set of classes with a special meaning, which will be explained below. The class `Behavior` describes the behavior of other objects, and it provides the information necessary for compiling methods and creating and running instances. The `ClassDescription` class is an abstract subclass of `Behavior`, which adds a number of facilities implemented by the other two subclasses, `Class` and `Metaclass`, which play a crucial role in class management in Smalltalk. These classes give high expressive power to the language, because they allow meta-programming facilities. In fact, the Smalltalk environment (and in particular the class browser) is described in Smalltalk itself. So, class manipulation (e.g., creation, definition of new methods and variables, storing and recovering, etc.) is made through these classes.

In order to fully understand what a metaclass is, it is convenient to remember that each class in Smalltalk is also an object, and therefore an instance of a certain class. Classes whose instances are classes themselves are called metaclasses. Given a class C its metaclass is accessed by sending the message `class` to C. So, for instance, to access the metaclass of `Point2D` we must use the expression

```
Point2D class
```

Metaclasses have the following peculiarities, illustrated in Figure 19.6:

- A metaclass only has one instance (overlapped class).
- All metaclasses are instances (dashed lines) of a special class in the hierarchy, called `Metaclass`.
- The inheritance hierarchy for metaclasses is a replica of the one for their instances (i.e., classes).
- The metaclass `Object class` inherits from a special class called `Class`.

As Figure 19.6 shows, two parallel class hierarchies are connected by an inheritance relation between `Object class` and `Class`. An important relation between a class and its metaclass is that former's class methods correspond to the latter's instance methods. In this way, when a message is sent to a class, the selection of the method to be executed is made by first traversing the class methods until the class `Object` is reached, and then by looking for an instance method in the hierarchy starting from the class `Class`. For instance, when the message `new` is sent to the class `Particle` (see Figure 19.5), the search is first carried out on the class methods of `Particle`, `Point2D`, and `Object`, and then carried out on the instance methods of `Class` and `ClassDescription`. Finally, the appropriate method is found in `Behavior`.

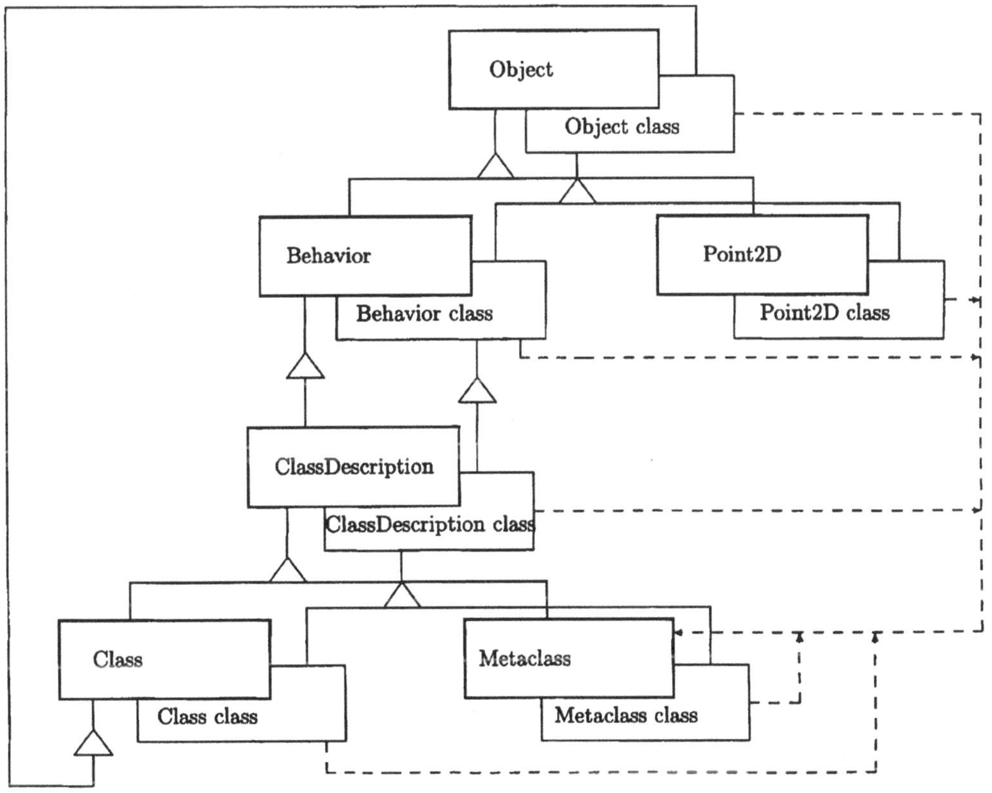

FIGURE 19.6 The Metaclass Hierarchy.

19.3.5 Class Library

The Smalltalk class library provides a rich hierarchy of classes, giving a standard functionality to the programming environment. To give a general view of this library, we have organized this section grouping classes according to their functionality. Thus, we describe the common protocol inherited for every class in the system, the main kernel objects, classes representing magnitudes, collections, streams, and processes. We do not include in this description the kernel classes rooted by `Behavior`, as these were covered in Section 19.3.4. We refer the reader to a specialized bibliography for a complete view of these and many other excluded classes.

19.3.5.1 The Common Protocol

As mentioned, every Smalltalk entity is an object, and consequently the corresponding protocol will be inherited from the `Object` class.

`Object` is an abstract class which defines the common protocol of all objects. A default behavior is given for most of this protocol, but every subclass can redefine it. Basically, it provides methods to test the functionality of an object, copy and compare objects, print and store objects, access the parts of an object, and error handling.

In order to obtain information about an object, several methods can be used. Thus, the class to which an object belongs can be obtained by sending it the `class` message. We are able to know if an object can respond to a message with a given selector by using `respondTo:`. Analogously, we can also know when an object is an instance of a given class (`isMemberOf:`) or one of its subclasses (`isKindOf:`).

Two different models of equality can be used in Smalltalk. The message '==' tests if the receiver and argument refer to exactly the same object, whereas the message '=' only tests whether the receiver has the same content as the argument. The messages '~~' and '~=' are the corresponding opposites.

Three different copying methods can be applied to an object: `copy`, `shallowCopy`, and `deepCopy`. The default behavior of the two first methods is the same. All three return a copy of the receiver, and they differ in the way the instance variable copy is made.

The method `printOn:` is used to obtain a printable representation of an object, where the argument refers to the stream containing this representation. The default behavior provided by `Object` adds the class name of the receiver to the stream. Note that all classes described in this chapter redefine this method conveniently. A string representation of the receiver from which it can be reconstructed may be obtained by using the `storeOn:` method.

A class can be created in such a way that its instances can manipulate indexed instance variables. These variables have no name, and they are accessed by an index. The methods for accessing and storing are: `at:`, and `at:put:`, where the first argument is the index.

One of the most used methods is `new`. It is sent to a class in order to create a new instance, and is usually redefined as a class method. However, it does not belong to the class protocol of `Object`, but is an instance method of the `Behavior` class. Remember that the `Object class` class is a subclass of `Class` class (Section 19.3.4), and this one (indirectly) inherits from `Behavior`. There is another method in `Behavior` class, called `basicNew`, with the same behavior as `new`, but which must not be overridden. When a class includes indexed instance variables the methods `new:` and `basicNew:` are used instead, where the argument indicates the number of indexed instance variables which will contain the created instance. The subhierarchy rooted by `Behavior` includes other methods to obtain information concerning the structure of a class (variables and methods), its relationship with other classes in the full hierarchy (subclasses and superclasses), its instances, etc.

A family of instance methods is also provided by the protocol of the `Object` class for the management of basic error conditions. Among these, we could highlight the following: `doesNotUnderstand:`, which reports to the user that the receiver does not understand the argument as a message; `error:`, which has a string as an argument, and reports an error notification indicated by the string; `subclassResponsibility`, used to define deferred methods, in order to report an error to the user when they are not overridden.

19.3.5.2 Kernel Objects

The common protocol for logical values is given by the abstract class Boolean. The implementation depends on the specific value of the boolean expression receiving the messages. Thus, Boolean has two subclasses, True and False, both with only one instance, the respective pseudo-variables true and false (see Section 19.3.1.2). These two classes provide the specific implementation for the usual methods to manipulate logical expressions, including logical connectives. Also included in these classes are the methods ifTrue:, ifFalse:, ifFalse:ifTrue:, and ifTrue:ifFalse:. So, for instance, the implementation of the last one in the class True is:

```
ifTrue:   trueAlternativeBlock  ifFalse:   falseAlternativeBlock
  ↑ trueAlternativeBlock value
```

whereas in the class False it is:

```
ifTrue:   trueAlternativeBlock  ifFalse:   falseAlternativeBlock
  ↑ falseAlternativeBlock value
```

In this way, the message lookup mechanism gives us an efficient implementation with no additional primitive operations. This technique, which consists of dividing the common protocol of an abstract class according to a classification of its potential instances, is very usual in Smalltalk.

Boolean expressions can also be used to control iterative structures. In fact, the messages whileTrue: and whileFalse: are defined to describe loops, by using a block (see Section 19.3.1.4) as an argument containing the sentences to be iteratively executed. The receivers of these messages are also blocks returning a boolean expression when they are evaluated. In this way, the corresponding methods do not belong to the class Boolean, but the class BlockContext. Thus, for instance, the implementation of whileTrue: is the following:

```
whileTrue: aBlock
  self value
    ifTrue: [aBlock value.  self whileTrue: aBlock]
  ↑ nil
```

19.3.5.3 Magnitudes

Magnitude is an abstract class with a common protocol for all objects that can be compared along a lineal dimension. Among others, Number, Date, Time, and Character are subclasses of Magnitude. Its protocol includes <, <=, >, >=, between:and:, min:, and max:. Some of these methods are deferred (i.e., they are defined in terms of the subclassResponsibility message), and the others are based on them. An example of this situation concerns the usual comparison operations:

```
between:  max and:  min
  "Answer whether the receiver is less than or equal to the argument, max,
   and greater than or equal to the argument, min."
  ↑ self > min and:  [self <= max]

<= aMagnitude
  "Answer whether the receiver is less than or equal to the argument."
  ↑ (self > aMagnitude) not

> aMagnitude
  "Answer whether the receiver is greater than the argument."
```

```
    ↑ aMagnitude < self

  < aMagnitude
    "Answer whether the receiver is less than the argument."
    ↑ self subclassResponsibility
```

Note that only the method < must be implemented by the subclasses.

The `Date` class adds an additional protocol that supports date management. An instance of `Date` represents a specific day in a month and a year. The class protocol includes methods to create dates in several ways and manipulate them conveniently (adding a number of days to a specific date, period of time between two dates, etc.) Similarly, the `Time` class is also provided as a subclass of `Magnitude`, in order to represent and manipulate times.

Another interesting class is `Character`, which has exactly 256 instances each one associated with a code in an extended ASCII character set. In the specific protocol there are testing methods for identifying the type of a character (`isLowerCase`, `isUpperCase`, `isDigit`, `isLetter`, `isAlphaNumeric`, `isSeparator`, `isVowel`), and methods providing conversions of a character (`asciiValue`, `asUpperCase`. `asLowerCase`, `asSymbol`).

Like everything in Smalltalk, numerical values are also represented by objects. However, unlike other objects that may change their internal state. A number's only state is its value, which should never change. This particularity is shared by the `Character` class. Numbers are classified into different subclasses. The class hierarchy is rooted by the `Number` class, an abstract class with the common protocol, which includes the standard operations. Its subclasses represent different kinds of numbers: `Float`, `Fraction`, and `Integer`. The last one is also subclassified in order to obtain an efficient implementation. These classes are widely used in the examples provided in this chapter.

19.3.5.4 Collections

The basic data structures in Smalltalk are found within a quite wide class hierarchy rooted by the abstract class `Collection`. An instance of this class represents a group of objects organized in a certain way. Methods in `Collection` permit adding, removing, testing occurrences, and enumerating elements. Figure 19.7 shows a functional hierarchical representation according to how the elements are dealt with in the collection (whether they can be ordered or not, accessed to by key or not, etc.) One of the most useful classes representing collections is `OrderedCollection`. This allows us to describe the usual abstract data types like stacks, queues, lists, etc. In the example shown in Figure 19.9 (the `initialize` method) the instance variable `orbits` is an ordered collection representing the orbits that different satellites can have around a given celestial body. Other important classes in this hierarchy are `Array`, `Dictionary`, `Set`, `Bag`, `String`, or `Symbol`. The first of these is a clear example of a class containing indexed instance variables, as was described in Section 19.3.5.1. So, to access an instance variable of an array, the method `at:` and `at:put:` have to be used:

```
| a |
a ←  Array new: 3.
a at: 1 put: Display.
a at: 2 put: Transcript.
a at: 3 put: Processor.
...
(a at: 2) show: 'Hello'
```

In order to illustrate the use of methods in the `Collection` class, a simple example is presented in Figure 19.8. This shows a very simple hierarchy involving two classes which inherit from `Particle` and model a simplified planetary system where planets (`CelestialBody` class) can have satellites following

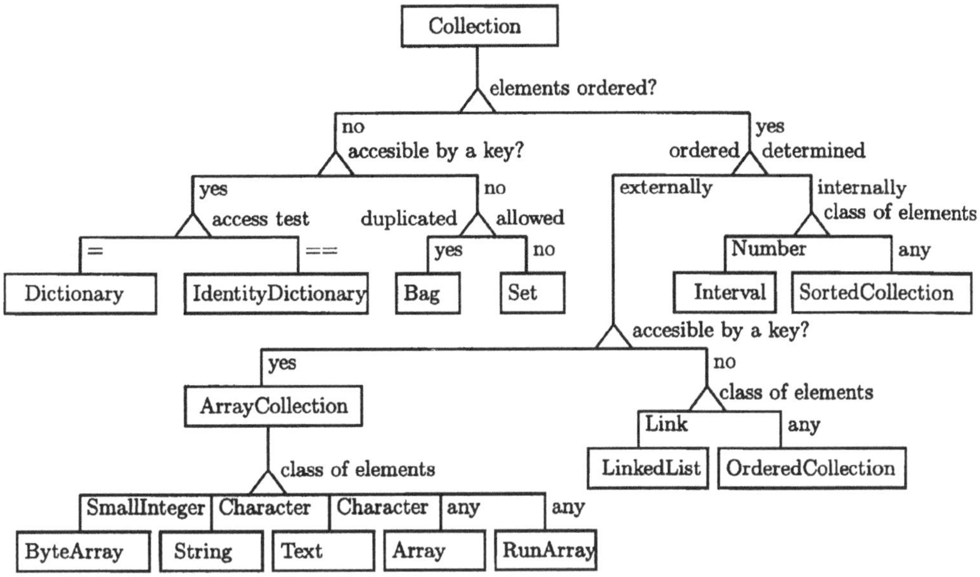

FIGURE 19.7 The `Collection` class.

an `Orbit` (we have assumed circular orbits). The relationship between the classes is described using an OMT-like notation, where we have distinguished instance from class variables (methods).

The protocol and implementation of the two classes `CelestialBody` and `Orbit` are given in Figures 19.9 and 19.10, respectively. `CelestialBody` inherits from `Particle` and redefines the class method `x:y:mass:` and the instance methods `rotate:wrt:` and `printOn:`. Thus, a celestial body is a particle with zero or more orbits, represented by the instance variable `orbits`, which is an ordered collection (see `initialize` description), grouping instances of the `Orbit` class. Each orbit consists of a satellite (again, an instance of the `CelestialBody` class) and its rotation period. The method `add:period:` adds objects to this collection by invoking the `add:` method on the ordered collection. A number of other methods use the collection to manipulate the objects grouped in `orbits`, by means of the `do:` iterator.

The following example creates a celestial body with a star, a planet and a subsystem composed of another planet and a satellite:

```
| star planet subsystem satellite |
satellite  ←  CelestialBody x: 5.3 y: 6.4 mass: 2.
subsystem  ←  (CelestialBody x: 5 y: 6 mass: 5)
                       add: satellite period: 28.
planet  ←  CelestialBody x: 10 y: 10 mass: 20.
star  ←  CelestialBody x: 0 y: 0 mass: 100.
star add: planet period: 150; add: subsystem period: 360.
star runTimes: 30
```

The temporary variable `star` stores a simple planetary system, and the final expression causes the system to progress 30 ticks. A careful analysis of the implementation in Figures 19.9 and 19.10 should be enough to understand this example.

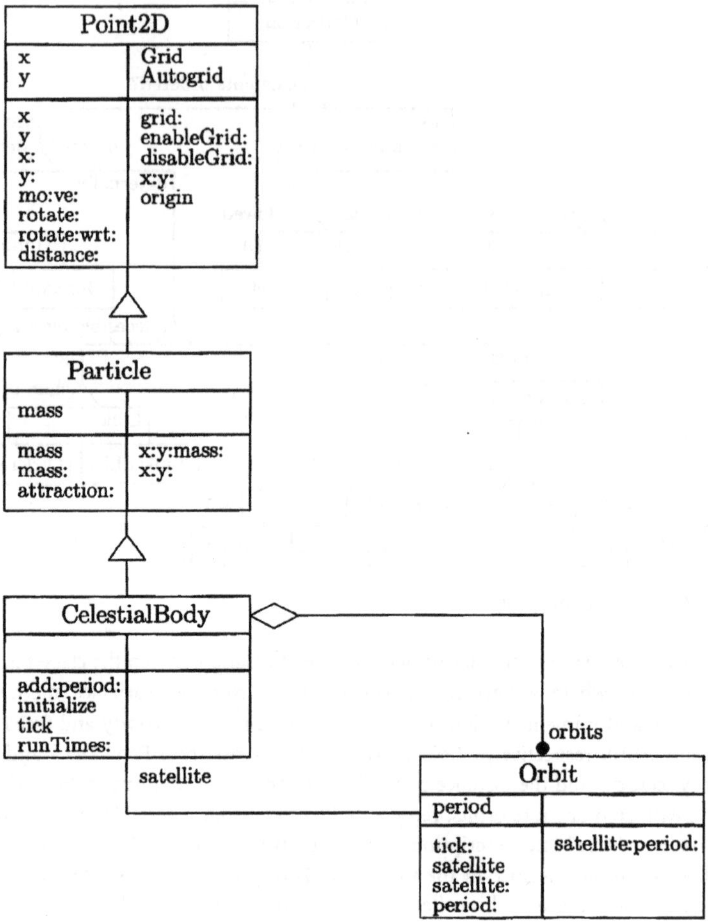

FIGURE 19.8 A simulation of a planetary system.

19.3.5.5 Streams

Class `Stream` is an abstract class that represents the ability to maintain a position reference in a collection of objects. Thus, `Stream` instances refer to a collection and a position inside them. This approach permits interruptible accessing to all of the elements in the collection, in a given order. The method of maintaining the position reference and the accessing mode (input or/and output) determines all its subclasses. The most useful messages are `next`, for accessing to the following element in the collection (the position reference is increased); `nextPut:`, for storing the argument as the next accessible element; and `nextPutAll:`, similar to the previous one, but using a collection as the argument. Typical examples of streams are instances of `ReadWriteStream` and `FileStream`. The argument used in the different implementations of the `printOn:` method is a stream, which is manipulated by means of the previously mentioned methods. For instance, the `printOn:` version described in Figure 19.10 causes the argument `aStream` to be a stream containing the character `'{'`, followed by a stream representation of the satellite and the period (separated by a hyphen), and finishing with the character `'}'`.

```
CelestialBody implementation description

class name                   CelestialBody
superclass                   Particle
instance variable names      orbits

class methods

  instance-creation
  ◇ x: coordX y: coordY mass: aNumber
      "Answer a celestial body with mass aNumber and coordinates
       (coordX,coordY) snapped to grid if necessary, initializing
       conveniently its orbits"
      ↑ (super x: coordX y: coordY mass: aNumber) initialize

instance methods

  accessing
    add: aCelestialBody period: aPeriod
      "Add to the receiver a new orbit with aCelestialBody and aPeriod"
      orbits add: (Orbit satellite: aCelestialBody period: aPeriod)
  printing
  ◇ printOn: aStream
      "Append to aStream a printable representation of the receiver"
      super printOn: aStream.
      aStream nextPutAll:  '==['.
      orbits do: [:anOrb |
                          anOrb printOn: aStream.
                          aStream nextPut:  $ ].
      aStream nextPutAll: ']>'
    runTimes: aNumber
      "aNumber of ticks are produced on the receiver, and the effect
       is visualized on the Transcript"
      Transcript cr; show: self printString.
      aNumber timesRepeat: [ self tick.
                             Transcript cr; show: self printString]
  private
    initialize
      "Set orbits to an empty ordered collection"
      orbits ← OrderedCollection new
  transforming
  ◇ rotate: aNumber wrt: aCenter
      "Move the receiver by applying a rotation of aNumber radians
       with respect to aCenter. All its orbits also rotate"
      super rotate: aNumber wrt: aCenter.
      orbits do: [:anOrb | anOrb satellite rotate: aNumber wrt: aCenter]
  timing
    tick
      "Simulate the ticks of a clock, by sending tick: to every orbit"
      super rotate: aNumber wrt: aCenter.
      orbits do: [:anOrb | anOrb tick: self]
```

FIGURE 19.9 The `CelestialBody` class.

19.3.5.6 Processes

A process in Smalltalk is a sequence of actions to be executed by the virtual machine. A new process is created by sending the `fork` message to a block (i.e., `fork` is an instance method of the `BlockContext` class), and the actions to be performed by the new process are specified by the block's expressions. The `fork` message is used to create and schedule the execution of a process, like the `value` message (Section 19.3.1.4), and it has a similar effect on a block. The difference is that after evaluating a block the system has to wait for every expression in the block be totally evaluated (sequential execution), whereas actions to be performed by a process can be concurrently executed with other actions after the `fork` has been made. The following example creates and schedules a process, which displays numbers from 1 to 1000 at the center of the screen (denoted by the global reference `Display`):

```
Orbit implementation description
------------------------------------------------------------
class name                    Orbit
instance variable names       satellite
                              period

class methods
------------------------------------------------------------
  instance-creation
    satellite: aCelestialBody period: aNumber
      "Answer an orbit with aCelestialBody as satellite and aNumber as period"
      ↑ self new satellite: aCelestialBody; period: aNumber

instance methods
------------------------------------------------------------
  accessing
    satellite
      "Answer the satellite"
      ↑ satellite
  printing
  ◇ printOn: aStream
      "Append to aStream a printable representation of the receiver"
      aStream nextPut: ${.
      satellite printOn: aStream.
      aStream nextPut: $-.
      period printOn: aStream.
      aStream nextPut: $}
  private
    period: aNumber
      "Change the period to aNumber"
      period ← aNumber
    satellite: aCelestialBody
      "Change the satellite to aCelestialBody"
      satellite ← aCelestialBody
  timing
    tick: aCenter
      "Rotate the satellite with respect to aCenter and
       also provoke a tick on the satellite"
      satellite rotate: (Float pi * 2) / period wrt: aCenter.
      satellite tick
```

FIGURE 19.10 The `Orbit` class.

```
[ 1 to:  1000 do:
        [:i | i printString displayAt: Display center ]
] fork
```

Other methods are also available in the `BlockContext` class for manipulating processes. The instance method `forkAt:` also creates and schedules a process to execute actions, but assigns it a priority: the argument. A third way to create a process, but without scheduling, is the block method `newProcess`.

Processes in Smalltalk-80 are instances of the `Process` class, which include methods to `resume`, `suspend`, or `terminate` a process. This is possible because a scheduler is always available to track the processes in the system. The scheduler can also be directly manipulated by means of the global reference `Processor`. When a process receives the `resume` message, its state becomes *ready*. The only process whose actions are currently being carried out is in the state *active*. When the active process terminates, another *ready* process becomes *active*. It is possible to change the active process by sending the `yield` message to `Processor`. The following example creates two processes. The first one shows the current time on the mouse position 100 times, and it is continuously yielding control to the other process, which coincides with that of the previous example, but that also yields control in each iteration:

```
[100 timesRepeat:
        [Time now printString
```

```
                displayAt: Sensor cursorPoint.
            Processor yield ]
] fork.
[ 1 to: 1000 do:
    [:i | i printString displayAt: Display center.
         Processor yield ]
] fork
```

Another important class concerning concurrency in Smalltalk is `Semaphore`. Instances of this class are used as a simple way to synchronize processes. The methods `wait` and `signal` are responsible for this. The former suspends the receiver (and its state becomes *blocked*) until the semaphore receives the corresponding `signal` message. If one or more processes are suspended on a semaphore, a `signal` message resumes the first one. The following example describes a concurrent version of the *quicksort* approach to sort ordered collections. This should be defined as an instance method in the `OrderedCollection` class:

```
concQuickSort
  "Answer a sorted copy of the receiver by a concurrent quicksort"
  | aux first lessThan greaterThan aSemaphore |
  aux ← self copy.
  aux size <= 1 ifTrue: [↑ aux].
  first ← aux removeFirst.
  aSemaphore ← Semaphore new.
  [lessThan ← (aux select: [:elem | elem <= first]) quickSort.
   aSemaphore signal] fork.
  [greaterThan ← (aux select: [:elem | elem > first]) quickSort.
   aSemaphore signal] fork.
  aSemaphore wait; wait.
  ↑ lessThan , (OrderedCollection with: first) , greaterThan
```

This method divides the tail of the receiver collection into two other collections, which contain the elements less than and greater than the head element, respectively. Following this, both collections are concurrently sorted. Partitioning and sorting are done by creating two processes synchronized by the same semaphore. Note that each process sends a `signal` to the semaphore. This allows us to know when the collections are already sorted, in order to construct the result. While the two collections are being sorted, the invoking process is suspended (by the two `wait` messages). There is another way to suspend a process, which is provided by the `Delay` class. Instances of this class can be used to suspend the active process for a period of time. When the instance is created the period of time is specified (in seconds or milliseconds), and the suspension is carried out when it receives the message `wait`.

19.4 Smalltalk Extensions

We have briefly explained the main and significant characteristics of Smalltalk, such as it was initially defined. However, today there are a wide variety of extensions concerning other fields. In this sense, the interaction with databases has been one of most frequent extensions of Smalltalk systems. Examples of these are: GemStone/S (by GemStone), VisualAge for Smalltalk (by IBM Corp.), VisualWorks (by ParcPlace), ObjectStudio (by CinMark Systems, Inc.), etc. From a more general point of view, client-server applications can be developed in these systems, where most of them permit to generate server applications in an efficient way. Another field widely explored in the context of Smalltalk is distributed systems. ParcPlace-Digitalk provides Distributed Smalltalk which allows the building of multi-tiered applications compliant with CORBA (Common Object-Request Broker Architecture). Other systems are strongly adapted to particular operating systems: Dolphin Smalltalk (by Object-Arts), Smalltalk MT (by Object Connect), VisualWorks (by ParcPlace-Digitalk), Smalltalk Express (by ObjectShare, Inc.), Smalltalk Agents (by Quasar Knowledge Systems, Inc.), etc. Some of these systems provide visual programming environments, Internet features (web servers, plugins), version management, etc.

Currently, the research is focused on fields such as integration with other languages (C++, Java), object-oriented concurrency (Concurrent-Smalltalk), typing, and multiple inheritance. The integration with other languages is already being covered by some products, which offer the composition of heterogeneous systems (i.e., systems described in different languages). Types and multiple inheritance have also been considered in some Smalltalk implementations, but only from an experimental point of view.

References

[1] *Byte Special Issue, The Smalltalk-80 System*, 6(8), 1981.

[2] Goldberg, A., *Smalltalk-80. The Interactive Programming Environment.* Addison-Wesley, Reading, MA, 1984.

[3] Goldberg, A. and Robson, D., *Smalltalk-80. The Language and its Implementation.* Addison-Wesley, Reading, MA, 1983.

[4] Goldberg, A. and Robson, D., *Smalltalk-80. The Language.* Addison-Wesley, 1989.

[5] Krasner, G., The Smalltalk-80 Virtual Machine, *Byte*, 6(8), pp. 300–320, 1981.

[6] Krasner, G., *Smalltalk-80. Bits of History, Words of Advice.* Addison-Wesley, 1983.

[7] Lalonde, W. and Pugh, J., *Inside Smalltalk, Vol. I.* Prentice-Hall, Englewood Cliffs, NJ, 1990.

[8] Lalonde, W. and Pugh, J., *Inside Smalltalk, Vol. II.* Prentice-Hall, Englewood Cliffs, NJ, 1991.

[9] Linderman, M., *Developing Visual Programming Applications Using Smalltalk.* Prentice-Hall, Englewood Cliffs, NJ, 1996.

[10] Lorenz, M., *Rapid Software Development with Smalltalk.* Prentice-Hall, Englewood Cliffs, NJ, 1995.

[11] Mével, A. and Gueguén, T., *Smalltalk-80.* Eyrolles, Paris, 1987.

[12] Skublics, S., Klimas, E., and Thomas, D., *Smalltalk with Style.* Prentice-Hall, Englewood Cliffs, NJ, 1996.

[13] Smith, D., *Concepts of Object-Oriented Programming.* McGraw-Hill, New York, NY, 1991.

[14] X3J20 Committee for NCITS, Working Document for Programming Language Smalltalk, 1996. Unpublished.

20

Ada 95: An Object-Oriented Programming Language for Real-Time and Distributed Systems

Luis Joyanes Aguilar
Pontifical Salamanca University

Francisco Gutiérrez
University of Malaga

The Ada language, whose current version is known as Ada 95, is a high-level programming language directed to large systems development in which correction, efficiency, and ruggedness are specially important characteristics.

The first language version known as Ada 83 started to develop in 1974 promoted by the U.S. Department of Defense, and in 1983 the first language standard was published with a document called *Reference Manual for the Ada® Programming Language.*

Ada 83 has been considered as an object-oriented language par excellence, which implies it counts with some of the main characteristics of an object-oriented language, including abstraction, encapsulation,

0-8493-3135-8/99/$0.00+$.50

modularity considered to be fundamental, and some other secondary characteristics such as typing, genericity, and concurrency.

In 1995 a revised Ada Standard, ANSI/ISO/IEC-8652: 1995 commonly known as Ada 95, was approved. The revision added a number of facilities to Ada 83, possibly the most important of which was support for OOP.

The language foundations are available in several sources, especially emphasizing *The Ada Reference Manual* (RM) and *The Ada Annotated Reference Manual* (ARM). With modern features such as object-oriented programming and enhanced interfacing capabilities, Ada 95 will enable the flexible and reliable development of major applications in the coming years. The new standard marks an important milestone in Ada's history. This characteristic has been possible because the enormous contribution from some of the world's finest software engineers and programming language experts has gone into the revision effort, reflecting both current and anticipated user requirements.

Ada is a programming language of special value in the development of large programs which must work reliably. This applies to most defense application domains, especially for real-time systems and distributed applications.

20.1 Main Ada Characteristics

Important aspects of Ada 95 include (Rational, 1995)*:

- *Object-oriented programming* — Ada 95 includes full OOP facilities giving the flexibility of programming by extension which enables programs to be extended and maintained at lower cost.
- *Hierarchical libraries* — The library mechanism now takes a hierarchical form which is valuable for the control and decomposition of large programs.
- *Protected objects* — The tasking features of Ada are enhanced to incorporate a very efficient mechanism for multitask synchronized access to shared data. This is of special value for hard real-time systems.

These enhancements to Ada make Ada 95 an outstanding language. It adds the flexibility of languages such as C++, Smalltalk, or Java, to the reliable software Engineering framework provided and proven by Ada 83 over the past ten years. Ada 95 is a natural evolution of Ada 83. Upward compatibility has been a prime goal and has been achieved within the constraint imposed by other requirements and the enhancements have been made without disturbing the existing investment in the Ada 83 program and programmers. The Design Goals, Language Summary, and Language Changes can be looked up in RM.

20.2 Evolution from Ada 83 to Ada 95

Ada 95 is a revised version of Ada updating the 1983 ANSI Ada standard (ANSI, 1983) and the equivalent 1987 ISO standard (ISO, 1987) in accordance with ISO procedures. The revised ISO standard was published on February 15, 1995. The official definition for Ada 95 is in the *Reference Manual for the Ada Programming Language* (RM, 1995)**. Ada's main goals are:

- Reliability
- Simplicity
- Modularity
- Efficiency
- Portability (between machines with different architectures)

---

* Rational: Hypertext Ada 95 Rationale, 1995. URLs.http://lgl.epl.ch/Ada/rat95-preface.html

** http://www.adahome.com/rm9x-toc,html
http:// lglwww.epfl.ch/rm95/

A prime goal of the design of Ada 95 has thus been to give the language a more open and extensible feel without losing the inherent integrity and efficiency of Ada 83. The additions in Ada 95 which contribute to this more flexible feel are the type extension, the hierarchical library, and the greater ability to manipulate pointers or references. As a consequence, Ada 95 incorporates the benefits of object-oriented languages. Ada 95 remains a very strongly typed language. Another area of major change in Ada 95 is in the tasking model where the introduction of *protected objects* allows a more efficient implementation of standard problems of shared data access.

The major new features of Ada 95 are

- Programming by extension (tagged types)
- Class wide programming
- Abstract types and subprograms
- Hierarchical libraries
- Protected objects
- Interfacing with other languages
- Multitasking
- Generic parameters
- Dynamic binding (dispatching)

20.3 Program Structure

An Ada program is made up of one or more *program units.* A program unit can be (Wheeler, 1996):

- *A subprogram,* which defines executable algorithms; both procedures and functions are subprograms
- *A package,* which defines a collection of entities
- *A task unit,* which defines a computation that can occur in parallel with other computations
- *A protected unit* (*object*), which can coordinate data sharing between parallel computation (this did not exist in Ada 83)
- *A generic unit,* which helps make reusable components (C++'s templates are similar)

Program units normally consist of two parts:

1. The *specification,* which contains information that will be visible to other programs units and defines the interface for a program unit (it is similar to the contents of C "*.h*" files)
2. The *body,* which contains implementation details that need not be visible to other parts (it is similar to the contents of C "*.c*" files)

20.4 Packages

The package is Ada's basic unit for defining a collection of logically related entities. These are the basic modeling units in both Ada 83 and Ada 95. They provide the possibility of obtaining other object properties such as abstraction, encapsulation, and occultation, and the definition for *abstract data types* which are the direct ancestors of classes (objects).

The package consists of two distinct parts, *package specification* and *package body.* These parts can be compiled separately. The package *specification* is its declaring part containing all the elements that will be visible to the user. Among other declaring elements we can find type definition, variable declaration, constants and subprograms, tasks, or protected objects specifications (*public part*). In addition, there is a *private* or *hidden part* in which a complete type definition or the specification of certain operations that cannot be used from the outside are provided.

The *specification* is split into two distinct parts: a *public part* and a *private part*

The package body lies mainly in the definition of all subprograms, tasks, or protected objects that occur in the corresponding specification. It can have a declaring part and an initialization part, but both are hidden from the package user.

```
--Package specification
package TAD_table_persons is
   type Person is
        record
           name:string(1..32);
           age:integer;
     end record;
   type table is private;
   procedure create_table(t: in out table);
   procedure insert_table(t: in out table; p:Person);
   procedure delete_table(t: in out table; p:Person);
   function empty(t:table) return boolean;
   --rest of de operations that are considered necessary

private
--private part non-visible to the user
--private type table is implemented
   type table is ....;
end TAD_table_persons;

--package body
package body TAD_table_persons is
--declarative part if any object needs to be declared, it not visible
--implementation of the specified operations in the package
--specification
--operation implementation is hidden from the user

procedure create_table(t:in out table) is
--declarative part
begin
--procedure body
end create_table;

procedure insert_table (t: in out table; p: Person) is
--declarations
begin
--procedure body
end insert_table;

--rest of implementations of specified operations and of any
--that you wish to hide completely because it is used just by the
--package operations and is not used by its users

end TAD_table_persons;
```

20.4.1 With and Use Clauses

A compilation unit contains either the declaration or the body of a program unit, preceded by the necessary context clause ("with" or "use" clauses). The clause *with* and *use* makes available the contents of a unit to the following program unit.

`with unit_name` — Makes available to the unit all the public components of the imported unit, however, if the imported unit is a package when components of the package are used in a program, they must be prefixed with the package name.

use package_name — Permits public components of the package to be used without having to prefix their name with that of the package name (visibility).

Example:
Assume two packages P1 and P2 that export a Test procedure acting on different types:

```
package P1 is
  procedure Test (i: Integer);
end P1;

package P2 is
  procedure Test (i: float);
end P2;
```

You could use it as follows:

```
with P1, P2;
use P1, P2;
procedure Demo is
  begin
    Test(1);          -- is P1.Test(1)
    Test(5.0);        -- is P2.Test(1.0)
  end Demo;
```

20.4.2 Private and Limited Private Types

The package specification has a *visible part* that makes up the usable information in the outside of the package and a *private part* that regroups the implementation details to which package users cannot gain access (but necessary for the compiler). These two parts are divided by the key word `private`. Therefore, the following example shows the specification of a complex number management package:

```
package  Numbers_Complex is
  type Complex is private;
  I: constant Complex;
  --deferred constant, the initial value cannot be given
  --in the visible part, the details of type are not known
  function "+" (X, Y: Complex) return Complex
  function "-" (X, Y: Complex) return Complex
  function "*" (X, Y: Complex) return Complex
  function "/" (X, Y: Complex) return Complex

private
    --the user cannot gain access to these declarations
  type Complex is
    record
      Real  : Float;
      Imag  : Float;
    end record;
  I: constant Complex := (0.0, 2.0);
    end Numbers_Complex;
```

The Complex type is referred to as *private type*. In the visible part its presence is announced and the complete definition is provided in the private part.

When declaring a type as private, other packages can use only the operations that you provide and the assignment (:=) and equality (=) operations. It is possible to remove these properties declaring the type as limited private; the type is then known as limited type. A limited private type is a private type that does not even define the default assignment and equal-to operations. Here is how Account would be defined as a limited private type.

Type Account is limited private:

1. *Private type objects* can be declared, passed as parameters, compared to verify their equality, and be assigned to other objects with the same type.
2. The type *limited private* objects declaration cannot include an initial value, a constant cannot be declared outside the defining package, but it can be declared subprograms with limited type as parameters.

20.5 Class and Objects

The class concept, as discussed above, was already present in Ada 83.

Ada doesn't have its own construction for the class implementation from which objects sharing both structure and behavior can be defined. It does count with packages that allow you to simulate class construction, providing the definition of a type, in general private, and of a series of functions or procedures whose parameters count at least with a defined type instance in the package, that is, in Ada terminology, they are the class primitive operations or methods (in Smalltalk). The defined type inside the package is register type, so that its components represent the class attributes.

Objects are entities with internal state and externally visible operations that read or modify this state. Each object is an instance of a class. A class is the implementation of an Abstract Data Type, which defines the behavior of the set of objects that are instances of the class. Ada does not have a class construct for its implementation from which objects sharing both structure and behavior can be defined.

In Ada, classes are expressed using user-defined types and the package construct, which may export one or more types with their primitive operations. The primitive operations of the type include subprograms declared in the same declaration part — the package specification — and having the type in question as the type of a parameter or of the result. In defining a class, the following conventions are used:

- The class is defined in terms of a package which has the class name prefixed with `class_`.
- The package has a single private type which takes the class name and is used to declare instances of the class.
- Procedures and functions are used to define the behavior of the class.
- The implementation of the private type is defined as a *record* type, the components of which define the structure of the class.

Example:

```
package Class_account is
   type Account is private;
   procedure Deposit (A: in out Account);
   procedure withDraw (A: in out Account; Amount : out Money);
   function Balance (A: Account) return Money;

private
   type Account is tagged
     record
        Initial_Balance : Money;
        Owner: String (1..25);
     end record;

end Class_account;
```

Another example:

```
Package Class_Person is
   --the type Person is totally visible
```

```
Type Person is tagged
   record
      Name: String(1..32);
      Age:Integer;
   end record;
-- primitive operations must be after
--the type and must have a parameter or return type of the
--type to which they belong
function obtain_name (p: Person) return string;
function obtain_age(p:Person)return integer;
procedure change_age(p:in outPerson; a:integer);
-- in fact it has no much sense to define this operation, since
-- the type is visible and it could be performed by direct
--assignation to the register component
end Class_Person
```

In Ada 95 new style, the new data type is usually defined as tagged type (extensible or tagged types), both being defined as private types (non-visible) or visible types. Its important to note that every object of tagged type has a hidden component or tag used as the type indicator; it is precisely this tag that will determine the operation that will be executed when issuing a message to an object. Note: Ada 95 does not allow putting together public and private attributes within the same type. However, private attributes and members can be achieved by using a combination of private types and child library.

20.6 Genericity

The generic units are parameterized units which allow you to define an algorithm regardless of the handled objects type. This is the main problem in reusing code of previously written functions or procedures, as they are limited to process specific types of values. Ada 95 permits the definition of generic packages or subprograms. The actual parameters to be used are supplied by the user of the package or subprogram.

The declaration of a generic unit is split into two components: a specification part that defines the interface to the outside world, and an implementation part that defines the physical implementation. In the specification part, the parameters to be used in the unit are specified between the *generic* and the prototype line of the package or subprogram.

Here's an example of a generic procedure that swaps its arguments:

```
generic                                   -- Specification
   type Item is private
procedure Swap (X, Y : in out Item);      -- Prototype swap

procedure Swap (X, Y : in out Item) is    -- Implementation swap
   Temp: Item;
begin
   Temp := x;
   x := Y;
   y := Temp;
end Swap;
```

To use this procedure the user must first instance a procedure that will operate on a particular type. This is accomplished by the declaration:

```
procedure Swap-Year is new Swap (Year);   -- Instantiation
      ...
Swap-Year (One-Year, Two-Year);
```

The following example gives us the specification of a sort generic unit of a table (array sort):

```
generic
   type Index is (<>);
   type Component is private;
   type List is array (Index) of Component;
   with function "<" (X, Y : Component) return Boolean is <>;
procedure Sort (A_sORT : in out List);
```

The generic parameters are the array index type, the component type, the array type itself, and a comparison function. This comparison function has its own value by default (clause *is* <>), meaning that if the user does not supply a value, the predefined comparison must be used (if available). The advantages of these properties are obvious; from a written algorithm, it is possible to obtain instantaneously the sort functions of any data type, using any comparison criteria. Therefore, for instance, the following is a procedure that sorts a list of real numbers in ascendent order:

```
type Int is range 1..10;
type Arr is array (Int) of Float;
procedure Sort_Up is new Sort (Int, Float, Arr);
```

If you wish to sort in descendent order, inverting the comparison criterion is enough:

```
procedure Sort:Down is new Sort (Index => Int,
          Component => Float,
          List => Arr,
          "<" => ">");
```

Example:
Creating a template of a generic class table

```
Package Class_Person is
   type Person is tagged private;
   --now type Person has private attributes and members
   --the only way to initialize the components is by using a
   --primitive operation with visibility on private members

   --Especification of the generic unit
generic
   --generic parameters
   type element is private;
   --it can be any type with the assignation defined
package TAD_table_generic is
   type table is private;
   procedure create_table(t: in out table);
   procedure insert_table(t: in out table; e:element);
   procedure delete_table(t: in out table; e:element);
   --operations also depend on the generic parameters
   function empty(t:table) return boolean;
   --rest of operations that are considered necessary
   private
--private part not visible to the user
--it implements the private type table
   type table is array(1..100) of element;
   --the array is of elements that is a parameter and depending on
--the value it takes, the table will store one thing or another

end TAD_table_persons;
```

```
--package body
package body TAD_table_persons is
--declarative part if it is needed to declare any object.., it is
--not visible implementation of specified operations in the package
--specification operation implementation is hidden from the user

procedure create_table(t:in out table) is
--declarative part
begin
--procedure body
end create_table;

procedure insert_table (t: in out table; e:element) is
--declarations
begin
--procedure body
end insert_table;

--rest of implementations in the specified operations and of any
--that you wish to hide completely because it is used just by the
--package operations and not used by its users

end TAD_table_persons;
```

In order to create a generic instance and obtain an integer and persons table, those types are passed as parameters:

```
package TAD_table_integers is new TAD_table_generic(integer);
package TAD_table_persons is new TAD_table_generic(Persona);
--type Person is supposed to be defined and visible where the instance
--is performed
```

20.6.1 New Characteristics of Generic Units

In Ada 95, modifications performed in the generic units are directed to the possibility of using new generic parameters, in order to add the same object-oriented characteristics addition to overcome some errors that could occur in the instantiation mechanism of generic units in Ada 83 in terms of the parameters.

Three parameter types are mainly added: tagged types, derived types, and instantiations of generic packages. In addition, as something new, it is allowed to indicate whether or not a generic parameter corresponds to a restricted type.

20.6.1.1 Tagged Type Parameters

Its interest focuses on the possibility of using types extension in the genericity, an addition allowing you to add new components, the characteristic of which mixing inheritance is based. It provides the possibility of "simulating the multiple inheritance" which allows us to define types derived from others and, in turn, to have visibility upon other types.

```
with Data_Works; use Data_Works;      -- exports the type Data_Work
generic
   type Person is tagged private;
package Worker_Type is
   --A person who works has some additional data
   type Worker is new Person with private;

   procedure Introduce (W: in out Worker; D: in Data_Work);
   function Data_of (W: Worker) return Data_Work;
```

```
private
   type Worker is new Person with
     record
        Data_own: Data_Work;
     end record;
end Worker_Type;
```

In fact, this is not multiple inheritance because it does not inherit data from two tagged types, it inherits from what will be the one that will be passed as a generic parameter and contains an object from another.

20.6.1.2 Derived Type Parameters

This case is similar to the above-mentioned, although you have to consider that the type of the real parameter must be of a type derived directly or indirectly from that specified in the generic unit definition. Let's distinguish whether or not the base type or derived types are tagged:

```
type D is new Base;
--the formal parameter can be Base or derived from Base, but it not
-- tagged

type D is new Base with private;
--in this case they must also be tagged
```

In the case of both generic parameters tagged and derived you can indicate if they can be non-restricted, if they have discriminant, or they can be abstract.

```
type T is abstract tagged private;
-- it can be or not of tagged abstract as well
type T(i:index) is abstract tagged private;
-- it must also have a discriminant of index type
type T(<>) is tagged private;

--it can be non-restricted
```

20.6.1.3 Parameters as Instances of a Generic Package

This is a new generic parameter type that provides some important characteristics. It simplifies the import of complete abstractions since not only a type is imported through them, but also all operations, without the need of their enumeration.

There are two ways of indicating a parameter of that type:

```
with package P is new PB(<>);
--points out that the current parameter must be the package instance
--PB generic
with package P is new PB(P1,P2,....);
--in this case it must be the generic parameter PB instance
--specifying the required parameters to carry out the instance
```

With the use of these generic parameters the language has received a greater capability of being reused, as well as errors and mistakes existing in Ada 83 which have been overcome. You could not specify whether the type of the formal parameter was non-restricted, which obviously influenced both in the definition and the implementation of the corresponding operations.

20.6.2 New Forms of Using Pointers and References

In Ada 95, pointer types have extended to subprogram handling obtaining a greater flexibility when accessing the objects.

The main characteristic which has been incorporated into the language is the possibility of accessing objects already declared through pointers, objects not created by using *new* for dynamical memory allocation, that is, to be able to handle them. General pointers have been created for that purpose. General pointer type objects can be assigned the address of any object with the type the pointer refers to, as long as that object had been declared as aliased, so that it will be handled by means of that pointer; that is, it is allowed access to read and write the object. To assign the aliased object address to the pointer object, the attribute *Access* must be used.

```
type char_ptr is access all character;
CP:char_ptr;
C: aliased character;
--C object is initialized
CP := C'Access;
--C can be handled by means of pointer CP
```

In addition, it is provided the possibility of read-only access by means of the definition of constant pointer type.

```
type pointer_constant_character is access constant character;
PCC: pointer_constant_character;
CC:aliased constant character := 'a';
--CC can be accessed through the pointer because the constant
--pointer has only-read access
```

The flexibility these pointers provide is great since they can access elements of composite type declared as aliased, you declare collections of objects with different sizes (for example, a character string array with a different number of characters), etc.

Another important contribution to the language in this aspect has been the possibility of declaring pointers to subprograms. This provides another form of late binding, invoking subprograms in dereferencing the value access.

```
type Function_Mathematics is access function (F:FTB) return FTB;
--FTB is subtype FTB is Float_Type'Base;
F:Funcion_Mathematics;
Value:FTB := 2.6;
Result:FTB;
F := Sqrt'Access;
Result := F(Valor);
--is an indirect call to Sqrt as abbreviation for
--Result := F.all(Value)
```

20.7 Inheritance

Ada 83 did not totally support inheritance property, although it supported derived types, that to some extent, were similar to inheritance concept. Ada 95 incorporates a new form of type declaration that supports inheritance.

Inheritance lets us define types as extensions of existing types; the new types are *derived types*, while the extended types are usually called "base types." Inherited operations can be overridden with new definitions of those operations. Derived types can also add new operations and attributes that apply only to them and not their base types.

Type extension in Ada 95 is carried out by using tagged record types. The types that can have parents or children are termed *tagged types*. The keyword "tagged" is a part of their definition.

There is a simple way of defining extensible data types. A record type can be declared to be a tagged record which allows it to be extended later. A tagged record type declaration is very similar to an ordinary type declaration. That is, it is encapsulated inside the package specification, is defined by means of a record, and is included in the key word `tagged`.

```
package Class_Person is
   type Person is tagged private;
   --now type Person has private members or attributes
   procedure initialize(p: in out Person; n:string; e:integer);
   --the only way to initialize the components is by means of
   --a primitive operation which has the visibility upon
   --private members
   function obtain_name(p:Person) return string;
   --rest of operations considered opportune
private
   type Person is tagged
     record
       Name : String(1..32);
       Age :Integer;
     end record;
end Class_Person;
```

The object declaration of the previous type is performed similarly to the variable declaration of any other type, and always in the unit declaration part in which such a type is visible (i.e., to which the package Class_Person has been imported).

```
with Class_Person;
--starting unit in which type Person objects are to be defined
--declaration part of that unit
use Class_Person;
Johnny: Person;
--it cannot be initialized by means of a normal assignation, because
--components are private
```

With these characteristics, a tagged type is accomplished (class in other language terminologies) that can be a hierarchy base, that is, derived tagged types or derived classes can be defined from it, thus creating true class or tagged types hierarchies.

The definition of a class derived from the last one is based on the definition of a derived type, that is, the derived class is defined making use of the keyword *new* followed by the base class name, in this way inheriting all base class attributes and functions, also with the possibility of adding new attributes and new primitive operations.

It is important to take into account that the descendent type has no direct visibility upon what was private in base, if it is encapsulated in a package other than the base, or what is otherwise more convenient if you want the application to be more maintainable. Then, in order to be able to access those attributes or operations, inherited operations that were visible in the base must be used.

```
with Class_Person; use Class_Person;
package Class_Student is
   --this type descents from person
   type Student is new Person with private;
   procedure initialize(st:Student; n:name; a:age);
   --it needs a primitive procedure that invokes the procedure
   --to initialize the base type to be able to initialize the private
   --components that have been inherited from the base type, since --
   --base private members are not visible in its descendents

private
   type Student is new Person with
     record
       Carrier: String(1..50);
       Course: integer;
```

```
      Num_expdte: string(1..6);
    end record;

  end Class_Student;
```

Type conversion is always allowed from derived classes to the base, and additional components of descendent type are ignored in the base, in case they exist.

```
P:Person:
S:Student;
P := Person(S);
--explicit conversion, aditionals components are ignored
```

20.7.1 An Inheritance Application

A typical class hierarchy is normally: Figure, Circle, Triangle, and Ellipse.

```
package Figure is
  type Point is
      x, y : Float;
  end record;

  type Figure is tagged
    record
      Origin : Point;
    end record;

  function Area (F : in Figure) return Float;
  function Perimeter (F : in Figure) return Float;
  procedure Draw (F : in Figure);
  type Circle is new Figure with
    record
      Radius : Float;
    end record;
  function Area (C : in Circle) return Float;
  function Perimeter (F : in Circle) return Float;
  function Draw (F : in Circle) return Float;

  type Triangle is new Figure with
    record
      Base : Float;
      Height : Float;
    end record;

  function Area (T : in Triangle) return Float;
  function Perimeter (T : in Rectangle) return Float;
  procedure Draw (T : Rectangle);

  type Equilateral_Triangle is new Triangle with null record;

end Figure;
```

20.8 Abstract Types (Class)

Ada 95 also provides the possibility to define abstract types or classes. Such types encapsulate a series of characteristics that are to be defined in descendent types, but they are not to be defined in the abstract type. Some abstract class operations have no implementation.

Abstract types are defined as tagged preceding the key word tagged of the key word **abstract** and must have at least a *primitive abstract subprogram*, which cannot be directly invoked and whose body does not exist in the abstract type, but in some or all descendent types. Like other languages, abstract

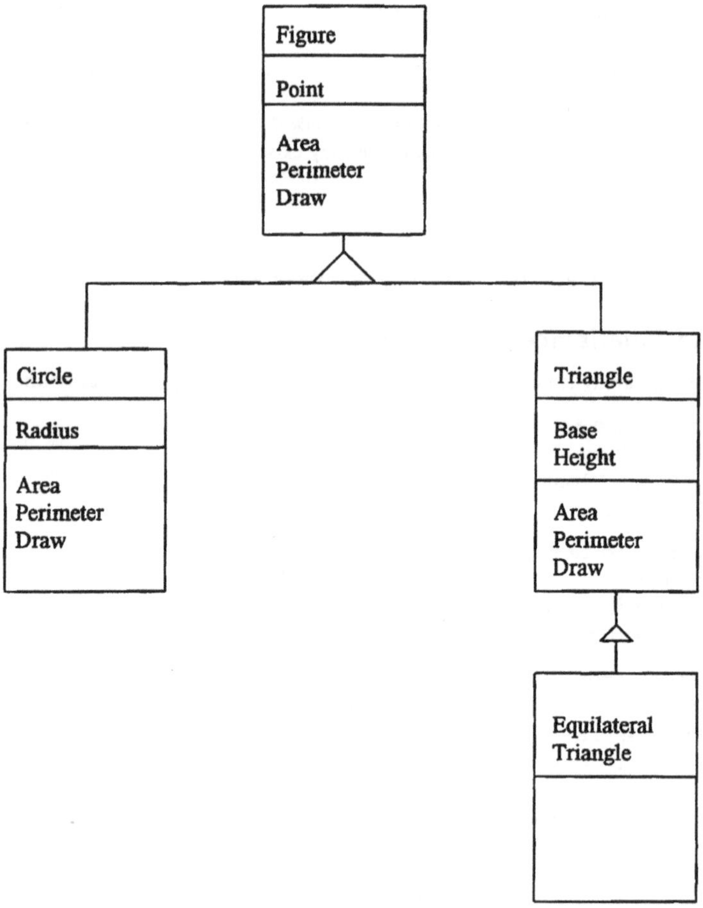

FIGURE 20.1

types cannot be used to declare its objects, they are actually types whose goal is to embrace the common characteristics to all types pertaining to a hierarchy which is the base. Therefore, an abstract type is used as a base class to define new derived classes that are concrete, for example, from those that objects can be created, as long as all the primitive abstract operations had already been implemented.

Subprograms can also be declared as *abstract*; a call to such subprograms would have to dispatch to an overridden version of the subprogram. To *declare* a subprogram as *abstract*, place the phrase "is abstract" before the last semicolon in its definition.

Rule (Wheeler, 1997):

- If you have an abstract subprogram for a given type, the type unit must also be abstract.
- When you later create a non-abstract type that descends from an abstract type, you must define all of its abstract subprograms.

C++ vs. Ada 95:
Abstract subprograms are equivalent to ending a C++ function declaration with "=*0*".

Example:
An abstract type representing a set of natural numbers; an example from RM, 95, Section 3.9.3;*

* http//:www.adahome.com/rm9x/rm9x-03-09-03.html.

```
package Sets is
   subtype Item_Type is Natural;
   type Set is abstract tagged null record;
   function Empty return Set is abstract;
   function Union (Left, Right : in Set) return Set is abstract;
   function Intersection (Left, Right : in Set) return Set is abstract;
   function Unit_Set (Item : in Item_Type)return Set is abstract;
   procedure Take (Item : out Item_Type; from: in out Set) is abstract;
end Sets;
```

Example:

```
An abstract class representing a chess pieces
package cpieces is
type colour_type is (whites, blacks);
--enumerated type
type piece is abstract tagged private;
--private abstract type that embrace the common characteristics
--of an application pieces that implements the chess game
--reduced there are only three types of pieces)

procedure initialize(p:in out piece; x1,y1:integer;
                              p:colour_type);
--it needs a procedure to initialize the components
function valid (x1, y1:integer; p:piece) return boolean
                                             is abstract;
--it is not implemented for that type, it is abstract since the
--movement validity depends on the piece type

procedure move (x1,y1:integer; p:in out piece);
--it is implemented, it is not abstract, it is assumed that once
--checked if the movement is valid, move is simply
--to change pieces coordinates, then all are implemented
--the same way
function colour (p:piece) return colour_type;
procedure draw(p:piece) is abstract;
--abstract, each piece is represented differently, it is not
--implemented for that type

type tower is new piece with private;
--descendent types can be defined in the same package
--or another
function valid(x1,y1:integer; t:tower) return boolean;
procedure draw(t:tower);
--descendent type of piece, neither new attributes are added
--nor new operations, but if abstract operations
--of base type are defined

type bishop is new piece with private;
function valid(x1,y1:integer; a:bishop) return boolean;
procedure draw(a:bishop);
--similar to the last one

type queen is new piece with private;
function valid (x1,y1:integer; d:queen) return boolean;
procedure draw(d:queen);
```

```
--similar to the last
private
     type piece is abstract tagged record
        x,y :integer;
        colour:type_colour;
     end record;
type tower is new piece with null record*;
type bishop is new piece with null record;
type queen is new piece with null record;

end cpieces;
```

20.9 Polymorphism (Dynamic Dispatching)

In Ada 95, the dynamic polymorphism is obtained from the redefinition of primitive operations in the derived classes and by using class wide types, a new notion that is incorporated into the language precisely for this purpose.

For each tagged type T there is an associated type T′ class; this type comprises the union of all types in the tree of derived types rooted at t. For example, in the previous example, Triangle class is a class that includes the types triangle and Equilateral Triangle.

The type T′ class is a non-restricted tagged type, or its tag has no defined value. It will have values from whatever type in the hierarchy whose root is T, since it comprises the union of all of them.

Every time a type of the hierarchy to the type T′ class is assigned, that is, the implicit conversion of the corresponding type to class wide type is performed, the tag associated to T′ class is given a value, consequently, it will already have a concrete type.

The fact that type T′ class is non-restricted forces it to be initialized by using an object of the type you wish, either of base type or derived, when an object of that type is declared .

```
The type piece'class is a class wide type corresponding to the hierarchy
defined in the above example.
Whitetower:tower;
p18:pieza'class:= Whitetower;
--tag of object p 18 takes tower type value, that is the value
--of tag Whitetower
```

With the use of these objects you can obtain the polymorphism, that is, the dynamic binding between an operation and the object for which it is activated.

In fact, in Ada 95 every primitive operation is polymorphism-sensitive, as long as such an operation has already been defined in derived classes of the base in which it is specified for the first time.

Therefore the operation has to be invoked with a class wide type object (already initialized, as we have discussed before), and depending on the tag value, the operation appropriate for the corresponding type is invoked. This form of binding is known as *dispatching*:

```
draw(p18);
--binding between the object and the operation is dynamic and
--the primitive operation
--corresponding to the type tower will be invoked
```

By manipulating objects through references, you still can get more flexibility. Then a general access type to a class wide type is defined, so that any variable of this type could designate any value of the class wide type.

```
type p_pieces is access all piece'class;
--access type to a class wide type
```

* The null record is shorthand for 'record null; end record'

```
piece18:p_pieces := new tower;
--an object of any kind of the hierarchy can be assigned
draw(piece18.all);
--dynamic binding since piece18.all refers to the pointed object
--per piece and whose tag has the value tower
```

Dynamic dispatching is simply the process of determining at runtime exactly which routine to call, and than calling it. Every value that is tagged type includes an invisible "tag" that tells Ada the actual type. This tag is used to figure out which routine to call. Because of the compilation rules Ada imposes, Ada can guarantee that dynamic dispatching will always find a subprogram to call.

20.10 Initialization, Finalization, and Copy

Like other object-oriented languages, Ada 95 incorporates the possibility of controlling the initialization and finalization of objects in certain classes implicitly, as well as redefining the assignation.

Therefore classes are allowed to redefine a series of primitives referring to that aspect, as long as such classes are derived from controlled and limited controlled classes, which are private abstracts and limited private types, respectively, defined in a library *Ada.Finalization*. Such classes include abstract procedures called Initialize (to control initialization), Finalize (to control finalization), and Adjust (to define assignation). The latter is only defined in the controlled type. The library specification is the following:

```
package Ada.Finalization is
   type Controlled is abstract tagged private;
   procedure Initialize (Object: in out Controlled);
   procedure Adjust (Object: in out Controlled);
   procedure Finalize (Object: in out Controlled);

   type Limited_Controlled is abstract tagged limited private;

   procedure Initialize (Object: in out Limited_Controlled);
   procedure Finalize (Object:in out Limited Controlled);
private
...
end Ada.Finalization;
```

Procedures have the following characteristics:

1. *Initialize*
   - It must have a parameter in out, a class object, for which is defined.
   - It is implicitly invoked after creating an object and as long as its explicit initialization has not been performed.
   - This procedure performs an initialization with default values of the object created.
2. *Finalize*
   - It is a procedure with a parameter in out of the class type for which it is defined.
   - It is implicitly invoked before the object destruction, in two occasions: when the object exceeds its scope (in order to free dynamically assigned memory to it) and before an object assignation in order to delete it and give it new values.
3. *Adjust*
   - It is a procedure with a parameter in out of the class type for which it is defined.
   - It is implicitly invoked after the assignation and is applied to the object modified.

Example (above chess pieces):

```
with cpieces,ada.finalization;
use cpieces, ada.finalization;
```

```
package class_chessboard is
   type chessboard is new controlled with private;
   --descendent type of the type controlled, its object
   --initialization can be controlled as well as its finalization and
   --copy by means of the definition of the primitive operations
   --initialize, finalize y adjust
   procedure initialize(t:in out chessboard);
   procedure adjust(t:in out chessboard);
   procedure finalize(t:in out chessboard);
   function square_empty(t:chessboard; x1,y1:integer) return boolean;
   procedure move(t:in out chessboard; x1,y1,x2,y2:integer;
                        prop:colour_type);
   procedure draw(t:chessboard);
   procedure erase(t:in out chessboard);
private
   type p_pieces is access all piece'class;
   type achessboard is array(1..8,1..8) of p_pieces;
   type chessboard is new controlled with
     record
       bchess: achessboard;
     end record;
   --container type or class, contain objects or references to
   --objects of other tagged types
end class_chessboard;
```

The implementation of the operations initialization, finalization, and copy for the last example is the following:

```
procedure initialize(t:in out chessboard) is
   --it initialize a simplified chess chessboard which only has
   --towers, queens and bishops
begin
        t.bchess(1,1) := new tower;
        t.bchess(1,3) := new queen;
        t.bchess(1,5) := new bishop;
        t.bchess(8,4) := new bishop;
        t.bchess(8,6) := new queen;
        t.bchess(8,8) := new tower;

        --the board elements are general pointers to type piece'Class

   initialize(t.bchess(1,1).all,1,1,whites);
   initialize(t.bchess(8,8).all,8,8,blacks);
   initialize(t.bchess(1,5).all,1,5,whites);
   initialize(t.bchess(8,4).all,8,4,blacks);
   initialize(t.bchess(1,3).all,1,3,whites);
   initialize(t.bchess(8,6).all,8,6,blacks);
   --the operation is invoked to fix the initial position of each
   --piece, dispatching is performed
end initialize;

procedure adjust(t:in out chessboard) is
--it is defined the copy for the board that appears on the left of the
--assignation, to avoid that copied board squares to
--point the same memory addresses
begin
for i in 1..8 loop
```

```
        for j in 1..8 loop
          if t.bchess(i,j) /= null then
          declare
            pt:p_pieces := t.bchess(i,j);
          begin
            if pt.all'tag = torre'tag then t.bchess(i,j) := new tower;
                    --each element tag is checked to
                    --assign a new objet with the same tag
                    -- it had
          elsif pt.all'tag = alfil'tag then t.bchess(i,j) := new bishop;
            else t.bchess(i,j) := new queen; end if;
            t.bchess(i,j).all := pt.all;
          end;
          end if;
    end loop;
end loop;
end adjust;

procedure finalize(t:in out chessboard) is
--it frees dynamically assigned memory to every square of the board
begin
  for i in 1..8 loop
      for j in 1..8 loop
        if not square_empty(t,i,j) then free (t.bchess(i,j)); end if;
        --free is a unchecked-deallocation generic procedure instance
        --to free dinamically assigned memory
      end loop;
  end loop;
end finalize;
```

20.11 Child Libraries

This new Ada 95 characteristic allows us to add components to an existing package without the need to modify the original package; in addition, a private type can be shared by more than one library and the possibility to breakdown a system into encapsulated subsystems of compilation modules without broadening the user's visibility. Child libraries can also be used to simulate the existence of protected members in a base type, that is, members only accessed by descendent types and not by users.

There are two types of libraries: public and private. Both characteristics are very similar although there are some outstanding differences between them giving a different meaning and usefulness to each one.

20.11.1 Public Child Libraries

These child libraries are mainly used to broaden an existing library giving it greater visibility to the user. What gives more strength to these libraries is the visibility that private parts or their implementation have upon the private part or hidden from the parent library. It is worth emphasizing that visibility of the parent private part does not exist in the child library public part because it would disturb the parent abstraction, thus allowing you to export private characteristics through their renaming in the child library. Besides a library does not need a clause *with* upon the parent to be compiled, the parent parts cannot be used without the need of the clause *use*.

This mechanism will bring about a library hierarchy in which children, in turn, can have new children with visibility upon them, and not upon their parent.

A public child library is declared by means of a package whose name is the library name followed by a point and a new identifier.

We have next, some examples of the use of public libraries. The type interface which represented the chess board is to be broadened, in order to permit going back in the game and choosing the best action. Therefore a child library in which new primitive operations are specified and which have access to the private part of the base type is created from the last one, trying to avoid modifying the library already created which would also mean to recompile it as all the user libraries.

```
package class_chessboard.broadened is
    procedure go_back(t:in out chessboard;
                              x1,y1,x2,y2:integer;prop:type);
    procedure obtain_action_optimum(t:in out chessboard;
                                         x1,y1,x2,y2:integer;prop:type);
end class_chessboard.broadened;
```

As we can see, all operations are primitive operations of the board type and the child library does not need the parent with and has direct visibility upon its elements. Another important use of child libraries is to provide access to private parent members to the descendent types (simulate protected members), as well as the possibility that several libraries share a private type. Therefore the chess pieces library is to be modified in order to locate them in a different package. Child libraries are to be used so that primitive operations of descendants can directly access private parent members.

```
package cpieces is
  type colour_type is (whites, blacks);
  type piece is abstract tagged private;
  procedure initialize(pie:in out piece; x1,y1:integer;
                         p:colour_type);
  function valid (x1, y1:integer; p:piece) return boolean
                                                is abstract;
  procedure move (x1,y1:integer; p:in out piece);
  function colour (p:piece) return colour_type;
  procedure draw(p:piece) is abstract;

  private
    type piece is abstract tagged record
      x,y :integer;
      colour:colour_type;
    end record;

end pieces;

package cpieces.tower is
  type tower is new piece with private;
  function valid(x1,y1:integer; t:tower) return boolean;
  procedure draw(t:tower);
  --these functions can access private members
  --of the base type
  private
    type tower is new piece with null record;
end cpieces.tower;

package cpieces.Bishop is
  type bishop is new piece with private;
  function valid(x1,y1:integer; a:bishop) return boolean;
  procedure draw(a:bishop);
  private
    type bishop is new piece with null record;
end cpieces.bishop;
```

```
package cpieces.queen is
   type queen is new piece with private;
   function valid (x1,y1:integer; d:queen) return boolean;
   procedure draw(d:queen);
   private
      type queen is new piece with null record;
end cpieces.queen;
```

The three child libraries share the private type.

20.11.2 Private Child Libraries

The declaration of a private child library is similar to a public one but preceded by the word private. However, the interpretation of these private child libraries is different from the public. Their goal is to breakdown a system in terms of implementation without giving additional visibility to the user. The visibility rules for these libraries are similar to those of the public, although with two very important new rules. The first rule is that a private child library is visible only within a subtree of the hierarchy whose root is its parent; even more is only visible to the specifications of the public children, although visible to their bodies or private parts. The second rule is that the visible part of a private child can access the private part or hidden from the parent, without damaging its parent abstraction since it cannot export private characteristics from the parent to the user because that part itself is not visible to it.

In order to make use of this library hierarchy it is important to take into account that the clause *with* applied to a child library automatically implies a clause *with* over all its ancestors, otherwise, a clause *use* for a library implies that child libraries for which clause *with* exists and can be accessed by their name without the need of any qualification or the use of the clause use.

20.12 Protected Objects

At the beginning of this chapter it was said that protected objects incorporate the object concept to the concurrent part of the language. In fact, a protected object generally encapsulates data items that are to be shared by several tasks, via protected subprograms or protected entries, by providing the possibility of creating systems with less task overload. A protected unit may be declared as a type or as a single instance.

A protected type is a passive data object that provides protection of data consistency even when multiple tasks attempt to access its data. Protected types can be considered to be a very advanced form of "semaphore" or "monitor." A protected type contains data that access only through a set of protected operations defined by the developer.

There are three kinds of protected operations (Wheeler, 1997):

1. *Protected functions*, which provide read-only access to the internal data. Multiple tasks may simultaneously call a protected function.
2. *Protected procedures*, which provide exclusive read/write access to the internal data. When one task is running a protected procedure, no other task can interact with the protected type.
3. *Protected entries*, which are just like protected procedures, except that they must add a "barrier." A barrier is some boolean expression that must become true before the caller may proceed. The barrier would usually depend on some internal data value protected by the protected type. If the barrier is not true when the caller makes a request, the caller is placed in a queue to wait until the barrier becomes true.

A protected object, the same way as package or tasks, consists of a specification and a body, which provide the access protocol and the operation implementation, respectively.

Upon a protected object a series of operations that can be written or read can be performed. The reading operations are functions which can be executed simultaneously over the protected object. However, there are two types of operations that can modify the object and that are the procedures and inputs, similar to the tasks, but they must be accompanied by a condition, called barrier, and then met so that the entry can be executed. These two types of operations must be executed in mutual exclusion, that is, they cannot be executed simultaneously with any type of operation upon the protected object.

The protected object access protocol is complex and barriers have an important role. In order to access an object there are two types of process queues waiting for executing an operation upon it. At first every task must pass the first barrier to access the object, that is, a task invokes an object operation and depending on the object, it will be executed or not. If the operation invoked is a function and other functions are being already executed, this task call will be served at that time.

If a procedure is invoked, it will only be executed when there is no operation being executed on the object, therefore, the task performed may keep waiting in a queue of tasks outside the object. The input call is treated like that of a procedure in terms of mutual exclusion, but what's more, the barrier must be associated to such an input, that is, it must be true, since the barrier will be blocked in a waiting queue associated to such an input.

Anyway, it is important to consider that, to a certain extent, the task queues associated to the inputs have priority over the external queue, since every time the not read-only operation execution finishes over the external queue, the barriers that have been modified during the operation execution and have task queues, will be again evaluated, and if they become true the first task in the queue will appear. Therefore, we will go to the next tasks in the outside only when we finish executing o or more functions (those that can never modify the tasks) upon the object or when no barrier has been opened after the execution of another type of operation or there is no task in the object input queues.

Therefore protected objects provide a data-oriented approach to synchronization in addition to providing the efficiency of a monitor to which some high-level conditions are added for performing operations. Therefore, protected objects can be considered as true objects whose additional characteristic is to be shared by different tasks without inconsistency and synchronization problems.

20.13 Exceptions

An *exception** represents a kind of exceptional situation, usually a serious error. That is the exception provides a comfortable approach to deal with all that is considered as "abnormal" or "exceptional" in the program development.

An exception can be declared by the user, although certain exceptions are predefined as `Storage-Error` (insufficient memory) or `Constraint_Error` (non-valid error assigned to a variable).

An exception can be *raised* at runtime, which calls the attention to the fact that an exceptional situation has occurred in raise explicitly through the `raise` statement. A program block can declare an *exception handler* which will receive control, if the cited exception is yielded in the block considered.

If we anticipate that an exception may occur as a part of our program, then we can write an exception handler to deal with it. For example, assume we write:

```
begin
Result  := A/B;                  --sequence of statement
exception
when Constraint_Error =>
  Result  := Float 'Large;       --do something
end;
```

* Section 11 of the Ada RM: http//:www.adahome.com/rm9x/rm9x-toc-11.html.

If an exception is dealt with locally, it is propagated to the caller unit, until it encounters an appropriate exception handler, or the exception type of the main program stops the exception. A special clause, with others, allows dealing with all exceptions.

The following is an example of what a main program could be and to guarantee its own halt before any unexpected thing could occur in the program.

```
Procedure Main is
begin
  Do_the_work;
exception
  When others => Cleaning;
end Main;
```

Several handlers can be written between exception and end (Barnes, 1996):

```
begin
     --sequence of statements
exception
     when constraint_Error | Program_Error =>
  put ("Constraint or Program Error occurred");
  ...
     when Storage_Error =>
  put ("Run out of space");
     when others =>
  put ("Something else went wrong");
end;
```

20.13.1 Declaring and Raising Exceptions

Before you can raise or handle an exception, it must be *declared*. Declaring exceptions is just like declaring a variable of type exception. Exception declarations are generally placed in a package declaration. Here is an example:

```
Anomaly: exception
```

Therefore, raising an exception is to use the raise statement, `raise Anomaly;` it causes the suspension of the normal exception and it points out and enables the exception called Anomaly. The effect is to interrupt the program unit execution in which the exception is caused.

A response to an exception is performs (an exception is treated) by adding one or more exception sequences at the end of the program unit.

```
exception
sequence of exception

exception
     when Constraint_Error => statements;
  .
  .
  .
     when Anomaly => statements;
     when others => statements;
  ...
```

20.13.2 Handling and Propagation Exceptions

If an exception is raised and is not handled, the program stops. To handle exceptions, you must define, reasonably enough, an *exception handler.*

When an exception is raised, the program will abandon what it was doing and look for a matching exception handler in the sequence of statements when the exception was raised. An exception propagates throughout the sequence of called units, until a unit is found (exception handler) that provides control over the exception. If a program does not provide the exception handling and an execution error causes the exception activation, the program finishes in a non-handler exception error message.

Very often, a program unit will not be able to handle an exception. Even though sequences are provided, they cannot cover all the exceptions sensitive to being created during the execution. In any case the program block or unit is terminated and it is said that the exception has been *propagated.*

Example:

```
with TEXT_IO;
use TEXT_IO;
procedure BLACK is
   ERROR :exception;

procedure VERT is
begin
   null;
raise ERROR;
   null;
end VERT;

procedure BLUE is
begin
   VERT ; null;
exception
   when ERROR =>
         PUT_LINE (("Exception within BLUE procedure");
end BLUE;

begin
   BLUE;
exception
   when ERROR => PUT_LINE ("Exception within black procedure");
end BLACK;
```

The exception ERROR is raised in the procedure. VERT is treated in the BLUE level procedure and level BLACK error does not exist.

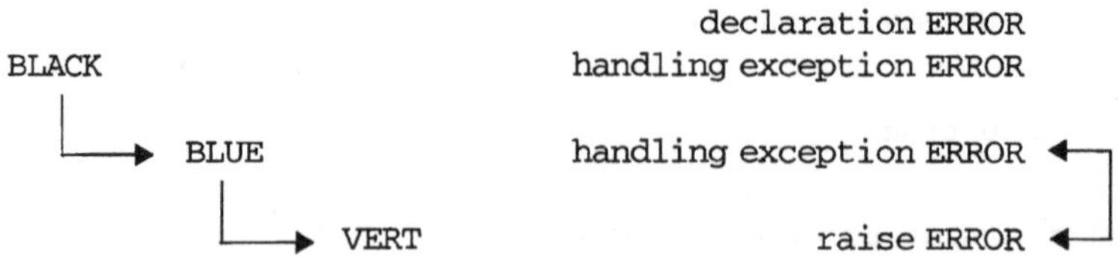

20.14 Conclusions

Ada 83 provided limited support for OOD and OOP, but the need for additional support for this style of development had already been recognized. In 1995 a raised Ada standard, ANSI/ISO/IEC-8652:1995, commonly known as Ada 95, was approved. The revision added a number of facilities to Ada 83, possibly the most important of which was supported for OOP.

Ada is officially defined in its Ada 95 Reference Manual. Four main areas were perceived to be worth paying attention:

- Object-oriented programming
- Program libraries
- Interfacing to other languages such as C, FORTRAN, COBOL, and I-code; there are versions to generate Java class files
- Tasking; multiple parallel threads of control can be created and communicated

There are many Ada compilers among which we can note: Rationale, Intermetric, GNAT, and Tanin. There are also many Ada-related tools* and on-line reference documents.**

Among the great advances Ada offers for the next decade we find the following:

- Better tools for object-oriented programming — tagged types and controlled types
- Better for programming overall — hierarchical libraries and child units
- Better tools for concurrent programming protected types
- Better for parameterized software components — formal packages
- Earlier multilanguages programming — interfaces
- Distributed programming within the language — remote types and subprograms
- Support for the HOOD methodology and others; the HOOD methodology that was selected by the Europeans Space Agency

In short, the ISO Ada 95 standard opens more avenues for Ada in the construction of reliable software, as well as for the development of real-time systems and distributed applications.

References

ANSI, 1983. ANSI/MIL-STD 1815A ISO/IEC 8652:1983.

ANSI/ISO/IEC 8652:1995, 1995. (The ISO standard was published on February 15, 1995).

Barnes, J. 1996. *Programming in Ada 95.* Addison-Wesley, Wokingham, U.K.

Booch, G. 1996. *Software Engineering with Ada,* 2nd ed. Benjamin/Cummings, Menlo Park, CA.

Cohen, N.H. 1996. *Ada as a Second Language,* 2nd ed. McGraw-Hill, New York, NY.

Culwin, F. 1997. *Ada, A Development Approach,* 2nd ed. Prentice-Hall, Europe.

English, J. 1997. *Ada 95: the Craft of Object-Oriented Programming.* Prentice-Hall, Europe.

Fayard, D. and Rousseau, M. 1996. *Ver Ada 95 par l'exemple.Langage, Technique et Pratique.* De Boeck & Larcier, Paris.

Intermetrics. 1995. *Ada 95 Reference Manual.* Intermetrics, Cambridge, MA.

Joyanes, L. 1996. *Programación Orientada a Objetos. Conceptos, Modelado, Diseño e Implementación,* (*Object-Oriented Programming: Concepts, Modeling, Design and Implementation*). McGraw-Hill, Madrid.

Joyanes, L. and Díez, M.L. 1998. *Programación en Ada 95: Un en foque orientado a objetos para sistemas distribuidos y de tiempo real,* (*Programming in Ada 95. An Approach Object-Oriented for Real-Time and Distributed Systems*). McGraw-Hill, Madrid.

Roseu, J.P. 1995. *Mèthodes de gènie logiciel avec Ada 95.* InterEditions, Paris.

Smith, M.A. 1996. *Object-Oriented Software in Ada 95.* International Thomson, London, UK.

Taft, T. 1996. *Programming the Internet in Ada 95.* Proceedings Ada Europe '96, Montreux, June.

Taylor, B. 1995. *Ada 95 Compatibility Guide in Ada Yearbook 1995.* Ratcliffe, M., Ed., IOS Press, Oxford, U.K.

Wheeler, D. *Ada 95. The Lovelace Tutorial.* Springer-Verlag, New York.

* http://www.adahome.com/resources/tools/tools.html.

** http://www.adahome.com/resources/reference.html; http://info.cam.org/rgada; http://lglwww.epfl.ch/Ada; http://lglwww.epfl.ch/Ada/LRM/9X/rm9x/rm9x.toc.html.

Webliography

<Ada RM>
http://www.adahome.com/rm9x/rm9x-toc.html

<Ada compilers>
http://www.adahome.com/Resources/Compilers/Compilers.html

<GNAT compiler>
http://www.adahome.com/Resources/Compilers/GNAT.html

<Ada-related tools>
http://www.adahome.com/Resources/Tools/Tools.html

<Reference documents>
http://www.adahome.com/Resources/References.html

<Ada Quality and Style: A Guide to Professional Programmers>
http://www.adahome.com/Resources/References.html#style

<Ada FAQ>
http://www.adahome.com/FAQ/programming.html#title

<comp.lang.ada newsgroup FAQ>
http://www.adahome.com/FAQ/comp_lang_ada.html#title

<Magnus Kempe Home of the Brave Ada Programmers (HBAP)>
http://www.adahome.com/

<Public Ada Library (PAL)>
http://wuarchive.wustl.edu/languages/ada/pal.html

<Ada Information Clearinghouse Home page>
http://sw-eng.falls-church.va.us/

<SIG Ada>.SIGAda, a Special Interest Group of ACM
http://info.acm.org/sigada/

<Ada 95 Booch Components>
http://www.ocsystems.com/booch

<GNAT compiler>
http://www.gnat.com

<Ada Rationale>
http://www.adahome.com/LRM/95/Rationale/rat95html/

<Ada home>
http://www.adahome.com

<The ASIS WG Home Pages> (the current Definition of ASIS for Ada 95 as ISO Working Draft)
http://www.acm.org/sigada/WG/asiswg/asiswg.html

<The APIS Implementation for GNAT>
ftp://lglftp.epfl.ch/pub/ASIS/
http://such.srcc.msu.su/asis

<Validate Ada 95 Compilers>
http://sw-eng.falls-church.va.us/AdaIC/forms/vcl95.shtml

<Home of the Brave Ada Programmers>
http://lglwww.epfl.ch/Ada

<Ada Internet Resource List>
http://www.cera.com/ada.htm

<The Public Ada Library>
http://www.cnam.fr/Languages/Ada/PAL

<GNAT compiler>
ftp://cs.nyu.edu

<Walnut Creek>
http://www.cdrom.com

<Ada-UK>
http://www.adauk.org.uk

<Ada-Belgium>
http://www.es.kuleuven.ac.be/~dirk/ada-belgium

<Ada-Europe>
http://lglwww.epfl.ch/Ada-Europo

<Ada-Spain>
http://www.ceselsa.es/~fperez/adasp.html

<ACM SIGAda>
http://www.acm.org/sigada

<DBRG University of Geneve>
http://cuiwww.unige.ch/db-research/Enseignement/analyseinfo/Ada95/BNFindex.html

<Reference Cards Paul Pukite>
http://wuarchive.wustl.edu/languages/ada/userdocs/html/cardcat/refcards.html

<Swiss Federal Institute of Technology Lausanne Switzerland>
http://lglwww.epfl.ch/Ada

<Server de l'IUT d'Orsay (France) >
http://www.int-orsay.fr/pub/Ada

<Swiss Federal Institute of Technology in Lausanne, Switzerland>
http://lglwww.epfl.ch/Ada/Tutorials

<Smith M.A.>
ftp://ftp.bton.ac.uk/pub/mas/ada95
http://www. bton.ac.uk/ada95/home.html

21

Modula-3

Samuel P. Harbison
Texas Instruments, Inc.

Farshad Nayeri
Critical Mass, Inc.

21.1 Introduction

Modula-3 is a modern, general-purpose programming language. It provides excellent support for large, reliable, and maintainable applications. Its clean syntax and semantics, along with its support for object-oriented programming (OOP) and parallelism, make Modula-3 an excellent teaching, design, and implementation language. Compared to other languages with a roughly equivalent feature set (e.g., Ada, C++, and Java), Modula-3 is much simpler and safer from runtime misbehavior.

Like C++, Modula-3 is a "hybrid" object-oriented language, supporting both object-oriented programming and procedure-oriented programming. While objects are only one of the central features of Modula-3, support for OOP was designed into the language from the beginning. Hence, objects are exceptionally well integrated with, for example, the facilities for modules, parallelism, and separate compilation. Modula-3 supports a single-inheritance object model, with flexible encapsulation and optional garbage collection.

Modula-3 was designed as a joint project of Digital Equipment Corporation's Systems Research Center (SRC) and the Olivetti Research Center. The designers were Luca Cardelli, Jim Donahue, Mick Jordan, Bill Kalsow, and Greg Nelson. Digital and Olivetti published the first description of the language in August 1988. The language has remained unchanged since a few final adjustments were made in 1990, and high quality implementations and libraries have been developed. Indeed, Modula-3 enjoys compatible free and commercial implementations on a wide variety of platforms. Many of the features of Modula-3 have been adopted in later language designs, such as Python and Java.

While Modula-3 is not as popular as C++ or Java outside academia, most projects that have used it (in either commercial or non-commercial settings) have found it to be a very productive environment for systems programming (Nayeri, 1997a). Among systems implemented in Modula-3 are distributed object systems, extensible operating systems, multi-platform windowing systems, 911 call center applications, and augmented reality applications. There is even a Java Virtual Machine implementation entirely in Modula-3.

0-8493-3135-8/99/$0.00+$.50

21.2 Modula-3 Overview

The primary goals in the design of Modula-3 were simplicity and safety. Modula-3 corrects deficiencies of previous language designs (such as Pascal, Modula-2, and C/C++) for practical software engineering. In particular, Modula-3 keeps the simplicity of type safety of the earlier languages, while providing new facilities for exception handling, concurrency, OOP, and automatic garbage collection. Modula-3 is both a practical implementation language for large software projects and an excellent teaching language.

Programming can be a difficult, complicated, and risky activity, only made worse by programming languages that are themselves difficult, complicated, and risky. Modula-3's designers selected features proven through experience in other languages; especially, features that support good program structure (modules, objects, threads) and those that support robustness (garbage collection, isolation of unsafe code, and exceptions). They simplified and unified the underlying language concepts, discarding features that did not pull their own weight.

Since most readers will be familiar with programming language concepts, we will give a very brief overview of the underlying concepts in Modula-3, followed by a more extensive treatment of its distinctive features. Object-oriented programming is considered later, after the other facilities on which OOP largely depend have been described. The Further Information section specifies where you can find a complete language definition.

21.2.1 Modules, Interfaces, Statements

A Modula-3 program consists of a collection of *modules*. An *interface* includes the specification for a module, which is strictly separated from its implementation. Interfaces define what a module does, whereas an implementation defines how the module does its task. A module may *export* one or more interfaces, meaning that it implements the facilities specified in those interfaces. Module M may *import* interface I to get access to its facilities, in which case we call M a *client* of I (and of the module implementing I). Interfaces may also import other interfaces, but they do not automatically export the names from imported interfaces. Interfaces may contain any declarations except procedure bodies or non-constant variable initializers.

Modules contain procedure bodies and may contain other declarations. Each module has an initialization part that can contain statements executed during program initialization. Programmers who use an object-oriented style heavily will wish to structure their programs as collections of object types (classes). Encapsulating each object type in its own interface/module pair is the customary way of doing this. However, this convention is not enforced by the language, leaving flexibility for grouping of multiple object types in the same interface.

Modula-3 also provides a facility for generic programming based on interfaces and modules. You can write interfaces and modules that are dependent on interface parameters, and then instantiate actual interfaces and modules from the generic ones.

21.2.2 Statements and Expressions

Modula-3 has a typical range of statements, such as assignment and procedure call, plus a few interesting additions.

Conditional statements include `IF-ELSIF-ELSE`, as well as a `CASE` statement. In addition, there is a type-conditional statement (`TYPECASE`) that makes use of runtime type information.

Looping statements include `FOR` (with an index variable local to the loop), `WHILE`, `REPEAT` (with the test at the bottom), and `LOOP` (with no test). Loops can be aborted with the `EXIT` statement.

Exceptions are thrown with `RAISE` and can be caught with the `TRY-EXCEPT` statement. The interesting `TRY-FINALLY` statement intercepts exceptions (and `EXIT` and `RETURN`), executes user-defined clean-up code, and then continues with the exception or other transfer of control.

The `LOCK` statement provides synchronization between threads.

Expressions follow C (rather than Pascal) conventions, including the short-circuiting of boolean expressions.

21.2.3 Declarations and Types

There are five kinds of declarations in Modula-3. TYPE, CONST, and VAR define data types, constants, and variables, respectively. Variable declarations may omit the data type when it is the same as the type of the initialization expression. PROCEDURE declares procedures (and procedure types when used with TYPE). EXCEPTION declares exceptions. The list of exceptions raised is part of the specification of a procedure.

Modula-3's built-in integer types include INTEGER and CARDINAL, the latter being a non-negative subrange of INTEGER. The type WORD.T (from a standard interface) is an unsigned integer type. There are three sizes of floating-point types, REAL, LONGREAL, and EXTENDED, with typical IEEE representations of 32, 64, and 128 bits.

BOOLEAN is an enumeration type consisting of FALSE and TRUE. General enumeration types are also provided, as are arbitrary subranges of both integer and enumeration types.

The type SET OF T is a set type implemented as a bit vector for efficiency. The type T must have no more than about 256 elements (so T may be CHAR but not INTEGER).

ARRAY and RECORD types are provided. Arrays are normally of fixed size with integer or enumeration indices, but there is an open (variable-sized) array type used for dynamically allocated arrays and for array parameters to procedures. Enumeration and integer types may be packed into bit fields within records or arrays.

Text processing is supported by the character type CHAR and the string type TEXT. Values of type TEXT are dynamically allocated and immutable. Arrays of CHAR can also be used for string processing.

The type REF T is a pointer to a value of type T. Values of type REFANY may be pointers to any type; runtime type information prevents erroneous pointer conversions. Dynamically allocated values are normally subject to garbage collection, but the types UNTRACED REF T and ADDRESS may be used to create uncollected values on the heap.

Object types (classes) are all descended from the fundamental object type ROOT (or UNTRACED ROOT).

To describe the semantics of programs, a *subtype* relation is defined between certain types. The notation T <: U means that type T is a subtype of U and every value of type T is also a value of type U. The subtype relationship is used to define type compatibility, assignment compatibility, and parameter-passing compatibility. Class inheritance can give rise to the subtype relationship: if object type A descends (inherits) from object type B then A <: B. Other examples of subtype relationships include: subranges are subtypes of their parent type (integer or enumeration); REF T is a subtype of REFANY; ROOT is a subtype of REFANY; and a fixed array type is a subtype of an open array type whose element type is the same.

21.2.4 Example

Below is a simple example of a Modula-3 program that uses a sorting module. The program does not use OOP facilities. First, we create the interface to an insertion sort procedure. To make the example more interesting, we will also keep track of how many times the sorting procedure is called and will make that information available through a function. Interface Sort exports a procedure, InsertSort, which takes a single by-reference (VAR) parameter that is an array to be sorted, and a function, TimesCalled, which takes no parameters and returns a non-negative integer. The open array parameter v will accept any array of integers.

```
INTERFACE Sort;
  PROCEDURE InsertSort(VAR v: ARRAY OF INTEGER);
  PROCEDURE TimesCalled() : CARDINAL;
END Sort.
```

The main module of a program is by convention named Main. This module imports the Sort interface and calls the InsertSort procedure. The variable a is declared and initialized using an array constructor. The notation ". ." in the constructor indicates that the last value is repeated to fill out the array. Within Main, the names InsertSort and TimesCalled must be qualified with the interface name; there is another form of IMPORT that makes them visible directly.

```
MODULE Main;
IMPORT Sort;
TYPE
  TestArray = ARRAY [1..10] OF INTEGER;
VAR
  a := TestArray{1,9,3,5,4..}; (* array constructor *)
  n : INTEGER;
BEGIN
  Sort.InsertSort(a);
  ...
  n = Sort.TimesCalled();
  ...
END Main.
```

Now we can show the implementation of the Sort interface. In the InsertSort procedure, the open array parameter v will have array indices that go from FIRST(v), which is always zero, to LAST(v), which will be 9 in this case. The FOR loop variable i is automatically declared local to the loop body and is read-only; its type is INTEGER, as determined from the upper and lower bound expressions. The variables temp and j are declared and initialized in an inner block, and their types are taken from the initialization expressions. The INC and DEC statements add 1 and subtract 1, respectively, from their arguments.

```
MODULE Sort;

PROCEDURE InsertSort(VAR v: ARRAY OF INTEGER) =
BEGIN (* Sorts V[0]..V[LAST(V)] into ascending order. *)
  FOR i := FIRST(v)+1 TO LAST(V) DO
    VAR
      temp := v[i];
      j := i-1;
    BEGIN
      WHILE j >= FIRST(v) AND v[j] > temp DO
        v[j+1] = v[j];
        DEC(j);
      END;
      v[j+1] := temp;
    END
  END;
  INC(times);
END InsertSort;
```

The module also provides the implementation of the TimesCalled procedure, which uses a variable, times, that is local to the module (i.e., not visible to any other module). It does not matter that the variable is declared after the InsertSort procedure that uses it, as Modula-3 allows declarations in a module to be written in any order, eliminating the need for forward declarations.

```
VAR times : CARDINAL := 0;
PROCEDURE TimesCalled() : INTEGER =
BEGIN
  RETURN times;
END TimesCalled;

BEGIN
  (* No initialization code needed *)
END Sort.
```

21.2.5 Safe and Unsafe Programming

Safety is a principal goal of Modula-3. The majority of the language is safe, in the sense that the compiler guarantees that runtime invariants (e.g., variables' values, array indices, and the validity of pointers) are not violated. Contrast this with Appendix F in the ISO C (1989) standard, which lists 97 different circumstances in which the behavior of a C program is undefined at either compile time or runtime. Modula-3 guarantees safety through a combination of compile-time analysis and occasional runtime checking.

However, systems programming can be unsafe by its very nature. Network layers, legacy systems, storage allocators, or collectors often require "bit twiddling." In Modula-3 unsafe features include the ability to perform arbitrary type coercions, to perform arithmetic on pointers, and to call the `DISPOSE` procedure to free dynamic memory allocated with `NEW`.

To use the unsafe language features, you must insert the modifier `UNSAFE` in your interface or module declaration; otherwise, the compiler will restrict you to the safe language subset. Modula-3 does not permit a safe module or interface to import an `UNSAFE` interface. To bridge the gap from unsafe code to safe code, an `UNSAFE` module may export a safe interface. In this case, the programmer makes an implicit assertion that the calls exported in the safe interface are, in fact, safe. Nelson (1991) contains an interesting discussion of this nontrivial responsibility in the description of the Modula-3 I/O system.

Strict separation of safe and unsafe code also aids portability, because the unsafe code is just what will need to be examined when moving to a new system. In contrast, languages such as C and C++ do not enforce strict safety, so problems can creep in seemingly safe and portable code. Java takes another approach by disallowing unsafe operations altogether which forces the programmer to go outside of the Java language for many systems programming.

21.2.6 Exceptions

Modula-3's exception mechanism encourages programmers to write more robust programs. An *exception* is an event that suspends normal program execution and causes control to be transferred to a *handler* for that exception. If there is no enclosing handler in the current procedure, the call stack is successively unwound until a context containing a handler is found. After the exception is handled, execution resumes after the handler who may be quite far from where the exception was first *raised*. Good exception handling mechanisms are important for writing robust code.

As an example of exception use, we reproduce (somewhat abridged) one of the built-in I/O interfaces supplied with Modula-3. The `Wr` interface defines a generalized output stream of characters (a "writer"), of type `T`. The `Wr` interface includes a `PutText` procedure to write out a text string, and this procedure can raise the `Failure` exception (`Wr.Failure`) if an error occurs. This `Failure` exception happens to carry with it an arbitrary pointer as an argument.

```
INTERFACE Wr;
  TYPE T <: ROOT; (* T is an unspecified object type *)
  EXCEPTION Failure(REFANY);
  PROCEDURE PutText(wr: T; t: TEXT) RAISES {Failure };
  PROCEDURE Close(wr: T) RAISES {Failure};
  ...
END Wr.
```

Now, suppose there were a `FileStream` interface to open a file and return an output stream for it. (The actual Modula-3 facility is somewhat different.) It also might use the `Wr.Failure` exception to signal problems.

```
INTEFACE FileStream;
  IMPORT Wr;
  PROCEDURE OpenWrite(filename: TEXT) : Wr.T
    RAISES {Wr.Failure};
  ...
END FileStream.
```

Here is sample client code that opens a file, writes out a line, and closes the file.

```
IMPORT Wr, FileStream;
...
VAR wr := FileStream.OpenWrite("file.txt");
Wr.PutText(wr, "Hello.");
Wr.Close(wr);
```

There is a potential problem with the code as written. If the PutText procedure raises its exception, then processing will be short-circuited and the Close procedure will never be called. If we wish to handle the exception from PutText, we must write the following code. (The parameter r is set to the REFANY parameter passed with the Failure exception.)

```
TRY
  Wr.PutText(wr, "Hello.");
EXCEPT
  Wr.Failure(r) => (* Do something, then continue *)
END;
Wr.Close(wr);
```

If, as is often the case, we do not really want to handle the exception but we wish to be sure to call Close when an exception occurs, then we can use Modula-3's convenient TRY-FINALLY statement:

```
IMPORT Wr, FileStream;
...
VAR wr := FileStream.OpenWrite("file.txt");
TRY
  Wr.PutText(wr, "Hello.");
FINALLY
  Wr.Close(wr);
END;
```

The effect of TRY-FINALLY is to execute PutText followed by Close. However, if PutText raises an exception, the statement after FINALLY will be immediately executed, after which the original exception will be re-raised. The TRY-FINALLY statement would also intercept RETURN or EXIT statements that could be placed between TRY and FINALLY, ensuring that the cleanup code is executed before the RETURN or EXIT propagate further.

As illustrated in the FileStream interface, exceptions are declared in the signature of methods and procedures, so that the compiler can check to make sure that you are properly handling all the exceptions that may be raised from a procedure, function, or method call.

21.3 Object-Oriented Programming in Modula-3

Modula-3 provides both object-oriented and traditional programming models. However, unlike languages that evolved through the later addition of objects, Modula-3's OOP facilities were carefully woven into the original language definition, in particular, into the type system. Although OOP support is fairly straightforward — it is a single-inheritance model with garbage collection — Modula-3 provides one unique innovation, *opaque types*, whose interface can be revealed differently to different clients

Below is a simplistic example that implements the abstraction of a geometric point. This sort of point has an (unchangeable) position and provides two methods that return the point's X and Y coordinates. The interface illustrates several things. Object types in Modula-3 are normally paired with interfaces, which are a more powerful encapsulation mechanism and which permit the inclusion of multiple object type declarations and non-OOP facilities, such as the New procedure in this case. The primary object type is customarily named simply T, a convention that associates the interface name (SimplePoint) to the principal object type implemented in the interface (SimplePoint.T). In C++ terminology, all object type methods are *virtual*, meaning they can be changed in descendant types. Method specifications are linked to actual code by assigning to them a specific procedure with a compatible signature, as illustrated. Modula-3's designers consciously decided not to provide user-defined initialization or finalization methods, so the New procedure shown is a common convention for creating and initializing object types. (Distinguished `init` methods are also common.) All object types in Modula-3 are dynamically allocated.

```
INTERFACE SimplePoint;
  TYPE T = OBJECT
         X, Y : REAL; (* Per-object data *)
      METHODS
         PosX() : REAL := PosXProc;
         PosY() : REAL := PosYProc;
      END;
  PROCEDURE New(x, y: REAL) : T;
  PROCEDURE PosXProc(self: T);
  PROCEDURE PosYProc(self: T);
END SimplePoint.
```

Here is sample code that creates and uses points defined by the `SimplePoint` interface:

```
IMPORT SimplePoint;
VAR
  a := SimplePoint.New(10.0, 20.0);
  x, y: REAL;
...
x := a.PosX();
y := a.PosY();
```

The `SimplePoint` module simply must provide bodies for the method procedures. The built-in NEW procedure, used within the user-defined New procedure, allocates a dynamic type and allows its components to be initialized. No "dispose" procedure is needed because points will be garbage-collected when they are no longer referenced.

```
MODULE SimplePoint;
  PROCEDURE New(x, y: REAL := 0.0) : T=
  BEGIN
    RETURN NEW(T, X := x, Y := y);
  END New;

  PROCEDURE PosXProc( self: T) : REAL =
  BEGIN RETURN self.X; END PosXProc;

  PROCEDURE PosYProc(self: T ) : REAL =
  BEGINRETURN self.Y; END PosYProc;
END SimplePoint.
```

21.3.1 Opaque Types and Partial Revelation

The `SimplePoint` interface did a poor job of hiding its implementation from clients. The `X` and `Y` object variables are needlessly exported, as are the `PosXProc` and `PosYProc` procedure names. Instead of the usual convention of providing "public" and "private" parts of class definitions, Modula-3 provides a much more flexible generalization. The second implementation of the `SimplePoint` interface below declares a *partially opaque* type, which reveals only methods that can be called on the object, but not the object's representation. The notation `TYPE T<:Public` means that `T` is a subtype (descendant) of the `Public` type. (The name `Public` is arbitrary.) The data and methods of `Public` will be a prefix of the data and methods of `T`. However, there may be several intermediate subtypes between `Public` and `T` — we cannot tell at this point. `Public` provides the necessary methods, but does not include the object type's data, nor does it supply procedures for the methods. (The methods are abstract at this stage.) This change in the interface does not change the way the interface is used.

```
INTERFACE SimplePoint;
  TYPE
    T <: Public;
    Public = OBJECT
      METHODS
        PosX( p: T) : REAL; (* X position *)
        PosY( p: T) : REAL; (* Y position *)
      END;
  PROCEDURE New(x, y: REAL) : T;
END SimplePoint.
```

The new SimplePoint module supplies the missing details of SimplePoint.T by revealing that T is a direct descendant of Public, specifying the internal data, and overriding the method procedures. The OVERRIDES keyword makes the programmer's intention explicit.

```
MODULE SimplePoint;
  REVEAL
    T = Public BRANDED OBJECT
        X, Y : REAL;
      OVERRIDES
        PosX := PosXProc;
        PosY := PosYProc;
      END;
  (* The definitions of New, PosXProc,
    and PosYProc are as before. *)
END SimplePoint.
```

This was still a fairly simple example of the revelation of types, but you can imagine the power of encapsulation of this flexible revelation system. In fact, Modula-3 permits arbitrarily long sequences of partial type declarations, partial revelations, and full revelations. It requires only that all types are eventually completely revealed, considering all the separately compiled interfaces and modules in a program.

Consider a more complicated example taken from the Modula-3 I/O system. We will look at the type structure for Wr.T, the object type that represents an abstract output stream. The top-level interface Wr defines Wr.T to be an object type. ROOT is the ultimate ancestor of all garbage-collected object types, thus saying T is a descendant of ROOT simply says it is some kind of object type without revealing any of its methods. This let's the compiler distinguish the opaque type Wr.T from other opaque types so it can enforce type safety.

```
INTERFACE Wr;
  TYPE T <: ROOT;
  PROCEDURE PutText(wr: T; t: TEXT);
  ...
END Wr.
```

The Wr interface does not reveal any methods for Wr, but a second interface, WrClass, reveals additional information, in particular the data and methods needed to do class-independent buffering. Although Wr.T is completely revealed (using = instead of <:) in WrClass, a new ancestral type, Private, is introduced between ROOT and Wr.T. The structure of Private is still not revealed.

```
INTERFACE WrClass;
  IMPORT Wr;
  TYPE Private <: ROOT;
  REVEAL Wr.T = Private BRANDED OBJECT ... END;
END WrClass.
```

Although it is not yet apparent, writers are *thread-safe.* (See the next section on concurrency.) That means several concurrent threads of control can use the same writer without damaging its internal representation (although the resulting output might be interleaved in arbitrary ways). Safety is achieved because each writer is locked while its representation is being manipulated, so only one thread has access at a time. In order to allow clients more explicit control over locking, a separate interface, `UnsafeWr`, is provided to make the lock visible and supply different output procedures that do not themselves lock the writer. Clients can therefore lock the writer around a sequence of I/O calls for more efficiency and for control over the interleaving of output across threads. Because not all clients will be well behaved, this is an `UNSAFE` interface. (If the client does not lock the writer, then the writer's data structure may be damaged when the I/O procedures are called.) If a module imports `UnsafeWr`, then the compiler now knows that `Wr.T` is a subtype of `Thread.Mutex` and thus inherits the locking methods.

```
UNSAFE INTERFACE UnsafeWr;
   IMPORT Wr, Thread;
   REVEAL Wr.T <: Thread.Mutex; ...
END UnsafeWr.
```

Finally, the implementation of all the interfaces is combined in a single module, `WrRep`. For efficiency, `WrRep` uses unsafe features of the language, and so is declared `UNSAFE`. However, since it exports safe interfaces, it must ensure that the I/O operations are in fact always safe when invoked through the safe interfaces (Nelson, 1991), *even when some clients do not cooperate.* This completes the revelation of `Wr.T`.

```
UNSAFE MODULE WrRep EXPORTS Wr, WrClass, UnsafeWr;
   IMPORT Thread;
   REVEAL Private = Thread.Mutex BRANDED OBJECT ... END;
   (* Lots of code ... *)
END WrRep.
```

21.4 Concurrency

Built-in support for concurrent programming — the management of multiple, simultaneous control flows — is another way in which Modula-3 distinguishes itself from most other object-oriented languages. Concurrency is useful in many programming situations: when you want to take advantage of multiprocessor computers, when you want to allow background processing during slow user interactions, or when you are handling naturally asynchronous tasks.

Modula-3 adopts the *thread* model, in which concurrent "threads of control" are managed within the same program and address space, each with its own local call stack but with shared access to all global data. Threads are typically much more efficient than *processes,* which have separate address spaces.

Thread support is provided in the standard interface `Thread`. The technique for starting and stopping threads is sketched in the code below. (Not all details are shown.) The user type `Closure` must override the `apply` method of `Thread.Closure` to designate the procedure that will be started by `Thread.Fork`. `Closure` can additionally hold any parameters to be passed to the thread code. The `apply` method returns a `REFANY` parameter which is then returned by `Thread.Join`, this return parameter is used by the programmer as needed.

```
IMPORT Thread;
TYPE Closure = Thread.Closure OBJECT ...
     OVERRIDES apply := ...
END;
VAR t1, t2: Thread.T;
   c1, c2 := Closure;
   result1, result2: REFANY;
...
(* Store parameters in c1, c2 (not shown) *)
```

```
t1 := Thread.Fork( c1 );
t2 := Thread.Fork( c2 );
...
Thread.Join( t1 );
Thread.Join( t2 );
```

The object type Thread.Mutex, a mutual-exclusion semaphore or "lock," supports synchronization between threads. Locks may be created and stored in data structures, or object types may be derived from Thread.Mutex, providing a built-in object lock and avoiding an extra object allocation. The two styles are shown below. The statement LOCK mu DO ... END locks mu and executes the statements following DO. If code within DO...END raises an exception, or attempts to RETURN or EXIT, then mu will be unlocked as control exits the LOCK statement. This feature of LOCK helps guard against deadlocks caused by failing to unlock a lock.

```
TYPE
  ObjectIsLock <: Thread.Mutex;
  RecordHasLock = RECORD mu: Thread.Mutex; ... END;
VAR
  OiL: ObjectIsLock;
  RhL: RecordHasLock;
...
LOCK OiL DO
  (* Operate on OiL object *)
END;
...
LOCK RhL.mu DO
  (* Operate on RhL record *)
END;
```

The Thread interface also provides condition variables and procedures to "alert" (interrupt) running threads (Nelson, 1991).

There is a Network Objects package for Modula-3 which provides a state-of-the-art distributed object system, allowing Modula-3 objects to be exported across address spaces and computers (Birrell et al., 1994). It provides complete network transparency for accessing objects, and can be the foundation for creating robust distributed applications.

21.5 Implementations, Tools, and Libraries

Practical use of a language depends on the infrastructure of tools and libraries that are provided with it or for it by third parties. Modula-3 has benefited by having a high quality, portable, and freely available compiler and runtime system developed by Digital's Systems Research Center, *SRC Modula-3*. (Critical Mass Modula-3 [Nayeri, 1997b] is a commercial implementation, source-compatible with SRC Modula-3.) In addition to a compiler, SRC Modula-3 provides software to manage separate compilation with minimal recompilation of modules. Two garbage collectors are provided: a portable stop-and-copy collector and a conservative, multi-threaded, incremental collector. This software has been improved over the years into an industrial-strength system, and it has been ported to both Windows and UNIX environments. Not only does it provide a rapid way to begin using Modula-3, but it also has served as a standard reference implementation for the language and libraries, enhancing portability of Modula-3 programs. See Further Information below for the location of the software.

Modula-3 specifies several interfaces that every implementation must provide. They include Text (operations on text strings); Thread (synchronization primitives); Word (unsigned integer operations); Real, LongReal, and ExtendedReal (properties of floating-point types); RealFloat, LongRealFloat, ExtendedFloat (numerical operations on floating-point numbers); and FloatMode (control of floating-point behavior). In addition, SRC Modula-3 provides several interfaces that have become *de facto* standards: `Fmt` and `Lex` (text formatting of numbers); `Pkl` (support for persistent data storage); `Math`, `Stat`, `Random` (mathematical and statistical functions); `Sequence`, `List`, `Table`, and `Bundle` (data structures); `Rd`, `Wr`, `Stdio`, and `FileWr` (stream-oriented I/O interfaces); and interfaces for C and operating system compatibility (Horning et al., 1993).

The Network Objects package (Birrell et al., 1994) provides a state-of-the-art distributed object system, allowing Modula-3 objects to be exported across address spaces and computers. M3Tk is a meta-programming system for Modula-3, a toolkit for parsing and analyzing Modula-3 programs.

Finally, Trestle, VBTkit, FormsVBT, and FormsEdit are software packages that let you develop operating system-independent graphical user interfaces for UNIX and Windows (Brown and Meehan, 1993; Nelson, 1991).

21.6 Summary

Modula-3 is a modern, general-purpose programming language. It provides excellent support for large, reliable, and maintainable applications. Modula-3's OOP support comprises a single-inheritance model with automatic garbage collection and the ability to define partially opaque object types across separately compiled modules. Standard libraries extend this object model to distributed networks of computers. Compared to other languages with a roughly comparable feature set, Modula-3 is easier to learn and safer from runtime misbehavior.

References

Birrell, A., Nelson, G., Owicki, S. and Wobber, E. 1994. Network objects, Research Report 115. Systems Research Center, Digital Equipment Corporation, Palo Alto, CA, February.

Brown, M. H. and Meehan, J. R. (eds). 1993. *VBTkit Reference Manual toolkit for Trestle* and *The FormsVBT Reference Manual.* Systems Research Center, Digital Equipment Corporation, Palo Alto, CA. (Available in the SRC Modula-3 distribution.)

Boeszoermenyi, L. and Weich, C. 1995. *Programming with Modula-3: An Introduction to Programming with Style.* Springer-Verlag, New York, English version.

Cardelli, L., Donahue, J., Glassman, L., Jordan, M., Kalsow, W. and Nelson, G. 1992. Modula-3 language definition, *Sigplan Notices,* 27(8):15-42, August.

Harbison, S. P. 1992. *Modula-3.* Prentice-Hall, Englewood Cliffs, NJ.

Horning, J., Kalsow, B., McJones, P. and Nelson, G. 1993. *Some Useful Modula-3 Interfaces.* Systems Research Center, Digital Equipment Corporation, Palo Alto, CA.

Nayeri, F. 1997a. *Modula-3 at Work.* At http://www.cmass.com/cm3/projects.html.

Nayeri, F. 1997b. *CM3.* At http://www.cmass.com/cm3/.

Nelson, G. (Ed). 1991. *System Programming with Modula-3, Prentice-Hall Series in Innovative Technology.* Prentice-Hall, Englewood Cliffs, NJ.

Sedgewick, R. 1993. *Algorithms in Modula-3.* Addison-Wesley, Reading, MA.

Further Information

The standard reference for Modula-3 is contained in Nelson (1991) and was reprinted in Cardelli et al. (1992). Nelson (1991) also contains a description of how Modula-3 got many of its features, a detailed description of the I/O system, and tutorials on thread programming and the use of the Trestle window system. There are two textbooks on Modula-3, (Boeszoermenyi and Weich, 1995) (Harbison, 1992), and a version of Sedgewick's classic text on algorithms with examples in Modula-3 (Sedgewick, 1993).

Considerable up-to-date information for Modula-3 and its implementations may be found on the internet. A good beginning place is the Modula-3 Web Resource Page, *http://www.m3.org/,* or the Modula-3 home page, *http://www.research.digital.com/SRC/modula-3/html/home.html.* An online version of the language definition is available at *http://www.research.digital.com/SRC/m3defn/html/m3.html.* There is also a USENET newsgroup, *comp.lang.modula3.*

The SRC Modula-3 implementation is available from *ftp://gatekeeper.dec.com/pub/DEC/Modula-3/*. Commercially supported application development environments that use Modula-3 are available from Critical Mass, Inc., *http://www.cmass.com/*. That site also contains a list of commercial and educational systems that have been built using Modula-3.

A complete, annotated Modula-3 bibliography may be found at *http://www.research.digital.com/SRC/modula-3/html/bib.html*.

22

The Object Pascal Language (in Borland Delphi 3)

Marco Cantù
Wintech Italia SrL

In recent years, many alternative object-oriented extensions of the Pascal language have been proposed. The latest version and probably the most successful is the Object Pascal language found in Borland Delphi™.

Delphi's Object Pascal is the latest incarnation of the Borland family of Turbo Pascal compilers, based on extensions of the ANSI Pascal language, and so widespread to define a *de facto* standard.

Object Pascal has all the features of modern object-oriented programming (OOP) languages, and its heritage is in Eiffel and C++, which makes it very similar to Java (although the syntax is Pascal based).

Object Pascal is a proprietary language, so it has no standard. Borland tends to extend the language at each release of Delphi. This paper is referred to Object Pascal as found in Version 3 of Borland Delphi.

0-8493-3135-8/99/$0.00+$.50

22.1 Introduction to the Key Features

Object Pascal includes all the standard notions of OOP languages: the definition of class types, inheritance among class types, and polymorphism. Object Pascal is a strongly typed language, and objects are defined as instances of class types. The language favors compile-time type-checking extensively, much more than C++. This is partly due to the fact that the Pascal language is more strongly typed than the C language. For example, in Pascal, predefined and ordinal types are not compatible, and Boolean, Integer, and Char values are not compatible. There are, however, some pitfalls in the form of variant records and the free usage of pointers and casting.

These problems are due to the fact that Object Pascal is not a pure OOP language. It is, instead, a typical example of a hybrid language, which allow programmers to use all the traditional ANSI Pascal and Turbo Pascal programming techniques as well as the OOP approach.

22.1.1 The Object Reference Model

Some traditional OOP languages, such as C++, allow programmers to create objects on the stack, the heap, and the static storage. In these languages a variable of a class type corresponds to an object in memory.

Lately, there seems to be a trend to use a different model, often called an "object reference model." In this model every object is allocated dynamically on the heap, and a variable of a class type is actually a reference or a handle to the object in memory (technically implemented as a pointer). Object Pascal adopts this reference model, introduced in the past by Eiffel, and used today also by Java.

22.1.2 The Visual Programming Support

One of the most peculiar element of Delphi's Object Pascal is the support for visual programming. It is very important to notice that this support is built into the language, and is not only due to the development environment (although the two elements are strongly related). Object Pascal support for visual programming is based on the notion of property — a sort of "virtual class field" on the notion of "published" class elements — and on the extensive Runtime Type Information (RTTI) produced by the compiler.and available to other programs.

22.1.3 Windows Operating System Integration

Finally, the Pascal language has been extended to obtain a close integration with the Windows operating system. For example, the *message* keyword allows a method to respond to a Windows message directly, and the *interface* support is closely tied to COM, Microsoft's Common Object Model.

22.1.4 Notes on Pascal

Before looking into the OOP features of Object Pascal, let's make a brief mention of a few noteworthy features of the basic language, Pascal, not commonly found in other languages.

One of them is the inclusion of the data type constructors as *subranges*, enumerated types, and sets. It is important to mention these data types constructors, because Delphi generates runtime information for them, and the environment takes full advantage of their definitions. For example, Delphi's Object Inspector automatically lists the possible values of enumerated types.

Among predefined data types there are Booleans and strings. In ANSI Pascal strings used to suffer from a 255-character limit. In Delphi 2 Borland introduced long string, which are dynamically allocated, reference-counted, and use the *copy-on-write* technique. These strings are also type compatible with Windows string data type.

Delphi 2 also introduced in Pascal the C++ single-line commenting convention, //. Other comments are written within braces, or the parenthesis-star characters combination.

Instead of using braces for programs blocks, Pascal uses the *begin* and *end* keywords. A final noteworthy element is that Object Pascal code is not totally case insensitive.

TABLE 22.1 The Definition and Initialization of Class Type Variables.

```
var
 Obj1, Obj2: TMyClass;
begin
 // assign a newly created object
 Obj1 := TMyClass.Create;
 // assign to an existing object
 Obj2 := ExistingObject;
```

22.2 Classes, Objects, and References

Object Pascal programming is based on the definition of new class types. This is enforced by the visual development environment, since for every new form defined at design time Delphi automatically defines a new class, and every component visually placed on a form is an object of a class type available in or added to the system library. Of course the language allows you to define new classes (and also new components, or visual classes), and provides constructors, destructors, and many other features are explored in this section.

22.2.1 Objects as References

As already mentioned, in Object Pascal a class type variable does not provide the storage for the object, but it is only a pointer or reference to the object in memory. Before you use the object, you must allocate the memory for it by creating a new instance or by assigning to the variable an existing instance, as shown in Table 22.1.

As you can see in Table 22.1, Object Pascal requires each variable to be declared in a *var* block, which can be local to a function or global (even if eventually accessible and visible only inside a source code file or unit). The call to *Create* invokes a default constructor available for every class, unless the class redefines it (as described later).

If the object reference model seems to require more work for the programmer, keep in mind that in languages such as C++ you often have to use pointers to objects and references to objects. By only using pointers and references, for example, you can get polymorphism.

The object reference model, instead, makes the pointers the defaults, but does a good job hiding them. Java is an even better example of this behavior then Object Pascal, since it totally hides the notion of pointers, but the basic approach is the same among these two OOP languages and many others.

22.2.2 Defining New Classes

Now that we have seen how to create objects of the existing class, we can focus on the definition of new classes. A class is simply a collection of methods operating on some local data. In Object Pascal the syntax of the class declaration is Table 22.2.

As shown in the Table 22.2, methods are defined with *function* and *procedure* keywords, depending if they have a return value of not, and methods that require no parameters have no open and close parenthesis. Inside the class definition methods can only be declared, they are then defined in the *implementation* portion of the unit, using the dot notation, to specify which class they belong to.

22.2.3 Accessing the Current Object

As in most OOP languages, in Object Pascal methods are different from global functions and procedures because they have a hidden parameter, a reference to the object for which the method has been invoked. This reference to the current object is indicated using the *self* keyword.

Table 22.2 The Definition of a New Class and of Some of its Methods

```
type
  TDate = class
  private
    dd, mm, yy: Integer;
  public
    procedure Init (d, m, y: Integer);
    function Month: Integer;
    function Day: Integer;
    function Year: Integer;
  end;

procedure TDate.Init (d, m, y: Integer);
begin
  dd := d;
  mm := m;
  yy := y;
end;

function Date.Day: Integer;
begin
  Result := dd;
end;
```

22.2.4 Creating and Destroying Objects

Once you have created and used an object, you need to destroy it to avoid using unnecessary memory. This is particularly important because objects are not allocated on the stack, so when a class type variable goes out of scope the object it refers to remains in memory. Object Pascal has no garbage collection algorithm — it uses a reference counting approach — but this is limited to strings (a predefined type) and to interface type variables.

As an alternative to manual objects tracking and deallocation, Delphi supports the idea of an owner object: the owner of an object becomes responsible for destroying all the object it owns. This makes handling the object destruction very simple and straightforward. The ownership mechanism is not directly built into the language, though, but it is available in the *TComponent* class of the standard library, called VCL, which is the base class for all components or visual classes.

22.2.5 Constructors

The *Init* method of the class shown in Table 22.2 is a class initialization procedure, and it can be considered as a constructor. It is actually possible to turn it into a constructor by replacing the *procedure* keyword with the *constructor* keyword. When a constructor is applied to a class type, the system automatically creates a new object of that class type, allocating memory for it, and then executing the initialization code it provides. When a constructor is applied to an existing class type variable, only the initialization code is executed.

Object Pascal uses a specific keyword, *constructor,* because in the languages there is no method overloading (so it is not possible to have multiple constructors with the same name). However, since constructors have custom names, it is possible to provide several constructors anyway.

In Object Pascal each class has the default *Create* constructor, based on the fact that every class inherits from a common ancestor class, *TObject,* which provides a do-nothing *Create* constructor.

Unless you override it with a constructor having the same name, and eventually different parameters, this constructor is simply inherited by each class. *TComponent* derived classes, however, redefine the *Create* constructor with one parameter — the owner of the newly created object.

It is very important to notice that in Object Pascal constructors can be declared as virtual, to activate dynamic binding for them. This is required by another language feature, the class type references, which can be used to create a new object of the class they refer to at runtime, by calling a virtual constructor, as described in Section 22.5.4.

22.2.6 Destructors

A destructor has the opposite role of a constructor, and is called when an object is destroyed. A destructor is a method marked with a specific keyword, *destructor*, and when it is called, after executing the related code, the system destroys the object by deallocating its memory.

Object Pascal uses a standard virtual destructor, called *Destroy*, defined in the common base class *TObject*. This destructor is usually called indirectly, using the standard *Free* method (defined in *TObject* as well). This method checks if the object reference is not *nil* before destroying the object. Setting the references of deallocated object to nil, however, is a programmer's responsibility.

As mentioned in Section 22.2.4, all objects are dynamic, so you are supposed to call *Free* for each object you create, unless it has an owner responsible for its destruction. In theory you can declare multiple destructors, which makes sense because you call destructors in your code (there is nothing automatic).

22.2.7 Class Encapsulation (Access Specifiers)

A common element of OOP language is the presence of access specifiers indicating different levels of class encapsulation. Object Pascal has the *public*, *protected*, and *private* access specifiers, but also a few extra ones.

A *public* field or method is visible by every other class, a *protected* field or method is visible only by derived classes and by all the classes defined in the same source code unit. A *private* field or method has no external visibility, besides the classes defined in the same source code unit. Using a C++ terminology, classes defined in the same source code unit in Object Pascal can be considered as *friend* classes.

Compared to most other OOP languages, Object Pascal has two more access specifiers, *published* and *automated*. The system generates extensive RTTI information for published fields and methods, so that other classes in the system can access these elements searching them by name in an internal table. It is also possible to query a class for a list of its published fields and methods (although this is accomplished only through undocumented and unofficially supported techniques).

The last access specifier, *automated*, is used to build the OLE Automation interface of an object, that is, an interface visible outside of the boundaries of the application and available to other applications.

The default access specifier for a class is *published*.

22.2.8 Units and Scope

An important element of Object Pascal, related to the access specifiers just mentioned, is the idea of unit or module. In Object Pascal, each source code file is called *unit* and marked with this keyword. Each unit is divided in two parts, the *interface* and the *implementation*, marked by these two keywords.

The interface portion of a unit is visible to other units, and has the same role of a header file. A unit can refer to the identifiers declared in the interface portion of a different unit by means of a *uses* statement. In other words, a *uses* statement corresponds to an *include* statement referred only to the interface of the unit, not its complete source code.

The interface of a unit generally includes type declarations, which comprise the declaration of the class or classes defined in the unit, and also globally allocated variables visible from other units. The implementation portion of a unit must include the declaration of all the methods of the classes declared in the interface portion (with the only exception of *abstract* methods). It can also include further types and globally allocated variables, which will not be visible outside of the unit.

It is illegal to write actual code in the interface portion of a unit.

Units also define "namespaces." In case of a clash by two global names, defined in two different units, it is possible to prefix the name with the unit name.

22.2.9 Class Method and Data

OOP languages generally allow to have some methods and data which relate to the class as a whole, not to specific objects. Object Pascal has only class method, which is indicated by the *class* keyword. Class method can be applied both to an instance of a class type or to the class type itself. Class methods do not have the *self* hidden parameter.

Object Pascal does not directly support class data, or data not replicated but shared among the objects of a class type. Usually class data is replaced by adding global variables to the implementation portion of the unit which defines the class. There are no real drawbacks to this approach.

22.3 Properties

As mentioned in the introduction, properties are one of the most peculiar features of the Object Pascal language, and they constitute one of the key foundations onto which Delphi's visual programming environment is built. The best definition of a property is "a typed virtual field."

22.3.1 Properties Definitions

A property is invariably an element of a class, and is indicated by a name, a type, optional reading and writing mechanisms, and other optional specifiers. A property can be the public or published name of some private data (thus mapping directly to a field), but often a property defines access functions to read or modify this data, eventually producing side effects (such as a refresh of the output). Actually access functions are not restricted to reading and writing a corresponding private field, but can do anything a method can do. Some properties even rely on operating system level features for storing their data, and the read and write operations are translated to Windows API level calls.

In Table 22.3 there are the definitions of properties using different approaches. The *Size* property maps to the *FSize* field in reading (that is, when it is used in an expression), and maps to the *SetSize* method in writing (that is, when it is used on the left side of an assignment). This means that the compiler converts a statement such as:

```
Obj1.Size := Obj2.Size * 2;
to the following code:
Obj1.SetSize (Obj2.FSize * 2);
```

In the same Table 22.3, the *MinHeight* property maps to two methods and the Handle property is a read-only property.

In my opinion, properties are a sound OOP encapsulation mechanism. In fact, you can use properties to provide a simple and uniform access to class information and still be able to change the implementation behind a property by changing its access methods or replacing a direct data access with an access method.

Table 22.3 Examples of the Definition of Properties in Object Pascal

```
property Size: Integer
  read FSize
  write SetSize;

property MinHeight: Integer
  read GetMinHeight
  write SetMinHeight;

property Handle: THandle
  read GetHandle;
```

Properties must have a data type and can be part of the published interfaces of a class. Published properties are important, because they provide a way of interacting with objects at design time. In the Delphi environment, the Object Inspector is the tool programmers can use to interact with the published properties of a component or class.

22.3.2 Method Pointers and Events

Another addition to the Object Pascal language is the idea of a method pointer. A method pointer is a sort of function pointer (that is a variable holding the address of a function or procedure) that refers to an object method. Still, a method pointer is not simply a function pointer, because it encapsulates both the address of the method to call (the code portion) and the object to apply the method to (the data portion).

Method pointers really matter in Delphi. In fact component events are properties which have a method pointer type. For example, when a programmer defines an event handler for the *OnClick* event of a button component, the button will delegate the event handler to the form hosting the component. This means the *OnClick* event of the button component, or the *OnClick* method pointer stored inside the button class, will refer to a method of the form. When the button has to fire the event, it simply calls the method which handles it. This is the code, often invisible, you can use to assign a method of a form to the event of a component:

```
MyButton.OnClick := Form1.OnButton1Click;
```

This shows in practice how to assign a method (as *Button1Click*) to a method pointer type property (as *OnClick*). This operation can be done both at design time (usually with few mouse clicks) and at runtime (with the code above).

22.3.3 Component Streaming

A topic strictly related to properties and events, and another key element of Delphi's visual environment, is component streaming. The class library, in fact, includes support for streaming (through *TStream*-derived classes). Besides saving other types and blocks of binary data, the streaming support work on the published properties of TPersistent-derived classes. Streaming a component to a file does not save a snapshot of its internal memory representation (its binary image) but of its published interface. Notice that the streaming involves both properties and events.

The corresponding objects can later be automatically rebuilt loading them from the file. Streaming objects is fundamental for Delphi visual architecture. You create and set attributes of objects at design time, and these objects are *loaded* when the form is displayed. Notice that the language has been extended with some properties specifiers (such as *default* and *stored*) to support persistency. The result of streaming a form to a file is a custom Windows resource format, which can be embedded into the executable file of an application. These files are binary files, marked by the DFM extensions, which can be converted in a textual description by several means.

Among other things, the availability for a textual description of the streamed objects helps the development of source code tracking tools and of automatic code generators.

22.4 Classes and Inheritance

Inheritance among classes is one of the foundations of OOP. Object Pascal uses no keyword to express inheritance, but a special syntax: the base class name appears within parenthesis after the *class* keyword:

```
type
   TDog = class (TAnimal)
```

All the public and protected fields and methods of the base class maintain their visibility. Private fields and methods of the base class, instead, are not visible (unless both the base and the derived class are defines in the same unit).

22.4.1 The Mother of All Classes

As already mentioned, all the classes in Object Pascal have a common base class, called *TObject*. Technically if a class specifies no base class, it inherits directly from *TObject*. Since Object Pascal lacks multiple inheritance, all the classes form a single huge hierarchical tree. The *TObject* class handles RTTI and has some other limited capabilities.

22.4.2 Base Class Constructors and Initialization

In Object Pascal, it is the programmers responsibility to initialize the base class subobjects. This is generally done by adding a call to a base class constructor inside the constructors of a derived class. This is not compulsory, though. On this respect Object Pascal is simpler than other OOP languages, but there are more chances of providing a erroneous initialization that might lead to runtime problems.

22.4.3 Accessing Methods of the Base Class

When writing a method of a class, or overriding a method of the base class, a programmer can refer to any method of the base class by using the *inherited* keyword. This keyword precedes the name of the base class method to call. In certain circumstances, it is simply possible to use the *inherited* keyword without further specification to access to the base method begin redefined, or a handler of the same message.

22.4.4 Subtype Compatibility

Object Pascal class types are strongly typed, which means that objects of different classes are not type-compatible. There is an exception to this rule: objects of derived classes are compatible with the type of their base class, as in many OOP languages. The subtype compatibility is directly available for class type variables, thanks to the object reference model (all class type variables are size compatible, regardless of the size of the objects they point to). Moreover, in Object Pascal all the class types are type-compatible with the *TObject* type, because they all derive from it.

22.4.5 Late Binding (and Polymorphism)

When different classes of a hierarchy redefine a method of their base class, it is very powerful to be able to refer to a generic object of one of these classes (thanks to the subtype compatibility) and call a method, which results in a call of the method of the proper class. To accomplish this the Object Pascal compiler supports late binding, but only for methods for which this is specifically requested. As already mentioned Object Pascal allows defining virtual constructors.

In Object Pascal late binding is introduced with the *virtual* or *dynamic* keywords (the difference between the two is only a technical implementation difference, favoring size of speed). In derived classes, redefined virtual and dynamic methods must be specifically marked with the *override* keyword (this forces a compiler check on the method signature). This is a peculiar aspect of Object Pascal, and the rationale behind it is that this allows for more changes in the base class, since the eventual name clash of a new virtual or dynamic method with an existing method of the derived class won't create too much harm.

A third related keyword, *message*, allows binding a method to a operating system message. This is something most OOP languages really lack. In Table 22.4 there is an example.

22.4.6 Abstract Methods and Classes

When building a complex hierarchy, programmers often need to introduce methods in higher level classes, even if the methods are not yet defined for that specific abstraction. Object Pascal, as many OOP language, implements a specific mechanism to support this definition of abstract methods, that is, virtual or dynamic methods without an actual implementation. Object Pascal uses the *abstract* keyword to mark these methods.

TABLE 22.4 The Code Used to Handle a Windows Message Directly Inside the Class Defining a Form

```
type
  TForm1 = class(TForm)
    procedure WMMinMax (var Message: TMessage);
      message wm_GetMinMaxInfo;
  end;
```

Classes having at least one of the abstract methods are often called abstract classes. Strangely enough Object Pascal allows the creation of instances of abstract classes (although the compiler emits a warning message). This exposes a program to the risk of calling an abstract method an event that generates a runtime error and terminates the program.

22.4.7 Multiple Inheritance and Interfaces

Some OOP languages support multiple inheritance, which is inheriting a class from more than one base class. Object Pascal has no support for multiple inheritance, but it allows the definition of interfaces, or pure abstract classes. Interfaces are types which list methods, similar in all to abstract virtual methods, but they have no data and no method implementation.

In Object Pascal a class can inherit from only one base class, but can implement multiple interfaces. In this case the class must compulsorily provide the implementation of all the methods of the interfaces it declares to implements.

Contrary to other languages which share a similar feature, like Java, in Object Pascal these interfaces are strongly mapped to Microsoft's COM, although it is technically possible to use them in plain non-COM programs. Interfaces form a hierarchy separated from classes, and every interface inherits from *IUnknown*, in the same way any class inherits from *TObject*. The actual mapping of the methods of the class into the methods of the interfaces the class implements, and the techniques used to solve the eventual name clashes, is one of the more convoluted parts of the Object Pascal language.

22.5 Other Features

22.5.1 RTTI

In strongly typed OOP languages the compiler does all the type-checking, so there is little need to keep information about classes and types in the running program. However, there are cases (as the type downcast, from a base class type to a derived class type) which require some type information. Object Pascal has two operators for downcast, the type check, obtained with the *is* keyword, and the actual cast, obtained with the *as* keyword:

```
if AnAnimal is TDog then
  ...
ADog := AnAnimal as TDog;
```

If the object (*AnAnimal*) happens not to be compatible with the type it is being converted into (*TDog*), the system raises an invalid cast exception.

Besides the support for the safe downcast, the Object Pascal compiler generates extensive RTTI for classes and their published interface. Actually the *published* keyword governs most of the RTTI generation. All the idea of properties, the streaming mechanism (the form files), and the Delphi environment, starting from the Object Inspector, rely heavily on class RTTI.

The TObject common base class has (among others) the ClassName and ClassType methods. ClassType returns a class type variable, an instance of a special class reference type (see Section 22.5.4).

Table 22.5 Examples of Exceptions Handling Code

```
// exceptions handling block
function Divide (A, B: Integer): Integer;
begin
 try
  Divide := A div B;
 except
  on EDivByZero do
   ...// handle a specific type of exceptions
 end;
end;

// finally block
function ComputeBits (A, B: Integer): Integer;
var
 Bmp: TBitmap;
begin
 Bmp := TBitmap.Create;// allocation
 try
  // unsafe operations
 finally
  Bmp.Free;// protected de-allocation
 end;
end;
```

22.5.2 Exceptions Handling

The basic idea of exceptions handling is to simplify the error handling code of a program, providing a standard built in mechanism, with the goal of making programs more robust. Object Pascal uses the *raise*, *try*, and *except* keywords, corresponding to C++ language *throw*, *try*, and *catch* keywords with similar capabilities. The exception mechanism is based on objects, and exceptions are handled based on their data type. You can see an example of an exception handling block in the first part of Table 22.5.

Because objects are not allocated on the stack, Object Pascal diverges from the C++ implementation of exceptions handling, providing the *finally* keyword which marks a block of code to be executed in any case (an example is in the second part of Table 22.5). In Delphi exception classes are generally derived from the *Exception* class. The system, by default, automatically handles exceptions of subclasses of *Exception*.

22.5.3 Container Classes

Object Pascal has no support for generic programming or templates. Container classes are generally built as containers of objects of the *TObject* class or by building type-specific containers (using the *TList* of *TContainer* classes of the library). A few techniques have been devised to make generic lists more type-safe.

22.5.4 Class References

The class references construct is something not available in many other OOP languages. A class reference is a variable holding a class as value (not the class name, but the class itself). A class reference type relates to the specified class and its subclasses, with the usual type compatibility rule. You can apply to a class reference every class method, but also a class constructor, as shown in Table 22.6.

If *Create* is a virtual constructor it is possible to use the last statement of Table 22.6 to create any object of a class derived from TMyClass, and actually call the proper overridden constructor. This is a very powerful technique used by Delphi to re-create the streamed objects and components (from DFM files).

Table 22.6 An Example of the Use of a Class Reference to Create an Object

```
type
 TMyClassRef = class of TMyClass;

var
 MyObj: TMyClass;
 MyCRef: TMyClassRef;
begin
 TMyClassRef := TSubclass;
 MyObj := TMyClassRef.Create (...);
```

22.5.5 The Visual Component Library (VCL)

Although this paper is a discussion of the Object Pascal language as found in Borland's Delphi, it is relevant to point out at least a few features of the class library which are integrated with the product. In standardized languages there is a clear-cut distinction between standard class libraries and compiler specific libraries. In this case such a distinction is impossible, although, for example, the definition of the *TObject* common base class falls into the runtime library support, and it has been discussed as part of the language. A few notes on the VCL library are worthwhle from the language perspective. The central element is the correspondence between the idea of component and the idea of class. A component is nothing but a class derived from the *TComponent* base class.

For this reason the VCL is, at the same time, a library of components which can be visually used in the development environment, at design time, and a class library which can be used in the source code as the class library of any other OOP language. In other words, every operation done in the development environment corresponds to code being executed. As such, everything which can be done at design time, can also be done at runtime, using specific code. Examples are the dynamic creation of new components/object, the association of a new handler to an event, and the access to the list of the published properties of a component.

Because components are simply classes derived from *TComponent*, it is very easy to build new components and install them in the library, making them available also at design time. The important thing to notice is the notion of language-based components, which is shared by the JavaBeans model. This differs highly from the generic language-independent component models, such as DCOM or CORBA, and is way more integrated into the language and generally quite powerful.

Language-based component models have a fundamental role in promoting code reuse at an intermediate level, and the large market of VCL-based components is a demonstration of this. The language-independent component models, instead, tend to be more suitable for application integration and large projects development.

22.6 Conclusions

The Delphi development goal was "easy visual programming," without giving up too much power, as some of the competing visual development environment tend to do. By creating an object-oriented language with specific features for visual programming (as the idea of properties) as a foundation of the development environment, Borland has achieved these two often contradicting goals: power and visual development. Although Delphi's development environment is often regarded as the key to the success of this product, in reality it is the Object Pascal language behind the tool which deserves this role.

23

Python

Guido van Rossum
Corporation for National Research Initiatives (CNRI)

23.1 Introduction

Python is an interpreted, object-oriented, high-level programming language with dynamic semantics. Its high-level built in data structures, combined with dynamic typing and dynamic binding, make it very attractive for Rapid Application Development, as well as for use as a scripting or glue language to connect existing components together. Python's simple, easy to learn syntax emphasizes readability and therefore reduces the cost of program maintenance. Python supports modules and packages, which encourages program modularity and code reuse. The Python interpreter and the extensive standard library are available in source or binary form without charge for all major platforms, and it can be freely distributed.

This chapter gives the reader an introduction to the language as well as an overview of the main tools and libraries available. Python is compared to a number of other languages, and a comprehensive list of further reading material, on-line and off-line, is included. The version described is Python 1.5; it was released at the end of 1997. Since its inception, around 1990, Python has evolved steadily but carefully, and no major incompatibilities exist between recent versions.

23.2 Application Areas

Python is a complete, general programming language with many properties that make it an ideal language for Rapid Application Development and Rapid Prototyping. Its dynamic properties dramatically reduce the time required to deliver a working application. This makes it well suited to the development of applications for which a short lead time is important. Examples of such application areas abound: World Wide Web scripting, Graphical User Interface prototyping, application testing, database applications, image processing, and steering of large scientific applications.

0-8493-3135-8/99/$0.00+$.50

In all these and similar areas, "getting results quickly" is not so much dependent on the execution speed of the program but on the time it takes a programmer to write the program. The apparent contradiction in the examples of processor-intensive applications like image processing or scientific computing is easily explained: Python is used here as a "glue" or "scripting" language, which controls the sequencing and parameters for pre-built components. Python is easily extended with modules written in C or C++ (or other languages, from Fortran to Java). Extension modules make it possible to create object-oriented Python interfaces to almost any existing component, making that component scriptable through Python. Python extensions can define new Python object types so that the Python program can accurately reflect the data types used by the component. For example, the "Numerical Python" extension defines an object type for the space-efficient storage of multidimensional arrays of numbers, which can be passed efficiently to a variety of numerical, scientific, image processing, and graphical libraries.

Developing an application as Python typically takes one third to one tenth of the time that it would take to develop the same application in a "classic" object-oriented language like C++. Python is easy to learn and easy to use, so the cost of programmer training can be reduced. Its simple, clear syntax is very readable, further reducing the cost of program maintenance. It has even been said that Python code reads like pseudo-code, such as would be used to explain an algorithm in a textbook or to sketch the control flow of an application; except Python would be executable pseudo-code. It may be possible to write bad code in any language; Python, however, certainly encourages the writing of good code. It does this through a variety of mechanisms: packages and modules, classes, exceptions, high-level data types, polymorphism, operator overloading, and familiar notations for common operations.

Since there is no compilation step, the edit-test-debug cycle is incredibly fast. Debugging Python programs is easy — a bug or bad input will never cause a segmentation fault. Instead, when the interpreter discovers an error, it raises an exception; when the program does not catch the exception, the interpreter prints a stack trace. A source level debugger allows inspection of local and global variables, evaluation of arbitrary expressions, setting breakpoints, stepping through the code a line at a time, etc. The debugger is written in Python itself, testifying to Python's introspective power. On the other hand, often the quickest way to debug a program is simply to add a few print statements to the source. The fast edit-test-debug cycle makes this simple approach very effective.

Another factor in Python's usefulness is an extensive library of standard modules and packages. The Python library provides standard, portable ways to perform a wide variety of tasks. For example, it supplies implementations of many common Internet protocols and conventions (e.g., HTML, CGI, HTTP, and FTP), a powerful library of string matching operations based on Perl regular expressions, and a portable GUI library based on Tk, the GUI toolkit that comes with the Tcl language. Above and beyond the portable standard library, there are platform-specific modules that provide interfaces to native facilities; for example, on the Windows platform there are interfaces to COM and DCOM and to the Win32 user interface primitives. There are also numerous third-party libraries, including a CORBA compliant RPC interface (ILU, by Xerox PARC) and interfaces to most commercial databases. Many of these can be downloaded freely from the Python Web site.

This brings us to a final aspect of Python, the helpful on-line user community. Python users and developers meet on-line in the Python newsgroup, visit the Python Web site, and contribute to a variety of topical mailing lists. The yearly International Python Conferences (started in 1994 as half-yearly Python Workshops) help community members put faces to e-mail addresses, and contribute significantly to the further development of the language, its library, and applications.

23.3 Python in a Nutshell

There are several tutorials that teach Python to someone with prior programming experience in an afternoon or two; references are provided at the end of this chapter. This section is not a full tutorial, it gives just enough of a taste of Python to be able to assess the power of the language.

While Python is an object-oriented language, you can get started without using the object-oriented features. A programming style using functions and variables instead of classes and instances works well for small programs. The example below defines a function of two arguments to calculate the greatest common divisor using Euclid's well-known algorithm:

```
def gcd(a, b):
   "Greatest Common Divisor of a and b."
   while b != 0:
      a, b = b, a%b
   return abs(a)
```

Block structure in Python is indicated as indentation, allowing for better readability. The amount of indentation used is up to the programmer as long as it is consistent within each block (an editor with an auto-indent feature is all you need). The quoted string literal at the start of the function body is a doc(umentation) string; it can be used for automatic generation of printed documentation or on-line help. Most definitional constructs (functions, classes, modules) can have a doc string. There are also regular comments and these start with a hash (#) mark.

The body of the while statement contains a parallel assignment. The value of b is copied into a, and at the same time a%b, the remainder of dividing a by b, using the values of a and b before the assignment, is stored in b. The while statement terminates when b is zero (! = is Python's not-equal comparison operator). At this point abs(a), the absolute value of a, is returned.

Here is a somewhat larger example that computes the list of prime numbers less than a given maximum:

```
def primes(max):
   "List of prime numbers < max."
   primes = [2]
   # Loop over odd numbers from 3 up to max
   for i in range(3, max, 2):
      for p in primes:
         if p*p > i:      # i is a prime number
            primes.append(i)
            break
         elif i%p == 0:  # i has divisor p
            break
return primes
```

The value [2] used to initialize the list of known primes is a list constructor; it creates a list of one element, the integer 2. The list is later extended one prime number at a time, in the statement primes.append(i). Python's for statement iterates over a sequence (for example, a list). The flexible built-in function range(start, stop, increment) returns an arithmetic progression of integers; range(N) is shorthand for range(0, N, 1). For example, range(5) yields the list [0, 1, 2, 3, 4] — a list of five elements starting at zero (Python uses zero-based indexing everywhere). The break statement breaks out of the nearest loop. It is used to skip scanning the remaining prime numbers already calculated when it is determined that i definitely is or is not a prime number. The if statement probably speaks for itself; elif is short for "else if," and of course a plain else: <block> clause is also supported.

23.3.1 Object-Oriented Programming

The core concept for object-oriented programming in Python is the class. A class definition contains the class name, an optional list of base classes (allowing multiple inheritance), and the body of the class. The body can contain both data attributes (class variables) and methods. The example below defines a class with two methods:

```
class Person:

def __init__(self, name, age):
   self.name = name
   self.age = age

def celebrate_birthday(self):
   self.age = self.age+1
```

For a method, the object on which the method is invoked is not implicit (as in C++), but explicit as the first argument — usually called self. Attribute access is done using a dot (.) between the object and the attribute. Methods that are invoked implicitly by the interpreter are indicated using an underscore convention. For example, the __init__ method is invoked when a new instance is created, i.e., it is the constructor. A new instance of the class can then be created using a functional notation:

```
john = Person("John", 41)
john.celebrate_birthday()
```

Python is not a statically typed language: there are no type declarations for the method arguments, nor are the attributes of an instance declared. Instead, the presence of an attribute is checked at the time the attribute is accessed.

This dynamism is the basis for both polymorphism and late binding. Attributes are bound at the latest possible time, when they are accessed. Late binding is not only restricted to methods, it applies for all attributes. Polymorphism is an immediate result of the late binding. If a method expects an instance of a certain class, an instance of a derived class can be passed at runtime. When the attribute is accessed, the interpreter checks the instance itself, then the class, then the base classes. Furthermore, polymorphism is not restricted to the inheritance relationship. Suppose L is a list of objects with a retail price tag. The total of all the items in the list can then be computed as follows:

```
sum = 0
for item in L:
   sum = sum+L.price()
```

The code works regardless of the inheritance relationships between the items. Instead, each item must support a price method which should return a numerical value. This allows the implementation of generic algorithms without requiring templates or type casts as in C++ or Java.

Because there is no static typing, errors in the program are detected at runtime. Rather than aborting the program, the interpreter raises exceptions. The exception mechanism in Python works similar to that of C++ or Java.

23.3.2 Object-Oriented Scripting

The main goal of script programming is to develop small programs in a short time. In order to do so, the scripting language must support complex functionality built-in, and the turn-around times during development must be short.

Python comes with a standard library that supports various application areas. For text manipulation, functions ranging from regular expressions up to SGML parsers are available. For Internet programming, the core functionality is in the socket support (implemented in C), with application protocols such as FTP and HTTP built on top (in Python). Operating system functionality and file access is exposed in a platform-independent way.

In addition to the library, scripts often make heavy use of advanced data structures. Python supports three built-in data structures for common application problems: tuples, lists, and dictionaries. Tuples and lists are integer-indexed arrays and support concatenation and slicing, and dictionaries are indexed with arbitrary values and implemented as hash tables. In the example above, the list L could have been constructed like this:

```
# Assume that Butter, Milk and Meat are
# classes with appropriate constructors.
L = [Butter(10.3), Milk(amount=4)]
L.append(Meat(type='pork', amount=8))
```

Here is a simple class that uses a dictionary to build up an index of the word occurrences in a file. It is presented without further explanation.

```
import string

class Indexer:

  def __init__(self):
    self.index = {}

  def scan_file(self, file):
    lineno = 0
    for line in
file.readlines():
      lineno = lineno + 1
      self.scan_line(line,
                     lineno)

  def scan_line(self, line,
                lineno):
    words = string.split(line)
    self.index_words(words,
                     lineno)

  def index_words(self, words,
                  lineno):
    for word in words:
      if
self.index.has_key(word):

self.index[word].append
                   (lineno)
      else:
        self.index[word] =
                   [lineno]

  def print_index(self):
    words = self.index.keys()
    words.sort()
    for word in words:
      print word, ":",
self.index[word]
```

23.3.3 Modules and Packages

In order to structure the library and the application, Python uses a module concept similar to the one of the Modula family of languages. A module is a source code unit stored in a single file (named *module*.py). Using the import statement, other modules can load the module, and then access the objects defined in the module. Modules are a good approach to code reuse.

Modules also provide namespace management. Each module has its own namespace, which is used for all functions, classes, and other objects (like global variables) defined in the module. If module A defines an object named X, its author does not need to worry about an unrelated module B that might also define an object named X; they are distinct objects, and users explicitly choose which object they use by writing A.X or B.X.

A collection of related modules can be grouped together in a directory, this is called a package. A module inside a package can be referenced by its qualified name, *package.module*. Packages can contain subpackages. There is a renaming facility that allows using shorter names (from *package* import *module*). Packages are a relatively new feature first introduced in Python 1.5.

The Python interpreter first translates the module into platform-independent byte code, and it stores this byte-code into a file for future use. The byte code is then executed. This approach reduces the time between development cycles, because expensive compilation steps to machine code are avoided. The byte code is stored in a file just for efficiency (to avoid reparsing the same module over and over), and the program will work whether the byte code is available on disk or not.

Having the source code parser available at all times gives an additional advantage. It is possible to execute source code that was created at runtime, e.g., constructed by the program, entered by a user, or downloaded from a remote location. This is different from languages like Java, which require the compilation to byte code prior to the execution. A customizable mechanism known as *restricted execution* allows a program to establish flexible security in the context of untrusted code.

23.3.4 Extensibility

Python supports both extensions to the library as well as embedding the interpreter into another application. Extension modules are machine code files, usually obtained from compiling C or C++ code. Using extension modules, it is possible to access libraries written in other languages.

Most operating systems allow dynamic loading of shared libraries into an already running program. When available, Python uses this mechanism to import extension modules from separate files, thus allowing the addition of extension modules to an installation without the requirement to relink the interpreter. This makes distributed management and independent distribution of third party extension modules possible.

Embedding is the process of enhancing an existing application with a Python interpreter. This is usually done to allow the user of the application to enhance it by providing Python code. Embedding the Python interpreter increases the total program size by about 300KB, depending on the number of modules made available to the application.

Closely related to the combination of Python code and compiled code like C is the issue of packaging. Usually, a Python installation consumes one file per module, thus reducing the amount of I/O performed at application startup. If this is undesirable, a mechanism called *freezing* allows the integration of all those files into one. This is done by copying the relevant byte code into the resulting program image. Any mix of frozen and external modules is possible.

23.4 Existing Applications and Packages

This section presents a powerful argument for using Python — the large collection of existing Python applications and modules available for use.

23.5 Graphical User Interfaces (GUI)

The Python language itself is not tied to a particular user interface paradigm; it runs as well in an embedded system as on the desktop. Depending on the operating environment, different extension packages are available to add a GUI to a Python program.

Perhaps the most commonly used GUI package for Python is **Tkinter**. This is an object-oriented interface to the Tk toolkit that comes with the Tcl language. Tkinter is well supported on Unix, Windows, and Mac platforms, although its Unix origins and its nature as a platform-independent package mean that it does not always support the latest user interface style guidelines on the latter platforms. Here is a simple "Hello world" program written using Tkinter:

```
from Tkinter import *
root = Tk()
def bye():
  print "Goodbye world"
  root.quit()
b = Button(root, text="Hello world", command=bye)
b.pack()
root.mainloop()
```

On each of the major platforms, there is also an interface to the platform's "native" GUI toolkit. On Unix, there is an interface to the X11/Motif library. On Mac, there is an interface to the Mac toolbox, and on Windows, there are interfaces both to the Win32 GUI APIs and to the MFC library. The latter comes with a complete Integrated Development Environment, dubbed PythonWin. These are all third-party add-ons, maintained by volunteers, and available for free.

Other GUI solutions also exist. For example, there is wxPython, an interface to the portable GUI toolkit wxWindows (written in C++). In general, as soon as a GUI library becomes popular, someone creates a Python interface for it.

Related to GUI programming are Python's third-party interfaces for OpenGL, a vendor-neutral 3-D graphics library, and GD (GifDraw), a free library to create images in the popular GIF format. There is also support for other image file formats, in the form of PIL (Python Image Library) by Fredrik Lundh.

23.5.1 Web and CGI Programming

The standard Python library has good support for Web and CGI programming. At the lowest level, there is the built-in socket extension module, which provides cross-platform access to the basic Internet protocols. Layered on top of this are modules that implement object-oriented interfaces to the Internet's main user-level protocols, e.g., ftplib, httplib, and nntplib define classes that represent connections using FTP, HTTP, and NNTP, respectively. (Similar modules for other protocols such as SMTP and SNMP are available as third-party add-ons.)

The sgmllib and htmllib modules provide scanners for (simplified) SGML and (full) HTML: A simple text-based HTML formatter is provided as an example application of the latter.

Python is an excellent language to write CGI scripts; the standard CGI module takes care of most details of interfacing with the http server, and makes the form contents available as a dictionary-like structure. There are also third-party solutions for CGI scripting that enhance the performance of CGI scripts and automate the generation of HTML, e.g., for database report generation.

Another ambitious project is Grail, which is a full featured Web browser implemented in Python, using the Tkinter GUI library. Grail supports applets (active content) written in Python.

23.5.2 Numeric Extensions to Python

The Numeric Extensions to Python (NumPy) add powerful multidimensional array objects to Python. These new objects give Python the number crunching power of numeric languages like Matlab and IDL while maintaining all of the advantages of the general-purpose programming language that is Python. NumPy was originally developed by Jim Hugunin, and it is being distributed independently from the main Python interpreter and library. It is currently being maintained by Lawrence Livermore National Laboratories. Discussion of NumPy generally takes place on the mailing list of the Matrix Special Interest Group (accessible via the Python Web server).

The NumPy extensions add two new object types to Python, and they include a number of extensions that take advantage of these two new objects:

1. Multidimensional Array Objects
   - Efficient arrays of homogeneous machine types (floats, longs, complex doubles, ...)
   - Arbitrary number of dimensions
2. Sophisticated structural operations
   - Universal Function Objects
   - Supports mathematical functions on all python objects
   - Very efficient for Array Objects
3. Simple interfaces to existing numerical libraries
   - Linear Algebra (LAPACK)
   - Fourier Transforms (FFTPACK)
   - Random Numbers (RANLIB)

23.5.3 Commercial Databases

There are third-party modules that interface to various commercial or semi-commercial databases. The Database Special Interest Group maintains the specification for a generic database API, and collects pointers to the database specific interfaces on the Python Web site. At the time of writing, there are conforming interfaces for the following databases: ODBC, Oracle, Informix, Solid, and MySQL. There are also (non-conforming) interfaces to Sybase and mSQL.

23.5.4 SWIG

SWIG (Simplified Wrapper and Interface Generator, developed by David Beazley) is a program development tool designed to make it easy to build scripting language interfaces to C/C++ programs. Its primary audience is scientists, engineers, and programmers who would like to build interactive C/C++ programs, but who would rather work on more interesting problems than figuring out how to extend their favorite scripting language or using an excessively complicated programming tool. SWIG is not Python specific, although its support for Python is very strong (and has motivated a number of SWIG features). Other languages supported include Tcl, Perl, and Guile (a Scheme dialect).

In a nutshell, SWIG turns C/C++ declarations into a working scripting language interface. C functions become commands, C variables become scripting-language variables, etc. By using ANSI C/C++ syntax, SWIG is easy to use, requires no modification to underlying C code, and is relatively simple to apply to existing applications.

23.6 Comparing Python to Other Languages

Python is often compared to other interpreted languages such as Java, JavaScript, Perl, Tcl, or Smalltalk. Comparisons to C++, Common Lisp, and Scheme can also be enlightening. In this section I will briefly compare Python to each of these languages. These comparisons concentrate on language issues only. In practice, the choice of a programming language is often dictated by other real-world constraints such as cost, availability, training, and prior investment, or even emotional attachment. Because these aspects are highly variable, it seems a waste of time to consider them much for this publication.

23.6.1 Java

Python programs are generally expected to run slower than Java programs, but they also take much less time to develop. Python programs are typically three to five times shorter than equivalent Java programs. This difference can be attributed to Python's built-in high-level data types and its dynamic typing. For example, a Python programmer wastes no time declaring the types of arguments or variables, and Python's powerful polymorphic list and dictionary types, for which rich syntactic support is built straight into the language, find a use in almost every Python program. Because of the runtime typing, Python's runtime must work harder than Java's runtime. For example, when evaluating the expression a+b, it must first inspect the objects a and b to find out their type, which is not known at compile time. It then invokes the appropriate addition operation, which may be an overloaded user-defined method. Java, on the other hand, can perform an efficient integer or floating point addition, but requires variable declarations for a and b, and does not allow overloading of the + operator for instances of user-defined classes.

For these reasons, Python is much better suited as a "glue" language, while Java is better characterized as a low-level implementation language. In fact, the two together make an excellent combination. Components can be developed in Java and combined to form applications in Python. Python can also be used to prototype components until their design can be "hardened" in a Java implementation. To support this type of development, a Python implementation written in Java is under development, which allows calling Python code from Java and vice versa. In this implementation, Python source code is translated to Java bytecode (with help from a runtime library to support Python's dynamic semantics).

23.6.2 JavaScript

Python's "object-based" subset is roughly equivalent to JavaScript. Like JavaScript (and unlike Java), Python supports a programming style that uses simple functions and variables without engaging in class definitions. However, for JavaScript, that is all there is. Python, on the other hand, supports writing much larger programs and better code reuse through a true object-oriented programming style, where classes and inheritance play an important role.

23.6.3 Perl

Python and Perl come from a similar background (Unix scripting, which both have long outgrown), and sport many similar features, but have a different philosophy. Perl emphasizes support for common application-oriented tasks, e.g., by having built-in regular expressions, file scanning, and report generating features. Python emphasizes support for common programming methodologies such as data structure design and object-oriented programming, and it encourages programmers to write readable (and thus maintainable) code by providing an elegant but not overly cryptic notation. As a consequence, Python comes close to Perl but rarely beats it in its original application domain; however, Python has an applicability well beyond Perl's niche.

23.6.4 Tcl

Like Python, Tcl is usable as an application extension language, as well as a stand-alone programming language. However, Tcl, which traditionally stores all data as strings, is weak on data structures, and executes typical code much slower than Python. Tcl also lacks features needed for writing large programs, such as modular namespaces. Thus, while a "typical" large application using Tcl usually contains Tcl extensions written in C or C++ that are specific to that application, an equivalent Python application can often be written in "pure Python." Of course, pure Python development is much quicker than having to write and debug a C or C++ component. It has been said that Tcl's one redeeming quality is the Tk toolkit. Python has adopted an interface to Tk as its standard GUI component library.

23.6.5 Smalltalk

Perhaps the biggest difference between Python and Smalltalk is Python's more "mainstream" syntax, which gives it a leg up on programmer training. Like Smalltalk, Python has dynamic typing and binding, and everything in Python is an object. However, Python distinguishes built-in object types from user-defined classes, and it currently does not allow inheritance from built-in types. Smalltalk's standard library of collection data types is more refined, while Python's library has more facilities for dealing with Internet and www realities such as e-mail, HTML, and FTP.

Python has a different philosophy regarding the development environment and distribution of code. Where Smalltalk traditionally has a monolithic "system image" which comprises both the environment and the user's program, Python stores both standard modules and user modules in individual files which can easily be rearranged or distributed outside the system. One consequence is that there is more than one option for attaching a GUI to a Python program, since the GUI is not built into the system.

23.6.6 C++

Almost everything said for Java also applies for C++, just more so. Where Python code is typically three to five times shorter than equivalent Java code, it is often five to ten times shorter than equivalent C++ code. Anecdotal evidence suggests that one Python programmer can finish in two months what two C++ programmers cannot complete in a year. Python shines as a glue language, used to combine components written in C++.

23.6.7 Common Lisp and Scheme

These languages are close to Python in their dynamic semantics, but so different in their approach to syntax that a comparison becomes almost a religious argument: Is Lisp's lack of syntax an advantage or a disadvantage? It should be noted that Python has introspective capabilities similar to those of Lisp, and Python programs can construct and execute program fragments on the fly. Usually, real-world properties are decisive: Common Lisp is big (in every sense), and the Scheme world is fragmented between many incompatible versions, where Python has a single, free, compact implementation.

Acknowledgments

Much of the section "Python in a Nutshell" was adapted from a description of Python by Martin von Löwis. I am grateful to everyone in the Python community who contributed to the design and implementation of Python, whether in the form of contributed code and fixes, criticism, or simply by being a satisfied user.

Further Reading

Books

The following books on Python have been published:

- *Internet Programming with Python*, by Aaron Watters, Guido van Rossum, and James Ahlstrom, MIS Press/Henry Holt publishers, 1996.
- *Programming Python*, by Mark Lutz, O'Reilly & Associates, 1996.
- *Das Python-Buch*, by Martin von Löwis and Nils Fischbeck (in German), Addison-Wesley-Longman, 1997.

O'Reilly expects to publish at least two more Python books whose working titles are *Learning Python*, by Mark Lutz and David Ascher, and *Using Python*, by Fredrik Lundh.

On-Line Resources

The official Python Web site at http://www.python.org serves as a central switchboard for all Python-related on-line resources, including a FAQ (frequently asked questions list) and a plethora of on-line documentation. It incorporates the Python ftp site, ftp://ftp.python.org, which contains the official Python source distributions, binary distributions for many platforms, and a comprehensive collection of third-party software. The Web and ftp sites are mirrored at a number of locations around the world.

A second Python-oriented Web site is the Python Starship site, a site for and by Python developers: http://starship.skyport.net (this URL may change, but the official Python Web site will always link to it). There are also a growing number of commercial sites for Python users; the official Python web site will link to these.

The official Python manual set consists of the following pieces:

- Python Tutorial
- Python Library Reference Manual
- Python Language Reference Manual
- Extending and Embedding the Python Interpreter
- Python/C API Reference Manual (new with Python 1.5)

These manuals can be printed from the LaTeX and FrameMaker sources that come with the Python source distribution. However, it is usually easier to browse them on-line at the Python Web site, download them from the Web site as PostScript (for printing) or HTML (for local on-line browsing).

Another excellent on-line tutorial is *The What, Why, Who, and Where of Python*, by Aaron Watters; it is UnixWorld Online Tutorial article No. 005, and accessible via the URL; http://www.unixworld.com/unixworld/archives/95/tutorial/005.html.

The Usenet newsgroup for discussion of all Python-related subjects, including the occasional Monty Python joke, is comp.lang.python. It is gatewayed into a mailing list (python-list-request@cwi.nl) for those who prefer mail to news. The Python Web site contains a list of other Python-related mailing list, including those of Special Interest Groups (SIGs). The newsgroup and most mailing lists are archived, and the Web site contains the archives or at least links to them.

24

BETA: A Block-Structured, Concurrent Object-Oriented Language

Ole Lehrmann Madsen
Aarhus University

24.1 Introduction

The BETA programming language has been developed in the Scandinavian tradition for object-orientation based on Simula. In this tradition, support for modeling and design have been important design goals for programming language design. There has thus been two accompanying design criteria for BETA. BETA should be a useful tool for modeling concepts and phenomena from an application domain, and it should be an efficient tool for implementing such models. To support modeling and design, a conceptual framework was developed together with the BETA language. The conceptual framework is a set of conceptual means for understanding knowledge about the real world. It includes means such as concepts and phenomena, identification of objects, identification of classes, classification, generalization/specialization, multiple classification, reference- and part-of-composition, etc. For a further description of the conceptual framework, see Madsen et al. (1993).

In this paper we concentrate on presenting the BETA language. Another important design goal for BETA has been simplicity and unification of language constructs. BETA is a small language, but the generality and power of the language makes BETA as expressive and often more expressive as mainstream languages like C++ and Java.

BETA is a statically typed language as Simula (Dahl et al., 1968), Eiffel (Meyer, 1988), C++ (Stroustrup, 1986), and Java (Arnold and Gosling, 1996). As most other object-oriented languages it is influenced by Simula, but perhaps to a higher degree than other languages, since BETA is one of the few languages that has adapted the Simula notions of block-structure, active objects, and the inner mechanism.

0-8493-3135-8/99/$0.00+$.50

A main characteristic of BETA is that it unifies abstraction mechanisms like class, procedure, function, generic class, type, process, and exception into one abstraction mechanism called pattern. A pattern may then be used as a class, procedure, function, etc. A pattern used as a class is often called a class pattern, a pattern used as a procedure is often called a procedure pattern, etc. An instance of a class pattern corresponds to an object in most object-oriented languages. An instance of a procedure pattern corresponds to a procedure activation record in most languages. An instance of a process pattern corresponds to an active object (process).

Besides keeping the language small, this unification has given a systematic treatment of all abstraction mechanisms and led to a number of new possibilities. For a class, it is possible to define subclasses. For a pattern it is similarly possible to define subpatterns, and when a pattern is used as a class, a subpattern is quite similar to a subclass. A pattern may also be used as a procedure (a procedure pattern). A subpattern of a procedure pattern is then a new possibility compared to most other languages. Subpatterns of procedure patterns make inheritance possible for procedures.

Most object-oriented languages support virtual functions. In BETA a pattern may be virtual and a virtual pattern used as a procedure (virtual procedure pattern) corresponds to virtual functions. A virtual class pattern is a possibility that is not available in most languages. Virtual class patterns may be used for parameters patterns with other patterns, and it is an alternative to template classes and generic classes.

As already mentioned, BETA is a block-structured language. This means that patterns can be arbitrarily nested. Nesting of procedures is well known from, e.g., Algol and Pascal, but the possibility of nesting classes is less common. Simula supported nested classes, C++ has a limited support for nested classes (Madsen, 1996) and recently nested classes (called inner classes) were added to Java.

BETA has active objects in the form of coroutines as known from Simula. In addition BETA supports concurrent active objects. Synchronization between active objects may be done using semaphores. However, a semaphore is a very low-level mechanism, and it is mainly used as a primitive to build higher level abstraction mechanisms such as monitors and Ada-like rendezvous. The pattern abstraction combined with the inner mechanism is a powerful means for defining concurrency abstractions.

The Mjølner System (Knudsen et al., 1994; The Mjølner System, 1998) is a professional environment for supporting object-oriented development with BETA. In addition to professional software development, the Mjølner System is well suited for teaching. The Mjølner System supports multiplatform development for Windows NT, Windows 95, Macintosh, and Unix. The system includes libraries and frameworks for GUI construction, 2-D graphics, meta-programming, basic data structures (such as containers), and interfaces to external languages. The system includes a number of tools such as a CASE tool, an interface builder, a source code browser, an integrated text- and structure editor, a debugger, an object browser, and a compiler. The CASE tool supports a subset of UML that corresponds to the abstraction mechanisms of BETA. This makes it possible to freely alternate between design using UML and programming using BETA. The tight integration with a CASE tool is one example of how BETA may be used to support design as well as implementation. The Mjølner System also supports a multiuser persistent object store based on type orthogonal persistence and a distributed implementation of BETA. For further details about the Mjølner System, see The Mjølner System, 1998.

In the rest of this paper the central mechanisms of BETA will be presented.

24.2 Patterns, a Unification of Abstraction Mechanisms

BETA does not distinguish between class, procedure, and other abstraction mechanisms. They are all unified into the general abstraction mechanism called pattern. A pattern may then be used as a class, procedure, etc. A pattern used as a class is often referred to as a class pattern. The definition of a class Person with data-items name, address, age and methods display, and changeAddress may in BETA look as follows:

```
Person:
   (# name,address: ^text;
     age: @ integer
     display: (# do name[] -> screen.putLine; ... #);
     changeAddress:
        (# newAddress: ^text
        enter newAddress[]
        do ...
        exit this(Person)[]
        #)
   #)
```

The pattern person is an example of a class pattern. Display and changeAddress are examples of procedure patterns. Let S be a reference to a Person:

```
S: ^Person
```

then the methods in S may be invoked as follows:

```
S.display;
'3966 Duncan Place, Palo Alto, CA94303'
   -> S.changeAddress
   -> S1[]
```

where S1 is declared as

```
S1: ^Person
```

The general form of a pattern declaration is:

```
name: super
   (# attributes
   enter input-parameters
   do imperative-list
   exit output-parameters
   #)
```

where

- *Name* is the name of the pattern.
- *Super* is a possible superpattern. If super is not specified, then the pattern is a subpattern of object.
- *Attributes* is a list of attributes where an attribute may be a data-item (like instance variable) or pattern.
- *Input-parameters* is a list of input parameters.
- *Imperative-list* is a list of imperatives that can be executed.
- *Output-parameters* is a list of output parameters.

An attribute may be a pattern. Such a pattern is often a procedure pattern (corresponding to a non-virtual procedure in Simula and C++), but it may also be a class pattern. The use of nested class patterns will be further discussed in Section 24.4.

Most parts of an object-descriptor may be empty, including super, attributes, enter-part do-part, and exit-part.

The class pattern person has no super, enter-part. do-part and exit-part.

The procedure pattern Display has no super, enter-part, and exit-part. The procedure pattern change-Address has no super.

amic reference variable

:r to instances of Person or subpatterns of Person, i.e., BETA supports subtype
ıer object-oriented languages.
nay be used to create instances of a pattern

ın instance of pattern Person is created and the [] operator specifies that a
nce is the value of the expression &Person[].*
nay be accessed through remote invocation

: a static part object:

together with the enclosing object and is a fixed part of this object. Whereas
ıle like S may refer to subpatterns of Person, a static part object like R refers
son. An attribute like R is thus type exact in the sense that its type (a pattern
(compile-time).
n of person is shown in the following example:

```
s: ^text;
r;

 -> screen.putLine;
 [] -> screen.putLine;
creen.putint;

ss:
:es: ^text
ıddress []
:ess [] -> address []
Person) []
```

/.

ective part objects support *whole-part composition* and dynamic references
ion (see Chapter 18 in Madsen et al., 1993).

attern Invocation

ınction between value assignment /equality and reference assignment/equality. If S is
reference to the object and S denotes the value of the object. For details see Madsen

ıvocation. An instance of S.display is created followed by an execution
ː instance of S.display being created plays the role of a procedure-
ıre-activation records are objects.

```
› Alto, CA94303'
```

ern invocation with input- and output-parameters: an instance of
ł966 Duncan Place, ...' is assigned to the enter-parameter newAddress,
ıngeAddress instance is executed and the exit-value this(Person)[] is
ș(Person)[] is a reference to the enclosing Person object.
enter- and exit-values, as illustrated by the following two procedure
ı*:

```
ṣ: ^text
ıddress [])
[]; newAddress [] -> address []
```

```
 ^text
nto street, city and state *)
te)
```

```
:aster Street, ...')
lress

ṣtreet [],theCity [],theState [])
```

.te are declared as follows:

```
ṣtate: ^text
```

ɔf Person:

```
;
ry: @integer;... #);
ıp: ^EmployeeList... #);
 ... #)
```

tterns of Person, and Manager and WhiteCollar are subpatterns of
ther class-based object-oriented languages.
fine subpattern hierarchies for procedure patterns

```
> screen.putint; INNER #)

group.display; INNER;... #)
```

ment.

Execution of displayEmployee takes place as follows:

1. The do-part of display is executed, i.e., name and age is displayed on the screen.
2. When inner is executed in display, the do-part of displayEmployee is executed.
3. In the do-part of displayEmployee, salary is first printed on the screen.
4. Execution of inner in displayEmployee is empty.
5. When execution of the do-part of displayEmployee has finished, the control returns to after inner in displayPerson.
6. When execution of the do-part of display is finished, execution of display is finished.

As mentioned in Step 4 above, execution of inner in displayEmployee is the empty action when executing displayEmployee. Consider a subpattern of displayEmployee

```
displayWhiteCollar: displayEmployee (# do ... #)
```

If displayWhiteCollar is executed then this will happen as described above for execution of displayEmployee, except for step 4 where execution of inner in the do-part of displayEmployee will imply that the do-part of displayWhiteCollar is executed. A possible inner in displayWhiteCollar will be the empty action.

24.3 Virtual Patterns

The procedure pattern attributes of Person in the previous examples are non-virtual corresponding to non-virtual procedures in Simula and C++. A pattern attribute may also be declared to be virtual. In the following example a virtual pattern print has been added to Person*

```
Person:
  (# ...
    print:< (# do ...; INNER #)
  #)
```

In subpatterns of person, the virtual patterns may be further bound

```
Employee: Person
  (# ...
    print::< (# ... #)
  #)
```

A major difference between BETA and other object-oriented languages is that virtual procedure patterns are not redefined. A subpattern can only define a specialization of the virtual patterns from the super pattern. Consider

```
E: ^employee
```

When executing

```
E.print
```

execution starts with the display defined in person. When inner is executed, the display in employee will be executed. The print attribute for an Employee is a subpattern of the display attribute defined in Person.

We may continue to further bind print in subpatterns

* Note: Person also has a non-virtual pattern display which in the following will be compared with the virtual pattern print.

```
WhiteCollar: Employee
   (# ...
     print::< (# ... #)
   #)
```

It is relevant to compare the non-virtual patterns display, displayEmployee, etc., with the virtual pattern print. For non-virtual patterns the pattern being referred is statically bound at compile-time, whereas for a non-virtual pattern the actual pattern is bound at runtime.

Consider

```
P: ^Person; E: ^Employee
```

Assume that P refers to an instance of Person and that E refers to an instance of Employee. The two imperatives:

```
P.display
P.print
```

will then produce the same result. Execution of

```
E.display;
```

will (only) display the Person attributes whereas the two imperatives

```
E.displayPerson
E.print
```

will give the same result.

Assume now that P refers to an instance of Employee, then

```
P.display
P.print
```

gives a different result. P.display will only display the person attributes, whereas P.print will display person and employee attributes. The virtual pattern print thus (almost) corresponds to standard object-oriented virtual functions as introduced by Simula and is now a main characteristic of most object-oriented languages.

There is, however, a major difference between virtual functions in BETA and most other languages. In most object-oriented languages, a virtual function may be redefined in a subclass. This is not the case in BETA where a virtual pattern is not redefined but extended to a more specialized behavior.

There is a trade off between security and flexibility. With traditional virtual functions it is always possible to redefine the behavior defined in a super-class. In BETA it is not possible to redefine the behavior of a super-class. The behavior can only be extended. This makes it possible to establish invariants in a super class stating that certain code is always executed. The traditional semantics gives more flexibility.

In general, code may be executed before and after or in a loop

```
myClass:
   (# ...
     foo:< (# do A1; INNER; A2 #);
     bar:<
        (#
     do B1;
          (for i: ... repeat C1; INNER; C2 for);
          B2
     #)
   #)
mySubClass: myClass
   (# foo::<
```

```
        (#
        do (* A1 has been executed #);
           I1;
           (* A2 will be executed *)
        #);
     bar::<
        (#
        do (* Initially B1 has been executed;
           * for each iteration of the for-loop,
           * C1 has been executed
           *)
           I2;
           (* For each iteration of the for-loop,
           * C2 will be executed;
           * for the last iteration B2 will be executed
           *)
        #)
     #)
```

24.3.1 Final Bindings

BETA also supports final bindings of virtual patterns as shown in the following version of employee:

```
employee: person
   (# ...
      print:: (# ... #)
   #)
```

Here the virtual pattern print is extended through a final binding. This means that print is no longer virtual and that it cannot be further bound in subpatterns of employee.

As in Simula, BETA supports virtual as well as non-virtual patterns. The reason is that this makes it possible to explicitly define which part of a class pattern can be redefined in a subpattern. If all procedure pattern attributes are virtual, it is much harder to make subpatterns. A common problem in object-oriented software construction is that programmers are not explicit about which procedures of a class are intended to be redefined in subclasses. In Simula, C++, and BETA the programmer has to explicitly decide which attributes are virtual and if it is meaningful to redefine a virtual attribute in subclasses. Although this problem can be handled through careful documentation, the distinction between virtual and non-virtual attributes makes the interface of a class to its possible subclasses much clearer. The price for this is, of course, less flexibility. However, for maintenance including use of application frameworks we prefer to sacrifice the lesser flexibility.

Final bindings are a natural link between virtual and non-virtual attributes, since the programmer may specify that a virtual can no longer be extended in subpatterns.

Final bindings are also useful in connection with parameterized patterns as discussed below, since they improve the possibilities for compile-type checking.

24.3.2 Virtual Class Patterns

Since patterns can be used as procedures as well as classes, the virtual concept also supports virtual class patterns. In BETA parameterized classes corresponding to templates in C++ and generic classes in Eiffel are supported by virtual class patterns. In the following example, a generic List pattern is shown:

```
List:
   (# element:< object;
      insert:
         (# e: element
```

```
            enter e[]
            do ...
            #);
        ...
    #)
```

The declaration

```
element:< object
```

specifies a virtual pattern attribute of List. Element is a pattern and may (almost) be used as a non-virtual.

In pattern insert, Element is used to specify the qualification of the reference e. Element is declared as virtual object. This means inside pattern List the only property known about the pattern Element is that it is a subpattern of Object. Since Object is the most general of all patterns, Element can be any pattern. This means that any object is legal as an input parameter to List.

Consider declarations

```
L: @ List; P: ^Person; E: Employee; S: Student; T: ^Text;
```

We may then insert elements into L:

```
P[] -> L.insert;
E[] -> L.insert;
S[] -> L.insert;
T[] -> L.insert;
```

As already said, the pattern Element in L is qualified as Object, we may insert any object into L. List is thus very similar to a template class in C++. Note, there is nothing special about List. It is a normal pattern and a template as in C++.

Suppose that we want to restrict the possible members of a given list. This may be done be defining a subpattern of List and then bind Element appropriately:

```
PersonList: List(# element::<Person #)
```

In PersonList, element has been further bound to Person, which means that in instances of PersonList, we know that Element is at least a Person or a subpattern of Person. Consider declarations:

```
PL: @ PersonList;
```

We may insert elements:

```
P[] -> PL.insert; E[] -> PL.insert; S[] -> PL.insert;
```

It is, however, not legal to insert a text as in

```
T[] -> PL.insert;
```

since Text is not a subpattern of Person.

We may continue to define subpatterns of PersonList to restrict the possible members of the list:

```
EmployeeList: List(# element::< Employee #)
```

In a list

```
EL: @ EmployeeList
```

we may now only insert employees:

```
E[] -> PL.insert;
```

It is no longer possible to insert Person or Students.

In [Thorup, 1997] virtual patterns has been suggested as an extension to Java.

24.3.2.1 Structural Equivalence

One weakness with virtual patterns that was recognized from the beginning was the strong reliance on name equivalence for patterns. One of the motivating examples for virtual class patterns was the Pascal array type which was modeled as follows:

```
Array: Type(# index:< IndexType; element:< Type #)
```

Pattern Type is supposed to model any Pascal type and IndexType is supposed to model Pascal index types. An actual array may then be declared as follows

```
myArray: Array(# index::SomeIndex; element::SomeType #)
```

where SomeIndex is some IndexType and SomeType is some type. It is possible to partially specify an array type as in the following example where the index is specified

```
myArray1: Array(# index::SomeIndex #);
```

A subpattern of myArray1 may then bind element:

```
myArray2: myArray1(# element:: SomeType #);
```

It is, however, also possible to bind the index and the element in the reverse order:

```
myArray3: Array(# element:: SomeType #);

myArray4: myArray3(# index::SomeIndex #);
```

The strict type rules of BETA imply that myArray2 and myArray4 are not the same type. In the original design of BETA this was foreseen as a problem, and it was considered to introduce a from of structural equivalence for patterns. The equivalence problem, however, rarely appeared in practice and no structural equivalence mechanism was introduced. As the amount of BETA code is growing, the problem has appeared more often. The typical example* is two libraries defining lists of text as in the following example. Image that TextList1 is defined in one library and textList2 by another library.

```
TextList1: List(# element::< Text #);
TextList2: List(# element::< Text #)
```

When using the two libraries together, it is not possible to exchange text lists.

The original structural equivalence mechanism considered for BETA was the following:

- Two patterns P1 and P2 are structural equivalent if the following conditions are fulfilled:
- P1 and P2 are direct or indirect subpatterns of some pattern P.
- P1 and P2 only contain bindings of virtual patterns defined in P, i.e., no new data-items or patterns are defined.
- Corresponding virtual in P1 and P2 are either bound to the same pattern or bound to patterns that are structurally equivalent.

Consider declarations

```
L1: ^ TextList1; L2: ^TextList2
```

L1 may then be used as a textList2 or vice versa. This could either be an implicit rule or an explicit syntax like

```
L1 [] as TextList2 -> L2[]
```

could be used. Structural pattern equivalence is not supported by the current version of BETA.

* Gilad Bracha recently inquired about this example.

24.3.2.2 Subtype Substitutability, Static Type Checking, and Covariant Subtyping

Languages, like Simula, C++, Eiffel, Java, and BETA, are often referred to as statically typed languages. The reason is that most type checking can be carried out at compile-time. This is opposed to languages like Smalltalk, CLOS, and Self where most type checking is carried out at runtime, and they are therefore referred to as dynamically typed languages. There are, however, some forms of dynamic type checking going on in most statically typed languages. One example is **reverse assignment**. Consider declarations:

```
P: ^Person; E: ^Employee
```

The legality of the assignment

```
E[] -> P[]
```

may be checked at compile-time, since E is known to be a subpattern of Person.

The reverse assignment

```
P[] -> E[]
```

is legal if P refers to an instance of Employee or a subpattern of Employee. This cannot, in general, be verified at compile-time. In most statically typed languages, this is checked at runtime. With virtual class patterns, a similar situation may arise.

Consider declarations:

```
PL: ^PersonList; P: ^Person
```

and the expression

```
P[] -> PL.insert
```

At a first glance, it might appear that the legality of this assignment may be checked at compile-time, since PersonList is declared to contain instances of pattern Person. PL may, however, refer to an instance of a subpattern of PersonList, e.g., EmployeeList. Consider the following code:

```
&EmployeeList[] -> PL[]; ...; P[] -> PL.insert
```

As PL refers to an instance EmployeeList, the call

```
P[] -> PL.insert
```

is illegal because insert of PL requires an Employee. It is therefore necessary to check the legality of this by means of a runtime check.

The virtual class pattern mechanism of BETA is an example of what is called covariant subtyping. In general, it is not possible to have subtype substitutability, static typing, and covariant subtyping without introducing restrictions. The restrictions may be in the form of type exact variables, final bindings, or forbidding invocations of virtual functions with parameters qualified by virtual class patterns (Torgersen, 1997). In Madsen and Møeller-Pedersen (1989), Madsen et al. (1990), and Madsen (1996) the virtual pattern mechanism and typing issues related to virtual class patterns is discussed.

24.4 Block Structure

Algol 60 introduced the notion of block structure, which essentially means that procedures may be arbitrarily nested. Simula extended this to also allow arbitrary nesting of classes, and BETA has followed this tradition. The previous examples have already shown several examples of nested patterns. Pattern Person contains patterns Display and changeAddress. Person is a class pattern and Display and change-Address are procedure patterns. This use of nested patterns is not particularly interesting since it corresponds to a class with local procedures. In this section we will show examples of nested class patterns. Such examples have, to a great extent, been documented in the literature (Madsen and Møeller-Petersen, 1992; Madsen et al., 1993; Madsen 1994 and 1996; and Østerbye, 1990). In many of these examples it is shown how nested class patterns may be used as an alternative to multiple inheritance. In the following we show examples of how nested patterns may be used as an alternative interfaces as found in Objective-C (Thorup, 1999) and Java.

In BETA an interface may be defined as a class pattern that only contains the signature of virtual procedure patterns. Consider an interface Printable that may be defined for objects that can be printed to a screen, file, or text. Printable may be defined as follows:

```
Printable:
   (# Print:< (# do INNER #);
     Separator:< (# ch: @char enter ch do INNER #);
     Medium:< (# S: stream enter S[] do INNER #);
   #);
```

where stream* is a superpattern for text, file, and screen:

```
stream: (# ... #);
text: stream(# ... #);
file: stream: (# ... #);
screen: @ stream(# ... #);
```

The idea is that this interface supports printing to a text, file, or screen. The actual stream may be set by the Medium operation. Items to be printed may be separated by some character that can be set by the Separator operation.

If we want a Person to be printable we may define a subpattern of Printable as an attribute of Person as shown in the following example:

```
Person:
   (# name, address: ^text;
     age: @integer;
     ...
     asPrintable: Printable
       (# Print::<
         (#
         do name[] -> theMedium.putText;
           theSeparator -> theMedium.put;
           address[] -> theMedium.putText;
           theSeparator -> theMedium.put;
           age -> theMedium.putInt;
           theMedium.newline;
         #);
       Separator::< (# do ch -> theSeparator #);
       Medium::< (# do S[] -> theMedium[] #);
     exit this(asPrintable)[]
     #);
   theMedium: stream;
   theSeparator: @char
#);
```

* The Mjølner libraries contains such patterns. As can be seen screen is not a pattern but a singular object.

The subpattern asPrintable specifies an implementation of Printable for pattern Person. Note that all of the operations, Print, Separator, and Medium, make use of data-items (variables) in the enclosing Person object. Consider declarations

```
P: @Person; S: ^Printable;
```

We may then obtain the Printable interface by executing

```
P.asPrintable -> S[]
```

and execute expressions like

```
screen[] -> S.medium; ';'-> S.Separator; S.print;
```

The reference S may refer to any Printable object, i.e., a Printable interface may be declared within several class patterns. The combination of nested class patterns and block structure in this case handles access to the state of the actual object implementing Printable.

Using these techniques, it is possible to define several interfaces. Another example may be an interface like Sortable:

```
Sortable:
   (# key:< (# K: @integer do INNER exit K#);
      lessThan:<
         (# item: ^Sortable; aBoolean: @boolean
         enter item[]
         do (key < item.key) -> aBoolean;
            INNER
         exit aBoolean
         #)
   #)
```

Person may then define a nested subpattern of Sortable:

```
Person:
   (# ...
      asPrintable: Printable(# ... #);
      asSortable: Sortable
         (# key::< (# do (* convert name into key *) #);#)
   #);
P: @Person;
sortList: @ List(# element::Sortable #);
P.asSortable[] -> sortList.insert;
```

Note that in this example the operation lessThan is specified in the Sortable interface and need not be specified in asPrintable within Person.

The above technique of using class patterns with procedure pattern signatures to define interfaces and then to implement these interfaces as nested patterns is also applied as technique for supporting the Common Object Model (COM) in (Rogerson, 1997) BETA.

24.5 Concurrency

A BETA object may be active in the sense that it may have an associated set of imperatives executed as an active thread. An active BETA object may be a non-preemptive lightweight process, in the sense that control transfer between active objects is only carried out when specific control operations are executed. This form of active object is similar to the Simula notion of coroutine. For details about coroutines in BETA see Madsen et al. 1993.

An active BETA object may also execute in true concurrency. The following example includes three objects: a bank account of a person (Joe), an object representing Joe, and one representing a bank agent:

```
(#Account: ...;
  JoesAccount: @ Account;
  bankAgent: @ |
    (#
    do cycle(# do ...; 400->JoesAccount.deposit; ... #)
    #);
  Joe: @ |
    (#
    do cycle(# do ...; 150->JoesAccount.withDraw; ... #)
    #)
do bankAgent.fork;{start concurrent execution of bankAgent}
  Joe.fork;{start concurrent execution of Joe}
#)
```

The details of `Account` will be given later. The "|" following "@" in the declarations of `Joe` and `bankAgent` describe that these objects are active objects. The do-parts of these objects contain a `cycle` imperative that executes a list of actions forever. The `bankAgent` deposits money on Joe's account and Joe withdraws the money. Since the `bankAgent` and `Joe` execute concurrently, access to the account must be synchronized.

The basic mechanism for synchronizing access to shared objects is the semaphore. A semaphore is a low-level mechanism and should only be used to define higher level synchronization abstractions. The pattern mechanism of BETA makes it easy to define synchronization abstractions like monitor and Ada-like rendezvous. The inner mechanism is especially useful here. In the following pattern `Account` is defined by means of a monitor pattern:

```
Account: monitor
  (# balance: @integer;
    deposit: entry
      (# amount: @integer
      enter amount
      do balance + amount -> balance
      #);
    withdraw: entry
      (# amount: @integer
      enter amount
      do balance - amount -> balance
      #)
  #)
```

Account is a subpattern of monitor and the operations `deposit` and `withdraw` are subpatterns of pattern `entry` defined within `monitor`. The definition of `monitor` and `entry` ensures that `Account` behaves like a monitor. Pattern `monitor` is defined in the following way:

```
monitor:
(# mutex: @semaphore;
   entry: (# do mutex.P; INNER; mutex.V #);
   init:< (# do mutex.V; INNER #)
  #)
```

A `monitor` object has a semaphore attribute, `mutex`, that is controlled by the abstract superpattern `entry`. Any operation inheriting from `entry` can only execute its do-part (via `inner` in `entry`) if the `mutex` semaphore is not blocked. When the operation completes it releases the semaphore after returning from `inner` in `entry`. Thus all details of the `monitor` implementation are hidden in the abstract `monitor` pattern.

The next example shows a concurrent BETA program using Ada-like rendezvous for communication. Three concurrent objects: Buf, Prod, and Cons are defined. Buf is a buffer that can hold one char. Prod and Cons are a producer- and consumer object, respectively. They just repeatedly produce/consume a character.

A produced char is transferred to the buffer by invoking the Put operation. Similarly a char is obtained from the buffer by the consumer by invoking the Get operation. The buffer can only hold one character at a time, so a new char cannot be delivered (via Put) before the previous char has been obtained (via Get).

The buffer is implemented by an active object in the form of an Ada-like task that controls which operations it is willing to accept. The do-part of Buf is a cycle-imperative that alternates between accepting on its in-port and on its out-port. The Put operation is associated with the in-port since it is declared as a subpattern of in.entry. The Get operation is in a similar way associated with the out-port.

An imperative

```
in.accept
```

blocks the Buf-object until a Buf.put has been executed. Similarly when Buf.put is executed by Prod, Prod is blocked until Buf executes in.accept.

```
(# Buf: @ | System
   (# in, out: @Port;
     ch: @char; (* holds the buffer element *)
     Put: in.entry(# c: @char enter c do c -> ch #);
     Get: out.entry(# c: @char do ch -> c exit c #);
     do cycle(# do in.accept; out.accept #)
     #)
  Prod: @ | System
     (# do cycle(#do ...; aChar -> Buf.put; ... #)#);
  Cons: @ | System
     (#do cycle(#do ...; Buf.get -> aChar; ... #)#);
do Prod.fork; Buf.fork; Cons.fork
#)
```

The patterns System, Port, entry, and accept are abstractions implemented by means of semaphores using patterns and inner. In Madsen et al., 1993 a number of more elaborate examples of implementing concurrency abstractions are shown, including a complete implementation of a monitor (as in Vaucher, 1975) and Ada-like rendezvous.

24.6 Final Remarks

In this paper we have tried to give an overview of BETA and describe the most common mechanisms. There are a few mechanisms that have not been discussed.

- As mentioned in the introduction, patterns may also be used to define exceptions. More precisely, virtual procedure patterns are used to support the so-called static exception model introduced in Knudsen (1984). In Madsen et al. (1993) details of how static exceptions are supported in BETA are described.
- BETA does not have any rules for information hiding like private, public, and protected. Instead the so-called fragment system may be used for this. The fragment system is used for modularizing BETA programs. It makes it possible to split BETA code into interface modules and implementation modules and hide private attributes. For details see Madsen et al. (1993).
- A pattern is a first class value in the sense that patterns may be passed as parameters and returned as the result of procedures. A so-called pattern variable may refer to patterns and be assigned different patterns. For procedure patterns this corresponds to procedure pointers, but in the form of closures. As patterns can be classes, a pattern variable may refer to class pattern closures, i.e., class patterns can also be passed around. For details see Madsen et al. (1993).

Finally, the best way of getting to know BETA is to obtain the Mjølner System. A free personal version is available from The Mjølner System (1998).

Acknowledgments

BETA was designed by Bent Bruun Kristensen, Birger Møller-Pedersen, Kristen Nygaard, and the author. Many people have influenced the design of BETA, see Madsen et al. (1993) for a long list. During the last 10 years, the main influence has been from developers and users at Mjølner Informatics and Aarhus University.

References

Arnold, K. and Gosling, J. 1996. *The Java Programming Language.* Addison-Wesley.

Dahl, O.J. Nygaard, K. and Myrhaug, B. 1968. Simula 67 Common Base Language, Technical Report Publ. no. S-2, Norwegian Computing Center, Oslo.

Goldberg, A. and Robson, D. 1983. *Smalltak-80: The Language and its Implementation.* Addison-Wesley.

Knudsen, J.L. 1984. Exception handling — a static approach, *Software Pract. Exper.*, May, 429-49.

Knudsen, J.L., Löfgren, M., Madsen, O.L. and Magnusson, B. 1994. *Object-Oriented Environments — The Mjølner Approach.* Prentice-Hall, Englewood Cliffs, NJ.

Kristensen, B.B., Madsen, O.L., Møller-Pedersen, B. and Nygaard, K. 1983. Abstraction Mechanisms in the BETA programming language. In Proc. POPL'83, Austin, TX.

Madsen, O.L. 1995. Open issues in object-oriented programming – a Scandinavian perspective, *Software Pract. Exper.*

Madsen, O.L., Magnusson, B. and Møller-Pedersen, B. 1990. Strong Typing of Object-Oriented Languages Revisited, in Proc. OOPSLA'90, Ottawa, Canada. Also in Knudsen, J.L., Löfgren, M., Madsen, O.L. and Magnusson, B. 1994. *Object-Oriented Environments — The Mjølner Approach.* Prentice-Hall, Englewood Cliffs, NJ.

Madsen, O.L. An Overview of BETA, in Knudsen, J.L., 1994. *Object-Oriented Environments — The Mjølner Approach.* Prentice-Hall, Englewood Cliffs, NJ.

Madsen, O.L., Møller-Pedersen, B. and Nygaard, K. 1993. *Object-Oriented Programming in the BETA Programming Language.* Addison-Wesley/ACM Press.

Madsen, O.L. and Møller-Pedersen, B. 1989. Virtual classes, a powerful mechanism in object-oriented languages, OOPSLA'89.

Madsen, O.L. and Møller-Pedersen, B. Part Objects and their Locations, *Tools.*

Meyer, B. 1988. *Object-Oriented Software Construction.* Prentice-Hall, Englewood Cliffs, NJ.

Østerbye, K. 1990. Parts, Wholes and Sub-Classes. In Proc. European Simulation Multiconference.

Rogerson, D. 1997. *Inside COM — Microsoft's Component Object Model.* Microsoft Press.

Stroustrup, B. 1986. *The C++ Programming Language.* Addison-Wesley.

The Mjølner System, http://www.mjolner.com.

Thorup, K.K. 1997. Virtual types for Java, ECOOP'97, *Springer Lecture Notes in Computer Science,* Vol. ??.

Thorup, K.K. 1999. Objective-C, *Handbook of Object Technolog.*, Zamir, S., Ed., CRC Press, Boca Raton, FL.

Torgersen, M. 1997. Virtual Types can be Statically Safe, Proc. FOOL '97.

Vaucher, J. 1975. Prefixed procedures, a structuring concept for operations, *INFOR,* 13(3), Oct.

IV

Object-Oriented Frameworks

Saba Zamir
Senior Information Technology Consultant

A framework defines a specific method by which multiple objects are used in conjunction to perform one or more tasks that cannot be performed by any single object. An object-oriented framework provides a way of capturing a reusable relationship between objects, so that those objects do not have to be reassembled within the same context each time they are needed. A singular object within the framework has the capability of being replaced by another similar object, without loss of functionality. Frameworks can be purchased and/or reused. Thus, predeveloped programming expertise can be aptly utilized in the development of future projects. The effort required to develop a new application is proportional to the difference in functionality between an existing framework and the new application.

This section contains chapters that describe these concepts in greater detail.

Second, frameworks are by their nature incomplete. Whereas an application design has all of the components it needs to execute and perform its task, a framework design will have places within it that need to be instantiated by adding concrete solutions to a specific application problem. A framework does not cover all of the functionality required by a particular domain, but instead abstracts the common functionality required by many applications, incorporating it into the common design, and leaving the variable functionality to be filled in by the framework user.

Due to these differences, framework design focuses on providing flexible abstractions that cover the functionality required by applications within a domain and making the framework easy to use. These abstractions in turn provide ways in which application developers can customize the framework. Object-oriented technology is a natural fit for frameworks. Just as a subclass is a specialization of a parent class, an application can be thought of as a specialization of a more general framework. One of the ways to use a framework is to specialize the generic classes that are provided in the framework into application specific concrete classes.

There is yet to be an established standard for designing and developing frameworks. The purpose of this chapter is not to propose a standard, but instead to identify some of the key issues and techniques that affect framework design. Hopefully, as framework development becomes more common and better understood, standard approaches will emerge. We assume that the reader is already familiar with object-oriented design, so we will focus on the factors that differ between regular application vs. framework development. Several properties, such as ease of use and flexibility, have been identified in the frameworks literature as aiding the reuse of the framework. We discuss several techniques, such as the benefits of using inheritance, composition, and the use of hooks which help a framework attain these properties. Some key terms are defined in Section 25.2 and the benefits of using frameworks are described in Section 25.3. Sections 25.4, 25.5, and 25.6 form the core of this chapter, describing the issues to consider when designing frameworks and methodologies for doing the actual design. Section 25.7 briefly discusses framework deployment issues. Section 25.8 summarizes the chapter and lists some of the open issues in framework design.

25.2 Concepts and Properties of Frameworks

Before discussing framework design, we define some concepts and terms associated with frameworks, starting with the roles involved in framework technology and a more in-depth look at the parts of a framework.

25.2.1 Users and Developers of Frameworks

Three different roles can be associated with the development and use of frameworks:

1. *Framework designers* or framework developers, develop the original framework.
2. *Framework users,* sometimes called application developers or framework clients, use (reuse) the framework to develop applications.
3. *Framework maintainers* refine and redevelop the framework to fit new requirements.

The different roles are not necessarily filled by different people. Often the framework designer is also one of the framework users and framework maintainers.

25.2.2 Framework Concepts

Several different parts can be identified within an application developed from a framework as shown graphically in Figure 25.1. Applications are developed from frameworks by filling in missing pieces and customizing the framework in the appropriate areas. Application development is discussed in Chapter 26.

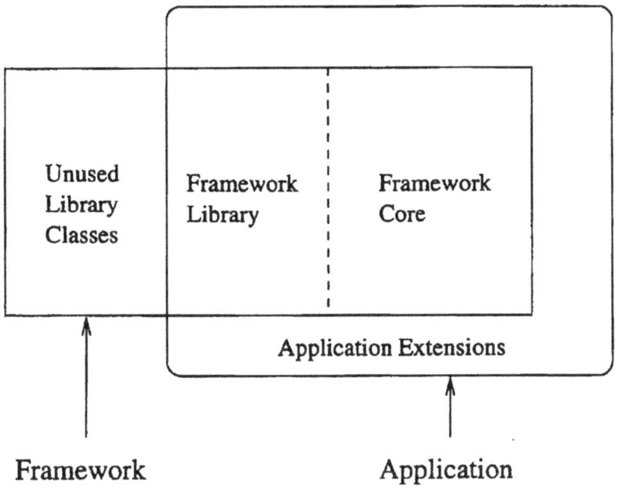

FIGURE 25.1 Application developed from a framework.

The parts of a framework are

- Framework Core — The core of the framework, generally consisting of abstract classes, defines the generic structure and behavior of the framework, and forms the basis for the application developed from the framework. However, the framework core can also contain concrete classes that are meant to be used as is in all applications built from the framework.
- Framework Library — Extensions to the framework core consisting of concrete components that can be used with little or no modification by applications developed from the framework.
- Application Extensions — Application specific extensions made to the framework, also called an *ensemble* [10].
- Application — In terms of the framework, the application consists of the framework core, the used framework library extensions, and any application specific extensions needed.
- Unused Library classes — Typically, not all of the classes within a framework will be needed in an application that can be developed from the framework.

A simplified example of the HotDraw framework [18] is shown in Figure 25.2. HotDraw is a framework for building graphical editors, such as class diagram editors, written in Smalltalk.

The core of the HotDraw framework consists of classes that define the interactions and interfaces of the *key abstractions* of the framework. Some of the key abstractions in HotDraw are `Figures` (along with `CompositeFigures` and `Drawings`), which represent items within a diagram such as lines and boxes, `Tools` which plug into the `DrawingController` to handle user actions such as moving `Figures` around on the screen or creating new `Figures`, and `DrawingViews` which handle the display for the application.

Some of the pre-built components supplied with HotDraw in its framework library consist of `SelectionTool` for selecting and moving `Figures` and `RectangleTool` for creating `RectangleFigures` within a `Drawing`. These are tools that may be useful in any application, but do not necessarily need to be included in every application built from the framework. Common `Figures` are also provided, such as `RectangleFigure` for representing rectangles and `TextFigure` for text labels.

HotDraw applications often require new application specific `Tools` and `Figures` to be derived. As an example, two application specific classes are shown in Figure 25.2. The complete application allows Object Modeling Technique (OMT) [31] class diagrams to be drawn and edited, but only two classes are shown

HotDraw, `DrawingController` is an example of a frozen class. The `Tools` used may vary, but the `DrawingController` remains a constant underlying mechanism for iteration.

25.2.4 Framework Categorization

Several different means of classifying frameworks have been proposed. Here we present three relatively orthogonal views of frameworks. A framework can be categorized by its scope, its primary mechanism for adaptation and the mechanism by which it is used. The scope defines the area to which the framework is applicable, whether a single domain or across domains. The adaptation mechanism describes whether the framework relies primarily upon composition or inheritance for reuse. Finally, the means of usage describes how the framework interacts with the application extensions; by either calling the application extensions, or having the extensions call the framework.

25.2.4.1 Scope

The scope of the framework describes how broad an area the framework is applicable too. Adair [1] defines three framework scopes.

- *Application frameworks* contain horizontal functionality that can be applied across domains. They incorporate expertise common to a wide variety of problems. These frameworks are usable in more than one domain. Graphical user interface frameworks are a typical example of an application framework and are included in most development packages.
- *Domain frameworks* contain vertical functionality for a particular domain. They capture expertise that is useful for a particular problem domain. Examples exist in the domains of operating systems [8], manufacturing systems [32], client-server communications [6], and financial engineering [11].
- *Support frameworks* provide basic system-level functionality upon which other frameworks or applications can be built. A support framework might provide services for file access or basic drawing primitives.

25.2.4.2 Customization

The means of customizing is another way in which frameworks can be categorized. Johnson and Foote [20] define two types of frameworks, white box and black box. While this is an important dichotomy, a framework will often have elements of both black box and white box frameworks rather than be clearly one or the other.

- *White box frameworks,* also called *architecture-driven frameworks* [1] rely upon inheritance for extending or customizing the framework. New functionality is added by creating a subclass of a class that already exists within the framework. White box frameworks typically require a more in-depth knowledge to use.
- *Black box frameworks,* also called *data-driven frameworks* [1], use composition and existing components rather than inheritance for customization of the framework. Configuring a framework by selecting components tends to be much simpler than inheriting from existing classes, so black box frameworks tend to be easier to use. Johnson argues that frameworks tend to mature toward black box frameworks.

25.2.4.3 Interaction

Andersen Consulting [34] differentiates frameworks based on how they interact with the application extensions, rather than their scope or how they are customized.

- *Called frameworks* correspond to code libraries (such as the Eiffel libraries [26] or Booch's libraries [5]). Applications use the framework by calling functions or methods within the library.
- *Calling frameworks* incorporate the control loop within the framework itself. Applications provide the customized methods or components which are called by the framework ("don't call us, we'll call you"). In this chapter we will be primarily focusing on calling frameworks, although much of the material applies to called frameworks as well.

25.2.5 Desirable Properties

Frameworks are meant to be reused to develop applications, so reusability is very important. Software reusability means that ideas and code are developed once, and then used to solve many software problems, thus enhancing productivity, reliability, and quality. With frameworks, reusability applies not only to the code, but also the design. A good framework has several properties such as ease of use, extensibility, flexibility, and completeness [1] which can help to make it more reusable.

25.2.5.1 Ease of Use

Ease of use refers to an application developers ability to use the framework. The framework should be both easy to understand and facilitate the development of applications; therefore ease of use is one of the most important properties a framework can have. Frameworks are meant to be reused, but even the most elegantly designed framework will not be used if it is hard to understand [5]. In order to improve the user's understanding of the framework, the interaction (both the interface and the paths of control) between the application extensions and the framework should be simple and consistent. That is, the hooks should be simple, small, and easy to understand and use. Additionally, the framework should be well-documented with descriptions of the hooks, sample applications, and examples that the application developer can use.

25.2.5.2 Extensibility

If new components or properties can be easily added to a framework, then it is extensible. Even if a framework is easy to use, it must also be extensible to be truly useful. A simple parameterized linked list component may be completely closed and easy to use, but its reusability is enhanced if it can be easily extended to include new operations.

25.2.5.3 Flexibility

Flexibility is the ability to use the framework in more than one context. In general, this applies to the domain coverage of the framework. Frameworks that can be used in multiple domains, such as graphical user interface frameworks, are especially flexible. If a framework is applicable to a wide domain, or across domains, then it will be reused more often by more developers. However, flexibility must be balanced with ease of use. In general, a framework with many abstract hooks will be flexible, but will also be either difficult to understand, require too much work on the part of the application developer to use, or both.

25.2.5.4 Completeness

Even though frameworks are incomplete, since they cannot cover all possible variations within a domain, relative completeness is a desirable property. Default implementations can be provided for the abstractions within the framework so they do not have to be re-implemented within every application, and application developers can run the framework to gain a better understanding of how it works. The framework library can provide the implementations of common operations, which the developer can choose, making the framework easier to use as well as more complete.

25.2.5.5 Consistency

Consistency among interface conventions, or class structures, is also desirable. Names should be used consistently within the framework. Ultimately, consistency should speed the developers understanding of the framework and help to reduce errors in its use.

25.3 Benefits and Concerns of Building a Framework

The design of any type of framework requires the consideration of many issues. The first, and possibly the most important, decision is whether or not a framework is needed. Although frameworks have benefits such as design reuse, there are also drawbacks, such as the increased cost of building a good object-oriented framework as compared to a single application.

25.3.1 Benefits

1. **Reuse.** Quite simply, the main benefit of frameworks is the ability to reuse not only the implementation of a system, but the design as well. The framework helps to reduce the cognitive distance [24] between the problem to be solved and the solution embodied in a software system. Once a framework has been developed, the problem domain has already been analyzed and a design has been produced which can be reused to quickly develop new applications.
2. **Maintenance.** Since all applications developed from a framework have a common design and code base, maintenance of all the applications is made easier.
3. **Quality.** The framework not only provides a reusable design, but also a tested design proven to work, therefore forming a quality base for developing new applications.

25.3.2 Concerns

1. **High Cost.** Building a framework is often significantly more costly than developing a single application. A great deal of time is spent defining and refining the abstractions that form the core of the framework.
2. **Shifting Domains.** The domain in which the framework is to be built must be relatively stable and well-understood. If the domain changes, then, unless the framework can be easily modified to fit the new domain, much of the effort put into development will be lost.
3. **Evolution.** Any changes to the framework will affect the applications developed with the framework. If the architecture or any interfaces change then upgrading applications to use the new framework may be costly. If the applications are not upgraded, then the advantage of having a common code base is lost.

Typically, the best candidates for frameworks are applications that are developed repeatedly, with minor variations [35]. Domains that change rapidly, or are new enough not to have a base of existing applications, are generally not good candidates for frameworks.

25.4 Design Process

Frameworks should be developed from "scratch." It is unlikely that an application can be transformed into a framework in a straightforward manner. Frameworks, just like most reusable software, have to be designed to be reusable from the very beginning.

As Booch [5] suggests, object-oriented development in general and framework development in particular requires an iterative or cyclic approach in which the framework is defined, tested, and refined a number of times. Additionally, small teams or even individual developers are recommended for framework development so that each member of the development team has a good overall understanding of the framework.

Standard software development methodologies are not sufficient for developing object-oriented frameworks [30]. For example, traditional methods do not take into account the need to design the hooks of a framework which provide for the flexibility and extensibility of the framework. They tend to focus on the functional requirements. Hooks are also requirements of a framework, but they are quasi-functional. They do not perform functions within the system, but instead allow the framework to be customized to support a wide range of functionality. Hooks should be considered throughout the process of requirements analysis through to testing [9].

While there is no agreed upon standard for designing frameworks, some techniques have been proposed [19, 30, 34, 35]. The proposed approaches are still immature and provide guidelines rather than a fully defined methodology. Each of the approaches can be characterized by several general steps: analysis, design and implementation, testing, and refinement.

These steps are the traditional stages of software development, but each is tailored to the design of frameworks. Typically, the framework is not built during a single pass, but through multiple iterations of the steps.

25.4.1 Analysis

As with any type of software development, the first stage is the analysis of the problem domain. In the case of frameworks, this requires a domain expert. The expert identifies the size of the domain that the framework covers, the abstractions that will be incorporated within the framework, and how variations between applications within the domain will be dealt with.

One of the key decisions that needs to be made when building a framework is deciding on how large a domain it will cover. Does the framework apply to a large domain, a narrow part of a domain, or even apply to several domains? There are benefits and drawbacks to frameworks that cover a large domain or a large part of a domain vs. small frameworks which cover a narrow part of a domain. A wide framework will be reusable in more situations, and thus be flexible, but may be unwieldy and difficult to maintain. Building a widely applicable framework is a significant undertaking, requiring lots of resources.

Narrow frameworks may be insufficient for an application, and developers will have to add significant amounts of additional functionality to produce an application. Narrow frameworks are also easily affected by changes in the domain. While a wider framework might be able to evolve, a narrow framework may no longer be applicable. On the other hand, narrow frameworks do tend to be smaller and less complex and therefore easier to maintain. They are also potentially easier to use in other contexts because they are not all encompassing of a particular domain. Finally, using a large framework often requires using all of the functionality within it, regardless if it is needed or not. Having several smaller frameworks instead of one large one allows framework users to only take the functionality they need. In general, the benefits of building small frameworks outweighs the drawbacks, so small frameworks are typically recommended.

After the domain of the framework has been determined, analyzing the domain of the framework helps to determine the primary or key abstractions that will form the core of the framework. For example, graphical drawing framework, such as HotDraw, will contain abstractions for representing the drawing, the figures the drawing contains, and the graphical tools used to manipulate the figures.

Examining existing applications within a the domain of the framework is a useful means of identifying the abstractions [19]. In order to gain domain expertise, a framework designer may also want to build an application within the domain if the designer is not already an expert in the domain [35].

Developing scenarios for the operation of the framework and reviewing them with potential users of the framework is another recommended analysis approach [34]. Scenarios help to define the requirements of the framework without committing developers prematurely to any design decisions. The scenarios can be abstracted into use cases [17] to help identify the primary abstractions and interaction patterns the framework needs to provide.

The hot spots, the places of variation within the framework, also need to be identified. Again, examining existing applications will help identify which aspects change from application to application and which remain constant.

25.4.2 Design and Implementation

The design determines the structures for the abstractions, frozen spots, and hot spots. The design and implementation of the framework are often intertwined. Abstractions can be difficult to design properly the first time and parts of a framework may have to be redesigned and reimplemented as the abstractions become better understood [30]. Parts of the framework may undergo redesign even while other parts are being implemented.

In order to refine the abstractions, reviews of the design are recommended [34]. Reviews examine not only the functionality the design provides, but also the hooks and means of client interaction provided by the framework.

Specific techniques that aid in the design of frameworks will be discussed later in this chapter. However, some general guidelines have been identified through experience by framework developers working on the Taligent frameworks and ET++. In order to develop easy-to-use and flexible frameworks, Taligent [35] suggests:

- Reducing the number of classes and methods users have to override
- Simplifying the interaction between the framework and the application extensions
- Isolating platform-dependent code
- Doing as much as possible within the framework
- Factoring code so that users can override limiting assumptions
- Providing notification hooks so that users can react to important state changes within the framework

Some additional general design advice proposed by Birrer and Eggenschwiler (1993) is to:

- Consolidate similar functionality into a single abstraction
- Break down larger abstractions into smaller ones with greater flexibility
- Implement each key variation of an abstraction as a class (and include it in the framework library)
- Use composition rather than inheritance

At this stage, the specific hooks for each hot spot must also be designed and specified. The hooks show specific ways in which the framework can be adapted to an application, and thus are an important part of the framework. Hooks can be described in an informal manner or a semi-formal manner using templates [12].

Often, trade offs must be considered when designing the hooks and structuring the hot spots in general. Frameworks cannot be arbitrarily flexible in all directions (i.e., they only bend in certain ways and bending them in other ways will break them). Some of the required flexibility can be determined by examining existing applications. Often the framework designer has to rely on experience and intuition to make these trade offs. Subsequent testing may require changes in the structure of the hot spots. Further trade offs occur between flexibility and ease of use. The most flexible framework would have very little actually defined and thus require a great deal of work on the part of the framework user. The framework should incorporate as much functionality as it can and all the interfaces should be clearly defined and understandable, sometimes at the expense of flexibility.

25.4.3 Testing

There are two types of testing that a framework can undergo. First, a framework should be tested in isolation; that is, without any application extensions. Testing the framework by itself helps to identify defects within the framework, and in so doing it isolates framework defects from errors that might be caused by the application extensions, or in the interface between the framework and the application extensions. Andersen Consulting has followed an approach of requiring framework designers to produce a test plan that provides a minimum of 50% block coverage of the framework with a goal of 70% coverage [34]. It is important to catch defects in a framework since any defects will be passed on to all applications developed from the framework. Defects in the framework force users to either fix the defects themselves, or find a work around, both of which reduce the benefits of using the framework.

Second, the true test of a framework really only occurs when it is used to develop applications. Designers never truly know if a framework can be reused successfully until it actually has been. Using the framework serves as a means of testing the hooks of the framework, or the points where interactions between application extensions and the framework occur. Using the framework also helps to expose areas where the framework is incomplete and helps to show areas where the framework needs to be more flexible or easier to use. The applications produced from this kind of testing can be kept as examples of how to use the framework and are also valuable for regression testing when parts of the framework change.

25.4.4 Refinement

After testing, the abstractions of the framework will often need to be extended or refined. Building a framework is a highly iterative process, so many cycles through these steps will be performed before the final framework is produced. A rule of thumb among framework developers is that three separate applications must be developed from a framework before it is ready for deployment and distribution. After the core has been successfully developed and implemented, the framework library can be further developed to make the framework more complete.

25.5 General Framework Development Techniques

25.5.1 Abstract and Concrete Classes

A good framework often has a core of abstract classes which embody the basic architecture and interactions among the classes of the framework. Not all of the core classes need to be or should be abstract, but the ones involved in hot spots generally are. For example, HotDraw has classes for `Figure` and `Tool` which must be customized to use. Framework designers derive new classes from abstract classes by filling in the methods deliberately left unimplemented in the abstract classes or by adding functionality. The abstract classes should be flexible and extensible. These classes capture the properties of key abstractions, but just as importantly, they capture the interactions between elements of the framework as well. The `Figure` class interacts with many classes to provide its functionality, such as `Tool`, `Drawing`, and `DrawingView`, and this interaction is defined at the level of the `Figure` class. Any classes derived from it will follow that interaction.

A framework will generally have a small number of these core classes [14], but will also have a number of concrete classes which form the framework library. These concrete classes inherit from the abstract classes but provide specific and complete functionality that may be reused directly without modification in an application developed from the framework. HotDraw provides a number of `Figure` classes within the library that can be easily reused. However, the library can also contain parameterized object instances, such as the `Tool` instances provided with HotDraw. Library components may also be composed of a number of core classes rather than derived from one exclusively. Providing these concrete classes makes the framework both more complete and easier to use. If concrete classes are not needed in a particular application, then they can simply be excluded from the application.

25.5.2 Hot Spots and Frozen Spots

As mentioned earlier, frameworks contain hot spots which are meant to encompass the variability between applications within the domain of the framework. Hot spots provide the flexibility and extensibility of the framework and their design is critical to the success of the framework.

Two questions to consider about a hot spot are [30]

- What is the desired degree of flexibility, remembering that flexibility has to be balanced with ease of use?
- Must the behavior be changeable at runtime, in which case composition is preferred over inheritance?

Pree's hot spot approach [30] defines several metapatterns which aid in hot spot design. Each metapattern defines a set of relationships between template methods and hook methods within an abstract base class. Template methods define the flow of control for the framework and either perform actions directly or defer functionality to hook methods. Hook methods are left unimplemented within the framework and are specialized by the application developer to fit the needs of the application. Design patterns also help in structuring hot spots as described in Section 25.6.3.

Each hot spot will likely have several hooks associated with it. The hooks describe how specific changes can be made to the framework in order to fulfill some requirement of the application [12]. Figure 25.3 shows the `Tool` hot spot and three hooks within it. There are three main ways in which a framework can be modified using hooks and each of these are illustrated in the three hooks depicted in Figure 25.3.

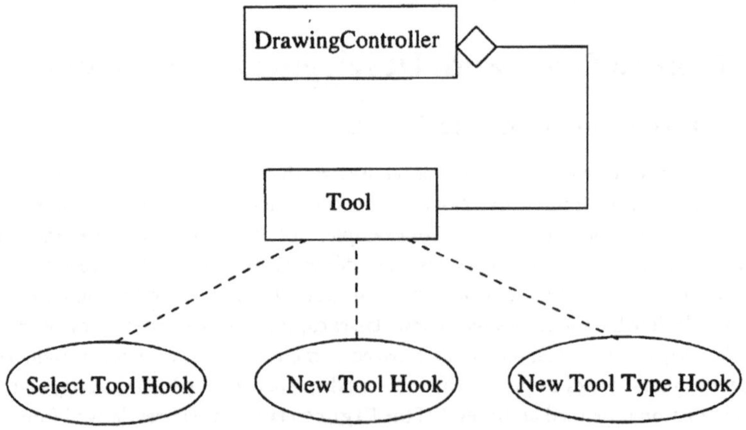

FIGURE 25.3 Hooks for the Tools hot spot.

1. Several pre-built components can be provided within the framework library which can be simply used as is in applications, such as the `Select Tool Hook`. If there are a limited number of options available, then the components provided may be all that is needed.

2. Parameterized classes or patterns can be provided (such as the use of template and hook methods) which are filled in by framework users. The `Tool` class in HotDraw is an example of a parameterized class and the `New Tool Hook` describes how the parameters must be filled in.
3. When it is difficult to anticipate how a hot spot will be used, or if a lot of flexibility is needed, then new subclasses are often derived from existing framework classes and new functionality is added, corresponding to the `New Tool Type Hook`.

25.5.3 Composition and Inheritance

Inheritance and composition are the two main ways for providing hooks into the framework. Composition is often recommended over inheritance as it tends to be easier for the framework user to use (data-driven as opposed to architecture-driven), but each has strengths and weaknesses. The type of customization used in each case depends upon the requirements of the framework.

25.5.3.1 Composition

Composition typically involves the use of callbacks or parameterized types. The class of the framework to be adapted will have a parameter to be filled in by the application developer which provides some required functionality. Because the customization is done by filling in parameters, the framework user does not need an in-depth knowledge of how the particular component operates. In HotDraw, the `Tool` class is parameterized so that new `Tools` can be quickly and easily produced. The main parameter for customizing the `Tool` class is the command table shown here for the example `OMTClassFigure` tool.

Reader	Figure	Command
`DragReader`	`OMTClassFigure`	`MoveCommand`
`ClickReader`	`OMTClassFigure`	`ExpandCommand`

The `OMTClassTool` shown here has two entries in its command table which determines what actions it takes depending upon the context in which the tool was used. The `Reader` determines the type of use, such as `DragReader` or `ClickReader`. The `Figure` is the type of figure selected by the tool and the `Command` is the action to take on the `Figure` using the `Reader`. So, if the `OMTClassTool` is dragged on the `OMTClassFigure` then it will invoke the `MoveCommand` which moves the `Figure`. `Tools` can be easily produced by combining different `Commands`, `Readers`, and `Figures`. The separation of `Readers` and the `Commands` from the `Tool` class also makes the individual `Readers` and `Commands` more reusable. Many `Tools` will have actions for dragging and clicking the mouse and they can all use the same `Reader` classes.

Composition also allows the component used to be changed dynamically. The `DrawingController` class in HotDraw uses composition for this purpose. The class has a slot for the `Tool` that is currently being used, but there are many different `Tools` in a typical HotDraw application and the user changes `Tools` frequently. The tool that is currently in the `DrawingController` class may have to be changed at runtime, so `Tool` was made into a separate class with each tool having the same interface so that it can be made the current tool whenever the user selects it.

When composition is combined with a large number of existing concrete classes within the framework library, adapting the framework becomes a simple matter of choosing the right components and connecting them together. Composition tends to be the easier of the two types of adaptation to use. A developer should understand the interface to the component, the functionality the component provides, and little else about the inner workings of the framework. More generally, the developer simply needs to understand which existing concrete component performs the desired function.

25.5.3.2 Inheritance

Inheritance involves specializing methods from an abstract class, or adding functionality to an abstract class. Inheriting from a class requires a considerable understanding of the abstract class and its interactions with other classes, thus it can be more error prone and more difficult to use than composition. The advantage of inheritance is extensibility. An application developer can easily add completely new functionality to a subclass of an existing class, which is not as easily accommodated with composition.

New `Figures` in HotDraw are derived by inheritance. New `Figures` often require added functionality or instance variables that cannot be anticipated by the framework developers and inheritance provides the means by which the new methods and variables can be added. For example, the `OMTClassFigure` in Figure 25.4 is derived from `CompositeFigure` and adds two new methods, `addvar` and `addmethod`. These methods are used to add new variable and method text labels to the class box. It also contains `TextPopupFigures` derived from `TextFigures` for the text labels. The `TextPopUpFigures` contain an additional attribute `desc` which holds a description or code fragment and a method `popupdesc` for displaying the description. Since none of this functionality was contained in HotDraw before, and it is impossible to anticipate the full range of additional functionality that might be needed in a `Figure`, it must be added by inheritance.

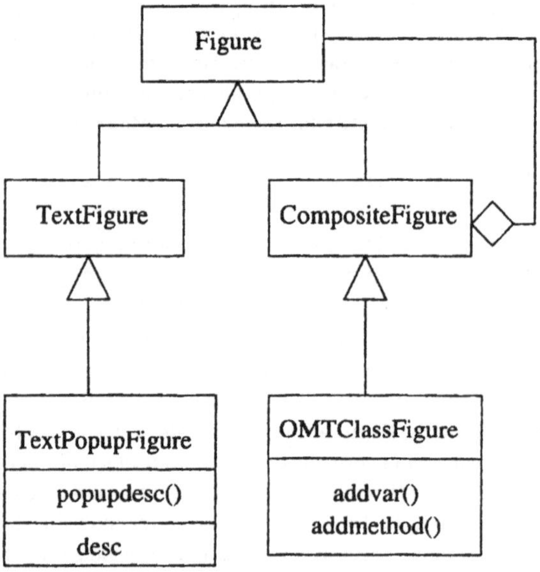

FIGURE 25.4 Inheritance diagram for `OMTClassFigure`.

Often the abstract class will provide default methods that need to be overridden in a child class. `Hook` methods are an example of this. The method is called by another template method, but the specific functionality is class specific and cannot be pre-determined. HotDraw provides a step method for `Drawings` that is used for animation, but it is left empty by default since no one method can account for the complete variety of possible ways to animate a `Drawing`.

25.5.3.3 Composition vs. Inheritance

Composition is generally used when interfaces and uses of the framework are fairly well defined, whereas inheritance provides flexibility in cases where the full range of functionality cannot be anticipated.

Composition forces conformance to a specific interface and functionality which cannot be easily added to or changed. All `Tools` use `Readers` to determine the location of the mouse pointer and what action is being taken, and invoke `Commands` to perform actions on `Figures`. In practice this works fairly well and covers the range of actions needed to be performed by `Tools`. When something outside of this paradigm is required, however, the `Tool` class itself must be subclassed to provide the extra functionality.

It has been proposed that frameworks start out as white box frameworks that rely upon inheritance. As the domain becomes better understood and more concrete support classes are developed, the framework evolves to use more composition and becomes a black box framework [20]. The step method for animating `Drawings` was mentioned above. While it is currently blank, and must be overridden through inheritance, it may be possible to provide a number of standard ways to animate `Drawings`. Instead of providing a new `Drawing` class for each standard type of animation, it would be better to move the animation routines into their own class using the Strategy design pattern [13] which can be linked into the `Drawing` class as needed.

Beyond components that developers have to connect, a framework might gain the ability to decide how to connect components itself. This could possibly be done dynamically or by using a development tool, freeing the developer to simply choose the components needed without doing any programming.

25.5.4 Framework Families

Much in the same way that an individual class is a specialization of a more abstract class, one framework may be a specialization of a more abstract framework. There are two reasons why such a family of frameworks might be built.

First, a specialized framework can provide more support for special cases within the domain. Abstract frameworks provide the basic services and interactions, while the specialized frameworks extend that to provide more specialized support. The abstract framework provides flexibility while the specialized frameworks provide more completeness and ease of use.

Second, framework families are a means of dealing with complexity. Instead of including all possible options within a single, complex framework, related options can be bundled into specialized frameworks.

An alternate approach for producing framework families is to develop an initial problem solution and then to generalize it [23]. For example, a framework that is developed to solve a graphing problem might be generalized into a more abstract framework. The generalized framework is then abstracted again into a more abstract problem. This process continues until the most general problem solution is found. The generalization approach quite naturally produces a framework family with the most abstract and flexible framework at the top of the "family tree" and the more specific framework at the bottom. Unfortunately, it is not always clear what a more general solution to the problem would be, or what the most general solution is.

25.6 Specific Development Techniques

25.6.1 Domain Analysis

Domain analysis techniques, such as FODA [21], focus on finding the requirements for an entire domain rather than just for a single application. Domain analysis [2] identifies the concepts and connections between concepts within a domain without determining specific designs. The analysis can help to identify the variant and invariant parts of the domain and the primary abstractions needed for a framework. In the Feature Oriented Domain Analysis technique, the generic parts of the domain are abstracted from existing applications by removing all of the factors that make each application within the domain different. The abstraction is done to the point where the product produced from the domain analysis covers all of the applications. Differences are factored out by generalizing existing parts of applications, or aggregating the variant aspects into more generic constructs. The resulting concepts are then the primary invariants of the framework. Variations within the domain are captured in FODA by refining the common abstractions through specialization and decomposition. Parameters are defined for each refinement which capture the variant aspects. The refinements and parameters can then form the basis for the hooks of the framework.

25.6.2 Software Architecture

All software systems, including frameworks, must have a solid foundation at the level of *software architecture* [29]. Software architecture studies the higher level issues involved in software design, such as the organization of the system, physical distribution of subsystems, performance, and composition of design elements [33]. Architecture consists of components, the pieces of software such as UNIX filters or object-oriented classes, and the connectors that allow them to communicate with each other, such as UNIX pipes or object-oriented methods.

25.6.2.1 Architectural Styles

An architectural style [33] defines the types of components and connectors that can exist within a particular style, and the rules of how they can be composed. These rules can aid in application development from a framework by helping to describe the types of applications that can or cannot be built, and general rules for their structure.

For example, HotDraw uses the object-oriented architectural style. The components within HotDraw are classes and the connectors are the messages that are passed between classes. Object-oriented architectures allow flexible structures in which objects can collaborate with other objects in arbitrary ways to provide functionality, but each object must know about the objects it collaborates with beforehand, unlike filters in the pipe and filter architecture. However, HotDraw is a framework for graphical drawing applications rather than a command line filter and is well suited to the object-oriented style.

25.6.2.2 Domain Specific Software Architectures

Domain Specific Software Architectures [36] are closely related to object-oriented frameworks. By focusing on a specific domain, a DSSA can provide more specialized components and connectors than architectural styles and even provide components that can be used within applications, just as is done with frameworks. A DSSA consists of three things:

1. A software architecture with reference requirements and domain model
2. Infrastructure to support it
3. Process to instantiate/refine it

The reference requirements define the requirements that an application has within the domain. The domain model is a lexicon of terms within the domain, such as objects, relationships, or even actions that occur within the domain. The infrastructure can refer to tool support provided to build an application within the domain, as well as pre-built components than can be used within applications.

A DSSA can be provided as a framework (which satisfies the architecture and some of the infrastructure requirements), but it can also include such things as fourth generation languages or application generators. However, the requirements for a DSSA apply equally well to object-oriented frameworks, and suggest that frameworks should be part of a larger package that includes requirements, tool support, and a process for using the framework.

25.6.3 Design Patterns

A design pattern captures some of the expertise of object-oriented software developers by describing the solution to a common design problem that has worked in the past in several different applications. The description of the solution will detail the benefits and drawbacks of the pattern and perhaps name alternatives. Design patterns have been associated with object-oriented frameworks from their inception even though they are not limited to use in frameworks. They are appropriate for designing parts of frameworks and particularly designing hot spots within frameworks because many design patterns enhance flexibility or extensibility.

Three levels of design patterns have been identified [7]. Architectural patterns describe a general high-level architecture that can form the basis of a framework or application, and are closely related to architectural styles. However, many patterns use a particular style and are not styles themselves. The patterns identify specific components and connectors that are used in the architecture. For example, the HotDraw framework uses the object-oriented architectural style, and the Model-View-Controller architectural pattern [7] described briefly in Figure 55.8. As shown in Figure 25.5 the `Drawing` forms the basis of the model, `DrawingView` corresponds to view and `DrawingController` corresponds to the controller. Using the pattern gives the framework flexibility by separating the display (`DrawingView`) from the user input mechanisms (`DrawingController`) and the internal representation of the drawing (`Drawing`). New views or types of views can be easily added, new user input mechanisms can be implemented or even removed so the application becomes a simple display.

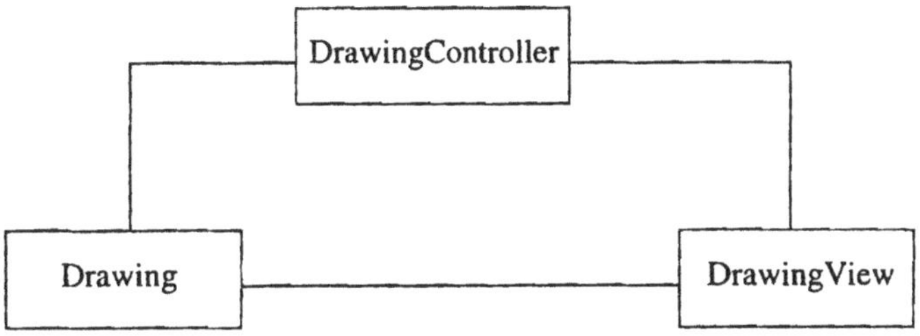

FIGURE 25.5 The MVC pattern in HotDraw.

At the next level down, the patterns are specifically called design patterns. These patterns do not form the basis for an entire framework, but help to structure specific parts of a framework. They are especially useful in adding flexibility to hot spots in the framework. The Composite Pattern [13] is used in HotDraw as shown in Figure 25.7 to help structure the Figures hot spot. Basically, `CompositeFigure` is made a subclass of `Figure` with the same interface as `Figure`, but also may contain any number of `Figures`. `Drawing` is a specific type of `CompositeFigure`. `CompositeFigures` will respond to the same methods that are invoked on `Figures`, so that they can be treated interchangeably with ordinary `Figures`. This allows flexible and arbitrary collections of new `Figures` and nested `CompositeFigures` developed for an application rather than forcing a flat model in which `Drawings` can only contain simple `Figures`.

HotDraw also incorporates the Observer Pattern [13] to provide a means in which Figures can be linked to each other, also within the Figures hot spot. Figure 25.8 shows a sample HotDraw application in which two `OMTClassFigures` are connected by a `LineFigure`. When one of the `OMTClassFigures` is removed, the `LineFigure` should be removed as well by the application. In order to provide this feature, the Observer Pattern is used. `LineFigure` is made a dependent of each `OMTClassFigure` it is connected to and when one `OMTClassFigure` is deleted, the framework automatically sends the class the appropriate deletion message. The `OMTClassFigure` then notifies each of its dependents so that they can take the appropriate action, deleting itself in this case. Notifications can also be sent to dependents whenever a given `Figure` changes, giving application developers an easy-to-use mechanism through which one `Figure` can reflect changes in another.

The lowest level patterns are called *idioms*. Idioms tend to be implementation language specific and focus on specific low-level issues. For example, an idiom might describe how exception handling can be provided in a specific language.

Model-View-Controller

Context: Interactive applications with a flexible human-computer interface.

Problem: User interfaces are especially prone to change requests, and when the functionality of an application changes, the user interface must change to reflect that. Additionally, different users require different interfaces, such as keyboard vs. menu and button. If the user interface is tightly tied to the functionality of the application, then it becomes difficult to change and maintain. The following forces influence the solution:

- Different windows display the same information and each must reflect changes to the information.
- Changes to the user interfaces should be easy, including supporting different look and feel standards.

Solution: Divide the application into three areas: processing, output, and input. The three components that incorporate these areas are called the model, the view and the controller.

- Model: encapsulates the data and functionality of the application.
- View: displays the data within the model. Multiple views can be attached to a single model to display the data in different ways, or to display different parts of the data.
- Controller: receives input from the user and invokes methods within the model to fulfill user requests. Each view can have its own controller and controllers can be changed to provide different means of input.

FIGURE 25.6 The model-view-controller architectural pattern.

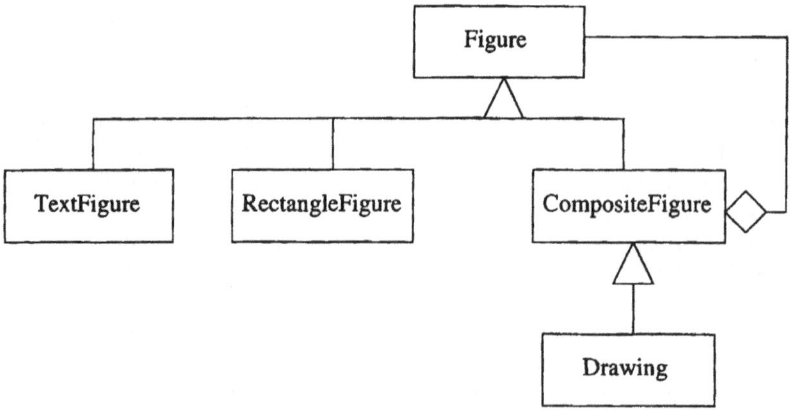

FIGURE 25.7 The composite pattern in HotDraw.

25.6.4 Open Implementation

Open implementation [25] is another technique for supporting flexibility. Software modules with open implementation can adapt their internal implementations to suit the needs of different clients. The modules themselves support several different implementation strategies and provide a strategy control interface to allow client modules to help choose or tune the implementation strategy that best suits the client. For example, a file system might support several different caching strategies and allow the caching strategy to be tuned based on the usage profile of the application. The application provides this information to the module with open implementation, perhaps indicating that it will perform a sequential scan of a file, or

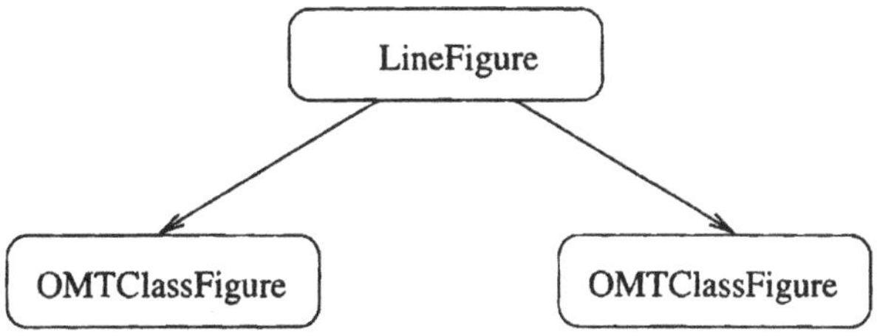

FIGURE 25.8 The observer pattern in HotDraw.

random access. Typically, the strategy selection information is provided during the initialization of the module.

This notion can be applied in particular to the framework library. Allowing clients to help select the implementation strategy can help applications to tune a library class or module for efficiency, making it more suitable for a wider variety of applications.

Four styles of open implementation interfaces have been identified [22]:

1. Style A — No control interface is provided which is the same as providing a black box component or module. The client has no means of tuning the implementation so this approach is best used when only one implementation of a component is appropriate.
2. Style B — The client provides information about how it will use the component, typically through setting parameter values when initializing the component. The component itself is responsible for choosing the best implementation strategy based on the information provided. The approach is easy for clients to use, but it does not give them much control over the component.
3. Style C — The client specifically specifies the implementation strategy to use from a set of strategies. The component has no control over the selection, and this approach is the same as providing several interchangeable components. It is best used when the component cannot select the appropriate strategy through declarative information, as in style B.
4. Style D — The client actually provides the implementation to use. The component simply provides the interface, but no implementation. In frameworks, abstract classes are used in a similar way, defining the interface, but leaving the implementation of methods to the application developer. It is best used when the set of possible implementations cannot be predetermined.

25.6.5 Contracts

One of the difficulties in any type of framework is ensuring that the framework receives or produces the correct information. Integrating classes is an issue in any application development, and using a framework is in part an integration issue. Therefore, it is critical that the interfaces to the framework, both the methods of the framework that are called by an application and the methods of an application that the framework calls, be clearly defined.

25.6.5.1 Simple Contracts

Simple contracts as proposed by Meyer (1988) are a means of specifying the pre-conditions required by a method or operation and the post-conditions that a method ensures. Specifying and enforcing conditions can help to cut down on the level of defensive programming needed within a framework, or any piece of reusable software. For example, a reusable component within the framework library does not have to handle every possible exception or error condition in the input if the pre-conditions for the component's methods are clearly identified and enforced.

As Meyer argues, clearly specifying the conditions helps application developers since they do not have to guess what the framework does, and they can handle errors that might best be handled by the application. Forcing the framework to handle every possible exception can reduce performance and make the framework less attractive for use.

Further, some means of enforcing the contracts may help reduce the number of errors application developers make when using the framework. In Eiffel, contracts are built into the language. In other languages, Hollingsworth (1992) proposes that separate classes be built to represent contracts. These classes will ensure that the pre- and post-conditions are met for the framework to operate correctly. These contract classes could be included with the release of a framework and used during the development of an application and removed to improve efficiency when the application is released.

25.6.5.2 Behavioral Contracts

More complex behavioral specifications have been proposed [15]. Also called contracts, they cover not only the interactions between two classes, or the conditions placed on one method, but on the total interaction between multiple classes, often involving multiple methods to perform some task. The specification is flexible in that one contract can specialize another, and contracts can be composed of other contracts. When actually using the contract, a conformance declaration is produced which states how the classes involved fulfill the contract.

Specifying behavioral contracts within a framework helps to capture design information that might be needed by application developers. Figure 25.9 shows the ExecuteTool contract used in HotDraw which details how `Readers`, `Commands`, and `Tools` interact in order to perform the task. When the `Tool` executes, it first initializes the `Reader` with the mouse `sensor` and the `Command` to be executed. Afterwards, it sends the `manipulate` command to the `Reader` which in turn actually executes the command on the `Figure` found at the current location of the mouse. When the user is finished using the tool (i.e., lets go of the mouse button during a drag operation) the `Tool` sends the effect message to the `Reader` which performs any clean up operations needed, including sending the effect message to the `Command`. When application developers add a new `Reader`, `Command`, or `Tool` class to an application developed from HotDraw, they need to conform to this contract. The contract makes the information explicit, thus the application developer does not need to synthesize this information from the source code, which may not even be possible if the source code of the framework is not available.

25.7 Framework Deployment

Once an object-oriented framework has been implemented, refined, and tested to the point where it is stable, it is ready to be deployed by application developers. There are a number of questions to be considered when deploying a framework. First, what sort of aids for learning the framework are provided? Andersen Consulting has used three different approaches [34]:

1. Roll out sessions — Sessions are held after a framework has reached a certain phase in its development in order to introduce users to the current set of features. This approach has the advantage of gradually introducing the users to the framework as it is developed.
2. Example Applications — Examples help to show specific ways in which the framework can be used. Examples can also potentially be modified and used in a new application being developed.
3. Reference Documentation — Documentation that describes the purpose of the framework, how to use it, and how it is designed can and should be provided. Documentation techniques will be covered in the next chapter on using object-oriented frameworks.

```
contract ExecuteTool
    Tool supports[
        s:  Sensor
        execute() ↦ Reader → initialize(s,Command); Reader →
            manipulate(s);
        Reader → Effect ]
    Reader supports[
        c :  Command
        initialize(sensor,c) ↦ Δc {command = c}; c → initialize
            (sensor.mousepoint)
        manipulate(sensor) ↦ c → execute(sensor.mousepoint)
        effect ↦ c → effect ]
    Command supports[
        initialize(loc)
        execute(loc)
        effect ]
end contract
```

FIGURE 25.9 The ExecuteTool behavioral contract.

Additionally, a framework developer might be involved with application development as well. When the framework designer is also involved in using the framework, application developers can use the designer's expertise with the framework. The framework designer may also gain insights into how the framework can be modified or improved.

Second, will the framework be distributed as source code or a binary executable? Binary executables do not allow developers to modify the framework, but instead require them to rely on the interfaces provided. This may make future upgrades of the framework easier to incorporate into existing applications if the interfaces do not change, and will protect the framework code against tampering. However, developers cannot fix any errors they encounter in the framework and are forced to devise workarounds. Additionally, developers cannot examine the binary implementation to help to understand the framework as they can with source code.

Third, how will changes to the framework be handled? When bugs are fixed or new features are added to the framework, how will existing applications be affected? Ideally, only the internal implementations of framework components will change, leaving interfaces and hooks the same, but this is not always possible. This issue will be examined more fully in the chapter on using object-oriented frameworks.

25.8 Summary and Open Issues

Object-oriented frameworks provide the means for reusing both the design and implementation of a system or subsystem. As such, they provide tremendous leverage for the application developer. The design of similar applications do not have to be repeatedly constructed out of existing or new code components, but instead an existing design can be customized quickly to provide the desired functionality. Due to the common design base, several applications developed from the same framework can also be maintained more easily.

However, frameworks are more difficult to design and develop than single applications. Frameworks must be general enough to capture the commonalties of all the applications that might be built within the domain of the framework, and they must also be flexible enough to allow for the variations that exist between those applications. All of this generality and flexibility has to be made easy to use for application developers if the framework is to be a success.

There are no mature framework development methodologies. There are, however, guidelines and promising techniques for aiding in the development of frameworks and several of these have been presented. Domain analysis can be used to identify the commonalties and variations (frozen and hot spots) in the domain. Inheritance and composition can be used to provide different sorts of ease of use and flexibility. Design patterns and open implementation techniques help to structure the framework and to provide the right types of flexibility.

Providing such a methodology is one of the key open issues in the area of object-oriented frameworks. A framework development process needs to focus on the identification of hot spots and frozen spots. How are the right abstractions for the framework determined and how should they be structured? It also needs to focus on building flexibility and ease of use into the framework, which in essence is designing the hot spots of a framework.

Some techniques are available for developing flexibility in a framework, but there is very little help for deciding on which trade offs to make. Which part of the framework should be made more flexible and how will it affect the other parts? Does flexibility need to be sacrificed for more ease of use? While there are guidelines for making frameworks easier to reuse, there is no criteria quantifying just how easy they should be to reuse.

Object-oriented frameworks are a key means of moving software development away from the traditional means such as continuously redeveloping commonly used code or trying to reuse and fit together unrelated and often mismatched components. Frameworks provide the components and the context, together with an overall structure and design, to ensure component compatibility and provide a powerful form of software system reuse.

References

[1] Adair, D., Building object-oriented frameworks, *AIXpert*, Feb. 1995.

[2] Arango, G. and Prieto-Diaz, R., *Domain Analysis Concepts and Research Directions*, IEEE Computer Society, 1991.

[3] Beck, K. and Johnson, R., Patterns generate architectures, pp. 139–149. In *Proceedings of ECOOP 94*, 1994.

[4] Birrer, A. and Eggenschwiler, T., Frameworks in the financial engineering domain: an experience report, pp. 21–35. In *Proc. ECOOP 93*, 1995.

[5] Booch, G., Designing an application framework, *Dr. Dobb's J.*, 19(2), 24–32, 1994.

[6] Brown, K., Kues, L., and Lam, M., HM3270: An evolving framework for client-server communications, pp. 463–472. In *Proc. 14th Annu. TOOLS Conf.*, 1995.

[7] Buschmann, F., Meunier, R., Rohnert, H., Sommerlad, P., and Stal, M., *Pattern-Oriented Software Architecture: A System of Patterns*. John Wiley & Sons, Chichester, England, 1996.

[8] Campbell, R.H., Islam, N., Raila, D. and Madany, P., Designing and implementing choices: an object-oriented system in C++, *Commun. ACM*, 36(9), 117–126, 1993.

[9] Cline, M.P., Pros and cons of adapting and applying patterns in the real world, *Commun. ACM.*, 39(10), 47–49, 1996.

[10] Cotter, S. and Potel, M., *Inside Taligent Technology*, Addison-Wesley, Reading, MA, 1995.

[11] Eggenschwiler, T. and Gamma, E., ET++ SwapsManager: using object technology in the financial engineering domain, pp. 166-177. In *Proc. OOPSLA 92*, 1992.

[12] Froehlich, G., Hoover, H.J., Liu, L., and Sorenson, P., Hooking into object-oriented application frameworks. In *Proc. 1997 Int. Conf. on Software Engineering*, 1997

[13] Gamma, E., Helm, R., Johnson, R., and Vlissides, J., *Design Patterns: Elements of Reusable Object-Oriented Software*. Addison-Wesley, Reading, MA, 1995.

[14] Gangopadhyay, D. and Mitra, S., Understanding frameworks by exploration of exemplars, pp. 90–99. In *Proc. 7th Int. Workshop on Computer Aided Software Engineering (CASE-95)*, 1995.

[15] Helm, R., Holland, I.M., and Gangopadhyay, D., Contracts: specifying behavioral compositions in object-oriented systems, pp. 169–180. In *Proc. ECOOP/OOPSLA 90*, 1992.
[16] Hollingsworth, J., *Software Component Design-for-Reuse: A Language Independent Discipline Applied to Ada*, Ph.D. thesis. Department of Computer and Information Science, The Ohio State University, Columbus, Ohio, 1992.
[17] Jacobson, I., Christerson, M., Jonsson, P., and Overgaard, G., *Object-Oriented Software Engineering — A Use Case Driven Approach*. Addison-Wesley, Wokingham, England, 1992.
[18] Johnson, R., Documenting frameworks using patterns, pp. 63–76. In *Proc. OOPSLA 92*, 1992.
[19] Johnson, R., How to design frameworks, *Tutorial notes from OOPSLA 1993*, 1993.
[20] Johnson, R. and Foote, B., Designing reusable classes, *J. Object-Oriented Program.*, 2(1), 22–35, 1988.
[21] Kang, K., Cohen, S., Hess, J., Novak, W., and Peterson, A., Feature-Oriented Domain Analysis (FODA) Feasibility Study. (CMU/SEI-90-TR-21, ADA 235785), Pittsburgh, PA, Software Engineering Institute, Carnegie Mellon University, Pittsburgh, PA, 1990.
[22] Kiczales, G., Lamping, J., Lopes, C.V., Maeda, C., Mendhekar, A., and Murphy, G., Open implementation design guidelines, pp. 481–490. In *Proc. 19th Int. Conf. on Software Engineering*, Boston, MA, 1997.
[23] Koskimies, K. and Mossenback, H., Designing a framework by stepwise generalization, pp. 479–497. In *Proc. 5th European Software Engineering Conf., Lecture Notes in Computer Science 989*, Springer-Verlag, New York, 1995.
[24] Krueger, C.W., Software reuse, *ACM Comp. Surv.*, 24(6), 131–183, 1992.
[25] Maeda, C., Lee, A., Murphy, G., and Kiczales, G., Open implementation analysis and design, pp. 44–53. In *Proc. 1997 Symp. on Software Reusability in ACM Software Engineering Notes*, 22(3), 1997.
[26] Meyer, B., *Object-Oriented Software Construction*. Prentice-Hall, Englewood Cliffs, NJ, 1988.
[27] Meyer, B., *Reusable Software — The Base Object-Oriented Component Libraries*. Prentice-Hall, Englewood Cliffs, NJ, 1994.
[28] O'Connor, J., Mansour, C., Turner-Harris, J., and Campbell, G., Reuse in command-and-control systems, *IEEE Software*, 11(5), 70–79, 1994.
[29] Perry, D.E. and Wolf, A.L., Foundations for the study of software architecture, *ACM SIGSOFT Software Eng. Notes*, 17(4), 40–52, 1992.
[30] Pree, W., *Design Patterns for Object-Oriented Software Development*. Addison-Wesley, Reading, MA, 1995.
[31] Rumbaugh, J., Blaha, M., Premerlani, W., Frederick, E., and Lorenson, W., *Object-Oriented Modeling and Design*, Prentice-Hall, Englewood Cliffs, NJ, 1991.
[32] Schmid, H.A., Creating the architecture of a manufacturing framework by design patterns, pp. 370–384. In *Proc. OOPSLA 95*, 1995.
[33] Shaw, M. and Garlan, D., *Software Architecture — Perspectives on an Emerging Discipline*. Prentice-Hall, Englewood Cliffs, NJ, 1996.
[34] Sparks, S., Benner, K., and Faris, C., Managing object-oriented framework reuse, *IEEE Comp.*, 29(9), 52–62, 1996.
[35] Taligent, *The Power of Frameworks*. Addison-Wesley, Reading, MA, 1995.
[36] Tracz, W., Domain-specific software architecture (DSSA) frequently asked questions (FAQ), *ACM Software Engineering Notes*, 19(2), 52–56, 1994.
[37] Vlissides, M. and Linton, M.A., Unidraw: a framework for building domain-specific graphical editors, *ACM Trans. Inform. Sys.*, 8(3), 237–268, 1990.

26

Using Object-Oriented Frameworks

Garry Froehlich
University of Alberta

H. James Hoover
University of Alberta

Ling Liu
University of Alberta

Paul Sorenson
University of Alberta

26.1 Introduction

Often it is difficult to reuse a software component outside of its original context. Object-oriented frameworks can provide the context in which the component is meant to be reused and thus allow for a significant amount of reuse. An object-oriented framework is the reusable design of a system or subsystem implemented through a collection of concrete and abstract classes and their collaborations [2]. The concrete classes provide the reusable components, while the design provides the context in which they are used. A framework is more than a collection of reusable components. It provides a generic solution to a set of similar problems within an application domain. The framework itself is incomplete and provides places called hooks where users can add their own components specific to a particular application.

Developing an application from a framework differs from developing an application on its own. The framework already supplies the architecture of the application, and users fill in the parts left incomplete by the framework. A framework typically includes the main control loop and calls application extensions to perform specific tasks. Unlike the reuse of pure function libraries, framework users give up control of the design. In return, users are able to develop applications much more quickly, and a single framework can form the basis for a whole family of related applications. Since frameworks can be complex and difficult to learn, documenting all aspects of the framework is important to aid in the user's understanding of the framework and to make the framework easier to use.

In this chapter we discuss techniques and concepts related to using frameworks. Many users will use a framework as it was meant to be used, but others will want to use the framework in new, non-standard ways. Still, others will want to evolve the framework to incorporate new capabilities. Although the focus

0-8493-3135-8/99/$0.00+$.50

of this chapter is mainly on using the framework as it was meant to be used, we discuss issues related to many other aspects of use.

The next section introduces some terms and concepts important to framework use. Section 26.3 discusses some of the advantages and disadvantages of using a framework. Section 26.4 describes how frameworks affect application development. Section 26.5 discusses the difficulties with using multiple frameworks and Section 26.6 describes some issues in evolving frameworks. Section 26.7 presents a number of different documentation methods and how they aid in the use of frameworks. Finally, some conclusions and a brief discussion of some open issues are presented in the last section.

26.2 Terms and Concepts

Not everyone will use a framework in the same way. In this initial section we discuss the ways in which a framework can be used, and the different types of users of frameworks.

26.2.1 Ways to Use a Framework

There are a number of different ways in which to use a framework. Each of them require a different amount of knowledge about the framework and a different level of skill in using it. Taligent (1995) defines three main ways in which frameworks can be used.

1. **As is** — The framework is used without modifying or adding to it in any way. The framework is treated as a black box, or maybe as a collection of optional components that are plugged together to form an application.
2. **Complete** — The framework user adds to the framework by filling in parts left open by the framework developers. Completing the framework is necessary if it does not come with a full set of library components.
3. **Customize** — The framework user replaces part of the framework with custom code. Modifying the framework in such a way requires a detailed knowledge of how the framework operates.

26.2.2 Users of Frameworks

In addition to the different ways to use a framework, different people will use a framework with different goals [6].

1. **Regular user** — Many users will use a framework in the way that it was meant to be used. They will use it as is, or they will complete the framework as the framework designer intended. A regular user needs to know only enough about the framework to enable them to use it effectively and typically do not require an in-depth knowledge of the framework.
2. **Advanced user** — Some users will want to use the framework in unexpected ways, ways in which the framework developers never anticipated nor planned. They will use the framework in the same way as regular users, but they will also customize the framework or try to add completely new and unanticipated functionality to it. Needless to say, the advanced user needs a deeper understanding of the framework.
3. **Framework developer** — A framework can evolve by adding functionality or fixing errors, specialized frameworks can be derived by adding specialized classes, or the framework can be generalized to accommodate a wider domain. The framework developers performing these activities need to know all of the details of the design and implementation of the framework and must keep in mind how changes will affect applications already developed from the framework.

4. **Developer of another framework** — Some users simply want to learn how the framework achieves its flexibility, and they need to know about the design and the decisions behind it.

Of the four types of users, the first is probably the most common. A framework is designed for a particular type of application and will be most successful when it is used to build that type of application. As an example consider a framework for building graphical user interfaces. Most users simply want to build a user interface for their application, and will use the framework as intended. A few users will push the interface paradigm to develop custom interface styles. Even fewer will be interested in evolving the framework.

26.3 Advantages and Disadvantages of Using Frameworks

Frameworks provide tremendous leverage for developers of new applications. For example, a framework represents a flexible design that can be easily and quickly extended to develop applications. However, frameworks are not appropriate for every application. Here we give some advantages and disadvantages of using a framework.

26.3.1 Advantages

- **Reusing expertise** — The single biggest advantage of using a framework is that it captures the expertise of developers within that domain. The framework developers are generally experts within the domain and have already analyzed the domain to provide a quality, flexible design. That expertise can be transferred to the application developers simply by using the framework.
- **Decreased development time** — The problem domain does not have to be analyzed again, and the framework often provides a number of components that can be used directly in an application. Users familiar with the framework can develop new applications from a framework in much less time than without the framework. However, there is the disadvantage of learning the framework as discussed below.
- **Enhanced quality** — The framework should have a well thought out, quality design. Applications developed from the framework will inherit much of the quality design, although poorly developed applications based on high quality frameworks are still possible.
- **Reduced maintenance cost** — If a family of similar products are developed from a single framework, then maintainers will only have to learn one standard design and will be able to maintain the whole product line more easily.

26.3.2 Disadvantages

- **Framework mismatch** — Committing to a particular framework can be inconvenient if the requirements of the application are incompatible with the design of the framework. It can be disastrous if the incompatibilities are found late in the application development cycle. Unfortunately, knowledge of what the framework can and cannot do primarily comes from experience using the framework, although clear documentation helps to alleviate this problem. Prototype projects can help familiarize users with what a framework can be used for without jeopardizing an important project.
- **Learning curve** — Using a framework requires some amount of learning, just as with any relatively complex tool or technique. A complex framework can require a great deal of time to learn and may not be appropriate if very few applications will be developed from it. The cost of the initial period of learning is lessened if several applications are developed from a single framework.

- **Lack of design control** — The framework already has a design specified and implemented and any applications developed from it have to conform to that design. Application developers give up most of their control over the design, but this loss is more than offset by the advantages of using a framework.

26.4 Building Applications from Frameworks

Much like framework design, there are no well-defined methodologies for developing applications from frameworks. The problem is made worse since individual frameworks will often require different processes for using them. Rather than defining a methodology, we provide some general techniques for using object-oriented frameworks.

26.4.1 Example Framework

In this section we will use the HotDraw framework [15] which is intended for developing structured graphical editors written in Smalltalk. A view of a HotDraw application is shown in Figure 26.1. The major elements of HotDraw are the `Tools` arranged in a toolbar which are used to manipulate `Figures` within a `Drawing`. The tools provided in HotDraw include the selection tool for moving and manipulating figures, the deletion tool for removing figures, and many tools for drawing different types of basic figures such as circles or rectangles.

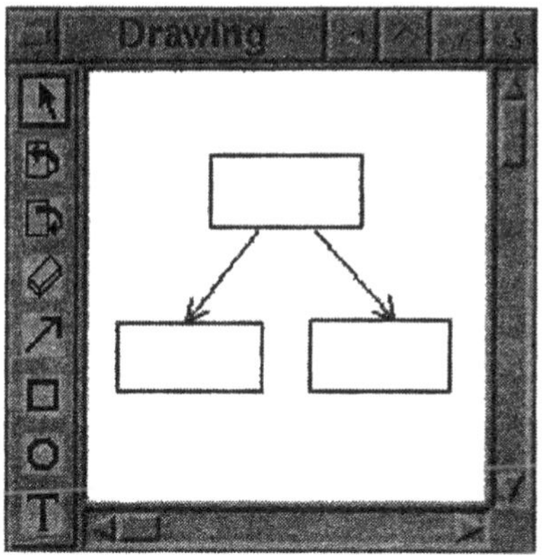

FIGURE 26.1 HotDraw.

As an example of an application built from a framework, we used HotDraw to construct a graphical display application for the Responsive Corporate Information Model (RCIM); [25] manager prototype. RCIM is an aid to corporate strategic planning. It manages several alternative and/or interrelated plans consisting of the goals, objectives, and action plans of the business. The plans can be represented as diagrams, and the display application draws and lays out those diagrams automatically to give a graphical depiction of the plans. An example of a plan is shown in Figure 26.2.

26.4.2 Analysis

As with any type of software development, one of the first stages involved in developing applications from frameworks is analyzing the requirements of the application. If the users are already familiar with

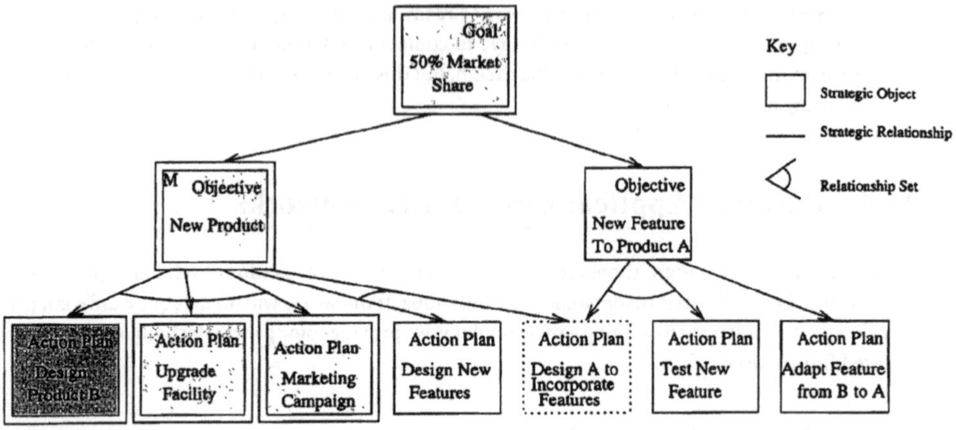

FIGURE 26.2 Example of an RCIM strategic diagram.

the framework, then the requirements can be cast immediately in a form that is compatible with the framework.

If the users do not already have a framework, then they will have to find one that supports the application requirements. Frameworks already exist in many areas such as client-server communications [5], operating systems [8], graphical editors [28], and graphical interfaces [29]. A framework can be chosen by viewing the documentation, or through other user's experiences. In particular, the documentation covering the purpose and intended use of the framework should indicate if the framework is compatible with the requirements. The documentation should also list any limitations of the framework. By looking at the hot spots of the framework (see Chapter 25), users can check to see if the framework has the desired flexibility. By looking more closely at the hooks of the framework, users can try to map the functional requirements met by the hooks with the requirements of the application. Non-functional requirements have to be matched to the capabilities given in the description of the purpose of the framework. Additionally, the framework determines the types of requirements that can be met. If the chosen framework supports a restrictive set of system functionalities, then any system developed from the framework may also be restrictive unless significant changes are made to the framework itself, which is a dangerous practice to follow.

In the RCIM graphical display application we have several general requirements. Two views are provided: the Strategic Object View which displays all of the Strategic Objects and Strategic Relationships connected below a given root object, and the Constraint Object View which displays a single Strategic Object and all Constraint Objects and Constraint Relationships connected to it. All strategic and constraint objects are represented using graphical icons that are combinations of text and polygons. Objects go through a number of different states depending on the current state of the plan and each state has a different look, some of which can be set to blink to attract attention when inconstancies in the plan arise. All relationships are represented using lines. Multiple views can be open at the same time and each view should be kept consistent with one another. Additionally, each view has a distinct layout associated with it which is performed automatically by the program.

Since HotDraw is a framework for manipulating and displaying diagrams, it proved to be a good platform upon which to build a graphical display application for the diagrams. HotDraw provides `Figures` to represent the objects and relationships. It provides hooks for animation to perform the blinking, and it allows multiple views to be associated with a single underlying drawing each of which is updated to maintain consistency across views. While the display application does not make use of the `Tools`, HotDraw's support for tools and figure manipulation allows us to extend the display application into a graphical editor with little difficulty. The only major requirement not supported is automatic layout, which might be a problem if the required layout strategy is incompatible with the framework. At this point, we can look at the hot spots to see if the framework can be extended, or into the design of the framework itself. It turns out that layout routines can be added to the `Drawing` class with little difficulty, but this requires a more advanced use of the framework.

26.4.3 Learning to Use the Framework

One of the first difficulties faced by users of any framework is learning how to use it. Frameworks are typically complex and abstract, making them difficult to learn. Learning how to use a framework given only the code and interface descriptions is a daunting task and makes framework use unattractive. A framework should be easier to use as the basis for an application than building a new application without the framework, so some means of lowering the learning curve is needed. Some approaches are

- **Framework developers as users** — When the framework developers are also the ones developing applications and maintaining the framework, they are already experts on the framework and require little, if any, time to learn it. They can also pass on their expertise to new developers on an informal basis when it is needed. As long as the framework developers do not leave and take their expertise with them, this approach can be affective for in-house frameworks. However, for frameworks that will be distributed to other users, other methods are needed.
- **Tutorial sessions** — Framework developers can hold tutorials in which they show potential users what the framework can be used for and how it can be used. Often the developers go through examples which help to make the abstract details of the framework more concrete and understandable. Sessions can also be held as the framework is being developed in order to gradually expose users to new concepts in the framework [23].
- **Tool support** — A good tool can make a framework much easier to use. With it, regular users generally do not have to learn all the details about the framework since the tool will dictate how and where adaptions can take place. The tool will perform the tedious tasks of integrating components into the framework, leaving users free to focus on design. A simple example of this is the `ToolBuilder` tool which comes with HotDraw [15]. It allows users to build new tools simply by filling in the appropriate parameters and then automatically integrates the new tool into an application. More complex tools such as the one provided for OSEFA [22] help users to develop complete applications by allowing them to select from existing components or sometimes to add their own components. However, the tool also constrains how the framework can be used, so it is not as valuable to advanced users that want to use the framework in new ways. Existing tools also tend to be tied to individual frameworks and cannot be used with other frameworks, or be used to integrate more than one framework together.
- **Documentation** — Good documentation can aid users in learning the framework. It can be used to not only capture the design details and design rationale of the framework, but also to help users to learn the framework. Each type of user can be accommodated by different types of documentation. Documentation is discussed in detail later in Section 26.7.

26.4.4 Design and Implementation

Learning how to use the framework is closely related to using the framework during application design and implementation. However, some knowledge of how to use the framework is necessary before application system design can start.

Since the framework should already define an abstract design of the application and provide much of the implementation, users have much less work to do at this stage. Frameworks are used as a whole rather than piecemeal. When building an application from a framework, the framework core will form the basis for the application. Regular users will not have to do much additional design as they will follow what is already present in the framework. A calling framework defines the main execution loop. It forms the core of the application and it calls application extensions. The user assumes an assemblers role of providing pieces required by the framework in order to complete the application rather than building an application that calls functions within the framework. Advanced users will likely extend or modify the framework, but the additional design has to be constrained to fit the existing design of the framework.

If hooks are defined for the framework, then all users can follow them to adapt the framework. Hooks can provide support for choosing components to customize the framework, for completing the framework by filling in parameters or patterns of behavior, or by allowing new behavior to be added, with some customization. If hooks are not provided, then the user has to discover how the framework can be adapted through other documentation or communication with the framework developers or other users.

There are three general ways in which frameworks can be adapted to an application without modifying the framework itself. The framework may come with library components that can be used directly within the application without modification. The components have the advantage of already being developed for the framework and so should integrate smoothly. All that the user must do is select the components and connect them to the framework. Tools can be provided for the framework to make the connection and configuration automatic. The RCIM graphical display application makes use of several existing `Figures` within HotDraw to compose other `Figures` as shown in Figure 26.3. The `RCIMObject` figure is composed of existing `RectangleFigures` and `TextFigures`.

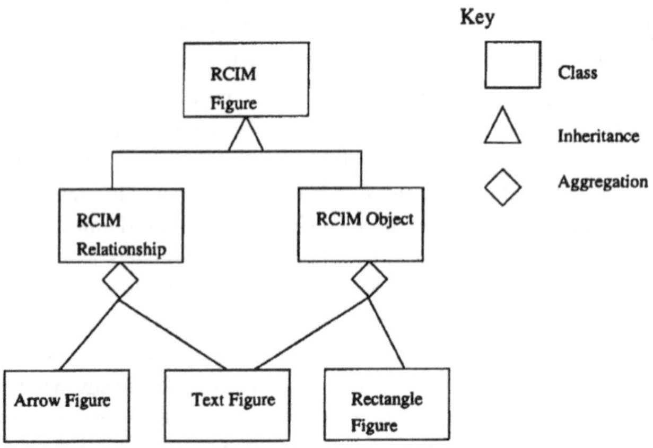

FIGURE 26.3 Composing figures in HotDraw.

When existing components are not available, new ones must be developed and fitted to the framework. How the new components are developed depends on whether the hook into the framework is done through composition or inheritance. With composition, the user is generally provided with an interface that the framework requires and develops a component that conforms to that interface. With inheritance, an abstract class is provided which the user "subclasses" and fills in with methods or parameters. The graphical display application requires strategic objects in certain states to blink, and so it uses the animation hook provided by HotDraw within the `Drawing` class. `Drawing` does not provide the required animation, so as shown in Figure 26.4, a new class `RCIMDrawing` is derived from `Drawing`. The `step` method of `RCIMDrawing` is then filled in to perform the desired animation.

When the framework does not already contain the desired functionality, then it has to be added. However, the addition of new functionality is specific and local to the application, and does not become part of the framework itself. If the new functionality is applicable to many different applications then

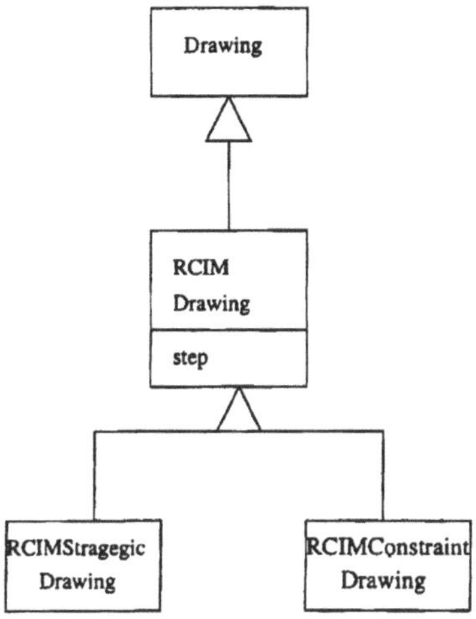

FIGURE 26.4 RCIMDrawing class.

the framework must evolve in order to include the functionality. Extending the framework with new functionality is a more advanced use of the framework and requires a greater understanding of the design of the framework. While configuring and completing the framework allows regular users to treat much of the framework as a black box, extending the framework requires that the advanced user understand both the structure and behavior of the framework. New functionality has to fit into the existing structure and behavior by preserving the state of the framework. In the RCIM display application, the framework can be extended to provide automatic layout capabilities. The layout occurs at the level of the `Drawing` so we investigate the `Drawing` class and its interactions to see how to integrate the layout capabilities. Layout needs to occur when figures are added or deleted, and the layout routines are inserted into the framework's flow of control at those points after the framework has completed its normal processing. The `RCIMDrawing` class is modified to call the layout algorithms at those points. Layout is provided as a separate class, since it is important to be able to provide different layout algorithms for different types of drawings, and it is connected to the `RCIMDrawing` as shown in Figure 26.5. The `Layout` class also directly interacts with the `Figures` within the drawing in order to reposition them.

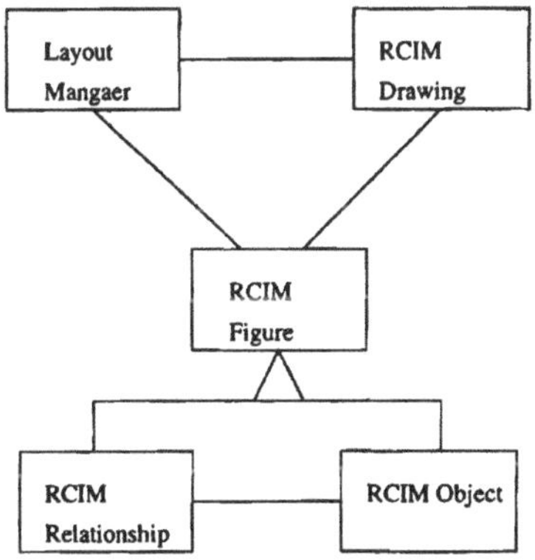

FIGURE 26.5 Inclusion of layout in the RCIM display application.

Because the layout algorithm is a general extension to the framework, it might be added to the framework itself for other applications to use. New hooks can also be added to the addition and deletion methods of the `Drawing` class to indicate that the class can be extended easily at those points.

26.4.5 Testing

Applications developed from frameworks can be tested just as any other application. The framework itself may come with tests predefined to determine if the application extensions are integrated properly with the framework. However, additional tests for the application specific functionality will always be needed. If errors are discovered, they can occur in three different places.

1. **In the interface to the framework** — The framework may require a specific interface or that certain conditions be met by application extensions. Pre- and post-conditions on all framework interfaces can help to highlight these errors when they occur and make them easier to track down.
2. **In the application** — Some errors will be within the application extensions. These errors tend to occur within the new functionality added to the framework.
3. **In the framework** — The framework itself may have errors within it. Framework errors are probably the most difficult to find, since users will be unfamiliar with the fine details of the framework. When they do occur, developers have one of three difficult choices: fix the error (which may not be possible if the source code is not available), devise a work around, or stop using the framework.

26.5 Using Multiple Frameworks

Thus far we have focused on developing an application from a single framework. However, a single framework will not always cover every aspect of the application to be developed. Since small frameworks are generally preferred over large ones, sometimes more than one framework will be used in a single application. The same general techniques for using single frameworks apply, but two new problems arise: framework gap and framework overlap [23].

Framework gap occurs when there are holes between the functionality provided by two different frameworks. One framework may expect data in a particular format that the other framework does not provide. Alternatively, one framework may expect some amount of processing to be done that the other framework does not do. In order to fit the frameworks together, application extensions have to be made to one or both to fill in the gaps. The extensions will do data conversion or extra processing so that the frameworks interface correctly.

Framework overlap is a more serious problem. In framework overlap, two frameworks provide the same functionality, or expect control over the same resources. An example of framework overlap occurs when two frameworks contain the main event loop for the application. To use the frameworks together, the overlapping functionality of one of the frameworks has to be removed or turned off, which may not always be easy or even feasible.

26.6 Evolving Frameworks

Just like any other software, frameworks evolve. However, little work has been done on framework evolution. We define evolution as any changes to the framework itself as opposed to additions or extensions made to the framework for specific applications. Frameworks evolve to fix errors, to add new functionality, or to restructure for more flexibility or ease of use. For example, the `Tool` class in the HotDraw framework has evolved to become more structured and easier to use by switching from requiring inheritance to a parameterized class. Frameworks also evolve as a normal part of the development process as more experience is gained in using them.

A problem faced by all reusable software is the potential side effects of changing the framework code for applications already built from earlier versions of the framework. In order to take advantage of the new features or fixes within the framework, the application has to be fitted to the new framework. If the application is not changed, then multiple versions of the framework have to be maintained, which undermines the ease of maintenance gained by basing a product line on a common framework. Ideally, the evolved framework can simply be inserted into the application and no changes will have to be made. The interfaces of the framework should be fixed and rarely changed [26]. The hooks, which can be viewed as a special type of interface, should also remain relatively constant in order to make the upgrade easier. Obviously, this applies to frameworks which are used as is or completed. Applications which customize the framework by replacing parts of it will require much more work to fit into the new framework. Two means of evolving frameworks are refactoring and using design patterns.

26.6.1 Refactoring

Refactorings [19] are ways of restructuring a framework. They are behavior preserving transformations for evolving a framework, producing semantically equivalent references and operations. Refactorings, for example, cover aspects of creating new abstract superclasses, creating aggregate classes, changing class names, changing variable references and method calls, changing inheritance hierarchies, moving methods between classes, and grouping classes together. Complex refactorings, such as moving a method between classes, are made up of smaller refactoring steps, such as updating all references to the method. Tool support is provided for the refactorings, and it aids in ensuring that all required changes are made. Using a refactoring guarantees that the behavior of the framework is preserved, although the interfaces and class structure may change. They are used for consolidating and simplifying the interfaces and functionality of the framework to make it easier to both use and refine.

26.6.2 Using Design Patterns

Design patterns can also be used to help evolve frameworks as a means of increasing flexibility. Johnson claims that as frameworks mature, they evolve from using inheritance to using composition [14]. Many design patterns focus on composing classes together, and providing flexible and extensible solutions, so they are valuable for determining possible directions for framework evolution.

An example of using patterns to evolve a framework comes from the telecommunications domain [13]. The initial framework is a white box framework that relies heavily on inheritance. Experience gained from using the framework helped them to identify areas where the framework could be made more flexible. Once they identified the type of flexibility required, they were able to apply appropriate design patterns to restructure the framework. Unlike refactorings, evolving a framework in this way does not guarantee that the behavior of the framework is preserved, but it does allow other types of changes to be made, such as extensions to the functionality of the framework.

26.7 Documentation

Framework documentation can aid in all aspects of framework use. Since the framework developers will not always be available, documentation becomes the means through which users can learn about the framework and refer to for information about the framework. A framework will typically have few developers and many users, so it is important that the documentation be made both understandable and up to date. Johnson (1992) proposes that three types of documentation are needed for frameworks.

1. *The purpose of the framework* — A description of the domain that the framework is in, the requirements it is meant to fulfill, and any limitations it has.
2. *The use of the framework* — A description of the way the framework builder intended the framework to be used.
3. *The design of the framework* — A description of the structure and the behavior of the framework.

Framework documentation should not just consist of class diagrams describing the detailed design of the framework. While advanced users will require that information, learning all of that information will require too much effort for regular users, thus making the framework impractical for general use. Documentation describing what the framework is for and how it can be used will aid regular users in both learning and using the framework. The additional documentation shows users those parts of the framework they need to know about and those which they can treat as a black box in order to make efficient use of their time. Examples are also valuable to show for what the framework can be used. Each of these types of documentation are discussed in the following subsections.

26.7.1 Purpose

There are no standard methods for documenting the purpose of a framework. Generally a high-level overview of the framework is needed which serves as an introduction to the framework. The introduction can be used to help quickly decide if the framework is appropriate for the intended application. As a rough guideline, the purpose should include:

- Domain — The domain that the framework covers should be defined as clearly as possible. It is often difficult to pin down the exact domain that the framework covers, so giving examples of applications that can and have been built with the framework is a useful technique [15].
- Requirements — The functional and non-functional requirements that the framework fulfills.
- Limitations — Any limitations or assumptions about a framework's environment should also be stated, if possible. Putting the limitations up front prevent users from finding out halfway through a project that the framework they have chosen cannot support their requirements.

26.7.2 Intended Use

Beyond the general purpose of the framework, regular users are interested in how to use the framework. Documentation describing the intended uses of the framework helps users to learn the framework and develop applications. Documentation of intended use should identify the problems that the framework solves or that users will face when using the framework, how to think about the problem in order to understand how to solve it, and the actual solution [2]. Documentation also captures the framework developer's experience and knowledge of how the framework can be used. These are valuable insights that otherwise would have to be gained by users through trial and error since this knowledge is not captured explicitly in the design and implementation of the framework. Several methods have been proposed for describing the intended use. In the following subsections, we introduce three documentation methods: motifs/patterns, cookbooks, and hooks.

26.7.2.1 Motifs/Patterns

Johnson (1992) proposes that the experience and knowledge of framework developers about how the framework can be used should be captured by a series of patterns. Lajoie and Keller (1995) call these patterns motifs in order to avoid confusion with design patterns (discussed later in this section).

Each motif has the following parts:

- Name — The name identifies the motif and gives an indication of what problem the motif is intended to solve.
- Description of the problem — A brief description acquaints the user with the purpose of the motif. From the description, a potential framework user should be able to decide whether or not the motif matches the problem they want to solve.
- Description of the solution — The longest and most detailed section of the motif describes various potential ways of solving the problem. The description tends to be general and high level enough to accommodate a range of solutions. Often brief examples help the user to understand the solution.
- Summary of the solution — Finally, the motif ends with a brief summary of how the problem is solved. It also points to other motifs which solve related problems.

The series of motifs starts with a general overview of the framework. The overview describes the purpose of the framework, what problems it is appropriate for, and it also gives a brief process for using the framework. For example, the following simple outline is given for using HotDraw: "*To design a drawing editor using HotDraw, first list the atomic elements of the diagram. Each one will be a subclass of Figure. Decide whether the drawing needs to be animated. List the tools that will be in the palette and make a subclass of DrawingEditor with a tools method that returns an array of the tools making up the palette*" [15].

The motifs provide a high-level narrative of how to solve various problems that application developers may encounter when trying to use the framework. The descriptions are informal and easy to read, but often they leave out detailed information that a user may require. They are valuable for understanding the key concepts behind the framework. Each motif also links to other motifs, starting with the initial motif that describes the framework. The collection of motifs form a directed graph that moves from very general to more specific information about the framework and provides a way in which users can learn about the framework gradually without being overwhelmed by the details right away.

Lajoie and Keller (1995) combine the idea of design patterns with Johnson's patterns to provide a more complete description of a framework. In their strategy, motifs point to design patterns, contracts [12], and micro-architectures to help provide the developer with an understanding of the architecture of the framework in the context of the problems it was meant to solve.

Beck (1994) proposes a slightly different style of pattern. Each pattern starts out with a brief problem description. The next part describes the context of the pattern. The context is the set of constraints that affect the solution to the problem. Often these constraints conflict with one another and may seem to rule out a solution altogether. The description of the context is meant to give an understanding of exactly what the problem is and why the solution is structured in a certain way within the framework. The solution then describes what to do to solve the problem.

26.7.2.2 Cookbooks

Cookbooks for describing how to use frameworks have been around almost as long as frameworks themselves. At least two styles of cookbooks have been used. Krasner and Pope (1988) use a tutorial style in describing the basics of the Model-View-Controller framework in Smalltalk. The first parts describe the framework in general and subsequent parts describe specific parts of the framework in more detail. Finally, several examples using the framework are provided.

The second, and more common, type of cookbook is related to patterns. A cookbook of recipes [27] is provided, with each pattern describing a problem and a series of steps to follow to solve the problem. Each recipe consists of the following parts:

- Strategy — The first section introduces the recipe, describes the problem it is meant to solve, and may include some of the limitations of the solution. It provides all of the information needed to understand the context of the solution.

- Basic steps — The actual solution is captured as a sequence of steps to carry out. These steps include using development tools as well as actual code. Often a simple example is included to help demonstrate the solution.
- Variants — Solutions that are essentially the same as the one given in the basic steps, but differing in some small way, are provided. The variants help to capture some of the alternative or advanced uses of the framework.
- See also — The final section directs the user to other descriptions that are related to the current description.

The recipes are provided as a catalog and indexed by their name. Unlike motifs there is no reading order specified, so they form more of a reference than a learning tool. Like motifs, descriptions are informal so they are easy to read and usually easy to understand. The steps provided are more focused than the general notes given in a motif, therefore they provide more support to novice users.

26.7.2.3 Hook Descriptions

Since cookbooks and motifs are loosely structured narrative descriptions, they sometimes face the problem of being imprecise or lacking information needed by the user. Hook descriptions [9] provide a semi-formal template for describing the intended use at a detailed level. The template helps to prompt the developer for all the required information and the semi-formal language makes the descriptions more precise.

The sections of the template detail different aspects of the hook, such as the components that take part in the hook (`participants`) or the steps that should be followed to use the hook (`changes`). The sections serve as a guide to the people writing the hooks by showing the aspects that should be considered about the hook, such as how using it affects the rest of the framework (constraints). The format helps to organize the information and make the description more precise and uniform. This aids in the analysis of hooks and the provision of tool support for them. Each hook description consists of the following parts:

- Name — A unique name, within the context of the framework, given to each hook.
- Requirement — The problem the hook is intended to help solve.
- Type — An ordered pair consisting of the method of adaption used and the amount of support provided for the problem within the framework.
- Area — The area(s) and parts of the framework that are affected by the hook.
- Uses — The other hooks required to use this hook; the use of a single hook may not be enough to completely fulfill a requirement that has several aspects to it, so this section lists the other hooks that are needed to help fulfill the requirement.
- Participants — The components that participate in the hook; these are both existing and new components.
- Changes — The main section of the hook which outlines the changes to the interfaces, associations, control flow, and synchronization among the components given in the participants section; while the changes focus on the design level, so as not to overly constrain the developers, sometimes changes to the code itself must be included. All changes, including those involving the use of other hooks, are intended to be made in the order they are given within this section.
- Constraints — Limits imposed by using the hook, such as configuration constraints.
- Comments — Any additional description needed.

Not all sections will be applicable to all hooks, in which case the entry not required is simply left out. For example, a hook that does not use any others will have no Uses declaration. An example of a hook is shown below.

Name: `Create a New Composite Figure`
Requirement: `A new figure is needed which is composed of other figures, such as a text label within a rectangle.`
Type: `Enabling, Pattern`
Area: `Figures`
Uses: `SetFigures, SetConstraints`
Participants: `CompositeFigure, NewComposite`
Changes:

```
new subclass NewComposite of CompositeFigure
property NewComposite.figures
NewComposite.figures = SetFigures
property NewComposite.figure_constraints
NewComposite.constraints = SetConstraints [NewComposite.figures]
NewComposite.constraints overrides CompositeFigure.constraints
  returns set of NewComposite.figure_constraints
```

The `Create a New Composite Figure` hook describes how to create new figures which are composed of other more basic figures within HotDraw. This hook was used to create the `RCIM Figures` within the RCIM graphical display application. The hook uses functionality provided by the framework by filling in parameters so its type is an enabling pattern. In this case the parameters are the figures contained in the composite figure and the constraints between the figures. `NewComposite` is defined as a subclass of the existing class `CompositeFigure`. `NewComposite` adds the `figures` and `figure_constraints` properties (instance variables in this case) and uses them to hold the component figures and constraints. The additional hooks `SetFigures` and `SetConstraints` are used to fill in the figures and constraints for the new class. For example, `RCIM Object` defines two component classes: `Text Figure` and `Rectangle Figure`. It also defines graphical constraints between the component figures so that the position of the text label remains constant with respect to the location of the rectangle when the location of the entire composite figure is changed. Finally, the `constraints` method is provided to return the set of constraints defined for a class so that they can be evaluated when needed.

Hooks are characterized along two axes: the *method of adaption* used and the *level of support* provided. The method of adaption is used to fulfill the requirement and describes the basic mechanism used to extend or adapt the framework. The level of support indicates how the change is supported within the framework, such as using provided components or requiring developers to produce their own components. For example, removing a feature, such as the use of tools in HotDraw, may be well-supported and simply require turning off a switch in the framework, or may be less well-supported and require the modification of one or more methods.

A hook's method of adaption quickly gives an application developer an idea of what the hook does. Its support type indicates how difficult it may be to use. The types can also serve as a basis for locating a desired hook. For example, if a developer needs to extend the framework in a particular area, they could retrieve all of the hooks that add a feature to that part of the framework. Each type indicates the issues that both the hook writer and the application developer must consider. For example, removing a feature such as the use of tools in HotDraw will often have an impact on other features of the framework, such as the ability for the user to manipulate the figures in a diagram.

26.7.2.4 Method of Adaption

There are several ways that a developer can adapt a framework and each hook uses at least one of these methods.

Enabling a feature that exists within the framework but is not part of the default implementation is one common means of adapting a framework. Hooks of this type often involve using pre-built concrete components that come with the framework which may be further parameterized. The hook needs to detail how to enable the feature, such as which components to select for inclusion in the application, which parameters to fill in, or how to configure a set of components. The constraints imposed by using the feature, such as excluding the use of another feature, are also contained in the hook.

Disabling a feature may be required if the default implementation of the framework has some unwanted properties. This is different from simply not choosing to enable a feature. Disabling a feature may be done through configuration parameters or by actual modification of framework code. The hook description shows how to do the removal and it also shows the effects of the removal. For example, removing the use of tools from HotDraw significantly affects the capabilities of the rest of the framework.

Replacing or overriding an existing feature is related to disabling a feature, with the addition that new or pre-defined components are provided in place of the old. If the replacement requires the application developer to provide new classes or components then it is important to describe the interface and behavioral obligations that any replacement must fulfill. The replacement may also be a pre-defined component that the developer simply puts in place of the original component.

Augmenting a feature involves intercepting the existing flow of control, performing some needed actions, and returning control back to the framework. Unlike replacing behavior, augmenting simply adds to the behavior without redefining it. The framework builder can point to places in the control flow where a change to fulfill a particular requirement might be made, perhaps but not always, by providing stub methods that can be overridden by developers. The hook describes any state that needs to be maintained, where to intercept the flow of control, and where to return it.

Adding a new feature or service to the framework is another common adaptation and probably the most difficult to support. Unlike enabling a feature, where the developer is using existing services, possibly in new ways, adding a feature involves adding something that the framework was not capable of before. These additions are often done by extending existing classes with new services or adding new classes, and adding new paths of control with the new services. The hook shows what new classes or operations are needed, and indicates where to integrate them into the framework and how they interact with old classes and services. The framework builder may also provide constraints that must be met by the new class or service and which may limit the interfaces that the new class can use to interact with the framework.

26.7.2.5 Level of Support

Another important aspect of hooks is the level of support provided for the adaption within the framework. There are three main levels of support types for hooks.

The *option* level provides the most support, and it is generally the easiest for the application developer to use. A number of pre-built components are provided within the framework and the developer simply chooses one without requiring extensive knowledge about the framework. This is the black box approach to frameworks [14]. Most often, components are chosen to enable features within the framework or to replace default components. If the solutions are alternatives, then the hook is a single option hook. If several alternatives can be used at once, then the hook is a multi-option hook. For example, several existing tools can be incorporated into an application based on HotDraw using a multi-option hook.

At the *pattern* level, the developer supplies parameters to components and/or follows a well-supported pattern of behavior. Unlike option hooks, there are no complete pre-defined components to choose from, but support is generally provided for the feature through parameters to components. The simplest patterns occur when the developer needs to provide parameters to a single class within the framework. The parameters themselves may be as simple as base variables, or as complex as methods or component classes. Some common tasks may require the collaboration of multiple classes, and they may also have application specific details. For these, a collaboration pattern is provided in which the developer follows to realize the task. Both pattern and option hooks are well suited for normal users of the framework because they do not require a complete understanding of the design of the framework.

At the *open-ended* level hooks are provided to fulfill requirements without being well supported within the framework. Open-ended hooks involve adding new properties to classes, new components to the framework, new interactions among components, or sometimes the modification of existing code. These modifications often, but not always, are for more advanced users that have a greater knowledge of the design of the framework so that they are aware of potential problems the modification may cause. Because they are open-ended, the developer has to be more careful about the effects changes will have on the framework.

26.7.2.6 Hooks and Motifs

The level of detail and semi-formal notation makes the hooks more suitable for partial automation than motifs or cookbooks. Well-defined hooks at the option or pattern level might be fed into a tool which automatically applies them when selected and their participants are filled in by the user. Hooks can provide the basis for a flexible tool that can be applied to more than one framework. The tool can also be open-ended, since hook descriptions can be modified as the framework evolves, or new hooks can be added as they are documented over time.

However, this level of detail provided by hooks is not as useful for novice users who are just learning the framework. Hooks require a certain level of knowledge about the framework, and thus may be confusing at first. Also, the hook descriptions do not present the forces involved in a solution or trade offs involved in alternate solutions.

Motifs and hook descriptions can be combined to provide a more complete description of the intended use of the framework. Their strengths complement each other nicely. A motif provides a general, relatively high-level description of a problem and its constraints, perhaps giving an overview of a particular hot spot within the framework. The motif can then refer to a number of more detailed and precise hook descriptions which are used to actually adapt the framework to an application.

26.7.3 Design

Documentation of the design is most useful to advanced users, maintainers, and framework developers, since they need to know the details of the framework. Regular users may also need to understand some of the design of a framework. While normal methods such as Booch's method [3], the OMT [21] or their unified effort, UML [4], can be used to document the design of a framework, they are often not sufficient for a full description. The problem with traditional notations is that the collaborative relationships between the core classes of the framework are not made explicit [11]. In any object-oriented software, understanding the collaborations is important, but in frameworks it is crucial since frameworks are meant to be reused. The collaborations describe how the classes interact and often comprise much of the complexity of the framework. In order to better represent these collaborations, several specialized methods for documenting the design of an object-oriented framework have been developed. The following methods are briefly described in this section: multiple views, exemplars, design patterns, metapatterns, reuse contracts, and behavioral contracts.

26.7.3.1 Multiple Views

Campbell and Islam (1992) document the design of frameworks by providing several different views of the design. Each view captures a different aspect of the design and together they provide a view of both the structure and behavior of the framework. The views are:

- Class hierarchies — Inheritance hierarchies explicitly show the root abstract classes and all derived concrete library classes.
- Interface protocols — The interface protocols are the methods that each class in the framework makes public. The protocols list the methods along with their return values and parameter types.

- Synchronization — Path expressions specify the order in which methods of a class must be invoked. For example, the initialization method of a `Figure` must be invoked before it can be moved or resized. Path expressions can also define methods which should not be invoked together.
- Control flow — Message passing in the runtime behavior of the framework is represented using control flow diagrams. Each diagram presents the classes and methods invoked in a particular operation and the sequence in which messages occur.
- Entity relationship model — The relationships between objects in the framework and the cardinality of those relationships are shown using ER diagrams. Optional and mandatory links can also be expressed.
- Configuration constraints — A framework may have components that are not meant to be used together but are included in the framework library for the purposes of completeness. Components are labeled with a type attribute and a Venn diagram is used to show which types can or cannot be used together in a single application.

There are many views in this approach and integrating all of the information can be a problem, so this method is not as popular as some of the others. However, none of the other methods describe configuration constraints which can be important.

26.7.3.2 Exemplars

An exemplar consists of at least one instance of a concrete class for every abstract class in the framework [11]. Collaborations between the objects are explicitly and formally represented, so the collaborations cannot only be viewed, but the entire exemplar can be executed as well. A visual tool allows framework users to interactively explore the relationships between the instances and thus learn the interconnections between the main classes of the framework. The exemplar is provided by the framework developers with the framework and application developers can use the exemplar by following several steps.

1. Exploration — This visual tool is used to explore the framework. The tool shows the static relationships between classes. It also allows the user to observe message passing between the objects to provide an understanding of the runtime behavior of the framework. The user has the advantage of actually being able to see the framework execute in a limited way to gain a deeper understanding of how the framework works.
2. Selection — After the framework user has gained an understanding of the framework through exploring the exemplar, the user can select objects from the exemplar that need to be replaced or modified to fit the requirements of the application being built.
3. Finding alternatives — The tool allows the user to explore the inheritance hierarchy for a selected object. It displays the abstract class and the framework library classes derived from the class that correspond to the object and the user can select the one that is needed for the application. By restricting the search to the inheritance hierarchy of the selected object, the tool cuts down on the number of classes the user has to search through.
4. Adaptation — If no appropriate replacement class exists within the framework, then a new one has to be created. The replacement can, for example, be a subclass of the existing abstract class corresponding to the object selected, or it can be a composition of more than one existing class.

An object of the replacement class can then be inserted into the exemplar model, and it can be executed to see if it has the desired behavior. Framework users repeat this process for every object they wish to replace and can, in part, prototype the application by selectively replacing objects. The authors call this process *Design by Framework Completion.* By substituting classes directly, application developers are able to use the framework as is, but there is no direct support for extending the framework in new ways. However, the understanding of the framework gained by exploring the exemplar helps developers to use the framework in new ways.

26.7.3.3 Design Patterns

A design pattern [10] is a solution to a common software design problem in a given context. Design patterns are valuable because they capture the expertise of software developers, expertise that can be used in education, in design, and in the documentation of object-oriented systems. Many frameworks are designed using design patterns and the patterns used serve as a form of documentation for the framework.

Design patterns consist of four general parts, although the exact format often varies between pattern authors.

- Pattern Name — The name gives a brief image of the pattern. The name is important because it becomes a part of a developer's vocabulary. The name provides a means of describing a potentially complex set of classes and their collaborations in a single word or two. In effect they can become an important and standard means of communication between and among framework developers and framework users.
- Problem — The problem is a description of both the problem that the pattern is meant to solve and the context in which the pattern is applicable. The context is often described as a set of conditions that must apply before the pattern can be used.
- Solution — The main part of the pattern describes the static structure of the pattern and the collaborations between the classes it contains. The solution is a template rather than a specific implementation. Since the problem descriptions are general, the template approach typically allows for a range of variations to fit the specific problems to be solved in an application or framework.
- Consequences — Every pattern has some effect on the overall design of a framework or application, and the consequences section describes those effects. Knowing the limitations of the design patterns that a framework uses helps users decide if the framework is appropriate and can prevent users from trying to use the framework in inappropriate ways.

Design patterns aid in the understanding of frameworks in several ways. First, they provide a description of the design. The description includes both the classes and the collaborations between the classes which is crucial to understanding the framework. The patterns can also make a complex design much easier to understand since they raise the level of granularity at which the design is viewed. Instead of viewing a framework as a collection of low level classes, the framework can be viewed as a collection of interwoven patterns, each of which contains several classes that interact in standard ways. The patterns provide a shared vocabulary between framework developers and framework users that can help users to more quickly gain an understanding of the overall structure and behavior of the framework.

Second, each design pattern specifically states the problem it solves and the context in which it is used so it can help to convey the intent of the design [2]. The record of why certain design decisions were made can help the user to understand how the framework can be used, and how it should not be used (what would break the framework). The design patterns can also help maintainers during evolution of the framework to understand the assumptions behind the design and to change the design if the assumptions no longer hold. Finally, a kind of tutorial can be provided using design patterns to help users to learn the framework. An initial problem the framework solves is stated and the design pattern used is described. Subsequent problems and pattern descriptions build on earlier descriptions to slowly build up a view of the architecture and behavior of the framework.

Finally, design patterns can be used to explore or visualize the design of an existing framework [18]. By using a visual tool, users can view the framework classes within a design pattern and even watch the execution of the framework through the patterns. However, research into visualization of design patterns is still in an early stage, and users must find and identify the patterns within the framework themselves, limiting the usefulness of the approach as a learning tool.

26.7.3.4 Metapatterns

Metapatterns [20] use meta-abstractions to describe ways of designing flexible connections between classes. They are called metapatterns because a design pattern can usually be described using a combination of metapatterns. However, the metapatterns do not capture the specific problem and context information inherent in design patterns.

Each metapattern identifies a relationship between a template method which is defined in the framework, and a hook method that is left open for the application developer to complete. The class that contains the template method is called the template class and the class that contains the hook method is the hook class. Hook methods and hook classes are not the same as the hooks described earlier. Hooks are a means of adapting a framework, whereas hook methods are something to be adapted. A simple example of a metapattern used in HotDraw occurs between the `DrawingController` and the `Drawing`. In order to animate a drawing (such as having a `Figure` blinking in the RCIM graphical display application) the `DrawingController` calls the hook method `step` in `Drawing`. It is an example of the 1:1 connection pattern since each `DrawingController` is associated with a single `Drawing`.

Metapatterns can help document frameworks in the same way as patterns, and they can be an aid to advanced users and framework evolvers. Because not every part of the framework will have a corresponding design pattern to describe it, metapatterns can be used to help document the other areas.

26.7.3.5 Reuse Contracts

Reuse contracts [24] form a specialization interface between a class and subclasses developed from it. They consist of a set of descriptions of abstract and concrete methods that are crucial to inheritors while hiding implementation specific details. Specialization clauses can be attached to methods. They consist of a set of methods that must be invoked by the method being specialized, documenting all *self* method invocations of a method. The methods within the specialization clause are called hook methods and have the same purpose as Pree's hook methods (methods to be filled in by application developers).

Reuse operators formally define how abstract classes are used by defining relationships between the reuse contract of an abstract class and the reuse contract of its subclass. Three reuse operators are defined:

1. Refinement — Overriding method descriptions to refine their functionality; new hook methods are added to the specialization clause of the method being overridden while keeping all of the existing hook methods. The specialization clause is extended and the behavior of the method is refined. The inverse of refinement is called coarsening. Coarsening is used to remove hook methods from a specialization clause.
2. Extension — Adding new method descriptions to a reuse contract; the new methods contain functionality specific to a framework library, or application class. If the new methods are all concrete, then the extension is concrete, otherwise it is abstract. The opposite of extension is cancellation in which unwanted method descriptions are removed from the reuse contract.
3. Concretization — Overriding some abstract methods within the contract with concrete ones; this is often done by application developers when producing an application. The opposite of concretization is abstraction in which concrete methods are defined as abstract. Abstraction is useful for forming abstractions when developing frameworks.

Reuse contracts can help to specify what methods need to be specialized in an abstract class, and define operators for creating new classes from an abstract class. In that way, they define how the class can be used. However, they primarily document how a subclass relates to its parent class, defining and documenting the changes between the classes. Reuse contracts are useful when frameworks evolve. The effects of changes to a parent class can be propagated down to all of its child classes through the reuse contracts. Using the relationships between reuse contracts defined by the operators, the contracts can indicate how much work is needed to update child classes, including those in previously built applications, when a framework changes.

26.7.3.6 Behavioral Contracts

Behavioral contracts [12], are used to help design a framework and are also valuable for learning the framework and ensuring that the framework is correctly used. The contract defines a number of participants, corresponding to objects, and defines how they interact. They form templates which can be similar to design patterns. Each contract consists of the following parts.

- Contractual obligations — The obligations define what each participant must support. The obligations consist of both type obligations (variables and interfaces) and causal obligations. The causal obligations consists of sequences of actions that must be performed and conditions that must be met.
- Invariants — The contract also specifies any conditions that must always be kept true by the contract, and how to satisfy the invariant when it becomes false.
- Instantiation — Pre-conditions form the final part of the contract which must be satisfied by the participants before the contract can be established.

Behavioral contracts can aid both regular and advanced users in understanding how objects in the framework collaborate. A general contract can often be used in a new context, much like a design pattern, and thus new framework developers will be interested in them as well. An example of a contract is given in Chapter 25.

26.7.4 Examples

Examples provide another means of learning the framework and complement all of the other types of documentation. The examples can be complete applications developed from the framework, or smaller examples to demonstrate how a particular hot spot can be used, or how a given design pattern works. The examples are valuable because they make an abstract framework concrete and easier to understand. They provide a specific problem and show how the framework can be used to solve that problem. Examples are also valuable to framework evolvers for regression testing of the framework.

An example application might also be modified into a new application if it is similar enough to the desired application. However, examples cannot cover every possible use of the framework and so the other forms of purpose, intent, and design documentation are all still necessary.

26.8 Conclusions

Frameworks provide a means of capturing the knowledge of domain experts and packaging this expertise in a form that can be used by many different users. Regular users who are not experts in the domain can build quality applications based on the framework simply by configuring pre-defined components within the framework, or by completing parts of the framework left open.

Individual applications can be developed more quickly and easily using the framework since it provides much of the implementation of the application already. Entire product lines can be quickly developed from a single framework and can be more easily maintained due to the common design and code base.

Documentation is important for supporting all types of framework use. Documentation should describe the purpose of the framework in order to aid users in deciding whether or not to use the framework. It should describe how to use the framework to aid regular users to quickly develop applications from the framework. It should also describe the design of the framework to aid advanced users, maintainers, and developers of new frameworks. Examples can be used to both explain ways in which the framework can be used, and to test the framework when it evolves.

Tool support is one of the most promising areas that needs to be investigated. Many uses of the framework can be described as standard patterns and tools can make a framework much easier to use by incorporating those patterns and performing all of the tedious work associated with them. Tools can make the use of a framework less error prone. However, tools also have to allow for non-standard extensions to be made to a framework, which is much more difficult to support.

Issues of integrating multiple frameworks remain open. As frameworks become more popular, applications will be developed using more than one framework and problems of integrating those frameworks will arise.

Techniques for framework evolution also need to be devised. Little work has been done concerning how frameworks evolve and the effects of evolution on applications. Anyone who has used a graphical user interface framework and had to change their application when a new version of the framework broke the application can appreciate the need to devise methods of evolving frameworks that require little or no changes to the application extension interfaces.

References

[1] Beck, K., Patterns and software development, *Dr. Dobb's J.*, 19(2), 18–22, 1994.

[2] Beck, K. and Johnson, R., Patterns generate architectures, pp. 139–149. In *Proc. of ECOOP 94*, 1994.

[3] Booch, G., *Object-Oriented Analysis and Design with Applications.* The Benjamin/Cummings Publishing Company, Redwood City, CA, 1994.

[4] Booch, G., Jacobson, I., and Rumbaugh, J., *The Unified Modeling Language for Object-Oriented Development.* Rational Software Corporation, (`http://www.rational.com/uml/`), 1996.

[5] Brown, K., Kues, L., and Lam, M., HM3270: An evolving framework for client-server communications, pp. 463–472. In *Proc. of the 14th Annu. TOOLS (Technology of Object-Oriented Languages and Systems) Conf.*, 1995.

[6] Bulter, G. and Denomme, P., Documenting frameworks. In *Proc. of the Eighth Annu. Workshop on Institutionalizing Software Reuse (WISR)*, 1997.

[7] Campbell, R.H. and Islam, N., A technique for documenting the framework of an object-oriented system. In *Proc. of the 2nd Int. Workshop on Object-Orientation in Operating Systems*, 1992.

[8] Campbell, R.H., Islam, N., Raila, D., and Madany, P., Designing and implementing choices: an object-oriented system in C++, *Commun. ACM*, 36(9), 117–126, 1993.

[9] Froehlich, G., Hoover, H.J., Liu, L., and Sorenson, P., Hooking into object-oriented application frameworks. In *Proc. of the 1997 Int. Conf. on Software Engineering*, 1997.

[10] Gamma, E., Helm, R., Johnson, R., and Vlissides, J., *Design Patterns: Elements of Reusable Object-Oriented Software.* Addison-Wesley, Reading, MA, 1995.

[11] Gangopadhyay, D. and Mitra, S., Understanding frameworks by exploration of exemplars, pp. 90–99. In *Proc. of 7th Int. Workshop on Computer Aided Software Engineering (CASE-95)*, 1995.

[12] Helm, R., Holland, I.M., and Gangopadhyay, D., Contracts: specifying behavioral compositions in object-oriented systems, pp. 169–180. In *Proc. of ECOOP/OOPSLA 90*, 1990.

[13] Hueni, H., Johnson, R., and Engel, R., A framework for network protocol software. In *Proc. of OOPSLA'95*, 1995.

[14] Johnson, R. and Foote, B., Designing Reusable Classes, *J. Object-Oriented Program.*, 2(1), 22–35, 1988.

[15] Johnson, R., Documenting frameworks using patterns, pp. 63–76. In *Proc. of OOPSLA 92*, 1992.

[16] Krasner, G.E. and Pope, S.T., A cookbook for using the model-view-controller user interface paradigm in Smalltalk-80, *J. Object-Oriented Program.*, 1(3), 26–49, 1988.

[17] Lajoie, R. and Keller, R.K., Design and reuse in object-oriented frameworks: patterns, contracts, and motifs in concert. In *Object-Oriented Technology for Database and Software Systems*, Alagar, V.S. and Missaoui, R., eds., pp. 295–312. World Scientific Publishing, Singapore, 1995.

[18] Lange, D.B. and Nakamura, Y., Interactive visualization of design patterns can help in framework understanding, pp. 342–357. In *Proc. of OOPSLA'95*, 1995.

[19] Opdyke, W. and Johnson, R., Refactoring: an aid in designing application frameworks and evolving object-oriented systems. In *Proc. of Symposium on Object-Oriented Programming Emphasizing Practical Applications*, 1990.

[20] Pree, W., *Design Patterns for Object-Oriented Software Development*. Addison-Wesley, Reading, MA, 1995.

[21] Rumbaugh, J., Blaha, M., Premerlani, W., Eddy, F., and Lorenson, W., *Object-Oriented Modeling and Design*. Prentice-Hall, Englewood Cliffs, NJ, 1991.

[22] Schmid, H.A., *Creating the Architecture of a Manufacturing Framework by Design Patterns*, pp. 370–384. In *Proc. of OOPSLA'95*, Austin, TX, 1995.

[23] Sparks, S., Benner, K., and Faris, C., Managing object-oriented framework reuse, *IEEE Comp.*, 29(9), 52–62, 1996.

[24] Steyaert, P., Lucas, C., Mens, K., and D'Hondt, T., *Reuse Contracts: Managing the Evolution of Reusable Assets*, pp. 268–285. Proceedings of OOPSLA'96, 1996.

[25] Tse, L., *A Responsive Corporate Information Model*, Ph.D. thesis, University of Alberta, Edmonton, AB, Canada, 1996.

[26] Taligent, *The Power of Frameworks*. Addison-Wesley, Reading, MA, 1995.

[27] *VisualWorks Cookbook*. Release 2.5, ParcPlace-Digitalk Inc., Sunnyvale, CA, 1995.

[28] Vlissides, M. and Linton, M.A., Unidraw: A framework for building domain-specific graphical editors, *ACM Trans. Inform. Sys.*, 8(3), 237–268, 1990.

[29] Weinand, A., Gamma E., and Marty, R., ET++ — an object-oriented application framework in C++, 46–57. In *Proceedings of OOPSLA'88*, 1988.

27

Development and Extension of a Three-Layered Framework

António Rito Silva
INESC/IST Technical University of Lisbon

27.1 Introduction

An object-oriented framework is a reusable design expressed by a set of classes [5]. These classes constitute a skeleton which provides a generic solution for a class of problems. This skeleton can be fleshed out to support application specific needs [20].

Frameworks have proven to be a powerful tool for software development [10]. However, some problems have been pointed out:

- Understandability — Frameworks are designed, after a domain analysis, by experts in a particular domain, as result of this activity, a large set of classes and interactions is designed. Framework users may be non-experts in the particular domain, however, they have to be able to understand the framework so they can use it.
- Inconsistent Specialization — Frameworks offer flexible ways of specializing abstract classes. However, not all the combinations of specialized classes are consistent. It is the responsibility of framework users to choose the right combinations.
- Combinatorial Explosion — Frequently, the specialization of a framework class requires the specialization of other classes in an uncontrolled manner. The number of classes that need to be specialized to construct a solution is variable and may be large.

0-8493-3135-8/99/$0.00+$.50

This chapter describes a three-layered framework with separation of concerns that presents solutions for the problems above.

27.2 Three-Layered Framework Architecture

Figure 27.1 depicts the three-layered framework architecture. A box represents a group of classes. Solid and dashed arrows represent, respectively, integration and customization relationships.

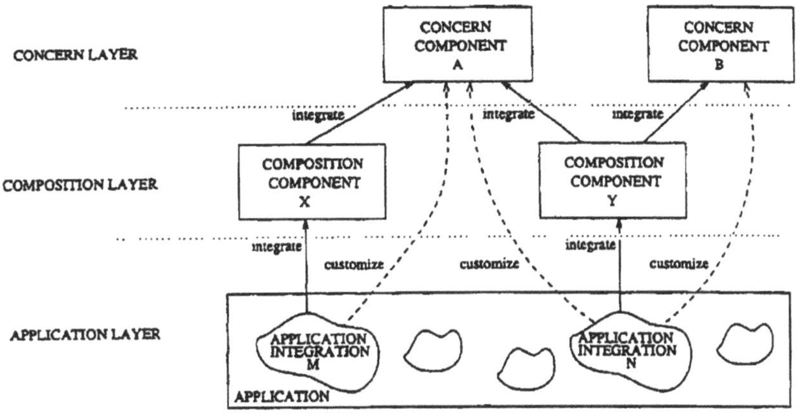

FIGURE 27.1 Three-layered framework architecture.

The Concern layer contains components which offer solutions for specific minimal problems. The Composition layer contains integration components which are responsible for the combination of concern components. At the Application layer composition components are integrated within the application and concern components are specialized according to the application specific requirements.

27.2.1 Concern Layer

Concern components are responsible for offering a solution for a minimal problem (concern). The minimal characteristic allows, and simplifies, the composition of concern components thus increasing reuse.

Concern components should hold the following properties:

- Independence — The solution provided by a concern component should be independent of those provided by other components. This property reduces the number of dependencies between concern components allowing independent concern components' instantiation. From a software engineering perspective, this property enforces modularity of concern components.
- Abstraction — A concern component should abstract a set of solutions to allow component customization. Each solution is called a concern policy. This property increases framework flexibility because the component can be specialized according to application specific needs. From a software engineering perspective, this property enforces extensibility of concern components.
- Explicit Interface — The concern component should provide an interface to be used in the composition of concern components. This property reduces the explosion of combinations

as it reduces the number of visible elements of each concern component. From a software engineering perspective, this property enforces encapsulation of concern components.

In order to build concern components holding the properties above, a domain analysis should be done for each concern.

- Independence — To achieve independence a careful identification and separation of domain concerns should be done. The identification process should verify whether and how concern algorithms can be decoupled.
- Abstraction — To achieve abstraction a domain analysis should be done for each concern. As a result of the domain analysis a significant set of policies should be abstracted and described by abstract classes. Afterwards, the policies may be made concrete by specialization of the abstract classes.
- Explicit Interface — To achieve an explicit interface the domain analysis should, in addition, identify the variable and stable parts of each concern. The stable part should be encapsulated by an interface. The variable part should be "objectified" for future specialization.

27.2.2 Composition Layer

Composition components are responsible for integrating concern components and to make inter-concern dependencies consistent. Composition components should also offer a simple interface for final integration in the application and hide the particularities of inter-concern dependencies from programmers at the application layer.

Composition components should have the following properties:

- Consistency — The combination of concern components may result in the integration of incompatible concern policies. So, the different concern components should be consistently integrated in a composition component disallowing the combination of incompatible concern policies.
- Minimal Interface — Composition components should offer a minimal interface to the programmer at the application layer. This minimal interface allows composition components to be smoothly integrated in the application so that the programmer can easily, almost transparently, integrate the composition component within the application.

In order to build composition components holding the properties above the composition activity should support:

- Consistency — This property is achieved by applying design solutions which avoid incompatible combinations [13] and by writing the necessary code to integrate components.
- Minimal Interface — To achieve a minimal interface the composition component should aggregate the explicit interfaces of each of the concern components in an interface, which hides all aspects deemed non-relevant for the application programmer.

27.2.3 Application Layer

In the application layer composition components are integrated in the final application and concern policies may be customized:

- Integration — A composition component is integrated in the application through its minimal interface. This can be done using a design solution, like the Proxy pattern [4] or the Surrogate pattern [8] which decouples an object's interface from its implementation.

- Customization — Concern components, which are integrated in the composition component, may be customized by specializing their variable parts according to application specificities. Variable parts were isolated in classes at the concern layer such that customization becomes a well-defined and localized procedure.

27.3 Framework for Object Concurrency and Synchronization

To illustrate the three-layered framework architecture, this section presents a fragment of a framework for heterogeneous concurrency, synchronization, and recovery in distributed applications [16], which is implemented in C++ on top of the ACE environment [14]. The framework architecture has the properties discussed in the previous section. The described fragment, framework for object concurrency and synchronization, supports several policies of object concurrency and synchronization.

The diagrammatic notation will use Booch class diagrams [2]. A dotted cloud represents a class and if it is an abstract class a triangular adornment should appear inside the cloud. Containment relationship is represented by a line with a black circle in the container side. Uses relationship is represented by a line with an open circle in the using side. Inheritance relationship is represented by an arrow pointing to the base class. A template class is represented by a dotted cloud with a dotted rectangle, the template arguments. A dotted cloud with a solid rectangle represents a template instantiation.

27.3.1 Concern Layer

The framework considers two concern components: object synchronization and active object. Object synchronization component supports variations of optimistic and pessimistic synchronization policies for object invocations. Active object component defines an object with an internal activity which selects pending invocations for execution.

A concern component is a particular case of a design pattern [4], which has the concern layer properties of independence, abstraction, and explicit interface. Concern component description is twofold: pattern and implementation description. The pattern description emphasizes the design abstraction implemented in the component and its properties. The implementation description emphasizes on how the pattern is implemented in the concern layer. Some of the classes in the pattern description are not implemented by the concern layer, so they do not appear in the implementation description. Moreover, the implementation description may introduce new classes to support further combination at the composition layer.

The pattern description uses the object-oriented design patterns format in [4]. How the concern component accomplishes the properties required for the concern layer is also described. Note that contrary to the common description of design patterns which emphasizes the pattern known uses, this description emphasizes the properties associated with the concern layer.

27.3.1.1 Object Synchronization Component

The Object Synchronization component implements the Customizable Object Synchronization pattern which is described in [18].

27.3.1.1.1 Intent

The Customizable Object Synchronization pattern abstracts several object synchronization policies. It decouples object synchronization from object functionality (sequential part).

27.3.1.1.2 Structure and Participants

The Booch class diagram in Figure 27.2 illustrates the structure of the Customizable Object Synchronization pattern.

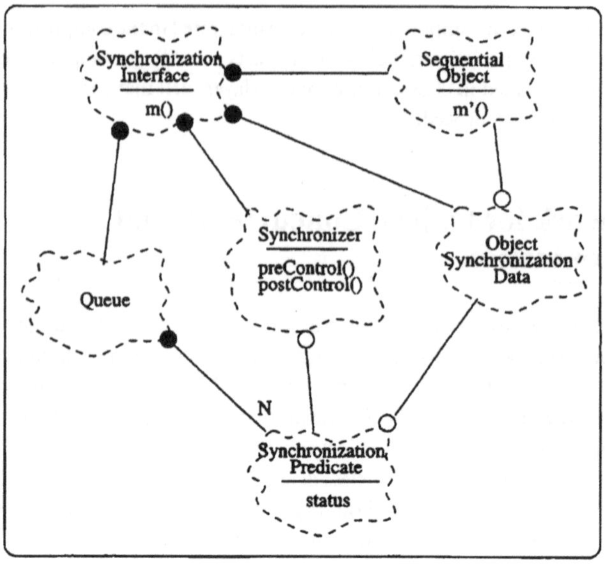

FIGURE 27.2 Pattern structure.

The main participants in the Customizable Object Synchronization pattern are

- `Sequential Object` — It contains the sequential code and data, where accesses should be synchronized.
- `Synchronization Interface` — It is responsible for the synchronization of invocations to the `Sequential Object`. It uses the services provided by the `Synchronizer`, and it creates a `Synchronization Predicate` object for each invocation.
- `Synchronizer` — It decides whether an invocation may continue, stop, or should be delayed. Operations `preControl` and `postControl` control the order of invocations.
- `Queue` — It contains `Synchronization Predicate` objects of pending invocations. It is passed to each new `Synchronization Predicate` by the `Synchronization Interface`.
- `Synchronization Predicate` — It identifies the invocation and contains its current status, (attribute `status`), which can be pre-pending, executing, post-pending, and terminated. It also defines the synchronization semantics of an invocation, which determines whether the invocation should proceed, be delayed, or terminated.
- `Object Synchronization Data` — It provides global object synchronization data. It may use the `Sequential Object` to get synchronization data. It is passed to each new `Synchronization Predicate` by the `Synchronization Interface`.

27.3.1.1.3 Collaborations

When method `m` is invoked, a `Synchronization Predicate` object is created by the `Synchronization Interface`. Afterwards, it invokes `preControl` and `postControl` on the `Synchronizer`, respectively, before and after method `m'` is executed on the `Sequential Object`. `preControl` synchronizes an invocation before execution and an error may be returned, preventing invocation execution, otherwise access is delayed or resumed. `postControl` verifies if an invocation already done is correctly synchronized with terminated invocations. To evaluate synchronization conditions (operations `preControl` and `postControl`), the `Synchronizer` interacts with `Synchronization`

`Predicate`. The `Synchronization Predicate` may use the synchronization data in other pending invocations, iterating on `Queue`, or in the `Object Synchronization Data`.

27.3.1.1.4 Implementation Description

The Booch class diagram in Figure 27.3 illustrates the structure of the Object Synchronization component.

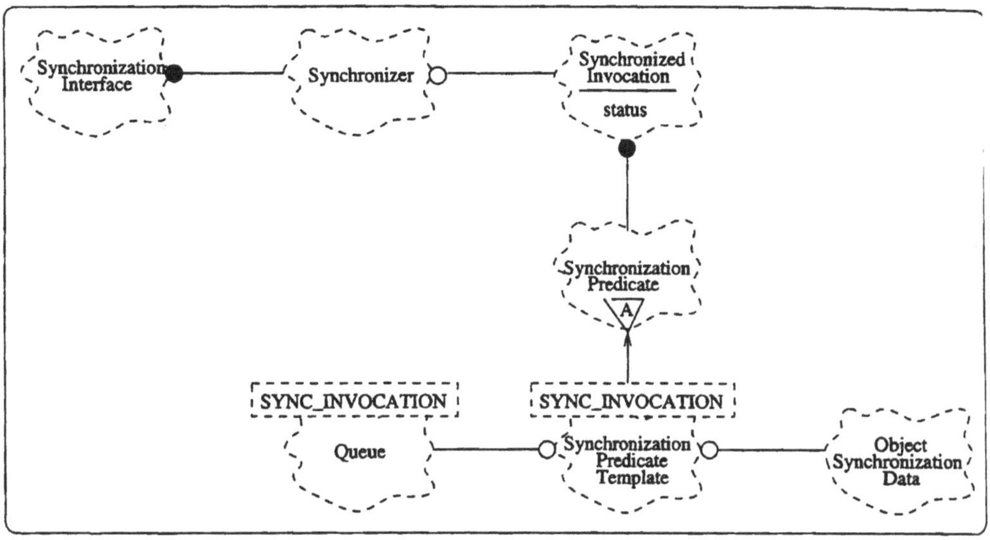

FIGURE 27.3 Component structure.

Comparing with the pattern description, class `Sequential Object` is missing. It will be defined at the application layer. Some containment relationships of `Synchronization Interface` are also missing. Subclasses of `Synchronization Interface`, to be defined at lower layers, will contain `Sequential Data`, `Queue`, and `Object Synchronization Data`.

New classes, `Synchronized Invocation`, and `Queue<SYNC_INVOCATION>`, to support combination at the composition layer were introduced. `Synchronized Invocation` contains the common part of invocations, their `status`. To avoid template propagation `Synchronization Predicate` was defined as an abstract class having `Synchronization Predicate Template` as a subclass. `Synchronization Predicate Template` uses `Queue<SYNC_INVOCATION>`, the containment relationship in the pattern description will be defined at the composition layer.

27.3.1.1.5 Properties

The Object Synchronization component has the properties required by concern components:

- Independence — Object synchronization is decoupled from object functionality which is implemented in `Sequential Object`. It will be shown at the composition layer that it is also independent of the concurrency concern.
- Abstraction — Synchronization policies can use two different generic algorithms: pessimistic, when the object is expected to have high contention; and optimistic, when the level of contention is expected to be low. The component supports pessimistic policies, which synchronize invocations before access (operation `preControl`), and optimistic policies, which synchronize invocations after access (operation `postControl`). These policies are abstracted by `Synchronizer`. The component also supports several object specific customizable policies, e.g., readers/writers or producer/consumer, which are abstracted by `Synchronization`

`Predicate` and `Object Synchronization Data.`

- Explicit Interface — The component's stable part is the participant's interactions which are encapsulated by `Synchronization Interface.` This follows the object-oriented design principle stating that variations should be "objectified" such that polymorphism can be used.

27.3.1.2 Active Object Component

The Active Object component implements the Active Object pattern described in [7].

27.3.1.2.1 Intent

The Active Object pattern decouples method invocation from method execution. An active object holds an internal activity which selects pending methods for execution.

27.3.1.2.2 Structure and Participants

The Booch class diagram in Figure 27.4 illustrates the structure of the Active Object pattern.

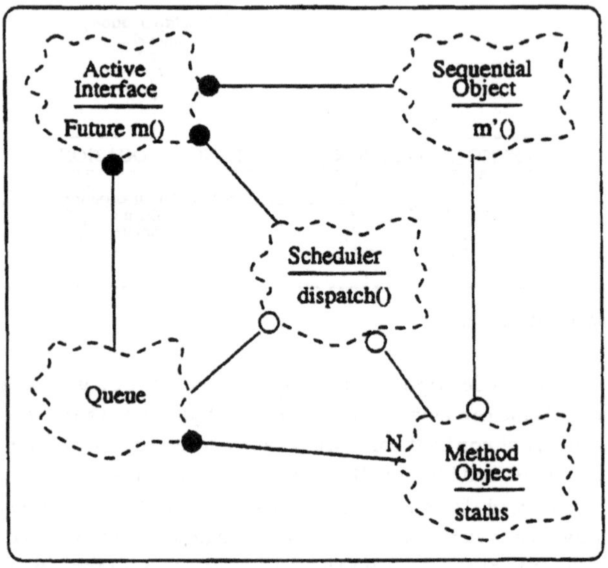

FIGURE 27.4 Pattern structure.

The main participants in the Active Object pattern are

- `Sequential Object` — It contains the sequential code and data which are shared by concurrent activities.
- `Active Interface` — It is responsible for decoupling method invocation to the `Sequential Object` from method execution. It creates a `Method Object` for each invocation.
- `Scheduler` — It triggers the execution of `Method Objects` associated with pending invocations (operation `dispatch`).
- `Queue` — It contains the `Method Objects` of pending invocations.
- `Method Object` — It identifies the invocation and contains its current status, (attribute `status`), which can be pending, executing, and terminated. It contains the context necessary to execute the invocation.
- `Future` — A call to an active object is asynchronous. It is returned to the caller for future synchronization.

27.3.1.2.3 ***Collaborations***

When method `m` is invoked a new instance of `Method Object` is created and inserted in the `Queue`. A `Future` object is returned to the caller. Afterwards the caller has to synchronize with the `Future` to obtain the result values.

The `Scheduler` selects a pending `Method Object`, using its internal activity, and starts its execution. `Method Object` execution proceeds on the `Sequential Object`.

27.3.1.2.4 ***Implementation Description***

The Booch class diagram in Figure 27.5 illustrates the structure of the Active Object component.

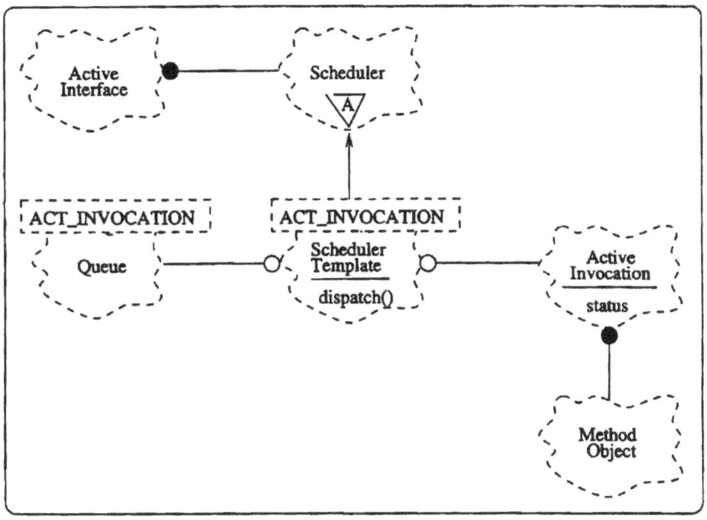

FIGURE 27.5 Component structure.

The rational behind the implementation at the concern layer is similar to the Object Synchronization implementation.

27.3.1.2.5 ***Properties***

The Active Object component has the properties required by concern components:

- Independence — Active Object decouples object concurrency from object functionality which is implemented in `Sequential Object`. It will be shown at the composition layer that it is also independent of the synchronization concern.
- Abstraction — It supports a single policy of object concurrency, active object. It does not need to abstract passive object policy since `Sequential Object` is already passive.
- Explicit Interface — The component's stable part is the participants interactions which are encapsulated by `Active Interface`.

27.3.2 Composition Layer

The framework has two composition components: active synchronized object and passive synchronized object. The former integrates object synchronization component with active object component, while the latter adapts (integrates) the object synchronization component for passive objects.

Invocations should have the semantics of the composition. Figure 27.6 shows the use of inheritance (multiple) to adapt/compose invocations. For instance, `Active Synchronized Invocation` holds a `Method Object` and a `Synchronization Predicate`. The new classes should be redefined to support the composition semantics, e.g., garbage collection of terminated invocations.

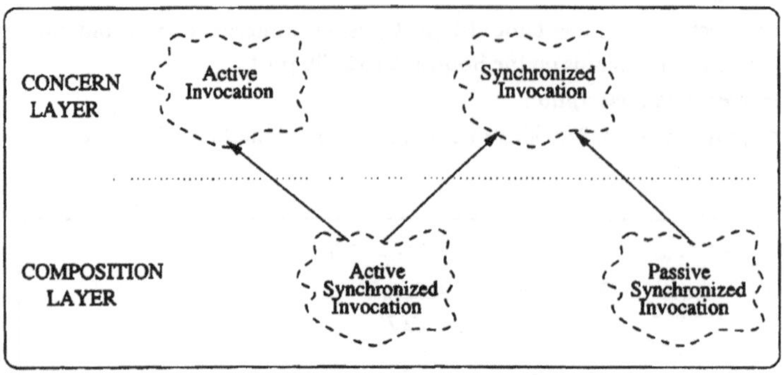

FIGURE 27.6 Active and passive invocation hierarchy.

Figure 27.7 shows the interface hierarchy. Inheritance (multiple) is also the chosen composition technique.

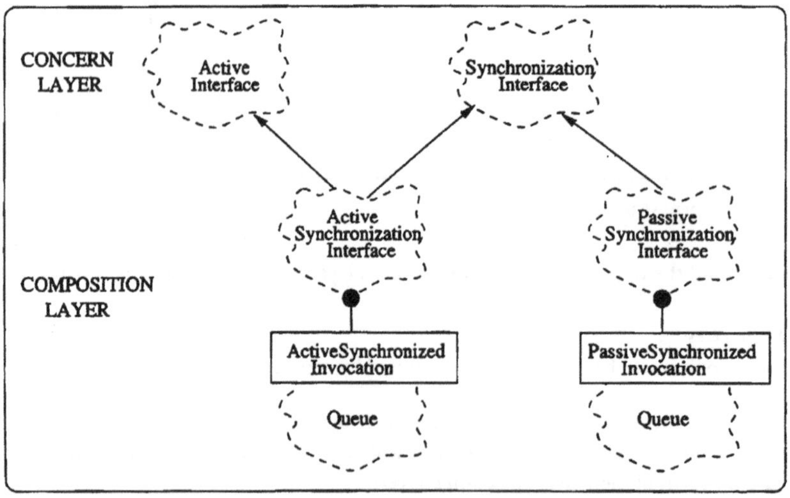

FIGURE 27.7 Active and passive interface hierarchy.

A `Queue` object is defined to be shared by components. It corresponds to `Queue`, Queue<SYNC_INVOCATION> and Queue<ACT_INVOCATION> classes described in Figures 27.2–27.5. The new subclasses should be redefined to support the composition semantics and properties, e.g., minimal interface.

27.3.2.1 Passive Synchronized Object Component

This component has the properties required by composition components:

- Consistency—Invocations to passive objects proceed using the caller activity. So, the `Passive Synchronization Interface` is concurrently accessed by several activities which may result on data corruption. This is a consistency problem which results from integrating synchronization in a passive object. The following code shows the implementation of mutual exclusion in methods `preControl` and `postControl` to consistently integrate Object Synchronization with Passive Object. It also implements delay and awake of invocations in the passive context. Identifier names have been shortened.

The code below defines the `Passive Synchronization Interface` where the ACE library [14] is used to support mutual exclusion.

```
// defines a passive synchronizer interface
class Pass_Sync_Int : private Sync_Int
{
public:
  // defines a passive synchronized object
  // Synchronizer is passed to superclass constructor
  Pass_Sync_Int(Synchronizer* sync);

protected:
  // creates an invocation
  Pass_Sync_Inv* createInv(Sync_Pred_T<Pass_Sync_Inv>* pred);

  // defines preControl
  X_Status preControl(Pass_Sync_Inv*);
  // defines postControl
  X_Status postControl(Pass_Sync_Inv*);

private:
  // invocation queue
  Queue<Pass_Sync_Inv> queue_;

  // ACE synchronization mechanisms
  ACE_Mutex mutex_; // mutex
  ACE_Mutex cond_mutex_; // mutex for condition
  ACE_Condition_Mutex cond_; // condition
};
```

Execution of `preControl` on the `Synchronizer` is a mutual exclusion implemented by `mutex_`. When necessary, invocations are delayed in `cond_`.

```
// pre-control phase
int Pass_Sync_Int::preControl(Pass_Sync_Inv* inv)
{
  X_Status status; // execution status
  do
  {
    // begin mutual exclusion
    mutex_.acquire();

    // verify compatibility
    status = sync_->preControl(inv);
```

```
      // end mutual exclusion
      mutex_.release();

      // if there are incompatibilities wait
      if (status == DELAY) {
        cond_.wait();
        cond_mutex_.release();
      }
    }
    while (status == DELAY); //retry

    // return result
    return status;
}
```

Execution of `postControl` on the `Synchronizer` is also a mutual exclusion. When necessary invocations are delayed in `cond_` and awaken whenever another invocation finishes execution. Awaken invocation should re-evaluate synchronization conditions.

```
// post-control phase
int Pass_Sync_Int::postControl(Pass_Sync_Inv* inv)
{
  X_Status status;
  do
  {
    // begin mutual exclusion
    mutex_.acquire();

    // verify compatibility
    status = sync_->postControl(inv);

    // end mutual exclusion
    mutex_.release();

    // if there are incompatibilities wait
    if (status == DELAY) {
      cond_.wait();
      cond_mutex_.release();
    }
    else
      // only if CONTINUE or ERROR
      // awake pending invocations
      cond_.broadcast();
  }
  while (status == DELAY); //retry

  // return result
  return status;
}
```

- Minimal Interface — Class `Passive Synchronization Interface` defines three operations, `createInv`, `preControl`, and `postControl`, to be used by the final application programmers. Note, from the code above, how invocation execution retry is hidden from final programmers.

27.3.2.2 Active Synchronized Object Component

This component has the properties required by composition components:

- Consistency — To consistently integrate Active Object and Synchronization Object components a subclass of `Scheduler` should be defined. The `Active Synchronization Interface` should also support a mutual exclusion on accesses to `Synchronizer`.
  Since `Scheduler` is responsible for selecting and dispatching the execution of pending invocations its integration with object synchronization requires the definition of a subclass `Sync_Scheduler`.

```
class Sync_Scheduler : public Scheduler_T<Act_Sync_Inv>
{
public:
  // defines a Scheduler for active synchronized objects
  Sync_Scheduler(Queue<Act_Sync_Inv>* queue, Act_Sync_Int *int);

protected:
  // scheduler dispatch
  void dispatch();

private:
  // active synchronization interface
  Act_Sync_Int* int_;
};
```

  This class is responsible for invoking `preControl` and `postControl` on the `Synchronizer`. The code below shows operation `dispatch` of the `Sync_Scheduler`. Note that the invocation is done through the interface (`int_`), the interface acts as a Mediator Pattern [4] between the components.

```
void Sync_Scheduler::dispatch(void)
{
  // get first of pending invocations
  Act_Sync_Inv* inv = queue_->first();

  // pre-control
  // if active invocation status is pending
  if (inv->getActStatus() == Act_Inv::PEND)
    // evaluate preControl
    if (int_->preControl(inv) == CONTINUE)
      // if execution can proceed

      // execute method object
      inv->execute();

  // post-control
```

```
  // if active invocation status is terminated
  if (inv->getActStatus() == Act_Inv::TERM)
    // evaluate postControl
    int_->postControl(inv);
}
```

The code below defines the `Active Synchronization Interface`. Contrary to the passive case, it is not necessary to explicitly re-execute the synchronization code while the result is `DELAY`: this is done by the `Sync_Scheduler`. Furthermore, mutual exclusion is easily provided by the internal scheduler activity and invocation wait is implemented by moving the invocation to the end of the queue.

```
// pre-control phase
int Act_Sync_Int::preControl(Act_Sync_Inv* inv)
{
  X_Status status;

  // it is not necessary to define a mutual
  // exclusion, synchronization code is being
  // executed by the scheduler internal activity

  // verify compatibility
  status = sync_->preControl(inv);

  // if there are incompatibilities move invocation to end of queue
  if (status == DELAY)
    moveEnd(inv);

  // return result
  return status;
}

// post-control phase
int Act_Sync_Int::postControl(Act_Sync_Inv* inv)
{
  X_Status status;

  // it is not necessary to define a mutual
  // exclusion, synchronization code is being
  // executed by the scheduler internal activity

  // verify compatibility
  status = sync_->postControl(inv);

  // if there are incompatibilities move invocation to end of queue
  if (status == DELAY)
    moveEnd(inv);
  // only if CONTINUE or ERROR
  // Sync_Scheduler will awake pending invocations

  // return result
```

```
    return status;
}
```

- Minimal Interface — The programmer at the application layer only needs to invoke `createInv` method of `Active Synchronization Interface`. Invocation of methods `preControl` and `postControl` are responsibility of the `Sync_Scheduler` and hidden from the final application programmer.

27.3.3 Application Layer

At the application layer composition components are integrated in the application and concern components are customized.

27.3.3.1 Integration

Figure 27.8 shows the integration of composition components with a buffer object. Programmers decide which component to use, `Active Synchronization Interface` or `Passive Synchronization Interface`, and by inheritance they define their own, respectively, active and passive synchronized interfaces (in Figure 27.8 the Proxy Pattern [4] is applied).

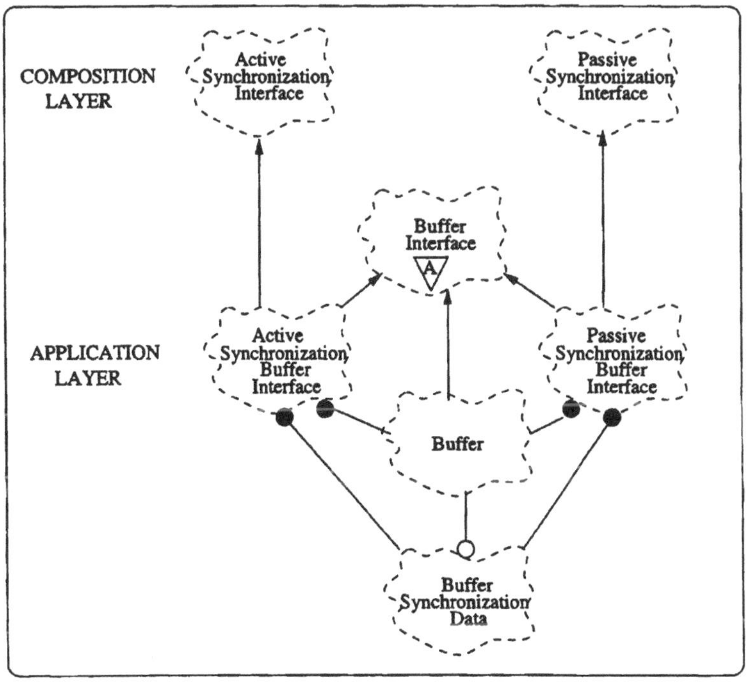

FIGURE 27.8 Application layer integration.

Note that `Buffer` corresponds to `Sequential Object` and `Buffer Synchronization Data` is a subclass of `Object Synchronization Data` in Figures 27.2–27.4.

The code below shows the constructor of a passive synchronized buffer. A `Pessimistic Synchronizer` and a `Buffer Synchronization Data` are created. The constructor of an active synchronized buffer is similar.

```
Pass_Sync_Buffer_Int::Pass_Sync_Buffer_Int(int size)
  : Pass_Sync_Int(new Pess_Synchronizer()),
  Buffer_Int(size),
  buffer_(new Buffer(size)),
  syncData_(new Buffer_Sync_Data(buffer_))
{ }
```

A synchronized put invocation on a passive buffer is presented below. The programmer only needs to create an invocation and bound the execution on the Buffer with operations preControl and postControl. Put_Pred is the synchronization predicate.

```
void Pass_Sync_Buffer_Int::put(int val)
{
  // creates a predicate initializing it with the object synchronization data
  // information about arguments may be included
  Pass_Sync_Inv* inv = createInv(new Put_Pred<Pass_Sync_Inv>(syncData_));

  // pre-control
  preControl(inv);

  // invocation proceeds on sequential object
  buffer_->put(val);

  // post-control
  postControl(inv);
}
```

A synchronized put invocation on an active buffer only needs to create an invocation. The Sync_Scheduler will dispatch the invocation. Put_Pred and Put_Method are, respectively, synchronization predicate and method object. A Future object is created, where the caller synchronizes immediately after invocation.

```
void Act_Sync_Buffer_Int::put(int val)
{
  // defines a future object
  Future future;

  // creates a predicate initializing it with the object synchronization data
  // and creates a method object initializing it with buffer and future
  Act_Sync_Inv* inv = createInv(new Put_Pred<Act_Sync_Inv>(syncData_),
                                new Put_Method(buffer_,future,val));

  // synchronize in future
  future->wait();
}
```

27.3.3.2 Customization

In the previous example the following classes were customized: Pess_Synchronizer, which defines a pessimistic policy of synchronization; Buffer_Sync_Data, which defines the buffer synchronization data; Put_Pred, which defines the put synchronization predicate; and Put_Method, which defines the put method object.

27.4 Framework Features

The three-layered framework presents some characteristics which are orthogonal to the implementation language: object classification, layered description, and layered knowledge. Any framework emphasizing separation of concerns benefits from having these features.

27.4.1 Object Classification

In the framework, objects can be classified according to their properties:

- *Stable Objects* represent the objects which are encapsulated within concern components and do not need to be specialized. In the example there are no stable objects, the participant's interactions is the stable part.
- *Variable Objects* represent the objects which need to be specialized for integration or customization:

  1. *Integration Objects* are variable objects used for integration at composition and application layers. `Interface` and `Invocation` objects are examples of integration objects. `Sync_Scheduler` is also an integration object since it integrates the `Scheduler` of Active Object component with the `Synchronizer` of Object Synchronization component.
  2. *Customizable Objects* are variable objects used for policy customization. Two kinds of customizable objects were identified: application- and object specific. The former rely on the application semantics, e.g., synchronization policies can use two different generic algorithms: pessimistic, when the object is expected to have high contention, and optimistic, when the level of contention is expected to be low. An example of an application specific object is `Pess_Synchronizer`. Object specific objects rely on the object semantics, its structure and operations. Examples of object specific objects are `Put_Pred`, `Buffer_Sync_Data` and `Put_Method`.

27.4.2 Layered Description

As a consequence of its structure, the framework can be described in terms of its layers improving framework understanding.

- *Concern Layer* has two descriptions: pattern and implementation. The former describes the overall concern solution. The latter presents the details of implementing the concern component. Pattern description can be completely independent of implementation details, emphasizing the abstraction properties and the resulting extensibility by describing the supported policies and showing how they are implemented using the customizable objects. It is also possible to include some implementation hints reducing the gap to components descriptions. For instance, Figure 27.9 shows the pattern description completely independent of implementation details, corresponding to the pattern description reducing the gap to implementation shown in Figure 27.2. Note that queue is replaced by `pending` relationship and some containment relationships are not presented because they are used for initializations only. For the sake of space limitations, in this chapter we only used the pattern description which reduces the gap between descriptions.
- *Composition Layer* describes how concern components are integrated as well as the consistent combinations of concern policies. For the latter a table can be drawn. The minimal interface which will be used by final programmers should also be described.

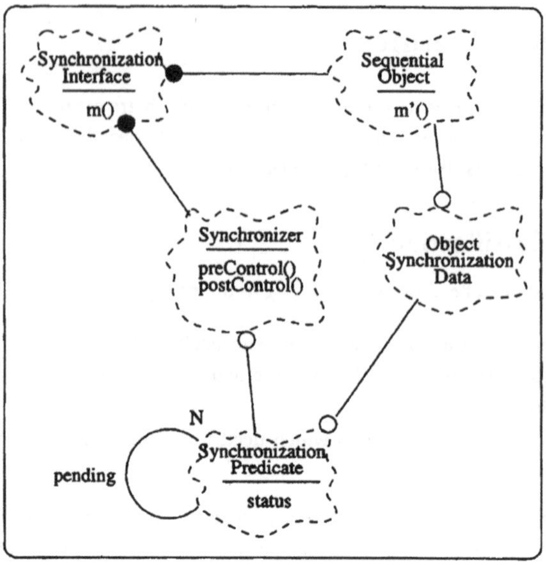

FIGURE 27.9 Pure pattern structure.

- *Application Layer* describes how composition components are integrated in the application and which customizable objects should be instantiated.

27.4.3 Layered Knowledge

Associated with the layered description there is a layered knowledge allowing different framework programmers expertise:

- *Concern Programmer* is responsible for the definition of concern components and he should be an expert on the particular domain.
- *Composition Programmer* is responsible for the integration of concerns components. Knowledge of composition techniques and of consistent policy combinations is required.
- *Application Programmer* integrates the composition component interface within the application and customizes the concern component. The concern pattern description emphasizing customization can be used. Moreover, pre-defined application specific customizable objects may be used as well as generic object specific customizable objects. For instance, a pessimistic synchronizer for the former and read/write synchronization predicates for the latter.

27.5 Discussion

The approach is centered on the domain semantics. The domain analysis allows us to abstract groups of policies and identify the stable and variable parts of the concern, but there is an open issue whether separation of concerns is scalable. This is an issue of current research work. However, we have successfully applied the three-layered architecture in a larger framework than the Object Concurrency and Synchronization framework as will be described in the Conclusions.

The problems described in the Introduction are solved by the three-layered architecture:

- Understandability — The three-layered architecture offers layers of knowledge and description which improve understandability. Moreover, the application programmer only needs to understand the concerns required by the application due to the independence property of concern components.

- Inconsistent Specialization — The composition layer is responsible for a consistent combination of structures and policies. Composition components encapsulate these combinations from the application programmer, which only needs to specialize the customizable objects.
- Combinatorial Explosion — Combinations in the three-layered architecture are done at component's granularity, reducing the combinatorial explosion. Integration objects are specialized in the composition layer as a whole, limiting the number of new subclasses that need to be defined. The specialization of customizable object at the application layer also limits the number of new classes due to the independence property of concern components.

27.6 Related Work

The work in [1] defines two properties required by scalable software libraries: minimal building blocks and combination generators. Three-layered framework minimal building blocks are the concern components which are combined in the composition layer. We do not follow the generation approach since concern combination is not trivial, requiring tailoring in a case by case basis.

Our approach is centered on the domain semantics while others emphasize the composition techniques. The OOram method [11] describes components in terms of role models and provides a synthesis mechanism which combines roles models. In [12] the OOram techniques are extended with the specialization relationship. These approaches may be applied to the description of the three-layered framework, where the concern component corresponds to a role model and synthesis generates composition components.

Reflection is a composition technique which is provided in languages [3] and operating systems [21]. Reflection supports meta-objects which define the semantics of objects. Incremental definition of objects is achieved by changing object's meta-objects. In [9] it is presented as a reflexive framework which decomposes fine-grained behavior into objects and their subsequent composition into object models. This approach differs from ours in the composition techniques used and it does not address composition problems.

In [13] the problem of framework inconsistent specialization is addressed. Design solutions which cope with this problem are presented, e.g., the Abstract Factory pattern [4]. These solutions can be used in the composition layer.

27.7 Conclusions

A three-layered framework with separation of concerns is presented and its qualities discussed. The top layer is formed by concern components which may be described as object-oriented design patterns [6]. The qualities of the concern layer — independence, abstraction and explicit interface — allow the definition of minimal components which can be reused by combination at the composition layer and customized at the application layer. The intermediate layer, composition layer, contains integration components which are responsible for the combination of concern components. The qualities of the composition layer — consistency and minimal interface — allow the consistent integration of concern components and their smooth integration in the application. At the application layer the concern components are customized and composition components constructively integrated in the application.

The three-layered framework extends the traditional framework approach which directly specializes the framework and does not distinguish composition from customization and integration in the application. The three-layered approach emphasizes concern composition as a separated stage in the process of developing and using the framework. From this separation results a reduction of combinatorial explosion, consistent specialization, and better understandability.

The three-layered framework was defined in the context of an approach to the Development for Distributed Applications with Separation of Concerns (DASCo) described in [15, 17]. The DASCo method identifies a set of concerns in the solution space. A constructive, stepwise, development process is defined by establishing solutions for each concern and integrating concerns solutions. In DASCo the concerns of concurrency, synchronization, recovery, replication, naming, configuration, and communication were identified.

This chapter presents a small framework to illustrate the approach, but the proposed architecture has already been proven to work on a larger three-layered framework for heterogeneous concurrency and synchronization policies for distributed applications [16]. This framework considers the other concern components, besides Object Synchronization and Active Object:

- Object Recovery — It abstracts several object recovery policies [19].
- Concurrency Generation — It abstracts several concurrency generation policies, and it associates activities with method execution.

The framework allows multiple compositions, as Passive and Active Synchronized Recoverable Objects, both, passive and active objects can associate a new activity with method execution. This framework is publicly available from the DASCo page `http://albertina.inesc.pt/~ars/dasco.html`.

Currently the framework is being extended with the concern components for replication, configuration, naming, and communication.

Acknowledgment

Thanks to Luís Gil and João Martins for the work done on the implementation of the object synchronization framework. I also thank my colleagues, Francisco Rosa and Teresa Gonçalves for their comments which helped to improve this chapter.

References

[1] Batory, D., Singhal, V., Sirkin, M., and Thomas, J., Scalable software libraries, 191–199. In *ACM SIGSOFT '93*, Los Angeles, CA, 1993.

[2] Booch, G., *Object-Oriented Analysis and Design with Applications.* The Benjamin/Cummings Publishing Company, Menlo Park, CA, 1994.

[3] Chiba, S. and Masuda, T., Designing an Extensible Distributed Language with a Meta-Level Architecture, 482–501. In *ECOOP '93*, Kaiserslautern, Germany, 1993.

[4] Gamma, E., Helm, R., Johnson, R., and Vlissides, J., *Design Patterns: Elements of Reusable Object-Oriented Software.* Addison-Wesley, Reading, MA, 1995.

[5] Johnson, R.E. and Foote, B., Designing Reusable Classes, *JOOP*, 1(2), 22–25, 1988.

[6] Johnson, R.E., Documenting Frameworks using Patterns, 63–76. In *OOPSLA '92*, Vancouver, Canada, 1992.

[7] Lavender, R.G. and Schmidt, D.C., Active object: an object behavioral pattern for concurrent programming. In *Pattern Languages of Program Design 2*, Vlissides, J.M., Coplien, J.O., and Kerth, N.L., eds., 483–499. Addison-Wesley, Reading, MA, 1996.

[8] Martin, R., *Designing Object-Oriented Applications Using the Booch Method.* Prentice-Hall, Englewood Cliffs, NJ, 1995.

[9] McAffer, J., Meta-level Programming with CodA, 190–214. In *ECOOP '95*, Aarhus, Denmark, 1995.

[10] Moser, S. and Nierstrasz, O., The effect of object-oriented frameworks on developer productivity, *Computer*, 29(9), 45–51, 1996.

[11] Reenskaug, T., Wold, P., and Lehne, O., *Working With Objects: The OOram Software Engineering Method.* Manning Publications Co., Greenwich, CT, 1996.

[12] Riehle, D., Describing and composing patterns using role diagrams, 137–152. In *Proc. of the Ubilab Conf. '96,* Zurich, Switzerland, 1996.

[13] Ruping, A., Framework Patterns. In *EuroPLoP '96,* Kloster Irsee, Germany, 1996.

[14] Schmidt, D.C., The ADAPTIVE communication environment: an object-oriented network programming toolkit for developing communication software. In *11th and 12th Sun User Group Conf.,* San Jose and San Francisco, CA, 1994.

[15] Silva, A.R., Sousa, P., and Marques, J.A., Development of distributed applications with separation of concerns, 168–177. In *APSEC '95,* Brisbane, Australia, 1995.

[16] Silva, A.R., Pereira, J., and Marques, J.A., A framework for heterogeneous concurrency control policies in distributed applications, 105–114. In *IWSSD '96,* Schloss Velen, Germany, 1996a.

[17] Silva, A.R., Hayes, F., Mota, F., Torres, N., and Santos, P., A pattern language for the perception, design and implementation of distributed application partitioning, presented at the OOPSLA'96 Workshop on Methodologies for Distributed Objects. 1996b.

[18] Silva, A.R., A quality design solution for object synchronization. In *EuroPar 97,* Passau, Germany, 1997a. In press.

[19] Silva, A.R., Pereira, J., and Marques, J.A., Customizable object recovery pattern. In *Pattern Languages of Program Design 3.* Riehle, D., Martin, R., and Buschman, F., eds., Addison-Wesley, Reading, MA, 1997b. In press.

[20] Wirfs-Brock, R., Wilkerson, B., and Wiener, L., *Designing Object-Oriented Software.* Prentice-Hall, Englewood Cliffs, NJ, 1990.

[21] Yokote, Y., The Apertos Reflective Operating System: The concept and its implementation, 414–434. In *OOPSLA '92,* Vancouver, Canada, 1992.

V

Object Technology Standards and Distributed Objects

Messaoud Benantar
IBM Corporation

Juan Manuel Cueva
Oviedo University

Since its inception, computer programming has taken a natural pace of evolution, from using complex machine instructions to high-level comprehensible procedural language abstractions. Further advances have led to the development of different programming styles that attempt to mimic the way things compute in the real world, including modular programming and most notably programming with abstract data types. Finally, object-oriented programming and component-based software emerged as a natural way of modeling real-world entities and computations.

Similarly, deployment of applications has evolved from a single address space computation; to cooperating processes on a single host machine; to remote address spaces linked over a network media and protocols, giving rise to the client-server paradigm of computation. At the core of this paradigm is the natural aspect of distributing computational services that can be sought from remote clients.

Distributing objects and software components over a network, thus, became the next step in the process of this evolution. Two major distributed object technologies have emerged in recent years: The Common Object Request Broker Architecture (CORBA) from the Object Management Group (OMG) and OLE with its core technology of Component Object Model (COM) from Microsoft. In this section you will find descriptions of these technologies, along with descriptions of SOM and DSOM.

28

CORBA: Toward an Open Distributed Object Computing Architecture

Julio García-Martín
Polytechnical University of Madrid

In order to overcome the problem of interoperability among separately-developed systems in a distributed heterogeneous context, in 1991, the consortium OMG (1991) specified an abstract distributed architecture named CORBA. Since then, the successive revisions of CORBA have ended by molding a mainstream framework technology with a large number of common services and features. An overview of the CORBA model is now presented. This work also includes a wide description of the main CORBA features and CORBA components.

28.1 Introduction

The real world is concurrent rather than sequential (Wegner, 1990). Nevertheless, it is under a distributed interpretation as the real-world concurrency of applications is naturally modeled. Distributed programming emerged to provide a suitable conceptualization for the interactions among entities within the multiple-process applications. In the early seventies, long before the boom of networked computing, many studies on concurrent programming had already pointed out the success of distribution to describe the real world. In opposition to the shared memory based models, the autonomy provided by distributed

0-8493-3135-8/99/$0.00+$.50

designs meant a powerful conceptual property to develop concurrent software and concurrent executions. If the real world appears to us as a collection of physical autonomous entities, our software applications should be able to capture this circumstance.

Today, the development of distributed object applications still represents a step forward in establishing new modeling foundations on collaborative systems. If we look back at the past, we can see that the advantages pointed out two decades before have been confirmed today. First, because distributed computer systems faithfully reflect how human organizations interact and collaborate. Secondly, because the collaboration among distributed systems allows the fulfillment of common activities, which makes it feasible for us to take more profit of resources, a more balanced distribution of responsibilities, and likewise, a better adjustment of the necessities.

During the last decade, the massive use of the Internet, corporate intranets, and the WWW services has stressed even more the interest in distributed programming and collaborative systems, restating the problem of interconnectivity in terms of computers and software components that networks and protocols support and connect. The theoretical non-limited scalability of distributed models allows systems to grow autonomously without compromising further changes or enlargements. However, and opposite to this non-limited scalability, the fact of distribution yields us to deal with more heterogeneous computer environments. For example, it is very common that an enterprise using mainframes might invest in UNIX or VMS workstations because of new requirements. The lowest cost of PC systems running Microsoft Windows, IBM OS/2, MacOS, etc., might persuade the company to install cooperative intranets running different operating systems. The usage of graphical design tools will require different platforms than in the case of compilers or database systems. Besides, networks and protocols underlying and connecting systems are just as diverse as computers. As a consequence, particular investment policies, personal affinities with vendors, and other immeasurable circumstances will end by making up a *Babel's Tower* of languages, resources, machines, operating systems, and network protocols.

As an answer to the problem of interoperability between heterogeneous systems, in 1989, the consortium *Object Management Group* (OMG; Object Management Architecture Guide, 1990), was formed with more than 600 software developers, computer companies, and end users. Because there is more and more diverse networked activity, the OMG posed the adoption of new standards in the area of distributed computing, which allows us to overcome the complexity introduced by the heterogeneity of computer environments.

The OMG embraced the object orientation as the OMG specification model. On the one hand, objects technology had already shown its ability to describe the real world. On the other hand, the background obtained from the client/server age should mean a source of experiences to reuse. Primarily, the OMG's attention was focused on describing the *Object Request Broker* (ORB; Object Management Group, 1991), a middleware entity based on the object-oriented model. Based on the concept of "*bus of software*," the ORB succeeded in defining a hardware- and software-independent object framework. This framework does not only determine an object-oriented design tool, but it also includes a collection of services and facilities for the management of the client/server interaction within the distributed applications.

In order to fix a standard description for the ORB's model, in 1993, the OMG's committee specified the *Common Object Request Broker Architecture* (CORBA; Object Management Group, July 1995). The proposal allows two distributed systems to interoperate despite their heterogeneous architectures. Moreover, CORBA automates many common network-programming tasks as well as provides flexible foundations for higher level services, which simplifies distributed application development.

28.2 The OMG Project: An Interface-Based Distributed Object Model

28.2.1 Antecedents

Traditionally, the interactions between two heterogeneous systems required the mutual knowledge of the characteristics addressing their activity. Due to this, the systems involved in the interaction are forced to define some kind of matching (or mappings) between protocols and applications, from one system to the other, or both. In general, this approach does not provide flexible solutions and means a considerable human effort and a waste of time. When the systems involved are more than two, the situation becomes even worse, having to deal with a many-to-many interactions/adaptations problem.

During the previous decade, the client/server model and the Remote Procedure Calls (RPC) (Birrell and Nelson, 1984) become the *de facto* standard frameworks for distributed computing. Using some features borrowed from object-oriented programming, the client/server model extended the benefits of object-oriented technology across process and machine boundaries to encompass entire networks. Distributed object programming made remote objects appear to programmers as if they were local objects, making the location boundaries between two distributed applications disappear. On its side, the traditional RPCs allowed a "procedural" integration of application services. The RCP succeeded in adding platform transparency to the applications. However, it did not provide a similar level of abstraction as objects did, nor the benefits obtained for the use of inheritance. Very often, both proposals were used together in a common integrated framework.

In spite of the integration achieved by concurrent programming, object orientation, and other communication technologies, this approach did not succeed in overcoming the computing barriers due to the use of different languages, machines, network protocols, etc.

28.2.2 The OMG

In 1989, the most important software developers together with computer companies and end users formed the OMG.*

The characteristics outlining the OMG proposal are reflected in the following main points:

- The OMG's Objective — To develop, adopt, and promote standards for the development and use of object technologies, and particularly, distributed object applications in the context of heterogeneous environments.
- The OMG's Proposal — Primarily, the OMG was focused on the specification of the Object Management Architecture (OMA; Object Management Architecture Guide, 1990), a conceptual distributed object model. Secondly, the OMG specified the CORBA (Object Management Group 1991, July 1995), an open abstract distributed architecture over which distributed systems can interoperate despite their heterogeneous features.
- The OMA's Specifications Process — Every year, the OMG members join in order to make advances in the OMA's specifications process. The OMG's technical activities are focused within the OMG Task Forces and special interest groups. The OMG Task Forces determine the new proposals to be described and discussed. The method to divulge new proposals is known as OMG Request For Proposal (RFP).** The OMG RFP processes are used to adopt new specifications. These new specifications must fit into the OMG proposal and work with the others previously adopted.
- The OMA's Proposal-Acceptation Process — Under an OMG RFP, the Task Forces inform the OMG Technical Committee (TC) about the new proposals. During a period, members and other participants discuss the new proposals. After that, the Task Forces and the TC must accept or reject proposals and suggestions. At the last stage of the process, the OMG Board of Directors (BD) decides the proposal to be firmly included into the OMA specifications.

Even when, as a basic principle, the OMG only produces specifications, software developers are fully licensed to implement the OMG specifications without previous permission.

* Constituted as an international non-lucrative organization, the OMG is today one of the most active collaborative groups.

** Several OMG RFPs are currently inactive (Object Management Group, January, June, and August 1996).

28.3 The Object Management Architecture (OMA)

The OMA proposal is a conceptual distributed object model over which the rest of the OMG specifications will be described. In the OMA, the description unit is not the object but the object's interface. An interface defines the boundary layer that establishes a contract between clients and the supplier of the services (server or servant). In this manner, an object system is defined as a collection of objects in such a way that service providers are isolated from their clients by well-defined interfaces. The role played by interfaces consists of encapsulating the functionality provided by the servers.

28.3.1 The OMA Concepts

The main concepts underlying the OMA model are the following:

- Object — It refers to any identifiable encapsulated entity that is able to provide one or more services for the clients that request them.
- Request — Events with the following associated information — an operation name, the identity of target object, zero or more parameters, and an optional context for the request.
- Object Reference — An identifier associated with a concrete object. One object can be accessed through multiple references.
- Types — An entity identifiable by means of a predicate, which defines the possible values. Any value satisfying the predicate belongs to the type.
- Interfaces — A set of operations (services) that a client can execute over an object. They are specified using the interface description language (IDL). The principal interface of an object consists of all inherited operations.
- Operations — They are identifiable entities denoting a service. The signature for a given operation consists of several specifications (such as the arguments, the result, the raised exceptions, additional contextual information, etc.).
- Implementation Model — It is divided into two models:
  - Execution Model — The program code implementing a service is called method. The method execution starts by means of the method activation.
  - Construction Model — An object implementation must include the complete information needed to create an object.

At the highest level of abstraction, the OMA is composed of an Object Model and a Reference Model. The Object Model defines how objects distributed across a heterogeneous environment can be described. It contributes to the static part into the OMA distributed programming, making explicit both the object functionality (i.e., the object's operations) and attributes. Besides, the OMA establishes the definition of data types that are used by operations and attributes. On the other side, the dynamic meaning of the interactions taking place between clients and servants is provided by the Reference Model.

The OMA embodies OMG's vision for the component software environments. This architecture shows how standardization of components interfaces will penetrate up to (although not into*) application objects in order to create a plug-and-play component software environment based on object technology.

28.3.2 The OMA Object Model

In the OMA Object Model, an object is an encapsulated entity with a distinct immutable identity whose services can be accessed only through well-defined interfaces. An OMA interface is the boundary layer that separates a client of an object service from the supplier of the object service (an object implementation). This relation between interfaces and implementations can be seen as a *contract*, in which the implementation of a servant agrees to respond to a given request with certain results. Both clients and

* Therefore, it is not an intrusive model.

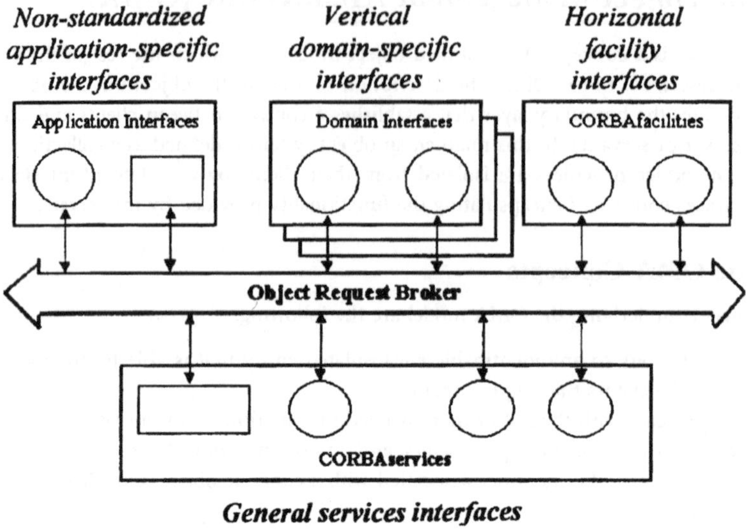

FIGURE 28.1 The ORB.

servants agree on the information that will be exchanged in a given operation. Finally, the clients delegate into OMA objects to perform services on their behalf. Along the process of interaction, the object implementation and location will remain hidden for the clients. As commented above, the role played by interfaces is crucial in the OMA system, and they are going to reside in the center of the CORBA specifications dealing with aspects relative to:

- How to describe interfaces
- How to store and manage interfaces
- How to map to concrete programming interfaces into diverse programming languages
- How object implementations relate to and support an interface

28.3.3 The OMA Reference Model

The Reference Model assumes the responsibility of defining the dynamic meaning of interactions between clients and servants. In order to do this, the OMA Reference Model defines the ORB. By using the concept of *bus of software* (see Figure 28.1), an ORB provides a platform-independent object framework. Moreover, the ORB model supplies foundations in support of some important transparential properties will be very important for interoperability among programming languages, platforms, and representations. Let us remark that this framework does not define only an interface-based design schema, but it also provides a collection of components and facilities responsible for managing client/server interactions. The ORB's components allow distributed objects to make and respond to requests transparently by supplying those mechanisms that distributed objects need to interact.

28.3.4 The Object Request Broker (ORB)

An ORB introduces a homogeneous object-computing stage between two heterogeneous computing interactions. Based on the client/server model, the ORBs mediate between clients and objects residing on different computers. This way, when two heterogeneous systems interact through an ORB protocol, they assume a role (i.e., the client or the servant) inside a virtual common architecture. When a distributed system exports its services, these are presented to the other systems under a common appearance. To do this, any software component providing services is described as a server (i.e., an object) by means of a common description syntax that is provided by The OMG IDL. On the other hand, any system which requests a service must adopt the role of client into the ORB's protocol. As in the case of the server, clients are described as IDL components.

More intuitively, an ORB is an object layer that mediates between a client and its target objects. This mediation will involve several actions:

- To deliver the request from the client context to the server context
- To invoke the method on the target object
- To deliver results back to the client, if any

Figure 28.1 shows the structure of an ORB. As a bus of software, objects in transit support the interactions between heterogeneous systems. Under the ORB model, mappings for languages or network protocols only will involve a many-to-one application from each system to the ORB. Because the ORB's programming model is interface-oriented, the OMG IDL provides language constructs for interface definition, encapsulation, inheritance, polymorphism, and other object-oriented concepts also applicable to interfaces. Additionally, the mechanisms needed to connect clients and servers operating on different locations are also supplied.

In order to establish a standard for the ORB's model, in 1993, the OMG's committee specified a CORBA (Object Management Group, March 1995).* In the CORBA model, the ORB makes software systems able to overcome the computing barriers due to the use of different languages, machines, and network protocols. The architecture provided by an ORB not only established a common space where objects interact, but it also introduces a higher degree of flexibility and transparency in those interactions (Vinosky, 1997). These transparential properties are described now:

- Location transparency — The distributed applications can be seen as an object-based application, in which remote objects appear to programmers as if they were local objects.
- Programming language transparency — The client and the server may be written in different programming languages.
- Platform transparency — The client and object implementation programs may be executed on different types of computing hardware with different operating systems.
- Representation transparency — Applications interacting as client object and server object through an ORB protocol can be using different low-level data representations due to the use of language, hardware, or compiler differences. The ORB converts different byte orders, word sizes, floating-point representations, etc., which allows the applications to ignore the differences due to different data representations.

28.4 CORBA

CORBA is able to solve the problem of interoperability between separately developed systems in a distributed heterogeneous environment, enabling the applications to use combinations of hardware and software components from different systems. Besides, CORBA automates many common network-programming tasks, which simplifies distributed application development, providing flexible foundations for higher level services. The CORBA ORB architecture is shown in Figure 28.2.

To this end, CORBA** specifies the following components:

- A concrete object model (ORB Core)
- An abstract language to describe object interfaces (OMG IDL)
- Abstract programming interfaces for implementing, using, and managing objects (stubs, skeletons, dynamic invocation and dispatch, object adapters, etc.)

* A few years later, CORBA succeeded to provide many foundations, services, and facilities for systems interoperability and software portability.

** "The CORBA specifications provide the foundations for the most comprehensive platform for systems interoperability and software portability that is foreseeable in today's computing market" [Smidch].

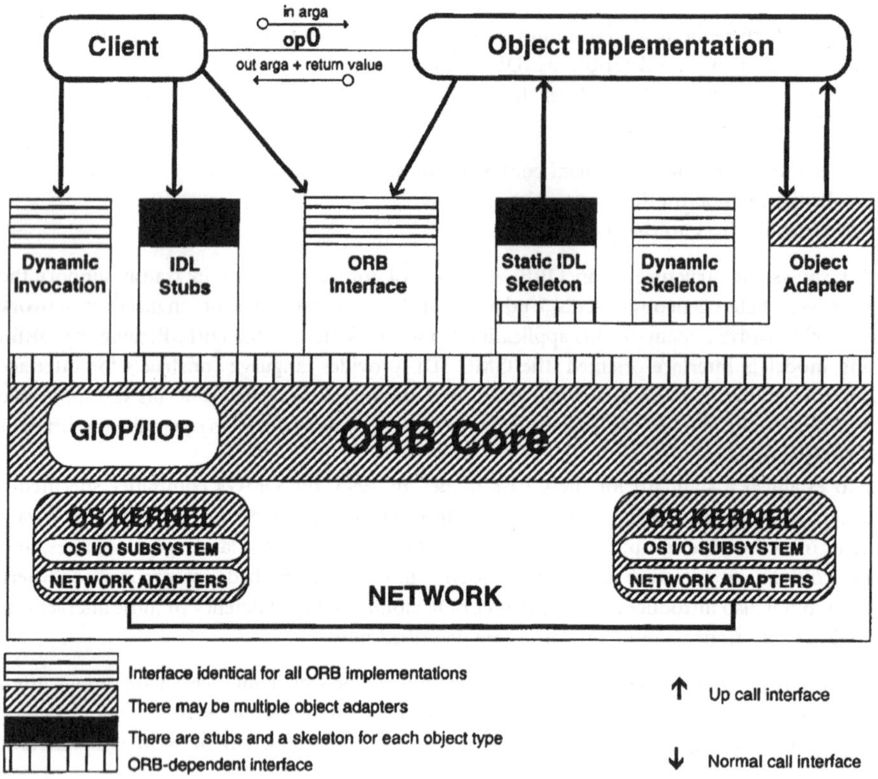

FIGURE 28.2 The CORBA ORB architecture.

- An interface repository
- Language mappings for the most common programming languages (object-oriented or not)
- An ORB-to-ORB architecture and several bridge-based facilities to ensure interoperability between products from different vendors (GIOP and IIOP standards)

28.4.1 ORB Core

As mentioned before, an ORB mediates between a client and its target objects. Across this interaction process, the ORB delivers requests from clients to objects, invokes the methods and, finally, delivers the result back to the client. In order to fulfill this mediation, an ORB must hide the following information:

- Object location — The location of the target object; this location can be different from client location.
- Object implementation — The client is ignorant of how the target object is implemented, which is the programming language it was written in, and which are the operating system or hardware characteristics.
- Object execution state — The client does not need to be aware of the current state of the object (if activated or not). It is the ORB, which transparently will start the object execution when it was required.
- Object communication mechanism — The client does not know what communication mechanisms (TCP/IP, shared memory, local method calls, etc.) the ORB uses to deliver the client request to the object and return the response to the client.

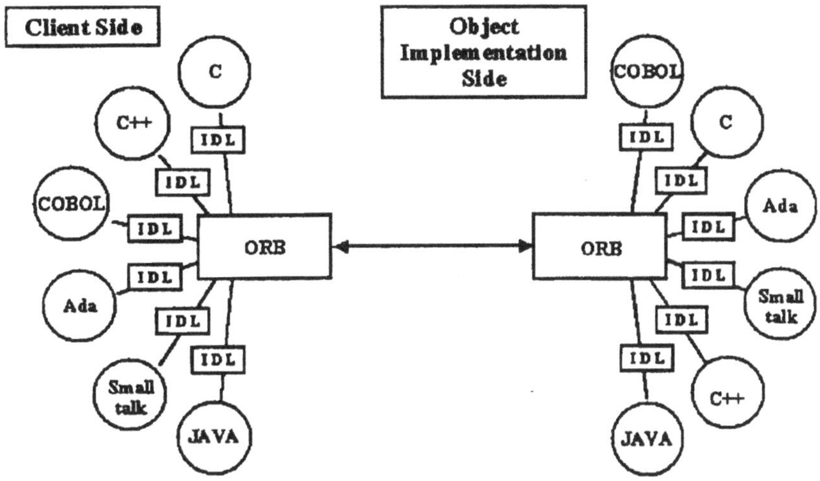

FIGURE 28.3 The role of the OMG IDL.

- Object creation — When a client creates an object, it gets an object reference. Actually, there are no real client operations for object creation in CORBA, it is done by invoking creation requests (common operation invocations).
- Directory service — CORBA specifies two standard Object Services in order to provide object references to the clients. On the one hand, the *Naming Service* allows clients to obtain object references by name. On the other hand, the *Trading Service* allows them to do it by properties. These services do not create new objects.

28.4.2 OMG Interface Definition Language (OMG IDL)

The ORBs are responsible for defining those interfaces acting on behalf of distributed objects. They are also responsible for adjusting the interactions between interfaces and object implementations. Once the conceptual layout has been fixed, the next is to find a concrete common interface representation. To this end, CORBA proposes the standard interface language named OMG IDL.

Interfaces for objects are defined using the OMG IDL. The IDL is not a real programming language but an interface description language. Therefore, IDL interfaces cannot execute on their own, they must be associated to concrete implementations.

These associations are carried out by mappings from interfaces to concrete programming languages. Objects written in different languages can communicate with other objects through the services provided by their IDL interfaces. This communication can be done even if any of the objects are implemented in a non-object-oriented language (just by mapping the IDL to that language). This language independence property is one of the most important and original features in the CORBA model.

In order to favor an easier use of the language, the OMG committee decided IDL syntax remained as close as possible to the syntax used by the most widely known languages. Therefore, IDL interfaces are quite similar to classes in C++ or interfaces in Java. An IDL interface definition example is shown in Figure 28.4.

The object interface *Account* specifies its attributes and a signature with the operations defined by the interface. On its side, each operation is described with a name and several parameters. From this interface the IDL compiler will generate some object-oriented code for a concrete language. The access to the *Account* object will be carried out through those operations defined on the interface. As direct access to the attributes is not allowed, only the operations *Deposit* and *Withdrawal* can be executed. A read-only attribute specifies that only reading operations are allowed. On the other hand, the parameters

```
//Define the Account interface.
interface Account {
  //Attributes related to the account balance and account owner
    attribute float balance;
    readonly attribute string owner;

//Operations
  void Deposit (in float amount, out float newBalance);
  void Withdrawal (in float amount, out float newBalance);
}:
```

FIGURE 28.4 The account-interface example.

```
//Define AccountService by inheritance.
interface AccountService : Account {

//Define a sequence of Account object references
  typedef sequence <Account, 10> AccountList;

//Attributes related to the account balance and account owner
  attribute AccountList accountFluctuation;

//AccountService operations
  AccountList Fluctuation (in string userName);
}:
```

FIGURE 28.5 An interface-inheritance example.

are tagged with a prefix (*in*, *out*, or *inout*). This determines the directionality associated with the parameters during the passing-parameters procedure. The tagged information improves the documentation provided by the interfaces and helps the target languages to generate the corresponding code. As the functionality in an IDL interface is rigorously fixed, the information provided to the clients is as much as they need.

The use of an interface-based programming style is the key for achieving sound distributed designs in CORBA. As the IDL is an interface language, several well-known drawbacks caused by using real object languages can be avoided. Much closer to object design than object implementation, interfaces are free of the side effects that members' redefinition might cause. The derived IDL interfaces inherit the operations and types defined on their base interfaces (i.e., systems are extensible*). As interfaces do not contain data members, no collision will affect the forthcoming derived classes. In Figure 28.5, an example is shown with interfaces inheritance.

With respect to the data representation, the OMG IDL provides a set of types (or types constructions) that are similar to those found in the most common programming languages. IDL types are classified into three groups: basic types, constructed types, and the object reference type. Additionally, IDL supports template types, similar to those used in C++. These template types are usually classified into the subset of constructed types. Figure 28.6 presents the hierarchical classification of the IDL types. In addition, the following sections present a deeper description for the IDL data types.

At this moment, the OMG has standardized language mappings for the most common implementation languages** (such as C, C++, COBOL, Ada, Smalltalk, Java, etc.). Figure 28.3 presents the role of OMG IDL in CORBA.

* This interface-based programming style agrees with the so-called *Open-Closed Principle* (Meyer, 1989).

** For more information about the languages mapped to CORBA, visit the OMG home page on the WWW at http://www.omg.org/.

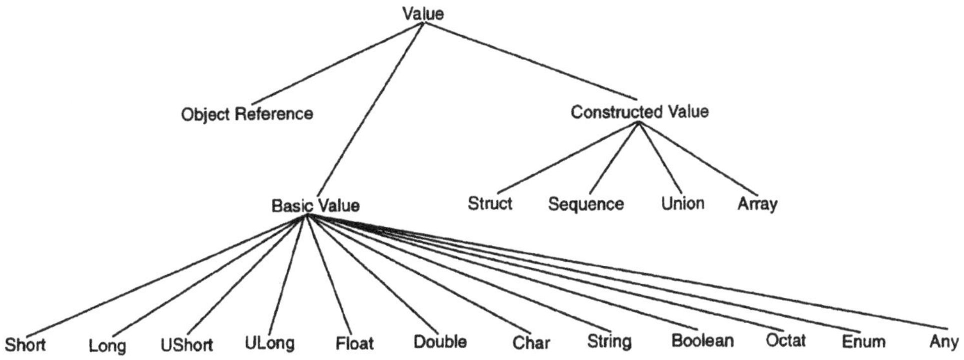

FIGURE 28.6 The OMG IDL types classification.

28.4.2.1 Built-In Types

OMG IDL supports the following built-in types:

- *long* (signed and unsigned) — 32-bit arithmetic types
- *long long* (signed and unsigned) — 64-bit arithmetic types
- *short* (signed and unsigned) — 16-bit arithmetic types
- *float, double*, and *long double* — IEEE 745-1985 floating point types
- *char* and *wchar* — character and wide character types
- *boolean* — Boolean type
- *octet* — 8-bit value
- *enum* — enumerated type
- *any* — a tagged type that can hold a value of any OMG IDL type, including built-in types and user-defined types.

28.4.2.2 Constructed Types

OMG IDL also supports constructed types:

- *struct* — aggregation construct (similar to structs in C or C++)
- *union* — a type composed of a type discriminator and a value of one of several possible OMG IDL types that are specified in the union definition; OMG IDL unions are similar to unions in C/C++, with the addition of the discriminator that keeps track of which alternative is currently valid.

28.4.2.3 Template Types

Similar to C++, OMG IDL supports some template types. It uses a static polymorphism, and therefore, the characteristics determining a template type must be defined at declaration time. There are three main template types:

- *string* and *wstring* – string and wide-character string types; both bounded string/wstring and unbounded string/wstring can be declared (i.e., *string <20>* or, in the unbounded case simply *string*).
- *sequence* — it is a dynamic-length linear container. On declaration time, the sequence maximum length of the sequence, as well as the basic type can be specified (for example, both *sequence <Account>* and *sequence <short, 12>* are allowed).

28.4.2.4 Object Reference Types

OMG IDL object reference types refers to the name of defined interface types. Figure 28.5 shows an example of object references. The interface named *AccountService* contains the definition of a type named *AccountList*. The *AccountList* is defined as a bounded sequence of Account object references. Sometimes, the term object reference may also be used to denote the abstract concept of an object's identity and location. One might say, for instance, that an object reference is passed from a client to a server as a parameter in an invocation.

28.4.3 Interface Repository

Because the application must know the types of values to be passed as request arguments, every CORBA application requires access to the OMG IDL type system. Many applications require only static knowledge of the OMG IDL system. In this case, the translation rules can be in charge of compiling IDL specifications into code for the application's programming languages. There are some applications, however, for which static knowledge of the OMG IDL type system is impractical. In this case, the CORBA Interface Repository allows the OMG IDL type system to be accessed and written at runtime.

Using the IR interface, applications can traverse an entire hierarchy of OMG IDL information, allowing applications to discover (by programming) type information at runtime. This way, it supports CORBA dynamic invocations (Gokhale and Schmidt, 1996). In order to do this, CORBA defines the Dynamic Invocation Interfaces (DII). Analogously, there exist Dynamic Skeleton Interfaces (DSI), which allow servers to be written without having skeletons for the objects being invoked (compiled statically into the programs).

28.4.4 Stubs and Skeletons

Clients to invoke operations on target CORBA objects use *stubs.* Therefore, a stub is a mechanism that effectively creates a service request on behalf of a client. A stub is not a CORBA object itself, but instead it represents a CORBA object. It is responsible for propagating requests made on itself to the real target object.*

When the target object resides in a remote process, the stub is responsible for packing the request with its parameters into a message and sending the message to the remote process across a network. After that, it receives the reply message from the object, unpacks the operation results from the message, and returns them to the calling program.

On its side, a *skeleton* is a mechanism that delivers requests to the CORBA object implementation. A skeleton takes the form of an abstract class with abstract methods that correspond to the operations in the IDL interface. The skeleton is responsible for unpacking a request, delegating the parameters to the appropriate method, and packing any results into a reply message, which are finally sent to the stub. As with the stub, the interface of the skeleton is isomorphic to the IDL interface, implying that the stub and skeleton have identical interfaces.

28.4.5 Object Adapters (OA)

The *Object Adapters*** glue CORBA objects implementations to the related ORBs. An object adapter is responsible for adapting the interface of a real implementation to the interface expected by the clients (see Figure 28.7). By assuming this interposing responsibility, OAs allow the ORB functionality maintains to be much simpler than they would be in another case, not compromising the ability of CORBA to support diverse object implementation styles. Each OA provides access to the services of an ORB (such as activation, deactivation, object reference management, etc.) used by a particular interface of object implementation.

Usually, different programming languages need different OAs. For this reason, CORBA provides multiple OAs. Though CORBA allows the use of multiple OAs, the standard only provides one — the Basic Object Adapter (BOA). The ORB core may provide the BOA functionality, by the BOA, or by the two in combination. In the case that an ORB is not able to provide a determined functionality, as it is the case of some specialized objects (OODBs, library-based objects, etc.), it may adapt the interactions on behalf of the ORB.

---

* Stubs are sometimes called *proxies* (Gamma et al., 1995).

** Several network patterns such as Adapter and Proxy (Gamma et al., 1995) have been used in CORBA.

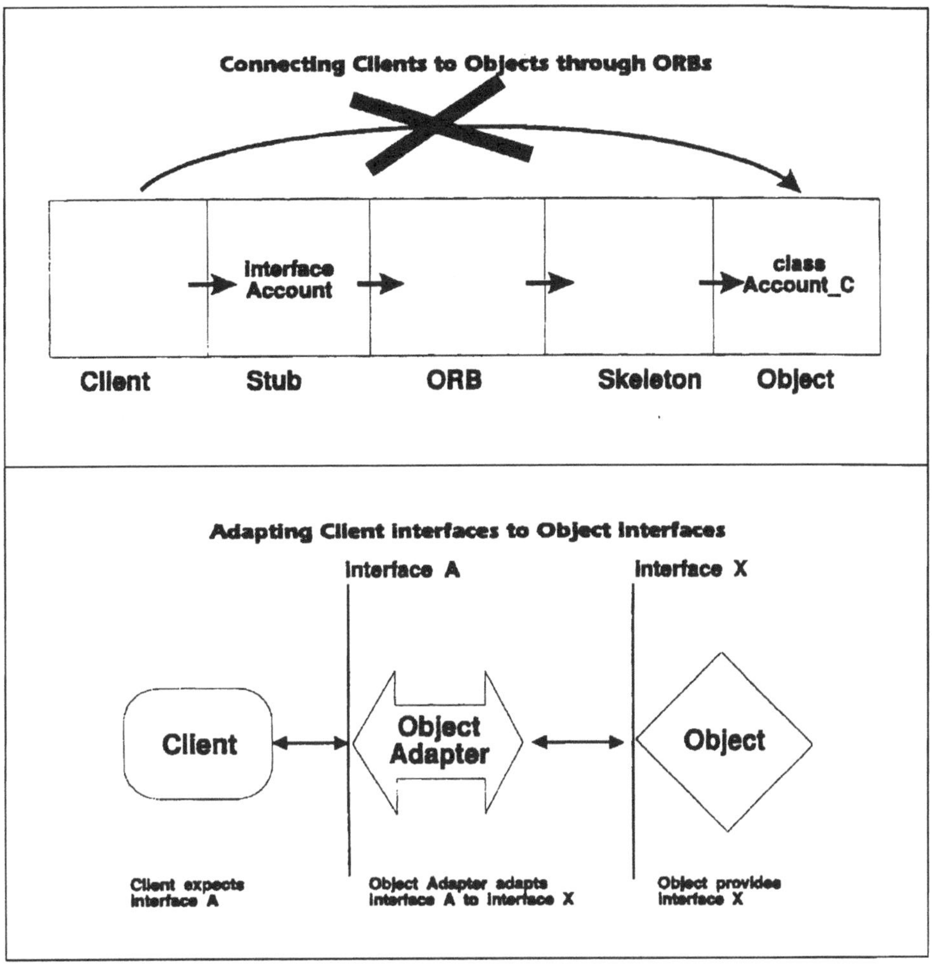

FIGURE 28.7 Object programming in CORBA.

As the BOA was thought to support multiple languages, the BOA specification introduced certain vagueness in several areas, such as the registration of the programming language objects as CORBA objects. Finally, it turned into a non-trivial portability problem between BOA implementations. Recently, a Portability Enhancement RFP has posed the need of solving this drawback in order to adopt a specification for a standard Portable Object Adapter (POA).

28.5 The ORB-to-ORB Interoperability

As the OMG's first attention was focused on establishing specifications for the ORBs, the first CORBAs 1.X only served to standardize several common object services and facilities. Despite the wide gap filled by these versions toward a CORBA standardization, it was not enough to solve the complex problem of interoperability. Certainly, because CORBA did not mandate any particular data formats or protocols for ORB communication, the early ORB implementations were not capable of interoperating. Once the OMG specifications for ORB interaction were fixed, it remained to establish new specifications for a standard ORB-to-ORB architecture. To fill this gap, the OMG introduced some new interoperability facilities in the CORBA 2.0 version. Under the new specifications:

- Two ORBs residing in a same domain (that is, with the same object references and the same OMG IDL type system) could interoperate directly.
- If ORBs resided in different separate domains, CORBA provided a bridge-based interoperability. In this case, the role of the bridge should be to map ORB-specific information from one ORB domain to the other.

The CORBA 2.0 meant the introduction of a general ORB interoperability architecture based on the General Inter-ORB Protocol (GIOP).

By means of some extra interoperability features, the CORBA 2.0 allows a direct ORB-to-ORB interoperability and bridge-based interoperability. This way, the new CORBA made it possible so that multiple ORBs could integrate into larger hierarchies, allowing a transparent access to CORBA object servers. In addition to the GIOP description, the OMG described the Internet Inter-ORB Protocol (IIOP), a canonical request format and standardized request dispatching, to determine how GIOP can be implemented using TCP/IP. It is mandatory that any CORBA 2.0 ORB must support the GIOP and IIOP standards.* The OMG GIOP specification includes the following components:

- The Common Data Representation (CDR) — It defines representations for all OMG IDL data types. It includes dynamic-length types, such as struct, sequence, enum, and the CORBA Object Reference. The specification takes into account byte ordering and alignment. Receiver-makes-right semantics avoids unnecessary translation of messages between machines of the same byte order. The point of CDR is that all GIOPs share a common data representation, so to bridge this part of the message should be easy.
- A Common Message Format — GIOP messages are specified following a common format. A message includes a GIOP header, a request header, and a request body.
- A Common Message Header — It contains the message length, the GIOP version, the byte order, and the type of GIOP message.
- GIOP Messages — There are seven different types of GIOP messages. They support all of the functions and behavior required by CORBA, including exception reporting, passing of operation context, and dynamical object relocation and migration. The messages meet the needs of the object-oriented CORBA semantics in the most efficient way possible, and they are managed transparently with regard to the applications.
  1. Request (sent by client) — A server operation request.
  2. Reply (sent by object) — It is the answer to an operation request.
  3. CancelRequest (sent by client) — The client indicates to the server the cancellation of an operation request.
  4. LocateRequest (sent by client) — To determine (1) if a particular object reference is valid, (2) if a current server is capable of servicing requests, or (3) if not, a new address for requests for that object reference.
  5. LocateReplay (sent by object) — The server reply to a LocateRequest.
  6. CloseConnection (sent by servers) — To inform clients that the server intends to close the connection and will not provide further responses.
  7. MessageError (sent by either) — They are sent in response to any GIOP message non-interpretable.
- Transport Assumptions — It is established that some requirements on the GIOP message transport. GIOP requires:
  1. A connection-oriented protocol
  2. A reliable delivery; participants must be notified of disorderly connection loss
  3. The model for initiating a connection must meet certain requirements
  4. Together with TCP/IP protocol (mandatory for IIOP), other usual targets
  5. Other protocols mapped by GIOP (such as IPX and OSI), if any

* See Figure 28.2.

In addition to standard interoperability protocols, standard object reference formats are also necessary for ORB interoperability. CORBA specifies a standard object reference format called Interoperable Object Reference (IOR). An IOR stores information needed to locate and communicate with an object over one or more protocols.*

28.6 Present and Future with CORBA

Since 1993, the successive overhauls of CORBA have extended the initial OMA model to provide more foundations for higher level distributed object collaborations as well as more object services and object facilities. More recently, the versions have established new specifications to automate common network-programming tasks.

The CORBA 1.1 extended the original OMA framework with the mechanisms used by request invocations, which allowed clients to call to remote servers via ORBs (OMG, 1991). The CORBA 1.2 served to standardize several common object services (OMG, 1995).** This way, CORBA 1.X versions were mainly focused on establishing the foundations to perform transparent remote requests from client applications to servers. In addition to the OMG IDL, several IDL mappings (such as C, C++, and other common languages) were also specified [OMG 91, OMG 93].

The later CORBA 2.0 meant the introduction of a general ORB's interoperability architecture based on the GIOP (OMG, March 1995). By these extra features supported by the CORBA 2.0, it was able to provide a direct ORB-to-ORB interoperability and bridge-based interoperability and a standard format for object references.

Today, a wide variety of CORBA products exists, complete or quasi-complete versions for the standard CORBA 2.0 (OMG, July 1995). Most commercially available ORB products already support IIOP and IORs having been tested to ensure interoperability. Interoperability testing is currently done by ORB vendors rather than by an independent conformance-testing body.***

For a long time, the OMG Committee activity was channeled throughout the OMG Task Forces groups. They were in charge of establishing which new issues to treat, as well as how the objectives reached were fixed. This regulated organization allowed the OMG's to maintain a common technical orientation about CORBA specifications, against interested proposals and external influences coming from concrete ORB vendors**** or software developers. In 1996, with a solid corpus of CORBA already established, the OMG reorganized itself to give users of the CORBA components the power to set their own technical directions. Because of the new orientation, the OMG TC split into two committees:

1. Domain Technical Committee (DTC) — Focused on vertically oriented technologies (i.e., domain specific), the DTC makes up task forces addressing issues such as financial, manufacturing, medical, business, and telecommunications.
2. Platform Technical Committee (PTC) — Focused on horizontally oriented technologies (i.e., domain-independent), the PTC makes up task forces addressing issues such as ORB/Object Services (ORBOS) (OMG, March 1996) and common facilities.

This separation responds to the need of separating the most domain-specific groups, with a broader set of objectives, from the domain-independent groups, which must follow the OMG's guideline maintained until now. Figure 28.8 shows the current OMA organization.

* For example, an IOR continuing a IIOP information stores hostname and TCP/IP port number information.

** The functionality of these services was established with independence of vendors-interests or concrete-environments.

*** Excepting the so-called OMG CORBAnet (OMG, May 1996), which facilitates testing ORB interoperability and proves commercial viability.

**** For more information about the upper layers of the OMA see (Soley, 1995) or visit the OMG home page on the WWW at http://www.omg.org/. For other information about other CORBA issues, see Vinoski (1997), Schmidt and Siegel (1996).

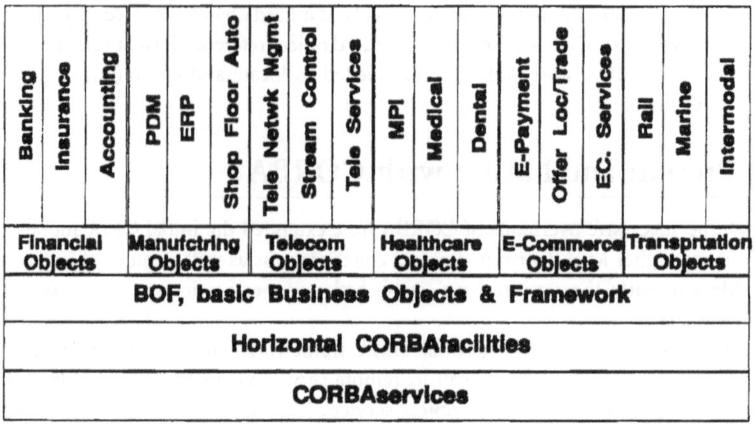

FIGURE 28.8 Domains in the OMA project.

Nevertheless, and in spite of the new OMA structure, the integrity of the project is ensured by the existence of an Architecture Board (AB). The AB is a technical board committee composed of ten elected members and a chairperson, with the power to reject RFP technologies that do not fit into the OMA. Even though CORBA was started from scratch, it has been able to incorporate and integrate legacy systems (Vinoski, 1997), which is one of its most profitable advantages. As CORBA is not mandated by implementations, a well-designed ORB does not require components and technologies already in use to be abandoned. This way, existing protocols and applications, such as DCE [X] or Microsoft COM, can be integrated rather than replaced.

28.6.1 The OMG's Future Challenges

CORBA has come a long way, but many issues still remain unsolved. Even though the experience acquired along CORBA's life has clarified some flaws in the model, this better comprehension of the problem has brought out other flaws.

In practice, most of the existing ORBs do not support dynamic invocation yet. Besides, CORBA does not comply well with type-oriented paradigms [X] and IIOP specification lacks sophisticated security and runtime support [X]. It has been proven that conventional implementations of IIOP incur considerable overhead when used for performance-sensitive applications over high-speed networks. This is the case in some application domains, such as avionics, telecommunications, and multimedia, which require real-time guarantees from the underlying networks, operating systems, and middleware components to achieve quality service requirements.

Even if lower level middleware implementations (such as ORBs and message-oriented middleware) are now reaching maturity, the semantics of higher level middleware services (such as the CORBA's Common Object Services and Common Facilities) are still vague, under-specific, and non-interoperable. In this sense, emerging industry middleware standards (like CORBA, DCOM, or Java RMI) to eliminate distributed software complexity today are very risky. As a final remark, the usual skills required to successfully produce distributed middleware remain a "black art" [X]. Because of this, the next-generation distributed applications should take a higher profit from old concepts as reusability, efficiency, and reliability, as well as capture and specify the patterns that underlie the successful distributed software components and frameworks that already exist [X].

In the early future, the continuous increase of networked activity is going to determine an even wider heterogeneous landscape. In this situation, the CORBA proposal represents the most feasible solution for cooperative organizations, software-services suppliers, telecommunications enterprises, financial and business companies, and end users.

Acknowledgments

I would like to thank Javier Galve and Julio Mariño for their excellent comments and suggestions. I would also like to express my deep appreciation to Eva González for her multiple reviews of early versions of this article.

References

Birrell, A. D. and Nelson, B. J. 1984. Implementing remote procedure calls, *ACM Trans. Comp. Syst.*, Vol. 2, pp. 39–59, February.

Gamma, E., Helm, R., Johnson, R. and Vlissides, J. 1995. *Design Patterns: Elements of Reusable Object-Oriented Software.* Addison-Wesley, Reading, MA.

Gokhale, A. and Schmidt, D. C. 1996. The performance of the CORBA dynamic invocation interface and dynamic skeleton interface over high-speed ATM networks, pp. 50–56. In *Proc. GLOBECOM '96,* (London, England), *IEEE,* Nov. 1996.

Martin, R. C. 1996. The open-closed principle, *C++ Rep.*, Vol. 8, Jan.

Meyer, B. 1989. *Object O. Software Construction.* Prentice-Hall, Englewood Cliffs, NJ.

Netscape Communications Corporation. 1996. New Netscape ONE Platform Brings Distributed Objects To the Internet and Intranets, July 29, 1996. Press release. URL: http://home.netscape.com/newsref/pr/newsrelease199.html.

Object Management Architecture Guide 1.0, 1990. OMG 90-9-1.

Object Management Group. 1991. *Draft Common Object Request Broker: Architecture and Specification,* 91-1-1.

Object Management Group. 1995. *The Common Object Request Broker: Architecture and Specification,* 2.0 ed. July.

Object Management Group. 1995. *CORBAServices: Common Object Services Specification,* Revised Edition, 95-3-31 ed., March.

Object Management Group. 1995. ORB Portability Enhancement RFP, OMG Document 1995/95-06-26 ed., June.

Object Management Group. 1995. Systems Management: Common Management Facilities, Volume 1, Version 2, OMG Document 1995/95-12-02 through 1995/95-12-06 ed., December.

Object Management Group. 1996. Messaging Service RFP, OMG Document orbos/96-03-16 ed., March.

Object Management Group. 1996. OMG Unveils CORBAnet Initiative, May 13, Press release. URL: http://www.omg.org/pr96/corbanet.htm.

Object Management Group. 1996. Control and Management of A/V Streams Request For Proposals, OMG Document telecom/96-08-01 ed., August.

Object Management Group. 1996. Objects-by-value Request For Proposals, OMG Document orbos/96-06-14 ed., June.

Object Management Group. 1996. Common Business Objects and Business Object Facility RFP, OMG Document cf/96-01-04 ed., January.

Rosenberry, W., Kenney, D. and Fischer, G. 1992. *Understanding DCE.* O'Reilly and Associates, Sebastopol, CA.

Schmidt, D. C. and Fayad, M. E. 1997. Lessons Learned: *Building Reusable OO Frameworks for Distributed Software, Communications,* Vol. 40, October.

Schmidt, D. C. URL: http://www.cs.wustl.edu/~schmidt/.

Siegel, J. 1996. *CORBA Fundamentals and Programming,* John Wiley & Sons. New York.

Soley, R. M., Ed., 1995. *Object Management Architecture Guide,* Third ed. John Wiley & Sons, New York.

Vinoski, S. 1997. CORBA: Integrating diverse applications within distributed heterogeneous environments, *IEEE Commun. Mag.*, February.

Wegner, P. 1990. Concepts and paradigms of object-oriented programming, *OOPS Messenger,* Vol. 1, Num. 1, August.

29

OMG Interface Definition Language and its SOM Extensions

Messaoud Benantar
IBM Corporation

Mohamed Kodeih
IBM Corporation

29.1 Introduction

An Interface Definition Language, or simply IDL, is a descriptive language that consists of a set of declarations only. When processed by an IDL compiler, the declarations are translated into language specific bindings for use by the interface implementation, commonly known as the server, and the caller of the interface referred to as the client. The bindings are also sometimes called a stub and a skeleton for use by the client and the server, respectively. The goal behind an IDL is to provide for a language-neutral means of declaring an interface to a server's operations. Generally, this interface is fully described in terms of its operations signatures including a name for each operation, its type, and the input and output parameters. Furthermore, IDL relieves the caller of the interface from being tightly bound to the operations as implemented by the server, thus allowing client programs to become more insulated from modifications in the server implementation. IDL predates object technology in that the Remote Procedure Call, known simply as RPC, protocol used in the Distributed Computing Environment architecture also uses its own IDL to define a server's interface (Open Software Foundation, 1993). In the next sections we discuss the fundamental language elements that make up an OMG IDL specification. Subsequently, we describe the major IDL extensions as implemented by the IBM System Object Model (SOM).

29.1.1 OMG IDL

OMG IDL follows lexical rules similar to those of C++. Its syntax is a subset of the ANSI C++, with additional constructs and keywords to support the operation invocation mechanism and the needs of a distributed model of programming (OMG, 1995; Otte, 1996; and Mowbray, 1995). Each operation's

0-8493-3135-8/99/$0.00+$.50

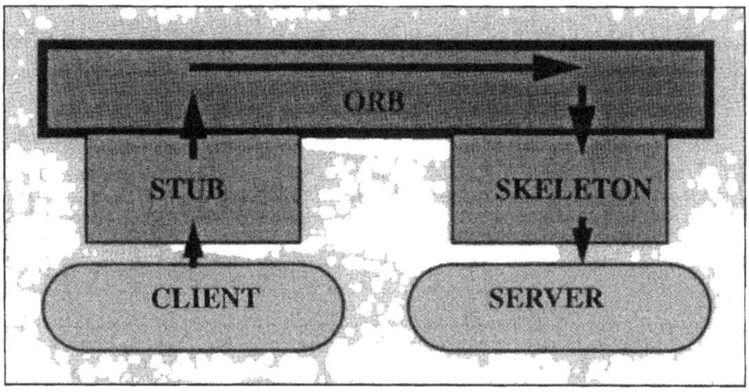

FIGURE 29.1 The interactions between the client/server programs, the emitted IDL bindings, and the ORB.

parameter is specified with a type and a direction qualifying the parameter as an input, output, or both an input and a side-effected output.There is no means for a client to directly access the implementation of an interface, and thus, the concept of encapsulation is implicit in an IDL definition. As such, there is no notion of public and private parts of an interface. Current OMG specifications include bindings for a number of languages such as C, C++, Smalltalk, Ada, and Java. Each interface definition is emitted into a class in the target programming language. The language bindings emitted by an OMG-based IDL compiler define the links between a client program and a communication infrastructure known as the Object Request Broker, or simply the ORB, on one hand, and the server program and the ORB, on the other hand. As depicted in Figure 29.1, the client program functions, or method calls resolve to the stub that represents the server program to the client. The stub then interacts with the ORB, which, possibly, sends the request to another remote ORB, residing either on the client's platform or on a different one. Using the skeleton, the remote ORB dispatches the request in the server (note that while in Figure 29.1 the interactions are depicted in a one-way, the flow goes in both directions as the client expects responses from the server).

29.2 OMG IDL Lexical and Syntax Definitions

A language is constructed from building blocks, called tokens, that make up the units from which a statement from the language can be defined. OMG IDL uses the ISO Latin-1 (8859.1) character set standard for the generation of its tokens. A statement can be made from the combination of five kinds of tokens: identifiers, keywords, literals, operators, and token separators. An identifier is an arbitrarily long sequence combining alphabetic, digit, and the underscore ("_") character. The first character, however, must be alphabetic. Identifiers are case insensitive in that upper- and lower-case letters are treated as the same letter, but an identifier is required to be spelled in the same manner throughout the whole specification. Literals of different types including Integer, Character, Floating-Point, and String, all follow similar rules as in the C language.

To accomplish a particular semantic, the elements of a language statement are tied together through special tokens called keywords that follow the grammar, or the syntax, rules defined by that language. The keywords are special identifiers recognized in the language to underscore a particular semantic other than simply defining an identifier. Figure 29.2 lists a few of the OMG IDL reserved keywords that may not be found in common languages.

29.3 OMG IDL Specification

An OMG IDL specification formally consists of one or more module definitions, interface definitions, type definitions, constant definitions, or exception definitions. Each of these definitions in itself represents

any default in out inout attribute

interface exception module sequence

Object octet string context oneway

FIGURE 29.2 A subset of the OMG IDL keywords.

a naming scope. Generally, a *module* makes up the outermost scope for defining multiple interfaces of a single specification (see OMG, 1996 for a complete syntax.) Figure 29.3 shows an example of a specification written in OMG IDL.

An interface declaration, although formally not required by an IDL specification, is the core element of a specification. It describes the elements of an interface to which both the implementor and the user adhere. An interface declaration begins with the interface header followed by the interface body. The header consists of the keyword *interface* followed by the interface identifier, then possibly followed by an optional inheritance specification, as it is the case with interface *book* of Figure 29.3 directly inheriting from interface *PaperMedia*, while indirectly inheriting from interface *bookstore*. Note that the definition for interface *bookstore* is part of the *bookstore.idl* file and thus the file had to be included at the top of the specification. The interface body may contain constant declarations, type declarations, exception declarations, and attribute declarations, as well as operation declarations.

29.4 Inheritance

An interface can be derived from another interface called a base interface; e.g., interface *book* inheriting from interface *PaperMedia*. Note that a *forward* declaration for interface *PaperMedia* is needed in the example of Figure 29.3 as interface *book* refers to interface *PaperMedia* prior to *book*'s definitions. A derived interface may declare its own elements such as operations, exceptions, attributes, and constants. In addition elements of the base interface can be used in the derived interface as if they were elements of that interface provided they are not redefined. The name resolution operator :: can be used in the derived interface to explicitly refer to an element of the base interface. Attributes and operations are not allowed to be redefined in the derived interface. An interface may simultaneously inherit from multiple base interfaces. Multiple inherited elements can be unambiguously referred to in the derived interface by using the name resolution operator ::. It is not, however, allowed to inherit from multiple interfaces declaring the same attribute or operation name.

29.5 Type Declaration

OMG IDL provides for type declarations similar to C language. In addition to the keywords *struct*, *union*, and *enum*, the keyword *typedef* is used to associate an identifier with a particular data type. The named type is identified through its specifier keyword. Three kinds of type specifiers are used. Basic type specifiers include Integer Types identified through the keywords *long*, *short*, *signed*, and *unsigned*. Floating point types are specified using the keywords *float* and *double*. The *char* type specifier is an 8-bit quantity that can represent any ISO Latin-1 (8859.1) character. In preparation for transmission some data elements may be transformed into other representations. In order to explicitly avoid this conversion, the type *octet* can be used to guarantee that a sequence of characters being transmitted will reach its destination at the current representation. The *boolean* type specifier is used to denote an item that takes

```
#include <bookstore.idl>

#include <periodicals.idl>

module books_and_magazines {

  typedef sequence<string> Authors;

  interface PaperMedia;

  interface book: PaperMedia {
            Authors GetAuthors(in string title);
            string ISBNcode();
  }

  interface magazine: PaperMedia, periodicals {

    enum category { science, sports, entertainment};

    exception UnknownCategory {long ErrCode};

    raises Unknown_Category;

    attribute category kind;

    unsigned short GetCurrentIssue(in category kind);

  }

  interface PaperMedia: bookstore {

    string GetTitle();
    float Price();
  }
} // end module books_and_magazines
```

FIGURE 29.3 A typical OMG IDL specification.

only one of the values TRUE or FALSE. Type specifiers can also refer to a constructed type that can be a structure, a union, or an enumeration.

Finally, a specifier may be of a template type which includes sequences and strings. A *sequence* is a one-dimensional array with a maximum length, statically known at compile time, and a current length varying at runtime and not exceeding the maximum length. A sequence can also be thought of as a structure whose elements are a maximum length, a current length, and a buffer to hold the elements of the sequence. If no maximum size is specified, the sequence buffer is dynamically allocated by explicit programming, and its maximum and current length are set. It should be noted that the only form of recursive type specifications allowed in OMG IDL is by using the sequence type such as depicted below.

```
struct record {
  unsigned long key;
  sequence<records> next_records;
}
```

A *string type* is similar to a sequence of characters. It can be bounded by specifying a maximum size such as in *string<MAX_SIZE>*, or unbounded by simply using the *string* type alone such as in the example of Figure 29.2. In addition multidimensional, fixed-size arrays can be defined by an OMG IDL specification and their types can be used as type specifiers.

29.6 Attribute Declaration

Besides declaring different data types, an interface definition may declare one or more attributes. Declaring an attribute of some type is equivalent to declaring a pair of accessor functions; one to set the value of the attribute, and one to retrieve it. For instance the attribute kind in interface magazine of Figure 29.3 is equivalent to declaring two operations.

```
_set_kind(in category value)
category _get_kind()
```

The optional *readonly* keyword may precede the keyword *attribute* to indicate that only the retrieve operation can be applied to that attribute. The attribute type cannot designate an array declarator. Like operations attributes are inherited by the derived interface. It should be noted that declaring an attribute is the only means of defining a data member of an object in an OMG IDL specification.

29.7 Operations and Parameter Declaration

An operation declaration consists of three required parts: a return type, a name identifying the operation, and a list of parameters. Every operation should be preceded by a return type; e.g., the ISBNcode operation of the book interface where the type of the returned value of the operation is a string. An operation not returning any value should be preceded with the keyword *void.* Optionally you may see a method declaration proceeded by the *oneway* keyword as shown below to indicate an asynchronous method which conveys a best-effort semantic to the ORB in delivering the method to a remote target object. Here the method is not guaranteed delivery. A one-way operation must specify a return type of void as no return value is expected. The call to such a method returns to the client immediately.

```
oneway void myMethod(in string aMessage)
```

An OMG IDL parameter declaration consists of a required directional attribute followed by the parameter type, followed by the identifier naming the parameter. A directional attribute can be the keyword *in* indicating that the parameter is passed from the caller; i.e., from the client to the server. It can be the keyword *out* to indicate that the parameter is an output from the server to the client, or it can be *inout* to indicate a bidirectional parameter, one that is an input from the client that is also side-effected by the server and becomes an output. When an unbounded string or sequence is passed as an *inout* parameter, upon return the buffer length of either the string or the sequence cannot exceed its value at the input.

29.8 Name Scoping

Like in most programming languages, a file containing an IDL specification forms the outermost naming scope of the translated unit corresponding to that file. A scope becomes more specific as a module, an interface, a structure, a union, an operation, or an exception declaration is encountered as each of these forms a nested scope. Name scoping affects identifiers that define types, declare constants, enumerations, exceptions, interfaces, attributes, or operations. Names of these types are immediately available for use in their defining scope and in any nested scopes. Explicit name scoping allows for unambiguously redefining identifiers in nested scopes. An identifier that is redefined in a nested scope still can be referred to within that scope by simply qualifying it by *<name-scope>::identifier,* where name scope, in turn, can be a simple identifier referring to a module name, an interface, a structure, a union, an operation, or

```
interface ...
{
  OMG IDL statements ...

  #ifdef __SOMIDL__
  implementation
    {
    SOM IDL statements ...
    }
  #endif
};
```

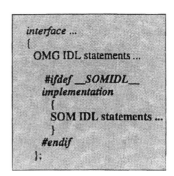

FIGURE 29.4 SOM IDL interface skeleton.

an exception name, or it can be a complex name scope of the form <name-scope>::identifier. For a qualified name that begins with ::, the scope resolution process starts at the file scope and continues down the nested scopes until the identifier is located. As a result of this name scoping, every identifier can be referred to with a global name in an IDL specification. A nested scope is said to go out of scope when the end of its definition is encountered.

29.8.1 SOM Extensions to OMG IDL

OMG IDL is a language used to specify interfaces. Since it is a declarative language, it does not convey any implementation specific information to the IDL-based compiler. With OMG IDL, interface implementation decisions are made at the programming language level. SOM IDL extends OMG IDL by providing constructs allowing the developer to specify, at the IDL level, how an interface should be implemented (IBM, 1996 and Lau, 1994). These extensions are mainly used at the IDL level to exercise control over the interface implementation in order to allow for more flexibility and achieve better performance.

29.8.1.1 Class Implementation Specification

The main SOM extensions to IDL are a set of implementation oriented statements that specify how a class is to be implemented. Such statements — called modifiers — are used to specify the following:

- List the methods of the class in certain order so as to maintain a release to release binary compatibility
- Specify whether a class is an abstract or a concrete class
- Specify the factory of the class, the type of the class proxy, and the class metaclass
- Define initialization functions that will be invoked at the time of class instantiation
- Specify a particular method resolution policy
- Indicate a specific memory management policy at the module level, class level, or method level
- Define a specific parameter passing mechanism such as pass by value
- Specify whether a method should override an inherited method and whether a method is allowed to be overridden by a derived class

The skeleton of a SOM IDL interface is shown in Figure 29.4. Bold statements depict SOM IDL extensions. The *#ifdef* is used so that the OMG IDL portion of the interface can be compiled with an IDL compiler that is not SOM based.

SOM IDL modifiers are used inside the implementation statement. Figure 29.5 shows an SOM IDL description. It consists of a single method described in OMG IDL and three SOM IDL instance variables. SOM IDL instance variables offer an alternative way to using attributes, and they differ from attributes in making the instance variables access private to the interface. They also offer the flexibility of using non-OMG IDL data types.

```
interface Name
{
   string get_name();
#ifdef __SOMIDL__
implementation
{
   string first, middle, last;
}
#endif
};
```

FIGURE 29.5 SOM IDL description of the Name interface.

29.8.1.2 Controlling Re-Implementation of an Inherited Method

SOM IDL defines a set of modifiers that can be used to specify whether an inherited method should be overridden or not. The *override* modifier is used in a derived class (or a subclass) to specify that a method should be re-implemented by this class. The *nooverride* modifier is used to disallow re-implementing a method in a derived class.

29.8.1.3 Maintaining a Release to Release Binary Compatibility

Object-oriented programming languages such as C++ introduced a problem of maintaining a software upward compatibility. In C++, upward compatibility might be broken when a change is made to a class, such as introducing a new method. This is because a change to a class may require re-compilation of the client program and re-compilation may not be possible in cases where the source code is not available. This problem is referred to as the fragile base class problem.

The fragile base class problem does not exist in cases where a software is implemented in a procedural language. This is due to packaging the software as a dynamic link library (DLL.) A DLL allows a function implementation to be modified without requiring the client code to re-compile or link, provided that the function interface remains intact. This capability is possible since a client program does not have to link to the DLL until runtime. Therefore, DLLs provide a convenient mechanism for upward compatibility as long as the DLLs represent a procedural code.

This capability provided by DLLs fails when the DLL represents code written in an object-oriented language such as C++. The example in Figure 29.6a-e illustrates the reason. First, the class provider defines the class Name as shown in (a) that consists of two data members (first and last name) and their get and set operations. A client code that uses this class is shown in (e). When the client code is executed, it first links dynamically with the DLL of the class in (a); then produces the output "John Doe." Note that when the code in (a) is executed, it assumes the memory layout shown in (c). Next, the developer changes the class by adding a data member and its get and set operations as shown in (b). The addition of the new data member changes the memory layout as shown in (d). Now, when the client code is executed, it links dynamically with the DLL of the modified code and produces an error. This is because the client code has no knowledge of the memory layout change that occurred after adding the new data member to the class. The setLast("Doe") call assumes the memory layout as shown in (c) and assigns the value "Doe" to the second location. However, the second location belongs to the second data member which is the middle name as shown in (d). In order for the client code to execute correctly, it should be re-compiled with the class header file even though the class maintained the same interface.

To address this problem, SOM IDL introduced the *releaseorder* modifier statement which is used by the SOM compiler to create the storage layout of the class. This statement lists every method name defined in the IDL, including the get and set methods that are automatically generated for each attribute. The order of the method names in the releaseorder list should be maintained. When a method is deleted,

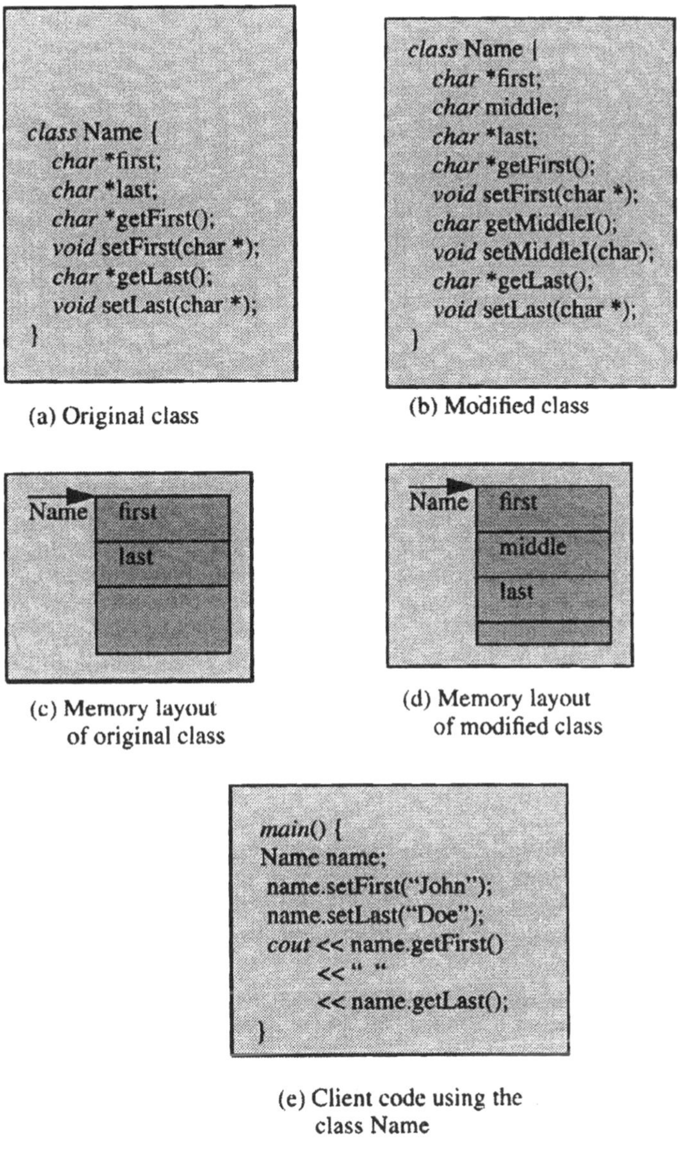
class Name {
char *first;
char *last;
char *getFirst();
void setFirst(char *);
char *getLast();
void setLast(char *);
}
(a) Original class
class Name {
char *first;
char middle;
char *last;
char *getFirst();
void setFirst(char *);
char getMiddleI();
void setMiddleI(char);
char *getLast();
void setLast(char *);
}
(b) Modified class
Name
first
last
(c) Memory layout of original class
Name
first
middle
last
(d) Memory layout of modified class
main() {
Name name;
name.setFirst("John");
name.setLast("Doe");
cout << name.getFirst()
<< " "
<< name.getLast();
}
(e) Client code using the class Name

FIGURE 29.6 Example of error encountered in modification of class definition using C++.

its name should not be removed from the list. When a new method is added, its name should be added to the end of the list. If these rules are followed, then adding or removing attributes or methods to or from the class should not require the client code to be re-compiled.

SOM can accommodate many interface changes without affecting the binary interface to a class library and without affecting the client programs. Examples of such changes are adding new methods, adding or deleting instance variables, relocating methods in the class hierarchy, and restructuring the class hierarchy by adding a new parent class. Typically, these changes are made as the software evolves.

Figure 29.7 shows the original and modified versions of the Name class rewritten in SOM IDL.

```
interface Name {
    attribute string first;
    attribute string last;
    #ifdef __SOMIDL__
    implementation {
    releaseorder: _get_first,
                  _set_first,
                  _get_last,
                  _set_last;
    };
    #endif
};
```

(a) Original Name class in SOM IDL

```
interface Name {
    attribute string first;
    attribute char middleI;
    attribute string last;
    #ifdef __SOMIDL__
    implementation {
    releaseorder: _get_first,
                  _set_first,
                  _get_last,
                  _set_last;
                  _get_middleI;
                  _set_middleI;
    };
    #endif
};
```

(b) Modified Name class in SOM IDL

FIGURE 29.7 An SOM IDL releaseorder example.

29.8.1.4 Defining an Abstract Class

OMG IDL interfaces are emitted into classes in the target programming language. There are cases where it is useful to define an emitted class as an abstract class. This is typically done when the abstract class is intended to be used as a base class from which many subclasses will derive. SOM IDL introduces the modifier *abstract* to specify that an interface should be emitted as an abstract class. The emitted abstract class is not instantiable. An attempt to instantiate the class will result in the throwing of an exception.

29.8.1.5 Specifying a Factory and a Proxy for a Class

SOM IDL introduces modifiers which allow the user to associate the factory and proxy properties with a given object. The modifiers *factory* and *proxy* are used to specify a factory object and a proxy object, respectively.

A factory object is used to create other objects. It is useful in cases where the client has a reference to some parent class and wants to create an instance of a class derived from this parent class. Provided that the client does not have a reference to, or a definition of, the derived class. A factory object is also useful in a distributed environment where it is used to ensure local remote transparency of objects. A client can use a factory object to create a remote object. The factory object in this case creates the object at the remote location and transparently returns its reference to the client.

A proxy object is very useful in a distributed environment and acts as a local representative of a remote object. Usually, a user does not need to explicitly specify a proxy for a remote object, since the ORB will automatically create one. However, SOM IDL introduces the proxy modifier to give the user more control over the behavior of proxies. One instance where the developer may want to customize his own proxy is to add a cashing mechanism to the proxy in order to improve performance.

29.8.1.6 Metaclasses

In SOM, a class is treated as a first order object. For that reason it is called a class object. Since a class in SOM is also an object, it must be an instance of some class which defines the implementation of that object. The class of a class object is called a metaclass. Like any class, a metaclass has its own attributes and methods. Typically, class methods create new instances of the class and accumulate runtime statistical information about these instances. Class methods that create instances of a class are called factory methods. Factory methods are used as an alternative to factory objects to create objects.

Like any object, a class object can have its own state which can be modified at runtime. The runtime change of a class object state allows the definition of object implementation to be modified at runtime. In other words, a class can be composed and customized dynamically. Using metaclasses, new components can be created from existing components and existing components can be customized at runtime. This customizing can vary depending on the environment. For instance, in one environment, a component is made persistent; while, in another environment it is made secure. The persistence and security properties can be added to the component dynamically.

As an example, the SOM3.0 Toolkit provides a metaclass called SOMMBeforeAfter which can be used by a class to invoke a method before and a second method after the invocation of each method defined by the class. This "before/after" behavior can be used to add properties to the class. The example in Figure 29.8a-c shows how the interface of the SecureAccount class (shown in (c)) is composed from the

```
interface Secure : SOMMBeforeAfter
{
  #ifded __SOMIDL__
  implementation {
   somBeforeMethod: override;
   somAfterMethod: override;
  };
  #endif
};
```

(a) Interface for Secure metaclass

```
interface Account {
  attribute float balance;
  void withdraw(float amount);
  void deposit(float amount);
  #ifdef __SOMIDL__
  implementation {
   releaseorder: ...
     ....
  };
  #endif
};
```

(b) Interface for Account class

```
interface SecureAccount : Account {
  #ifded __SOMIDL__
  implementation {
   metaclass = Secure;
  };
  #endif
};
```

(c) Interface for Secure Account class

FIGURE 29.8 A metaclass example.

```
interface Name : SOMObject
{
   string get_name();
#ifdef __SOMIDL__
implementation
{
   string first, middle, last;
   somDefaultInit: override, init;
}
#endif
};
```

FIGURE 29.9 Example of an initialization method.

interface of the Account class (shown in (b)) and the interface of the Secure metaclass (shown in (a)). Note that in the Secure interface the *override* modifier is used to specify that the somBeforeMethod and somAfterMethod should be overridden by the Secure class. These methods implement behavior which ensures secure access to instances of the SecureAccount class. The SOM compiler emits the necessary code to intercept all methods invoked on the SecureAccount instances. When a client invokes the withdraw method on an object of class SecureAccount, the method somBeforeMethod is invoked first. This method might check if the client is authorized to access the object in which case it allows the withdraw method to be executed next. If the client has no permission to access the object, the execution of the the withdraw method is skipped (Benantar et al., 1996). Execution of somAfterMethod follows the execution of the withdraw method. An implementation of the method somAfterMethod in this example might be to perform an auditing function reflecting the transaction

29.8.1.7 Defining Initialization Methods

SOM IDL allows object developers to define initialization methods. These methods are used at object creation to initialize the state of the object. While object initialization can be achieved through factory methods or through factory objects, initialization methods are used in cases where simpler design and better performance is required.

Figure 29.9 shows an example of an initialization method called somDefaultInit. This method is initially defined by the interface SOMObject. Note the use of the *init* and *override* modifiers. The *init* modifier specifies that somDefaultInit is an initialization method that should be invoked upon object creation. The *override* modifier specifies that this method should be overridden by the Name interface.

29.8.1.8 Method Resolution

A client code invoking a method on an object may not have all the information about the specific object on which the method is to be invoked. Even the method name and signature might not be known. Method resolution is a runtime activity which determines that method is to be invoked on which object.

SOM IDL provides the developer with the following method resolution mechanisms listed in the order of increased flexibility and decreased efficiency: *offset* resolution, *name-lookup* resolution, and *dispatch-function* resolution.

The developer can specify that a method resolution is offset or name-lookup by qualifying the method with the modifiers *offset* and *namelookup*, respectively. The dispatch function resolution mechanism does not have a corresponding SOM modifier. Instead, SOM Toolkit provides a method called *somDispatch* which can be used to perform a dispatch-resolution on a method.

Offset Resolution – This mechanism is the least flexible, the most time efficient, and the easier to use. It is the least flexible since it requires that the method name and the class name be known at compile time. In addition, the method should be declared in the IDL specification of the class. This resolution is the fastest since it uses a technique similar to C++ virtual function resolution. Like C++ virtual function resolution, offset resolution determines the method to invoke by looking up the address of the method from a table associated with the class to which the method belongs.

Offset resolution is the default method resolution for C and C++ bindings.

Name-Lookup Resolution — This technique offers more flexibility at the expense of less speed. It can be used in the following cases:

1. The name of the method is not known at compile time.
2. The name of the class defining the method is not known at compile time.
3. The method is introduced to the class interface at runtime.

Typically, this resolution is used when the same method is defined in multiple classes and the user wishes to decide at runtime which instance of one of these classes to use.

Name-lookup resolution is similar to the resolution techniques employed by Objective-C and Smalltalk.

Dispath-Function Resolution — This technique is the slowest but the most flexible. Using this method resolution, the user can defer until runtime the determination of the method name, the method argument list, and the class name.

The criteria used in selecting which method to invoke does not have to be based on the receiving object. Instead it could be arbitrary and decided by the programmer. For example, the programmer might decide to base the selection criteria on some method argument value.

29.8.1.9 Specifying a Memory Management Policy

SOM IDL supports the memory management policy defined by the OMG standard. This policy is described as follows:

> When a client object performs a local or a remote method invocation on another object (called the target or server object), ownership of memory belongs to the client object. Specifically, the caller object is responsible for providing storage and freeing the provided storage for the *in* and *inout* parameters and for initializing pointers for the *out* parameters. While the target object carries the responsibility of allocating storage for the method's *out* parameters and for method's result.

OMG memory management policy is the default policy supported by the SOM IDL compiler. This policy serves a large range of applications. In addition to the default policy, SOM IDL provides the developer with a set of modifiers that offer the flexibility of controlling the ownership of memory at the method parameter level. The *object_own_paramer* and *object_own_result* modifiers allow the developer to choose to assign memory ownership for a specific method parameter to the target object. The *object_owns_result* allows the developer to relegate to the target object the ownership of memory associated with the method results. The *dual_owns_parameter* can be used to give the ownership of memory associated with a method parameter to both the caller and target objects. This policy is only meaningful in a remote call where each object maintains a copy of the storage allocated for the parameter. In this case each object is responsible for freeing its own copy. The *dual_owns_result* is similar to *dual_owns_parameters* except that it applies to the method's results.

29.8.1.10 The SOM Compiler

The SOM compiler translates an SOM IDL specification producing code in a target programming language such as C or C++. The SOM compiler generates the following files in the target programming language: implementation template or skeleton file, implementation binding file (contains bindings for use by the class developer) and a usage binding file that contains bindings for the class user. Figure 29.10 illustrates the steps followed in developing a SOM application.

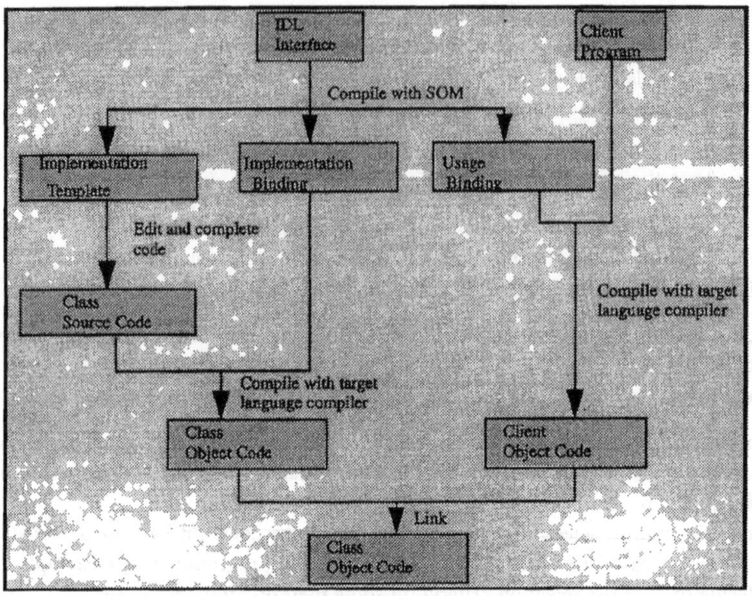

FIGURE 29.10 SOM development process.

References

Benantar, M., Nadalin, A. and Blakeley, B. 1996. *Use of DSOM Before/After Metaclass for Enabling Object Access Control.* In *Distributed Platforms,* Schill, A., Mittasch, C., Spaniol, O. and Popien, C., Eds. Chapman & Hall, New York.

IBM. 1996. SOMobjects Developer's Toolkit 3.0, User's Guide, IBM.

Lau, C. 1994. *Object-Oriented Programming Using SOM and DSOM.* Van Nostrand Reinhold, New York, NY.

Mowbray, T. and Zahavi, R. 1995. *The Essential CORBA.* John Wiley & Sons, New York, NY.

OMG. 1995. *The Common Object Request Broker: Architecture and Specification.* OMG, July.

Open Software Foundation. 1993 *OSF DCF Application Development Guide.* PTR Prentice-Hall, Englewood Cliffs, NJ.

Otte, R., Patrick, P. and Roy M. 1996. *Understanding CORBA.* Prentice-Hall, Upper Saddle River, NJ.

30
Systems Object Model (SOM)

Lourdes Tajes-Martines
Oviedo University

Maria de los Angeles Diaz-Fondon
Oviedo University

30.1 Introduction to SOM

SOM is an object-oriented technology born with the goal of establishing a mechanism which allows object interoperability regardless of the programming language or operating system used. SOM uses a foundation based on the concept of class interface and class implementation. A class is characterized by an interface, a set of methods which define its behavior. Instances of classes are called objects. Objects will answer to invocations to any method defined in the class interface of the object.

A class interface is implemented by a set of procedures which will be executed in response to invocations to methods of the class. This is completely transparent for clients. Clients are only aware of the services offered by the server object.

To hide implementation details, SOM uses a strict separation of the definition of the interface of a class from its implementation; that is, between methods supported by the class and the procedures implementing these methods.

Thus, clients are immune to changes in the procedures implementing the methods of the classes used. Recompilation or reloading of the client is not needed as binary class libraries can be constructed, packed, and distributed to clients. Clients can use classes in the libraries without restrictions imposed by the implementation language or operating system used to create them. SOM provides clients with

0-8493-3135-8/99/$0.00+$.50

tools to create instance objects of a class, create subclasses using inheritance in a class hierarchy, and invoke methods on objects. SOM has a runtime environment which supports these operations.

To separate the class interface from its implementation, SOM requires performing two steps in order to define a class. The programmer first describes the interface offered by the class to the outside using a SOM interface definition language. Once the interface is defined, the programmer can implement the classes in any programming language.

Thus, SOM is a binary standard for objects, with language and operating system neutrality, designed to solve the problem of the tight binary coupling existing between an application and the classes it uses.

Left out initially in SOM are other goals such as using and communicating objects living in different address spaces, even in different machines. Nevertheless, there has been an evolution in SOM in order to allow this kind of object interoperability. Distributed SOM (DSOM) is a tool which has been developed based on SOM. Both are now intimately bound, making a clear distinction between SOM and DSOM difficult.

30.2 Interface vs. Implementation

In SOM, class interfaces are strictly separated from their implementations. This is key to properties like object interoperability and language and operating system neutrality. Objects written in different languages and platforms can also communicate, and client objects are immune to changes in the implementation of server objects.

A class interface defines the methods offered by instance objects of the class. This is the only part of an object known publicly by others, and the only thing needed to use it.

The implementation of a class defines the actual code of the procedures and/or functions implementing the exported methods of the interface. Clients are neither aware nor interested in this part of the class definition. The code of the procedures can be then changed without subsequent recompiling or reloading of the client programs.

Thus, when a programmer defines a SOM class, the class interface and the implementation are defined apart. The class interface is defined with a formal interface definition language (IDL). This language is independent from the programming language used to implement methods and variables of the object.

The IDL specification file (.idl) includes the name of the interface or the name of the class and the ancestor classes, the name of the attributes of the class, and the signatures (method name, type and order of arguments, and return type if it exists) of the new methods. Class implementation is performed in the language chosen by the programmer of the class after the interface is defined.

Compilation of the interface makes the association between the interface file and the implementation file. This interface file is the input file of the SOM compiler. Below is an example of an interface file:

```
#include <somobj.idl>              /* Include IDL of father class */
interface solid:SOMobject          /* solid inherits from SOMObjects
                                   by its interface */
{
float volume();/* Headers of the methods */
void cost(in float base, in float volumecost); /* name and arguments */
};
Then a class sphere is defined, inheriting from solid.
#include <solid.idl>
interface sphere:solid
{
attribute float radius;     /* attributes of a class. Generates a pair of
set/get functions to handle the attribute*/
#ifdef __SOMIDL__
implementation /* implementation aspects of the methods */
{
```

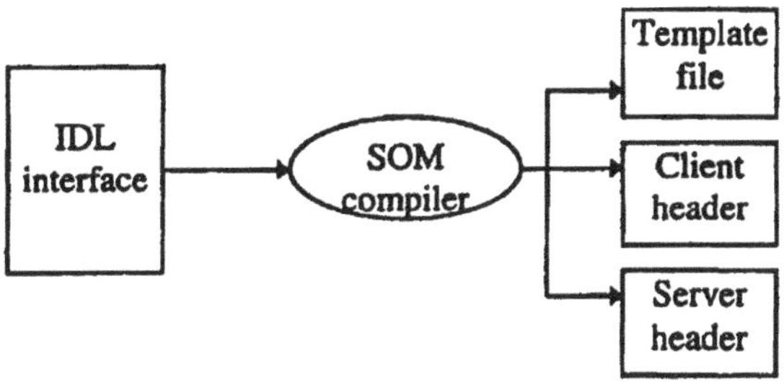

FIGURE 30.1 SOM Compiler input and outputs.

```
volume:override;    /* specialization of volume by overriding.
implementation of volume will be changed */
};
#endif
};
```

The SOM compiler will analyze the .idl file and will call a generator for the output language called emitter (Figure 30.1). This emitter generates a set of files written in the output language chosen. A compilation for the above interface will look like

```
> sc -s "xc;xh;xih" solid.idl
> sc -s "xc;xh;xih" sphere.idl /* Only when all steps for the creation of
solid are completed */
```

The set of files generated by the compiler is (Figure 30.2):

- Binding files for programmers; these will be included using `#include` sentences in the implementation skeleton.
- An implementation skeleton or template file for classes; in this file the SOM compiler adds a stub procedure for every method defined in the interface file. Initially these stubs are empty except for some initialization or debugging sentences. An example of a compilation of class solid is:

```
#include <solid.xih>
SOM_Scope float SOMLINK volume(solid somSelf, Environment *ev)
/* stub for the volume method */
{
   solidMethodDebug("Solid", "volume"); /* for debugging */
}
SOM_Scope float SOMLINK cost(solid somSelf, Environment *ev, float base,
float volumecost)
/* stub for the volumecost method */
{
   solidMethodDebug("Solid", "cost");
}
```

The class programmer will add the code to implement the method. The skeleton is written in the language chosen among the ones supported selecting the appropriate compilation options. In this example, only the cost method should be implemented because the volume method will be implemented by descendant classes. Implementation for cost will be like:

```
SOM_Scope float SOMLINK cost(solid somSelf, Environment *ev, float base,
float volumecost)
/* stub for the volumecost method */
{
```

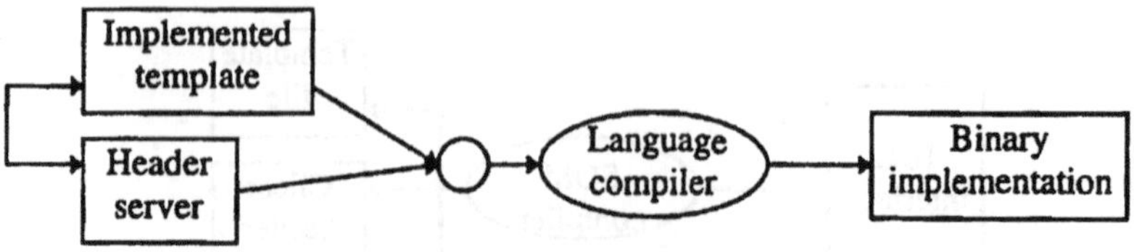

FIGURE 30.2 Binary code generation.

```
    solidMethodDebug("Solid", "cost");
    printf("%f",((base+volumecost)*somself->volume(ev)));
}
```

- Binding files for client programs; these are included in the client program and depend on the language used for the client.

With these binding files, SOM encapsulates implementation details supplying a set of stubs for the methods of the class expressed as macros and functions. These stubs are an abstract API for object access, and they offer a simpler interface to SOM objects customized for a particular programming language.

This way, C programs can invoke methods by using ordinary procedure calls. C++ bindings offer SOM objects as if they were C++ objects. C++ programs can invoke methods in SOM objects using the same syntax for methods invoked on C++ objects.

30.3 Description of SOM

SOM works as an intermediate element between a client and the implementation of the objects it uses (Figure 30.3). SOM allows the communication of them regardless of the operating system or programming language used. The client is only concerned with the interface of the server objects. SOM will provide the internal mechanisms needed to find the object implementing a method, deliver the arguments, invoke the method, and return the results.

From a client's point of view, SOM provides the following:

- Static Invocation Mechanisms — These mechanisms translate client method calls into calls to SOM's runtime support. This runtime will deliver the call to the server. They offer static interfaces to the server methods, and define how to invoke these methods. They work like the stubs in RPCs. From the client side, it makes a local call. The stub will do whatever is needed to call the procedure implementing the method to invoke. This includes argument marshaling.
- Dynamic Invocation Mechanisms — They solve the problem of lack of compile time information about which method to invoke; for example, when the method has been introduced later at runtime. Static bindings are not possible in these cases. Dynamic invocation mechanisms will find at runtime the procedure implementing the method, discover which arguments are needed, invoke it, and return results.
- Interface Repository — Keeps information about all interfaces defined in the system. SOM has means to dynamically query, store, and modify the information in the repository.

From a server's point of view, SOM is seen as:

- Server Stubs — They are the counterpart of client stubs in the object implementing the methods. They provide static interfaces to these methods. These stubs as well as client stubs are generated by the SOM compiler.
- Dynamic Invocation Interface — Provides runtime binding mechanisms for those servers handling calls to methods without information at compile time or have been introduced dynamically into the class. Those methods cannot use stubs.

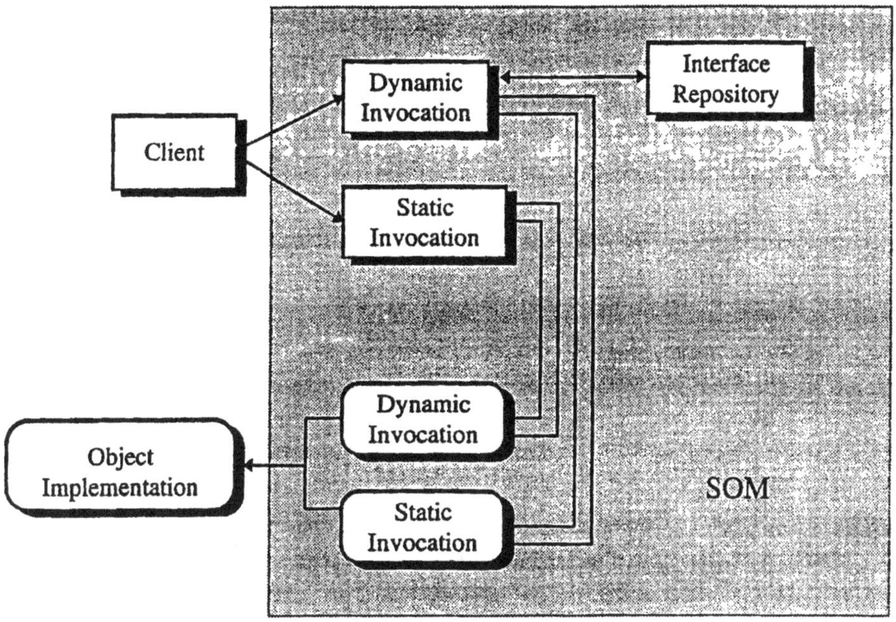

FIGURE 30.3 SOM architecture for method invocation.

30.4 Basic Elements of the SOM Toolkit

30.4.1 SOM Compiler

The SOM object development toolkit includes a SOM compiler. The SOM compiler is used to construct classes with separate steps for the interface definition and the implementation. The class interface specification file is the input to the compiler. It contains all the information needed by the client in order to use the class, such as the name of the attributes and the signature of the methods. The file is written using the IDL. The compiler generates a set of binding files as an output. The binding files help with the implementation and use of SOM classes, offering programmers a simpler interface to SOM.

30.4.2 Runtime Library

The SOM runtime environment is composed of a set of objects and global data structures keeping information about the state of the environment. The runtime library includes functions that can create and handle these objects, as well as invoking methods on objects. Using the library, it is possible to use SOM classes from any programming language with minimal capabilities: make calls to external procedures, store a pointer to a procedure and call the procedure, and map IDL types into types of the language. Classes are represented in the runtime environment as class objects. The runtime environment should be initialized by any application using SOM. The initialization creates all the basic class objects of SOM: SOMObject, SOMClass, SOMClassMgr, and an instance object of the latter class named SOMClassMgrObject. Once created and loaded, these objects offer the application programs the ability to invoke methods on these class objects, such as methods to create or free other instance objects.

30.4.3 Set of Class Libraries

SOM supplies a set of class libraries to help the development of object-oriented applications: DSOM, Interface Repository, Emitter Library, and Metaclass Library.

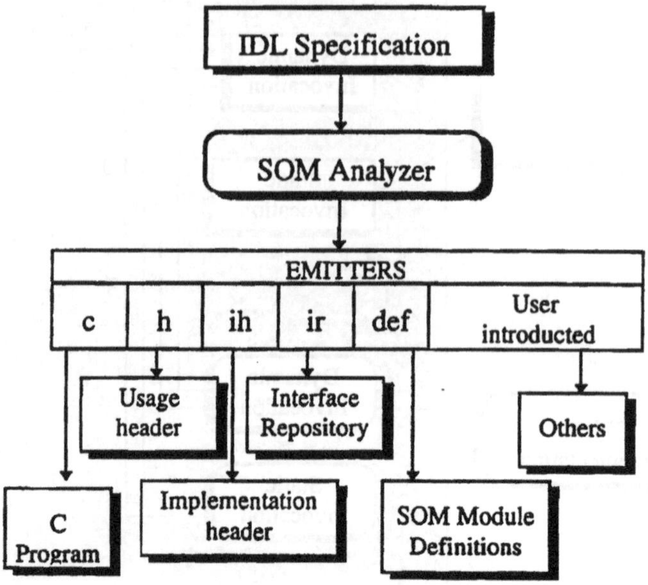

FIGURE 30.4 SOM compiler structure.

30.4.3.1 DSOM

DSOM is a set of SOM classes allowing the invocation of methods located in other address spaces or even in remote machines. Communication between objects is achieved transparently by DSOM using an Object Request Broker (ORB). Chapter 31 is devoted to DSOM.

30.4.3.2 Interface Repository Framework

It is a set of classes implementing the CORBA standard to allow runtime access to the information repository. The interface repository is simply a database created and maintained by the SOM compiler. This database contains all the data about the IDL description of the classes. With this information, a client can make dynamic invocations to objects not known at compile time.

30.4.3.3 Emitter Framework

The emitter framework is a set of classes implementing the last step in the compilation of an interface. The first step is an analysis of the interface file. The information discovered is fed into the emitter, which generates the implementation skeleton and the binding files in the chosen language. New emitters can be added to the framework to generate code for a new language (Figure 30.4).

30.4.3.4 Metaclass Framework

This is a special set of classes. They provide functions used by designers of SOM classes to modify the semantics of object creation and invocation.

30.5 SOM Object Model

The object model of SOM is an advanced model. Classes define the properties of objects, which are runtime entities with a set of methods and instance variables. Every class has a method table called method instance table. This table is shared by every instance object of the class. It contains pointers to the procedures implementing the supported methods.

SOM classes are represented as runtime objects called class objects. This differs from many object-oriented languages, in which classes have meaning only at compile time. There are some advantages to this runtime representation, such as the possibility to access or modify class information at runtime.

SOM's object model has encapsulation, multiple inheritance with ambiguity resolution mechanisms, polymorphism, metaclasses, different method resolution modes, and dynamic class creation. SOM also provides a base class hierarchy used to generate the remaining set of classes and metaclasses.

30.5.1 Inheritance

SOM classes can be derived from others, inheriting the interface of the ancestor classes. Any method available in an ancestor class is also available in the subclass. This is the common inheritance mechanism used in CORBA. A property not present in CORBA is that subclasses also inherit procedures implementing the methods which can be overridden or specialized in some cases. This is called inheritance by specialization. Last, classes can introduce new methods, attributes, and instance variables which will be inherited by any descendant class. This is called inheritance by addition.

SOM also supports multiple inheritance. A class can be derived from multiple ancestor classes. This kind of inheritance has some clashes or ambiguities. SOM offers some facilities to solve them.

- Many possibilities for the same name — This conflict appears when two ancestors of the class define different methods using the same name. This feature is also known as overloading, and is not always a problem. SOM's runtime API allows two different methods with the same type. Nevertheless, the IDL language forbids the static definition of classes with method overloading because of resolution anomalies.
- Alternative implementations for the same inherited method — It is possible to inherit the same method or variable from multiple superclasses; for instance, if there is a common ancestor. In this case, only one of the implementations of the method or variable is inherited. For variables this is not a problem, as the implementation of a variable is basically the location where the variable is stored inside the object. This location cannot be overridden, but classes can override methods so that different parents could have different implementations for the same method. The base object SOMClass provides a procedure which implements inheritance. This procedure resolves at runtime these kinds of conflicts when choosing the ancestor which is written first in the IDL definition of the list of ancestors.
- Multiple calls to methods in the parent — In an OO paradigm, subclasses can override inherited methods with special purpose code. This code could provide a specialized management or make calls to parent methods to allow ancestor classes to participate in the execution of the method.

30.5.2 Metaclasses

Classes are runtime entities, just as normal objects. Classes are instances of SOM metaclasses. A metaclass is a class defining a set of potential classes. It can be seen as the type of a class. Metaclasses of a class define the class methods; that is, the methods a class can execute. These methods are also called factory methods, or constructors. Factory methods do things such as create new instances of a class, keep the count of instances of a class, etc. They also facilitate the inheritance of instance methods from the ancestor classes.

30.5.3 Method Resolution

Method resolution is the mechanism used to determine which procedure to call in response to a method invocation. SOM supports three different mechanisms to resolve methods with increased flexibility and computational cost.

30.5.3.1 Offset Resolution

It is very much like C++ virtual functions, in which the method to invoke is determined at compile time. This is the fastest mechanism, but the one with more restrictions:

- The name of the method should be known at compile time.
- The name of the class introducing the method should also be known at compile time.
- The method invoked should be part of the static interface of the class.

Using offset resolution for a method invocation on an object, SOM makes a search in the method table of the class implementing the interface until the slot for the method is found.

30.5.3.2 Name-Lookup Resolution

Name-Lookup resolution is much slower than offset resolution, but more flexible. Contrary to offset resolution, it can be used when the name of the method invoked is not known at compile time. The arguments and the name of the class introducing the method should be known at compile time, though. Methods introduced at runtime into the class interface can be also invoked using this resolution.

In any case, name-lookup resolution is performed by the class to which the object receiving the invocation belongs. The class object should have a method which is called to perform this resolution. This method is in charge of finding the desired method. To resolve the method, the class object gets a pointer to the procedure implementing the method. A search based on the name and the arguments of the procedure is possibly performed on data structures of the class and its ancestor classes. This type of resolution supports polymorphism, but based on the protocols supported by an object, rather than polymorphism based on the derivation, as in the above case.

30.5.3.3 Dispatch-Function Resolution

This is the slowest resolution, but the most flexible. Dispatch-function resolution should be used when neither the name of the method, nor the signature are known at compile time. The dispatch function allows a class implementor to establish a set of rules known only in the class implementing the method. These rules will be used to find and invoke the procedure implementing a method.

The programmer of a class creates a method to be called when dispatch-function resolution is used. The programmer codes the particular mechanism used in the class to find a method.

30.5.4 Base Class Hierarchy

SOM object hierarchy is a tree with only one root. SOM offers three primitive basic classes. The rest are derived from these basic classes.

30.5.4.1 Class Object SOMObject

This is the root class for all SOM classes. Every class derives directly or indirectly from SOMObject. Methods in this class are always inherited by any class, providing behavior common to every SOM object.

30.5.4.2 Class Object SOMClass

SOMClass is the parent class for all SOM metaclasses. As with SOMObject, methods in this class provide the common behavior for all SOM class objects. For example, the mechanism used to solve inheritance clashes is inherited by all class objects from here. SOMClass has class methods to create new instances and methods in a class, and to dynamically obtain and update information about a class and its methods at runtime. As any SOM object, SOMClass inherits from SOMObject, so all class objects inherit the common set of base methods included in the object class SOMObject.

30.5.4.3 Class Object SOMClassMgr and Object SOMClassMgrObject

SOMClassMgrObject manages the information about classes. It keeps a runtime registry or directory with all SOM classes used by the current process. It is also in charge of the dynamic loading and unloading of classes located into class libraries.

Figure 30.5 depicts the relationships between SOM classes, metaclasses, and objects at runtime.

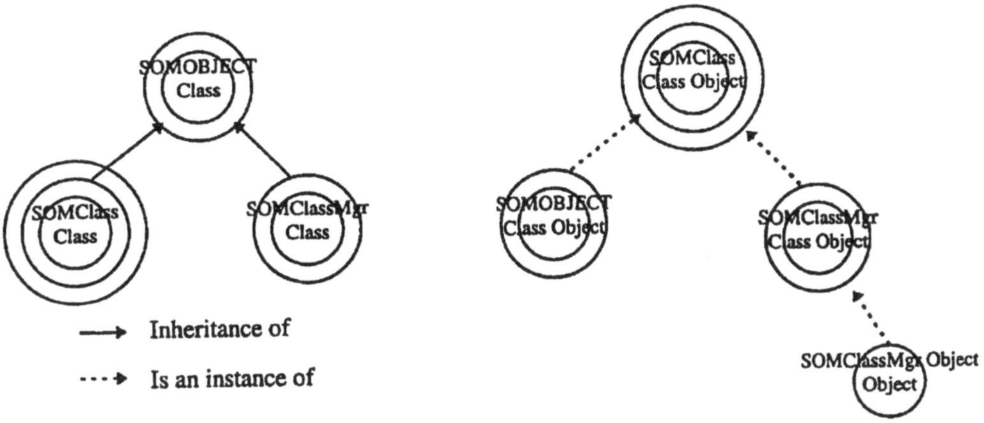

FIGURE 30.5 SOM basic class hierarchy.

30.5.5 Dynamic Class Creation in SOM

SOM supports dynamic creation of class objects to be added to the environment at runtime. Then, methods can be invoked on these objects to create instance objects, etc. Resolution for methods of classes created dynamically is performed by SOM's runtime machine.

30.6 Class Implementation in SOM

SOM definition classes can be made by any programmer. Interface is defined separately from implementation to achieve language independence. Complete definition for a SOM class involves compiling the interface file and obtaining the template implementation file and binding files.

SOM compiler can also update the implementation file, showing the changes made later in any class interface. These changes can involve the addition of new methods or commentaries and changes in prototype of the methods. These changes do not interfere with the code existing for the procedures of the methods.

30.6.1 Implementation and Kinds of Methods

The implementation of a method involves the addition of code to the body of the method's procedure in the implementation file. Along with code in a language like C or C++, the class implementator can employ any of the functions, methods, or macros provided by SOM for class and object manipulation.

30.6.1.1 Static Methods

This is the default type for methods in SOM. Static methods are similar to virtual functions in C++. Each static method has a slot in the method table of the object. It can be overridden by any descendant class.

30.6.1.2 Non-Static Methods

They are similar to C++ non-static member functions. They have a slot as well in the method table, but it cannot be overridden by descendant classes. Nevertheless, descendant classes can hide the inherited method and define another with the same name and behavior.

Offset resolution is mostly used for these methods, but it can also be used for the other methods. The procedure chosen in this case is determined by the interface of the object invoking the method.

30.6.1.3 Dynamic Methods

They differ radically from the methods above. Rather than being declared in an IDL file, they are added to a class object at runtime using SOM-defined functions for this task. Only name-lookup or dispatch-function resolution can be used for these methods.

30.6.1.4 Direct-Call Procedures

They are similar to C++ static functions. They neither have a slot in the object's method table nor are they known by SOM class objects. Bindings to call them directly are generated instead.

30.6.2 Class Libraries in SOM

SOM distributes classes in binary form as class libraries which are loaded and unloaded dynamically following application requirements. Client programs using these libraries will not need recompilations because of changes in the libraries, if these changes follow some restrictions: (1) syntax of existing interfaces must not be changed and (2) addition of new methods must be done at the end of the existing ones.

30.6.3 Types of Class Libraries

In order to use the classes, a set of programs must be provided to help the user create the classes and objects she needs. A program can use a class library containing one or more known classes in one of the following ways:

- The client program will contain static references to the class if the programmer uses SOM bindings. The operating system will automatically resolve these references at program loading time by loading the referenced classes.
- Another possibility is that the client program does not contain static references to the class. This happens if the programmer uses SOM dynamic mechanisms. The SOM class manager class (SOMClassMngr) provides a method to ask the SOMClassMngrObject object to dynamically load the class library at runtime and to create the class object.

30.7 SOM Clients

30.7.1 Client Programs

Client programs are those which use SOM classes implemented independent of the program. These programs can be written in C, C++, or any other language, not dependent of the language in which the classes used are implemented. By using a SOM class, the program can make operations like creating class objects, creating class instances, or invoking methods of an object. Nevertheless, a client program cannot internally use inheritance to subclass a new class from other SOM class. Many of the operations used in a client program come with the binding files which are included in the client in the form of functions or macros for a specific language. Although these functions facilitate the use of a SOM class, a client program can use SOM classes without including the header files or using the provided bindings. That may be the case of clients not written in C or C++, or clients that do not have enough information about which files have to be statically linked at compile time.

A client program written in a specific language can use a SOM class if this language can make calls to external procedures, store a pointer to a procedure and invoke that procedure, and map IDL types into native types of the language.

30.7.2 Class Declaration

An object variable conforming the interface of a class must be declared by a client program in order to use the SOM class, but in SOM all objects are defined as runtime entities, so the size is not known at compile time. Thus, memory for the object must be reserved dynamically, with the variable declared as a pointer to the object. SOM bindings for some languages provide macros which hide the definition of the pointer to the programmer.

```
SOMObject obj;/* SOM supplies a macro to the C programs
         that hides the pointer definition*/
SOMObject *obj;// In C++ programs
```

30.7.3 Methods Invocation in SOM

In SOM, operations on an object are always made using a reference to an object and invoking the desired method. To obtain a reference to an object, an object variable matching the class interface must be declared. When invoking operations there are two possibilities: static and dynamic invocation. The client chooses which one to use. In any case, the server object is not aware of any of these mechanisms, but only of the call for a service.

30.7.3.1 Static Invocation

This is the best mode for those clients who know all the invocation details at compile time. That is, the object involved, the name of the method to invoke, and the arguments. The SOM compiler supplies binding files for clients written in some languages. These files contain the stubs generated by the IDL compiler for the methods of an object, thus making this mode easier to use.

30.7.3.2 Dynamic Invocation

This is the mechanism used when part of the information needed to perform the invocation is not known at compile time. This information must be obtained at runtime. Dynamic invocation mode always makes some previous steps before invoking any method. First, the class interface is retrieved, and then the procedure implementing the method to invoke. At last, if needed, the list of arguments for the procedure is created, a request is created, and finally the invocation is performed.

30.7.4 Objects Creation

Creation of objects of a class results from the invocation of an instance creation method of the class defining the interface of the desired object. Thus, the class object as well as all ancestors must be created before. The result is a new object instance of the class which will answer to invocations of its interface methods. Once created, the object will exist until explicitly deleted or until the process that created it no longer exists.

30.7.4.1 Static Creation

SOM supplies a set of macros and operators customized for the language used. These macros and operators perform object creation functions automatically. These operators create any class object not existing before and then invoke the class method responsible for memory assignment and instance creation.

```
solid *s;
s = new solid();
```

30.7.4.2 Dynamic Creation

If bindings are not used in the client program, or the class to use is not known at compile time, SOM provides another mechanism with which to create objects. Objects whose class is not known at compile time are declared of a generic type SOMObject. Its creation will not be done until its class is looked up. Once the class is known, the method somNew of the object class is invoked to create the instance. The programmer must make sure that the class object is already created and create it if that is not the case.

```
SOMObject *o;
o = (SOMObject*) (ClassName->somNew());
```

30.7.5 Invocation of Methods

Once an object is created, client programs can invoke interface methods of the object. The invocation can be static or dynamic.

30.7.5.1 Static Method Invocation

The pointer to the procedure implementing the method is commonly acquired using offset resolution, but the client can call the method in any of two ways. If binding files are included in the client, the invocation can be performed using the `macro_methodname(object, arguments)`, or using the operator `object→methodname(arguments)`. These are part of the bindings. One of the arguments is a value of the type `(environment *)` which passes environment information between the calling and called methods. Method invocation is similar to a normal procedure call.

When two classes introduce or inherit methods with the same name, the above mechanism is ambiguous. The bindings have the macro classname_methodname to be used instead, which is the way used in CORBA. Below is an example of a static invocation using bindings.

```
#include <solid.xh>
main()
{
...
x = solid→volume(args); /* volume is defined in solid.xh */
...
}
```

The client can be written in a language for which SOM has no emitter for header files. These clients must use SOM generic functions to invoke methods, instead of the handy macros supplied by the bindings. When given a pointer to an object and the token for a method (position in the method table), the SOM procedure somResolve returns a pointer to the procedure implementing the method or an error if it is not supported. somResolve finds the procedure looking in the method table of the object's class. To get the token for a given method, somGetMemberToken can be used.

30.7.5.2 Dynamic Method Invocation

This kind of invocation can use name-lookup or dispatch resolution to get the pointer to a procedure implementing a method. somResolveByName or somFindMethod are functions which return a pointer to the desired procedure from the pointer to an object and the name of the method. Then the desired method is invoked by calling the procedure. Dispatch resolution must be used if the signature is not known at compile time. Once the signature is gotten, a va_list type variable is constructed with the arguments and a method such as somDispatch is used.

30.7.6 Operations on Class Objects

In addition to operations on instance objects, operations on class objects are sometimes needed. For example, creating instance objects requires the existence of a corresponding class object.

30.7.6.1 Static Class Creation

Class objects are normally created the first time a macro to create instances of this class is called. Sometimes this class object must be created explicitly, as in the case of a language with no SOM bindings for a given class, and, consequently, with no macros for it. The class object must be created using SOM generic methods, as well as the instance objects.

For C and C++ with the class name known at compile time, the procedure *classnameNewClass* creates a class object for a given classname. This procedure initializes the SOM environment if necessary and creates the class object. It also creates objects for the ancestor classes and metaclasses, returning a pointer to the object created. Then, the client can reference the class object using the macro *_classname* or *classnameClassData.classObject.*

30.7.6.2 Dynamic Class Creation

First, the SOM environment should be initialized. Then, the method somFindClass of the class manager object which creates the desired class should be invoked.

30.7.7 Example of a Client Program

Any client program can use an implemented class. The client program includes the header file generated before to use objects and methods in the class.

```
#include <sphere.h>
int main(int argc, char **argv)
{
/* Declare a variable pointing to an instance of class sphere */
sphere *obj;
Environment *env = somGetGlobalEnvironment();
/* Create an instance of class sphere */
obj = new sphere;
/* Set radius to 5.5 */
obj->_set_radius(env, 5.5);
....
/* base and costvolume data must be gotten here */
/* Invoke method cost */
obj->cost(env,base,costvolume);
/* Free the instance */
obj->somFree();
return(0);
}
```

30.8 SOM Benefits

SOM gives reusability and flexibility by means of the following properties.

30.8.1 Upward Binary Compatibility

This is achieved because SOM encapsulates classes so that clients are not aware of the implementation details of the classes used, but only of the services instance objects offer. This way, changes in the implementation do not require recompilation of the client. SOM's runtime machine avoids this by supporting of the object model and dynamic linking between the client and the class library. These are the changes allowed:

- Add new methods to classes
- Change the size of an object by adding or deleting instance variables
- Modify the class hierarchy by inserting a new parent class above any class in the hierarchy
- Relocate methods in the class hierarchy

30.8.2 Language Neutrality

Classes in SOM can be implemented in different languages and can be used in clients implemented in other languages (Figure 30.6).

30.8.3 Use of Object-Oriented Technology in Procedural Languages

Classes and objects implemented with SOM technology can be used from clients implemented in procedural languages. These languages are extended with OO technology and customers using them before need not learn a new language. SOM will generate bindings customized for the client language, translating method invocations into client language's procedure calls. On the other side, classes implemented with SOM technology can use object-oriented or procedural languages. Use of a procedural language as a class implementation vehicle is useful to programmers used to a particular language.

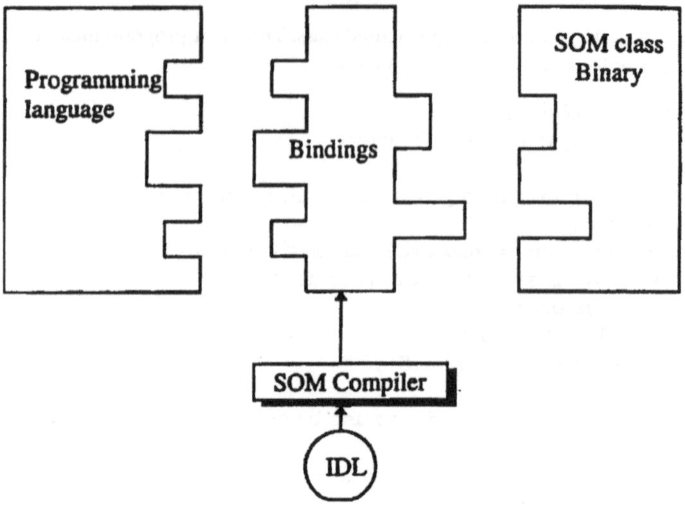

FIGURE 30.6 Language neutrality.

30.8.4 SOM and the CORBA Standard

SOM follows specifications conforming the architecture of the OMG CORBA standard in these aspects:

- SOM class interfaces are described with the Interface Definition Language IDL, which is an extension of CORBA's IDL.
- SOM bindings for the C language are compatible with CORBA's C bindings.
- All the information about a SOM class is available at runtime through an interface repository as defined in CORBA.

Further Information

Orfali, R., Hadkey, D. and Edwards, J. 1997. *Instant CORBA.* Wiley Computer Publishing, New York.
Mowbray, T. J. and Zahavi, R. 1994. *The Essential CORBA.* Wiley Computer Publishing, New York.
Otte, R., Patrick, P. and Roy, M. 1996. *Understanding CORBA: The Commnon Object Request Architecture.* Prentice-Hall PTR, Englewood Cliffs, NJ.

These books describe the theory and principles of standard object technology, systems architecture integration, frameworks, and OMG standards including CORBA. Because SOM is a technology following CORBA standards, these are very interesting books for understanding SOM philosophy.

IBM Corporation. 1996. *SOMobjects Developer Toolkit. Version 3.0. Programming Guide.* Volumes 1 and 2.
IBM Corporation. 1996. *SOMobjects Developer Toolkit. Version 3.0. Programming Reference.* Volumes 1 to 4.

This is the most important and full document written about SOM by IBM Corporation. It is a complete guide where SOM architecture is explained. Also, the design, implementation, and use of classes are shown. It is an essential reading for those people who wants to start in SOM implementation. Some notions about the SOM IDL language, compilation process, and the most common errors are introduced.

IBM Corporation. 1994. Object Technology Products Group, *IBM's System Object Model (SOM): Making Reuse a Reality.* Austin, TX.

It is a very short paper giving some general ideas about SOM and DSOM. The main advantages obtained with their use are shown.

IBM Corporation. 1994. Object Technology Products Group, *IBM's The System Object Model (SOM) and the Component Object Model (COM): A Comparison of Technologies from a Developer's Perspective.* Austin, TX.

This paper establish a brief comparison between the two main object interoperability technologies implemented and extended.

System Object Model, URL : http://info.gte.com/ftp/doc/activities/x3h7/by_model/SOM.html

In this Web page there is a short view about SOM technology. Basic concepts like objects, their operations, methods, state, and lifetime are briefly explained. Some basic ideas in object-oriented technologies like binding, polymorphism, types and classes, inheritance, and others are introduced as well as SOM's implementation of these characteristics.

InterOperable Objects, *Dr. Dobb's J.,* October 1994.

An interesting article about relationships between objects. Different objects technologies are described.

Orfali, R., Hadkey, D. and Edwards, J. *The Essential Client/Server Survival Guide.* Wiley Computer Publishing.

This interesting book introduces client/server programming techniques.

Sessions, R. *Object Persistence,* Prentice-Hall, Englewood Cliffs, NJ.

Some notions about CORBA's object persistence service are explained. There is also a practical introduction to SOM/DSOM.

Lalonde, W. and Pugh, J. 1995. Using SOM in VisualAge and IBM Smalltalk, *J. Object-Oriented Programming,* February.

This article includes an example of using a SOM class written in C++ in a Smalltalk application.

Westerfeld, K. 1996. Extending OS/2's user interface, *Byte,* February.

This article has a practical approach. The use of SOM to replace the OS/2 Workplace Shell is shown.

Wayner, P. 1994. Objects on the march, *Byte,* January.

Although the article is about object technologies and operating systems it includes, among other topics, a comparison of SOM and COM.

Nance, B. 1993. OS/2's System Object Model, *Byte,* January.

This is an introduction to SOM and the reasons for its origination.

31

Distributed Systems Object Model (DSOM)

Raúl Izquierdo Castanedo
Oviedo University

31.1 Introduction

IBM's Distributed System Object Model (DSOM) allows interaction between objects in different address spaces. Objects can collaborate with instances located in some other process in the same machine, but they also can collaborate with objects even living in another machine. The location of each object does not matter to the client object, which accesses them in the same way regardless of its local or remote situation.

DSOM extends SOM bringing *location* independence. SOM brought *implementation* independence. A SOM object can communicate with any other SOM object regardless of its implementation language. An object implemented in C++ can communicate with another object implemented in C and vice versa. The combination can be extended to any other language with CORBA bindings (Java, Smalltalk, etc.). Together they (SOM/DSOM) offer the possibility to communicate objects regardless of their implementation language and their location.

DSOM, besides being an extension to SOM, is also an Object Request Broker (ORB) which complies with the Common Object Request Broker Architecture (CORBA) 1.1 specification published by the Object Management Group (OMG) and X/Open. It also complies with the CORBA Internet Inter-ORB Protocol (CORBA IIOP) specification, which allows interaction with other CORBA IIOP compliant ORBs. That is, objects using DSOM ORB can communicate with any other object located in any other IIOP ORB.

DSOM allows for an application to use local and remote objects indistinctly. Programs do not know which object is local and which is remote. Objects can even be redistributed from one execution to another. One object which first was local could be remote in the next execution and vice versa. The application does not need to be modified and neither does the source modification nor recompilation.

DSOM also uses the SOM compiler, Interface Repository, language bindings, and class libraries. This means that non-distributed SOM applications can be transformed to be distributed easily. In fact, DSOM has been constructed using SOM.

0-8493-3135-8/99/$0.00+$.50

31.2 DSOM Basics

In DSOM an object exists in one single process called the object server. The clients can communicate with this object via normal method calls which are transparently transformed into remote method calls by DSOM runtime.

In a DSOM application at least four processes cooperate and each of them could be local or remote. The first player is the client program. It is the main beneficiary of the DSOM system and can create local/remote instances and access them in a transparent way. Thus it is the final user of every class developed with DSOM.

When creating local instances the client offers them its address space, but when using remote instances it needs someone else to offer an address space for them. Once the remote instance has been created it also needs a way to communicate. The server program (which may be the default provided by DSOM or a customized server) plays this role. The default server listens to client requests to locate and create objects and provides them with an address space.

The third player is in charge of providing a way to localize resources (services or instances). The name server provides a Naming Service used by DSOM applications and by DSOM itself to provide Factory Service, which is used by clients to create remote objects. This subject will be further explained in Section 31.3.

The last player is the DSOM daemon, called *somdd*, which runs on the same machine as the servers. Its mission is to establish the initial connection between the client and the server.

The DSOM runtime, uses some files which must be properly configured before execution.

- The Interface Repository files are used by both the client and the server processes. These files contain the IDL declarations of the classes used in the application and are maintained using the SOM compiler. This Interface Repository is the same one specified for CORBA.
- The Implementation Repository files contain information used by the daemon to start servers and by the servers themselves.
- Naming Service files that store information for the Naming Service and the DSOM Factory Service; this information includes which application classes are supported by each server.

The following describes the usual sequence of events when running a DSOM application. In this sequence it is shown how all the processes and the files mentioned above all play together. The first step is to update the Interface Repository with the IDLs used in the application. The next step is to register application servers and classes in the Implementation Repository. After that the *somdd* daemon must be started on every machine with a server located on it. The daemon will activate the required servers consulting the Implementation Repository. Finally, the client application will use the Naming Service to locate a server capable of creating instances of a required class. The *somdd* daemon of the corresponding machine will establish the initial connection with the desired server.

When running DSOM applications a client object communicates with the server via a proxy object. A proxy object is a local representative for the remote object, an intermediary. The proxy has the same interface as the remote object it substitutes, that is, it responds to the same methods. There is a proxy for every non-local object to which a client has access.

The client object uses a reference to the proxy object instead of a reference to the remote object. The client invokes methods on the local proxy object who redirects them to the server object. When the server object finishes its work it sends the return value back to the proxy, which in turn gives it to the client object (see Figure 31.1).

That is how location transparency is gained. The client object *always* communicates with local objects; whether directly invoking the server (if it is in the same address space) or a local proxy who transparently communicates with the real server. The client does not need to know if the request reached the server directly or indirectly.

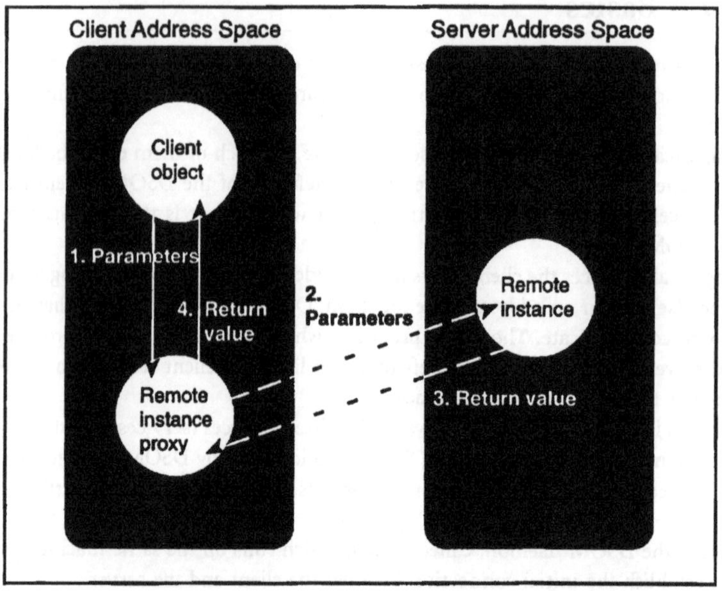

FIGURE 31.1 Instances communication using proxies.

31.3 Creating Objects

Since DSOM hides whether an object is remote or local, programming a client in DSOM is almost the same as doing it in SOM (see Chapter 30). However, a client application needs to know how to create, locate, and destroy remote objects. DSOM provides these services through the DSOM ORB object. This object is a CORBA-compliant ORB interface created during DSOM initialization.

The ORB provides services such as obtaining references for object services, obtaining object identifiers, or given an identifier, obtaining the object and creating an argument list to use with the Dynamic Invocation Interface. Creating an object is done in two steps. In the first phase the client has to get a remote factory using the Name Service. Once the client has access to a convenient class factory it asks to create an instance invoking one of its methods. A factory is just an object with the mission to create new objects. That is, objects are created by other objects instead of being created by specific language constructions (like *new* in C++). This allows location independence when creating objects.

There are two ways to get access to a class factory. The first one is used when the client knows the factory it needs to reach a server object. The factory is advertised in the Naming Service and can be accessed using standard Naming Services methods. The client can use the method *resolve*, which has the following IDL signature:

```
SOMObject resolve(in Name x);
```

This method returns the object attached to the name.

In the second case the client uses the Naming Service to get an adequate factory by specifying its desired properties. When a server is registered in the Implementation Repository an entry is created in the Naming Service with the server properties. There are three default properties besides any other that could additionally be included. These properties are

- *class* — Specifies the class of the object to create.
- *alias* — Declares the alias of the server where the factory is located.
- *serverId* — Implementation Id of the server where the factory is located.

Using these properties, and others that may optionally be added, the client can query the Naming Service using the following method:

```
SOMObject find_any(in Constraint c, in unsigned long distance);
```

The *find_any* method returns the first object found with properties satisfying the constraint. The constraint is a string containing the expression the desired object must match. For example, if a client in C wants to get a factory to create *Date* instances, it would write:

```
factory = _find_any(enc, &ev, "class == 'Date'", 0);
```

The *find_any* and *resolve* method can return either a local or remote object.

Once the client gets the factory, it is able to ask for a new instance. The OMG COSS Life Cycle Service Specification does not define any interface for an object factory. This means that the signature of the creation method depends on each factory. It is the application writer's responsibility to know the name of the method that creates the new instance. It could be *somNew* (the common name in DSOM), but it could be any other like *createInstance.*

Besides creating objects, a client would want to locate an already created object. The Naming Service is used to announce any type of object. Instead of locating a factory, the client would directly locate the created object specifying its properties (supposing the object was previously published in the Naming Service).

The reference obtained using the object factory or the Naming Service is a local object as far as the client is concerned, but it actually could be a proxy for a remote object, as explained in the introduction. The DSOM runtime automatically creates a proxy every time an object is returned by some remote operation. Thus in an address space there will be as many proxies as remote objects accessed by the local objects it contains.

31.4 Invoking Methods

The DSOM runtime (to which the proxies belong) is responsible for transmitting the parameters from the client address space to the server address space. It is also responsible for sending back the return value of the method's invocation, unless an exception occurs. If an exception is thrown or a system exception occurs while processing a method, no return values or *out* parameters will be returned to the client. In this case DSOM returns only USER_EXCEPTIONS declared in IDL using the clause *raises* in the method's signature. If an exception not declared in the method's signature is thrown, DSOM produces a system exception.

When a pointer to an object is returned to a client from a server method invocation, the pointer to the remote object is transformed into a pointer to a proxy for that object (created in the client side). Equally, when a client passes as a parameter reference to a proxy DSOM translates that reference appropriately. Accordingly, two situations arises.

1. If the reference to the proxy passed as parameter corresponds to an object in the server address space, the reference is translated to a reference to the "real" local object (local from the server point of view).
2. If the proxy represents an object in another address space, a new proxy is created in the server side as it was done in the client side. Now both client and server (each one on its own address space) have a proxy representing the same object located in a third address space.

Passing an object as a parameter which is not a proxy but a local object is only allowed in a remote invocation if the process making the call is a server. Client-only processes cannot pass local objects as parameters in remote invocations.

31.5 Memory Management

When making remote method invocations, it is necessary to establish the responsibilities relative to memory management between the client, the server, and the DSOM runtime which communicates them.

The runtime is comprised of the moment when the client locally invokes the proxy methods until the remote server object receives the parameters as if they were from a local method invocation. Thus there is a client-side runtime (in charge of sending the parameters to the server-side runtime and receiving back the return value for the client) and a server-side runtime (in charge of receiving the parameters, locally invoking the server object and sending back its return value).

When using the default memory-ownership policy, the DSOM runtime of each side behaves as the object in the other side. That means that the runtime within the client behaves like a server object and performs the memory allocations and deallocations that a server object would do on a local method invocation. The runtime in the server-side would reproduce the allocations and deallocations of memory the same way the client object would do it on a local invocation.

The default memory-ownership policy specifies that the caller is responsible for releasing every parameter and the return value after the call is complete.

The default attribute-accessors *get* and *set* generated by the SOM Compiler do not follow the default memory-ownership policy. Thus when managing attributes of non-scalar types in a DSOM application, the implementor should provide its own implementation of *get* and *set* adhering to the default policy.

The Default Memory Allocation Responsibilities state that the parameter or return value should be allocated by the caller or the target depending on the parameter mode. The client is responsible for providing storage for *in* and *inout* parameters and for initializing pointers used to return *out* parameters. The target object is responsible for allocating memory for the return value and for any other storage necessary to hold the *out* parameters. DSOM runtime in the client-side will allocate memory in the client address space corresponding to the memory allocated in the server.

The sequence of memory related events that occurs during a single remote method invocation (using the default memory-management policy) is:

- The client allocates and initializes *in* and *inout* parameters and initializes the pointers used in the *out* parameters. Then it makes the local method invocation to the client-side DSOM runtime (the proxy).
- The client-side runtime passes the parameters to the server-side runtime.
- The DSOM runtime in the server-side allocates memory in the server process corresponding to the memory allocated and initialized in the client address space. Now the parameters are in the address space of the server object. Then the server object is invoked locally by the runtime.
- The target object allocates memory needed for *out* parameters and for the return value. When the server object finishes its work returns to the server-side runtime.
- The runtime releases any memory allocated to hold the parameters and the memory used by the return value after sending it to the client-side runtime.
- The client-side runtime allocates memory for the return value and the *out* parameters received. Then it returns control to the client.
- The client finally has the result value and the parameters in its own address space and has the responsibility of deallocating them.

31.6 Releasing Objects

The method *somFree* is used to destroy objects. When *somFree* is invocated on a proxy object, it forwards the invocation to the server. After *somFree* is executed the proxy and the server object it represents are both destroyed.

There are two other methods involving object destruction. The first is *somdTargetFree* which is used to release the remote object, but not the proxy. On the other side the *release* method frees the proxy, but not the target object. The *release* method can be invoked on any SOM object, not only proxies. If the object on which *release* is invoked on is not a proxy, the request is just ignored.

Basically the guideline is to use *somFree* to release objects created by the client. If the client just obtained a proxy for an existing object (because the object was created by another process or by DSOM itself) then the client must only release the proxy. The remote object could be accessed by other clients.

31.7 Location Transparency

The target of location transparency is to obtain programs which do not depend on the location (address space) of the objects they manipulate. Most parts of the code should operate without changes independently of the situation on which the objects have to act. Code which relied on local objects properties would fail when redistributing the application objects.

There are some guidelines which must be followed to easily obtain transparent programs. Generally, it will not be transparent applications which rely on specific implementation details. Any communication from an object without using method invocations is not transparent (for example, accessing instance data directly).

One guideline involves using SOM Class objects. Class objects have methods for inquiring about objects memory requirements. They also has some methods that cannot be distributed because they use parameters difficult to marshal. Thus Class objects are not completely transparent and they should be used with caution. To access the class of an object the macro *SOM_GetClass* should be used instead of the usual *somGetClass* method. The macro sends the request to the remote object to obtain a handle to the remote class instead of a handle to the local class of the proxy (which is returned by *somGetClass*).

Using factory objects to create new instances is another guideline when obtaining location transparency. A factory object is used to create other objects (local or remote) and the factory itself can either be local or remote. When a new object is created using a factory the location of the returned object is unknown. It is even possible to create local instances in one execution and remote ones in another.

About method invocation, the guideline is to consider that every method could produce an error. When working with an object it can be a proxy for a remote object, so the method invocation produces a data transmission over a net (LAN or even WAN). This adds new error possibilities to the process of invoking a method. For example, the object server could be killed, the communication could be broken, etc.

When passing objects as parameters it is necessary to consider another guideline. CORBA objects are accessed through references and these references are generated and resolved by the ORB using the SOMOA (SOM Object Adapter) and SOMDServer. If an object is passed as a parameter a reference is created to it and passed by the object adapter. If the process does not have an object adapter (it is a pure client), a reference for its objects cannot be passed to remote objects.

This is just an enumeration of the most important rules. For a more thorough list of guidelines for achieving local/remote transparency see IBM Corp., 1996.

31.8 A DSOM Example Application

In this final part we will assemble a basic application using DSOM. This application is an example of the subjects shown in this chapter. Two goals will be fulfilled in the example. The first one is to implement an application that can be reused by any other application coded in any programming language with SOM bindings in a totally transparent way. The application will not need to know in which language the class has been implemented. The class could even be reimplemented later in another programming language without needing to recompile any client. In the next execution the new version would be used without them being aware of the change. The second goal of the example class is to allow reuse not only by applications instantiating it into its own address space, but also by applications that wish to create or access the instances located in another address space (that is, another process or even another remote machine).

The construction of the complete example application will be split in two parts. The first one will show a class implementation in accordance with the established goals. The second part will cover the implementation of a sample client using that class. It is not necessary to build a sample client to show how to create local instances of the class and another sample client showing how to create remote instances. As it will be shown, in DSOM the client avoids having to hardcode the location of the instances. The same sample client can play both roles.

The sample class will be a simple *Tokenizer.* The mission of our class is just to group together a sequence of input characters transforming it into a sequence of tokens. This simplified example codes an extremely poor lexical analyzer, which is only capable of recognizing two kinds of tokens: identifiers and numbers. The client application just gives a string with the input characters to the *Tokenizer* instance and asks it for the tokens found.

To build the sample class, it is necessary to carry out the two typical phases found in any CORBA compliant ORB. The first phase is to declare the class interface in an IDL file (see Chapter 28, Section 28.4.2). The interface of a class exposes the services offered by its instances independently of the implementation language. The interfaces of the classes composing the application are saved in the Interface Repository for future use. The second phase is to implement the class in the desired programming language with SOM bindings.

The declaration of the *Tokenizer* class in IDL is:

```
#include <somobj.idl>
interface Tokenizer: SOMObject
{
   exception NO_TOKEN
   (
      string reason;
   );
enum Token {Ident, Num};

   // Sets the text to be scanned
   void setInputString(in string text);

   // Gets the current token (non-destructive)
   Token getToken() raises(NO_TOKEN);
   string getLexeme() raises(NO_TOKEN);

   // Advances the current token
   void nextToken();

   // can we use 'getToken()' and 'getLexeme()'?
   boolean isTokenAvailable();

#ifdef __SOMIDL__
   implementation
   {
         releaseorder: setInputString, getToken, getLexeme, nextToken,
   isTokenAvailable;
         somDefaultInit, somDestruct: override;

         string input;      /* Input text to be scanned */
         string lexeme;     /* Position of current lexeme in input */
         int token;         /* Type of current lexeme (string/num) */
         int length;        /* Length of the lexeme */
         dllname = "tokenizer.dll";
      };
#endif
};
```

The first item declared in the *Tokenizer* IDL file is the exception raised by some methods of the class as an indication of an abnormal operation. Such an exception is thrown when the *Tokenizer* is asked for a token in a situation when there is not one available. This could happen if an input has not been assigned to the analyzer or if it was assigned but it has been exhausted (no more tokens left in the input sequence). The exception contains a string which tells the exact reason for the error.

Following the exception, an enumerated type is declared with the two kinds of tokens the analyzer can detect. The *Tokenizer* considers a number as a sequence of one or more decimal digits. It considers an identifier as any sequence of characters beginning with a non-decimal-digit and delimited with a space character. Any sequence of space characters is discarded.

The method *setInputString* sets the input characters to be analyzed by the *Tokenizer*. Once the *Tokenizer* is given an input, it is ready to be asked for the tokens found in it. Using *getToken*, a client receives the first token (number or identifier) and with *getLexeme* it gets the group of characters composing it. A client can invoke these two methods as many times per token as required as it is a non-destructive read. After processing the token, the client can invoke the method *nextToken* to analyze the rest of the input. The method *isTokenAvailable* informs of the availability of a token. Asking for a token when this method returns *false* will raise an exception.

In the second half of the IDL interface implementation specific information is defined. This part is a proprietary extension of SOM/DSOM to the standard CORBA IDL. Only SOM compilers define the macro __SOMIDL__. So these declarations are included inside an optional part which will only be compiled if the file is processed by a SOM compliant compiler.

In the implementation section, it is noticed that the methods *somDefaultInit* and *somDestruct* are overridden in this class. These methods serve as constructor and destructor of the class, respectively, and are originally declared in the class *somObject* which is the parent of *Tokenizer*. In SOM/DSOM every class has *somObject* as its parent (directly or indirectly through other parent).

This section continues describing the instance variables of the class together with their types. At the end of the interface the clause *dllname* points out the name of the DLL file where the class implementation is located. This DLL is the target of the next phase in constructing the sample class.

The second phase consists of creating the DLL with the class implementation. This DLL will be responsible for carrying out the services promised in the IDL. In this example it has selected C as the implementation language.

It is not necessary to start the implementation of the DLL from scratch. The IDL compiler will generate header and template files for us. The header files, in addition to other macros and constants, contain basically the equivalent in C of the types found in the IDL file. The template file for the *Tokenizer* implementation contains the skeletons of the class' methods with empty bodies. The work begins editing the template file and adding the bodies to perform the desired behavior. The final implementation of the tokenizer (contained in the file *tokenizer.c*) is shown below.

```
#define Tokenizer_Class_Source
#include <tokenizer.ih>
#include <ctype.h>
#include <string.h>

static void raiseException(Environment *ev, char *reason);

SOM_Scope void SOMLINK somDefaultInit(Tokenizer somSelf, somInitCtrl
*ctrl)
{
   TokenizerData *somThis;
   somInitCtrl globalCtrl;
   somBooleanVector myMask;
   TokenizerMethodDebug("Tokenizer","somDefaultInit");
   Tokenizer_BeginInitializer_somDefaultInit;

   Tokenizer_Init_SOMObject_somDefaultInit(somSelf, ctrl);

   _input = _lexeme = 0;
   _token = _length = 0;
}
```

```
SOM_Scope void SOMLINK somDestruct(Tokenizer somSelf, octect doFree,
somDestructCtrl *ctrl)
{
   TokenizerData *somThis;
   somDestructCtrl globalCtrl;
   somBooleanVector myMask;
   TokenizerMethodDebug("Tokenizer","somDestruct");

   Tokenizer_BeginDestructor;
if (_input != 0)              /* If input assigned, release it */
     SOMFree(_input);

   Tokenizer_EndDestructor;
}

SOM_Scope void SOMLINK setInputString(Tokenizer somSelf, Environment *ev,
string text)
{
   TokenizerData *somthis = TokenizerGetData(somSelf);
   TokenizerMethodDebug("Tokenizer","setInputString");

   if (_input != 0)         /* If input assigned, release it */
     SOMFree(_input);

   /* Cheking params omitted here (NULL, empty, etc) */

   _input = (string) SOMMalloc(strlen(text) + 1);
   strcpy(_input, text);

   _lexeme = _input;
   _length = 0;

   _nextToken(somSelf, ev);
}

SOM_Scope Token SOMLINK getToken(Tokenizer somSelf, Environment *ev)
{
   TokenizerData *somthis = TokenizerGetData(somSelf);
   TokenizerMethodDebug("Tokenizer","getToken");

   if (_isTokenAvailable(somSelf, ev))
     return _token;

   if (_input == 0)
     raiseException(ev, "No input defined");
   else
     raiseException(ev, "No more tokens");
}

SOM_Scope string SOMLINK getLexeme(Tokenizer somSelf, Environment *ev)
{
   TokenizerData *somthis = TokenizerGetData(somSelf);
   TokenizerMethodDebug("Tokenizer","getLexeme");
   if (isTokenAvailable(somSelf, ev))
   {
     string s = (string) SOMMalloc(length+1);
     strncpy(s, _lexeme, _length);
     return s;
   }
```

```
    if (_input == 0)
      raiseException(ev, "No input to scan");
    else
      raiseException(ev, "No more tokens");
}

SOM_Scope boolean SOMLINK isTokenAvailable(Tokenizer somSelf,
Environment *ev)
{
    TokenizerData *somthis = TokenizerGetData(somSelf);
    TokenizerMethodDebug("Tokenizer","isTokenAvailable");

    return (_length > 0);
}

SOM_Scope void SOMLINK nextToken(Tokenizer somSelf, Environment *ev)
{
    TokenizerData *somthis = TokenizerGetData(somSelf);
    TokenizerMethodDebug("Tokenizer","nextToken");

    _lexeme += length;           /* Skip current lexeme */
    while (isspace(*_lexeme)) _lexeme++;           /* Skip spaces */
    char *p = _lexeme;
    if(isdigit(*p)) {
      while (*p && isdigit(*p)) p++;
      _token = Tokenizer_Num;
    }
    else {
      while (*p && !isspace(*p)) p++;
      _token = Tokenizer_Ident;
    }

    length = p - _lexeme;
}

static void raiseException(Environment *ev, char *reason)
{
    NO_TOKEN *ex;

    ex = (NO_TOKEN *) SOMMalloc(sizeof(NO_TOKEN));

    ex->reason = (string) SOMMalloc(strlen(reason) + 1);
    strcpy(ex->reason, reason);

    set_exception(ev, USER_EXCEPTION, ex_NO_TOKEN, ex);
}
```

The major part of the code was generated automatically by the IDL compiler. The manually added bodies have been written in cursive for an easier identification.

The *somDefaultInit* method is the constructor of the *Tokenizer.* In this example its only job is to initialize the instance variables to express that there is no input assigned, thus there is no token available. The class destructor is the *somDestruct* method which just releases the memory allocated for the input string.

With *setInputString* the client sets the input to be scanned by the *Tokenizer.* After releasing any memory used by a preceding input, the method asks for memory to save a copy of the input for successive analysis. Finally, it calls *nextToken* to get the first token ready. *GetToken* and *getLexeme* just returns the current token after checking with *isTokenAvailabe* that there is actually a token ready. If these methods cannot return a token they just raise a NO_TOKEN exception as published in their interface. They both carry over this process by invoking a common function *raiseException* which sets up the environment variable according to the desired exception to be thrown.

The current token can be accessed repeatedly using *getToken* and *getLexeme.* To scan for the next token the *nextToken* method must be used. From that moment on, the methods *getToken* and *getLexeme* will return the new token and the old token will be definitively lost.

Finally, the *Tokenizer* source file is compiled and transformed into a DLL called *tokenizer.dll* (the one mentioned in the IDL file). One last thing must be remarked about the implementation of the *Tokenizer* class. It must be noted that no assumptions about its future use have been prematurely included in the source file. No source line in the code presents *Tokenizer* as a class designed to be used locally, nor have restrictions showing that it has specifically been designed to be used by remote clients. A reusable class has been achieved that can be used in any local or remote application developed in the future independently of the implementation language. The *Tokenizer* class won't even know who is requesting its services. It could be some client directly or, as seen before, just a proxy playing the role of intermediary.

Now for the second part of the DSOM example. The following program shows how to use the class *Tokenizer* from a client program.

```
#include <somd.h>
#include <tokenizer.h>

int checkEnvironment (Environment *env);

void main(int argc, char *argv[])
{
   Tokenizer tok;
   Environment env;
   ExtendedNaming_ExtendedNamingContext enc;
   SOMObject tokFactory;
   string lexeme;
   int token;

   SOM_InitEnvironment(&env);
   SOMD_Init(&env);

   enc = (ExtendedNaming_ExtendedNamingContext)
 _resolve_initial_references(SOMD_ORBObject, &env, "FactoryService");

   tokFactory = _find_any(enc, &env, "class == 'Tokenizer'", 0);

   tok = _somNew(tokFactory);

   _setInputString(tok, &env, "abc 123 abc");
   while (_isTokenAvailable(tok, &env))
   {
      token = _getToken(tok, &env);
      lexeme = _getLexeme(tok, &env);
      somPrintf("Token: %d Lexeme: %s\n", token, lexeme);
      SOMFree(lexeme);

      _nextToken(tok, &env);
   }

   /* Exception raised -> asking for a token when not available */
   _getToken(tok, &env);
   checkEnvironment(&env);
   /* The last line reports a "NO_TOKEN" exception */
   _somFree(tok);
   _release(tokFactory, &env);
   _release(enc, &env);
```

```
    SOMD_Uninit(&env);
    SOM_UninitEnvironment(&env);
}

int checkEnvironment(Environment *env)
{
    string exceptionName, reason;
    NO_TOKEN *nt;

    /* check if exception raised */
    if (env->_major == NO_EXCEPTION)
        return TRUE;

    exceptionName = somExceptionId(env);

    if (env->_major == USER_EXCEPTION)
    {
        /* An exception generated by the tokenizer */
        nt = (NO_TOKEN *) somExceptionValue(env);

        somPrintf("USER EXCEPTION [%s] detected\n", exceptionName);
        somPrintf("Reason: [%s]\n", nt->reason);

        SOMFree(nt->reason);
    }
    else
    {
        /* An exception generated by DSOM */
        somPrintf("SYSTEM EXCEPTION [%s] detected\n", exceptionName);
    }

    somdExceptionFree(env);

    return FALSE;
}
```

A client using DSOM must include the file *somd.h.* This header file contains several types, global variables, and function prototypes necessary to communicate with the DSOM runtime.

The invocation of *SOMD_Init* initializes DSOM. This function must be called before any other DSOM call. As part of the initialization, it creates global objects used in other DSOM runtime functions. One of this objects is SOMD_ORBObject which will be used later in the client.

The next three sentences are all relative to the creation of a *Tokenizer* instance. The objective is not to tie the client application to a concrete location of the *Tokenizer.* That is, we do not want a client who can only use *Tokenizers* located in their same address space. In the same way, we do not want the client to be forced to work with remote *Tokenizers.* We want a client who *can* use remote *Tokenizers.* That is why we use *class factories.* Class factories are just objects in which we delegate to create instances. The instances returned by class factories could be local objects or proxies for objects in a remote address space.

That is the reason for using class factories instead of the usual macro *<className>New()* supplied by SOM. This macro always creates a local instance. If we later wanted to redistribute the objects that build up our application, we would have to modify every source where a remote object is created. With class factories we just distribute the objects. The next time the application is executed the affected factories will simply return a proxy instead of the object returned previously.

So the first step is to find the class factory that creates *Tokenizer* objects. With the *resolve_initial_references* function we ask the SOMD_ORBObject for a reference to the *factory service.* This service allows us to find the appropriate factory to create instances of a specified class. Once we have access to the factory service we use the function *find_any* to get a factory suitable for creating instances of class

Tokenizer. The string containing the search condition could have included more tests based on different properties of the desired factory.

Finally we have a reference to the class factory. Now it is time to ask it for a new instance of a *Tokenizer.* In this example the method *somNew* applied on the factory will return the expected instance or a proxy for the object. However, the name of the method which returns the instances could be any other, depending on the implementation.

From this point in the source until the deallocation section at the end of *main* the program is identical to its SOM counterpart. This example just passes to the *Tokenizer* a string to be scanned and successively gets the tokens found on it (three in this case).

An example is given after the *while* of how to detect exceptions raised on a method invocation. We ask the *Tokenizer* for the current token when there is none available. The *Tokenizer* will complain, an exception will be raised, and it will come back in the environment variable. This variable also should be checked after any invocation of a method that can be the source of exceptions. In a real program we should also have checked the environment inside the *while* loop. Although we know that user exceptions cannot happen in the loop, there is always the possibility of a system exception (communication lost, etc.).

Checking the environment variable is done inside the function *checkEnvironment.* The attribute *major* of the environment shows if an exception was received. If an exception occurred it could either be a user exception (declared by the methods in the IDL file) or a system exception (reserved for system events). This function identifies both categories printing their names. In the case of a user exception it also prints the reason given by the *Tokenizer* to raise the exception.

There is only one task left. We must release all the resources used by the program. First we release the *Tokenizer.* The *somFree* function will delete the object and, if it is remote, it will also delete the proxy. It is important not to mistake the function *somFree* with another SOM function with the same name but with another capitalization, *SOMFree.* The first, as mentioned above, deletes *objects* (and proxies if needed). The second one just releases memory blocks allocated with *SOMMalloc.* Comparing it to C++, the *somFree* function would be equivalent to the *delete* operator, and *SOMFree* would be the SOM counterpart to *free.*

Once the *Tokenizer* is released, there are still two other objects to handle. Remember we asked for a factory finder, and using it we obtained the factory itself. There is an important difference between the *Tokenizer* and these two objects. We did not create them. They were there, available for any program, and we just got a reference to each of them. We do not have to release the objects themselves but the proxies we have acquired. That is why we use *release* instead of *somFree.* This function only releases proxies. The remote objects stay alive, possibly offering services to other clients (through other proxies to them located in other address spaces).

A SOM programmer could conclude that DSOM basically is the same stuff (at least from the codification viewpoint) just changing the way objects are created, with the drawback that this task is rather cumbersome. But in fact there is a way to achieve the same functionality in just one invocation. The DSOM function *somdCreate* creates an instance from an unspecified server and returns a reference to it (or to its proxy).

The sample program written above shows the most general way to create an instance. It is the most arduous but also the most powerful. The programmer has full control over the properties of the desired factory through the *find_any* function. On the other hand, with *somdCreate* the programmer has no control over the server selected to create the instance. It is just a server capable of creating instances of the required class, and in this client that is just what we need. In the example program we do not make use of the extended possibilities of the general approach (as will be the case in most of the instantiations), so the client example could be rewritten using *somdCreate* achieving the same functionality (some unmodified lines are not rewritten).

```
#include <somd.h>
#include <tokenizer.h>
```

```
int checkEnvironment (Environment *env) { ... }

void main(int argc, char *argv[])
{
   Tokenizer tok;
   Environment env;
   string lexeme;
   int token;

   SOM_InitEnvironment(&env);
   SOMD_Init(&env);

   tok = somdCreate(&env, "Tokenizer", TRUE);

   _setInputString(tok, &env, "abc 123 def");
   while (isTokenAvailable(tok, &env))
   {
      [...] /* loop unmodified */
   }

   _getToken(tok, &env);
   checkEnvironment(&env);

   _somFree(tok);

   SOMD_Uninit(&env);
   SOM_UninitEnvironment(&env);
}
```

Compare the first version of the client (using the class factory) with this new version using *somdCreate*. The only new line added is the *somdCreate* itself (remarked in bold). In contrast, five lines have been removed. Three of them are the location of the factory service (*resolve_initial_references*), the query for a suitable factory (*find_any*), and the instance creation (*somNew*). The two other omitted lines are the invocations of *release* on the factory service proxy and on the class factory proxy. No other line of the client was modified.

The reason to include the first version was to show the general approach and what really happens inside *somdCreate*. After all, object creation is one of the main differences between SOM and DSOM from the developer viewpoint. Other improvements included in DSOM are totally transparent to a SOM developer (for example, the proxies' job).

Now the only drawback found in the original client has gone away. A DSOM client is as easy (or as difficult) to code as a SOM program, so it seems that there is no reason to develop an application making it SOM compliant but not DSOM compliant. With no additional effort an application is achieved that can be redistributed even without recompilation.

References

IBM Corporation. 1996. *SOMobjects Developer Toolkit. Version 3.0. Programming Guide*, Volumes 1 and 2.

Futher Readings

Orfali, R., Hadkey, D. and Edwards, J. *The Essential Client/Server Survival Guide*. Wiley Computer Publishing, New York.

Orfali, R., Hadkey, D. and Edwards, J. *The Essential Distributed Objects Survival Guide*. Wiley Computer Publishing.

In the first book the authors offer a general guide on the client/server programming techniques. The second book extends the first one on the chapters related to object-oriented client/server programming. It dedicates many chapters to CORBA and to the comparison of CORBA with OLE/COM.

IBM Corporation. 1996. *SOMobjects Developer Toolkit. Version 3.0. Programming Guide,* Volumes 1 and 2.
IBM Corporation. *SOMobjects Developer Toolkit. Version 3.0. Programming Reference,* Volumes 1 to 4.

This is the most important and full document written about SOM by IBM Corporation. It is a complete guide where SOM architecture is explained. Also, the design, implementation, and use of classes are shown. It is an essential reading for those people who want to begin in SOM/DSOM implementation. Some notions about the SOM IDL language, compilation process, and the most common errors are introduced.

Sessions, R. *Object Persistence.* Prentice-Hall, Englewood Cliffs, NJ.

In this book the author introduces the CORBA's *object persistence service.* Roger Sessions was one of the fathers of the persistence service. The first half of the book is a practical introduction to SOM/DSOM.

Lalonde, W. and Pugh, J. 1995. Using SOM in VisualAge and IBM Smalltalk, *J. Object Oriented Programming,* February.

An easy introduction to the SOM bindings with Smalltalk. The authors implement a SOM class in C++ and show how this class can be reused in any Smalltalk application.

Wayner, P. 1994. Objects on the march, *Byte,* January.

Although this article is about object technologies and operating systems, it includes, among other topics, a comparison of SOM and COM.

Nance, B. 1993. OS/2's system object model, *Byte,* January.
Udell, J. 1993. IBM's assault on distributed objects, *Byte,* November.

An introduction to SOM and DSOM, respectively. In the first article SOM is presented together with the reasons that originated it. In the second article it is shown that DSOM is a natural extension of SOM in the search of distribution.

Orfali, R. and Hadkey, D. *Client/Server Programming with Java and CORBA.* Wiley Computer Publishing, New York.
Vogel, A. and Duddy, K. *Java Programming with CORBA.* Wiley and Sons, New York.

These books combine CORBA with the Java programming language. They both make a general introduction to CORBA followed by a series of practical example programs.

Orfali, R., Hadkey, D. and Edwards, J. 1997. *Instant CORBA.* Wiley Computer Publishing, New York.
Mowbray, T. J. and Zahavi, R. 1994. *The Essential CORBA.* Wiley Computer Publishing, New York.

These books describe the theory and principles of standard object technology, systems architecture integration, frameworks, and OMG standards including CORBA. Because SOM is a technology following CORBA standards, these are very interesting books to help in understanding SOM philosophy .

IBM Corporation. 1994. Object technology products group, *IBM's System Object Model (SOM): Making Reuse a Reality.* Austin, TX.

This is a very short paper giving some general ideas about SOM and DSOM. The main advantages obtained with their use are shown.

IBM Corporation. 1994. Object technology products group, *IBM's The System Object Model (SOM) and the Component Object Model (COM): A comparison of Technologies from a Developer's Perspective.* Austin, TX.

This paper establishes a brief comparison between the two main object interoperability technologies, implemented and extended.

32

Component Object Model (COM)

Fernando Alvarez-Garcia
Oviedo University

Dario Alvarez-Gutiérrez
Oviedo University

32.1 Introduction

Component Object Model (COM) is a specification defined by Microsoft about how to create components and how to build applications that use these components. Before talking about COM, we must define the concept of component. A component is a functional unit that follows the encapsulation principle defined by object orientation. To provide their functionality, components expose sets of functions which potential clients can invoke. This is the only means clients have to use components.

Like any other specification, COM defines several standards that permit component interoperability:

1. A binary standard for invoking component functions
2. A component can have several interfaces, which are groups of functions
3. A base interface called *IUnknown* that provides:
   - A way for components to dynamically discover the interfaces supported by other components (*QueryInterface*)
   - Component lifecycle control based on reference counting (*AddRef* and *Release*)
4. A mechanism to univocally identify component classes and their interfaces (GUIDs*)

* GUIDs (Globally Unique Identifiers) are identifiers taken from DCE/OSF UUIDs and identify interfaces, component classes, etc.

0-8493-3135-8/99/$0.00+$.50

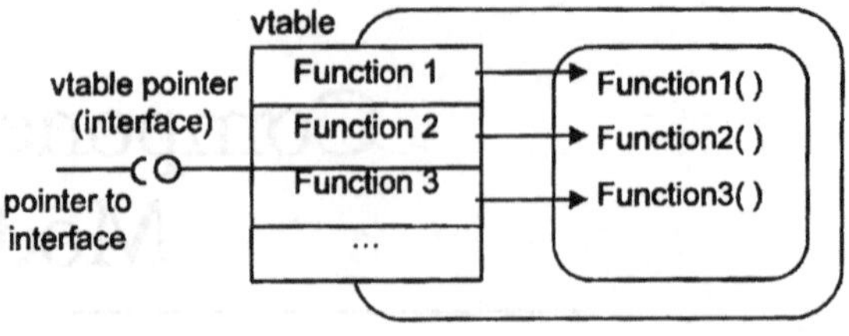

FIGURE 32.1 Memory layout for a COM component.

COM is now available for Microsoft Windows enviroments and is now being ported to other platforms. Since it is a binary standard, it does not depend on any programming language.

From now, we will use interchangeably the terms component class and component instance (COM terms) and class and object (terms used in object-orientation literature), respectively. Sometimes we will only use the term component, but the context will clarify when are we talking about a component class and when we are talking about a component instance.

32.2 Interfaces

An interface provides the connection between a client and a component. COM makes a very precise definition of an interface: an interface is a well-defined memory structure made up of an array of function pointers, called virtual table or for short, vtable. Every element of the array stores the address of a function implemented by the component. For COM, everything but this are all implementation details and are not concerned with its vision of an interface. It is the responsibility of the component class programmer to correctly implement all of the component functions.

From a client point of view, a COM component is simply a set of interfaces. Clients can only communicate with components by means of any of its interfaces. In fact, if a client wants to communicate with a component, it must obtain a pointer to any of its interfaces (we will see later how to do this) before any possible interaction.

Figure 32.1 shows the memory structure of a COM interface. This memory structure is the same as those generated by some C++ compilers for abstract base classes. This is the case of the Microsoft C++ compiler. Anyway, every language able to invoke functions by means of pointers (like C, C++, Ada, etc.) can use components with the memory structure shown above.

It is interesting to notice the double indirection used to access the array of function pointers. We can imagine a client using several component instances via the same interface. These several instances could share a unique array of pointers to save memory space.

Interfaces in COM are immutable. Once an interface is public, it will remain intact. If the programmer of the component wants to improve it (adding more functions), he must add a new interface with the improved functionalities. Modifying an interface is not allowed. That is the way COM manages versions.

Every COM interface is univocally identified by its IID (Interface Identifier). An IID is a GUID for interfaces. COM interfaces also have a symbolic name, always beginning with I, for identification purposes at compile time. These names are defined in header files provided by the interface designer using the Interface Description Language (IDL). Figure 32.2 shows a component supporting three interfaces, with symbolic names IA, IB, and IC.

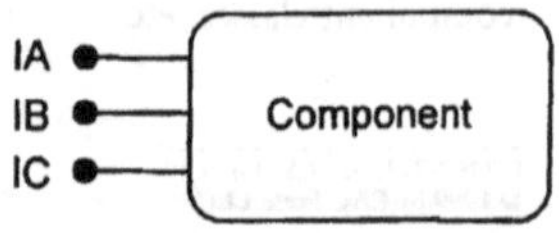

FIGURE 32.2 A component with three interfaces.

Interfaces permit clients to communicate with different component classes in the same way. If two or more component classes support the same interface, a client could use the same code to communicate with them. This is how polymorphism is achieved in COM.

Almost every interface function return has a return value or an HRESULT value. An HRESULT type is a COM predefined data structure composed by four fields: success or failure of the invocation, a

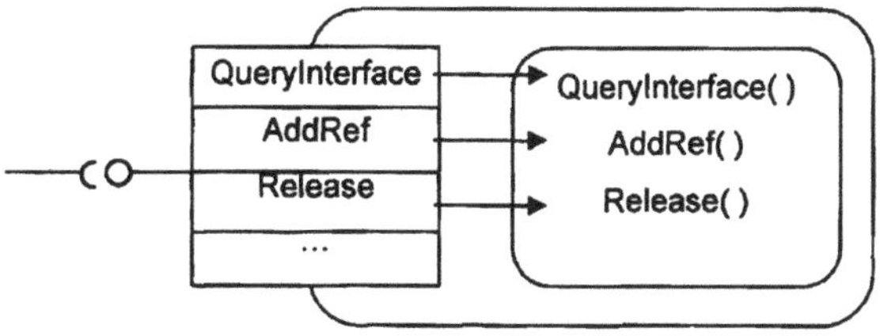

FIGURE 32.3 A IUknown interface with its functions.

return code, information about the origin and type of the return code, and a fourth field reserved for future use.

32.3 The IUnknown Interface

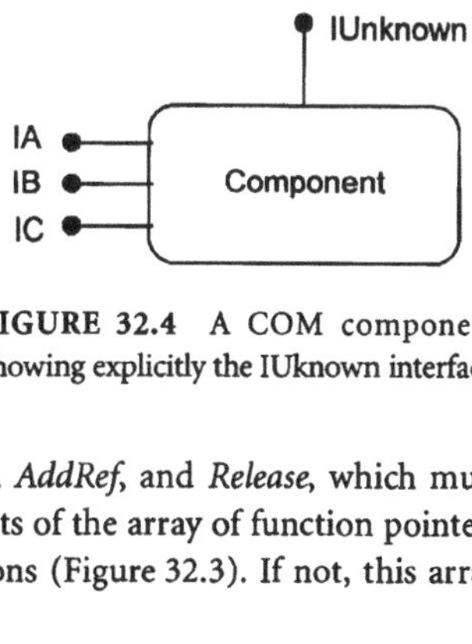

FIGURE 32.4 A COM component showing explicitly the IUknown interface.

We have said that everything a client wants to do with a component is made by means of its interfaces. Therefore, clients need a mechanism to know if a component supports a given interface before it could use it. The mechanism provided by COM is the *IUnknown* interface. Clients will ask the component using the *IUnknown* interface if it supports a certain interface.

IUnknown is the heart of COM. *IUnknown* is used for interface resolution at runtime, for component lifecycle management, and for aggregation (we will see this later). Every COM interface inherits from *IUnknown*, so every component supports the *IUnknown* interface. *IUnknown* declares three functions: *QueryInterface*, *AddRef*, and *Release*, which must be implemented by every interface. To be exact, the three first elements of the array of function pointers of every interface must be occupied by pointers to this three functions (Figure 32.3). If not, this array of pointers is not considered a COM interface.

If every COM component supports the *IUnknown* interface, we can add it to the set of interfaces it exports, as shown in Figure 32.4.

32.3.1 QueryInterface

It is used to know, at runtime, if a component supports a given interface. If the component supports the interface, *QueryInterface* returns a pointer to it (more exactly, a pointer to the structure described). Once the client has obtained the interface pointer, it can interact with the component invoking the interface functions.

COM forces *QueryInterface* to always return the same interface pointer value when asked for a given interface, regardless if the interface derived from *IUnknown* used to ask the component. The reason is that a client could test if two different pointers point to the same component instance. *QueryInterface* also permits programmers to add new interfaces to components as they evolve, and without any recompilation of the client code. Old clients could continue using old interfaces as newer clients could use the improved ones.

32.3.2 AddRef and Release

AddRef and *Release* look after the lifecycle control of components. They both coordinate to implement a memory management technique called reference counting. Every COM component must maintain a number called reference count. Every time a client obtains an interface reference, the reference count is incremented. Every time a client finishes using an interface, the reference count is decremented. When the reference count reaches zero, the component eliminates itself from memory.

Every invocation to *AddRef* must have a corresponding invocation to *Release* when the interface is no longer needed. The use of these functions must be done carefully, because some functions make an implicit call to *AddRef* before returning. COM implementations must support 31-bit counters for the reference count.

32.4 Component Creation (Class Factories)

To access the functionality provided by a component class, clients must obtain a pointer to any of its interfaces. Before, we had to create an instance of the component class. COM clients cannot create components directly. Clients must use special components, called Class Factories, which exist only for the purpose of creating component instances. More exactly, a given class factory creates only component instances of a specific component class, identified by its Class Identifier or CLSID (a CLSID is a GUID for component classes). We can summarize the steps a client must follow for creating a component below:

1. The client must obtain a component creation interface of the class factory identified by the CLSID (it actually obtains an interface pointer).
2. The client instructs the class factory (using the interface obtained in Step 1) to create a component instance, and obtains, as a return value, a pointer to the requested component interface.

As mentioned, the first step consists of obtaining a pointer to an interface of the class factory, given a CLSID. The COM library provides a function called *CoGetClassObject* to do this. Given the CLSID of the component class we want to create an instance, some information about the server in which it resides, and the IID of the class factory interface desired. *CoGetClassObject* will return a pointer to the interface of the class factory.

There is a standardized class factory interface for creating component instances: its name is *IClass-Factory*, and it has two functions called *CreateInstance* and *LockServer.*

- *CreateInstance* — Creates an instance of the component class associated to the class factory and returns an interface pointer to the interface requested. It is important to note that *CreateInstance* does not take the CLSID as a parameter, because *CreateInstance* can only create component instances corresponding to a unique CLSID, and this CLSID is a parameter for *CoGetClassObject.*
- *LockServer* — A client uses *LockServer* to keep a server in memory even if it is not serving any component. A server usually unloads itself from memory when it has no components to serve, but a client can block it in memory to avoid several load and unload operations, improving the performance this way when instantiating components.

Figure 32.5 shows a component instance creation scenario. There is an easier but less flexible way to create components. The COM library has a function called *CoCreateInstance* for creating components. For a given CLSID, *CoCreateInstance* creates a component instance, returning a pointer to the interface requested in the invocation. Of course, *CoCreateInstance* does not create the component directly. Internally, *CoCreateInstance* creates a class factory which finally creates the component.

In most cases, clients will create components using *CoCreateInstance,* excepting when:

- The client wants to create the component not using *IClassFactory* but using another creation interface (i.e., *IClassFactory2* interface adds licensing capabilities to components)
- The client wants to create a set of components (all of them instances of the same component class) all at once, avoiding creation and deletion of a class factory for each one

32.5 Reusability

One of the main objectives of an object model is to enable component designers and programmers to reuse and extend components provided by other developers as parts of their own components. To achieve reusability COM supports two mechanisms that enable components to reuse other components. As a

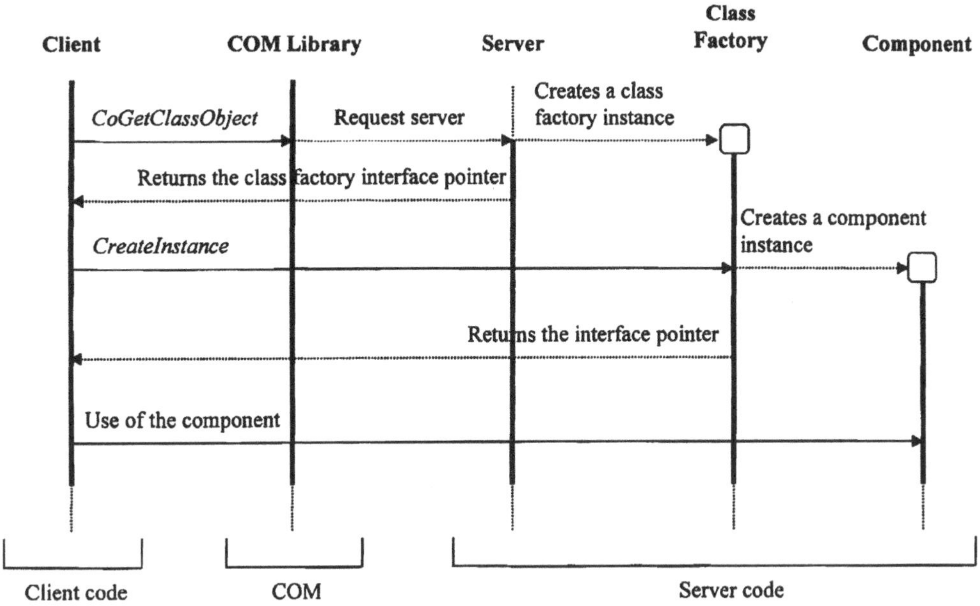

FIGURE 32.5 A scenario showing the creation of a component instance.

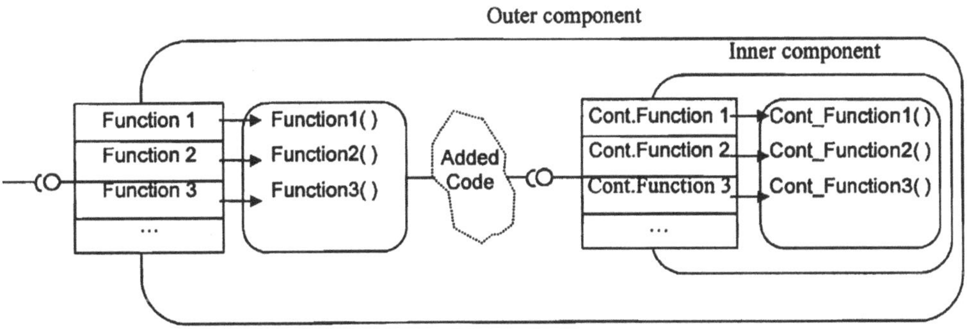

FIGURE 32.6 Component containment.

convention, the component being reused is called the inner component, and the component using the inner component, the outer component.

1. Containment/Delegation — the outer component behaves as a client for the inner component. The outer component contains the inner object (see Figure 32.6). When the outer component wants to use the functionality of the inner component, it delegates implementation to the inner component interfaces. In other words, the outer component uses the services of the inner component for its implementation. Furthermore, the outer component could specialize the inner component interface, adding code after and before the invocations of the functions of the inner component.
2. Aggregation — it can be understood as a specialization of containment. The outer component exposes the inner component interfaces as if they were implemented by the outer component (see Figure 32.7). Aggregation is very useful when the outer component always wants to delegate invocations to one of its interfaces to the same interface in the inner component, because these

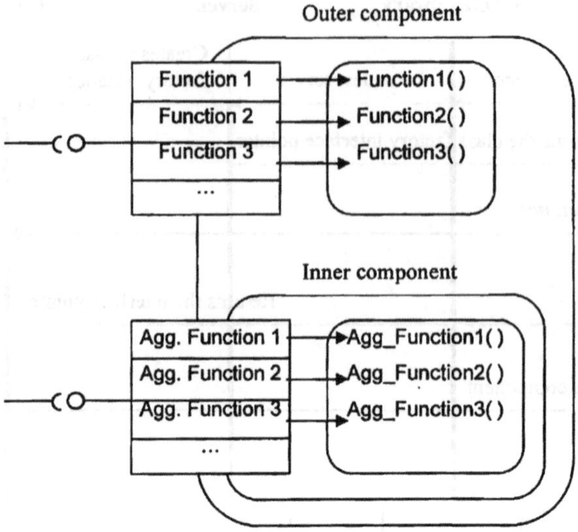

FIGURE 32.7 Component aggregation.

invocations are forwarded automatically to the inner component interface. Extra code in the outer component is thus avoided. The client is not aware of the existence of two different components respecting the encapsulation principle.

Containment is easy to implement; it is just a component containing another one. Aggregation is more complex. It is necessary that *QueryInterface* work transparently with all the interfaces the outer component exposes, independently of the component that supports them (the inner or the outer). COM provides support to achieve the desired transparency.

32.6 Component Servers

A component server is a binary code (commonly packed in Windows as an EXE or a DLL) which hosts one or more class factories and the implementation for the corresponding components.

A COM server should have a structure with some overall responsibilities:

- Register the classes it serves — Every class supported has to be registered into an information repository (the registry for Windows environments). The CLSID for every class is associated with the pathname of the DLL or EXE server. When a client requests creation of an instance of the class, COM uses its CLSID to find the server in the registry. This registration is normally done once at installation time.
- Implement a class factory — The server should implement a component with a component creation interface for each class hosted. This interface *IClassFactory* is used by COM library functions to create instances, but can also be used directly by the client. Other interfaces for component creation can be implemented. For example, *IClassFactory2* is a standard interface that adds licensing support.
- Booting mechanism (entry point) — An initial entry point should be provided to start the server and create the class factory(s). Once the class factory in the server is started, the server can now be used to create instances.
- Unloading mechanism (exit point) — Analogously, the server should provide a way to terminate itself when its components are no longer used.

How these features are implemented depends on the kind of server considered.

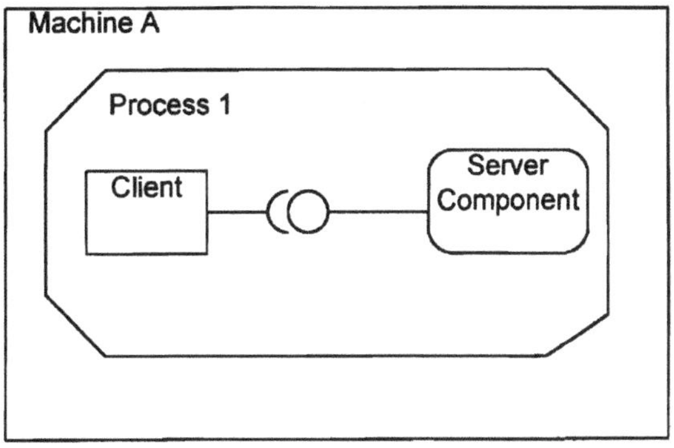

FIGURE 32.8 A client using an in-process component.

32.6.1 In-Process Servers

An in-process server is implemented as a DLL. A DLL executes in the same address space of the client. So, the code for the component in the server is directly accessible by the client.

Once an interface is acquired, its use is reduced to direct calls to the functions of the interface, as the functions will be in the same address space of the client. No intermediate actions are used for the call in this case (Figure 32.8).

Booting — To initialize a server in a DLL, a function should be exported to allow COM to create the class factory for a class, for example, in response to a *CoGetClassObject* call requested by a client of the class. Besides, a class factory interface should be returned to the client. This function is called *DllGetClassObject.*

Registration — A *DllRegisterServer* function is commonly exported to supply external programs with a means to register the components in a server DLL. An inverse function, *DllUnRegisterServer,* unregisters the components.

Unloading — A DLL cannot unload itself. COM performs this, but COM needs a way to know when to do it. An exported function *DllCanUnloadNow* tells COM whether the server is still serving clients or not. If not, COM can safely unload the DLL from memory.

32.6.2 Out-Process Servers

These servers are implemented as EXE files and execute in a process (and address space) different from the client process. When the server is located in the same machine where the client is, it is called a local server. If it is located in another machine on the net, it is a remote server.

The client uses an interface by simply making calls to its functions. So, these functions are required to be located in the same address space where the client is. As the server is in another address space, a mechanism must be provided which transparently receives server requests, forwards the calls to the EXE server, accesses the component, and then returns results.

The client uses a proxy component in its address space, which mimics the external appearance of the target server component. From a client's point of view, a normal interface of the component is used by making calls within its own address space.

The proxy component receives the call and is in charge of delivering to the server EXE. To communicate with the server, lightweight procedure calls (LPCs) are used for local servers, and remote procedure calls (RPCs) are used for remote servers. These procedure calls are performed by the operating system. A marshaling process is required in order to use these calls. Marshaling packs the parameters of the call in an appropriate way for a subsequent transmission to the server. The call reaches a stub in the server. The stub receives the call, unmarshals the data, and invokes the requested function in the server

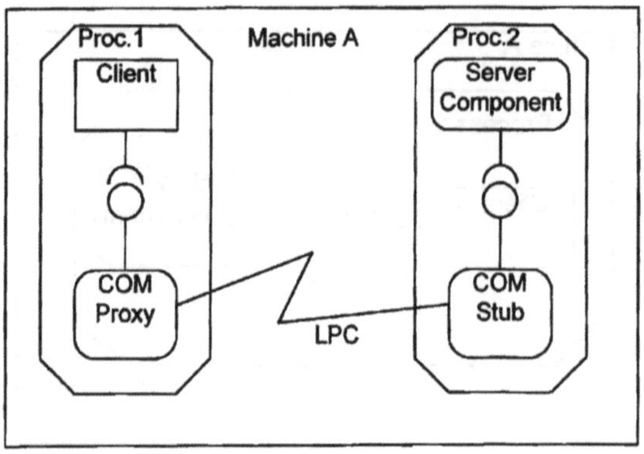

FIGURE 32.9 A client using a local out-process component.

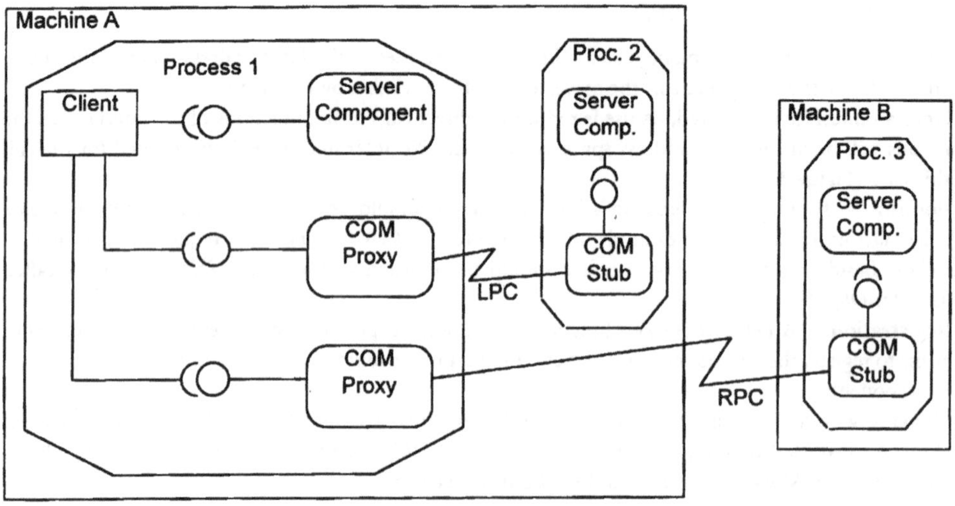

FIGURE 32.10 A client using an in-process, a local out-process, and a remote out-process server.

component, as it shares the address space with the server. Parameters are returned making the inverse journey. From the server component to the stub; from the stub to the proxy and finally the proxy returns results to the client. This situation is depicted in Figure 32.9.

With this architecture, the client and the server component do not have to care in which address space the other party is located. Clients work without modification with an in-process or an out-process server component and vice versa. Figure 32.10 shows a client using the three types of servers: an in-process server, a local out-process server (which uses LPCs), and a remote out-process server (which uses RPCs).

32.6.2.1 Proxy and Stub Generation, Marshaling/Unmarshaling, IDL Language, and the MIDL Compiler

To use an EXE server, COM needs the proxy/stub pair which implement transparent communication between client and server components. This proxy/stub pair is implemented as a DLL that maps as an in-process server for both the client and the server.

Proxy/stub DLLs can be coded by hand, but it is easier to generate them with an automatic mechanism. Interfaces are described using a generic language called Interface Definition Language (IDL). Using a

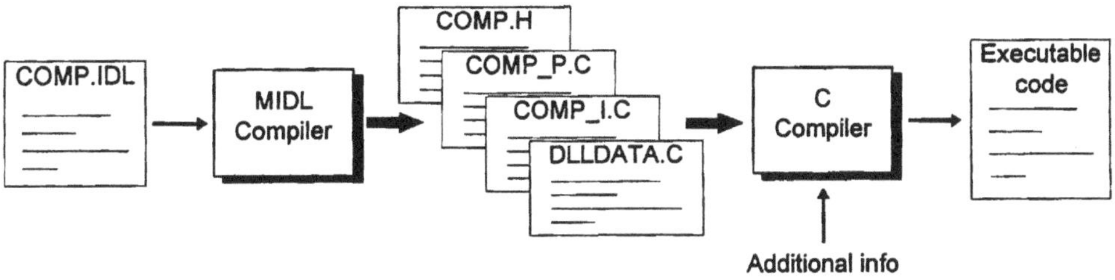

FIGURE 32.11 Using the IDL compiler.

compiler such as MIDL with the interface definitions, code for proxies and stubs is generated (among other things) to create the corresponding DLL. This code also performs the parameter marshaling/unmarshaling for the majority of data types.

The IDL language used is based on the RPC specification language from OSF/DCE, with extra nonstandard extensions added by Microsoft to support certain COM features.

```
// Interface IExample
[
  object,
  uuid(8389ABA0-D8F1-11D0-A617-080000526267),
  helpstring("IExample interface"),
  pointer_default(unique)
]
interface IExample : IUnknown
{
  HRESULT F1([in] short n, ...);
  HRESULT F2([out, retval] float f...);
  ...
};
...
// Component definition
[
  uuid(AAB12B40-D8F1-11D0-A617-080000526267),
  helpstring("Example of component")
]
coclass MyComponent
{
  [default] interface IExample;
}
object: specifies a COM interface
uuid: assigns an IID for the interface
helpstring: defines a help string for the item
pointer_default: used to choose the default handling for pointers
interface: denotes an interface

uuid: assigns a CLSID to the component class
coclass: defines a component class
```

Figure 32.11 shows a typical use of the IDL compiler. The IDL file is fed into the compiler. The MIDL compiler generates files compatible with C and C++. The .H file contains declarations for the interfaces, the _I.C file declares the GUIDs used, the _P.C file has code implementing the proxy/stub for the interfaces, and the DLLDATA.C is used to generate the DLL containing the proxy/stubs. COM has to find in the information repository the DLL implementing the proxy/stub pair for a given interface. Code that registers this information can also be generated into the DLL by the IDL compiler.

Booting — An EXE is an autonomous entity, which may be already activated in memory. This makes COM use a procedure to activate an EXE server different from the one used for a DLL server. COM maintains an internal table associating CLSIDs with the EXE server implementing them (the corresponding class factory interface, precisely). When a client requests creation of a component of a given class, COM searches the CLSID in this table. If not found, COM finds it in the registry and launches the associated EXE. Being an autonomous program not able to export functions to be used as a DLL, the EXE itself must create the class factories when launched and indicate to COM which classes (with its class factories) it supports so that the classes get included in the table. The COM function *CoRegisterClassObject* is used for this purpose. After this, the executable does not need to be launched (only if it is desired).

Registration — The EXE can be coded to have control over the regular registry of its components, so that registration can be done at any time. The EXE can have command line options to indicate registering or unregistering of components, but this is usually used only once at installation or uninstallation.

Unloading — The count of components used can be monitored, and being an EXE, it should self-terminate when it reaches zero. The entries in the internal COM table for its classes should be deleted using *CoRevokeClassObject.*

32.7 Dynamic Invocation

The static invocation mechanism using interfaces is very good when using components from code written in languages such as C++. This static invocation prevents many errors, as compile time type checking facilities of the language can be used. Nevertheless, it is required to know all the information about the component at compile time, usually by including some kind of header files. The MIDL compiler generates these header files for C and C++ languages as part of the compilation of an IDL specification for interfaces and components. This procedure is too inflexible sometimes. What is needed is a way to invoke functions in a component without knowing the function nor the parameters and its types beforehand.

Components should provide a dynamic invocation mechanism. Functions and parameters supported by a component could be discovered at runtime using this mechanism; then they would be invoked. This flexibility comes with a cost in the form of a much slower invocation time.

The IDispatch interface — Dynamic invocation is achieved in COM making components support and having a standardized interface named *IDispatch.* Basically, this interface allows a client to invoke a component function using its name and arguments passed as parameters to *IDispatch.* So, *IDispatch* has functions to return information about the functions supported in the component (*GetIDsOfNames, GetTypeInfoCount, GetTypeInfo*) and to invoke them dynamically (*Invoke*). A COM component with the *IDispatch* interface is called an Automation Server, and a client who knows how to use the *IDispatch* interface is an Automation Controller. Thus, an Automation Controller can use any Automation Server through its *IDispatch* interface. Inversely, any Automation Controller can use an Automation Server.

Dispinterfaces and DISPIDs — The set of functions which are accessed dynamically through *IDispatch::Invoke* is called a dispinterface. They define the dynamic interface of the component, different from the normal interfaces supported. Usually these dynamic functions map to functions of normal interfaces. To be able to invoke these functions dynamically using their name, the component should implement a table, which maps every function name with a number called the DISPID. The *GetIDsOfNames* function returns the DISPID associated with a given name. This DISPID is passed as an argument to the *Invoke* function, which in turn invokes the desired function of the dispinterface.

Dual interfaces — At first, implementation of *IDispatch* is left to the programmer. One method is to define a normal interface inheriting from *IDispatch,* with the functions intended to be invoked dynamically. Then, implementation of *Invoke* is simply a matter of forwarding calls to the functions of

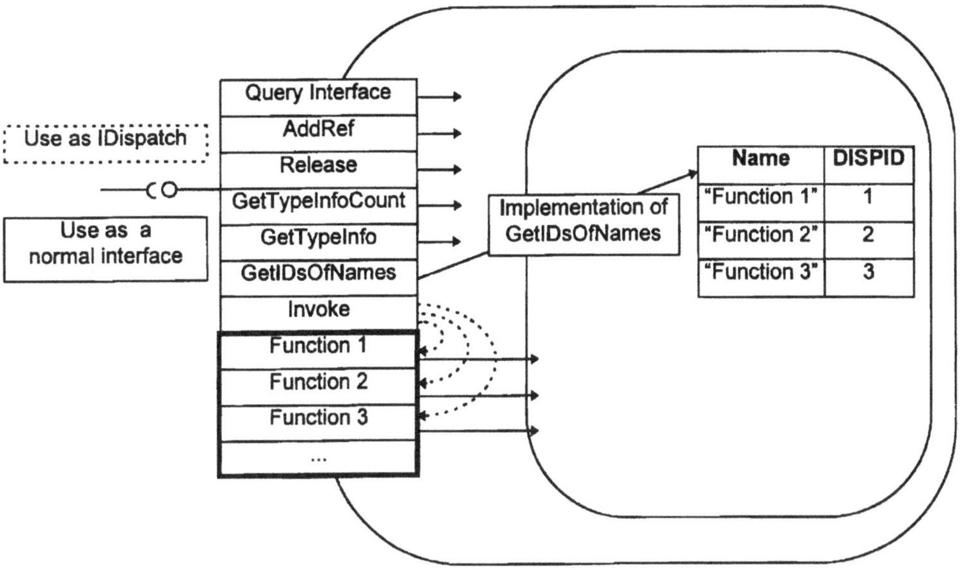

FIGURE 32.12 A dual interface.

this interface (Figure 32.12). This kind of interface is a dual interface, as it can be used dynamically as a dispinterface through *IDispatch* or statically as a normal interface.

With a dual interface, an automation controller such as a scripting language (Visual Basic for instance), can connect to a component dynamically (slower) or statically. For example, a Visual Basic component declared to be of generic type Object will be used through its dispinterface. If it is declared to be of a given component type, Visual Basic is able to use it with the normal interface.

Invoke in detail, DISPPARAMS and VARIANT — Essentially, the call to *Invoke* must provide the dispinterface function to use and the expected parameters as well. To indicate the function to use its DISPID is used, which can be obtained using *GetIDsOfNames*, but the parameters of the function can be of varying length and types. To represent the parameters, *Invoke* uses a DISPARAMS-type structure. Basically, this structure holds the number of parameters being passed and a list with the parameters. Types of the parameters must be known, so a generic type VARIANT is used to represent any type. A VARIANT is simply the union of a COM-prefixed set of different types. Due to this, a dispinterface can only use parameters with a type selected from those defined in this structure.

Additional parameters of Invoke — Languages like Visual Basic use methods and properties. Methods are functions and properties are variables that hold a value. COM interfaces only have functions, properties are simulated with a pair of Set/Get property functions. Nevertheless, the IDL can define properties for a dispinterface as well, being referenced from C++ with functions prefixing them with put_ and get_. But a property can have the same name as a function, and hence have the same DISPID. An additional parameter is needed to tell *Invoke* how the name is being used: as a function, as a property to be put by value, as a property to be put by reference, or as a property to get. The rest of the parameters for *Invoke* carry localization information, the returned result, and a structure with information about exceptions possibly produced when executing the function.

More flexible use of dispinterfaces — Flexibility due to the dynamic use of dispinterfaces makes it possible to use the interface without an exact knowledge of the number or types of the parameters. If a server component wants to make it easier to use the interface when programming the functions, it is very useful to recover errors as much as possible, for example, making type conversions when a parameter is passed with an incorrect type as in the case of using an integer when a float is expected.

Using dispatch interfaces in out-process servers — Another feature of these interfaces is that when they are used as out-process servers, no proxy/stub pairs generation is needed. As only VARIANT parameters are used, a system library (OLEAUT32.DLL) does the marshaling. This and other features of the Automation mechanism are partly owed to the fact that Automation and the *IDispatch* interface evolved together with Visual Basic to support this functionality.

32.8 Type Libraries

A client can use a dispinterface without knowing it completely at compile time, only knowing how to use *IDispatch.* Any server with a dispinterface can be controlled without (at first) knowing anything more. However, in order to use a dispinterface correctly, a mechanism is needed to help discover this information (names of functions, number and types of parameters, etc.) at runtime. This mechanism is based on type libraries. Information about components, interfaces, etc., is described in an IDL definition. A type library holds the same information described in the IDL, but structured in a way that allows the client's program to query it at runtime. A type library is stored using a file or an EXE or DLL resource.

32.8.1 Creating Type Libraries

To create a type library it is easier to let the IDL compiler do the work. The IDL language has extensions that indicate which information has to go to the type library and later generate the right file. As any other COM element, every type library is identified with a GUID called LIBID. There is also an option, which indicates in the definition how to generate a help file and/or a short help text for every element in the library.

32.8.2 Using Type Libraries

To query a type library the library function *LoadRegTypeLib* is used. *LoadRegTypeLib* finds the type library using the registry and returns an *ITypeLib* interface. Using this interface, information about any component or interface held in the type library can be queried, obtaining an *ITypeInfo* interface. Through this interface all the information about the interface or component is extracted. A characteristic example of client programs using this mechanism is object browsers. Another advantage is that languages such as Visual Basic can have complete information of a dual interface and thus are able to use the interface faster through the normal interface part of the dual interface.

32.9 Information Repository

To be able to perform certain tasks, COM needs a repository holding some information. For example, COM provides a library function to create an instance of a class of components. Internally, this function should locate where the file serving (in-process or out-process) the class of components requested is. The kind of information making this functionality possible is stored in a repository. The Windows registry is used to physically store this information when using Windows environments. Next, the structure of this specific registry used to store some COM information is described, as an example of the information needed. COM provides a set of library functions or component interfaces to manage this repository without knowing its internal structure; but for some specific tasks, a direct use of Windows registry functions might be needed.

Structure of the Windows registry — It is organized as a hierarchic tree. Entries in the tree that can have subentries are called keys. Other entries are named values. A key can have a default value. The root of the tree is a key (Figure 32.13).

Registering components and servers — At least, COM should know the server for every class of components so that instances could be created. What is needed is basically to map every CLSID with

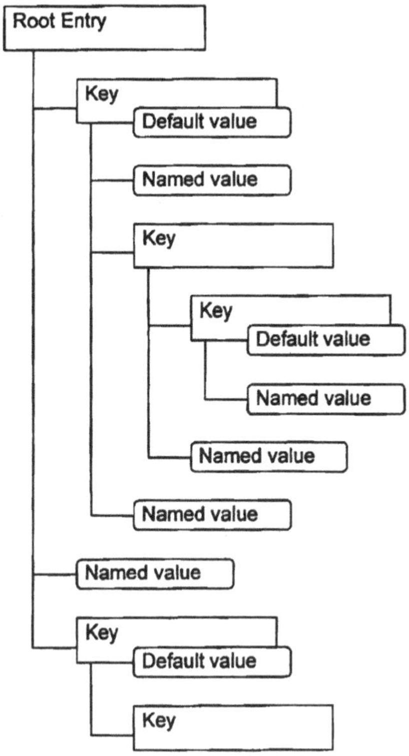

FIGURE 32.13 Structure of the Windows™ registry.

the corresponding server. Every component is represented under the key *HKEY_CLASSES_ROOT/CLSID*, using the CLSID in string format as a key. The default value for the CLSID is a friendly name for the component to help with its identification. Under the CLSID for a component class information about it is included. The name of the in-process server uses the InProcServer32 key. The out-process server uses LocalServer32 (Figure 32.14).

Interfaces and proxy/stub pairs — When using local servers, COM must locate the DLL of the component implementing the proxy/stub functions for an interface. Interfaces are registered apart from components implementing them, under the key HKEY_CLASSES_ROOT/Interface. Every interface uses its IID as a key, with the name of the interface used as the default value. The *ProxyStubClsid32* key shows the CLSID of the component class which in-server process implements the proxy/stub for the interface (Figure 32.14).

Creating components by name, ProgIDs — In order to have a way to create components using a friendlier name than CLSID, ProgIDs are used. A ProgID is a friendly name for a CLSID, so that it is possible to establish a mechanism to create a component using a name instead of having to know a CLSID beforehand. Information to map a ProgID with the CLSID of the component is stored using every ProgID as a key under *HKEY_CLASSES_ROOT.* The convention for ProgIDs is Program.Component.Version, but it is just a convention. There is also a version-independent ProgID which represents the component in general. A ProgID key has a default value with the friendly name of the component and contains the CLSID for the component. Version-independent ProgIDs have a CurVer key with the ProgID of the current version of the component (Figure 32.15).

Type libraries — The file where the type library is stored is the most important information about type libraries. Type libraries are represented under *HKEY_CLASSES_ROOT/TypeLib*, using the LIBID as a key. Every version of the library is a subkey, with a language specifier under which the Win32 key

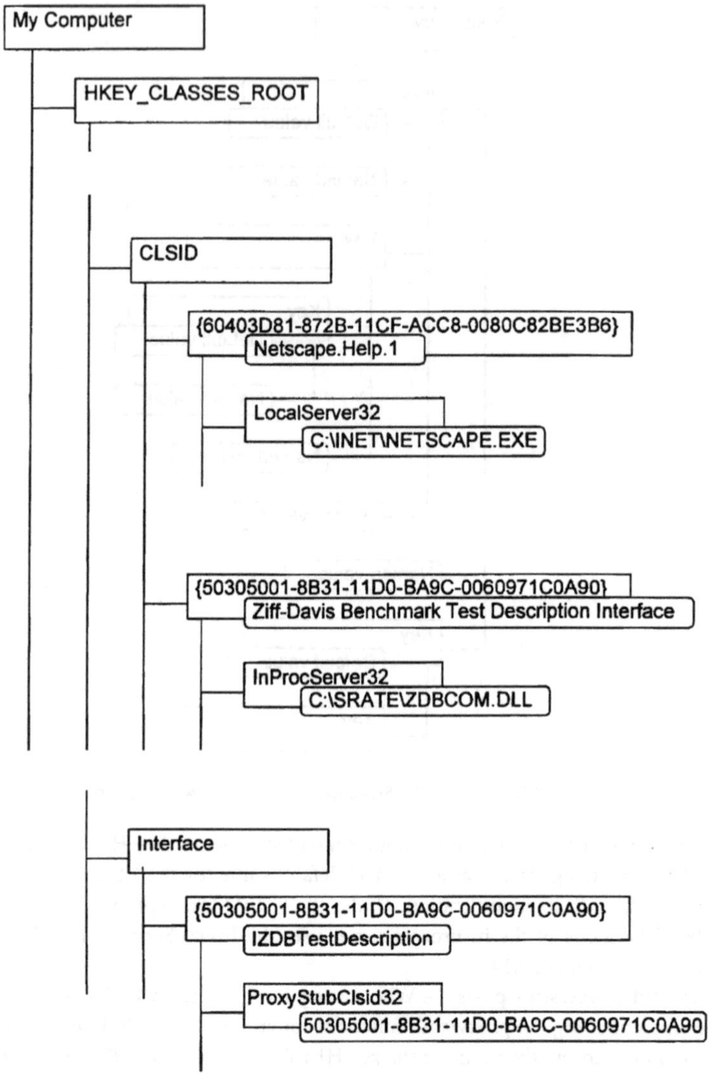

FIGURE 32.14 Information for components, servers, interfaces, and proxy/stub pairs.

holds the name of the file for the type library. The component should be associated with its type library (if it exists), including in the CLSID branch of the component a TypeLib key holding the LIBID for the type library (Figure 32.16). There is much more additional information about the above and other aspects. For example, licensing information, component categories, etc. There are also many inverse associations to speed, among other things, registry searches; for example, to pass faster from a ProgID to its CLSID and vice versa.

32.10 DCOM

What is DCOM? DCOM, or Distributed Component Object Model, is an extension of the described COM. DCOM extends COM in various ways. First of all, a simple change in the registry allows out-process servers to be located transparently in remote computers. Neither clients nor servers require

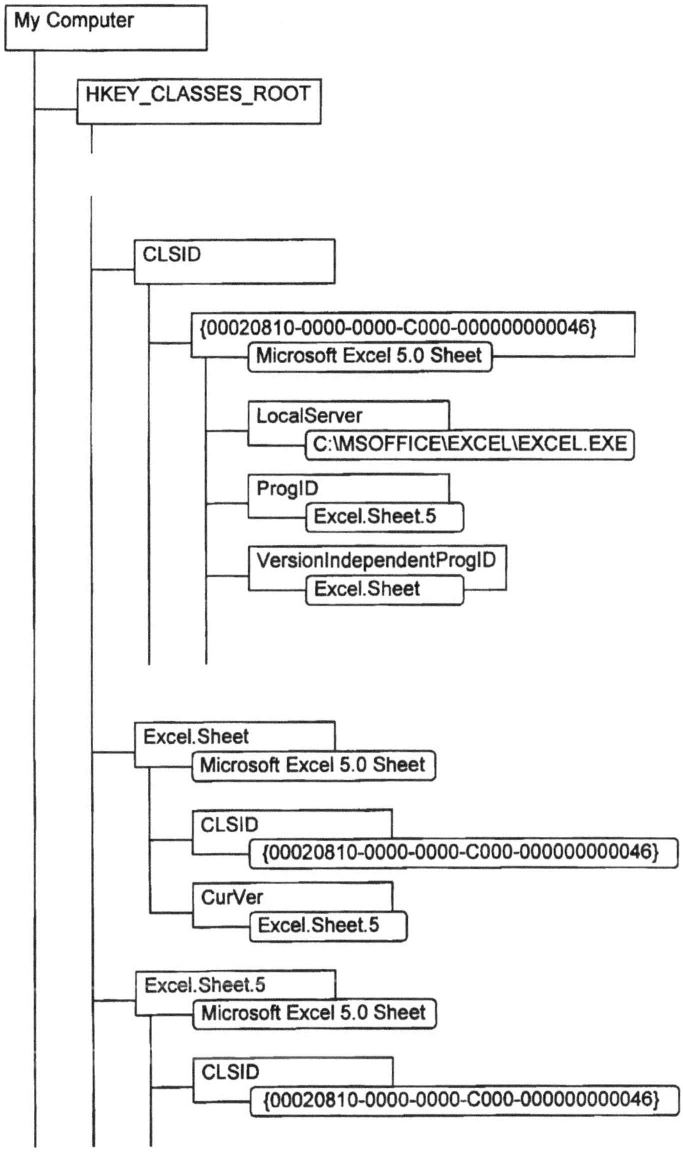

FIGURE 32.15 Information for ProgIDs.

modification. Besides, DCOM runs in different platforms like Windows 95, Windows NT, Macintosh, and UNIX, and introduces security support for components.

32.11 ActiveX

COM is a component infrastructure that can be used to develop complex environments, such as compound document architectures. For example, Microsoft's ActiveX (formerly OLE) is developed as a well-defined set of interfaces that must be supported by COM components to interact in ActiveX style. That is, an ActiveX component is simply a COM component, which supports a certain set of ActiveX interfaces.

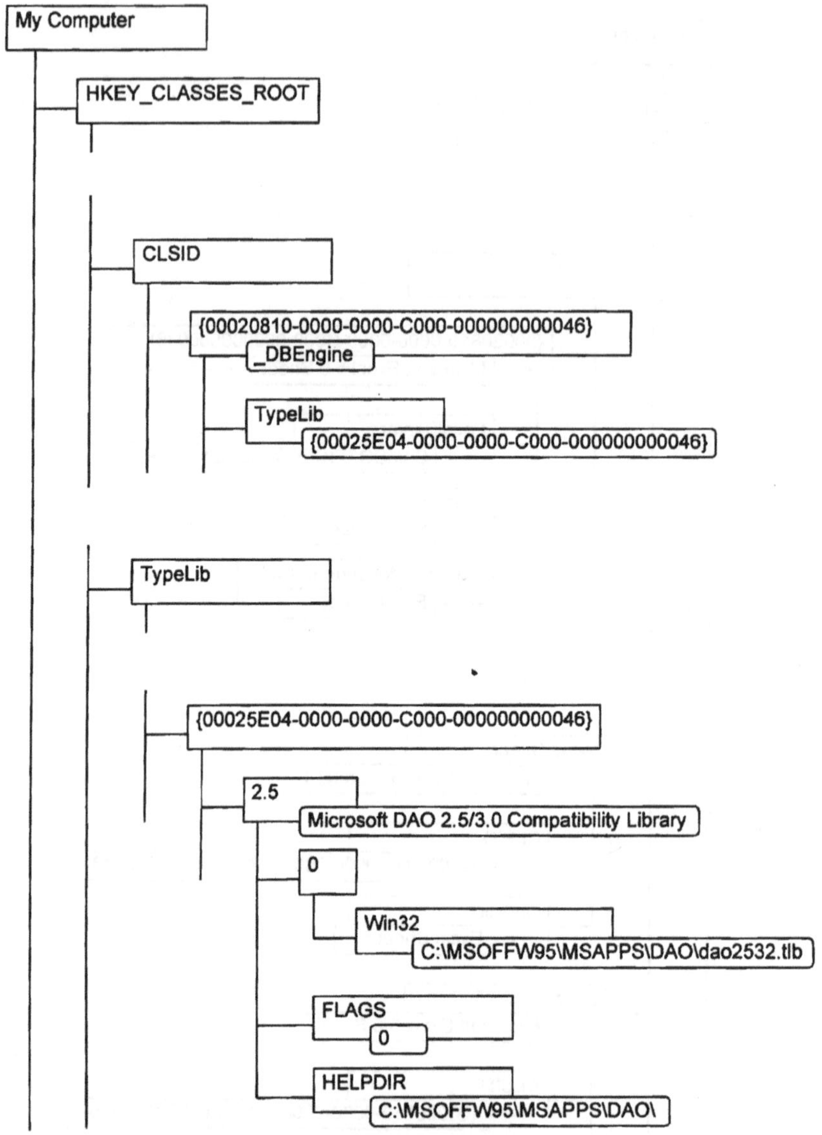

FIGURE 32.16 Information for type libraries and components.

COM was developed to support Microsoft OLE 2 compound document architecture. So, it is difficult to draw the line separating COM features from OLE features. In this chapter we have described the features that are commonly accepted as being part of COM.

Further Information

COM is a rather new subject, so books about COM are just beginning to appear. The ultimate source information for COM is the current Microsoft technical documentation. It is sometimes not very clear and difficult to understand. It accompanies different Microsoft developer products and can be reached via the World Wide Web through the Microsoft site http://www.microsoft.com.

One of the first books covering just COM is *Inside COM* by Dale Rogerson. This book introduces the COM architecture incrementally as well as programming techniques for implementing components. It is rather comprehensive but very easy and fun to read. It is also worth to notice that the author is affiliated with Microsoft. Any book covering OLE or ActiveX should address COM at some point. One of the best books on this subject is *Inside OLE, 2nd edition*, by Kraig Brockschmidt. *Essential Distributed Objects Survival Guide*, by Robert Orfali, Dan Harkey, and Jeri Edwards, has sections devoted to COM and OLE. While describing COM and OLE architectures, the book also compares them to other distributed object architectures and standards, such as CORBA and OpenDoc.

VI

Object-Oriented Databases

Douglas McDavid
IBM Global Services

Saba Zamir
Senior Information Technology Consultant

An Object Database Management System (ODMS) is a *traditional database system*, in addition to being an *Object* System. It stores and manages *objects*, instead of data. Thus, an object-oriented DBMS allows the storage, retrieval, and access of not just data as we know it, but of objects that can be considered data, such as sound, video, and graphics. These databases often feature multimedia application development platforms, and allow companies to process and display information in highly original ways. Object database management tools significantly increase the amount and kind of data that is available to be processed. Thus, the quality of the decision making process of the corporate environment is greatly improved.

In this section, you will find descriptions of the key components of object-oriented databases, along with a chapter that compares object-oriented to traditional relational databases.

33

Persistence in Object-Oriented Databases

Setrag Khoshafian
Technology Deployment International

Data manipulated by an object-oriented database (Khoshafian, 1993) can be either transient or persistent. Persistence is the ability of objects to persist different transactions or program invocations. Figure 33.1 illustrates transient and persistent objects. In this example some transient objects are referencing persistent objects. Transient data are valid only inside a program or transaction executed in a process (or a thread); they are lost once the process (or thread) terminates. Persistent data are stored in persistent storage. Various program invocations can access and modify the state of the same object. These objects persist across transactions, system crashes, and sometimes even media crashes. By contrast transient objects are accessible only within a single program invocation, or a single transaction. As soon as the process (or thread) executing the program terminates the transient objects are no longer accessible — they cease to exist. Persistence therefore is essential in database management systems, object-oriented or otherwise. In fact persistence can be analyzed from a programming language perspective and a database perspective.

33.1 Persistence and Programming Languages

Most object-oriented languages do not support persistence. Object orientation provides primitives to create, instantiate, and manipulate objects. The internal state of objects is stored in instance variables. Each object has a protocol, the messages to which it responds. Encapsulation deals with the protection of the data stored in the instance variables of an object. Therefore it is not surprising that object

0-8493-3135-8/99/$0.00+$.50

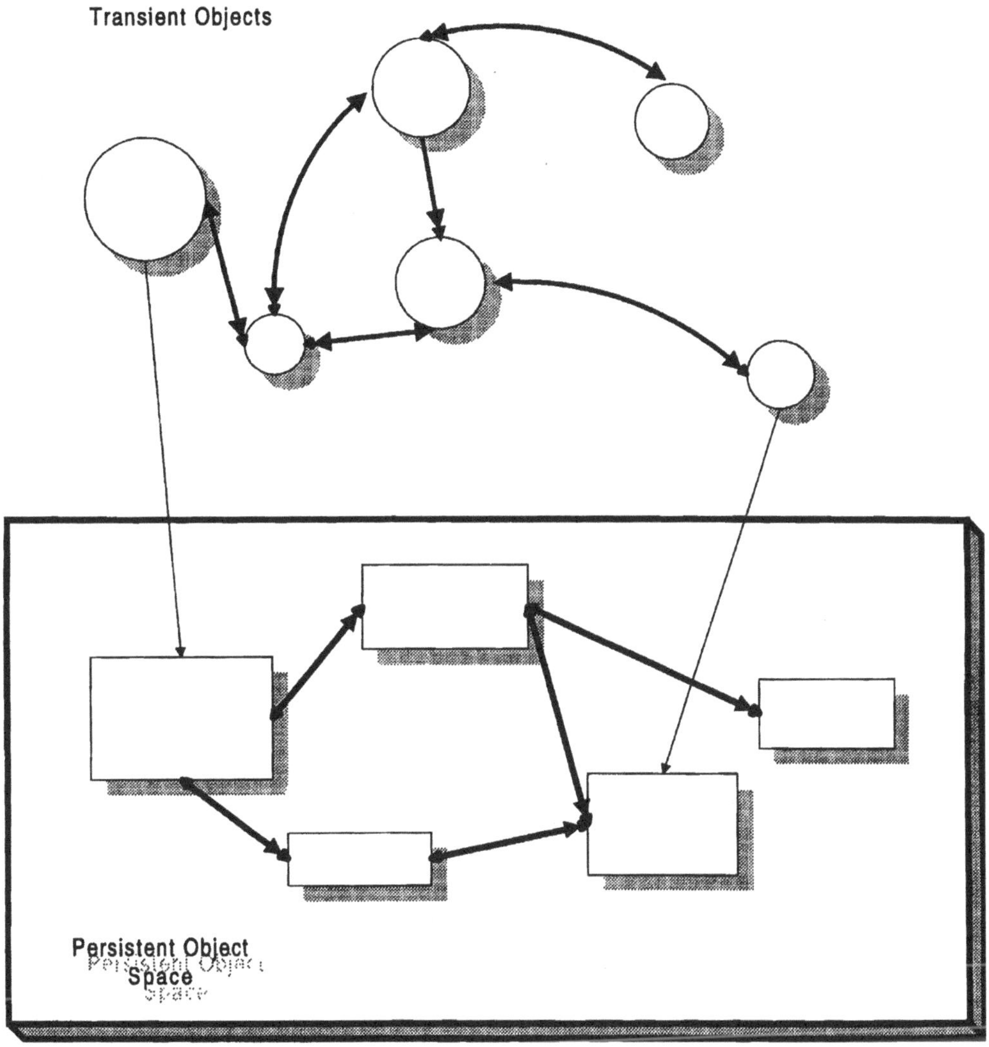

FIGURE 33.1 Persistent and transient objects.

orientation, even from its earliest days, has concerned itself with the persistence of objects between various program invocations.

To achieve persistence of the state of objects in a program, software engineers have traditionally relied on three basic strategies:

1. Repositories for records of values — The most commonly used strategy to "store and retrieve" values is to use persistent repositories. For example, operating system files or even a database management system can be used to store either structured text or records, which do not contain object references or (virtual) memory addresses ("pointers"). No special provisions are needed for this.
2. Saving the image of a session — This strategy saves the object states, variables, and the environment parameters in one huge operating system file. The file is retrieved and used with an application, such as an interpreter. The user can make modifications and save the file again.

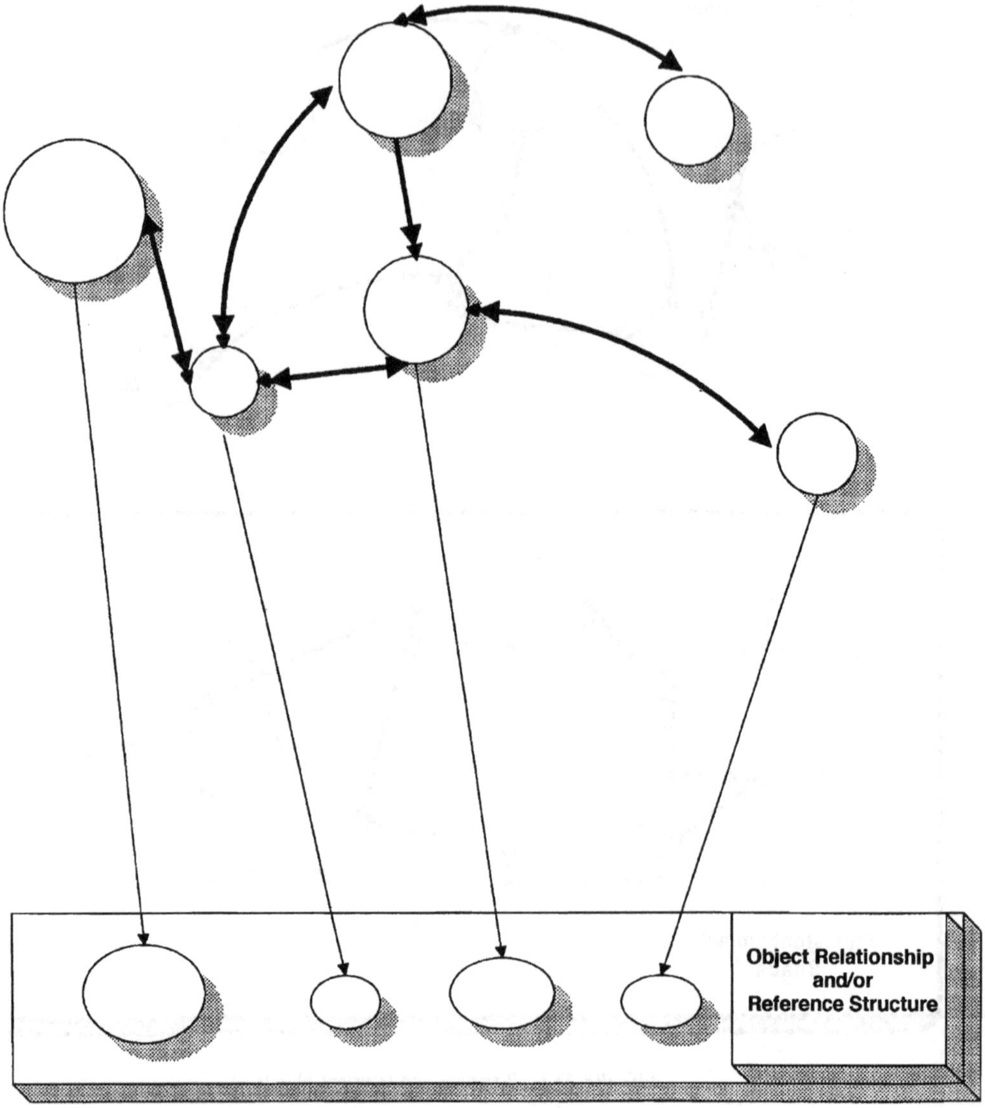

FIGURE 33.2 Serialization.

3. Serialization — An object can potentially contain references (pointers) to other objects. Given an object O1, if all the objects accessible (*reachable*; see definition below) from O1 are connected, the result is a directed graph which can potentially contain cycles. This is illustrated in Figure 33.2. Serialization is a technique where the graph structured objects (potentially involving circular references) are flattened or "serialized" onto a persistent storage, such as an operating system file. Then subsequently a "de-serialization" step converts the objects back from the storage, for instance a file, onto objects.

Each of these strategies has problems. The first allows the persistence for only some types of objects — literals or structured values that do not contain object references or pointers. The second is inefficient and provides limited ability to share objects concurrently. These strategies do not deal with the fundamental property of persistence, which is the ability to make the instance of any type (or class) persistent. Serialization is the more advanced technology and has many uses in modern applications. However, it is not a solution for large collections of objects that are concurrently shared under transaction control.

33.2 Any Type of Object (Instance of Any Class) Could Persist

The main philosophy behind introducing persistence to programming languages is to make persistence orthogonal to the type of objects. In other words, any type of object should be allowed to persist. The classical example of persistent programming languages is PS-Algol (Atkinson et al., 1983). The most important contribution of this prototype language that extended the then popular Algol procedural language was to demonstrate how persistence of an "object" could be orthogonal to the type. Simply stated this means any object could persist, even if that object is a collection of references or a record with pointers. Pointer types (which represent in-RAM or virtual memory addresses) are the most difficult types to make persistent. By its very nature a reference or a pointer type in a conventional or object-oriented language is a transient reference to an object. Its lifetime is limited to the execution of the program in which it gets created. Therefore persistence attempts to relax this constraint and allow many program invocations manipulate the *same* object.

In addition to conventional languages, there have been many attempts and products which have incorporated persistence into the object-oriented language. Conventional programming language, such as C or Pascal, as well as object-oriented database languages, such as C++, Smalltalk, and more recently Java, have been extended with persistence. The object-oriented database ODMG 2.0 standard (Cattell et al., 1997) specifies persistent bindings for the three aforementioned object-oriented languages: C++, Smalltalk, and Java. In addition to persistence other database concepts which have been incorporated in these object-oriented languages include transactions, querying for bulk data, recovery, and more.

33.3 Advantages of Persistence for Programming Languages

The advantages of extending an object-oriented language with database capabilities, and especially persistence, are many. One immediate consequence is that it might potentially alleviate the impedance mismatch which exists between programming languages and database management systems. For instance, in applications using relational databases the data retrieved from the DBMS using a database query language such as SQL is manipulated using a host programming language such as C. Often SQL statements are embedded in C programs to read database record values into C variables. Here is an example of embedded SQL:

```
strcpy (stmt, "SELECT * FROM ACCOUNT");
strcat (stmt, "WHERE ACCOUNT_NUMBER = ?");
EXEC SQL PREPARE S1 FROM :stmt;
EXEC SQL DESCRIBE S1 into :sqlda;
EXEC SQL DECLARE C1 CURSOR FOR S1;
printf ("Successfully successfully declared cursor.\n");
EXEC SQL OPEN C1 USING :account;
EXEC SQL FETCH C1 USING DESCRIPTOR :sqlda;
EXEC SQL CLOSE C1;
```

The variable SQL is a C structure; the variable account is an integer valued C variable. The example shows that EXEC SQL statements are interspersed with C statements. This embedded approach has several problems. Conventional programming languages such as C are procedural. Database query languages are higher level and more declarative. Therefore development environments that involve both types of languages mix (mismatch) these different programming paradigms. Furthermore, the data types in the different languages (SQL and C for instance) are not the same and have to be mapped onto one another. Therefore dealing with two models and two types we have a mismatch; we need to go from one model to the other in the same program and often in the same procedure. We have to map types and objects between the two models. The mismatch has many implications. It results in source code modules that are hard to understand, maintain, and debug.

33.4 Persistence in Databases

The term persistence is rarely used in traditional database literature. Rather the term used is the database which connotes the resilient, concurrently shared object space. The function of a database management system is to allow the concurrent access and update of persistent databases. In order to guarantee the long-term persistence of the data, database management systems employ various transaction management, concurrency, as well as recovery strategies against transaction, system, or media failures. A fundamental relationship between concurrent sharing and persistence in databases exists. Transaction updates must persist, but since the persistent database is concurrently accessed and updated, the database management system must concern itself with potential conflicts and the consistency of the persistent data objects. This is typically achieved through concurrency control and recovery strategies.

The data manipulated by an object-oriented database can be either transient or persistent. Transient data is only valid inside a program or transaction; it is lost once the program or transaction terminates. Persistent data, on the other hand, is stored outside of the "context" of a program and thus survives various program invocations. For example, personnel databases, inventory databases, and databases on sales people, accounts, or items all contain persistent data.

33.5 Levels of Persistence

There are several levels of persistence. The least persistent objects are those created and destroyed in procedure or methods locally. Next we have objects that persist within the workspace of a transaction but are invalidated when the transaction terminates (aborts or commits). Transactions are typically executed within a session. The user establishes his/her login and sets different environmental parameters within a session, such as paths, display options, etc. Several transactions could be activated within the same user, some of them concurrently. These transactions will all share the session objects (i.e., the objects which persist for the duration of the session). When the user terminates his/her session, however, the session objects are invalidated. The only type of objects that persist across transactions (and sessions for that matter) are permanent objects which typically are shared by multiple users. These objects (databases) persist across transactions, system crashes, and even media crashes (e.g., hard disk crashes). Technically these are the recoverable objects of the database. We often use the term persistent objects to identify this most persistent category of objects with an understanding that there are actually several levels of persistence.

33.6 Alternative Strategies for Defining Persistent Classes

Several strategies indicate which objects should become persistent. For an object to be persistent it must be an instance of a class that can generate persistent instances. In the terminology of ODMG 2.0 these classes are called persistent capable classes. A persistent capable class is a class whose instances can become persistent objects. Therefore if a class is not persistent capable, it will not be possible to create persistent instance of the class, and for that matter, any of its subclasses. There are a number of ways for specifying persistent capable classes. In fact various OODBMSs might have different conventions for specifying persistence capability. The persistent Java binding of the ODMG 2.0 standard, for instance, leaves it to the implementation of the OODBMS to specify persistent capable Java classes. There are several mechanisms for specifying persistent capable classes. The two most common are

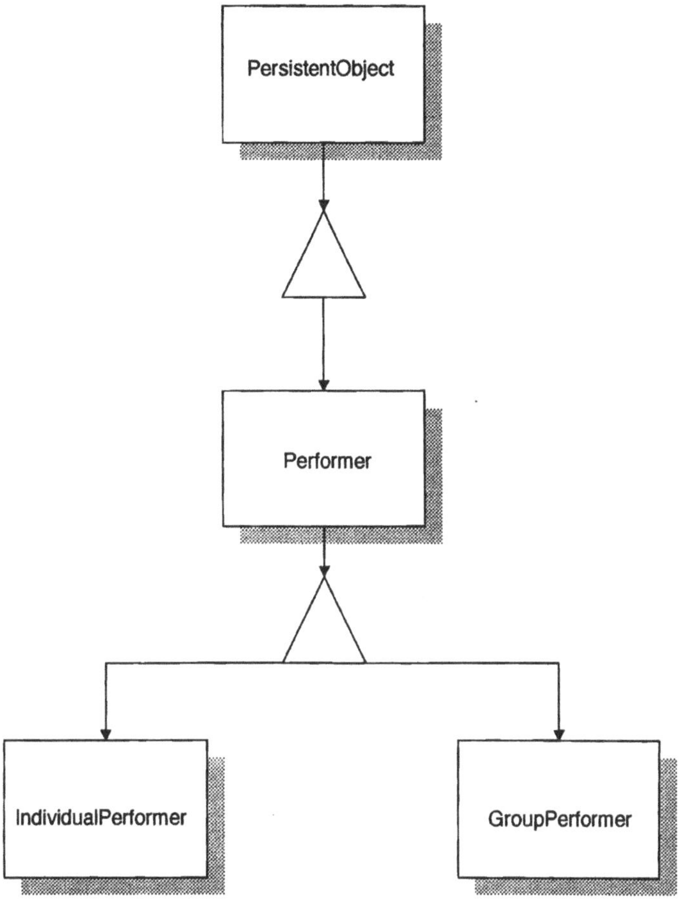

FIGURE 33.3 Persistence through inheritance.

1. Persistence through inheritance — With this approach the persistent classes are defined by their inheritance from a root persistent class, say, PersistantObject. This is illustrated in Figure 33.3. Every class which has persistent instances must be a descendant of this persistent root class. Thus, Performer, which is a direct descendant of PersistantObject and represents the most generic class of folders, can have persistent instances. Transitively so can IndividualPerformer and GroupPerformer. The classes that are reachable through the PersistantObject root using inheritance hierarchies therefore represent the templates of the persistent object space in the database. In various database management system products, the name or specific features of the root persistent class differs but the main function is usually the same. Among other things the PersistantObject class provides useful methods shared by all persistent objects. Some of these methods follow:
   - Constructors new with various parameters to instantiate and store persistent objects; these parameters include the location of the object: where the created object should be stored, access rights on the object, etc.
   - Methods to destroy the persistent object or delete it from the persistent object space
   - Methods to Read the state of an object, or the current values of its instance variable; given a reference to an object or the object identity, these methods read the object from the database into variables in the programming language environment

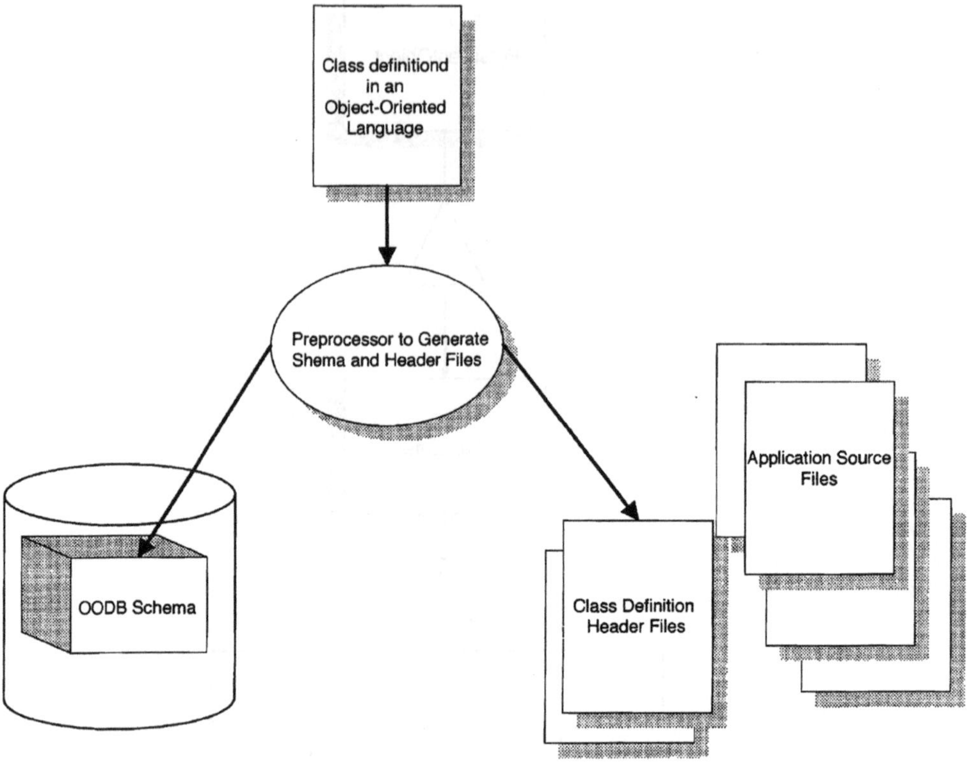

FIGURE 33.4 Preprocessing class definition to generate OODBMS schemata.

- Methods to Write, or Save, the modifications to object state back to the database
- Methods to Lock and Unlock the object to provide explicit congruency control on the object by the user

In the ODMG 2.0 C++ binding specification, a persistent capable class must inherit from the class d_Object. This class specifies a number of methods including methods to create new instances and delete them. For example, the class Performer can be defined as:

```
class Performer: public d_Object{
public:
         d_String           name;
         d_Boolean          available;
...
};
class GroupPerformer: public Performer{
...
};
```

2. Pre-processed or classes — With this approach, class definitions in an object-oriented language are pre-processed by a pre-processor provided by the object-oriented database vendor. The pre-processor introduces the meta-data in the database management system and, typically, also generates header files to be used by the database application. This is illustrated in Figure 33.4. There are, at least, two strategies to achieve this:
   - Use a data definition language to specify the persistent classes — One option is to use a different data definition language. This language can contain various database data definition constructs.

Some examples of such constructs include relationships, integrity constraints (e.g., unique keys), specification of physical database design (e.g., indexes), etc. The approach here is similar to the SQL DDL. In fact the ODMG 2.0 specifies an Object Definition Language (ODL) that is itself an extension of the IDL language of OMG. In fact many ORB implementation use a similar strategy, generating object-oriented language header and skeleton source files from IDL interface specifications.

- Pre-process class definitions in an object language — The other alternative is to define the meta-data in an object-oriented database binding for the object-oriented language. The persistent class definitions could include database specific constructs. These could be specified via constructs or classes (including template classes) supported by an OODBMS vendor, or they could potentially be specified through minor extensions to the object language. In either case, the persistent meta-data classes need to be pre-processed. The pre-processing defines the meta-data in the database and also generates header and potentially source files (skeletons). The application code then can be written using these classes. The generated object code then gets linked with the runtime libraries of the object-database to generate the application executable.

33.7 Defining Persistent Objects

Just because a class is persistent does not automatically mean all the instances created by the class are persistent. It could be the case, but not always. There are a number of mechanisms for specifying persistent objects.

1. Persistent extensions — The notion of a persistent extension has always been a fundamental assumption in database management systems. In conventional DBMSs (such as relational), when the user defines a schema using a data-definition language (such as the DDL of SQL), persistent extensions define both a structure and an extension. In object-oriented languages users define the structure of objects through the class construct. A class is like a type in a conventional programming language, except that the class specifies the behavior (operations, or methods) of objects, as well as their structure. Most object-oriented databases also use classes to define the structure of objects and their methods. The most essential function of a database management system is to allow users to store, manipulate, and iterate over bulk data. Because a class represents a category of objects all of the same "type," it is useful to have persistent class extensions and treat the class as an Abstract data Type constructor *and* as the container of all its instances.

   Object-oriented database management systems which support persistent extensions typically have iterators or other constructs to traverse (navigate) the persistent instances of the class. Object-oriented databases that support persistent extensions have at least three methods by which an object is created:

   - Every time an instance of a persistent class is created it is automatically inserted into the extension.
   - Specify an object as persistent the moment the object is created; this could be specified, for example in the NEW, constructor of the object.
   - Require an explicit Write or Save operation to save the object to the persistent database.

   Persistent extensions are very well defined and an established concept. It is so fundamental in relational databases, and hence, object-relational databases support it as well. It is also supported in many object-oriented databases. The ODMG 2.0 ODL has a special key word extent that can be used in the definition of a class to indicate the class will have an extension. In fact, the C++ binding of the ODMG 2.0 standard supports the interface of extensions through the template class d_Extent<T> , where T is a persistent capable class. This template class provides a number of interface methods to access and manipulate the extension as a collection of objects:

```
template <class T> class d_Extent
{
public:
```

```
    unsigned long cardinality() const;
            ...
    d_ref<T>
    select_element(const char * OQL_pred) const;
            ...
    d_extent<T>&
    operator=(const d_Extent<T> &);
};
```

2. Persistence through reachability — The approach in this strategy is to have one or more persistent database roots and make every object reachable from these roots persistent. Programming or database languages typically incorporate different type constructors for tuples (record, aggregate, structure, etc.) and collection objects (set, bag, list, array, etc.). Starting with some persistent, typically uniquely named, database "roots," reachability can be defined transitively using this collection/aggregation model. More specifically, if O is persistent, then every property of O is also persistent. Properties of O could be:

   Relationships with other objects or object-valued attributes; reachability here implies all the objects referenced by the persistent object are also persistent.

   The property could be a collection or set of objects or a many-relationship. In this case all the elements of the collection or the many relationships are also persistent.

   Thus with reachability we start with persistent roots and navigate, via object valued attributes, collection valued attributes, or relationships, to other objects, making every reachable object a persistent object in the database. Figure 33.5 illustrates persistent through reachability.

   Persistence through reachability is very popular. It is used in a number of object database implementations. In fact both the Smalltalk and Java binding in ODMG 2.0 specify persistence through reachability. It is elegant because as soon as an object gets created and becomes accessible from a persistent ancestor it becomes automatically persistent. When the transaction that created the object commits, other subsequent accesses and transactions will see the persistent object. Persistent through reachability can work in conjunction with other persistent object-space definition techniques.

3. Persistent instances — Given a persistent capable class, there are a number of alternative approaches that can be used to render particular instances, maybe all, of the class persistent. As mentioned above, one is to impose the restriction whenever an instance of a persistent capable class — a class in the schema — is created, it is automatically rendered to be persistent. Every object that gets created is in the persistent extension of the class. This has been the case in traditional database technology. A table defined in SQL presents both the intention (structure) and extension (the tables). There is no concept or capability to create a "row" in SQL that is not persistent. An alternative approach, as discussed in (2), is to have objects become persistent through reachability. Here also there are variations. For example, we require that in order for an object to become persistent it must both be created through a persistent constructor new and, at the same time, become reachable from a persistent root. On the other hand, we can have a strategy where objects become persistent if and only if they are reachable from a persistent root. There are other alternatives.

   One mechanism is to have a persistent instance strategy and render particular instances persistent either by explicitly declaring them to be persistent or by making an existing object persistent through a function call. With this approach persistence is not a property of classes; rather the user can construct databases, or storage extents, and "place" persistent objects in them. The specification of declaring which objects (instances) are persistent can potentially be completely independent of the class definition. This is of course almost an anomaly in database technology, where the bulk of the functionality is dedicated to the management of large collections of objects with meta-data. Here potentially each object can carry its own definition ("meta-data"). Potentially this approach does not even need the pre-processing phase of generating meta-data.

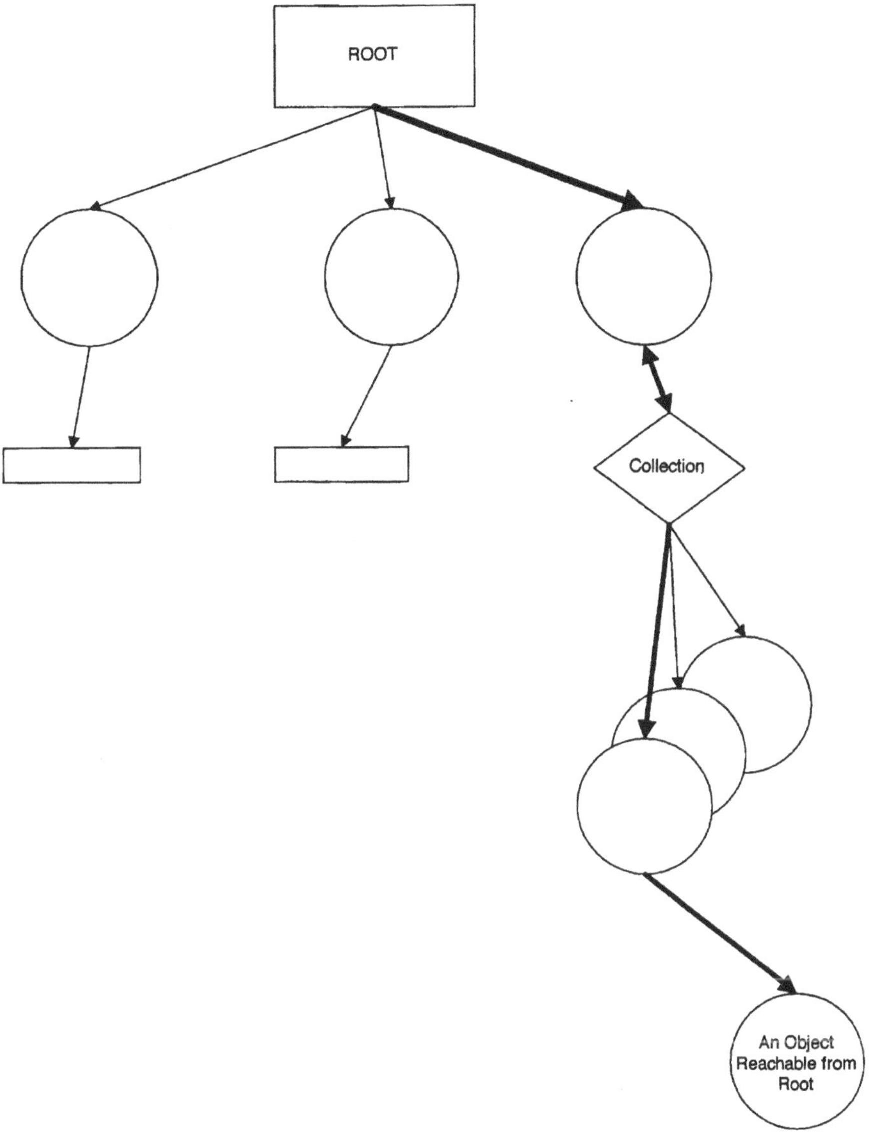

FIGURE 33.5 Persistence through reachability.

This mechanism works well with the persistence through reachability approach. Some entry point(or root) objects will have either references to other objects or contain sets of other objects. These objects will also be persistent through reachability. For instance if the sales person John is an entry point or a root then objects reachable from John such as his customers or his office are all persistent. However, unlike schema (or meta-data) based approaches, the persistence property is associated with particular instances.

It should also be pointed out that not all object-oriented systems are class based, where every object is the instance of a class. There are delegation based actor models, where there is no distinction between classes and objects, and persistence in this context applies only to objects.

4. Persistent and transient properties (or members) — Persistent object-oriented systems allow some of the properties to be always transient, even if they pertain to a persistent object. Thus the declaration of the peristent capable class will indicate:
   - The pP persistent properties that will be used to store and retrieve persistent attribute values or persistent relationships
   - The tP transient properties that can contain transient attributes, pointers, and transient relationships

   When a persistent object is read from persistent storage to the working space of an application, the tP transient properties need to be re-initialized and set to point to values or structures of the current application working space, in the context of an application session.

33.8 Persistent Object Spaces and Object Identity

As mentioned earlier, one of the most fundamental aspects of persistence in object-oriented systems is the ability to make references or object pointers persistent. Persistent languages should support persistence of any type of object. Object references (and referential sharing) are supported through the strong notion of object identity. What is object identity? Identity is that property of an object that distinguishes it from all other objects. The identity of an object should be independent of the location of an object, the name of an object, the state (values of attributes) of an object, or the class of an object.

Conceptually, each instance of a class, each object, has an identity. The identifier is associated with the object at object creation time and remains associated with the object irrespective of any state or type modifications undergone by the object. Each identifier can be associated with one and only one object. Furthermore, if there is an identifier in the system it *must* be associated with an object. In other words, an object and its identifiers are indistinguishable. The identifier uniquely identifies the object and the object remains associated with an identifier throughout its lifetime.

Therefore, each object is a triplet:

1. The object is an instance of a class; this indicates the object's type
2. The object has an identity; a unique identifier that gets associated with the object
3. The object has a state; the state of an object is the object value of its instance variables — its based valued properties and its relationships to other objects.

33.9 Persistent Objects in Various Spaces

Object-oriented programming languages have persistent specifications in ODMG 2.0 that extend the language with persistence. At a given time an application is accessing only a strict subset of the entire persistent object space, that is concurrently shared by many application sessions. There are therefore potentially many "copies" of the same object accessed in various application sessions.

The persistent objects in the database need to be somehow mapped to application objects that are manipulated in the address space of the application session. Furthermore, when the object states or object relationships of persistent objects are updated in an application transaction that commits, then they need to be saved back to the persistent concurrently shared database. There are many approaches to achieve this. Here we briefly mention three popular strategies.

1. Reading and writing objects through methods — The most straightforward approach is to have a number of methods to explicitly read a persistent object into an object in the application's address space, possibly make modifications, and then through a method explicitly write the object back to the persistent shared database.
2. Pointer swizzling — This is an elegant and seamless approach. When object references (pointers) are accessed or traversed, the underlying object database system brings the accessed object from the persistent storage into the (virtual) memory address space of the application program. This

is done automatically by the underlying OODBMS system. The converse, writing the object back to persistent storage, is called unswizzling. This approach works very well with reachability.

3. Object tables — Another approach is to maintain an object table that maps each object reference or object identity onto a memory address. Thus each object access will require first a lookup in the object table, and then an indirection through an object table that has to go through an extra level of indirection to access the object in the address space of the application. Here the objects can be accessed either through methods, where given a reference to an object (its identity) the method returns the object's memory address, or the implementation of the object system can make this seamless for the user application which is similar to the pointer swizzling scheme.

33.10 Implementing Object Identity

One of the most important aspects in understanding the implementation of the persistent object system is the implementation techniques for object identity (Khoshafian and Copeland, 1986). Several implementation strategies have been used to support object identity, including the use of identifier keys and the use of a virtual or physical address as identity. These strategies can be used as the underlying implementation techniques supporting the more complete object identity concept.

A powerful technique for supporting identity is through surrogates, or globally. Surrogates are system-generated, globally unique identifiers completely independent of object state or object address. Surrogates are persistent identifiers and can be used to access objects in persistent store. Surrogates should not be re-used. Conceptually an object identity associated with an object is independent of the object's name, state, type, or location address. The surrogate implementation strategy directly reflects the value, location, type, or name independence of object identity. With the surrogate strategy, each object of any type is associated with a globally unique surrogate at the instant it is instantiated. This surrogate is used to internally represent the identity of its object throughout the lifetime of the object. The surrogate implementation strategy uses indirection — given a surrogate we must still find the address of the object indicated by the surrogate. Object database implementations often use a data structure such as a B-tree or a hash-table to accelerate the surrogate to physical object storage access. Therefore each object in an application session has:

- A memory address: in the application session
- A persistent secondary storage address
- A surrogate, implementing object identity

33.11 Case Study: Persistent Java for Jasmine

The previous sections provided an overview of the basic concepts associated with persistence. We provide a brief description of a product that supports persistent Java for an object-oriented DBMS. This section therefore illustrates how some of the aforementioned constructs are manifested in an actual product that enables persistent programming in Java.

Jasmine™ (Khoshafian et al., 1998) from Computer Associates and Fujitsu is a next generation object-oriented database system. It integrates a number of key technologies that are going to be crucial for advanced applications in the next millennium. These technologies include distributed computing, multimedia, Internets/Intranet, and visual rapid application development environments.

pJ™ from Technology Deployment International, Inc. (TDI, 1997) is a Java persistence layer for Jasmine. pJ allows persistent database applications to be developed entirely in Java. All the persistent database capabilities and features of Jasmine are encapsulated in pJ Java classes.

pJ comes with a runtime library and a Java class hierarchy for persistent Java application development. Some of these classes include:

- Database — This class provides the methods to connect/disconnect with a persistent database. It also has methods for transaction control, querying, and looking up persistent objects with given object name.
- DBContainer — It defines a root abstract class for persistent object containers. It has an *oid* instance variable and various methods to activate a set from a persistent store like to get the oid of the persistent collection, to handle exceptions, etc.
- OQLQuery — It defines a class to prepare and execute an OQL query.
- Transaction — This class supports the transaction control functionality for Java applications. It has methods to start, commit, and start transactions.

These and many other classes are used to implement the methods of persistent Java classes as well as applications. Java classes that need to be made persistent capable are processed by pJ's Java Persistence Processor (JPP). This pJ utility generates two files: one for the Jasmine database to create the schema and the other which consists of augmented Java class definitions of the original classes that are extended for persistence. Using the augmented class definitions and the pJ utility classes, developers can implement the body of the methods for the persistent Java classes.

The overall structure of a persistent Java program will be:

```
public class persistent-application {
  public static void main(String args[]) {
    Database pDatabase = new Database();
    if (pDatabase.open(aDBName, ... )) {
      <persisetnt application-code>
      pDatabase.close();
    }
  }
```

After developing all the persistent application it is compiled with the Java compiler JAVAC. The pJ libraries — packages — need to be imported. Here is a declaration that imports the pJ packages:

```
import pJ.jasmine.*;
```

The byte code that is generated by the Java compiler uses the pJ runtime library, and probably other Java libraries, when it is executed on a Java virtual machine. During the execution of the application by the Java virtual machine, the pJ runtime libraries handle all the interfaces to the underlying Jasmine object-oriented database engine including database connections, transactions, querying, etc. Figure 33.6 shows a runtime system configuration in the simplest form. The Java database classes are made persistence capable by pJ's JPP, as discussed above.

We use a simple example to illustrate how to write database applications in Java using pJ. This example is part of an application for designing music CDs. We give one class definition and two trivial Java programs making use of this persistent Java class.

The Java source defining the Song class is shown below. It acts as both a Java class definition and a database schema definition. While the Java code is very simple and most of it is self-explanatory, we point out that, by stating that Song implements PRI, it indicates to JPP that it needs to be made persistence capable.

```
import java.io.*;
import java.awt.*;
import sun.audio.*;
import pJ.jasmine.*;
public class Song implements PRI {
  public static final int POP =1;
  public static final int ROCK =2;
```

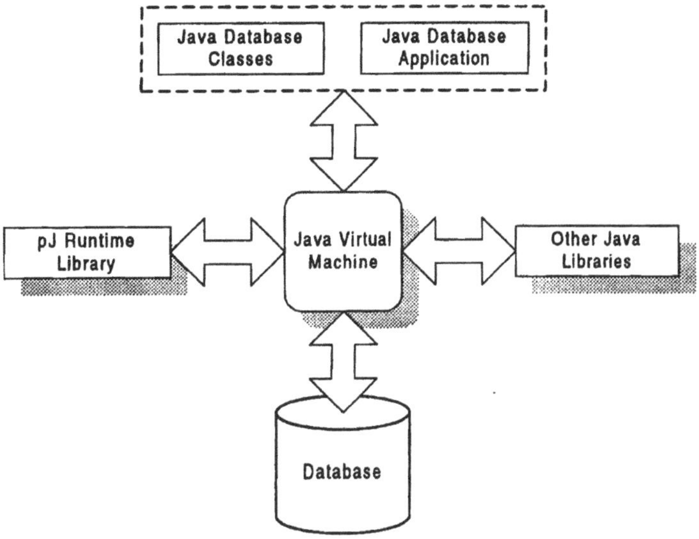

FIGURE 33.6 The pJ and Java environment.

```
public static final int COUNTRY =4;
public static final int JAZZ =8;
public static final int CLASSIC =16;
public static final int HEAVYMETAL =32;
public static final int FIRSTYEAR =1900;
public static final int LASTYEAR =2000;
public static final int THISYEAR =1997;
protected String name;
protected int style;
protected String performer;
protected String album;
protected MMImage picture;
protected MMAudio sound;
protected int year;
protected int length; // in seconds
protected String description;
public Song(String n, int t, String p, String a,
      String i, String s, int y, int l, String d) {
  name = n;
  if (POP <= t && t <= HEAVYMETAL) {
    style = t;
  } else {
    style = POP;
  }
  performer = p;
  album = a;
  description = d;
  if (FIRSTYEAR <= y && y <= LASTYEAR) {
    year = y;
  } else {
    year = THISYEAR;
  }
```

```
        length = 1;
        picture = new MMImage(n);
        sound = new MMAudio(n);
        try {
          picture.importData(i);
          sound.importData(s);
        } catch (FileNotFoundException e) {
          System.out.println("FileNotFound exception");
        } catch (IOException e) {
          System.out.println("IOException");
        } catch (SecurityException e) {
          System.out.println("SecurityException");
        }
      }
      public Image getImage() {
        Image ii =null;
        MMImage mm = picture;
        if (mm != null) {
          ii = mm.createImage();
        }
        return (ii);
      }
      public AudioStream getAudio() {
        AudioStream aa =null;
        MMAudio mm = sound;
        if (mm != null) {
          aa = mm.createAudio();
        }
        return (aa);
      }
    }
```

Persistent objects can be created using the persistent object creation method generated by JPP. Persistent objects are also created through reachability. For example, by having a persistent object referencing a transient object, the transient object becomes persistent upon transaction commit.

In addition to being a Java persistence facility, pJ also provides strong multimedia database (Khoshafian and Baker, 1996) as well distributed Web-centric application development facilities. Multimedia data, such as images and sounds, are encapsulated as MMImage and MMAudio objects, which are persistent Jasmine objects. They are used in Java applications as if they were ordinary Java objects. It is also worth pointing out that Java classes such as MMImage and MMAudio are made persistence capable by pJ itself. For client server applications, pJ comes with built-in support for Java Remote Object Invocation (RMI). One can easily write an application in such a way that the Java can either run locally with the database, or remotely as a client communicating with an RMI server, as the comments in the sample code indicate. Furthermore, using the client/server support of pJ, a database application can be activated from within a Web browser as an applet and all the Java code can be downloaded dynamically from the server. Finally, we show a simple Java program that retrieves all of the Song objects from the database and plays the music using the AudioPlayer class from the package sun.audio.

```
import java.util.*;
import sun.audio.*;
import pJ.jasmine.*;
public class playSongs {
  public static void main(String argv[]) {
    Database aDatabase;
    if (argv.length == 1) { // argv[0]: RMI server name
```

34

Object Database Management

Mary E.S. Loomis
Hewlett-Packard Laboratories

34.1 Introduction

Object Database Management Systems (DBMSs) are fundamental elements in the broad suite of object technologies, yet they remain relatively unfamiliar to many people who consider themselves quite expert in the object technology field. A DBMS, the technology that manages databases, is classic "middleware." The DBMS sits between application programs and data storage. More obvious to the majority of object technologists are the OO programming languages (e.g., Java, C++, Smalltalk, Eiffel), OO methods (e.g., UML, OPEN, SOMA), and object interaction technologies (e.g., ActiveX/DCOM, CORBA IDL/ORBs, IBM's SOM/DSOM).

0-8493-3135-8/99/$0.00+$.50

An object DBMS provides the same kinds of functionality for objects that the previous generations of DBMSs have provided for records. Perhaps a primary reason that object DBMSs have remained relatively unfamiliar to the growing masses of object programmers and analysts is that with some effort, relational DBMSs (e.g., Oracle, Informix, Sybase, DB2) can also be used to store objects. Because many companies already have significant experience with relational DBMSs, their first inclination is typically to use that kind of DBMS with their object applications. It is important that the decision of what kind of DBMS to use be made with full understanding of the alternatives, and using an object DBMS is an important alternative.

My objective in writing this chapter is to describe how object and relational DBMSs are the same and how they are different, so that developers and managers will be better informed about their trade offs. In some situations, the best decision is clearly to use a relational DBMS with object applications. In other situations, an object DBMS is clearly a better choice. Better understanding of trade offs should lead to better designs and implementations, which should result in better applications for all of us to enjoy.

34.2 Several Kinds of Applications have Driven the Object DBMS Market

A fundamental characteristic of an object DBMS is that it uses an object programming language as its primary interface to applications. By contrast, a relational DBMS uses its own language, SQL, which can be embedded in other programming languages. Only very recently have relational DBMSs supported embedding of SQL in object programming languages; they have concentrated instead on the more conventional languages, e.g., COBOL and C. Therefore, the first users of object DBMSs were application developers using C++ or Smalltalk who wanted persistent storage for their application objects. The relational DBMSs did not meet these programmers' language interface needs.

The first big market approached by the object DBMS vendors was the Computer-Aided Design (CAD) vendors. CAD products traditionally used the underlying file system (typically Unix) for persistent storage of the data associated with designs. As the CAD vendors increasingly addressed their users' needs for shared access to that design data, the CAD vendors began to write their own database mechanisms. Most of them did not use relational DBMSs, because they could not get the levels of performance their products needed.

Obviously the relational DBMSs were well able to deliver satisfactory performance for the kinds of applications in which they were usually deployed — on-line transaction processing (OLTP) and decision support systems (DSS). However, the characteristics of the CAD data and applications are quite different from the OLTP and DSS characteristics. One source of the performance problems was the complexity of representing and accessing the design models in the tabular form required by relational DBMSs. Another source was the mismatch between the relational DBMS's client-server model and the typical CAD application's characteristic of focusing the bulk of its data processing on the desktop. We will return to these performance issues later. At about the same time, many of the CAD vendors were moving from use of the C programming language to use of C++. The early object DBMS products became an attractive alternative for CAD vendors to use.

A second big market for the object DBMS vendors was the network management area. The products used to manage large computer and telecommunications systems require access to information about the elements in those networks and their configurations and interconnections. Object DBMSs were recognized as a good fit for the database needs of network management. In the CAD case, there was synergy between the two concurrent factors of moving to C++ and needing shared databases, at a time when relational DBMSs provided neither the C++ interfaces, nor sufficient performance for CAD data. In the network management case, there was synergy between the same two concurrent factors. Programmers were moving to C++ and they encountered significant complexities (and associated performance problems) representing their network configuration models in relational databases.

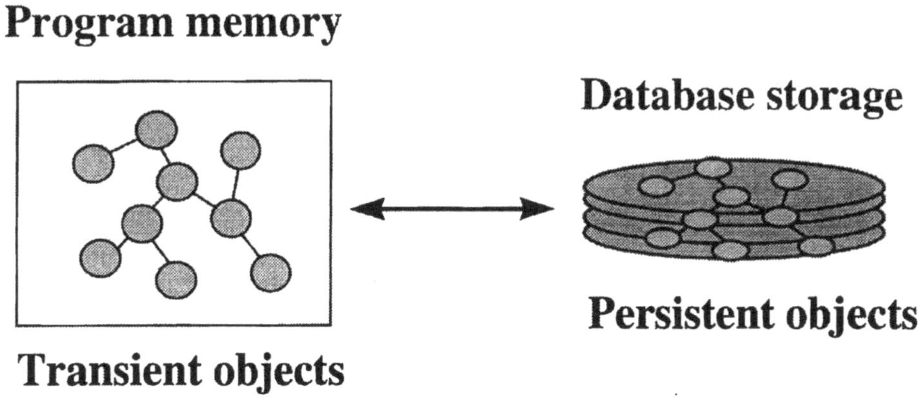

FIGURE 34.1 Making objects persistent.

More recently, explosion in use of the Internet and access to multimedia data using Web-browsing technologies have provided additional boosts to the object DBMS market. An object database is well suited to storage of web pages, because the inter-page links and multimedia content are the kinds of data that can be relatively simply represented in an object database. By contrast, representing these relationships and data types in a relational database can be quite complex.

Let's look more carefully now at these database technologies, using the approach of comparing and contrasting the object and relational DBMS approaches. This discussion will not get to the level of detail of comparing particular products, rather the two families will be discussed in general terms. Thus some of the specifics that apply to particular products of interest may not be covered. However, understanding the characteristics and trade offs between the two families will provide the foundation for quite easily progressing to understanding particular products.

34.3 Objects can be made Persistent as Records on Files

A primary reason to use an object DBMS is to make objects persistent. A store of persistent objects is called an *object database*, and the system that manages them is the *object DBMS*. We will use the term *object* as simply a short-hand for *instance of a class*. Persistence is required if an object created using a programming language variable is to be retained and accessible after the creating run-unit terminates. Applications typically do not require that all the objects they create become persistent, but commonly many objects will be accessed by either other applications or other executions of the same application. An object DBMS stores objects on non-volatile memory (Figure 34.1). Those objects persist even when the power supply is turned off.

An application programmer could also write objects to a file, using an operating system function or utility. This is a non-database way to make data persistent. Smalltalk provides a fileOut method that writes the snapshot of the current Image to a file. The Image contains the current state of all the objects created by the Smalltalk run-unit. There is a corresponding fileIn method for later accessing that Image and making it current.

C++ does not provide such a method, so the programmer is responsible for ensuring that objects are written to the file in a way that preserves their structure. A record in a file is flat, i.e., just a string of bits, which may or may not be grouped together in various ways to represent different simple data types, like integer, real, character, etc. If a class has internal, non-flat structure, for example, an embedded array or linked list or tree, then the programmer must write code to transform that multidimensional structure to a flattened sequence of fields which can be written in a record (Figure 34.2). Alternatively, the code might transform the class's multidimensional structure to a multiple flat records. Whatever

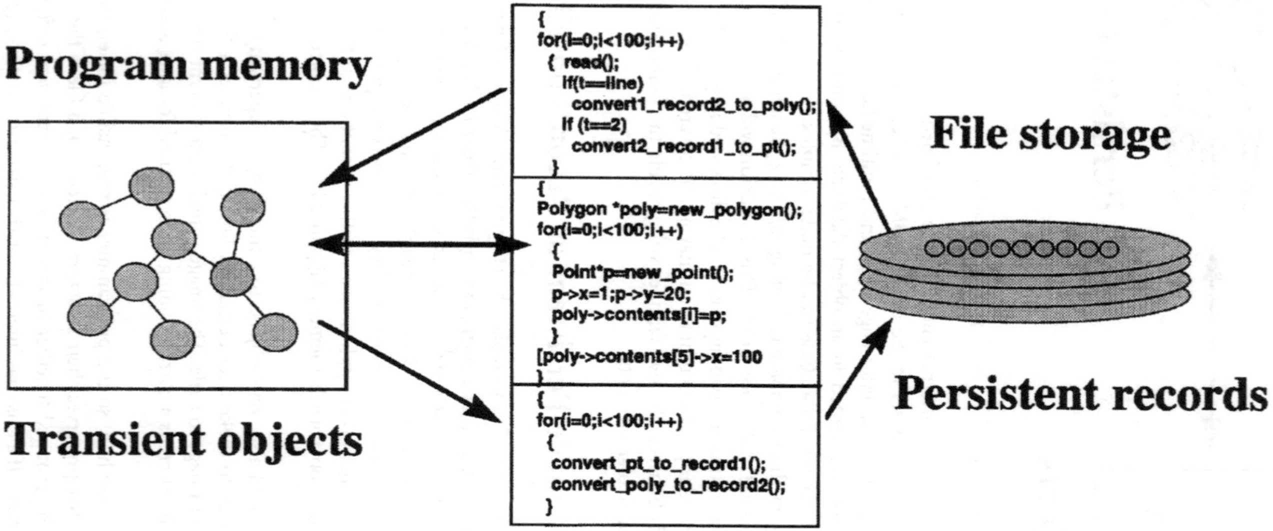

FIGURE 34.2 File system transformations.

technique is used to transform an object into a file record or records, any application that reads that object from the file must include the corresponding code to re-structure the object from its flattened form.

While the logic and code to implement these transformations can become quite complex, the enduring challenge is to keep the pair of transformations consistent. If for any reason a programmer changes the flattened structure written to the file, it is imperative that the code expecting to read the file and create an object be changed accordingly. Not keeping paired transformations consistent has been the source of many nasty bugs. The representation of the class on the file must be treated as a controlled interface.

While the file system provides persistence, it does not provide sharability. DBMSs provide functionality to ensure that multiple applications and run-units can access the same data concurrently, without interfering with each other. The DBMS serves as a middleware layer between applications and the file system, coordinating multiple applications accessing data in the same file. The DBMS also manages the distributed database situation, where the objects needed by an application are stored in multiple files, resident on multiple nodes of a network. Because the DBMS provides this functionality, each programmer does not have to.

It is convenient to consider the DBMS alternatives for object persistence in four categories: relational DBMS, object DBMS, object-relational gateway, and extended-relational DBMS. Each of these has its own strengths and weaknesses, relative to providing persistent, sharable objects. Products are commercially available in each category.

34.4 Using a Relational DBMS to Manage Shared Objects

One alternative is to store objects in a relational database, e.g., using Oracle, Sybase, and DB2. These DBMSs provide SQL access to data, with robust functionality for transaction management, security, backup and recovery, etc. Many tools are available to help in the design, implementation, and administration of relational databases and the applications that access them. A primary indicator that a relational DBMS may be the most appropriate alternative for storing objects is if the data already reside in a relational database. In this case, an application written using an object programming language would access data that other applications previously had stored using SQL. Even if the data are already in a relational database, there are some situations when it is appropriate to periodically copy those data to an object database for access by object applications.

There are potentially three issues when using a relational DBMS to store objects. First, just as in the direct use of records on files to get object persistence, the application programmer must write the code to transform objects to rows in relational tables (Figure 34.3). Because relational table rows are flat, multidimensional object structures must be flattened. Because relational table rows reference each other only by the values stored in their fields, the programmer must encode any inter-object links, references, or pointers into field values. Depending on the complexity and dynamics of the class hierarchy, these transformations will be more or less difficult to design, implement, and maintain.

A second potential issue is performance, for two reasons. If the transformations between class structures and relational tables are complex, then processing those transformations will take time. This processing can be expensive if table joins are required to reconstruct inter-object links, references, or pointers from field values. The other source of potential performance problems comes from the fact that many relational DBMSs are optimized for OLTP applications. OLTP applications tend to have high volumes of short, value-based accesses, each of which touches only a relatively small number of table rows. For example, the classic OLTP transaction is a debit or credit to a particular bank account. If the application has other characteristics, then the optimization for OLTP-style accesses won't be of benefit. For example, a non-OLTP-style access navigates long sequences of inter-object linkages, perhaps to construct maps from network configuration data.

A third potential issue is use of SQL to access objects. SQL is the database language interface provided by a relational DBMS. If developers want to use SQL, then this is a non-issue. If developers do not want to use SQL, then this can be a big issue. A large number of object programmers would prefer to stick

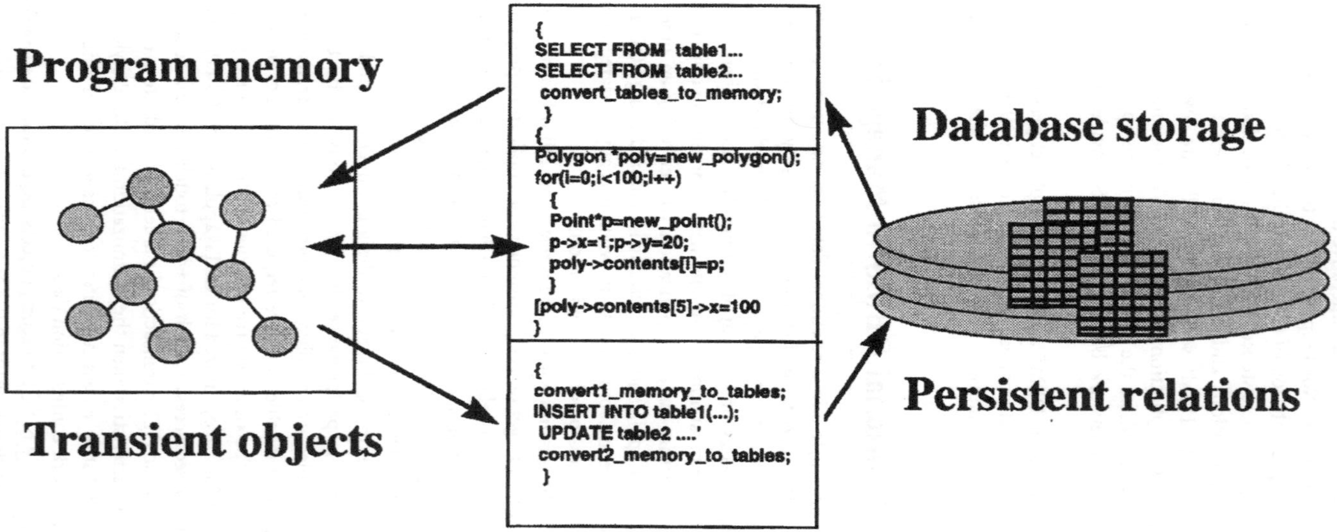

FIGURE 34.3 Relational database transformations.

with their object programming language and to use that language to manipulate objects, whether those objects are persistent or not.

34.5 Using an Object DBMS to Manage Shared Objects

Another alternative for managing shared objects is to use an object DBMS. A primary difference between an object DBMS and a relational DBMS is their language interfaces. While a relational DBMS uses SQL, an object DBMS uses an object programming language. Use of the same language implies that both the object DBMS and the object programming language compiler (or interpreter) use the same object model. In contrast, a relational DBMS has its own model, the tabular model of relations. Examples of commercially available object DBMSs are Gemstone, Objectivity, ObjectStore, and VERSANT. There are many others.

Potential advantages of using an object DBMS stem from two sources: its use of the object programming language and its architecture. Because an object DBMS uses an object programming language as its application interface, the object programmer uses the same language syntax to access all objects, regardless of whether they are persistent or transient. Such an interface is sometimes described as being *seamless*. For C++ or Smalltalk programmers who do not want to use SQL, a seamless interface to an object database is a real advantage. The seamless interface via C++, Smalltalk, or Java is not an advantage for developers who do want to use SQL or SQL-based tools. For this reason, the major object DBMS products now also support SQL access to persistent objects.

Application performance can also benefit from the object DBMS using the object programming language as its interface and therefore the same object model as the programming language. The argument here is the inverse of the discussion above about the second potential issue in using a relational DBMS to store objects. Using a consistent object model for both the programming language and database access enables the application to avoid transformation processing. Inter-object links, references, and sometimes pointers can be stored directly in the object database. If the application navigates long sequences of inter-object linkages, an object DBMS may deliver significantly better performance than a relational DBMS.

Another major difference between object and relational DBMSs is their architectures. Not all the relational DBMSs have the same architecture, nor do all the object DBMSs. However, there is enough in common within each of these types that some general statements can be made. Nearly all DBMSs today use a client-server architecture. They differ in how much of the database processing responsibility is allocated to the client and to the server processes, respectively.

Relational DBMSs typically do very little processing on the client side, with most of the database functionality on the server side. Object DBMSs typically assign more of the responsibility to the client side. Some execute the great majority of their functions on the client side while others have a more balanced assignment of processing. If the application is heavily client-oriented, then a DBMS that does more of its processing on the client side may deliver better performance than if the application continually must access a server database. There may also be performance advantages if the object DBMS moves objects from persistent storage directly into an application's address space, without using a database buffer space, thereby avoiding later copying from the buffer to application variables.

34.6 Using an Object-Relational Gateway to Manage Shared Objects

The third alternative for object persistence with sharability is to use an object-relational gateway. Such a gateway is a middleware layer that maps classes to relations (Figure 34.4). The software enables a program written in an object programming language to store and retrieve objects in a relational database, without having to code all the details of the logic that maps those objects to and from table rows. Two examples of object-relational gateway products are Persistence and ObjectLens. Persistence maps between

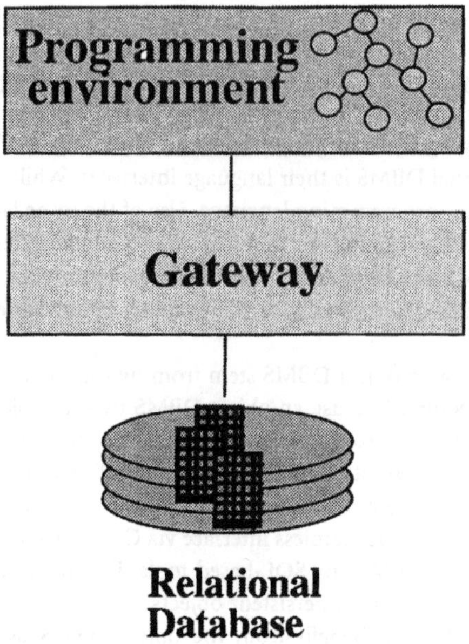

FIGURE 34.4 Object-relational gateway.

C++ or Java and a variety of relational DBMSs. ObjectLens maps between Smalltalk and relational DBMSs.

A primary advantage of using an object-relational gateway is that it can significantly ease the programming burden of using an object programming language to access data that already reside in a relational database. One way to think of such a gateway is as a library that encapsulates the mapping logic, plus the logic of managing connections to the DBMS. Many application development organizations that use relational DBMSs and C++ or Smalltalk write this type of library themselves, so that the code becomes more sharable among their programmers. The object-relational gateway vendors provide commercial sources of these libraries.

There are two potential issues in using an object-relational gateway: performance and mapping complexity. If the processing required to execute the object-relational mappings does not disappear, the mappings still must be executed. Development time can be improved, because the application programmer can leverage the code provided by the gateway, but runtime execution of the mappings is still required. Performance probably will not be much different from the case of using the relational DBMS directly.

It may be difficult to represent complex mappings between classes and tables, depending upon the expressive capabilities of the object-relational gateway. In some cases, the developer may need to write mapping code, while also using the gateway for some of its other functionality.

34.7 Using an Extended-Relational DBMS to Manage Shared Objects

The fourth alternative for object persistence with sharability is to use an extended-relational DBMS. There is a definite trend for the relational DBMS products to incorporate object management capabilities. The DBMS vendors are extending their relational products to interface well with object programming languages and to be able to manage some of the semantics of the object model. Two example extended-relational DBMS products are the Informix Universal Server and Oracle Database Version 8.

Two early extensions of "traditional" relational DBMS capabilities were stored procedures and BLOBs. By using augmenting SQL with programming logic constructs (e.g., looping, conditionals), the developer could define procedures to be compiled and executed by the DBMS. The big advantage is that these procedures become sharable by the multiple programmers who use the relational database with that code under database administrator control. However, it can still be relatively difficult to determine whether the logic that a particular programmer needs has already been coded in a stored procedure, or to determine which stored procedures affect a particular relational table. Only recently have the ISO/ANS SQL committees addressed standardization of SQL extensions for declaring procedures.

BLOBs extend SQL to understand the data type *binary large object.* This extension enables the programmer to store data in a relational database that otherwise would not "fit" in the set of conventional SQL data types. However, the logic to interpret the contents of the BLOBs must be encoded into the programs that access them. Thus a BLOB is quite a primitive type, with no inherent semantics.

More recent extensions to the relational model that are now being revealed in extended-relational DBMS products include subtables, structured data types, and inter-table relationships. The subtable construct approximates subclassing. Structured data types, e.g., arrays, accommodate some non-flat rows. Inter-table relationships are used to represent inter-object references directly, rather than indirectly, by pairings of field values. Each of these extensions brings the relational model closer to being able to represent the semantics of an object model.

As the extended-relational DBMS products increasingly embrace object semantics, it becomes more difficult to distinguish them from object databases. One big difference in philosophy persists, the application programming interface. The relational DBMS community views SQL as the *lingua franca* of persistent data. SQL is headed in the direction of becoming a full-function object programming language. By contrast, the object DBMS community views the object programming languages as the most appropriate interfaces to objects. Nonetheless, nearly all the object DBMS vendors have added some or all of the SQL interfaces to their products.

It is difficult to talk about the extended-relational DBMS products in general, because they still are quite different from each other. The unifier will be standardization of SQL to object declaration and manipulation capabilities. Some time will pass before all the products adhere to the standards, especially as they are still evolving. Meanwhile, we will focus on comparing object DBMSs and relational DBMSs. To understand a particular extended-relational DBMS, try to determine how it compares to these two end-member types.

34.8 Summarizing the Differences

The primary difference between an object DBMS and a relational DBMS is that one supports an object model and the other the relational table model. Because an object DBMS supports an object model, it uses an object programming language directly to provide access to persistent objects. The result is a relatively seamless interface between the database and the programming language space. The programmer can use basically the same syntax for both persistent and transient objects.

Because a relational DBMS supports the relational model, it uses SQL for defining and manipulating databases. SQL is highly tuned to table structures. The relational architectural model is that the database is quite separate from any particular application program, and it should be considered a separate resource. The programmer should use the database language to encode database work, and he should use some other programming language for other kinds of operations.

34.9 Mapping Type Hierarchies to Relational Tables

Before considering the architectural differences between object and relational DBMSs in more detail, let's look at an example of mapping a type hierarchy to relational tables. This is a simple example, but illustrative of some of the choices the developer must make if objects are to be stored in relational tables.

The choices made for mapping between the object and relational logical structures (which we will call *schemas*) determine the logic of the code required to access the stored data.

Consider an extremely simple type hierarchy with supertype Employee and subtypes HourlyEmployee and SalariedEmployee. Assume that each of these types has its typical attributes and methods. Let's assume we are designing a relational database to store instances of the classes that implement these types in some object programming language.

One mapping that immediately comes to mind is to map each type to a table. The result here would be three tables, i.e.,

1. Employee (*socNo*, empName, birthDate, deptNo)
2. HourlyEmployee (*socNo*, hourlyRate, overtimeRate, maxOvertimeHrs)
3. SalariedEmployee (*socNo*, monthlyRate, bonusPct)

The fields that form the primary key in each table are underscored. These three tables capture the data in the original three types, but lose some of the meaning or semantics. Lost are

- The type-subtype relationship between the tables — If less meaningful names were given to these tables, it would not be obvious that each row in HourlyEmployee must have a corresponding row in Employee, and that a row in Employee must have one and only one corresponding row in either HourlyEmployee or SalariedEmployee.
- The mutual exclusiveness of the subtypes — It is not at all obvious (again, especially with less meaningful naming) that a socNo value that appears in a row in HourlyEmployee cannot appear in a row in SalariedEmployee.
- The relationship between the Employee type and the Department type — This is now encoded in the presence of the deptNo in the Employee table, and must match a value for a corresponding field in some Department table.

If these semantics are lost from the table definitions, how are they enforced in the database? This is the programmer's responsibility. Each application program that adds, deletes, or changes rows in these tables must be aware of the constraints and code accordingly. Otherwise, as the semantic constraints are violated, the result is called a *corrupted database.*

Another alternative that avoids the first set of losses above is to map each leaf type to a table. The result here would be two tables, i.e.,

1. HourlyEmployee (*socNo*, empName, birthDate, deptNo, hourlyRate, overtimeRate, maxOvertime-Hrs)
2. SalariedEmployee (*socNo*, empName, birthDate, deptNo, monthlyRate, bonusPct)

This mapping still suffers from the loss indicated above. It becomes the programmer's responsibility to ensure that a socNo value that appears in a row in HourlyEmployee does not appear in a row in SalariedEmployee.

Yet another alternative is to flatten the type hierarchy into a single table:

Employee (*socNo*, empName, birthDate, deptNo, hourlyRate, overtimeRate, maxOvertimeHrs, monthlyRate, bonusPct)

Now the challenge is for the programmer to ensure that only the correct combinations of fields have null and non-null values. A row for an hourly employee should have null values for the monthlyRate and bonusPct fields. A row for a salaried employee should have null values for the hourlyRate, overtimeRate, and maxOvertimeHrs fields. Typically a typeCode field would be included in the table layout, so that the program could easily test which type of employee is represented by a particular row. A typeCode field, e.g., empType, would be a clue that there is a subtype relationship buried in the table.

While this is a simplistic example, it illustrates the loss of semantics that occurs when mapping from one type system to another simpler type system. To preserve the semantic constraints and consistency

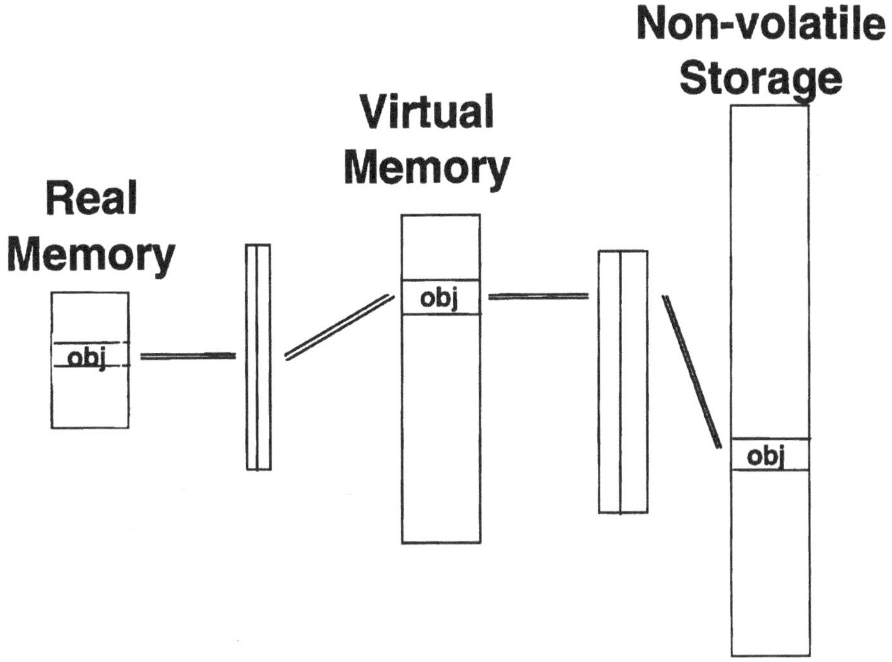

FIGURE 34.5 Extending virtual memory.

of the richer type system, the logic must be added to the simpler system. This "adding on" is done by the application programmer when the system involved is a relational DBMS.

Other issues arise when taking an existing relational database structure and mapping its semantics to a class hierarchy. It is typically insufficient just to look at the database table structures, especially if poor naming schemes have been used. It may be necessary to examine application code to detect type-subtype relationships and inter-type associations.

34.10 Memory Models: Single-Level vs. Multi-Level

Now let's turn to architectural considerations. One way to think of an object DBMS is as a means of extending virtual memory into the network. Operating systems extended real memory to virtual memory, freeing programmers from many of the considerations of managing main memory. The operating system took on the responsibility of mapping from the program's address space to the available real memory space, using mechanisms like paging. Similarly, an object DBMS extends virtual memory to include non-volatile storage, whether that storage is local to the processor or elsewhere on the network (Figure 34.5). The object DBMS takes on the responsibility of mapping object references across these "spaces." When an application program references an object, the combination of the language runtime and the object DBMS runtime fetch that object, whether the object is already in the program's address space or stored in a local database or in a remote database. The benefits to the application programmer are similar to the benefits enjoyed when a user clicks on a url on a Web page. The details of following all the various physical links involved in finding the way to that next page are hidden from the user and are managed by code specialized for that task.

A relational DBMS takes a somewhat different approach. If the DBMS manages distributed databases, then it may mask the details of whether the requested data are stored in a local database or a remote database. However, because SQL is used to access persistent data and a programming language is used

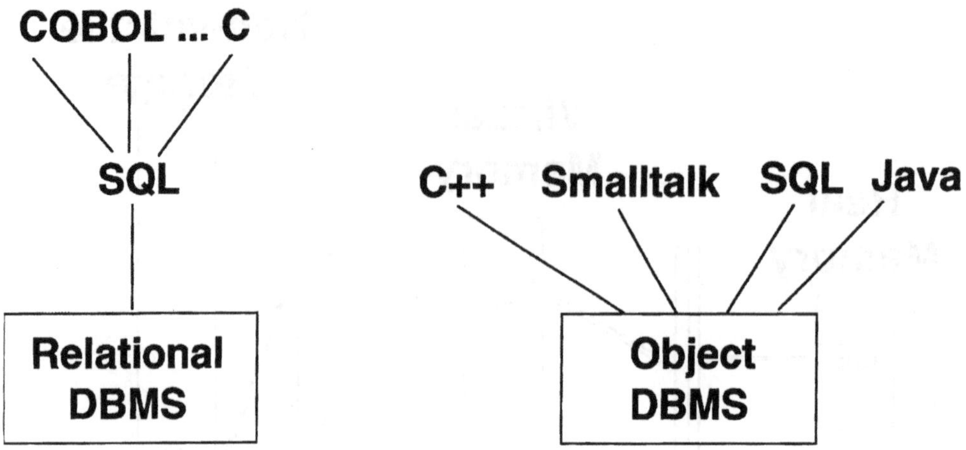

FIGURE 34.6 DBMS language bindings.

to access transient data, the programmer must constantly be aware of whether the desired data are currently in program variables or still on disk.

The object DBMS single-level memory approach necessitates a very close relationship between the DBMS runtime and the programming language runtime. The DBMS retrieves objects from the disk and places them in address space that is also accessible by the programming language, say C++. Otherwise, C++ could not be used directly to access the objects. Typically such a DBMS uses the C++ memory layout for objects as the layout scheme for those objects on disk. This tight binding has the benefit to the programmer of a seamless interface, as discussed above, and a performance benefit by avoiding transformations between the in-memory and on-disk layouts.

34.11 Supporting Multiple Programming Languages

Another challenge of this tight binding between the object DBMS and the programming language is the difficulty of having a single database support multiple programming languages. A fundamental characteristic of a relational database is that its contents can be accessed by applications written in any of a variety of programming languages. This multilingual access is relatively straightforward to provide, because the relational DBMS uses its own scheme for record layouts, both in its buffers in main memory and persistently on disk. SQL is used to access these records, and SQL can be embedded in many different programming languages (Figure 34.6).

There are two basic approaches used by object DBMSs to support multilingual access, if they support it at all. One approach is to introduce a neutral layout scheme, then transform objects coming off disk into the layouts expected by whatever language requests them. When new objects are placed on disk, they are converted from the language format to the DBMS's neutral layout scheme. This approach introduces a performance penalty on each disk access, due to the conversion processing. This is also the approach used by the relational DBMSs and requested tables are converted from their storage form to programming language variables.

A second approach is for the object DBMS to store a persistent object according to the layout scheme of the programming language used to create the object. In the great majority of cases, that object will be accessed in the future primarily by that same programming language and no conversion penalty will be incurred. In those relatively rare cases where an application written in a different programming language needs to access the object, the DBMS will perform the layout conversion. It would complicate

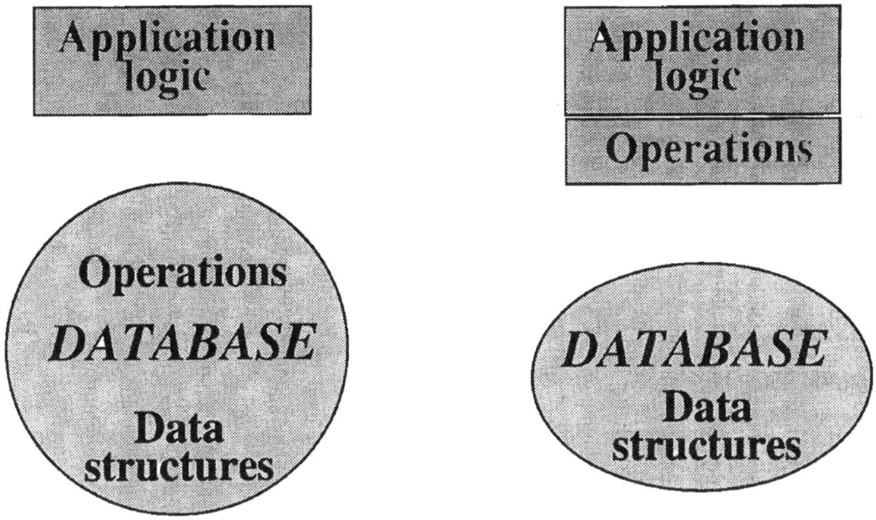

FIGURE 34.7 Storing object data structures vs. storing objects.

the DBMS's storage management tasks significantly to mix different layout schemes in the same physical database file, therefore, most object DBMSs do not. A physical object database typically stores only objects created with C++, or only objects created with Smalltalk, or only objects created with Java. This approach seems to be quite an acceptable solution for most customers. Increasingly, the object DBMS products allow an application program to open more than one physical object database, so conceivably the program could access objects that had been created in multiple programming languages.

34.12 Storing Objects or Storing Data Structures

We are not going to cover the details of how objects are actually laid out on storage by an object DBMS, primarily because each product has its own scheme. However, it is useful to understand which aspects of objects actually become persistent in an object database. One of the fundamental notions of object technology is that a type can have both state and behavior. The state is specified by *attributes* and the behavior is specified by *methods*. An implementation of a type is called a *class*. The state aspects of a class are represented by a *data structure* and the behavioral aspects are represented by *operations*. An object (i.e., instance of a class) populates the data structure with values for the attributes (sometimes called *instance variables*). The class' operations can be executed "on" any of the objects in that class.

Some object databases contain both aspects of classes, others contain only the data structures (Figure 34.7). In fact, the majority of object DBMSs that support C++ only store the data structures. The operations are defined in and managed by C++ and need to be included into application programs just like any other class libraries. The potential issue with this approach is that the operations need to be linked into the application programs wherever they execute. If the application is deployed on many different clients, and the implementation of a method changes, then that code must be redistributed to each of those clients. Moving to Java will simplify some of this problem.

The object DBMSs that support Smalltalk typically store and manage both the data structures and the method implementations. The operations can be executed in the object database, making it qualify as an *active database*. It is the dynamic nature of Smalltalk, as compared with the compiled nature of C++, that makes active Smalltalk databases far more prevalent than active C++ databases. The primary benefit of managing and executing operations in the database is easier version management. If the implementation

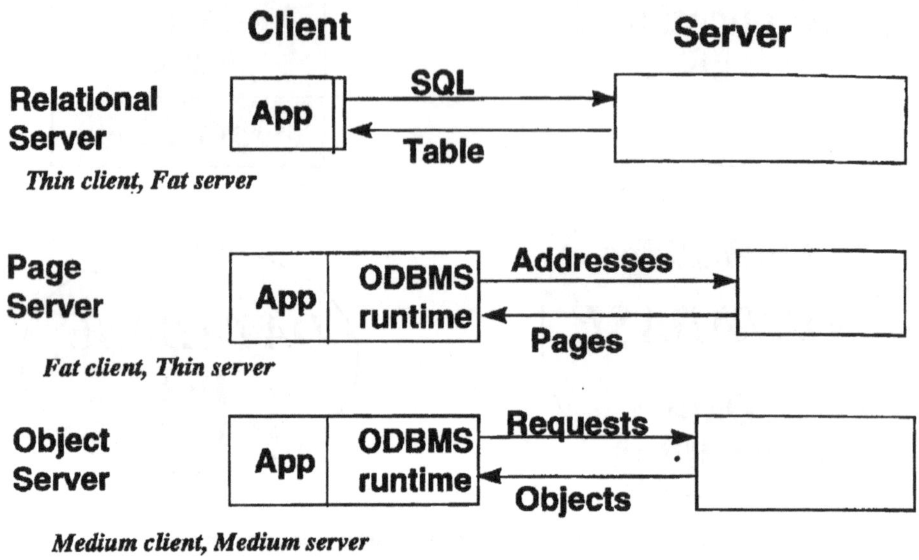

FIGURE 34.8 Client-server architectures.

of a method should be changed, say to optimize a complex algorithm, then that upgrade needs to be made only once. The improved operation then will be available to each of the application programs that invokes it on the database server, without having to redistribute the code to each of the clients.

34.13 Client-Server Models

Both relational and object DBMSs typically are architected according to a client-server model. Their functionality is partitioned in two, for purposes of distributing the execution across multiple processors. The client part executes on the same machine that runs the application program, and the server part executes on the same machine that has the database disks attached. In fact, this is far too simplistic a statement. Sometimes the disks are on the same machine as the application program. Sometimes the disks are distributed over multiple machines, or may even be network-attached storage with no conventional processor involved. Sometimes multiple processors reside in the same machine.

The typical relational DBMS client-server model is a thin client and a fat server (Figure 34.8). The client basically functions to trap each SQL statement encountered in an application program execution and to route that request to the server. For a query, the server handles parsing the request, determining a search strategy, finding the data, composing a response table, and delivering that response back to the client. The client buffers the response for access by the application program.

Some object DBMSs use a page-server approach, which differs significantly from the relational approach. These DBMSs place the majority of their functionality on the client, with only minimal functionality on the server — fat client and thin server. The fattest clients request pages by address; the thinnest servers deliver pages. A page is a physical unit of storage, and may contain many small objects, or a fragment of a large object. The client part of the DBMS must determine which are the appropriate pages to request, given references to persistent objects by the application program.

An architecture between these two extremes uses an object-server approach. These DBMSs have a more balanced distribution of functionality between the client and server — medium client and medium server. The client side is responsible for determining search strategies and makes requests to the server in terms of object references. The server determines which pages are needed.

34.14 Architecture Trade Offs and Performance

Which client-server architecture is most appropriate for a given situation? This question is usually answered from the perspective of performance. In general, the more an application localizes its object uses to a particular subset of the database, the better performance will come from the fat-client-thin-server approach of the page-server architecture. By contrast, the more an application needs to access a broad range of objects in the database, the better performance will come from the thinner-client-fatter-server approaches of the object-server or relational architectures. To complicate matters, a database typically supports more than one application, each of which may exhibit quite different access patterns to objects. A DBMS has but one client-server architecture, so trade offs must be made.

Consider a CAD application, where an engineer works on a particular design for an extended period. That design might occupy quite a bit of memory. A DBMS supporting the fat-client-thin-server approach will move the objects comprising the design to the client, where they will be directly accessible by the application program. The better clustered the design's objects are on database pages, the fewer pages need to be transferred from the server to the client. The thin-client-fat-server approach would probably require noticeably more trips to the server to access the design objects and to write them to disk when updated.

To speed performance, a fat-client-thin-server DBMS may link its client and the application into the same process. This avoids inter-process communication required to make objects accessible by the application, after those objects are in the client cache. The programming language runtime and the DBMS share the cache memory address space. By contrast, the relational approach keeps the client part of the DBMS in a separate process from the application, partly for the protection of its cache contents. The application copies records from the database cache into program variables as part of the data access sequence.

An OLTP application typically processes large numbers of independent queries or transactions, each of which targets just a few records from large volumes of data. The more the server can do to ferret out the qualifying records for each transaction, the better the performance of the application will be. The intent is for only the qualifying records to pass between the client-server boundary. The server may apply highly sophisticated indexing and filtering techniques. It could be unreasonable to assign this functionality to the client side.

Thus applications that navigate through relatively well-contained collections of objects tend to show better performance with the fatter-client approach. Such applications include CAD, word processing, spreadsheets, network traffic simulations, financial portfolio analyses, etc. Other applications that pinpoint relatively small numbers of objects from huge collections tend to show better performance with the thinner-client approach. These applications include OLTP and queries.

34.15 Querying Objects

Most "database people" expect to be able to query database contents using SQL, the *lingua franca* of database access. Relational DBMSs excel at this capability, differing from each other primarily in the particular optimization techniques they use. Object DBMSs are dramatically improving in their query capabilities. Many object DBMSs support at least a subset of the SQL SELECT statement, enabling value-based access to objects. Some support all of SQL, typically as specified in the ANS/ISO SQL 89 or 92 standards.

Querying objects based upon attribute values has been a controversial subject in the object database community. One position is that this functionality is obviously desirable, being a fundamental capability of databases. The position at the other extreme is that this functionality directly violates the principles of encapsulation, which imply that the state of an object should be accessible only through its methods. It appears that the first position is winning as nearly all object DBMSs support some form of query by attribute value. Meanwhile, SQL is being extended to include query by method-result value. The familiar

34.18 Research Directions

Database management has long been an area offering many intriguing research issues. Because the object model is so much richer semantically than the relational table model, object database management adds some degree of enrichment to these issues. Among the most important are:

- Incorporating rules and constraints into the object paradigm
- Semantics and implementation venues for views
- Security, especially when methods are involved
- High availability
- Replication
- New transaction models
- Derivation of database schemas (including method implementations) from object models
- Active databases (including method implementations) seamlessly integrated with static languages
- Performance, performance, performance

References

ANSI X3H2. *Database Language SQL*, X3.135-1992.

Cattell, R. 1991. *Object Data Management: Object-Oriented and Extended Relational Database Systems*. Addison-Wesley, Reading, MA.

Cattell, R. Ed. 1994 and 1996. *The Object Database Standard: ODMG-93*, Releases 1.1 and 2. Morgan Kaufmann, San Mateo, CA.

Loomis, M.E.S. 1995. *Object Databases: The Essentials*. Addison-Wesley, Reading, MA.

Further Information

Further information about object database management technology is available from a variety of sources. For details about particular products, consult their vendors. Visit their booths at trade shows like OMG's Object World and ACM SIGPLAN's OOPSLA (Object-Oriented Programming Systems, Languages, and Applications) Conference. Ask the vendors for names of reference accounts, then talk with these users.

The primary sources of experience-related and tutorial-level publications about object database management technology include *Component Strategies*, formerly *Object Magazine*, the *Journal of Object-Oriented Programming*, and *Distributed Object Computing*. Tutorial presentations about object databases are commonly found at object technology conferences, especially OOPSLA and Object World.

Peer-reviewed research results are reported in *ACM Transactions on Database Systems*, and in the proceedings of research-oriented conferences, including ACM SIGPLAN's OOPSLA Conference, ACM SIGMOD's Conference, and the Conference on Very Large Databases (VLDB). Results are also reported in *IEEE's Data Engineering* newsletter.

35

Object-Oriented vs. Relational and Extended Relational Databases

Mario Piattini Velthuis
University of Castilla-La Mancha

35.1 Evolution of the Database Management Systems

Since computers were introduced in the sixties to automate enterprise management, using COBOL programs, the Information Systems (IS) evolution has considerably affected data management, demanding an increase in performance.

Slowly, the computing center of gravity has moved from process to data structuring. We passed from process-oriented information systems to data-oriented systems, in which data acquired a privileged role. In the late sixties and seventies the first generation of databases appeared in network and hierarchical products like IBM's IMS and Cullinet's IDMS. These products, although efficient, presented procedural languages which constrained the programmer to navigate the database (a record at a time), lacking physical/logical independence which produced a loss of flexibility.

When, in 1969, Dr. Codd proposed the relational model (Codd, 1970), hardly anybody thought that an "elegant mathematical theory without any possibility to have an efficient implementation in commercial products," would become, in the eighties, a mandatory feature for every DBMS product. The relational model marks the second generation of databases with products like ORACLE, DB2, INGRES, INFORMIX, SYBASE, etc. These products are characterized by a better physical/logical independence, greater flexibility, and specification languages (acting on sets of records).

From the beginning of this decade we see the birth of a new database generation (the third) that not only manages data, but also supports complex objects, multimedia information, and knowledge management with incredible performance (Cattell, 1991). In this generation we can find active, deductive, temporal, multimedia, fuzzy, intelligent, multidimensional, etc., databases, and above all, object-oriented databases.

0-8493-3135-8/99/$0.00+$.50

35.2 New Requirements for Databases

From the enterprise side, companies in these days must be "open" in a broad sense. If they want to survive they must support organizational flexibility, change adaptation, intercompanies extensions, integrated processes and management, etc. In real competitive markets they must offer their clients greater quality and flexibility, offering products and services with the greatest quality/price ratios. It is fundamental to alieneate IS architectures with corporative strategies and critical success factors. Companies must be redesigned and databases, as the core of IS, are affected by these changes and must offer an adequate support for the new organization.

Also new areas of application for databases have appeared. The first generation products solved administrative tasks (accountability, personnel management, seat reservations, etc.), but they were not suitable to attend to unplanned queries as in a decision making process. Relational products changed this situation and increased the application fields of the databases. There are still several cultural, scientific, and industrial areas where database technology is scarcely represented due to the special requirements they pose.

- CASE (Computer-Aided Software Engineering) — These tools require the management of hundreds of information, charts, diagrams, code, etc., associated with different lifecycle phases. They need DBMSs capable of version management, activity features, etc.
- CAD/CAM/CIM (Computer-Aided Design/Computer-Aided Manufacturing/Computer Integrated Manufacturing) — These systems manage complex objects related to all phases of a production plant.
- GIS (Geographical Information Systems) — These systems use information codified from maps, and are used in military, environmental, urbanistic, and transport researches.
- Document systems, that have their own software management systems (Information Retrieval Systems) — They must be integrated with traditional databases.
- Scientific applications — They include satellite data management or genetic research.
- Health systems — Associated personnel need a different kind of patient information, like radiographs, analysis results, etc.
- Computer-Aided Publishing and OIS (Office Information Systems) — They must handle text, images, voice, audio, etc.
- Education and training — This sector has experimented with very big changes, with the introduction of CD-ROM, "virtual classes," etc.
- Electronic commerce — Internet Society forecasts that in 1999 there will be more than 200 million Internet users who could access electronic shopping, video on demand.

These systems need new features not presented in actual databases like unique identity, complex objects, references and relationships, object hierarchies, big data blocks, change facilities, version control, etc. In order to attend these demands, existing database products have been extended and new products have appeared since the late 1980s.

35.3 "Extended" Relational DBMSs vs. "Pure" Object-Oriented DBMSs

Two different approaches can be followed to implement the new generation of DBMS products. The first of them is to "extend" RDBMSs (in an evolutionary manner), in order that they could support object-oriented concepts. The second approach is supported by more "purist" experts that think that ODBMSs must offer a real object model not being "polluted" by relational concepts.

The first approach can be found in the *Third Generation Database System Manifesto* by Stonebraker et al. (1990) and elaborated on by The Committee for Advanced DBMS Functions, and it is logically propagated by the main RDBMS vendors.

This manifesto is articulated in three principles refined in thirteen propositions. The first principle asserts that third-generation DBMSs must support objects (data and functions) with a rich type system, inheritance, and rules. The second principle serves to guarantee that third-generation DBMSs subsume second generation DBMSs, not losing any achievement made by relational systems as non-procedural access and data independence. The third principle wants to assure that third-generation DBMSs are open to other systems and that they continue to support the "intergalactic dataspeak" language SQL.

The second, more "revolutionary," option is exposed in *The Object-Oriented Database System Manifesto* by Atkinson et al. (1989), in which thirteen Golden Rules and five optional features are given. The first eight rules come from the object technology arena (complex objects, object identity, encapsulation, types/classes, inheritance, dynamic binding, computationally complete language, and extensibility), and the last five come from the database technology field (persistence, support for very large database, concurrency control, recovery, and query). The optional features are multiple inheritance, type checking and type inferencing, distribution, design transactions, and versions. This manifesto was published by a distinguished group of researchers and has established the principles followed by ODBMS products like O2, ObjectStore, Objectivity, ITASCA, GemStone, SERVIO, etc.

Besides using a different approach, there are also various differences between the two manifestos like:

- Object identity is required for objects in the *Object-Oriented Database System Manifesto* whereas the *Third-Generation Manifesto* states that "unique identifiers should be assigned by the DBMS only if a user-defined primary key is not available."
- (Updatable) views are essential for the *Third-Generation Manifesto*, but no reference of them is made in the OODBMS Manifesto.
- Multiple inheritance is optional for OODBMS Manifesto but *The Third-Generation Manifesto* signers think that "multiple inheritance is essential."

The purist approach is attacked by relational expert Chris Date, because of the lack of a logical basis, as the relational model. He and Hugh Darwen have recently published a new proposal called the *Third Manifesto* (Darwen and Date, 1995), reinterpreting the relational model on an object-oriented vision. They equal relational domains to object-oriented classes, and propagate that products support user-defined domains that include structure and behavior. They reject SQL unequivocally (as a "perversion" of the relational model), proposing the D language. In Camps (1996), the evolution of the meaning given to the "domain" in the relational model community from its beginning is analyzed.

The debate between evolutionary and revolutionary approaches is a matter with an economical and commercial basis which is not negligible, and it has been prolonged to the standard arena. On the evolutionary hand we find SQL3, elaborated by ANSI and ISO, and supported by the main relational vendors. On the revolutionary hand, a consortium supported by the main "purist" object-oriented vendors, ODMG (Object Database Management Group), has defined a different version of the standard known as ODMG-93, the latest can be found in Cattell (1997). For a more complete description of the standards landscape see Thompson (1995).

As Taylor (1992) remarks, the two approaches concern more companies than users, because both are converging, the future database is, in fact object-oriented, keeping all the advantages of relational

TABLE 35.1 Comparison Between Extended-Relational and Pure Object-Oriented Database Systems

	Extended Relational		"Pure" Object-Oriented
Approach	Evolutive		Revolutionary
Manifestos	Third generation database system Manifesto	Third manifesto	Object-oriented database system manifesto
Stand/Lang.	SQL 3	D	ODMG-93
Products	Oracle 8, Informix/Illustra, UNISQL, DB2/2, Sybase, Ingres, etc.	—	O2, Objectivity, ONTOS, ITASCA, Gemstone, etc.

databases. In the next section a comparison between relational and object DBMSs is given, not distinguishing between extended-relational or "pure" object-oriented.

Besides manifestos, while considering implementation approaches two types of RDBMS extensions can be identified:

1. Implementing an object layer above an RDBMS, as Hewlett-Packard's OpenODB. In this case, the "machinery" (technology related to concurrence, I/O management, recovery, transactions, etc.) is relational, but the model view by users and applications can be object-oriented, Friedman (1993). The main advantage of this approach is coexistence of relational and object technology (programs developed under different paradigms could be executed on the same system), but performance is sacrificed because of the need to convert relational data to objects and vice versa.
2. Object-Relational DBMSs, Stonebraker (1996), that combine OO and the relational model, in an integrated manner.

35.4 Characteristics of ODBMSs

The characteristics of these kinds of systems came from the confluence of database technology and object technology (Fong et al., 1991). ODBMSs incorporate the basic concepts of the object-oriented paradigm like encapsulation, generalization, aggregation, object identity, dynamic binding, polymorphism, etc., and the basic functionality of databases such as security, concurrency, recovery, query language, etc.

Others features presented in ODBMSs are

- Extensibility (users can define new classes and modify existing classes dynamically) — This aspect is essential for new applications as CAD/CAM or CASE, where schema evolution is the norm.
- Class libraries — These define elements with a high level of functionality that can be integrated in the database. Some libraries suffer from limited functionality because of the compatibility with the model supported by the ODBMSs.

In this section we summarize the main differences between relational and object DBMSs. Extended RDBMSs are incorporating some of the features that we cataloged as object DBMS characteristics. One must take into account that the differences discussed here are general and not related to a specific product that could offer a better support.

Data model — There are several aspects that must be considered when comparing relational to object-oriented database models. The relational model offers a solid theoretical foundation for database design, and it is a landmark in the database history, but it shows some weaknesses for supporting the requirement imposed by new applications. Repetitive groups are not allowed in the relational model, enforcing the normalization of relations, splitting data related to the same entity. Object models offer a greater correspondence between relations and "real-world" entities, meanwhile the relational model has only one primitive (the relation) for representing entities and relationships. Another important consideration is that relational model is valued-based, while object-model is identity-based; objects can be different although all their attributes are equal. ODBMSs are characterized for "break the wall", or that the preceding database technology generation has risen between data (which reside in the database) and processes (which are in the program applications developed using SQL embedded in third or fourth generation languages). In ODBMSs models objects combine data and operations in an encapsulated form. We have been recently assisting, in the RDBMSs world, to the diffumination of the border between applications and data. Nowadays, part of the code that resided exclusively in applications can be stored in the database (Kent, 1990). Latest versions of RDBMSs products support triggers, rules, and stored procedures. As a consequence of these features, ODBMSs reduce the existing distance in a relational development between conceptual modeling (usually carried out in a variation of the ER model) and the logical model. The object-oriented paradigm provides a unique underlying model, implemented in the ODBMS, to which applications can have direct access.

Three-level architecture — ANSI (1975) proposed today's classical three-level architecture for databases, with this architecture databases are given physical/logical independence. In ODBMSs this independence is a little lost, because views are not usually supported. Today there are some interesting researches in this area, for example, Bertino (1992) or Souza (1995).

Persistence — In object-oriented programming languages objects are transient, their life is associated to the program that creates them, and they reside in main memory. In RDBMSs information is permanent because it must be deleted explicitly. In ODBMSs persistence must be orthogonal to data types — every element of the system, independently of its type, must be capable of becoming persistent by itself.

Data language — In RDBMSs there is the "impedance mismatch" problem between SQL (the data language) and the host languages (COBOL, C, FORTRAN, etc.). ODBMSs solve the problem adopting extensions to C++ or Smalltalk in an integrated form. In past years, RDBMS products lack a complete data language, as ODBMSs (with C++ or Smalltalk). In December 1996, ANSI/ISO approved the SQL/PSM (Persistent Stored Modules) that extend SQL converting it in a complete language. Regarding query languages, objects are considered "white boxes" in RDBMSs and "black boxes" in OOPL, but in ODBMSs they are "gray boxes," because of the difficulty in strictly following the encapsulation principle and not allowing direct access to attributes. First ODBMSs did not offer high-level query languages like SQL, but they have quite improved since the early 1990s, and today ODBMSs incorporate good object query languages as Object SQL or OQL. Another characteristic of ODBMSs is the possibility of "navigation" through the database.

Optimization and performance — Relational experts have dedicated more than two decades to refining optimizers, this has been possible because of the good solid foundation of the relational model (algebra, calculus). ODBMS optimization is more difficult, because of the lack of algebra, and also in some of them, because of the navigational languages. According to several benchmarks (see, for example, Cattell and Skeen, 1992) ODBMSs are superior to RDBMSs when big main memories are available and navigation through complex objects is required. Strategies such as swizzling (converting OIDs in memory addresses) allow ODBMSs to perform more like hierarchical DBMSs than RDBMSs. RDBMSs are most suitable when handling millions of simple records.

Security — RDBMS security is usually positive and explicit (the creator of a table, or someone who has the appropriate privilege must grant you the adequate access to data: select, insert, etc.). ODBMSs do not support, in general, good models of security, but some interesting proposals can be found in Rabitti et al. (1988) and Fernandez et al. (1992). These proposals use not only positive and explicit authorization, but also implicit (i.e., if you have the privilege to select a class you are allowed to select all the class' objects) and negative (e.g., you cannot access the object that represent the manager). The maturity of secure features in RDBMSs is also demonstrated by the existence of Trusted RDBMSs that implement mandatory access control (MAC). There are prototypes of ODBMSs that also support this kind of policy, see Oliver and Von Solms (1995), but, for the moment, any commercial product offers this possibility.

Concurrency control and recovery — As it is known, RDBMSs use transactions as units of work and recovery. In RDBMSs, applications transactions are inspired from bank models and last only a few seconds, but new applications (as CAD/CAM) require long transactions that can last hours, days, or even weeks. Another novelty is nested transactions where a transaction is divided into smaller units that can be recovered without affecting other transactions.

Application Programming Interfaces (API) — ODBMSs as RDBMSs must offer support for several languages. Most ODBMSs have evolved from persistent OOPLs, but today most of them are multilanguage. However, RDBMSs still offer more bindings to different programming languages.

Application development tools — It is essential that DBMSs provide different kinds of development tools (forms and report generators, screen painters, etc.). RDBMSs are more mature in this sense than ODBMSs.

Monitoring and administration tools — RDBMS vendors and third parties (like Platinum, etc.) offer lots of tools to administrate, tune, and monitorize databases. ODBMSs are poorer in this aspect. It is also necessary to have more experience with really big object databases to improve these tools.

Multimedia data support — In RDBMSs multimedia data is stored using blobs (binary large objects). They called them complex objects but they are only a bit of a collection without structure as its complexity is only reflected by the size. ODBMSs understand the complex nature of multimedia objects, allowing better query support and better storage and recovery. If RDBMSs vendors adopt SQL/MM proposals, extended RDBMSs will support real multimedia complex objects.

Distribution — Although distribution aspects are orthogonal to the data model (relational or object-oriented) supported by the DBMS, ODBMSs are better suited for applications to be deployed in a distributed computing environment, especially in heterogeneous systems, because of the capability of the object model to integrate the others (relational, hierarchical, etc.).

Version control and configuration — Version control is a characteristic of ODBMSs, due to its use in areas like CAD/CAM, CIM, etc. In ODBMSs versions can be integrated with the object model and an automatic version management is provided. In relational systems versions must be handled by a level built above the relational model, see Roddick (1995) for more details.

35.5 Conclusions

We have presented a very summarized comparison between relational, extended relational, and object-oriented DBMSs. Today the market is dominated by relational DBMSs, extended-relational products are just appearing (Oracle 8, Informix/Illustra, ...), and "pure" object-oriented products have less than 5% of the market (reduced to very special applications like CAD/CAM, etc.).

New applications and the market pressure have forced relational vendors to improve their products which have become "universal servers" (Norman and Bloor, 1996). In two or three years' time we will see the market dominated by extended relational products in which relational concepts are mixed (more or less orthogonally) with the main principles of the object-oriented paradigm (complex objects, generalization, dynamic binding, encapsulation, etc.) and presumably "pure" object DBMSs will keep their special "niche" (Miranda, 1997).

References

ANSI 1975. ANSI/X3/SPARC Study Group on DBMS, *ACM SIGMOD FDT Bull.*, 7 (2).

Atkinson, M. et al. 1989. The object-oriented database system manifesto, pp. 40-57. In *Proc. First Int. Conf. of Deductive and Object-Oriented Databases*, Kyoto, December.

Bertino, E. 1992. A view mechanism for object-oriented databases, pp. 136-151. In *Proc. Third Int. Conf. on Extended Database Technology.*

Camps, R. 1996. Domains, relations and religious wars, *SIGMOD Rec.*, 25 (3): 3-9.

Cattell, R.G.G. 1991. What are next-generation database systems?, *Commun. ACM,* 34(10): 31-33.

Cattell, R.G.G. et al. 1997. *The Object Database Standard: ODMG 2.0.*, Morgan Kaufmann Publishers, San Francisco, CA.

Cattell, R.G.G. and Skeen, D. 1992. Object operations benchmark, *ACM Trans. Databases,* 17 (1).

Codd, E.F. 1970. A relational model of data for large shared data banks, *Commun. ACM,* 13 (6).

Darwen, H. and Date, C.J. 1995. The third manifesto, *SIGMOD Rec.*, 24(1): 39-49.

Fernandez, E.B., Gude, S.E. and Song, H. 1994. A model for evaluation and administration of security in object-oriented databases, *IEEE Trans. Knowledge Data Eng.*, 6(2): 275-292.

Fong, E., Kent, W., Moore, K. and Thompson, C., Eds. 1991. *X3/SPARC/DBSSG OODB Task Group Final Report,* NIST Technical Report.

Friedman, J. 1993. New options for object databases. New routes to choose from, *Object Mag.*, March/April: 67-71.

Kent, W. 1990. The leading edge of database technology. In *Information System Concepts: An In-Depth Analysis,* Falkenberg, E.D. and Lindgreen, P., Eds., Elsevier Science Publishers, New York.

Kim, W. 1995. Object-oriented database systems: promises, reality and future. In *Modern Database Systems,* Kim, Ed., Addison-Wesley, Reading, MA.

Miranda, S. 1997. Invited Conference. *BIWIT'97, Basque International Workshop on Information Technology*, Biarritz, IEEE Computer Science Press.

Norman, M. and Bloor, R. 1996. To universally serve, *Database Program. Design*, 9 (7): 26-35.

Olivier, M.S. and Von Solms, S.H. 1995. A taxonomy for secure object-oriented databases, *ACM Trans. Databases*, 19(1): 3-46.

Rabitti, F., Bertino, E., Kim, W., and Woelk, D. 1988. A model of authorization for next-generation database systems, *ACM Trans. Databases*, 16 (1): 88-131.

Roddick, J.F. 1995. A survey of schema versioning issues for database systems, *Inform. Software Technol.*, 37 (7): 383-393.

Souza, C. 1995. Design and implementation of object-oriented views, pp. 91-102. In *Proc. Int. Conf. and Workshop on Database and Expert Systems Applications* No. 978, Lecture Notes in Computer Science.

Stonebraker, M. 1996. *Object-Relational DBMSs: The Next Great Wave.* Morgan Kaufmann Publishers, San Francisco.

Stonebraker, M. et al. 1990. Third-generation database system manifesto, the committee for advanced DBMS function, *SIGMOD Rec.*, 19(3): 31-44.

Taylor, R. 1992. The coming convergence of object and relational databases, *Object Mag.*, Sept/Oct: 16-18.

Thompson, C. 1995. The changing database standards landscape, In *Modern Database Systems*, Kim, Ed., ACM Press-Addison Wesley, Reading, MA.

Further Information

A very good introduction to object and relational databases is presented in *Object Data Management. Object-Oriented and Extended Relational Database Systems* 2nd edition by R.G.G. Cattell (Addison-Wesley, 1994). This is one of the most complete books on object-oriented DBMS. It covers their characteristics in an exhaustive manner.

Other excellent books about object-oriented databases are *Object-Oriented Database Systems: Concepts and Architectures*, by Elisa Bertino and Lorenzo Martino (Addison-Wesley, 1994) and *Object Databases. The Essentials* by Mary Loomis (Addison-Wesley, 1995).

Modern Database Systems. The Object Model, Interoperability and Beyond by Won Kim (ed.) (ACM Press, Addison-Wesley, 1995) is an interesting recompilation composed of different articles on ODBMS about models, languages, views, security, query processing, standards, distribution, etc.

The Object Database Handbook by D. K. Barry (John Wiley & Sons, 1995) is particularly helpful for its practical approach in the ODBMS selection, including valuable checklists for comparing products.

Recently Michael Stonebraker published *Object-Relational DBMSs: The Next Great Wave* (Morgan Kaufmann Publishers, 1996) which is the first book about object-relational DBMSs.

Proceedings of the SIGMOD International Conference on Management of Data and Proceedings of the OOPSLA (Object-Oriented Programming Systems, Languages, and Applications) are published annually by ACM, the Association for Computer Machinery. Proceedings of the International Conference on VLDB (Very Large Data Bases) are published annually by Morgan-Kaufmann Publishing. These proceedings document the latest developments in the field of databases each year.

There are several journals that report advances in extended relational and object databases. One of the most important is *Database Programming and Design* (monthly). For subscription information contact Miller Frieman Inc., P.O. Box 51247, Boulder, CO 80323-1247. Phone (800)289-0169 (outside U.S. (303) 678-0439). Another is *SIGMOD Record*, a quarterly publication of the ACM Special Interest Group on Management of Data. For subscription contact ACM, P.O. Box 12115 Church Street Station, New York, NY 10257, or visit http://www.acm.org/sigmod/.

VII

Patterns

Saba Zamir
Senior Information Technology Consultant

Patterns, as eloquently described by one of my contributors, Linda Rising, is "a way of documenting experience by capturing successful solutions to recurring problems." A pattern consists of a description and a structural diagram that illustrates the implementation of the pattern. A pattern is at the very core of the object-oriented paradigm, it encourages "reuse" of prior documented experience to help resolve current problems.

Currently, design patterns, analysis patterns, coding patterns, organizational patterns, and many other types exist. This section contains chapters that describe major existing patterns.

36

Software Patterns

Martin Fowler
Independent Consultant

I have a vivid memory of the evening I flew into Seattle in fall 1992. We were flying above clouds, but the peak of Mount Rainier poked through the cloudbase, a very beautiful sight. Seattle airport was quiet and I was both excited and apprehensive. I was on my way to my first OOPSLA conference. While waiting at the airport I struck up a conversation with another Englishman on his way to OOPSLA. Bruce Anderson was an old OOPSLA hand, and friendly to a newbie like me.

He talked about the workshop he was running. The idea was to collect ideas to form an architecture handbook for software. There were plenty of lessons which practitioners had learned about software, but had never written down. Engineering disciplines have handbooks that describe set and proven ways to do certain things. Software people tend to work from a blank sheet of paper all the time. The workshop sounded very interesting, sadly he told me that you needed to book ahead of time to get in.

That workshop, and its predecessor at the 1991 OOPSLA, were the primordial soup from which a new community of software writers had sprung. The idea of an architecture handbook has spread to yield many books looking at different aspects of software. The form and content of these books is different in many ways. Yet they share a common theme, taking working ideas from practical experience, distilling them into manageable chunks, and spreading them around.

At that workshop was Erich Gamma. He had become familiar with a number of software frameworks and had written a Ph.D. dissertation which pulled out the common pieces of design. These were exactly the kinds of things an architecture handbook needed. At the workshop he met Richard Helm and John Vlissides and they agreed to collaborate.

Kent Beck and Ward Cunningham, two Smalltalk developers well-known for inventing CRC cards, had read some books by the architect Christopher Alexander. They felt that his idea of "pattern" was a good way to write these ideas. Alexander's approach was to describe a problem, discuss the various issues involved in solving it, and give a solution. The patterns were observed from buildings that Alexander enjoyed. Kent worked with Ralph Johnson to document Hotdraw, the Smalltalk diagramming framework, using patterns. Ralph also joined Erich, Richard, and John to work on their project. This group soon became known as the Gang of Four.

0-8493-3135-8/99/$0.00+$.50

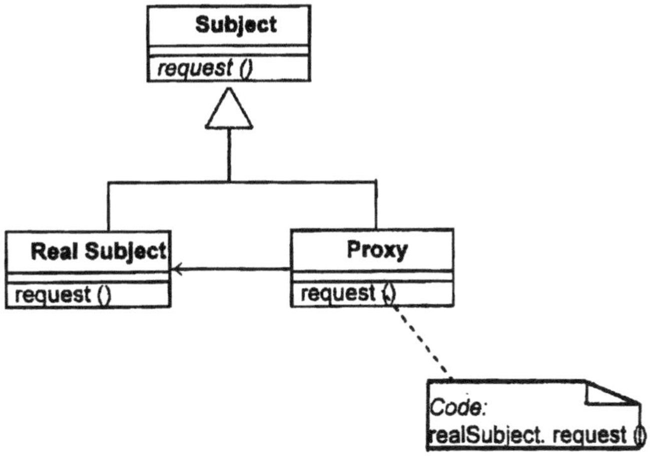

FIGURE 36.1 A class diagram of the Proxy pattern (UML notation). (From Gamma et al. 1994. *Design Patterns: Elements of Reusable Object-Oriented Software.* Addison-Wesley, Reading, MA, and Fowler, M. 1997. *UML Distilled: Applying the Standard Object Modeling Language.* Addison-Wesley, Reading, MA. With permission.)

After these workshops I heard many more mutterings about the idea of software patterns. In the following year a group of those interested in the subject got together in Colorado to decide where to take the ideas further. They formed the Hillside Group which was devoted to encouraging the development of patterns.

The Hillside Group ran a conference the following year called Pattern Languages of Programming (PLoP). It attracted a wider group of people who were interested in exploring these ideas, but the object community really sat up and took notice at OOPSLA 94 when the book that the Gang of Four had been working on finally came out. I remember ambling over to get a copy. The line ran the length of a hall. Patterns had arrived.

36.1 Design Patterns

The Gang of Four book (as it is generally known) has become one of the most widely referenced and used books in software development (Gamma et al., 1994). It contains 23 patterns. Each pattern is described in the same basic form. The form opens with a short description of the pattern, or the intent. Thus the intent of the Proxy pattern is to "Provide a surrogate or placeholder for another object to control access to it." They follow the intent with an example of the kind of problem that the pattern solves. With the problem clear they move onto the solution. For a proxy the example problem is that of a document which needs to lay text on a page with graphics. At the beginning you do not actually need the graphic to display, but you do need to know what space the graphic takes up. Since the graphic object is expensive to create the proxy helps by pretending to be the graphic, but not taking as much time to create. The proxy knows enough to describe how much space it takes up, but delegates any other questions to the real object, which would then need to be created.

The pattern describes the solution with a class diagram and a statement of the responsibilities of the various classes. Also it discusses when the pattern is useful and its positive and negative consequences. There are also several pages that discuss how to implement the pattern with sample code in C++ and Smalltalk.

The result is a cogent discussion of a design that is applicable to many situations. Although the motivation is in graphics, proxies are probably most widely used in networking. For anyone who thinks they might need a proxy this pattern is ideal. A reader gets guidance on when proxies are useful and an in-depth discussion of how to design and build it, and a discussion that includes the various trade offs that you need to make when doing this in practice.

The Gang of Four book was the first book of design patterns, but it was not the last. The POSA book (Buschmann et al., 1996), which I'll talk about more in Section 36.7, includes many design patterns. Also there have been a couple of books on more specialized design topics.

Doug Lea has written a book on patterns for concurrent programming in Java. Although there is much I like about Java, I expect to see a lot of people get burned with multi-threaded programming. Java makes it easy to create threads, and gives people the core structures you need for locking; but many Java developers are not aware of the many issues involved in concurrent programming, and won't be aware of the many subtle bugs that are just waiting for a concurrent program in which to breed. Doug's book is essential to dealing with these kinds of problems, and if you are ever tempted to create a thread, you should read his book at least twice before you do. As it is I fear that Brian Foote is right when he says that threads are likely to be the GOTO of the nineties. One problem you may have with Doug's book is that the patterns are not obviously separated in their elements. If you find this a problem you should take a look at Doug's home page <http://gee.cs.oswego.edu/dl/cpj/index.html>.

In a similar vein is Mowbray and Malveau's work on patterns for CORBA development (Mowbray and Malveau, 1997). Here I cannot give a strong recommendation on the content, since I'm not an expert on CORBA, nor have I done anything other than recently buy and skip over the book. Mowbray is well known in the CORBA community, so you should certainly take a look if you are working with CORBA.

36.2 Coding Patterns — Idioms

Design patterns are common design level constructs. Coding patterns are language specific patterns. Actually the boundary between the two, like most pattern boundaries, is somewhat fuzzy, but certainly things fit as coding patterns that you would be very reluctant to call design patterns.

Indeed coding patterns were a source of inspiration for the Gang of Four, in particular the coding patterns in Jim Coplien's work (he referred to them as *idioms*; Coplien, 1995). His book on advanced C++ is one of the classics on the language. In this book he described a number of idioms which are important techniques in using the language. One example is the handle-body idiom. Consider trying to build a string class. Rapidly you begin to mire yourself in the complexities of pass-by-reference and memory management issues that can make such a class very awkward. The handle-body idiom splits the class into two parts. The body holds the behavior of the string and its representation (a character array or whatever). However, classes that use a string do not refer to the body directly, instead they see the handle. The handle class contains a reference to the body and delegates behavior to the body, but does little else. If you use an assignment to create more than one reference to a string, a second handle object is created that points to the same body. This effectively means that handles are always passed by value and are therefore much easier to deal with. Built upon this idiom are several others that make memory management easier. Essentially they treat the handle as a smart pointer that helps to manage a reference count to the body, thus reducing memory problems. This idiom is a very valuable technique in dealing with memory issues in C++.

The most complete work on coding patterns thus far is Kent Beck's work for Smalltalk (Beck, 1996). Kent's patterns range from design level issues, to use of Smalltalk's class libraries, and how to format Smalltalk code. An example of these is the *Converter Method.* This pattern deals with the conversion of objects from one form to another, such as converting an integer to a real number. The Smalltalk way of doing this is to provide a method called asReal. The method creates a new real number object that has the same value as the originating integer. Kent's pattern includes a discussion of why this pattern is useful, some of the problems that appear with this pattern (which can be solved with a different pattern), and a naming convention for Converter Methods. It is a valuable pattern both in writing new Smalltalk code and in understanding how the standard image works.

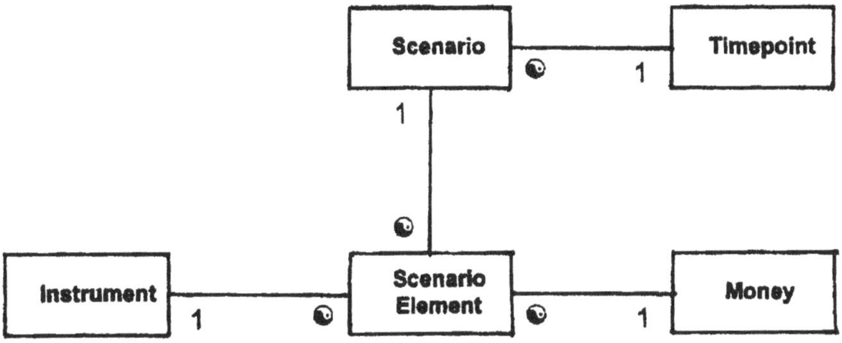

FIGURE 36.2 The Scenario pattern. (From Fowler, M. 1997. *Analysis Patterns: Reusable Object Models.* Addison-Wesley, Reading, MA. With permission.)

One of the saddest things about Kent's book is the timing of its publication. As I write this, Smalltalk's future looks bleak. Kent's patterns deserve a wider audience, not just because they are well written, but also because they are applicable to more than just Smalltalk. Many Java programmers would get a great deal from this book, and I think it is worth a read for any OO programmer.

36.3 Analysis Patterns

I must confess a preference here, having written a book on analysis patterns, they are a subject dear to my heart. Analysis Patterns come from understanding domains and building conceptual models — models that reflect how people think about their domain.

Again I will start with an example. Consider a trading company that trades stocks. It needs to be able to calculate the value of a portfolio of its stocks. It also needs to know about how that value changes over time. To do this it is not enough to give each stock a price, a stock needs to be given a price history so the portfolio can be valued over time. For risk management purposes, even this is not enough. Risk management involves asking questions about what might happen, and considering how this would affect a portfolio. What if tech stocks dropped 10%, how about a big rise in the utility sector? When looking at risk a trader needs to value the portfolio against a number of hypothetical combinations of market factors.

This scenario simply collects together a group of prices for instruments that would coexist in some hypothesis. Any real situation is a scenario at a point in time, the current scenario is just the prices as at this moment. The trader can create alternative scenarios by taking a group of stocks and adjusting the prices according to his judgment. He then values the portfolio with this scenario to see the effects. The class diagram in Figure 36.2 shows the outline conceptual structure for this pattern. The pattern text also discusses how scenarios can be linked together so people can make adjustments on a group of stocks and how people can assemble scenarios from pieces of other people's scenarios.

My book contains patterns from several domains: healthcare, corporate finance, trading, organization, accounting, and planning. They come from my own consulting experience and, as such, reflect the hodge-podge of things on which I have worked. I'm hoping that more people will start writing analysis patterns books so that we can cover a wider field of analysis ideas.

One important lesson I learned from working with analysis patterns is that their use does not confine themselves to the traditional vertical domains. I picked this up when I was working for a large manufacturing company on a project to build some high-level financial analysis software. The problem was to take a high-level problem, such as sales are down last year, and dig deeper to find the causes for this problem. We found that many patterns that I had discovered for an earlier project in healthcare were remarkably applicable. Essentially both problems were about recording observations about things, using a diagnostic process to determine the root cause observations from the immediate symptoms. This use of healthcare patterns in corporate finance showed us how analysis patterns often cross domains, and thus are more reusable than one might immediately think.

Although I would like to think of my work as the paramount effort on analysis patterns, its only fair to point to a couple of other books that tread along these lines. David Hay predated me by a year or so with his book on data model patterns (Hay, 1996). He is not involved in the patterns community and did his work independently (as in fact did I for most of it). His patterns are also very much data model patterns using a relational data modeling style. However, he does have a very conceptual orientation to his patterns, and thus object developers will find quite a few valuable ideas in there. Several of his ideas are similar to mine, but there are also significant differences, which reflect our different experiences; for example, he has much more on manufacturing than I do. Of course using them in an object-oriented context will require some translation, but the conceptual ideas are worth the effort.

One of the first to work in an analysis direction with patterns was Peter Coad, who published a paper on the subject in the CACM. His patterns book [Coad] is, however, quite different from mine or David Hay's book. Again Peter Coad works independently from the patterns community.

On the surface, Coad's patterns look rather superficial, indeed they carry that same superficial superficiality that characterizes much of his work. Indeed when I read the book I found myself thinking "this is nice for teaching newbies, but has little to offer me." If you have this reaction, jump forward to Chapter 6. In this chapter he talks about how you can use the patterns to help you ask questions of the domain and thus help you to model it. It is a striking technique. I have not heard too much about how well it works, but it is certainly worth looking at.

36.4 The Patterns Community and PLoP

I've referred to the "patterns community" a couple of times now, so I suppose I should explain what it is. The patterns community grew out of the original group of people who worked in the architecture handbook workshops.

The Hillside Group organized the first PLoP conference in 1994, just before the Gang of Four book was published. It was little publicized but still well attended. Since then it has had little publicity but a big attendance. The conference is there for pattern writers, to help them to get to know each other, talk about patterns, and to give each other feedback on their work. The patterns community includes people who are involved in PLoP and other events that the Hillside group supports.

PLoP is a most unusual conference. The usual academic conference has authors submit papers to a program committee which will reject many papers and only accept the good ones (if it is a prestigious conference). Most papers are little altered between submission and the conference, although some conferences do some shepherding to improve a paper's presentation. At the conference a book is produced of all the accepted papers (the proceedings) and each paper is presented by the author with a talk to the rest of the conference. The papers usually have to show new research and demonstrate originality.

In PLoP the authors submit their work to the conference but papers are not judged at that point. Instead a shepherd is appointed to work with the author to improve the paper and make it as good as possible. The shepherd only rejects the paper if he feels that the paper does not have much promise, i.e., he judges the potential as much as the current state.

At the conference the author participates in a writers workshop. Authors of about eight papers work in a group together for most of the conference. Each paper in the group is workshopped by the group. The workshop is run along the following lines

1. One of the members of workshop (not any of the current paper's authors) acts as a moderator.
2. One of the authors reads a section of the paper. This gives the rest of the group a chance to hear the author speak and get a sense of the tone of the paper. After this point the author must remain silent and only listen to what other people have to say until the clarification step.

3. The members of the workshop talk about the things that they like about the paper. Sometimes this is divided into separate stages: positive comments about the form and positive comments about the content. The author must remain silent during this step.
4. The members of the workshop talk about things that would improve the paper. Sometimes this is divided into separate stages: suggestions about the form and suggestions about the content. The author must remain silent during this step.
5. The author may ask questions to clarify any statement made during the earlier stages, she cannot try to refute a criticism, only ask for clarification.

The whole workshop lasts about an hour, so in effect the author gets to listen to her peers discussing her paper for an hour. I have always found this very useful. The whole spirit of the workshop is not to debate the paper, but to help the author to make the paper better. That is why PLoP is primarily an authors' conference.

Papers are not published at the conference, since they are works in progress. Authors can further revise them and, if they wish, submit them for the PLoPD book series. Such papers are first reviewed to see if they are of a sufficient quality, then the editors make a personal choice from those that remain. For the first two PLoPD books all the papers of the right quality were accepted, for the third book there was only room for half of the quality papers.

36.5 Project Management Patterns

The patterns community has long had an interest in project management and the human issues of software engineering. Thus we have seen several patterns papers on project management at PLoP, although nobody yet has tackled a book on the subject.

Two of these papers are Jim Coplien's *A Generative Development Process Pattern Language* and Ward Cunningham's *EPISODES: A Pattern Language of Competitive Development.* Coplien's patterns were gathered by looking at a series of hyperproductive projects, many with AT&T, but also a few outside. He was looking for common themes, particularly some that went against the conventional wisdom, a wisdom that says that formal process is an essential part of software development. He looked at smaller projects, typically no more than a dozen developers, that still achieved results that you would only expect from a larger project. The resulting patterns are essential reading for anyone involved in object-oriented project development.

Ward's patterns originated during his experience developing a financial system in Smalltalk. Ward developed a process that was geared to Smalltalk's development strengths. Smalltalk has a very rapid cycle time between edit, compile, and run. Smalltalk also makes it much easier to carry out changes to the core architecture of the system, even after it has been delivered (a process Ward refers to as *architectural substitution*). Ward's principal experience was a small product company that needed to build releases rapidly to take on their competition. Sadly, Ward has not written down a full writeup of his patterns, although Kent Beck is working on a book with very much the same philosophy.

The two pattern languages are fascinating to read together, there are many agreements and some disagreements. As such the patterns make for an interesting study in the details of project management. In this field in particular we need more examples of patterns from particular projects, or groups of projects. Such patterns can give us a great deal of insight into effective project management and development process techniques.

36.6 Pattern Languages

I see I have used another new term into the book, that of a pattern language. Patterns can be published alone or in groups. A paper to PLoP can easily be just a single pattern. Often authors wish to talk about several connected patterns that seem to come together. The Gang of Four book contains twenty-three patterns. A book like the Gang of Four book is a pattern catalog, it consists of many patterns, but there is no deep structure to how the patterns are organized. You could easily come up with several ways of rearranging the patterns which would make just as much sense as the Gang's patterns.

A pattern language also has several patterns, but here the way that the patterns are organized is crucial. The idea is that each pattern in the language, as it is applied, sets up the context for the following patterns. Not only do the patterns only make sense when used together, but furthermore, the patterns need to be considered in a certain order. Certain choices made early in the pattern language govern the later decisions.

This sounds rather like methodology, and indeed one of the arguments about pattern languages is that they present an approach to teaching how skilled developers go about their work, without the necessary trappings of a conventional methodology. *Caterpillar's Fate* (Kerth) represents an excellent example of an experienced project leader describing his process in this form. Patterns are not the only way of doing this, of course, but they do accentuate the rationale behind the process, explaining why each step is the way it is.

36.7 Architectural Patterns

Patterns are often small scale things. Most of the patterns I've discussed thus far involve just a few concepts. Their importance lies in the fact that they are either at the heart of a development (such as the analysis and project management patterns) or that a single pattern may appear all over a development (such as design or coding patterns). Architectural patterns try to look at the big picture and to capture the key issues at the highest level of thinking about software systems. Thus far the best known of these is the work of a group of researchers and developers at Siemans (Buschmann et al., 1996).

The POSA book focus lies in the architectural patterns, although they do have quite a few design patterns as well. The architectural patterns are all on a large scale. An example is a discussion of the pipes and filters architecture, which is particularly well known to Unix programmers. Buschmann et al. discusses the key classes in such an architecture, their responsibilities, scenarios illustrating the dynamics, implementation advice, and a summary of the benefits and liabilities.

36.8 Where We Are

Patterns is still a very young field in software engineering. Although there are now several books and a couple of regular conferences, it is still a field that has been around for only a few years. I believe, however, that patterns are essential to software's future development.

One of the problems that we are beginning to see is patterns proliferation. The Gang of Four book was one book, and the patterns in it are all of value. As more patterns appear we will undoubtedly see poor patterns, or those that are not useful, as well as good ones. How can we tell the difference? Naturally authors only write patterns that they think are good. The patterns community is certainly disinclined to set itself up as a certifier of patterns, even if it could.

I do not feel I can tackle this issue in general, but I can offer my personal thoughts. I may have written *Analysis Patterns*, but I do not think its going to be the last word on the subject. All of the patterns in that book are ones that I currently think will be useful. However, I'm sure that there are a few rotten apples lurking in the barrel, I just do not know which ones they are. By publishing these patterns in a book I am bringing all of these ideas out into the light, where many people can discuss them. As that discussion unfolds, as people try out the patterns in the book, I hope to see articles that will say which patterns are good, which ones are flawed, and which ones are plain wrong. This discussion will only increase our knowledge of our profession. Whatever the book's value as a source of useful patterns, it has a further value as a stimulus to others to talk about patterns. Over the last few years we have spent a lot of time talking about methodologies and arguing for one notation or another. This argument is boring, and has little value to me as a developer. Arguing about the patterns is much more productive and much more influential for me. At some stage someone, possibly me, will come out with a book that collects all the arguments together and establishes a new baseline for further discussion. Thus we will slowly walk our way toward an engineering handbook.

Patterns are useful now and many developers I know have found their professional skills greatly improved by a knowledge of patterns. If that were their only benefit it would be great indeed. Yet for the future of our profession, patterns are even more important. At the heart of any engineering there is science. In a recent discussion about patterns and academia, Ralph Johnson argued that the current pattern writers are like the early specimen hunters in biology who recorded the many and varied things they found, but did not necessarily come up with any way to make sense of what they saw. Such observation of things is an essential first step in science. Before Kepler and Newton could pronounce their laws, they needed de Brahe to make the observations. Patterns provide the specimens of things that seem to work. Only when we have enough of these can we truly move to more general principles of software, and then maybe some science will be present in computer science.

References

Beck, K. 1996. *Smalltalk Best Practice Patterns.* Prentice-Hall, Englewood Cliffs, NJ.

Buschmann, F., Meunier, R., Rohnert, H., Sommerlad, P. and Stal, M. 1996. *Pattern-Oriented Software Architecture: A System of Patterns.* John Wiley & Sons, New York.

Coplien, J.O. 1992. *Advanced C++ Styles and Idioms.* Addison-Wesley, Reading, MA.

Coplien, J.O. *Generative Development Process Pattern Language,* pp. 183-237. In [PLoPD1], 1995.

Coplien, J.O. and Schmidt, D.C. ed. 1995. *Pattern Languages of Program Design.* Addison-Wesley, Reading, MA.

Cunningham, W. 1996. *EPISODES: A Pattern Language of Competitive Development,* pp. 371-388. In [PLoPD2].

Fowler, M. 1997. *Analysis Patterns: Reusable Object Models.* Addison-Wesley, Reading, MA.

Fowler, M. 1997. *UML Distilled: Applying the Standard Object Modeling Language.* Addison-Wesley, Reading, MA.

Gamma, E., Helm, R., Johnson, R. and Vlissides, J. 1994. *Design Patterns: Elements of Reusable Object-Oriented Software.* Addison-Wesley, Reading, MA.

Hay, D. 1996. *Data Model Patterns: Conventions of Thought.* Dorset House, New York.

Kerth, N. *Caterpillar's Fate: A Pattern Language for the Transformation from Analysis to Design,* pp. 293-324. In [PloP1].

Lea, D. 1997. *Concurrent Programming in Java: Design Principles and Patterns.* Addison-Wesley, Reading, MA.

Mowbray, T.J. and Malveau, R.C. 1997. *CORBA Design Patterns.* Wiley, New York.

Vlissides, J.M., Coplien, J.O. and Kerth, N.L. ed. 1996. *Pattern Languages of Program Design 2.* Addison-Wesley, Reading, MA.

37

Pattern Template Library

Jiri Soukup
Code Farms Inc.

37.1 Introduction

The prime purpose of *design patterns* as introduced in (Gamma et al., 1995) was to bring some system and reusability into the design of software architecture. A properly recorded pattern provides a textual description, a structural diagram, and describes situations suitable (or not suitable) for this pattern. By cataloging patterns and giving them generally recognized names, we avoid duplications, and improve communication among programmers. In my opinion, the most important parts of the pattern description are the structural diagram (because it determines how to implement the pattern), and the description of its intended purpose (because this explains the reasons for the pattern's existence).

When you browse through the structural diagrams in (Gamma et al., 1995), it is hard not to notice how they resemble traditional data structures. They work with collections, lists, and reference pointers among classes, and the only difference is that design patterns also employ inheritance. This may not be true of absolutely every design pattern, but it certainly is true of patterns intended for software architecture, or so-called *structural patterns.* I see design patterns as an OO generalization of the traditional data structures. For an example, see pattern *Composite* in Figure 37.1.

Another curious thing about design patterns is that they were originally intended as a high-level design concept, and the idea of representing them as reusable C++ classes seems to deny this original purpose. Typically, patterns use abstract collections without specifying whether these are implemented as arrays, lists, hash tables, or as special trees. This is an implementation detail which is supposed to be irrelevant when thinking in the terms of patterns.

There are two problems with this view, however. There is no point in designing a software architecture if we do not implement it in code, and having pre-coded patterns would definitely help just as it helps to have pre-coded collections and other data structures. The second problem is that, unless you have the OO diagram of the architecture, the original design intent and its patterns are buried in the manual

0-8493-3135-8/99/$0.00+$.50

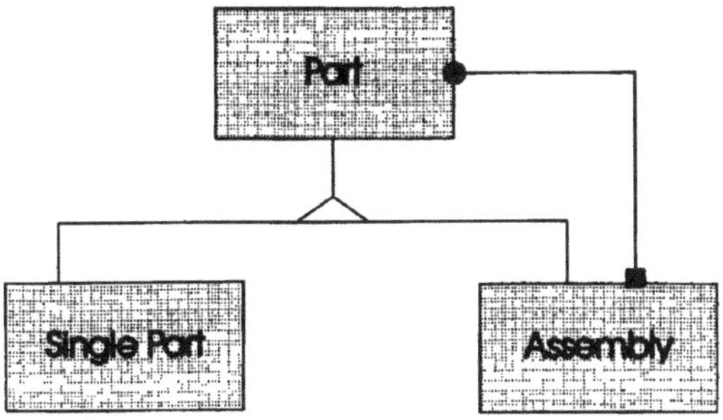

FIGURE 37.1 Pattern *Composite* is an elegant way of describing a multi-level hierarchical composition. Single parts are derived from Part, while Assembly, which by itself is a Part, consists of several Parts, some of which can again be Assemblies. All this is expressed by one collection and two inheritance relations.

implementation. It is usually very hard to figure out what patterns have been used by just reading the code.

For these reasons, I recommend working with *abstract* and *concrete* patterns, which are an analogy of the abstract and concrete data structures (Soukup, 1996). Abstract patterns are the patterns listed in (Gamma et al., 1995), and concrete patterns are those abstract patterns where the collections and other features have been implemented in some particular way. Usually, there can be several concrete patterns for one abstract pattern, but often one of the concrete patterns provides the most efficient, practical implementation.

It would be nice if we could implement concrete patterns as generic C++ classes (templates), and store them in a class library just like collections or string classes. The way to do this is the main subject of this article. After several years of experimenting with the idea, I implemented such a library using two basic ideas: (1) all patterns are based on intrusive data structures and (2) with one exception, all patterns and data structures are represented as manager classes. Section 37.2 will explain both of these concepts.

The Pattern Template Library (PTL) was released only two months prior to submitting this article. It is sold over the Internet at http://www.CodeFarms.com. There is no long-term experience with this approach yet, even though the library is already used in a variety of applications.

37.2 Underlying Principles

37.2.1 Intrusive Data Structures

Let's start with an example of a simple data structure (in my view, any data structure is also a pattern, even if it does not use inheritance), where every Department contains several Employees, while each Employee knows its Department — see Figure 37.2. This relation is often called *aggregate*, or *one-to-many*

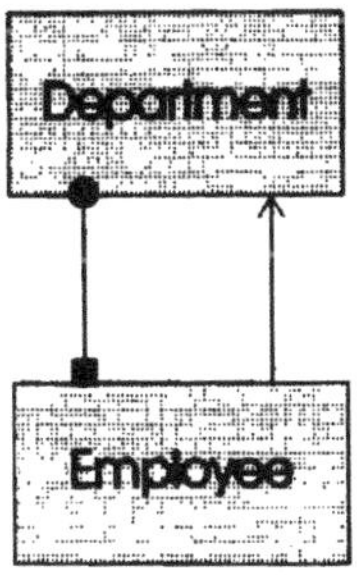

FIGURE 37.2 Class diagram of the Aggregate (1-to-many relation). Every Department has several Employees, and each Employee knows its Department.

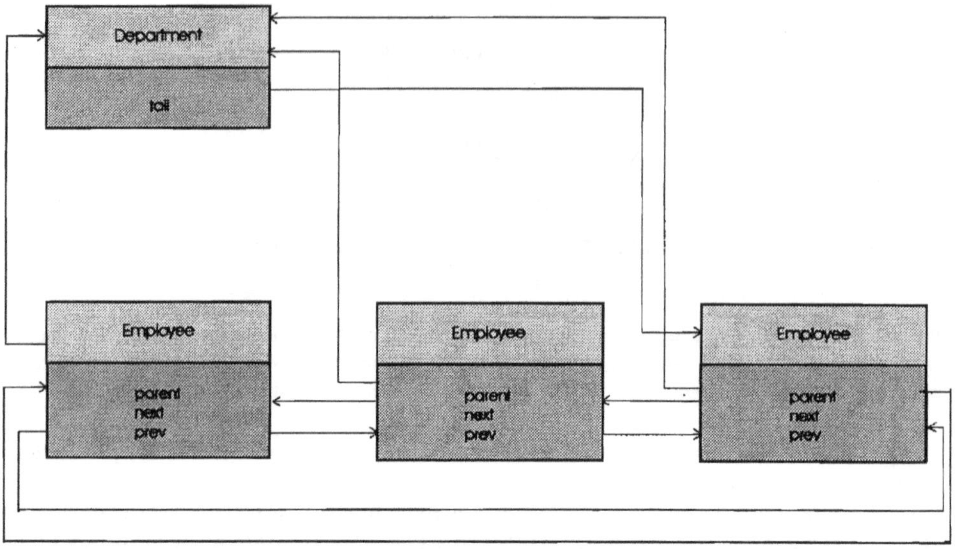

FIGURE 37.3 Implementation of the Aggregate from Figure 37.2, using embedded (intrusive) pointers.

relation, and since it expresses a hierarchy of objects, it is one of the most frequently occurring data organizations. If you design this particular aggregate from scratch, you would likely code it with pointers embedded in the participating classes as shown in Figure 37.2. There are several ways of implementing the list. Instead of the usual NULL-ending list, all classes in the library use circular lists (rings). As explained in Chapter 39, rings allow fast runtime checking of data integrity.

The pointers that form the data structure in Figure 37.3 are embedded (inserted) into the participating objects, and for this reason this implementation is called *intrusive*. Note that practically all existing class libraries are non-intrusive. Their *containers* form data structures with auxiliary objects which only point to the application objects. Figure 37.4 shows a situation where a container holding several Employees is a member of the Department. This arrangement is usually considered to be non-intrusive because Employees do not store any pointers, but it is really just half-intrusive, because the container itself is a member of class Department.

If the aggregate is one of the most frequently required data organizations, why is it that with the exception of Code Farms libraries, no class library (MFC, tools.h++, STL) provides this data organization? The reason is that all of these libraries are container-based, and the aggregate is inherently intrusive. Note that Figure 37.4 is not equivalent to Figure 37.3, because the parent pointer is missing. If you add this pointer to class Employee, both Department and Employee are modified regardless of how you implemented the list.

There are situations when containers are better, and there are situations when intrusive data structures are better. For a detailed comparison, see (Soukup, 1997). Containers are easier to implement with templates, but as you will see intrusive data structures are not much more difficult. Intrusive structures are better for implementing design patterns, because design patterns often include two-way communication, which is inherently intrusive.

37.2.2 Manager Classes

In Figure 37.4, the functions which manipulate the relation are assigned to the container. When implementing the aggregate (Figures 37.2 and 37.3), most programmers would assign these functions arbitrarily to classes Department or Employee, depending on where the function could be most naturally implemented. For example,

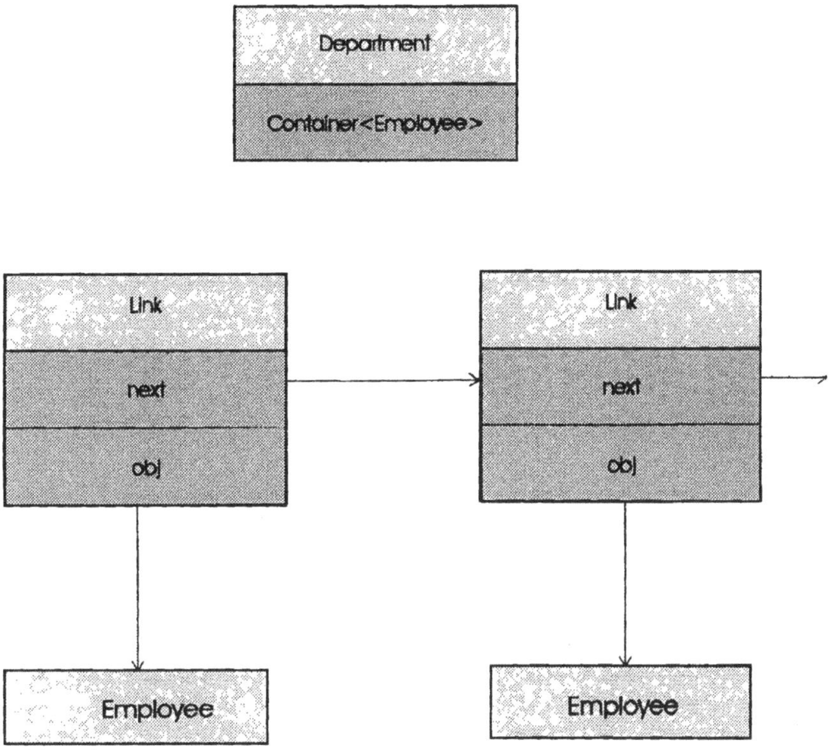

FIGURE 37.4 Indirect list (container) which assigns several Employees to one Department, but it needs no pointers or other data in the Employee class. This data organization is not equivalent to that from Figure 37.3, because the parent pointer is missing.

```
Employee* Employee::nextEmployee(){ return next;}
Department* Employee::myDepartment(){ return parent;}
void Department::addEmployee(Employee *e){ ... };
Employee* Department::firstEmployee(){
  Employee* e = NULL; if(tail)e = tail->next; return e;}
```

It may look completely natural and logical to distribute the functionality of the aggregate between the Department and Employee, but if Department and Employee participate in several other data structures, this leads to poor architecture where every class depends on every other class; if one class changes all other classes have to be recompiled. Such spaghetti++ code should be avoided, but how? One possibility is, for every data organization (or pattern), introduce a new class which will manage the organization, and assign the functions which control the pattern to this class. For more details, see Soukup (1994 and 1997). Typically, the manager class contains little or no data, but it has all the functions that manipulate the data structure. To provide fast access to the internal pointers, this class must be a friend of the classes that participate in the pattern. For example, we can introduce class DEaggregate — see also Figure 37.5:

```
class DEaggregate {
  public:
    Employee *nextEmployee(Employee *e){return e->next;}
    Department *myDepartment(Employee *e){return e->parent;}
    void addEmployee(Employee *e){ ... }
```

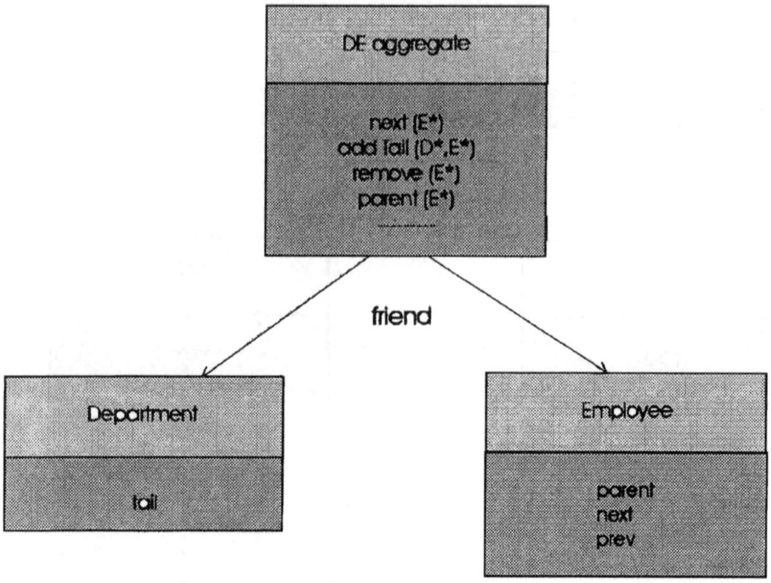

FIGURE 37.5 Class diagram of the aggregate between Department and Employee, implemented with the manager class *DEaggregate.*

```
    Employee *firstEmployee(Department *d){
      Employee* e = d->tail; if(e)e = e->next; return e;}
    ...
  };
  class Department {
  friend class DEaggregate;
    Employee *tail;
    ...
  public:
    ...
  };
  class Employee {
  friend class DEaggregate;
    Department *parent;
    Employee *next;
    Employee *prev;
    ...
  public:
    ...
};
```

Instead of coding the aggregate again for every new application, it makes more sense to design a generic aggregate with C++ templates and store it in a class library. The pointers that we need in the application classes such as Employee, can be injected through inheritance. In the following code, class P is the application class which will be the parent of the aggregate, and class C is the class which will be the child of the aggregate. The integer parameter i, with default 0, prevents conflict when applying the same pattern to the same participating classes several time (e.g., for multiple lists). The following three classes will be stored in a library:

```
//represents the aggregate, has all the functions,
//stores no structural pointers
template<class P, class C, int i = 0> class Aggregate {
public:
  C *next(C *c){return (AggregateChild<P,C,i>::c)->next;}
  P *parent(C *c){return (AggregateChild<P,C,i>::c)->parent;}
  void addTail(P *p,C *c);//add c as a tail under p
  void remove(C *c);//remove child c from its parent
  C *head(P *p){ C* c = (AggregateParent<P,C,i>::p)->tail;
                                    if(c)c = c->next; return c;}
  ...
};

//through inheritance, injects pointers into the parent class
template<class P, class C, int i = 0> class AggregateParent {
friend class Aggregate<P,C,i>;
  C *tail;
public:
  AggregateParent(){tail = NULL;}
};

//through inheritance, injects pointers into the child class
template<class P, class C, int i = 0> class AggregateChild {
friend class Aggregate<P,C,i>;
  P *parent;
  C *next;
  C *prev;
public:
  AggregateChild(){parent = NULL; next = prev = NULL;}
};
```

In essence, this is the way the PTL is constructed. The application inherits AggregateParent and AggregateChild, and since we have only one aggregate between Department and Employee, we can use the default value for parameter i:

```
class Department: public AggregateParent<Department,Employee> {
  ...//no members or functions related to the aggregate
};

class Employee: public AggregateChild<Department,Employee> {
  ...//no members or functions related to the aggregate
};

Aggregate<Department,Employee> myAggregate;
```

37.2.3 Iterators

A class library usually provides one or several iterators for each data organization. The iterator permits you to traverse the data using ++ and -- and other operators. However, if you try to destroy objects while traversing a list, most libraries will crash:

```
class Department { ... };
class Employee { ... };

Employee *e;
Aggregate<Department,Employee> agg;

//create a department with 10 employees
Department* d = new Department;
for(i = 0; i<10; i++){
```

```
        e = new Employee;
        aggr.addTail(d,e);
    }

    //disconnect and destroy all employees
    AggregateIterator<Department,Employee> it;
    for(e = it.start(d); e; e = ++it){//crash on the second pass
        aggr.remove(e);
        delete e;
    };
```

The reason for this crash is that most iterators remember the current object, and they use its *next* pointer to get to the next object on the list. If the current object is destroyed within the loop, the next call to ++ attempts to use pointer next on an invalid (already destroyed) object, which results in a crash.

The cure for this problem is to let the iterator remember not the current object, but the next object on the list. Then, even if the current object is removed, you still get the next one correctly. This is the method used throughout the PTL. The improved iterator still is not bullet proof though. For example, if you perform the following operation, it will crash:

```
Employee *e, *nxt;
for(e = it.start(d); e; e = ++it){
    if(...){
        nxt = aggr.nextChild(e);
        aggr.remove(nxt);
        delete nxt;
    }
    ...
};
```

It is possible to design an iterator which permits the application to remove or add objects at any position while traversing lists, even in multiple loops. In this case, the Aggregate class keeps a list of all active AggregateIterator instances. Functions Aggregate::addTail() and Aggregate::remove() run through all active iterators and check whether the change affects the next object that should be stored by the iterator, and if it does, it makes an appropriate correction. This is the way the iterators work in the C++ Data Object Library, see Soukup (1988). The PTL does not use such super-smart iterators. When running with multiple threads, the central list of all active iterators causes a dependency among otherwise independent threads.

PTL permits three styles of traversing the data. The first style combines a for(..) loop with functions start() or end:

```
Department *d;
Employee *e;
AggregateIterator<Department,Employee> it;
...
for(e = it.start(d); e; e = ++it){
    ...//runs through all e under d
}

for(e = it.end(d); e; e = --it){
    ...//runs through all e under d
}
```

The second style uses convenient macros ITERATE() or RETRACE(), which hide the underlying for() loops:

```
Department *d;
Employee *e;
```

```
AggregateIterator<Department,Employee> it;
   ...
ITERATE(it,d,e){
     ...//runs through all e under d
}

RETRACE(it,d,e){
     ...//runs through all e under d
}
```

The third style uses function next(), but you have to handle the end of the loop yourself. Don't forget, we are working with a ring:

```
for(e = aggr.head(d); e; e = aggr.next(e)){
   ...//runs through all e under d
   if(e == aggr.tail(d))break;      //end condition
}
```

Multiple loops are permitted in all three styles, ++ and –– can be used within the same loop.

37.3 Best Practices

37.3.1 User Interface and STL

Standards in programming are just as important as in any other science, and when designing new libraries or software, one should adhere to existing standards whenever possible. Since the Standard Template Library (STL) has been established for C++, why is the PTL using a different interface?

The main reason is that STL is based on indirect containers, while PTL uses intrusive data structures. As the result of this conceptual difference, there are certain PTL operations that STL cannot perform, and some STL functions which in PTL must have a different syntax. For example, the next() operation is natural to the PTL aggregate, but cannot be performed or needs access to the parent in STL. Also there is only a small overlap between the two libraries in what classes they provide. It is better to think about PTL as an extension of STL rather than as its competition. Both libraries can be used simultaneously on the same project.

The two libraries are also different in how they control their data structures. For example, in STL, class Collection represents both the parent and the manager of the collection. If you want class Department to keep Employees, Department typically keeps the collection as a member. The outside world needs a custom coded function Department::addTail(Employee*) in order to add an Employee to the collection.

```
class Employee {
   ...
};

class Department {
   Collection<Employee> employees;
   ...
public:
   void addTail(Employee *e){employees.addTail(e);}
};

int main() {
   Department *d; Employee *e;
   ...
   d->addTail(e);//logic: adding e to d
}
```

Compare this with the PTL implementation, where control is provided by the manager class which is *outside* of the two classes participating in the collection. Note the different syntax which may first appear weird, especially if you are used to the STL syntax. If you think about it more though, the PTL syntax makes more sense.

```
class Employee : public CollectionChild<Department,Employee>{
   ...
};

class Department : public CollectionParent<Department,Employee>{
   ...
};

int main() {
   Department *d; Employee *e;
   Collection<Department,Employee> employees;
   ...
   employees.addTail(d,e);      //logic: add e to 'employees' under d
}
```

Exercise: Assume that each Department keeps two or three separate collections of Employees, and try the two implementation styles.

There is one additional, philosophical reason for the difference between the interfaces. Personally, I believe in a simple, compact interface, and nine years of experience with the Data Object Library convinced me that it is the right choice. Perhaps my memory is poor, but I have problems memorizing all the functions in STL, and always having the STL manual beside my terminal is not practical. The Data Object Library interface is more universal. With about one fifth of the functions and operators, it proved to be satisfactory even in a great variety of performance sensitive applications. PTL follows the same philosophy, and its interface is similar to the interface used by the Data Object Library. Perhaps, a new standard will be needed for intrusive libraries.

37.3.2 Available Classes

37.3.2.1 Collection or Linked List: Collection<Parent,Child,i>

Collection is just like the Aggregate which we discussed extensively above, except that the Child does not keep a pointer back to its Parent. Each Parent maintains a doubly linked, intrusive, circular list of Children. Depending on how you interpret this pattern, Collection can be used as a linked list, collection, sorted collection, or a set. It is one of the basic building blocks of numerous data structures and patterns. Besides the usual functions that control this data structure, the interface allows you to merge or split collections and sort them on demand. Integer index i, which is 0 by default, is used only for multiple collections with identical participating classes.

37.3.2.2 Aggregate or One_to_Many: Aggregate<Parent,Child,i>

This is the data organization discussed above. Each Parent keeps a doubly linked, intrusive, circular list of Children. This pattern is derived (inherits) from COLLECTION; aggregates can be merged, split, or sorted just like collections. Some interface functions require fewer parameters than for the collection, because in the aggregate the Child always knows its Parent.

37.3.2.3 Array Container or Basic Dynamic Array: ArrayContainer<Item,i>

This is a dynamic array in its classical container form. It is not implemented as a pattern. The data and all functions that control it are in the same class, and no intrusive data is involved. This array has been included for completeness, and also as a building block for some more complex patterns such as Flyweight. Note that this array can be used in several different ways. For instance, you can control its order, sort it, use it as a simple collection, array of pointers, as a stack, and many other things.

This class keeps an array of objects, which you can access with the operator [] as if it were a real array. The array starts with a certain size (either default or specified by the constructor), and as you access it, it automatically increases its size as needed. You can control how the array will grow or shrink, and how it will be initialized. This is one of the classes that has a close relative in the STL. When using the Template Manager, the Pattern() statement is not required; an object of type ArrayContainer<> is typically a member of an application class.

37.3.2.4 Intrusive Array: Array<Holder,Item,i>

This is the same dynamic array as ArrayContainer<>, but treated as a pattern (intrusive data structure), which assigns the array to the Holder class. You as the user do not have to worry about whether the array is a member, inherited, whether there are other arrays, etc. The access is as for other intrusive patterns. For example, if Register keeps an array of integers, you have:

```
class Register:: Pattern(Register) {
   ...
};
int main() {
   Register* r = new Register;
   Array<Register,int> myArray;
   ...
   myArray.array(r)[8] = 134;
```

37.3.2.5 Pointer Array: PtrArray<Holder,Item,i>

Both ArrayContainer<Item> and Array<Holder,Item> can store arrays of pointers just by declaring ArrayContainer<Item*> or Array<Holder,Item*>. For convenience and the clarity of interface, PTL provides a special array class which stores pointers. PtrArray<Holder,Item> is derived from Array<Holder,Item>, is equivalent to Array<Holder,Item*>, but has some additional functions, different initialization, and modified count control.

37.3.2.6 Composite: Composite<Parent,Child,i>

This pattern describes a multi-level hierarchy of objects, and it is internally derived from Collection<Parent,Child>. If you want a container-based Composite, design it yourself with the PtrArray<Parent,Child>. Class Parent must inherit from Child, and both Parent and Child must have function

```
virtual int C::isComposite();
```

which returns 0 for the Child and 1 for the Parent. If you use the Template Manager, both the inheritance and the special function are provided automatically. Since Composite is derived from Collection, hierarchical subsets can be sorted, split, or merged, and their order can be controlled. In addition to the forward and backward iterator, Composite also has functions which permit traversal of the entire hierarchy: depthFirst(), and breadthFirst(). Function dissolve() disconnects a given subtree.

37.3.2.7 Flyweight: Flyweight<Keeper,HeavyWeight,CalculatedState,StoredState,i>

In an attempt to improve clarity, we are using terminology different from Gamma (1995). In this pattern the Keeper class keeps a non-intrusive container of relatively large objects (HeavyWeight) which can be referenced by an index. The index can be unsigned int, unsigned short, or unsigned char, the operation is transparent. In a typical application, a line of text is stored as an array of small integers (lightweight, unsigned char) that index into an array of larger objects that can actually draw the characters for the printer. Some data is calculated on the fly (CalculatedState), for example, the x,y position of the character within the given page. The Flyweight class can be used in a variety of situations, with light characters stored in arrays or more complex data structures such as B-trees. Its design also permits switching between multiple Flyweights (for example, when handling different fonts).

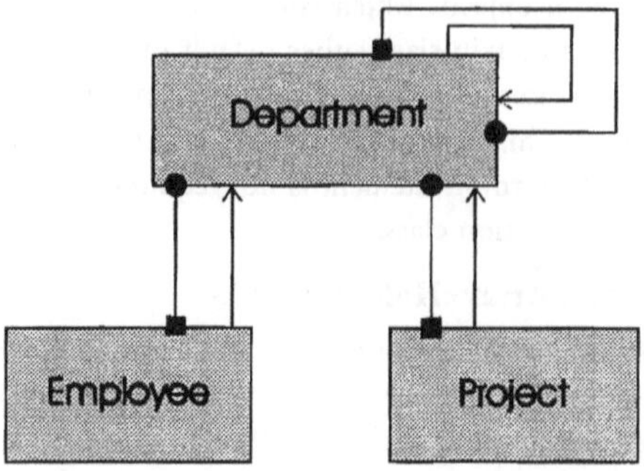

FIGURE 37.6 Three Aggregates used simultaneously. We have a tree of Departments, where each Department has several Employees and several Projects. Both Employees and Projects are always assigned to only one Department.

Our Flyweight<> does not provide storage of the lightweight characters — the application must do that — but it takes care of everything else including the communication between the Keeper and the HeavyWeight and the calculation of the CalculatedState.

37.3.2.8 Finite State Machine: FSM<F,S,I,T,D>

A generic pattern for the Finite State Machine was not included in Gamma (1995), and it is not in any commonly used class library. Yet, it is a very important pattern, and many applications depend on its efficient implementation. The PTL allows you to create and dynamically modify your own finite state machines, while maintaining a high runtime performance. The template has the following parameters:

F = Your finite state machine class
S = Base class for all your state classes
I = Base class for all your input classes
T = Type for the internal tables, must be unsigned and able to accommodate MAX(numInputs,numStates,numFuncts)
D = Integer id when using multiple parallel FSMs (as for other patterns)

The FSM assumes that you have a special class for each of your states, with a common base state class, S. Similarly, you must have a special class for each of the input stimuli, with one common input base class, I. In many applications, these two classes will be just an integer or a byte.

Your FSM class (myFSM) can have an arbitrary number of transition functions that look like this: S* myFSM::f(S*,void**), and the same function can be assigned to several transitions. The assignment of both functions and of target states is performed dynamically, while executing your program.

The FSM<> class keeps internally two (ni × ns) tables, where ni is the number of inputs, and ns is the number of states. One table stores the index of the target state, the other table indexes the transfer functions. Entries in both tables are of type T (usually 1 byte).

37.3.3 Complex Inheritance Statements

Once you understand the concept of manager classes, the PTL is easier to work with than any of the container libraries. The only thing that can get complicated is the inheritance statements, especially when some of the classes participate in more than one pattern.

Figure 37.6 shows an example of such a situation where Departments form a tree and each Department has its own sets of Employees and Projects. The class diagram represents this situation as a combination of three aggregates: Department-Department, Department-Employee, and Department-Project. A program using this data organization would typically start like this:

```
#include <aggregat.h>
class Department;
class Employee;
class Project;
class Department:     public AggregateParent<Department,Department>,
                      public AggregateChild<Department,Department>,
                      public AggregateParent<Department,Employee>,
                      public AggregateParent<Department,Project>{
   ...
};
class Employee: public AggregateChild<Department,Employee>{
   ...
};
class Project: public AggregateChild<Department,Project>{
   ...
};
//-----------------------------------------------
Aggregate<Department,Department> departments;
Aggregate<Department,Employee> employees;
Aggregate<Department,Project> projects;
```

You can imagine that when using 25 classes which participate in 15 patterns, these inheritance statements grow complicated. At the same time, the information contained in these statements is already available from three Aggregate definitions. If we know that class Aggregate works with classes AggregateParent and AggregateChild (and that information can be stored in the library), then it is simple to conclude that

```
from line1:
   Department must inherit AggregateParent<Department,Department>
   Department must inherit AggregateChild<Department,Department>
from line2:
   Department must inherit AggregateParent<Department,Employee>
   Employee must inherit AggregateChild<Department,Employee>
from line3:
   Department must inherit AggregateParent<Department,Project>
   Project must inherit AggregateChild<Department,Project>
```

From the viewpoint of the application programmer, the inheritance statements are an unnecessary duplication. This leads to the idea of generating the inheritance statements automatically.

37.3.4 Template Manager

Instead of coding the inheritance statements by hand, we can write a template manager which will read the declarations of the patterns and generate the inheritance statements. This simple program has only 450 lines excluding comments, and its source is already part of the PTL. This is not a code generator, it only makes the handling of templates more elegant and safe.

To make the template manager simple, we reserve two keywords: *pattern* and *Pattern*. The first keyword will mark all pattern declarations so that the template manager can find them easily.

```
//-----------------------------------------------
pattern Aggregate<Department,Department> departments;
pattern Aggregate<Department,Employee> employees;
pattern Aggregate<Department,Project> projects;
//-----------------------------------------------
```

The second keyword will be a cover name for the combined inheritance statements required for the given class. The Template Manager will generate these Pattern(.) expressions in the form of a macro.

From the application programmer's point of view, all the inheritance triggered by the use of the library becomes transparent.

```
class Department: Pattern(Department) {
   ...//everything as before
};
class Employee: Pattern(Employee) {
   ...//everything as before
};
class Project: Pattern(Project) {
   ...//everything as before
};
```

If we have the Template Manager which already generates code (we allowed the devil to put one foot in the door), we can improve two more things:

1. We can let the Template Manager decide which header files must be included and store this information in file *pattern.h*. We then do not have to worry which files to include, even when we change the architecture. We always include pattern.h.
2. We can hide the long templates for iterators under more sensible names which refer to the instance of the patterns. For example, instead of

   ```
   AggregateIterator<Department,Department,0> it;
   ```

   you can write

   ```
   pattern_iterator_departments it;
   ```

The last line uses the name *departments*, because this iterator is associated with

```
Aggregate<Department,Department,0> departments;
```

Note the improved clarity of our original code:

```
#define TEMPLATE_MANAGER
#include "pattern.h"//provides all required header files

class Department;
class Employee;
class Project;
class Department: Pattern(Department) {
   ...//everything as before
};

class Employee: Pattern(Employee) {
   ...//everything as before
};

class Project : Pattern(Project) {
   ...//everything as before
};

//these statements are the roadmap to all patterns/relations
//-----------------------------------------------
pattern Aggregate<Department,Department,0> departments;
pattern Aggregate<Department,Employee,0> employees;
pattern Aggregate<Department,Project,0> projects;
//-----------------------------------------------
```

The Template Manager may include any functions or members into the body of the class. For example, if file pattern.h includes the following macros

```
#define Pattern(A) Pattern##_##Project
#define Pattern_Project                                  \
  public AggregateChild<Department,Project>              \
  {                                                      \
  friend class Aggregate<Department,Project,0>           \
  /##/
```

The application code

```
class Project : Pattern(Project) {
  ...
};
```

turns into

```
class Project : public AggregateChild<Department,Project,0>
{
  friend class Aggregate<Department,Project,0>
  ...
};
```

Note how the original '{' is eliminated by the hidden comment '//' at the end of the macro, a new '{' is inserted into a new location, and the friend statement is inserted inside the body of the class. All these tricks are not essential, they only make the use of templates more readable.

Prior to compiling your program, you run the Template Manager on any section of your code which includes *pattern* statements. Typically, this can be your entire source (if this is a relatively small program), your main header file, or a special header file where you keep all the *pattern* declarations. The Template Manager generates file pattern.h. You do not have to generate this file again when debugging your program, unless you remove or add a new pattern, or change some of the patterns definitions. *Important*— You can use the library with or without the Template Manager. The syntax is identical.

37.3.5 Complete Example

This presentation would not be complete without one full, running example where you can see the library in full action. The following problem deals with class Product, which represents a complex mechanical device built as a hierarchy of Assemblies. Each Assembly is composed of simple Parts and lower level Assemblies (pattern Composite). Parts can be: Plate, Bolt, and Nut. Each Bolt keeps a pointer to its corresponding Nut. Each Plate keeps a one-to-many relation with the associated Bolts (pattern Aggregate), and the Product also keeps a list of all Plates (pattern Collection). This is a little framework which resides in memory. The standard class diagram (I miss special symbols for patterns) is in Figure 37.7. The following code creates a fictitious product composed of complex parts, and prints the entire assembly.

```
//-------------------------------------------------------------
#include <iostream.h>
#define TEMPLATE_MANAGER
#include "pattern.h"
class Part;
class Plate;
class Bolt;
class Nut;
class Assembly;
class Product;

class Part  : Pattern(Part) {
protected:
  int mPartNo;
```

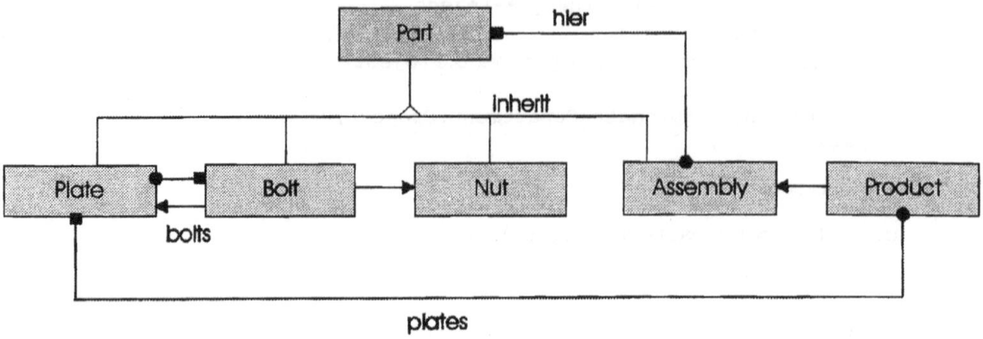

FIGURE 37.7 The standard class diagrams have no symbols for patterns. This architecture includes patterns Composite<Assembly,Part> hier, Aggregate<Plate,Bolt> bolts, and Collection<Pròduct,Plate> plates. I use blobs with the name of the pattern to show which classes participate in each pattern.

```
public:
   Part(int n){mPartNo = n;}
   virtual void prt(int k){};
};

class Plate : public Part, Pattern(Plate) {
                              //  inheritance of Part is not part of composite
   int mx,my;
public:
   Plate(int n,int x,int y)  :Part(n){mx = x; my = y;}
   void prt(int k);
};

class Bolt : public Part, Pattern(Bolt) {
                          //inheritance needed, Part not a part of composite
   int mDiam;
   Nut *mpNut;      //knows its own nut
public:
   Bolt(int n,int d,Nut *np)  :Part(n){mDiam = d; mpNut = np;}
   void prt(int k);
};

class Nut : public Part {//no Pattern(..), is not in any pattern
   int mDiam;
public:
   Nut(int n,int d):Part(n){mDiam = d;}
   void prt(int k);
};

class Assembly : Pattern(Assembly) {//covers even inheritance from
Part
public:
   Assembly(int n)  :Part(n){}
   void prt(int k);
};

class Product : Pattern(Product) {
   char *mpName;       //product name
   Assembly *mpAssembly;  //to the root assembly
public:
```

```
    Product(char*name,Assembly*root){mpName =name;mpAssembly =root;}
    void prt(); //print the composition of the entire product
};

void Plate::prt(int k){
    for(int i = 0; i<k; i++) cout << " ";
    cout << "Plate No." << mPartNo << " x = "
         << mx << " y = " << my << "\n";
}

void Nut::prt(int k){
    for(int i = 0; i<k; i++) cout << "   ";
    cout << "Nut No." << mPartNo << " diam = " << mDiam << "\n";
}

void Bolt::prt(int k){
    for(int i = 0; i<k; i++) cout << " ";
    cout << "Bolt No." << mPartNo << " diam = "
         << mDiam << " -> "; mpNut->prt(0);
}

void Assembly::prt(int k){
    pattern_iterator_hier it;
    Part *pPart;
    for(int i = 0; i<k; i++) cout << "   ";
    cout << "Assembly No." << mPartNo << "\n";
    ITERATE(it,this,pPart){
        pPart->prt(k+1);
    }
}

void Product::prt(){
    Plate *pPlate;
    //  first print the assembly hierarchy
    cout << "Product = " << mpName << "\n";
    mpAssembly->prt(1);
    cout << "list of all plates:\n";
    pattern_iterator_plates it;
    ITERATE(it,this,pPlate) pPlate->prt(1);
}

int main(void){
    pattern Composite<Assembly,Part,0> hier; //hierarchyofAssemblies
    pattern Aggregate<Plate,Bolt,0> bolts;     //1-to-many
    pattern Collection<Product,Plate,0> plates; //all plates
    Product *pProduct;
    Assembly *pRootAssembly;

    //short names permit a table-like form of creating the data
    Assembly *a1,*a2; Plate *p; Bolt *b; Nut *n;

    //create a complex product from plates, bolts, and nuts
    pRootAssembly = new Assembly(1000);
    pProduct = new Product("myProduct",pRootAssembly);
    a1 = new Assembly(1100); //  assembly one
p = new Plate(1110,34,22); plates.addTail(pProduct,p);
                                                  hier.addTail(a1,p);
n = new Nut(1101,10);                             hier.addTail(a1,n);
b = new Bolt(1102,10,n); bolts.addTail(p,b);      hier.addTail(a1,b);
```

```
n = new Nut(1103,10);                                   hier.addTail(a1,n);
b = new Bolt(1104,10,n); bolts.addTail(p,b);            hier.addTail(a1,b);
   a2 = new Assembly(1100); //assembly two
p = new Plate(1120,72,12); plates.addTail(pProduct,p);
                                                        hier.addTail(a2,p);
n = new Nut(1105,8);                                    hier.addTail(a2,n);
b = new Bolt(1106,8,n); bolts.addTail(p,b);             hier.addTail(a2,b);
p = new Plate(1130,14,14); plates.addTail(pProduct,p);
                                                        hier.addTail(a2,p);
n = new Nut(1107,6);                                    hier.addTail(a2,n);
b = new Bolt(1108,6,n); bolts.addTail(p,b);             hier.addTail(a2,b);

   //nut & bolt for the root assembly, not linked to any plate
   n = new Nut(1501,8);      hier.addTail(pRootAssembly,n);
   b = new Bolt(1502,8,n); hier.addTail(pRootAssembly,b);
   hier.addTail(pRootAssembly,a1);
   hier.addTail(pRootAssembly,a2);
   pProduct->prt();
   return 0;
}
```

The program generates the following output:

```
Product = myProduct
   Assembly No.1000
      Nut No.1501 diam = 8
      Bolt No.1502 diam = 8 -> Nut No.1501 diam = 8
      Assembly No.1100
         Plate No.1110 x = 34 y = 22
         Nut No.1101 diam = 10
         Bolt No.1102 diam = 10 -> Nut No.1101 diam = 10
         Nut No.1103 diam = 10
         Bolt No.1104 diam = 10 -> Nut No.1103 diam = 10
      Assembly No.1100
         Plate No.1120 x = 72 y = 12
         Nut No.1105 diam = 8
         Bolt No.1106 diam = 8 -> Nut No.1105 diam = 8
         Plate No.1130 x = 14 y = 14
         Nut No.1107 diam = 6
         Bolt No.1108 diam = 6 -> Nut No.1107 diam = 6
list of all plates:
   Plate No.1110 x = 34 y = 22
   Plate No.1120 x = 72 y = 12
   Plate No.1130 x = 14 y = 14
```

37.3.6 Error Handling

The library detects two types of errors:

1. During attempts to perform an operation which would corrupt data integrity a warning message is issued, and the operation is bypassed (not executed). For example, this happens if you want to insert object A into a list before object B, but B is not in any list.
2. Data is corrupted beyond repair, and the program will crash sooner or later. An error message is issued, and the library throws exception using class PTLerrorHandler. For example, this happens for an Aggregate, if object A is one of the children of B, but the parent pointer on A does not point to B.

37.4 Research Issues and Summary

More research is needed to provide smart iterators which would work in a multi-threaded environment. One possibility would be to keep a separate list of active iterators for each thread. Probably, an addition to the STL will be needed with special attention to intrusive data structures.

Another suggestion: Design patterns which have the same structural diagram should, perhaps, be considered to be the same abstract pattern. Otherwise, one concrete pattern may implement more than one abstract pattern, which is counter-intuitive.

The existing PTL is only a seed of the library I envision today. Our company encourages anybody with good pattern classes coded in the PTL style to add them to the library, which we hope will grow to include all major patterns.

37.4.1 Summary

The PTL is unique in two ways: (1) it lets you use design patterns as if they were ordinary collections and (2) it provides intrusive data structures not available in other C++ libraries. The library has been implemented with pure C++ templates (no code generation necessary). The optional Template Manager only simplifies complex inheritance statements.

References

Gamma, E., Helm, R., Johnson, R. and Vlissides, J. 1995. *Design Patterns — Elements of Reusable Object-Oriented Software.* Addison-Wesley, Reading, MA.

Soukup, J. 1994. *Taming C++, Pattern Classes and Persistence for Large Projects.* Addison-Wesley, Reading, MA.

Soukup, J. 1996. Quality patterns (implementing patterns), *The C++ Rep.*, Vol. 8, No. 9, Oct., pp.34-47.

Soukup, J. 1997. Intrusive Data Structures, two-part article submitted to *The C++ Report* in June, 1998.

Soukup J. 1999. Coding and Debugging three-times Faster, in *Handbook of Object Technology,* Zamir, S., Ed., CRC Press, Boca Raton, FL.

Further Information

For more information, look at the Code Farms' Web site, *http://www.CodeFarms.com.* The site lets you browse the PTL documentation, or download a free demo copy which includes the full documentation in HTML format.

38

Patterns Mining

Linda Rising
AG Communication Systems

38.1 Introduction

The Design Patterns text, Gamma (1994), appeared in October 1994 and started a wave that swept across the software community. At first there were patterns for object-oriented software and now there are analysis patterns, system test patterns, organization and process patterns, Smalltalk patterns, customer interaction patterns, and patterns for many domains and interests.

A pattern is a way of documenting experience by capturing successful solutions to recurring problems. This documentation is complete in the sense that the context for the problem, the forces that weigh upon the problem-solver, the rationale, and the resulting context of applying the solution must all be carefully recorded. A pattern is more than a simple heuristic that leaves users without a sense of when it is appropriate to follow the guideline. This additional information makes the pattern useful. An example of a pattern template can be found on the AG Communication Systems Patterns Home Page (AGCS). The template shows the information that must be documented to produce a useful pattern.

What every corporate group in the world wants, however, is not a book of patterns written by someone outside the company, but a collection of patterns that reflect the company's way of doing business. The business goal is a handbook of best practices that documents the things the company has done well. This handbook would ensure that corporate wisdom would be recorded and shared with current and future employees. It is almost certain that no one person already has all this knowledge, so everyone in the company would become more knowledgeable about the business and the whole organization would improve.

This sounds wonderful, but how is it accomplished? Obviously, such a handbook does not appear overnight but requires considerable investment. Will the people who know the business willingly create patterns and, in so doing, perhaps, make themselves less valuable to the organization? In these days of downsizing and re-engineering, this may not be likely. Will roving patterns reporters identify the corporate citizens with the requisite wisdom and coerce them into revealing their secrets? How will these pattern gatherers identify knowledge holders, interview them, write useful patterns, document them in a handbook, and ensure that the knowledge is successfully transferred to others?

0-8493-3135-8/99/$0.00+$.50

These are open questions. People in and outside the patterns community are interested in answers, but, in the meantime, some of us are experimenting in our own companies. We are patterns pioneers, striking out to learn from our own experience.

In March 1995, I presented the notion of patterns to our vice president and his staff. There was almost unanimous approval for the idea and a real interest in a corporate handbook of best practices patterns. Since that time, along with David DeLano (DeLano, 1997), my fellow patterns miner, we have tried to solve the problem of developing this handbook in many different ways. This chapter will share some of our successes and failures and hopes for the future of our work.

First, let me introduce my company. AG Communication Systems is based in Phoenix, AZ. It is a joint venture of Lucent Technologies and GTE and is a leading developer and manufacturer of advanced telecommunications products and services, including switching, intelligent network, access and wireless products.

My role at this company is an unusual one. I'm the patterns champion or the self-proclaimed patterns "princess." I "do" patterns all day long! In the following chapter I will share my experience by describing the following techniques: mining by interviewing, mining by borrowing, mining by teaching patterns writing, mining in workshops, mining your own experience, mining in meetings, and mining in classes.

38.2 Underlying Principles

Patterns as a technology is in its infancy with few theoretical underpinnings. Most work published about patterns is based on practice. Indeed, the whole thrust of patterns derives from experience. The Design Patterns text, Gamma (1994), is a collection of object-oriented design best practices that shares what four expert designers have seen. There is no presentation of design methodology or theory. It is a catalog of twenty-three patterns that have solved real problems in many settings.

Those of a theoretical bend have been looking to undergird the patterns movement with a formal infrastructure, just as formal methods investigators have been attempting for decades to similarly make software engineering tractable. Both movements have been unsuccessful in making inroads in the software development community. At this time, no theoretical approaches have been developed for patterns mining. It is an attempt by practitioners to document their best practices.

38.3 Best Practices

38.3.1 Mining by Interviewing

The first pattern mining efforts at AG Communication Systems were begun after a visit from Jim Coplien and Bob Hanmer of Bell Labs. They had been doing pattern mining with the developers of the 4ESS®, a member of the AT&T electronic switching system product line. This activity was in response to a concern by AT&T management about the imminent retirement of some long-time developers on the 4ESS. Their pattern mining took the form of interviewing these experts and recording the information they gathered in pattern form. Over 100 patterns have been mined. Some have been documented in the Addison-Wesley PLoPD series (Adams, 1996).

We were inspired to experiment with this mining tactic. We taped one-hour interviews with a couple of experts on the GTD-5®. We returned to our desks to translate what was recorded and document that information as a pattern. After the patterns were documented, we tried, with varying degrees of success, to return to our sources to verify that what we had written really captured the speaker's intent. This is a long, slow, difficult process.

Usually the company gurus, the people everyone recognizes as having the best domain understanding and the greatest knowledge of company history, are extremely busy people. Most developers are tied to a project, and when that project finished, they have a little breather between projects and a little time as the next project gears up. Gurus are always tied to several projects. They are in constant demand. They never have a breather. Even though they recognize the need to transfer what they know to others, they often do not have the time for the interview and the subsequent review. Ralph Johnson (1996) once suggested that we take these people off-site, away from interruptions, for a day or a weekend. This suggestion has been documented as one of a collection of patterns for introducing patterns into the workplace (OOPSLA, 1996). This solution is difficult to implement. Gurus have no free time, even for trips at company expense!

The related problem with interviewing gurus is asking the right questions. Some we have used:

What would you share as a mentor?
What would be lost to the company if you left tomorrow?
What problems have you solved successfully on several projects?
What do you say repeatedly at project meetings that never gets documented?

Gurus are strong, extremely knowledgeable people and steering them toward useful information takes skillful interviewing techniques. I do not feel that we have learned how to do this effectively. On the few occasions when we have shared an hour with a guru, the information we have gathered has not been as useful as we had hoped.

A positive result of our experience is that we have learned that everyone is anxious to share their knowledge. No one seems to be afraid of becoming less valuable to the company. In fact, sharing successes makes these contributions visible, when, in many cases, that accomplishment would have been lost completely. These stories are a valuable part of the patterns. Roger Shank (1990) has written a fascinating book that helps explain this. He states:

> "People need to talk, to tell about what has happened to them, and they need to hear about what has happened to others, especially when the others are people they care about or who have had experiences relevant to the hearer's own life."

Stories are documented in the pattern rationale. Stories always draw readers in. They love to hear a personal account of what went wrong or what went right on an earlier release of a product. The people at my company have a tremendous respect for each other. I think that is why the patterns work has been so successful. Shank supports our observation:

> "We can tell people abstract rules of thumb which we have derived from prior experiences, but it is very difficult for other people to learn from these. We have difficulty remembering such abstractions, but we can more easily remember a good story. Stories give life to past experience. Stories make the events in memory memorable to others and to ourselves. This is one reason why people like to tell stories."

Using patterns to mine patterns is very effective. When you tell people about a pattern, invariably, they will have a story about the pattern, which can be added to the pattern document, or they will have a disagreement with the solution. Usually this means the context is too broad. The story the dissenter will tell helps narrow the context and improve the pattern. Context in a pattern is related to Shank's statement about contexts for stories:

> "People need a context to help them relate what they have heard to what they already know. We understand events in terms of events we have already understood. When a decision-making heuristic, or rule of thumb, is presented to us without a context, we cannot decide the validity of the rule we have heard, nor do we know where to store this rule in our memories. Thus, what we are presented is both difficult to evaluate and difficult to remember, making it virtually useless. People who fail to couch what they have to say in memorable stories will have their rules fall on deaf ears despite their best intentions and despite the best intentions of their listeners. A good teacher is not one who explains things correctly but one who couches explanations in a memorable format."

38.3.2 Mining by Borrowing

Since AG Communication Systems creates telecommunications systems and since AT&T (now Lucent Technologies) was our parent, we were privileged to share in the patterns that Coplien and Hanmer had gathered on the 4ESS. We are examining these patterns and learning what we can from them. Mining by borrowing is appropriate for companies in the same domain who can share information. Unfortunately, except in a joint venture setting, this is a rare occurrence. Domain knowledge is regarded as proprietary, even when the information is of a truly general nature. Since domain-specific patterns are being published, these patterns provide a base that can be extended with proprietary patterns.

I recently attended a seminar by Peter Senge, author of *The Fifth Discipline* (1994). We talked about the problem of companies sharing information and he told me an interesting story. Senge had been working as a consultant with Ford. There had been some successes as a result of this work. A high-level executive at Ford had suggested sharing these successes with Chrysler. His fellow executives were horrified and asked him why he would even consider sharing information about success with a competitor. The answer is especially important for members of the patterns community. He said he could not imagine *not* sharing, because that would hamper their own success. Senge's new approach required not only a change in the way Ford operated but also a change in attitude toward Chrysler. To translate this to patterns, sharing what we know with others increases our own understanding. In many cases, we find that what we have learned is not domain-specific but applies across the industry. We share what we know and we all improve. Drawing a boundary at organizational lines hampers the work of the whole community.

This is a new way of doing business. Clearly, we are not giving away trade secrets. Details of product information are not handed over to competitors. Senge's notion of learning organizations and the changes it makes in the way we work and the ideas captured in patterns are solutions to problems that appear anywhere. To share the best of us with the rest of us means that we all improve.

David Armstrong's *Managing by Storying Around* (1992), is a collection of management observations that apply across many domains. The author is vice president of Armstrong International, a manufacturer with offices throughout the world. He has taken one of the oldest forms of communication, storytelling, and turned it into a powerful management tool. Here is his answer to the sharing question:

> "If a story helps a competitor, so be it. A better competitor forces us to be better. Besides, what I really think will happen is our competitors will read our stories and become frustrated because they cannot do business the way we do."

Mining by reading is a form of mining by borrowing. Books by experienced people are fertile ground for patterns mining. In April 1996 we enjoyed a visit from Jim McCarthy, author of *The Dynamics of Software Development* (1996). Jim was not familiar with patterns but his book contains a collection of guidelines that resemble patterns. To illustrate the close relationship, I translated one of his guidelines to a pattern. The result, "Don't Flip the Bozo Bit!" can be found on our external Web site (AGCS). It describes the problem of software development teams casting someone as a bozo. After that, no one listens to that person, so the team has lost a contributor. The guideline warns that everyone must be a part of the development effort and that team members must be constantly aware of this possibility and "get everyone's head into the game!" McCarthy also cautions us about flipping the bozo bit on ourselves. Other patterns I have documented are "It is a relationship, not a sale!" and "Enrapture the customer!" These are included in a collection of customer interaction patterns on our external Web site (AGCS).

38.3.3 Mining by Teaching Patterns Writing

Coplien and Hanmer brought not only the report of patterns mining on the 4ESS but also a patterns writing class they had been teaching at sites within AT&T. By learning how to write patterns, participants learn a lot about patterns and they also produce one. This is an effective way to start patterns mining in an organization. Some writers are so eager, especially if appropriate reward mechanisms are in place, that they continue to write after the class has ended. At AG Communication Systems, we reward pattern writers with a patterns publication. After several patterns have been written, we look for publishing opportunities for the enthusiastic contributor. This approach is appealing to frustrated writers within the development community. Unfortunately, these folks are a minority. Most engineers do not like to write. As Ralph Johnson (1995) has noted:

> "You'll find that most people are not good at finding patterns. Fortunately, you do not need (or want) most people to be doing that. You want to make everybody feel included and wanted, but ultimately people will sort themselves out into those who will want to work on finding patterns and those who do not…your organization's real job is to get a product finished, and patterns are a means to that end. Most people should just get on with their work."

Sometimes pattern writers come from unlikely places. Most of those who have followed the patterns activity know that a building architect, Christopher Alexander, is responsible for the patterns movement. In his work, *The Timeless Way of Building* (1979), he writes:

> "Every person has a pattern language in his mind. …Your pattern language is the sum total of your knowledge of how to build. The pattern language in your mind is slightly different from the language in the next person's mind; no two are exactly alike; yet many patterns, and fragments of pattern languages, are also shared."

Alexander was talking about building cities, towns, neighborhoods, and houses, but his words can apply to any product. Creation involves patterns that are, to some extent, shared by other creators. This phenomenon of shared patterns can be seen in a writers class where a pattern written by one person is recognized by another participant. There is a sense that the pattern captures an important or essential element of the domain. This feeling is a response to something Alexander calls the "quality without a name." This quality is what makes the pattern live. As Alexander notes:

> "The fact is that we feel good in the presence of a pattern which resolves its forces. …people who come from the same culture do to a remarkable extent agree about the way that different patterns make them feel."

The patterns writing class introduces the writers workshop. This process is documented on our external Web page (AGCS). The approach was introduced to the patterns community by Richard Gabriel. Writers workshops, interestingly enough, are for writers. This helpful medium enables a writer to hear feedback from colleagues in a non-threatening setting. Everyone in a writers workshop should also be a writer and, therefore, equally sensitive to comments. Writing patterns is difficult and those who have struggled to capture their experience in a pattern are in a good position to help others who have chosen the same path.

38.3.4 Mining in Workshops

When Jim McCarthy visited us, he told the story of a problem-solving workshop technique used by management at Microsoft. Managers would gather around a conference table and someone would begin by describing a problem and asking for help in its solution. Someone else would propose a solution: "We had that problem on Project W and we resolved it by doing X." Another would respond, "Yes, we also had that problem and we did Y." After a few proposals, someone would summarize, "What we are talking about is Z!" At that, notebooks would open and managers would start writing. What was being observed and captured was the essence, a high-level extraction, of the solution to the problem. They are capturing patterns.

Always on the look-out for new pattern mining approaches, I thought we might try patterns mining in a workshop format. By happy coincidence, as we were debating this approach, we were also teaching a patterns writing course. A pattern written by Mike Sapcoe, a system tester, provided the opportunity we were seeking. I was glad to see Mike's system test pattern, our first in this area. Ray Fu, the coach for system test, was interested and supported us.

We sat in a room with a dozen of our best system testers and asked them to talk about recurring problems with known solutions. We typed furiously while the discussion raged around us. We were lucky to have the assistance of Greg Stymfal, a member of our patterns community with system test experience and effective facilitation skills. This role is critical in corralling a room full of old hands. The result of our trial with workshops is a paper that will be published in the pattern series by Addison-Wesley (Delano and Rising, 1997) and is also available on our Web site (AGCS).

Since the time of publication, the patterns have grown considerably and continue to grow. Patterns are living things that change as we learn more about the problem, the context, the solution. Some may completely outlive their usefulness as procedures and other technologies change. These patterns should be gracefully retired as new ones spring up to replace them. As Alexander (1979) has observed:

> "As people exchange ideas about the environment, and exchange patterns, the overall inventory of patterns in the pattern pool keeps changing. ...Of course, this evolution will never end."

We grow the system test patterns by repeating the workshop experience, each time with a new set of testers. We present the existing patterns and ask for feedback, again, typing energetically to keep up with the comments. Everyone agrees with the solutions in the patterns and many testers can help us improve the patterns with new stories. We have also split some patterns into two or more smaller patterns and spawned new patterns. During this workshop process, the testers learn the existing patterns and we learn how to improve them. In this new training approach the trainers and the trainees both learn.

Our goal is to have all system testers go through the system test patterns workshop experience. We will then teach the patterns to our coaches and the rest of the corporate development community. This should ensure a more uniform view of problems faced by system test and the solutions of our experienced system testers.

The system test patterns are valuable because they document the way we do business. One challenge we face in publishing articles about our patterns is that the best patterns contain stories about real projects. Unfortunately, these stories contain sensitive or proprietary information and cannot be shared outside the company. Removing this information usually leaves a thumbnail sketch of a pattern, which may not have much credibility. This publishing restriction is found across the industry. Because most members of the pattern community are not in academia, there is little incentive to publish anything. We at AG Communication Systems are lucky. We are rewarded for external publication. Nonetheless, the publishing dilemma is a problem we face as the patterns community grows and more patterns are uncovered.

38.3.5 Mining Your Own Experience

The extraordinary thing about patterns is the underlying premise that we all have something to share and we all can learn from each other. Mining your own experience is something we can all do. When Jim Coplien and Bob Hanmer taught that first patterns writing class at our company, I had my first opportunity to mine my own experience.

Everyone in the class was anxious to produce something worthwhile, since Jim Coplien, patterns and C++ guru, would read it. Each of us combed our past for some nugget of expertise to document and share with the group. I finally decided to write a brief summary of my Ph.D. work. I had spent years doing the research and the requisite statistical analysis (Rising and Calliss, 1994) to say one simple thing: each software module should contain one design decision. The intent of this pattern is that whatever a module is, function or procedure, package, class, or even an entire subsystem, it should be viewed by a user as providing a single service or capability. It should be possible to state: The module does this. This comprises one component of information hiding as described by David Parnas (1972). Information hiding is hiding a single design decision behind a minimal interface. The pattern, "Single Design Decision," can be found on our external patterns home page (AGCS).

38.3.6 Mining in Meetings

For the last couple of years, I have noticed that the world is increasingly one big mother lode of patterns. I see patterns in everything I do. This reminds me of learning to type when I found myself mentally typing every conversation. When I learned French and German, I mentally translated every conversation. Sounds like a pattern.

It certainly makes meetings more interesting. I treat every meeting as a pattern mining opportunity. I serve on a team with George Jester, someone who knows our company and the people in it very well. Our team gives many presentations to our vice-president's staff and we have experienced what works and what does not when it comes to effective presentations for upper management. During post mortem sessions of some of our not-so-successful presentations, George has provided interesting analyses that I have captured as presentation patterns. Some have been written as exercises in pattern writing sessions and can be seen on the Phoenix Patterns Group Home Page (Phoenix).

I also took potential pattern notes at a team meeting when David Saar, one of our business and marketing leaders, gave a presentation to help our product development team prepare for its customer interaction meetings. AG Communication Systems, like many companies, has chosen the path of self-directed work teams. As a consequence, developers are asked to play a variety of new roles. One is to interact more closely with the customer. These patterns can be seen on our external Web site (AGCS).

Some customer interaction patterns appear obvious, for instance, "Mind Your Manners!" Unfortunately, as Jim Coplien has noted: "Common sense is so uncommon!" Many times we are tempted not to document "common sense," thinking that "everyone knows that!" In reality, of course, Coplien is right, not everyone does know that. How many times has a customer trouble report been written for something that everyone should know? Another patterns guru, Kent Beck (1996), has commented:

> "The patterns that I have written with the broadest impact were the ones that I was tempted not to publish because — everyone knows that. "

38.3.7 Mining in Classes

My coach, Tom Snelten, attended a business simulation course where a game, Tango, was played by teams. Business decisions were made and business cycles were played out. The instructor, Brent Snow, had prepared some supplemental materials for our business leaders: "Hiring and Retaining The Best and The Brightest, A Compendium of 25 Strategies and Best Practices." As Tom read through this document, he saw that these strategies and best practices were clearly the beginnings of patterns. On his recommendation, I took the course and spent time after class talking with the instructor. Brent and I have agreed that we will write a paper that presents these patterns.

Peter Senge's book *The Fifth Discipline* (1994) describes a collection of system archetypes. One archetype, "Shifting the Burden," addresses the problem of attacking symptoms without understanding the root cause of the problem. As a result, our solutions, while they appear effective, are superficial at best, and may make the problem worse.

I saw this archetype in action in the Tango course. I was part of a team that played the role of a company in simulated business cycles. My team, Gamma, made a decision to develop our personnel competence. In the previous round of the simulation, we had lost a key person to a more capable company and had been unable to follow through on some of our plans. Can't you hear fists pounding in the board room? "We won't let that happen to us again! We're going to meet that challenge head on!" Sad to say, that is exactly what our team or company did. We did meet that challenge. Our competence increased tremendously. Unfortunately, as a result of our focus on increasing competence, Gamma nearly went bankrupt! We weren't even aware of what we had done until the end of the simulation cycle when we found we were barely able to pay our taxes. After that, each year was spent trying to keep our heads above water. We never did fully recover. I learned that a company can borrow on its accounts receivable — good for the shortterm — but a painful way to do business. If this can happen in one round of a game with three smart people looking at all the parameters, imagine the potential for disaster in a large corporation or state or federal government.

One pattern I mined from the Tango class is "What have you done for me lately?" The essence of this pattern is that a company cannot bank points with developers who have high expectations. These "high flyers" want continual growth in competence and, therefore, demand on-going experience on challenging projects. These individuals are not satisfied with opportunities presented in previous years. They must be challenged each and every year or they will leave the company.

38.4 Research Issues and Summary

There is a lot of work to be done in the area of patterns mining. We are at the gateway to uncharted territory. Software developers are having successes with patterns but there is little research to develop solid theory. There are several unexplored but useful topics that call for investigation. As I see it, our most important task is the development of a model for patterns mining and training. Some members of the patterns community feel the best way to capture and use patterns is to employ a categorization scheme and search engine that allows problem solvers to find the right pattern for a given situation.

I have developed my own model for this process, which matches that of other engineering disciplines that have a handbook of best practices. Certified professional engineers in these disciplines are trained in the best practices of the field and apply them when creating products. I think we are a long way from having a well-defined handbook, but we can certainly begin to make progress in that direction. As we add to our fledgling handbook, we provide training in the patterns we have at that point and continue to add to the handbook and offer more training.

We also need to know more about how people successfully develop software. This broad topic should include all techniques at every stage of the software lifecycle as well as all the organizational and managerial factors that affect notable achievement. These components will determine the scope of our handbook of best practices.

We must learn from related disciplines. Others have tried to show how people learn, how people solve problems and how components are stored and retrieved. In an age of increasing specialization, we must join hands across academic and practical boundaries to share what we know and expand our viewpoint. As Weinberg (1996) has noted, "None of us is as smart as all of us!" This could be the most powerful outcome of the patterns movement — real sharing across disciplines that would enable us all to be better at what we do. What a challenging and hopeful prospect.

References

Adams, M., Coplien, J., Gamoke, R., Hanmer, B., Keeve, F. and Nicodemus, K. 1996. Fault-tolerant telecommunication patterns, *Pattern Languages of Program Design 2*, pp. 549-562. J. Vlissides, N. Kerth, and J.O. Coplien, eds. Addison-Wesley, Reading, MA.

AGCS Patterns Home Page: http://www.agcs.com/patterns.

Alexander, C.A. 1979. *The Timeless Way of Building.* Oxford University Press, New York, NY.

Armstrong, D. 1992. *Notes from Managing by Storying Around: A New Method of Leadership.* Doubleday Dell Publishing Group, Inc., New York, NY.

Beck, K. 1996. Posting to the patterns listserver.

DeLano, D. 1998. Pattern mining, in *Best Practices: A Patterns Handbook,* Rising, L., Ed., Cambridge University Press, U.K.

DeLano, D. and Rising, L. 1998. A pattern language for system test, in *Pattern Languages of Program Design 3,* Martin, R., Riehle, D., and Buschmann, F., Eds., Addison-Wesley, Reading, MA.

Gamma, E., Helm, R., Johnson, R. and Vlissides, J. 1994. *Design Patterns: Elements of Reusable Object-Oriented Software.* Addison-Wesley, Reading, MA.

Johnson, R. 1995. Electronic mail exchange with the author.

Johnson, R. 1996. Personal conversation with the author.

McCarthy, J. 1996. *Dynamics of Software Development.* Microsoft Press, Redmond, WA.

OOPSLA, 1996. Introducing patterns into the workplace, http://www.agcs.com/OOPSLA/intro.html.

Parnas, D. L. 1972. On the criteria to be used in decomposing systems into modules, *CACM,* 15(12):1053-1058.

Phoenix Patterns Group Home Page: http://www.radsoft.com/patterns/.

Rising, L.S. and Calliss, F.W. 1994. An information-hiding metric, *J. Sys. Software.,* 26:211-220.

Senge, P.M. 1994. *The Fifth Discipline.* Currency Doubleday, New York, NY.

Shank, R. C. 1990. *Tell Me A Story.* Charles Scribner's Sons, New York, NY.

Weinberg, G. 1996. Electronic mail exchange with the author.

Further Information

There is an immense amount of information about patterns (and everything else) on the World Wide Web. A good place to start is the AG Communication Systems Patterns Home Page: http://www.agcs.com/patterns. There are patterns, published papers, a sample pattern template, information about writers workshops, information about the patterns conference in Arizona, ChiliPLoP, and links to a host of other pattern sites around the world.

The Pattern Languages of Program Design (PLoP) conference is held annually at Allerton House near Champaign, IL. Many patterns from the first three PLoP conferences and the first EuroPLoP conference in 1996 have been published by Addison-Wesley:

Pattern Languages of Program Design. 1995. J.O. Coplien and D. Schmidt, eds. Addison-Wesley, Reading, MA.

Pattern Languages of Program Design 2. 1996. J. Vlissides, J.O. Coplien and N. Kerth, eds. Addison-Wesley, Reading, MA.

Pattern Languages of Program Design 3. 1998. Addison-Wesley, Reading, MA.

Information on other patterns books can be found at: http://st-www.cs.uiuc.edu/users/patterns/books/.

Information on the patterns conferences: PLoP, EuroPLoP, UP, and ChiliPLoP can be found at: http://st-www.cs.uiuc.edu/users/patterns/conferences/ and http://www.agcs.com/patterns/chiliplop/index.html.

OOPSLA (Object-Oriented Programming Systems, Languages, and Applications) is sponsored by ACM SIGPLAN and held annually in October. It is the premiere object-oriented conference, attracting thousands of attendees. There are typically several patterns workshops, tutorials, presentations, and papers.

Information on the many patterns listservers can be found at: http://st-www.cs.uiuc.edu/users/patterns/Lists.html.

VIII

Application of OO Technology

Saba Zamir
Senior Information Technology Consultant

This section contains chapters that illustrate the application of the object-oriented paradigm to real-life situations and problems. The scope of the chapters contained here varies from practical techniques that allow you to code C++ faster and better, to requirements modeling, transaction analysis, project management, and transitioning enterprises to Object Technology.

39

Coding and Debugging C++ Three Times Faster

Jiri Soukup
Code Farms Inc.

39.1 Introduction

The original question which started this project actually was: Is it possible, by using a better design methodology, to develop and maintain serious C++ programs at least three times faster? Eight years later, and after selling the technology to over 500 companies, the answer is affirmative.

Coding and debugging three times faster? You must be thinking that this is a hoax or a silly exaggeration. If this were true, the new technology would change the way software is designed today. The ideas (this involves more than just one idea) are quite simple, and the practical experience is that experienced programmers routinely improve their efficiency 5 to 10 times. Removing spaghetti++ is one of the most important ideas involved in this effort.

This project reflects my own experience with several state-of-the-art VLSI CAD systems, combined with the results of a private survey, which asked software managers what would help them most to increase software productivity. There are several major problems which I like to call the five evils of today's C++ programming.

39.1.1 The Five Evils of the Today's C++ Programming:

1. Spaghetti++ is the name I like to give to networks of objects linked with pointers and function calls (messages). These networks of interdependent classes are often complex and difficult to

0-8493-3135-8/99/$0.00+$.50

understand. This is an OO equivalent of spaghetti code. This term was introduced with structured programming, and it describes the situation where numerous "go to" statements form an incomprehensible network. Once the code is difficult to understand, it is difficult to debug and maintain, and the probability that some errors are still hidden in the code is relatively high.

2. Hard to find pointer errors were the number one problem reported by the software managers. "If you could prevent this type of error," several of them said, "my life would be much easier". These pointer errors crash the program a long time after the error occurs, and they are extremely difficult to find. They are usually caused by the premature destruction of objects connected in lists, or by some other subtle ways that mess up internal data structures. Chapter 3.2, page 91 in Soukup, 1994 describes an encounter with such an error, which stalled the entire software development of a 100+ people company for 3 days and nights.
3. A poor record of architecture shows that if you build software using more than just trivial data structures, the existing class libraries such as STL, MFC, or tools.h++ do not leave a simple record of the data structure in your code. Collections and lists are spread throughout your class definitions, and recovering the original design intent (the software architecture) from the code is tedious. This complicates both debugging and maintenance, and makes it difficult to move programmers among projects. This problem is the prime reason for the popularity of OO diagrams. The situation is similar to the popularity of flow charts before the advent of structured programming. The reason is the same though; because the code is messy, we need a graphical representation in order to understand the code logic. Isn't it better to write clean code in the first place? Often, as the code evolves, the documentation (and the OO diagrams) are not properly updated, and programmers are naturally reluctant to use anything but the code for information about the architecture and algorithms when dealing with history software.
4. Wrong tools — The existing programming methodology is generally sloppy. Programmers often produce software which is full of errors, and then demand smart tools to help them clean up the mess. This is the reason for the popularity of interactive debuggers and packages such as Purify. It would save a lot of unnecessary work if the software was designed correctly by construction, at least its main part or the sections that are difficult to debug. This of course is a programmer's dream. If we can improve our existing practices in this direction, it would certainly improve software productivity.
5. Persistent data — Many application programs have to store internal data for later use, and my experience is that programs that do not have to do this are exceptions. For example, batch compilers do not store any data, but note that incremental compilers do. Using a database system is often not the ideal solution, because of the cost and performance involved. Libraries such as MFC or tools.h++ provide persistent data, but the user must code serialization functions which read/write all classes to disk. These serialization functions are a major liability. The slightest mismatch between the read and write functions will crash the program, and they involve lots of code. For example, I have seen a business application consisting of 100,000 lines of C++, where serialization functions represented about 20% of the code. The complexity of these functions practically stopped the evolution of the system, because the developers feared to touch this part of the code. Note that neither the C++ language nor the STL library support persistency.

These five evils are C++ specific. For example, in Smalltalk, internal data is automatically persistent, and both Smalltalk and Java avoid hard pointer errors. However, these languages suffer from the spaghetti++ symptom just like C++, and exhibit additional problems like performance, higher probability of error when using data structures, etc.

39.2 Underlying Principles

We realized that correcting any of the five evils will improve software productivity, but not by the factor of two or three. That can be achieved only by a simultaneous attack against all five points. In this paragraph, I will shortly describe the measures which we took to correct each problem. Note that some of the measures which we introduce help to improve more than just one evil.

39.2.1 Cure for Spaghetti++

This consists of two steps:

1. Instead of building data structures with the usual containers, which store pointers to the objects instead of the objects themselves, we use intrusive data structures formed by pointers embedded directly in the application objects.
2. We represent data structures and design patterns with special manager classes. The details of this new technique are described in Section 39.3. This arrangement has a very positive impact on software architecture. It eliminates dependencies among classes participating in the same data structure, avoids complex inheritance trees, provides generic classes for design patterns and complex data structures, manages pointers transparently (just like Java, but this was in existence long before Java), and helps with rapid prototyping (just like in Smalltalk).

39.2.2 Cure for Hard Pointer Errors

Intrusive data structures and pattern classes transparently manage the pointers that form all data structures. In addition to this, our internal lists are implemented as rings, not as NULL ending lists. This helps to detect whether an object is connected to some data structure. Pointers on new objects are initialized to NULL. When an object is taking part in a data structure, none of its pointers can be NULL, and when the object is disconnected, its pointers are set back to NULL. Only an object with all its pointers equal to NULL can be safely destroyed.

Similar checking is also used when adding an object to any data structure. If the relevant pointers on an object are not NULL, it means the object is already part of another list or other data structure, and cannot be safely added unless it is disconnected first. Note that this check is very inexpensive — only one "if" statement for any access call. This type of checking is possible only for intrusive data structures, it cannot be used for the usual containers.

39.2.3 Cure for the Insufficient Record of the Architecture

Each class relation is represented as a pattern class, and the code line which invokes this pattern serves as a record of that relation. If lines invoking pattern classes are presented as one block of code, possibly as a separate include file (see the code example in Section 39.3), they represent the logic of your data structure just like a database schema. There is a simple one-to-one mapping between these lines and the OO class diagram. From these lines, you can automatically generate the OO diagram and, from a given OO diagram, you can generate this section of the code.

Having a clear and compact record of the software architecture also provides flexibility when modifying data structures. Removing or adding a new data structure can be achieved by removing or adding a single line of code, and if the change implies additional changes (for example, a different syntax for some functions) the compiler tells you where the changes are required.

39.2.4 Cure for the Wrong Tools

All the measures that we introduced thus far lead to code where, once it compiles, most of the silly mistakes related to the data structures manipulation have been removed. Manager classes are set up so that the compiler catches most errors in the use of the data structures. Remaining data related errors are caught at runtime by the checking for NULL pointers. Most importantly, errors caused by premature deallocation and messed up data structures are eliminated. Obviously, it does not eliminate all errors. For example, it cannot detect errors in the logic of your algorithm, or if you force a completely wrong value onto a pointer. For example, if you have class MyClass { ... };

```
MyClass* ptr = (MyClass*)1234;
```

(Actually, even this type of error often gets detected when checking whether the pointers inside this "object" are NULL, but it is not guaranteed.)

When I use this system, I never have to walk through my data structures with a debugger. I can rely on this part of the code to be solid, and if something does not work, I get a message about what is wrong, and I fix it, without searching for the error.

Having a clear record of the architecture (the lines which instantiate pattern classes, and are like a database schema) helps to keep a high point of view when debugging, without getting lost in low implementation details. Note that it takes about twice as long for a program coded in this style to pass through the compiler, but once it compiles, the debugging is much faster. The need for error checking tools such as Purify has been significantly reduced. The part notorious for errors (data structures) is now correct by construction.

Is this different from C++ class libraries, such as STL, MFC, or tools.h++? These libraries encapsulate data structures, and therefore reduce the possibility of low level pointer errors. However, these libraries are not intrusive, and therefore cannot use the checking for NULL pointers, which is pivotal in our approach. Also, when using these libraries, the invocation of the data structures is spread throughout the applications classes. There is no central code which represents "the data structure schema."

Summing up, instead of tools to find errors introduced by the programmer, we provide tools that help to create code where the toughest errors are eliminated automatically.

39.2.5 Cure for Missing Data Persistency

Automatic persistence can be added to any class library, and this section describes two possible methods of implementing this. In both cases, the new() operator must be overloaded. Also, one or several root objects data must be given when storing the data to disk. When restoring the data to memory, the library returns new pointers to these root objects.

Method A — Starting from the root objects, the library traverses all the internal data structures (object closure), collects all objects, and stores them to disk either as a plain block of bytes or using serialization. Serialization functions can be either user coded or generated automatically. Then when restoring the data, pointers are converted (swizzled) to reflect the new locations of the objects. Some libraries convert pointers to object IDs before storing data to disk (as done for example by Rogue Wave), but another possibility is to use the pointer values as object IDs and store the objects in their original form (Code Farms).

Method B — The library allocates pages of memory, and uses these pages for the allocation of all objects. Part of each page is a special bitmap, where each bit corresponds to one potential pointer location in the page. The bit map occupies only $1/32$ of the page for a 32-bit architecture. When storing data to disk, entire pages are simply copied to disk without fragmentation to individual objects, which is extremely fast. When restoring data to disk, the library walks through the bit map, detects the location of the pointers, and converts them to new locations with a few arithmetic operations. (Only the Code Farms library includes this method.)

Note that the positions of pointers even within complex C++ objects can be detected without detailed knowledge of the metamodel, using a simple programming trick described under Section 39.3.

39.2.6 Improving the Entire Design Cycle

It is interesting to see what the proposed measures will do to the overall design cycle:

1. The architecture design can use pattern classes, and produce a data structure schema which can be plugged directly into the code. If the architects prefer to work only with pictures (OO diagrams), the schema code can be generated automatically. This guarantees that the architecture is not misinterpreted by the coders, and that changes immediately and correctly propagate to the code.

2. Coding is rapid, and a prototype can be used in the production code without complete recoding, because even the prototype is already safe. There is no need to prototype in Smalltalk and then implement in C++ or some other language. Then new methodology makes prototyping in C++ just as easy as prototyping in Smalltalk, but it provides the safety of type protection and the speed of C++. Prototypes can even be used to evaluate performance.
3. Coding is faster, because it does not deal with low-level data structure handling. This is true about the use of any class library. However, the main time saving is in automatic persistency. Coding persistent data from scratch and getting it running safely is a major undertaking, which usually takes many months to complete. Our library gives you all this in a matter of minutes.
4. Compilation takes longer now, because the pattern classes use the compiler for detection of some errors. This does not represent a significant increase in overall design time — the time to compile is always much shorter than debugging.
5. Debugging is rapid, more thorough, and can proceed at a higher level. The need for tedious traversal of the data with the debugger is significantly reduced. Notorious pointer errors which are normally the main subject of debugging are caught here automatically.

What has been said is not a proof, but it gives you a general feeling that it may be possible to develop software three or more times faster. This number (three times) is actually an understatement assuming users who are not familiar with all the features of this library. Personally, I now routinely design and debug software 5 to 10 times faster, and if you ask me to code in the "normal" C++ style, it feels like going back to FORTRAN.

39.3 Best Practices

39.3.1 Intrusive Data Structures

One of the essential ingredients of the approach described in the previous section was the replacement of the indirect containers which are common today by intrusive data structures. What are intrusive data structures, and how do they differ from containers?

A list-based collection can be implemented in two styles, see Figure 39.1. In the intrusive version, a Holder object points to the beginning of the list, which consists of Elem objects. Each Elem object has the "next" pointer to the next object on the list. In the container version, the Holder object points to a list of Link objects, where each Link points to an Elem object. As Dr. Stroustrup pointed out when reviewing Soukup (1997), even containers are, internally, based on an intrusive list.

When using array-based collections, the situation is similar. The array can store entire Elem objects, or just pointers to Elem objects. Why is it that most existing libraries (STL, MFC, tools.h++) use indirect, container based collections? They are obviously more complicated.

The usual explanation is that one Elem object can be simultaneously in several containers. I suspect, however, that the true reason is the ease of implementation. Generic class libraries are easier to implement in the indirect (container) form, especially when using templates.

There are some additional reasons: For example, you can add a container of Elem object to your existing program, and the Elem class does not have to be recompiled. However, if you add an intrusive collection, you are adding a "next" pointer to each Elem object, and class Elem must be recompiled.

On the other hand, intrusive data structures give you better performance, both in the terms of used memory and in CPU time. For example, the intrusive version of the list from Figure 39.1 is faster when traversing the list, and adding or removing objects from the list. It also needs less memory, because it needs only one pointer per Elem objects, while the container uses two pointers in each Link object. Actually, the container uses four more bytes or the allocation overhead for each Link object (most allocators need this overhead for each independently allocated object). Allocation and initialization of objects is generally expensive in C++, and unless you use a special cache of List objects, the container version of your program will be significantly slower primarily due to the allocation.

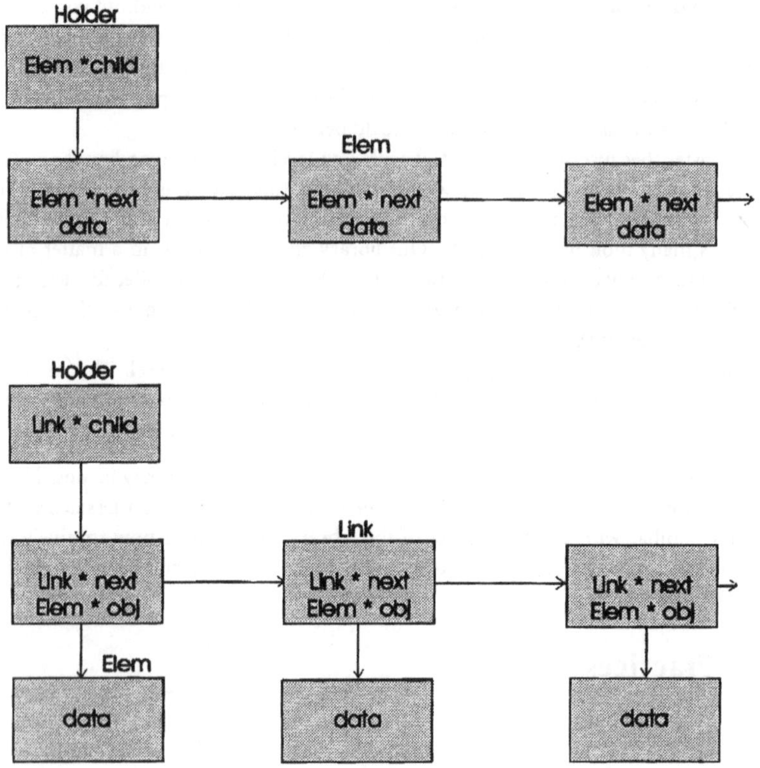

FIGURE 39.1 Intrusive list (top), and the indirect container (bottom). The intrusive list inserts pointer "next" into the application class; the container only points to the participating objects.

It make sense neither to claim that intrusive data structures are better than container, nor the other way. Simply, each design style is more suitable for different applications. However, there is one critical question which must be answered: Is it possible to insert pointers into existing classes in some acceptable, elegant way? Adding pointers manually each time we add or remove a data structure would be error prone and tedious. One possibility is to use inheritance. For example, we can do this:

```
template<class T> class Link {
   T *next;
   ...
};
class Elem : Link<Elem> {
   ...
};
```

The inheritance inserts the "next" pointer into class Elem. This is the approach used in another chapter in this volume, called Pattern Template Library. Another possibility is:

```
#include "generate.h"
class Elem {
   INCLUDE(Elem);
   ...
};
```

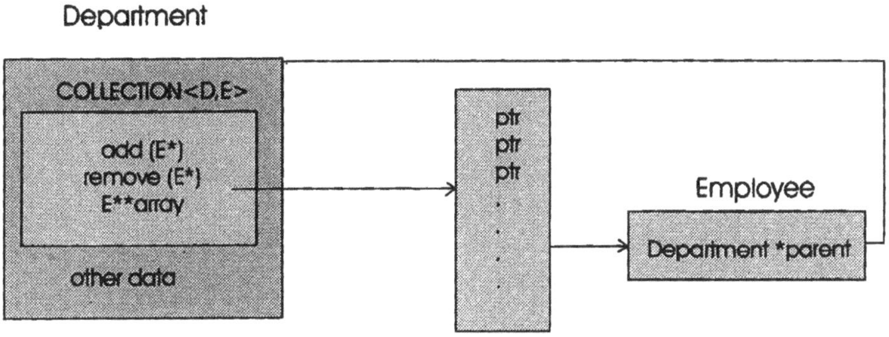

FIGURE 39.2 When creating a hierarchy with an array-based container, class Department includes the COLLECTION as a member. A pointer to the parent Department is inserted into every Employee. This shows that even when using a container, some intrusive pointers may be required in many practical applications.

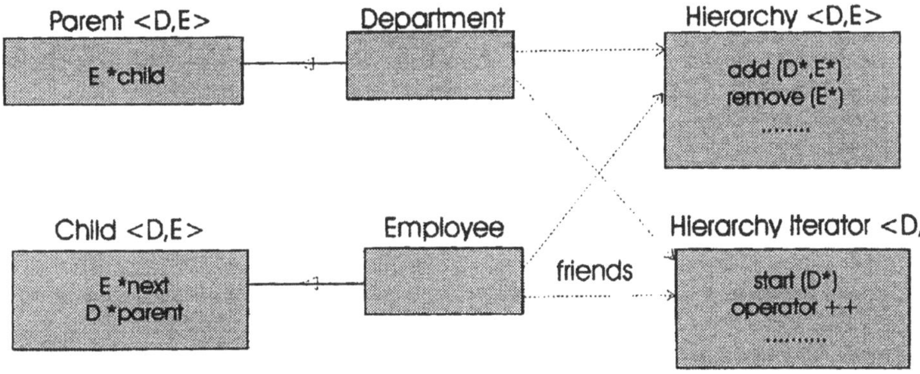

FIGURE 39.3 Intrusive hierarchy based on inheritance requires three library classes: Parent, Child, and Hierarchy. Class Hierarchy manages the relation and, usually, does contain any relational data.

where file generate.h is automatically generated and specifies all the list and other data structure pointers required for class Elem. This example assumes that class Elem participates in two lists, list1 is singly linked, list2 is doubly linked:

```
FILE generate.h:
   #define INCLUDE(A) INCL##A
   #define INCL_Elem          \
   Elem *next_list1;          \
   Elem *next_list2;          \
   Elem *prev_list2
```

Even though this approach is more difficult to implement, it is more elegant and easier to use, if you can live with the step of automatically generating file generate.h every time you recompile your program. This method has been successfully used in the C++ Data Object Library by Code Farms.

Figures 39.2–39.4 show graphically what happens in three different implementations, if you need a Department/Employee hierarchy, where every Employee knows its own Department. When you use an array-based container COLLECTION<D,E> as in Figure 39.2, class Department includes the COLLECTION as a member. Even though the COLLECTION itself is non-intrusive, and therefore does not

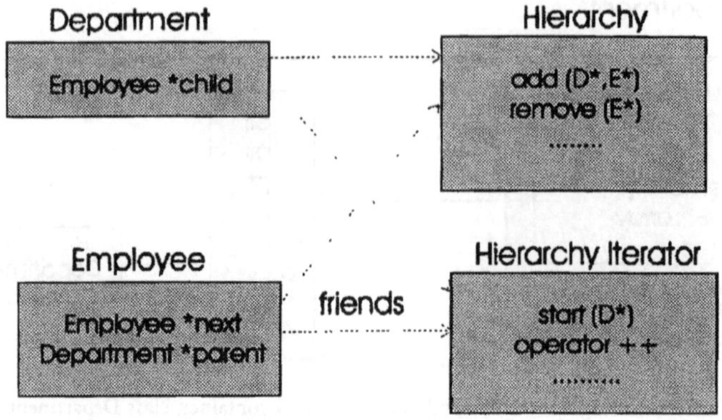

FIGURE 39.4 When the code generator injects the required pointers, the design is simpler than in Figure 39.3. Fewer classes are involved, and objects are simpler and there is no layering effect caused by the inheritance. The Hierarchy class manages the relation just like the Hierarchy class in Figure 39.3.

require additional pointers inside class Employee, each Employee still needs a pointer to its parent Department. Talking about non-intrusiveness of the container class is, in this case, a little mockery. Both classes, Department and Employee, must be recompiled after adding this data organization.

39.3.2 Manager Classes

When using the intrusive data structures based on inheritance (Figure 39.3), the library contains two classes that form the hierarchy relation — Parent and Child. The pointer to the parent is already contained in the Child class. Department inherits Parent, and Employee inherits Child. The Hierarchy class is a special class, which manages the data structure. Manager classes such as the class Hierarchy here are usually complemented by an iterator class (or classes) which provide the interface for traversing the data. Note the difference. In Figure 39.2, we needed one library class (COLLECTION), and we had to modify class Employee manually. In Figure 39.3, we needed three library classes (Parent, Child, Hierarchy), but no manual modification was necessary.

Figure 39.4 shows what happens when the code generator injects the objects into the application classes Department and Employee. No inheritance is involved, classes Department and Employee are simple, and only one library class is required (Hierarchy). The following code fragment demonstrates that, in spite of the bad reputation of code generators, this approach produces an elegant, easy-to-read application code. Note that the INCLUDE(..) statements are always the same regardless of whether the particular class is involved in one list or in several complex data structures:

```
#include "generate.h"

class Department {
   INCLUDE(Department); //always the same
   ...
};
class Employee {
   INCLUDE(Employee); //always the same
   ...
};
HIERARCHY(hier,Department,Employee); //Macro hides class Hierarchy
...
Department* dp = new Department;
Employee* ep = new Employee;
```

```
hier.add(dp,ep); //add ep to hier under dp
hier.del(ep); //delete ep from hier

hier_iterator it(dp); //create an iterator
ITERATE(it,ep) {
   ..traverses through all Employees under dp
}
```

Note that *hier* is the instance of the manager class, and it represents the relation between the Department and the Employee. This code is conceptually similar to using inheritance based intrusive data based on templates (Figure 39.3):

```
class Department;
class Employee;

class Department: public Parent<Department,Employee> {
   ...
};
class Employee: public Child<Department,Employee> {
   ...
};
Hierarchy<Department,Employee> hier; //declares the hierarchy
...
Department*    dp = new Department;
Employee*      ep = new Employee;
Hierarchy_Iterator<Department,Employee> it;

hier.add(dp,ep); //add ep to hier under dp
hier.del(ep); //delete ep from hier

for(ep = it.begin(dp); ep; ep = ++it){
   ..traverses through all Employees under dp
}
```

The manager classes can be designed with an interface which is similar to the STL, but it cannot be exactly the same due to the differences in the overall concept (intrusive data vs. containers). The iterators can be identical. Note that the iterator classes in the STL library are built on a similar concept as the manager classes for the intrusive data structures.

Intrusive data structures permit the implementon of smarter iterators than you may expect. For example, you may be able to perform operations like this:

```
Hierarchy_Iterator<Department,Employee> it;
Employee ep;

for(ep = it.begin(dp); ep; ep = ++it){
   hier.del(ep);        //remove ep from the hierarchy
   delete ep;           //destroy ep
}
```

and the loop will continue properly without crashing. Another level of sophistication is to be able to remove or add a new object anywhere in the hierarchy while traversing it in multiple loops, and still obtain logical, predictable behavior:

```
Hierarchy_Iterator<Department,Employee> it1, it2;
Employee ep1, ep2;

for(ep1=it1.begin(dp); ep1; ep1= ++it1){
   for(ep2=it1.begin(dp); ep2; ep2= ++it1){
      if(...){
```

```
            hier.del(epp);  //epp is some general Employee, not ep2
            delete ep;      //destroy it
         }
         else {
            epp = new Employee;          //create a new Employee
            hier.insert(ep2,epp);        //insert it after ep2
         }
      }
   }
```

When using iterators with these capabilities, class Hierarchy<...> must keep a list of all active iterators, and when the data structure is modified (inside functions such as add(), del(), or insert()) the active iterators are informed about the change, and a quick check determines whether the change affects the data stored inside the iterator. This is the method used in Ver.5.0 of the Data Object Library by Code Farms.

When I introduced manager classes in Soukup (1994), I called them "pattern classes," because they manage entire data structures or design patterns. Unfortunately, this name did not catch on, and the term "manager class" seems to be more accepted today. One important advantage of manager classes is that they provide a clear record of the software architecture; the application classes and their relations (manager classes) are orthogonal, independent entities. For example:

```
//----------- application classes ------------
class Department :
   public TreeNode<Department>,
   public HierarchyParent<Department,Employee>,
   public CollectionParent<Department,Project>
{
   int deptNo;
   ...
};
class Employee :
   public HierarchyChild<Department,Employee>,
   public HierarchyChild<Project,Employee>
{
   long salary, startingDate;
   ...
};
class Project :
     public HierarchyParent<Project,Employee>,
     public CollectionChild<Department,Project>
{
   long dueDate;
   ...
};
//--------------------------------------------

//----------- software architecture ------------
Tree<Department> departments;
Hierarchy<Department,Employee> employees;
Collection<Department,Project> projects;
Hierarchy<Project,Employee> worksOn;
//--------------------------------------------
```

In this case, Departments form a tree. Departments have Employees and Projects, each Employee knows its parent Department, but the Projects do not. Each Employee works on exactly one Project, and each Project keeps the list of Employees that work on it. The architecture definition is clear and concise, and translates directly into the OO diagram shown in Figure 39.5.

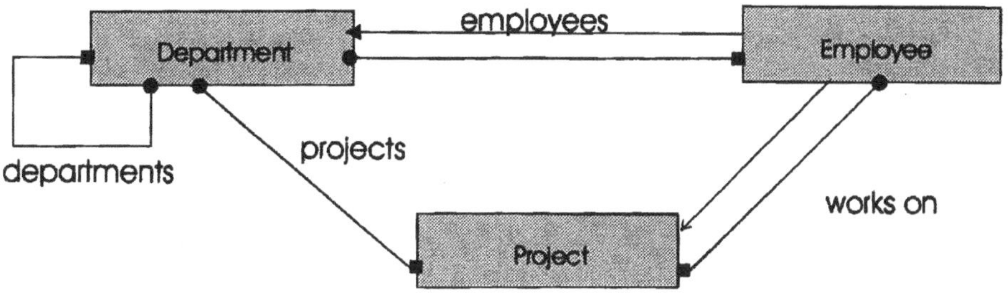

FIGURE 39.5 OO diagram derived from the manager classes for classes Department, Employee, and Project. Note that the Hierarchy relation must be represented as a collection plus the parent pointer.

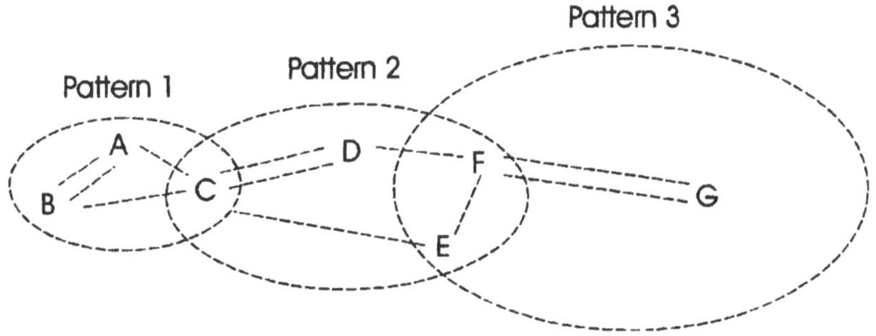

FIGURE 39.6 When functions managing data structures and patterns are assigned to application objects (or to members or base classes of application objects), the dependency graph may easily form large clusters (top diagram). When these data structures or patterns are represented by manager classes (bottom diagram), the dependency is reduced, usually removing all cycles in the dependency graph.

39.3.3 Class Dependency

Another important property of manager classes is that they decrease dependency among the application classes. If you implemented this architecture with standard containers, you will most likely end up with a knot of classes that depend on each other, and cannot be compiled independently. However, if you use manager classes, and decide to remove collection "projects," only classes Department and Project must be recompiled, class Employee can stay as it is. For 3 classes this does not sound like a big deal, but if your design involves 15 classes, it makes a difference, whether after changing one data structure you have to recompile all 15 classes, or just 2 of 3 of them.

Figure 39.6 expresses this graphically. When functions that control data structures are assigned to application objects or to classes that become members or are inherited by application objects (which is the common practice today), the dependency graph encompasses all classes. When each pattern (or data structure) is represented by a manager class, the dependency is reduced. For example, if class E changes, only the manager classes P2 and P3 must recompile with it. Or when pattern P1 is replaced by another pattern, classes A, B, and C must recompile.

39.3.4 Integrity Checking — Rings

Another important idea which I briefly mentioned above, is the possibility of integrity checking by examining whether the data structure pointers are NULL. This is possible only when working with intrusive data structures, and when all internal lists are implemented as rings, not as NULL ending lists. For example, in the container from Figure 39.1 (bottom diagram), the only way to tell whether a certain Elem is used in the container is to run through all Links and check whether the obj pointer points to the particular Elem. A check like that is too expensive to be used for every add() or del() operation on the list.

On the other hand, if we want to detect whether an Elem participates in an intrusive list (Figure 39.1, top diagram), all we have to do is to check whether its pointer(s) have an agreed initial value (which means "disconnected" or "unused") or are assigned to valid pointer values.

When working with lists, the values of NULL is used for two purposes: pointers on new objects, which are not connected to any data structure are initialized to this value, and the last object on the list points to NULL. If we use a different value for each purpose (for example 0 and -1), this would permit additional validity checking. Another possibility is simply to avoid the END_OF_LIST value by implementing all lists as rings, and use NULL solely to mark initialized (unused) pointers. In a valid ring, all pointers have non-zero values, and in a new object, which is not connected to any data structure, all pointers are then initialized to NULL. Only objects that have all pointers equal to NULL can be safely destroyed. This arrangement guarantees that we destroy only objects that are completely disconnected from all data structures, and that prevents a large category of hard to solve pointer errors.

Here I should credit Michael Palcewski who, many years ago and after endless discussions, convinced me that rings are better than NULL ending lists. Operations on rings are actually more elegant, because the end points represent less of an exception from the algorithmic point of view. Also, one object can effectively serve as both the head and the tail of the list. This can be seen from the following code:

```
template<class P,class C> class Hierarchy;
template<class P,class C> class HierarchyChild;

template<class P,class C> class HierarchyParent {
   friend class Hierarchy<P,C>;
   C *child;  //the child represents the tail of the list
};

template<class P,class C> class HierarchyChild {
   friend class Hierarchy<P,C>;
   C *next;
   P *parent;
};

template<class P,class C> class Hierarchy {
public:
   C *tail(P *p){return p->child;}
   C *head(P *p){C* c = p->child; if(c)c = c->next; return c;}
      void insert(C *c,C *n);  //insert n after c, under the same parent
   ...
};

template<class P,class C> void Hierarchy<P,C>:: add(C *c,C *n) {
   if(n->next){ ... // error, n is already in a hierarchy }
   else if(c->next == NULL){ ... // error, c is not in a hierarchy }
   else {
      n->next = c->next; c->next = n; n->parent = c->parent;
      if(c->parent->child == c)c->parent->child = n;
   }
}
```

The tail and the head of the list are derived from the single pointer, "child." Note the simplicity of the insert() function due to the use of the ring. We do not need special code for inserting an object at the beginning or end of the list. Also note that intrusive data structures have a natural tendency to implement sets (groups of objects where each object can appear at most once), while the indirect containers have a tendency to implement bags (groups of objects where one object can be included several times).

39.3.5 Data Browser

When debugging a program with complex data structures, it is important that you deal with entire sets of objects, rather than with individual pointers and fields. To complement the regular debugger, the C++ Data Object Library provides a special browser, which can be called from the application code for any given object. The library displays the object and all its links in the associated data structures. The user may then navigate to adjacent objects, and conveniently traverse the entire data. For example, assume that you have the following architecture (I modified the syntax used in the library slighly, in order to make it more compatible with the text of this chapter):

```
#include "generate.h"

class Department {
  INCLUDE(Department);
  int deptNo;
  ...
};

class Employee {
  INCLUDE(Employee);
  long salary, startingDate;
  ...
};
TREE(departments,Department);
HIERARCHY(employees,Department,Employee);
NAME(emplName,Employee); // equivalent of the String class
UTILITIES(util); // disk saving utilities, include also the browser

Department *dp;
...
util.debug(dp,"Department");
```

Then the call to util.debug( ) enters the browser and, the program displays on the screen:

```
object = 1109331950 type = Department:
1: 1109331890   employees.child->Employee
2: 0            departments.child->Department
3: 1109332204   departments->parent->Department
  deptNo = 114;
select pointer (-n retrace n steps, 0 exit):
```

This tells you that you are at the Departments No.114 which starts at memory location 1109331890, and which uses three data structure pointers. Pointer (1) leads to the tail (child) Employee under the "employees" hierarchy. Pointer (2) leads to the tail (child) in the "departments" tree, and 0 means this is currently a leaf of the tree. Pointer (3) leads to the parent within the "departments" tree.

If you type 1, you selected to move to the first Employee of this department, and you may see on the screen something like this:

```
object=1109331890 type=Employee:
  1: 1037304370 emplName.name->Employee=Green J.
  2: 1109331866 employees.next->Employee
  3: 1109331950 departments->parent->Department
    salary=3200 startingDate=190395
  select pointer (-n retrace n steps, 0 exit):
```

The interface lets you retrace several steps, which is important in case you walk into one of the dead ends in your data structure. This tool is invaluable when debugging and testing large data sets. It lets you traverse the data quickly and in a more meaningful way, than you can do it with a standard debugger.

39.3.6 Persistent Data

Thus far I explained all the ingredients of our design methodology, except for one: Automatic persistence. Persistent data is the data which survives one program run, and is usually implemented through a disk storage of some or all memory resident data used by the program.

The literature and even the C++ language itself treat data structures and data persistency as two independent issues, but the truth is that the two subjects are closely related. Data structures depend on pointers, and the storage and recovery of pointers is the key issue when storing/restoring data from the disk. To make things worse, in C++, there are two types of pointers which must be converted: (1) Ordinary pointers that form your data structures, and that you either included as members of your classes, or that got there transparently through the library you are using and (2) virtual function pointers, which are invisibly inserted by the compiler to your classes, and which are essential to the execution of virtual functions.

39.3.7 Virtual Function Pointers

Look at these two simple classes:

```
class A {
   int a;
public:
   virtual int fun(){return a;}
};

class B: public A {
   int b;
public:
   virtual int fun(){return b;}
};
```

If you check the sizes of the two classes, you will get sizeof(A) = 8, sizeof(B) = 12, even though class A stores only one integer (4 bytes), and class B stores only 2 integers (8 bytes). The additional space of 4 bytes is needed for the virtual function pointer. The C++ language does not specify where this pointer should be, and different compilers insert the pointer in a different position within the object.

For example, the Microsoft compiler puts it in the beginning of the object, while the Cfront compilers (e.g., older Sun compilers) put it at the end of A in this case. Borland compiler uses only a short, 2-byte offset instead of a full pointer. To make this even more complicated, when multiple inheritance is used, there can be several such pointers in a single object. For more details, look at Chapter 8 in Soukup,1994.

39.3.8 Interface for Persistent Data

Our objective is to store/restore the memory data in a single command, without a need to manually code the serialization functions. For example, the Data Object Library does it in this style:

```
UTILITIES(util);//utility class which manages persistency

Department *root;
void *v[1]; char *t[1];
...
v[0] = root;              //you must provide a root of the data
t[0] = "Department";  //and confirm its type
util.save("myFile",1,v,t);  //save data to myFile
...
util.open("myFile",1,v,t); // retrieve the data from the disk
if(strcmp(t[0],"Department")){ ... }; // error
root=(Department *)(v[0]); // root of the new data
```

Note that if this code was part of a single run, you end up with two copies of the entire data image — one with the old root, and one with the new root.

39.3.9 Finding Pointers in Objects

As I explained above, we need to know where, in any object, all the pointers are. We also need to identify data structure pointers and virtual function pointers, because they must be treated differently. (There can also be virtual class pointers, see [Soukup, 1994], but I do not want to go to this level of detail here.)

In 32-bit architectures, 4-byte pointers must start on addresses that are multiples of 4. For example, an object of size = 20 bytes and starting at the address 43024 has only 5 potential locations for pointers: 43024, 43028, 43032, 43036, and 43040. If we overload the new( ) operator so that new memory is always initialized as 0, we can easily detect all three types of the pointers. The following program demonstrates the idea. It is not necessary to overload new( ) with calloc, but all memory must be initialized to 0.

The program works with three images of the same class: p1 and p2 just have memory initialized to 0 and non-zero values must be v.f. pointers (same for both p1 and p2) or virt.class pointers (different for p1 and p2). Pointers which are non-zero in p3, but zero in p1 (or p2) are data structure pointers. The data structure implementation must provide a constructor(Alloc2*), which sets all data structure pointers to a non-zero value (not shown in this code sample):

```
#include <iostream.h> // Microsoft version
#include <malloc.h>

// classes to identify special constructors
class Alloc1 {int dummy;}alloc1;
class Alloc2 {int dummy;}alloc2;

class Employee {
    ...
public:
    Employee(){...} // normal constructors and functions as usual
    virtual void f(){}

    Employee(Alloc1 *s){} // all memory pre-initialized to 0
    Employee(Alloc2 *s){...} // data structure ptrs set to non-zero
    void* operator new(size_t size){return calloc(1,size);}
};

template<class T>void prtPtrs(T* t){
    char** p1=(char**)new T(&alloc1); // first object vf ptrs only
    char** p2=(char**)new T(&alloc1); // second object vf ptrs only
    char** p3=(char**)new T(&alloc2); // object with data ptrs

    cout << "object=T, size=" << sizeof(T) << "\n";
    for(int i=0; i<sizeof(T); i=i+sizeof(T*), p1++, p2++, p3++){
        if(!(*p3))continue; // no pointer in this location
        if(!(*p1))cout <<
                    "address=" << i << " data structure pointer\n";
        else if((*p1)!=(*p2))
                cout << "address=" << i << " virt.class pointer\n";
        else cout << "address=" << i << " virt.fun pointer\n";
    }
}

int main(){
    Employee e;
    prtPtrs(&e);
    return 0;
}
```

39.3.10 Updating Hidden Pointers

The hidden pointers used by the compiler (v.f. pointers and virt. class pointers) can be updated with the following trick without knowing where they are, as long as you know the type of the object. If you retrieve an old image of the object from the disk, and feed it into new() as if it were a newly allocated memory, operator new() will reset the hidden pointers to their correct values, while leaving the remaining bytes intact. This action is controlled by the static variable allocControl. When this is NULL, normal allocation is required. When it is not NULL, this is just a call to update the hidden pointers on the given object:

```
#include <iostream.h> // Microsoft version
#include <malloc.h>

class Alloc1 {int dummy;}alloc1;

class Employee {
   ...
public:
   ...
   static Employee *allocControl;
   Employee(Alloc1 *s){} // all memory pre-initialized to 0
   void* operator new(size_t size){return calloc(1,size);}
};
Employee* Employee::allocControl = NULL;

template<class T> static void updateHiddenPointers(T *t){
   T::allocControl = t;
   T* p=new T(&alloc1);
   T::allocControl = NULL;
}

int main(){
   Employee* e;
   ...
   // here e is an object image with incorrect hidden pointers
   updateHiddenPointers(e);
   // now the hidden pointers are up to date
   return 0;
}
```

39.3.11 Collecting All the Objects

Now that you understand how to access pointers within objects, it is easier to explain how automatic persistency works. As I mentioned above, the Data Object Library provides two different storage mechanisms. The first method assumes that in addition to the position of all pointers, we also know the type of the objects to which the pointers lead. How to obtain this information is again beyond the scope of this chapter.

When you call util.save(...) with one or several root objects, the library saves the root object as two records:

Record 1: A header indicating object type, its size, current address, and the size of the array (= 1 for a single object).

Record 2: Flat binary image of the object.

After this, the library follows all pointers present in the object, and because it knows the type of the target objects, it can write these to disk and proceed like this recursively until all objects are written to disk. In this process it is essential to secure that each object will be written to disk just once. Besides wasting lots of disk space, without this, the algorithm could run into an infinite loop. The speed of checking whether an object has been written out to disk is critical for the performance of the algorithm, and even hashing, normally considered to be fast, is not fast enough for this purpose. The Data Object Library is using a special intrusive (of course) arrangement which is very fast.

Let us assume that we have N objects, at least 4 bytes each, and we allocate two arrays of void pointers R[N], A[N]. We remember the size S of the used part of these arrays, and start with S = 0. After we write an object to disk, we copy the first 4 bytes of the object to R[S], remember the address of the object in A[S], and replace(!) the first 4 bytes of the object by a 4-byte integer equal to S. Then we increase S by 1.

When checking whether an object starting at address p has been written to disk, we proceed like this:

```
void *R[N], *A[N]; int S;
...
(unsigned int)* i = (int*)(p); // first 4 bytes of the object as int
if((*i)<S && R[i] == (void*)p){ ... object already written to disk ... }
else { ... object not written to the disk yet ... }
```

After writing all objects to the disk, we have to reset their first four bytes back to their original values, which is again very fast:

```
int i; void **v;
for(int i=0; i<S; i++){
   v=(void**)(A[i]);
   *v=R[i];
}
```

Obviously, the disk storage process cannot be interrupted. Some objects would be invalid, with the first four bytes overwritten by some integer index.

Besides writing each object to the disk as a flat array of bytes, as described above, the Data Object Library has an option of recording the object in an ASCII format which outputs each object hierarchically as if using the usual serialization (Microsoft MFC, Rogue Wave tools.h++). The difference is that the serialization functions in the Data Object Library are generated automatically, and they are transparent to the user. This is another subject that I have to skip because of the limited scope of this chapter.

The advantage of the ASCII representation is that it is portable among different architectures. The flat binary representation is not, unless you do some byte swapping within the object image, depending on the hardware architecture.

39.3.12 Memory Blasting

If you do not need portability among different platforms, the Data Object Library has a much faster method for storing data to disk, which is called "memory blasting." It combines allocation of objects with disk storage, and vaguely resembles the Object Store database. It works like this.

The library runs its own memory manager, which allocates pages of memory (the application specifies how large page), and overloads all new() operators so that new objects are allocated from these pages. When the page size is a power of two, the swizzling of pointers is especially fast. Note that these pages are not system pages as in Object Store. Dependency on system pages makes the algorithm less portable.

Each page has a small bit map ($^1/_{32}$ of the page for a 32-bit architecture) where each bit represents one potential location of a pointer within the page. When allocating a new object, the library uses the algorithm which detects the positions of all pointers within the object (as described above), and marks these pointers in the bitmap. Saving of data to disk is lightning fast — the library just moves entire pages of memory to the disk, including the associated bitmaps.

When retrieving the data back from the disk, again, we read entire pages to memory, and we can walk through the bitmap, detect positions of all pointers, and convert them to the new object locations. Note that this again runs without fragmenting the process to individual objects, and is therefore very fast.

The update (swizzling) of each pointer takes only several arithmetic operations. The library keeps two arrays: A[] for the old potential page locations, and B[] for the corresponding new page. For example, if the page size is 2**12 = 4096, it may look like this:

```
i    A[i]   B[i]
0    0      0          old pages starting between 0-4095
1    0      0          old pages starting between 4096-8191
....
10   0      0          old pages starting between 40960-45055
11   45072  41004      old pages starting between 45056-49151
12   49232  48804      old pages starting between 49152-53247
13   0      0          old pages starting between 53248-57343
....
```

When converting the old pointer value, we use shift to determine index i of the old page. For example, the old pointer 45080 shifted by 12 to the right gives 11, where A[11] tells us the beginning of the old page was 45072. The offset in the old page was 45080-45072 = 8, therefore the new pointer value will be 41004+8 = 41012.

Note that the shift may give you either the correct page index, or the index of the next page. For example, old pointer 49156 shifted by 12 gives you index i = 12, but because A[12] = 49232 is bigger than 49156, the index must be 11, and the offset is 49156-45072 = 4084. On the other hand, the old pointer 49312 shifted by 12 gives also index i = 12, but because 49312 is bigger than A[12], the offset is 49312-49232 = 80. For the full description of the algorithm, see Soukup (1994), Chapter 8.

Memory blasting was added to the Data Object Library in the early 1990s on the request of Mark Kramer from Zycad Corporation, who also invented this algorithm.

39.3.13 Practical Experience

The ultimate proof that the suggested measures indeed lead to a threefold improvement of efficiency is in practical experience. For this reason, I collected several stories of real-life commercial projects, which used the proposed methodology, and generated high quality software in an unusually efficient manner.

39.3.13.1 User Experience No. 1

In the early 1990s, High Level Design Systems in Santa Clara, CA, developed a VLSI CAD system which, along with other features, allowed its users to transfer between different commercial CAD systems while designing the same silicon chip. Until that time, chip designers had been locked into the CAD system which they selected.

The heart of the HLDS system was the internal database, called Pillar, which supported the data conversion, fast algorithms, and the graphical display of vast layout data. This database was designed by a single person (Mark Bales) and was operational in three months. Mark used the methodology described in this chapter, and implemented Pillar with the Data Object Library. Using other methods, a project like this would have required three man years. Pillar stores data to disk using memory blasting.

In 1997, HLDS was purchased by Cadence Design Systems for $99 million.

39.3.13.2 User Experience No. 2

MultiQuest Corporation in Schaumburg, IL, developed a graphical object-design tool supporting the Unified Modeling Language (UML) ahead of Rational, including many advanced features such as user customizable code generation and reverse engineering. This CASE system consists of 100,000 lines of C++, with 500 classes 7 levels deep, and 52 data organizations represented by manager classes recommended in this chapter (Data Object Library). It runs under Windows 95/NT, Sun Solaris, HP, and Apple Macintosh.

The original system was developed by two people in six man/years using the Data Object Library; a negligible effort compared to the resources that went into Rational Rose. The original system stored the data in ASCII format, which was later replaced by a custom format that was better suited to this particular application. The representation of data structures through manager classes is still in use.

When UML was announced, Naresh Bhatia completely redesigned the entire system in one year. Without using manager classes, he reported, this would be totally impossible. I consider this a good indicator that my claims of improved maintenance are not exaggerated.

In 1997, MultiQuest was purchased by Cayenne Software, which is now selling the system under the name PepperSeed.

39.3.13.3 User Experience No. 3

In 1995, Fulcrum Technologies in Ottawa, Ontario, Canada, was interested in the Data Object Library, and I was asked by Mike Heffernan to code a simple syntax processor, which would demonstrate the capabilities of the library. I received a specification which included two classes, a tree, a collection, several string and pointer links, and no persistence, and I designed, coded, and debugged the entire program in 1.5 days, and e-mailed the 630 lines of code plus comments to Fulcrum.

Fulcrum purchased the library, and I have not heard from them for a while. About half a year later, I received a letter from Fulcrum congratulating me to my contribution to the new, just released Fulcrum product. I thought first this was a mistake, but learned later that my syntax processor worked perfectly, and was included in the released software without anybody ever touching it, and is still probably there.

This is a good example of how the proposed methodology permits fast prototyping and, at the same time, produces solid, industrial grade software.

39.3.13.4 User Experience No. 4

In 1996, a group of 4 programmers at Fulcrum Technologies designed the first prototype of a web crawler which internally used 41 classes and 19 data organizations represented by manager classes. The data (potentially the order of Gbytes in size) was stored to disk in two parts: (1) the structural data using the algorithm described above, and (2) the large volume of text using the PAGER organization (essentially a virtual array, not discussed in this book). I participated in this design as a consultant/contractor.

After experimenting with the first prototype, the company modified the specification and added more stringent requirements for its performance. About one half of the architecture changed, but it took us only one day, and the new version was running.

I quote this as another example how the new methodology improves software maintenance, allowing fast and safe changes of the architecture.

39.3.13.5 Unsolicited Quotes

Occasionally, happy users send me e-mails expressing the benefits of the new methodology better than I could do it myself. For example,:

> "Thanks for writing your book and promoting better ways of designing software. This stuff is so cool I have a hard time not wanting to teach my wife C++ just so I can tell her about it." (Ross Jekel)

> "I have found your library to be very reliable and bug free (memory corruptions, etc.). It has been very addictive to code with. It simplifies coding immensely." (Sebastian Ishaq)

> "F.P.Brooks, Jr. argued in 'No Silver Bullet — Essence and Accidents of Software Engineering' that no new development tool would arise that would yield a 10x increase of programming productivity in 10 years. In his book, J. Soukup presents methods which, in our mind, qualify as silver bullets." (J. Hoffman, manager of a team using the Data Object Library).

39.4 Research Issues and Summary

The general trend in the C++ and the OO programming is to avoid code generation. Libraries built on templates are recommended by gurus. The methodology described here does not depend on code generation, even though it was demonstrated mostly on the C++ Data Object Library, which uses a code generator. The key ideas — which are the use of intrusive data structures, rings instead of NULL ending lists, and manager classes representing relations — can be implemented with templates, as was demonstrated in the recently released library by Code Farms. For details, see Chapter 37.

The only feature which I recommend in this chapter and which is missing in Chapter 37 in order to make software development three times faster than it is today is automatic persistence. The idea is to separate persistency from data structures and patterns, by providing a smart, persistent pointer class, which could be used with any class library and make it instantly persistent. In Code Farms, we are currently working on a new product with the tentative name Persistent Pointer Factory, which will do exactly that.

In order to make any library persistent, normal pointers will have to be replaced by this special persistent pointer:

```
//old version
class SomeClass {
   ...
   char *p;
   SomeClass *next;
   ...
};

//new version
class SomeClass {
   ...
   PersistentPtr<char> p;
   PersistentPtr<SomeClass> next;
   ...
};
```

39.4.1 Summary

This chapter describes several ideas which, when jointly applied to C++ software development, result in threefold (or more) improvement of software productivity.

These ideas are:

- Representation of data organizations by manager classes
- Use of intrusive data structures instead of containers which are common today
- Using rings instead of NULL ending lists
- Having a library which provides automatically persistent data

These speed up and qualitatively improves all parts of the design cycle:

- The architecture is recorded in a form that can be used in the final code; immediate feedback both ways, no possibility to misinterpret the architecture.
- Rapid coding of high quality, errorless code. Easy evolution and modification of the code.
- It takes longer to compile the code, but many errors are conveniently discovered at this stage. This tremendously speeds up debugging and produces more reliable code.
- Debugging is much faster because pointer and allocation errors are practically eliminated. The clear record of architecture helps to debug at a higher, conceptual level.
- Maintenance is improved, because the architecture is clearly recorded in the code, and because the data and its organization are orthogonal. Changes are easy to introduce and safer.

References

Hoffman J.W. and Weininger J. 1997. Taming C++ (book review), *The C++ Rep.*, Feb., Vol. 9, No. 2, pp. 66-67.

Soukup, J. 1994. *Taming C++, Pattern Classes and Persistence for Large Projects.* Addison-Wesley, Reading, MA.

Soukup, J. 1997. *Intrusive Data Structures,* two-part article submitted to the *C++ Report* in June.

Vadaparthy K. 1997. Data object library, three-part series to be published in the fall of 1997 by the *J. Object-Oriented Program.*

Further Information

Additional details can be obtained from the documentation of the C++ Data Object Library distributed by Code Farms Inc. (see *http://www.CodeFarms.com*). The library comes in full source, which may be of interest if you are concerned about implementation details. At this Web site, you can also access free of charge the documentation for the Pattern Template Library.

40

Requirements Modeling

Daniel A. Rawsthorne

BDM Air Safety Management Company

40.1 Introduction

Software Engineering is a discipline whose purpose is to translate user needs into software products. Most software development projects fail to accomplish this. Why? According to Booch (1996), "it is because of: (1) a failure to properly manage the risks, (2) building the wrong thing, or (3) being blindsided by technology." Being more specific, Chonoles (1996) says that "developing the wrong system, a system that is not needed, is a more serious risk than any arising from technological or methodological issues."

In either case, it is clear that misunderstanding the requirements of a system is one of the most common sources of failure for software projects. To underscore this, requirements management is given great weight in all software development standards ([ISO, 1991 and Space and Naval Warfare Systems Command, 1994], for example). In fact, the first Key Process Area (KPA) in the Capability Maturity Model for Software (CMM), is the Requirements Management KPA. So, we are all convinced that Requirements Management is crucial. How is this chapter going to help?

The purpose of this chapter is to describe requirements modeling in an object-oriented environment. Requirements modeling is important because an analyst needs to have formal, methodical, control of the requirements of the system. An analyst also needs a formal way to validate that the "right" system is being developed. This chapter describes a way to do these things in an OO environment, by developing a Requirements Model.

It is important to note that this chapter is only about Requirements Modeling, and how it might be used within an effective Requirements Management process. There are many aspects of Requirements Management that will not be discussed, including requirements prioritization, trade off analysis, configuration control, traceability, etc.

0-8493-3135-8/99/$0.00+$.50

40.1.1 What Are Requirements?

Before we can embark on a study of the Requirements Model, we must know what requirements *are*. There are two similar definitions:

1. A Requirement is a characteristic of a system that must be present for the system to be acceptable to the Customer;
2. Or, more pragmatically, a Requirement is something that the Customer tests for in the final product.

These definitions are simple, but there is a hidden assumption — that a system *can* be built that will satisfy the requirements. This assumption is made by the Customer when the requirements are initially stated, and is made by the Developer when the requirements are accepted. If this assumption is not present, then a statement like "I want an aluminum ladder that will allow me to climb to the moon in 20 minutes" could be considered a legitimate requirement. Clearly, it is not.

Once it is agreed that this tacit assumption is being made, we have opened the door for Requirements Analysis, which is a process that is intended to do two things:

1. Prove that the stated requirements are consistent
2. Prove that the stated requirements are possible to accomplish

This process should be a cooperative one, involving both the Customer and the Analyst. The goal is to provide a common understanding of the requirements, including how they will be verified or tested. One cannot say that "legitimate" requirements exist until this common understanding is reached. This is one of the driving forces behind ISO-9000 — that system specification is not complete until the Customer and Analyst (or, more generally, the Developer) agree on the requirements and the validation criteria for these requirements.

This concept of requirements is different from what most of us are used to. Typically, we think of the requirements as being supplied by the Customer at the beginning of a project, probably as part of the Statement of Work (SOW). Historically, this has always caused us problems, as unrealistic or inconsistent requirements were often part of the contract and difficult to change. The modern thinking is different. We still receive a "requirements" document as part of the SOW, but we now consider it only an input to the Requirements Analysis process, with the "actual" requirements specification being the result.

40.1.2 What is a Requirements Model?

The bottom line is that we want a requirements specification that is consistent, unambiguous, testable, and possible to meet. In order to increase our chances of getting such a specification we do requirements modeling, which develops a model of the system's desired behavior. This model can come in various forms, but it represents the same idea no matter what the form. A Requirements Model is telling us: *If you build a system that looks and acts like this, you will succeed.*

We think of the Requirements Model as a living, breathing, version of the requirements specification. It can be examined, analyzed, manipulated, and played with in ways that allow it to be validated as correct, consistent, unambiguous, and testable. It is a model that indicates what a successful system *could* look like — it may not be unique. That is, there can be many Requirements Models that are based on the same initial set of requirements. The goal is to produce a Requirements Model that not only satisfies the stated requirements, but satisfies the unstated ones as well.

We can build such Requirements Models in a number of ways. In this chapter we describe how to build one using object-oriented technology. There are two parts to this description. First, we will describe the types, aspects, and forms of the model that we are likely to use. Second, we describe a strategy to use in order to elicit and model the requirements.

The Requirements Model is used to describe the Customer's requirements. Because there is basically no limit to what the Customer can require, we have the need to be extremely flexible with this model. This means that there can be many different forms of this model, at different levels of abstraction. It also means that the model need not be complete — there may be pieces of the system that the Customer has no requirements for — and, hence, can go undocumented in the Requirements Model.

Even though there can be many different aspects of Requirements Models, there is a relatively straightforward strategy for developing them. We present the basics of this strategy later in this chapter, describing how to elicit and document an object-oriented Requirements Model.

40.1.3 Uses of the Requirements Model

Before getting to the meat of this chapter, however, we will briefly discuss the potential uses of the Requirements Model. There are many of them, some obvious, some not so obvious.

1. The first, and most obvious, use of the Requirements Model is as a form of Analytic Model. In this role the Requirements Model is used to assist the Designers in developing the system.
2. The second, and most important, use is to view the Requirements Model as a communications medium to use with the Customer. In this role the Requirements Model is used to validate requirements with the Customer.
3. Since the Requirements Model is a living, breathing, version of the requirements, it is an ideal source of test material. When the test developers use the Requirements Model as the source for requirements to test, it improves the probability that the developers are building the system that the testers think they are testing.
4. Finally, the Requirements Model is a good source of training material. There are always decisions that must be made in order to resolve ambiguity, and the decisions are more likely to be consistent if all the developers are trained using the Requirements Model.

40.2 Diagrams Representing the Requirements Model

We wish to develop and document a Requirements Model. We document the Requirements Model by presenting diagrams representing particular aspects of it. There is a single Requirements Model, but there can be many diagrams describing it. One reason for this is that the Customer can have many different kinds of requirements. Another reason is that there are different aspects of the model that need to be represented. In an object-oriented context there are three basic aspects of the Requirements Model that need to be represented: behavioral, structural, and constraint.

- *Behavioral aspects* — This is how objects interact to accomplish behavior. This aspect describes the system's dynamic relationships.
- *Structural aspects* — This is how objects are connected. It usually includes inheritance, associations, aggregations, and other static relationships between objects and classes.
- *Constraint aspects* — They describe speed, size, or other constraints. They are usually quite free-form, and may be used to modify or amplify diagrams representing either structural or behavioral aspects.

The following sections describe some common diagrams used to model these aspects of the Requirements Model.

40.2.1 Straight Text

The most common way we encounter requirements is in straight text. Though text is technically not a "diagram," it is used for the same purpose — to describe requirements for the system. Therefore, we consider textual description as a form of diagram (albeit a strange one).

Requirements are presented to us by the Customer in textual form, and it is our job to analyze them for consistency, unambiguity, and possibility. The major strength of straight text is that it can be used to express arbitrary requirements. The major weakness of straight text is that it is ambiguous and hard to analyze.

TABLE 40.1 Sample Textual Requirements

2.7.1-5	The Build 2 support system shall provide the capability to test Build 2 operational releases.
2.7.1-5.1	*Threshold*: Provide the capability to create, modify, and configuration manage baseline simulations of the operational Build 2 upon request.
2.7.1-5.2	*Threshold*: Exercise all inputs and outputs of the operational Build 2 with the baseline simulations upon request; the intent is to have baseline simulation capability equal to or better than test NAS.
2.7.1-5.3	*Threshold*: Provide levels of testing sufficient to identify a problem down to the lowest level software components and data items, and the ability to specifically test corrections to these components and items.

The following is from an Operational Requirements Document (ORD) published by the FAA. The document has over 700 requirements of this sort (Table 40.1).

If possible, we would like to avoid textual requirements, primarily because of the inherent ambiguity. One of the main uses of Requirements Modeling is to convert such textual specifications into a model that can be analyzed and validated. However, we often must convert these models back to text in order to communicate with Users and get them validated. We hope that our Customer is familiar with the modeling, but often the Customer must deal with a User community that is not.

40.2.2 Use Cases

Use Cases are very popular, and are used to describe how a system is used by a User, or by extension, how an object (or group of objects) is used by other entities. Use Cases were introduced by Ivar Jacobson, and have been adopted (or, at least, tolerated) by every popular object-oriented methodologist as a good way to capture behavioral information.

The usual form of a Use Case is structured text, often accompanied by a scenario diagram. It is not our mission here to describe the differences between Use Cases, scenarios, transactions, etc., but only to present the basic idea. This idea is that the most important thing to know about a system is how it will be used, and this knowledge must permeate the development process.

The development of Use Cases is one of the most straightforward, and effective ways, to elicit and capture this information. This is often done as the first step of Requirements Modeling. Table 40.2 is an example of a Use Case (more precisely, a scenario) involving a Customer's use of a gas pump.

Use Cases have many formats and notations. For a good discussion of them, see Harwood, 1997. As noted, Use Cases are often accompanied by scenario diagrams.

TABLE 40.2 A Simple Scenario

- Pump asks customer to select method of payment; customer selects "credit"
- Pump asks customer to insert card
- Customer slides card through card reader; pump reads card
- Pump verifies card account with Corporate Credit; CC notified pump "OK"
- Pump asks customer to select grade; customer selects "Plus"
- Pump activates "Plus" valve
- Pump tells customer "Pump On"
- Customer removes nozzle
- Pump displays initial unit cost, total cost, gallons dispensed
- Customer depresses nozzle and pumps gas; pump updates display
- Customer releases nozzle and replaces nozzle on pump
- Pump disables valve and tells customer "Pump Off; Receipt Printing"
- Pump prints receipt
- Pump tells customer to take receipt; customer removes receipt

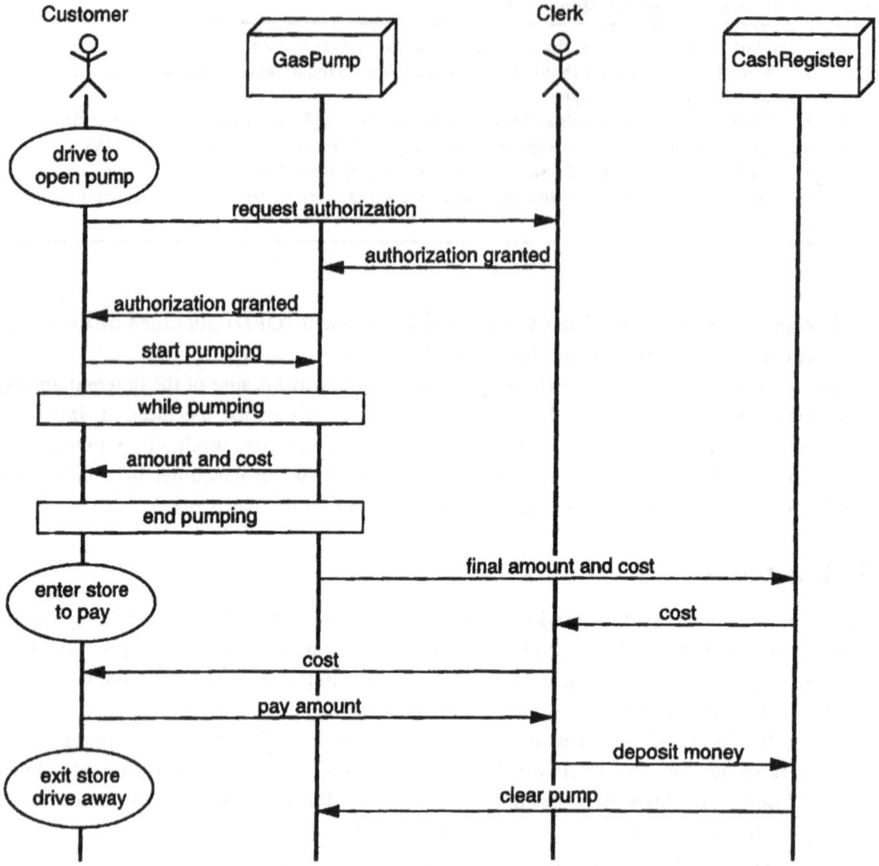

FIGURE 40.1 Sample Scenario diagram.

40.2.3 Scenario Diagrams

Scenario Diagrams are graphical depictions describing how objects interact in order to carry out their responsibilities. They are more precise than text, are easily understood, and can be used to capture complex patterns of interactions. As such, they are one of the best ways to capture behavioral information for a system.

There are many different notations that can be used for Scenario Diagrams. Figure 40.1 is the notation of the Object Modeling Language (OML) (Firesmith et al., 1996). It represents the same scenario that the textual scenario from the last section documented.

The Scenario Diagram is one of my personal favorites. It is an easily understood notation, can be used to provide information at different levels of abstraction, and is precise enough to allow for adequate analysis and validation.

40.2.4 State Transition Diagrams

One of the definitions of an object is that it is a well-defined entity with state. There are many objects that "live" in the problem domain or the logical architecture whose behavior can be well described by a State Transition Diagram (STD). It seems that STDs can be used as an efficient way to summarize a

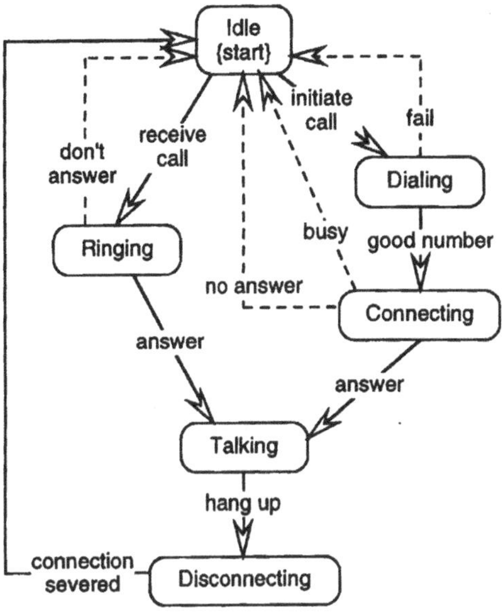

FIGURE 40.2 Sample STD.

lot of Use Cases or scenarios. Some methodologists say that STDs are unnecessary if one is using Use Cases, but I disagree.

It is unlikely that a set of Use Cases could be more precise, concise, or easily understood than the STD (Figure 40.2), which represents the behavior of a telephone. This STD is in the notation of the OML (Firesmith et al., 1996).

An STD indicates the states that an object can be in, and the ways it transitions from one to another, independent of the interactions it is involved in. In this way STDs complement Use Cases and Scenario Diagrams; STDs take a single object's point of view, while Use Cases and Scenarios take a more global point of view. STDs are often used to summarize an object's behavior after identifying a number of scenarios. It is extremely useful when an object has a (relatively) small number of distinct states, but is involved in a (potentially) large number of interactions.

40.2.5 CRC Cards

CRC Cards were developed by Cunningham and Beck (1989), in the late 1980s in order to aid in the training of object thinking. It was soon realized that they were appropriate and useful for object-oriented analysis. Their purpose is to identify the objects in the system, their responsibilities, and the other objects they collaborate with in order to carry out their responsibilities.

The derivation of CRC cards is as much a part of the method as the cards themselves. CRC cards are usually developed in highly collaborative, collective sessions. Most methodologists referring to "the CRC method" are referring to the sessions as much as they are referring to the cards.

Table 40.3 shows part of the analysis of a drawing package. It indicates that there is a SelectTool, which is a (inherits from) Tool. It has two sets of responsibilities, each with its own collaborators.

CRC cards are used in much the same way that Use Cases are. While Use Cases are developed to explore the fundamental *behavior* of a system, CRC cards are developed to explore the fundamental *architecture* of a system, and determine the responsibilities associated with each element of this architecture. As such, they can be seen as a structural model, with links to behavior, as represented by the responsibilities.

TABLE 40.3 Sample CRC Card

SelectTool	
Tool	
1. select/deselect Shapes select_new_shapes add_selected_shape delete_selected_shape toggle_selected_shapes	SelectedShapes Document
2. move/resize selected shapes resize_selected_shapes move_selected_shapes select_drag_shape	SelectedShapes Page

Many successful developments start with either CRC analysis, Use Case analysis, or both. I like to use CRC cards augmented with Use Cases for my initial attempts at a Requirements Model. The CRC Cards define the structure, and the Use Cases (scenarios) show how the collaborations take place.

40.2.6 Category Diagrams

In object-oriented technology, objects are usually considered to be the fundamental unit of functionality. However, it is often the case that we need to document entities that are "larger" than objects in our diagrams. This need arises during decomposition, as we decompose our system, and it arises during design, as we organize our entities.

These "big" entities are referred to as Categories within the UML, and we do so here as well. A Category is defined as a collection of objects (or subcategories) with associated interactions, Use Cases, or other semantics. That is, they represent "complete" models for the subsystems imbedded in our system.

There are a number of notations available for Categories. Figure 40.3 comes from the UML. It represents the subsystem decomposition of a ViewGraph System, and indicates dependencies between some of the Subsystems.

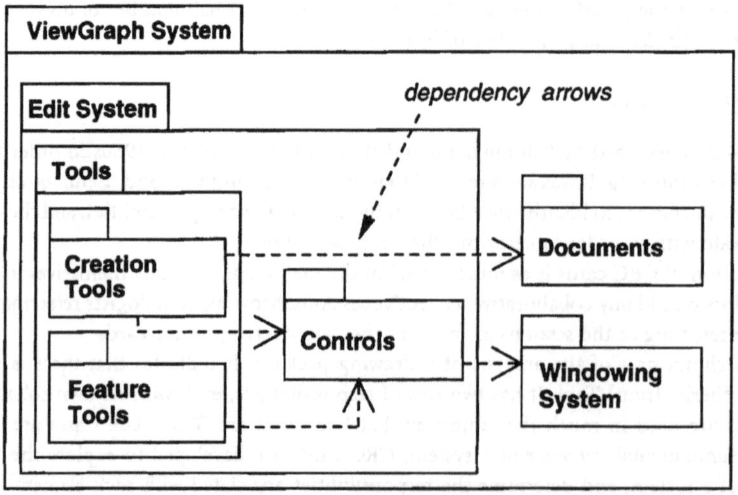

FIGURE 40.3 Sample Category diagram.

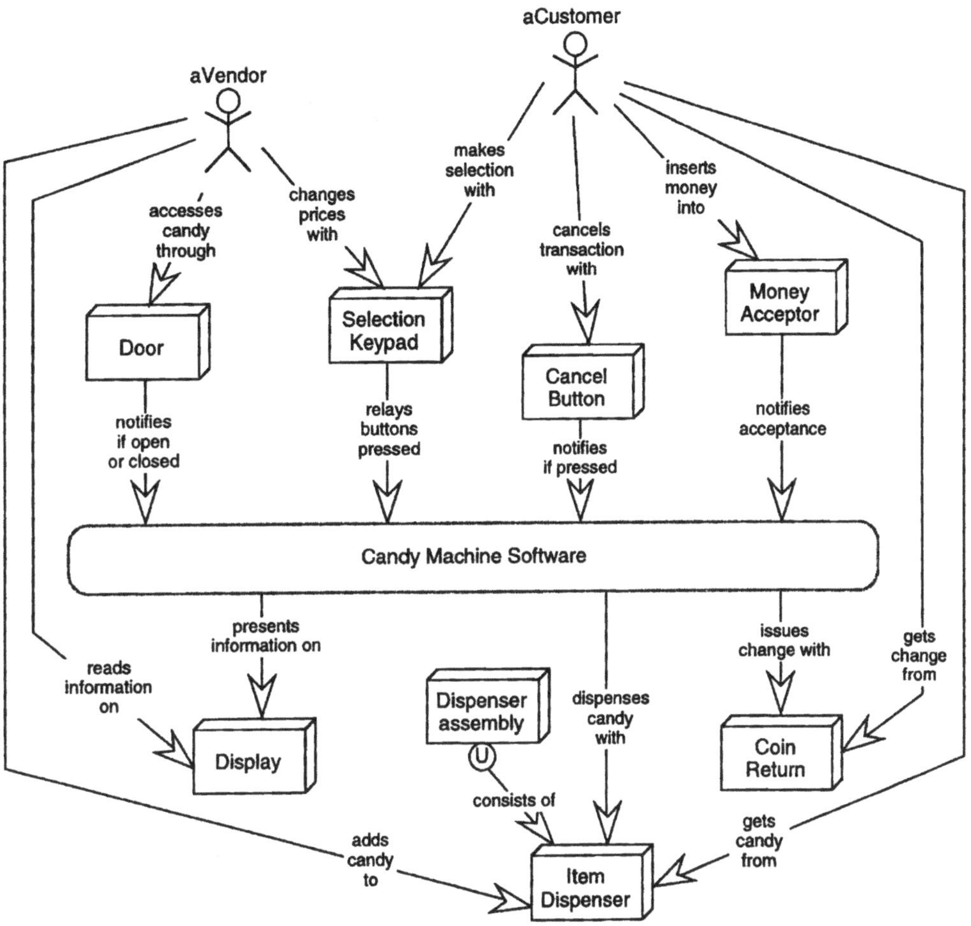

FIGURE 40.4 Sample Context diagram.

Category Diagrams are very useful to indicate the top-level architecture of a system. I find them particularly useful for developing a top-level architecture and describing it to my Customers, Users, and Development Team.

40.2.7 Context Diagrams

No system operates in a vacuum; there are always actors and external objects that interact with it. The interactions of the system with these entities are usually described with Use Cases, but this is often an insufficient description for the Customer.

Most people like to see boxes and arrows indicating who does what to whom. The Context diagram is the diagram that illustrates this, and it is an excellent model to introduce a model to Customers and Users. It is often used to describe and define the "players" that appear in Use Cases.

The Context diagram (Figure 40.4) is in the OML notation, and represents the major "players" involved in a Candy Machine.

I really like this model. I have never seen a better way to introduce a system to others at such a high level of abstraction. When coupled with Use Cases it can really tell the story of the system.

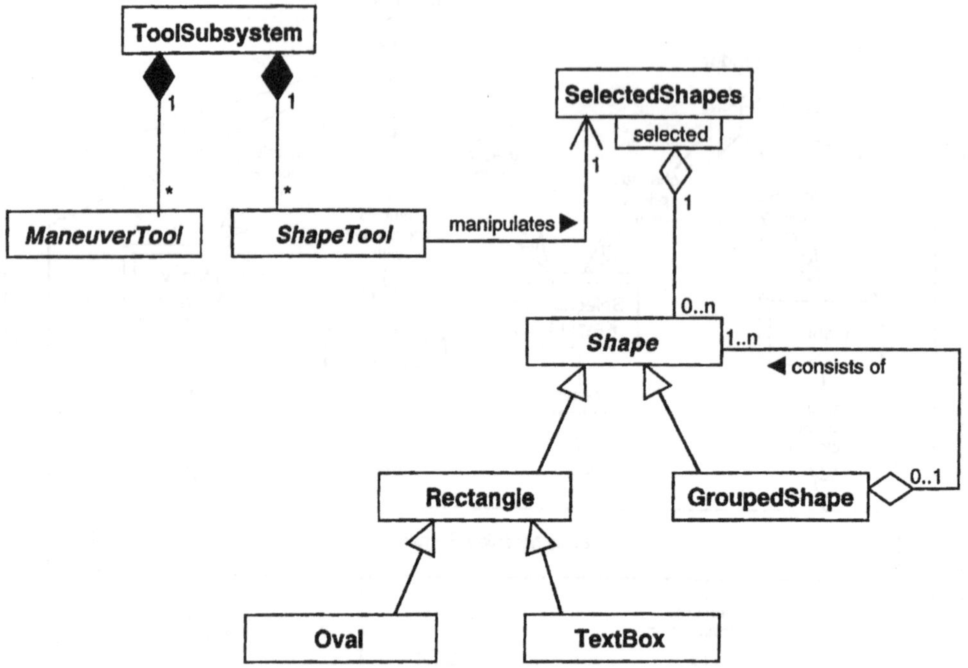

FIGURE 40.5 Sample Class diagram.

40.2.8 Class Diagrams

The Class diagram is usually the first object-oriented model of which one thinks. Every methodology has a Class diagram and they are all basically the same. The contents of the Class diagram are the Classes and the relationships between them.

These relationships usually consist of inheritance, aggregation, and association. The Class diagram (Figure 40.5) is in the UML notation, and represents some of the basic classes that exist in the ViewGraph system.

Class diagrams are commonly used to document the design of a system. However, they may also be used to document portions of the Requirements Model by showing how a system could be constructed that would satisfy the requirements. I believe that the Class diagram is more useful for Design than Requirements Modeling, but it can be used when the Requirements Model is highly complex, and it includes a number of internal structural elements.

40.2.9 Collaboration Diagrams

Objects interact with other objects in many ways. For any two objects (or classes) there is a set of messages that can pass between them. This set constitutes a contract between these two entities, and defines the interfaces between them. A collaboration diagram shows the Classes in a system, and the sets of interactions between them. The Collaboration diagram (Figure 40.6) is in the OML notation, and indicates some of the collaborations involved in the Candy Machine.

Generally speaking, collaboration diagrams are more useful for Design than Requirements modeling. In this, it is similar to the Class diagram. However, also similar to the Class diagram, the Collaboration diagram is useful when the Requirements Model is complex and involves many interacting entities in the logical architecture.

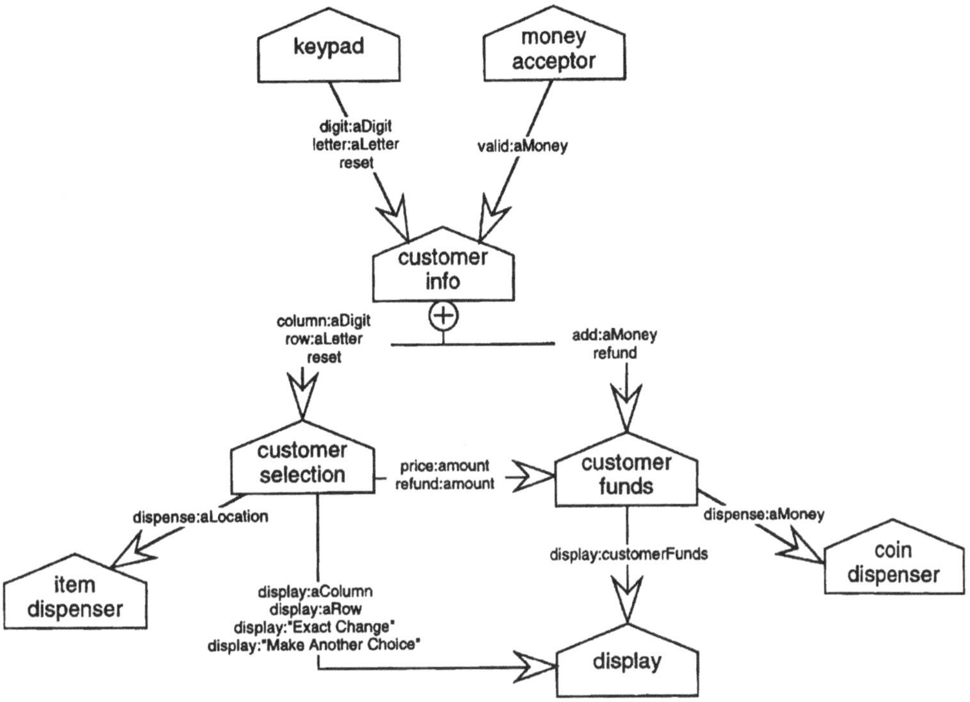

FIGURE 40.6 Sample Collaboration diagram.

40.2.10 Diagram Summary

There are a number of diagrams that can be used to document the Requirements Model, as we have just described. Table 40.4 summarizes the previous sections, listing the diagram name, whether it is used for Behavior or Structure, and presents a brief evaluation.

When developing a Requirements Model, you must choose the diagrams you will use to document it. There are many factors to consider in making these choices. Chief among these are

- *Customer needs* — What can the Customer understand? What diagrams does the Customer find intuitive? What diagrams "speak" to the Customer?
- *Domain needs* — What kind of domain is it? Are the requirements inherently behavioral, as in many real-time applications? Are the requirements inherently structural, as in many MIS applications?

Because Requirements Modeling is so important, it is crucial to be flexible. Often, requirements analysts feel the need to develop their own notations, based on the needs of the Customer and the domain. I hope that the diagrams I have presented here will either be adequate in themselves or provide sufficient guidance to enable adequate custom development of diagrams.

40.3 Development of the Requirements Model

In the preceding sections of this chapter we have seen some sample diagrams that can be used to document the Requirements Model. Now that we know what sorts of diagrams can be used to document the Requirements Model, we need to know how to develop the model itself. In this section we present a series of strategies that can be used to develop a Requirements Model.

TABLE 40.4 Summary of Notations, and their Uses

Diagram	Used For	Evaluation
Straight text	Everything	Most common; used to communicate with Users; usually augmented with more formal models; usually necessary to document constraints
Use cases	Behavior	Very Popular; good first step; helps frame the problem
Scenarios	Behavior	For decomposing functional behavior; very useful when there are a relatively small number of logical entities
State transition diagrams	Behavior	Useful with a large number of interactions, but few states
CRC cards	Structure	Very good for initial decomposition of system; work well with Scenarios
Category diagrams	Structure	Used to show relationships between "large" entities; good way to indicate Subsystem structure
Context diagrams	Structure	Shows how externals interact with the system; great diagram for indicating overall structure
Class diagram	Structure	Common structure model; shows connections in system; more useful for design
Collaboration diagram	Structure	Shows how connections between entities will be used to pass messages; more useful for design

40.3.1 General Context

Each of the strategies presented here is used within the context of Requirements Modeling. We assume that there is a system that needs to be built. This system may or may not have a initial, formal specification as different development projects start at different points. For example, the analyst may start with a 600-page written specification (some government contracts) or the plaintive call "I need a way to ..." from the user down the hall. Usually, the development team is not completely sure of what the system should be.

There are a number of common forces to consider when conducting, or preparing to conduct, requirements modeling. Some of the more powerful are

- There is a need for common understanding of the requirements for the system.
- The requirements for the system will change, so maintaining a common understanding is difficult.
- There is a great temptation to start designing the system before its requirements are understood.
- There is often a perceived need to start "real" development (coding).

These forces permeate the strategies given in this chapter. When there are other, more specific, forces at work, we will list them with the individual strategies.

There are a number of specific roles to be played within the requirements modeling process. The most important for our purposes is the Analyst, whose job is to provide an understanding of the requirements to the development team. In particular, we assume that the analyst's job is to develop, document, and maintain the Requirements Model.

There is an identifiable Customer (or surrogate) who can be used to provide the customer's needs and wants to aid in evaluation and validation of software products produced. Providing a Customer to play this role is a responsibility of the "purchaser" of the system, and is strongly recommended in ISO 9000-3 (ISO, 1991, paragraph 4.1.2). The existence of such a Customer is crucial to successful development of a system, and it is unlikely that successful requirements modeling can be conducted without one.

There is an identifiable Domain Expert who can be used to provide knowledge of the problem domain and aid in evaluation and validation of software products produced. The responsibility of the domain expert is to understand the domain within which the system will live, and communicate this information to the analyst. The domain expert knows what will and won't work within the domain, and is quite often a member of the development team, rather than a Customer.

The fundamental relationships between these three are

- The Analyst extracts needs and wants from the Customer, and validates them for feasibility with the Domain Expert
- The Analyst extracts domain knowledge from the Domain Expert, and focuses it on the information relevant to the needs and wants of the Customer
- The Analyst documents all this information in the diagrams that represent the Requirements Model

There are a number of other roles that have responsibilities within these strategies, including prototypers, the development team, and the test team.

40.3.2 The Strategies

Requirements Modeling is a complex process, and it is not the purpose of this paper to describe how the subprocesses described in these strategies should be organized within the development activities; that is a management responsibility that is outside the scope of this chapter. Rather, the purpose of the strategies in this chapter is to show how the subprocesses relate to each other in a technical, rather than managerial, sense.

The names of the strategies that are presented here are *Develop Requirements Model, Understand the Domain, Understand the Requirements, Document Structure, Document Inheritance, Document Behavior, Document Constraints, Scavenge Abstractions, Validate the Models, Identify Reuse Candidates, Develop Prototypes,* and *Develop Acceptance Criteria.* These strategies are interrelated in two ways:

- There are activities that execute the processes captured in the strategies, and the strategies follow each other in ways that depend on the development process used. As noted above, this paper does not concern itself with this sort of organization.
- These strategies *use* each other in a number of ways, which are indicated within the strategies themselves. Figure 40.7 summarizes these "uses" relationships.

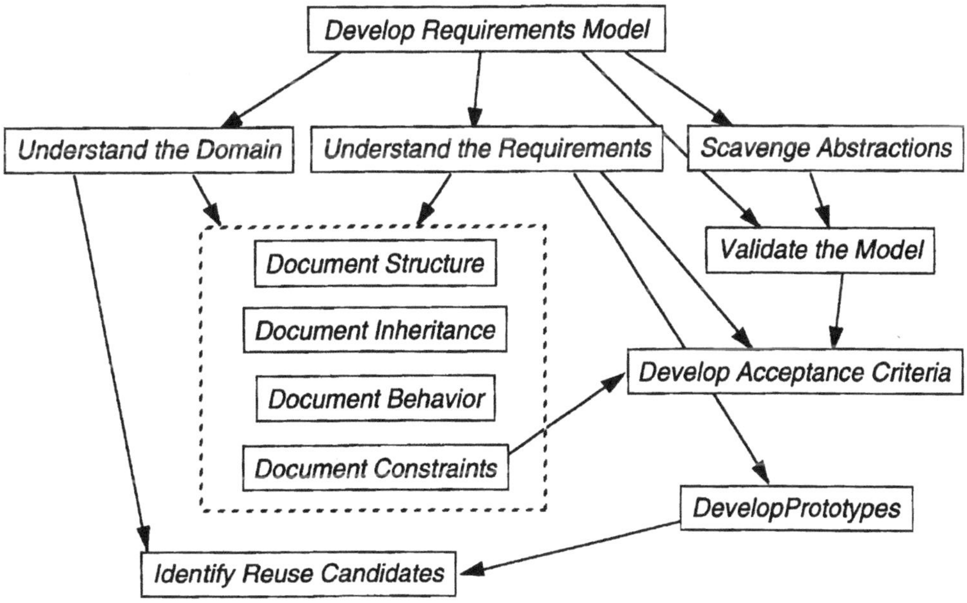

FIGURE 40.7 Relationships between the strategies.

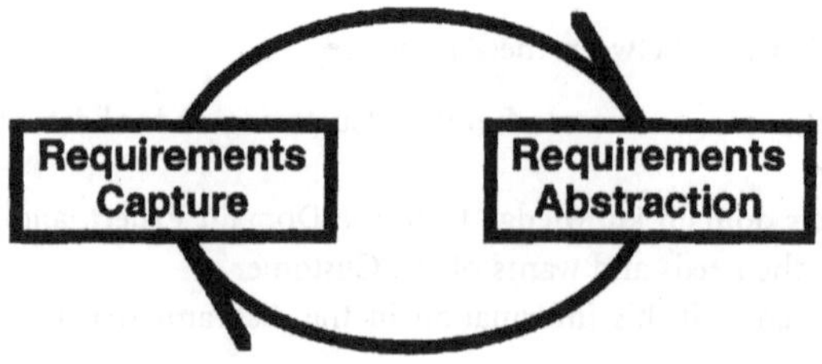

FIGURE 40.8 Requirements Modeling is an Iterative Process.

This presentation is brief and consists of strategies documented in a simple form*. This is because we believe that strategies should provide a minimally sufficient set of directions, and leave as much leeway as possible to the Analyst. As noted above, these strategies are not specific to any development paradigm; for example, they are equally applicable to either a waterfall development, an iterative development, or a rapid development process.

40.3.2.1 Develop Requirements Model

Problem: How does an analyst describe a required system to a software development team?

Context: See General Context.

Solution: Provide an analytic model using a robust Requirements Modeling process. This Requirements Model should not only adequately describe the system to be built, but should also capture and present common features in the problem domain that could possibly be exploited during design.

There are two distinct, though intertwined, (meta)processes involved in Requirements Modeling: Requirements Capture and Requirements Abstraction. The directions for their use are quite loose and informal, and mostly left up to the discretion of the analyst. The simplest way to use them is a simple iteration, as in Figure 40.8.

Requirements Capture is the specification of what the system must do. This specification must be captured in a set of diagrams that are both adequate and correct (including structured text). The focus is on important behavior and constraints (from the customer's point of view), and the process consists of the analyst's attempts to *Understand the Domain, Understand the Requirements,* and *Validate the Model.*

Requirements Abstraction is the extraction of similarities and patterns inherent in the requirements and expression of them in refinements of the Requirements Model. The result is the identification of analytic patterns (both behavioral and structural) that are inherent in the system, and that may be exploited by the designer (these diagrams are seldom textual). What the analyst does is *Scavenge Abstractions* and *Validate the Model.*

40.3.2.2 Understand the Domain

Problem: How does an analyst produce or modify the Requirements Model based on the relevant aspects of the problem domain?

Context: The Requirements Model may or may not already exist. There is an identifiable Domain Expert who can be used to provide knowledge of the problem domain.

Forces:

- The Domain Expert likely knows more about the domain than is relevant to the system.
- The Analyst wishes to extract all relevant information from the Domain Expert.

---

* This form is also referred to as "pattern form" and these strategies could also be referred to as design patterns. I prefer to think of this as a set of strategies, but it could also be referred to as a pattern language.

Solution: Work with the Domain Expert to develop or extend the Requirements Model. There are three basic types of requirements: structural, behavioral, and constraint. It is usual that structural and behavioral requirements are documented directly in the diagrams representing the Requirements Model, while the constraint requirements either augment these diagrams or are given separately (in text).

For behavioral and structural requirements, the Analyst views the domain as a set of interrelated entities, and the Domain Expert will help the Analyst determine what these entities are, and what the relationships are between them.

The Analyst and Domain Expert work together to determine those relationships that are "natural" within the domain, and that are relevant to the system being developed. There are three types of relationships to be captured:

1. Structural relationships — The analyst must *Document Structure*
2. Inheritance relationships — The analyst must *Document Inheritance*
3. Behavioral relationships — The analyst must *Document Behavior*

It is the job of the Analyst to focus the Domain Expert on the problem as it has been communicated by the Customer. It is the job of the Domain Expert to understand the domain within which the system lives, and provide this understanding to the Analyst. One of the difficult tasks of the Analyst is to balance the (limited) need for information with the (vast) amount of information available.

It is our experience that the Domain Expert provides primarily structural and inheritance relationships that occur within the system, and interaction relationships only secondarily. The Domain Expert also helps the analyst *Document Constraints* on the system.

Another aspect of understanding the domain is the identification and evaluation of potential software reuse candidates. The Analyst is seeking existing software products that can be reused during development of the system. Other systems that operate over the same problem domain are considered part of the domain, and they are identified and evaluated as part of this analysis. The Analyst and Domain Expert must *Identify Reuse Candidates.*

40.3.2.3 Understand the Requirements

Problem: How does an Analyst produce or modify the Requirements Model based on the Customer's needs and wants?

Context: The Requirements Model may or may not already exist. There is an identifiable Customer (or surrogate) who can be used to provide the Customer's needs and wants.

Forces:

- The Customer often does not know exactly what is needed.
- The Customer often does not know what is possible within the domain.
- The Customer often has unreasonable expectations.

Solution: Work with the Customer to produce or modify the Requirements Model. There are three basic types of requirements: structural, behavioral, and constraint. It is usual that structural and behavioral requirements are documented directly in the diagrams representing the Requirements Model, while the constraint requirements either augment these diagrams or are given separately (in text).

The Analyst views the system as a set of interrelated entities, including those that reside within the domain, and those that are specific to the system. The Customer will help the Analyst determine what these entities are (particularly those specific to the system), and what the relationships are between them.

These relationships are those that allow the system to satisfy the Customer's wants and needs, and the Analyst and Customer must work together to prioritize and manage them in developing the Requirements Model. There are three types of relationships that are captured:

1. Structural relationships — The analyst must *Document Structure*
2. Inheritance relationships — The analyst must *Document Inheritance*
3. Behavioral relationships — The analyst must *Document Behavior*

It is common that the Customer's needs and wants are elicited, expanded, or clarified by having the Analyst (or prototyper) *Develop Prototypes.* Additionally, when the Analyst is eliciting requirements from the Customer, the Analyst must constantly be looking to *Develop Acceptance Criteria.*

It is the job of the Analyst to extract specific needs and wants from the Customer, and communicate to the Customer what the Domain Expert has said is common within the domain, what is possible/impossible, etc. The Customer must work with the Analyst to develop a set of specific requirements for the system that are consistent with the way the Domain Expert understands the domain. It is our experience that the Customer primarily provides interaction relationships between the entities that have been identified by both the Customer and the Domain Expert. The Customer will also help the analyst *Document Constraints* on the system.

40.3.2.4 Document Structure

Problem: How does the Analyst refine the structural relationships within the Requirements Model?

Context: The Requirements Model exists, and the Analyst has access to an Expert (either a Customer or a Domain Expert) to aid in developing these relationships.

Forces:

- The Expert likely has a different view of structure than the Analyst.
- The Analyst must provide structural diagrams understandable by both the Expert and the development team.

Solution: Work with the Expert to identify and document the different types of structural relationships that should exist in the system. There are a number of different types of structural relationships that can exist between entities, and different methodologies use different names for them. The following paragraphs attempt to describe common understandings of these relationships, and use no specific naming conventions.

Aggregation — This refers to a relationship between classes, and indicates when an instance of one class is made up of instances of other classes, and this relationship is (relatively) fixed. For example, a Car is always made up of an Engine, a Body, four Tires, etc.

Subsystem — This refers to a relationship between objects, and indicates when one object is made up of other objects. The internal objects are distinct (though may be of the same class), and are "known by name" to the system. Typically, we think of a system as a one-of-a-kind decomposition of an object into other objects. For example, the Menu subsystem consists of FileMenu, EditMenu, ViewMenu, …

Container — This refers to a relationship between an object or a class (the container, or a class of containers) and a class (the class of the contained objects), and indicates that one object holds a number of other objects, each of the same class and virtually indistinguishable to the container. For example, TodaysTransactions is a container that is a list of all the Transactions executed today, the ClassRoom class is a container of Students, etc.

In both aggregations and containers there is the concept of multiplicities, when one entity can own a number of objects of the same class. These multiplicities are normally captured within the Requirements Model.

One of the more complicated things about structural relationships is based on the fact that a given entity can "belong" to a number of others within the system. For example, in a model that involves Members and Clubs, it is clear that a Club is a container of Members, and that any particular Member can belong to more than one Club. This information must be captured in order for the system to be adequately understood.

During this process the Analyst must keep in mind that it is a Requirements Model, not a design model, that is being constructed. As such, it is more important to understand the structural relationships between individual objects than it is to generalize them to relationships between classes.

40.3.2.5 Document Inheritance

Problem: How does the Analyst refine the inheritance relationships within the Requirements Model?

Context: The Requirements Model exists, and the Analyst has access to an Expert (either a Customer or a Domain Expert) to aid in developing these relationships.

Forces:

- The analytic and design concepts of inheritance are different.
- The Expert may misunderstand the analytic concept of inheritance.

Solution: The Analyst should work with the Expert to develop the inheritance portions of the models. Inheritance (in an analytic model, including the Requirements Model) is a simple, and often misunderstood, concept. Basically, it involves an entity's need to be similar to other entities in some way. These similarities are analytic, and have little to do with the inheritance of classes one finds in object-oriented languages.

For example, we could inherit based on objects needing to know similar information, needing to perform similar services (having similar responsibilities), playing the same or similar roles within the system, or based on looking alike in some other way that is relevant to the system. It is quite common for the Expert to refer to entities as abstractions; it is the Analyst who must determine when these abstractions are useful.

Typically, abstractions represent "placeholders," or entities that can be replaced by any of a set of objects within a particular context. For example, within an ATM system, the expert may refer to a Transaction, which could represent a DepositTransaction, WithdrawalTransaction, or some other type. In this case we would say that Transaction is an abstraction from which the others inherit. Abstractions used as placeholders typically occur quite naturally in the domain.

Inheritance is also used to indicate when one object is an "extension" of another. For example, a CancerPatient is an extension of a Patient, so we could say that CancerPatient inherits from Patient. Often, objects found in the system are extensions of objects in the domain — extended to provide specific system functionality.

During this process it must be kept in mind that one captures inheritance based on how an entity behaves in the system, not inheritance based on implementation constructs.

40.3.2.6 Document Behavior

Problem: How does the Analyst refine the behavior documented in the Requirements Model?

Context: The Requirements Model exists, and the Analyst has access to an Expert (either a Customer or a Domain Expert) to aid in developing these relationships.

Forces:

- It is often difficult for the Expert to express behavior of the system in object-oriented terms.

Solution: Work with the Expert to develop or refine the Requirements Model based on behavior of the entities in the system. Most object-oriented systems accomplish their functionality by having entities interact. It is crucial that the Requirements Model capture these interactions in order that the designers and testers have an adequate understanding of the system.

Most methodologists agree that one should capture these interactions, and we earlier presented a number of diagrams used to capture them, including Use Cases, Scenarios, and STDs. Many interactions are part of the domain, and involve typical behavior within the domain. For a particular system, however, it is more important that the interactions that provide the system-specific behavior be determined.

This is possibly the most important process the Analyst and Expert can perform. Without adequate definitions of the interactions needed for the system to accomplish its required functionality, it is doubtful that the system can be developed effectively.

40.3.2.7 Document Constraints

Problem: How does the Analyst augment the Requirements Model with constraints concerning the system?

Context: The Requirements Model already exists, and there is an identifiable Expert (either Customer or Domain Expert) who can be used to provide system constraints.

Forces:

- Constraints seem to be everywhere, and it easy to overlook them.
- Constraints are not fun to find and document.

Solution: The Analyst must work with the Expert to find and define the constraints on the system. The Analyst and Expert view the system as a set of interacting entities, and they must define constraints in terms of this view. Therefore, the forms these constraints take is, in large measure, determined by the forms of the diagrams used to document the structure and behavior of the system.

In general, we view constraints as augmentations, or comments, on the behavioral and structural diagrams defining the Requirements Model. Some constraints, such as overall CPU footprint, must be defined at the system level itself, while others are assigned to specific objects, subsystems, interactions, etc., within the system.

One of the most common kind of constraint concerns speed of calculation; in particular, speed of a certain algorithm, or process, the system must carry out. This kind of constraint can be documented as a comment to the interaction(s) used to carry out the requirement. Another common kind of constraint concerns the sizes of Containers; for example, that a list must be able to contain up to 2000 members. This kind of constraint can be documented as a comment on the structure diagram showing the relationship.

In most cases, the Analyst and Expert should try to assign the constraint to a particular behavioral or structural diagram of the Requirements Model at as detailed a level as possible. However, sometimes we may have a separate (usually textual) portion of the Requirements Model that documents constraints. I have found it useful to have a matrix showing the constraints and the pieces of the model to which they pertain.

40.3.2.8 Scavenge Abstractions

Problem: How does an Analyst identify and capture patterns of structure and behavior within an existing Requirements Model?

Context: There is an existing Requirements Model.

Forces:

- This strategy tempts one to do premature class design.

Solution: The Analyst must examine the existing diagrams representing the Requirements Model to determine similarities in structure and behavior. Basically, we are looking for similar "shapes" in the existing graphical depiction of the model.

When similarities are identified, abstractions (both objects and responsibilities) are developed to act as "placeholders" for the objects and responsibilities that play similar roles within the Requirements Model. These abstractions are assembled into abstract diagrams that represent the ones being analyzed.

One of the major strengths of object-oriented technology is inheritance. During requirements modeling both structural and behavioral responsibilities of the system are discovered and captured in diagrams. In order to provide consistency and reuse within the application; similarities between these responsibilities should be identified and captured within the diagrams. Typically, these similarities are encapsulated within abstract objects and responsibilities, and disseminated throughout the system via inheritance.

This process is an extension of what we do already — extract class abstractions by looking at objects. In this process we extend this to look for patterns of behavior between objects, or patterns of structure among objects. We note that many of the design patterns found thus far (Gamma et al., 1995) are precisely such abstractions.

40.3.2.9 Validate the Model

Problem: How does the Analyst validate the Requirements Model?

Context: There is an existing Requirements Model. There is an Expert that can be used to evaluate and validate the model.

Forces:

- Validation forces a thorough understanding of the requirements.
- Validation is often seen as tedious; it is often easier to agree with a model than study it closely.
- It is difficult maintaining consistency among the various diagrams representing the model.

Solution: The Analyst must work quite closely with the Expert to validate the Requirements Model. The first, and most important, thing to do is assure that the person(s) doing the validation understand the notation used in the diagrams that represent the Requirements Model. Have the analyst(s) that produced the diagrams present during the validation process in order to explain any subtleties and resolve any misunderstandings about the meaning of the diagrams.

Review all portions of the Requirements Model in an orderly fashion. This includes all constraints that have been documented as comments, or augmentations, to the diagrams. Make notes about all issues or questions that arise. For each feature of the Requirement Model being evaluated, determine whether or not a test case will be needed to validate this feature or constraint in the final system. If it is determined that a test case is not necessary, document this fact. If it is determined that a test case will be necessary, *Develop Acceptance Criteria* to provide the framework for one. In a very real sense, the criteria are as much a part of the specification as the Requirements Model itself.

Appropriate parts of the Requirements Model can be validated by either a Domain Expert or a Customer. Any Requirements Model should be validated by both as being complete before it is used as a starting point for design. In many cases the Requirements Model has been developed with the assistance of the Customer or Domain Expert. The Analyst should *not* assume that validation will be automatic in these cases.

The best way to validate something is to develop and agree on criteria that will validate the finished product. In many ways the criterion *is* the requirement, as it provides a way to determine whether the product meets the requirement. Validation of the model often means validation of the acceptance criteria.

Once the Requirements Model has been reviewed, prepare an action plan to resolve the issues and questions that arose. This action plan should involve attempts to *Understand the Domain* and *Understand the Requirements*, and refine the Requirements Model based on these understandings.

40.3.2.10 Identify Reuse Candidates

Problem: How does an Analyst identify software artifacts that can be reused within the current system?

Discussion: It often happens that the Customer wants to have an existing system reused within the new one. It is the Analyst's job to determine if these software products can be reused in a cost-effective manner. In general, it is the job of the development staff to determine if there are artifacts (libraries, patterns, existing analyses, etc.) that can be reused to aid in the development.

Context: The Analyst has access to a Domain Expert to aid in evaluation.

Forces:

- Reuse is often defined as reuse of code; other products are ignored.
- Reuse is often confused with recycling; the cost effectiveness is ignored.

Solution: The Analyst must identify and evaluate software products for potential reuse. The Analyst should work with the Domain Expert to identify existing products in the domain that have potential applicability. There are a number of software products that should be evaluated for reuse: code, plans, models, tests, etc. Each should be evaluated for applicability to the system being developed. At the very least, existing systems should be studied to better understand the problem domain.

Each product's applicability must be determined on a case-by-case basis. Remember that if any significant part of a product needs to be reworked (the definition of significant ranges from 5 to 25%, according to the literature), it is probably more cost effective to rework the whole product than attempt reuse.

It must be noted that much of the information being evaluated may not be expressed in an object-oriented fashion. In order to convert these products to object-oriented ones, we recommend looking at the patterns in Kerth, 1995.

40.3.2.11 Develop Prototypes

Problem: How does the Analyst determine or refine requirements through prototyping?

Context: The Requirements Model may or may not already exist. There is an identifiable Customer (or surrogate) that can be used to help develop and evaluate prototypes for applicability.

Forces:

- Prototyping is often confused with rapid development.
- A prototype is worth a thousand requirements.
- There is natural pressure to reuse the prototype within the system.

Solution: With the aid of the Customer, an Analyst develops prototypes to explore limited sets of requirements. This exploration is not limited to user interface issues; these requirements could include algorithms, structural relationships within the system, etc. Remember that a prototype is a simulation of a portion of the system, and may be developed in many ways. In fact, prototyping on paper or in some other non-software medium can be quite useful.

If possible, use a simulation tool that guarantees that your Customer will not expect reuse of the prototype in the finished product, expect to throw away the prototype. If the Analyst believes that the prototype has some reuse possibility, it should be evaluated in the same way as we would *Identify Reuse Candidates.*

Requirements for a system are often not fully expressed, nor are they fully understood. Prototyping often aids the Customer in formalizing or solidifying the system's requirements.

40.3.2.12 Develop Acceptance Criteria

Problem: How does the test team develop a set of acceptance criteria that will be used to evaluate and validate portions of the system?

Discussion: When the Analyst is working with the Expert, he must constantly ask the questions: How do we know that we have done it right? and How do we test for that? These questions could be integrated when trying to *Understand the Domain,* when trying to *Understand the Requirements,* and when trying to *Document Constraints,* or they could be asked in special sessions with the Expert. In any case, the refinement and documentation of acceptance criteria is done by the test team as part of this strategy.

Context: Particular requirements have been identified that require acceptance criteria. There is an Expert identified who can aid in evaluation and validation of the criteria. There is a test team (which could be the analytic team) whose responsibility it is to develop the system's tests based on these criteria.

Forces:

- It is difficult to define testable requirements.
- A product cannot be tested without testable requirements.

Solution: The Analyst should develop acceptance criteria, validate them with the Customer and the test team, and document them as part of the Requirements Model.

There are three basic types of requirements: behavioral, structural, and constraint. When it is identified that a requirement requires a test case, criteria for this test case should be developed by the Analyst in conjunction with the Expert and documented as part of the Requirements Model. In some real sense, the requirement is not complete until the criterion exists, is documented, and validated by the Expert.

The test team must make sure that the requirement is testable, and that the acceptance criterion is sufficient to derive a test from. It is possible that the statement of a requirement fully defines its acceptance criterion, but the Analyst must make sure that the criteria are sufficient and documented as such.

The basic idea is that the Analyst and the Expert have determined the need for a test, and they work with the test team to outline and prepare acceptance criteria that will be used to develop the test. Acceptance criteria definition is one of the most important steps in requirements modeling. Without knowledge of the criteria that will be used to validate the system, it is impossible for the Analyst to be sure that the Requirements Model of the system is correct.

40.3.3 Development Summary

The strategies just presented provide the basic processes necessary to produce a good Requirements Model. They must be executed within a set of activities determined by analyzing the system, the customer, and the domain. The result of using these strategies is a Requirements Model, represented by a set of diagrams, that meets the needs of the customer, the domain, and the development team.

40.4 Summary

Software Engineering is a discipline whose purpose is to translate user needs into software products, and it is one of the most important processes involved in Software Engineering. In this chapter I have done two things:

1. Provided examples of common diagrams used to model requirements
2. Outlined a series of strategies that can be used to develop an object-oriented Requirements Model.

I hope that this chapter has helped you understand the importance of the Requirements Model, and that it has given you the guidance you need to develop them yourself.

References

Beck, K. and Cunningham, W. 1989. A laboratory for teaching object-oriented thinking, *SIGPLAN Notices*, Vol. 24(10), October.

Booch, G. 1996. *Object Solutions: Managing the Object-Oriented Project.* Addison-Wesley Publishing Company, Menlo Park, CA.

Booch, G., Rumbaugh, J. and Jacobson, I. 1997. *Unified Modeling Language*, Version 1.0. Rational Software Corporation.

Chonoles, M.J., Schardt, J.A. and Magrogan, P.J. 1996. Object-Oriented Conceptualisation, Report on Object-Oriented Analysis and Design, Sept.

Firesmith, D., Henderson-Sellers, B., Graham, I. and Page-Jones, M. 1996. *OPEN Modeling Language (OML) Reference Manual*, Version 1.0. OPEN Consortium.

Gamma, E., Helm, R., Johnson, R. and Vlissides, J. 1995. *Design Patterns: Elements of Reusable Object-Oriented Software.* Addison-Wesley, Reading, MA.

Gause, D.C. and Weinberg, G.M. 1989. *Exploring Requirements: Quality Before Design.* Dorset House Publishing, New York.

Harwood, R.J. 1997. Use case formats: requirements, analysis and design, *J. Object-Oriented Program.*, Jan.

International Organization for Standardization, 1991. *ISO 9000-3: Guideline for Application of ISO 9001 to the Development, Supply, and Maintenance of Software.*

Kerth, N. 1995. Caterpillar's fate: a pattern language for transformation from analysis to design. In *Pattern Languages for Program Design,* James C. Coplien and Douglas C. Schmidt, eds. Addison-Wesley, Menlo Park, CA.

Space & Naval Warfare Systems Command. 1994. *MIL-STD-498: Software Development and Documentation.*

Whitenack, B. 1995. RAPPeL: A requirements analysis process pattern language for object oriented development. In *Pattern Languages for Program Design,* James C. Coplien and Douglas C. Schmidt, eds. Addison-Wesley, Menlo Park, CA.

Further Information

One of the classic discussions of why requirements modeling is important is found in *Exploring Requirements: Quality Before Design,* written by Gause and Weinberg. This book should be on every software developer's bookshelf.

Virtually every book on object-oriented development contains information that is relevant to Requirements Modeling. Among others, a good list of books contains:

- *Object-Oriented Analysis and Design with Applications,* by Grady Booch
- *Object-Oriented Analysis,* by Peter Coad and Ed Yourdon
- *Object-Oriented Software Engineering,* by Ivar Jacobson et al.
- *Object-Oriented Modeling and Design,* by Jim Rumbaugh et al.
- *Designing Object-Oriented Software,* by Rebecca Wirfs-Brock et al.

The IEEE Computer Society Technical Council on Software Engineering has sponsored (and will continue to sponsor) conferences on Requirements Engineering. There have been two International Conferences in Requirements Engineering (ICRE '94 and ICRE '96), and each of them had a few papers on object-oriented techniques. Look to this forum in the future.

41

Object-Oriented Project Management

Richard T. Dué
Thomsen Dué & Associates, Ltd.

41.1 Executive Summary

The successful introduction and use of Object Technology organization requires effective project management. Unfortunately, one of the leading deficiencies in organizations today is the availability of skilled Information Technology project managers. Effective project management is not about having expertise with an Object methodology nor is it about being a skilled lead analyst or an object-oriented programming wizard. Instead, project managers must be skilled at delivering the project through their estimating, scheduling, monitoring, risk analysis, contingency planning, communications, conflict resolution, and change management abilities. This chapter describes how a project manager can select the appropriate object-oriented development methodology, the appropriate estimating and scheduling technique, and how to effectively document the project lifecycle.

41.2 Key Points

- The systems development methodology must match the systems development maturity of the organization.
- The first job of a project manager is the development of the Project Charter.

0-8493-3135-8/99/$0.00+$.50

- The project manager must use the appropriate estimating and scheduling technique.
- Projects involve the ongoing negotiation of time, money, people, scope, tools and techniques, and quality.
- The Project History Manual contains a summary of the key documentation of a project's origin, development, current status, and proposed enhancements.

You must note beside
That we have tried the utmost of our friends;
Our legions are brim-full, our cause is ripe.
The enemy increaseth every day;
We at the height are ready to decline.
There is a tide in the affairs of men
Which, taken at the flood, leads on to fortune;
Omitted, all the voyage of their life
Is bound in shallows and in miseries.
On such a full sea are we now afloat,
And we must take the current when it serves,
Or lose our ventures.

Julius Caesar
Act IV, Scene 2
William Shakespeare

Brutus explained to Cassius that even the best led, best planned, equipped, and staffed projects can only be executed successfully at certain times and places. The success or failure of Object Technology projects depends upon the project manager's awareness and response to the project's environment.

41.3 Project Management Strategy

For nearly twenty years I have been using the ideas of Dr. Richard Nolan (1979) to analyze the ability of organizations to employ new Information Technologies. I have found that Information Technology professionals all over the world have been able to use his evolutionary stages of growth learning curve to help explain the success and failure of Information Technology projects in their organizations. The key concept of Dr. Nolan's model is that the types of technology that can be successfully implemented in an organization depend upon the ability of the organization to understand and utilize the technology. This means that although a technology may be highly productive in certain organizations and in certain situations, it will fail in other organizations and in other situations. As with any other type of learning curve, it is not possible to jump from the novice stages of learning to the expert level; nor is it possible to skip any of the necessary stages of learning. The amount of time that has to be spent on learning can, however, be shortened by the use of effective coaches and teachers. It is imperative that an organization understand its ability to use a new technology and to plan for its progression through the learning curve stages.

Object Technology can only be successfully introduced into organizations that have reached the necessary level on the Information Technology learning curve. I have modified Dr. Nolan's original model to reflect the learning stages which organizations will have to pass through as they try to implement Object Technology projects (Table 41.1).

The stages of learning start with the development of simple, procedural programs, as a small group of innovators in the organization tries out object-oriented programming languages. These innovators are usually found within the information processing department, although they may come from the ranks of the users or even from senior management. The next stage of learning sees the application of Object Technology in the development of large and complex systems. After the inevitable failures of

TABLE 41.1 Nolan's Model Updated for Object Technology

Stage One — Initiation Risk Level — Minimal. There is no plan, no budget, no real expectations, and no productivity measurements.	The initial implementation of Object Technology; characterized by lack of methodology and project management. Management is generally unaware of the project. Concentration on object-oriented programming languages and the development of code.
Stage Two — Contagion Risk Level — Very high. Unrealistic expectations, rapidly increasing costs.	The spread of Object Technology throughout the organization; characterized by inappropriate use of the technology and the increasing number of project failures. Management becomes aware of the increasing amounts of resources being consumed by the new technology. Management finds that the new technology is poorly planned, often over budget, and has produced still more "islands of automation" in the organization.
Stage Three — Control Risk Level — Very High. Unless senior management is able to recognize that the new technology is asset and not an expense, the technology will be abandoned.	The situation reaches a critical point. Senior management insists on centralized control over any further implementation of object-oriented technology. The innovators in the organization become extremely frustrated. Management is still generally concerned with deploying the new technology to decrease costs. The organization makes its first attempt to use an object-oriented analysis and design methodology, but is more interested in control than in productivity. Many organizations may see senior management order the abandonment of object-oriented technology in favor of the next cost reduction "silver bullet."
Stage Four — Integration Risk Level — Medium. Management may become impatient with the amount of time and resources required.	The redevelopment and integration of existing projects; characterized by movement to system development methodologies. Management realizes that Information is an important business asset that requires a substantial investment in education, training, planning, and implementation.
Stage Five — Administration Risk Level — Medium. Personnel with traditional skills may not be able to adapt to a reuse culture.	Formal management of reuse of the requirements, systems design, and Class libraries. Use of proven frameworks, patterns, and programming idioms.
Stage Six — Maturity Risk Level — Low. All levels of the organization have passed through the learning curve.	Management recognizes that the Enterprise Object model is the key asset of the business. The Enterprise Object Model evolves to become the organization's business and MIS systems.

many of these large projects, the next stage sees senior management either ordering the abandonment of Object-Oriented Technology or instituting a program of centralized control over any subsequent projects. The fourth stage of development sees the rework of the systems that have been developed to date to standardize operating platforms, languages, interfaces, and storage management systems. The fifth stage involves the utilization of proven frameworks and patterns of business classes to develop integrated, interorganizational systems. In my opinion, the sixth stage of organizational maturity will be the progression to Enterprise Object models. This stage involves the use of Business Process and Enterprise Object simulations. Eventually these Enterprise simulation models will evolve into being the actual operational and MIS systems of the organization.

41.4 Process-Orientation vs. Project-Orientation

In addition to learning curve factors, successful project management requires that the organization must also understand its strategic approach to projects within the organization as a whole. Project management is easier to implement in project-oriented organizations than in process-oriented organizations. An organization is considered to be project-oriented if the majority of the organization's revenues come from the sum of the individual projects it undertakes. Examples of project-oriented organizations include architectural firms, consulting firms, advertising agencies, and engineering firms. An organization is considered to be process-oriented if the majority of its revenue comes from the sum of the individual processes that it performs. Examples of process-oriented organizations include banks, government agencies, insurance companies, and utilities.

Many individuals working in process-oriented organizations have little or no exposure or experience with project management. The work that they are involved with today varies little from the work which they performed yesterday or the work which they will perform tomorrow.

Unfortunately, many individuals working on Information Technology projects received their training and experience in data *processing* not data *projecting*. These managers, analysts, and programmers have become adept at performing the ongoing processes of computer operations, maintenance, analysis, design, and programming, but have little experience or training in managing or participating in projects.

Capers Jones, in a recent CompuServe forum posting, identifies this problem as:

> "From our assessments to date, management is the weakest link in the software engineering chain. If you consider what programmers and software engineers are supposed to do — design, code, and debug — many of them can do this pretty well. But consider what project managers are supposed to do — plan, estimate, measure, and control — most of them cannot do any of these at all.
>
> The bulk of the disasters and failures that you read about are because management messed up the project very early on with sloppy planning and estimating, and did not know how to dig themselves out of the problems later."

Any attempt to implement Object Technology in an organization in the absence of effective project management principles will inevitably result in failure. This does not necessarily mean that the individuals involved in the effort were poor programmers or analysts or hackers; nor does it mean the Object Technology is just another failed "silver bullet." Instead, it means that process-oriented individuals were trying to undertake a project-oriented activity without understanding what is involved in proper project management.

41.5 Situational Factors

Unfortunately, there are a number of situational factors that can hinder an individual or group of participants in a large organization from moving to a new approach. In actual situations the following factors can influence an individual manager's approach to motivation:

1. The manager's personality and past experience — Despite the best of intentions, people are still bound by the limitations of their personalities and by their past experiences. A person with a traditional Information Technology background is going to find it very difficult, if not impossible, to shift to the Object Engineering approach. In my own experience, I typically find that personnel with a traditional background are often quick to adopt the terminology of the Object Technology paradigm, but that they continue to try to develop systems in the traditional manner. Object Technology is only viewed a new tool or technique and not as a fundamentally new approach.
2. The expectations of superiors — Again, despite the best intentions of an individual, their actual behavior will be guided by the expectations of their superiors. If their superiors are entrenched in traditional approaches, it is highly unlikely that a subordinate will be able to apply Object Technology in their organization.
3. Subordinate's characteristics, expectations, and behavior — In this case, a well-intentioned manager will find it very difficult to introduce a new approach to subordinates that have had some success in the past with traditional approaches.
4. Task requirements — It is highly unlikely that an individual will be able to apply an Object Technology approach in the middle of an emergency response to a critical failure of a mission critical system.
5. Organizational climate and politics — The overall reaction of the organization to innovation will affect the efforts of any one individual to introduce a new paradigm.

TABLE 41.2 Why Good Individual Contributors Make Poor Managers

A Good Programmer/Analyst	A Good Project Manager
Seeks optimal solutions	Seeks pragmatic solutions
Strives for accuracy	Strives for workability
Deals with things	Deals with people
Focuses on processes	Focuses on outcomes
Works with laws	Works with situational rules
Specializes to improve	Generalizes to improve
Succeeds individually	Succeeds through others

Adapted from Gilbreath, R.D. 1986. *Winning at Project Management*, p. 52. John Wiley & Sons, New York.

6. Peers' expectations and behavior — The actions of any one manager are influenced by the expectations and behavior of their colleagues. The introduction of a new approach can be easily viewed as a criticism of the approaches used by other managers in the organization. It is unlikely that one manager would be able to introduce a new approach without the support of his or her peers.

Another obstacle to the introduction of a new Information Technology paradigm can be the personality differences between the desirable characteristics of a traditional Information Technology professional and an Object Engineering project manager (Table 41.2).

The common tendency to appoint a person who is expert in the technology to the job of project manager will inevitably lead to the frustration of the technical expert and the loss of technical expertise to the organization. Instead, the project manager is more likely to be drawn from the ranks of the traditional users of information systems. Training a user in project management and the Object paradigm will be much easier than trying to get a technologist to change his psychological makeup while also trying to get him to abandon his long-established traditional approaches to information systems development.

41.6 New Functions and Roles

Object Technology may require the creation of some new job categories. The implementation of the layered class library approach, for example, will require pattern and framework designers, class constructors, business systems analysts, and enterprise modelers (Table 41.3).

41.6.1 Pattern and Framework Designers

These highly experienced abstract thinkers are needed to identify and specify the productive, successful patterns of classes that provide basic information modeling services. Pattern designers will evolve clusters of patterns common to many different types of information systems. There will probably be a relatively small number of these people in the world. I expect that this work will largely be carried on through consortia approaches such as Taligent, Sematech, and the Object Management Group. Framework designers will evolve clusters of classes that are common to specific domains. These frameworks will be used as templates of good practice within a particular market sector or industry.

TABLE 41.3 Classifications and Responsibilities of New Job Categories

Job Classification	Responsibility
Enterprise modelers	Workflow and business process re-engineering models
Business systems analysts	Information systems models
Pattern and framework designers	Information model templates at various levels of abstraction
Class constructors	Class components

41.6.2 Class Developers

As the body of proven patterns is developed, object-oriented programmers will be required to implement the classes specified by the pattern and framework designers. Again I expect that this will be a relatively small number of people who will be working for commercial class vendors. Class developers will use CASE tools to generate much of the required code, although there will certainly be a continuing need for experienced, creative expert programmers.

41.6.3 Business Analysts

Business analysts will be required to introduce, assemble, and implement collections of patterns and frameworks within individual organizations. A large number of these people will be required to implement and to innovate unique and creative information systems.

41.6.4 Enterprise Modelers

Enterprise Modelers will be required to work with senior management to assemble and implement workflow models for business process re-engineering projects. This relatively small group of people will be drawn from the senior ranks of business analysts and consultants.

41.7 New Approaches to Evaluation and Pay

Object Technology will require new approaches to the evaluation and compensation of information systems personnel. Traditionally, systems personnel were rewarded on their ability to create new code, new designs, and new documentation. Object Technology requires rewarding people for reusing code, designs, and documentation. The traditional measure of productivity, lines of code, will have to be replaced by a new set of performance metrics.

41.7.1 The New Performance Metrics

41.7.1.1 Lifecycle Shape

How has the performance of this individual changed the shape of the systems development lifecycle curve? Traditionally, most of the resources required to develop a new information system are consumed by construction (programming, testing, and documentation). One of the problems with this approach is that the cost of finding and fixing errors to the system requirements specifications increases exponentially with each successive step in the traditional waterfall method. On a relative scale, the cost of finding and fixing errors during the initial specification phase is 100 to 100,000 times less then the cost of finding and fixing errors after the system has been implemented. If the shape of the lifecycle curve can be altered by concentrating the investment of resources in the early stages of system specification and design, there is the potential for enormous cost savings and productivity increases.

41.7.1.2 Business Value

How has the performance of this individual increased the profits of the organization? Traditionally, there have been no links between the performance of the information systems personnel and the profits of the organization. The shift to Object Technology, however, can result in the assembly of enterprise simulations. The performance of these simulations can be directly mapped to the performance and financial success of the organization.

41.7.1.3 Percent of Reused Functionality

How has this individual optimized the use of information system functionality? The real benefits of Object Technology are obtained from the reuse of requirements, designs, documentation, and code. The appropriate way to measure an individual's reuse of previously developed technology is to calculate the ratio of reused functionality to required functionality.

41.7.1.4 Return on Investment

How has this individual optimized the return on the investment in their training, tools, and overhead? Recognition of people and models as the primary assets of the organization means that these two assets must be measured by traditional financial asset measures.

In addition to measuring an individual's contributions, a similar, but expanded set of productivity metrics must also be used to measure the progress of the entire enterprise.

41.7.2 A Dashboard of Productivity Metrics

41.7.2.1 Profitability

What is the direct effect of the organization's investment in Information Technology (IT) on the organization's profitability? Measures should include return on investment and quantified indications of the value added by each process in the IT department to the total value of the organization.

41.7.2.2 Customer Satisfaction

What is the effect of the organization's investment in IT on the satisfaction of the organization's ultimate customers? Ultimate customers are the final end users of the organization's products and services. They are not clients or users within the organization. In my own training and consulting practice, I have rarely encountered any IT organization that felt their real customers were outside the enterprise. Most managers have told me that their job is merely to keep some internal user happy and that any attempt by IT to directly contact ultimate customers would not be allowed. Usually this approach results in the IT department picking up costs for other departments which they could not justify themselves. The internal user appears to be more productive by shifting these costs, but the overall organization is actually less productive. The efforts of IT managers must be measured by the marketplace and not by internal politics or power plays.

41.7.2.3 Time to Value

How long does it take to turn IT investments into profits? Many organizations now feel that their IT investments must be profitable within three to six months. IT managers no longer have the luxury of embarking on multi-year infrastructure projects. The need to drastically reduce the time to value means that IT managers will have to use new systems development strategies. The traditional waterfall and information engineering approaches will have to be replaced with 80/20 development (provide the 20% of the code that satisfies 80% of the requirements), or with "just good enough" systems, or with entirely new system development paradigms like the use of object-oriented frameworks and patterns. These new strategies will require the use of new methodologies, techniques, tools, and most likely new IT personnel who are able to work with these new approaches.

41.7.2.4 IT Value Added

How much value is added by IT to the organization? How much value is being given by the IT department to the organization's ultimate customers? Is this value increasing over time?

41.7.2.5 Business Alignment

Are the organization's investments in IT understood and supported by the managers in the main functional areas of the business? For instance, some organizations have gone as far as to insist that every line of code (or Function Point) has to have an identified owner within the organization who is independent of the IT department. Is the IT department organized by business function? What cross-training and career paths exist for IT employees and employees in the rest of the organization? How effective are these programs?

41.7.2.6 Employee Satisfaction

What are the cross-industry comparative rates of employee turnover and compensation? What is the rate of increase in the intellectual capital of the organization? How effective are the organization's training and education programs? How is the organization meeting employee demands for experience with up-to-date technologies?

41.7.2.7 Productivity and Quality

What is the actual level of productivity and quality of the organization's IT personnel when compared to the best industry practices? Productivity and quality measurements and comparisons must be based upon technology neutral measures such as function points.

41.7.2.8 Improvement Rate

How quickly are all of the IT productivity metrics showing improvement?

41.7.2.9 SDLC Shape Change

How is the organization changing the shape of its System Development Lifecycle? Ideally, the length of the cycle should be decreasing while an increasing percentage of the cycle is spent on planning and modeling compared to a decreasing percentage spent on coding, documentation, and testing. A realistic goal is a shift to 80% planning and modeling within an overall three to six month project time frame. This radical SDLC shape change (most organization's today spend 5% or less of the SDLC on planning and modeling) will require new methodologies, techniques, tools, and people. This critically important metric will be extremely difficult to establish as fewer than 3% of today's IT organizations even have an appropriate, repeatable systems development methodology in place.

41.7.2.10 Learning Rate

How long does it take to introduce new technologies into the organization? What is the participation rate and how long does it take to reach a critical mass of users?

41.7.2.11 Rework Change Rate

What is the rate of improvement in finding and fixing errors? Is there a shift in error identification and elimination of errors from the end of the system development lifecycle to the beginning of the cycle?

41.7.2.12 Reuse

What is the rate of reuse of proven methods, techniques, tools, plans, documentation, designs, requirements specifications, patterns, frameworks, project management activities, and code? What is the rate of increase of reuse?

41.8 Project Management Tactics

The first step in undertaking a project is the selection of a full time project manager. The required qualification for this job is that the person is experienced in project management. This does not necessarily mean someone who is an expert in Object Technology methodologies or programming languages. The project manager must be qualified to plan, organize, staff, control, and manage the delivery of the project. This requires skills in scheduling, estimating, monitoring, risk analysis, contingency planning, conflict resolution, and change management. The project manager must be skilled in communications and in making presentations. The first task of the project manager is the development of a Project Charter.

Project Charter

- Business statement
- Description
- Context model
- Methodology
- Project resource estimates and schedules
- Quality assurance
- Post implementation review
- Risk analysis and contingency plan

The Project Charter is a formal document that contains the following clauses:

41.8.1 Business Statement

The business statement provides the rationale for undertaking this particular project. It identifies the business owner of the project and the project champion. The business owner of the project is the user who is responsible for identifying the benefits of the project. The business owner is also responsible for paying for the development and operating costs of the project. The project champion is the most senior manager in the organization who has the most to gain from the success of the project. The project champion is responsible for resolving political questions and priority conflicts.

If the project manager is unable to identify a business owner and project champion for the project, no further activity should be undertaken. In the case of an Object Technology project, the absence of the owner and champion does not mean that Object Technology is not useful, nor does it mean that our organization has inadequate analysis or programming skills. It simply means that the business case for undertaking the project has not been made in this particular organization at this particular time.

41.8.2 Description

The description of the project including the business reasons for undertaking the project.

41.8.3 Context Model

The Context model is a schematic diagram of all the relationships among the information sources and users of project. The project is represented in the Context diagram as a black box. The sources of information and the users of the system are connected to the black box by lines that represent the type of services that will be supplied or used. The Context diagram represents the environment in which the project will operate. The Context diagram must be validated with representatives of the information providers and users.

In my own modeling work, I interview all of these sources and users of information, develop the Context diagram, and then review and validate the diagram with the people I interviewed. One affective way to accomplish this validation in an Object Technology project is to specify these relationships by the Design by Contract approach. These Object Technology service contracts are drawn up as a part of the Use Case or CRC modeling activities. The validated Context diagram and the related service contracts become the requirements specifications, test plans, and the acceptance criteria for the project.

41.8.4 Methodology

This section of the Project Charter identifies the project development methodology that will be used for the project and specifies the business case reasons for its selection. The methodology identifies the tasks that must be accomplished, the order in which they need to be performed, and the expected outputs of each task. The Project Charter must justify the selection of methodology. The justification must show why the method is appropriate to the type of project and why the project manager feels that the organization is able to use the methodology. Some Object Technology projects require object-oriented programming methodologies; others require Object-Oriented Analysis and Design methodologies. Not all organizations have reached the necessary maturity to successfully apply revolutionary object-oriented design methods. These organizations may have to rely on evolutionary approaches. The project manager must show in which stage of maturity the organization is able to operate and which stage of maturity this project requires. For example, in an organization that is only capable of using evolutionary object-oriented programming methodologies, the development of an Enterprise Object model will not be possible.

41.8.5 Project Resource Estimates and Schedules

Once the development methodology has been selected and justified, the resources necessary to undertake each of the tasks can be identified and assigned to the project. Assignment of the actual resources, including the actual staff (identified by name), is critical to developing the project schedule. Project resources include office space and support services, project manager and development staff, management, stockholders, and users of the system. A realistic project schedule must demonstrate that the actual resources required for the development, approval, and implementation of the project are available.

The project schedule must be expressed in terms of actual calendar dates. The consequences of changing the start dates or substituting project resources must be identified. Obviously, a seven-day task, which is scheduled to begin on December 24, is not going to be reviewed and approved on January 1. In the U.S., April 14 is obviously not a good day to schedule the start of a new project in a tax accounting firm. Amazingly though, the impact of the actual calendar dates on the availability of resources and key personnel and the duration of the project is seldom taken into consideration.

There are four major project scheduling techniques that can be used by the project manager:

1. Milestone — Work is done on the project until a set date. The output and status of the project are evaluated and a new milestone is set. The milestone technique is best used in unique research projects. Typically none of the participants have any experience in the project area. There is no record of any previous experience and no proven methodology in place. Detailed estimates are only attempted for the immediate tasks. Milestones are set for very short intervals, typically one or two weeks. Milestone projects involve high risk of failure. The only useful output may be the participants' learning experience.
2. Gantt Chart — The Gantt chart technique uses bar charts to show the estimated duration of all of the tasks in the project. Detailed estimates are only done for immediate tasks, but rough estimates are made for subsequent phases of the project. The Gantt chart technique is typically used on projects where there is some experience with each of the tasks involved in the project, but where there is uncertainty as to how the tasks are interrelated.
3. Critical Path — The critical path technique uses a network diagram to show the tasks in the project and their interrelationships. The critical path is the longest series of sequentially related tasks in the network from the beginning to the end of the project. If the project is going to be completed on time, every task on the critical path must be completed on schedule. Tasks that are not on the critical path may take longer than expected without affecting the completion date of the overall project as long as the delay does not change the critical path itself.

   Critical path projects require an experienced project team and the use of a proven methodology. One of the weaknesses of the critical path approach, however, is that the network only shows the tasks which have to be performed. It does not show the schedule of resources that will be required to undertake the tasks. For example, it is possible that one person could be scheduled to be working full time on several different tasks on the same day. Typically, a Gantt chart must also be constructed to shows the schedule of actual resources and personnel.
4. PERT — The Project Evaluation and Review Technique uses a network diagram which shows the tasks in the project and their interrelationships. The PERT technique requires the use of three different estimates for the accomplishment of each task. Estimates are obtained from the actual people who will be doing the work, for the typical time a task will take, the most optimistic time, and the most pessimistic time the task will take. These three estimates are then used in the following equation to derive the expected duration for the task:

   ```
   Expected Duration = 3D (Optimistic Estimate + (4 × Typical Estimate) +
   Pessimistic Estimate)/6
   ```

   Once the expected duration has been calculated the following equation is used to compute the task duration variation:

   ```
   Task Duration Variation = 3D((Pessimistic Estimate – Optimistic
   Estimate) = 16) **2, where **2 means squared or raised to the power of 2.
   ```

The standard deviation of the duration of the entire project can then be computed by taking the square root of the total of all of the individual task duration variations that are found on the critical path of the network diagram.

The PERT technique provides the project manager with a probability estimate for a range of values of the actual duration of the project. For example, 95% of the time, the actual completion date of the project will be found in the range of dates between two standard deviations above and two standard deviations below the expected completion date. This range of values for the completion date of the project represents the results of all of the tasks on the critical path experiencing the normal mix of optimistic, pessimistic, and typical durations.

The PERT technique can only be used when the participants in the project all have sufficient experience with the technology and the methodology to be able to generate realistic pessimistic, typical, and optimistic estimates of task durations.

The project manager can use Table 41.4 to identify the type of scheduling technique that is appropriate for the project:

The project manager ranks each of the project's characteristics on a relative scale of how predictable they are. For example, the project manager must answer the following questions:

- Can we predict the structure of the project?
- How stable will be the technology during the duration of the project?
- How big will the project be?
- How proficient are the users in their area of the business?
- How proficient are the users, developers, and senior management in working on projects?

Finally the project manager, with the help of the project sponsor, ranks the stability of the environment in which the project will be undertaken. For example, the project manager must answer the following questions:

- What is the competition doing in this area?
- What is happening to the economy?
- What is happening to the profitability of the organization?
- What other projects will be competing for resources with this one?

If the sum of these evaluations indicates that the project is highly predictable, then the preferred scheduling tool is PERT. If the sum of the evaluations indicates that the project is highly unpredictable, then the preferred scheduling tool is the milestone. A mix of predictable and unpredictable characteristics indicates that either the critical path or Gantt chart technique is appropriate.

Unfortunately, the current state of the art in Object Technology (stages one and two of the learning curve) often indicates that the best scheduling technique available to the project manager will be the milestone approach. This means that the best estimate of the project we have can only tell us about the tasks we expect to undertake in the next week or two. Not only are we unable to estimate a final completion date, we are probably unable to even say if the project can be completed.

TABLE 41.4 Identifying Scheduling Techniques

Project Characteristics	Predictable	Technique
Pre-defined structure		PERT
Stability of technology		
Project size	o--------------------->	Critical path
User proficiency	(Swing the arrow according	Gantt chart
Developer proficiency	to the sum of predictable	
Environmental stability	and unpredictable factors)	Milestone
	Unpredictable	

In many organizations, however, the scheduling technique that is employed is what I refer to as the "poker technique." Management sets a deadline before the project begins; the project manager has to decide if this estimate is a bluff or a serious bid. As the project unfolds, both management and the project management play their new cards (new crash deadlines are mandated by senior management, phased implementations are proposed by the project team, etc.). In the end, however, the poker technique can only result in all of the players losing their stakes. The project is either abandoned or limps to completion over budget and under scope.

Once a schedule has been developed, it will now be necessary for the project manager to negotiate the six variables of project management:

1. Time — Can deadlines be changed?
2. Money — Can more money be budgeted?
3. People — Can different people be used?
4. Scope — Can the scope be modified?
5. Tools and techniques — Can new technology be used?
6. Quality — Can the quality be changed? Unfortunately, quality is often lowered without any formal negotiation in order to compensate for problems with the other five variables.

Negotiation of these six variables will be an ongoing task for the project manager over the life of the project.

41.8.6 Quality Assurance

This section of the Project Charter contains the plan that will be followed to insure the quality of the project. This section will almost be a mini project charter, since it includes the identification and justification of the quality assurance methodology and the resource estimates and schedule. Provision for an independent, external review of the project should be included. Typically, 1 to 3% of the project's schedule and budget should be allocated to quality assurance activities.

41.8.7 Post Implementation Review

This section identifies the procedures and resources that will be required to undertake the post-implementation review. The productivity metrics and project documentation necessary to perform this review must be identified and included in the project plan.

41.8.8 Risk Analysis and Contingency Plan

Once the project schedule has been developed, the project manager must identify all of the risk factors that could adversely affect the schedule. A plan for minimizing each of the major risks must be developed. A contingency plan (what do we do when despite our best efforts to minimize the risk the problem still happens) must also be drawn up by the project manager. Risk analysis and contingency planning will be an ongoing activity for the project manager over the life of the project.

After completing the Project Charter, the next task for the project manager is to begin work on the Project History Manual.

41.9 Project History Manual

The Project History Manual (Dué and Gallo) is a summary and an index of the detailed documentation of all of the significant events in a project from its inception until replacement or abandonment. The manual has four major sections:

1. Project origin — The summary or index of strategic plans, auditor reports, and project proposals which lead to the development of the project. This section deals with why the project was initiated.

2. Project development lifecycle — The executive summary of the project's development lifecycle. The project charter becomes the first part of this section of documentation. A revised cost benefit study and a quality assurance report for each major phase of the project are included. This section deals with how the project was developed.
3. Project maintenance — This section identifies the key users of the project and all major maintenance activities. It contains periodic system effectiveness reviews that contain recommendations for enhancement or replacement of the system. This section deals with what the system actually accomplishes.
4. Project enhancement — This section contains the Project Charters for all recommended enhancement activities. This section deals with the what next aspects of the system.

The Project History Manual has four major audiences:

1. Senior management — The manual is a summary of the background and status of each project. It is a critical input for planning and control.
2. Financial control and audit — The manual provides the dynamic cost benefit history of the project. It contains approval and sign-off documentation.
3. Quality assurance — The manual provides a history of quality control reports and problem resolutions.
4. Systems users — The manual provides the background on why the system was developed, what maintenance activity has taken place, how problems were resolved, and what enhancements have been proposed.

In my experience, the project history manual should be initiated by the project manager. Upon completion of the development phase of the project, however, the project history manual becomes the property and responsibility of the owner of the project.

41.10 Problem Checklist

The following checklist can be used by the project manager to insure the success of Object Technology projects:

TABLE 41.5 Object Technology Project Problem Checklist

Problem	Cause	Remedy
Lack of project management	Common in stages one and two of the technology learning curve; common in process-oriented organizations	Acquire the services of a professional project manager
Lack of a systems development methodology	Common in stages one and two of the technology learning curve	Select a development methodology that conforms to the characteristics of the project and the maturity of the organization
Unrealistic deadlines	Common in process-oriented organizations	Prepare a project charter; negotiate the six project variables
Unrealistic expectations	Common in stages one to three of the technology learning curve.	Prepare a project charter
Frequent change requests	Common in turbulent project environments	Treat each change request as a mini project
Project manager spends most of his time reacting to problems	Common in turbulent project environments	Prepare risk analysis and contingency plans before the project starts

References

Dué, R.T. and Gallo, J.G. Stressing Project Accountability Via Sound Systems Documentation and a Project History Manual, Computer Security, Auditing and Controls, pp. A-5–A-8. Management Advisory Publications, Wellesley Hills, MA, Vol. 14, No. 2.

Nolan, R.L. 1979. *Managing the Crises in Data Processing, Harvard Bus. Rev.*, March-April, pp. 115-126.

42

Transactional Analysis (TA) as Applied to the Human Factor in Object-Oriented Projects

Bhuvan Unhelkar
Case Digital, Inc.

Most of us Managers are prone to one failing:
A tendency to manage people as though they were modular components

DeMarco and Lister, 1987

Abstract

Object orientation is rapidly becoming an issue of management rather than technology. At OOPSLA'95 (Austin, TX) as well as at OOPSLA'96 (San Jose, CA), there were special panels to discuss topics related to human relations or "soft factors" in project management. In an object-oriented development environment, these issues include parallel team organization, quality, reusability in OO, and its implications for management, rewarding structures, morale building, and legal issues — to name but a few. Transactional Analysis (TA) is a popular yet simple approach to handling human relations issues with potential for application in software projects. This is a discussion of the application of the principles of TA in the development of an object-oriented software.

0-8493-3135-8/99/$0.00+$.50

42.1 Soft Factors in OO Development

42.1.1 The Human Factor

Jaron Lanier (1997), in discussing "the frontier between us," in the commemorative issue of *Communications of the ACM* on the first 50 years of computing states:

> The easiest predictions to make about the next 50 years of computer science are those centering on the computers, not the people. It's when people are brought into the equation, however, that the business of prediction becomes difficult.... The biggest surprise from the first 50 years of computers is that computation turns out to be a cultural object in its own right, with all its warts and semicolons.

This consideration of the "human factor" in computing has permeated all aspects of software development including project planning, analysis and design, testing, and quality assurance, and is now considered instrumental in the overall success or failure of a project. This human factor influence on a project starts with the recruitment process and formation and 'gelling' of the team, through to keeping the team productive and motivated, and concludes with the completion of a project and/or, as it happens so often, the departure of a team member. Meyer (1995b) has given a lot of importance to the *non-*technical role of a project manager, which essentially deals with the "soft factors" in managing technical teams. Goldberg and Rubin (1995) discuss the importance of team formation (its structure and operation, pp. 280) in carrying out a successful reuse program in an object-oriented environment. However, team formation and operation is not a simple task, mainly because it does not seem to follow logic. It was interesting to listen to Constantine (1996), during the panel discussion on these "soft issues" at OOPSLA'96, wherein he said:

> "It is easier to communicate with machines and solve the problems; But with people, it is difficult. This is mainly so because people are very difficult to 'generalize'."

However, handling this "difficulty" is precisely at the heart of success or failure of a particular project. Lack of management considerations has led to more project failures than have technical issues. For example, Greatrex (1996) in a KPMG report presented at the IT Project Management conference in Auckland in April 1996 discusses results from a survey of over 250 companies in the Pacific region for failure of their IT projects. The results indicate that in 32% of the cases it was inadequate project management that led to the failure of projects. Other major factors were failure to define objectives (17%) and inadequate communication (20%). Only 7% of the projects surveyed failed due to technical reasons.

Project management (especially with respect to human relations) issues mentioned above are what Constantine (1995) calls *soft factors* or what DeMarco and Lister (1987) call *sociological factors.* In developing a financial market's enterprise (discussed in Chapter 43) using object-oriented techniques, we gave due importance to these soft or sociological factors in the project. This resulted in a considerable goodwill within the project team and also produced all major releases of the product within time. However, it was important to maintain the right balance between emphasizing the soft factors vs. driving the project through technology.

42.1.2 Balancing Sociology with Technology

The technologist plays a crucial role in combining money and technology to create business value. One has to only add *people* to money and technology, to arrive at the repository of tools that an IT manager has at his or her disposal to create business value. Creation of this value, however, is always a balancing act. Given a certain set of resources (in terms of time and money), they could be directed toward handling the technical factors (hard factors), or alternatively, toward sociological factors (soft factors). This is shown in Figure 42.1.

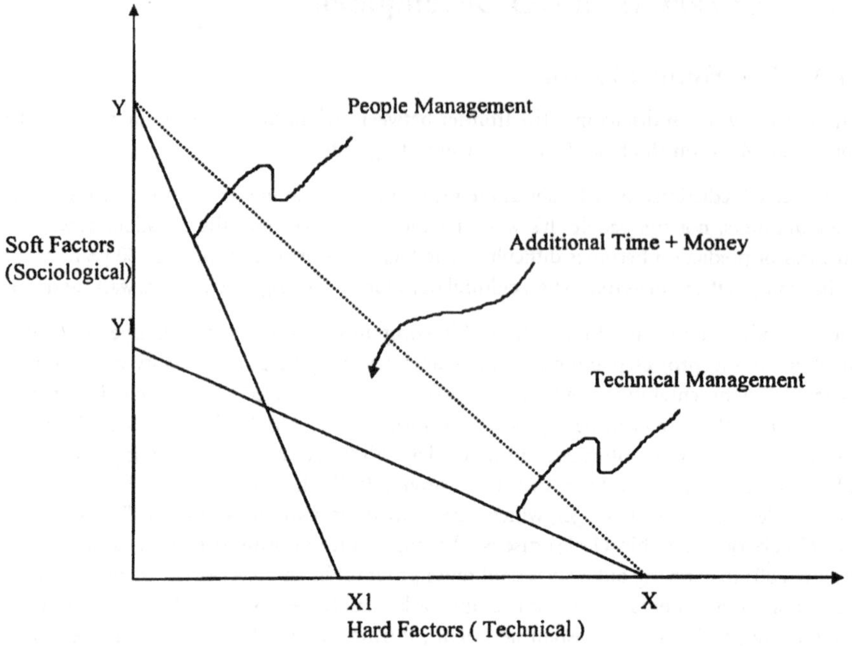

FIGURE 42.1 Balancing sociology in project management. (Adapted from Unhelkar, B. 1996. *Proc. IT Project Management by AIC Conf.*, Auckland, New Zealand, 15-17 April.)

Within certain limits, either of these two approaches can lead to success. However, as per the survey results discussed at the beginning, technical factors contributed to only 7% of the failures. If additional resources are available to a project, then both the soft and hard factors can be handled appropriately and the overall project would comprise the entire area of the triangle X-O-Y, as shown in Figure 42.1 above. However, whenever the resources are scarce and there is a balancing act to be performed, then it is important to develop and apply a corresponding *soft* approach to management. This would result in a shrunken area Y-O-X1 which indicates added emphasis on the people management factor. The other alternative of X-O-Y1 indicates a hard technical approach at the cost of soft factors. This has been shown as a non-prudent approach to project management in the software industry, and it is not recommended.

42.1.3 Soft Issues Specific to OO

Software development efforts continue to be necessarily non-linear in the sense that it is difficult to identify a one-to-one relationship between productivity and the number of hours spent in designing and coding a system. Sometimes the productivity may be very high, and at other times the productivity chart may be going down. In object-oriented software development, issues such as these are further complicated because of new concepts such as reuse by inheritance and polymorphism.

The soft factors specific to an object-oriented project can be summarized as follows:

1. Parallel team organization (loosely coupled subsystems can be developed in parallel)
2. Reusability (need to encourage both producer and consumer of reusable designs and code)
3. Length of employment (long-term employment tends to encourage reuse and quality)
4. Senior management support (due to the paradigm shift implicit in OO)

These factors, while based on the object-oriented technology, are more of an organizational nature. As Goldberg and Rubin (1995, p. 5) correctly state :

> "Objects are not new. They were tested, were found to work, and are still around. But they continue to be used successfully only where appropriate organizational and management contexts are created."

Our attempt at Dow Jones was to continue to provide this context so that the development was destined to be successful right from the beginning.

42.1.4 Support from a Methodological Framework

Our task was further facilitated by the modular or "contract-driven" nature of the OPEN methodological framework (see Chapters 2 and 3 by Henderson-Sellers), which was the framework adopted by our team for all over developments. Indeed, Henderson-Sellers et al. (1996) have addressed the management issues of software development by providing an "open ended" methodological framework which enabled us to treat a given situation at an appropriate level of technicality. The modular nature of the methodology allowed us to incorporate soft activities within the overall framework easily, making our approach to software development "human centric."

42.2 Principles of Transactional Analysis (TA)

42.2.1 Place of TA in Psychology

As a science, psychology is quite new. However, since the advent of Sigmund Freud on the scene in 1890, it has turned into a disciplined inquiry with applications in various fields. McWalters (1991) gives an excellent overview of the different schools of thought in the field of psychology. They are: Psychoanalytical (Sigmund Freud), Behaviorist (B.F.Skinner), Cognitive (Jean Piaget), Humanist (Carl Rogers), and Transpersonal (Ken Wilber). Out of these various schools of thought, the psychoanalytical school of thought has received immense attention in the last 100 years. There have been a number of psychologists like Carl Jung (Archetypes) and Fredrick Perls (Gestalt) who have tried to build on what Freud created, and whose work has received world wide acclaim.

While summarizing Freud, McWalters (1990) discusses the twentieth century psychologist Eric Berne, who is credited with providing "us with a revision of Freud's personality theory." Berne's approach to psychology is called Transactional Analysis (TA for short).

TA has been popularized by well-known works (Berne, 1964; Harris, 1969; and James and Jongeward, 1971) and, at the same time the rigors of its scientific approach documented in the form of an advanced text book of psychotherapy (Berne, 1972). Its application to management was made popular through books like *The OK Boss* (James, 1975) and *Practical TA in Management* (Morrison and O'Hearne, 1977). In the following sections the basics of TA are considered. This is followed by how these principles can be applied in forming and managing teams within areas of object-oriented software development. Just as object technology is not new, but has become popular after more than two decades due to the availability of cheaper hardware and need for complex and quality software systems, similarly TA is not new (it is also more than two decades old), but it is found to contain all the ideal elements for a soft factors approach to technical development and project management in the area of object technology.

The basics of TA consist of the ego states, the life positions, and the games. These are discussed in the following sections, followed by the way these principles were applied in the OO development at Dow Jones.

42.2.2 The Ego States

The basics of TA include the ego states and life positions. Ego states are what make up a personality. Each person has within himself three ego states. These are

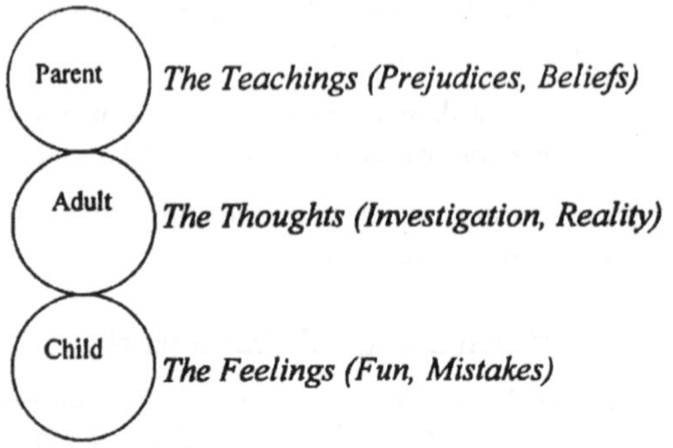

FIGURE 42.2 The ego states of a person (manager).

1. The Parent,* which essentially comprises the taught concept of life
2. The Adult, which is the thought concept of life
3. The Child, which is the felt concept of life

These three parts of a personality are shown in Figure 42.2.

Structurally everyone has a Parent, Adult, and a Child ego state. Unlike Freud's concepts of Superego, Ego, and Id, the P-A-C (Parent, Adult, Child) according to Berne (1961) are phenomenological realities. The difference in people is not of structure, but often lies in the dynamics of these ego states. These characteristics of the ego states can be summarized as follows:

1. Ego states are phenomenological realities.
2. Everyone is structurally the same (everyone has a P-A-C).
3. We differ functionally.
4. Each ego state is important when expressed at the right time and place.
5. It is the function of the Adult to decide the appropriateness of expression.

Furthermore, according to Berne (1961), once a person has a firm grasp of the psychological and social meaning of the terms Parent, Adult, Child, he/she is in a position to use them in day to day transaction in whatever capacity he/she might be functioning. This could be as a teacher, a transactional analyst, a social scientist, or as in our case, a project manager managing object-oriented development.

When a project manager is confronted with a decision making process, data from all three parts of his personality states come in play. The Parent data brings in righteousness as well as prejudices and deals with such parental precepts as "work before play," "work hard," or "never leave a job undone" (further details in Berne [1972]). These data have organizational value for the team, but they are archaic and do not deal with external reality. The Child brings in fun and joy, laughter and parties, and is concerned with the plan for the weekend. It has motivational importance but does not care for objective reality. The Adult is the *reality tester.* It is free from the prejudices and rigidity of the Parent as well as from the emotional and carefree approach of the Child in understanding what is real out there. However, a person need not ignore her Parent or Child — only correctly identify it as such. In the decision making process the Adult of an individual's personality functions like a computer. It takes into account the three sources of data (the Parent and Child within a person and the Adult reality) before arriving at the final decision.

If the three aspects of the personality are kept separate and the Adult is left in the executive decision making process, then the decisions bear greater resemblance to the demands of the reality, and they are made accurately and faster. However, it is when the Adult is *contaminated* by the Parent (prejudices,

* Ego states are referred to by initial capitals.

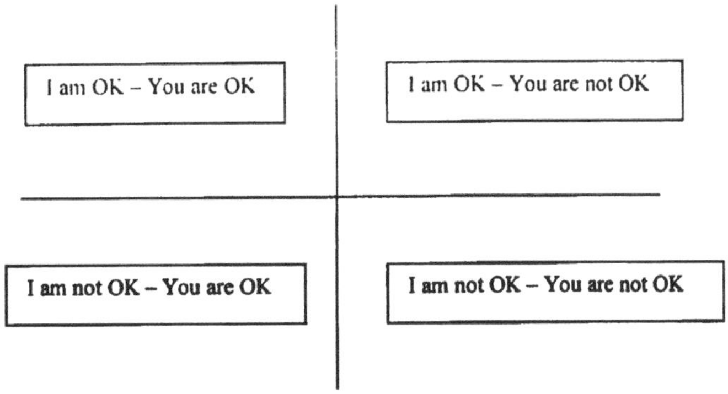

FIGURE 42.3 The life positions in TA.

parental precepts) and/or the Child (fun, personal preferences) that inappropriate decisions are taken, resulting in a loss of harmony for the team.

The aim of TA is to *de*-contaminate the Adult, i.e., to separate the Parent and the Child from the Adult, so that the manager does not confuse the external reality with what lies in his Parent and/or Child, enabling him to take appropriate decisions and manage the team.

42.2.3 Life Positions

The emergence and display of ego states is based on life positions. Positions are the view of a person of the world and the people within the world (Berne, 1961, p. 85). The possible views have been classified by Berne into four *life positions.* These life positions are as shown in Figure 42.3.

As shown in the above figure, the four life positions are

1. *I am OK — You are not OK* — This is mostly didactic, and the person tends to respond from a position of superiority. The active ego state is Parent most of the time.
2. *I am not OK — You are OK* — This is a team member that is always feeling inferior. The active ego state is the adaptive Child.
3. *I am not OK — You are not OK* — This person shuts himself out from the team, and in the extreme case the withdrawal is complete; unable to figure out ego states.
4. *I am OK — You are OK* — This is the position of good leaders and motivators. These are the people that maintain universal respect for themselves and others even in utmost adversity. The active ego state is Adult most of the time, but Parent and Child are allowed uncontaminated display.

These positions are different from feelings in that they are formed early in the childhood and remain with the person for the entire life. While feelings are transitory, life position remain the same. Furthermore, a person tends to come back to his or her original position irrespective of the external reality. In fact, since the world view is projected through the positions, external influences do not shake the position but instead strengthen them. Thus, all experience is selectively interpreted by the individual which fortifies his/her position. It is also worth mentioning that organizations also have their own personalities, and therefore their own positions.

42.2.4 Games

There are various ways in which we structure our time. In TA terminology this structuring of time can be divided into withdrawal, ritual, activity, pastime, intimacy, and games (Berne, 1964). Out of these possible ways of structuring time, ritual, activity, pastime, and games have a role to play within the work environment. The other two ways of time structuring are usually outside the work environment.

Furthermore, ritual, activity and pastime get work done in a formal, rigid way whereas games tend to be basically dishonest and destructive in work (as well as in other social situations). However, since most of the working time is involved in some form of games, it is essential to carefully develop full understanding of the nature of games. This will reduce their negative impact on the functioning of the team. Berne (1964) defines a *Game* as a series of complementary ulterior transactions progressing to a well defined payoff. They have a concealed motivation, and are almost always destructive in human relations (teams, in this case).

Some of the examples of games have been succinctly described by Berne (1964) in *Games People Play.* In their attempt at structuring time they tend to encourage teams to make progress, and keep on making progress without delivering. These types of team games have a relationship with the teams in IT that keep progressing without producing a single product. The key to producing products and delivering them on time is the use of Adult by the team leaders and members of the team. This approach has been extremely successful in the development undertaken at Dow Jones.

42.3 Application of TA in OO Project

42.3.1 Creating a Utopian Team

Understanding our ego states, life positions, and games within our project environment made a direct impact on the way the project teams were formed and managed. Object-oriented systems are usually built by putting together different subsystems. Division of the project into subsystems, that can then be assigned to individual project teams for development, is considered by Meyer (1992) as one of the two major responsibilities* of a project manager. This Activity is also supported by the OPEN methodological framework.

Once the teams in an OO development are organized in parallel, the next step is to maintain cohesion within the teams so that they would continue to remain motivated during and after the project. Thomsett (1994) develops on Constantine's (1989) excellent description of the various ways in which teams could be organized in a software development project. The four possible team structures include:

1. *Closed* — Wherein the team follows the traditional hierarchical structure and is good for traditional development and maintenance such as payroll or accounting systems;
2. *Open* — Here the teams perform as collaborators. There is very little hierarchy and no tradition. The lack of hierarchy is particularly appealing to new programmers.
3. *Random* — These teams are innovative. They would be made up of very few people (3 to 4) and they are put together to achieve a short-term breakthrough goal. Obviously, due to lack of structure, they cannot be expected to perform in a cohesive manner for a long time.
4. *Synchronous* — These are, as Constantine (1995) calls them, Utopian (out of the world) teams. They perform on total understanding and harmonious alignment. This is the team structure that every project manager would hope to achieve.

Our aim was to create a Utopian team which would be able to function coherently and with minimum control. In terms of TA, it had to be a team wherein all members would function with an *I am OK — You are OK* life position. The team members would also suspend there Child tendencies until it would be appropriate to let them out and instead, would work using the Adult part of their personality.

42.3.2 Recruitment — The Best Fit Approach

Since we were aware of what we wanted from our team members, it was easy to start looking for those qualities right from the recruitment process. We had given careful consideration to our recruitment procedure and we were consciously looking for people who have a "strong Adult" and who would operate

* The other one is being in charge of the latest Demo.

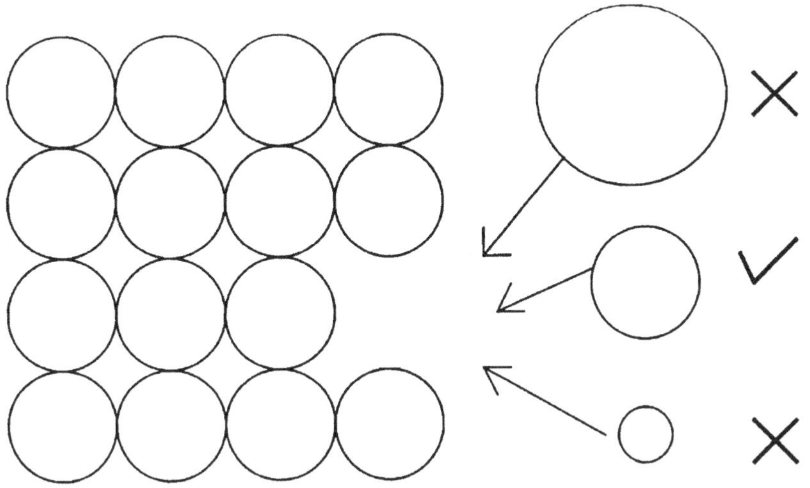

FIGURE 42.4 Recruiting the people that maintain the homogeneity of the team.

from the OK position. We had a set of questions which were used in all tests and interviews to provide us with an indication of the type of person the candidate was.

Following this procedure resulted in a team that was *not* necessarily made up of the best technical people. We realized that at times we had to let go of a technically superior person because, based on our interviews, we realized that the person would not fit in very well with the existing team members. The end result of this process of selection was a team that fit very well, and a team that was in the right direction toward becoming a Utopian team. We called this approach "The Best Fit Approach" and it can be shown as in Figure 42.4.

42.3.3 Moving Away from a Hierarchical Organization

Once we had the right people with us, it was essential to continue to encourage them to remain productive. We decided to do away with the traditional hierarchical way of showing the structure of the team. While Hammer and Champy (1994) have discussed "flattening the pyramid of the organizational structure" in their re-engineering approach, we found the same idea appealing in re-doing our team structure. In order to understand our structure, you have to look at the team from *above.* A typical team with a leader and five members, when viewed from above, would look a little like that in Figure 42.5.

Development can benefit by viewing the team organization from the top (the vertical view), because it does not carry the hierarchical notion of traditional team structures. This is a flat *circular* arrangement with many advantages in terms of organization and communication. For example, communication is now facilitated between not only the leader and members (L-P1, L-P2, etc.) but also among members (P1-P2, P2-P3, P4-P5, etc.). The position of the leader is not seen as superior (but as seen from the top view), but is seen at the same level as the other members of the team. The leader is the facilitator in this case. Thus this model of team structure caters to the static as well as the dynamic aspect of its functioning. The improvement in communication can be used to handle another major cause of project failures (*viz.* inadequate communication, 20% as discussed by Greatrex, 1996).

42.3.4 People in Reusability

Fafchamps (1994) of Hewlett-Packard Laboratories states "it is now obvious that reuse is not just a technical issue, it is also a people issue." This people issue of reusability was very well brought out by

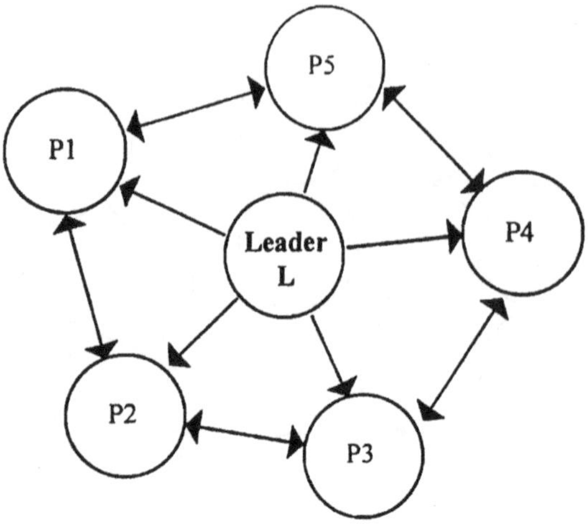

FIGURE 42.5 Flattening the pyramid, and viewing it from top. (Adapted from Unhelkar, B. 1996. *Proc. IT Project Management by AIC Conf.*, Auckland, New Zealand, 15-17 April.)

Meyer (1995a) wherein he compared it with the philosophical problem of "to have or to be." Reuse programs, Meyer (1995a) further stated, were based on rewarding the users ("with" reuse) but did not concentrate on the producer ("for" reuse) of reusable code.

Thus, for reuse to succeed, proper management structures should be put in place which would reward the producer of reusable code. This effort has been specifically mentioned in the fountain model of Henderson-Sellers and Edwards (1994) wherein there is a specific activity of generalization/specialization before the code is accepted in library. This requires the producer to put in effort which is visible only at a later stage, when the code is reused.

This indicates that it is not just the product-based reuse that can achieve results, but the processes themselves should be based on reusability. The team organization should reflect these reuse-based processes. One required element of this reused-based process is the development of an appropriate reward system. In functional development, rewards are given at the completion of major milestones. However, in OO development (especially due to reusability) there is a need to think ahead, beyond the immediate problem and to separate current needs from general ones. This requires the management system to compensate those developing reusable classes either by providing lump sum payments for contributions accepted into the organization's reuse library or by providing royalty payments based on actual class reuse (Kreindler, 1993).

One other approach to team organizations which would provide just rewards to teams producing reusable code is discussed by Henderson-Sellers and Pant (1993). It is the creation of a common role with the responsibility for both the teams producing reusable software code (the "producers" of Meyer [1995a]) and the teams reusing the code produced. This is similar to Thomsett's (1990) recommendation of a linchpin role, except that instead of vesting the responsibility with a particular role (person), the same is achieved in an organizational fashion.

While we did not have a detailed monetary reward structure in place, it was still possible to recognize reuse efforts through our bonus system. More importantly though, the peer recognition for large scale reuse and the recognition from the rest of the organization when the product was produced in time was considered to be a precious reward for reuse. With our OK teams, it was easier to encourage both "for" and "with" reuse as programming teams did not mind reusing designs and code written by other members of the team. Furthermore, teams also generalized their own code to enable subsequent teams to reuse it.

42.3.5 Games in an OO Project

We discussed earlier on that "games" are a way of structuring time. Games are not necessarily productive, and they are almost always ulterior in nature. Because software development is a team event wherein all the nuances of social psychology as presented by TA contribute, it is obvious that games exist within these development teams. During the course of our project at Dow Jones, we discovered a few games. They are discussed here briefly along with their antidotes (Unhelkar, 1995):

Use it or lose it — Constantine (1995) mentions the need of some programmers to use every available feature of the language, resulting in a highly complex code with functionality present only because of a corresponding language or tool feature. We actively discouraged use of features for the sake of using them. A routine requiring the programmers to justify the need to use a particular OO feature (or language specific feature) was set up as an antidote to this game.

Cowboy programming — These are games played by people who disregard methodologies. Dodani (1994) and Suzudrich (1993) discuss examples of situations where the cowboy programming game could be played. We publicized in detail within the project the fact that we were using methodologies only as a road map (see Unhelkar and Mamdapur, 1995) and that methodologies were not there to strangle creativity.

Flour mix — This is the creep factor so often discussed in IT project management. In this case, it is a game played by the developer in that he wants to add one more functionality before delivering the system, and then to satisfy that functionality he needs one more resource. The development goes on like mixing the flour/dough for bread (Unhelkar, 1996). The time boxed approach to development (Graham, 1995) was used as one of the possible antidotes to this game. The Next Release Maybe (NRM) approach proposed by Meyer (1995) in which the requirement of the functionality is accepted, but only on the condition that it will be provided *not* in this release, but the next one, was also utilized to help break up this game.

Meetingitis — Meyer (1995) discusses this problem in which the development team spends hours in meetings. It is a game that provides tools to structure time for workers who do not know what to do with their time, but is unproductive and self-defeating. Timing the meetings beforehand can help in breaking this game. This is precisely what we did with our team meetings. We would always set times *before* we started a meeting, and stick to it.

Deadline — Development teams play this game in many situations. When the team wants to look busy, it tries to approach the development with a *Harried* (games described by Berne [1964]) approach. It appears to the onlooker that the team will die if it does not meet the deadline. The deadline comes and passes by, and the team is still there. So it brings in the next deadline. Deadlines could be excuses for not following a proper methodological approach and thereby courting disasters. We followed the methodology as a reference, and we were successfully able to produce results on time.

42.3.6 Additional Soft Factors

In addition to the discussion on using TA for team building, there are a number of other soft factors which continue to influence the success of object-oriented projects. For example, Cox (1992) has discussed the problems of copyright and royalty payments associated with a set of reusable components. Since OO software is meant for reuse, Cox (1992) proposes that instead of selling copies of software packages, royalties should be paid on a usage basis.

Reusability influences people. For example, experience with reuse facilitates further smoother and easier reuse. Lim (1994), while discussing the effect of reuse on quality, productivity, and economics says, "Finally, we have found that reuse allows an organization to use personnel more effectively because it leverages expertise. Experienced software specialists can concentrate on creating work products that less experienced personnel can then reuse."

DeMarco and Lister (1987) have discussed the effect of the environment on the quality of work produced. This is defined by them as the environmental factor or "E-Factor." The frequency and types of disturbances (e.g., telephones, paging), the sitting arrangements (privacy, group discussions), etc., have been correlated by them to productivity and quality. The influence of these factors cannot be discounted in producing quality code, and it has a significant role in object-oriented development as well.

42.4 Conclusions

This discussion started with the need to consider soft factors in the management of a software development project — typically an object-oriented project. After arguing for a "balanced" approach to managing an OO project, some specific requirements of an OO project were discussed.

This was followed by an introduction of the principles of TA. This included the ego states, life positions, and games. The discussion then moved to the use of these principles in order to recruit and "gel" a team together. The organizational and motivational aspect of reusability in OO projects was discussed.

Finally, additional soft factors which influenced our project indirectly were also discussed. It is hoped that by sharing these soft factors, project managers will be prepared for them beforehand, and thereby able to manage a successful project.

Acknowledgments

This is contribution number 97/12 of the Centre for Object Technology, Applications and Research (COTAR), Australia. Thanks to Professor Brian Henderson-Sellers (Swinburne University, Melbourne) and Dr. Julian Edwards (OO P/L, Sydney) for constructive comments and criticisms.

References

Berne, E. 1961. *Transactional Analysis in Psychotherapy,* pp. 23-24. Grove Press, First Evergreen Edition.

Berne, E. 1964. *Games People Play.* Penguin.

Berne, E. 1972. *What Do You Say After You Say Hello?: The Psychology of Human Destiny.* Transworld Publishers, London.

Constantine, L. 1989. Teamwork paradigms and the structured open team, *Proc. Embedded Systems Conf.,* Miller Freeman, San Francisco.

Constantine, L. 1995. *Constantine on Peopleware.* Yourdon Press, Prentice-Hall, Englewood Cliffs, NJ.

Constantine, L. 1996. Panel on Soft Issues and other Hard Problems in Software Development, (Ward Cunningham, Luke Hohmann, Norman Kerth), *OOPSLA'96,* San Jose, CA, 6-10 Oct.

Cox, B. J. 1992. What if there is a silver bullet?, *J. Object Oriented Programming,* Vol. 5, No. 3, pp. 8-9,76

DeMarco, T. and Lister, T. 1987. *Peopleware: Productive Projects and Teams.* Dorset House Publishing Company, New York.

Dodani, M. 1994, Archaeological designers, *J. Object-Oriented Prog.* May.

Fafchamps D. 1994. Organizational factors and reuse, *IEEE Software,* Sept., Vol. 11, No. 5, pp. 31-41.

Goldberg, A. and Rubin, K. 1995. *Succeeding with Objects: Decision Frameworks for Project Management.* Addison-Wesley, Reading, MA.

Graham, I. 1995. *Migrating to Object Technology.* Addison-Wesley, Reading, MA.

Greatrex, C. (KPMG Director). 1996. Achieving excellence through effective management of your IT project, *Proc. ITProject Management by AIC Conferences.* Auckland, April.

Hammer, M. and Champy, J. 1994. *Reengineering the Corporation.* Allen and Unwin.

Harris, T. 1969. *I am OK, You are OK.* Pan Books, London and Sydney.

Henderson-Sellers, B. and Pant, Y. 1993. When should we generalize classes to make them reusable? *Obj. Mag.,* 3, 4, 73-75.

Henderson-Sellers, B. and Edwards, J. M. 1994. *Book Two of Object-Oriented Knowledge: The Working Object.* Prentice-Hall, Englewood Cliffs, NJ.

Henderson-Sellers, B., Yap, L.-M. and Fung, M. 1995. Methodology modeling: The role of business rules and quality in methodologies, *Rep. Object Anal. Des.,* Vol. 2, No. 4, Nov-Dec, pp. 10-12.

James, M. 1975. *The OK Boss*. Addison-Wesley, Reading, MA.

James, M. and Jongeward, D. 1971. *Born to Win*, NAL Penguin, New York.

Kriendler, J. 1993. Cultural change and object-oriented technology, *J. Object-Oriented Prog.*, Feb., Vol. 5 No. 9, pp. 6-8.

Lanier, J. 1997. The frontier between us, *Comm. ACM*, 40, 2, 55-56.

Lim, W. C. 1994. Effects of reuse on quality, productivity, and economics, *IEEE Software*, Sept., Vol. 11, No. 5, pp. 23-30.

McWalters, M. 1990. *Understanding Psychology*, Chapter 1 — Human Nature, pp. 18-23. McGraw-Hill Australia.

Meyer, B. 1992. Public communication, presentation at the Object-Oriented Special Interest Group of the Australian Computer Society (New South Wales Branch), Sydney, October 21.

Meyer, B. 1995a. *Object Success*. Prentice-Hall, Englewood Cliffs, NJ.

Meyer, B. 1995b. Object technology: What's in it for management, *Proc. Object'95 by AIC Conf.*, March.

Morrison, J. and O'Hearne, J. 1977. *Practical Transactional Analysis in Management*. Addison-Wesley, Reading, MA.

Szudrich, M. 1993. Opinion: Methodologies for mediocrity, *Informatics*, Publication of Australian Computer Society, Vol. 1, Issue 5, July.

Thomsett, R. 1990. Managing implications of object-oriented development, *ACS Newslett.*, October 5-7, pp. 10-12.

Thomsett, R. 1994. When the rubber hits the road: A guide to implementing self-managing teams, *Amer. Prog.*, December, pp. 37-45.

Unhelkar, B. 1995. Managing objects, managing people: a peopleware perspective of object-oriented development, *Proc. Object-Orientation by AIC Conf.*, Johannesburg, South Africa, 3-5 July.

Unhelkar, B. 1996. Developing the vital leadership skills required of an IT project manager. *Proc. IT Project Management by AIC Conf.*, Auckland, New Zealand, 15-17 April.

43

Developing Risk Management Applications for Financial Markets using OPEN: A Case Study

Bhuvan Unhelkar
Case Digital, Inc.

Abstract

Object orientation is extremely beneficial in the development of complex and dynamic applications like the risk management applications for financial markets. OPEN (Object-oriented Process Environment and Notations), a full lifecycle object-oriented methodological framework, is able to guide such a development. A case study of the first major release version of TELAN (TELerate ANalytics — an analytical application for managing financial risks) developed for Dow Jones (erstwhile Dow Jones Telerate) by their Analytics Development Group (ADG) in Sydney is presented here. TELAN has won Computerworld Object Developer's Award (CODA) for "Best object-oriented development across the organization."

43.1 The Financial Markets and Object-Orientation

43.1.1 Background of Financial Markets

The sophistication of today's derivatives and risk management markets is such that it demands a crucial role from the software systems that are used by the traders and end users. These requirements from

0-8493-3135-8/99/$0.00+$.50

software in today's financial markets go way beyond the traditional need for a banker or trader to identify and measure the risk to which their money is exposed (Unhelkar and Lindblom, 1995). As the J.P. Morgan document (Morgan, 1995) on RiskMetrics™ states:

> These developments, along with technological breakthroughs in data processing, have gone hand in hand with changes in management practices — a movement away from management based on accrual accounting toward risk management based on marking-to-market of positions. Increased liquidity and pricing availability along with a new focus on trading led to the implementation of frequent revaluation of positions, the mark-to-market concept.

This is the "Value-at-Risk" or *VAR* methodology of risk management, as compared to the traditional banker's "Asset-Liability-Management" or *ALM* approach. The resultant complexity of the problem, due to the *VAR* approach, makes it an ideal situation for the use of object-oriented design techniques. As Davidson (1994) reports, "the market's complexity and rate of change is the kind of problem to which the technology (object) is best suited." James Martin, as quoted by Burns (1997), agrees: The process of modelling has become "...exceptionally sophisticated in the area of derivatives designs...," Martin notes. Object technology facilitates this process of sophisticated designs.

Granularity (Unhelkar, 1997), which is the ability of object-oriented designs to determine the average size of a class, provides an opportunity to the designers to express their systems in an extremely malleable form. These "granularity-conscious" designs lend themselves to various reusable combinations which result in a large number of different views of the system. These views, or various combinations of the classes, are in a position to satisfy the demands of the traders. Additional technical advantages of finer granularity (e.g., decomposing the classes into persistence (data storage) and manipulative (calculations), see Haythorn, 1994) also make object technology a worthwhile contributor in the financial markets' software development.

The object-oriented approach to software development using the OPEN methodological framework (see Chapter 2, OPEN: Object-Oriented Process, Environment and Notation: The First Full Lifecycle, Third Generation OO Method by Henderson-Sellers), together with the concept of granularity to produce reusable and malleable designs, was tried out by the Analytic Development Group (ADG) within Dow Jones. After a brief introduction to the company and the group, a discussion of the development is presented in the following sections.

43.1.2 The Dow Jones Business

Dow Jones is in the business of providing real-time data to the financial markets on its proprietary network. In addition to the real-time data, there is a large demand for historical data, which are used for analytical purposes. The source for the data on financial markets is as follows:

1. Collecting the data at the local exchanges
2. Existing historical data within the company
3. Data purchased from third party information vendors

These data are then a marketable commodity which could be used for various purposes such as analysis or prediction. After the data have been collected/purchased from various sources, they are massaged into a format that can be used to deliver them to customers, both in-house and external. This format depends on a number of considerations including the speed of delivery required and the available bandwidth on the network and the cost of delivery, as well as the security issues related to accessing client networks. This massaged delivery of data is provided to the clients through the various *feeds* of Dow Jones.

With increasing demand for sophistication, many of these feeds are combined together into a cohesive platform called Telerate Workstation (TW). The TW interface further massages the feeds by providing the same data through a cohesive platform interface. The users are able to access these data in order to satisfy their needs for more data on the financial instruments, as well as a need for better presentation.

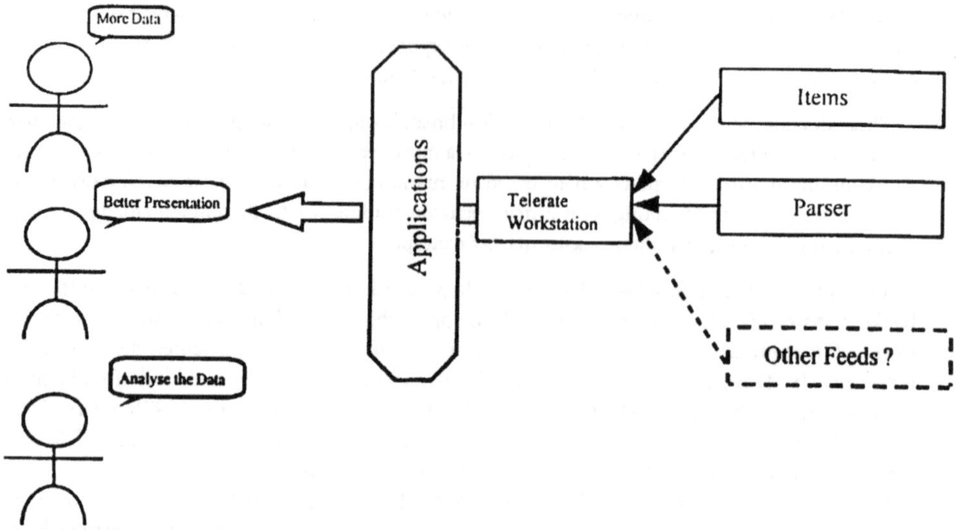

FIGURE 43.1 Adding value to data through application development by ADG. (From Unhelkar, B. 1996b. *Proc. Business Intelligence by AIC Conf.* Sydney 23-30 April.)

The data can be downloaded by the clients on to their own machines, and viewed through applications like Excel spreadsheet. This is shown in Figure 43.1.

In Figure 43.1, Items and Parser are the names of two of Dow Jones' feeds which are providing specific data to the clients. The dotted box indicates the possibility of additional feeds which can be taken in by the TW platform. The applications attempt to satisfy the threefold needs of the clients: more data, better presentation, and more analysis of the data.

43.1.3 The ADG

It is the analysis of the data (in addition to more data and better presentation) that provides the competitive edge to the traders in today's financial markets. Traders in the markets make decisions based on *probabilities* and these probabilities are worked out using highly sophisticated mathematical models like, for example, the Black-Scholes and the Binomial pricing models, described by Ritchken (1996).

In order to satisfy the need for *analyzing* the data in order to make correct pricing estimations, analytical applications are acquired through third parties, or built in-house by Dow Jones. One of the various groups responsible for building the applications in-house is the ADG, based in Sydney. This group works in association with mathematicians and market experts within the organization and builds products to their specifications. The group also associates with other developing teams within the organization including teams at New Jersey, Toronto, and Hong Kong.

The analytical products (or applications) developed by ADG attempt to satisfy the "analytical" needs of the clients. These applications take the data from the TW, and then analyze them and present them to the users to enable them to make informed judgments, as well as storing their transactions and positions in order to determine where they stand, on a day-by-day basis.

Cooper (1996), in discussing J.P. Morgan's RiskMetrics™ product quotes Jacques Longerstaey, their vice-president of market risk research: "We have had a lot of feedback from clients saying: "Thanks for the Risk Metrics data, but how do we use it?" It is this "how do we use it?" question that ADG is trying to answer through its developments. However, instead of developing a spreadsheet type product, which would not be able to change according to the changing user needs, and which may not provide the sophistication required of analytical products within the markets, the ADG has adopted the object-oriented approach in the development of all of their products enabling them to produce sophisticated and malleable systems. In following the object-oriented approach the team was greatly benefited by utilizing the OPEN methodological framework (mentioned earlier in Chapters 2 and 3) and formal industrial strength tool MeNtOR (discussed in greater detail in Chapter 42 by this author) in designing and documenting the development. These tools and methodology, however, were used as a "reference" at every step of the development. Sometimes the development followed the methodology to the last activity and task, whereas at other times the methodology did not map with the actual road ahead. However, just as we do not blame the street directory for pot holes or accidents on the road, the team did not blame the tools it used when hiccups occurred in the development (For greater details on this philosophy of using a methodology as a "road map" see Unhelkar and Mamdapur, 1995a).

For and *with* reuse* were a part of the overall strategy, the teams were organized in parallel (i.e., one team for each subsystem), and the management approach was based on due consideration to "soft factors" (see Chapter 42). This resulted in a speedy and timely delivery for each iteration of the software releases. This culminated in the group's winning the Computerworld Object Developer's Awards (CODA); (for details see Unhelkar, 1995c, as reported by Keith Power) and receiving accolades both within and outside the organization. The reason for the success of object-oriented techniques in financial markets development is further elaborated.

43.1.4 Reasoning for Object Orientation

In the world of financial markets, knowledge of the latest market rates and trends is considered necessary, but not sufficient. Large corporate traders, banks, and business houses who have invested in the financial markets need to know the risks to which they are exposed. However, their positions are made up of varied instruments including government bonds, forwards and futures, options and swaps, etc. Furthermore, these positions are not restricted to one country or to one currency.

With ever increasing sophistication in the markets due to round-the-clock trading across the globe, traders trade in multiple currencies and in many different markets. Furthermore, the methods used to price instruments also differ from country to country and sometimes from region to region. Finally, there is a need for the financial developers to keep up with the exotic derivative products which keep inundating the markets and with the traders who conjure up new ways of trading every day. Shimko (1996, p. 100) of J.P. Morgan, in justifying the need for exotic derivatives, says that

> "These derivatives help those with naturally complex risk exposures by converting these exposures to simple and manageable entities, and they also help create these exposure more efficiently."

The above-mentioned requirements for sophistication and complexity provide an ideal opportunity for application of the object-oriented approach to software development to produce systems that are flexible, that span multiple markets, and that help manage risk through exotic option pricing. Object-oriented development, due to its ability to handle complexity (by modularizing) and short time to delivery (reusability and iterative development), was very well suited for adoption by ADG for its software products. As Duffy (1993) states,

> "It is increasingly rare to find a derivative trading operation that doesn't use some software created with a version of object-oriented programming." "This new form of program design," Duffy further reports, "can wrap around a pricing model like a transparent film, allowing traders and programmers structuring new deals to reuse program information without the time and effort of writing new code."

With this thinking in the industry, ADG found it ideal to use object-oriented techniques in the development of its products, which comprise its risk management enterprise.

* *For* reuse is when the design keeps future reuse in mind; *With* reuse is when the design considers what can be used *now* from the available repertoire of reusable designs.

43.2 Development of Risk Management Enterprise

43.2.1 Need for TELAN

A need was felt by the market experts for a software system in the area of financial risk management which would utilize newer development techniques like OO, and therefore, change according to the changing needs of the users quickly. This new system was meant to replace an earlier C/DOS product which was used by the existing traders to analyze data. This resulted in the market justification for the development of TELAN (Telerate Analytics). TELAN is a suite of object-oriented applications developed with the initial purpose of replacing an existing C/DOS product and then extending the functionality to incorporate sophisticated analysis across multiple markets and currencies.

A risk management system is meant to provide a wide range of users with the opportunity to be *in control* and *anticipate* the possible profit/loss scenarios for a wide range of inputs. An ever increasing computer-literate group of users coupled with a greater variety and complexity of products that now exists in the derivatives markets implies that systems are required not only to identify the risks but also to *explain* them to the end-users, in an easy to understand GUI (graphical user interface), so that they *understand* the products and participate in the decisions made by their banks (Unhelkar and Lindblom, 1995). In order to satisfy the need of a system that is flexible, capable of catering to the rapidly changing market demands, with reduced delivery time, we produced TELAN.

43.2.2 TELAN Product Details

TELAN comprises three major areas of analysis:

1. Observing the markets as they are, including their sensitivities, arbitrage etc.; this is called the *Market Watch*
2. Analyzing the historical trends of prices and yields of various instruments called *Historical Analysis*
3. Recording trades on a group of instruments and managing their positions called *Portfolio Management*

Each of these applications provides a number of analytics on the data to enable the user to view the markets in different ways. The system follows the "plug-and-play" architecture, easily facilitated by its OO design, resulting in an iteratively developed product, which can be marketed in different combinations.

The first release of TELAN is primarily for use by the fixed interest market, essentially trading in bonds, forwards, and swaps for the Australian, New Zealand, Japanese, and U.S. markets. It combines the real-time Telerate data feed (providing spots, volatilities, etc.) with bond pricing and charting for viewing of data, performs various "what-if" scenarios for single and group of instruments, performs historical analysis, and provides some simple portfolios for management. It provides sophisticated tabular analysis and charting which gives an instant view of instrument prices, price variations with respect to variation in one of the other factors, and real-time access to volatility rates.

The initial releases of TELAN perform preliminary risk analysis (which is being extended for more sophisticated analysis as this is being written). Parameters used in pricing options such as spot rate, volatility, or strike rate (which are entered in the columns on the table), can be varied over user-specified ranges and the position of the deal can be analyzed via tabular reports and sophisticated graphics. While the system itself is extremely easy to learn, it is also supported by detailed online help which is context sensitive. Later versions will also have an online tutorial. The status bars provide a short and instant description of the cursor position.

TELAN is also scalable. The modular design makes it easy to scale the system upwards to permit position management to be integrated with the existing applications. Finally, the architecture is open enough to allow third party software to be released on Telerate's analytical platform by means of DLLs, should that be dictated by the marketing requirements.

TELAN is meant to be a global analytical product, comprising a suite of applications which would include multiple currencies and many markets in its analysis. The ever changing nature of the financial markets, together with the need to incorporate varied financial instruments in its analysis, made the

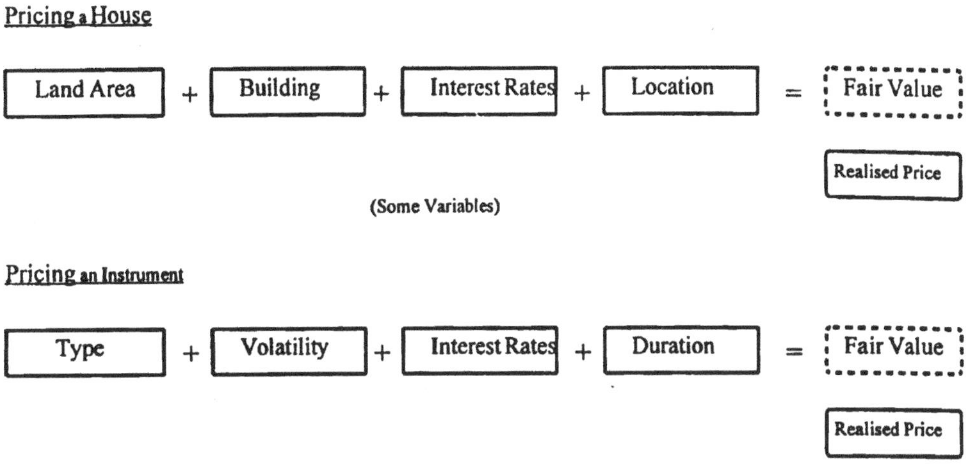

FIGURE 43.2 Pricing an instrument. (From Unhelkar, B. 1996b. *Proc. Business Intelligence by AIC Conf.* Sydney 23-30 April.)

requirements for this product extremely complex and dynamic. This complexity can be understood by examining the basic building block of a system.

The building block of a risk management system is an "Instrument." Pricing an Instrument requires careful consideration to all aspects of design before a "good" risk management software can be produced. This is discussed next.

43.2.3 Pricing the Instrument

One of the basic activities in managing risks in financial markets is understanding what is the current "worth" or value of the portfolio. This is similar to understanding the risks associated with an investment property by ascertaining its current value. This analogy can be further developed in order to understand how pricing an instrument in financial markets compares with the pricing of a house. This has been appropriately discussed and presented by Unhelkar (1996b) and is briefly described as follows.

Some of the factors that make up the fair price of a house are the land area, type of building, current interest rates, and the location of the house, to name a few (see Figure 43.2). Changes in these factors are reflected in the fair price of the house. However, the fair price of the house is not necessarily the actual price at which the house is sold or purchased. The difference in the fair value and realized price indicate the profit/loss. The *potential* for such a profit or loss is the *risk* to which the owner's equity is exposed. Similarly in financial markets, some of the factors that influence the fair value of an instrument are the type of the instrument (a bond or an option, and which type of bond, etc.), its volatility (rate of change of price), interest rates, and duration. The influence of these factors on the price and its comparison with house price is shown in Figure 43.2.

While the above example presents the case of pricing a simple house, in real life there are various *types* of houses which have corresponding nuances in their pricing formula. Similarly, in real-life financial markets, there are various types of instruments that are priced in slightly different ways. For example, there are bonds (which are government, semi-government, or corporate) which are priced in a certain way, and then there are currencies (currency spots, forwards, futures, swaps, etc.) which are priced in a different way. Options are financial instruments which do not actually deal with buying or selling something, but provide an *option* or a *right* to buy or sell a particular currency or bond or some other underlying Instrument. These are again priced differently. Some of the various types of instruments that could be priced in TELAN have been shown through a screen shot of the "Instrument Selector" for TELAN, as in Figure 43.3.

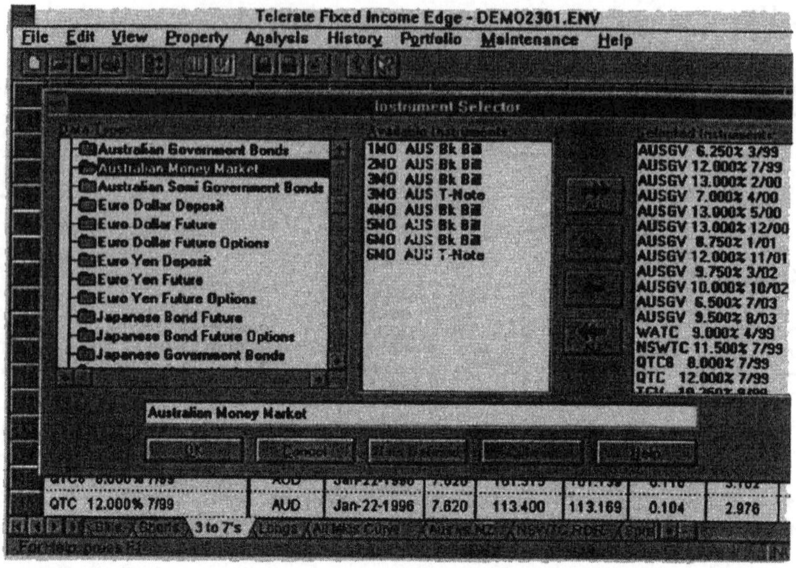

FIGURE 43.3 Various types of instrument. (From Unhelkar, B. 1996a. *Proc. Object'96 by AIC Conf.* Sydney, 8-10 May and Unhelkar, B. 1996b. *Proc. Business Intelligence by AIC Conf.* Sydney 23-30 April.)

The instrument selector is showing various Australian instrument types (e.g., money markets, semi-government, and government bonds) Japanese bond-futures, etc. Each of the instrument types shown above have a slightly different way of calculating prices. Thus there is a considerable amount of commonality in the way these instruments are "priced." The object-oriented approach within the OPEN methodological framework enabled the designers to abstract these common functionalities and put them together in a higher level abstract class.

43.2.4 Breadth of TELAN

The instrument types (or data types) shown in the TELAN screen (Figure 43.3) relate specifically to fixed income markets. The design of TELAN, however, has incorporated a wider enterprise level approach. Therefore, instead of developing solution for a narrow domain, the wider area of financial markets was investigated and the design reflected this *generalized* enterprise development approach. The various markets within this domain encompass the Fixed Income, Bonds, FRA/Swaps, Commodities, Equities, and Energy markets. Analyzing and documenting the requirements for these markets was made possible by the use of Activities within OPEN and documenting them within MeNtOR.

OPEN/MeNtOR was followed in development of all systems within the enterprise. Apart from the benefits that a well thought out methodology provides, this continuity in using the same methodology over more than one project also resulted in immense benefits to the company in terms of large scale reuse, shorter time to delivery, ideal team organization, better quality, and overall excellence in project management (Unhelkar, 1995b). The resulting goodwill within the company, especially the feeling of trust in the sales and marketing departments, also helped the image of the group. Finally, as shown in the metrics section later, this same environment also helped in arriving at correct productivity figures and using them to estimate the requirements for new projects accurately.

43.2.5 The Reusable Architecture

In order to produce an enterprise model for the financial markets development, it was essential to produce a robust reusable architecture for the development at ADG.

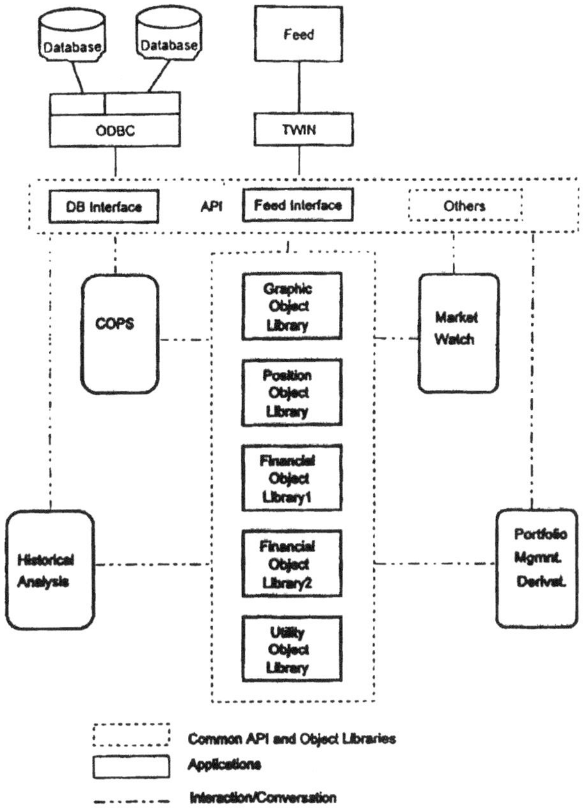

FIGURE 43.4 The reusable architecture for Dow Jones' Analytical Enterprise. (Adapted from Aung Thurein, Project Manager, ADG.)

Instead of producing a single product, or handling one project, ADG took the enterprise wide development approach, resulting in analysis of a wider domain and production of various libraries (e.g., Graphics, Position Keeping, Financial). The final products are then derived from these libraries, as shown in Figure 43.4.

While the financial markets are moving toward object technology for designing their complex application, a key question is how objects should be stored (Davidson, 1994). Financial organizations are usually accommodating objects in relational databases. This is because object-oriented technology is still evolving (as compared with relational technology, as far as data storage is concerned), and because "financial organizations tend to be conservative in their approach to computer systems," says Jeffrey McIver, Director of Financial Engineering at systems supplier Infinity International Financial Technology (see Davidson, 1994). The same issues were experienced and investigated by ADG, and eventually the data made persistent in a relational database (Microsoft's SQL server). In order to maintain transparency to the database, the interface to the database is through ODBC (Object Data Base Connectivity — a Microsoft product for connectivity to databases). The feed interface is the TW interface discussed earlier, which provides access to the live data of Telerate, as shown in Figure 43.4.

43.2.6 TELAN Subsystems

The concept of subsystems in OPEN is specifically aimed at handling the complexities of OO designs. This was put to good use in designing TELAN. The technical design of the system is divided into various subsystems of importance that include the GUI, Maths, Utility, Instrument, and the Printing subsystems.

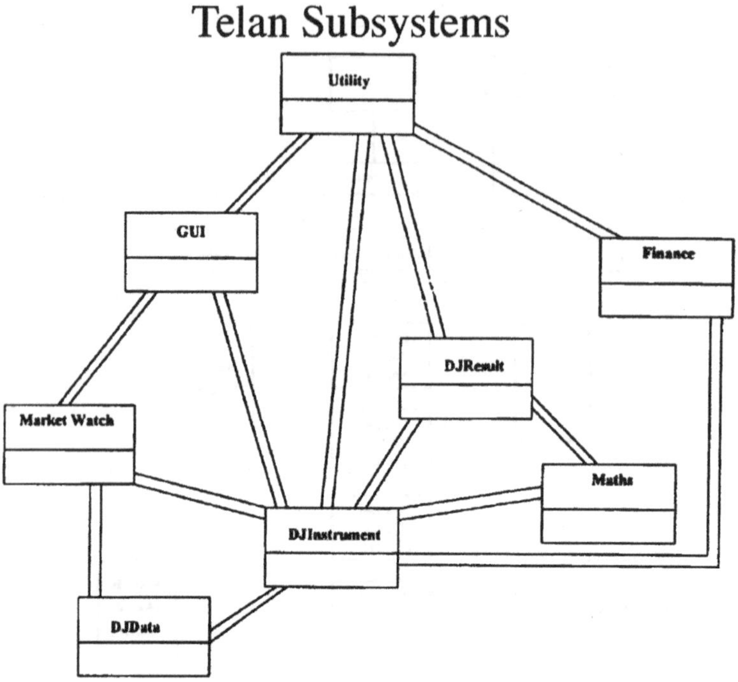

FIGURE 43.5 TELAN subsystems — loosely coupled. (From Unhelkar, B. 1995c. Objects please financial developers. In *Computerworld,* by Keith Power, 6 October, Vol. 18, No. 14, pp. 1, 38.)

to name but a few. These modules are very loosely coupled and therefore have very little dependence on each other. This facilitates parallel development, wherein it is possible to develop many modules of the system (which are loosely connected) at almost the same time. TELAN also uses the Dynamic Link Libraries from TW (the feed platform described earlier on). Once again the modularity of the design has made it easy to integrate TELAN with the platform application. These subsystems are shown in Figure 43.5.

Not all of these subsystems start from scratch. In fact, TELAN reuses a large amount of design and code produced during the earlier Telerate Currency Options (COPS) development and therefore this new development is, in a way, an augmentation of the COPS class library. Many of the TELAN subsystems are extensions of the reusable class libraries shown earlier in Figure 43.4 (the reusable architecture). For example, the GUI subsystem for TELAN was designed as an extension from the COPS table described earlier. This enabled a similar look and feel for TELAN, as for COPS, and also provided large scale reuse advantage. Another subsystem, called the Utility subsystem, was hardly a specific part of TELAN. It provided various data and time calculations, specific to financial markets, many of which were written earlier during the development of COPS. Thus, the Utility subsystem was reused extensively during the development of TELAN. It was also augmented by newer classes which the team came across during TELAN development.

43.2.7 Fine Granularity in TELAN

Granularity is a concept explored in detail during the research conducted by this author (see Unhelkar, 1997). The opportunity to experiment practically with some of the results from the research was provided by the TELAN development. Fine granularity in TELAN was evident in both areas of reuse. In *with* reuse, TELAN was reusing a large amount of fine granular designs and code from COPS development. At the same time, TELAN was also producing fine granular designs. One such design was the Instrument

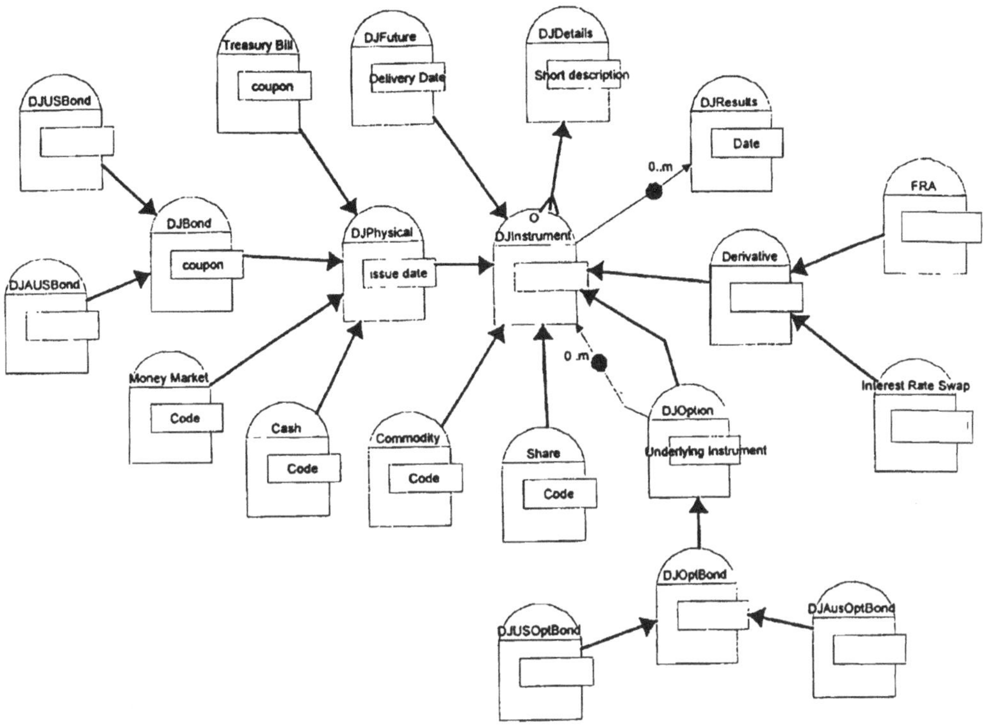

FIGURE 43.6 TELAN — Fine granular Instrument subsystem.

subsystem (shown as DJInstrument in Figure 43.6; it was decided to name the potentially reusable subsystems and classes with a prefix of DJ for Dow Jones to make it more attractive for other users across other development sites in the U.S. and Hong Kong to reuse).

The starting point for this design is the DJInstrument class (observe that this is different from the subsystem DJInstrument, however, since subsystems do not have a corresponding implementation entity, there was no confusion). This *initial* class contains attributes and methods that apply to all instruments (current and future) in the financial world. This implies that the class contains the bare minimum attributes and functions. All other types of Instruments (e.g., Options, Shares, Commodities, Futures, and a set of Physical Instruments — Bond, Treasury Bills, Money Markets) are derived from the main instrument. This design is taking advantage of the object-oriented approach wherein it is utilizing the concept of granularity, and it is consciously being designed as a fine granular system. Newer instruments, as they appear on the markets, could then be derived from the existing classes.

An example of such a derivation is the Options module, shown in Figure 43.7. Observe here that various types of options are derived from the basic DJOption class. The design has the potential to extend into many new varieties of options that are not yet in the market.

While the above two designs demonstrate the usage of object-oriented techniques and especially the advantages of finer granularity for reusability and extensibility, it is also important to show an additional advantage of finer granularity, as described in the next section.

43.2.8 Separating Calculations from Data (Additional Use of Granularity)

Davidson (1994), in criticizing the object-oriented approach for ignoring data persistence, states "OO programming languages more or less ignore the issue of storage. In fact, in the basic object model, a

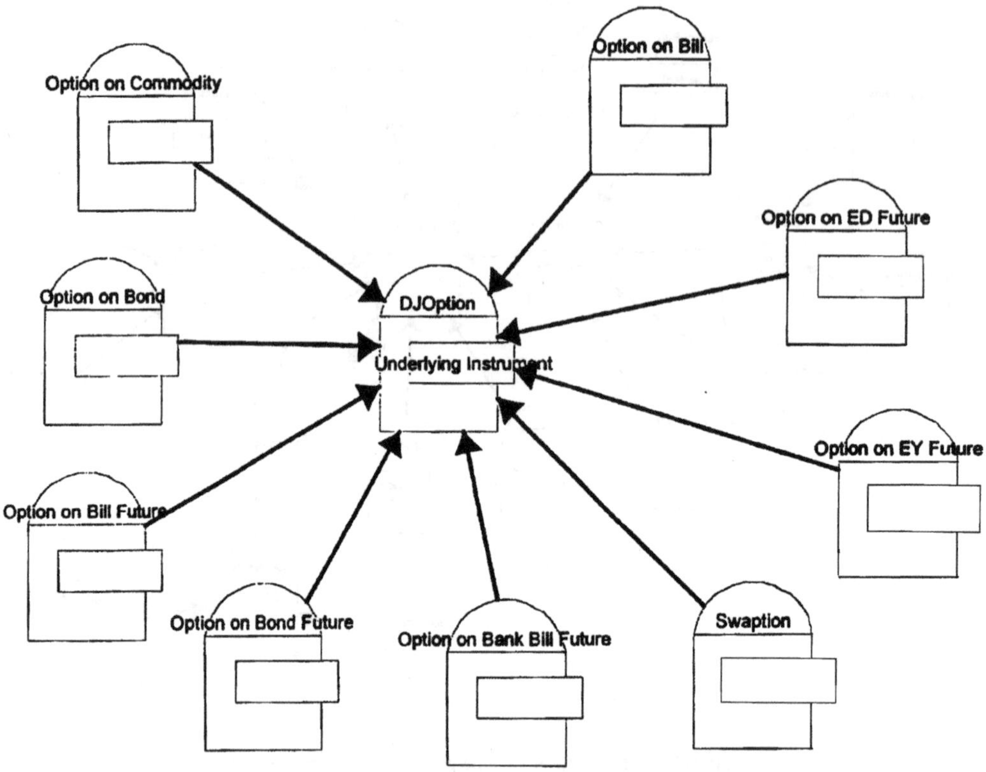

FIGURE 43.7 TELAN — Fine granular Option subsystem.

system is conceived of as a dynamic collection of objects, not put away on disk but always active ...." This, of course, is not true of practical commercial strength software systems. There is always an issue of storing data, and usually those data are kept in relational systems, as discussed earlier.

Haythorn (1994), in discussing the difference between an object-based and an object-oriented system, has given an excellent example of how the functionality of a system in an object-oriented system can be "decomposed" such that the data of the system are stored separately from the rest of the system. Such a separation can be achieved by creating an abstract data type which is clearly responsible for only the data storage aspect of the system, and whose implementation can be changed without affecting the rest of the system. Separating a class into two classes, and making one of them responsible for storage and retrieval of data, is essentially a decision of decomposing the functionality of a system into smaller sized (or separate) classes. This is precisely a granularity decision. These types of granularity decisions have been taken in the development of TELAN and an example of such a design is shown in Figure 43.8.

Note how the DJInstrument class, which is the higher level abstract class, deals with the DJResults class in order to perform the calculations which would produce the results required for pricing an instrument. As far as the functionality is concerned, DJInstrument could itself have handled the storage of data, as well as the calculations performed by DJResults. However, due to the granularity decision, the functionality was "split," leaving the DJResults class completely buffered from the database and the related storage issues, which are being handled by DJInstrument.

43.2.9 Reuse in TELAN's Views

We discussed earlier the large scale reuse occurring in TELAN's subsystems. One of the subsystems is the GUI subsystem which provides the various "views" of TELAN. Thus, at the heart of the TELAN

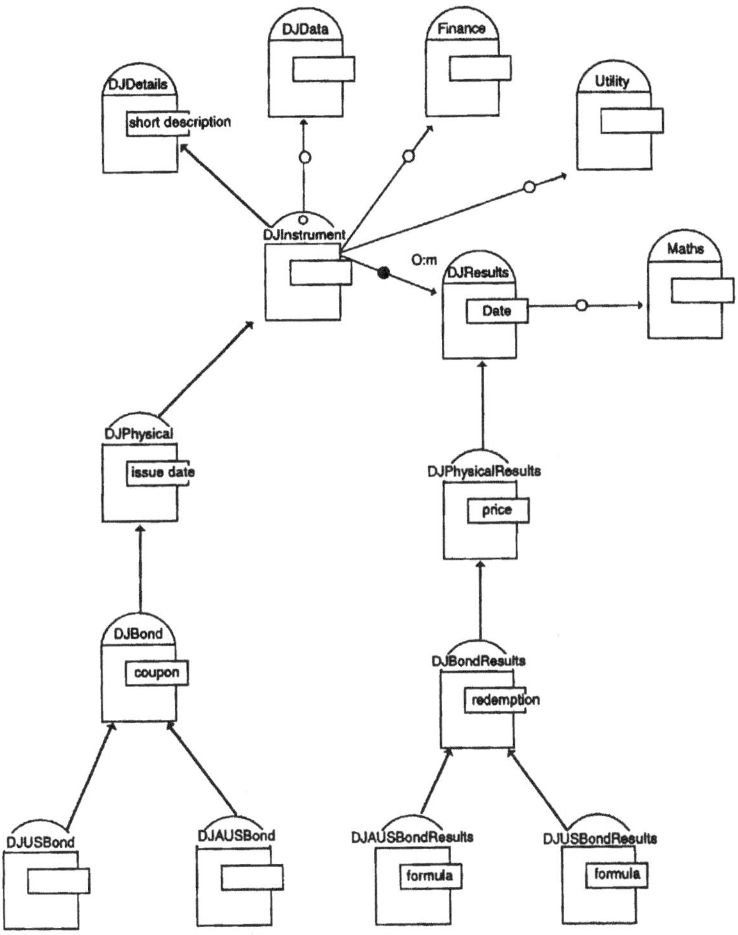

FIGURE 43.8 A fine granular design that separates data from calculations.

presentation is the view, which is essentially a table that has been reused from the earlier COPS development.

Figure 43.9 shows the main view of the TELAN system. It displays details of instruments, details of pricing, sensitivity, etc. The values are calculated based on the data entered by the user and/or selected from the online feed. Many views of the TELAN system are similar to views in other systems developed by ADG. This similar "look and feel" is an additional selling point for the products, and has been a result of derivation from the same set of reusable GUI classes provided by the Graphics Object Library shown in the reusable architecture of Figure 43.4.

Apart from the technical advantage of reusing code, this reuse also provided opportunity for the marketing and sales staff to promote the ease of use (and ease of learning) of the system. A financial market's client that has already used one of our earlier products would be familiar with the interface, and therefore would be able to start using TELAN straight away. Quality is also enhanced, as the views in the earlier products had already undergone rigorous testing, making it unnecessary to retest the reused classes for TELAN. Instead, the effort of testing and quality assurance was concentrated on the modified or inherited classes and testing their integration.

The discussion up to this point has focused on object-oriented design issues within the OPEN methodological framework, in the development of products by ADG. It has shown the advantages of

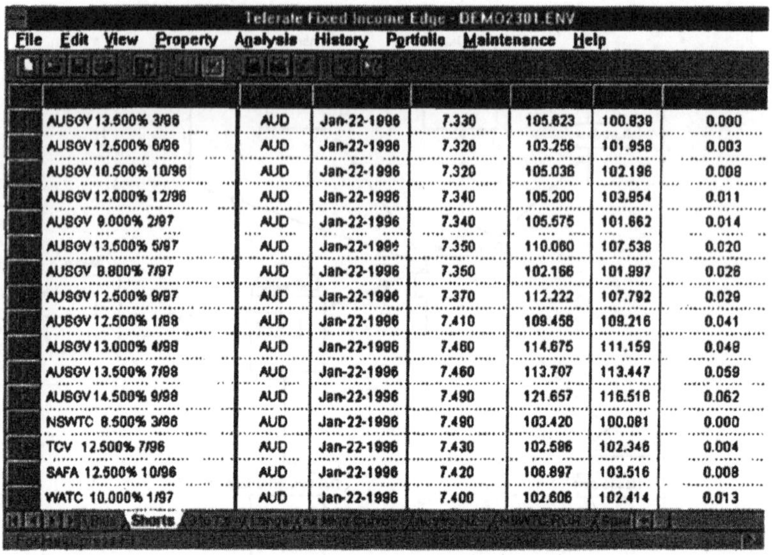

FIGURE 43.9 TELAN Normal View.

reuse, especially in the context of finer granularity as applied to the problems of designing and producing financial markets software. Additional advantages of finer granularity were also shown in separating calculations from data. The rest of this chapter deals with issues related to project estimation based on metrics, and how they were used to arrive at the productivity factor for ADG, and thereby provide correct estimates for the subsequent project.

43.3 Metrics Matters

The development described in this case study used the fine granular designs coupled with prudent management, in order to succeed. Metrics played a crucial role in managing this development. As Lorenz and Kidd (1994) correctly state, "if we are to estimate and manage our efforts, we must measure our progress effectively." This is precisely what we did in the development of our financial market's enterprise.

43.3.1 Data from Earlier Development Efforts

In order to arrive at the productivity factor for the group, data from the earlier COPS development turned out to be of immense value. In order to estimate the size of COPS, the ADG team considered multiple issues related to object-oriented metrics. Lines of Code (LOC) was not considered good enough for the reasons given by Jacobson et al. (1992) and Lorenz and Kidd (1994). These reasons include incorrect measurement of reused code, no weighting for complexity of code, no consideration of language complexity (or ease), etc. Due to these reasons it was decided by the team to use the metrics proposed by Henderson-Sellers and Edwards (1994) to measure the systems. The earlier COPS product was measured as shown in Figure 43.10.

Note that the weighting factors W_A (= 1) and W_M (= 10) were derived empirically. While the design and coding effort for the methods was placed at 10 times the effort required of an attribute, this was arrived at purely by the previous experience of the managers. There was no attempt made to justify these numbers in greater detail, and there was no need to do so either. If the weighting factors are kept the same, then the results over a number of projects are not affected. It is only when cross-domain, cross-language comparisons are required that these weighting factors assume importance. That, however, is a topic requiring further research, and it is outside the scope of the current discussion.

How "big" is COPS ?

(Size estimate based on above Metrics)

Weighting Factors:

$W_A = 1$, $W_M = 10$

(Factors kept Constant over projects)

	Attributes	*Methods*
class 1	12	9
class 2	10	8
....		
class 220		
	------------	------------
Totals =	2,266	4,576

Total Size *S* of system = 48,026

Average Size of a Class = 218.3

Total Usecases (Scenarios) = 10

FIGURE 43.10 Measuring size of COPS. (From Unhelkar and Mamdapur, 1995b).

The classes were all listed in an Excel spreadsheet, and the attributes and methods of all the classes were totaled to provide total attributes as 2266 and the total methods as 4576. Since at the time of measuring the total number of classes were 220, this provided the total size of the system as 48,026 and the average size of a class as 218.3, as shown in Figure 43.10. The total number of use cases for this system was 10.

43.3.2 Productivity Factor of ADG

The productivity factor for ADG was calculated based on the COPS data gathered over a period of approximately 10 months. Since the total person-months used in development of COPS was 55 (this was arrived at by using a very simple log, no time sheets were maintained as it would have otherwise affected the spirit of the development, cf. DeMarco and Lister's (1987) study on improved productivity with *no* estimation) and the size of COPS, as shown in Figure 43.10 was 480 units, it gave ADG a productivity of 8.73 average S-units* per person-month, as summarized below:

- Size of COPS = 480 S-units (we dropped two zeros for convenience)
- Person-Months spent on development = 55 (simple personal log, no timesheets)
- Average S-Units per Person-Month = 8.73

These figures are valid only when the development environment is similar, with the technical and managerial skills not changing rapidly over time. The development environment in our case was indeed similar (e.g., the language or the development methodology had not changed) and so were the skill sets

* S-Unit stands for Size Units. There is no industry accepted name for this size metric. Since it is used only for comparison purposes, and since it is not LOC, we have decided to call it S-Unit. This name, of course, is subject to change depending on industry acceptance and usage of this metric.

of the programmers involved in this development. These are the caveats to be considered by any development team that plans to use this metrics.

43.3.3 TELAN Project Estimations

When the requirements for the new TELAN system were drafted, they were put together in the MeNtOR documentation (see Chapter 42) which would hold the Scenarios for the system. These Scenarios (including the business and technical scenarios) totaled 25. An *estimate* of the total number of classes that TELAN will have was made based on these Scenarios as well as technical and commercial judgment. The total classes required were estimated at 550. This led to the estimate of the size of the new system, and thereby the person-month required, as summarized below (Unhelkar and Mamdapur, 1995b):

- Total Use Cases/Scenarios describing the functionality of the system = 25
- Total *estimate* of Classes = average class/scenario (22) × total scenarios (25) = 550
- Number of Classes reused from earlier COPS project = 100
- New Classes to be Coded = 450

  Need to Convert this to S-Units and Apply the Productivity Factor
- $W_A = 1$; $W_M = 10$
- Average Attributes/Class = 10.2
- Average Methods/Class = 20.8
- Total Number of Classes N = 450
- Entering the Above values in the Equation:

$$S = \sum_{i=1}^{N=450} S_i = \sum_{i=1}^{N} \left(AW_A + MW_M\right)_i = \left(10.2 \text{ x}1 + 20.8 \text{x } 10\right) \text{x} 450 = 98235$$

- Person-Months Required = 982.35/8.73 = 112.5 or 9.38 person-years

These translated into approximately nine programmers for a year. The first major release of TELAN development utilized 10 programmers working for approximately 1 year. Thus, surprisingly, the details of our estimate came out correct, providing valuable information in turn about the productivity of the group and guidelines in controlling future development.

43.4 Conclusions

Considering the way the financial markets are influenced by software, there appears to be an open-ended development opportunity in this field. Unlike the accounting or payroll software, wherein all the basic principles have been "bedded" down, and there is hardly any window for improving the process, in "financial markets" software the analytical development can only attempt to match the imagination of the traders and brokers within the markets.

However, while the risk management applications continue to remain complex, it is not always that such complexity has paid off. At times, these systems have resulted into inordinate losses to the traders (Irving, 1996) and therefore they have reverted back to the simpler risk options. The software systems, which provide for the needs of such traders, have to also respond accordingly. This is made possible through the use of the flexible object-oriented approach discussed in this case study. The TELAN risk management application discussed here (due to its object-oriented nature) has many of the advantages of an object-oriented design. These advantages include reusability, scalability, and quality, to name but a few. Granularity of object-oriented designs, as applied in this product development, has also produced substantial results in terms of reusability and improved productivity. As this is being written, TELAN continues to expand with more and more analytical applications being added to it in order to satisfy the demands of the users for risk management.

Acknowledgments

This is contribution number 97/10 of the Centre for Object Technology, Applications and Research (COTAR), Australia. Thanks to Professor Brian Henderson-Sellers (Swinburne University, Melbourne), Dr. Julian Edwards (OO P/L, Sydney), and Mr. Andrew Powell (Dow Jones, Sydney) for constructive comments and criticisms.

References

Burns, A. 1997. Bridging the canyon, an interview with James Martin. In *The Information Age*, pp. 20-23. The official publication of The Australian Computer Society, August.

Cooper, G. 1996. J.P. Morgan plans software sales, *Risk Mag.*, Vol. 9, No. 3, March, pp. 7.

Davidson, C. 1994. Objects of debate, *Risk Mag.*, Vol. 7, No. 6, June.

DeMarco, T. and Lister, T. 1987. *Peopleware: Productive Projects and Teams.* Dorset House Publishing Company, New York.

Duffy, M. 1993. Object lesson, *Risk Mag.*, Vol. 6, No. 9, Sept., pp. 126-130.

Haythorn, W. 1994. What is object-oriented design?, *J. Object-Oriented Prog.*, Vol. 7, No. 1, Mar-April, pp. 67-76.

Henderson-Sellers, B. and Edwards, J.M. 1994. *Book Two of Object-Oriented Knowledge: The Working Object.* Prentice-Hall, Englewood Cliffs, NJ, (pp. 419, granularity of documentation; pp. 428, the granularity at which reuse is operated ranges across classes, frameworks, and subsystems).

Irving, R. 1996. The ghosts of 1994, *Risk Mag.*, Vol. 9, No. 3, March, pp. 19-22.

Jacobson, I., Christerson, M., Jonsson, P. and Overgaard, G., *Object-Oriented Software Engineering: A Use Case Driven Approach.* Addison-Wesley, Reading, MA.

Lorenz, M. and Kidd, J. 1994. *Object-Oriented Software Metrics.* Prentice-Hall, Englewood Cliffs, NJ.

Morgan, J.P. 1995. *RiskMetrics™ — Technical Document,* Third Edition. Morgan Guaranty Trust Company, Global Research, 26 May 1996; Publicly available by e-mailing *guldimann_t@jpmorgan.com.*

Ritchken, P. 1996. *Derivative Markets: Theory, Strategy, and Applications.* HarperCollins, New York.

Shimko, D. 1996. When to use exotic derivatives, *The Handbook of Exotic Options,* p. 100. I. Nelken, ed.

Unhelkar, B. 1995a. The MOSES experience: A case study, printed in *Object Mag.*, SIGS New York, Vol. 5, No. 3, June, pp. 50-55.

Unhelkar, B. 1995b. Development of telerate currency options using MOSES: A case study (tutorial), Presented at *OOPSLA'95 Conference,* Tutorial No 51, Merging OOAD Methodologies: COMMA project and its first results. Austin, TX, 15-19 October.

Unhelkar, B. 1995c. Objects please financial developers, Interview in *Computerworld,* by Keith Power, 6 October, Vol. 18, No. 14, pp. 1, 38.

Unhelkar, B. 1996a. Using object technology for strategic modeling and business process re-engineering. In *Proc. Object'96 by AIC Conf.*, Sydney, 8-10 May.

Unhelkar, B. 1996b. Effect of object-oriented technology on modeling an enterprise. In *Proc. Business Intelligence by AIC Conf.*, Sydney, 29-30 April.

Unhelkar, B. 1997. Effect of granularity of object-oriented designs on modelling an enterprise and its application to financial risk management, Ph.D. Thesis, University of Technology, Sydney; *Note:* Although these ideas were presented at numerous conferences, they were finally put together in this thesis.

Unhelkar, B. and Lindblom, S. 1995. Software in derivatives-based risk management, *Asia Risk Manager, J. Asian Treasury Risk Management,* Hong Kong, May, pp. 16-17.

Unhelkar, B. and Mamdapur, G. 1995a. Practical aspects of using a methodology: A road map approach, ***ROAD,*** Vol. 2, No. 2, July-August, pp. 34-36, 54.

Unhelkar, B. and Mamdapur, G. 1995b. Role of OO metrics in managing the development of a financial markets analytical product: A case study, In *Proc. ACOSM'95 Second Australian Conf. on Software Metrics,* Sydney, Australia, Jeffery, R., Ed., pp. 168-177. Australian Software Metrics Association, 22-24 November.

44

Transitioning Large Enterprises to Object Technology

Robert Marcus
AMS Center for Advanced Technologies

44.1 Introduction

The past five years have witnessed the most rapid software technology changes since the advent of computers. The growth of the Internet and Web is enabling global communication and exchange of data at a level that would not have seemed possible in 1980. In response to these developments, there has been an accelerated growth in network bandwidth and the deployment of online computers.

This new technology infrastructure is causing many large organizations to consider dramatic restructuring of their business processes and underlying computing architectures. These transformations are often necessary to maintain competitive advantage or to ensure long-range survival. Another important driver of change is the concern about the viability of some existing systems due to Year 2000 problems and the rising costs of maintenance.

Many different types of technology are playing a role in the transition process. Some examples of new software technology that are not directly related to object technology include application packages (e.g., SAP), groupware (e.g., Lotus Notes), the Web, data warehouses, and middleware.

However, object technology is often considered the key driver for architectural changes because it cuts across so many aspects of software development and integration. In addition, it is a relatively mature technology with a range of tools, languages, methodologies, and experienced technologists available.

Object technology has been gradually evolving for over 20 years. Similar to many new technologies, it started slowly and then gathered increasing momentum as more developers became aware of its

0-8493-3135-8/99/$0.00+$.50

potential. The technology has also suffered through the usual hyperbole over its capabilities. Currently most organizations are convinced of the value of object technology but have learned that it requires disciplined planning to achieve the maximum benefit.

In this chapter, I will discuss the issues involved in the transition of large enterprises to object technology. I will begin with an overview of current large enterprise computing environments, the future vision of improved processes, and the problems that must be overcome. I will compare and contrast several strategies for addressing these problems. The specialization of the strategies to object technology will be described in detail with a strong focus on methods of enhancing reuse. Finally, I will present a summary of strategy planning, lessons learned, pitfalls to be avoided, and conclusions based on extensive industrial experience.

44.2 Overview of Enterprise Environments

44.2.1 Current Enterprise Architectures, Transitions, and Goals

Large enterprise computing environments are usually a mixture of many different platforms, databases, and applications. These systems have usually developed over the course of many years without centralized planning. Typically applications were based on the needs and preferences of a particular functional area resulting in a set of incompatible "stove pipes." Many older applications tightly integrate user interface, business logic, and database access layers into a monolithic package. Often newer applications will also merge different layers in order to enable higher performance and/or rapid development.

The lack of common standards for data representation and naming has created a major problem for cross-functional processes in the enterprise. The extraction and loading of data is further complicated by the bundling of data access code with business logic and user interfaces. In order to share data between applications it has often been necessary to create complicated data transformation programs that are difficult to maintain. In other cases, error-prone manual processes are used for the movement of data.

In many large enterprises, the majority of the computing software budget has gone into time-consuming maintenance activities which add limited value but are necessary for business or technical reasons. The "Year 2000" crunch is the most visible example of this problem. New projects are often very large multiyear efforts based on a step-by-step "Waterfall" model. Typically these steps include analysis, design, development, testing, deployment, and maintenance. Unfortunately, as the pace of business and technology changes increases, this long software cycle has not been adequate to meet enterprise needs.

44.2.2 Transitions

The combination of costly legacy systems maintenance and slow new systems development has led many organizations to consider adopting new processes for software engineering. The desire for rapid change has sometimes resulted in major disasters when inadequate technologies have been adopted as "silver bullets" for software problems. Experience has shown that transitions in large organizations must be done carefully based on detailed analysis and evaluation of alternative approaches. It is very important to view the transition as an incremental process that can be viewed at various levels.

The lowest level is the underlying technologies, which will be the basis of the change. Technologists will often get very excited about the new capabilities of software such as the World Wide Web, Java, or object databases. In many cases, it is possible to build prototypes or smaller applications very quickly with the new technologies. However, in enterprise computing environments it is not sufficient for software to work well in isolated applications.

To succeed in the long run, it is necessary for new technology to work well at a higher architectural level. Software components must be able to interoperate with other systems in the enterprise. There should be well-defined interfaces for accessing functionality and data. Any new applications that use the new technology must be maintainable, manageable, and scalable. If legacy systems are being replaced it is necessary to plan carefully for a smooth transition. In particular, the issues of data extraction and movement can cause serious problems. Even if new software technology can be integrated into the enterprise architecture, it is not guaranteed to provide value at the business level.

To gain the full benefit of technology transitions, it is necessary to change the business processes to take maximum advantage of the new capabilities. In particular, the planned improvements in business processes should be major drivers in the technology transition. If there is limited business value associated with introducing a new technology or architecture, then it should probably be given low priority when resources are constrained. One of the main goals of object technology is to create software systems that can support rapid business process changes. Software development could also be considered a business process when evaluating the potential benefits of object technology.

The ultimate level where many transitions succeed or fail is the cultural changes that are required when introducing major new technologies. This can be especially true in software development when the pace of change is increasing rapidly. In many organizations, there is a great deal of tension between developers using older technologies and proponents of the newest software techniques. It is critical to handle these cultural issues in large enterprise because developers from many different backgrounds must work together to ensure the success of major transitions.

44.2.3 Goals for the Future

There is a growing industry consensus on many of the high level goals for future software development processes and architectures. The basic structures that many technologists believe can provide the context for higher productivity are frameworks. For examples see Lewis, 1995. Frameworks are skeletons of application functionality based on generic designs. A good framework should allow easy customization and the ability to embed new components for extended capabilities. There are several frameworks that are currently available for basic technology such as user interfaces and data access. Object technology has played a key role in many of these frameworks and component architectures.

One of the main advantages of frameworks is the ability to provide standards interfaces and communication between components. Often a framework will also include a scripting language to allow developers to easily customize, embed, and interface components. A good framework should also provide a set of services. These services should handle requirements such as security and component management for the application developer. Enterprise level frameworks should also support components for accessing legacy systems and data.

The key next step for increasing productivity is the development of domain specific frameworks. These frameworks include domain knowledge and higher level business objects in the application skeleton. They can also provide standard representations and formats for domain data. These capabilities will allow business developers to quickly create families of applications by customization of a basic package. In the next few years there will be many domain frameworks developed inside enterprises and by external vendors.

The use of frameworks, object technology, and new software development tools is enabling a fundamental change in the software development process. Many organizations are striving to move away from the sequential waterfall model to an iterative process with short-term demonstrable deliverables. This change will have several benefits. The shorter cycle time will reduce the chances of major requirement changes in the middle of the project. It will also provide a focus and measurable progress metric to the development effort.

To achieve the goal of rapid iterative lifecycle, several organizations are exploring organizational changes in their software development groups. A common strategy is to divide developers into component builders and component assemblers. The component builders will typically use a high performance advanced object-oriented language such as C++. The assemblers will take a new application by customizing components within a framework and use a scripting language to provide connections and interfaces between components.

The most difficult goal of the transition is to achieve frameworks for cross-functional process in large enterprises. This requires that data, interface, and communication standards be instituted across divergent organizations. In general, this level of integration can supply very high productivity but will be very difficult to achieve for technical and cultural reasons. It will take many years of controlled planned effort to achieve this goal. In the following sections, I will discuss some of the general and object technology specific strategies that can help in the migration to enterprise frameworks.

44.3 General Strategies

There are several general strategies that have been used by large organizations for introducing new technologies. In practice, these strategies are often combined and modified over time but are useful for characterizing organizational structures. In this section I will describe four basic approaches: (1) Laissez Faire, (2) Swat Team, (3) Centralized, and (4) Coordinated.

The "Laissez Faire" strategy is to allow a new technology to be introduced by independent groups and individuals based on local needs and interests. Centralized support is often limited to supplying training and informational resources. This approach is often used in the early stages of an emerging technology.

The "Swat Team" approach assumes that a group of technology experts have been assembled internally or brought in as consultants. This group is available to provide support and mentoring to projects when requested. In some cases, the support group will also write software components that can be made available to projects for possible reuse. In general, the Swat Team will interact with projects on a case-by-case basis and not have a process for ensuring cross-project communication. This approach is often employed when a new technology becomes increasingly important to the organization.

The "Centralized" approach requires the establishment of a group that will be responsible for driving the new technology into the organization. This group will set standards and choose products that must be followed by all projects. In some cases, project schedules and deliverables will also be under centralized control. Elements of this approach are used when a technology is perceived as a critical component of future enterprise architectures.

The "Coordinated" approach is a combination of the vertical support provided by the Swat Teams and the horizontal perspective of the Centralized strategy. To achieve the maximum benefit, the Coordination group must work closely with projects as part of the enterprise's software development process. The Coordination group can supply the project with expertise and reusable components. Members of the Coordination group should work with the projects to refine frameworks and develop future reusable components (Table 44.1).

44.4 Specialization to Object Technology Transitions

In this section, the general strategies for technology transitions will be specialized to the domain of object technology. Individual components of object technology can be handled by different approaches. For more extensive transformations, I will present a cross-strategy approach based on a transition lifecycle.

44.4.1 Laissez Faire

In most large organizations, the initial encounters with object technology are driven by individual or small groups. Early adopters of new technology will often bring in an object language or tool for evaluation. If the tool or language increases productivity, it will often be used in small projects or proof-of-concepts demonstrations. Over time more groups will learn about the new technology and start new pockets of usage. This is a relatively low risk approach for departmental applications. Many organizations began object technology deployment using this approach with Smalltalk in the early 1990s.

TABLE 44.1 General Strategies for Introducing New Technologies

Strategies	Description	Advantages and Benefits	Disadvantage and Costs	Risks
Laissez Faire	Local initiative; informal reuse among projects; vertical approach	Low cost, low risk; easy way to explore the technology	No structure, duplicated efforts; training and tool purchase are main cost	Can produce opposing camps of technologists and methodologists
Swat Team	Central team of providing support and software; available on request; vertical and horizontal separated	Improves productivity with new technology; helps new projects get started; reduces duplication of effort	Limited focus on sharing between projects; requires training and paying for upgraded skills of Swat Team	Lack of coordinated effort across projects; limited use of Swat team by projects, often only when necessary
Centralized	Centralized group controlling standards and/or projects; horizontal approach	Consistency across the enterprise; coherent strategy; costs can be reduced by standards	Often too rigid; limited local initiative can produce resistance from projects	Potential for major mistakes due to wrong centralized decision
Coordinated	Team of technology and reuse experts some of whom are located with specific projects; part of the project process; vertical and horizontal simultaneously approach	Supports projects while encouraging reuse; can provide extensive reuse due to cooperation between coordinators and project staff	Requires more extensive planning to succeed; can be more costly in terms of resources and skills required; not necessary when the technology does not have to satisfy any project specific requirements	Requires organizational restructuring; coordinators must be technically knowledgeable but also able to work well with project and domain experts

Another facet of object technology that won early support was object-oriented analysis and design. Many methodologists and system analysts became convinced that object modeling was superior to earlier structured approaches. Often projects would use object analysis and design even when the implementation language and database were non-object-oriented. This approach required additional training but seemed to increase project quality without requiring extensive software purchases. There were computer-aided software engineering (CASE) tools developed to support various methodologies, but in general they were not essential for applying object techniques.

In many organizations, the downside of the Laissez Faire strategy became apparent as the use of object technology spread. Often opposing camps would develop centered around particular tools, languages, or methodologies. Many new projects expended a great deal of effort in battles between advocates of alternate technologies. Training and purchase costs escalated as the number of tools proliferated. This is the point where organizations typically began to evaluate alternate strategies.

With all of its faults, Laissez Faire strategies are still appropriate for organizations that are still at the earliest stage of introducing object technology. It can also be used for initial evaluation of leading edge object tools and software. There should be some well-defined process for deploying technology that proves successful in these early tests.

44.4.2 Swat Team

As a new object technology spreads through a large organization, it usually becomes necessary to have a group of experienced people (Swat Team) that can serve as a resource to new users. This group can provide informational, mentoring, support, and trouble-shooting services to many projects. The Swat Team often employs external consultants and contractors. In a more advanced approach, this expert team can also attempt to supply components and frameworks for project reuse. Some large organizations have created Object Technology Centers or Labs to provide a centralized location for object expertise.

The Swat Team can play a critical role in supporting the introduction and efficient use of new object technology especially on crucial pilot projects. Frequently the introduction of an object methodology requires initial training and support by an experienced practitioner. The use of expert mentors in object languages such as Smalltalk, C++, or Java is also a common practice. In more advanced computing environments, the growing use of distributed object systems based on the Object Management Group or Microsoft architectures is driving the creation of new Swat Teams. There are some niche areas such as object databases or legacy system wrappers where experts can also provide valuable support to individual projects.

The most sophisticated role for a centralized group of experts is the creation of reusable components and frameworks. Ideally projects would take the reusable output of the Swat Team and use it as a foundation for creating new applications. This type of approach has achieved success on Microsoft Windows desktops where the Component Object Model (COM) has provided a framework for the assembling of applications using reusable controls.

However, the construction of reusable frameworks and components has not been as easy to achieve in the business or higher level application domain. This is partially due to the wide divergence in requirements, practices, and environments within large enterprises. To avoid this problem, many organizations have chosen to sacrifice business process flexibility by installing monolithic application packages such as SAP. In general, it has been difficult for centralized groups within large organizations to independently produce and deploy reusable object-oriented software into projects.

44.4.3 Centralized

In order to overcome the problems caused by excessive diversity, many large enterprises have set up central groups with the responsibility of mandating standards in object technology and other areas. This group is also frequently asked to create enterprise object deployment guidelines. To foster reuse, software and informational repositories are often created and administered centrally.

The Centralized approach has produced efficiencies by avoiding unnecessary variations in areas such as tools, languages, and databases. It is essential when deploying major infrastructure components such as distributed object systems or system management. The Centralized staff must be knowledgeable about industry trends and often uses the services of external analysts, consultants, and standards groups.

In contrast to the Swat Team, the Centralized group does not need detailed technical expertise and generally will not provide support to specific projects. The focus of the group is on the horizontal aspects of object technology deployment. To be successful the group must add value to the overall organization without unnecessarily constraining local flexibility.

There are two problems that seem to occur with the Centralized approach. The first is an attempt to be overly ambitious in setting global directions. This results in statements of direction based on technology that is not mature enough to handle project requirements. The Open Software Foundation's Distributed Computing Environment and X-Windows are examples of technologies that were often proclaimed to be standards but never achieved widespread acceptance. In object technology, attempts to develop standard Enterprise Object Models and business class libraries have had limited success.

The second problem for centralized direction is the premature choice of standards in parts of object technology where there is a great deal of contention. This often can create a negative response on the part of projects which feel that their productivity or freedom is being reduced unnecessarily.

Some common areas where this conflict occurs are in the choice of CASE or user interface tools. The choice of a single object language has proven particularly controversial since language enhancements and new languages are constantly appearing. It is critical that the Centralized group understand and appreciate the concerns of application projects.

44.4.4 Coordination

The goal of the Coordination strategy is to combine the horizontal approach of the Centralized approach with the vertical support provided by the Swat Team. A Coordination organization must contain technical experts in object technology who can provide value to application projects. These experts should be responsible for ensuring that projects practice reuse whenever possible. In addition, these experts should understand the problem domain in enough detail so that they can leverage current project work for future efforts in similar domains. It is important that a process for close continuing cooperation be set up between projects and the Coordination group. For example, some organizations have practiced co-location or even rotation of staff as a way of achieving this goal.

The Coordination group can also include individuals who are focused on purely horizontal aspects of the transition to object technology, for example, the deployment of common services in areas such as security, data modeling and integration, and legacy system interfaces. Their work should be done in close consultation with the members of the group who have been working with application projects. This helps to ensure that enterprise standards and directions are realistic and will improve overall productivity.

The Coordination approach has achieved some very successful results in the area of developing reusable object frameworks for specific application domains. Several organizations have found that it requires at least three projects before a team of developers working together can produce a truly robust reusable domain framework. Once this goal is realized the productivity improvements on future projects are often dramatic. However, it should be noted that there are still many open questions about the proper scope of frameworks and interfacing frameworks across domains.

The Coordination strategy requires more extensive planning and resources than the other approaches. It is not necessary if object technology is expected to play a relatively minor role in future enterprise-computing architectures. Niche object technologies that will be used by a small group of projects may be better handled by a less costly strategy.

44.4.5 Combined Strategies

In most enterprises, a combination of the basic strategies will be used depending on the maturity of specific technologies and enterprise development groups. There is even a strategy lifecycle that seems to occur frequently in the deployment of new technologies.

The initial phase is marked by a Laissez Faire approach as the technology undergoes initial evaluation. Early evaluators develop expertise and become the nucleus of an informal Swat Team for supporting new users. If the technology is making a significant impact, this Swat Team is usually incorporated into official groups. If the new technology is being deployed across the enterprise or there are competing alternatives, a Centralized group is established or expanded to provide guidance and guidelines for the new technology. Finally if significant cooperation among diverse groups is required to maximize the benefits of the new technology, a Coordination team is sometimes established. In general, different parts of object technology can be in any of the above phases at a given time.

44.5 Reuse and Specific Object Technologies

44.5.1 Reuse Strategies

Reuse is often considered one of the main benefits of the transition to object technology by providing faster development, better quality, and reduced maintenance. For example, see B. Meyer, 1994. Table 44.2 describes the typical impact of the individual strategies on reuse.

TABLE 44.2 Impact of Individual Strategies on Reuse

Strategies	Impact
Laissez faire	Limited reuse based on individual initiatives
Swat team	A library of generic reusable components can be built and distributed by the Swat Team; projects will usually not produce reusable domain components or frameworks without incentives
Centralized	Use of specific class libraries and standards can be mandated; projects will often resist centralized control
Coordinated	Coordinators should be a part of the project team; they should be responsible for introducing reusable components and working within the project toward future reuse at the framework and component levels

44.5.2 Basic Technology

44.5.2.1 Language Class Libraries

Class libraries are the most common level of reuse in object technology. The extent of reuse usually depends on the language and the focus of the libraries. In particular, user interfaces, collections, and object wrappers of existing systems have been areas where class libraries have been very successful.

Among languages, Smalltalk implementations have typically supplied a large number of reusable class libraries which has greatly increased developer productivity. C++ has not been as successful as a language for implementing class libraries. Some of the C++ language features such as multiple inheritance, explicit memory management, and compiler dependencies have made class libraries difficult to use and maintain. Initially Java seems to have avoided the problems of C++ and will be capable of supporting reusable class libraries to the same degree as Smalltalk.

However, class libraries in all object-oriented languages seem to be prone to the "fragile base class problem" due to the use of inheritance. This problem results when developers extend the capabilities of an existing class library by subclassing. Changes made to base classes in the next version of the library will often produce errors in the new derived classes. To overcome this problem, it is often necessary to distribute the source code for class libraries.

44.5.2.2 Components

In object technology, components are collections of objects that have well-defined properties and interfaces, and can be embedded into frameworks or containers. Increasingly components are being employed as the basic unit of reuse. The properties and interfaces allow manipulation of underlying capabilities. The larger granularity of components compared to individual classes seems to be easier to reuse. The enhancement of functionality by composing or aggregating components avoids the fragile base class problems of inheritance.

In the marketplace, the reuse of desktop components based on Microsoft's COM has been very successful. There are a large number of vendors producing and selling COM components. Components for the Java language called JavaBeans have been defined by Sun's Javasoft group. It appears likely that JavaBeans will also become a widespread way of disseminating reusable components.

44.5.2.3 Distributed Objects

The Object Management Group (OMG) has produced an Interface Definition Language (IDL) that can be used to specify interfaces to reusable objects and services. Theoretically this could provide a means of creating classes and services that could be reused by many applications in a distributed environment. In practice, the limited use of the OMG's object request broker has meant that the services and classes are usually confined to a single project or application.

The use of distributed components is still in an early phase. Microsoft has developed a Distributed Component Object Model (DCOM) which will be integrated with the Microsoft Transaction Server (MTS) on Windows NT. Javasoft is developing a similar infrastructure based on Java Remote Method Invocation (RMI), Enterprise JavaBeans, and a Java server "Beanstalk." With these technologies, it is possible that the component approach will repeat its desktop success on the network.

44.5.2.4 Object Databases

Object databases have been used successfully to provide persistence support for object-oriented applications. The initial implementations of object databases used proprietary data models that often were tightly linked to specific languages and applications. The Object Data Management Group (ODMG) was formed to provide standards such an Object Query Language (OQL) across databases. However, in general, there has not been much reuse across applications even when the same object database is used.

44.5.3 Architecture

44.5.3.1 Java

The Java program language has the potential for providing extensive new dimensions of reuse due to its portability and ability to support dynamic loading of mobile code. At present, many reusable Java classes have been developed and included in the Java Development Kit. Java wrapper interfaces to back-end resources such as relational databases, middleware and legacy applications have been defined. Distributed Java communication using the Web and RMI permits access to Java interfaces and mobile code. The most critical question for the future of reuse is whether platform-specific versions of Java will achieve success due to the desire by developers to gain greater performance. For example, a Java library optimized for Microsoft Windows might have a great deal of appeal even if it constrained the possibilities for more general reuse.

44.5.3.2 Adaptability

Several years ago when technology and business requirements were not changing so rapidly, it was possible to sustain a longer software development cycle. Due to resource limitation and the difficulty of modifying legacy systems, it was very important to design a system carefully to guarantee functionality and performance. The time to add new functionality to existing systems was considered a problem but not a fatal flaw.

In today's competitive business environment with rapidly changing technology components, it is essential to architect systems to be flexible and adaptable. Object technology was promoted as a solution to this problem. In practice, it has been found that some type of framework for linking objects and components is necessary for adaptability.

44.5.3.3 Frameworks

Frameworks provide a skeleton that allows components to be added and customized to produce applications. There are several ways that frameworks can be utilized by developers. A "white box" framework permits visibility and modification of its internal structure. In contrast, a "black box" allows customization only through strictly defined interfaces.

The conventional wisdom is that it takes developers several iterations to develop a robust application-area framework. In general, early versions of a framework used a white box approach and migrated to a more black box implementation as the domain become better understood.

44.5.3.4 Patterns

Patterns are an attempt to capture design knowledge in a structured format. The basic idea was invented by Robert Alexander for the domain of architecture and has been embraced by many object-oriented designers and developers. Patterns have been used as a method for capturing the design of an existing framework. Recently there has been a move toward using patterns as a tool in the initial design of the frameworks.

44.5.4 Software Development Process

44.5.4.1 Organizational Change

The use of frameworks and components is causing some organizations to separate developers into multiple categories. One common approach is to have a small skilled group responsible for framework and component development. A larger less experienced set of developers assemble applications by composing components within the framework. Typically the framework builders will use a powerful object-oriented language while the application programmers will use a scripting or 4GL language.

44.5.4.2 Process Change

The traditional analysis and design approach for software systems has been based on modeling application domains independently of previous existing models. When a framework is used, many of the generic classes, components, and designs in the domain are already captured. It is necessary to use an incremental approach focused on the specific features of the new application.

It is critical that software development processes be changed to support incremental development based on extensive reuse. In particular, developers should be rewarded on the basis of delivering functionality quickly using existing components, rather than for producing extensive new code over longer periods of time.

44.5.4.3 Reuse Repository

A repository is often used by application development environment as a way of storing and retrieving reusable components and classes. Many proprietary repositories have been created for specific tools and there have been attempts to provide standards for interchange between repositories. This is still an area requiring further research.

44.6 Planning, Lessons Learned, and Pitfalls

A global plan for the introduction of object technology into a large organization should use a multiyear approach. A generic outline based on the specialized strategies outlined above is

First year — Laissez Faire
Second year — Swat Teams
Third year — Centralized standards
Fourth year — Coordination teams in local domains
Fifth year — Coordination across domains

Typically organizations that are considering a major transition to object technology will not be starting at the beginning of this cycle. Most commonly object technology will have been deployed using a Laissez Affaire approach. Often a group of experts in specific technologies may have already formed informal Swat Teams. The purpose of the multiyear plan is to build a sustained infrastructure on top of these initial foundations.

Some general lessons learned from the experience of large organizations that have undergone transitions to object technology are

- Going totally to object technology quickly usually does not work and can be a recipe for disaster.
- CASE tools for object modeling are not fully mature but are getting better.
- Object languages and tools reduce development time. At the present time, Smalltalk provides more rapid development than Java. However, developers using Java are more productive than those using C++.
- Applications using object languages are easier to maintain especially if they provide automatic memory management ("garbage collection"). C++ may provide problems in maintenance due to lack of garbage collection and complex language features.
- New software development processes and methodologies are required.
- Education and training is crucial.

Some specific lessons from personal experiences at Hewlett-Packard, Boeing, and American Management Systems are

- Even at an early stage in the introduction of object technology, it is useful to set up an object technology interest group for the purpose of exchanging information and experiences among different parts of the enterprise. This initial group can be relatively informal but can serve as a foundation for later structured cooperation. In Hewlett-Packard, there was an object interest group formed in 1986. A similar group was established at Boeing several years later by Smalltalk users.

- A useful next step for structuring the introduction of object technology is to select some members of the interest group to serve as technology focal points. These individuals can distribute information and answer questions about object technology across the enterprise. They can also serve as the points of contact for external vendors and experts. In Boeing, the Computer Services Architecture Standards Board appointed Coordinators of Object Technology. In American Management Systems, the Center for Advanced Technologies has an Object Lab Director who plays a similar role.
- A useful method for getting an organization up to speed in object technology is to bring in outside speakers who can describe the basic technology, the products and tools available, and implementation strategies. At Boeing, there was an extensive series of presentations on all aspects of object technology by leading experts. These talks raised awareness among managers and provided valuable knowledge and insights to technologists.
- Once the capabilities of object technology are understood and a critical mass of knowledge is in place, the next step is usually a period of enterprise strategic planning. This is when strategies similar to those described in this chapter (i.e., Laissez Faire, Swat Team, Centralized, and Coordinated) are evaluated and chosen. In Boeing, there was an extensive study done by a group of leading object technologists representing all major company organizations. This study produced a comparison of alternate approaches and a recommended multi-year strategy. A similar study was done by the U.S. Department of Defense in 1993, see Diskin, 1993.
- The establishment of a Swat Team is often one of the first steps in an object technology transition strategy. This team is usually located in the Corporate Advanced Technology Center. At American Management Systems, an "Object Core" group was started that developed a set of reusable class libraries in Smalltalk and C++. These libraries were used successfully by projects in many different business units. As experience in object technology became available across the company, the Object Core was moved into the Telecommunications business unit to bring them closer to their primary customer. The most successful use of the class libraries was as part of a framework installed by a major telecommunications company. The methodology for using the framework was a Coordinated approach with developers on specific projects working closely with the architects of the underlying general object classes and frameworks. The use of the Coordinated framework approach across multiple domains or business areas remains an open problem.

44.7 Conclusions

In conclusion, here are some final thoughts on the transition to object technology in large organizations:

- There are major benefits from a successful transition to object technology
- Be patient, don't expect miracles
- It can be a long expensive transition
- It should be combined with other technology transitions
- The transition will happen even if it is not planned or controlled
- It is not guaranteed to be a great success
- An effective strategy can produce a new generation of adaptable systems

References

Diskin, D.H. 1993. Managing the Transition to Object-Oriented Technology for Department of Defense Information Management Systems, Defense Information Systems Agency.

Lewis, T. 1995. *Object-Oriented Application Frameworks.* Prentice-Hall, Englewood Cliffs, NJ.

Meyer, B. 1994. *Reusable Software: The Base Object-Oriented Component Libraries (Object-Oriented Series).* Prentice-Hall, Englewood Cliffs, NJ.

IX

Object-Oriented Metrics

Douglas McDavid
IBM Global Services

Saba Zamir
Senior Information Technology Consultant

Metrics imply using a specific set of measurements on items or processes. Metrics allow the quantitative measurement of the success or failure for the item or process that is being measured. Metrics also help identify and quantify trends, estimates and improvements or lack thereof for the process.

Metrics in object-oriented development is a fairly new field. OO metrics can be used to formulate units of measurement for OO products (code, models, test cases), processes (OO analysis and design), and the activities of the people involved in formulating/implementing these products and processes.

This section contains chapters that identify some of the work that has been done in this field.

45

Object-Oriented Metrics

Simon Moser
Swinburne University of Technology

Brian Henderson-Sellers
Swinburne University of Technology

45.1 Introduction

Before we plunge into the details of the topic, let's briefly summarize the main reasons for using software metrics at all. As industrial practice "proves," one can also survive without metrics. So, what are they good for?

To answer this question, we have to be aware of the main parameters of the software production process (in fact, the parameters of any production process): (1) time, (2) cost, and (3) the earned value in form of a product. The ultimate goal of process management (Humphrey, 1989) is to have these three parameters under control. The activity of control, however, consists of three steps:

1. Knowing where one stands
2. Aiming where we wish to go
3. Going there (and reapply the problem solving steps periodically while going)

Obviously, Step 1 is directly related to measurement, i.e., you cannot "know" a thing unless you can measure it. As we will see later, Step 2 of control is also linked to measurement. The answer to our question, therefore, is that metrics are a prerequisite to process control.

This immediately raises the question: What and how should we measure in the (object-oriented) software development arena with respect to the three parameters?. Here are some answers:

0-8493-3135-8/99/$0.00+$.50

Time — This parameter is most easily measured since everybody can identify and record a fulfilled or missed deadline.

Cost — In software development this parameter is, to a very high degree, proportional to personnel effort measured in work-hours (some marginal fixed costs might also occur, but are ignored here for simplicity's sake). Therefore, cost can be easily measured, in theory, as the sum of all the work-hours spent. Practical problems, however, occur because reported and actual work-hours spent on a certain process are only coincidentally the same. One good way of determining the extent of this personal effort is to use the Personal Software Process (PSP) as proposed by Humphrey (1995). Given such a basis, the defined and measured personal process of a software engineer created through the application of PSP will allow the parameter of cost to be a more objectively measurable entity. Additional fuzziness is, however, also introduced by the usually "fuzzy" definition of the overall software processes. Nevertheless, we will treat the problem of measuring cost as "solved" in the following text.

Product — This parameter, which in its final form is the net output of a production process, is the most difficult to measure in the software and systems context. While, for the process of building a wall, you can easily measure both the quantity and quality of the product (e.g., by measuring the square meters for quantity, and the kilogram/square meter for one aspect of quality, i.e., solidity), we are left with a large but rather obscure set of "experimental" measures in the software arena. The following text will focus on this as yet essentially virgin territory.

In order to become aware of some of the pitfalls associated with software metrics and to know about some of the more basic concepts of measurement (cf., also Section 45.2 and Fenton (1991), let us begin with a hypothetical metrics project context statement:

> Members of a specific software development team have been selected to participate in a measurement experiment. We measure their weights on a three-valued scale of "light-medium-heavy" and the number of lines of code they wrote last Tuesday. Management is (for some reason) interested in both personal and professional characteristics: specifically, how many are overweight, how productive this team is (their Christmas bonus depends on this), and the correlation of weight to productivity.

That this is an ill-conceived experiment is perhaps self-evident, but this is precisely the bog that a lot of software metrics literatii seem to wallow in. Let us look at some specific problem areas.

Problem area #1: Lacking precision of definition — We can almost certainly count the number of lines of code (LOC) written on a given day, but only if we are very careful to define what we mean by both "line of code" and "write." Do we allow for multiple statements on a single line or for comment lines, and do we permit major modifications to be equivalent to a pristine construction? These questions will lead us into the area of models of software and models of software models, i.e., metamodels, upon which metrics can be precisely defined (Section 45.3).

Problem area #2: Ill-defined goal-metrics links — Although we can measure the weights of the developers, it is a wrong or insufficient metric for our experiment. Whether a given person is overweight must have something to do with the characteristics of both weight and height. But we have made no measurements of height. To avoid using such ill-chosen metrics like simply weight for capturing the aspect of overweight, we present the Goal-Question-Metric (GQM) framework and a table of recommended metrics in terms of a metrics multidimensional framework (MMDF) to choose from in Section 45.4.

Problem area #3: Unification of internal and external variables — Based on the assumption that productivity equals LOC per day, we may assume a causal link simply on faith (or maybe guesswork). We have unified the software-internal concept of LOC with the more vague notion of product size.* But

* Even though when we use LOC we always measure software size, the reverse is not true, i.e., when we want to measure software size we need not always measure it with LOC. This fact should clarify the non-identity of LOC and the notion of "size." Software size is used to express an amalgamation of sheer volume, complexity, difficulty and quality found in software with personal and contextual variations of weightings for those aspects. We therefore claim that software size is an external variable.

there is a major difference between internal and external variables (see Fenton, 1994). An internal variable such as LOC can, in principle, be measured objectively such that all measurers would come up with the same value for the variable of LOC. In contrast, variables such as size, quality, maintainability, etc., are all external variables in the sense that they involve people's personal viewpoints. Just as the distance of a walk may seem too long to some people and rather short to others, a certain piece of code may be maintainable for Sally and a nightmare for John. Nevertheless, even when we quantify external variables using internal variables (see the GQM approach in Section 45.4) we must not unify the two notions.

Problem area #4: Small samples, fast conclusions — The management may wish to define productivity in terms of LOC written per day. If we simply use this one measure of LOC last Tuesday as a measure of productivity then we are guilty of yet another sin. A variable such as productivity cannot be evaluated by a spot measurement; it has to be derived from a number of measurements. Any "averaging" type of measure (mean, median, mode etc.) is of this type. The greatest difficulty comes when we try to make industry-level statements. Any statement that pertains "on average," should always be tested in this vein — not by a single experiment* but by a statistically valid, sufficiently large sample of experiments. Of course, a major difficulty in devising such experiments is being aware of all the other extraneous variables that might affect the result, such as the people involved, the development environment, etc., The metrics that survive this degree of validation should then be clearly stated as being tested in a specific environment, i.e., a set of specific values for the "extraneous variables." The more specific the values, e.g., all projects taken from just one company, the more precise will be the observations, but also the less "industry-level" they will be. We will discuss the "tricks" of such statistical data analysis in Section 45.5.

Problem area #5: Non-allowed mathematical operations — Do you know the average gender of the population of Melbourne? Do you know the result of adding 3 apples and 5 oranges? If you do not, then you are correct in not knowing. Every measurement is made using a certain scale and dimension, i.e., unit of measurement. If we want to apply mathematical operations, we have to be sure that the rules of the dimensional units are not violated. In our fictional experiment, the request for correlating height to productivity is in conflict with the scale for the measurement of height, which is ordinal, i.e., consisting of the ordered discrete values of "small," "medium," and "tall." As correlation involves operations such as multiplication, which is meaningless on ordinal scales, the request for correlation becomes meaningless. We will discuss more of those issues related to measurement theory (Zuse, 1991) in Section 45.5.

45.2 Basic Software Metrics Concepts

In the introduction we have learned about distinguishing external and internal variables of software and of the process of software development. For the practical reason of imposing some sort of cognitive order on to the vast field of software metrics, there are some more categorizations, or metrics dimensions, of which one might be aware. We present these categories in arbitrary order.

45.2.1 *a priori* vs. *a posteriori* Metrics

Note that for every external variable there are always two paths to quantification: (1) *a priori* and usually product-based measurement and (2) *a posteriori* and usually process-based measurement. The external variable of maintainability, for example, may be quantified by the product-based metric "LOC per module" (with the rationale that less LOC per module are more maintainable). It can, however, also be captured by the process-based *a posteriori* metric "work-hours per maintenance request" (which assumes some standard "maintenance request," a problematic assumption; however, not discussed here). The

* It is frequently observed in the metrics literature that most metrics are "validated" by a single experiment which, probably, leads to the observation that "for every positive validation there is a negative validation" (Curtis, 1979). The discussion here shows that this approach is untenable.

a posteriori measure will tell us the "real" maintainability, i.e., our product *was* more maintainable when the average effort spent per request *was* lower compared to that of some other product. It does not, however, tell us anything about the reasons why this was the case. The product-based *a priori* metric, on the other hand, may capture one aspect of the "reasons." An analogy states: In medicine we may empirically observe causal patterns like "smoking correlates with lung cancer"; exactly what the chemical and physical processes look like is not relevant. Using statistical correlation, we may similarly observe the extent and quality of a possible causal link between LOC per module and work-hours per maintenance request.

45.2.2 Product vs. Process Metrics

Measurable characteristics may be of two different natures: either product or process. A product measure is a value obtained from a static analysis of a software artifact. It can thus be taken from the requirements, the early design, or from the code. Variables such as staffing levels, effort, or productivity ratios, in contrast, cannot be derived from the software artifacts alone. They can only be extracted by also looking at the records of the artifact's production process. This is the definitional distinction of product and process software metrics. We use the distinction as a mere structuring aid and immediately make use of it by now being able to state clearly that object-orientation has brought little new as yet with respect to process metrics (see, e.g., Haynes and Henderson-Sellers, 1996). We therefore recommend sticking to the two basic process measures of time and effort and to try to measure them as accurately as possible (see Section 45.4, the GQM approach, for some more comments on process metrics; the rest of the chapter will be focused on product metrics).

45.2.3 Dynamic vs. Static Measures

Metrics values usually vary over time. The amount of requirements, code size, effort, and team size, among other variables, will change. Metrics that deal with this change are called dynamic metrics according to Lorenz and Kidd (1994). They contain a time rate of change (a d/dt term) and reflect some dynamic model (e.g., of acceleration, growth, or decrease) in order to fully understand what is happening. The most prominent examples of dynamic metrics are requirements change rates (e.g., y measuring new and changed requirements per time interval) or staffing growth rates. Despite being of interest, we have to admit that, in the object-oriented area, we are not aware of any data or experience worth mentioning with respect to dynamic metrics, although some embryonic proposals can be found in De Champeaux (1996). We will not, therefore, provide any further information on this topic here.

45.2.4 Analysis and Design Metrics

Every system (be it a software system or not) is characterized by two viewpoints: (1) the black box viewpoint (also known as the external or user viewpoint) and (2) the white box viewpoint (also known as the implementation viewpoint). For our purpose, we define the term analysis artifacts as the set of all models and descriptions that reflect the black box view. Other terms for those artifacts may be requirements or specifications. Examples of such artifacts are business models or specifications in the ultimate form of a "user manual" (which may be overly verbose but, nevertheless, describes a system from a black box point of view). Unfortunately, analysis is the only non-agreed-upon term among the software engineering community (notice the irony). Therefore, readers who are not comfortable with our definition are invited to retain that meaning while using their personally preferred name. Design, on the other hand, is the set of all artifacts dealing with the white box view of a system from high-level (but internal) system architecture models to the ultimate form of "code." Note that we do not distinguish, in this context, between design, which is a model of the code, and the actual code. With respect to metrics we may make use of those definitions and categorize the product metrics further into analysis and design metrics.

45.2.5 Metrics of Size vs. Quality Metrics

The two external variables of system (or software) size and quality, even though intuitive themselves, are often used as yet another means of metrics categorization. While metrics of size help to distinguish between "big" and "small" systems, quality metrics do the same for the "good" and "bad." Metrics of size are typically defined on an open-ended scale, e.g., counting the lines of code can, theoretically, yield results up to infinity. Quality metrics, on the other hand, typically are dimensionless numbers, e.g., a defect ratio which may be defined as the ratio of defective lines of code per total lines of code. Quality metrics may then be interpreted using the pattern of "0% = worst, 100% = best" or vice versa.*

Intriguingly enough, the distinction between size and quality metrics is further complicated by the fact that a metric of size can also serve as a quality measure if it is mapped to some scale of quality. The scale of quality here typically is the binary scale of "bad" and "good," but can be more refined. The LOC metric can, for example, be used for measuring the quality of object-oriented methods (= functions) by applying the mapping of "good" = 1-14 LOC and "bad" = 15-∞ LOC. The problem here is to find the right threshold values for the mapping in a particular context, an area of metrics sadly neglected. A practical application of such a mapping is typically that of an alarm system, where "bad"-rated values raise an alarm and attract attention (see Lewis and Henry, 1989; Kitchenham and Linkman, 1990; Lorenz and Kidd, 1994; and Henderson-Sellers, 1996). Most often corrective actions should then be taken to improve the situation.

45.2.6 Estimation vs. Measurement

The desire to forecast costs is a major driving force in the derivation of quantitative, i.e., metrics-based, models. The main idea is that internal characteristics of product or process, that can be collected objectively at some time T_1, can be used as predictors for the same or other internal characteristics at some later time T_2. Just as the distance measured on a map will predict the duration of a journey by car (if we know, by empirical observation, the correlation** between the map distance and the duration), the measured size of a modeled system can predict the development effort, to give one important example. This approach, however, requires collecting reasonable amounts of data and looking for, again context-specific, correlations. For instance, we should clearly state that some data are only from COBOL MIS environments in the U.S. or from real-time developments using Assembler from company XY. Then the derived relationships can be used sensibly within their declared environment. Globally applied statements such as "McCabe's cyclomatic complexity predicts the cost and reliability of coded software within a ±-5% range" must be regarded with skepticism.

Note that the "alarm" usage of quality metrics (see subsection above) is just a variant of estimation. While, for example, some LOC value for a newly coded method itself is neither good nor bad, we may have had bad experiences with high LOC values when undertaking the subsequent processes of method testing, debugging, and maintaining. We only estimate or guess that methods with high LOC values will turn out as troublemakers in those subsequent processes.

In order to introduce yet another important notion, the one of estimation error or error probability, we elaborate further on the "LOC as a predictor for badness" example. We may take our past experience and compare the two statistical LOC distributions (mean and standard deviation) of the methods rated "bad" and of those rated "good." Eventually we may observe that the distributions differ significantly. We may then choose a threshold value between the two mean values (see Section 45.5 on how to do

* In a suite of metrics used together, we highly recommend to use the same interpretation scheme for all quality metrics.

** Note that the term correlation, here, is used in an extended sense. We do not only refer to the extent of "linked behavior" between two parameters, but also to the actual linking function that may have been determined using regression techniques. It is the linking function that is used as a predictor function in the estimation process. In our "map — car journey" example the linking function is equal to the notion of "expected average travel speed."

that). We should be aware, though, that there always remains a probability for still erroneously rating "good" methods as "bad" and vice versa. This error probability is inherent in any estimation (or alarm) type of metrics application and its extent can only be determined using statistical means. We claim that error probability is the main quality criterion for metrics-based estimation* and invite practitioners and researchers to be very skeptical with "models" that do not explicitly state those probabilities in a statistically sound way.** Ignoring those probabilities, or rather risks, can lead to completely inappropriate managerial and technical behavior.

In the case where we do not have a significant difference there are still several possible explanations, not just one. The first, and most obvious, may be that LOC actually do not predict "badness" well enough. A second explanation may be that measuring "badness" using a binary scale (thus leaving vast room for interpretation and personal taste) is not appropriate. Finally, it may be that the data are of poor quality. In the latter case the data should clearly be thrown away and not the correlation hypothesis. If exclusion of the second and third reasons make us assume the first reason, still note that we must not conclude, from a single failed statistical experiment, that LOC is not a good measure in general. It is just not suited for predicting "method badness." Also note that you may not transfer the property of non-predictiveness from the internal to the external characteristic (do you remember pitfall #3 from Section 45.1). When LOC does not predict "badness," this does not mean that the external notion of size is not related to the external notion of trouble-making methods. Thus, maybe some other metric of size will do the job better.

45.3 A Review of Product Metrics and Underlying Metamodels

In this section we will present metrics and underlying metamodels that meet two requirements. First, the metamodels are truly object-oriented, and second, they are formally sound and validated to some degree. This prevents the reader from having to browse through definitions of well-known traditional metrics such as Function Points, Software Science Metrics, Lines of Code, Cyclomatic Complexity, and of merely experimental metrics whose use is not yet clear. We are aware of the fact that some of the traditional metrics may be useful for object-oriented environments if used with caution (see discussion of FP in Section 45.3.1). In addition to the two requirements we limited ourselves to metrics that are independent of the programming language used. Therefore, metrics like "number of friend classes" (C++-bound) or "number of pool variables" (Smalltalk-bound) are not mentioned here.

The two main sources used for the following collection of metrics were Henderson-Sellers' (1996) comprehensive overview of the topic and Lorenz and Kidd's (1994) practice-oriented approach. We will present the metrics within the orthogonal categories of analysis/design and size/quality metrics and assess them with respect to their usage of development process control. This means with respect to (1) *tracking* the quantity/quality of the product, and (2) *estimating* effort, time, and quantity/quality of future stages of the process and product.

45.3.1 Object-Oriented Analysis Metrics of Size

The most widely used conventional analysis (= black box) metric of size are Function Points (IFPUG, 1994). In the context of object-oriented systems, however, several proposals to replace Function Points have been made. Here is a list of the most promising approaches.

* We are aware of a number of other estimation techniques such as bottom-up estimation, expert round-table, and Delphi methods, but will not discuss them here, where the context is object-oriented metrics.

** We usually indicate error as a percentage bandwidth, e.g., ±20%, around the estimate into which the effective result will fall with a 95% probability. Other equally sound forms of error indication may, however, also be used.

45.3.1.1 Number of Domain Classes

Name and origin: #DC, first broadly discussed in (Lorenz and Kidd, 1994).

Measurement: #DC is very basic to object-oriented systems. It can be easily measured, even without tool support, on object-oriented domain models that were established using any of the emerging analysis modeling approaches (Rational, 1997 and Firesmith et al., 1997).

Metamodel: Behind #DC stands a metamodel of classes that captures the key types of "things" appearing in the real world. The metric's metamodel ignores the associations or relationships between the classes and their features. It assumes some "standard average size" of classes.

Usage: #DC can be used for tracking the analysis process. Tracking the overall software process using this metric is, however, not recommended because it can only reflect relatively major changes to the system (the creation, deletion, or replacement of entire domain classes). Estimation of the post-analysis effort can be accomplished using #DC as a predictor but empirical studies (Moser et al., 1997) suggest that it predicts effort with less accuracy than other measurement approaches at the analysis stage. Empirical studies have shown that #DC also correlates with the #C (number of classes) metric at the design level in certain contexts (Haynes and Henderson-Sellers, 1996). The estimation error of estimates making use of this correlation is, however, not published.

45.3.1.2 Number of Atomic Scenarios

Name and origin: Task Points (Graham, 1995).

Measurement: Task Points are the simple count of the so-called "atomic" task scripts (a more formal form of use cases) in an object-oriented analysis model. As #DC, it can be easily measured.

Metamodel: Behind the Task Points, also a well-formed metric, is a metamodel of task scripts (or usage patterns of a system) that capture the system's behavior in the real world. This metamodel can be viewed as "orthogonal" to the #DC metamodel as it does not include any structural information about the system.

Usage: Task Points are suggested for tracking and estimating the overall software process. No empirical data can, however, be reported on the practical use of it.* We included the metric in this review because of its simplicity and well-formedness and suggest it as a starting point for controlling behaviorally complex systems (in contrast to #DC which seems to be suited for controlling structurally focused systems like IS [information systems] or other database applications).

45.3.1.3 The System Meter

Name and origin: System Meter (Moser, 1995).

Measurement: The System Meter, put simply, is a token count of all objects (behavioral and structural) appearing in a system model. Its measurement procedure is very fine-grained and requires formally denoted models and automated tools.

Metamodel: Behind the System Meter is a generic metamodel of model objects (also called description objects) and the dependency relationships between them. It may capture notions appearing in the real world as well as in other systems. The metric is currently defined for two layers of analysis models: (1) preliminary models (functionalities and subject areas) and (2) detailed domain models (class model, use-case model, and state-transition model). We speak of the PRE System Meter for the first layer and of the DOME System Meter for the second.

Usage: The PRE System Meter is used for very early estimates. It delivered results of slightly lower error (±34%) than #DC (±40%) in an industry-based field study (Moser, 1996). We would not

* An object-oriented metrics club was founded in 1995 to support the collection of Task Points (and other object-oriented metrics) data in industry. Contact Bezant Object Technologies, 6 St. Mary's St., Wallingford, Oxon, OX10 OLE, England, *100073.1340@compuserve.com*, +44 1491 826 005 for more information.

recommend it as a means of process tracking except at the very first preliminary analysis stages. The DOME System Meter, on the other hand, was statistically demonstrated to deliver significantly more accurate estimates (±9%) than any other approach in a broad context of projects (including the traditional Function Point approach with an observed ±20% error). It can also be successfully used for project tracking at a requirements oriented level. Even though it can be applied for estimation of the technical processes, it cannot be applied for tracking them directly.

45.3.2 Object-Oriented Analysis Quality Metrics

At the time of writing, we are not aware of any sound and validated quality metrics at the analysis level. A possible *a posteriori* measure could be the percentage of analysis artifacts "not thrown away." Here the expression not thrown away would be defined as "still appears as in the first signed-off requirements model." Such a percentage could be measured using any of the three metrics of size just presented. In a similar manner more *a posteriori* measures can be defined, but still need validation in the context of object-orientation.

45.3.3 Object-Oriented Design Metrics of Size

45.3.3.1 Number of Method Sends

Name and origin: #ms, (Lorenz and Kidd, 1994).

Measurement: #ms is equal to the number of atomic messages sent within a method's implementation body. A hypothetical message body like `if (x > 0) do-this; else do-that;` is counted as 5 message sends: 1. `if (<exp>) <true-body>;`, 2. `x > 0`, 3. `do-that`, 4. `else <false-body>;`, 5. `do-this`.

Metamodel: The metamodel behind this metric views a system or a component as simply a set of message sends. This approach, even though better adapted to modern syntactical and lexical conventions, is similar to the old-style approach of perceiving a software system as a set of code lines. Structural and logical complexity is ignored. This metamodel, though, is handy in devising fine-grained derivatives such as ratios of unchanged vs. changed message sends, etc.

Usage: An upper threshold value of 9 may be used to indicate alarm for methods coded in any object-oriented language. A system-wide summation of all #ms values can be used as a measure of design size (and thus be used for tracking the technical design process).

45.3.3.2 Number of Instance or Class Methods

Name and origin: #im, #cm (Lorenz and Kidd, 1994).

Measurement: #im equals to the number of newly introduced or redefined methods that instances of a class can understand, and #cm the number a class can understand (both regardless of eventual method access restrictions such as "private" or "protected").

Metamodel: In the context of these metrics, a system or component is perceived as a set of methods, i.e., functional abstractions. The assumption is that every method is equal, i.e., the metrics do not differentiate between different kinds of methods. While this assumption simplifies measurement, it prohibits a fine-grained application of the metric for estimation and progress tracking purposes.

Usage: Upper threshold values of 20 for #im and 3 for #cm may be used to indicate alarm for individual classes. When assessing sets of classes (systems or subsystems) use 12 as an upper threshold for the average #im per class. The average threshold for #cm remains 3. Use those thresholds only for non-interface and non-generated classes. Interface classes, as well as generated classes, usually require higher thresholds that need to be determined in a certain context (e.g., use an upper threshold of 40 for individual GUI-classes). A system-wide summation of all #im and #cm values can be used as a measure of design size (and be used for tracking the technical design process).

45.3.3.3 Number of Instance or Class Variables

Name and origin: #iv, #cv (Lorenz and Kidd, 1994).

Measurement: #iv equals to the number of newly introduced data variables that instances of a class contain, and #cm the number a class contains (both regardless of eventual access restrictions such as "private" or "protected," even though access restrictions on variables are recommended).

Metamodel: This is a rather limited view of a system or component in the sense that it reduces the focus on the data part of a system. We therefore recommend not using this metric as an estimation or progress tracking measure, but restrict its application to alarm type cases.

Usage: Upper threshold values of 3 for #iv and 1 for #cv may be used to indicate alarm for both individual classes and class averages. Again, interface classes, as well as generated classes, usually require higher thresholds that need to be determined in a certain context (e.g., use an upper threshold of 9 for GUI classes).

45.3.3.4 Number of Classes

Name and origin: #c (Lorenz and Kidd, 1994).

Measurement: #c is the number of classes that make up a system. Usually the reused classes (from frameworks, class libraries, language systems [such as Smalltalk]) are not counted unless they are heavily modified.

Metamodel: In the context of this metric, a system or component is perceived as a set of classes, i.e., data abstractions. The same remarks as for the "number of methods" metric apply to an even larger extent.

Usage: The number of technical or design classes can be used to track the process of design. However, one has to be careful about using this white box metric in the interaction with the user and customer who takes on a "black box" point of view. The user will be bothered with the "appearance" and maybe destruction of classes that will not affect the functionality as visible to him. In unfortunate cases, the user will panic and set upper limits for #c while he should only do so for #dc. It is unwise, in general, to use design metrics in the interaction with customers. Use them for controlling the technical processes only. BTW: Much of the "troubles" reported with LOC, which is a design metric, also stem from this misuse.

45.3.4 Object-Oriented Design Quality Metrics

45.3.4.1 Percentage of Commented Methods

Name and origin: %cm (Lorenz and Kidd, 1994).

Measurement: We calculate %cm as the ratio of those methods (instance and class methods) which have a comment and the total number of methods (=#im + #cm). Usually, simple variable access methods and GUI methods are not taken into account.

Metamodel: The metamodel in this context is an enhancement over the "number of methods" metamodel in that we differentiate between the commented ones and the uncommented ones. While this is still a coarse approach, it provides sufficient information for assessing some parts of the understandability aspect in coded systems.

Usage: There is a lower threshold of 65% recommended for individual classes as well as for averages on class sets. Note that such a threshold may be lower for special purpose and generated classes, because they may contain lots of "tiny" access methods.

Also at the design level we observe an almost total lack of validated metrics of quality. While there are a few proposals for measuring the important structural quality aspects of coupling and cohesion (Chidamber and Kemerer, 1994 and Henderson-Sellers et al., 1996), none of the proposals has undergone positive and sufficient empirical validation.* Recent studies have even shown that current cohesion measurement research at the class level has led to a dead end (Avotins, 1996) and that new approaches must be sought (see Section 45.7).

45.4 Relating Management Goals to Metrics

45.4.1 The GQM Approach

Management of any production process is simplified if some measures of progress toward a quality product are collected and analyzed. In manufacturing, tolerance limits are prescribed and individual components assessed against these "standards." Excessive product rejections suggest that the process producing them is at fault. Costs are tracked during the process and compared with estimates made initially ("variances"). In introducing a software measurement program, an initial question is often: What is to be measured? A more appropriate question is: What is the goal which we want to attain? For example, is the goal to increase programmer productivity; to decrease the number of defects reported per unit of time or to improve the efficiency of the overall development process. Until that goal is defined, recommendations on the optimum measurement program cannot be made.

A widely used framework here is the "Goal/Question/Metric" paradigm of Basili and Rombach (1988). As its name suggests, the first step of selecting metrics is to identify the goal, 'G', (as illustrated above). This leads to questions, 'Q', such as how to increase code quality, decrease enhancement schedules. In turn, these questions help to elucidate the appropriate metrics, 'M', which need to be collected. GQM evaluates the goals and questions, thus leading to choice of an appropriate metric. The problem with the application of this approach to OO metrics is that the set of metrics available may be empty. Thus a complementary activity is the one of identifying simply the 'M' component of 'GQM' independently of specific goals and questions. A major first step there is the identification of a number of "potentially useful" metrics in some systematic manner. We present such a systematic manner (covering object-oriented and some traditional metrics) in the form of a so-called Metrics Multidimensional Framework (MMDF) as described below.

45.4.2 A Metrics Multidimensional Framework

Henderson-Sellers et al. (1993) have undertaken some preliminary normative (theoretical) work which is presented here in a more mature form. The aim is to provide metrics practitioners and researchers with a systematology for metrics. The systematology has three main dimensions within which metrics are positioned: (1) the external characteristic the metric assesses, (2) the level of granularity at which the metric is applicable, and (3) the lifecycle phase at which the metric is available. We briefly describe each dimension in three tables before presenting the framework "filled" with metrics:

It is clear that the reasons for any individual using metrics in an OO development environment may vary. The motivation may be managerial or technical; it may be focused on reuse or on productivity; it may be of concern to code maintainability or to deriving early lifecycle estimates of the whole system. Henderson-Sellers et al. (1993) argue that the most frequent metrics purposes can be identified and described as combinations of characteristic/lifecycle phase/granularity. The relevance of each measure is then assessed for each such combination. This approach should lead to a minimal set of metrics, because combinations with a satisfactory quantification should no longer be a focus of metrics research. A minimal set of metrics is desirable for practical managerial purposes. Identification of this key set of

* Note that the metric LCOM (Lack of Cohesion in Methods) as proposed by Chidamber and Kemerer (1994) is shown to be invalid theoretically. A revised and mathematically correct cohesion metric for object-oriented systems is described in Henderson-Sellers et al. (1996). The empirical linkage of this new metric to *a posteriori* characteristics, however, is still the subject of future research.

TABLE 45.1 The External Characteristics Dimension of the MMDF

External Characteristic	Comments and Typical Usages
Quality	This is an overall characteristic which enables us to distinguish the "good and the bad"; as quality has many facets we have identified several sub-characteristics
Understandability	= "Effortlessness" of understanding some piece of software or software model; this characteristic can help to predict the effort of introducing new development or maintenance personnel to the specifics of a piece of software
Provability	= "Effortlessness" and "thoroughness" with which an artifact can be validated; this characteristic can help to predict the effort of validating a software artifact (in the context of executable software this characteristic is also known as "Testability")
Maintainability	= "Ease" of enhancing and changing a piece of software or software model; this characteristic can help to predict the effort of making changes to a piece of software
Reusability	= "Effortlessness" of picking a component out of its original context and plugging it into some new environment; this characteristic can help to predict the effort of producing new systems based on existing systems
Correctness	= Ratio of "correct" parts within a piece of software or software model; this characteristic can help to predict the effort of corrections to be made
Completeness	= Ratio of the "original" parts of a component and the same component with "add-ons" later; this characteristic can help to predict the effort of enhancements to be made
Size	This is an overall characteristic which enables us to distinguish the "small and the big"; size has two subcharacteristics
External size	= Size as perceived by users of a piece of software or software model, i.e., the size of the "interface" or "functionality" of the system
Internal size	= Size as perceived by the implementers of a piece of software

TABLE 45.2 The Granularity Dimension of the MMDF

Granularity	Comments and Typical Usages
System (S)	This level of granularity treats the system as a single entity; product metrics gathered at this level are usually related to process metrics dealing with the system as a whole (e.g., overall effort) or other system-level product metrics
Part (P)	The term "part" is understood here as anything between (and including) a single class and the whole system; product metrics gathered at this level typically relate to process metrics that deal with parts of the overall system (e.g., increments, subsystems, etc.)
Class (C)	This level of granularity looks at a single class; product metrics at this level typically relate to process metrics of detailed tasks associated with a single class (e.g., validation/testing of a class) or are used as "alarms"
Method (M)	This most fine-grained level of granularity looks at a single method; method-level product metrics typically are used as "alarms" to attract attention within some task

metrics is strongly supported by the MMDF approach and should improve the current, more *ad hoc* and uncoordinated (OO) metrics research effort since the MMDF permits the identification of useful metrics but also, perhaps more importantly, of poor and/or irrelevant metrics.

We present the MMDF for use in the (M) step of the GQM approach as three separate matrices (Figures 45.1, 45.2, and 45.3), one for each system lifecycle phase. The metrics contained therein are not only purely object-oriented.

A brief look at this MMDF immediately unveils an area of total neglect: the measurement of analysis quality with *a priori* measures that can be related to empirical measures that are measurable *a posteriori*. The facts are even worse, as you will discover, in the System Use MMDF that also empirical measures for assessing software product quality are not available with sufficient coverage of the characteristics dimension.

The MMDF for design includes thresholds that may be used for alarms. The source for those thresholds mainly is Lorenz and Kidd (1994). We recommend using these thresholds with care and possibly redefining thresholds specific for your environment by applying the procedure given in Section 45.6.

TABLE 45.3 The Life-Cycle Dimension of the MMDF

Lifecycle Stage	Comments and Typical Usages
Analysis	Analysis is defined as the time of system life from its "birth" until the detailed requirements/specifications are released and understood in a first signed-off version. There may exist higher level requirement models (such as business models) but we will consider them as belonging to one single phase in this chapter. Metrics applicable at this phase typically deal with size from a user point of view and are used to control the development process from this viewpoint.
Design (design + coding + test)	Design is defined as the time of system life from analysis until the tested software system is accepted and used by the customer. Be aware of the fact that the requirements are not thrown away during design, but kept (and maintained[a]) as a part of the system documentation for acceptance reference. Metrics applicable at design therefore include the analysis metrics. In order to purge our framework from redundancies, we will, however, only consider the newly emerging metrics here. Design metrics typically deal with the size/complexity and quality from a programmer's point of view and are used to control the development process from this viewpoint.
System use	System use is defined as the time of system life from first signed-off implementation until the system's "death."[b] Be aware of the fact that during system use neither the requirements nor the design (code) are thrown away, but remain maintained. Metrics applicable at this stage therefore include the analysis and design metrics. In order to purge our framework from redundancies, we will, however, only consider the newly emerging metrics here. Metrics applicable at this phase typically are *a posteriori* metrics that assess the "real" system's characteristics (e.g., how much effort was spent on defect removal per class in the first year of use, etc.). These metrics typically give feedback to the earlier metrics.

[a] The term "maintain" here refers to the activities of (1) adding new artifacts and (2) deleting artifacts. We consider change as a combination of deletion and addition.

[b] The "death" of a system is often not a "natural" and complete one. First, the real-world system behind a software system often remains alive, which means that some of the analysis artifacts remain alive. Second, a system may evolve into a new system (often called a new release or version) as soon as some substantial parts of the specifications change or grow. Even though a large part of the analysis (and also maybe implementation) artifacts remain alive, we "declare" the old system as "dead." In the assessment of the "new" system it is then crucial to differentiate between the reused and newly developed parts. We will, however, not be able to give detailed advice here.

Also note that the thresholds given here will probably not be suited for special purpose classes or partially generated classes (e.g., for GUI classes for which Lorenz and Kidd use different thresholds). Also note that the thresholds given here were derived heuristically rather than using sound statistical procedures.

Of course more metrics at the system usage stage than are included in the above MMDF have been proposed (e.g., the testing effort per class), but there are either not enough data or none at all available to support any application of those metrics in the object-oriented arena.

One last word of caution to finish this section. When applying metrics to some real-world development process one may observe that the stage, i.e., analysis, design, and system usage, is not unambiguously determinable for the system as a whole. While certain parts may have already passed customer acceptance others are still "waiting" at the analysis stage. Furthermore, there are versions of the same system that revert to earlier stages for extension and modification. We urge you to be aware of those lags and, whenever possible, to exploit feedback from more mature components.

45.5 Best Statistical and Mathematical Practices

Metrics practice will typically involve the following tasks:

- Correlating two (or more) metrics using regression techniques
- Calculating key numbers involving basic mathematical operations applied on the metrics
- Defining context-specific alarm thresholds

In this chapter we will briefly present the techniques and prerequisites of each of these tasks related to statistics, mathematics, and measurement theory.

Metric	Quality						Size	
	Understandability	Provability	Maintainability	Reusability	Correctness	Completeness	External	Internal
#DC							SPC 40%	Not applicable
Task Points							SPM ??%	
PRE System Meter							SP 30%	
DOME System Meter							all 10%	
Function Points (IFPUG, 1996)							all 20%	

Legend:

level of granularity: S=System, P=Part, C=Class, M=Method (here interpreted as "Use Case")
all=applicable at all levels

percentages: approximate error level for correlation with the corresponding empirical metric (cf. the System Use MMDF, below)

FIGURE 45.1 The analysis MMDF.

45.5.1 Correlation Using Regression

Correlation, in its pure sense, tries to provide us with a measure for the extent to which two variables behave similarly, e.g., between the height and weight of persons. In a broader sense, correlation can be defined as "the dependency between two variables." Regression, on the other hand, typically tries to derive an approximation function between two variables in a certain context that can then be used for prediction. It can therefore be considered a form of correlation analysis in its broader sense. We will not explain regression formulae here but refer the reader to any standard statistics textbook (e.g., Kennedy and Neville, 1976). Instead we will state two prerequisites:

1. The number of value pairs from *a posteriori* analysis of projects should, theoretically, at least be 30 (you can perform regression with less value pairs but the stability of the gained regression function will be insufficient). In practice you can start with 5 value pairs, but then, we recommend to use the regressed function with great caution only.
2. The scale types of the two involved metrics should at least be of interval type (see Section 45.5.2 for details about scale types) .

Two constraints once a regressed function is about to be used are:

1. The context of the correlation/regression, i.e., the set of characteristics observed in the sample set, should be clearly stated.
2. The correlation/approximation error should be calculated in a statistically sound way and clearly indicated.

Metric	*Quality*						*Size*	
	Understandability	*Provability*	*Maintainability*	*Reusability*	*Correctness*	*Completeness*	*External*	*Internal*
#ms (per method)				all >9	CM >9			all
#im (per class)	C >20 SP >12	C >20 SP >12	C >20 SP >12		C >20		SPC	
#iv (per class)				C >9 SP >3				SPC
#cm (per class)	SPC >3	SPC >3	SPC >3				SPC	
#cv (per class)	SPC >1			SPC >1				SPC
#c							SP	
v [McCabe, 1976]	M > 1		M > 1	M > 1	M > 1			all
#DC/#c						S <20%		
%cm	SPC <65%							

Legend:
level of granularity: S=System, P=Part, C=Class, M=Method, all=applicable at all levels

(higher level application is achieved by taking the arithmetic mean)
percentages: not available at the time of writing
thresholds: <x = alarm when value is below x, >y = alarm when value is above y

FIGURE 45.2 The design MMDF.

Metric	*Quality*						*Size*	
	Understandability	*Provability*	*Maintainability*	*Reusability*	*Correctness*	*Completeness*	*External*	*Internal*
Development effort							all	all
#Problem reports					SPC >2		SPC	
#Reuses				SPC <2			SPC	

Legend:
level of granularity: S=System, P=Part, C=Class, M=Method, all=applicable at all levels

(higher level application is achieved by taking the arithmetic mean)
thresholds: <x = alarm when value is below x, >y = alarm when value is above y

FIGURE 45.3 The system usage MMDF.

TABLE 45.4 Scale Types and Allowed Mathematical Operations

Scale Type	Typical Measurement	Example	Allowed Operations
Nominal	Labeling, categorizing	Human gender (male, female)	Counting
Ordinal (Likert)	Rating, ranking	Test marks (1, 2, ..., 6)	Median, comparison
Interval	"Measurement" on a continuous scale but without fixed point 0	Temperature in Celsius or Fahrenheit	Mean, variance
Ratio	"Measurement" with a fixed point 0	Temperature in Kelvin, Distances	Ratios, percentages
Absolute	Counting	Number of classes	Any operation

45.5.2 Mathematical Operations

This is the area where measurement theory plays its role. For every measurement we have to be aware of its scale and scale type (Zuse, 1991). Without going into too much detail, we may identify two rules to be obeyed.

45.5.2.1 Dimensional Correctness

This rule has to be checked in two situations: (1) when values are added/subtracted and (2) when values are compared using comparison operators (equal, greater than, etc.). In both cases we have to assure that we do not mix "apples" with "oranges," i.e., the scales or units of measurement of the involved measures have to be the same.

45.5.2.2 Scale Types and the Validity of Mathematical Operations

This rule has to be checked with every operation trying to be applied to a value or set of values. In order to check the rule, we first have to identify the scale type of the value's scale. We may do this by asking ourselves how the measurement was accomplished by using Table 45.4.

Note that the entries under "allowed operations" accumulate from top to bottom. Therefore, for example, counting is also allowed in ordinal scales, etc.

In the early days of any scientific or engineering discipline, unknown and unquantified factors may be introduced. Metrics which require subjective assessment, often characterized by the use of a 3 or 4 point Likert scale, are, however, *not* of an interval type and therefore cannot be used for correlation. Metrics with subjective weightings, in which not only are Likert scales used, but the mapping from that scale to a numerical scale itself is fuzzy, have no scientific validity and should be avoided if at all possible. For practitioners, it may be the safest approach to use only simple counts (like counting classes, methods, message sends, or, on the process side, person days, etc.). Any mathematical and statistical operation can then be applied safely.

45.5.3 Defining Alarm Thresholds

Typically the task of finding an alarm threshold is used in situations where one has to guess from an observation whether an item belongs to the population of "good" items or to the population of "bad" items. For example, we may want to use the number of message sends in a method to guess if the method will be hard to maintain ("bad") or not ("good").

The first step, in such a situation, must be to test whether the observation, the application of a metric, allows a significant population distinction. If we only have few samples, which is what we usually have in the software area, then we should use the W-test, a modified Wilcoxon test (see Kennedy and Neville, 1976), to test if the mean values of the two populations differ significantly. In our example, we take a set of methods that are "good" and another set containing "bad" methods (obtaining this ordinal scale measurement is another problem area not covered here), measure the number of message sends for each methods and calculate the means μ_{good} and μ_{bad} of the two populations. Even if they differ, we still are not sure if the difference is by accident or "real". Therefore, we will have to choose a hypothesis (e.g., $\mu_{good} < \mu_{bad}$), a certainty level (e.g., 95%) at which the decision is to be made, and then calculate a test

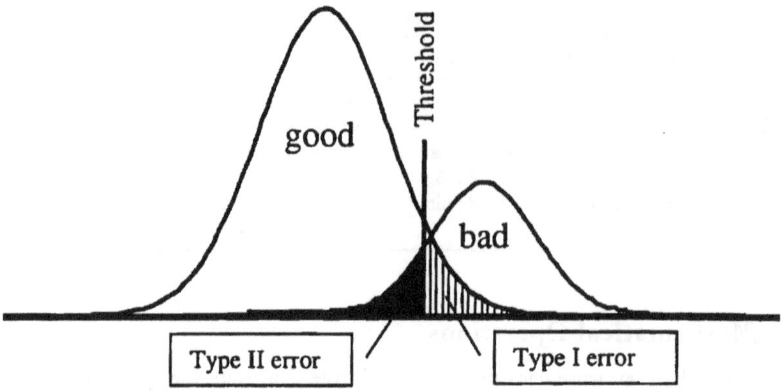

FIGURE 45.4 Type I and II errors for a threshold distinguishing between "good" and "bad" populations.

value, W in the case of the W-test, and compare it to so-called quantiles. Only if the test value exceeds the quantile can we accept* the hypothesis (with the chosen certainty). Otherwise, the hypothesis is not accepted, and it is useless to attempt the second step of finding a threshold.

The second step, once step one is successfully passed, then tries to find the "best" value for a threshold for distinguishing the two populations of "good" and "bad" items each with its known distribution. We assume the situation where all items yielding a higher measured value than the threshold are assessed to belong to the "bad" population (Figure 45.4).

Given any threshold we can make two kinds of errors: (1) type I error, assessing a "good" item as "bad" or (2) type II error, assessing a "bad" item as "good".

The threshold definition procedure depends on the cost or severity of each error type. If type I errors are more costly or severe then one tries to reduce primarily this one, and vice versa. In both cases one uses the Gaussian probability distribution function of the relevant population — the "good" population for type I and the "bad" population for type II — for error minimization. For example, we may have observed that methods which are difficult to maintain (= the "bad" ones) have a mean number of message send values of 40 and the "good" ones have a significantly lower mean. If the standard deviation for the "bad" population is 10, we can choose a threshold that reduces the type II error to 2.5% by subtracting 2 times the standard deviation from the mean. In that case the threshold would be 20 and we have optimized for low type II error probability and ignored type I errors (the vice versa procedure works analogously).

The trickiest situation is when the overall type I plus II errors need to be minimized. In this case we have to take the relative frequencies, f_1 and f_2, of the two populations into account as well as a relative weight of severity, s_1 and s_2, of the two error types (both, frequencies and severities, should add up to 100%). For a given threshold T we can then calculate the overall alarm error E_T as

$$E_T = \left(f_1 \times s_1 \times \left(1 - \Phi_{\mu 1,\sigma 1}(T)\right)\right) + \left(f_2 \times s_2 \times \Phi_{\mu 2,\sigma 2}(T)\right) \quad (45.1)$$

where $\Phi_{\mu,\sigma}(T)$ stands for the $[-\infty,T]$-integral of the Gaussian distribution function with mean μ and standard deviation σ (Kennedy and Neville, 1976). By numerical optimization we may find the optimum T for which E_T is minimal. This situation, with the different frequencies and severities of the populations diagrammed as different heights of the distribution curves, is shown in Figure 45.4. Finding the optimum threshold is equal to shifting the threshold line until the weighted sum of the type I and II errors is

* Strictly, we construct a null hypothesis (e.g., $\mu_{good} = \mu_{bad}$) as well as the alternative and test the null hypothesis. If we find reason to reject the null hypothesis, that is tantamount to accepting the alternative.

minimal. The optimization for only one error type can be considered as a special case with the frequencies and error severities of the two populations both set to 0% or 100%, respectively.

Similar to the use of regressed estimation or prediction functions, we state two conditions that every given threshold has to fulfill: (1) the context of the threshold, i.e., the set of characteristics observed in the sample set from which the observed populations were taken, should be clearly stated, and (2) the threshold error E_T with the assumed frequencies and error severities should be clearly indicated.

45.6 Research Directions

As quite obvious from the MMDF matrices presented in Section 45.4, metrics research in the object-oriented environments is still valuable. Whereas there are some sound approaches for measuring size at analysis and design level, measurement of software quality is still mostly "terra incognita." One of the possible approaches could be to quantify recent results of research in cognitive program comprehension including debugging and maintenance (Cant et al., 1994; 1995). Their cognitive complexity model (CCM) can be described qualitatively in terms of a "landscape" model which depicts the two techniques of chunking and tracing which programmers use concurrently and synergistically. In chunking, the software engineer divides up the code mentally into logically related chunks, e.g., an iterative loop or decision block. In tracing, other related chunks are located in order to understand the "starter" chunk. Having found that code, programmers will once again chunk in order to comprehend it.

Quality may then be defined as the "ease" of chunking and tracing. Some of the current research ideas are based on the hypothesis that the ease of chunking is correlated to high cohesion and ease of tracing to low coupling. Coupling and cohesion, once properly captured as metrics, are *a priori* product-based design metrics. Empirical validation will then have to be undertaken and those future metrics matched with *a posteriori* process-based metrics of quality. There is a long way to go, so we had better start now!

45.7 Conclusions

Despite the lack of a large number of validated object-oriented metrics, especially in the area of assessing quality, we encourage the reader to use the approaches presented in Section 45.3 which are mainly focused on system sizing and, as an application, on cost estimation. The task of choosing the right metrics in a certain organizational context should be guided by the GQM and MMDF approaches presented in Section 45.4. A world-wide Internet-based interest group (e-mail to *see@csse.swin.edu.au*) that collects data on both object-oriented and conventional software metrics to support all aspects of software estimation has recently been founded. It is open for all practitioners and researchers to support the application and development of measurement-based software project management.

Acknowledgments

This is contribution number 97/8 of the Centre for Object Technology Applications and Research (COTAR). Simon Moser wishes to acknowledge financial support from the Swiss National Science Foundation. We wish to thank our reviewers, Houman Younessi and Vojislav Mišič, for their help in improving form and contents of this chapter.

References

Avotins, J. 1996. *An OO Method for Evolving and Evaluating OO Design Metric Models.* Monash University, Department of Software Development, November.

Basili, V. R. and Rombach, H. D. 1988. The TAME project: toward improvement-orientated software environments, *IEEE Trans. Soft. Eng.*, 14(6), 758-773.

Cant, S. N., Henderson-Sellers, B. and Jeffery, D. R. 1994. Application of cognitive complexity metrics to object-oriented programs, *J. Object-Oriented Prog.*, 7(4), 52-63.

Cant, S. N., Jeffery, D. R. and Henderson-Sellers, B. 1995. A conceptual model of cognitive complexity of elements of the programming process, *Inf. Soft. Technol.*, 37(7), 351-362.

Chidamber, S. and Kemerer, C. 1994. A metrics suite for object oriented design, *IEEE Trans. Soft. Eng.*, 20(6), 476-493.

Curtis, B. 1979. In search of software complexity. In *Workshop on Quantitative Software Models*, pp. 95-106, IEEE, New York.

De Champeaux, D. 1996. *Object-Oriented Development Process and Metrics*, Prentice-Hall, Upper Saddle River, NJ.

Fenton, N.E. 1991. *Software Metrics: A Rigorous Approach.* Chapman and Hall, London.

Fenton, N.E. 1994. Software measurement: a necessary scientific basis, *IEEE Trans. Soft. Eng.*, 20, 199-206.

Firesmith D., Henderson-Sellers B. and Graham I. M. 1997. *The Open Modeling Language (OML) Reference Manual.* SIGS Books, NY.

Graham, I. M. 1995. *Migrating to Object Technology.* Addison-Wesley, Wokingham, U.K.

Haynes P. and Henderson-Sellers, B. 1996. Cost estimation of object-oriented projects. In *The American Programmer,* Vol. 9, No. 7, Arlington, MA.

Henderson-Sellers, B. 1996. *Object-Oriented Metrics — Measures of Complexity.* Prentice-Hall, Englewood Cliffs, NJ.

Henderson-Sellers, B., Moser, S., Seehusen, S. and Weinelt, B. 1993. A proposed multidimensional framework for object-oriented metrics, measurement — for improved IT management, *Proc. First Australian Conf. Software Metrics, ACOSM '93,* J.M. Verner, ed. 24-30.

Henderson-Sellers, B., Constantine, L. L. and Graham, I. M. 1996. Coupling and cohesion (toward a valid metrics suite for object-oriented analysis and design), *Object-Oriented Syst.*, 3(3), 143-158.

Humphrey, W. S. 1995. *A Discipline for Software Engineering.* Addison-Wesley, Reading, MA.

Humphrey, W. S. 1989. *Managing the Software Process.* Addison-Wesley, Reading, MA.

Kennedy, J. B. and Neville, A. M. 1976. *Basic Statistical Methods for Engineers and Scientists* (2nd ed.). Harper & Row, NY.

Kitchenham, B. A. and Linkman, S. J. 1990. Design metrics in practice, *Inf. Soft. Technol.*, 32, pp. 304-310.

Lewis, J. and Henry, S. 1989. A Methodology for integrating maintainability using software metrics. In *Proc. Conf. on Software Maintenance,* pp. 32-39. Miami, Oct. 16-19, IEEE, Piscataway.

Lorenz, M. and Kidd, J. 1994. *Object-Oriented Software Metrics.* Prentice-Hall, Englewood Cliffs, NJ.

McCabe, T. J. 1976. A complexity measure, *IEEE Trans. Soft. Eng.*, Vol. 2, pp. 308-320.

Moser, S. 1995. Metamodels for object-oriented systems, *Software — Concepts and Tools,* No. 16, Springer International, Heidelberg, 63-80.

Moser, S. 1996. *Measurement and Estimation of Software and Software Processes,* Ph.D. Thesis, University of Berne, Switzerland.

Moser, S., Henderson-Sellers, B. and Mišič, V. 1997. Software Cost Estimation based on Business Models, submitted for publication.

Rational Inc. 1997. *Unified Modeling Language (UML) V1.0,* Santa Clara, CA (http://www.rational.com).

Zuse, H. 1991. *Software Complexity: Measures and Methods,* Walter de Gruyter, Berlin.

Further Information

We would like to comment on three sources of further information about object-oriented metrics that are in the list of references.

1. Henderson-Sellers (1996) gives a comprehensive overview of research done and experiences made. A rigorous approach, based on measurement theory and sound statistical practices, is promoted. This book provides the researcher and practitioner with many valuable insights and pointers to further information sources. It also connects metrics to the broader concepts of methodology, project management, software lifecycle models, etc.

2. Lorenz and Kidd (1994) take a more practitioner-oriented approach. Their main contribution is a comprehensive list of metrics, most of them backed by empirical data, and a discussion of their practical use for assessing design quality, which is the focus of the book.
3. Moser (1996) in his Ph.D. thesis focuses on the estimation application of metrics of size. He suggests a new metric for object-oriented systems, the System Meter (an evolution of Function Points), that is independent of human rates and takes reuse into account. In an industry analysis covering 36 projects, the new metric delivers significantly more accurate estimates than Function Points. A practical guide for using the new approach is contained in appendix E of the thesis.

46

Metrics Used for Object-Oriented Software Quality

Thomas Drake
Coastal Research & Technology, Inc.

46.1 Introduction

Today, programming is more complicated than ever before. Projects are bigger, last longer, cost more, and are more difficult to manage. Yesterday's methods are just not adequate for today's software development environments. This is why software measurement is so important at leading edge software development companies and organizations, particularly with the increasing use of object-oriented software development languages, environments, and tools.

Because object-oriented programming is relatively new, there is no common agreement on the precise nature of the appropriate metrics for measuring object-oriented software development. However, there has been a lot of progress in evolving a more generally accepted and common set of metrics for the object-oriented programming approach. This includes metrics at the system, class, and method level. Most of the object-oriented measures that are proposed or included in automated tool technology are measured at the class and method level.

Typically, the object-oriented approach is largely aimed at developing highly reusable, flexible, low maintenance systems. Increasing numbers of developers are creating whole software systems using the Java, C++, Smalltalk, and Eiffel object-oriented languages, plus others.

0-8493-3135-8/99/$0.00+$.50

Object-oriented methodologies require significant effort early in the development cycle to identify objects and classes, attributes and operations, and relationships. Encapsulation, inheritance, and polymorphism require object-oriented designers to carefully structure the design and consider the interaction between the various objects. The result of this early analysis and design process is a blueprint for implementation. Thus, it becomes even more important to ensure the creation of quality object-oriented designs.

Typically, the analysis and the design phases in the development of object-oriented systems are iterative in nature. Given a set of requirements, we are often required to revisit the analysis and make changes to the design several times. "When do you decide that the design is complete?" or "Is the quality of the design good enough?" or "How does the design compare with other designs from similar domains?" are difficult to answer questions for most object-oriented software development designers.

One way to ensure quality and meaningfully discuss quality issues is to measure for the "presence of quality" characteristics in the object-oriented artifact of interest. However, quality is not easy to evaluate; since it is a multifaceted concept that means different things to different people and is subjective by nature. In addition, the issue of quality needs to be addressed from the viewpoint and context of those who are interested in the information, and the outcome and quality that is appropriate and useful for the object-oriented development approach.

The demand for quality software continues to intensify due to our society's increasing dependence on software and the devastating effect that a software error can have in terms of life, functional catastrophe, financial loss, or time delays. Today's software programs do everything from controlling home appliances to monitoring and managing life- and mission-critical operations. Large and complex software systems are required to provide commercial services ranging from billing, managing complex telephone systems, and process controls in manufacturing plants, to vital services like monitoring patient health care, and controlling and managing national defense systems. We have become very dependent on our software intensive information technology systems.

Software systems like these and many others must ensure consistent, error-free operation every time they are used. This demand for increased software quality has made quality more of a discriminator between products than ever before. In a marketplace of highly competitive products, the importance of delivering quality is no longer an advantage, but a necessary factor for success. While there is uniform agreement that we need quality software, there is little agreement on how, when, and where to measure and assure quality.

The demand for greater capability, capacity, robustness, user friendliness, and adaptability to new environments has increased the complexity of modern day software. This demand, when coupled with the need to deliver quality products in compressed development cycles to overcome competition and meet customer demand, has pushed the software industry to adapt new and innovative ways for developing software. In addition, the software industry must also deal with the need to maintain legacy software and new products that are often developed from scratch every time, with no support for systematic and high-level reuse. The result of all of these demands and pressures is an industry in which change is constant and innovation is a way of life.

Weaknesses and flaws in the traditional software development processes and methodologies have much to do with the current problems of the software industry. Until recently, structural and functional development approaches and methodologies were dominant, with C and FORTRAN as two of the more popular "structured" programming high-order languages used for functional software implementation. The functional approach to software design and development essentially separates functions (or procedures) and data into different spaces. However, traditional functional programming languages like C provide few constructs to support encapsulation, structuring, or layering, which can eventually lead to the development of rigid and monolithic software that is difficult to maintain, adapt, scale up, and extend.

Much expectation has been placed on the object-oriented software development paradigm as "the answer" with its concepts of encapsulation, inheritance, and polymorphism. This "new" paradigm supposedly addresses many of the problems with the traditional structured approaches. Why?

Proponents would argue that object-oriented programming languages support constructs and mechanisms for encapsulating data and operations into a single unit. This extends existing functionality through inheritance and dynamic identification of operations to execute at runtime, and provides significant flexibility in developing reusable, maintainable, and extensible software.

The benefits of using the object-oriented approach, coupled with the deficiencies in traditional methodologies and programming languages, have been compelling enough for companies and developers to adopt this approach. The result is that there has been a steady shift in recent years toward adopting object-oriented methodologies and programming languages for the development of new software products.

The object-oriented approach to software design and programming is expected to have a major effect on software development for many years to come. Numerous software companies have either transitioned or are in the process of transitioning to the object-oriented approach. Given the growing acceptance of the object-oriented paradigm and the use of object-oriented programming languages for software development, it is extremely important that the methods and techniques of object-oriented design and analysis and the associated quality attributes measures are well defined. The number of methodologies that are being used for object-oriented analysis and design is growing rapidly. As the discipline matures there is a growing need to assess the effectiveness of the various approaches and the quality of the products they produce in order to select a set of object-oriented activities that will result in the highest quality product. To make object-oriented software development an engineering process, we should be able to measure the process and products at various stages in the development cycle. This requires one to address both the process of software development and the products that are developed.

Process-based models and metrics are used to measure the effectiveness of a software development process and deal with issues such as process repeatability, response to change, and process automation. The application of a process model as a means to measure software development has been effective in streamlining and making consistent what was previously considered an art and a chaotic process. Process models are based upon the assumption that to consistently produce quality software, a well-defined and well-calibrated process becomes necessary. It also provides for risk mitigation.

In contrast to process models and metrics, product models and metrics concentrate upon measuring the attributes of products. These attributes would include being able to specify and measure desirable software characteristics such as reusability, flexibility, and scalability. To develop a quality end product, quality not only needs to be included in all of the artifacts that lead to the end product, but it also must be measurable in each of the intermediate artifacts produced by a process. Numerous models and metrics have been suggested to assess the qualities of software products.

Software quality is still a vague and multifaceted concept that means different things to different people. This makes its direct assessment very difficult. To better define quality, researchers have developed indirect quality models that attempt to measure software product quality by using a set of quality attributes, characteristics, and metrics. An important assumption in defining these indirect quality models is that internal product characteristics influence the product's external quality attributes, and by evaluating a product's internal characteristics some reasonable conclusions may be drawn about these attributes.

Some of the earliest software product quality models suggested software product qualities as a hierarchy of attribute factors, quality release criteria, and analysis metrics. International efforts have also led to the development of a standard for software-product quality measurement in the form of ISO 9126. All of these models vary in their hierarchical definition of quality, and they share common problems. The most serious problem is that the models are vague in their definitions of the lower level details and metrics needed to obtain a quantitative assessment of product quality. Thus, these models offer little help to software developers who need to design, develop, and deliver quality products.

In addition, the emergence of the object-oriented development approach has had one additional major drawback for measuring software quality. Traditional software product metrics that evaluate product characteristics such as size, complexity, performance, and quality level do not necessarily apply as well to object-oriented development because of some fundamentally different notions (encapsulation, inheritance, polymorphism) inherent in object-oriented software development. At a minimum, these traditional measures must be augmented by metrics that are specific and appropriate to the object-oriented software development framework. This shift has led to the definition of many new metrics to measure the software products of the object-oriented approach.

A further complication is the fact that many of the metrics and quality models currently available can be applied only after a product is complete, or nearly complete. They rely upon information extracted from the implementation of the product. This provides information too late to help improve internal product characteristics prior to the completion of the product. Thus, there is a need for metrics and models that can be applied in the early stages of development, particularly during requirements and design, to ensure that the analysis and design have favorable internal properties that will lead to the development of a quality software product. This measurement approach would give developers an opportunity to fix problems, remove non-conforming design attributes, and eliminate unwanted complexity early in the development cycle. This should significantly reduce rework during and after implementation.

So, is object-oriented development really different? Object-oriented software design and development are popular concepts in today's software development environment. The object-oriented approach is often heralded as the silver bullet for solving software problems. While in reality there really is no silver bullet, object-oriented development has proved its value and worth for software-intensive systems that must be maintained and modified. However, object-oriented software development requires a different approach from more traditional functional, "top-down" design constructs, structural decomposition, and data flow development methods. This includes the associated software metrics used to evaluate object-oriented software. Fortunately, the object-oriented approach does lend itself to early "quality" assessment and evaluation.

Though several new object-oriented metrics for design and development are available, the metrics vary in what they measure and when they are applicable. Many of the newer metrics have only been validated with small and sometimes unrealistic data sets; therefore, the practical applicability and effectiveness of the metrics on large complex projects such as those encountered in an industrial environment is not known. Also, there are few significant studies that provide empirical values for metrics on real-world projects, or that show how to compare metric results between different designs.

The concepts of software metrics are well established, and many metrics relating to product quality have been developed and used. With object-oriented analysis and design methodologies gaining popularity, perhaps it is time to seriously begin investigating object-oriented metrics with respect to software quality. We are interested in the answer to the following questions:

- What concepts, approaches, and structures in object-oriented design affect the quality of the software?
- Can traditional metrics measure the critical and unique object-oriented structures?
- If so, are the threshold values for the metrics the same for object-oriented designs as for more traditionally structured designs?
- Which of the many new metrics found in the literature are useful for measuring the critical concepts of object-oriented structures?
- What correlated set of quality metrics permits the ability to measure variability over time?

While metrics for the traditional functional decomposition, top down orientation, and data analysis design approach measure the design structure or data structure flow independently, object-oriented metrics must be able to focus on the combination of function and data as an integrated object. The evaluation of a metric's utility as a quantitative measure of software quality is fundamentally based on the measurement of a software quality attribute. The metrics selected, however, must be useful in a wide range of models. The object-oriented metric criteria should be used to evaluate the following key attributes:

- Efficiency/Optimization — Are the object-oriented constructs *efficiently* designed and *optimized*?
- Complexity/Entropy– Can the design and software constructs be used more effectively to decrease the architectural *complexity* and avoid or mitigate *entropy*?

- Understandability/Comprehension — Does the design increase the psychological complexity and therefore make it less *understandable*?
- Reusability/Portability — Does the design quality support *reuse* and *portability*?
- Testability/Maintainability — Does the structure support ease of *testing* and *maintainability*?

Finally, if the goal is to assess the external quality attributes of the product rather than simply collect individual metrics, there must be a well-defined way to connect the two. There are no known comprehensive and complete models or frameworks that evaluate the overall quality of designs developed using an object-oriented approach, based on its internal design properties, but some metrics appear strongly correlated.

Also, the measurement of quality should largely be automated and the process of evaluation should be non-intrusive to a developer. Most previously defined object-oriented metrics have little support in terms of automated tools to collect and analyze the data. For metrics to be actively used in the real world, easy-to-use automated tools are a must. It is also equally important that the tools are flexible and adaptable in order to meet different requirements and goals.

A search for "object-oriented metrics" on the Internet will return a significant number of "hits" related to such metrics. One of the most extensive sites is located at http://dec.bournemouth.ac.uk/ESERG/bibliography.html, and there are many others. The reference list at the end of this chapter also represents a starting point for further inquiry; it is not meant to be exhaustive in any way.

This chapter provides a context for some of the most frequently used object oriented metrics as well as additional metrics that are appropriate for use in object oriented development at large. The focus here is decidedly applied and reflects a practitioner's perspective.

The author has personally analyzed some 20,000,000 lines of code from object-oriented software including C++ and Java, and a number of patterns with respect to the use of metrics have emerged. A single or isolated software metric is seldom useful. From 5 to 15 well-chosen metrics seems to be a practical upper limit; additional metrics above fifteen seldom provide a significant return on investment. In addition, it is the combination of various metrics that provides for the analysis of the "velocity and acceleration" between them and offers real utility over time.

What are some of the key object-oriented metrics? Unless noted, all specified measures are for individual methods/members.

- Number of use cases and user based scenario scripts
- Method/member size (range is <30–150 LOC)
- Number of classes
- Members/methods per class (max of 30)
- Public members/methods per class (max of 15)
- Private members/methods per class (max of 10)
- Protected members/methods per class (max of 5)
- Friend functions per class (max of 10)
- Friend classes per class (max of 5)
- Inline members/methods per class (max of 15)
- Virtual members per class (max of 15)
- Explicit inline functions per class (max of 50
- Comment percentages (40-60%)
- Volume or program size (3200 or less)
- Physical source statements (62 per method/member)
- Logical source statements (38 per method/member)
- Lines of code (62 is the "magic" mean)
- Purity ratio (0.85 or greater)
- Level of effort (100,000 or less)
- Span of reference between variables (max of 10)
- Executable statements (max of 50, with ideal of 25 or less)

- Maximum nesting depth (5)
- Average variable name length (25)
- Cyclomatic complexity (McCabe; 7 or less)
- Depth of inheritance tree (maximum of 5)
- Number of children
- Coupling between objects
- Number of instance variables per class
- Number of unique messages sent
- Number of classes inherited (derived classes)
- Number of classes inherited from base classes
- Estimated errors per member/method (range of 3-8 per KLOC)
- Number of problem reports per class
- Number of problem reports per use case
- Reuse ratio
- Estimated time to develop (max of 7 hours per method/member function)
- Number of executable test paths per method/member (100 or less, max of 1000)
- Average number of logical branch links per path for method/member (25 or less, max of 50)

Metrics are almost always interrelated. Attempts to influence one metric usually have an impact on others. To be relevant and useful, metrics must be gathered systematically and regularly — preferably in an automated manner with the use of tool technology. Metrics must be correlated with respect to the code, grounded in the particular application domain, and tracked consistently over time. This correlation must take place before we can make meaningful decisions based on the metrics.

Object-oriented software metrics are different from some of the traditional software metrics because of localization, encapsulation, information hiding, inheritance, and object abstraction techniques. Several object-oriented software metrics are related to the class-instance relationship (number of instances per class per application). Other metrics for object-oriented software include weighted methods per class that focus on the complexity and number of methods within a class, the depth of the inheritance tree as a measure of how many layers of inheritance make up a given class hierarchy, and the number of children for a given class. Another measure between object classes counts the number of other classes to which a given class is coupled. And yet another is the size of the set of methods that can potentially be executed in response to a message received by an object. Another metric is the lack of cohesion in methods. This is a measure of the number of different methods within a class that reference a given instance variable.

One approach to identify a set of object-oriented metrics is to focus on the primary, critical constructs of object-oriented software. A body of literature and a number of object-oriented software analysis and measurement tools support the metrics listed or cited in this chapter for object-oriented software. These metrics can evaluate the fundamental object-oriented concepts of methods, classes, coupling, and inheritance. In addition, these associated metrics focus on the internal object structures, the external measures of the interactions among entities, the measures of the efficiency of an algorithm, as well as the psychological and task level activity measures that affect the ability of a programmer to create, comprehend, modify, and maintain software.

With all this being said, there is still some considerable disagreement in the field about software quality metrics for object-oriented systems. Some researchers and practitioners contend that traditional metrics are inappropriate for object-oriented systems. However, there are valid reasons for applying traditional metrics if it can be done and where it is appropriate. The traditional metrics have been widely used, they are well understood by researchers and practitioners, and their relationships to software quality attributes is essentially known and are very relevant at the method and member function level.

In an object-oriented system, traditional metrics are generally applied to the methods that comprise the operations of a class. A method is a component of an object that operates on data in response to a message and is defined as part of the declaration of a class. Methods reflect how a problem is broken into segments and the capabilities other classes expect of a given class. Three traditional metrics would include the McCabe Cyclomatic Complexity, size, and comment percentages/word counts.

46.2 Cyclomatic Complexity (VG1)

Cyclomatic Complexity (McCabe) is used to evaluate the complexity of the control flow algorithm in a method. A method with a low cyclomatic complexity is generally better, although it may mean that decisions are deferred through message passing. Cyclomatic complexity cannot be used to measure the complexity of a class because of inheritance, but the cyclomatic complexity of individual methods can be combined with other measures to evaluate the complexity of the class. In general, the cyclomatic complexity for a method should be 7 or below this indicates that class-level inheritance decisions are deferred through message passing.

46.3 Size/Volume

The size of a method is used to evaluate the ease of understandability of the code by developers and maintainers. Size can be measured in a variety of ways. These include counting all physical lines of code, the number of statements, and the number of blank lines and the use of variants of the Software Science or Halstead metrics. Thresholds for evaluating the size measures vary depending on the coding language used and the complexity of the method. However, since size affects ease of understanding, large routines will always pose a higher risk in the attributes of understandability, reusability, and maintainability.

46.4 Comment Percentage/Comment Words

The line counts done to compute the Size metric can be expanded to include a count of the number of comments, both online (with code) and stand-alone. The comment percentage is calculated by the total number of comments divided by the total lines of code less the number of blank lines. Ideal comment percentages should be 40 to 60% and no lower than 25%, with an average of eight comment words per comment line.

Many different metrics have been proposed for specifically measuring object-oriented software systems. Relevant object-oriented software metrics should provide analysis of structures, which if improperly designed could negatively affect the design and integrity of the code.

In addition, most object-oriented metrics primarily apply to the concepts of classes, coupling, and inheritance. Multiple definitions are given for some of the object-oriented metrics listed in this chapter, since researchers and practitioners have not reached a common definition or counting methodology. In some cases, the counting method for a metric is determined by the software analysis package used to collect the metrics.

46.5 Class

A class is a template from which objects can be created. This set of objects share a common structure and a common behavior manifested by the set of methods. Three class metrics described here measure the complexity of a class using the class' methods, messages, and cohesion.

46.6 Method

A method is an operation upon an object and is defined in the class declaration as Weighted Methods Per Class (WMC). The WMC is a count of the methods implemented within a class or the sum of the complexities of the methods (method complexity is measured by cyclomatic complexity). The second measurement is difficult to implement since not all methods are accessible within the class hierarchy, due to inheritance. The number of methods and the complexity of the methods involved is a predictor of how much time and effort is required to develop and maintain the class. The larger the number of methods in a class, the greater the potential impact on the related children, since children inherit all of the methods defined in a class. Classes with large numbers of methods are likely to be more application specific, thereby limiting their possibility for reuse.

46.7 Message

A message is a request that an object makes of another object to perform an operation. The operation executed as a result of receiving a message is called a method. Response for a class (RFC) is the set of all methods that can be invoked in response to a message to an object in the class or by some method in the class. This includes all methods accessible within the class hierarchy. This metric looks at the combination of the complexity of a class through the number of methods and the amount of interaction with other related classes. The larger the number of methods that can be invoked from a class through messages, the greater the complexity of the class. If a large number of methods can be invoked in response to a message, the testing and debugging of the class becomes complicated since it requires a greater level of understanding on the part of the tester. A worst case value for possible responses will assist in the appropriate allocation of testing time. A maximum of 30 members or so per class is a useful threshold.

46.8 Cohesion

Cohesion is the degree to which methods within a class are related to one another and work together to provide well-bounded behavior. Effective object-oriented designs maximize cohesion since it promotes encapsulation. Lack of cohesion of methods (LCOM) measures the degree of similarity of methods by data input variables or attributes. Any measure of separateness of methods helps identify flaws in the design of classes. There are at least two different ways of measuring cohesion. One can calculate it for each data field in a class and then calculate the percentages of the methods that use that data field. The standard measure is to average the percentages then subtract from 100%. Lower percentages mean greater cohesion of data and methods in the class. Methods are more similar if they operate on the same attributes. You can also count the number of disjoint sets produced from the intersection of the sets of attributes used by the methods. High cohesion indicates good class subdivision. Lack of cohesion or low cohesion increases complexity, thereby increasing the likelihood of errors during the object-oriented software development process. Classes with low cohesion can probably be subdivided into two or more subclasses with increased cohesion.

46.9 Coupling

Coupling is a measure of the strength of association established by a connection from one entity to another. Classes (objects) are coupled primarily in three ways:

1. When a message is passed between objects, the objects are said to be "coupled."
2. Classes are coupled when methods declared in one class use methods or attributes of other classes.
3. Inheritance introduces significantly tight coupling between superclasses and their subclasses.

Since good object-oriented design requires a balance between coupling and inheritance, coupling measures focus on non-inheritance coupling. Coupling between object classes (CBO) is a count of the number of other classes to which a class is coupled. It is measured by counting the number of distinct non-inheritance related class hierarchies on which a class depends. Excessive coupling is detrimental to modular design and prevents reuse. The more independent a class is, the easier it is to reuse in another application. The larger the number of couples, the higher the sensitivity to changes in other parts of the design; this makes maintenance more difficult. Strong coupling complicates a system since a module is harder to understand, change, or correct by itself if it is interrelated with other modules. Designing systems with the weakest possible coupling between modules can reduce complexity. This improves modularity and promotes encapsulation. Thresholds are typically 10 or so maximum class couples.

46.10 Inheritance

Another design abstraction in object-oriented systems is the use of inheritance. Inheritance is a type of relationship among classes that enables programmers to reuse previously defined objects including variables and operators. Inheritance decreases complexity by reducing the number of operations and operators, but this abstraction of objects can make maintenance and design difficult. The two metrics used to measure the amount of inheritance are the depth and breadth of the inheritance hierarchy — depth of inheritance tree (DIT).

The depth of a class within the inheritance hierarchy is the maximum length from the class node to the root of the tree. This is measured by the number of ancestor classes. The deeper a class is within the hierarchy, the greater the number methods it is likely to inherit, making it more complex to predict its behavior. Deeper trees constitute greater design complexity, since more methods and classes are involved, but have greater the potential for reuse of inherited methods. A support metric for DIT is the number of methods inherited (NMI). This author has found that a maximum depth level should not exceed five with a depth of two as a system tree summary average.

The number of children (NOC) is the number of immediate subclasses subordinate to a class in the hierarchy. It is an indicator of the potential influence a class can have on the design and on the system. The greater the number of children, the greater the likelihood of improper abstraction of the parent; this may be a case of misuse of subclassing. The greater the number of children, the greater the reusability, since inheritance is a form of reuse. If a class has a large number of children, it may require more testing of its methods, thus increasing the testing time.

46.11 Coverage

What about coverage analysis for measuring object-oriented software? Several tool technologies assess the "testedness" of an object-oriented module. These tools also can create a coverage trace result and present the results in graphic, textual, and tabular reports. They do this by providing both branch and method-invocation (call-pair) coverage in a single test run to identify which part of the object-oriented source code has been tested, both at the unit/object level and the system integration level. Branch coverage is used for unit and system testing, tracking the number of times each segment of a method has been exercised. Testing coverage determines if each method invocation has been exercised. Testers can then efficiently concentrate on untested code. This reduces the likelihood of defects and improves product quality.

The coverage results can be displayed in comprehensive visual reports. Detailed call trees and digraph displays allow us to instantly grasp large, complex programs. This quick overview approach spotlights untested logical segments and/or method invocation in order to pinpoint untested methods, segments, classes, modules, and units. For example, applications built with Java must be thoroughly tested at the applet level. Thousands and thousands of people on the Internet may use them and even the smallest defect could cause catastrophic complications. The financial stakes leave no margin for error. As the Internet expands and continues its exponential growth, network-centric developers operate under ever increasing constraints of time and quality requirements. Only automated software testing can ensure the rapid development of software that is sufficiently error-free to meet this demand.

The major advantages of using automated tool technology to determine the quality of the code include the following:

- Reliable verification of test suite thoroughness
- Rapid identification of unexercised code (produces reliable code)
- Easy management of large, complex "industrial-strength" functionality
- Easily accessible graphical coverage reporting with immediate reference to source code
- Point-and-click visual display of call-tree
- Class hierarchy analysis
- Individual method digraph ability to do branch coverage (C1)
- Method invocation (call-pair coverage; S1) in a single test run
- Efficient instrumentation
- Runtime data collection
- Class associated source-viewing capability

As object-oriented software development methods come into more widespread use, we must revisit basic questions of process and product quality assurance. The essential concepts and use of software metrics in quality assurance are well established. However, traditional metrics were developed and validated for a design methodology in which system functionality and data elements are distinguished. We need new metrics for object-oriented systems.

So what is the utility in the measurement of object-oriented software systems? Let us start with some measurement characteristics — maintainability, reusability, extensibility, testability, inheritance dependencies, comprehensibility, and reliability. What would be some of the measures for these characteristics? These metrics definitions include all of the following essential characteristics for object-oriented software development:

- Methods per class
- Depth of inheritance tree
- Number of children
- Coupling between objects
- Lack of cohesion in methods

In general, these metric definitions form the basis for emerging object-oriented software measurement tools to evaluate characteristics such as maintenance, development effort, complexity, and reuse.

Software measurement tools typically provide some minimal set of measures. System measures include the following:

- Contents of classes
- Depth of the hierarchy
- Width of the hierarchy
- Average number of subclasses
- Average number of methods
- Average number of variables

Class measures that characterize the classes include the following:

- Contents of number of class methods
- Number of instance methods
- Number of class variables
- Number of instance variables
- Number of subclasses

Method measures are oriented around individual methods and associated member functions that can describe the method in terms of the lines of code, the Cyclomatic Complexity number of McCabe, and various Halstead Software Science measures. Additional program structure information can also be quantified. Measures include the following:

- Program level and effort
- Program length
- Number of statements
- Number of executable lines
- Number of non-executable lines
- Maximum nesting
- Operator and operand frequency
- Average statement size
- Cyclomatic number
- Comment lines, comment words and percentages

The use of Kiviat diagrams lets us see the values that fall outside the minimum and maximum limitations. These limitations can be adapted to a particular application domain and software development environment. Other measurement tools can perform statistical analyses, including the ability to graph the results for the average for all metric values, median for all metric values, variance for all metric values, and standard deviation for all metric values. Many measurement tools also allow the inclusion of an evaluation of "critical" values and some statistics and the ability to define new metrics. Additionally, histograms, scatter plots, pie charts, and various types of trend analyses typically are available with many of the automated metric tool technologies.

Testing is an important and integral part of any object-oriented application development effort. The quality of an application is dependent on the levels of testing performed and its conformance to its functional requirements. One measure of testing an object-oriented application is to gather software metrics and locate early defects. The results of software metrics could be applied to evaluate both the complexity and the quantity of testing needed for an application. Early defect analysis can help to localize errors in an application. Overall, these measures help an application to achieve high reliability and reduce the resources required during application development. Several metrics in object-oriented technology can generate guidelines for controlling an application's design and reliability while still under development.

Software development involves a process that requires continuous states of improvement. To improve a software development process, we need data that represents the software process. Software metrics are the data that provide a view of the software process. Improving the software process and isolating areas that can impact a software product's functionality is the primary reason for calculating software measures or metrics. The metrics data makes it easy to schedule the application testing time frame and resources. Metrics data also can be used to forecast failure rate for a software application. As stated earlier, most metric types are reported and measured at the class level. Other types of metrics look at individual member functions.

Encapsulation metric — This category of metric determines the encapsulation characteristics of a class. Encapsulation for a class is a mechanism that allows data protection. The mechanism also allows us to follow the access rules in order to access member data for a class.

Percent public data members — This metric type measures the percentage of members of a class that have public access. This includes only data members. A high percentage of public data members implies that an encapsulation violation can occur. A high error count also is related to high percentage of public data members.

Protected data members — This metric type measures the percentage of members of a class that have protected access. This includes only data members. A high percentage of visible protected members implies that an encapsulation violation can occur.

Percent private data members — This metric type measures the percentage of members of a class that have private access. This includes only data members. A low percentage of data members with private access, in a class, implies that the chances of an encapsulation violation are high.

Percent friend members — This metric type measures the percentage of members in a class that have been declared with a friend. This includes both the data and methods declared with a friend.

Percent of public methods — This metric type measures the percentage of methods of a class that have public access. A high percentage of methods with public access can imply that a high proportion of data can change state because of public methods. State changes to data may lead to an increase in errors. Encapsulation of data is not recommended as a practice and can create design problems.

Protected methods — This metric type measures the percentage of methods of a class that have protected access. A high percentage of methods with protected access for a given class can imply that the public-derived classes can change the state of data.

Percent of private methods — This metric type measures the percentage of methods of a class that have protected access. A high percentage of methods with private access implies tighter encapsulation and fewer side effects.

Inheritance metric — This category of metric determines the inheritance characteristics of a class. Inheritance is a mechanism in which new classes can be derived from base classes. The derived classes inherit characteristics from their base classes.

Number of base classes — This metric type measures the total number of base classes for a given class. A high count in the total number of base classes signifies multiple inheritance and higher complexity.

Depth of inheritance — This metric type indicates the depth of a class within a class hierarchy. In case of multiple inheritance, the value of this metric is the maximum length or distance from the node or decision point to the root of the tree. This metric measures the number of classes that must be analyzed before a method of a particular class can be used. This metric can be defined as the total number of super classes for a given class. The depth of a particular class within its inherited tree represents its complexity. The complexity of a class is directly proportional to its depth in its inheritance tree.

Polymorphism metric — This category of metric determines the polymorphism characteristics of a class. It is a mechanism by which functions can be invoked using the same interface.

Number of virtual methods — This metric type measures the number of virtual methods declared in a given class. It is useful for classes with reuse potential.

Number of inherited virtual methods — This metric type measures the number of virtual methods inherited by a given class. If the base class represents a reusable class whose design and code can be reused, this measure becomes important.

Weighted methods per class — This metric type measures the number of methods in a class with equal weight. The value calculated by this metric is directly proportional to the complexity of a class.

Total number of methods per class — This metric type measures the total number of methods present in the current class and all the inherited methods. A higher number indicates more testing and an increase in complexity.

Class coupling — This metric type measures the possible number of classes a particular class uses. It can be designed for a particular class as the number of use and association relationships with other classes. A higher value for use and association with other classes represents higher complexity. It is difficult to change a class that has high values for class coupling.

Class complexity — This metric is an analysis of all complexity metrics reported; it determines the current complexity of the class.

Number of parameters per method — The number of parameters per method is a reflection of design. In C++ for example, methods declared for a class can have arguments specified for them. The number of arguments specified for a method can vary, depending on the functionality implemented by the method. Any number of parameters that are higher than the average are reported in this metric. A class that is simple to use, with an average number of parameters, becomes a candidate for reuse and can provide a foundation for derivation and future development.

Managers can use software measurement to get a handle on the product their programmers are creating. Using well-accepted measurement techniques, they can identify the most complicated parts of the software and allocate programming, testing, and maintenance resources accordingly. Developers can use measurement to help minimize the complexity of their code earlier in the programming process. This yields more maintainable and less error-prone software. Test engineers and quality assurance personnel can use software measurement to manage code reviews, inspections, and testing. Software measurement is an indispensable aid and guide whenever decisions have to be made.

The effectiveness of walkthroughs, code inspections, and similar techniques to identify programming and design errors early in the software lifecycle is well known. However, the process of reading code is time-consuming. So much so, that participants in a scheduled walkthrough or inspection often have a chance to read only a small portion of the code being discussed. Many development organizations have also adopted metric thresholds that are checked as part of the code inspection process. This ensures that overly complex code will not find its way into subsequent testing and maintenance phases. This approach is part of a good practice that mitigates risk on the development effort.

Software developed with an eye toward reducing complexity will usually be much easier to maintain after delivery. This translates directly into lower operation and support costs. If the complexity of maintenance modifications can be controlled, the result can be software with a longer lifetime. Such software can then be rewritten or heavily documented to aid maintainability. A great deal of software dies before its time simply due to entropy. The gradual degradation of the code's structure as corrections and enhancements are made. The complexity of a piece of software can be compared before and after a change is made. Changes that increase the complexity above a certain threshold may warrant special attention to verify that there is no better approach to the change.

What are some of the useful key static object-oriented measures? They are detailed below and in Table 46.1.

46.12 Software Science Measures

- Length
- Effort
- Volume
- Purity ratio
- Estimated time
- Estimated errors

46.13 Complexity Measures

- Cyclomatic complexity (McCabe)
- Essential complexity (McCabe)
- Extended cyclomatic complexity

46.14 IEEE Standardized Size Measures

- Physical source statements (PSS)
- Logical source statements (LSS)
- Nonexecutable statements
- Compiler directives
- Blank lines
- Comments
- Control flow nesting depth
- Span of data reference
- Average variable name length

TABLE 46.1 Code Measurement Standards for C++, JAVA (provides correlation for ~85% + of the code)

Static Measure (Definition)	Standard "Normalized" Value (range in parens.)
	Measurement Thresholds
Cyclomatic Complexity (statement-level control flow) Note: Case statement increases count by one	7 (1–12 max) NOTE: >15 is critically out of bounds
Database code	<10 (2–25 max) Note: > 50 is critically out of bounds
GUI -generated code	<5 (2–10 max) Note: > 20 is critically out of bounds
Purity Ratio (optimization level per function)	1.0 (.85–1.25 +) Note: <0.70 is critically out of bounds
Database code	> .60 (.60–1.0 +) Note: <0.50 is critically out bounds
GUI-generated code	> .50 (.50–1.0 +) Note: <0.30 is critically out of bounds
Volume (program size)	3,200 (<100–4,500 max) Note: >7,500 is critically out of bounds
Database code	5,000 (<3,200–7,500 max) Note: > 15,000 is critically out of bounds
GUI generated code	7,500 (<3,200–10,000 max) Note: > 20,000 is critically out of bounds
Effort (abstraction level of function)	100,000 per function (<10,000–300,000 max) Note: >500,000 is critically out of bounds
DB code	500,000 per function (<300,000–1,000,000 max) Note: > 2,000,000 is critically out of bounds
GUI-generated code	1,000,000 per function (<500,000–5,000,000 max) Note: >10,000,000 is critically out of bounds
Estimated Time to Develop in Hours (per function as an average)	4.5 (< 2–7 max) Note: >15 is critically out of bounds
Comment Percent of Code	60% (40%–60%+) Note: <20% is critically out of bounds
Functional Density (per source lines of code/LOC)	62 (<36–150 max) Note: >250 is critically out of bounds
DB code	125 (<75–250 max) Note: >500 is critically out of bounds
GUI-generated code	250 (<150–500 max) Note: >1,000 is critically out of bounds
Predicted Errors in Code (per 1000 lines of code/KLOC)	4 (<3–8 max) Note: >15 is critically out of bounds
	Performance Predictability
Executable One-Trip Paths (per function)	<100 (<50–1,000 max) Note: >5,000 is critically out of bounds
DB code	2,000 (<500–20,000 max) Note: > 50,000 is critically out of bounds
GUI-generated code	5,000 (<1,000–50,000 max) Note: > 100,000 is critically out of bounds
Average Number of Branch Links (per function)	25 (<15–50 max) Note: >75 is critically out of bounds

Unit values are based on a "standard" single function/method within the programming language.

46.15 Predictive Performance Measures

- Average number of logical branch links per executable path
- Number of actual executable paths per function method/member

For the higher-level class information, a class hierarchy table listing all base classes and their derived classes allows the user to easily identify which classes are derived from which other classes. Class size metrics can include the number of instance methods and variables, and the number of class methods and variables. Class inheritance measures can include class hierarchy, nesting level, and specialization indices.

Method size metrics can include the number of message sends and the number of statements or expressions. Method internals can include the McCabe Cyclomatic Complexity and use analysis for accessing methods.

46.16 Process Measures

Additional key process metrics that can also be collected and analyzed include the following:

- Schedule and progress regarding work completion
- Cost, schedule, and development progress

- Requirements traceability and requirements stability
- Design stability and complexity
- Computer resource utilization
- Funding and personnel resources regarding the work to be performed
- Product quality regarding the delivered products
- Fault profiles and predicted reliability
- Breadth of testing, complexity, and depth of testing
- Software development performance regarding the capabilities to meet program needs
- Technical adequacy regarding software reuse
- Use of standard data elements

Schedule — Tracks progress vs. schedule (event/deliverable progress).

Cost — Tracks software expenditures ($ spent vs. $ allocated).

Development progress — Indicates the degree of completeness of the software development effort. It also can be used to judge readiness to proceed to the next stage of software development.

Requirements traceability — Tracks requirements to code (% requirements traced to design, code, and test).

Requirements stability — Tracks changes to requirements (user/developer requirements changes and effects).

Complexity — Assesses code quality.

Breadth of testing — Tracks testing of requirements (% functions/requirements demonstrated).

Depth of testing — Tracks testing of code (degree of testing).

Fault profiles — Tracks open vs. closed anomalies (total faults, total number of faults resolved, and the length of time faults are open).

Reliability — Monitors potential downtime and time between failures (software's contribution to mission failure/degradation).

Design stability — Tracks design changes and effects (changes to design, % design completion).

If we understand the costs and time associated with finding and fixing defects at the different phases of the object-oriented lifecycle, we can begin to use that data to fine tune the associated processes, reduce costs, and shorten the time to market.

While gathering and using the software metrics may appear complicated, it is really quite simple if the organization understands what must be done and implements an effective, staged approach to software metrics. One of the keys to a good software metrics program is to understand what has worked well and adapt it to your environment and software application domain.

Software measures have been extensively used to help software managers, customers, and users to assess the quality of a software product based on its internal attributes such as a reflection of the larger development and lifecycle process. Many large software companies have intensively adopted software measures to better understand the relationships between software quality, software product internal attributes and the improvements in their software development processes. For instance, software product measures have successfully been used to assess software maintainability and error-proneness. Large software organizations such as NASA and Hewlett-Packard have been able to predict costs and delivery time via software product measures. Many characterization baselines have been built based on technically sound and empirically adequate software measures.

Given the emerging discipline of the object-oriented approach, determining appropriate measures for quality is still a moving target. The object-oriented approach does provide for powerful design mechanisms that have not been fully or adequately quantified by existing software measures.

Research and study that investigates formally and empirically the relationship between object-oriented design mechanisms such as inheritance, polymorphism, encapsulation, usage, and the different aspects of software quality at the product level such as reparability, understandability, and extensibility are still necessary and include the following:

- Object-oriented metrics vs. quality attributes (reliability, portability, maintainability)
- Automatic collection (analysis tools, object-oriented tools)

- Validation of object-oriented metrics (empirical and formal)
- Relationships between object-oriented technology product and process metrics
- Standards for the collection, comparison, and validation of metrics

Given that metrics for determining object oriented quality are still emerging, it is important to note that this very chapter may no longer reflect the current state-of-the-art and practice in the field of object-oriented technology measurement and quality. It will no doubt take a combination of researchers and practitioners from industry and academia sharing even more recent advances in the field, and the emergence and validation of perhaps even other yet unidentified measures from the future, to advance the state-of-the-art in measuring object-oriented software quality.

References

Barnes, G.M. and Swim, B.R. 1993. Inheriting software metrics, *J. Object-Oriented Prog.*, Vol. 6, No. 7, November/December, pp. 27-34.

Berard, E.V. 1993. *Essays on Object-Oriented Software Engineering*, Volume 1. Prentice-Hall, Englewood Cliffs, NJ.

Card, D.N. and Glass, R.L. 1990. *Measuring Software Design Quality*. Prentice-Hall, Englewood Cliffs, NJ.

Chidamber, S.R. and Kemerer, C.F. 1991. Toward a metrics suite for object-oriented design. In *OOPSLA '91 Conf. Proc., Special Issue of SIGPLAN Notices*, pp. 197-211, Vol. 26, No. 11, November.

Chidamber, S.R. and Kemerer, C.F. 1994. A metrics suite for object-oriented design, *IEEE Trans. Soft. Eng.*, Vol. 20, No. 6, June, pp. 476-493.

Dunn, R.H. 1990. *Software Quality: Concepts and Plans*. Prentice-Hall, Englewood Cliffs, NJ.

Fenton, N.E. and Pfleeger, S.L. 1997. *Software Metrics: A Rigorous and Practical Approach*, 2nd ed., International Thomson Computer Press, London.

Fichman, R. and Kermerer, C. 1992. Object-oriented and conventional analysis and design methodologies: comparison and critique, *IEEE Comp.*, Vol. 25, No. 10, October, pp. 20-39.

Grady, R.B. 1992. *Practical Software Metrics for Project Management and Process Improvement*. Prentice-Hall, Englewood Cliffs, NJ.

Grady, R.B. 1994. Successfully applying software metrics, *IEEE Comp.*, Vol. 27, No. 9, September, pp. 18-25.

Grady, R.B. and Caswell, D.L. 1987. *Software Metrics: Establishing a Company-Wide Program*. Prentice-Hall, Englewood Cliffs, NJ.

Halstead, M.H. 1977. *Elements of Software Science*. Elsevier, North-Holland, New York.

Henderson-Sellers, B. 1996. *Object-Oriented Metrics — Measures of Complexity*. Prentice Hall, Englewood Cliffs, NJ.

Hetzel, B. 1993. *Making Software Measurement Work: Building an Effective Measurement Program*. QED Technical Publishing Group, Boston, MA.

Horgan, J.K., London, S. and Lyn, M.R. 1994. Achieving software quality with testing coverage measures, *IEEE Comp.*, Vol. 27, No. 9, September, pp. 60-69.

Jenson, R. and Bartley, J. 1992. Parametric estimation of programming effort: An object-oriented model, *J. Syst. Soft.*, Vol. 15, pp. 107-114.

Jones, C. 1991. *Applied Software Measurement: Assuring Productivity and Quality*. McGraw-Hill, NY.

Keyes, J. 1992. New metrics needed for new generation, *Soft. Mag.*, Vol. 12, No. 6, May, pp. 42-56.

Khoshgoftaar, T.M. and Oman, P. 1994. Software metrics: charting the course, *IEEE Comp.*, Vol. 27, No. 9, September, pp. 13-15.

Kolewe, R. 1993. Metrics in object-oriented design and programming, *Soft. Dev.*, Vol. 1, No. 4, October, pp. 53-62.

Li, W. and Henry, S. 1993. Maintenance metrics for the object-oriented paradigm. In *Proc. First Int. Software Metrics Symp.*, pp. 52-60. Baltimore, MD.

Lorenz, M. and Kidd, J. 1994. *Object-Oriented Software Metrics*. Prentice-Hall, Englewood Cliffs, NJ.

Miller, G.A. 1956. The magical number seven, plus or minus two: Some limits on our capacity for processing information, *Psycholog. Rev.,* Vol. 63, No. 2, March, pp. 81-97.

Minkiewicz, A. 1997. Objective measures, *Soft. Dev.,* June, pp. 43-50.

Pfleeger, S.L. and Palmer, J.D. 1990. Software estimation for object-oriented systems. In *Fall International Function Point Users Group Conference,* pp. 181-196. San Antonio, TX, October 1-4.

Putnam, L. and Myers, W. 1992. *Measures for Excellence: Reliable Software on Time, Within Budget.* Prentice-Hall, Englewood Cliffs, NJ.

Stark, G., Durst, R.C. and Vowell, C.W. 1994. Using metrics in management decision making, *IEEE Comp.,* Vol. 27, No. 9, September, pp. 42-48.

Weller, E.F. 1994. Using metrics to manage software projects, *IEEE Comp.,* Vol. 27, No. 9, September, pp. 27-33.

Whitmire, S.A. 1994. Object-oriented measurement of software, *The Encyclopedia of Software Engineering,* pp. 737-739, Volume 2, Marciniak, J.J. ed., John Wiley & Sons, NY, pp. 737-739.

Wild, III, F.H. 1991. Managing class coupling, *Unix Rev.,* Vol. 9, No. 10, October, pp. 45-47.

47

BIT: A Method for Built-In Tests in Object-Oriented Programming

Yingxu Wang
South Bank University

Dilip Patel
South Bank University

Graham King
South Bank University

Shushma Patel
South Bank University

Built-in test (BIT) is defined as a new kind of software testing which is explicitly described in the object-oriented (OO) software source code as member functions. Software with BITs has two modes of operating: the normal mode for program execution and the test mode for debugging, testing, and maintenance. The BITs are inactive in the normal mode and can be activated in the test/maintenance mode.

The BITs are a new philosophy contributing OOP methodologies. By extending the inheritable structure and the reusability of OO software from code to tests by the BIT methods, the capability of object-oriented mechanisms, such as encapsulation, inheritance, and reusability, can be enhanced to the maximum. OOP supplemented by BITs can form a new programming method, which is useful for creating test reusable, easily maintainable, and robust code in an object-oriented environment.

In this chapter, the concept of BITs is introduced. The standard structures which incorporate the BITs into conventional OO software are analyzed. Reuse methodologies for BITs in OO software are developed

0-8493-3135-8/99/$0.00+$.50

TABLE 47.1 Comparison of Reuse Levels in Hardware and Software

Reuse Level	Software	Hardware
1	Non-structured and non-reusable code	Individual component
2	Reusable object	IC
3	Reusable OO framework	VLSI
4	Reusable BITs in OO software	Testable VLSI

at object and system levels. A case study is provided for showing how to create BIT and how to inherit and reuse the BITs in OO programming (OOP). The applications of BITs in test-reusable and easy maintainable OO systems development, control of dynamic inconsistency of OO software, and OO re-engineering of the enormous legacy software systems are introduced.

47.1 Introduction

Programming methodologies are an important area in software engineering research. In the 1970s the most significant progress in programming methodologies were the structured programming (Hoare, 1972) and abstract data types (ADTs; Liskov and Zilles, 1974). Since the 1980s we have experienced OOP (Stroustrup, 1986 and Snyder, 1987) in almost every software engineering branch. OOP has taken the best ideas in structured programming and ADTs, and combined them with several new mechanisms such as encapsulation, inheritance, and reusability. The most powerful feature of OOP is the availability of reuse by inheriting code and structure information at object and system levels.

In this chapter the authors query whether the capability of OOP has developed completely, and ask if there are any possibilities to further evolve OOP with new methodologies. To answer these questions, this chapter develops the BIT method for OOP by extending standard structures of object and OO software to incorporate the self-contained tests. Based on the BITs, test inheritability and reusability for OO software can be implemented for the first time. A set of mechanisms and metrics for software testability at the basic control structure, object, and system levels have been developed (Wang, 1996; 1997a,b). This chapter extends the development (Wang, 1997a) toward a pragmatic approach.

47.1.1 Software Reuse vs. Hardware Reuse

In analyzing the nature of software reuse, the authors found that a comparison with the practices in hardware reuse are quite useful and inspirational, because computer hardware technology has been developed earlier and is relatively more mature than that of software. Additionally it has been proven theoretically and practically in computer science that hardware and software are functionally equivalent (Hoare, 1995). Table 47.1 provides a comparison for reuse levels in both computer hardware and software.

Table 47.1 shows that the non-structured and non-reusable code, developed by the early software techniques, approximate to individual components in hardware. The reusable object is equivalent to the small scale integrated circuits (ICs). The reusable object-oriented framework is equivalent to the VLSIs. At the highest reuse level, the BIT method for OO software is equivalent to that of testable VLSI.

For hardware reuse level 4, it is noteworthy that in order to close the gap between design and testing teams and to cope with the continuously increasing difficulties in VLSI testing, testable design or design for testability has been a significant trend in VLSI design. The BITs provided in this chapter have been partially inspired by the testable VLSI and system techniques developed in hardware (Hess, 1982; Smith, 1982; and Wang, 1988).

47.1.2 Code Reuse vs. Test Reuse

Reuse methods are found to be particularly useful in software engineering to improve both software productivity and quality. The conventional concept of software reuse concentrated on code. Reuse is defined as the application of a piece of code in different software. It is the authors' view that reuse has a far broader application in the total lifecycle of software engineering, such as design, implementation, test (Wang, 1995; 1996; 1997a,b; and 1998), documentation, process (Wang, 1997c,d), and experience, etc.

For code reuse, the object is the lowest level component which is reusable in OOP. A framework is defined as a skeleton prototype of an application system which consists of structural information, code implementation, and system interface. It is the highest level reusable structure in OOP.

For test reuse, this chapter develops a novel method for embedding BITs into OO software. In the BIT approach, the tests of OO software are self-contained rather than in separate documents, thus the tests can be inherited and reused as is code in OO software development.

The methods for incorporating BITs into OO software at object, class, and system levels are developed in Section 47.2. The reuse methods of BITs in OO software at different levels are provided in Section 47.3. A case study is analyzed in Section 47.4 for the design, implementation, and reuse of BITs. Applications of the BIT method in a number of software engineering areas have been identified and introduced in Section 47.5.

47.2 Built-In Test in OO Software

Conventional testing of software is generally application specific and hardly reusable, especially for a purchased software module or package. Even within a software development organization, software and tests are developed by different teams and are described in separate documents. This makes test reuse particularly difficult. The testing of conventional object-oriented software focuses on the generation of tests for existing objects and systems; the BIT method draws attention to building testability into objects and systems during design and coding, so that OO software testing can be self-contained. The most interesting feature of the BIT method is that, for the first time, tests can be inherited and reused in the same way as that of code in conventional OO software. The BIT techniques also make the object-oriented systems more maintainable (Wang, 1998).

47.2.1 Built-In Test at Object Level

A structural prototype of an object in OOP is described below. An object consists of two structural parts: the interface and the implementation. The interface of an object is the only means of external access to the member functions contained in the object. The implementation of an object is the description of codes for all member functions.

```
Class class-name {
                    // interface
                       data declaration;
                       constructor declaration;
                       destructor declaration;
                       function declarations;
                    // implementation
                       constructor;
                       destructor;
                       functions;
                    } (object-name-list);
```

An object is reusable because of its natural encapsulation and inheritability. For creating BITs, it is noteworthy that the standard functions of constructor and destructor contained in an object are interesting reusable structures. The authors have found that these standard structures can be extended further to be able to incorporate reusable BITs in an object.

A prototype of a test-built-in object is developed as shown below. Based on the conventional object structure described above, the test declarations in the interface and the test cases in the implementation are embedded into the standard object. In this way, the BITs may be inherited and reused in the same way as that of standard and application specific member functions within the object.

```
Class class-name {
                    // interface
                       Data declaration;
                       Constructor declaration;
                       Destructor declaration;
                       Function declarations;
                       Tests declaration;    // Built-in test declarations

                    // implementation
                       Constructor;
                       Destructor;
                       Functions;
                       TestCases;            // Built-in test cases
                    } BITObject;
```

It is proposed that BITs should be a standard component in test-built-in object structures. The BITs have the same syntactical functions as that of the standard constructor and destructor in an object. Thus BITs may well fit into an object via C++ or any other OO language compilers.

The BIT object has the same behavior as that of the conventional objects when normal functions are called, but if the tests are called as that of member functions in the object, e.g.,

```
BITObject :: TestCase1;
BITObject :: TestCase2;
......
BITObject :: TestCaseI;
......
BITObject :: TestCaseN;
```

the object can be automatically tested and the corresponding results are reported.

47.2.2 Built-In Test at OO System Level

The same test-built-in method can be extended to the object-oriented system level. An OO software with BIT subsystem and classes are shown in Figure 47.1, where modules 1.n, 3.k, and 2.m are the BIT classes for the fully reusable, partially reusable, and application specific (non-reusable) subsystems, respectively. The subsystem 4 is a new BIT subsystem for the entire object-oriented system. Within each class, such as ASF_1, ASF_2, PRF_1, etc., the testable mechanisms described in Section 45.2.1 can be adopted in every object.

In this way, an ideal OO software which is testable, test inheritable, and reusable is implemented at object, class, and system levels. The testable OO software also possesses the feature of easy maintenance because of its self-containment of code and structure, as well as tests within a single source file. Thus the maintenance team and the end users of the OO software system are no longer required to redesign and re-analyze tests as well as the code and class structure for a BIT software system.

47.3 Reuse of Built-In Tests in OO Software

Reuse of BITs at object and object-oriented system levels can extend and maximize the benefits of inheritability provided by OOP. In this section, the normal and test modes of OO software with BITs are introduced. In the normal mode of an OO software with BITs, the static and dynamic behaviors of the objects and system are the same as those that are conventional. In the test mode, interestingly, the BIT subsystem, classes, and objects can be activated hierarchically from the top down or bottom up.

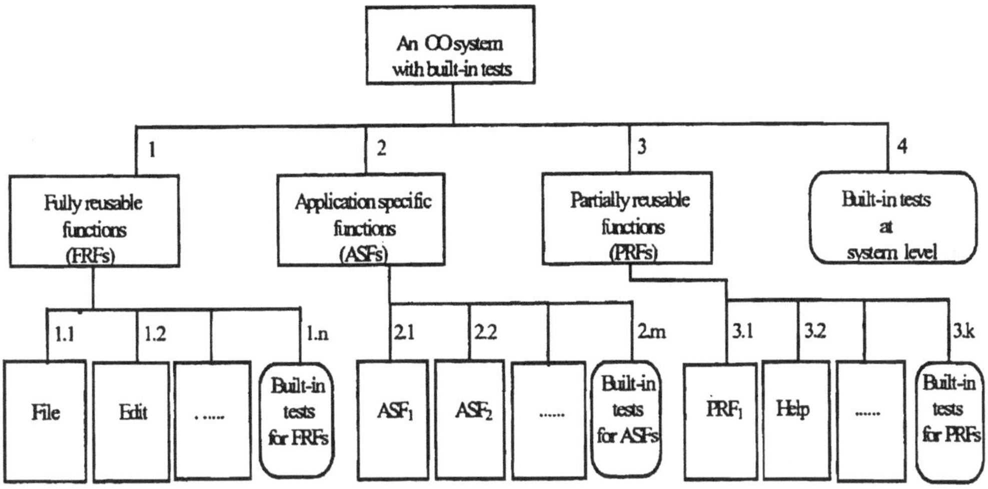

FIGURE 47.1 A prototype of test-built-in OO system.

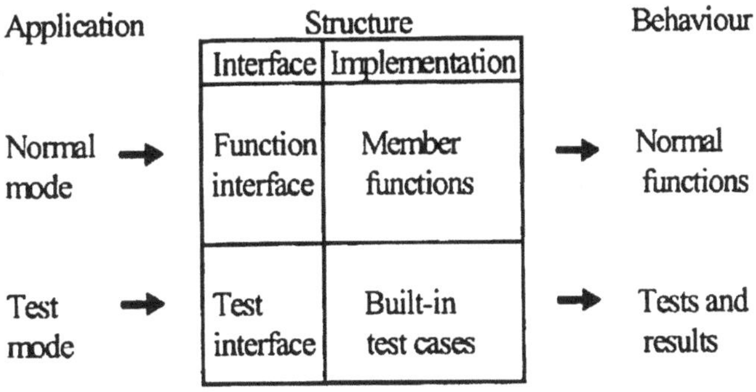

FIGURE 47.2 Reuse modes of a BIT object.

47.3.1 Reuse of Built-In Tests at Object Level

The reuse modes of a BIT object can be categorized into the normal mode and test mode as before and as shown in Figure 47.2.

47.3.1.1 Normal Mode of a BIT Object

In the normal mode, the static and dynamic behaviors of a BIT object are the same as those of the conventional objects. The member functions can be called by ObjectName::FunctionName; the BITs are standby and without any effect on the runtime efficiency of the object.

47.3.1.2 Test Mode of a BIT Object

In the test mode, BITs in a test-built-in object may be activated by calling test cases as member functions — ObjectName::TestCaseI. Each TestCaseI consists of a test driver and some test cases for the specific object. The test result can be automatically reported by the BIT driver.

47.3.2 Reuse of Built-In Tests at System Level

As in the BIT object, a test-built-in OO software as described in Figure 47.1 has two types of functions in the normal and test modes as shown in Figure 47.3.

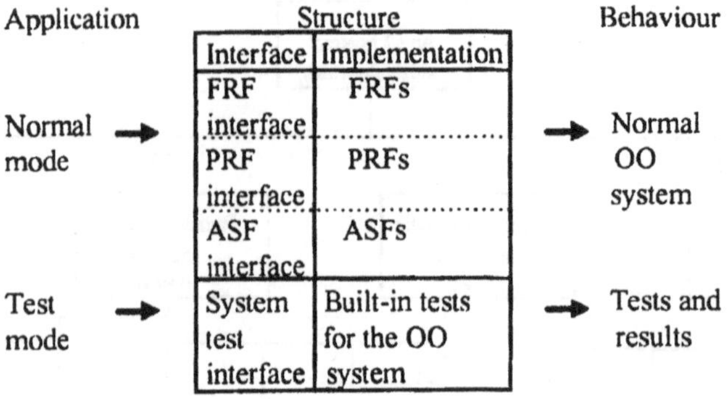

FIGURE 47.3 Reuse modes of an OO software with BITs.

47.3.2.1 Normal Mode of a BIT OO Software

In the normal mode, an OO software with BITs performs the same functions as that of the conventional software system with the same static and dynamic behaviors. The FRF, PRF, and ASF functions in the test-built-in OO software can be called by ObjectName::FunctionName; the BIT classes and subsystem are in standby and without any effect on the runtime efficiency of the test-built-in OO software.

47.3.2.2 Test Mode of a BIT OO Software

The test-built-in OO software has test mechanisms embedded at system, class, and object levels from top down as shown in Figures 47.1 and 47.3. In the test mode, the BITs can be activated by calling the test cases at the corresponding levels as member functions: ObjectName::TestCaseI. Each TestCaseI consists of a test driver and some test cases at the specific level. The test results can be automatically reported by the BIT driver.

47.4 Case Study

This section provides a case study of the application of the BIT method. A well-known example, the binary search, is given to show how to use the BIT method to develop test-built-in objects and software, and to demonstrate how BITs are inherited and reused in the same way as that of the conventional code. The test cases for the binary search algorithm are adopted from Cohen et al., 1986.

47.4.1 The Built-In Test Binary Search

A conventional subroutine of binary search with the BITs as special member functions in the object are shown below. Here the BIT object is implemented in two parts: the conventional functions and the BIT functions.

```
Class BITsBinarySearch {

////////////////////////////////////////////
// Interface
////////////////////////////////////////////

// Member functions
BITsBinarySearch();                             // The constructor
~BITsBinarySearch();                            // The destructor
int BinarySearch (int Key; int DataSet(10));    // The conventional object
void BIT1();                                    // The built-in-tests 1...3
void BIT2();
void BIT3();
```

```
//////////////////////////////////////////
// Implementation
//////////////////////////////////////////

// ========================================
// Part 1: The conventional function code
// ========================================
int BinarySearch (int Key, int DataSet(10))
{
// The conventional object
// Assume:  DataSet is ordered
//          LastElement -FirstElement >=0
//          and FirstElement >=0
// Input:   Key to be found in the DataSet
// Output:  TestElemIndex
Private:
  int bott, top, i;
  int found;

found = false;
Bott = 1;
Top = ArraySize (DataSet);    // The last element in DataSet
while (bott <= top) && (not found)
    {
    i = floor ((bott + top)/2));
    if DataSet(i) == Key
      Found = true;
      else if DataSet(i) < Key
          Bott = i +1
          else Top = i +1;
    }
if found == true
  return i;          // The index of the element
  else return 0;     // An indicator of not existence
}

// ========================================
// Part 2: The BITs
// ========================================

// BIT case 1
// ---------------------------------------
void BIT1()
{
// BIT case 1: Array size of 1, key in array
private:
  int DataSet(1) = {16};
  int Key = 16;
  int StdElemIndex = 1;
  int TestElemIndex;
  char TestResult1(5);
// Test implementation
  TestElemIndex = BinarySearch (Key, DataSet);
// Test analysis
  cout << "StdElemIndex1 = " << StdElemIndex << "\n";
  cout << "TestElemIndex1 = " << TestElemIndex << "\n";
  if TestElemIndex == StdElemIndex
```

```
        TestResult1 = "OK";
        else TestResult1 = "FALSE";
    cout << "TestResult1: " << TestResult1 << "\n";
}

// BIT case 2
// -------------------------------------------
void BIT2 ()
{
// BIT case 2: Even array size, key in array,
// not first or last
private:
    int DataSet(6) = {16,18,21,23,29,33};
    int Key = 23;
    int StdElemIndex = 4;
    int TestElemIndex;
    char TestResult2 (5);
// Test implementation
    TestElemIndex = BinarySearch (Key, DataSet);
// Test analysis
    cout << "StdElemIndex2 = " << StdElemIndex << "\n";
    cout << "TestElemIndex2 = " << TestElemIndex << "\n";
    if TestElemIndex == StdElemIndex
        TestResult2 = "OK";
        else TestResult2 = "FALSE";
    cout << "TestResult2: " << TestResult2 << "\n";
}

// BIT case 3
// -------------------------------------------
void BIT3 ()
{
// BIT case 3: Odd array size, key not in array
private:
    int DataSet(7) = {16,18,21,23,29,33,38};
    int Key = 25;
    int StdElemIndex = 0;
    int TestElemIndex;
    char TestResult3 (5);
// Test implementation
    TestElemIndex = BinarySearch (Key, DataSet);
// Test analysis
    cout << "StdElemIndex3 = " << StdElemIndex << "\n";
    cout << "TestElemIndex3 = " << TestElemIndex << "\n";
    if TestElemIndex == StdElemIndex
        TestResult3 = "OK";
        else TestResult3 = "FALSE";
    cout << "TestResult3: " << TestResult3 << "\n";
}
}
```

For the binary search function listed in Part 1, a set of ten or more test cases can be generated by using the equivalence partitioning technique or others. In the binary search example three of the test cases are adopted to show the method of BITs. It is significant that the BIT method can incorporate any test cases generated by the black box (functional) and/or white box (structural) testing methods as the BITs.

47.4.2 Mechanisms of the BIT Object

In the normal mode, the conventional functions described in Section 47.4.1 can be executed by calling:

```
BITsBinarySearch::
BinarySearch(int Key, int DataSet(10))(1)
```

In the test mode, the embedded BITs in the class can be reused by calling the following:

```
BITsBinarySearch::BIT1();
BITsBinarySearch::BIT2();
BITsBinarySearch::BIT3();
```

When the BITs are executed, testing results for the binary search function may be automatically reported as follows:

```
StdElemIndex1 = 1
TestElemIndex1 = 1
TestResult1 = OK

StdElemIndex2 = 4
TestElemIndex2 = 4
TestResult2 = OK

StdElemIndex3 = 0
TestElemIndex3 = 0
TestResult3 = OK
```

In case the *i*th test for the object had failed because of defect existence, code corruption, or runtime error, the report will be displayed in the following way:

```
StdElemIndexI = n
TestElemIndexI = n'// n'<>n, usually n'=0
TestResultI = FALSE
```

47.4.3 Inheritance and Reuse of the BITs in OOP

When a new object, DatabaseQuery, is developed based on the BITsBinarySearch, the BITs for the binary search algorithm described in Section 47.4.1 can be inherited and reused directly (Part 2, below) as that of the conventional member functions (Part 1, below). Also new BITs can be incorporated into the new object as shown in Part 3.

```
class DatabaseQuery: public BITsBinarySearch

{

/////////////////////////////////////////////
// Part 1: The inherited conventional functions
/////////////////////////////////////////////

int DatabaseQueryBinarySearch (int Key, int DataSet(10)) :
BITsBinarySearch::BinarySearch(int Key; int DataSet(10));

/////////////////////////////////////////////
// Part 2: The inherited BIT functions
/////////////////////////////////////////////
void BIT1() : BITsBinarySearch::BIT1();
void BIT2() : BITsBinarySearch::BIT2();
void BIT3() : BITsBinarySearch::BIT3();
```

```
/////////////////////////////////////////////
// Part 3: The newly developed BITs
/////////////////////////////////////////////

// BIT case 4
// ------------------------------------
void BIT4()
{
// BIT case 4: Even array size, key 1st element in array
Private:
      int DataSet (6) = {16,18,21,23,29,33};
      int Key = 16;
      int StdElemIndex = 1;
      int TestElemIndex;
      char TestResult4 (5);
// Test implementation
      TestElemIndex = BinarySearch (Key, DataSet);
// Test analysis
      cout << "StdElemIndex4 = " << StdElemIndex << "\n";
      cout << "TestElemIndex4 = " << TestElemIndex << "\n";
   if TestElemIndex == StdElemIndex
         TestResult4 = "OK";
         else TestResult4 = "FALSE";
   cout << "TestResult4: " << TestResult4 << "\n";
}

// BIT case 5
// ------------------------------------
void BIT5()
{
// BIT case 5: Even array size, key last element in array
private:
      int DataSet(6) = {16,18,21,23,29,33};
      int Key = 33;
      int StdElemIndex = 6;
      int TestElemIndex;
      char TestResult5 (5);
// Test implementation
      TestElemIndex = BinarySearch (Key, DataSet);
// Test analysis
      cout << "StdElemIndex5 =" << StdElemIndex << "\n";
      cout << " TestElemIndex5 =" << TestElemIndex << "\n";
   if TestElemIndex == StdElemIndex
         TestResult5 = "OK";
         else TestResult5 = "FALSE";
   cout << "TestResult5: " << TestResult5 << "\n";
}
}
```

In the new object DatabaseQuery listed above, the existing BITs developed in the BITsBinarySearch object can be activated by calling:

```
DatabaseQuery::BIT1(); // equivalent to BITsBinarySearch::BIT1
DatabaseQuery::BIT2(); // equivalent to BITsBinarySearch::BIT2
DatabaseQuery::BIT3(); // equivalent to BITsBinarySearch::BIT3
```

and the new tests supplemented in the DatabaseQuery object can be activated in the same way:

```
DatabaseQuery::BIT4(); // new BITs only in class DatabaseQuery
DatabaseQuery::BIT5();
```

It is interesting to note that in the BIT approach, software tests themselves are software too. As shown in Sections 47.4.1 and 47.4.3, the effort for BITs in the object BITsBinarySearch has been repaid by the ideal inheritability and reusability of tests in the case shown in Section 47.4.3 and all the subsequent reuse of the BITs in any related applications. Assuming that the existing software system can be re-engineered using the BITs method, the future software production will benefit strongly from the reuse of the BITs in software development, testing, and maintenance.

In the BIT approach, what the developer, end user, and maintainer inherit, is instant and self-testable. It is a kind of well-engineered software with high design quality, testability, reusability, and reliability. The BITs method has also found interesting applications in the software industry for re-engineering legacy systems.

47.5 Applications of the BIT Method

The BIT method has found a wide range of applications in software testing, development, and re-engineering. This section introduces applications of the BIT in maintainable OO software design, OO re-engineering of legacy software systems, and dynamic inconsistency control in OO software.

47.5.1 Maintainable OO Software Development

Testing is central in software maintenance. Tests are required in all the corrective, adaptive, perfective, and preventive maintenance (Lientz et al., 1978 and McDermid, 1991), because any existing, modified, improved, and safety-critical software, corresponding to the above-mentioned categories of maintenance, need systematic tests. This section demonstrates how the BITs can be applied to improve OO software maintenance. It also shows how the inheritable and reusable BITs can contribute to the implementation of easy maintainable OO software, with ready tests at object and system levels.

A fundamental problem in software maintenance is that the maintenance testing is generally application specific and hardly reusable, especially for a purchased software module or package. The BITs enable the OO software to be more maintainable for both existing and updated software based on the features of self-containment of code and structural information, as well as tests within a single source file. Thus the maintenance team and the end users of the OO software are no longer needed to redesign and re-analyze the code, class structure, and tests for a software system in maintenance.

According to the BITs solution for easy maintainable software development, maintainability of both existing and newly development OO software systems can be achieved by combining the source codes and their tests at object and system levels as shown in Sections 47.2–47.4.

Maintainable software is designed for operation in two modes — the normal and the maintenance mode. In the former mode, the software has the same behavior as the conventional system; in the latter mode, the BITs can be activated by calling a built-in test case, *TestCaseN*, at the corresponding level as member function: ObjectName::TestCaseN. As shown in Section 47.4, each test case consists of test drivers and test cases for a specific object. The test result can be automatically reported by the BIT drivers.

It is interesting to find a novel approach to implement an easy maintainable OO system, based on the BITs and reuse methods at object, class, and system levels. Combining the test-built-in method with the conventional OOP approach enables OO software to be highly maintainable based on the self-contained testing mechanisms. All corrective, adaptive, perfective, and preventive software maintenance can benefit from this approach.

47.5.2 Re-Engineering of Legacy Software Systems by the BITs

Re-engineering the legacy software systems with OO techniques has been an important trend in software re-engineering (McDermid, 1991; Sommerville, 1992; and Wang, 1997c). A new approach for OO re-engineering is developed in which the BITs can be incorporated into the conventional software during OO re-engineering. As a re-engineered OO system with the BITs is self-testable, test reusable, and easy maintainable, a BIT plus OO technology can be a significant re-engineering approach for the conventional OO or non-OO legacy systems.

Re-engineering of the legacy systems can be carried out in two ways. For the conventional non-OO software, re-engineering can be implemented by a combined OO and the BIT method. For existing OO software systems, re-engineering can be conducted by incorporating the BIT into the OO software and benefit from the highly testable, test reusable, and maintainable mechanisms of the BITs.

The BIT method is a new approach by which to extend conventional OO re-engineering methodologies. Incorporating the BIT method in OO re-engineering, both OO or non-OO legacy systems can be well re-engineered for higher design quality on system testability, maintainability, and reliability.

47.5.3 Software Inconsistency Control by the BITs

Software inconsistency can occur in any phase of the development process and in runtime applications. Avoidance of static inconsistencies in software design, implementation, and maintenance, as well as protection of dynamic inconsistencies of software at runtime, are important topics in software engineering research and in the software industry. This section presents a method to control the design and runtime inconsistency of OO software by the BIT.

47.5.3.1 Classification of Software Inconsistency

Two categories of software inconsistencies, the static and dynamic, have been identified by the authors in requirement engineering and software development. The former consists of design, implementation, and maintenance inconsistencies. The latter contains runtime, decay, random, environment, and configuration inconsistencies. These eight types of software inconsistency are formally defined below:

Definition 1 — Design inconsistency is defined as differences between user requirements and software specification.

Definition 2 — Implementation inconsistency is defined as differences between software specification and implementation.

Definition 3 — Maintenance inconsistency is defined as differences between user requirements and the changed implementation in corrective, adaptive, perfective, or preventive maintenance.

Definition 4 — Runtime inconsistency is defined as permanent differences between specified dynamic behaviors and real runtime behaviors.

Definition 5 — Decay inconsistency is defined as differences between original code and current code in system memory or storage.

Definition 6 — Random inconsistency is defined as temporary differences between specified dynamic behaviors and real runtime behaviors.

Definition 7 — Environment inconsistency is defined as differences of system behaviors under specified and real operation environments.

Definition 8 — Configuration inconsistency is defined as differences of system behaviors under specified and real setups.

47.5.3.2 Problems in OO Software Inconsistency Control

A summary of measures for protecting the static and dynamic inconsistencies is listed in Table 47.2. It shows that the conventional techniques for static inconsistency control are mainly formal methods, prototyping and testing; and those for dynamic inconsistencies are by inactive exception handling or system reset. The method of BIT is newly adopted as a key measure for both static and dynamic inconsistency, especially the latter.

TABLE 47.2 Inconsistency Protection Measures

No.	Type of Inconsistency	Category of Inconsistency	Protection Measures
	Static		
1		Design	Requirement engineering, formal methods, prototyping, review
2		Implementation	Testing, formal methods, field test, acceptance test, BIT
3		Maintenance	Testing, BIT
	Dynamic		
4		Run-time	BIT, exception handling
5		Decay	BIT, exception handling
6		Random	BIT, exception handling
7		Environment	BIT, adaptive testing, exception handling
8		Configure	BIT, post setup testing, exception handling

As shown in Table 47.2, a large proportion of software inconsistency is identified as dynamic inconsistency, such as the runtime, decay, random, environment, and configuration inconsistencies. The static inconsistencies have been relatively thoroughly studied in mathematical logics (Hatcher, 1982 and Hoare, 1985), formal methods (Harry, 1996), database systems (Ullman, 1987), etc. However, the dynamic inconsistencies are not easily detected, allocated, and handled, because they can only be realized at runtime.

47.5.3.3 Dynamic Inconsistency Control by BITs

By incorporating the BITs into an OO software system during development, the software dynamic inconsistencies can be detected, diagnosed, and handled at runtime. Examples are provided in this section for showing how to control dynamic inconsistency by the BITs.

Dynamic Inconsistency Detection by the BITs — Based on the BIT method, software inconsistency can be tested regressively at runtime for the first time. When the BITs at object, class, and system levels are executed, testing results for an OO software system can be automatically reported.

The BITs at different levels can be called in predesigned intervals or situations by the software system itself. The BITs can also be activated by users manually. In any case, if an inconsistency is detected at a specific level, an inconsistencies alarm will be generated for this level and levels higher.

Dynamic Inconsistency Diagnosis by BITs — In case a dynamic inconsistency is detected, the source and type of this inconsistency can be diagnosed and allocated based on a dynamic inconsistency detection report. Thus, detailed dynamic inconsistency, in terms of sources and reasons, can be allocated by the corresponding BITs automatically.

Dynamic Inconsistency Handling by BITs — After detection and allocation of any dynamic inconsistencies at runtime, a BIT at the system level will call a dynamic inconsistency handling subroutine, according to a predesigned dynamic inconsistency processing strategy, such as alarm, report, reset system, reload objects, reload data, reconfiguration, switch to standby system, replace hardware, etc.

Compared with the conventional dynamic software inconsistency handling techniques (exception → system reset), the detection, diagnosis, and handling of dynamic inconsistencies in the BIT approach is more active, accurate, and optimized. The BIT method is also suitable for controlling static inconsistencies, such as the implementation and maintenance inconsistencies.

The BIT method extends the software inconsistency protection ability from static to dynamic and from development to runtime application. By adopting the BIT approach, dynamic software inconsistencies can be detected, diagnosed, and handled as they occur. The BIT is useful for creating both dynamically and statically consistent, corrective, robust, and test reusable code in an object-oriented environment.

47.6 Conclusions

This chapter has reported the work in seeking new programming methodologies beyond the OOP theory. New methodologies supplementary to OOP in software development and OO re-engineering have been researched, and the BIT method has been developed. Fundamental reuse approaches of the BITs in OO software are demonstrated. A case study is provided for showing how to build-in tests and how to inherit and reuse the BITs in OOP.

It has been shown that the BITs method extends the reusability of conventional OO software from code to embedded tests. It is interesting to note that the tests of software are themselves software too in the BIT approach. The BIT method has found broad applications not only in new test-reusable and easy maintainable OO system development, but also in OO re-engineering of the enormous legacy software systems and the control of dynamic inconsistency of OO software. The BIT method can be fit into the conventional OOP techniques and OO compilers directly and has drawn much interest from the software industry.

Acknowledgments

The authors would like to acknowledge the support of the European Software Institute and the IVF Centre for Software Engineering. We would like to thank Geoff Staples, Ian Court, and Margaret Ross for their valuable comments.

References

Cohen, B., Harwood, W. T. and Jackson, M. I. 1986. *The Specification of Complex Systems.* Addison-Wesley, Reading, MA, pp. 15-22.

Harry, A. 1996. *Formal Methods — Fact File — VDM and Z.* John Wiley & Sons, England, pp. 57-88.

Hatcher, W. S. 1982. *The Logic Foundations of Mathematics.* Pergamon Press, Oxford, pp. 32-39.

Hess, R.D. 1982. Testability analysis: An alternative to structured design for testability, *VLSI Design,* Vol. March/April, pp. 22-27.

Hoare, C. A. R., Dijkstra, E. W. and Dahl, O. J. 1972. *Structured Programming.* Academic Press, New York.

Hoare, C. A. R. 1985. *Communicating Sequential Processes.* Prentice-Hall International, New York.

Hoare, C. A. R. 1995. Unified Theory of Computing Science, *OUCL Technical Monograph,* Oxford University Computing Laboratory.

Lientz, B., Swanson, E. B. and Tompkins, G. E. 1978. Characteristics of application software maintenance, *Commun. ACM,* Vol. 21, pp. 466-471.

Liskov, B. and Zilles, S. 1974. Programming with abstract data types, *ACM SIGPLAN Notices,* Vol. 9, pp. 50-59.

McDermid, J. A. 1991. *Software Engineer's Reference Book.* Butterworth Heinemann Ltd., Oxford, pp. 24.1-24.12.

Stroustrup, B. 1986. *The C++ Programming Language.* Addison-Wesley, Reading, MA.

Smith, K. 1983. Scan-path logic integrated on chip tests data array, *Electron. Int.,* Vol. 56, No. 15, pp. 85-86.

Snyder, A. 1987. Inheritance and the development of encapsulated software components, in *Research Directions in Object-Oriented Programming,* Shriver, B. and Wegner, P., Eds. MIT Press, pp. 165-188.

Sommerville, I. 1992. *Software Engineering* (4th ed.), pp. 427-437. Addison-Wesley, Reading, MA.

Ullman, J. D. 1987. *Principles of Database Systems* (2nd ed.), pp. 211-267. Pitman Publishing Ltd., London.

Wang Y., King, G., Patel, D., Court, I., Staples, G., Patel, S. and Ross, M. 1998. On built-in tests reuse in object-oriented programming, to appear in *ACM Software Engineering Notes (SEN).*

Wang Y., King, G., Court, I., Ross, M. and Staples, G. 1997a. On testable object-oriented programming, *ACM Software Engineering Notes (SEN),* July, Vol. 22, No. 4, pp. 84-90.

Wang, Y., Trujillo J. and Palomar M. 1997b. On a metric of software testability, *J. Spanish Computer Comp. Soc. (Novatica),* Vol. 125, Jan/Feb Issue, pp. 10-13.

Wang, Y., King, G., Court, I., Ross, M. and Staples, G. 1997c. On built-in tests in object-oriented reengineering, *ACM FSE/ESEC/WOOR'97 Proceedings on OO Reengineering,* Zurich, pp. x-y.

Wang, Y., Court, I., Ross, M., Staples, G. and King, G. 1997d. Software engineering process reuse in object-oriented framework development, *Technical Report SI-RCSE-WANG97-TEST25,* pp. 1-16.

Wang, Y., Staples, G., Ross, M., King, G. and Court, I. 1996. On a Method to Develop Testable Software, pp. 176-180. In *Proc. of IEEE European Testing Workshop (IEEE ETW'96),* Montpellier, France, June.

Wang, Y. 1995. On testable software and test reuse in OOP, *Technical Report of Oxford University Computing Laboratory,* OUCL-WANG-95002.

Wang, Y. 1988. Testability theory and its application in the design of digital switching systems, *J. Telecommun. Switching,* Vol. 17, pp. 30-36.

X

Business Objects

Dilip Patel
South Bank University

Saba Zamir
Senior Information Technology Consultant

Businesses have become intensively competitive. In order for corporations to gain strategic advantage over others, it is necessary for them to remodel their business processes, and translate these models rapidly and effectively into software implementations. Business Process Re-engineering (BPR) sets the stage for this need through the use of well-designed *business objects*. A *business object* encapsulates and integrates one or more *objects* that implement a business process. They are used to represent the business itself, and the nature and behavior of the processes that comprise that business. *OMG Business Objects* and *Business Application Architecture* is based on OMG's CORBA, and is intended to create a standard framework for identifying, developing, and utilizing such objects.

This section contains chapters that describe these concepts in greater detail.

X

48

Business Process Re-Engineering

Houman Younessi
Swinburne University of Technology

48.1 Introduction

Business process re-engineering (BPR), or at least its older sibling, "corporate planning" (Argenti, 1980), has been around for a long time and has been applied to business situations, quite independently of object technology. The principles, concepts, and approaches of BPR focus on re-orienting and optimizing the way business is done. Object technology too, has been around independently of BPR for some time. Its application in software development and information technology is well publicized. So why have we included a chapter on BPR in a book of object technology? The answer is because:

1. Object technology is a powerful modeling paradigm with important mechanisms for handling complexity. Any process redesign that deals with a complex problem domain can benefit immensely from such a modeling approach. Business is one such domain and thus BPR can benefit from its association with object technology.
2. Business improvement is the primary aim of most information technology offerings. The seamlessness offered by object technology allows us to ensure that the "purpose" for which the system is being developed is preserved throughout the development. Thus the transition from a business domain to a system domain (when IT is used as a BPR enabler) can be a lot smoother and much less prone to loss, than taking disparate approaches to business modeling and system modeling. In other words if a BPR exercise is conducted using object technology some of which changes are subsequently implemented through software, then the chances of the success of the system development effort in meeting the "purpose" for the development of the system is very much enhanced. This is due to the aligning of the strategy and its implementation thus achievable. As such we can say that object technology has been enriched by its association with BPR.

In this chapter we will start by introducing BPR and its basic underlying principles. We will then mount an argument that BPR needs, as its core, a rich and powerful modeling paradigm capable of

0-8493-3135-8/99/$0.00+$.50

handling complex real-world and also cognitively generated problem situations. Object technology is then presented as one such appropriate approach. Having introduced the basic concepts, in Section 48.3 we introduce a number of current approaches to *object-oriented* business process re-engineering. Section 48.4 will discuss current research issues, the way ahead, and then we will present a summary.

48.2 Underlying Principles

48.2.1 What is BPR?

Hammer and Champy (1993) define BPR as "the fundamental rethinking and radical redesign of business processes to achieve dramatic improvements in critical, contemporary measures of performance, such as cost, quality, service and speed." BPR therefore requires that enterprises take a comprehensive review of their entire existing operation and try to redesign it in a way that serves customers better (Jacobson, 1995). The three keywords in the Hammer and Champy definition are "radical," "redesign," and "processes." This implies that:

1. BPR advocates a radical and revolutionary reorientation of all elements of the business. This means that there is a need for an integrated and business centered approach to BPR. Otherwise stated, there has to be a central business-oriented purpose, a business strategy, around which BPR is conducted. In addition, the new approach for the implementation of such a purpose should represent a fundamentally, and radically better way of achieving the central purpose than the current approach. Gaining, for example, a 5% reduction in inventory costs is not what BPR is all about; a threefold reduction, and then if this is a strategic aim of the organization, might be.
2. BPR requires a redesign of the current business processes. This implies in turn that *evolving* the current processes is not what BPR undertakes. There is a need for a redesign of business processes either to achieve new goals and purposes or to achieve existing ones much more effectively.

48.2.2 BPR has a Process Focus

A process is defined as "*the collection of technologies and methods utilized within a particular context by an organization in order to produce a predefined outcome*" (Younessi, 1997). This definition implies that there are three dimensions of methodology, technology, and context underpinning a process. The methodological dimension in itself may be modeled or viewed from three distinct perspectives of structure, transformations, and causal relationships. As such, a system that is studied in accordance to one or a subset of these dimensions stands a real chance of not having been understood adequately. Such systems are a lot harder to model and improve.

Unlike its predecessors (e.g., traditional corporate restructuring which focuses primarily on the structural aspects of the business system and to a lesser degree on transformations, i.e., it has a "structural" approach), BPR has a process approach. By this we mean that in redesigning the business an appropriate BPR approach considers the business domain in need of redesign as a system that defines a process located in a business setting. This allows a process design approach to the problem situation, which by incorporating important system elements such as categories of stakeholders (e.g., customers), technologies available or attainable, and the current context of the business situation, provides a much richer picture of what there is and what is possible.

We therefore define BPR as: "taking a business focused, integrated and radical approach to designing a business system that implements a newly devised or aligned organizational strategy to achieve significant business advantage."

48.2.3 What BPR is Not

To be quite up front about it, BPR is not a new information technology. It is not a new product or a new system development approach that IT people can employ to produce software products faster and cheaper. It has very little to do with all of that.

BPR is also not a new reincarnation of the process improvement and TQM discussions of the late 1980s; although to be fair there is a lateral relationship between the two.

BPR is certainly not a phase or step in the software requirement engineering stage of the software development lifecycle, as it has sometimes been introduced. Although its lessons learned and outputs (say in form of "to be implemented" models) may be and should be used as a starting point for development of requirements for software products. Particularly if the latter are to be integral and strategic enablers of the overall new strategy.

BPR is not a fad. Although it may be seen as a new label for an old concept, through its introduction of a focus on the business process, BPR (when done correctly) provides a much stronger, more integrated, and holistic approach to organizational design. Such an approach remarkably increases the chances of repeatability of reorganizational successes. In as much, it has earned its place as more than just a label.

48.2.4 Why do BPR?

Re-orienting corporate processes has become an imperative for Western business. Why do organizations practice BPR? The answer that used to be given to this question in the mid to late 1980s was that Western business has to re-orient itself if it is to compete with the emerging industrial nations of particularly Asia (Rapkin, 1995; ERDC, 1989). Then it became popular to talk about the shifting profile of the third world, for long a major market for the Western industrialized nations (Simmons, 1988). The truth is that corporate West *has* to practice BPR and has to re-orient its business processes not just because of challenges mounted from Asia (Japan, Korea, Singapore, etc.) nor due to the changing face of the third world consumer markets, but because the time has come for it to change.

The fact is that for a substantial period of time, Western economy in general and the corporate world in particular, has not been able to add net economic value (Stern, 1995). Our corporations are not creating wealth. In other words the cost of capital utilized for production and marketing is generally greater than the after tax profits earned. The overwhelming majority of large corporations (over 85%) has shown a sustained negative net economic value-added since the mid-1970s, peaking (plummeting) to around $125 billion in 1991 (Stern, 1995). In contrast, the total market value of shares has increased dramatically in the same period (Wall Street Journal 1980-1995). This indicates a market condition in which hopeful investors are willing to reinvest or retain their existing investments in ventures for the hope of larger still, future earnings. On the contrasting side of this situation are the senior management of large organizations who, faced with the eventuality of having to deliver sooner or later, are now being forced to reverse this negative balance. While there was no real imperative to do so in the economically buoyant 1980s, the situation is now remarkably different in the harsh economic reality of the mid to late 1990s.

The organizations suffering most from this disease can be categorized into two segments:

1. **The rabbit.** These are organizations that grew out of the very buoyancy of the 1980s markets, rapidly developed over a short number of years, some of them to become multibillion dollar corporate giants. Examples of these organizations can be found most prevalently among information and financial industries.
2. **The dinosaur.** These are those organizations that are large, established, monolithic, sluggish and for a long time, comfortable. Examples of these may be found in the manufacturing, banking, insurance, and transport sectors.

The reason for the troubles of the former category is that throughout its growth, the rabbit never needed to stop to ensure that its processes were optimized and its dollars were serving it in the best way possible. There was more money coming in and growth was so phenomenally fast that there was no time to wait and "waste" time on "financial nit picking." Of course when in the late 1980s the situation drastically changed almost overnight, most of these organizations allowed their momentum (mainly attributable to their speed) to carry them still further. By the early 1990s, at around the time when the negative net economic value reached its lowest figure as reported above, the realization set in that something else had to be done. The attention of some senior managers was turned at this time to the business operation itself and how to increase "productivity." Discovering, in most cases, a very ill structured, hastily put together business process, with many duplications, omissions, and wasteful and reactively motivated implementation of business activities, they set out to rectify the situation. BPR began to be practiced in order to re-orient some of these companies.

The dinosaurs were also enjoying smooth sailing in the 1970s and 1980s economic waters. Markets were well defined, shareholders confident, and the creditors generous. The crash of 1987 changed all of that. Yet the momentum of these organizations (mainly attributable to their mass) carried them through to about 1991. Then they had to "sit up and listen."

Discovering the processes of their organizations to be relics of a non-mechanized, pre-information technology past, with many antiquated, unnecessary, inefficient practices, these organizations also saw the benefit of "streamlining" their businesses. A reorientation of business processes became a necessity. Recourse was seen in BPR.

48.2.5 Doing BPR

The issue is, therefore, really one of optimization. Businesses exist to make a profit. Profits are earned when the money made from sales exceeds the money spent on producing and marketing the goods or services. To increase profits either (1) sales must go up, (2) costs must come down, or (3) both. For sales to go up, the business must be customer focused (Kotler, 1995), as in final analysis, it is the happy customer who comes back and brings with him or her new potential customers. So a customer focus must be a central tenet of business engineering. This means that the system boundary of the business must be expanded to include those concerns that lead to customer focus. It also means that business engineers must model the internals of the business to support this requirement. To do this effectively, a process approach or view to the business should be taken. This allows modeling the system using systematic and robust modeling tools as used in engineering process design — tools such as object technology.

Also, to lower costs (including lower costs of credit) once again, the business must look at its operation in terms of a process. Only when a stable and well-defined model of the business is at hand can the business engineer decide on the course of action to be taken toward orienting the internal business processes to lowering of costs. Again, object technology will prove effective as a powerful modeling tool.

Once a rich model of the business process is obtained, the business engineer will turn to orient these internal processes toward lower costs. Two options are available:

1. Distinguish the common causes from special causes and redesign that aspect of the system (the business process) which is responsible for the special causes. This is called process improvement (TQM).
2. Distinguish that there is sufficient common cause perturbation, or conversely, sufficient process stability such that the present process will not (no matter how much we fiddle with it) produce the results we require. This is when a brand new process must be designed. This is at the heart of BPR.

If the new system is designed using systematic process engineering principles, is customer focused, and targeted toward the *real* aims of the business, then it has a good chance of contributing to lowering of costs *and* to customer satisfaction, hence to an increase in sales. Once these two aims are achieved, higher profits follow.

The essential elements of *doing* business (re-) engineering are as follows:

1. Identify and state the purpose for the business engineering project — This purpose must be *central, real, clear,* and *profit oriented.* By central we mean that it must be critical to the business operation. As an example of the importance of this we can note a major insurance conglomerate that went through a business re-engineering exercise which resulted in a significant and measurable improvement of certain of its processes, yet in six months the company was almost bankrupt.

The reason was the areas re-engineered were not central to the business. By real we mean that the concern must not only be central but also believed by influential stakeholders to be so. Its achievement must be part of the vision of the organization. To be clear, the purpose must be stated in terms of measurable entities, only then can we be assured of the achievement of our purpose. Profit oriented means that the purpose when achieved will significantly improve sales, lower costs, or both. To do this we said, customer orientation was essential.

2. Use the purpose identified to clearly define and model the problem situation — Although related, defining the problem is *not* the same as stating the purpose for business process engineering. Here an investigation into possible contributing factors is conducted and individual opportunities for redesign are identified. Sometimes it is useful to create a model of the present situation. This is done for a number of purposes including: understanding, communication, and analysis of the way things are. It must be stated that creation of such a model must not be allowed to stifle creativity, ingenuity, and a revolutionary approach to business process design. This can happen easily if the engineer's views become biased toward the existing way of doing things. In modeling problem situations, object technology will prove beneficial.
3. Commence analysis using the identified opportunities and context models created — Note that this analysis is possible only if a defined and clear model of the process exists. Ishikawa diagrams, root cause, and statistical analysis are among the main tools here. The purpose for this analysis is to identify and separate the common cause from special cause. Once the common and special causes are identified then a decision may be made whether to go for "gradual process improvement," that is the removal of special causes, or whether a whole new process is needed. If the latter is the case then we have a design task on our hands, the task of designing a new business process.
4. Design a new business process — This is when principles of process engineering such as maximization of cohesion, minimization of coupling, parallelism, piping, boundary value analysis, flow analysis, and process control may be applied to the design of a new business process. This new process is aimed to be fundamentally different in its internal characteristics (i.e., the structures, transformations, and interactions composing it), yet still fulfill the same purpose as the previous process, only better, and demonstrably so; or, to develop a new process that implements a new purpose, inspired by a new vision.
5. Model the new process — One central issue here is how do we capture and communicate this design? The answer is through creating a model of it. This is where object technology becomes an enabler.
6. Implement the model — Here the business engineer will decide on the performance of various tasks or roles. To do so a number of considerations such as the vision of the organization, best practices, current technology, funds, and human resources available become prominent. Another critical task here is to decide what level of automation and technology to use. In terms of information support technologies, the re-engineered organization is in as an enviable position as there is — through the application of object technology- a largely seamless path to the design and implementation of software systems.

48.2.6 Using Object Technology; Why is Object Technology Appropriate in the BPR Context?

If one is to take a formal approach to BPR, at a minimum one might expect an approach to include:

1. A notation that allows every method of approach, technology utilized, and context within which these methods and technologies are utilized within the enterprise to be specified. The deliverables from this analysis, in the form of business models, should capture the structures, transformations, and the interactions (dynamics) of the organization. In other words we need a modeling approach that can handle and model complex situations — one that provides ample coverage of modeling dimensions or views.

2. Models presented in a language which allows the "actors" in the enterprise (the CEO, executives, process owners/managers/operators, etc.) to engage in debate leading to change. Such a modeling approach has to generate models that are presented in terms of easy to understand, real-world, problem domain entities with which the stakeholders of the enterprise have a large degree of familiarity.
3. A process for the development of an information system that is integrated with the re-engineered organization. This implies seamlessness (impedance matching) between the business and information systems models, respectively.

Many authors (Henderson-Sellers, 1997; Jacobson, 1995; Taylor, 1995; and Younessi, 1995a,b) have suggested that an object-oriented approach might meet the expectations above of a formal approach to BPR. Specifically:

- Object-oriented concepts and notations allow one to represent and clarify the inner workings of an enterprise, capturing its structures, products, services, resources, dynamics, and transformations
- If coupled with simple, natural ways of enacting those models, the "actors" in the enterprise can engage in debate leading to change (for example, Jacobson adapts his idea of "use cases" to this purpose while Younessi et al. suggest various means within SBM of aligning the models with options for change)
- The pairing of object-oriented business engineering and object-oriented requirements engineering offers a relatively seamless transition from redefined process to the requirements for the information system.

48.3 Current Approaches

In this section we present, in alphabetic order of the last name of their originators, a number of leading, distinctive, or influential BPR approaches that explicitly utilize object technology as their modeling paradigm. It should be noted that there are a large number of other BPR approaches, not based on object technology, at various stages of development or utilization. These have not been presented here as we only concentrate on those approaches that are integrally related to the main topic of this handbook. Furthermore, there are potentially other extant object-oriented BPR approaches with which this author is not familiar at this time. For the omission of these from our presentation (I hope not many), I can only apologize and stress that I have in my selection utilized a number of criteria the most important of which are, distinctiveness, integrity (based on sound and homogeneous theoretical underpinnings), applicability, popularity, and availability.

48.3.1 Gale and Eldred (Future Strategy Business Planning®)*

Gale and Eldred (1996) present the future strategy business planning (fsbp®) methodology. This approach is described by the authors — a description with which this author agrees — as a methodology for enterprise modeling. This methodology is described as a seven-stage framework, which relies on a number of techniques, concepts, and underpinnings ranging from Shannon's theory of communications (Campbell, 1982) to object modeling (Jacobson, 1995). The stated aim is to build a methodology that takes a business centered, process focused approach to modeling of enterprises. The philosophical essence of the approach has been presented by the authors in the following terms:

- An enterprise must first have a strategic foundation as a basis for its being a vision of itself
- Given that vision, advantageous and efficient product/service solutions must be identified
- Given those product/service plans, competitive approaches to the process of their creation and delivery must be identified

* fsbp® and Future Strategy Business Planning® are registered trademarks of Future Strategies Inc.

- Knowing the products and how they will be produced, it is only now time to create the most efficient approach to management of the business processes — how you will organize; it is also time to consider the infrastructure necessary to support the enterprise's customers and its business processes — the technology architecture goes here (Gale and Eldred, 1996)

The following is a description of the seven stages of this methodology. Each stage, when conducted, results in the production of a single deliverable that documents and presents the findings, plans, and models arrived at in that stage. These deliverables, called books, provide the documentation and communication necessary to support the methodology. It should be noted, however, that there is no linear application intended through the linear presentation of the stages. In fact an intricate, and iterative interrelation, may arise between the stages as a result of enaction of the methodology.

Stage 1: The business definition stage — In this stage the business is defined in terms of its scope, position, key policies, and strategies. The industry, competitors, the market, and the available and forthcoming technologies are considered and analyzed in view of the strategic mandate of the enterprise in order to develop a base strategy. This view of the enterprise is then captured in terms of target markets, operations, structures, and relative industry position of the organization.

Stage 2: Market and product planning — In this stage the market for the organization is identified, their product sets are defined, and a sales plan is generated. This is done through identifying the market with the highest opportunity gradient and recognizing the set of products that the enterprise is positioned to deliver to it. Industry, competitor, market, and technology analyses are techniques used to develop this fundamental market strategy which is presented as a set of product definitions, sales programs, and pricing strategies.

Stage 3: Public policy strategy — This stage defines the position and image that the enterprise presents on national, regulatory, industrial, market, and other public issues. This is done through an analysis of social, geosocial, and sociopolitical issues and are presented as a series of key policy statements.

Stage 4: The enterprise model — This is the stage that defines the functions and business processes of the enterprise and their interrelationships. This is done — surprisingly, despite the stated object technology orientation of the methodology — through a largely functional approach. Initially the functions of the enterprise are defined, then they are decomposed into what the authors term "business processes." The next step is to define the interrelationship of these processes. Models of the functional view, abstract business processes, process dependency models and business process flows, as well as a hierarchical multilayer model are presented.

Stage 5: Business operations planning — There is realization of the enterprise model obtained in Stage 4. This stage models the functional, and organizational structures, the business resources, the business systems (people, methods, and technologies) of the enterprise and their relationships. The business operations plan is the output of this stage.

Stage 6: Infrastructure architecture — This stage defines the logical and physical views of the enterprise. The components of this stage are as follows:

- Define the design principles of the enterprise infrastructure
- Define the logical view
- Define the general physical view of the enterprise

The physical view will define the capabilities, technologies, and location and configuration of major structural elements of the physical infrastructure.

Stage 7: Infrastructure objects — This is the stage that considers the enterprise as a "global object space" defining an infrastructure that the authors of the methodology assert is organizationally, logically, and physically integrated. This stage also benefits from object technology as a primary modeling framework. The enterprise is modeled as an object-oriented environment along with all of its structures, transformations, and behavioral characteristics. A class hierarchy of objects composing the enterprise is created along with their relationships. The output, *fsbp Book 7: The Infrastructure Object Definitions*, contains the global object space architecture, object class hierarchy summary, object clustering descriptions, entity object relationship diagrams, and physical processing requirements.

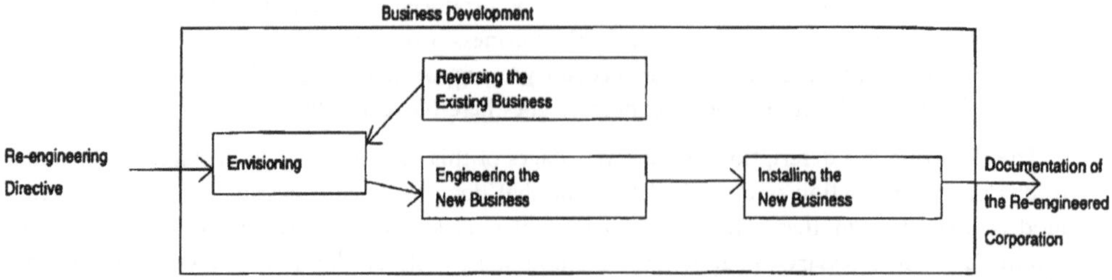

FIGURE 48.1 An overview of the main activities in a business process re-engineering project. (Adapted from Jacobsen et al. 1995. *The Object Advantage — Business Process Reengineering with Object Technology.* Addison-Wesley, Wokingham, U.K.)

The methodology, being one of enterprise modeling, does not provide a mechanism of comparing and assessing the efficacy, efficiency, and effectiveness of the enterprise model obtained as an output of Stage 7, nor does it provide a mechanism for the implementation of the model obtained.

Detailed description of the methodology and its underpinnings, along with examples, is available in Gale and Eldred, 1996.

48.3.2 Jacobson et al.

Jacobson et al. (1995) represent business process re-engineering as four primary activities, some of which are at least partially parallel, and some of which are iterated. The main activities of a re-engineering project, according to Jacobson, are shown in Figure 48.1.

The re-engineering project can start in many ways, broadly represented in Figure 48.1 as a "Re-engineering Directive" which explains why something must change and what the project is expected to achieve. The Directive triggers an activity termed "Envisioning" in which the new business enterprise or new processes are visualized. In order to achieve this, Jacobson argues that one must know the company's strategy and understand the existing business. Thus "Envisioning" triggers the "Reversing the Existing Business" activity which produces a model of the existing business. The tightly iterative Reversing/Envisioning activities result in an "Objective Specification," a vision of future business.

The "Objective Specification" is an input to the work of "Engineering the New Business" which involves creating one or more new processes, designing them, developing a supporting information system, and possibly simulating and iterating the models until a model of the redesigned company emerges. Finally, the re-engineering project will require "Installing the New Business," where the redesigned company is implemented in the real organization.

Jacobson et al. (1995) provide guidelines for all four activities. Underpinning the activities of "Reversing the Existing Business" and "Engineering the New Business" is formal modeling built around the notion of use cases and object models. To establish an understanding of what the business is meant to accomplish, one builds a use-case model consisting of actors and use cases. An actor is a representation of something that interacts with the business, whereas a use case specifies the flow of events that a particular actor wants to perform in the business. Use cases are a simple, natural way to identify business interactions. For each use case the objects and classes that are needed to execute that use case are identified. Subsequently various associations between objects and their classes are recognized (i.e., aggregates of objects, communication between objects, and inheritance between classes of objects). Worked exemplars of the method are available in Jacobson et al. (1995).

48.3.3 Taylor (Convergent Engineering)

Taylor's approach presented in his book *Business Engineering* with object technology (1995) presents an argument for utilization of the advantages of object technology to create a smooth path between the business model and the development of the information technologies that is presumed to be required to implement the business model. Termed "convergent engineering," the book argues that the seamlessness that is afforded the modeler by the utilization of object technology, will allow the business model to be transformed directly into the software systems that are to support it. The approach presented by Taylor is not defined rigorously in terms of stages and steps and is presented largely through a case study. It is really, in final analysis, a fairly general yet business-oriented approach to object-oriented requirements engineering of business systems. It utilizes generic modeling activities (e.g., object modeling) and techniques (e.g., creating class cards) available elsewhere as part of object technology, to model a problem situation that is business centered. As such the technique is best defined as a business motivated information technology requirements engineering methodology.

A BPR method we said has not only to be business centered and able to model business situations, it also has to offer specific activities and techniques to analyze, optimize, compare, and implement business systems. We also said that not all BPR exercises are IT enabled nor is IT the only enabler of BPR. There is a relationship between BPR and IT, but it is not a one to one relationship in that the latter is always the implementation mechanism of the models created by the former. The fact that it is possible to seamlessly trace the requirements of a system to the business strategy if an object-oriented approach is adopted for both BPR and information systems development is, albeit a fortunate and important one, still only a side benefit of doing BPR in the fashion recommended. The main aim of BPR should remain as it was stated earlier: "The taking of a business focused, integrated, and radical approach to designing a business system that implements a newly devised or aligned organizational strategy to achieve significant business advantage."

48.3.4 Younessi et al. (State Behavior Modeling, SBM)

Younessi et al. (1994, 1995a,b) represent business process re-engineering as a five-stage process, which adopts a number of the techniques of the Soft Systems Methodology (SSM; Checkland and Scholes, 1990). SSM is a systems-based, problem-solving methodology with a rich base of techniques for supporting the initial analysis of ill-structured enterprises, including the investigation of cultural issues. SBM advocates that the analyst should propose multiple relevant systems, each of which, when modeled, will support debate on the various perceptions that stakeholders have of the primary tasks and issues surrounding the operation of the enterprise. Further, the work of Wilson (1989) has provided insights into the means by which one might develop a model that accommodates various stakeholder views of the primary tasks which take place.

The five stages of SBM are presented schematically in Figure 48.2. As shown, the organization is investigated in *Stage 1*, using ideas such as those described by Checkland and Scholes (1990) under the headings of "analysis of the intervention," "social system analysis," and "political system analysis." With the insights so established it allows the naming, in *Stage 2*, of systems relevant to the tasks and issues considered by various participants as important to the organization's future operation. It is important to note that these are not present real-world systems, but named systems which participants believe may be relevant to understanding possible future processes of the organization. There may be many such system names. SBM prescribes the representation of each named relevant system as a "State-Behavior Definition" (Younessi, 1995a,b), a concise textual statement of the roles, states and behaviors, purpose and environment of each relevant system, somewhat akin the SSM's Root Definition with its CATWOE elements (Checkland, 1990).

At *Stage 3*, SBM provides a series of heuristics (Younessi, 1995a) which support the extraction of classes, attributes, operations, and the associations, aggregations, and inheritance structures required to construct an object model based upon each named relevant system (i.e., based upon the State-Behavior Definition). The models so constructed, termed "State-Behavior Models," can be represented in any class oriented-object notation (e.g., that of OML [Firesmith, 1997], or UML [Booch, 1995 and Rational, 1997]).

At *Stage 4*, SBM takes an approach similar to that advocated by Wilson (1989) for arriving at a model which accommodates the various views of the primary tasks. Specifically, the various object models developed at *Stage 3* are reviewed to identify classes which are common to all. Those about which there

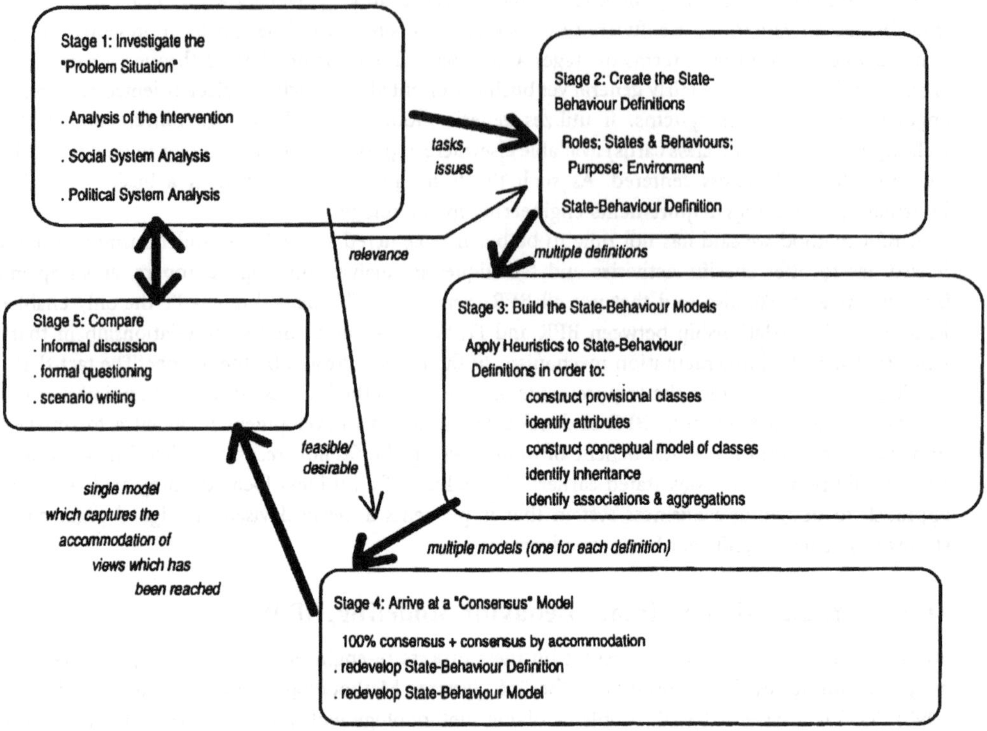

FIGURE 48.2 A schematic representation of the state-behavior modeling framework.

is not 100% consensus are then questioned as to desirability, determined by debate between the various stakeholders. Additional classes, agreed by this process, together with those common to all models, form a tentative "consensus" model. In order to improve the coherence of what is really only a collection of classes "glued" together, it is useful to utilize the pairing of the State-Behavior Definition and the State-Behavior Model, by developing a new State-Behavior Definition which attempts to be consistent with the tentative consensus model. From the new definition, one can develop a model which should be coherent, by recovering *Stage 3* starting with the new SBM Definition. Once this newly developed coherent consensus model is developed, the overall dynamic behavior of the model and its various components is investigated and modeled using a state-based dynamic modeling language.

Finally, in *Stage 5* one formally aligns the model with the real world, to identify the scope of change required to migrate to the re-engineered processes, and to arrive at recommendations and procedures for change. In undertaking this comparison, SBM adapts various comparison techniques, such as informal discussion, formal questioning, use-case generation, and scenario writing. Worked exemplars of the approach are available in Younessi (1995a,b).

48.4 Research Issues and Summary

Many BPR projects, even many of those that take a disciplined approach, still fail. We can attribute the reasons behind quite a few of such failures to one or more of the reasons enumerated below. This implies that if anywhere, these are the areas upon which research efforts must concentrate. Here we provide a description of these foci of concern and of current research in progress and future opportunities for work toward bringing forth improvements in these areas.

1. **Scope** — Contrary to our advice earlier in this chapter, most BPR activity has been traditionally confined to the business itself and has not included the greater environment and community in which the business resides. It has largely ignored, or at least has downplayed, the impact of the value chain, and the legal, social, and environmental aspects. In short most BPR implementations have taken a reductionist, narrow focus approach to the redesign of the "internals" of the organization and not a holistic, systems-oriented approach to placement of the newly designed organization into an environment in harmony with which these "internals" have been designed (optimized) in the first place. There has been much emphasis on efficiency with far less regard to efficacy, effectiveness, harmony, and desirability of the new business with respect to the environment within which it has to persist. This issue, we said, is central to the success of all BPR attempts, particularly those based on the object-oriented paradigm many of which, having emerged from a software system development parentage, have traditionally tended to be much more modeling focused, scientific/analytical, and as such reductionist in nature. Research in incorporating a holistic basis that extends beyond the confines of the business operations continues. The works of McHugh et al. (1995) and Younessi et al. (1995a,b) may be noted with the latter having taken an object-oriented approach. Related to the above issue is also the recognition that most modeling and design performed under the BPR banner has largely assumed the problem situation to be deteministic in nature or has at least modeled it as such. Business is, however, a human activity system and as it involves humans, is by nature non-deterministic. We need to recognize this fact and model business processes from this perspective. Some work has been done in this area (Graham, 1994), but much more is needed.
2. **Change management** — BPR is also about bringing forth change. Implementation of such change in itself is a major challenge. Change takes time, energy, and commitment: it must diffuse through and it must be accepted. These issues are also central to the success of a BPR exercise. Change management therefore must be integrally studied as part of the whole BPR question. Having a new business design is one thing, going bankrupt trying to implement the new business is another thing altogether. Many management researchers have and continue to study the issue of management of change resulting from introduction of BPR. The object-oriented BPR community also needs to integrate the logistics of change into their proposed approaches.
3. **Integration with IT** — Another related area of investigation and potential progress which is of particular interest to the object technology community is the linkage between BPR as a business design framework and object-oriented software system development. Work has been done (Henderson-Sellers et al., 1997; Taylor, 1995; and Graham, 1994) and continues to be done in this area. The use of business objects as the basis for requirements engineering (Fingar, 1996), the advent of business patterns (Hellenack, 1997), and business frameworks (Wooding, 1997) use of analysis patterns (Fowler, 1997) to implement reusable business patterns are all active research areas that together will work toward the realization of the seamless path from Mission Statement to the GUI on your screen.
4. **Measurement** — Another issue of current interest which can have a major impact on the future of BPR is the issue of benchmarking. How do we know that we have a good process? How do we know that we are doing the best we potentially can? How do we know where we stand with respect to our industry's best practices? How do we know if our industry's best practices are good enough? To answer these questions and many similar ones, we need more than just a benchmark, we need a yardstick. We need measurement. Current research in software metrics, particularly those that pertain to object technology (Henderson-Sellers, 1996), is a good starting point for such research. Well-founded metrics combined with well-designed, modular business objects and patterns modeled in a detailed and uniform fashion are all important ingredients in the future research in this area.

References

Argenti, P. 1980. *Practical Corporate Planning.* Allen and Unwin, London.

Booch, G. and Rumbaugh, J. 1995. Unified Method, Version 0.8, Rational Software Company Inc. (unpublished).

Campbell, J. 1982. *Grammatical Man; Information, Entropy, Language, And Life.* Simon and Schuster, New York, NY.

Checkland, P.B. and Scholes, J. 1990. *Soft Systems Methodology in Action.* Wiley, Chichester, UK.

EDRC (Economic and Development Research Center). 1989. *Key Indicators of Developing Asia and Pacific Countries.* Vol. 20. Oxford University Press, Oxford, UK.

Fingar, P. 1996. *The Blueprint for Business Objects.* SIGs Books & Multimedia, New York, NY.

Firesmith, D., Henderson-Sellers, B. and Graham, I. 1997. *OPEN Modeling Language: (OML) Reference Manual.* SIGS Books & Multimedia, New York, NY.

Fowler, M. 1997. *Analysis Patterns: Reusable Object Models.* Addison-Wesley, New York, NY.

Gale, T. and Eldred, J. 1996. *Getting Results with the Object-Oriented Enterprise Model.* SIGS Books and Multimedia, New York, NY.

Graham, I. 1994. *Migrating to Object Technology.* Addison Wesley, New York, NY.

Hammer, M. and Champy, J. 1993. *Reengineering the Corporation: A Manifesto for Business Revolution.* Harper Collins, New York, NY.

Hellenack, L.J. 1997. Object-oriented business patterns, *Object Mag.*, 6 (11):22-32.

Henderson-Sellers, B. 1996. *Object-Oriented Metrics: Measures of Complexity.* Prentice-Hall, Englewood Cliffs, NJ.

Henderson-Sellers, B., Graham, I. and Younessi, H. 1997. *The OPEN Process Specification.* Addison-Wesley, New York, NY.

Jacobson, I., Ericsson, M. and Jacobson, A. 1995. *The Object Advantage — Business Process Reengineering with Object Technology.* Addison-Wesley, Wokingham, UK.

Johansson, H., McHugh, P.P., Pendlebury, J. and Wheeler III, W. 1993. *Business Process Reengineering — Breakpoint Strategies for Market Dominance.* John Wiley & Sons, Chichester, UK.

Kotler, P. 1995. *Marketing Strategy.* Butterworth-Heinemann, Boston, MA.

McHugh, P., Merli, G., Wheeler, W.A., II. 1995. *Beyond Business Process Reengineering: Towards the Holonic Enterprise,* John Wiley & Sons, London.

Rapkin, D.P. and Avery, W.P. 1995. *National Competitiveness in a Global Economy.* Lynne Rienner Publishers, Boulder, CO.

Rational, UML semantics, Version 1.0; http://www.rational.com, January 1997 (unpublished).

Simmons, O.G. 1988. *Perspectives on Development and Population Growth in the Third World.* Plenum Press, New York, NY.

Stern Stewart & Co., Economic Value Added, http://www.spx.com/spxeva02.html, Stewart Stern Management Services, New York, 1995.

Stern Stewart Management Services, Stern Stewart performance 1000, New York, 1995.

Taylor, D. 1995. *Business Engineering with Object Technology.* John Wiley and Sons, New York, NY.

Wilson, B. 1989. A systems methodology for information requirements analysis. In *Systems Development for Human Progress,* H.K. Klein and K. Kumar, eds. Elsevier, Amsterdam, The Netherlands.

WSJ (Wall Street Journal) 1980-1997. Dow Jones and Company, Inc. New York, NY.

Wooding, P. 1997. Business frameworks, *Object Mag.*, 6 (11):50-54.

Younessi, H., Smith, R. and Grant, D. 1994. Systemicity: A rationale for revisiting object-oriented techniques. In *Proc. 5th Australasian Conf. on Information Systems.* Monash University, Victoria, Australia.

Younessi, H. and Smith, R. 1995a. Systemicity and object-oriented approaches to business process re-engineering. In *Proc. 1st Australian Systems Conf.*, Edith Cowan University, Western Australia.

Younessi, H., Smith, R. and Grant, D. 1995b. Toward a systemic approach to object-oriented analysis. In *Proc. 6th Australasian Conf. on Information Systems.* Curtin University, Western Australia.

Younessi, H. 1997. Software process improvement: an historical perspective. In *Software Process Assessment,* T.P. Rout, ed. Computational Mechanics Publications, Southampton, UK.

49

Perspectives on Design and Implementation of Business Objects

Dilip Patel
South Bank University

Islam Choudhury
South Bank University

Shushma Patel
South Bank University

49.1 Introduction

One of the main goals in business is to maximize profit. This requires better and efficient tools with which to manage and run the business. There has been a need to develop tools and techniques to help business work effectively, efficiently, and productively. Computerization has been seen to be the solution to most business problems. However, the concepts and ideas in business and that of information technology are very different. There needs to be a way of capturing the business knowledge and representing it in a form that can be understood by both the business and the computing professions. The concept of Business Objects attempts to address this issue.

Object-oriented programs and systems have been very successful in the development of applications, the reuse of code libraries, user interface development, and rapid prototyping. Objects are visible on the screen for users to manipulate as icons, windows, buttons, and boxes. Objects help to make software more reliable and reusable. To overcome the communication barrier and the problems with continual business evolution, the Object Management Group (OMG) has adopted the tools and techniques from the world of object-oriented technology, in developing the concept of business objects. In addition to the work of the OMG, a number of researchers and practitioners have addressed the idea of Business Objects with their own interpretations and implementations. It is accepted that the high-level semantics

0-8493-3135-8/99/$0.00+$.50

and the powerful features inherent to objects can be directly applied to the business itself. The types of objects within the business that can be modeled are customer, order, product, etc. Objects can also be used to represent business transactions and processes, such as sales order processing, purchase order processing, etc. This chapter gives a brief background and understanding of current research and future directions of business objects.

49.2 The Need for Business Objects

Global business competition and a shift from identical mass produced to tailor made products, the continual business changes with regard to people, government, technology, skills, etc., has led to rapidly changing business environments, which require the business to keep pace in order to survive. Companies have to compete in a climate where products and services have to meet customer demands, i.e., the best quality, low prices, exact specifications of requirements, short product delivery lead times, and long-term support. Businesses are continually re-assessing themselves in terms of their products, services, processes, suppliers, and customer concerns. A successful information strategy is crucial and must enable business flexibility by providing business solutions at a rate that matches the rapid changes in the business. It therefore requires user involvement and empowerment to dynamically change the various aspects of their business, as and when required, both efficiently and effectively. The software industry has failed to meet this challenge because of the complexity of the business domain and its continual evolution.

Generally there are three main points to bear in mind for a successful information system. First, the information system must capture the initial overall conceptual model, which requires a clear understanding of the business. Secondly, there has to be acceptance that business is in a constant state of flux. Finally, there must be a need to shift from an application view to a business view (Jacobson et al., 1995; Taylor, 1995; Partridge, 1996; Graham, 1995; and Martin and Odell, 1992). Mechanisms for achieving these are likely to utilize concepts of componentization, model-based specifications, and end-user solution composition. Such composition can be achieved through "business objects" which are self-contained and independently developed as "business concept components," "business process components," "business entity components," "business data components," "business systems components," "business people components," "business application components," and "business task components," or even small components such as "business code components." These components are specified in a business object model. The business object model can be used as a starting reference model to build various applications, as and when required. The model allows designers to concentrate on the business and develop and change the model as the business evolves.

49.3 Understanding Business Objects

To understand business objects, it is important to understand the concept of a "model." A model is basically a tool used to understand the relevant part of the world which is of interest, and to represent it using available and appropriate symbols to enable communication (Checkland, 1981). There are three types of models: the abstract or conceptual model, the representational model, and the instance model (Burkhart et al., 1992). These models have two main functions:

- To filter out irrelevant detail and thereby display only information that is essential to the task (this involves abstraction)
- To represent that information in a useful and appropriate way to address the goal of modeling.

Burkhart et al. (1992) define a model as:

"...the explicit interpretation of one's understanding of a situation, or merely one's ideas about that situation. It can be expressed in mathematics, symbols, or words, but essentially a description of entities, processes, or attributes and relationships between them. It may be prescriptive or illustrative, but above all, it must be useful."

In the computer science discipline the concept of a model is researched to find how a view of a given domain can be reflected in a computer system, and to develop languages and tools needed to describe such models. Current research in the area of business objects concentrates on providing strategies and tools for developing instance models. However, there is very little work done at the conceptual and representation levels. For business objects to succeed they must be modeled at all three levels. This is important, as one of the main objectives of business objects is to reduce the semantic gap between business and computer specialists.

The object-oriented paradigm provides the appropriate modeling constructs and symbols to enable the effective capture and representation of things within a business at the conceptual, representational, and instance levels. The object-oriented modeling constructs that are useful for business objects include objects, abstraction, encapsulation, instantiation, inheritance, specialization, polymorphism, composition, containment, and association. The abstraction, encapsulation, and representation of things meaningful to a business are referred to as business objects. A business object model is an object-oriented representation of a business domain, and it is both methodology and language independent.

49.4 OMG Business Objects

OMG and in particular, Business Object Management Special Interest Group (OMG BOMSIG) have devoted considerable time and resources in formalizing the idea of Business Objects.

The main work has focused on the following:

- Evaluating what business objects are, their roles, and how they are defined
- Developing guidelines for business object specifications
- Describing how the thousands of business objects which are developed can relate to each other in different scenarios
- Establishing acceptable behavior among business objects
- Establishing rules which apply to business objects
- Establishing the semantics that will define the relationships between objects
- Fostering industry-wide commitment to the concept of business objects.

The OMG BOMSIG are addressing the issues outlined above, and in particular, they have defined a working definition and a description of what is meant by the term "Business Objects." The definition and description are outlined in Section 49.4.1 below.

49.4.1 Business Object Definition and Description

The OMG BOMSIG define Business Objects as:

> A representation of a thing in the business domain, including at least its business name and definition, attributes, behavior, relationships, rules, policies, and constraints. A business object may represent, for example, a person, place, event, business process, or concept. Typical examples of business objects are: employee, product, invoice, and payment.

A business object abstraction, which models the real world, is represented by an object in the information system. Each such object in the information system is a component of that information system and must be supported by a technology infrastructure (Arrow et al., 1995).

Arrow et al. (1995) further elaborate the definition to a description as stated below:

OMG Business Objects represent the nature and behavior of real-world things or concepts in terms that are meaningful to the business. Customers, products, orders, trades, employees, vehicles, etc., are examples of business objects.

Business objects are of greater value than other representations because they allow a way of managing business complexity, understanding it, giving a high-level perspective, and packaging the essential characteristics of the business completely. Business objects are surrogates for the real-world concepts they represent. They can work together with other business objects and perform the required tasks or steps that make up business processes. These business objects can then be used to design and implement systems and still keep similar semantics to the business domain they are supporting. This allows the software systems to mirror the real world, hence, aligning the business to the information systems, which is the goal of many businesses.

Business objects allow an enterprise to communicate, model, design, implement, distribute, evolve, and market the software technology that will enable them to run their business. The implications of business objects include:

- *Communication* — Business objects provide common terms and ideas at a level of detail, which can be shared among business and technical people to articulate and understand the business in business terms.
- *Modeling* — Business objects have certain characteristics and behavior which enable them to be used naturally in modeling business processes, and the relationships and interactions between business concepts.
- *Design* — Business objects represent real-world things and concepts, which enable the design effort to be concentrated in manageable chunks.
- *Implementation* — Business objects have a late and flexible binding and well-defined interfaces so that they can be implemented independently.
- *Distribution* — Business objects are independent so that they can be distributed as self-contained units to platforms with suitable infrastructure. OMG Common Object Request Broker Architecture (CORBA) is an OMG standard which is required to implement a distributed-object business system.
- *Evolution* — Business objects can be used in a variety of roles and evolve with the needs of the business. They provide a means for integrating, migrating, and evolving existing applications.
- *Marketability* — Business objects have the potential to be commercially distributed and combined with business objects from other sources to facilitate a market in business objects.

More formally, a business object has a name, definition, attributes, behavior, relationships, and business rules. Business name is the term used by business experts to classify a business object. Business definition is a statement of the meaning and purpose assigned to a business object by business experts. Attributes are facts about the business object relevant to fulfilling its business purpose. Behavior is the actions a business object is capable of performing to fulfill its purpose, including recognizing events in its environment, changing its attributes, and interacting with other business objects. Relationship is an association between business objects that reflects the interactions of their business purposes. Business Rules are the constraints, which govern the behavior, relationships, and attributes of business objects.

49.4.2 OMG Standards for Business Objects

OMG has proposed an Object Management Architecture (OMA) by which various object components can communicate with each other (Figure 49.1).

The architecture basically consists of four components surrounding the Object Request Broker (ORB; OMG, 1992a):

- The Object Request Broker forms the communication backbone for a distributed object system.
- The CORBAservices provides services which are necessary for all objects, such as Lifecycle's move, copy, and destroy.
- The horizontal CORBAfacilities is divided into four parts: user interface, information management, systems management, and task management.
- The vertical CORBAfacilities applies to specifically one industrial domain such as finance, health, telecommunication, etc.
- The application objects represent functionality at the user level and are not standardized by OMG but left to the specialization by the users.

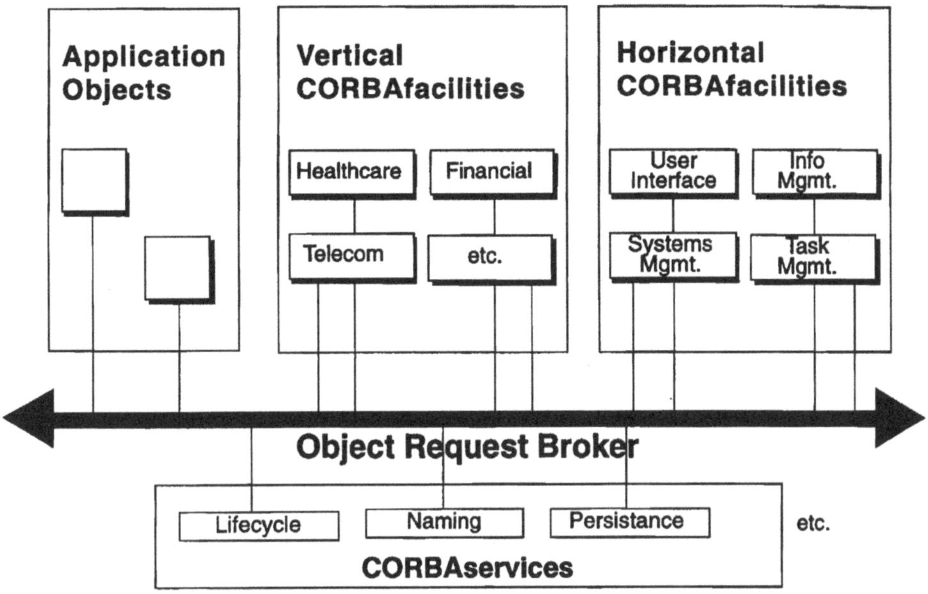

FIGURE 49.1 OMG Object Management Architecture. (From OMG. 1992a. Object Management Group 1992, http://www.omg.org/library/omaindx.htm. With permission.)

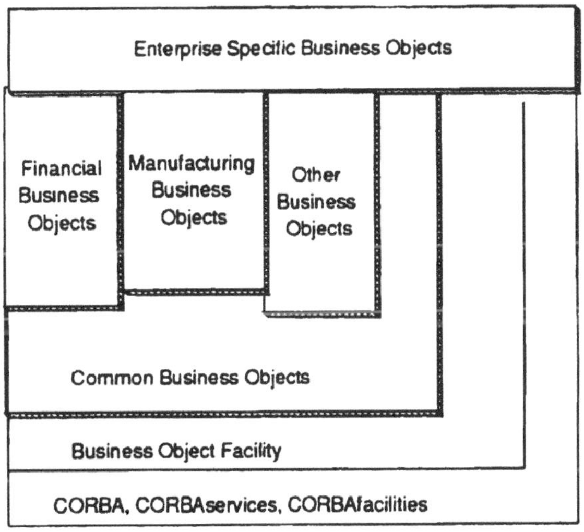

FIGURE 49.2 OMG Business Object Architecture. (From Casanave, C. 1997. *Business Object Design and Implementation, OOPSLA 95 Workshop Proceedings,* Sutherland, J., Patel, D., Casanave, C., Hollowell, G. and Miller, J. eds., pp. 7-28. Springer-Verlag, London. With permission.)

OMG BOMSIG (Casanave, 1996) takes the OMA further by giving a business perspective and incorporating the idea of business objects (Figure 49.2).

The OMG BOMSIG proposes a four-tier architecture on top of the OMA, which are:

- The Business Object Facility is what provides infrastructure such as the application architecture, services etc. This is required to support business objects operating as cooperative application components in a distributed object environment.

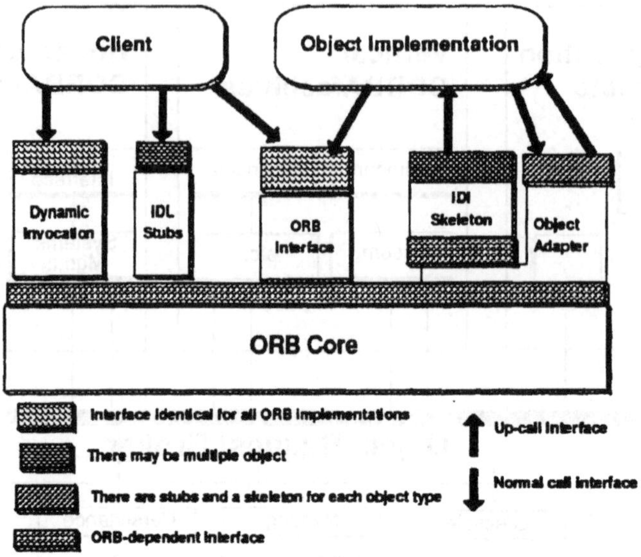

FIGURE 49.3 The structure of Object Request Broker Interfaces. (From *Object Management Group and X Open, OMG Document No. 91.12.1* Revision 1.1. John Wiley & Sons, New York. With permission.)

- The Common Business Objects are those objects which represent business semantics that are common across most businesses.
- The industry-dependent business objects are those which are shared by all, or many of the companies in a particular domain. For example, the telecommunications sector may share a business object which will not be found in the health-care sector.
- The enterprise specific business objects are general business objects found in all business domains. The OMG has yet to define business objects at this level.

49.5 Perspectives on Business Object Design

The term business objects have gained popularity with many researchers and practitioners as an important concept. This term has been interpreted in many ways, and this section discusses some of these issues which include: the infrastructure or object request broker perspective, business process modeling, reusability, component development, the change issue, genericity, enterprise modeling, and workflow perspective.

49.5.1 Infrastructure Perspective

A part of the description of business objects is that they can be effectively distributed as self-contained units across platforms with a suitably installed infrastructure. There is a need for standard infrastructures, which enables access, message passing, and routing among business objects. The infrastructure can be developed using ORBs, see Figure 49.3, which is the structure of the OMG ORB.

Business objects can then be linked by the broker business objects via an Interface Definition Language (IDL). The OMG has defined an architecture framework called OMA. The OMA provides a distributed object-oriented system which is a standard object request broker called CORBA. Other standard common distributed object systems also now exist, such as IBM DSOM (Distributed System Object Model), Sunsoft's DOE (Distributed Objects Everywhere), or Microsoft COM-OLE2 (Common Object Model-Object Linking and Embedding 2), which all use and support a client/server architecture. Business objects are implemented on top of these standard distributed systems. This allows any application program to access and manipulate the business objects.

Grotehen (1997) gives an example where business objects have been successfully implemented using OMA CORBA in the existing information technology environment of a bank, which is described in Section 49.6.3.

An example where business objects have been implemented with a non-standard infrastructure is that of Sims (1994), who suggests that business objects are high-level application components that appear as icons in the interface of an application. These can be assembled to build applications that implement some particular business process via cooperating business objects (CBO). CBOs are objects that can be used together at execution time in ways unplanned and unforeseen by their developers. The term application components means an object implementation that is the runtime manifestation of a business object through an IDL interface. Sims' (1994) infrastructure has been realized in the form of the NeWI (New World Infrastructure). NeWI supports business objects distributed over multiple communications protocols and aims to provide a runtime layer giving ease of programming for client/server, distributed object management, object-based user interfaces, and workplace integration using CBOs (McGibbon, 1994).

49.5.2 Business Process Modeling Perspective

Business processes are essential components of a business. They describe the set of activities needed to achieve the goals of the organization. These processes represent the flow of work and information throughout the business. The business processes are the complete interactions of business entities required to perform a business function. There may be different granularities of business processes ranging from order lifecycle to producing a sales report. Business processes can be represented as business objects but very little work has been done on this. Jacobson et al. (1995) suggests that business processes can be represented and modeled as "use cases." The use cases, as defined by Jacobson et al. (1995), allow one to model three types of business objects: interface object, control object, and entity object. The interface object essentially provides communication with the external environment. The control object represents tasks that can be carried out without direct contact with the external environment. The entity objects are the tangible products and things in the business. The interaction of these business objects, in essence, represents a business process.

SOMA (Graham, 1995) uses a more generic term than the use case called "task scripts." Task scripts are stereotypical use cases. The business processes are analyzed in terms of messages (semiotic acts) that conform to contracts and have goals. These goals are, in essence, business tasks which can be represented as objects in a Task Object Model (TOM). These tasks are examined to find the business objects (typically nouns in the task descriptions). These objects are directly related to actual business processes and are in a form which can be readily understood by users and domain experts. SOMA places emphasis on business objects as modeling constructs that are useful in requirement capture and business process re-engineering.

49.5.3 Reuse Perspective

Business objects can be stored either graphically or textually, thus allowing them to be developed, managed, accessed, and reused, as and when required. If reuse is to be achieved, it is important that the repository should represent Business Objects at the business level rather than only at the application or source code levels (Graham, 1997). The main benefits include:

- A base of understandable, implementation-independent, rigorously defined, reusable business objects
- Enable a library to extend into an enterprise model, in a bottom up, incremental fashion
- A semantically rich repository of business objects, which can be utilized by a wide spectrum of developers and users

49.5.4 Component Perspective

Cox (1987) suggested that the software engineering discipline should learn from the computer hardware industry in the development and assembly of components. Hardware designers reuse well-designed, cataloged components, allowing the number of components on a silicon chip to almost double every year. Plant and Wooding (1994) suggest that CBOs are fundamental stable components within a business from which specific applications can be developed, as and when required, by implementation and assembly of these components. They suggest that the idea of producing domain objects (components) as opposed to application specific ones is widely accepted. The key to improving productivity is by reusing them across multiple software applications. They further suggest that more work should be carried out to determine the scope, cost, and quality of these components, and investigate suitable domains, as well as look at the implications for consumers and suppliers.

Digre (1997) describes a component-based architecture which supports the intervention by users for reorganizing their business. Components hide the technological and implementation complexity, allowing business users to concentrate on the business problem domain. The proposed approach relies on the development of well-defined components (processes, workflow, rules, policies, presentation, etc.). These components can be specialized and/or assembled into applications. The approach would allow one to purchase tools and services off the shelf.

49.5.5 Change Perspective

In order to be competitive, the business must constantly keep up to date with changes and keep track of their products, suppliers, customer handling procedures, etc. The business objects strategy should be able to cope with these changes, thus enabling business solutions to be developed concurrently with the business change. Choudhury et al. (1997) suggest there should be a change dimension in the development of business objects. The change dimension should address the business drivers of change. This includes the factors that cause change such as legislative, policy, procedure, operational, people, technology changes, etc. It should also include factors to characterize, analyze, and measure change, such as context of change, focus of change, and scope of change. All business objects are continually evolving, therefore configuration management and version control must be part of the business object strategy.

49.5.6 Genericity Perspective

As mentioned in the above three sections, modeling at a business level is the key to a successful reuse program. This would allow the development of systems to keep pace with the business changes. If there is to be a move toward off-the-shelf components, one needs to view and develop business objects at an enterprise level. Figure 49.4 shows the genericity dimension within which this can be achieved. It is important to view the enterprise as components and view the business at different levels of genericity. Business object models can be built for any or appropriate levels within the hierarchy. As can be seen, each component can be specialized or generalized within the diagram. This gives developers an overall view to help them build appropriate business object models, which will fit into the overall enterprise model. This will aid in reuse of various models as the links between different models and different levels can easily be established. As the business evolves the models can be changed appropriately and still remain coherent.

49.5.7 Enterprise Modeling

An enterprise model offers the potential to serve as a basis for building a coordinated, responsive, long lasting set of business applications, which can be used in multiple projects over a period of time (Jackson, 1994). Shelton (1993) has developed an object-oriented method for enterprise modeling. His methodology, the Object-Oriented Enterprise Modeling (OOEM), allows one to build business objects at the enterprise level. He distinguishes business objects at different levels of an organization and has referred to them as

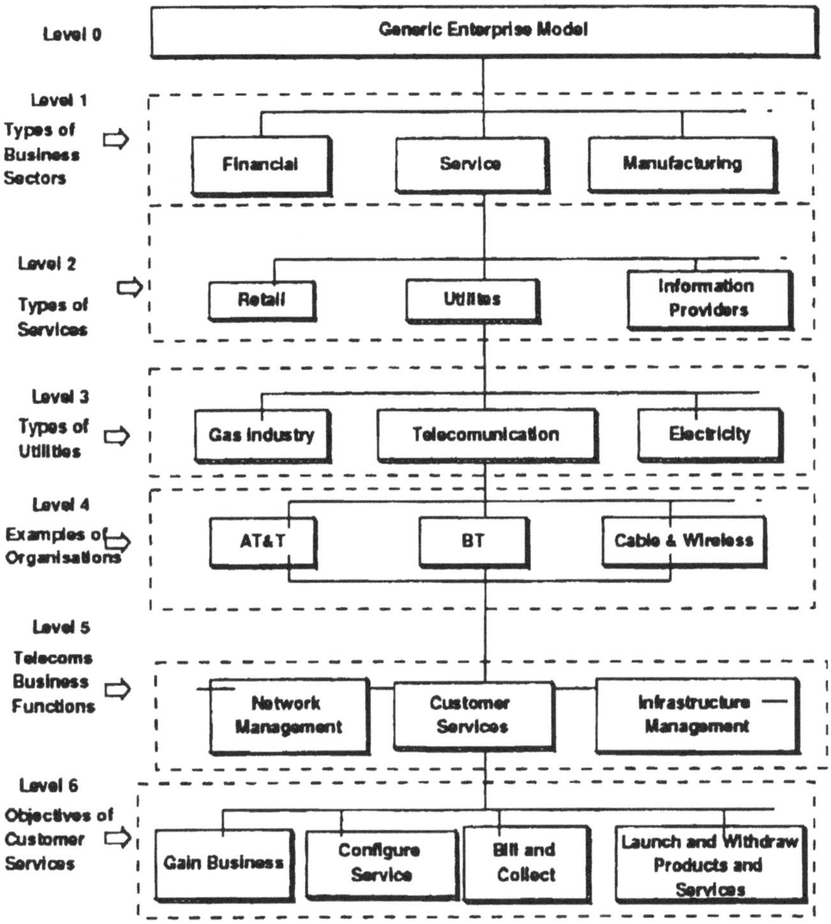

FIGURE 49.4 Genericity dimension. (From Choudhury et al. 1997. *OOIS97 Proc. 4th Int. Conf. on Object-Oriented Information Systems.* Springer-Verlag, London. With permission.)

business objects, application objects, and foundation objects within the Zachman framework (1987). He suggests that business objects are units of reusable specifications upon which designs can be based.

Cook (1996) supports this and suggests that business objects can be used to model all the significant processes and information of the enterprise. Also, duplication, contradiction, and bottlenecks will be eliminated and continual re-engineering will keep the business efficient and responsive to business change. Information systems can then be generated automatically from business object descriptions.

Choudhury et al. (1997) give an alternative perspective to enterprise modeling. They suggest that models should be built using a Generic Reusable Business Object Modeling (GRBOM) approach which takes into account infrastructure, business process modeling, reuse, component, change, and genericity.

49.5.8 Workflow Perspective

Business objects can be represented as business processes, therefore, the process creation part of workflow tools should incorporate business objects (Baker, 1996). The OMG is working toward a definition of workflow and developing a Workflow Facility, which provides management and coordination of objects that are part of a work process. The OMG Workflow Management Coalition (WfMC, 1996) has defined

Workflow as: "The automation of business process, in whole or part, during which documents, information, or tasks are passed from one participant to another for action, according to a set of procedural rules."

Workflow tools are made up of two parts:

- The processes execution and the controlling and monitoring of all the process instances active in the system
- The process creation, which includes a graphical tool for constructing (defining) processes, and support tools for deploying them.

49.6 Implementing Business Objects

Designing and implementing business objects is an expensive, time consuming, and difficult process. First, it must be established what business objects are, generally and specifically. Then, it is necessary to draft object diagrams containing suitable classes linked together appropriately. Having created a tailor made, bespoke business object model it may not be adaptable by other organizations. Hence, Choudhury et al. (1997) suggest that work must be carried out to build generic business object models which can be bought by organizations. This would allow an organization to adopt and extend the model for their specific needs. The advantage of this is that as the starting point was a generic model, the expectation is that organizations would contribute toward extending the model, over a period of time, based on their experiences. Many case studies will need to be done and evaluated in order to achieve this. At present, models are limited to data and process models based on a specific organization's understanding of the business. These are of little benefit to others. Another common limitation of these models is their choice of computer languages and databases.

Many researchers and practitioners have addressed the above issues and this section presents some results of the work on business object implementation by describing three different strategies for designing and implementing business objects.

49.6.1 Business Application Architecture

Casanave (1997) proposed a Business Application Architecture (BAA) based on the OMG's business object definition. He suggests that information systems should be built that can serve the enterprise and adapt to complex and dynamic business needs. Business objects are described as "information systems components" which represent the business model. He goes on to explain that business objects are not DBMS tables. Business objects will implement rules and processes that go beyond the scope of DBMS and are at a higher level. Business objects can be built with new technology or on top of existing and legacy software.

The BAA is an application architecture and a protocol for "cooperative business objects." BAA is not an architecture of the business but an architecture for how to represent and implement business concepts as business objects. It is the glue for binding the business model to the technology. Objects implemented in this way can interoperate with other business objects. BAA is not the standard business model but a standard way to represent any business model as a structure of executable distributed objects.

Casanave (1997) describes the BAA, see Figure 49.5, as being made up of the Business Object Model, Business Objects, and Business Object Presentation. The business objects are implemented as components which are executable representations of that object in the computer system. An application consists of programs that are composed of a set of cooperative business objects. A program may implement one or many presentations and processes that work with business objects. A business model is built using abstract business objects and processes and includes every person, place, thing, event, or transaction that needs to be captured in the information system. The business objects encapsulate the storage, metadata, concurrency, and business rules associated with a thing, process, or event in a business. The business processes are called business process objects and the actual things or concepts that make up the business

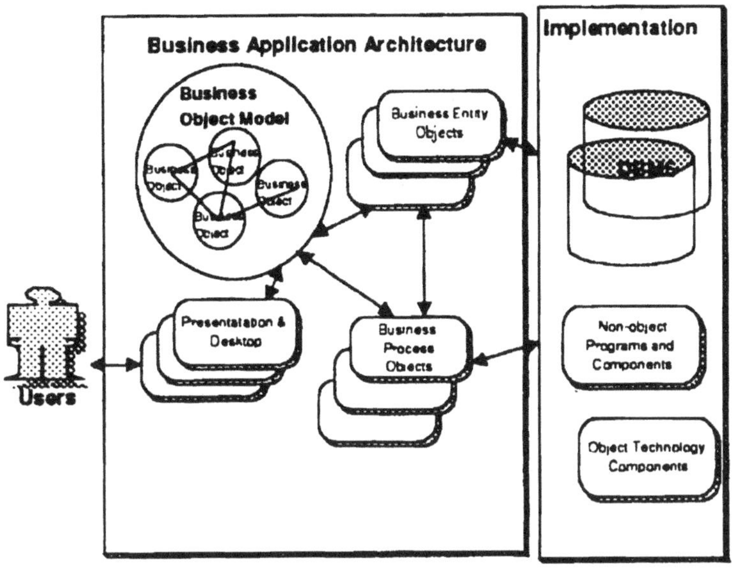

FIGURE 49.5 Business Application Architecture. (From Casanave, C. 1997. *Business Object Design and Implementation, OOPSLA 95 Workshop Proceedings,* Sutherland, J., Patel, D., Casanave, C., Hollowell, G. and Miller, J. eds., pp. 7-28. Springer-Verlag, London. With permission.)

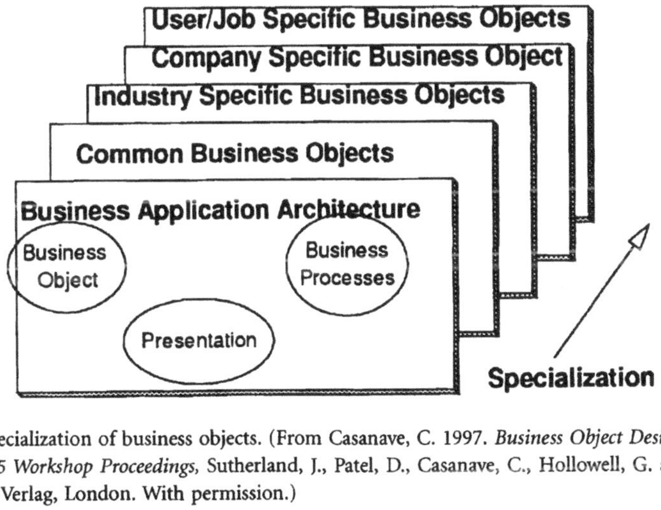

FIGURE 49.6 Specialization of business objects. (From Casanave, C. 1997. *Business Object Design and Implementation, OOPSLA 95 Workshop Proceedings,* Sutherland, J., Patel, D., Casanave, C., Hollowell, G. and Miller, J. eds., pp. 7-28. Springer-Verlag, London. With permission.)

are called business entity objects, the nouns of the model, such as the people, places, and things, and business events such as sales. The business object presentation can have multiple presentations for multiple purposes. The presentation is the user's view of the business object for a given purpose. The presentation communicates with the business objects by transferring information between the business object on behalf of the user and it also displays and manipulates the information.

Figure 49.6 shows how the generic business objects, business processes, and presentation defined in the BAA are specialized through common business objects, industry specific business objects, company specific business objects, and user/job specific business objects. For example, a business object might be specialized in a consulting company to be an "order for consulting services" object. A particular consulting company may add rules and attributes to that consulting-order object to enforce company policy. Finally, a particular department might further specialize the company's consulting-order object for a particular type of service.

He also suggests that the BAA has many advantages such as flexibility, and providing a single place to put business rules. The BAA works with legacy systems, and it also works with insufficient or transient standards. Moreover, it is scalable, reusable, ideal for business process re-engineering, and easy to use.

49.6.2 Object Business Modeling

Ramackers and Clegg (1997) discuss the requirements for a metamodel for "Object Business Modeling" which is a tool supported approach to exploit information systems by enterprise orientation and user involvement. They suggest that the combination of business modeling, business process re-engineering, workflow requirements, enterprise modeling, and object-oriented design can leverage the promise of reuse and flexibility at the business level by the semantic construct of business objects. Its goal is to create objects which can be developed, assembled, and tailored to the needs of the domain specialists and end users and hide many complexities of systems design through application and workflow generation.

Ramackers and Clegg (1997) suggest that the business model uses terminology which is close to the way business domain experts understand the business and end users express themselves when describing the organization. The main concepts are:

Actor — The responsible agents of action within an organization that are assigned as resources to one or more business units.

Object — Either material or information in nature. Information objects can be domain objects (similar to entity object (Casanave, 1997) which are the information concepts of a business or business objects which are aggregates of domain objects and precisely define the attributes, relationships, operations, and lifecycle state that are relevant for an actor in the context of a certain business process.

Process — A business process defines the chains of organizational activity threading through different business units.

Event — An event may be a state change of an object, a condition becoming true, a time event, or an external event (e.g., a phone call from a customer).

Rule — Business rules define precise conditions governing execution of processes.

Ramackers and Clegg (1997) provide support for the business model in the form of an integrated CASE tool which is capable of integrating many different, partially overlapping, "views" in a flexible manner. The tool makes modeling easier to understand for domain experts and end users, and it helps them in the transition to the implementation stage. The tool set consists of the following:

Process modeler supports business process re-engineering/workflow, object lifecycle processes to view and manipulate the business process model. **Object modeler** allows for the visualization and manipulation of *business objects and domain objects* which are modeled in two kinds of diagrams. The domain object model is the corporate object infrastructure for defining business objects. The business object model is the users view of a group of domain objects in the context of a certain business process. Such business object specifications can be tailored for each process step in which it is involved. Business objects can also be composed of existing predefined business object components. This allows for the reuse, development and evolution of business objects to support business requirements. **Organization modeler** models the departments and roles, organizational hierarchies, BAA and the goal of the business. **Rule Editor** manages the business rules such as policies, strategies, and work rules. It provides a natural language description of the rule so end users can understand them easily and a more formal one for analysts and domain experts. **Pattern Library** stores the business patterns that are developed which may be, for example, "order entry processing" or more generic ones such as "resource allocation" or "decision process." **Design Generator** (workflow, application) further generates a default design based on a set of preferences and once generated can be further specialized.

The tool supporting Object Business Modeling, as described above, is a very useful and powerful implementation of the business object concept. It allows end user and domain specialist involvement for developing a metamodel that can be easily understood, developed, and manipulated, for the effective and efficient use of object technology in corporate information systems.

49.6.3 Business Object Implemented on Top of CORBA

Grotehen (1997) describes an approach to show how OMG OMA and the OMG CORBA could be successfully employed in the existing legacy information systems of a bank. CORBA is used to define a layer of business objects above the legacy information system. This is done by first analyzing the business objects, secondly, specifying business object in CORBA-IDL, and then implementing the interfaces.

49.7 The Future

Business objects have great potential as they represent how an organization works at conceptual, representational, and instance levels. This allows a business to implement a variety of solutions that keep pace with changing business requirements. However, business objects have yet to mature, and considerable work needs to be done in the following areas:

- Standardize definition of Business Objects
- Develop a methodology to support modeling
- Develop enterprise models to enable reuse, etc.
- Develop configuration management tools

Business objects should be defined further and more accurately and precisely so that the user community will have a clear and concise understanding. Business objects must address business processes more directly. Business objects should be designed more rigorously so that they can be distributed. All possible levels of granularity of business objects must be defined and explanations must be provided on how to use business objects at different granularities.

Business object modeling and segmentation of business models into stable business object components are critical issues for the future. Business objects should be developed as reusable components which require organizations to be more sophisticated, in terms of developing, buying in, and using and reusing these components. Organizations should build enterprise models based on business objects that can be used as starting reference models for building their business applications. The model should conform to standards, which should be developed from object models from different industries. Due to the competitive nature of organizations, it will be difficult to extract confidential information to build enterprise models. However, we can foresee more of this information becoming public over time, especially if we can identify the right level of abstraction, generality, and granularity. The Massachusetts Institute of Technology is developing a handbook of organizational processes (Malone et al., 1997). When the book is published it will provide the information required to help build generic business object models.

49.8 Conclusions

This chapter has presented various perspectives on the design and implementation of business objects. The turbulent nature of a business has resulted in the need for adaptable business models that can reflect the business accurately in both business and computer terms. Business objects are a useful representation of business knowledge in terms that can be easily translated to an information system. Business objects should be modeled at an abstract or conceptual level, at a representational level, and at the instance level. A suitable methodology and development process should be used to build and link business objects at the different levels to maximize the potential benefits. Business objects are a suitable way forward for business organizations who wish to adopt object technology as their strategic solution to information systems development.

A business object model of an organization together with enterprise and industrial standard business object models will help organizations to develop solutions to various business problems. The applications that will be developed will meet the business requirements and the business model will evolve as the business changes.

References

Arrow, L., Barnwell, R., Burt, C. and Anderson, M. 1995. OMG Business Object Survey, *OMG Document 95-6-4*, Farmingham, MA.

Baker, M. 1996. Workflow meets business objects, *OOPSLA'96 Business Object Workshop II*, OOPSLA'96, San Jose, CA.

Burkhart, R., Fulton, J., Gielingh, W., Marshall, C., Menzel, C., Petrie, C. and Zoutekouw, D. 1992. The notion of a model. *Proceedings of the First International Conference on Enterprise Integration*, Petrie, C.J. ed., pp. 17-22.

Casanave, C. ed. 1996. OMG Common business objects and business object facility RFP, *OMG Document* CF/96-01-04, (www.omg.org).

Casanave, C. 1997. Business object architecture and standards, *Business Object Design and Implementation, OOPSLA 95 Workshop Proceedings*, Sutherland, J., Patel, D., Casanave, C., Hollowell, G. and Miller, J. Eds. Springer-Verlag, London, pp. 7-28.

Checkland, P.B. 1981. *Systems Theory, Systems Practice.* John Wiley & Sons, Chichester, U.K.

Choudhury, I., Sun, Y. and Patel, D. 1997. Generic reusable business object model — A framework and its application in british telecommunication plc. *OOIS97 Proc., 4th Int. Conf. Object-Oriented Information Systems.* Springer-Verlag, London.

Cook, S. 1996. Business objects for enterprise systems, *Proceedings: OOP'96*, pp. 195-7. SIGS Publishing, U.K.

Cox, B. 1987. *Object-Oriented Programming: An Evolutionary Approach.* Addison-Wesley, Reading, MA.

Digre, T. 1997. Business application components, *Business Object Design and Implementation, OOPSLA 95 Workshop Proceedings*, Sutherland, J., Patel, D., Casanave, C., Hollowell, G. and Miller, J. eds., pp. 151-165. Springer-Verlag, London.

Graham, I. 1995. *Migrating to Object Technology.* Addison-Wesley, U.K.

Graham, I. 1997. Object models, business models and business objects. In *Proc. Object Expo Europe, Java Expo*, pp. 35-44. SIGS, London, U.K.

Grotehen, T. 1997. Implementing business objects: CORBA interfaces for legacy systems, *Business Object Design and Implementation, OOPSLA 95 Workshop Proceedings*, Sutherland, J., Patel, D., Casanave, C., Hollowell, G. and Miller, J. eds., pp. 87-93. Springer-Verlag, London.

Jackson, M. 1994. The role of software architecture in requirements engineering, *The 1st International Conference on Requirements Engineering.* IEEE Computer Society Press.

Jacobson, I., Ericson, M. and Jacobson, A. 1995. *The Object Advantage. Business Process Reengineering with Object Technology.* ACM Press, New York.

McGibbon, B. 1994. Technical review: the New world infrastructure, *Object Manager*, September, pp. 9-11.

Malone, T.W., Crowston, K., Lee, J., Pentland, B., Dellarocas, C., Wyner, G., Quimby, J., Osborne, C. and Bernstein, A. 1997. Toward a handbook of organizational processes, Center for Coordination Science, Massachusetts Institute of Technology, (http://ccs.mit.edu/CCSWP198).

Martin, J. and Odell, J. 1992. Object-Oriented Analysis and Design. Prentice-Hall, Englewood Cliffs, NJ.

OMG. 1992a. Object management architecture, Object Management Group 1992, (http://www.omg.org/library/omaindx.htm).

OMG. 1992b. The Common Object Request Broker: An Architecture and Specification, *Object Management Group and X Open, OMG Document No. 91.12.1 Revision 1.1*, John Wiley & Sons, New York.

OMG. 1995. CORBAservices: Common object services specification, *OMG Document 95-3-31*, Farmingham, MA.

OMG. 1997. OMG Workflow Request for Proposal, http://www.omg.org/library/schedule/Workflow_RFP.htm.

Partridge, C. 1996. *Business Objects Reengineering for Reuse.* Butterworth-Heinmaan, Bath, U.K.

Plant, N. and Wooding, T. 1994. Common business objects: how feasible are they, *Object Manager,* December. pp. 15-18.

Shelton, R.E.A. 1993. Object-oriented method for enterprise modeling: OOEM. In *Proc. OOP'93,* Munich. SIGS, New York.

Sims, O. 1994. *Business Objects Delivering Cooperative Objects for Client/Server.* McGraw-Hill, Maidenhead, England.

Ramackers, G. and Clegg, D. 1997. Object business modeling, requirements and approach, *Business Object Design and Implementation, OOPSLA 95 Workshop Proceedings,* Sutherland, J., Patel, D., Casanave, C., Hollowell, G. and Miller, J. eds., pp. 77-86. Springer-Verlag, London.

Taylor, D.A. 1995. *Business Engineering with Object Technology.* John Wiley & Sons, New York.

WfMC. 1996. Workflow management coalition: Workflow Management Coalition: Terminology and Glossary, *Document Number WFMC TC 1011,* Issue 2.0, June 1996.

Zachman, J.A. 1987. A framework for information systems architecture, *IBM Syst. J.,* 26(3), pp. 276-292.

50

Business Object Wrapper Applications

Ian Graham
Chase Manhattan Bank

In this chapter, we will examine various proposed and actual strategies which meet the requirements of organizations facing migration and interoperation problems, emphasizing the concerns of a developer who wants to develop an object-oriented application that needs to use the services provided by applications that incorporate other programming styles. We shall also review various notions of business objects and business object models that have emerged over the past few years. We must ask whether the non-object-oriented features of old systems can be reused. If so, what are the fundamental issues in designing and building interoperation tools? Is it better to replace non-object-oriented features? If so, are there any rules or recommendations on migration techniques? How do you deal with those critical COBOL or Assembler applications? What is the role of object-oriented analysis and design techniques within this kind of migration? Is there a strategy that enables you to metamorphose an existing procedural application into an object-oriented application without disrupting services to the existing users?

This chapter will attempt to answer these questions based on such techniques as object wrappers, object request brokers (ORBs), and business objects. We will also cover such problems as how to wrap an old application which exists in a large number of different versions and explore briefly the ways in which object-oriented analysis in particular and object technology as a whole can be used as a migration technique.

50.1 Introduction

Many people and organizations are convinced of the wisdom of shifting their systems development activities toward an object-oriented style. This may be because they become aware of the benefits of object technology (OT), seen other companies succeeding in this way, or even for that worst of reasons — because OT is new and fashionable. Even in the latter, misguided, case these companies may gain from

0-8493-3135-8/99/$0.00+$.50

the experience because, even should the project in hand fail, they may gain a better understanding of existing systems and development practices through the construction of an object model. They have several reasons for replacing or extending older systems. For example, a package vendor may see the move to OT as closely tied to the move to an open platform and, in turn, see this as a way of achieving greater market share since there are usually potential customers who do not (and perhaps will not) own the proprietary platform on which the old product currently runs. They may wish to compete more effectively by adding value to the existing product with graphical user interfaces, management information system (MIS) features, or delivery on distributed platforms. User organizations may wish to take advantage of new standards, downsizing, and friendlier interfaces along with the benefits of the move to OT itself. Both types of organizations will be looking to slash maintenance costs, which can account for a huge proportion of the IS budget, and reduce time to market. However, while overnight migration is highly desirable, it is seldom possible. Furthermore, gradual migration may take too long for its benefits to be worthwhile. Often the solution is to reuse existing conventional components or entire systems and packages. So, there are several available options: interoperation, reuse, extension, and gradual or sudden migration. These options are closely related, but we will deal with interoperation first.

50.2 Interoperation of Conventional and Object-Oriented Systems

There are a number of scenarios in which an object-oriented application should interoperate with existing non-object-oriented systems. These include:

- The evolutionary migration of an existing system to a future object-oriented implementation where parts of the old system will remain temporarily in use
- The evolution of systems which already exist and are important and too large or complex to rewrite at a stroke and where part or all of the old system may continue to exist indefinitely
- The reuse of highly specialized or optimized routines, embedded expert systems, and hardware specified software
- Exploiting the best of existing relational databases for one part of an application in concert with the use of an object-oriented programming language and/or object-oriented databases for another
- The construction of graphical front ends to existing systems
- The need to build on existing "package" solutions
- Cooperative processing and blackboard architectures may involve agents which already exist working with newly defined objects
- The need to cooperate with existing systems across telecommunications and local area networks

The first issue this chapter addresses is how to tackle the migration of a vast system that is almost invariably very costly and tricky to maintain. The strategy I recommend is to build what is known as an object *wrapper.* Object wrappers can be used to migrate to object-oriented programming and still protect investments in conventional code. The wrapper concept has become part of the folklore of object-orientation but, as far as I know, the term was first coined by Wally Dietrich of IBM (Dietrich, 1989), though it is also often attributed to Brad Cox and Tom Love, the developers of Objective-C, but in a slightly different context. There are also claims that the usage was in vogue within IBM as early as 1987.

The existence of large investments in programs written in conventional languages such as Assembler, COBOL, PL/1, FORTRAN, and even APL has to be recognized. It must also be allowed that the biggest cost associated with these "legacy" systems, as Dietrich calls them, is maintenance. Maintenance is costly because, in a conventional system, may change to the data structure requires checking every single function to see if it is affected. This does not occur with object-oriented systems due to the encapsulation of the data structures by the functions that use them. However much we would like to replace these old

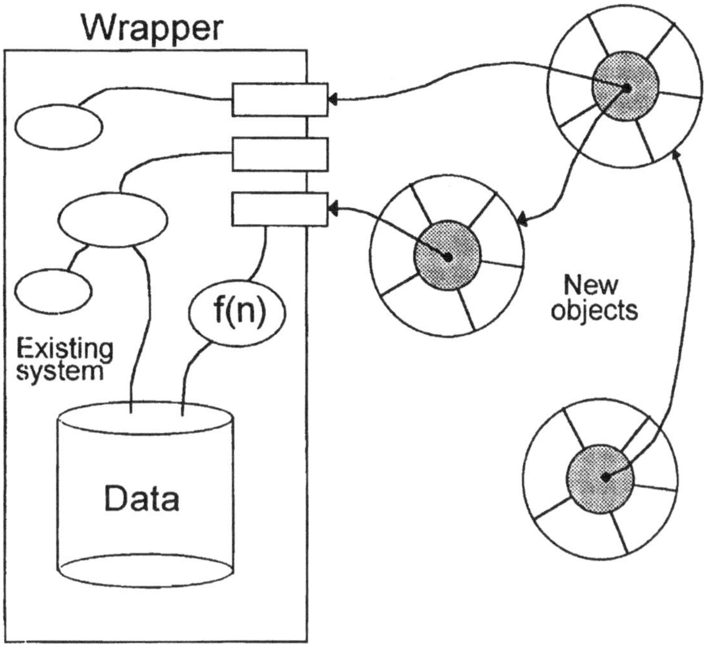

FIGURE 50.1 Object wrappers.

systems completely, the economics of the matter forbids it on any large scale; there are just not enough development resources. What we must do is build on the existing investment and more gradually to the brave new world of object-orientation.

It is possible to create object wrappers around this bulk of existing code, which can then be replaced or allowed to wither away. Building object wrappers can help protect the investment in older systems during the move to object-oriented programming. An object wrapper enables a new, object-oriented part of a system to interact with a conventional chunk by message passing. The wrapper itself is likely to be written in the same language as the original system, COBOL, for example. This may represent a very substantial investment, but once it is in place virtually all maintenance activity may cease. At least this is the theory.

Imagine that an existing COBOL system interacts with users through a traditional menu system, each screen offering about 10 options and with the leaf nodes of the menu tree being normal "enter, tab, and commit" data entry screens. This characterizes a very large number of present day systems. The wrapper must offer all the functions of the old system as if through the interface of an object, as illustrated by the "Gradygram" in Figure 50.1 where the small rectangles on the boundary of the wrapper represent its visible operations, which in turn call the old system's functions and thereby access its data too.* Effectively, the wrapper is a large object whose methods are the menu options of the old system. The only difference between this new object and the old system is that it will respond to messages from other objects. Thus far, this gives little in the way of benefits. However, when we either discover a bug, receive a change request, or wish to add a new business function the benefits begin; for we do not tinker with the old system at all but create a new set of objects to deliver the new features. As far as the existing

* The term *Gradygram* was coined to stand for the icons with operations indicated by small boxes on the boundary of a rectangle representing the object used by Grady Booch since his work on design for Ada in the mid-1980s. To this day, the Booch'93 method uses them for its module diagrams, but variants have appeared in several other methods.

users are concerned, they may see no different when using the old functions, although their calls are being diverted via the wrapper. Wrappers may be small or large but in the context of interoperation they tend to be of quite coarse granularity. For command-driven systems, the wrapper may be a set of operating system batch files or scripts. If the old system used a form or screen-based interface, the wrapper may consist of code that reads and writes data to the screen. This can be done using a virtual terminal. This is fairly easy to accomplish on machines such as the VAX, though it is not always possible with systems such as OS/400 where some specialist software or an ORB may be required. All new functions or replacements should be dealt with by creating new objects with their own encapsulated data structures and methods. If the services of the old system are needed, these are requested by message passing and the output is decoded by the wrapper and passed to the requester.

So much for the propaganda. Implementing wrappers is not as easy as it sounds in several respects. Much of the literature on wrappers is aimed at deriving the necessity ORBs. When these are not available, for whatever reason, developers have to face up to the implementation details directly. One such issue concerns granularity. Most of the theoretical arguments and a good deal of the practical experience of object-oriented programmers indicate that small objects are usually more reusable than large ones. Recall the usual set of guidelines for object design from your favorite text on the subject: interfaces should be small and simple; no more than about 17 operations per object; etc. However, with the legacy system we are faced with a *fait accompli;* the system is as it is. There are irreducibly large grain "objects" often present in the design of legacy systems. ORBs are specifically aimed at dealing with this kind of coarse grain reuse. The question is whether, without such a broker, we can still gain from the use of a hand-made wrapper. Some developers find that coarse grain objects arise naturally even with new requirements and deduce that object-oriented models are not always appropriate. Brice (1993), for example, found this in the context of geometrical image transformation software. The data structures were straightforward, but the processing required pages of equations to describe it and data flow models were found to be the most natural thing to use.* Here is a case where wrappers may be beneficial even with green field developments.

The wrapper approach to migration is not the only one available. Other options include the use of ORBs, employing object-oriented databases or proceeding in a completely *ad hoc* manner. The *ad hoc* approach is often the correct one, but there are so many ways of approaching a particular problem that few sensible generalizations can be made. The *ad hoc* approach was the only one available until the appearance of ORB and object-oriented databases (OODB) products. One leading financial institution, for example, built a straight through trading system to connect its front and back office systems using objects that effectively comprised self-describing data packets. The result was observed *post facto* to be an application specific ORB, but the work was completed before any stable commercial CORBA compliant distributed object management system had come to market. Furthermore, this application went beyond the CORBA specification by using self-describing data. Object-oriented databases are an ingredient of most ORB products but can be used alone to act as a repository for a handcrafted infrastructure. OODBs are discussed and compared by Cattell (1991), and Graham (1994) also gives a guide to the literature.

50.3 Data Management Strategies

One of the biggest problems with the concept of object wrappers concerns data management. Using the wrapper is easy until you need to split the storage of data across the old database and some of the new objects. The object wrapper approach seems ideal at first sight but closer examination reveals some severe data management problems. Where building a wrapper makes it necessary to duplicate or share data across the new and old system components, there are four conceivable strategies:

* Rumbaugh (1993) too has suggested using the data models in OMT to model numerical computation — a better use I think than that originally intended by Rumbaugh et al. (1991).

1. Carry a duplicate live copy of the common data in both parts of the system and keep both copies up to date. The problem with this is that storage requirements could double. Worse still, there are real integrity issues to worry about. It is almost certainly not a viable strategy for either migration or reuse of any commercial scale system. We will call this the *tandem* or *handshake* strategy because it requires constant synchronization of updates and retrievals. It only works when there is little or no overlap between the data of the old and new systems.
2. Keep all data in the old system and copy them to the new objects as required. Messages to the old system cause it to handle updates. This is known as the *borrowing* strategy because data are borrowed temporarily from the wrapper. It is similar to what is done in many existing conventional MIS applications where data are downloaded nightly from a mainframe to workstations and updates transmitted in batch too.
3. Copy the data to the new objects and allow the old system's data to go out of date. Again there may be integrity problems, and the wrapper may have to send messages as well as receive and respond to them, which greatly increases its complexity. Call this the *takeover* strategy by analogy with a company making a takeover bid for another.
4. Carve our coherent chunks of the database together with related functions. This is difficult and requires a sound method of object-oriented analysis capable of describing the old system as well as the new and/or a translation technique from original systems design documents such as DFDs. It seems the most promising approach to migration on balance. This is called the *translation* strategy because one must translate the design to an object model. It is easiest to do when the old system was originally written around critical data structures using a technique such as stepwise refinement. These structures and the programs that use them will migrate naturally to the objects of the new system. A refinement of this strategy is to reverse engineer a data model from the existing system and to identify all file access operations in relation to this model using, for example, a CRUD matrix approach. CRUD techniques are often used to organize conventional systems around their data structures. These calls can then be replaced as new objects are constructed around the entities. This improved version of translation can be called *data centered translation.* Whether it is feasible will depend on the difficulty of obtaining a data model and the complexity of the code in which the database calls are embedded. Reverse engineering tools may prove useful within this strategy and, as Reiss (1991) points out, the most useful tools would contain an understanding of the system semantics. When doing this, one should beware of normalized entities in any data model.

The habit of normalization is rooted deep in the data analysis community and one must be aware that normalized tables do not necessarily correspond to real-world entities. Take a look at any reasonably large data model and you will almost certainly find entities with strange, hyphenated names that correspond to absolutely nothing in the vocabulary of users. Thus, one must first denormalize to get rid of first normal forms which obfuscate the description of aggregate objects and then reconstruct objects that correspond to runtime joint operations. So far as reverse engineering is concerned, I would argue that a semantically rich version of object-oriented analysis is an indispensable tool and that its representations need not be as large or complex as Reiss maintains, if they are well structured and automated support is available. Such an approach is described in Chapter 7.

The above data management strategies may be variously appropriate according to whether we are migrating the system to an object-oriented implementation, reusing its components, extending it, or building a better or a distributed front end. Assuming that our chief aim is to migrate the old system to a new object-oriented one rather than merely to reuse its components, which strategies are feasible? The handshake strategy is flawed for all but the smallest systems, and then there must be little overlap between new and old components. The borrowing strategy may well involve tampering with the old system and is not usually viable for the purposes of system migration unless there is a clean separation between existing functions and new requirements. Borrowing does not permit data to move permanently outward across the wrapper boundary. This means that there will come a time when a huge step must be taken all at once to migrate the data out, unless a DBMS has been used for all data accesses. These strategies, as migration strategies, do grievous violence to the whole idea of building wrappers. Only the last two strategies promise to be feasible if our intention is to migrate the functions of the old system to a new one, and there are some systems where neither seems to be practical. It is also the case that the type of system, its structure, and the quality and type of its documentation will affect the choice of strategy. Dietrich's original application of the wrapper concept was to a solid modeling system of considerable complexity but whose intricacy resided in its code rather than in its data management. Furthermore, his primary concern was with the reuse of the functions of a stable system rather than its reconstruction. Hence, there has been little publicly documented experience of solving the problem under consideration here.

Strategy 4, translation, will work most often, provided that the old system can be decomposed around coherent data sets and if there are, for example, some existing DFDs from which to transform objects, by encapsulating their data stores. If not, one is faced with building a wrapper of much greater complexity using takeover, strategy 3. The latter is a far costlier option.

50.4 Practical Problems with Migration

Another problem arises when the old system exists and is maintained in multiple versions. For example, a commercial package for a particular industry may, over the years, have been adapted for the needs of particular clients. The cost of building a wrapper for each version is usually prohibitive. The wrapper approach will only work if there is a core system common to all the versions, and the modifications will have to be maintained separately in any case until they can be re-implemented. This was the situation on a project that I was involved with where there were around 70 versions of the product customized for particular sites scattered across the globe, with local, dedicated maintenance teams in many cases. Also, the decomposition of the existing system into coherent chunks was exceedingly hard because of the long modification history. The strategy adopted was to model the system using object-oriented analysis and first wrap the core system in such a way that *new* functionality (an MIS component) could be added using object-oriented methods, leaving the core system much untouched at this stage. One feature of the problem is particularly worthy of comment. It turned out that the hardware on which the system had to run, pending a move to UNIX at some future data, did not support an object-oriented language of any form. Thus, in the short-term, the new object-oriented components had to be implemented in a conventional language. To ensure that the new system could be fully object-oriented in the future, we had to find a way to minimize the cost. This led to the use of an object-oriented analysis approach and the conversion of its products to conventional code. It also led to the use of an ORB, NeWI, that was able to let the developers treat the system as object-oriented while still writing code in C. We also attempted to produce an object-oriented description of the existing system to clarify understanding and help carve out separate reimplementable chunks following a translation strategy. It emerged that treating some functions as objects instead of methods was useful. The bulk of the early effort went into designing additional features and their interface, via a wrapper, to the core of the existing system with translation tasks being deferred to the near future. Thus, it proved wise to proceed in these steps:

1. Build a wrapper to communicate with new object-oriented components using (most probably) the borrowing strategy
2. Perform an object-oriented analysis on the old system
3. Use translation or data centered translation to migrate
4. Utilize an ORB to implement.

Grass (1991) argues that wrappers work well for mature systems that are essentially frozen, in the context of a requirement to reduce the maintenance burden which she characterizes as "extremely aggravating" with the panache of understatement. Her main point is that ill-structured legacy systems are costly to understand and wrap. However, even this is worthwhile if the potential maintenance savings are large enough. Like Dietrich's, Grass' principal application (a parser for regular grammars) was complex functionally but not primarily a data intensive application.

One may conclude that, until much more experience has been accumulated, the best approach to migration of legacy systems with significant data management complexity is to build wrappers that support object-oriented front ends and to build the required new functions within the front ends. The tandem strategy can be used only when there is little overlap and separate databases will have to be maintained. The exceptions to this are when the existing system already has a coherent data centered structure that facilitates translation or when the benefits of the migration are large enough to justify the cost of building a very complex wrapper along the lines of the takeover strategy. If there is an existing DBMS this can be wrapped as a whole and maintained for a long time as the wrapped functions are gradually migrated. Then, at some point, one can move all the data at once to an object-oriented database if desired and eliminate the database wrapper. This is a special variant of the translation strategy where the database is one huge "coherent chunk." It is probably the ideal option for many organizations already obtaining satisfactory performance from their relational databases. A good wrapper for Oracle or Sybase, probably written in C++, is a very sound investment in terms of migration strategy.

Having decided to build a wrapper and a new front end, one needs tools for building them. There are no specific products offering wrapper technology for migration at present, but there are several ORB and GUI tools that may help with reuse.

A key problem faced by many IT departments exists when there is a mixture of essentially incompatible hardware and software that somehow has been made to work together over the years. Conceptually, it is easy to see that this "goulash" can be modeled as a system of large objects communicating by passing messages with parameters. The wrapper approach is appropriate when just one of these systems is to migrate to an object-oriented, open platform. Rather than build a wrapper for each old system, which would be expensive to say the least, it is better to wrap the communication system in some way. One approach to this problem is the ORB idea.

Microsoft's COM/Active X technology is beginning to exhibit features that let one treat existing applications as if they were wrapped. There are now several distributed object management systems (DOMS) that support wrappers, ranging from coarse grain ORBs like the ones from Iona Technologies and Expersoft to class libraries that help with finer grain wrapping and distributed object management.

In the product migration project referred to above, it turned out, for the reasons given, that there were no suitable software tools at the outset. Therefore our main tool was our object-oriented analysis approach itself. It was originally intended that the products we produced would conform to Object Management Group (OMG) standards including CORBA. In the outcome, the NeWI product was used to support both distributed object management and the use of C for object-oriented programming. The developers of NeWI were among the first people to coin the term "business object," which is a subject we will take up shortly (Simms, 1994).

Another requirement was for some sort of CASE tool or repository that would support the recording of object and structure definitions. No such tool could be found. Most existing tools allow the user to draw diagrams but are weak on the recording of textual information. The project ended up by creating its own repository tool based on existing AS/400 software. The approach was similar in some respects to that of the *SOMATiK* software, though lacking in the latter's code generation, graphical, and animation features.

We need to deal not only with the evolution of existing systems which are important and too large or complex to rewrite, but also with the evolutionary migration of an existing system to a future object-oriented implementation. This implies the need for techniques that will let us reuse components of existing functionally decomposed systems or even entire packages within our new or evolving object-oriented systems. To this issue we now turn.

50.5 Reusing Existing Software Components and Packages

Thus far we have considered the wrapper technique from the point of view of migration. Now we must also consider the problem of reusing existing components when there is no explicit need or intention to reimplement them in an object-oriented style. Dietrich's (1989) work has shown in principle how the reuse of highly optimized algorithms or specialized functions can be accomplished using the object wrapper strategy. This can be done by defining application level classes whose methods call subroutines in the old system. The legacy systems can be wrapped in groups or as individual packages, with the latter option offering greater potential for reuse.

There is also a need to build on existing "package" solutions. Once again a wrapper that calls package subroutines or simulates dialog at a terminal can be built. The alternative is to modify the packages to export data for manipulation by the new system, but this fails to reuse existing functional components of the old system. Also package vendors may not be prepared to support or even countenance such changes.

Some problems which must be solved in building such a wrapper are identified by Dietrich as follows.

- The designer is not free to choose the best representations for the problem in terms of objects since this is already largely decided within the old system. Here again there is a possibility that the wrappers will represent very coarse grain objects with limited opportunities for reuse.
- The designer must either expose the old system's functions and interface to the user or protect him from possible changes to the old system. It is very difficult to do both successfully. Generally, one should only allow read accesses to the old system, which tends to preclude the takeover data management strategy.
- Where the old system continues to maintain data, the wrapper must preserve the state of these data when it calls internal routines.
- Garbage collection, memory management, and compactification (where applicable) must be synchronized between the wrapper and the old system.
- Cross system invariants, which relate the old and new data sets, must be maintained.
- Building a wrapper often requires very detailed understanding of the old system. This is even more true when migrating but still a significant problem when reusing.

Because access to the internals of package software is seldom available at the required level of detail, the wrapper approach described above will not usually work. A better approach is to regard the package as a fixed object offering definite services, possibly in a distributed environment.

Whereas data centered translation is the best approach to migration and replacement of existing systems — while borrowing strategies fail to work — where reuse is the main concern, borrowing is a perfectly viable approach. If the existing system or package largely works, for the functions it provides, and can be maintained at an acceptable level of cost (however large that may be), then when new functions are required it may be possible to build them quite separately using an object-oriented approach and communicate with the old system through a wrapper. This wrapper is used to call the services of the old system and give access to its database. New functions are defined as the methods of objects that encapsulate the data they need, insofar as they are new data. When data stored by the old system are required, a message must be sent to the wrapper and the appropriate retrieval routines called borrowing the needed data. Updates to the existing database are treated similarly, by lending as it were.

It may well turn out that, in the fullness of time, the new object-oriented system will gradually acquire features that replace and duplicate parts of the old system. Data centered translation then becomes necessary instead of borrowing for the affected parts of the system. Therefore the step-by-step strategy recommended in the last section is indicated for many commercial systems projects.

We may summarize the conclusions of this chapter thus far in Table 50.1. In this table a "Y" indicates that a wrapper data strategy may be worth considering for a particular class of problem but not that it is guaranteed to work. An "N" indicates that it probably will not be suitable. A '?' means "that all depends." The four strategies defined above are compared with four possible reasons for building wrappers: migrating a complex legacy system to a new object-oriented implementation; reusing its components without changing the core system; extending its functionality without changing the core;

TABLE 50.1 Suitability of Data Communication Strategies for Different Purposes

Purpose	Migration	Reuse	Extension	Front End
Strategy				
Handshake	N	N	N	N
Borrowing	N	Y	Y	Y
Takeover	?	N	N	N
Translation	?	N	Y	Y
Data centered translation	Y	N	Y	Y

and building a possibly distributed front end to provide additional functions. Note that the last three purposes are very similar and the last two have identical Y/N patterns.

50.6 Combining Relational and Object-Oriented Databases

For developers and maintainers of commercial systems, many of which have a substantial data management component, exploiting the best of existing relational databases for one part of an application in concert with the use of an object-oriented programming language or even an OODB for another is a key issue. Generally, the interoperation of legacy relational databases and object-oriented programming languages is best viewed as a special case of the client/server model. The reason for considering an object-oriented database is that there are several commercial applications with which relational databases are very bad at dealing. Examples include bills of materials, document handling, and, in fact, any application where there are complex, structured objects. Older generation databases were just too inflexible to use for highly evolutionary applications such as text management. For these reasons it is still the case that most of the data owned by businesses are not in a computer system at all, up to 90% according to some estimates. Further, these data do not include the business and technical knowledge on which these organizations depend. As businesses strive for competitive edge there is an ever increasing demand to computerize all these data along with the need to build a knowledge base, and object-oriented databases offer a partial solution. On an application involving many complex objects, an object-oriented database can be 100 times faster than its relational equivalent and retains the flexibility of the relational approach in terms of schema evolution too. Furthermore, object-oriented databases offer enhanced facilities such as support for long transactions and version control. However, since most organizations have a monstrous investment in existing database systems, and since the relational approach works well for most record-oriented IS applications, it is imperative that moving to OODBs should not involve the abandonment of all the existing work.

There are two options available: a pure OODB or a relational system extended with object-oriented constructs. There are several pure object-oriented products in existence but they have not yet matured fully. Further, there is a class of applications where a relational system may be not only a more mature solution but a faster one — typically those involving few large joins such as ledger applications. One alternative is to continue with the relational model extended in various ways, as with products such as Illustra. The other is to try to make our new OODB applications interoperate with existing database systems. The first may give performance problems for certain applications, judging from early experiences, so the second is at least worth considering.

The obvious approach suggested in the foregoing is to build a generalized wrapper for the DBMS itself. For example, a C++ wrapper could be written for Sybase that converts between messages and SQL queries. Thus the object wrapper approach described above will go through in many cases and the interoperability considerations for database systems are not really any different from those discussed for general computer systems. One feature of database systems, however, does deserve separate attention, and that is the issue of data modeling, because modern database systems are nearly always based on a data model and such a model is based on real-world entities — bearing in mind my remarks about normalization above.

One of the great advantages of a conventional database management system is the separation of processes and data, which gives a notion of data independence and benefits of flexibility and insulation from change, because the interface to shared data is stable. The data model is to be regarded as a model of the statics of the application. With object-oriented, processes and data are integrated. Does this mean that you have to abandon the benefits of data independence? Already in client-server relational databases we have seen a step in the same direction, with database triggers and integrity rules stored in the server with the data. With an object-oriented approach to data management, it therefore seems reasonable to adopt the view that there are two kinds of business objects: *domain* (or *shared*) objects and *application* objects. As Daniels and Cook (1993) point out, objects that must be shared are nearly always persistent. Domain objects represent those aspects of the system that are relatively stable or generic and application objects are those that will be expected to vary from installation to installation or quite rapidly from time to time and which share the services of the domain objects. This approach resurrects the notion of data independence in an enhanced, object-oriented form. The domain objects are based on the data model and include persistent aspects of the model, constraints, rules, and dynamics (state transitions, etc.). The goal is to make the interface to this part of the model as stable as possible. The application objects (including the user interface objects) use the services of the domain objects and may interact through them. This approach is reminiscent of the approach taken in the KADS expert systems development method with its knowledge level, task level, and application level models of a domain (see Hickman et al., 1989). It is also compatible with Smalltalk's MVC pattern if we introduce non-business objects called *interface objects* to represent the controllers. The interface controls share access to the services of the application objects while the application objects share access to those of the domain objects. So-called "database aware" controls appear to give direct access to domain objects but may be implemented via intermediate application objects. Typically domain objects will be found in the domain or business model and will be maintained by a team separate from application development teams. They are the central repository for reuse of business objects.

The obvious candidates for domain objects are the denormalized relations or views of a legacy database wrapped with the behavior of the corresponding business objects. Where a database that offers the capability of storing procedures in the server, such as Sybase, is in use, this is even more straightforward though discipline is required to prevent access to data structures via SQL. All calls to the database must be stored via procedures representing the wrapper interface. In the extreme case this could be implemented by the database administrator closing off all access privileges to all users, except to the stored procedures. Developers should thus be able to refer to a clean, object-oriented conceptual model while designing their access operations from application objects.

How then should the object-oriented component of our database or data model interoperate with the relational part? Incidentally, I am assuming that you will eventually want to migrate all your old CODASYL and IMS applications to an object-oriented database.

The possibilities are as follows:

1. Object wrappers can be built for the relational system as a whole, treating it as an entire domain model. This approach offers minimal opportunities for the reuse of domain objects but may, nevertheless, be viable and the database wrapper can be replaced easily later.
2. Coherent chunks of the database can be wrapped individually, perhaps allowing a phased approach. The use of stored procedures and a published object model are highly beneficial here. Opportunities for reuse are maximized by this strategy where it is feasible.
3. SQL can be used to communicate with the relational system, which means that the new system must be able to generate SQL calls and interpret the resulting tables based on knowledge of the data dictionary and its semantics. This will usually involve the use of fairly complex AI techniques such as those used in natural language query systems such as Intellect.
4. The relational system could be addressed through an ORB provided it either conforms to the CORBA standard or a conformant wrapper is built. Once again, use of an ORB tends to deal with the legacy system as coarse grained and the reuse potential is not as high as Option 2 above.

A good example of interworking between relational and non-relational databases is provided by geographic information systems (GIS). Most GIS store two kinds of data — mapping data and data concerning the attributes of the objects mapped. The performance of relational systems is poor on mapping data because of their inability to store complex, structured objects and their need to do joins to reconstruct them. For this reason the mapping data are usually stored in a proprietary file system. The attribute data are often stored in a relational database and also often shared with other applications. In many applications a change to mapping data must be reflected in changes to the attributes and vice versa. This close coupling has been a significant task for product developers. Relational systems that support BLOBS (binary large objects) can be used but they cannot interpret the data. CAD systems developers have faced similar problems. The most recent geographic information systems, such as Smallworld, have opted for an object-oriented approach to storing mapping data.

Loomis (1991) identifies three problems and three approaches to object-relational interoperation. The three problems are to:

1. Build object-oriented applications that access relational databases
2. Run existing relationally written applications against an object-oriented database
3. Use an SQL-like query language in an object-oriented environment

The three approaches are to:

1. Convert the applications and databases completely to object-oriented ones
2. Use standard import-export facilities
3. Access the relational databases from the object-oriented programming languages

The first of these approaches is complicated and expensive, and works badly if some old system functions are to be reused or migration is gradual. The same problem referred to in Sections 50.2 and 50.3 arises, in that coordinating updates across heterogeneous databases is problematical. However, if you can do periodic downloads of data to the new system, the approach can be tolerated. This is exactly what we did when migrating from IMS to DB2 and building MIS extensions. The second approach relies on standards having been defined, which will depend on the application, e.g., standards exist in the CAD and VLSI design worlds but not in general. The best variant of this approach is to use an object-oriented database which supports SQL gateways to your relational databases, as does GemStone, for example. Here though, the application must provide a mapping between table and object views of data and, except for the simplest cases, this can be complicated. The third approach implies adopting Object SQL or SQL3.

Conventional databases let one store relations, such as "all the children who like toys," in a table, but not the rule that "all children like toys"; they also do not permit one to store the fact that when one field is updated another may have to be. Both of these kinds of relationship are easy to express in, for example, Prolog or in any knowledge based systems shell. For some time now relational database vendors have extended the relational model to allow database triggers to capture the latter kind of rule. In AI frame based systems the support for rules is more general and less procedural in style, but there is undoubtedly a trend to enriching the semantic abilities of databases in this way. Object relational databases, in addition, now offer facilities for defining abstract data types so that they can deal with complex data types exactly in the manner of an object-oriented database. At present no object-oriented database product known to the author offers explicit support for declarative rules.

One way to enhance interoperability, we are told, is to place system syntax and semantics in enterprise repositories. These days, nearly all new repositories are based on object-oriented database technology. In some cases a mixture of I-CASE and expert systems technology is used. See, for example, Martin and Odell (1992) for the arguments for this approach. Such repositories will store an interface library and this will help systems to locate and utilize existing objects.

All these developments suggest the need for a systems analysis technique which captures not just data, process, and dynamics but rules and facts of the type found in knowledge based systems. OODBs and extended relational databases will also make it imperative that business rules are captured explicitly during the analysis process. Certainly, I believe that the adoption of a sound approach to object-oriented analysis is a key part of any organization migration strategy.

50.7 Business Objects and Business Object Models

Arguments about whether object-oriented development is seamless or not, whether transformational approaches are better than roundtrip gestalt design, or disputes about the difference between essential and system models have beset attempts to explain object-oriented requirements engineering. I believe that lack of clarity about modeling is at the root of these disputes and has also led to a great muddle concerning the concept of a business object. In this section I want to explain my understanding of the meaning and status of modeling within object-oriented development. Then it will be possible to explain what a business object really is.

Modeling is central to software engineering practice and especially to object-oriented development. A model is a representation of some thing or systems of things with all or some of the following properties.

- It is always *different* from the thing or system being modeled (the *original*) in scale, implementation, or behavior.
- It has the shape or appearance of the original (an iconic model).
- It can be manipulated or exercised in such a way that its behavior or properties can be used to predict the behavior or properties of the original (a simulation model).
- There is always some correspondence between the model and the original.

Examples of models abound throughout daily life: mock-ups of aircraft in wind tunnels, architectural scale models, models of network traffic using compressed air in tubes or electrical circuits, and software models of gas combustion in engines. Of course *all* software is a model of something, just as all mathematical equations are (analytic) models.

Jackson (1995) relates models to descriptions by saying that modeling a domain involves making designations of the primitives of the domain and then using these to build a description of the properties, relationships, and behavior that are true of that domain. For example, if we take the domain of sending birthday cards to ones friends, we might make designations:

- p is a friend
- d is a date (day and month)
- $B(p,d)$ says that p was born on d

Then we can make descriptions like: for all p, there is exactly one B. Jackson suggests that modeling is all about ensuring that the descriptions apply equally well to the model and to the original domain. In the context of computer models this might mean that the instances of a class or the records of a database are made to correspond uniquely to domain instances of our friends. Most usefully, Jackson presents this concept as the M configuration shown in Figure 50.2.

The Domain and the Machine are different. In the domain friends do not reside in disk sectors. There are many things in the domain that are not in our model, such as our friends' legs or pimples. There are also things that go on in computers that we are not concerned with in a model, such as time sharing. The model comprises the features shared between the domain and the machine.

This understanding of what a model is can be applied to the problem of object modeling. We must understand clearly that a so-called Business Object Model (BOM) is both a model of the domain and a potentially implementable machine model, but we must begin with a model of the domain to understand and validate the requirements.

It is my thesis that object modeling is a very general method for knowledge representation. There is little that cannot be modeled with objects, provided, of course, that we do not restrict ourselves to the semantics of some particular object-oriented programmable language. We can model both the domain

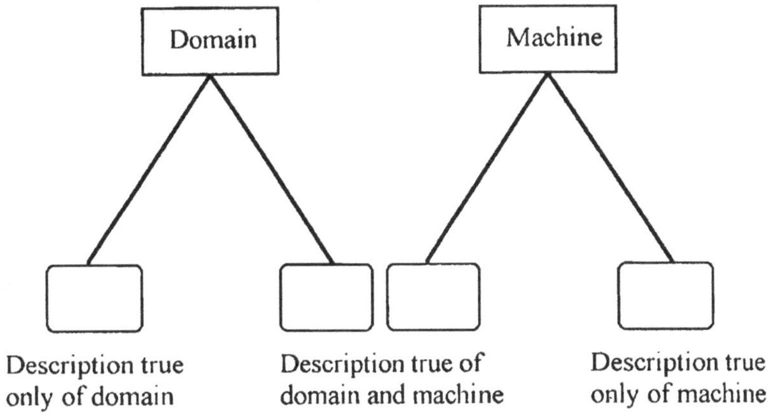

FIGURE 50.2 M is for "model." (From Jackson, M. 1995. *Software Requirements and Specifications.* Addison-Wesley, Wokingham, U.K. With permission.)

and the machine using objects. This is not to say that the world consists of our model objects, but it is to say that we can almost always model the domain as if it was made of objects. A good example is provided by Cook and Daniels (1994), who make a strong distinction between *essential* (i.e., domain) and *specification* models. They argue that the world is not made of objects citing by way of example the fact that the sun does not wake the birds up each morning by sending each one a message. However, if we want a correspondence between our domain and specification models it is quite permissible to model the sunrise event as recorded on a "blackboard" object in which each instance of the class Birds has registered interest. That is not what happens physically, but it is a good model insofar as object semantics do not include a broadcast metaphor. There are of course many exceptions where object modeling is inappropriate, but the sheer discipline of trying to model with objects is beneficial in terms of scientific parsimony and ordered thought. For example, I doubt whether the solution of a differential equation is best modeled with objects. Here another idea promoted by Jackson (1995) may be useful. He argues that one can recognize analysis patterns (which he calls problem frames) that recur and which imply suitable modeling methods. One example is the "simple IS frame" which indicates that a JSP approach is suitable. The arguments in this case are convincing, but generally I find that object modeling gives more chance of success than any other approach and that JSP can be accommodated as a technique within an OO approach. Kristen (1995), for one, does this within his KISS method.

Jackson's M metaphor provides us with an understanding of the correspondence between two words — the domain and the machine — in the example above. However, if we are to apply object modeling to a realistic business problem it turns out that this is often too simplistic a view. In practice we must build a linked series of models more reminiscent of a tasty *mmmmmm* than a single M. de Champeaux (1997) offers some support for this view. He distinguishes between two approaches to object modeling that he characterizes as constructivist (neat) and impressionist (scruffy). Scruffies do not emphasize the precise semantics of object modeling. They opine "the design fleshes out the analysis" without being precise about what this means. Precision is only introduced in the implementation models when the semantics of a language has to be faced. The neats are different. They want to "exploit the analysis computational model" and observe that analysis models are "nearly executable." Examples of approaches close to the spirit of the neats include those of Cook and Daniels (1994) and of de Champeaux (1997) himself. In both cases precision relies heavily on the use of state models, but this is not necessarily always the case. In SOMA, for example, there is a defined sequence of model transformations but state machines are only an optional technique. Let us examine this sequence in enough detail to illustrate the general idea.

We start by examining an entire business. If we try to build an object model of the business we soon find that it is too complex with too many people, departments, products, etc. The recommended technique is the activity grid, which is a matrix of the core business processes where the rows represent goals and the columns logical job description. Each cell of this grid can be regarded as a (process-oriented) business area. The model is usually underpinned by a value chain analysis. We can then zoom in on a cell (or group of cells) and again try to build an object model. At this scale we have a chance of succeeding. The model transformation merely takes us from the whole business to its component processes represented in natural language. Each area thus has a mission connected with executing the process and a number of definite, measurable objectives. The next recommended technique is to regard the business area as a network of communicating intelligent agents. The agents are modeled as objects that represent people, roles, systems, or aggregates (functional units). The agents communicate with each other and with external agents with objects representing customers, etc. Communication is interpreted as consisting of abstract "semiotic arts" or conversations. Each conversation is in support of a stated business objective. These conversations can be represented as messages with a definite structure: trigger; goal; offer/request; negotiation; task performance; and handover. We now transform this agent object model to a different one by focusing on the tasks that the messages contain, or we build the Task Object Model. Task objects can be thought of as generic use cases, although a more precise theoretical foundation exists. Tasks are decomposed into smaller atomic component tasks, exploiting the aggregation semantics of object modeling. Tasks can be specialization of reusable tasks from other projects, exploiting the inheritance semantics. Tasks can also be associated with each other. For example, one task may have to *precede* another. Finally, tasks can send messages to each other asking for help when exceptions arise. This is then a veritable object model, but it is *not* a model of a computer system in any sense.

We now transform the Task Object Model into a BOM. These is a creative transformation based on the usual noun/verb technique. We make the transformation seamless using an extension of the CRC card idea. The BOM represents those business objects referred to or implied by the task scripts. But what is its status? Is it a model of the world or a model of some system yet to be implemented? The answer is that it is both. It lies exactly in the middle of a Jackson M. It abstracts what is common to the business and a future implementation model, and it is potentially executable. Tools that allow execution of such models are already available with examples including ObjecTime, *SOMATiK,* and SES's ObjectBench.

Each business object is viewed as having its own thread of control. The BOM is inherently distributed in that no decisions about physical architecture have been made. When we begin to make such decisions we are transforming the model to an implementation object model (IOM). This too is a manual transformation wherein some very complex design decisions may be made. These decisions include distribution, sequentialization, and optimization, and de Champeaux suggests transforming the model in three steps corresponding to these issues. We must also select a language, messaging model, and persistence strategy during the design transformations. It is difficult to see how such complex transformations can be seamlessly linked back to the BOM when low-level languages are used and the need for tuning eliminates the use of code generation.

Several conclusions follows from the above argument. First among these is that object modeling cannot be seen as a single step consisting of a drawing of class diagrams and followed by refinement down to an implementation model. Such an approach — and remarkably, it is the one common to most of the well-known OO analysis methods — leaves out many domain issues that should not be ignored. There must be a sequence of models. Fortunately these can be object models in nearly every case and they can be linked together seamlessly until we come to implementation. At that stage we face a trade off between seamlessness and performance.

The argument also suggests the business object as the focal point of reuse, but our business objects are specifications not code, although they are executable specifications. This is a different view of business objects from the one emerging from the OMG currently. The latter tends to see business objects in the Common Facilities layer as though they were robust, reusable implementations, shielded only by IDL wrappers that cannot possibly contain a rich enough semantics to enable links back to the earlier models in the modeling sequence. Simms (1994) characterizes this as a confusion between components and

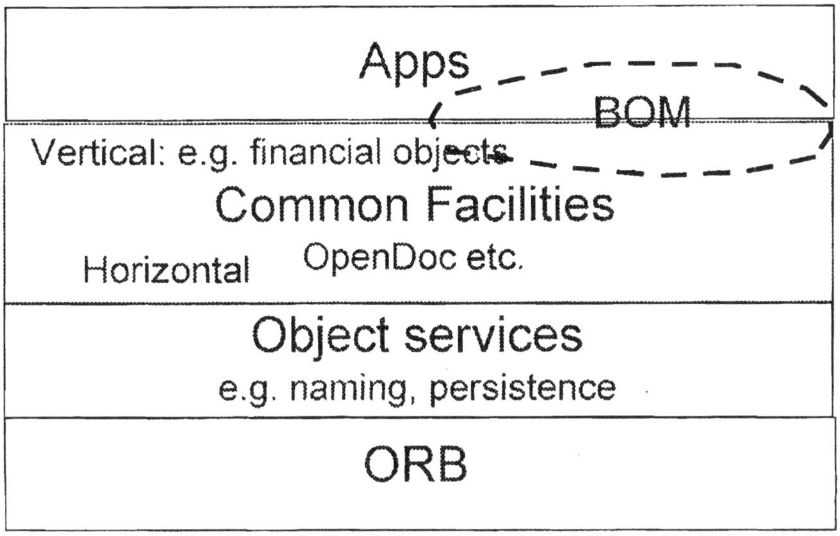

FIGURE 50.3 One possible architectural framework.

business objects, pointing out that business objects can be assembled from components but that they are by no means the same thing. This is an issue that needs to be explored very carefully before companies commit themselves to third party products masquerading as OMG business objects.

Figure 50.3 offers a possible architectural framework for a company adopting technology. It is broadly based on the OMG model but indicates that there will be minimal reliance on the OMG vertical common facilities. Creating a BOM for reuse in a vertical market is actually a far harder undertaking than it would seem at first sight. This is evident from the very few commercial offerings in the finance area, for example. Most commercial offerings are little more than rebadged data/process models. They are nearly always replete with false assumptions about business processes that reflect the practice of the (usually one) organization where they were first developed. Quite often they are closely tied to the semantics of a particular language, e.g., C++. Also, at the time of writing this chapter, the main contender in the banking sector is strongly associated with a relational database, leading to performance problems.

The alternative is to create your own BOM. This provides a tailor-made resource, gives you more control, permits performance optimization, and allows you to take advantage of new technology as it becomes available: WWW, Java, ODBMS, *SOMATiK*, etc. Of course there are costs. As noted already this is no simple matter. For one thing it is often hard to decide exactly what a business object is. In the Finance domain, for example, it is reasonably clear that financial instruments are good candidates for reusable business objects. However, there are well over 200 classes of this type and it is extremely difficult to form them into a robust, stable classification structure. Corporate actions are another good candidate, and here there are only about 42 classes. Even this number gives moderate complexity, as illustrated by the fragment of the hierarchy in Figure 50.4. Pricing algorithms too can be regarded as bona fide objects, even though they are just processes with light data structure. The reason for this is that instruments may be priced by many algorithms, so that the algorithm is not a method of the instrument. Events — such as trades, payments, cash flows, etc. — are more problematic. Trades have complex lifecycles that could be represented by state machines, but trades in different instruments often have quite different lifecycles. So, is the lifecycle a feature of the trade, of the instrument, or of the geographical location? Perhaps it is a feature of a "relationship" object. Customers, regulators, etc., are even more evidently not objects; instead, they are relationships between organizations, departments, and individuals. People are beginning to suggest that business processes are objects. If so, the question

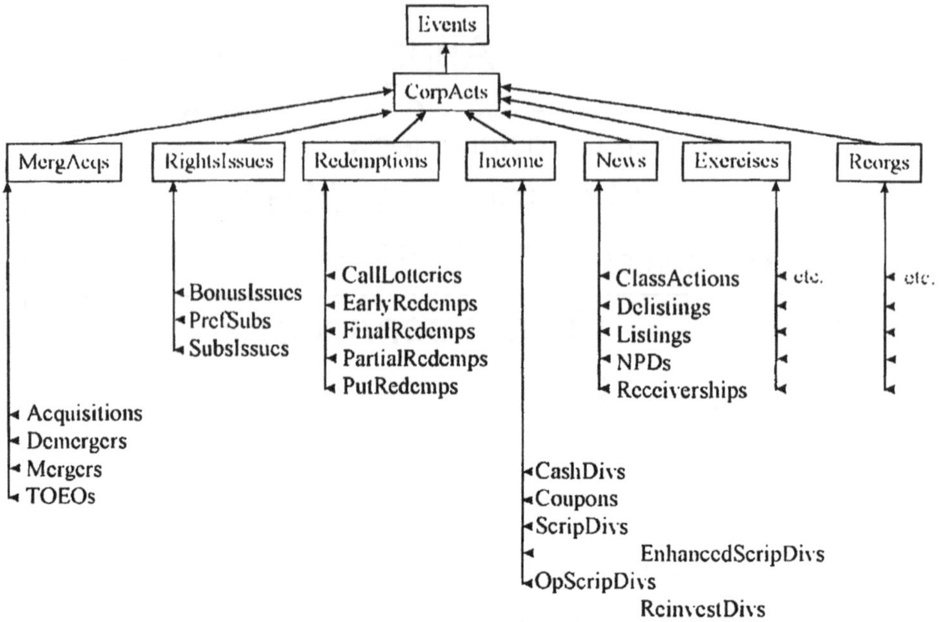

FIGURE 50.4 Part of the classification structure for corporate actions.

that is usually ignored is whether they have the same status as objects like instruments or are they part of the same model. The task modeling approach of SOMA is a step toward answering these questions, i.e., processes *are* objects but in separate object models.

50.8 What Needs to be Done?

The main conclusion to be drawn from this chapter is that an organization migrating to OT needs to establish an OO development method. This method should help establish a clear notion of what a business object is. It should have sufficiently rich semantics to capture business rules within objects. It should also have a clear process and a metrics suite.

Establishing a reuse program within the overall process is essential. The hairies and conscripts model (Graham, 1996) offers a managerial technique that encourages knowledge transfer between the reuse team and application developers.

Education and training of both users and developers is also critical. OO developers can be recruited and/or retrained and tools must be acquired. This includes language, databases, modeling/reuse tools, and especially middleware such as ORBs, gateways, and transaction monitors.

Teams must understand modeling. They should realize also that specification models include more than just business objects. They encompass business objectives and priorities, business processes (conversations), tasks (these are reusable objects too), business objects, links between business objects and tasks, implementation objects and components. The architecture should be the basis of the component library.

When choosing component and business object libraries, ask whether the model fits your business. Beware of data models in disguise. Make sure that performance is adequate. Take firm control over the specification of the objects, based on business needs. Use binary components only when you trust them completely. Buy or build the *right* middleware. Do not forget the business processes. Last but by no means least adopt a suitable method rather than just a notation of CASE tool.

50.9 Bibliographical Notes

Dietrich's (1989) paper is the original source on object wrappers and is well complemented by the analyses of Reiss (1991) and Grass (1991). Some of the panels in the OOPSLA proceedings (Meyrowitz 1989, 1990) contain useful insights. Some of the data management ideas explored here are taken up and explored further by Topper (1995).

SOMA is described in Chapter 7 and in detail by Graham (1995). The latter book I think coined the term Business Object Model for the first time to refer to business objects in the sense used in this chapter, while Sims (1994) first used the term business object to refer to objects that could be represented as graphical icons, which meant something to the business.

Much of the material in this chapter is based on articles that have appeared through the 1990s in various conference proceedings and in the journals, *First Class, Object Magazine,* and *Object Expert.* These articles are not included in the reference section.

References

Brice, A. 1993. Using models in analysis. *Computing,* 27th May, p. 41.

Cattell, R.G.G. 1991. *Object Data Management.* Addison-Wesley, Reading, MA.

Cook, S. and Daniels, J. 1994. *Designing Object Systems.* Prentice-Hall, Englewood Cliffs, NJ.

Daniels, J. and Cook, S. 1993. Strategies for sharing objects in distributed systems, *JOOP,* 5(8), 27–36.

de Champeaux, D. 1997. *Object-Oriented Development Process and Metrics.* Prentice-Hall, Englewood Cliffs, NJ.

Dietrich, W.C., Nackman, L.R. and Gracer, F. 1989. Saving a legacy with objects, in *Proc. OOPSLA 1989,* Addison Wesley, Reading, MA.

Graham, I.M. 1994. *Object-Oriented Methods, 2nd Edition.* Addison-Wesley, Wokingham, U.K.

Graham, I.M. 1995. *Migrating to Object Technology.* Addison-Wesley, Wokingham, U.K.

Graham, I.M. 1996. Hairies and conscripts: making reuse work. *Object Mag.,* 6(6), 82–83.

Grass, J.E. 1991. Design archaeology for object-oriented redesign in C++. In *TOOLS5: Proc. Fifth Int. Conf. on the Technology of Object-Oriented Languages and Systems.* Prentice-Hall, New York.

Hickman, F.R., Killen, J. and Lang, L. et al. 1989. *Analysis for Knowledge-based Systems.* Chichester: Ellis Horwood, U.K.

Jackson, M. 1995. *Software Requirements and Specifications.* Addison-Wesley, Wokingham, U.K.

Korson, T., Vaishnavi, V. and Meyer, B. (Eds.) 1991. *TOOLS5: Proc. Fifth Int. Conf. on the Technology of Object-Oriented Languages and Systems.* Prentice-Hall, New York.

Kristen, G. 1995. *Object-Orientation: The KISS Method.* Addison-Wesley, Wokingham, U.K.

Loomis, M.E.S. 1991. Objects and SQL, *Object Mag.* 1(3) 68–78.

Martin, J. and Odell, J.J. 1992. *Object-Oriented Analysis and Design.* Prentice-Hall, Englewood Cliffs, NJ.

Meyrowitz, N. 1989-90. *Proc. OOPSLA 1989,* Addison Wesley, Reading, MA.

Reiss, S.P. 1991. Tools for object-oriented redesign. In *TOOLS5: Proc. Fifth Int. Conf. on the Technology of Object-Oriented Languages and Systems.* Prentice-Hall, New York.

Sims, O. 1994. *Business Objects.* McGraw-Hill, London.

Topper, A. 1995. *Object-Oriented Development in COBOL.* McGraw-Hill, New York.

51

Managing Business Object Development Cycles

James Thomann
The Data Warehousing Institute

The main purpose of this article is to examine issues surrounding development, deployment, management, and maintenance of business objects. Specifically, we will examine the phases needed to develop business objects, and we will discuss the types of lifecycles used to deploy those objects. We will also look at the types of projects (developing, purchasing/customizing, quality management, maintenance) needed and consider issues of managing these projects. Most business IT centers are not ready for business objects, so we must explore what is required to introduce Object-Orientation (OO) into the enterprise. In addition, we will examine the role of the component library and associated standards, including the activities necessary to create, use, and maintain the library. Let's begin with a context setting by exploring what we mean by "business object."

51.1 What is a Business Object?

Any object can be classified as belonging to one of three types: Entity, Interface and Control.* An entity object contains the persistent information relevant to the business, its data. An interface object manages the communication that links the application to outside sources or receivers of information. Control

* These object types were first defined in *Object-Oriented Software Engineering*, Addison-Wesley, 1992.

0-8493-3135-8/99/$0.00+$.50

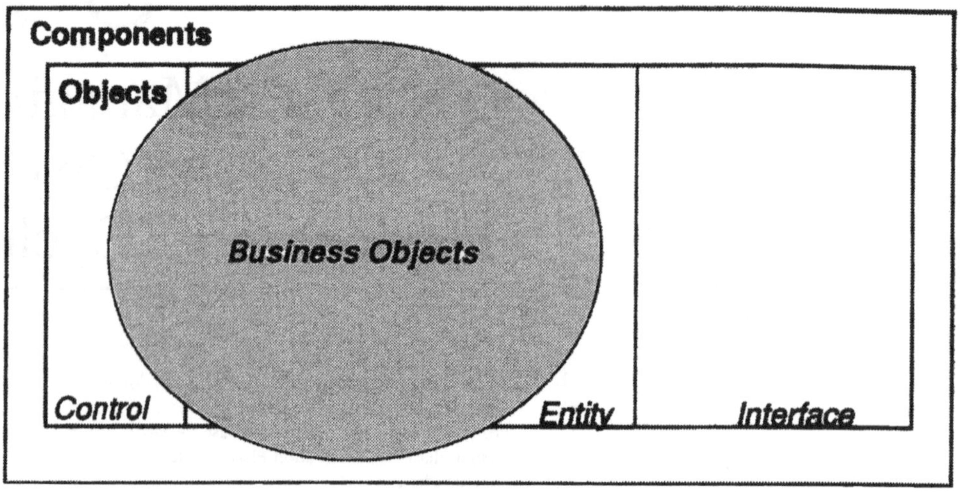

FIGURE 51.1 Component and object types.

objects are transient objects that contain behavior which does not naturally belong in entity or interface objects. We distinguish between these types of objects because it makes explicit the different possible uses of the objects in an application. By using these distinctions, the object developer will identify, design, and develop object classes that have well-defined data structures and functionality. Object typing also leads to the proper allocation of functionality to the appropriate object classes. This leads to a more robust collection of classes and objects where they have greater versatility, application environments are less volatile, and the impact of change is limited exclusively to affected object classes.

Business objects are most frequently implemented as entity objects (see Figure 51.1). As entity objects they represent the business memory required by the business processes they support. Some types of business objects may be implemented as control objects that represent key business processes or parts of business processes. A business object has a meaningful business name and contains essential business knowledge and rules. These objects must directly correspond to the organization/enterprise they support.

A business object, then, is a virtual representation of some real-world business thing, or a computer analog for that real-world thing. A technical object, by contrast, is one which implements behavior and/or memory requirements of the implementation environment. A technical object is a virtual representation of some thing in the computer environment.

An application is a set of business and technical objects bound together to produce specific business results in support of one or more business processes. Business objects may be built as part of application development or independently developed from an enterprise perspective. The choice of approach depends on an organization's strategies for technology investment and application development.

Along with objects, another structure being used to build applications is the component.* A component is a reusable application building block. Where an "object" is constrained by all the theory and rules of OO, a component is constrained only by the rules of the implementation environment. All "objects" are components, but not all components are objects in the purest sense (see Figure 51.1). The principles, methods, and models of OO analysis and design apply whether the "classes" are implemented specifically in an OO environment or in a more generalized component environment. All applications and many components are forms of business objects. The concepts presented in this chapter apply to business object development cycles for all business objects, including "pure" objects, components, and applications.

* This is especially being used in Microsoft Window's environments and defined in Microsoft's COM and DCOM architectures.

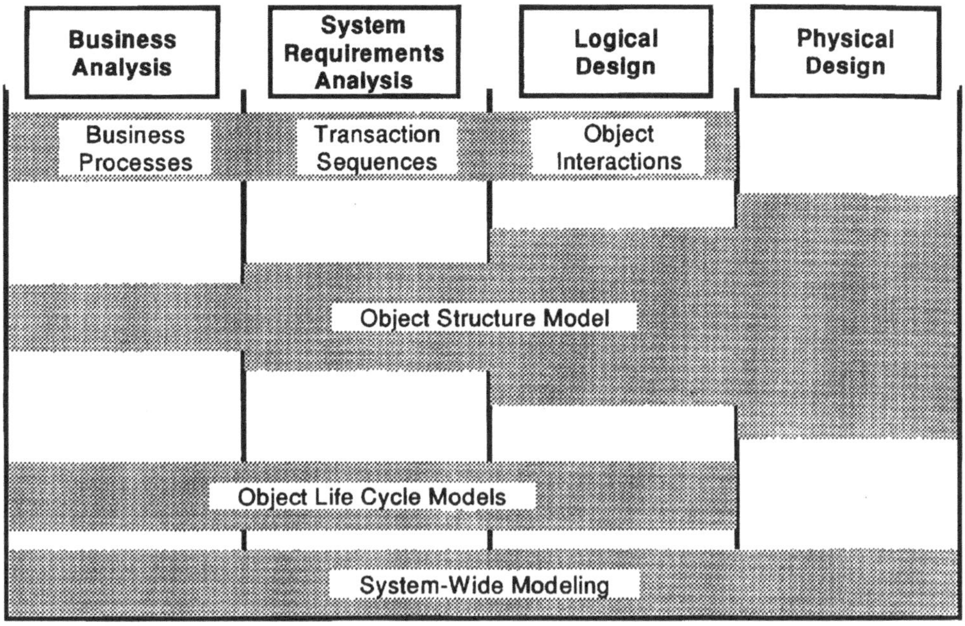

FIGURE 51.2 OO development phases and models used.

51.2 The OO Development Lifecycle

Whether developing individual business objects, components, or applications (new or upgrade), the fundamental parts of the development effort remain the same. Project organization configures the parts into a development process designed to meet the purpose and scope of the specific project. General configurations for common types of projects are called lifecycles, or systems development lifecycles (SDLC).

Each of the many lifecycles that organizes projects for business object development and deployment is composed of the same parts, called phases. Only sequence, degree of completeness, iteration, and dependencies vary among the lifecycles. Some lifecycles may also introduce specialized phases to meet their unique requirements. We will explore the lifecycles in greater detail later. Let's begin with an understanding of the phases fundamental to all of the lifecycles.

There are eight essential phases: planning, business analysis, system requirements analysis, logical design, physical design, construction, delivery, and support. The analysis and design phases build or refine a set of models. These models are integrated to define the complete set of information required. The main model is the object structure model. Business process models, transaction sequence models, object lifecycle models, system interaction models, and system wide models support this model.* Each of the phases is described below and associated with the models that it uses (see Figure 51.2).

* The names used for these models are taken from the methodology *Mainstream Objects* published by Prentice-Hall, 1995. The object structure model was adapted from Rumbaugh and Coad-Yourdon. The business process model is adapted from Hammer and Champy. The object lifecycle model is a form of state transition diagramming. The transaction sequence model is adapted from Jacobson's use-case model. The object interaction diagram was adapted from the Fusion method and from Jacobson. The system-wide model was adapted from Wirfs-Brock.

51.2.1 Project Definition and Planning Phase

Project definition establishes the scope and boundaries of the project. Scope setting is essential to clearly identify objectives and deliverables within the project domain and to be equally clear about that which is not a part of the project. Setting the proper scope is critical. Success of the entire development effort depends upon this. The scope may change during the project, but these changes must be consciously recognized, and their impacts assessed and actively managed. The system-wide model, context version, is used to model and validate the scope of the project.

Based upon a defined scope, project planning focuses on execution requirements, including time and resources. Project planning activities include feasibility assessment, cost/benefit analysis, lifecycle selection, staffing, and tentative budgeting and scheduling. Typically, detailed budgeting and scheduling are done only for the immediate next phase of the project.

51.2.2 Analysis Phases

The goal of the analysis phases is to define the requirements in business terms. This is done in two phases.

1. *Business analysis* — Business objects need to be grounded in the business realities. Business analysis seeks to understand the nature of the business within the domain defined by the scope. Specifically we seek to know: How is the business carried out today? What objects participate in conducting the business? What is the vision for carrying out the business in the future? Without this analysis, the essential business grounding is missing. Although important, this phase should never be overdone. It is meant to set up the next phase, system requirements analysis. The models used during this phase are the object structure model, the business process model, and the object lifecycle model.
2. *System requirements analysis* — System requirements analysis develops a business understanding of the needs for an application, business objects, and components. In other words, the business requirements for a computer system are defined here. This analysis is an extension of business analysis. Where business analysis looks at how the business currently operates, this phase identifies how the business needs to operate and details the role the system will play in supporting this operation. The models used during this phase are the object structure model, the transaction sequence model,* and the object lifecycle model.

51.2.3 Design Phases

The goal of the design phases is to produce the set of blueprints that will be used to build the business objects. Like analysis, design is performed in two phases.

1. *Logical design* — Logical design produces a specification of the hardware and software components necessary to meet the business requirements. This part of design should avoid specific implementation decisions as this is more appropriate to physical design. Component specification must occur within a known architecture, which may need to be developed as part of the logical design. Architecture serves as a mechanism to minimize dependencies among components and to localize impacts of change. The models used during this phase are the object structure model, the object lifecycle model, the transaction sequence model, the object interaction model, and the system-wide model, overview version.
2. *Physical design* — This phase is where all the technical decisions are made. The specific implementation environment is applied to the design to create the blueprints for construction. Decisions to be made here include operating environment, programming language(s), DBMS, GUI tools, middleware, etc. The models used during this phase are the version of the physical components object structure model and the system-wide model.

* Transaction sequence models are extensions of business process models when within this type of approach.

51.2.4 Construction Phase

Construction's goal is to build fully working applications, business objects, and/or components, along with all that is necessary to operate them. There are three main areas of activities, but these are not typically divided into actual phases.

- *Development* — This set of activities actually builds the application, business objects and/or components. The activities include object selecting, programming, aggregating, setting up, and using inheritance structures, etc. Adjustments are made to the physical design during this work as necessary to make things work.
- *Testing* — This set of activities is necessary to make sure that each requirement is fully met. Unit, integration, and system testing are all necessary. In addition, the developed system needs to be tested against the business requirements. The transaction sequences provide the basis for this testing. This forms the basis of the final acceptance testing.
- *Documentation* — Documentation requirements will vary, but items like user manuals, training designs and materials, and technical documentation must be completed. The models produced in the earlier phases can be used to form the basis of this work. This set of activities sees to the completion of the necessary items.

51.2.5 Delivery Phase

The main purpose of this phase is to put the developed application, business objects, and/or components into production. There are three main sets of activities for this phase.

- *User Training* — Both new and modified applications, business objects, and components will probably cause changes to the way business is being done. These changes need to be communicated in some form of training. The training should be developed during the construction phase. The purpose of this set of activities is to conduct the training and make sure that everything is done as intended.
- *Acceptance* — This is where the business purposes are certified, volume testing is done, and recovery and fallback plans are certified. This set of activities makes sure that the business and the operational needs are being fully met.
- *Cutover* — This set of activities puts the new application, business objects, or components into production and phases out the old ones.

51.2.6 Support Phase

This phase involves the day-to-day activities that keep everything doing what they are designed to do. It includes operation's activities and direct help to the users. This help is supplied through help desks and other means. It also involves tracking and fixing all problems. What does not belong here is making any changes to the applications, business objects, or components that will alter the original scope, functionality, and/or intents they were built to meet. These types of changes are really new development and need to be managed with the same structure and rigor that the originals were built with.

These phases are then packaged together into one or more lifecycles. There are a number of different lifecycles these phases can be packaged into. The typical waterfall lifecycle may be used for the development of OO applications, but it is frequently not the most appropriate choice. It should never be used for building business objects and components. The use of an iterative development and/or prototyping lifecycle is much better for development. In fact, OO provides many constructs that facilitate this type of a development approach.

To further understand the relationship of phases with lifecycles, look at the two lifecycles in Figure 51.3. The first is a prototyping lifecycle. The above phases are the basis for the phases in this lifecycle. The second is a lifecycle to purchase applications, business objects, or components. It too is based on the above phases, but the organization of these phases is different. Each lifecycle has also introduced specialized phases to meet unique requirements.

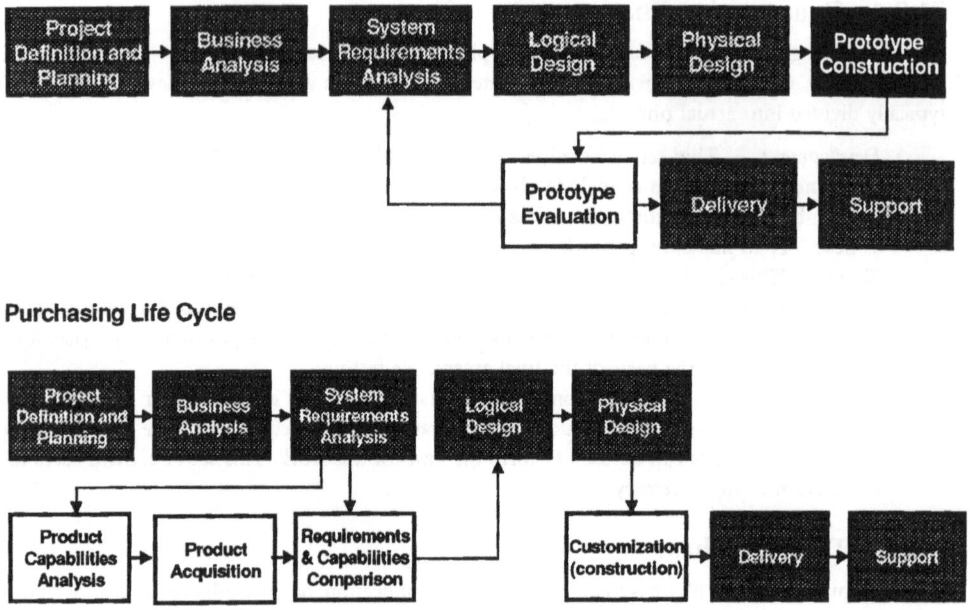

FIGURE 51.3 Sample development lifecycles.

A library of reusable objects — business and technical — and components is needed to support these kinds of lifecycles. Each development project should contribute to and use business objects and components from this library.

51.3 The Object/Component Library and Other Standards

The library of business objects and components is a major key to all the OO promises of reuse, standardization, accelerated development, etc. The library supplies the reusable pieces needed for application assembly and provides a repository for objects and components that are designed to be reused. Unfortunately it does not just happen. It must be set up. The objects — business and technical — and the components must be built or obtained and managed. Then, the objects and components must be accessible and used. Finally, they must be kept up to date. As the business changes, they must be changed to continue to meet the business organization's needs.

Another part of this library is the set of standards required by the organization. These standards should include the architecture that will help structure the applications, business objects, and components. The standards should also include the methods, lifecycles, models, techniques, object communications, etc., that will be used to build, obtain, and/or maintain the applications, business objects, and components. Of course, the business objects and components are also part of the standards.

In order to support the full business with this library, it may be necessary to support multiple versions of the objects and components. Every time a change is made to an object or component, a new version is required. It must be determined whether the new version will replace the old version or be used in addition to it. It must also be determined how the new version will be implemented. OO provides a number of constructs that can be used to implement and maintain multiple versions. Which of these constructs is best must be determined on a case-by-case basis.

Change is inevitable. The power of reusable business objects and components is that they help us apply the required changes to as small a set of pieces as possible and immediately make them available to a wide range of uses. OO and its powerful technology facilitate this, but it is based on the availability and usage of this library of reusable objects and components.

51.4 Planning and Managing the OO Development Project

A project brings together people and tools to produce a pre-defined set of results in a specified time period. The project is the formal vehicle that commits an organization to accomplish specified goals. The project also lays out how the results will be achieved, gives us the means to measure progress toward the goals, and plan what will be done next.

We have used projects for many years as the vehicle to build our applications. In building our business objects and components, no matter what the size, the project is still the key vehicle.

There are a number of types of projects that we use in developing applications, business objects, and components. By understanding these types we can better focus the activities and resources. The following types can provide the basis for any organization's set of project types.

- *Pilot projects* — These projects are used to prove the concept. They make sure we can support the business objectives, but only take a minimal investment of resources and time. The result of a pilot project can be viewed as the first prototype.
- *Business object/component development projects* — The aim of this type of project is to focus on creating the reusable building blocks for the organization. These projects help develop an organization's needed OO infrastructure.
- *Application development projects* — The aim of this type of project is to provide specific computer support to one or more business processes. These projects want to take advantage of the reusable business objects and components as well as build other reusable business objects and components.
- *Legacy application wrapping projects* — No organization can afford to just cast loose its investment in its legacy applications. In addition, there is a lot of business data, rules, and functionality buried in this legacy that we would want to reuse and migrate to more up-to-date implementations. These projects involve putting object wrappers around our important legacy applications and sharing the business data, business rules, and business functionality through these wrappers.
- *Purchasing/customizing projects* — There are many applications available for purchase that solve business problems. In the future, there will also be libraries of business objects and components available. None of these packages work right out of the box. They need to be customized to meet the organization's specific needs. Projects should be used to specify the requirements, select the package and customize it. The more these types of projects can be focused toward business objects and components the easier the purchasing and customizing process will become.
- *Quality Management Program* — Quality is important and best achieved through an evolutionary process. The quality program is a combination of measurements based on quality goals and special projects set up to continually meet these goals.

Once the project type is understood, project size is also a crucial issue. Time to delivery is becoming one of the crucial measuring points of success. More and more we cannot afford to get into large multi-year projects that deliver results to yesterday's needs. Object technology is conducive to shortening time to delivery, but it is only done because we choose to do it and take advantage of the constructs in OO that allow this to happen.

In addition to shorten time to delivery, we must also look to shorter life spans to what is developed. Change is speeding up and we must build to isolate the effects of that change. Some of the applications or objects will not be needed again because they support a one-time effort. For these objects, it is essential that they be developed quickly and with a limited budget since their short life span will not have any ROI otherwise. Others will need to change often because the business processes they are supporting are changing continually and we want to be able to extend the useful life span of these applications, business objects, and components. OO and the use of reusable business objects and components can be of great help here.

To make these shorter cycles work, we use short duration projects with time boxing and prototyping techniques. The availability of a library of reusable objects and components, along with OO technology,

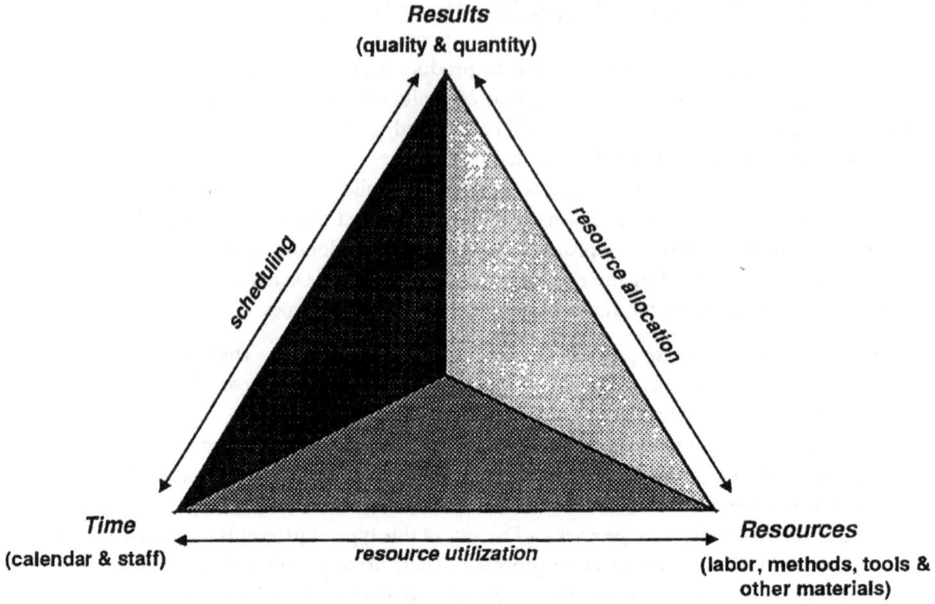

FIGURE 51.4 The project triangle.

enhance the use of these techniques. The advantages of projects using time boxing, prototyping, and OO include the following:

- The short duration helps get the application to those who need it in a timely manner.
- It forces the developers to discover and focus on the critical needs of the organization for business process support.
- It aids in scope management because if the time deadlines are to be met, then something must give.
- It helps us to manage our response to change. Since we are working with short duration, using prototyping, we will not see a lot of change that needs to be accounted for at the end of the project.

Planning and managing such projects is based on what is called the project triangle (see Figure 51.4). The points of the triangle represent results, resources (people, methods, OO tools, meeting rooms, budget, etc.), and time (project duration and schedule). Using this triangle we plan and manage projects that achieve the desired results — using the appropriate resources in the appropriate time. We plan and manage time utilization through the schedule (time ↔ results), resource utilization (time ↔ resources), and resource allocation (results ↔ resources).

In order to plan and manage our project we need to utilize the right lifecycle. The lifecycle is selected to be a good match between OO methods and the needs and goals of a particular project. Methods are the business processes of an IT organization. A business process is a set of activities that takes inputs and produces a product that is of value to the customer. A good method will:

- Clearly identify the intended product(s) and their customer(s), the necessary inputs and their sources, and the activities necessary to produce the product
- Contain a set of heuristics
- Contain a set of completeness and validation tests

There are many methods required for OO which include: analysis and design, testing, communication, coding, and maintenance. These methods need to satisfy the criteria listed above, then integrate together into a complete methodology. Organizations lacking such a methodology are unlikely to ever make the change to OO. The methodology helps define what exactly is necessary and provide a structure for getting it done.

Finally, we must also manage expectations of the organization. Depending on the type of project, the expectations that must be set up and managed are different. It is important that no matter what the project type, we must make sure that what is expected is reasonable and remains reasonable throughout the course of the project. The use of prototyping and the reusable business objects and components should help in managing the expectations.

51.5 Introducing OO into the Organization

Virtually every Information Technology (IT) organization will face the need to adopt object technology at some time in the near future. Yet the transition to objects is a difficult one. OO requires new approaches to application development and maintenance, and it demands fundamental changes in thinking patterns of IT professionals. Moving to objects is more than a technology problem. If an organization is to successfully adopt OO, it must make major human and cultural changes. The main challenges of migrating to object technology are not about technology, they are about *change.*

51.5.1 The Change Issues

Achieving organizational change is never easy. Organizations are, of course, composed of people, and people quite naturally resist change. At an individual level, change threatens the comfort zone. For the IT professional, that threat often comes in the form of current skills becoming obsolete and demanding that new skills be learned. The one-time expert becomes a novice, quite naturally resulting in fèar, discomfort, and resistance.

At an organizational level, the challenge is in changing culture. Culture establishes the set of values by which a group thinks, behaves, and acts collectively. Most organization cultures have evolved over time, are neither documented nor fully understood, and are sustained by inertia. Yet this fuzzy, partially understood force will directly affect an organization's ability to succeed with objects.

Changing people and culture also requires effective executive level sponsorship. All research into organizational change supports this need. The change to OO is no different. Without this high-level executive sponsorship, the move to OO is bound to fail.

Migrating to object technology demands simultaneous changes in people, culture, and technology. This is a major, complex, and difficult transition. Successful migration will employ the same principles that help with all complex undertakings such as a planned, systematic approach.

51.5.2 A Method for Managing Change

Fundamental to change management is the classic change model shown in Figure 51.5. The change model has three significant parts. The *desired state* describes what the organization wants to become. The *current state* objectively assesses where the organization is today. The *change process* describes how the organization plans to move from current to desired state.

Putting the change model to work would be quite simple if change were a one-time occurrence. IT organizations, however, face multiple, parallel, and continuous changes occurring at an ever accelerating rate. Migration of the organization to objects, or to any new technology, should follow these guidelines:

- Be selective about which changes you will implement. Create a realistic vision for the future, then *evolve* toward that vision.
- Do not try to implement all changes at once. Move in small steps and reassess your position after each step.
- Implement each change as a project. This implies all that is known about successfully executing projects such as known deliverables, constrained time, committed resources, and active management.

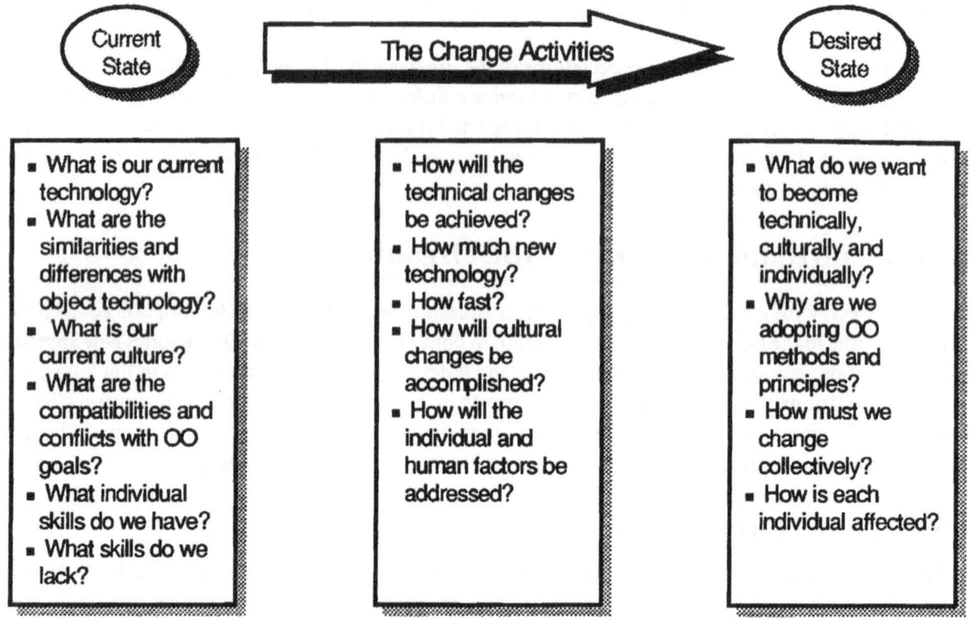

FIGURE 51.5 The classic change model.

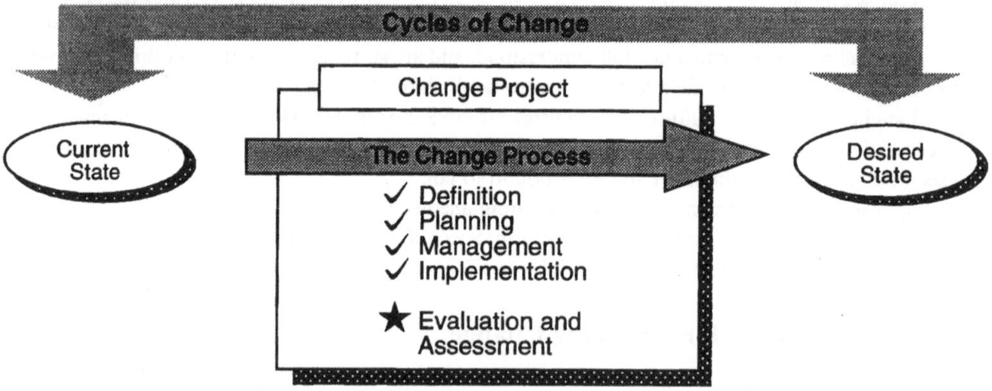

FIGURE 51.6 The enhanced change model.

Combining these principles with the classic change model, we have developed an enhanced change model (see Figure 51.6) to evolve an organization through multiple cycles of change. The change process is a formal project. Upon its completion the former desired state becomes a new current state. Following evaluation and assessment, a new change project is planned and executed.

51.5.3 Change Projects for Object Migration

Desired change must be engineered; it does not just happen. Object migration involves complex and difficult changes that must be carefully managed. Each change, or small set of related changes, is planned and executed as a project. Completion of the first change project will produce several important results:

- A new current state which includes some object components
- Understanding of the human and cultural issues
- Greater knowledge and better understanding of object technology
- Need and desire for a next change project

Many kinds of change projects are possible. Consider projects to implement OO methods, to address object data management, to acquire and implement object technology, to wrap legacy systems and data as objects, to inventory and manage object libraries, to establish OO standards, etc.

Each of the above examples is a significant change project with human, cultural, and technical considerations. Attempting to address everything at one time, in a single large project, is a certain path to failure. Multiple projects, each moving a step closer to the desired OO environment, are the only practical answer to the object migration challenge.

Begin the object migration journey by defining the longer term desired state. Next, partition the set of goals into a set of small projects. Sequence the projects in the way that makes most sense for your organization. Early projects need to produce some significant and meaningful results, while leveraging the organization's strengths and offering opportunities to learn and grow. Later projects build upon successes of earlier projects. Each project must have defined, measurable deliverables, and each project must address human and cultural needs, OO methods, and an effective training program.

51.5.4 People, Culture, and Object-Orientation

Object-orientation is an entirely different way of looking at and dealing with the world, the business, and the applications supporting that business. This difference makes the human and cultural issues among the greatest in the transition to OO. Long-established habits and behaviors will need to be replaced by a new set of "object-think" behaviors and patterns. The temptation to revert to old habits under pressure is a significant risk to object migration.

The change to "object-think" is both subtle and complex. Making this change in an organization demands support and nurturing. The changes must be:

- Well defined
- Openly discussed
- Thoroughly explored
- Extensively trained
- Fully and visibly supported, with opportunity to learn from mistakes
- Accepted by those whose jobs are changing
- Measured

51.5.5 Training for Object-Orientation

Although training is typical when introducing any new technology, the need for education is even greater when moving to objects. OO requires a substantial shift in the mindset of the software engineer — the transition to "object-think" discussed earlier. Effective OO education and training programs will:

- Deliver the right training at the right time
- Foster discussion among those making the transition together
- Offer opportunities to practice the necessary techniques and skills
- Focus on professional growth

Traditional training methods — composed primarily of classroom lecture, exercises, CBT, and books — are insufficient to master OO. These training methods fail to provide the discussion, practice, exploration, and discovery that are necessary to learn to think in object terms. Everyone is a skeptic, and the training program is the best opportunity to overcome doubt and resistance. Skeptics will need not only to have the value of OO illustrated through formal training, but also to experience it through individual and team accomplishments. An effective training program must include:

- A defined career path and skills acquisition plan for each staff member
- A standard OO business process (methodology) tailored specifically for your organization
- Formal training and review options (classroom, CBT, books, etc.)
- Guided training and mentoring
- Individual and group practice sessions
- Internal conferences where staff present their work and share their experiences
- Measurement of progress and success

The success you achieve in training your staff depends on how complete your program is. Overlooking any of the components increases the risk of reversion to old habits and behaviors.

51.5.6 The Fastrack to OO

Combining an intensive training program with a pilot project is a proven, effective way to transfer skills while working with real projects for your business. This technique, called Fastrack, has been used for nearly ten years to help develop skills in rapid application development (RAD), client/server systems development, and object-oriented systems development.

An OO-Fastrack program is based on a 12- to 16-week project that has two goals. The prime goal is the training of a project team in the use and practice of OO. The secondary goal is the delivery of an application. The project plan must account for all formal training required, as well as the work to produce project results. All formal training is done in a just in time (JIT) fashion, concentrating each training event on those skills required to achieve the next project milestone. Following the training event, the team performs the work to reach the next milestone under the guidance and mentoring of an experienced OO project leader.

OO-Fastrack is a sound way to meet several object migration objectives: training and education, an early project success, a tangible example of OO value, and real experiences with OO methods and techniques. Figure 51.7 illustrates the general components of such a project. Consider these guidelines to identify and organize a Fastrack project. A good Fastrack project is:

- Important enough to be visible, but not mission-critical
- Achievable in a short duration
- Achievable with a small team of four to eight people
- Staffed by a team dedicated to the project for its duration
- Planned that formal training activities are project events
- Led by an experienced mentor

Treat the OO-Fastrack as a radical, total-immersion approach to learning "object think." Total involvement in an OO development project, with support formal training, mentoring, and other team members is a most effective way to break the old habits and thinking patterns. Expect the first Fastrack to produce the mentors for future projects; the first step of your object migration journey.

51.6 Final Thoughts

OO concepts, techniques, and technology have great potential to respond effectively to many of today's IT pressures. The development, management, and usage of applications, based on business objects and components is where this potential is realized. To succeed in this effort, organizations require a solid understanding and implementation of OO methods and lifecycles, a library of reusable business objects and components, a solid project-based approach, and a clear transition path.

Yet making the transition to objects will produce new and different kinds of pressures. Plan the migration carefully, with attention to all of the factors discussed in this article. Then actively and objectively assess your readiness to carry out that plan. Fully understand the need to monitor, measure, reassess, and adjust the plan throughout your journey to object-orientation. If this is in place, the development, management, and use of business objects and components will be a practical and profitable undertaking for the organization.

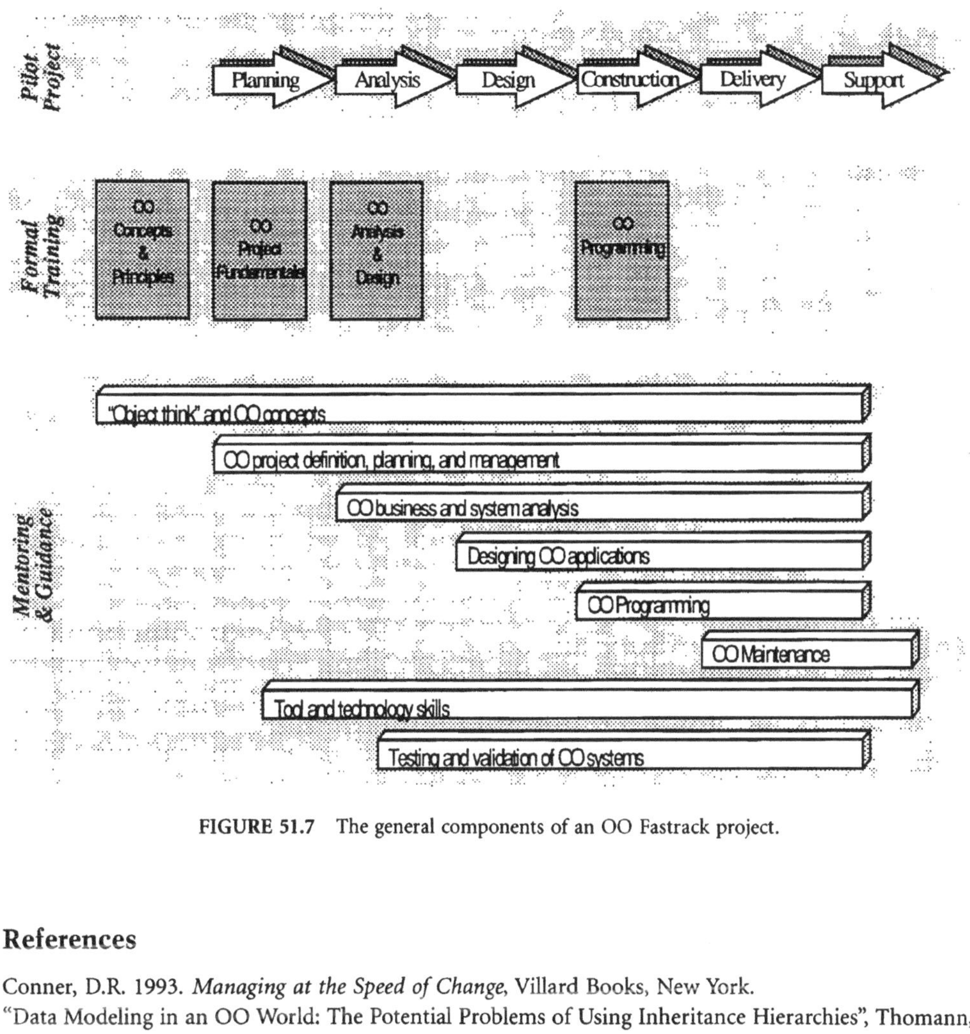

FIGURE 51.7 The general components of an OO Fastrack project.

References

Conner, D.R. 1993. *Managing at the Speed of Change*, Villard Books, New York.

"Data Modeling in an OO World: The Potential Problems of Using Inheritance Hierarchies", Thomann, American Programmer, Arlington, MA, October, 1994.

Mainstream Objects: An Analysis and Design Approach for Business, Yourdon, Whitehead, Thomann, Oppel and Nevermann, Yourdon Press, Prentice-Hall, Englewood Cliffs, NJ, 1995.

Object-Oriented Systems Design: An Integrated Approach, Yourdon, Yourdon Press, Englewood Cliffs, NJ, 1994.

Object-Oriented Software Engineering: A Use Case Driven Approach, Jacobson, Christerson, Jonsson, Overgaard, ACM Press, Addison-Wesley, Workingham, England, 1994.

Overcoming Resistance, Jellison, Simon & Schuster, New York, 1993.

Reengineering The Corporation: A Manifesto for Business Revolution, Hammer & Champy, Harper Business, New York, 1993.

Re-Engineering IT for OO, Thomann, *Data Management Rev.*, Brookfield, WI, December, 1995.

"The Challenge Facing the Information Systems Organization", Thomann and Wells, Connections Magazine, Reston, VA, Summer 1994.

The Fifth Discipline: The Art & Practice of The Learning Organization, Senge, Doubleday, New York, 1990.

Thomann and Wells. *Migrating to Object Technology: Challenges for the IT Organization*, Software Report, Darmstadt, Germany, 1997.

XI

Object-Oriented Intranets

Dilip Patel
South Bank University

Information is the most critical resource that a corporation can manage. Due to intense competition, it has become imperative for organizations to disseminate critical information within the organization, between affiliated partners, and out into the marketplace in a timely manner. The Intranet helps achieve this end by delivering informational resources to each individual's desktop with minimal cost, time, and effort. The intranet combines the resources of the corporation with Web technology, thereby compounding the resources available to corporations, and subsequently empowering their decision-making processes.

Intranets utilize business objects and object-oriented Web technology. This section contains chapters that describe these concepts.

52

Review and Perspectives of the Internet and Intranet

Dilip Patel
South Bank University

Yingxu Wang
South Bank University

Shushma Patel
South Bank University

This chapter reviews the origin of the Internet and its fundamental techniques, and looks ahead toward the trends of Internet technology. As a foundation of the Internet, principles of computer networks are introduced. The architecture, protocol, addressing system, and key services of the Internet are analyzed. The Intranet and Extranet are introduced as variations of the Internet. Perspectives on future Internet technology, infrastructure evolution, and new services are discussed, and their impact on network computing and object-oriented software construction are analyzed. Useful bibliography and Web site points are provided in the references.

52.1 Introduction

In the information age, computer networking and communication for information gathering, storing, processing, transmitting, and distributing is a basic requirement for business, society, and an individual's everyday life. The emergence of the Internet has profoundly influenced the way computer systems are organized to support the information processing demand.

The interconnection of multi-networks is called internetworking. Interconnecting separate networks enables worldwide resources, such as processing capability, hardware, software, and database, which can

0-8493-3135-8/99/$0.00+$.50

be shared and communication can be improved. The Internet has evolved from an academic curiosity to an essential tool for users in business and public communication. Worldwide electronic mail and the World Wide Web have been a daily reality for millions on the Internet.

52.1.1 Origin of the Internet

The Internet originated from the Advanced Research Projects Agency Network (ARPANET) in 1969 (Hafner and Lyon, 1996) directed by Charlie Herzfeld. Starting in the late 1960s, the Advanced Research Projects Agency (ARPA) of the U.S. Department of Defense, began stimulating research on the subject of computer networks by providing grants to computer science departments at many U.S. universities and companies. This research led to an experimental four-node network that went on the air in December 1969. It had subsequently grown to several hundred computers spanning half the globe, from Hawaii to Sweden. The ARPANET is a computer network that revolutionized communication and gave rise to the global Internet. In the early 1950s computing meant processing mathematical operations fast. Laboratories and companies put their machines to work doing large scale calculations. The initial idea of the ARPANET was to link computers at scientific laboratories across the U.S., so that researchers might share computer resources and files.

After the ARPANET technology had proven itself by years of highly reliable service, a number of computer networks, such as the NSFNET (Chinoy and Braun, 1992 and Claffy et al., 1994), MILNET, SATNET, and WIDEBAND, were set up in the 1970s and 1980s using the same technology. Thereafter many local area networks (LANs) were developed. Eventually, these led to the ARPA internet connected by the interface message processors (IMPs) with thousands of hosts and millions of users. This is the origin of the Internet acting as a network of computer networks.

It is predicted that by the year 2000, all organizations will be connected to their partners and customers via the Internet. The competitive advantage will come from the fact that, by using the Internet to distribute information, business can appear to have large outlets and maintain competitive advantage.

52.1.2 Coordination of the Internet

As an international, distributed, multi-vendor and multi-topology network of networks, the Internet has no central administration. However, some institutions are playing important roles for the coordination and evolution of the Internet which include: (1) the Internet Society establishes technical standards for the Internet (HTTP1); (2) the Internet assigned number authority (IANA) sets policy and controls the domain names assigned on the Internet (HTTP2); (3) the Internet Network Information Center (InterNIC) registers domain names on the Internet (HTTP3); (4) the World-wide Web Consortium (W3C) discusses future technology of the Web and its programming languages (HTTP4); and (5) a number of leading companies, such as Microsoft, Netscape, Sun Microsystems and CompuServe, are involved in developing and implementing Internet techniques.

52.2 Foundations of Computer Networks

The Internet is a worldwide computer network for interconnecting different local networks. To help to understand Internet techniques, this section introduces fundamental concepts and principles in data communications and computer networking.

52.2.1 Principles of Data Communications

Data communication networks were developed for transmitting digital information between telephone, computer, facsimile, and other data. Main switching techniques for data communication networks are described below.

52.2.1.1 Circuit Switching

Circuit switching selects a dedicated path between the source and destination in a switching network and seizes the path for the duration of communication. Circuit switching is the conventional technique used for telephone exchange. Circuit switching is inefficient for computer communication because of the nature of burst traffic between computers and the requirement of fast connection for computers.

52.2.1.2 Store-and-Forward Switching

Store-and-forward switching, also known as message switching, stores a message in the system until a channel is valid and seized, then the whole message is transmitted. Store-and-forward switching was used for telegram exchange and is not suitable for computer real-time communication.

52.2.1.3 Packet Switching

Packet switching selects an available route randomly in a network for different packets. At the sender end a message is split into a set of packets. Each packet has its own sequential identification as location in the message and the same message destination. On receipt packets are unpacked and assembled to form the original message according to their sequential identification, despite the order in which the packets arrive due to different routing and error control delays on the network. Packet switching is suitable for users who need to connect between many different computers and need the flexibility of this type of network.

52.2.1.4 ATM Switching

Asynchronous data transmission (ATM) is a digital switching technique in which the receiver and transmitter clocks are not synchronized. Each cell (data block) is preceded by a start bit pattern and terminated by a stop bit pattern, which are used by the receiver for synchronization.

ATM is a new and highly flexible technology oriented to rapid transmission of small message packets through a packet switched network. The data rate of ATM switching can be as high as one megabyte per second.

52.2.2 Principles of Computer Networks

Computer networks are designed to transmit information, share processing capability, and share data and program. The Internet is a special case of computer networks. This subsection introduces fundamental concepts on topologies of computer networks, local and wide area networks, and network operating systems.

52.2.2.1 Topologies of Computer Networks

Various network topologies exist to connect the nodes, such as servers, workstations, PCs, terminals, and peripherals in a network. Common configurations for local area networking are star, bus, and ring topologies. Configurations for wide area networking are mainly dependent on geographical distribution of a region, and the backbone structure of the switching networks. Topology of a wide area network is usually a partially connected network for nodes with some duplicated high-performance links between critical gateways.

52.2.2.2 Local Area Network

Local area network (LAN) is a computer network, which provides interconnection of computers, terminals, and other resources in a small area. Unlike the conventional central-controlled telephone-switching network, the LAN techniques rely mainly on the software approach that uses a protocol-based solution with a shared high performance data medium. The key LAN protocols are Ethernet and token ring for bus and ring topology networks, respectively.

Ethernet is a trade name for the Carrier Sense Multiple Access with Collision Detection (CSMA/CD) protocol. Ethernet was developed by Xerox Corporation in 1970 and adopted in the IEEE 802.3 Standard.

Ethernet protocol was designed for bus topology. In Ethernet every node is independent; no central network control is needed. Nodes may be added simply by tapping into the bus. It is suitable for networks with light traffic and with nodes distributed in a small area. When traffic is high or network propagation delay increases due to widely scattered nodes, network collisions and retransmissions will deteriorate Ethernet performance.

Token ring protocol (IEEE 802.5) is designed for ring topology of LANs. Token ring protocol uses a passed token (a bit pattern) to control access to a network. A node that holds the token at any given instant is the only one permitted to send a message on the ring. If it has no message to send, it passes the token to the next node. To transmit a message, it replaces the token with a busy token and adds the message to be sent. The message is then passed from node to node until it reaches its destination. The destination node receives the message and modifies the token with a copied token to acknowledge the sender. On receiving the copied token, the sending node places the original token back to the network, and the token passing continues. Token ring protocol performs efficiently at high traffic. It is noteworthy that a node is required to be responsible for detecting failures of the ring and initiating the ring when the network starts or reset. In a token ring LAN every node address is predetermined. Therefore it is difficult to add or remove nodes from the network.

A new wide-band protocol, known as fiber distributed data interface (FDDI), has been developed for over 100Mbps token ring topologies. Unlike the conventional token ring, FDDI uses a pair of rings operating in opposite directions.

52.2.2.3 Wide Area Network

Wide area network (WAN) is a computer network, which provides interconnection of LANs and independent computers at a regional, national, or international level. WAN can be implemented with conventional telecommunication networks or dedicated packet-switched networks. The Internet is a special case and a publicly available WAN based on packet switching technology.

Interconnection of LANs and WANs has been increasingly in demand over the last decade as information sharing has extended to the whole world. Bridges, routers, and gateways are used for network interconnection. A bridge is used for LANs using the same protocols. A router is used for dissimilar LANs by converting the format of message between different networks. A gateway is used for transmitting data from one type of network to another, e.g., from a LAN to a WAN or from one WAN to another. A gateway is adopted to implement more complicated protocol conversions between dissimilar networks.

52.2.2.4 Network Operating Systems

A network operating system (OS) implements protocols that are required for network communication and provides a variety of additional services to users and application programs. Network OS may provide support for several different protocols known as stacks, e.g., a TCP/IP stack and an IPX/SPX stack. A modern Network OS provides a socket facility to help the users to plug-in utilities that provide additional services. Common services that a modern network OS can provide include:

1. *File services* — File services transfer programs and data files from one computer on the network to another.
2. *Message services* — Message services allow users and applications to pass messages from one to another on the network. The most familiar application of message services is e-mail and inter-computer talk facilities.
3. *Security and network management services* — These services provide security across the network and allow users to manage and control the network.
4. *Printer services* — Printer services enable sharing of expensive printer resources in a network. Print requests from applications are redirected by the OS to a network station, which manages the requested printer.
5. *Remote procedure calls (RPCs)* — RPCs provide application program interface services to allow a program to access local or remote network OS functions.

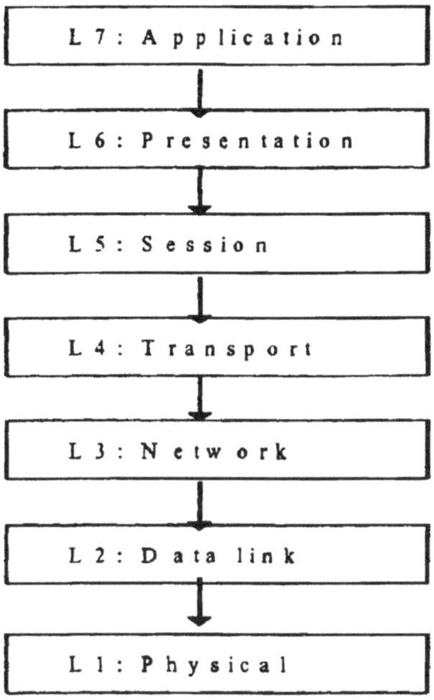

FIGURE 52.1 The OSI reference model.

6. *Remote processing services* — These services allow users or applications to remotely log in to another system on the network and use its facilities for program execution. The most familiar service of this type is Telnet, which is included in the TCP/IP protocol suite and many other modern network OSs.

52.2.3 The OSI Reference Model

The ISO open systems interconnection (OSI) reference model was developed in 1983 (Day and Zimmerman, 1983) for standardizing data communication protocols between different computer systems and networks. The OSI reference model is an important protocol framework for regulating multi-vendor, multi-OS computers interconnection in LAN and WAN environments. From bottom up the seven layers are: physical, data link, network, transport, session, presentation, and application as shown in Figure 52.1.

1. *The physical layer* — The physical layer provides a real communication channel for transmitting bit stream data. Mechanical, electrical, and procedural interfaces for different physical transmission media are specified on this layer.
2. *The data link layer* — The data link layer implements data frames in the sender end, acknowledges frames in the receiver end, and provides retransmission mechanisms when a frame is not successfully transmitted. The data link layer converts a raw transmission line on the physical layer into a line that is free of transmission errors to the network layer.
3. *The network layer* — The network layer controls the operation of a subnet by determining how message packets are routed from source to destination. It also provides congestion control, information flow counting, and packet size conversion between different networks.
4. *The transport layer* — The transport layer accepts data from the session layer, splits it up into smaller units for adapting to the network layer, and provides an interface between the session layer and the different implementation of the lower layer protocol and hardware.
5. *The session layer* — The session layer provides transport session establishment, synchronization, and data flow control between different machines modeled by the transport layer.

6. *The presentation layer* — The presentation layer converts the original data represented in vendor-dependent format into an abstract data structure at the sender end and vice versa at the receiver end. The presentation layer enables data to be compressed or encoded for transmitting on the lower layers.
7. *The application layer* — The application layer adapts a variety of terminals into a unified network virtual terminal interface for transferring different files between various file systems.

For detailed description of the OSI model, read (Day and Zimmerman, 1983; Tanenbaum, 1989; and Sloane, 1994).

52.3 The Internet

The Internet is a successful WAN technology. The scope of the Internet is continuing to grow. There are over 30,000 networks and 2 million computers interconnected via the Internet. Over 20 million users can be reached by electronic mail and have access to resources via the Internet.

Remarkable changes in the Internet are that it now services a large proportion of business users and individuals. In the 1970s and 1980s, the Internet was viewed as a specialized network serving the academic and research communities. In the early 1990s, the public began to take notice of the Internet capability and its potential ramifications. The Internet is now referred to as a standard computer communication infrastructure as that of telephone, facsimile, and postal mail.

This section discusses architectures, protocols, access, and addressing systems of the Internet. Some variations of the Internet, such as the Intranet and Extranet, are introduced.

52.3.1 Architecture

A hierarchical architecture of the Internet is shown in Figure 52.2. From bottom up, the Internet end users and their applications (known as clients) are incorporated into an Internet host, then to a subnet, local Internet, regional Internet, and national Internet. All national Internets are interconnected to form the worldwide Internet.

The addressing convention of the Internet is shown in the parentheses (Claffy et al., 1994). A formal description of the Internet addressing system will be provided in Section 52.3.3.3.

52.3.2 Protocols

The Internet protocol and a point-to-point protocol are described in this subsection to help understand the operation principle of the Internet.

52.3.2.1 Internet Protocol

There are a number of different protocol suites in use for WANs that operate similarly to the OSI reference model, such as IBM Systems Network Architecture (SNA), Novell IPX/SPX, DECNET, Appletalk, etc. The Internet has developed a protocol suite called Transmission Control Protocol/Internet Protocol (TCP/IP). TCP/IP provides a glue for the highly distributed Internet infrastructure.

Historically TCP/IP has been closely associated with the UNIX operating system and was developed ten years before the OSI model. With orientation to the Internet, TCP/IP has become the network connectivity protocol of choice for almost all the modern network operating systems in the last few years.

Figure 52.3 compares functional equivalency between TCP/IP and the OSI model. The TCP/IP design philosophy was to provide universal connectivity, with connection-independent protocols at the network layer. Thus TCP/IP does not address the data link and physical layers which determine the communication channels. There are no separate application, presentation, and session layers in TCP/IP; instead, a combined application layer is provided in TCP/IP, which has the functions of those layers.

The IP protocol is approximately equivalent to the OSI network layer. In a WAN, IP is presented on every node in the network. The role of IP is to segment messages into packets (up to 64 Kbyte) and

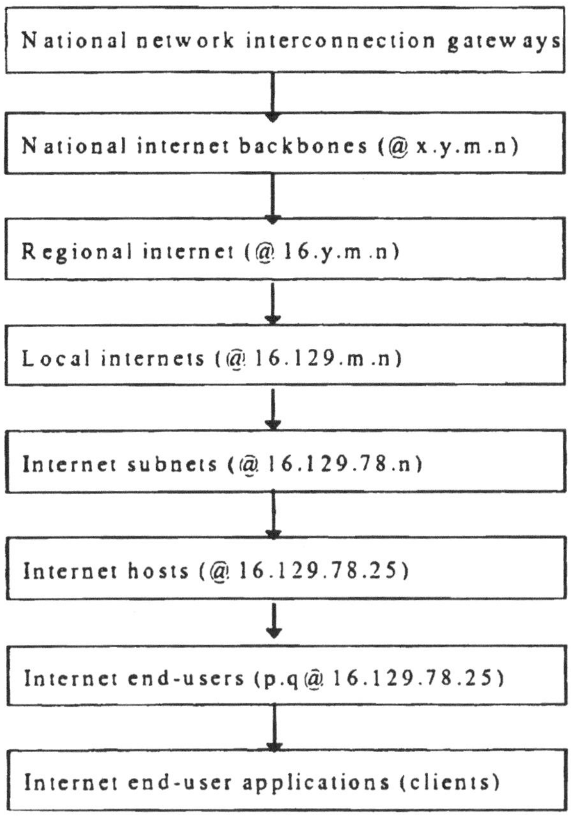

FIGURE 52.2 Model of the Internet Interconnection architecture.

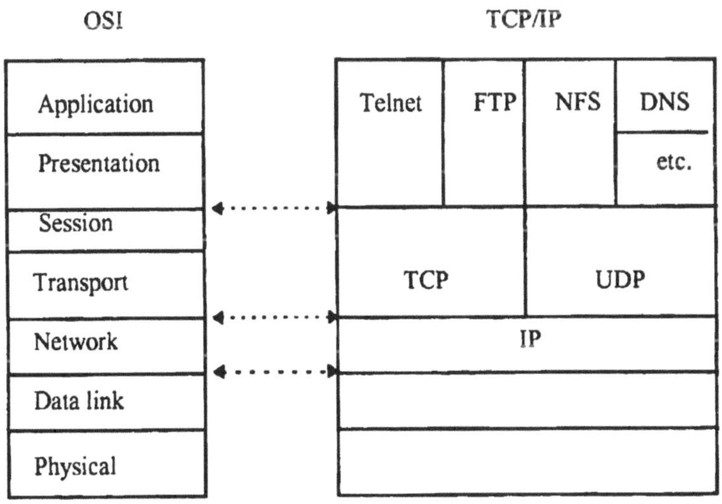

FIGURE 52.3 Comparison between the OSI model and TCP/IP.

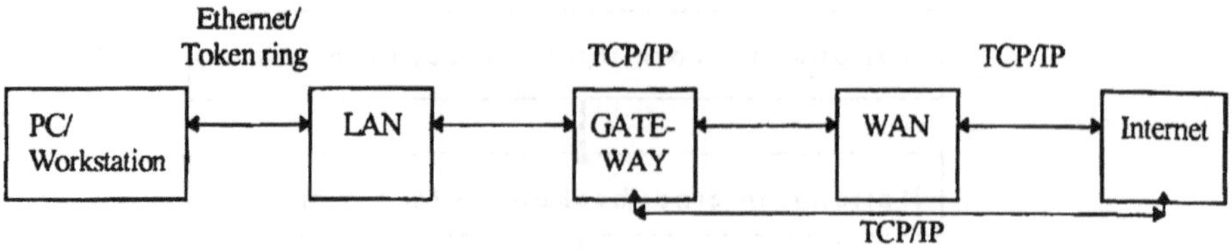

FIGURE 52.4 Connection via a LAN.

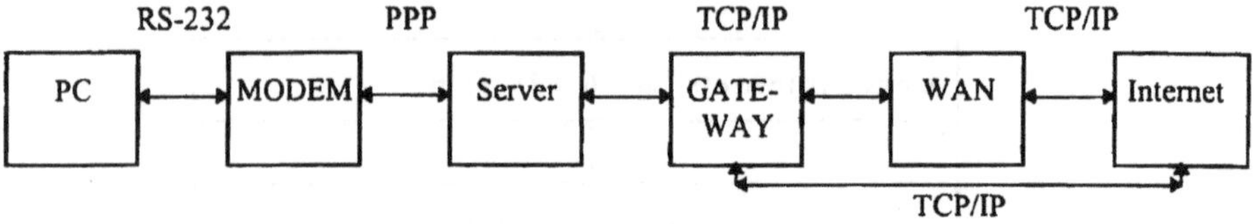

FIGURE 52.5 Direct connection via a modem.

then route and pass the packets from one node to another until they reach their destination. IP uses packet switching as its fundamental transmission algorithm. A message is transmitted from gateway to gateway by dynamic routed packets. IP routes packets to their destination network, but final delivery is left to TCP.

The TCP protocol fulfills the role of the OSI transport layer, plus some of the functionality of the session layer. TCP is designed to provide end-to-end connectivity. TCP is not required for packet routing, so it is not included on gateways. TCP provides an acknowledgment mechanism to enable messages be sent from destination(s) back to the sender to verify receipt of each packet that makes up a message.

52.3.2.2 Point-to-Point Protocol

Point-to-point protocol (PPP), or technically known as serial link internet protocol (SLIP), is used for individual computers via modems for telephone accessing to the Internet.

52.3.3 Access and Addressing System

This subsection describes interconnection of LAN and individual users onto the Internet. Access methods, the IP addressing system, and domain name systems are illustrated.

52.3.3.1 Access to the Internet

Users of a LAN can be connected to the Internet by the support of LAN and Gateway based on TCP/IP, as shown in Figure 52.4.

For individual users, as shown in Figure 52.5, PPP protocol can be adopted for telephone access to the Internet by a modem.

52.3.3.2 The IP Addressing System

The IP provides flexibility in route selection based on unique global addresses for every interconnected computer network and individual computer. IP addresses are 32-bit wide and are normally written as four decimal numbers (each representing a byte) separated by dots, as in 16.129.78.25. IP addresses consist of a network address (NA) and a host address (HA). All hosts with the same NA address are connected to the same physical network (e.g., a LAN or WAN). It is thus possible for routers to keep track of where to send a packet by inspecting only the network part of the destination address in the packet.

The size of NA and HA of the IP addresses vary between what is referred to as class A, B, and C networks as shown in Figure 52. 6.

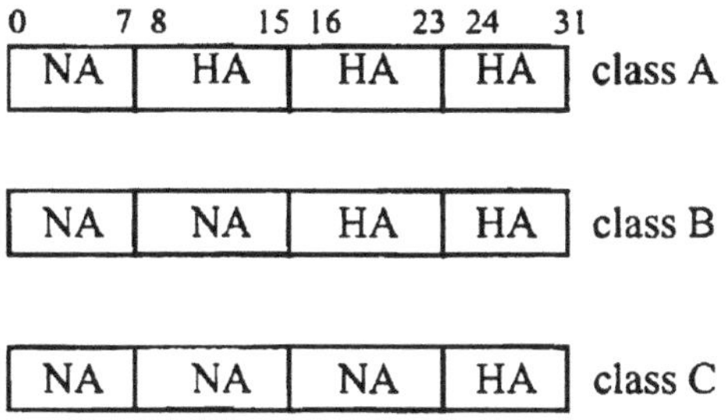

FIGURE 52.6 IP addresses: network address and host address.

The IP address space architecture originated with RFC791 (Postel, 1981), the initial Internet protocol specification that defined a pool of available network numbers. The InterNIC Registrar, on behalf of the Internet community, now formally registers these assigned network numbers in a database.

With the advent of RFC1366 (Gerich, 1992, 1993) in 1992, the InterNIC began to assign addresses according to the geographic location of requesters. The InterNIC also, in certain cases, delegates blocks of class-C IP network numbers to other authorities for future assignment. For example, the InterNIC assigned a large portion of the Class C space to Europe for future redistribution within the European network community.

52.3.3.3 Domain Name System

A domain name is an ordered textual label to show hierarchically structured user addresses on the Internet. A BNF specification for domain names (Rose, 1993) is

```
domain ::= label * (. label)
label  ::= (ALPHA | DIGIT) * (ALPHA | DIGIT |-|_)
ALPHA  ::= <a ... z | A ... Z>
DIGIT  ::= <0 ... 9>
```

Based on the definition of domain names above, an end-user's address on the Internet can be specified as follows:

user@domain
@subdomain.domain-type.country
@server.host.subnet.domain-type.country

Some common e-mail domain types on the Internet are described in Table 52.1. Observing Table 52.1, the authors predict that there will be another domain type on the Internet. It will probably be "pub" or "pc" for recognizing the increasing number of individual users with a personal computer for non-commercial access to the Internet.

TABLE 52.1 E-Mail Domain Type on the Internet

No.	Domain Type	Description
1	ac	Academic (U.K.)
2	co	Company or commercial (U.K.)
3	com	Company or commercial
4	edu	Educational institution
5	gov	Government (U.S.)
6	int	International organization
7	net	Internet gateway or administrative host
8	org	Non-profit organization
	......	......

52.3.4 Intranet

A variety of networking techniques have been developed for office automation since the 1970s. The mature and user-friendly characteristics of the Internet have drawn the attention of network designers and enterprise users to apply the Internet techniques in the office environment. This move led to the emergence of the Intranet.

52.3.4.1 Technology of Intranet

The Intranet is a private network using the same architectures, protocols, and tools applied on the Internet. The mechanism that distributes and shares information between computers on the Internet can be used in exactly the same way as in an enterprise local network. When this is not publicly accessible, it is called an Intranet (Stancic, 1996).

An Intranet provides enterprise-caliber server software, development tools, and packaged applications for Intranet computing, and migrates existing client/server applications to the WWW. A WebServer is the key of an Intranet application platform. Besides utilities for e-mail, transferring files, and online conferencing, Intranets can take advantage of many of the other innovative programs designed for the Internet. It is reported (Radke, 1996) that some of Internet programs, such as audio and video applications, even perform better on intranet environments because of faster data transfer rates on LANs.

52.3.4.2 Safeguard of Intranet

An Intranet may have highly classified information such as business plans, financial statements, and personal records. Protection for this internal information can be implemented by the following techniques:

- *Firewalls* — Firewalls are a kind of Intranet facilities that restrict the flow of information between a company's Intranet and the Internet in order to keep sensitive information private. Modern routers provide a high-speed packet filter mechanism for implementing a firewall. An Intranet manager can configure the filter in a router to block specific datagram by assigning its attributes of source/destination IP addresses, protocol, and/or source/destination protocol port numbers (Comer, 1995).
- *Encryption* — Encryption lets the Intranet owner decide who gets to see what and when. With encryption a company's proprietary information can be scrambled from its original form so only authorized users can see it.
- *Intrusion protection* — Intranet puts an electronic guard at the door of an Intranet. Users are inspected before entering in three ways: (1) by confirming the users are not using forgery to gain access; (2) by determining what the users should get access to once they are inside; and (3) by recording every move the users make.
- *Authentication* — Authentication assures the Intranet administrator that users are who they say they are. First, the user must enter the correct password. Then, a digital token confirms each user's identity automatically.

52.3.5 Extranet

An Extranet is an extension of the Intranet mechanism to a subset of Internet where the servers and clients share common interests in business. An Extranet improves coordination throughout a company and its partners and customers by providing information services covering all aspects of business and accessible by partners worldwide. Extranet creates a secure structure where a company can distribute key information to its partners and customers around the world, enabling them to access information critical to business wherever they need it.

For instance, a worldwide Extranet for a business travel management company, BTI, has been developed recently (IS Solutions, 1997). The Extranet connects over 3000 locations in 60 countries worldwide. This Extranet shows how secure Web-based technologies can improve knowledge and ultimately, profitability for a business and its partners.

TABLE 52.2 The Internet Services

No.	Services	Description
1	E-mail	Electronic mail
2	WWW	World Wide Web
3	FTP	File Transfer Protocol
4	Telnet	Telnet
5	BBS	Bulletin board services
6	Newsgroups	News groups
7	IRC	Internet relay chat

TABLE 52.3 E-Mail Services and Methods

No.	Category	Service	Method
1	One-to-one		
1.1		Text file	E-mail
1.2		Non-text file	E-mail attachment
1.3		HTML Web page	HTML mail
2	One-to-many		
2.1		Delivery	Multi-address sending/copy
2.2		Distribution	Mailing list

52.4 Application of the Internet

The Internet provides a variety of user-friendly services which cover all the functions of a WAN and a network OS as discussed in Sections 52.2.2.3 and 52.2.2.4. The Internet applications are distributed in academic, business, and public domains and are continuously growing.

There are two types of Internet service operators: Internet service provider (ISP) and online service provider (OSP). The ISPs provide internet access services for users for connecting to the Internet. The OSPs provide subscribers with internet access services as well as private services and protection. Such OSPs are AOL (America Online), Line One, MSN (Microsoft Network), Prodigy, etc.

The common Internet services are summarized in Table 52.2 and are described below.

52.4.1 E-Mail

E-mail is a method of sending text or non-text files between computers over the Internet. E-mail systems support one-to-one and one-to-many communication and management of communication files and address databases.

E-mail is one of the most popular services on the Internet. It has become a preferred way of many users to get in touch. Common e-mail services and methods are listed in Table 52.3.

52.4.2 WWW

World Wide Web (WWW) is an internationally distributed hypermedia network that uses graphical user interface (GUI) based hypermedia clients to hide complexities in accessing distant computer resources. WWW is one of the most exciting and fastest growing communication medium on the Internet. WWW provides a user-friendly point and click method of navigating data stored on the Internet. The only skill a user needs is to be able to use a mouse.

The WWW has changed the face of worldwide communications in the last decade. In 1989, Timothy Berners-Lee, a British software engineer, proposed a global hypertext project designed to allow physicists around the world to work together by combining their knowledge in a Web of hypertext documents. It was based on earlier work that was carried out at CERN, the European Particle Physics Laboratory in Geneva. In October 1990, Berners-Lee began writing the first WWW server and the first client, a wysiwyg hypertext browser/editor which ran in the NexTStep environment. The Web software was made available to a wider audience on the Internet by mid-1991. In 1994, Berners-Lee joined the Computer Science Laboratory at the Massachusetts Institute of Technology, as director of the WWW Consortium to realize the full potential of the Web and to ensure its stability through rapid evolution.

52.4.2.1 Hypertext and Hypermedia

Hypertext is a non-sequential, point-linked text document, which can be read by a hypertext viewer. Hypermedia is a hypertext document, which includes multimedia resources, such as pictures, sounds, animations, and video, as well as text.

52.4.2.2 HTTP Protocol

Web-related communication between dissimilar computers is regulated by the HyperText Transport Protocol (HTTP). All a user needs to know about HTTP is that it defines the format and syntax of Universal Resource Locator (URL).

URL is a Web address specifying where a Web resource can be found. URL is defined according to the syntax of the HTTP protocol. For example, a URL of xyz company's home page may be as follows: http://www.xyz.com/home/welcome.html. This URL means: using HTTP protocol to find a Web server identified by "www.xyz.com," open the directory "/home," and access the HTML format hypertext file "welcome.html."

52.4.2.3 Web Browser

A Web browser is a GUI-based WWW client software for online searching and viewing hypermedia files and documents on the Internet. Popular browsers are the Netscape Navigator, Microsoft Internet Explorer, Mosaic, etc.

52.4.2.4 Web Programming Language

A common Web programming language is the HyperText Markup Language (HTML). HTML is used for adding hypermedia symbols to documents so that, when accessed by a Web browser, the structure and links of the hypermedia document can be recognized and displayed. HTML is a hypertext variant of a Standard Generalized Markup Language (SGML). HTML gives users a way of making up the document so that the Web browsers know which part of the document is which, and linking the URLs represented by the anchors built into the hypertext.

52.4.3 FTP

File transfer protocol (FTP) is a method and protocol of two-direction file transmission between computers on the Internet. FTP is used for downloading or uploading files from remote computers.

1. *Download files* — By FTP, files and software distributed on the Internet can be downloaded onto a user's local PC.
2. *Upload files* — By FTP, files and software can also be submitted to a remote host on the Internet.

Downloaded software can be categorized as freeware and shareware. The former is a kind of public downloadable software without any expectation of payment. The latter is a kind of downloadable software which is with certain conditions attached for future payments.

52.4.4 Telnet

Telnet is a utility program that lets users of the Internet control a remote computer somewhere else on the Internet just as if you are sitting in front of it. Once remotely logged onto a computer on the Internet, users can launch programs and process files as on that of a local computer. For remotely logging in by Telnet, users have to specify the host machine's name and its Internet address.

52.4.5 BBS

Bulletin board service (BBS) is a network which primarily acts as a place to download and trade files. There are thousands of BBSs in the world. Major BBS providers are CompuServe, America Online, etc.

52.4.6 Newsgroup

Newsgroup messages are a kind of service on the Internet in which people join with common interests and are able to discuss issues with strangers, while retaining a comfortable degree of anonymity. Messages are grouped by topic into Newsgroups. You can discuss any problem with experts and people who have the same interests.

52.4.7 Internet Relay Chat

Internet relay chat (IRC) is an Internet service which supports conversation between people all over the world using a keyboard in real time, just like that of long distance telephone for voice. IRC was developed in Finland in 1988 to support live conversation. IRC has played a worthy part in transmitting news and informal chat in one-to-one or one-to-many mode.

52.5 Perspective on the Future Internet Technology

This section discusses the future trends of the Internet. The evolution of the Internet infrastructures and new services emerging on the Internet are introduced. The impact of object technology is covered.

52.5.1 The Internet Infrastructure Evolution

With widespread internationalization of the Internet, scores of countries now have fundamental interests in its evolution. The architectures and compatibility of national information infrastructure (NII) has become crucial.

52.5.1.1 The Future Information Superhighway

In 1996, President Clinton appointed an advisory committee on high performance computing and communications, information technology, and the next generation Internet. One of the committee's tasks will be to provide guidance on the next generation Internet Initiative. It is predicated that the speed of the future Internet information superhighway would be 1000 times faster than that of the present Internet, enabling the integrated wide-band services to be transmitted on the Internet.

52.5.1.2 The Future Network Infrastructure

As analyzed in Section 52.2, there were two types of techniques to support computer networking and internetworking — the computer network and data communication network techniques. The deregulation of the telecommunications industry and the convergence of voice and data networks may lead to the change of the future Internet infrastructure technology to ATM, Gigabit Ethernet, and ISDN.

- *ATM network* — The move to integrate voice and data means a switched network infrastructure is likely to emerge, helping the move toward ATM technology. As described in Section 52.2.1.4, ATM is a highly flexible technology for transmitting digital message at megabytes per second on hybrid packet switching networks. An ATM network enables faster and wider bandwidth transmission of data up to 2488.32 Mbps (Vetter, 1995).
- *Gigabit Ethernet* — The Gigabit Ethernet is a band-increased networking technology used to fulfill the demand for wide bandwidth data, voice and video integration (Kennedy, 1997).
- *ISDN network* — Integrated Services Digital Network (ISDN) is an emerging end-to-end CCITT standard for voice, data, and image services. The intention for ISDN is to provide simultaneous handling of digitized voice and data traffic on the same links and switching systems. An ISDN

network can be based on the ATM switching techniques to provide wide-band data transmission for both telecommunication and computer communication services (Lane, 1987).

52.5.2 Network Computing

Another major change on the horizon of network computing is the move from desktop environments to Webtops. A mirroring of Internet services from the desktop will allow real-time updating and manipulation of files that are a reflection of those same files on the Internet. The Web-browser of today will more than likely become the interface to many OSs, and the desktop will become a hypertext entity.

52.5.2.1 Network Computer

With the emergence of Internet computing, a much less powerful machine compared to the PCs and workstations, known as the network computer (NC), has been proposed by Larry Ellison, chief executive of Oracle. The concept of the NC is that it will run a lightweight OS, such as a JavaOS, and software will be distributed to the NC as and when required.

A Sun JavaStation is a typical thin client NC with only 8 M of main memory and no disk storage. The key NC applications are Internet-based, such as Web browser, e-mail, graphics presentation, word-processing, games, streamed video, spreadsheet, and object-oriented enterprise application frameworks.

However, many analysts agree that NCs are not PC-killers, but terminal replacements. In a Microsoft proposal, a NetPC will be compatible with PCs without end-user expansion slots. A hard disk will exist in a NetPC as a cache of information coming down from the network server. In a Zero Administration Initiative for Windows, Microsoft will support automatic updates of applications and the Windows OS, give network administrators central control of PCs, and allow users to roam between PCs with full access to their own data, applications, and environment.

52.5.2.2 Network Programming Language

Java is considered not only an ideal internet programming language, but also an alternative way in which online information is being accessed and distributed. As a network programming language, Java's philosophy is: write once, play anywhere. The idea behind Java is based on virtual machines, which can be traced back to the 1960s. However, what makes Java popular is its integration with the gigantic growth of the Internet.

Java compilers produce bytecode, a semi-interpreted pseudocode that can be converted into native object code by an entity known as a virtual machine (VM). The Java VM is currently implemented in the two most popular Web clients, Netscape Navigator and Microsoft Internet Explorer. A Java development kit consists of a Java compiler, debugger, interpreter (a JVM), and class libraries for software development. The Microsoft VM, which is based on the original JVM, is likely to be part of the Windows OS, which in turn will allow Java applets to be created and launched directly by the user. Once complied, a Java program can be executed by any computer where there is a suitable JVM installed. Developers are finding that they no longer have to worry about developing an application for a specific platform.

Java has also a key role to play in NCs toward a network-oriented computing mode, where data and programs are held on remote servers rather than on a user's local hard disk. For the first time in personal computing there is now a technology that is truly universal and architecture-neutral, which could potentially remove the need for perpetual software upgrades.

Java will be a powerful tool for applications in Intranet environments, especially where a variety of hardware platforms are in use, that is, where a greater degree of platform independence is required.

52.5.3 Object-Oriented Technology on the Internet

Along with the development of network computing mode on the Internet, object-oriented (OO) technology will play a major role on the Internet and get enhanced in the global network environment. In this subsection, the authors analyze the mutual impact of OO technology and Internet technologies, and they predict some important trends on OO programming and OO system development on the Internet.

52.5.3.1 Further Object-Orientation of the Internet

Modern Internet software implementation, application, and programming are dominated by Java and other OO programming languages and environment. By further object-orientation by means of OO components, tests, frameworks, and plug-ins, the Internet functionality organization and presentation will be more flexible and powerful.

52.5.3.2 Object-Oriented Software Construction

Conventionally, programming is to build software from scratch. Based on the technology of object-orientation and software component reuse, an interesting new approach to developing software — software construction — is merging in software engineering. The major difference between programming and software construction is that the former uses language statements as basic construction units, and the latter uses made-components (objects) as basic construction units in software development. It is interesting to note this fundamental difference is comparable to that in hardware development, in which systems can be built by using individual components at the lower level or by using integrated circuits (ICs) and very-large-scale-integrated-circuits (VLSIs) at the higher level.

The condition for enabling object-oriented software construction (OOSC) is the existence of rich and easily available object-bases like that of the standard IC/VLSI series in hardware technology. The global Internet provides OOSC technology an ideal environment for publishing, supplying, searching, acquiring, and testing ready-objects for software construction and integration. Thus OOSC will be a main trend in the future application of the Internet.

52.5.3.3 Object-Oriented System Design and Implementation

OO business application systems, such as OO enterprise frameworks and OO software engineering process models, can now be provided as plug-ins of the network operating systems on the Internet. These OO business application systems will provide optimized and reusable business models for improving operation of the existing software and IT industry.

In summary, the mutual stimulation and improvement between object-oriented technology and internet technology will largely change the current Internet toward a fully object-oriented internet. This will provide an ideal internet programming environment for OO software and system construction and integration, and provide reusable models for OO business application system improvement.

52.5.4 New Services on the Internet

As there will be continuous extension of the Internet application domains and evolution of the Internet infrastructure and performance, a wide range of new services will be innovated on the Internet. This subsection introduces some aspects of the trends on enhanced Internet communications, internet-based businesses, and education.

52.5.4.1 Enhanced Internet Communications

- *Internet telephony* — The idea of using the Internet as an alternative to the telephone network is getting some excited. This service needs multimedia computer support with soundcard, speaker, microphone, and sound control software. It requires 14.4 kbps or faster Modem in transmission. A few net phone programs have been developed, such as WebPhone and Internet Phone. Intel has successfully conducted an audio and videophone call through the Internet based on the H.323 technology, an international standard for Internet voice and video communication. For information about H.323 technology visit the Intel Website at www.intel.com.
- *Internet video conferencing* — Internet video conferencing is a service to enable Internet users to see whom one is talking to. The current techniques can only support semi-static picture transfer at 14.4 kbps. Microsoft NetMeeting can provide real-time voice and video conferencing. It can be used for document editing, whiteboard drawing and pasting, and background file transmission.
- *Web TV* — Intel has unveiled Intercast, a board that turns a PC into a television receiver. It also enables broadcasters to deliver data during the flyback and blanking parts of the program signal,

as Teletext services currently do. This sophisticated system should allow broadcasters to transmit at around four times the speed of the fastest current modems, allowing data to be delivered in the form of interactive WWW pages.

- *Mobile net access* — Mobile net access will provide truly wireless computing for transferring data, voice, and fax over the Internet.

52.5.4.2 Internet-Based Business

Internet-based business is another trend to reorganize an enterprise's activities based on the Internet technology and services. The Internet has full potential to provide interactive means for business operation in a wide range, such as publication, data search and retrieval services, banking, public services, marketing, advertising, entertainment, shop online, Internet payroll service, library, medical services, etc.

New technologies on network computing and OOSC and object-oriented business application models predicted by the authors will largely impact the operation mode of the IT industry. Organizations need to view the Internet as a productivity tool. The way an organization uses the Internet could determine whether it succeeds. Recently Angela Eager reported a Cisco Systems' view as to how and why the Internet will change the way that businesses run. Cisco did 35% of its business over the Internet and it saved £250 million in 1996 through its online activities. Its productivity has increased by 12.5%. As a consequence it has been able to pull back the amount invested in sales. For Cisco, the Internet has allowed it to "increase productivity without increasing the headcount" (Eager, 1997).

52.5.4.3 Internet-Based Education

Internet-based teaching will largely change the education system. The Internet can provide wide availability of good teachers, textbooks, teaching methods, information, libraries, and IT services for schools, higher education, and continuous education (Schrum and Lamb, 1997 and Brown and Williams, 1997).

52.6 Conclusions

The Internet is a mature and successful network interconnection technology. Initially a dedicated system, the Internet grew to serve the academic and research communities. More recently, there has been tremendous expansion of the Internet both internationally and in the business and public user domains. The commercial domain now makes up more than 50% of the connected base, and represents a large rate of growth. The Internet is now referred to as a standard computer communications infrastructure like that of the telephone, facsimile, and postal mail.

This chapter has reviewed the origin of the Internet and its fundamental techniques, and predicted some technical trends of the Internet. A remarkable change in the Internet is that it is now servicing a large proportion of business and public users. Due to the improvement of the future Internet information superhighway, the integrated wide-band services, such as video and digital telephone, will be publicly available on the Internet.

Another major change on the horizon of network computing is the move from desktop environments to Webtops. The Internet-based computing supported by NC and Java will provide a new mode of computing. The Internet enhanced OOSC approach will impact programming methodology and the IT industry fundamentally. The reusable object-oriented enterprise application models and frameworks as plug-ins on the Internet will help improving the modeling and operation of Internet businesses.

References

Atkins, J. and Norris, M. 1995. *Total Area Networking.* John Wiley & Sons Ltd., London.

Bort, J. and Felix, B. 1997. *Building an Extranet: Connect Your Intranet with Vendors and Customers.* John Wiley & Sons, London.

Browning, P. and Williams, J. 1997. Using the Internet in teaching and LEARNING: a UK perspective, *Comp. Geosci.,* Vol. 23, No. 5, June, pp. 549-557.

Chinoy, B. and Braun, H. W. 1992. The National Science Foundation Network, Technology Report GA-A21029, San Diego Supercomputer Center.

Claffy, K.C., Braun, H.W. and Polyzos, G.C. 1994. Tracking long-term growth of the NSFNET, *Commun. ACM*, Vol. 37, No. 8, pp. 34-45.

Comer, D.E., 1995. *Internetworking with TCP/IP, Vol. I: Principles, Protocols, and Architecture* (3rd ed.). Prentice-Hall International.

Comer, D.E. and Stevens, D. L. 1994. *Internetworking with TCP/IP, Vol. II: Design, Implementation, and Internals* (2nd ed.). Prentice-Hall International.

Comer, D.E. and Stevens, D. L. 1992. *Internetworking with TCP/IP, Vol. III: Client-Server Programming and Application.* Prentice-Hall International.

Day, J.D. and Zimmermann, H., 1983. The OSI reference model, *Proc. IEEE*, Vol. 71, Dec., pp. 1334-1340.

Eager, A. 1997. Cisco claims Internet is the key to success, *Inform. Week*, Issue No. 19, 10-23 December, pp. 10-11.

Englander, I. 1996. *The Architecture of Computer Hardware Systems Software: An Information Technology Approach.* John Wiley & Sons, New York.

Gerich, E. 1992. Guidelines for management of IP address space, Obsoleted by RFC 1366, InterNIC, Oct.

Gerich, E. 1993. Guidelines for management of IP address space, Obsoleted by RFC 1466, InterNIC, May.

Goralski, W.J. 1995. *Introduction to ATM Networking*, pp. 15-48. McGraw-Hill, New York.

Hafner, K. and Lyon, M. 1996. *Where Wizards Stay up Late: The Origins of the Internet.* Simon and Schuster, New York.

IS Solutions. 1997. Travel firm takes extranet route, *Internet Bus.*, Issue 3, April, pp. 14.

Kennedy, A.J. 1997. *The Internet and World Wide Web* (3rd ed.), pp. 389-406. Rough Guides Ltd., London.

Lane, J. 1987. *The Integrated Services Digital Network (ISDN).* The National Computing Centre Ltd Publications.

Postel, J.B. 1981. Internet protocol, Internet Request for Comments Series RFC 791, InterNIC, Sept.

Radke, H.D. 1996. Nets and Intranets with Win95 Getting Connected, Abacus, U.S.

Rose, M.T. 1993. *The Internet Message: Closing the BOOK with Electronic Mail.* Prentice-Hall, Englewood Cliffs, NJ.

Schrum, L. and Lamb, T.A. 1997. Computer networks as instructional and collaborative distance learning environments, *Educ. Technol.*, Vol. 37, No. 4, July-Aug., pp. 26-28.

Sloane, A. 1994. *Computer Communications: Principles and Business Applications.* McGraw-Hill Book Co., New York.

Stancic, H. 1996. Intranet: new solution for the internal communications, *Informatologia*, Vol. 28, No. 1-2, pp. 63-70.

Tanenbaum, A.S. 1989. *Computer Networks* (2nd ed.), pp. 1-46. Prentice-Hall International.

Vetter, R. 1995. ATM concepts, architecture, and protocols, in issue and challenges in ATM networks, *Commun. ACM*, Vol. 38, No. 2, February, pp. 30-38.

http://www.wia.org/pub/iana.html (Internet Assigned Number Authority, IANA)

http://info.isoc.org/ (Internet Society)

http://www.internic.com (Internet Network Information Centre, InterNIC)

http://www.w3.org/ (WWW Consortium, W3C)

http://www.netg.se/~kerfor/extranet.htm#books (Extranet — a reference page)

53

Business Objects and the Evolution of the Internet

Jeff Sutherland
IDX Systems Corporation

53.1 Introduction

> "The Web is considered at one level to be a web object, although documents on the web are quite different in many ways from objects in traditional distributed object-oriented systems. Will the two models continue to coexist, interacting weakly in certain cases, or will the relationship between the two worlds become well enough established for them to be regarded as one?"
>
> **Tim Berners-Lee, Director World Wide Web Consortium**

The World Wide Web (WWW) exists because of object-oriented systems. Berners-Lee was interested in hypertext systems at CERN in October, 1992. His boss said he could not justify any formal investment in a hypertext project, but that he was interested in the new Next machine and what it could do for CERN. If Tim would evaluate a Next machine, he could hack hypertext on it until Christmas. In one month, he had the first WWW browser and before Christmas the first content creator for the Web. Berners-Lee points out that each group implementing a commercial C++ browser after him took a year to do it (Berners-Lee, 1997). The uniqueness of the Next machine was the productivity of its visual environment for creating plug-and-play components; without it, the Web would not exist in its current form.

Most organizations will not build Web-based distributed object systems with a Next machine, but they will deliver them with Java. Productivity will depend on using a development environment with the Next machine characteristics, a tight integration of a visual development environment with component generation facilities more sophisticated than applet builders, and seamless coupling with object/relational databases and other Internet technologies. This chapter lays out the conceptual direction we are heading in building distributed, business object systems for the Web — the integration of components, objects, databases, and the Web.

0-8493-3135-8/99/$0.00+$.50

53.2 Underlying Principles

"It is well understood in biological evolution that change occurs sharply at intervals separated by long periods of apparent stagnation, leading to the concept of punctuated equilibrium. Computer simulations of this phenomenon suggest that periods of equilibrium are actually periods of ongoing genetic change of an organism. The effects of that change are not apparent until several subsystems evolve in parallel to the point where they can work together to produce a dramatic external effect" (JSOT, 1997).

Berners-Lee did not have a year to deliver a working system, and neither do most U.S. corporations in the Internet age. He was the first example of the Internet three-month product cycle, a phenomenon that is driven by Moore's law and Metcalf's law. Moore's law (chip density doubles every 18 months) has driven the personal computer hardware development cycle. Metcalf's law (the power of a computer network is the square of the number of nodes on the network) is driving shorter software development cycles and the exponential growth of users on the Internet. To live long and prosper in this brave new world, software developers will need to learn to deliver distributed object systems over the Internet/Intranet as fast as Berners-Lee delivered the first browser.

Technological change goes through periodic acceleration as a result of convergent discoveries. The pattern is the same for the adoption of eyeglasses in the 11th century as it is for the invention of the computer in the 20th century. It typically takes multiple inventions to enable a new technology and 20 to 30 years for acceptance and adoption. The personal computer, the mouse, the graphical user interface, the Ethernet, and the first widely used object-oriented language were all invented at Xerox Parc in the early 1970s (Kay, 1996). The Internet was developed in the 1960s and by the mid-1970s many government agencies, universities, and research facilities were connected to what was then called ARPAnet (Sterling, 1993). A design which led to TCP/IP was proposed by Vint Cerf and Bob Kahn in 1974 and the hypertext concept was created by Ted Nelson (1974) in the same year.

By the time these technologies had incubated for 20 years, it was evident in the early 1990s that the major thrust of computer-human interaction approaching the millenium was the use of hypermedia systems to augment the human mind, much as the telescope and microscope had augmented human vision (Sutherland, 1991). All that remained were the triggering mutations required to cause an evolutionary explosion of distributed object-oriented, graphical, hypermedia systems on the Internet. These mutations occurred in 1993. They were the Web browser, Java — the first computer language designed for dynamic distribution of objects on the Web — and Business Objects, an approach to re-engineering distributed software applications to support global re-engineering of corporate organizations.

53.3 Best Practices

53.3.1 The Java Revolution

"A revolution has got to leave the world with a totally different view of itself — its got to be a paradigm shift... When you've got a revolution like this, don't think about applets. We're talking about a situation where the whole content of your machine is going to have a totally different shape (to) it. As a result the whole society, the whole commercial environment around all software is going to look totally different" (Berners-Lee, 1996; Brickman, 1996).

"Java is the cleverest attempt at a Trojan horse yet. The Netscape browser grabs screen real estate, sort of like grabbing shelf space in the local supermarket, and Java delivers the goods right into the heart of Microsoft territory and breaks their lock on the desktop. No wonder Bill Gates announced a counterattack on Pearl Harbor Day last December. Internet World dresses him up as a WWII General and outlines his strategy in the March 1996, article, "Microsoft Declares War." Gates portrayed Microsoft as the suffering, innocent, American people while Netscape is billed as an unfeeling Japanese air strike on Pearl Harbor" (Sutherland, 1996).

The Netscape/Java combination is the first credible strategy to open up the desktop to competitive, non-Windows applications. As a result, every leading software and hardware vendor has rallied around Java. Microsoft has had to join the pack and support Java in Microsoft products. Every major C++ vendor will become a Java vendor to survive in the C++ marketplace. C++ currently owns about 42% of the market for development of object-oriented applications (*Object Magazine*, 1995). In the future, a substantial portion of the C++ market will turn into a Java market.

The popularity of Java has a significant impact on Smalltalk and C++ developers, because Java can be viewed as a crippled Smalltalk for C++ programmers. It avoids the complexity of C++ by introducing features that have been part of the Smalltalk environment for 20 years. More important, it can be seamlessly distributed over the WWW. It is free, totally portable, runs on every major hardware platform, and is supported by every major hardware and software vendor.

53.3.2 Java and Production Systems

Smalltalk is currently running in 15-20% of the production, object-oriented, client/server business applications (*Object Magazine*, 1995). Most of the rest are C++. Java is running in very few of these applications today because it is not robust, performance is poor, and Java development environments are not ready for prime time. It is useful primarily for applets on Web pages and not much else. In current development efforts for one of the leading Internet news providers, Individual, Inc., Java was used for building registration applets. Lack of tools, slow performance, and security restrictions prevented deployment of these Java tools on their Newspage sites.

While Java has been designed to deal with the security issues posed by the Internet, it cannot effectively deal with client/server development on corporate intranets. For example, consider the security restrictions that are built into the Java applet execution environment:

- A Java applet can communicate only with the server that distributed the applet to the client machine.
- A Java applet cannot evoke an executable on a client machine.
- A Java applet cannot write to ROM or disk on a client machine.

Consider one of the simplest of all client/server applications, updating a local computer clock to atomic time. A Java application, TickTock, calls the U.S. Naval Observatory atomic clock server (violating security restriction 1), evokes an operating system call on the local machine (violating security restriction 2), and writes the current time to the system clock (violating security restriction 3). This is one of the simplest of all client/server applications and it cannot be run as an applet.

Java's current perfomance and garbage collector limitations are similar to the first Smalltalks implemented in the 1970s. Nevertheless, Java compares well to other major object-oriented languages. Table 53.1 has been critiqued by members of the comp.lang.smalltalk, comp.lang.c++, and comp.object newsgroups. Despite isolated objections to particular entries in the table, the ratings are adjusted to reflect a widespread consensus of opinion in the newsgroups.

Much of the leading compiler talent on the planet is currently dedicated to providing good Java tools, improving Java performance, giving Java a state-of-the-art garbage collector, and generally getting Java ready for prime time. As can be seen from Table 53.1, with good tools, excellent performance, and a robust environment, Java will outrank Smalltalk as a software development language.

53.3.3 The Software Crisis

It is not news that there is a software crisis. The news is that it is getting a lot worse:

- It costs $70 billion/year to maintain 10 billion lines of legacy code in the U.S. alone (Lerner, 1994).
- 31% of new projects are canceled at a cost of $81 billion (*PC Week* 1995).
- 52.7% of projects are over budget for a $59 billion loss (*PC Week*, 1995).

TABLE 53.1 Smalltalk, C++, OOCOBOL, Java, and VB: The Good (1), the Bad (3), and the Ugly (2)

		ST	C++	OO COBOL	Java	VB
Flexibility	Dynamic binding	1	2	2	2	3
	Dynamic classes	1	3	1	2	3
	Multiple inheritance	3	2	2	3	3
	Roles/interfaces	2	3	3	1	2
	Function pointers/lexical closure	1	2	3	3	3
Ease of use	Class libraries	1	3	3	2	1
	Learning curve	1	3	2	1	1
	Speed of development	1	3	2	2	1
	Portability	2	3	3	1	3
Support	Tools	1	1	3	2	1
	Multiple vendors	2	1	3	1	3
	Internet aware	3	3	3	1	1
Performance		2	1	3	3	2
Productivity	Lines of code/function point	1	3	2	3	2
Risk	Garbage collection	1	3	3	2	3
	Memory leaks	1	3	1	1	1
	Overwriting memory	1	3	1	1	1
	Ready for prime time	1	1	2	2	1
TOTAL	(Low means best)	26	43	42	33	35

- Developer productivity has dropped 13% since 1993 (Yourdon, 1995).
- The ratio of best to worst organization software productivity has widened from 4:1 in 1990 to 600:1 in 1995 (Yourdon, 1995).

Java does not produce any more functionality per line of code than C++ (Jones, 1996). Its automated garbage collection might reduce lines of code required by 40% (*Object Magazine*, 1996). The elimination of pointers in the language significantly reduces debugging time and eliminates memory leaks, producing more robust applications.

Yet another computer language will not solve our software productivity problems. Only component-based development with scalable, advanced development environments can really help. We need enterprise solutions based on business object design and implementation (Sutherland, 1995). New approaches to software development and higher levels of engineering skill are required.

53.3.4 Business Objects and Business Process Re-Engineering

The global market has become an intensely competitive environment moving at an accelerated rate of change. Gradual improvements in productivity and enhancements in quality are no longer enough to maintain market leadership. Time to market of new products and rapid evolution of old products and applications are key success factors.

Accelerating product evolution requires re-inventing the processes that bring products to market and eliminating processes that do not add value. Since modern corporations have embedded many rules and procedures for product delivery in computer systems, the software applications that run the business must undergo significant change. To gain the strategic advantages of speed and flexibility, corporations must remodel their business processes, then rapidly translate that model into software implementations.

Business Process Re-engineering (BPR) sets the stage for continuous evolution of business processes to meet rapidly evolving business requirements. Implementation of software systems that support BPR requires Business Objects that can both simulate corporate procedures and translate smoothly into software objects. Well-designed Business Object implementations can be easily modified as the business changes.

53.3.5 Business Objects as Reusable Components

Early adopters of object technology asserted that packaging software in object classes would allow software to obtain some of the benefits of Moore's Law seen in IC chip fabrication (Cox, 1986). Some projects have achieved major productivity benefits. For example, a Maintenance Management System at General Motors originally written in PL/I was rewritten under EDS contract in Smalltalk and achieved a 14:1 increase in productivity of design, coding, and testing (Taylor, 1992). Detailed analysis of this project showed 92% fewer lines of code, 93% fewer staff months of effort, 82% less development time, 92% less memory needed to run, and no performance degradation.

While there are many isolated projects that used object technology to achieve dramatic productivity gains during the past decade, this success has not translated into broad improvements across the software industry. In 1995, the META Group reported that, "despite the promise of reusable objects, most IT organizations have realized a scant 10-30% productivity improvement from object technology (OT)." Failure to achieve larger productivity gains was attributed to:

- Data-centric, task-oriented application development
- Methodologies and cultures that do not promote reusability
- Few linkages between BPR-defined business processes and IT support initiatives (Meta Group, 1992)

While productivity gains from OT in recent years have been limited, some companies have been able to achieve dramatic returns on investment by bringing products to market sooner, with the flexibility necessary for rapid tuning of the products to meet changing market conditions.

For example, a recent analysis of return on investment (ROI) from object-oriented development of robotics software by Marcam Corporation showed a $56.5 million return on a $6 million investment. Return was calculated by multiplying the value of an improvement by the estimated probability of its occurrence and dividing by the cost of the improvement. The following spreadsheet was generated (*Software Magazine*, 1996):

TABLE 53.2 MARCAM ROI for OO Project (Corrected)

Perceived Advantage	Advantage Improvement	Probability of Occurrence	Incremental Cost	ROI
Time to market	$100 million	0.4	$3 million	$37 million
Flexibility	$100 million	0.2	$2 million	$18 million
Productivity	$2 million	0.8	$300,000	$1.3 million
Quality	$1 million	0.9	$200,000	$700,000
Other Costs	$0	—	$500,000	–$500,000
Code Size	$0	—	$0	$0
Reuse requirements	$0	0.9	$10,000	–$10,000
TOTAL			**$6 million**	**$56.5 million**

Business Objects are designed to support a clearly defined relationship between BPR-defined business processes and software implementation of these components. Using an object-oriented development methodology yields quick time to market and good object-oriented design allows for rapid evolution of Business Objects in response to market conditions. The bottom line is that OT is a necessary, but not sufficient condition for large returns on investment. It must be combined with focus on delivering Business Object Components that enable fast and flexible delivery of new or enhanced products in the marketplace. The Internet provides the first global infrastructure for rapid implementation of these capabilities.

53.3.6 The Need for a Business Object Architecture

As business models are renewed, software architectures must be transformed. A Business Object Architecture (BOA) is an effective solution for dynamic automation of a rapidly evolving business environment.

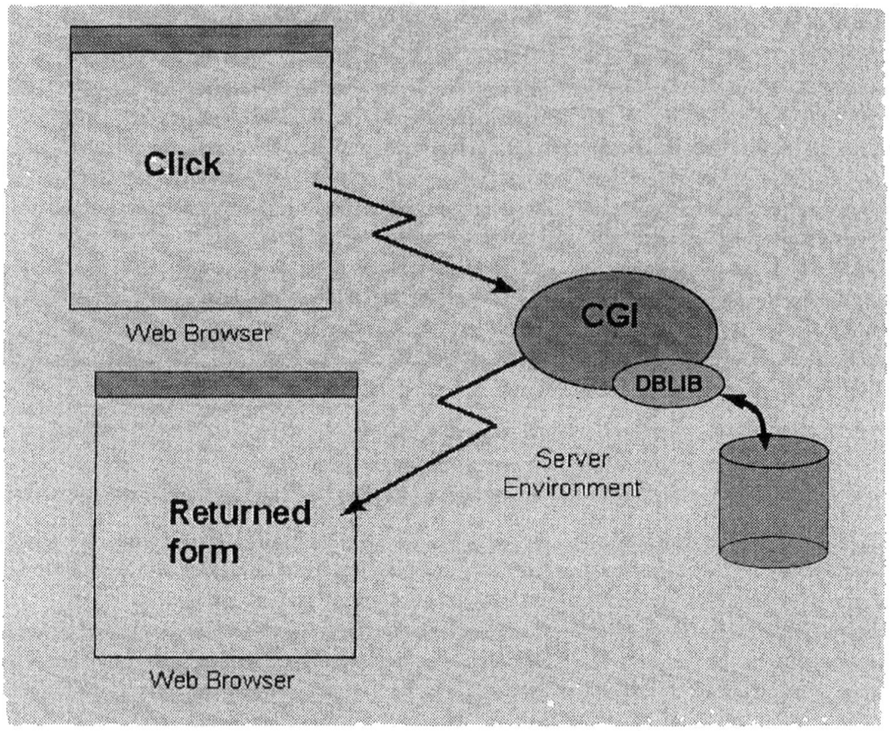

FIGURE 53.1 An order entry Business Object.

Dynamic change requires reuse of chunks of business functionality. A BOA must support reusable, plug-compatible business components. The two primary strategies now being used for implementing client/server systems to support re-engineering of business processes are visual fourth generation languages and classical OT. While both of these approaches are better than traditional COBOL software development, neither of them provides adequate support for implementation of Business Objects.

53.3.7 Building Business Object Components

A group of objects is the ideal unit of reuse. These groups of objects should behave as a higher level business process and have a clearly specified business language interface. Business components are encapsulated with a protocol that allows efficient communication with other objects on the network.

Consider a typical client/server application like an order entry system (Figure 53.1). This system takes a Purchase Order as input and produces a validated order as output. The internals of this component should be a black box to the external world. The resulting order is input for another subsystem or, alternatively, an exception condition is raised if the Purchase Order is not valid for processing.

To support plug-compatible reuse, a business component must be encapsulated in two directions. The external world must not know anything about component internals, and the internals must not know anything about external components, other than allowing interested objects to register for notification of specific events or exception conditions.

The internals of a business component are made of other encapsulated business components. For example, when a Purchase Order passes through the membrane of the Order Entry business object, an internal component must see it, validate it, look up customer information, inventory availability and catalog pricing, and build an order that is consistent with business rules and procedures. Each of these tasks is accomplished by embedded components, many of them communicating with external data sources.

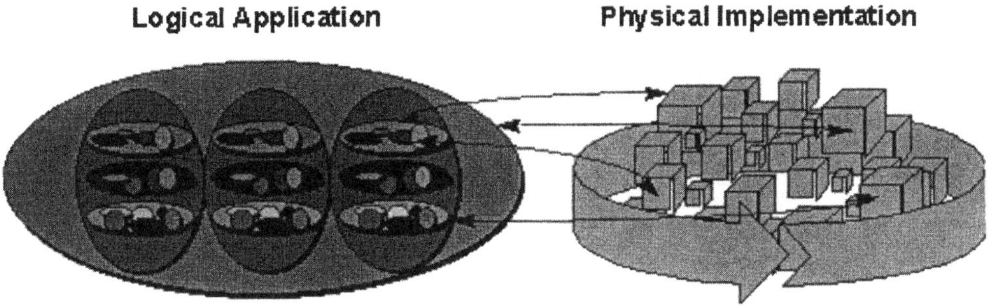

FIGURE 53.2 Client/server component.

External databases must be encapsulated as Business Objects or reuse will not be easily achievable. There must be a database access component that causes values from any kind of database to materialize as objects inside the business component. Whether object-oriented, relational, or other database access is required, a set of class libraries designed to automate this interface will result in a major savings in development resources (Sutherland et al., 1997).

An Order Entry business object will typically have multiple user interfaces. A clerk will take an order over the phone, enter purchase information, validate customer records and credit data, and review an order for consistency and customer acceptance. Other users may require different presentation screens. User interfaces are difficult and time consuming to build at the code level. Today, much of this process can be automated. They can be encapsulated as separate objects that communicate by message passing to the Order Entry object. Failure to do this will limit reuse and waste valuable programmer time on laborious, time-consuming maintenance tasks. Users can create interface objects with simple object-oriented tools. Subsequently, the programmer can easily snap user interface objects onto the Order Entry object.

A simple Order Entry client/server component (Figure 53.2) has at least three large-grained components, one or more presentation objects, a business component that models the business process, and a database access component that shields the application developer from database access languages, database internals, and network communications.

Business Object programmers focus their efforts on building business components, or large-grained Business Objects, which can be easily distributed on the network.

53.3.8 Distributing Business Objects

System evolution will invariably distribute these Business Objects to maximize network performance and processor utilization and to ensure proper control, integrity, and security of information. Business re-engineering implies implementing a distributed environment where components encapsulating business functionality can be migrated to nodes on the network that allow maximum flexibility, scalability, and maintainability of a Business Object system.

Business objects made up of nested components allow distribution of these components across a network. Figure 53.3 shows the logical application as a coherent set of nested client/server components. Deployment of this large-grained object may include distributing subcomponents across multiple heterogeneous computing resources in dispersed locations. Thus, an application designed on one processor is scattered across a network at runtime.

Developers of business information systems are beginning to take advantage of building applications with OLE components. At Object World in San Francisco, CA, Allied Signal won the Computerworld Award for best object-oriented application of 1995 (VMARK, 1995). They re-engineered the Supply Management Business Process that took 52 steps to purchase a single part, so it now requires only three steps to complete the same transaction. The old process required seven people and took nine weeks to

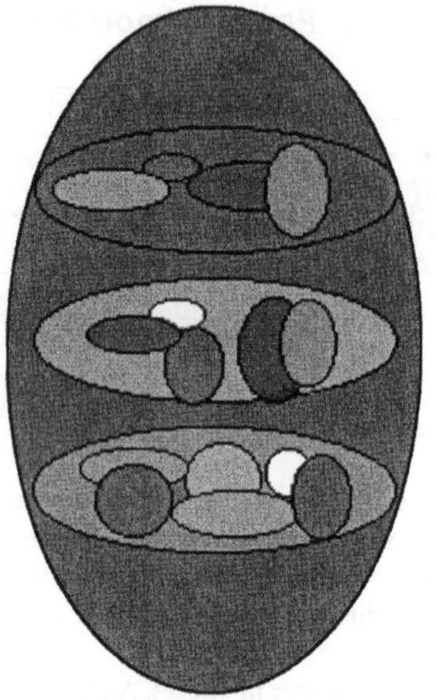

FIGURE 53.3 Application Business Object with nested client/server components.

produce an approved purchase order. The new Supply Management Specialist Tool (SMST), developed with the Object Studio (VMARK, 1995) advanced development environment, allows one person to complete the same process in nine minutes for established suppliers with long-term agreements in place. In the case of new suppliers, where a Request For Quote (RFQ) is required, the process takes nine days.

In this example (Table 53.3), cycle time of the process is reduced 2400:1 for established suppliers and 5:1 for new suppliers. Cost reduction of operational staff is 7:1. The impact of improvement in business efficiency leading to greater customer satisfaction and resulting market share is far greater than any reduced costs in operations overhead or development time, and it is the prime objective for the use of Business Object design tools to assure success of Business Process reengineering practice.

53.3.9 A Web-Based Solution for Business Object Architectures

To enhance competitiveness in an environment of accelerating change, businesses are turning to Web-based solutions for Intranet client/server applications. Some potential benefits are

- Thinner clients
- Reduced network costs
- Automated software distribution
- Lower development and maintenance costs
- Transparent portability dramatically reduces complexity
- Simpler technology for MIS to implement
- Infrastructure for distributed business object architecture

Building non-trivial client/server applications on the Web requires more than HTML programming. Current approaches are not object-oriented, CGI invocations must return a new screen on every

TABLE 53.3 Re-Engineering a Purchase Order Component

	Before	After	Improvement
Process steps	52	3	17.3
Staff	7	1	7
Time	9 weeks	9 min	2400

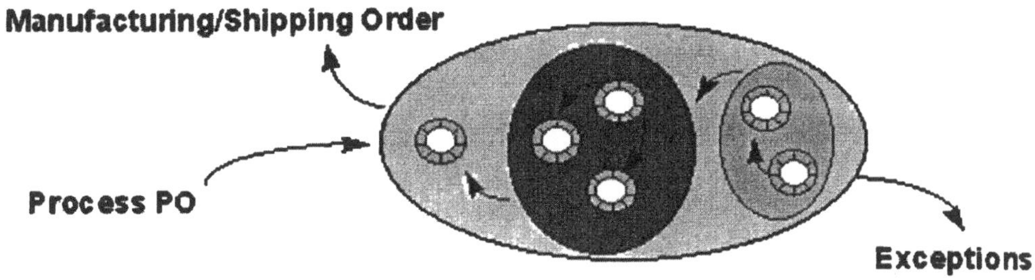

FIGURE 53.4 Typical CGI-based Web interaction.

interaction and context is lost. Every CGI access reopens the database, dramatically reducing performance characteristics of the application. Working around these problems requires a high level of technical skill and significant development resources not normally available to corporate MIS shops (Figure 53.4).

Current development in Internet companies is typically focused on an object-oriented implementation that improves maintenance and enables reuse. C++ CGI components are used to maintain open database connection for sessions, radically improving performance. Java applets communicate with the C++ components to maintain context between screen interactions (Figure 53.5).

The minimal environment needed for easily implementing client/server applications on the Web includes:

- Remote method invocation across the network, dramatically simplifying programming
- Java Applets or Servlets can initiate action (pull and push technology) and peer-to-peer communication is supported between applets and servlets; a simple example is the need for a servlet stock ticker that can update browser applet (Figure 53.6)
- Servlet/JDBC optimization of database performance and simplification of object to relational table mapping
- Database connections automatically held open for session and proper management of multiple simultaneous connections to the database

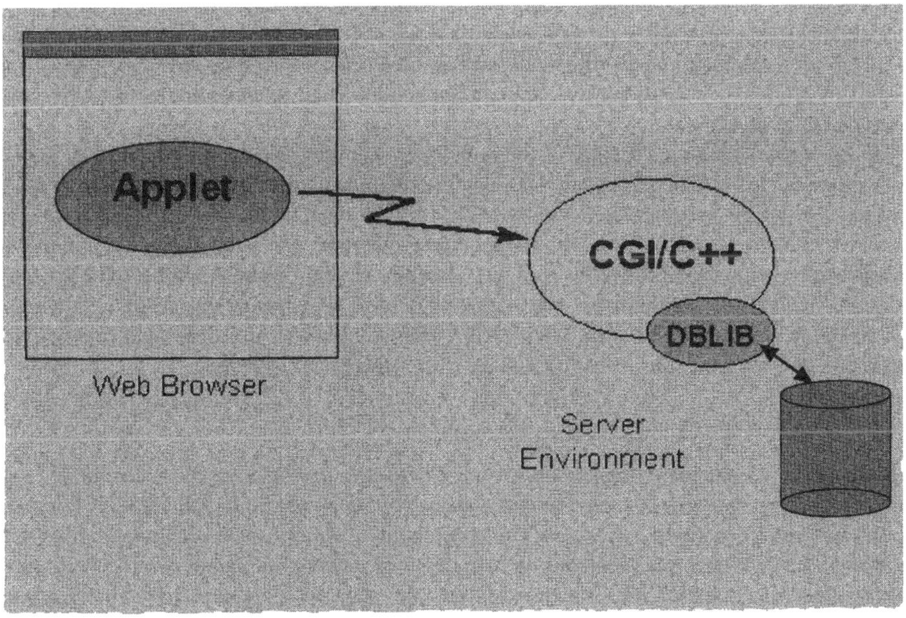

FIGURE 53.5 Enhanced Java/CGI implementation.

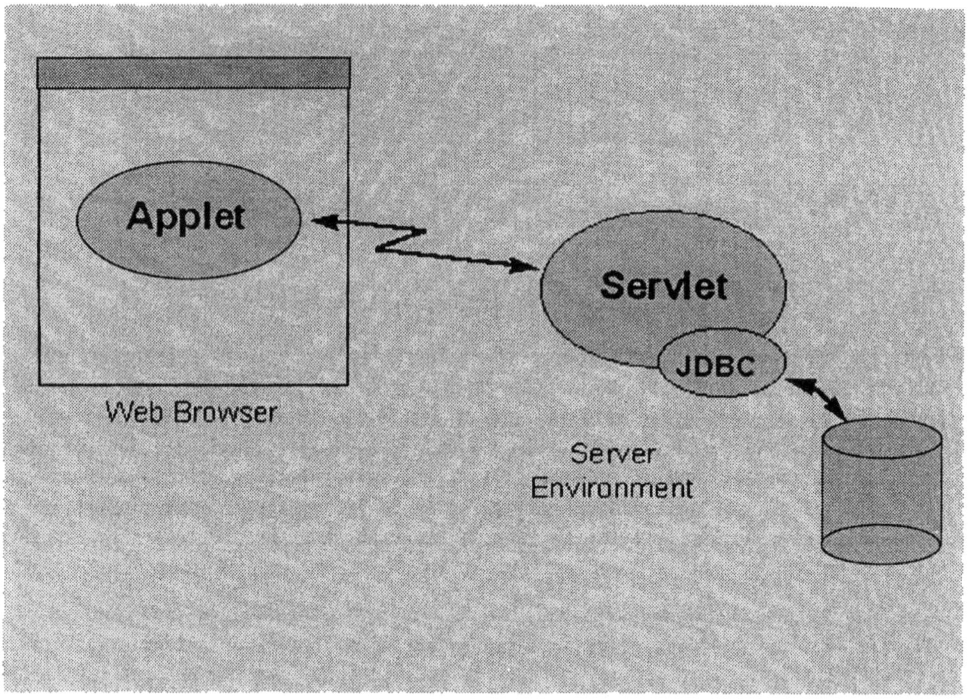

FIGURE 53.6 Applet/servlet RMI implementation.

53.4 Research Issues and Summary

The lack of tools to simplify implementation of business object systems on the Internet/Intranet is currently a major inhibiting factor for movement to Java-based client/server applications. The lack of a robust, bug-free Java integrated development environment is a second impediment. The third major handicap for building these applications is lack of a component-based environment required for building business object architectures.

Completion and industry acceptance of the evolving Sun Javasoft JavaBeans Specification (JavaSoft, 1996) is required for building standard Java components and Object Management Group (OMG) standardization of a Business Object Facility (OMG, 1997) is a core requirement for building standards-bases BOAs from Java components. The JavaBeans specification has stabilized and a recent OMG submission (informally called JBOF) of a Business Object Facility for building distributed object systems is promising (JBOF, 1997). This proposal will have a concrete implementation in Java and developers should review how it handles business rules, events, roles, constraints, assertions, and transactions — all the things that are requirements for large scale, distributed object systems.

53.4.1 ActiveX/CORBA Harmonization

One of the most encouraging developments for building distributed object applications for the Web is the emerging synergy between Java and Microsoft's ActiveX strategy based on OLE/COM. It turns out to be as easy or easier to use Java for creating COM components as it is to use Visual Basic or C++. In fact, Microsoft's COM architects state that Java is becoming the language of choice for COM component implementation. Microsoft has enabled every ActiveX component to look like a Java class to a Java application and every Java class to look like an ActiveX component to a Windows application (Chapell, 1996).

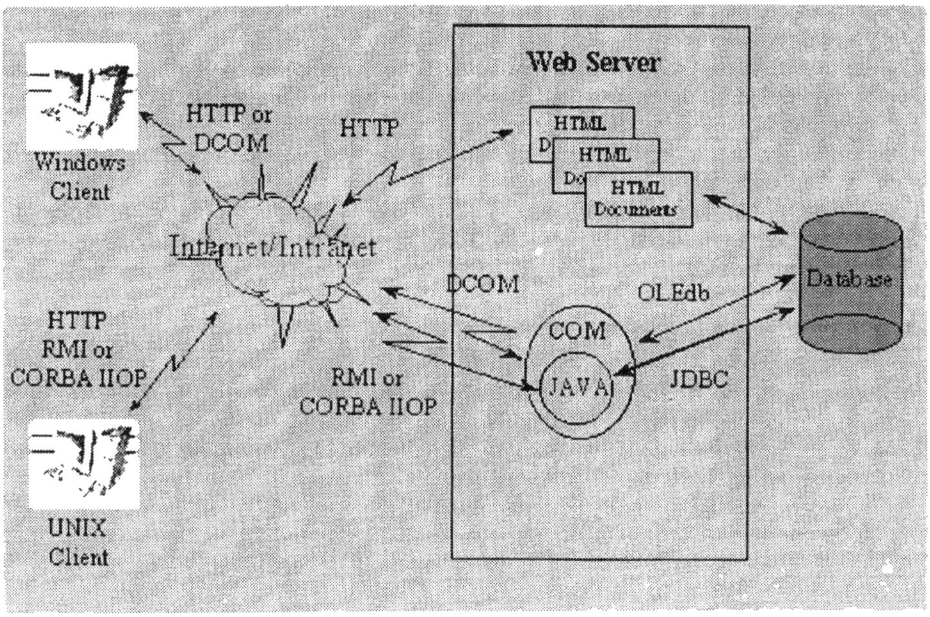

FIGURE 53.7 The environment we really need.

Java's support for garbage collection eliminates the need for reference pointer counting that is very tedious when building COM components in C++. It also hides some of the complexity of the COM interfaces. As a result, it is possible to supply seamless integration between ActiveX and Java components. If the vendors implement products properly, it will be possible to talk to the same component via DCOM or CORBA protocols.

Most CORBA-compliant ORB vendors deliver the capability for DCOM clients to access CORBA objects on the network. This is a primitive capability compared to the two-way interoperability between DCOM and CORBA. In 1997, only one vendor provides full interoperability. Users must be knowledgeable and careful when selecting CORBA middleware to ensure that required capabilities are supported.

53.5 Conclusions

Corporations that take advantage of BOAs will significantly shorten product cycles and Java will play a major role sometime before the year 2000 (Figure 53.7). Consulting groups that use Business Objects will significantly underbid their competition and deliver new systems on time and under budget. Because a BOA will allow software to change as rapidly as the underlying business processes, corporate viability will be enhanced by early implementation. Laggards will pay the price. They are already easily outmaneuvered in the marketplace by enterprises embarked on large scale implementation of global distributed object systems based on Internet technologies.

References

Berners-Lee, T. 1996. *The Axes of Revolution.* JavaOne Keynote slides, JavaOne. <http://java.sun.com/java.sun.com/javaone/keynotes/TBL/9605JAVA/slide1.htm>

Berners-Lee, Tim. 1997. *Of Webs and Objects.* Object World Keynote Address, Boston, MA, 6 March.

Brickman, Gary. 1996. News and comment from JavaOne, *JAVA J.* <http://www.gamelan.com/pages/javaone/javaone_article4.html#web>

Chappell, David. 1996. *Understanding ActiveX and OLE: A Guide for Developers and Managers.* Microsoft Press, Redmond, WA.

Cox, Brad. 1986. *Object-Oriented Programming: An Evolutionary Approach.* Addison-Wesley, New York.

Dennett, Daniel. 1995. *Darwin's Dangerous Idea: Evolution and the Meanings of Life.* Simon and Schuster, New York.

JavaSoft. 1996. *JavaBeans Specification, Version 1.00-A.* Sun Microsystems, 4 December. <http://splash. javasoft.com/beans/>

JBOF. 1997. OMG Joint Submission on BO RFP1 (formerly CF RFP4) by Data Access Technologies, Sematech, Prism Technologies, and IONATechnologies, 9 January. Related documents are bom/97-01-02 and bom/97-01-03. Available as document cf/97-01-05. <http://www.omg.org/library/schedule/CF_RFP4.htm>

Jones, Capers. 1996. *Programming Languages Table Monograph, Eighth edition,* Software Productivity Research. <http://www.spr.com/library/0langtbl.htm>

JSOT. 1997. *SCRUM Home Page.* Jeff Sutherland's Object Technology Web Site, Winchester, MA. <http://www.tiac.net/users/jsuth/scrum/index.html>

Kay, Alan. 1996. The early history of smalltalk. In *History of Programming Languages,* T.J. Bergin and Richard G. Gibson, Eds. ACM Press, New York.

Lerner, Moisey. 1994. Software maintenance crisis resolution: The new IEEE standard, *IEEE Software* 11:65-72, August.

Levy, Steven. 1993. *Artificial Life: A Report from the Frontier Where Computers Meet Biology.* Vintage Books, New York.

META Group, Inc. 1995. Making the case for use case, *Adv. Inform. Manage., File 324,* 13 February.

Nelson, Ted. 1974. *Computer Lib/Dream Machines.* self-published. Republished by Microsoft Press, Redmond, WA, 1987.

Object Magazine. 1995. Executive brief: Objects important to redesign, O-O 4GLs outracing Smalltalk?, 5:3:10 (June).

Object Management Group. 1997. *Common Facilities RFP 4: Common Business Objects and Business Object Facility,* OMG TC Document CF/96-01-04 <http://www.omg.org/library/schedule/CF_RFP4.htm>

PC Week. 1995. 16 Jan, p. 68.

Spertus, Mike. 1996. Garbage collection in C++, *Object Mag.,* 5:6 (Feb).

Sterling, Bruce. 1993. Internet. *The Magazine Of Fantasy And Science Fiction.* February, Cornwall, CT. <gopher://oak.zilker.net:70/00/bruces/F_SF_Science_Column/F_SF_Five_>

Sutherland, Jeff. 1991. *Hyperscope: The Next Step in Human/Computer Evolution.* Object Databases. Cambridge, MA.

Sutherland, Jeff. 1996. Road kill on the information highway: JavaDay, *Homepage J.,* February. <http://www.onemind.com/roadkill.html>

Sutherland, Jeff. 1995. Smalltalk, C++, and OO COBOL: The good, the bad, and the ugly, *Object Mag.*

Sutherland, Jeff et al. (Eds.) 1997. *Proc. the OOPSLA'95 Workshop on Business Object Design and Implementation.* Springer-Verlag, London.

Sutherland, J.V., Pope, M. and Rugg, K. 1993. The hybrid object-relational architecture (HORA): An integration of object-oriented and relational technology, In *Proc. of the 1993 ACM/SIGAPP Symp. on Applied Computing,* pp. 326-333. Indianapolis, IN, 14-16 Feb., Deaton, E. et al. Eds. ACM Press, New York.

Taylor, David. 1992. *Object-Oriented Information Systems: Planning and Implementation.* John Wiley & Sons, New York, pp. 320-322.

VMARK Software. 1995. *Allied Signal Company wins the Computerworld Object Application Award at Object World,* Press Release, 21 August. http://www.vmark.com/whatsnew/presrel11.html

VMARK Software. 1995. *Object Studio Product Literature.* http://www.vmark.com/products/objstud/objstud.html

What's the ROI on Objects, *Software Mag.,* May 1996. (Note that there are errors in the ROI calculation which have been corrected here.)

Yourdon, E. 1995. *Ed Yourdon's Guerilla Programmer.* July 1995 (No longer published. Back issues available from Cutter Information Corp.)

XII

Object-Oriented Analysis/Design Tools

Dilip Patel
South Bank University

This section contains chapters that highlight the value of case and modeling tools in the analysis and design phase of an object-oriented project.

54

Object-Oriented Analysis and Design Tools

D. Janaki Ram
Indian Institute of Technology
S. Srinath
Indian Institute of Technology
K.N. Anantha Raman
Indian Institute of Technology

54.1 Introduction

Computer Aided Software Engineering (CASE) tools are programs aimed at assisting developers manage the process of software development. CASE tools evolved over a period of time from being merely compiled code generators to sophisticated analysis and design tools. The emphasis on analysis and design became prominent in the structured paradigm of software development. There have been claims and counterclaims on the impact of CASE tools on the productivity of the developer and the quality of the software developed. However, there is a general perception that CASE tools did result in increased software quality and productivity.

As Object-Orientation (OO) started to establish itself as a new paradigm for software development, CASE tool support for OO also started appearing. However, OO software development methodologies are still evolving. A number of OO methodologies exist, at least 23 of which have been recognized by the Object Management Group (OMG; OMG, 1997). Some of the more widely known methodologies are Rumbaugh (OMT) (Rumbaugh et al., 1991), Booch (Booch, 1994), Unified Modeling Language (UML), Jacobson, Shlaer/Mellor (Shlaer and Mellor, 1993), Coad/Yourdon (Coad and Yourdon, 1990), OPEN Modeling Language (OML), Fusion (Coleman et al., 1994), etc.

CASE tool support for OO needs to address issues specific to OO development. Some of these issues include: (1) lack of clear boundaries between analysis and design, (2) no clear deliverables at the end of analysis, (3) lack of precise steps for providing automated support for methodologies, (4) existence of several methodologies with often confusing notations, (5) lack of an accepted standard lifecycle model, and (6) existence of multiple CASE tools focusing at different stages of the lifecycle.

Because of these issues, support for customizability and adaptability for a specific industrial environment becomes important during the design of a CASE tool. Vessey et al. (1992) identify three kinds of CASE tool support for methodologies: *restrictive* support, where the methodology is enforced on the user; *guided* support where the user is only encouraged to use the methodology; and *flexible* support,

0-8493-3135-8/99/$0.00+$.50

where adopting a methodology is completely in the hands of the user. Most OO Analysis and Design (OOAD) CASE tools may be classified as falling under the category of *flexible* support.

A plethora of CASE tools exist catering to various methodologies. Here, we present a compendium of forty-two CASE tools for OOAD. The tools have been classified and organized for easy reference. Most of the information about the tools were obtained from their respective home pages on the Internet. It is recommended that the user visit these home pages for the latest details. In the next section, we provide a taxonomy of the CASE tools for OOAD.

54.2 Taxonomy of the CASE Tools for OOAD

The first generation of CASE tools for OOAD are, to a great extent, only sophisticated drawing tools supporting a single notation. In a strict sense, it cannot be said that they supported the methodology, as there is no formal stepwise guidance, or error checking, to ensure that the steps of the methodology are being strictly adhered.

Since more than one methodology is in practice in industry, tools supporting multiple methods have come into existence. Some of these tools have started providing facilities for cross-migration from one notation to the other. These "multi-method" tools are often associated with a meta-design environment. Such tools are also called "meta-CASE" tools. They provide flexibility for the user to define his/her own methodology or modify an existing methodology. This appears to be an important trend, given that the methodologies are evolving, and do not define precise steps to be followed. They also allow the developer to use one's creative and intellectual abilities to customize the methodologies provided by the tool. Multi-method tools without such a meta-design environment are normally a bundle of methodologies, allowing the developer to choose a methodology from among them. However, the support they provide for a methodology may not be as comprehensive as that of a single method tool for the same methodology.

Often, a single CASE tool cannot cater to the entire lifecycle. When multiple tools have been employed at different stages of the lifecycle, an important issue is to integrate them appropriately to make them work together. CASE tool integration is provided by "model bridges," which adhere to specific standards for CASE data interchange (CDIF, 1997; OMG, 1997; IRDS, 1997; and JTC1/SC22/WG22-PCTE, 1996).

In the next section, we present various CASE tools for OOAD, which are classified broadly as (1) single method tools, (2) multi-method tools, (3) meta-CASE tools, and (4) model bridges. The above taxonomy is intended to help an organization select an appropriate CASE tool. Single method tools are suitable for small organizations which are focused in their domain requirements. Large, diversified organizations may find it economical to invest in multi-method tools which satisfy their methodology requirements. Meta-CASE tools are more suitable for organizations which require extensive customization in terms of the methodology adopted. Finally, organizations which require many CASE tools and interoperability among them might benefit from an appropriate model bridge. More details on constraints governing selection and use of CASE tools may be found in Goldberg and Rubin (1995) and Coad and Yourdon (1990).

54.3 Coding Scheme for OOAD Tools

A compendium of forty-two CASE tools for OOAD is provided here. A synopsis of all the tools for quick reference follows. The synopsis provides a multidimensional index of the tools based on different features, enabling one to quickly locate the tool with the desired features.

Broadly, the tools are classified as OOAD tools, meta-CASE tools for OOAD, and model bridges. OOAD tools are further classified into tools which support a single methodology and tools which support multiple methodologies. Each tool is provided with a quick reference index based on this classification. Tables 54.1 and 54.2 provide the index for each tool that has been included. The fields of Tables 54.1 and 54.2 are as follows:

Classification — OOAD tools are indicated by "O", meta-CASE tools are indicated by "M", and model bridges are indicated by "B".

TABLE 54.1 OOAD Tools — Synopsis

Tool	Classification	Index	Availability
ADvance	O	M1	C
BetterState	O	M2	CF
BOCS	O	M3	C
BridgePoint	O	S1	C
CRC	O	S2	CF
Classify	O	S3	C
EiffelCase	O	S4	C
EXCHANGE	B	1	C
Graphical Designer	M	1	C
Hardy	M	2	CF
HOOD	O	S5	C
HOODNice	O	S6	C
IONizer	O	S7	F
IPSYS ToolBuilder	M	3	C
Jack	B	2	F
Mac A&D	O	M4	C
Mesa	B	3	C
MetaEdit	M	4	C
Metaview	M	5	F
ModelMart	B	4	C

Index — The quick reference index helps locate the desired tool information. OOAD tools which support a single methodology have an "S" in the index, while those supporting multiple methodologies have an "M" in the index.

Availability — Commercial tools are indicated by "C". Freeware tools are indicated by "F". Some commercial tools also provide a *small project* version of the tool as freeware. Such tools are indicated by "CF".*

Table 54.3 relates individual methodologies and tools. The index of each tool is provided inside parentheses after the tool name. As mentioned earlier, some vendors use "methodology" and "notation" interchangeably. Since it is difficult to ascertain the full nature of the support provided, we have included whatever has been claimed by the vendors. However, it is important to note that a methodology support might be nothing more than just a notation support.

Table 54.3 indicates OMT (Rumbaugh, 1991) to be a very widely supported methodology. Booch and Jacobson follow closely. UML seems to have a pretty strong support, considering the fact that it was only recently released. Also, since UML is being released by the combined efforts of Booch, Rumbaugh, and Jacobson — who have a major share of the support — it seems likely that the popularity of UML is going to increase further and might eventually become the *de facto* standard.

54.3.1 Survey of OOAD Tools

The tools are classified into three broad classes as mentioned earlier: OOAD tools, meta-CASE tools, and model bridges. The list of tools is not exhaustive as many tools keep entering the market. As new paradigms like meta-CASE and CASE standards emerge, more tools might be expected to support these paradigms.

The tools are presented in the form of tables, one per tool. Each table lists a set of attributes, which indicate the tool features. Additional information, if any, are included as annotations. Any information that is not available is indicated as INA (for "Information Not Available"), and any attribute not applicable, is indicated as NA (for "Not Applicable").

TABLE 54.2 OOAD Tools — Synopsis

Tool	Classification	Index	Availability
Moose Workbench	O	M5	C
ObjChart	O	M6	C
ObjectCraft	O	M7	C
ObjectDomain	O	M8	C
ObjectGEODE	O	M9	C
ObjectMaker	M	6	CF
Object Modeler	O	M10	C
Objectory	O	S9	C
Object-Oriented Designer (OOD)	O	S10	F
ObjectTeam	O	M11	C
OEW	M	7	CF
OMW (LiveModel)	O	S8	C
OOram Professional	O	S11	CF
Paradigm Plus	M	8	C
PepperSeed	O	M12	C
Playground	O	S12	CF (shareware)
Pragmatica	M	9	CF
Rose	O	M13	CF
SoftBench	O	M14	CF
StP	O	M15	C
Together/C++	O	M16	C
VisualCASE	O	S13	C

A summary analysis of the forty-two CASE tools show the following interesting statistics:

- Microsoft Windows 3.1/95/NT and SunOS/Solaris are the most widely supported platforms (20 tools each). This is followed by HP-UX/9000 (16 tools). IBM AIX, comes third (8 tools).
- C++ is the most widely supported code generation language (23 tools). Smalltalk follows it (9 tools), although by a large interval. Java comes third (8 tools).
- Of the 42 tools, 14 (one third) are freely available, i.e., they are either freeware tools, or provide a small project version of the tool, for free. Meta-CASE has the largest proportion of freely available tools, 5 out of 9 tools; and multi-method OOAD tools have the least proportion, 3 out of 16 tools. It further suggests that meta-CASE tools are still in an evolutionary stage. Similarly multi-method tools are mostly commercial tools, suggesting that this approach is currently widely practiced in the industry.

54.3.2 OOAD Tools

These tools are provided in the form of tables. These help by looking at the tools along different attributes. More attributes and details are found as annotations. The attributes are informally divided into four groups. The first group comprises of the name of the tool, the vendor of the tool, the internet address for more information on the tool, and the cost. It is important to note that vendor's price of the tool is often not representative of the actual cost incurred for adopting the CASE tool for a particular environment. The actual cost could sometimes be higher by five to seven times the vendor's cost (Huff, 1992 and Iivari, 1996). The second group lists the platforms supported by the tool and the system requirements. The third group lists tool features like the product family, methodologies supported, details on code and document generation, repository, versioning, multiuser support, and meta-CASE support. Finally, the fourth group contains annotations describing more details about the tool.

TABLE 54.3 OOAD Tools — Methodologies

Methodology	Description	Tool(s)
BON	Business Object Notation, by Jean-Marc Nerson of SOL (Paris), and Kim Walden of Enea Data (Stockholm)	EiffelCase(O-S4)
Booch	Methodology developed by Grady Booch from Rational Software Corporation.	ObjectDomain(O-M8), Rose(O-M13), Graphical Designer(M-1), Mac A&D(O-M4), ObjectModeler(O-M10), PepperSeed(O-M12), StP(O-M15)
Coad and Yourdon	OOA methodology developed by Peter Coad from Object International Inc. and Ed Yourdon from Yourdon Press Inc.	Object Modeler(O-M10), Playground(O-S12), Together/C++(O-M16)
Fusion	Object Oriented Analysis and Design methodology, by Dereck Coleman et al.	Mac A&D (O-M4)
HOOD	Hierarchical Object Oriented Design from Lincoln Software	HOOD(O-S5), HOODNice(O-S6)
ION	Implementation Oriented Notation, developed by Colin Atkinson, of University of Houston, Texas	IONizer(O-S7)
Jacobson (tools which support use cases only are also included)	OOAD methodology by Ivar Jacobson, now in Rational Software Corporation.	ADvance(O-M1), Graphical Designer(M-1), MAC A&D(O-M4), Object Modeler(O-M10), Objectory(O-S9), ObjectTeam(O-M11), StP(O-M15)
Martin/Odell	Martin/Odell Object Oriented Information Engineering (OOIE), developed in 1993.	OEW(M-7), OMW(O-S8)
OML	OPEN Modeling Language, based on the COMMA metamodel, by Brian Henderson-Sellers, University of Swinburne, Melbourne, Australia	ObjectMaker(M-6)
OOram	The OOram Software Engineering Method developed by Trygve Reenskaug	OOram Professional(O-S11)
Rumbaugh (OMT)	Object Modeling Technique by Jim Rumbaugh, now in Rational Software Corporation	Classify(O-S3), IPSYS ToolBuilder(M-3), Graphical Designer(M-1), Mac A&D(O-M4), OOD(O-S10), ObjectDomain(O-M8), ObjectGEODE(O-M9), ObjectModeler(O-M10), Rose(O-M13), StP(O-M15), Together/C++(O-M16)
Shlaer/Mellor	OOAD methodology by Sally Shlaer and Steve Mellor, from Project Technology Inc.	BridgePoint(O-S1), Graphical Designer(M-1), Mac A&D(O-M4)
UML	Unified Modeling language — combining Booch, OMT, Jacobson, and other methods — from Rational Software Corporation	Graphical Designer(M-1), ObjectTeam(O-M11), PepperSeed(O-M12), Rose(O-M13), Together/C++(O-M16), VisualCASE(O-S13)

54.3.3 Single Method Tools

Single method tools cater to a single methodology. Often, single method tools would be developed by the developer of the method, but there are also third party tools (for example, OOD), which provide single method support. One of the common factors of most single method tools seems to be that the methodology assumes greater importance. The tools would normally be an aide for learning or adopting the methodology.

Out of the 13 tools that are listed here, 7 of the tools are developed by the proponents of their respective methodologies. OMT and HOOD have the highest support (2 tools each). Interestingly, both tools supporting OMT (Classify and OOD), are third party tools. Originally OMT was supported by OMTool, developed by Dr. James Rumbaugh, at General Electric (GE) Research and Development Center in Schenectady, New York. However, OMTool is no longer part of GE. It has been taken up by Lockheed Martin Corporation. We were not able to get the appropriate technical and support information for OMTool. The list of single method tools follows.

1. BridgePoint

Name of the tool	BridgePoint
Vendor	ProjTech Inc.
Product website	www.projtech.com
Cost	INA
Platforms supported	HP-UX 9.05 or 10.01, Sun Solaris 1 1.1.1 version B or later Sun Solaris 2 2.5 or later SGI-IRIX IRIX 5.3 or later
System requirements	INA
Product family	Consists of model builder, model verifier, and code generator. Model builder provides features like version management, multiuser support and automatic generation of derived products. Model verifier provides features like model execution, visual verification, and regression testing support. Code generator provides an archetype language which enables the user to have full user control over the design of the source code.
Methodologies supported	Shlaer/Mellor OOA methodology
Code generation	Yes
Languages	Any language
Reverse engineering	No
Document generation	No
Multiuser support	Yes
Versioning support	Yes
Prototyping	No
Meta-CASE support	No
Annotations	

2. CRC

Name of the tool	CRC
Vendor	Rational Inc.
Product website	www.rational.com/pst/products/cc.html
Cost	INA. Demo version may be downloaded from www.rational.com/demos
Platforms supported	Windows 3.1 or greater
Systems requirements	IBM AT, PS/2 or 100 percent compatible computer, 3 MB of hard disk space, 640 KB of RAM
Product family	No
Methodologies supported	CRC
Code generation	Yes
Languages	INA
Reverse engineering	INA
Document generation	INA
Multiuser support	INA
Versioning support	INA
Prototyping	INA
Meta-CASE support	INA
Annotations	Provides a graphical interface for creating and editing CRC cards, assigns responsibilities and collaborators to each of the classes generated, identifies class relationship hierarchies and group classes into subsystems at a higher education; it integrates with Rational Rose family of tools.

3. Classify

Name of the tool	Classify views
Vendor	Micram Technology GmBH
Product website	www.micram.de/classify

Cost	INA
Platforms supported	SunOS 4.1.x, Solaris 2.4, HPUX 9000 Windows NT, Sinix 5.2
System requirements	Objectivity/DB 3.8 Database Development System and X Windows System 11R4 or Open Windows
Product family	Consists of a set of tools. Classify/DB provides support for managing object models in a repository. Classify/Views is an OMT editor conceived to design, view, and edit object models. Classify/Dialogs is a GUI generator and editor used to customize the graphical appearance and functionality of applications based on Objectivity/DBTM databases. Classify/MetaPhase is a model browser.
Methodologies supported	OMT
Code generation	Yes
Languages	C++, Java
Reverse engineering	INA
Document generation	INA
Multiuser support	INA
Versioning support	INA
Prototyping	INA
Meta-CASE support	INA
Annotations	Supports ODL Data Definition Language of the ODMG and DDL Data Definition Language of Objectivity/DBTM. Also includes Metaphase TM Model and supports RTF Rich Text Format.

4. Eiffel Case

Name of the tool	EiffelCase
Vendor	ISE Eiffel
Product website	www.eiffel.com
Cost	INA
Platforms supported	Windows (NT,95,3.1), OS/2, Linux (a.out and ELF formats), Unix (Solaris, SunOS, HP 9000, IBM AIX, UnixWare, Silicon Graphics, Data General, Fujitsu, DEC OSF/1 etc.), VMS (Alpha as well as VMS)
System requirements	INA
Product family	No
Methodologies supported	Business Object Notation (BON)
Code generation	Yes
Languages	INA
Reverse engineering	Yes
Document generation	Yes
Multiuser support	INA
Versioning support	INA
Prototyping	INA
Meta-CASE support	INA
Annotations	Assists in preparing, documenting, and tracking identified object oriented system elements and their relationships from preliminary specifications to the programming phase.

5. HOOD

Name of the tool	HOOD
Vendor	Lincoln Software Limited
Product website	www.ipsys.com
Cost	INA
Platforms supported	VAX/VMS, Unix systems

System requirements	INA
Product family	No
Methodologies supported	HOOD
Code generation	Yes
Languages	Ada, C++
Reverse engineering	INA
Document generation	Yes
Multiuser support	Yes
Versioning support	INA
Prototyping	INA
Meta-CASE support	INA
Annotations	The tool adds to HOOD method by providing for requirements capture using CORE notation with requirements traceability to the generated code, and through Yourdon style structured analysis with Dataflow and State transition diagrams.

6. HOODNice

Name of the tool	HOODNice
Vendor	Intecs Sistemi
Product website	www.pisa.intecs.it/products/HoodNICE
Cost	INA
Platforms supported	SunOS 4.1.x, SunOS 5.3 or later and HPUX 9.x
System requirements	X11 R5 (MIT or Compatible), Motif 1.2
Product family	Consists of about 30 tools which can be activated directly from the OS shell or from the main interactive tools of the toolset. The major ones include HOOD Diagram editor (HDE) which provides graphical facilities for architectural design; the ODS Editor which supports textual notation of HOOD; the document generator; and reverse code generator which reconciles the design with the code, if it has been modified.
Methodologies supported	HOOD
Code generation	Yes
Languages	Ada, C, C++
Reverse engineering	No
Document generation	yes
Versioning support	INA
Prototyping	INA
Meta-CASE support	INA
Annotations	Has an open architecture that can be customized, extended, and integrated with foreign tools.

7. IONizer

Name of the tool	IONizer
Vendor	INA
Product website	www.ma.ultranet.com/jcdavis/ionizer.html
Cost	Freeware
Platforms supported	SunSparc running Solaris 2.x, RS6000 running AIX 3.2.x or 4.1.x, x86 PC's running Linux
System requirements	SunSparc with Solaris 2.x, OSF/Motif runtime installation, less than 1 MB of hard disk space. RS6000 with AIX 3.2.x or AIX 4.1.x with OSF/Motif runtime installation, less than 1 MB of hard disk space. x86 PC's having Linux with a.out or ELF version of Linux or compatible libraries for versions 1.1 and 1.2, respectively.

Product family	None
Methodologies supported	Supports Implementation Oriented Notation which complements OMT, Booch, OSA, Fusion, and others
Code generation	No
Languages	
Reverse engineering	No
Document generation	No
Multiuser support	No
Versioning support	No
Prototyping	No
Meta-CASE support	No
Annotations	It is an interactive diagramming tool for ION with many of the features which are usually found in painting and drawing software packages.

8. LiveModel

Name of the tool	LiveModel (formerly OMW)
Vendor	IntelliCorp
Product website	www.intellicorp.com/livemodel.html
Cost	INA
Platforms supported	INA
System requirements	INA
Product family	The Object Diagrammer, the Event Diagrammer, the Business Rule Editor, the Scenario Manager, the Report System
Methodologies supported	Martin/Odell Object Oriented Information Engineering (OOIE)
Code generation	Yes
Languages	C++, TCSI's OSP, SAP's R/3 and IntelliCorp's own Power-Model development environment
Reverse engineering	No
Document generation	Provided by the Report System
Multiuser support	INA
Versioning support	INA
Prototyping	INA
Meta-CASE support	No
Annotations	Formerly known as OMW, LiveModel provides the analyst with an environment for expressing business processes, in terms of business objects and execute and validate the model. Also provides support for business rules, expressed in structured English, and graphical support for expressing Event Diagrams. The rationale is to enable the business user to specify the business process and generate a software template that can be filled in by the software developer, obviating the need for the developer to understand the business process.

9. Objectory

Name of the tool	Objectory
Vendor	Rational Software Corporation
Product website	www.rational.com/products/objectory
Cost	INA
Platforms supported	Windows 95, NT 3.1, DOS 5.0 or 6.0 with Windows 3.1, HP 9000/700 with HP-UX 9.x, IBM RS/6000 with AIX 3.2.x Sun SPARC Solaris with Solaris 1 (SunOS 4.1.x), Sun SPARC Solaris 2 with Solaris 2.3
System requirements	INA
Product family	None

Methodologies supported	Jacobson's Use Cases
Code generation	
Languages	C++, Smalltalk
Reverse engineering	Yes
Document generation	Yes
Multiuser support	INA
Versioning support	Yes
Prototyping	INA
Meta-CASE support	No
Annotations	Objectory is now part of the Rational Rose family of products.

10. Object-Oriented Designer

Name of the tool	Object-Oriented Designer
Vendor	Professor Taegyun Kim at Pusan University of Foreign Studies Pusan, Korea
Product website	www.asset.com/WSRD/abstracts/ ABSTRACT_1332.html
Cost	Freeware
Platforms supported	Motif, SunSparc running SunOS, Unix
System requirements	X11-R5 and Motif-1.2 and C++-2.0. AT least 11 MB hard disk space
Product family	None
Methodologies supported	OMT
Code generation	Yes
Languages	C++, Java
Reverse engineering	Yes
Document generation	Obtained from the comments generated with the code
Multiuser support	No
Versioning support	No
Prototyping	No
Meta-CASE support	No
Annotations	Very user friendly, use of OOD requires knowledge of English and basic OMT graphical notation.

11. OOram Professional

Name of the tool	OOram Professional
Vendor	Taskon Technologies
Product website	www.sn.no/taskon/ooram.htm
Cost	US$4990 — an evaluation copy may be obtained from http://www.sn.no/taskon/order2.html
Platforms supported	Windows 3.11, Windows NT, Sun Solaris or HP-UX
System requirements	INA
Product family	None
Methodologies supported	OOram method
Code generation	Yes
Languages	INA, "various implementation languages"
Reverse engineering	Yes
Document generation	Yes
Multiuser support	INA
Versioning support	INA, provides a repository support for models
Prototyping	INA
Meta-CASE support	NO
Annotations	Supports model synthesis, such that different models may be put together into a more detailed and complex model. The tool is claimed to be best suited for applications like Bank/Finance, Telecommunications, Defense and, Offshore development.

12. Playground

Name of the tool	Playground
Vendor	Object International
Product website	www.oi.com
Cost	Registration fee $95
Platforms supported	Windows 95, Windows NT, Windows 3.1 with Win32
System requirements	16 MB RAM, 5 MB hard disk space
Product family	None
Methodologies supported	Coad and Yourdon
Code generation	No
Languages	NA
Reverse engineering	No
Document generation	INA
Multiuser support	No
Versioning support	No
Prototyping	INA
Meta-CASE support	No
Annotations	Useful for building basic object models and object interaction scenarios.

13. Visual CASE

Name of the tool	Visual CASE
Vendor	INA
Product website	login.eunet.no
Cost	INA, a free version is available for download
Platforms supported	Windows 95, Windows NT 3.51 and 4.0
System requirements	INA
Product family	None
Methodologies supported	Limited set of UML version 0.91
Code generation	Yes
Languages	C++ compatible with Visual C++
Reverse engineering	Yes
Document generation	Generates code comments compliant with Autoduck. (Autoduck is a source code parsing system that will generate Microsoft Word Documents)
Multiuser support	INA
Versioning support	INA
Prototyping	INA
Meta-CASE support	No
Annotations	Includes MFC library and object Toolkit library as a symbol library. Classes can be dragged from these libraries into any diagram for immediate use. Allows users to generate custom libraries, supports COM and ActiveX.

54.3.4 Multi-Method Tools

Multi-method tools support more than one methodology. These tools provide some flexibility to the user in terms of the methods that can be adopted. Some tools also allow intermixing of notations along the lifecycle. However, multi-method tools rarely provide support for methodologies in as much detail as that of a single method tool.

Some vendors have not specified the methodology support provided by their OOAD tools. In the absence of any further information, we have considered them to belong to the category of multi-method tools. This is because it is highly unlikely for single method tools not to specify their methodology support.

Among the 16 multi-method tools presented here, OMT has the widest support with 8 tools supporting it, Booch follows it with 6 tools supporting it, and UML follows Booch with 5 tools supporting it. The list of multi-method tools follows.

1. ADvance

Name of the tool	ADvance
Vendor	IC&C GmBH
Product website	www.io.com/~icc/products/advance/index.htm
Cost	
Platforms supported	VisualWorks 2.5, 2.5.1, 2.5.2 (with and without events), VisualWave 2.0a, and ENVY R3.01
System requirements	INA
Product family	None
Methodologies supported	Supports OMT and UML notations
Code generation	Yes
Languages	Smalltalk 2.0, integrates into any VisualWorks application
Reverse engineering	Yes
Document generation	No
Multiuser support	INA
Versioning support	No
Prototyping	No
Meta-CASE support	No
Annotations	Also supports Use Cases/scenarios.

2. BetterState

Name of the tool	BetterState
Vendor	Integrated systems Inc.
Product website	www.isi.com
Cost	INA, free version of the software called BetterState Lite is available
Platforms supported	Windows 95, Windows NT
System requirements	INA
Product family	None
Methodologies supported	INA
Code generation	Yes, a customizable code generator is also available
Languages	C, C++, Java, Delphi, C++ for MFC, Visual Basic, Perl, VHDL, Verilog HDL, CGI programs
Reverse engineering	No
Document generation	No
Multiuser support	No
Versioning support	No
Prototyping	No
Meta-CASE support	No
Annotations	The tool accepts conceptual design as input in the form of hierarchical state machines or petri nets and generates code.

3. BOCS

Name of the tool	Berard Objects and Class Specifier
Vendor	Berard Software Engineering
Product website	INA
Cost	$595
Platforms supported	Windows 3.1
System requirements	INA

Product family	None
Methodologies supported	INA
Code generation	Yes
Languages	C++, Smalltalk
Reverse engineering	INA
Document generation	Yes
Multiuser support	INA
Versioning support	INA
Prototyping	INA
Meta-CASE support	No
Annotations	A traceability tool provides tracing facility from requirements to design to code. More information may be had from info@bse.com.

4. MacA&D

Name of the tool	MacA&D
Vendor	Excel Software
Product website	www.excelsoftware.com/maca&dproducts.html
Cost	Product suite may be licensed by Single User, 5 User, or Unlimited User Site License; details about the latest prices for each may be found at http://www.excelsoftware.com/priceandordering.html
Platforms supported	Macintosh with System 7 or later, Solaris or HP-UX with Apple's MAE (Macintosh Application Environment)
System requirements	16 MB RAM, 15 MB hard disk space
Product family	MacAnalyst, MacA&D, MacTranslator
Methodologies supported	Supports Booch, OMT, Shlaer/Mellor, Coad/Yourdon, Fusion, or Jacobson notations
Code generation	Yes
Languages	C++, Object Pascal
Reverse engineering	INA
Document generation	INA
Multiuser support	Yes
Versioning support	Yes
Prototyping	Yes
Meta-CASE support	No
Annotations	A MacA&D Demo and Manual assists software designers in exploring software engineering methods or evaluating MacA&D products. It includes a set of diskettes with full product software and limited save capability. Software engineering documents for over a dozen sample projects are included using many popular methods.

5. Moose Workbench

Name of the tool	Moose Workbench
Vendor	Computer Systems Design group, Department of Computation at University of Manchester Institute of Science and Technology
Product website	INA
Cost	INA
Platforms supported	INA
System requirements	INA
Product family	INA
Methodologies supported	INA
Code generation	Yes
Languages	C++

Reverse engineering	INA
Document generation	INA
Multiuser support	INA
Versioning support	INA
Prototyping	INA
Meta-CASE support	INA
Annotations	It supports development of special purpose computer systems, for example, embedded reactive systems and application specific distributed systems. It supports a model-based approach which operates through an incremental development of a total system model leading eventually to the automatic synthesis of high-level language implementation source for both the hardware and software of the system. The implementation language for software and hardware is C++ and VHDL, respectively.

6. ObjectChart

Name of the tool	ObjectChart
Vendor	IBM
Product website	www.software.ibm.com/ad/objchart
Cost	INA
Platforms supported	INA
System requirements	INA
Product family	None
Methodologies supported	INA
Code generation	Yes
Languages	INA
Reverse engineering	INA
Document generation	Yes
Multiuser support	INA
Versioning support	INA
Prototyping	Yes
Meta-CASE support	No
Annotations	It supports an iterative process model; helps in modeling a system using a set of visual editors. Provides interactive executable models which simplify verification of the system's static and dynamic models; has an open architecture which supports incorporation of user developed code.

7. ObjectCraft

Name of the tool	ObjectCraft
Vendor	
Product website	www.oot.co.uk
Cost	INA
Platforms supported	INA
System requirements	INA
Product family	None
Methodologies supported	INA
Code generation	Yes
Languages	C++, Pascal
Reverse engineering	No
Document generation	Comments are embedded in the code
Multiuser support	No
Versioning support	No

Prototyping	No
Meta-CASE support	No
Annotations	Builds object oriented programs visually, by painting program objects, flow, interface, and database connections on the screen; has provisions for creating programs with database (Dbase) access to the programs.

8. ObjectDomain

Name of the tool	ObjectDomain
Vendor	Object Domain Systems Inc.
Product website	www.object-domain.com
Cost	Registration price $99
Platforms supported	Windows 95, Windows NT, Windows 3.1/3.11 with Win32s
System requirements	INA
Product family	None
Methodologies supported	Booch, OMT State, and Class diagrams
Code generation	Yes
Languages	Any language
Reverse engineering	Yes, from C++ code
Document generation	Yes
Multiuser support	INA
Versioning support	INA
Prototyping	No
Meta-CASE support	No
Annotations	TCL scripting language with extended commands to reference and manipulate the entire Object Domain model. The data extraction ability allows code generation for any language, model documentation to suit desired formats, and the development of utilities for conversion to and from other vendor's repository formats.

9. ObjectGEODE

Name of the tool	ObjectGEODE
Vendor	Verilog Inc.
Product website	www.verilogusa.com
Cost	
Platforms supported	OS: SunSparc SunOS, SunSparc Solaris, HP Series 9000/7xx-8xx, IBM RS/6000 and PowerPC, DEC Alpha/OSF1; RTOS:Microtec Research's VRTXsa, Integrated Systems' pSoS+, WindRiver's VxWorks, Enea Data's OSE, Chorus Systems' CHORUS, various flavors of UNIX
System requirements	INA
Product family	Consists of a set of tools; the ProjectOrganizer to organize all the components of the project and to integrate external tools; the OMT Editor for describing OMT analysis models and the passive data objects; the MSC Editor for building Message Sequence Charts during analysis and design phases; the SDL Editor for completing detailed SDL design models and for document generation; the SDL Simulator for rapid prototyping or verification and validation of design models; the Formal Verifier for conducting complete verification and validation through exhaustive simulations and including TTCgeN, a feature for automatic test cases generation in TTCN format; the Application Generator to provide code generation for the real-time parts of the system; the Design Tracer to graphically monitor the execution of the application on the target.

Methodologies supported	Integration of OMT, SDL (Specification Description Language), MSC (Messege Sequence Chart)
Code generation	Yes
Languages	C, C++
Reverse engineering	No
Document generation	Yes
Multiuser support	Yes
Versioning support	Yes
Prototyping	Yes
Meta-CASE support	No
Annotations	Provides APIs to access the various models or to directly invoke the ObjectGEODE editors from other environments. An interface is also provided for integrating ObjectGEODE with any configuration management environment.

10. ObjectModeler

Name of the tool	ObjectModeler
Vendor	ICONIX Software Engineering, Inc.
Product website	www.iconixsw.com/Spec_Sheets/ObjectModeler.html
Cost	$1495
Platforms supported	DOS, Windows 3.1, Windows 95, Windows NT 3.5x/4.0, HP-UX, Sun, SGI, Macintosh
System requirements	INA
Product family	None
Methodologies supported	Rumbaugh, Jacobson, Booch, Coad/Yourdon
Code generation	Yes
Languages	C++, Smalltalk, SQL
Reverse engineering	No
Document generation	INA
Multiuser support	Yes
Versioning support	Yes
Prototyping	INA
Meta-CASE support	No
Annotations	ObjectModeler is part of the ICONIX Powertools suite of tools; also provides for requirements traceability from the generated models.

11. ObjectTeam

Name of the tool	ObjectTeam
Vendor	Cayenne Software
Product website	www.cayennesoft.com
Cost	INA
Platforms supported	Windows 95 NT, UNIX
System requirements	INA
Product family	None
Methodologies supported	UML, Jacobson use cases
Code generation	Yes
Languages	C++, Java, Ada, Visual Basic, Power Builder, Fort, CORBA IDL, INFORMIX-NewEra, Smalltalk, DDL for various RD-BMs, embedded SQL DML code
Reverse engineering	Yes
Document generation	Yes, generates MS Word, Framemaker and InterLeaf documents
Multiuser support	Yes
Versioning support	Yes

Prototyping	No
Meta-CASE support	No
Annotations	Places emphasis on team development and iterative projects; also provides support for development of Embedded or Real-time Systems and IS Developers. ObjectTeam installation may be customized with Tcl. Support for third party tool integration is also provided.

12. PepperSeed

Name of the tool	PepperSeed
Vendor	Cayenne Software Inc.
Product website	www.cayennesoft.com/pepperseed/
Cost	Under $1000
Platforms supported	Windows NT/95, Macintosh
System requirements	INA
Product family	None
Methodologies supported	UML, Booch
Code generation	Yes, since code generator is written in Tcl, code generation is customizable by the user
Languages	C++
Reverse engineering	C++ reverse engineering
Document generation	Designs may be cut/pasted to MSWord and PowerPoint
Multiuser support	No
Versioning support	INA
Prototyping	No
Meta-CASE support	Supports UML metamodels
Annotations	Also supports graphical querying and Tcl scripting; designs may be exported to Microsoft's repository.

13. Rose

Name of the tool	Rose
Vendor	Rational Inc.
Product website	www.rational.com
Cost	INA
Platforms supported	Windows 95 or Windows NT
System requirements	80486 or pentium based PC with 16 MB RAM, 25 MB hard disk space, SVGA compatible display, pointing device with at least two buttons
Product family	Rational Rose/C++, Rational Rose/Fort, Rational/Java, Rational Rose/PowerBuilder, Rational Rose/Smalltalk, Rational Rose/SQLWindows, Rational Rose/Visual Basic, Rational CRC, Objectory
Methodologies supported	OMT, Booch, UML
Code generation	Yes
Languages	C++, Visual Basic, Java, PowerBuilder, Smalltalk, Forth, ADA
Reverse engineering	Yes
Document generation	Yes
Multiuser support	INA
Versioning support	Yes
Prototyping	INA
Meta-CASE support	No
Annotations	Supports Unified Modeling Language (UML), which includes use-case modeling, class and object modeling, component modeling, and distribution and concurrency modeling. Capable of generating SQL, DDL database schemas. Supports generation of CORBA/IDL.

14. C++ SoftBench

Name of the tool	C++ SoftBench
Vendor	Hewlett Packard
Product website	www.hp.com/sesd/products/ccppsoftbench/main.html
Cost	INA, a trial version of SoftBench is available for evaluation from http://www.hp.com/sesd/ordering/main.html
Platforms supported	HP-UX 9.0x or 10.0x, Solaris 2.3
System requirements	**On HP-UX:** X Window System version 11, Release 5; OSF/Motif Version 1.2 user interface; **on Solaris:** Open Windows 2.0
Product family	SoftBench (for C, FORTRAN, and Pascal)
Methodologies supported	INA
Code generation	Yes
Languages	C++, C, FORTRAN, Pascal
Reverse engineering	No
Document generation	No
Multiuser support	INA
Versioning support	INA
Prototyping	No
Meta-CASE support	No
Annotations	Some of the other features of SoftBench are Visually oriented, language-based tools, Graphical Performance Analyzer, a distributed debugging environment, full integration with emacs and vi, and links to middleware technologies like HP Odaptor data store and HP OODCE/9000.

15. Software Through Pictures

Name of the tool	StP
Vendor	Aonix
Product website	www.ide.com
Cost	INA
Platforms supported	IBM RS/6000; Sparc/Solaris; HP-UX; Digital Unix; DEC Alpha; OSF/1 3.2.SGI IRIX
System requirements	INA
Product family	Stp/OMT, Stp/Booch, StP/IM, Stp/SE, Stp/T
Methodologies supported	OMT, Booch
Code generation	Yes, a customizable code generator is also available
Languages	Smalltalk, C++, Java, Ada83, Ada95
Reverse engineering	Yes
Document generation	Automatic generation of RTF documentation
Multiuser support	INA
Versioning support	INA, a Design Repository is maintained, no information regarding version per se is available.
Prototyping	INA
Meta-CASE support	INA
Annotations	Integrates Jacobson's Use Cases with OMT and Booch models for capturing system requirements. Automated test case generation for design models is provided by StP/T.

16. Together/C++

Name of the tool	Together/C++
Vendor	Object International
Product website	www.oi.com
Cost	INA

Platforms supported	Windows 95 and Windows NT
System requirements	INA
Product family	None
Methodologies supported	Coad, OMT, UML
Code generation	Yes, source code formatting and commenting is user defined
Languages	C++
Reverse engineering	Yes, customizable; user can define a set of patterns to look for No which are defined as special Nolinks in the object model
Document generation	Yes, documentation in the form of Windows help files and HTML files are also available
Multiuser support	INA
Versioning support	Yes, works with standard version control systems like PVCS and MKS
Prototyping	INA
Meta-CASE support	No
Annotations	Provide an open high-level access to the object model with Information Export query language. Provides C++ interface to major subsystems. Can be easily integrated with the Borland C++ IDE.

54.3.5 Meta-CASE Tools

Meta-CASE tools provide a generic framework that can incorporate any methodology and its corresponding notation. In addition, they also provide features like creation of custom methodologies by the user. With the tool becoming independent of methodologies, the user now has greater flexibility in choosing and adapting methodologies. However, meta-CASE tools might not provide support to individual methodologies in as much detail as provided by the OOAD tools. In addition, often notation independence is claimed as method independence. Almost all meta-Case tools allow the user to create a set of custom notations to describe the OOAD model. However, the user might not be able to define a new set of steps and have the tool enforce the steps during the development process. Some tool vendors claim to provide support for intermixing of methods. This is almost always intermixing of notations from different methods rather than the methods themselves.

While a single methodology might not cater to the entire lifecycle, it is also quite unlikely that a meta-CASE tool can seamlessly integrate multiple methodologies to provide support for the entire lifecycle. But by enabling developers to share OOAD models from different methodologies, meta-CASE tools are probably the first step toward providing flexible support for the complete business process. The list of meta-CASE tools, follows.

1. **Graphical Designer**

Name of the tool	Graphical Designer
Vendor	Advanced Software Technologies Inc.
Product website	
Cost	INA, a 30-day evaluation copy may be obtained from http://davinci2.csn.net/~jefscot/eval.html
Platforms supported	Windows 95, NT, Solaris, HP-UX, SGI
System requirements	INA
Product family	GDPro, GDDraw
Methodologies supported	Use Cases, UML, Booch, Shlaer/Mellor, OMT
Code generation	Yes
Languages	Java, C++, Smalltalk (planned)
Reverse engineering	Yes, for Java, C++, C, and Smalltalk (planned)
Document generation	Yes, in ASCII, HTML, and RTF
Multiuser support	Yes

Versioning support	INA
Prototyping	INA
Meta-CASE support	Yes
Annotations	Provides integration with many third party tools. With the use of "Graphical Designer Scripts," one may design custom integrations. The drawing tool GDDraw provides application specific palettes containing commonly found objects in the application domain.

2. Hardy

Name of the tool	Hardy
Vendor	Artificial Intelligence Application Institute (AIAI), University of Edinburgh, U.K., and funded by Hitachi Europe Limited.
Product website	www.aiai.ed.ac.uk/~hardy/
Cost	Hardy is available free of charge for academic use. Cost for commercial use may be negotiated with AIAI. The cost would be around £4000 and would usually involve training at AIAI.
Platforms supported	Sun OS (Openlook, Motif), Windows 3.1, NT, OS/2
System requirements	INA
Product family	None
Methodologies supported	NA, Hardy is a metaCASE tool
Code generation	Yes
Languages	INA
Reverse engineering	No
Document generation	INA
Multiuser support	INA
Versioning support	No
Prototyping	No
Meta-CASE support	Yes
Annotations	Hardy is a customizable, hypertext-based diagramming tool developed by AIAI. It is integrated with NASA's rule-based object-oriented language CLIPS 6.0, enabling users to develop object-oriented applications. It can support any methodology, making it a metaCASE tool.

3. IPSYS ToolBuilder

Name of the tool	IPSYS ToolBuilder
Vendor	Lincoln Software
Product website	www.ipsys.com/tb.htm
Cost	INA
Platforms supported	Sun SPARC under Solaris 2 or SunOS 4, HP 9000/700 series under HPUX-9/UX-10 IBM RS/6000 under AIX 3
System requirements	
Product family	IPSYS TBK — ToolBuilder Kit, IPSYS TOOL FRAGMENTS, IPSYS ToolBuilder, IPSYS HOOD, IPSYS ENGINEER, IPSYS SSADM, IPSYS OMT
Methodologies supported	NA, IPSYS ToolBuilder is a metaCASE tool
Code generation	Yes
Languages	INA
Reverse engineering	No
Document generation	Yes
Multiuser support	Yes
Versioning support	Yes
Prototyping	Yes

Meta-CASE support	Yes
Annotations	IPSYS ToolBuilder from Lincoln Software is a metaCASE tool that may be used to build CASE tools. The ToolBuilder may be purchased as part of a family of tools which includes IPSYS HOOD, and IPSYS OMT CASE tools. Universities may get a discount up to 95% on these toolsets.

4. MetaEdit

Name of the tool	MetaEdit
Vendor	INA
Product website	www.jsp.fi/metacase
Cost	INA
Platforms supported	Windows 3.1 or later
System requirements	PC with at least a 386 processor and 4 MB main memory, EGA graphics adapter and display (VGA or better recommended), a mouse or pointing device, 2 MB free mass storage for the software
Product family	None
Methodologies supported	Offers a flexible framework which can incorporate any methodology
Code generation	Yes
Languages	INA
Reverse engineering	Yes
Document generation	Yes
Multiuser support	INA
Versioning support	Yes
Prototyping	INA
Meta-CASE support	Yes
Annotations	It provides a set of integrated methods by which the impact of changes in business practices on the supporting software systems can be monitored and analyzed. Consistency between business processes and system descriptions is maintained and enforced via the MetaEdit object repository.

5. Metaview

Name of the tool	Metaview
Vendor	Software Engineering Research group, University of Alberta, Canada
Product website	web.cs.ualberta.ca/softeng/Metaview/system/system.html
Cost	Freeware
Platforms supported	SunOS 4.1.x, SunOS 5.3 and 5.4 (Solaris), AIX 3.2.5 and 4.1
System requirements	X11 version 5 or later with motif: SICStus prolog version 2.1 (SICStus Prolog is available from www.sics.se)
Product family	None
Methodologies supported	NA
Code generation	INA
Languages	INA
Reverse engineering	INA
Document generation	INA
Multiuser support	INA
Versioning support	Yes
Prototyping	INA
Meta-CASE support	Yes
Annotations	Provides support for a generic repository; different software specifications and software development methods; graphical and conceptual views of the models; support for transformation from one model or method to another.

6. Object Maker

Name of the tool	Object Maker
Vendor	Mark V Systems Limited
Product website	www.markv.com/products.html
Cost	INA, an evaluation copy may be obtained from ftp://ftp.markv.com/pub/ObjectMaker
Platforms supported	INA
System requirements	INA
Product family	Object Maker TDK, Method Maker
Methodologies supported	Supports more than 30 notations
Code generation	Yes
Languages	INA
Reverse engineering	Yes
Document generation	Yes
Multiuser support	INA
Versioning support	Yes
Prototyping	INA
Meta-CASE support	Yes
Annotations	Supports more than 30 different notations. Allows the user to intermix notations inside a single project. Allows for customized notations, syntax rules, methods, syntax checking, semantic specification, and repository capture of all semantics, and other information and relationships important to the process and problem space.

7. Object Engineering Workbench (OEW)

Name of the tool	OEW
Vendor	Innovative Software GmbH
Product website	www.isg.de/OEW
Cost	INA, a small project version of OEW may be downloaded from http://www.isg.de/OEW/freedown.htm
Platforms supported	Windows, Windows NT, and OS/2; SUN Solaris 2.4 and HP-UX 10.0 releases are in beta-testing
System requirements	PC (486 or higher), 8 MB main memory, 10 MB disk space, 800*600 resolution monitor
Product family	None
Methodologies supported	Uses Martin/Odell notation, but is method independent
Code generation	
Languages	C++
Reverse engineering	Yes
Document generation	Yes, documents may be exported to RTF
Multiuser support	Yes
Versioning support	Yes
Prototyping	INA
Meta-CASE support	Some
Annotations	Caters mainly to development in C++. Supported compilers — Microsoft Visual C++, Borland BC++, Watcom C++, Metaware C++, Symantec C++, GNU C++, SUN C++, AT&T C++, and CenterLine C++. Also handles database schemes for ObjectStore and POET. Can integrate with any tool producing C++, RTF, or Clipboard. Interfaces with existing class libraries such as StarView, STL, MFC, OWL, Zinc, XVT, zApp, Open

	Interface, TurboVision, Rogue Wave, etc. Entity Relationship models from mainframe CASE tools like IEW and ADW are accepted by OEW.

8. Paradigm Plus

Name of the tool	Paradigm Plus
Vendor	Platinum Technology Inc.
Product website	www.platinum.com/clearlake
Cost	INA
Platforms supported	Windows NT, Windows 95, OS/2, Sun OS, Sun Solaris, HP-UX, AIX, IRIX; Databases Supported: DB2 for AIX, Informix, Microsoft SQL Server, ObjectStore, Oracle, OSMOS, Sybase, UniSQL Server, Versant
System requirements	40 MB hard disk space, 16 MB RAM (24 MB recommended), 80 MB of hard disk space, 24 MB RAM (32 MB recommended)
Product family	None
Methodologies supported	
Code generation	Yes
Languages	Ada, Borland C++, Delphi, Forte, Java, Persistence, PowerBuilder, Visual Age, Visual Basic, Visual C++, Visual J++, and VisualSmalltalk Enterprise
Reverse engineering	Yes
Document generation	Yes
Multiuser support	INA
Versioning support	Yes
Prototyping	INA
Meta-CASE support	Yes
Annotations	Provides an integrated view of object modeling, business process modeling, and object modeling. Supports Rapid Application Development. Supports Enterprise wide Component Modeling (ECM). Supports sharing of components via Paradigm plus repository and the World Wide Web.

9. Pragmatic

Name of the tool	Pragmatica
Vendor	Pragmatix Software Private Limited
Product website	www.novanet.net.au/~pragma/
Cost	INA, a shareware version is available
Platforms supported	Windows 95 or Windows NT4
System requirements	At least 8MB of RAM, at least 2MB of free disk space, download binary size is 1.04MB
Product family	None
Methodologies supported	NA, Pragmatica is a metaCASE tool
Code generation	Yes
Languages	C++
Reverse engineering	No
Document generation	Yes, available in RTF format
Multiuser support	INA
Versioning support	INA
Prototyping	No
Meta-CASE support	Yes
Annotations	User is allowed to create custom notations and change existing drawings to custom notations. Also arbitrary or informal drawings may be integrated into formal drawings. The software comes with a set of templates for some of the popular OOAD notations.

54.3.6 Model Bridges

A single CASE tool often cannot cater to needs all along the lifecycle of a project. Moreover, as CASE tools evolve or are upgraded with newer tools, they should be able to process all the data that were stored earlier without having to regenerate them. Similarly, data may have to be exchanged across different parts of an organization, each of which potentially use different methodologies and notations.

Such problems call for a standard for data interchange and representation. There has been some activity regarding standardization of CASE data and tools supporting these standards. Some of the standards organizations are CASE Data Interchange Format (CDIF), Portable Common Tool Environment (PCTE), Object Management Group (OMG), Information Resource Dictionary Standard (IRDS), etc.

Here, we provide a list of some of the tools which act as model bridges by providing support for one or more of the standards. The list of model bridges follow.

1. EXCHANGE

Name of the tool	EXCHANGE
Vendor	Software One, Inc.
Product website	www.software1.com/front.html
Cost	INA
Annotation	EXCHANGE is a meta-data interoperability too. It supports many CASE tools, dictionaries, and repositories. It operates on the export file created by the CASE tools. Of the many interfaces that it supports, CDIF is one of them. A list of all the supported interfaces may be obtained from http://www.software1.com/interfaces.html.

2. Jack

Name of the tool	Jack (Johannes' Adaptable CDIF Interface)
Vendor	Johannes Ernst
Product website	ftp://ftp.cdif.org/cdif/sw/Jack.tar.gz
Cost	Free for noncommercial uses
Annotation	Jack is a freeware tool which converts a given metamodel into a CDIF compliant metamodel. The user has to specify the metamodel and Jack converts it to support CDIF interfaces. However, a CDIF file describing the metamodel has to be sent to jernst@io.org, to obtain an interface header file called ci-objects.h, which has to be used to compile and generate the interface model. Presently, the main program does not do anything else other than writing the CDIF file to stdout. This method has to be changed to make the tool perform whatever is intended. Jack was originally written on a Macintosh using Metroworks CodeWarrior product. It now also supports Linux running gcc.

3. Mesa/Vista

Name of the tool	Mesa/Vista
Vendor	Mesa Systems Guild, Inc.
Product website	www.mesasys.com/vista/index.html
Cost	INA
Annotation	Mesa/Vista is an integrated process management tool which provides a flexible framework that can be tailored to support any system development process and any legacy project data. It provides support for project tracking and workflow management independent of any particular tool or process. Some of the other features it provides are perspective data filtering, multi-level security, consistent user interface for all data, event logging, plug-in modules, etc. It supports the CDIF interface standard.

4. ModelMart

Name of the tool	ModelMart
Vendor	Logic Works, Inc.
Product website	www.logicworks.com
Cost	INA
Annotation	ModelMart, from Logic Works is a mediator tool that mediates between models that are stored, enabling them to be shared across the enterprise. It works with the Logic Works ERwin tool, and is platform and network independent. The ERwin tool itself has a bidirectional support for the CDIF standard. This support is available through an add-in utility for ERwin that is available free of charge for currently licensed Logic Works customers. The utility is available for ERwin 2.5 and 2.6 and runs on Windows 95 and NT.

54.4 Conclusions

CASE support for OOAD is still an emerging field. This field is characterized by multiple methodologies and inexactly defined support. There have been efforts to improve the usage of OOAD case in the industry in the form of standardization of methodologies. However, it is debatable whether the area is ripe enough for one standard methodology. There is also a trend toward meta-level frameworks and standardization of CASE tool interfaces. Commercial support has just started for meta-CASE and interface standards. CASE tools for OOAD leave a number of issues open and it only remains to be seen which standards prevail.

References

Antonakopoulos, T., Agavanakis, K. and Makios, V. 1995. CASE tools evaluation: An automatic process based on fuzzy sets theory, *Proc. of the 6th IEEE Int. Workshop on Rapid System Prototyping*, 6, 140.

Assets in Domain: Object-Oriented Software Development. Available online at http://www.asset.com/WSRD/indices/domains/OBJECT_ORIENTED_SOFTWARE_DEVELOPMENT.html

Booch, G.E. 1994. *Object-Oriented Analysis and Design.* Benjamin/Cummins, Menlo Park, CA.

CDIF. 1997. *CASE Data Interchange Format.* Available online at http://www.cdif.org/

Cetus Links. 1997. *Object-Orientation.* Available online at http://www.objenv.com/cetus/

Coad, P. and Yourdon, E. 1990. *Object-Oriented Analysis.* Prentice-Hall, Englewood Cliffs, NJ.

Coleman, D., Arnold, P., Bodoff, S., Dollin, C., Gilchrist, H., Hayes, F., and Jeremes, P. 1994. *Object-Oriented Development: The Fusion Method.* Prentice-Hall, Englewood Cliffs, NJ.

Fowler, M. 1997. *A Survey of Object-Oriented Analysis and Design Techniques.* Available online at http://www.awl.com/cp/fowlerindex.htm

Goldberg, A. and Rubin, K.S. 1995. *Succeeding with Objects, Design Frameworks for Project Management.* Addison-Wesley, Reading, MA.

Huff, C.C. 1992. Elements of a realistic CASE tool adoption budget, *Commun. ACM,* 4, 45.

Iivari, J. 1996. Why are CASE tools not used?, *Commun. ACM,* 10, 94.

IRDS. 1997. *Information Resource Dictionary Standards.* Available online at http://www.irds.org

Kelly, S. 1997. *CASE Tools and Manufacturers.* Available online at http://www.jyu.fi/~kelly/meta/caselist.html

Kemerer, C.F. 1992. How the learning curve affects CASE tool adoption, *IEEE Software,* 3, 23.

Lamb, D.A. 1997. *CASE Tool Information.* Available online at http://www.qucis.queensu.ca/Software-Engineering/case.html

Metadata Coalition. 1997. *Metadata Coalition: For Metadata Interchange.* Available online at http://www.he.net/~metadata/

Object Management Group. 1997. Available online at http://www.omg.org

PCTE. 1996. *Portable Common Tool Environment.* Available online at http://www.dkuug.dk/JTC1/SC22/WG22/

Rumbaugh, J., Blaha, M., Premerlani, W., Eddy, F. and Lorenson, W. 1991. *Object-Oriented Modelling and Design.* Prentice-Hall International, Inc.

Scacchi, W. 1997. The USC ATRIUM Laboratory home page. Available online at http://www.usc.edu/dept/ATRIUM/index.html

Shlaer, S. and Mellor, M. 1993. *The Shlaer Mellor Method.* Available online at http://www.proj-tech.com/smmethod/smmethod.html

Software Engineering Institute. 1997. *Computer-Aided Software Engineering (CASE) Environments.* Available online at http://www.sei.cmu.edu/~case/

Strobart, S. 1997. The CASE tool home page. Available online at http://osiris.sunderland.ac.uk/ca1akh/case2/welcome.html

Van de Stadt, R. 1997. *Object-Oriented Methodologies.* Available online at http://www_trese.cs.utwente.nl/Docs/Methodologies/methodologies.html

Vessey, I., Jarvenpaa, S. L. and Tractinsky, N. 1992. Evaluation of vendor products: CASE tools as methodology companions, *Commun. ACM*, 4, 90.

55

Object–Oriented Modeling Tools

Boumediene Belkhouche
Tulane University

55.1 Introduction

In this chapter, we seek to establish a general framework for discussing modeling tools, rather than addressing the details of specific methods. This we do to avoid being overwhelmed by the sheer number and diversity of available methods. By establishing a basis of core concepts, we hope the reader is spared the idiosyncrasies of specific methods and can concentrate more effectively on the essence of OO modeling. Given that most major methods are introduced elsewhere in this handbook, no attempt is made here at being inclusive in the selection of illustrative examples.

The field of OO analysis and design is relatively young and is still unstable. The proliferation of development methodologies continues at a vigorous rate. No less than fifty methods (and probably many more) are being advocated, and the growth shows no sign of stability [13, 15, 16]. In fact, competing proposals are made regularly. This shows that no agreement is in sight yet. The field is rapidly evolving as evident by the recent and continuous proliferation of numerous OO development methodologies as well as the refinement of existing ones. A survey of the field suggests that the following issues remain to be addressed:

- *Lack of standard concepts* — All the OO development methodologies are based on similar overall concepts, but each of them has its own variations and interpretations. This introduces the possibility of misunderstanding. A set of common OO concepts may be needed to unify the field.
- *Lack of standard model* — Most OO methodologies are divided into a structural view, a behavioral view, and an architectural view. Except for the structural view, a consensus is yet to be reached.

0-8493-3135-8/99/$0.00+$.50

- *Development process* — While most OO methodologists would agree that an iterative and/or recursive development cycle is preferable for OO projects, the OO development lifecycle has yet to reach the stability comparable to other paradigms.
- *Formality* — OO introduced the notion of a single model type across the entire lifecycle. This opened the door for validations in earlier stages. Formality is desirable for its rigor. All the popular OO methods are informal, and formal approaches remain minimal [11].
- *Object orientation vs. component software* — The emerging field of software architecture raises the question of OO vs. component software, fueled by OO's failure to reach its predicted benefit of reusability. Component software are units that can be composed to form a system. Whether component software is a different approach or can be incorporated into OO still remains to be seen [19].

The discussion is structured as follows. In the rest of this section, we introduce general ideas associated with modeling in general, and OO modeling in particular. To this effect, we develop an abstract view of OO modeling and an OO metamodel. This foundation is used subsequently to address OO modeling issues. In Section 55.2, we identify and describe OO modeling principles and concepts. In Section 55.3, we present a general overview, and describe existing modeling constructs and tools for structural specifications. We also discuss the types of models generated. In Section 55.4, we describe modeling tools for the specification of OO behavior.

55.1.1 Role of Modeling

Depending on the area of interest, the term "model" may carry with it a specific meaning. In software development, it is used to mean an abstract representation of an entity, real or artificial. As such, the function of the software model is to describe the entity's *essential properties* at some desirable level of detail. It involves the construction of a structured representation of the subject being modeled. Hence, a model of an entity can be viewed as a representative instantiation that captures characteristics deemed relevant from a given perspective.

55.1.2 Models

Models are used as a basis for understanding and for communicating this understanding. They are also used for evaluation, negotiation, and further refinement. Consequently, models must be expressive, precise, and comprehensible. The nature and the expression of the descriptive properties vary according to the particular software development stage. Thus, at earlier stages (e.g., domain–related), the properties tend to be abstract and implementation–independent, whereas they tend to become constructive and operational near the implementation stage. These multi–level, stage specific descriptions entail the elaboration of at least three successive models [10]: (1) an essential model describing the problem domain, and ideally being a faithful map of the real–world situation under consideration; (2) a specification model describing the form and function of the model; and (3) an implementation model describing the data structures and the operational behavior of the model. On another dimension, interesting properties cover structural, behavioral, and architectural features leading to a comprehensive visualization of the system (see Figure 55.1).

In OO modeling, the typical approach is to use a number of different perspectives (views) complementing one another. Each perspective provides a different functionality of the system. The most common approach is to provide three distinct views of the system: the structural (static), the behavioral (dynamic), and the architectural. Conceptually, commonalities in most of the OO modeling methods are more prevalent than differences. However, there is a lack of a generic model, a shared understanding of the basic concepts, and a common vocabulary for discussing object–orientation. To address these issues, an abstract OO model was developed by [3]. This abstract OO model is a synthesis of several popular OO meth-

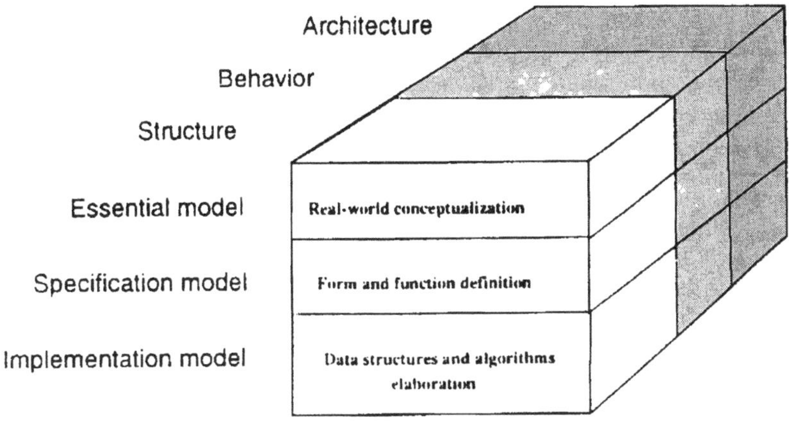

FIGURE 55.1 OO modeling dimensions.

ods [6, 13, 15]. It serves as a basis for understanding the fundamental OO framework. Figure 55.2 shows the components of the abstract OO model.

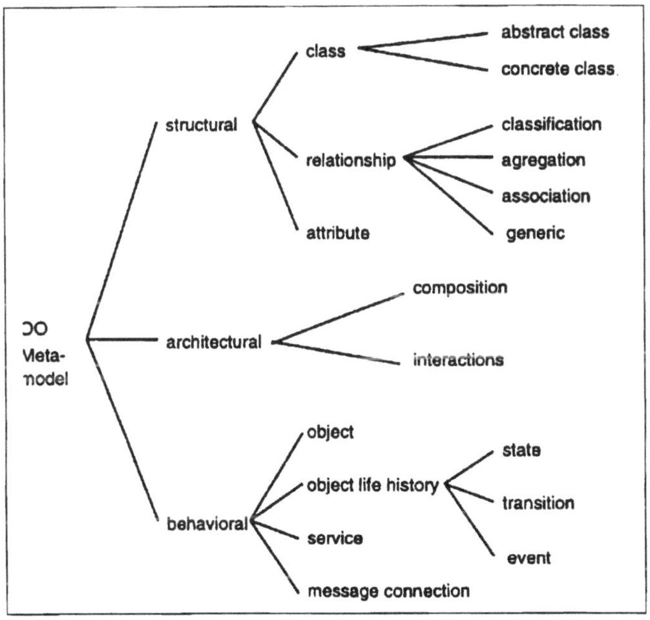

FIGURE 55.2 OO modeling metamodel.

55.1.2.1 Structural Model

The structural model captures the static structure of the problem domain. This is carried out by describing the classes and their relationships. Some common techniques used for structural view modeling include various class diagrams, object diagrams, and entity–relationship diagrams. The techniques used in structural modeling are well developed. The many different OO methodologies use essentially the same basic technique with some variations on concepts, notations, and namings. For example, the different dialects of the entity–relationship diagram are employed in many different methodologies. Even though variations exist in structural modeling across different methodologies, a unanimous pattern is beginning to emerge to the point where standardization efforts are being advocated [20]. Most OO methodologies provide constructs to express the static properties of a system such as classes, attributes, operations, relationships, inheritance, and composition [3]. The differences are relatively small and largely notational in richness. Almost all static models have, in one form or another, the concept of class, object, attribute, service, generalization/specialization relationship, whole/part relationship, and associations.

55.1.2.2 Behaviorial Model

The behaviorial model is intended to capture the dynamic aspects of the problem domain. It describes object behaviors and collaborations as they progress through time. Behavioral view modeling is commonly described by state transition charts, flow charts, timing diagrams, interaction diagrams, and event diagrams. Relatively speaking, the behavioral view is not as well developed as the static view. The unanimity that exists in describing the structure of a system is absent when it comes time to describe the behavior. The differences of concept and emphasis in behavior modeling techniques across different OO methodologies are greater than that of the structural view.

55.1.2.3 Architectural Model

It serves as a mechanism for aggregating groups of objects into higher levels of abstraction. A group contains a collection of distinct and discrete, but fairly cohesive classes according to some grouping criteria. The architectural view is aimed at decomposing a large system into manageable units. Some commonly used techniques for architectural view modeling include object decomposition, data flow diagrams, and functional decomposition. Sometimes the architectural decomposition is embedded within the structural and behavior model by providing mechanisms for architectural decomposition within the structural and/or behavior model. Some methods have separate architectural models while others incorporate them into the static and behavior models.

55.1.3 Characteristics of OO Modeling

While traditional software development approaches emphasize a hierarchical organization based on functionality, OO approaches use the concept of objects as the unit of organization, refinement through extensions as development process, and continuity between successive models. Consequently, the main task in OO is concentrated on the construction of a model of the problem domain, rather than software implementation. Its central theme is the process of discovering classes, objects, attributes, and operations, as well as the relationships among classes. Because of the need to capture structural, behavior, and architectural aspects, the prevailing trend in OO is a multi–model approach that employs different models to illustrate different aspects of the problem.

Typically, some descriptive medium is used to create a "picture" of a model, i.e., to specify it. Graphical notations and textual languages are the most commonly used media. The more expressive the notation is, the more profound the model properties. Expressiveness, as well as its formality, impacts the complexity and range of possible representational features as well as the analyses that can be performed on the model. Expressive models facilitate the understanding and the examination of what is to be constructed. As a communication and negotiation medium between analysts and customers, model construction is a critical component in the refinement of the specifications. Model validation and evaluation can be performed directly on the specification.

To develop a faithful model, the requirements must be understood in a fashion that is precise, unambiguous, explicit, and complete. Because requirements are often stated in informal languages, modeling tools that facilitate the expression of coherent of properties are needed. In general, no single technique can completely capture the problem domain. Thus, most methodologies employ *multiple views* by providing several perspective-based models. Regardless, modeling techniques must be able to produce specifications to form a solid foundation for design and implementation.

OO modeling uses the same conceptual model across analysis, design, and implementation. The line between analysis and design is blurred and even intertwined in some OO methodologies. The use of a single conceptual model across the entire development cycle results in smooth transition between the different phases. This smooth transition is sometimes referred to as a "seamless architecture" [24]. The single model approach across the entire software lifecycle promotes development continuity, early verification, and requirements tracing.

55.2 An Abstract OO Modeling Framework

As stated earlier, the diversity in the terminology and symbology makes an all-inclusive discussion of the fundamental OO modeling concepts tedious. To facilitate the task, a synthesis is presented here to relieve the reader from the peculiarities of each of the methods. Figures 55.2 and 55.3 will be used to describe OO modeling.

55.2.1 Principles

Four major principles underlie OO modeling: abstraction, encapsulation, polymorphism, and inheritance. Although not specific to OO modeling, *abstraction* is a key principle. It denotes the capability of capturing the essential properties of an entity without undue details. In a certain sense, abstraction allows the filtering of details not immediately necessary. Related to abstraction is the notion of *encapsulation*, which is defined as the hiding of implementation details. Encapsulation requires the packaging of the entity into one impermeable unit. An encapsulated entity can only be manipulated through a well-defined interface. In type theory, *polymorphism* means that an entity can assume many forms. In OO modeling, there are two kinds of polymorphisms: inclusion polymorphism and parametric polymorphism. Inclusion polymorphisms are based on the notion of subclassing, that is, objects having the type of a subclass have also the type of the superclass. Parametric polymorphism is supported by classes that are parameterized, that is, classes whose parameters may be type variables. Classification introduces a hierarchical taxonomy whereby elements high in the hierarchy are viewed (anthropomorphically) as ancestors (superclass) and lower elements are descendants (subclass). Thus, an *inheritance* relation is established among these elements. A subclass inherits properties from its superclass(es).

55.2.2 Concepts

The basic concepts in OO modeling are: classes and objects, relationships, interaction, and composition.

Classes and objects — Classification is a basic strategy of conceptual organization. The concept of a *class* is introduced to support this strategy. In OO modeling, classes are used as the unit of modularity to support the four major principles. A class is an abstract collection of objects that share some common properties. The concept of an *object* has been associated with various meanings, each of which is trying to justify the existence and superiority of object-orientation. Typically, these definitions identify real-world objects with object constructs in an attempt to demonstrate the "naturalness" of objects and their intrinsic fidelity in representing reality. For our purposes, an object is a structure that encapsulates both data and processes, and interacts with its environment through a well-defined interface. Objects are derived from classes through typing and instantiation. Thus, a class serves as a type which is then used to define objects (instances) of the class. Objects belonging to the same class share the same properties, behavior semantics, and relationships. The structure of a class consists of the class name, class attributes, and class operations.

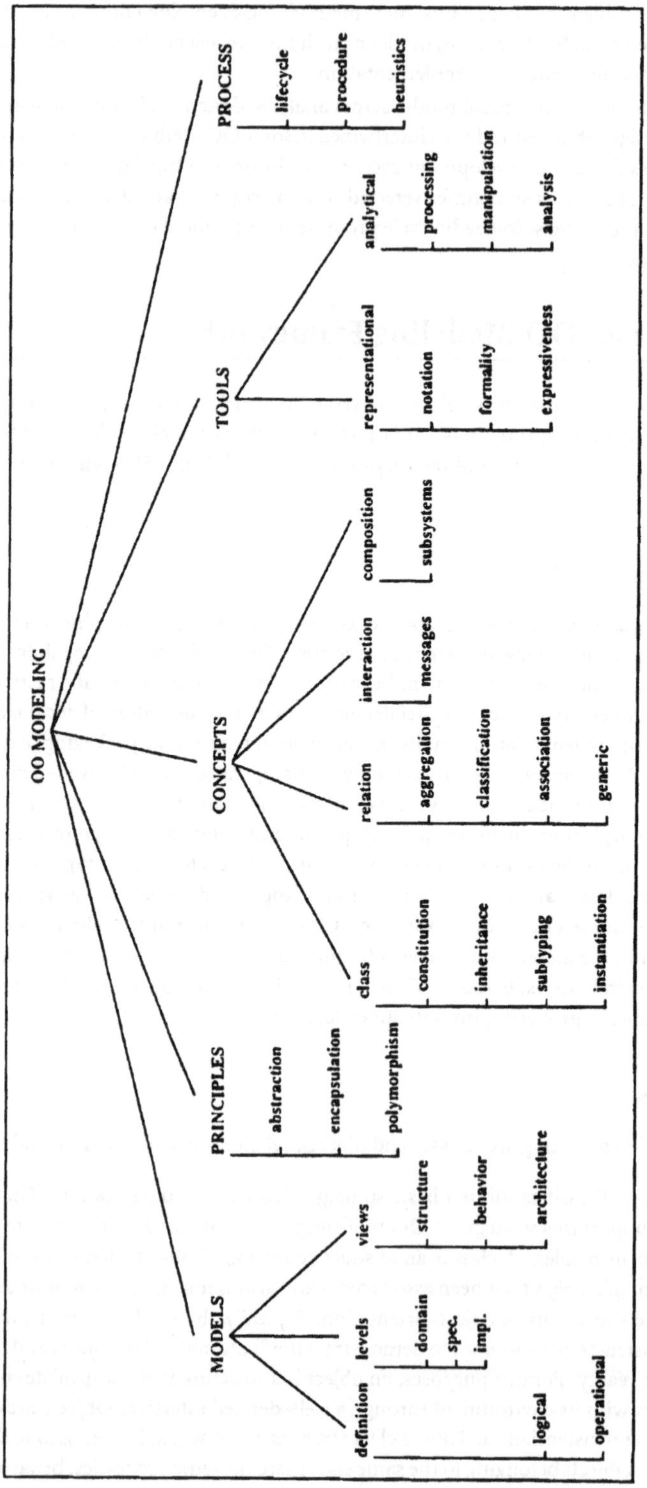

FIGURE 55.3 OO modeling.

The class name is used to uniquely identify the class. Attributes are the data elements encapsulated within the class and forming the state information associated with a class. Operations consist of functions and procedures that update, maintain, and convey information about the state of the class.

Relationships — Simply viewed, relationships are mathematical relations among sets of classes and objects. As such, they capture associations that may exit among objects. Besides their semantics, relationships have cardinalities which assume various values, such as optional, mandatory, one–to–one, one–to-many, many–to–one, many–to–many, and possibly other combinations. The following relationships are common:

- Classification (generalization–specialization) relationship — This relationship is used to describe the inheritance association between superclasses and subclasses. An example of such a relationship is that of a cat (subclass) and a feline (superclass).
- Aggregation (whole–part) relationship — This relationship is used to describe an aggregate class which is formed from a number of component classes. The component classes are parts of the aggregate class. An example of such a relationship is that of a bicycle (whole) and its wheels (parts).
- Instantiation relationship — This relationship refers to the case where a class is instantiated to create a specific object. An example of such a relationship is that of the class professor (type) and its instantiated object Professor Smith (instance).
- Association relationship — This relationship captures a general relation whose semantics is problem domain dependent. An example of such a relationship is that of employee vs. an employer and vice versa.

Interaction — Objects in an OO model interact and cooperate among themselves through the *message passing* paradigm. Two interacting objects, one a client and the other a server, exchange messages. Typically, the client sends a message to the server requesting a service. Upon receipt of the message, the service invokes the corresponding operation(s) to fulfill its task.

Composition — Software development in–the–large requires the integration of subsystems into larger ones. The principle of composition/decomposition has been used to support the formation of wholes from parts. In OO modeling, objects are viewed as a basic unit of composition. The architectural view is intended to model system composition.

55.2.3 Tools

The outcome of the conceptualization process needs to be expressed in some form. Representational tools are used to capture such an expression. The resulting expression is termed a specification of the model. Subsequently, analysis tools are applied to the specification to gain confidence in the model and to assert its properties.

Representational tools — The use of various diagrams is prevalent for the representation of OO models. The diversity of the diagrams is quite apparent, even though one can reduce them to some dialect of the ER notation. There are two types of notations used: graphical and textual. The graphical notation is dominant. It can be described as a graph consisting of nodes and arcs. Nodes of different shapes and forms represent mostly classes/objects, states, and systems. Arcs also come in different shapes and forms. They are mostly used to represent relationships. Constraints and cardinalities decorate arcs to associate semantics with arcs. Textual notation is used to augment the graphical one, and is incorporated within nodes and along arcs. The notation spectrum varies from a few symbols in some methods to a very large number in others. At the same time, except for a few timid attempts at providing some formality, the general trend favors informal definitions or definitions by examples. Two issues arise here: (1) the appropriate type and number of constructs needed to support OO modeling and (2) the formality of the notation. A third issue is the expressiveness of the notation. Even though this notion is well defined for formal languages, it is unclear how the OO modeling community is apprehending expressiveness and other linguistic issues. From recent proposals [2, 9, 10, 12, 20], there seems to be a rush into integrating what is the "best" of other methods. This strongly resembles the PL/1 approach. The field is still struggling with competing proposals. Section 55.3 provides a detailed description of the OO modeling tools.

Analysis tools — As an aid to the OO modeling process, analysis tools are needed to assess and help improve the quality of models. These tools are usually integrated in CASE environments (described in another chapter). Analysis tools are used to perform syntactic and semantic checking, testing, consistency and completeness checking, simulation, and other tasks.

55.3 Object-Oriented Modeling Tools

Models are used to express information. Modeling languages, whether graphical or textual, provide ways of expressing the models. The language serves as a mechanism to capture, abstract, and simplify the properties that are relevant to the system. Textual and graphical languages are the major form of OO modeling tools. They provide constructs to capture concepts, syntax, and semantics of OO models. A formal definition of the syntax of an OO model is shown in Table 55.1. This syntax provides an abstract framework that is instantiated differently by each of the methods.

TABLE 55.1 OO Model Syntax

OO_model	⟶	set_of_models
set_of_model	⟶	model | model set_of_models
model	⟶	classes relationships behavior
classes	⟶	class | class classes
class	⟶	class_id
		class_attributes
		class_operations
relationships	⟶	whole_part_relationship
	|	gen_spec_relationship
	|	instance_relationship
	|	association_relationship
behavior	⟶	state_transitions
	|	state_charts
	|	events
	|	csp_subsets

55.3.1 State-of-the-Art OO Modeling Tools

OO methodologies are approaches that incorporate a set of techniques, notations, and processes to facilitate the development of object-oriented systems. The proliferation and the sheer number of OO methodologies does not allow us to cover them all. The choice of just a few is not indicative of the merits, or lack thereof, of one over the others. We will cover Booch's object-oriented analysis and design [5], Coad and Yourdon's object-oriented analysis [7], Rumbaugh's OMT [21], Jacobson's object-oriented software engineering (OOSE); [17], Shlaer and Mellor's OOA/OODLE method [22, 23], Martin and Odell's object-oriented analysis and design [18], and the Fusion method [9]. In addition, UML [20], a new synthesis effort, will be discussed briefly. The survey is concentrated mostly on modeling tools support by each of the methodologies. The discussion is organized in the following fashion: (1) a general overview of the methodology; (2) the model(s) used to capture the system; and (3) the notation provided to describe the model.

55.3.1.1 General Overview

Booch's OO approach is one of the more popular OO methodologies [5]. The Booch method is an integrated approach that spans the analysis and design phases. Some implementation design is involved by allocating classes and objects to modules and processes to processors. No clear separation between analysis and design can be drawn. This is a multi–model approach with an iterative development process supported by a rich set of notations. The final product of this procedure is used directly for implementation. Booch bases his OO development method on the object–oriented conceptual framework that he describes as containing four major and three minor elements. These concepts are fairly standard OO concepts. The seven elements are abstraction, encapsulation, modularity, hierarchy, typing, concurrency, and persistence. Booch defines an object as having three characteristics: state, behavior, and identity. Relationships that exist between objects are either links denoting a client/server relationship, or aggregation denoting a whole/part hierarchy. A class is a set of objects that share a common structure and a common behavior. There are three basic kinds of relationships for classes: generalization/specialization, whole/part, and association. An association is defined as a semantic dependency. These three basic kinds of relationships can be further elaborated into six kinds of class hierarchies that may be directly supported by OO programming languages for implementation, and they include: association, inheritance, aggregation, using, instantiation, and metaclass.

Coad and Yourdon's modeling is part of comprehensive approach to object–oriented analysis, design, and programming [7, 8]. This is a comparatively simple method in terms of notation and documentation. It is based on one single multilayer model. Coad and Yourdon claim that their approach is a synthesis of three disciplines that have a solid basis in underlying principles for managing complexity: information modeling, object–oriented programming languages, and knowledge–based systems. From information modeling comes constructs analogous to attributes, instance connections, generalization–specialization, and whole-part. From object–oriented programming languages and knowledge–based systems come the encapsulation of attributes and exclusive services, communication with messages, generalization/specialization, and inheritance. Coad and Yourdon define several principles for managing complexity that form the foundations for their OO modeling concepts: (1) abstraction (procedural and data); (2) encapsulation; (3) inheritance; (4) association; (5) communication with messages; (6) pervading methods of organization (objects and attributes, whole and parts, classes and members); (7) scale; and (8) categories of behavior (immediate causation, change over time, similarity of functions).

Rumbaugh's OMT (Object Modeling Technique) is consistently praised as one of the most widely used object–oriented methods. It was developed at General Electric Research by Rumbaugh and his colleagues [21]. The method consists of several phases spanning the analysis–implementation stages. It includes: (1) an object analysis phase in which an object model is built; (2) a system design phase in which the architecture of the system is devised; (3) an object design phase in which the software model is realized; and (4) an implementation phase in which code is written. The notation used in each of the phases is quite rich and complex.

Jacobson's OOSE (Object-Oriented Software Engineering) is based on his commercial Objectory software development system. It is a result of his experience building large telecommunication switching systems using the concepts of signals and blocks. The basis for his OO modeling approach is the techniques of object-oriented programming, conceptual modeling, and block design. This is a comprehensive methodology encompassing the software lifecycle from analysis through testing. The development process revolves around the modeling and transformation of the models. One important characteristic of Jacobson's method is the notion of what he calls a use case, which is defined as a behaviorally related sequence of transactions performed by a user when interacting with the system.

The Fusion method was developed at Hewlett–Packard as a coherent and comprehensive approach to object–oriented software development across analysis, design, and implementation. This is a second–generation method developed by integrating and extending existing approaches including Booch, OMT, and CRC. The authors of Fusion choose the extended entity–relationship diagram as their notation for describing object structure. All the ER concepts are present in Fusion. Similarly to Fusion, Syntropy [10] is also a synthesis of earlier methods with the addition of concepts from the specification language Z to fully formalize the notation.

The object–oriented analysis and design method by James Martin and James Odell is based on information engineering and the Ptech method. Their book [18] exhibits a strong tie to the theoretical aspects of OO with a formal description and strong semantics correspondence to a set of well–defined OO concepts. This method spans the analysis and design phase with a distinction on the structural and behavior aspects. A set of diagramming notations is suggested but no process is given. Martin and Odell define five concepts as the fundamental ideas that underlie object–oriented technology: objects and classes, methods, requests, inheritance, and encapsulation.

Shlaer and Mellor developed the object-oriented analysis/recursive design method in several stages. In their initial method [22], they adapted the relational model as their basic development model. Subsequently, they refined this model to include more object–orientation concepts [23]. As part of their strategy, they advocate the notion of recursive design to develop software systems. The method emphasizes data modeling using relational theory, state modeling using state transitions, and process modeling using an action dataflow diagram formalism. Formal translation of each of the models into other forms is also supported.

The Unified Modeling Language (UML) is a recent effort at Rational to integrate state-of-the-art OO analysis and design into a comprehensive and coherent method [20]. Basically, UML is a synthesis of the Booch, Rumbaugh, and Jacobson methods. Thus, as far as the notation is concerned, it is derived, with enhancements, from these three approaches.

55.3.1.2 Models

Booch Model — Booch's model for object–oriented development is an elaborated multiview model that consists of logical and physical view on the static and dynamic semantics of the system. The following models are used throughout the analysis and design phases:

- *Logical model* — The logical perspective on the problem domain; it captures the problem domain without regard to implementation. This involves the class and object
- *Physical model* — The physical perspective on the actual software and hardware design and implementation of the system; this involves the module and process architecture
- *Static model* — Perspective on the static structure of the system; primarily depicts the class, object, module, and process structure
- *Dynamic model* — Perspective on the dynamic behavior of the system; primarily involves the state and state transition as well as object interactions

Coad/Yourdon Model — Coad and Yourdon's OOA model is a single multilayer model consisting of five overlapping layers. Each layer gradually presents more and more detail. The term class–&–object is defined by Coad and Yourdon meaning "a class and the objects in that class." The layers are as follows:

- Subject layer identifies groupings of related classes for complexity control.
- Class–&–Object layer shows the classes and objects.

- Structure layer shows the generalization/specialization (inheritance) and whole-part structure between classes and objects.
- Attribute layer shows the attribute of objects and its connections with other objects.
- Service layer shows services for an object and the messages it sends to request services from other objects.

OMT Model — Three models are generated in the analysis phase: (1) the object model which describes the structure of the model; (2) the dynamic model which describes the behavior of the model; and (3) the functional model which describes the functionality of the operations. Further modeling is carried out during the system design phase and the object design phase in order to organize the overall system into subsystems and to implement it.

OOSE Model — This methodology is based on model building and the transformation of models from one to the other. Jacobson introduced five different models to be used at different stages in the entire OOSE process. All five models are based on a use-case model [17]. The analysis stage consists of the requirements model and the analysis model aimed at understanding the system to be developed and building a logical model of the system.

Requirements Model — Derived from the requirement specification to capture the functional requirements of the system. This model completely defines the functional requirements of the system from a user's perspective. The requirements model uses actors and use cases to describe in detail each and every way of using the system from a user's perspective. Actors model external entities that interact with the system, while a use case is "a specific way of using the system by using some part of the functionality" [17]. The requirements model is composed of three models:

1. A use case model defined by actors and use cases. Actors represent entities in the environment that interact with the system. A use case is a particular way of using the system. This model captures the functionality of the system from a user's point of view. It is used throughout the entire OOSE development process.
2. Interface description describes the interfaces of the system associated with use cases.
3. A problem domain model composed of objects from the problem domain. This model is similar to the object model in other OO techniques.

Analysis Model — The building of the analysis model starts once the requirements model is approved by the user. The goal is to give the system a logical structure that is independent of the actual implementation environment. The analysis model is obtained by transforming the requirements model. It captures the system using three different types of objects associated with the three dimensions: information, presentation, and behavior. The objects are entity objects, interface objects, and control objects. Jacobson does not believe that the most stable system can be built by using only objects that correspond to problem domain entities, as is the case for most other OO methods. Hence the three different types of objects: (1) an entity object; (2) an interface object; and (3) a control object. There are three models generated after analysis: the design model, the implementation model, and the test model.

Martin/Odell Model — Martin/Odell's method aims to build two models that represent an aspect of reality in the problem domain. The two models are

1. *Object structure model* — It is specified by the object schemas to show the object structure, and it is concerned with object types, classes, relationships among objects, and inheritance. The following elements are modeled in the object schema: object types; object associations; generalization; and composition. The object schema consists of object types and associations; generalization diagrams; object–relationship diagrams; and composed–of diagrams.
2. *Object behavior model* — It is concerned with modeling the behavior of objects over time using two types of schemas. The following elements are modeled: event types; states; trigger rules;

control conditions; and operations. The behavior model consists of two schemas. The first is the object–flow diagrams. It describes the high–level process flow of objects similar to the concept of dataflow diagrams. The second is the event schema. It describes the behavior of the system.

Shlaer/Mellor Model — The Shlaer–Mellor approach is to partition the system under consideration into three domains: an application domain, an architectural domain, and an implementation domain. The application domain deals with the system from the user's point of view, the architectural domain provides the means to organize the system in its entirety, and the implementation domain is concerned with the implementation environment. Three major models are built out of the application domain: the information model which defines the structure; the state models which define the behaviors (lifecycles); and the action specifications which define processing associated with states.

Fusion Model — The Fusion method uses two different models to capture both the structural and behavior aspect of the problem domain. The object model shows the static structure of the system, while the interface models the system interface by describing its input and output communication. The object model shows the static structure of classes and their relationships. The notation for the object model is based on the extended entity relationship diagram. The following concepts are used in the modeling process to capture the problem domain: objects and classes; relationships and their properties/constraints; aggregation; generalization and specialization; leveling diagrams with aggregation; and system object model. An object model captures both the system and its environment. A system object model includes only those aspects that are within the system boundary by excluding all the classes and relationships that belong to the environment.

The interface model describes the behavior of the system by defining the input and output communication of the system. The description is in terms of events and the change of states that they cause. The interface model is composed of two components — the operation model and the lifecycle model. The following components are used: agents; event; system operation; and interface. In the interface model, the system is modeled as an agent that interacts with other agents in the environment. The environment is the set of agents with which a system communicates. The operation model defines the behavior of an individual system operation, while the lifecycle model describes behavior from the wider perspective of how the system communicates with its environment from creation until termination.

- *Operation model* — The operation model defines the behavior of individual operations. The effect of each system operation is characterized in terms of the state change it causes and the output events it sends. This is done by specifying the operation declaratively using pre- and post-conditions. The conditions are expressed as predicates. The model is expressed as a series of schemata, with at least one schema for each system operation. The schemata are structured text.
- *Lifecycle model* — The lifecycle model describes system communication over the lifetime of the system. It defines the allowable sequences of interactions that a system may participate in over its lifetime. The description is accomplished using lifecycle expressions, which are similar to a regular expression for a grammar. A lifecycle expression defines allowable sequences of events in the same way that a grammar describes the allowable sequences of symbols for a language.

Models After Analysis — Four models are used in the design stage. They are supported by the following notations:

- *Object interaction model* — Describes object interactions necessary to support a system operation; it uses a net style interaction diagram; one diagram is constructed for each system operation

- *Visibility model* — Used to depict object communication paths, for each class of objects, object references and the kinds of references are identified
- *Class descriptions* — Specifying class interface, data attributes, object reference attributes, and methods
- *Inheritance model* — Describes the inheritance structure between classes and subclasses

55.3.2 Modeling Tools

Except for differences in the strategies, the terminology, and maybe the level of abstraction, it is safe to state that most methods approach OO modeling from three orthogonal perspectives: the static perspective (structural model), the dynamic perspective (behavioral model), and the system perspective (architectural model).

55.3.2.1 Booch's Notation

Booch believes that a notation should be rich enough to ensure expressiveness. As a result, this method includes one of the largest sets of diagrams and notations. Some notations are labeled as essential while others are non–essential used to support "advanced concepts." Six different types of diagrams are used for analysis and design.

- *Class diagrams (Figure 55.4A(a))* — Used to show the classes and their relationships in the logical model of the system; class relationships among classes are shown in Figure 55.4C(a).
- *Object diagrams [Figure 55.4B(a)]* — Used to show the objects and their relationships in the logical model of the system
- *Module diagrams* — Show the allocation of classes and objects to modules in the physical model of a system; used in the design of the implementation
- *Process diagrams* — Show the allocation of processes to processors in the physical model of a system; used in the design of the implementation
- *State transition diagrams* — Used to show the states and state transitions for a given class; indicates the events that trigger state transitions and actions resulted from the transitions
- *Interaction diagrams* — Used to show interactions between objects during the execution of a scenario in the same context as an object diagram

55.3.3 Coad/Yourdon's Notation

Coad and Yourdon's notation is a relatively simple notation that uses the following notational components to illustrate the model.

- Class–&–Object; class and its objects; attributes and services are shown as components of a class–&–object diagram [Figure 55.4B(b)]
- Class; a generalization class from the problem domain; its specializations are the class-&-objects [Figure 55.4A(b)]
- Generalization–specialization structure, whole–part structure, instance connection, and message connection are links (relationships) that relate objects. Figures 55.4C(b) and 55.4D(b).
- Subjects are structures for composing subsystems

55.3.4 OMT Notation

OMT provides four major diagrams: the class diagram, the state–transition diagram, the object–interaction diagram, and the interaction diagram. The notations for class diagram capture the concepts

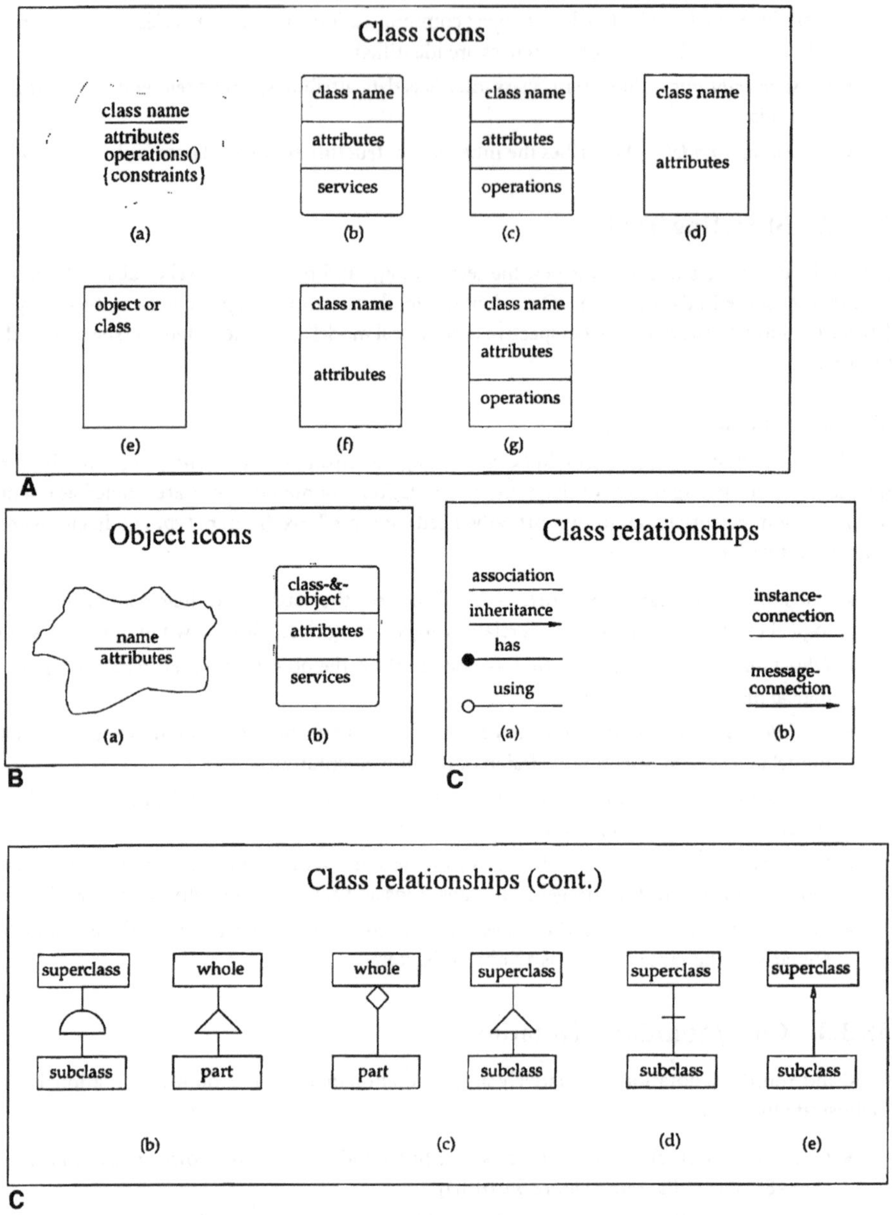

FIGURE 55.4 The use-case model is used to develop all other models.

of class, generalization, aggregation, associations and their types, constraints, and visibility properties. Figure 55.4A(c) shows the diagrams for classes and Figure 55.4D(c) the relationships.

55.3.5 OOSE Notation

A simple set of notation is used for the OOSE. In addition to this set of notations, each type of model has its own set of notations. The notation for OOSE consists of the following components associated with a particular model:

- **Associations** (Figure 55.5) are used to represent the different associations. Class associations are drawn with a dashed arrow, while instance associations are drawn with a full arrow.

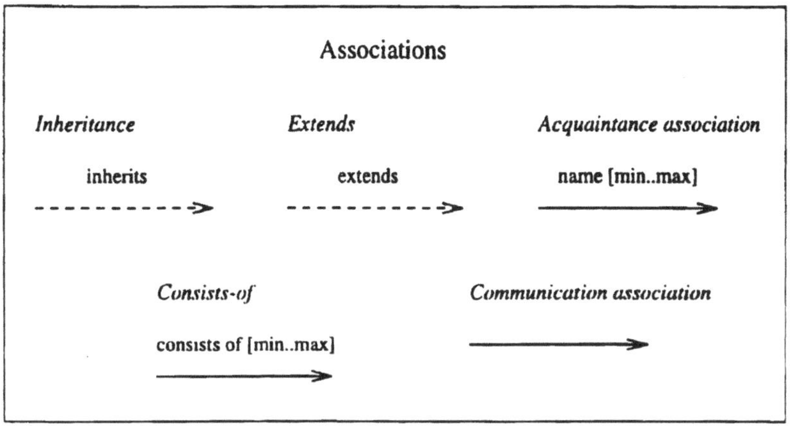

FIGURE 55.5 OOSE's association notation.

- **Use-case model** is used to represent actors and use–cases. Basically, it relates a user with a general context diagram.
- **Domain object model** is used to represent objects. It is represented as a circle with a label on the outside.
- **Analysis model** (Figure 55.6) is used to represent several objects, among them the interface object, the entity object, the control object, the attribute, and the subsystem.

55.3.6 OOA/OODLE Notation

Figures 55.4A(d) and 55.4D(d) show the notation advocated by Shlaer and Mellor. It is fairly basic notation for structural modeling. State diagrams and action dataflow diagrams are used to model the behavior.

55.3.7 Martin/Odell's Notation

Martin/Odell's notation for OOA is largely based on existing diagrams employed in conventional techniques. Its major components are shown in Figure 55.4A(e) (Class icons). They include classes and subclasses, relationships, transitions and communications, activities, events, triggers, and conditions.

55.3.8 Fusion's Notation

The object model, interface model, and operation model in the analysis phase all have their own notations. The model notation is shown in Figure 55.4A(f). The notation for the relationship superclass/subclass is shown in Figure 55.4D(c). The interface model notation defines a name and associates with it a regular expression. The operation model notation consists of structured text describing the operation name, the inputs/outputs, the behavior, and the communications.

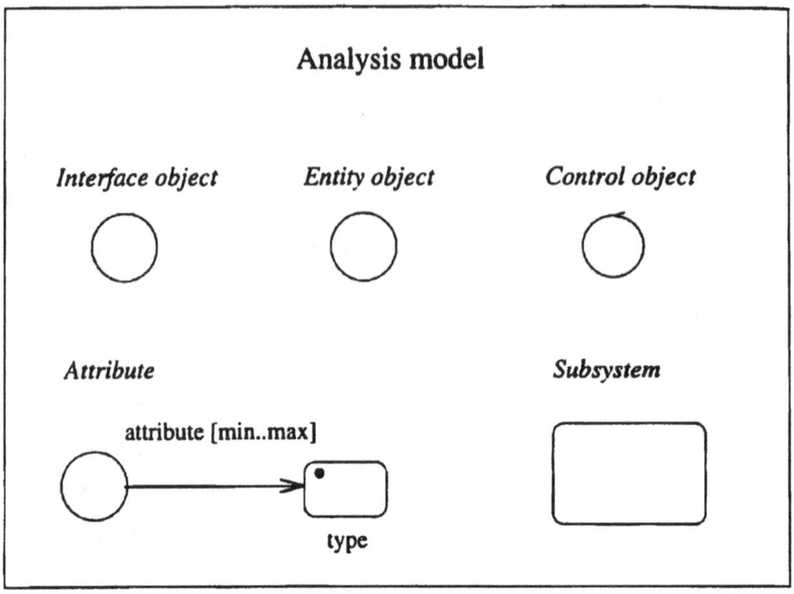

FIGURE 55.6 OOSE's analysis model notation.

55.3.9 UML Notation

Being a synthesis of three different notations (Booch, OMT, OOSE), the UML notation appears daunting, with a diagram for each of the large number of concepts. Because of its novelty, no experience has yet been reported concerning the effectiveness of the UML notation. Figure 55.4A(c) shows the class icon and Figure 55.4D(c,e) the class relationships.

55.4 Behavioral Modeling

The structural model shows the attributes and operations of classes as well as their associations and relationships. Behavior modeling is used to complement structural modeling by addressing the dynamic aspects of the system. Behavior modeling should capture the minimal constraints for valid behaviors to avoid committing to design and implementation decisions, as opposed to structural modeling in which a more encompassing model may be needed. Several techniques have been proposed for OO behavior modeling. They vary in terms of concepts and emphasis. There are basically two types of behavior modeling techniques in use across existing OO methodologies, the state–based and the event–based approaches. Other alternatives are textual descriptions using pre- and post-conditions and CSP–based formalisms. Pre- and post-conditions are a declarative approach defining what should be true before and after a state transition as well as invariants. An example of the use of pre- and post-conditions is the Fusion's operation model. The CSP–based approach, recently proposed [4], views an OO model as a system of concurrent objects. The state–, event–, and CSP–based approaches are described in the following subsections.

55.4.1 State–Based Approach

By far the most popular approach for behavior modeling in OO methodologies, state–based techniques have a well–understood formal basis rooted in finite state automata. The most commonly used notation is diagrammatic with nodes representing states of the system and directed lines connecting the nodes representing transitions between states. Each transition corresponds to an event. When an event occurs, the system changes state depending on its current state and the transition corresponding to the occurring event. A variety of state transition diagrams of varying detail are being used. Harel's statechart is one of the more powerful notations incorporating the concepts of superstate and substate as well as other improvements to manage complexity. This notation was adopted by many OO methodologies including Booch, Rumbaugh, Syntropy, and UML.

The main drawback of the state–based approach is that it requires all possible states of a system to be identified, resulting in what is sometimes referred to as the state explosion problem. OO methodologies avoid this problem by having separate state transition diagrams for each class instead of the whole system, thus neglecting object interaction modeling. Additional techniques augmenting the state–based approach are designed to capture object interactions explicitly.

55.4.2 Object Interaction Modeling

Although generically different in concepts and heuristics, they all identify a set of high-level behaviors involving a number of collaborating objects. Object interactions necessary to support this higher level behavior is then modeled explicitly. This approach enables the visualization of object interactions for a selected number of interobject behaviors. The various concepts used to identify this higher level of behavior is introduced next.

Mechanism based — A mechanism–based approach to behavior modeling attempts to visualize the interclass behavior. The term mechanism is defined by Booch (1994) as a structure whereby objects collaborate to provide some behavior that satisfies a requirement of the problem. Essentially, a mechanism–based approach is an extension of the state–based approach. An STD is constructed for each class of objects. In addition, some heuristics, based mostly on functionality, are used to identify mechanisms, some higher level behavior provided by aggregation of objects. This higher level behavior is then analyzed in terms of object interactions. Booch provides an interaction diagram to capture the object interactions for each mechanism.

System operation based — The Fusion method [9] introduced a new approach for behavior modeling by emphasizing system operations. A system operation represents an input event and its effect on a system. System operations are invoked by agents in the environment. In the analysis phase of Fusion, system operations and their allowable sequences are specified declaratively with a textual notation. This captures the behavior of the entire system within its operating environment. In the design phase, object interaction graphs are constructed for each system operation. An object interaction graph for a system operation shows the objects and their message passing relevant to support that particular system operation being modeled.

Use-case based — A use case is defined as a behaviorally related sequence of transactions in a dialog performed by a user when using the system. In OOSE, state transition graphs may be used to model the behavior of individual classes of objects over time. In addition, interaction diagrams are constructed for each use case to show the object interactions necessary for the support of the use cases.

Scenario based — In the OMT method, Rumbaugh (1991) defines a scenario as any sequence of events that occurs during one particular execution of an application. OMT uses a modified version of Harel's statecharts for modeling individual object behaviors. Scenarios are identified and event trace diagrams, essentially fence style interaction diagrams, are used to model the interactions between involved objects.

55.4.3 Tools for Object Interaction Modeling

The main notation for interaction modeling is diagrammatic. There are basically three types of interaction diagrams: net diagrams, fence diagrams, and timing diagrams. While notations may vary in many aspects for different interaction diagrams, the basic diagrammatic presentation style can be categorized into these three groups. Most existing methodologies incorporate one of the three basic styles, each adding some modifications to suit its particular flavor.

Net diagrams are based on object structure diagrams from the structural model. Object types are drawn in boxes as in the structural diagram. Directed lines are drawn among objects to indicate message connections. The messages may be labeled with a number for sequencing. Fence diagrams list objects on the top row and events as labeled arrows between the vertical lines representing objects. The flow of time is vertical from top to bottom. The event arrows represent the messages passing between objects. Like net diagrams, fence diagrams are able to show messages passing between objects and their sequencings.

In timing diagrams, objects are listed vertically on the left side and the horizontal axis is used to represent the passage of time. The thread of control passing between objects is shown alone with the messages sent. Timing diagram is the least popular notation.

The various approaches to interaction modeling allow the explicit capturing of interobject behaviors. As described earlier, they all use different concepts to extract and model behaviors involving more than one object. The similarity among them is substantial. However, there are problems associated with these types of techniques. This style of interaction modeling shows only a single thread of control. There is no way of combining different interaction models to show a wider view of behavior. Also, there is no way of showing iterations and repetitions, and, as pointed out by Carmichael (1994), it lacks a diagrammatic notation rich enough to be computationally complete. It may also be difficult to identify the interobject behavior of interest, which is largely heuristic. The diagrammatic notation may become difficult to construct and read for large interobject behaviors.

55.4.4 Event–Based Approach

Martin/Odell's (1992) approach for behavior modeling is based on the notion of an event. Events are used as the basic component for behavior description. The principal modeling tool for the event–based approach is the event diagram. An event diagram consists of four basic types of components: operations, events, triggers, and control conditions. As defined by Martin/Odell, an operation changes the state of an object; an event is the successful completion of an invoked operation; a trigger invokes an operation when an event occurs; and control conditions ensure that an operation is invoked only when certain conditions are met. The behaviors of the system therefore consist of the pattern of triggers that invoke operations, operation invocations that result in events, and events in turn create triggers. Their strength lies in their ability to describe the behavior involving a number of collaborating objects. Iterations and conditional behavior are supported. However, operations in the event diagram are not associated with their respective object classes. As a result, event diagrams can describe the behavior of the resulting systems involving collaborating objects, but collaborations between objects are not captured explicitly, as compared to object interaction modeling. Event diagrams capture behaviors of the whole system that are not tied to any particular class definitions.

The advantages of event diagrams are their ability to capture behavior of the entire system as a whole, at the expense of not having the ability to capture object interactions and individual object behaviors. There is no information describing which operations are from which classes.

55.4.5 CSP–Based Approach

Consider Figure 55.7. An OO behavior model is composed of a set of concurrent objects that communicate through message connections. When an operation in the initial object is invoked by a user, it will trigger a series of message–passing between objects necessary to complete the task of the system. Consistent with the OO principle of encapsulation or information hiding, individual objects are treated as black boxes. In this OO execution model, message communications are a major part of how an object can affect and be affected by other objects or entities outside of its black box boundary. This perspective fits nicely the CSP framework [14]. CSP is designed to enable the specification of synchronizations between multiple concurrent processes by synchronizing the processes' I/O. Multiple processes are multiple objects that must synchronize their I/O, or message communications, in order to interact with one another. In this CSP approach, only one single technique is needed to capture both object life history and object interactions. Systematic ways of composing smaller models into a larger one are a basic operation in CSP. Thus, a comprehensive view of the behavior of operations, objects, and systems is captured in one seamless formalism.

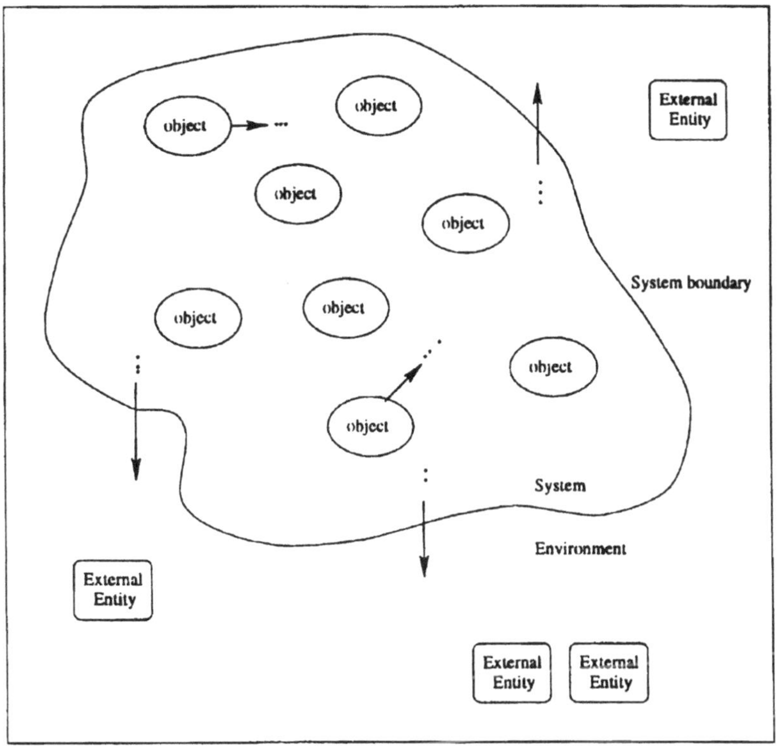

FIGURE 55.7 A CSP–based behavior perspective.

Here is an example to illustrate the use of CSP. The sensor system is composed of two objects, a sensor unit and an alarm unit. We specify the behavior for each of them and of the entire system as follows:

SENSOR = power_on → (power_off → SENSOR
| threshold_reached → alarm!activate → SENSOR)

ALARM = power_on → (power_off → ALARM
| alarm?activate → sound_alarm → ALARM)

SENSOR_SYSTEM = (SENSOR || ALARM)

Informally, the sensor engages in the action power_on followed by the action power_off and then behaves as a sensor again, or it engages in the action power_on, detects a threshold, sends an activation signal to the alarm, and then behaves as a sensor again. The alarm engages in the action power_on followed by the action power_off and then behaves as an alarm again, or it engages in the action power_on, detects an activation signal, sounds the alarm, and then behaves as an alarm again. The sensor system is quite simple; it is the parallel composition of the sensor and the alarm.

55.5 Summary and Conclusions

There is no lack of vitality in the development and synthesis of new OO methods. Despite differences of terminology, notation, and process, the field is converging toward a mutually understood general framework for OO modeling. This chapter conveys that framework. The current OO modeling methods that have impacted this development are: Booch method, OMT, OOSE, Coad/Yourdon method, CRC method, Shlaer/Mellor method, and Martin/Odell method. Other methods such as Fusion, Syntropy, UML, OPEN, and many more, are the results of synthesis work. They have consolidated the original concepts, and put them into practice. Even though they may constitute the OO methodology state of the art, there is probably a need for further design iterations for a method to gain wide acceptance. The experiment with UML will prove critical in the development of a "standard" OO method.

An overview of the field reveals a wide spectrum of concepts, constructs, and details, as exemplified by the range between, for example, the Booch method and the Coad/Yourdon method. The Booch method is a broad methodology that encompasses most aspects of the object–oriented analysis and design process. This method aims at establishing a foundation for implementation. The products of this method are the models of the system that can be directly used in the implementation stage for coding. A rich set of concepts, techniques, and notations is provided that some may find complicated and overwhelming. Multiple views of the system allow different aspects of the system to be expressed, which is supported by four static diagrams and two dynamic diagrams. Class and object relationships are also more elaborate than many other methods. The main strength of Booch's method lies in its flexibility as a result of the comprehensive set of notations. It includes interesting components such as the class utilities, which are subprograms not belonging to any class but available for use by all classes. However, this richness is a double-edged sword in that it is also the cause for difficulty in use because the techniques may not be apparent at first. On the other hand, the Coad/Yourdon method provides just enough strategies and notations to get the job done. Its simplicity is a strength, but it has also been criticized by some as being too simple. A set of heuristics is provided to guide the analyst through the five activities associated with the five layers of the single model. The output of this OO method is a set of graphical notations and templated textual documentation of classes and objects. No technique is provided to capture all the behavior aspects of the objects. Behavior is captured implicitly by naming operations on the classes and defining within the class by object state diagram and service charts. Interactions between objects are shown by the message connections only. Overall, a consensus toward this method is that while its simplicity is effective for small projects, it may not be suitable for larger systems.

Between these two is a wide range of methods. For example, OOSE emphasizes the concept of use case. Several fundamental differences in concepts characterize this method among others as well. OOSE first requires the identification of use cases. This notion is then used to extract objects. This two-step analysis approach to model building differs from most other OO methods that extract model objects directly from the problem domain. The two step approach derives objects from the use-case model rather than directly from the problem domain. This approach is claimed to be more robust and maintainable for future changes. Three different object types are used in the analysis model for structuring. Model transformation is the process and the distinctions between process and method are made. The notations are simple and easy to understand. The process is iterative, although the model–transformation approach requires that one model be stable before the development of the subsequent one. This is a well-structured method centered around the notion of use case which is the core that drives all the other model developments. However, the completeness and consistency of models are not addressed strongly in this method. The notations and models are not well defined in that the semantics of different models may not be clearly distinguishable. The three types of objects are used in analysis only, and they are all converted to blocks in the design stage.

Martin and Odell's method stresses a deep understanding of the object model concepts. The analysis method is driven by a philosophical view and attention is paid to the semantics of the techniques [6]. However, no process is clearly given on the use of the methods. The authors described a rich set of conceptual foundations without prescribing how to put them together into a process. In the structural modeling, object schema similar to the extended entity–relationship diagram is used. In the behavior modeling, the event diagram is used. However, the event diagram shows only the overall behavior of the system not tied to any particular class of objects. The object–flow diagram is a method for top down decomposition showing process and objects flowing between them, similar to the concept of dataflow diagram.

As an example of a second generation method synthesized from Booch, OMT, and CRC, Fusion incorporates a rich and coherent set of concepts and constructs, and a well–defined and clearly documented process for OO development. The structural model (object model) is extracted from the problem domain. The behavior model (interface model) is determined by looking at the input–output of the system, which is described by lifecycle and operation models using a specification language. The only graphical notation in the analysis phase is based on the entity–relationship diagram. Object interaction and inheritance relationship are delegated to the design stage. The Fusion method did not address the concept of a subject, instead, it includes the concept of leveling (aggregation) for complexity control in the object diagrams.

Conceptually, OO methods have been following a kind of "versioning" lifecycle of their own. A historical analysis shows that newer versions tend to include more new concepts, as these become widely used in the field. Thus, in the more established area of structural behavior, a consensus has already been reached. On the behavioral side, issues are still unsettled. It is unclear how the behavior of an OO model ought to be specified. Competing proposals, which can be reduced to the finite state automata model, are being advocated. It seems that there is a lack of deep understanding of the semantics of objects and object composition. Theoretical research dealing with the semantics of objects may provide insights on what constitutes the behavior of an object [1].

References

[1] Abadi, M. and Cardelli, L., *A Theory of Objects.* Springer-Verlag, New York, 1996.

[2] Belkhouche, B. and Chavarro, M., Analysis of object–oriented design, *J. Object–Oriented Program.*, 52–64, Feb. 1995.

[3] Belkhouche, B. and Mendoza, A., Object oriented analysis through a knowledge-based system. Technical Report, Department of Computer Science, Tulane University, Jan. 1995.

[4] Belkhouche, B. and Wu, J., Behavioral specification and analysis of object–oriented designs. Technical Report (submitted), Department of Computer Science, Tulane University, Mar. 1997.

[5] Booch, G., *Object-Oriented Analysis and Design.* Benjamin/Cummings, Menlo Park, CA, 1994.

[6] Carmichael, A., Ed., *Object Development Methods.* SIGS Books, New York, 1994.

[7] Coad, P. and Yourdon, E., *Object–Oriented Analysis.* Yourdon Press, Englewood Cliffs, NJ, 1991a.

[8] Coad, P. and Yourdon, E., *Object–Oriented Design.* Yourdon Press, Englewood Cliffs, NJ, 1991b.

[9] Coleman, D., et al. *Object-Oriented Development: The Fusion Method.* Prentice-Hall, Englewood Cliffs, NJ, 1994.

[10] Cook, S. and Daniels, J., *Designing Object Systems.* Prentice-Hall, Englewood Cliffs, NJ, 1994.

[11] Duke, D. and Duke, R., Toward a semantics for object–Z. In *VDM'90,* Springer-Verlag, New York, 1990.

[12] Firesmith, D., Henderson-Sellers, B., and Graham, I., *OPEN Modeling Language (OML) Manual.* SIGS Books, New York, 1997.

[13] Graham, I., *Object-Oriented Methods.* Addison-Wesley, Reading, MA, 1994.
[14] Hoare, C.A.R., *Communicating Sequential Processes.* Prentice-Hall, Englewood Cliffs, NJ, 1985.
[15] Hutt, A., Ed., *Object Analysis and Design: Comparison of Methods.* John Wiley & Sons, New York, 1994.
[16] Hutt, A., Ed., *Object Analysis and Design: Description of Methods.* John Wiley & Sons, New York, 1994.
[17] Jacobson, I., Christerson, M., Jonsson, P., and Overguard. G., *Object-Oriented Software Engineering: A Use Case Driven Approach.* Addison-Wesley, Reading, MA, 1992.
[18] Martin, J. and Odell, J., *Object-Oriented Analysis and Design.* Prentice-Hall, Englewood Cliffs, NJ, 1992.
[19] Nierstrasz, O. and Tsichritzis, D., *Object–Oriented Software Composition.* Prentice-Hall, Englewood Cliffs, NJ, 1995.
[20] Rational. UML notation guide. Technical Report, Rational Software Corporation, 1996.
[21] Rumbaugh, J., Blaha, M., Premerlani, W., Eddy, F., and Lornsen, W., *Object–Oriented Modeling and Design.* Prentice-Hall, Englewood Cliffs, NJ, 1991.
[22] Shlaer, S. and Mellor, S., *Object–Oriented System Analysis: Modeling the World in Data.* Prentice-Hall, Englewood Cliffs, NJ, 1988.
[23] Shlaer, S. and Mellor, S., *Object Lifecycles: Modeling the World in States.* Prentice-Hall, Englewood Cliffs, NJ, 1991.
[24] Walden, K. and Nerson. J.-M., *Seamless Object-Oriented Software Architecture.* Prentice-Hall, Englewood Cliffs, NJ, 1995.

XIII

Object-Oriented Application Development

Frank Budinsky
IBM Canada Laboratory

Application development using object-oriented programming languages involves many of the same tools and techniques that are used for procedural programming. The use of objects, however, enables new ways of building applications and places a number of unique requirements on the development environment. Object-oriented development has motivated several new kinds of tools that are commonly included in application development environments for object languages. Some examples of these include extensive class browsers, wizards/experts, and tools that support visual construction and scripting of components.

The chapters that follow describe features provided in commercially available development environments for three of the most widely used object-oriented languages: C++, Java, and Smalltalk. Chapter 56 describes C++ developments environments but also provides a thorough overview of features that are common to object-oriented development environments for any language. Chapters 57 and 58 focus mainly on the features specific to Java and Smalltalk environments, respectively.

56

C++ Commercial Development Environments

Frank J. Budinsky
IBM Canada Ltd.

Steven R. Dobson
IBM Canada Ltd.

> Upon leaving Cambridge, I swore never again to attack a problem with tools as unsuitable as those I had suffered while designing and implementing the simulator.
>
> — **Bjarne Stroustrup**

Good tools can make a tremendous difference in any software development effort. This chapter describes tools and techniques that are commonly used in commercial development environments to help make C++ programming easier. Features of these environments include extensive class libraries, smart compilation/make, class browsers, source code generators, GUI builders, and the visual construction and scripting of components.

56.1 Introduction

In recent years, the C++ programming language has emerged as one of the most popular languages for the development of object-oriented software. Along with this popularity, there has been an emergence of commercially available application development environments supporting C++. Like the C++ language itself, these environments cover a wide range of developers, from those working alone to create small local programs to those working in large teams to create complex programs for distributed enterprise environments.

Programs being developed using C++ are based on various technologies, both new and existing. For example, many C++ programs incorporate Graphical User Interface (GUI) or Object Linking and Embedding (OLE) technology; some may involve database connectivity, Internet (or intranet) access, and encapsulation of legacy code and data. Without native support for these technologies in the development environment, a developer may be forced to code at a low level and to a complex API, or to purchase third-party software; neither of which would be considered a selling feature for the environment itself.

0-8493-3135-8/99/$0.00+$.50

Some development environments overcome these shortcomings by including third-party software themselves. This approach is often much less costly for the manufacturer; however, in some cases it results in a component that stands out as poorly integrated with the rest of the product. Although manufacturers attempt to package these purchased components consistently with the rest of the product, often the only features that really appear well integrated are those that are natively supported.

Because C++ has such a wide range of uses, there is a correspondingly large variation in the requirements for tools and supported technologies in the development environment. As such, many manufacturers provide several versions of their product, usually designated as *standard*, *professional*, and *enterprise* versions. Although not identical, there are strong similarities in content between the products at similar version levels from different manufacturers. By factoring their products into versions of varying levels of function (and cost), manufacturers are attempting to meet the requirements of the large set of C++ users with solutions tailored to each customer set.*

56.1.1 Standard Development Environments

The *standard* version of a C++ development environment typically includes an integrated set of basic tools including an editor, compiler, debugger, make facility, and class browser. These environments are targeted at small- to medium-sized development efforts, and therefore do not include tools that are primarily important for large scale projects.

The standard products typically include an extensive set of general class libraries and/or support for automatic generation of code. The class libraries (or tools) supplied with these products typically support the development of applications using technologies such as the following:

- GUIs
- Components (e.g., COM/ActiveX)
- 2-D graphics
- Resources
- Exceptions
- Help (general and contextual)
- Internationalization (e.g., Unicode support classes)

Commercially available C++ development environment products that fall into this category include Microsoft Visual C++ Standard Edition, Borland Turbo C++, and Powersoft Watcom C/C++.

56.1.2 Professional and Enterprise Development Environments

Professional and *enterprise* C++ development environments are targeted at medium- to (very) large scale software development efforts. *Professional* versions typically include tools for database access, for customizing the development environment, and for creating industrial-strength, network-aware programs. *Enterprise* versions often extend this with tools for database design, program analysis and design, source control, application partitioning, and reporting facilities.

In addition to the class libraries and frameworks provided by standard development environment products, those supplied with the professional and enterprise products might include support for the development of applications using technologies such as:

- Internet/intranet
- Database
- Distributed objects
- Communications

* Product, service, and company names used in this chapter may be trademarks of their respective owners.

Examples of commercially available products in the professional or enterprise category include Microsoft Visual C++ (Professional and Enterprise Editions), Borland C++ Development Suite and C++ Builder (Professional and Client/Server Editions), Powersoft Optima++ (Professional and Enterprise Editions), IBM VisualAge for C++, and Symantec C++.

56.2 Features of the C++ Development Environment

Although application development using an object-oriented programming language shares many of the same problems as procedural programming, the use of objects both enables new ways of building applications and presents a number of unique requirements. The set of features provided in any C++ development environment can be divided into three categories:

1. Those that are specific to C++ development
2. Those that are common to development environments for any object-oriented language
3. Those that are common to application development of any kind

At a high level, the majority of the features in C++ development environments are of the second and third type. At a lower level, they typically have a number of details that are specific to C++. For example, a class browser or an object-oriented analysis and design tool can be considered common to development for any object-oriented language. However, a C++ implementation will need to deal with C++ specific features such as templated classes and multiple inheritance, while a similar tool for other languages may not. On the other hand, some C++ environments include tools that simply work at the file level (e.g., a source controller). This type of tool is likely to have no C++ specific details; the contents of the files just happen to contain C++ source code, rather than C, FORTRAN, or any other language source.

The following sections describe the set of tools that can be found in commercially available C++ development environments, to show how C++ applications are developed in practice.

56.2.1 The Primary Tools

Traditional C++ development environments are centered around a tool suite consisting of the following:

- A source editor
- A C++ compiler
- A debugger

The function behind each of these tools can range from very primitive to quite advanced, and the tools can run from working totally separately to being tightly integrated. The tools are used together in the edit, compile, and debug cycle to iteratively develop programs.

56.2.1.1 Editors

Although the program source is often entered using a number of tools, the basic text editor is still one of the staples of every C++ development environment. The degree to which conventional text entry is used during development typically depends on the level of sophistication of the environment and of the user. It may be used for initial program entry, or simply for augmenting and modifying a program source that has been automatically generated by another tool.

Some degree of "syntax awareness" has become standard in program editors. By making the editor aware of the syntax of the source code being edited, it is possible to dynamically parse the source as it is typed. This allows the editor to set the colors and fonts for certain language elements to make the code easier to read (for example, make all comments the same color).

Programmable editors are another common feature in C++ development environments. By allowing the editor to be programmatically configured and driven, it can be customized to suit a programmer's specific needs. For example, many source editors have built-in emulation for several popular editors, or can be programmed to emulate other editors. Another advantage of programmatically controlled editors is that they can be driven by other tools in the environment. For example, the editor can be automatically scrolled to show the line of code on which a compilation error has occurred. This kind of integration is described further in Section 56.2.3.

56.2.1.2 Compilers and Linkers

Because C++ is a statically typed object-oriented language intended to generate highly optimized source code, the compilation times can become very long. A well-designed *make* environment (see Section 56.2.2.1) can reduce compilation times by ensuring that only the affected files are recompiled when changes are made to a program. Unfortunately, this approach does not work well in many cases. For example, changing a comment in a common *include* file will result in recompilation of every file using it. To help with this problem, most C++ development environments support one or more of the following:

- Incremental compile
- Precompiled headers
- Incremental link

Incremental compilers recompile only those parts within a source file that are actually affected by other changes (as opposed to recompiling the whole file). By keeping track of changes at a finer level of granularity than the file level (which just uses time-stamps), superfluous compiles can often be avoided.

One approach stores the parsed source code as objects in an object database. This representation serves as the basis for the incremental compile mechanism. Also, by maintaining the parsed format instead of parsing it each time, the compile time is further reduced. Another advantage of this approach is that the compile-time information is available for other tools (e.g., browsers and analyzers) to use.

Another approach that can significantly reduce compilation time is to precompile unchanging header files that are included in the compilation. This reduces the overall compile time by the amount of time needed to recompile those pieces. This may even involve compiling the same pieces multiple times if a header is included in more than one compilation unit. Precompiled headers are almost essential when building applications that include many stable header files, such as applications using predefined class libraries and frameworks.

Instead of relinking all the object code needed to create an executable program, incremental linkers simply replace those pieces of the executable program that have changed. For large executable programs involving many object files, the resulting time savings can be enormous.

Most C++ development environments also provide support for assembly language programming. This is generally supported (by the C++ compiler) by allowing assembler instructions to be mixed in with the C++ source code, usually delineated by compiler keywords or directives. The excellent optimization provided by some C++ compilers often makes the need to write assembler instructions, for gaining optimum performance, unnecessary.

Although C++ is a compiled language, interpreters and virtual machines are also available for it. These are typically used to enable rapid turnaround during development, after which the software can be compiled for production use. Support is also provided for pieces of interpreted and compiled code to call one another.

56.2.1.3 Debuggers

C++ debuggers have been striving toward a number of goals. One such goal is tighter integration with the editor and other tools. Another goal is support for debugging beyond single-process environments. For example:

- Multi-threaded and multi-process debugging have become more essential as client/server programming is much more common.
- Remote debugging is required for those development environments that provide cross-platform support.
- Distributed debugging is the next technology to be required, as programs may consist of multiple objects communicating across a distributed network of machines.

A key improvement in debuggers has been the ease of use of the interface. For example, most debuggers are well integrated with the other tools in the development environment, allowing the user to simply click on a line of source code in an editor window to set a breakpoint. Another example is the ability to show calculated values in a program data monitoring window. Some debuggers are adding features to help analyze memory usage and point out memory leakages.

C++ programs must be compiled with certain compile-options that enable debugging. This is usually the default setting during development. Later, when the program is working correctly, it is recompiled with the debugging option disabled in order to create an optimized production version of the program.

56.2.2 The Essential Extensions

In addition to the basic components (editor, compiler, and debugger), any effective C++ development environment will include the following:

- A *make* facility
- Source code generators and/or class libraries
- A class browser

Without some level of support for this set of features, it would be quite difficult, if not impossible, to develop any nontrivial C++ application.

56.2.2.1 Project Management and Make

Source code is generally stored in files, so these files must be managed. Project management tools help to manage program files by:

- Helping to group classes into files
- Displaying and navigating the relationships between files
- Maintaining the information necessary for building the program from the source files

The Project Manager is often the heart of an interactive development environment.

In more traditional development environments, the information used to build programs is stored in *makefiles*, scripts that are interpreted by a "make" program in order to carry out the steps required to build a program. The script consists of a number of specified targets (i.e., the files to be built), the dependencies for each target, and the operation required to build them. Before building a particular target, the files in its dependencies list are first checked and built if necessary (i.e., if a file does not exist or is outdated according to its dependencies). This proceeds recursively until every target in the *makefile* has either been built or been determined to be up to date.

Often the *makefiles* are coded manually, but in some development environments, especially those that work with the notion of projects, they are automatically generated from information specified within the project and from information parsed from the source files (such as which files the project includes).

56.2.2.2 Class Libraries and Frameworks

The class libraries and frameworks that come with a development environment play a crucial role in producing standardized, quality code through reuse. Class libraries provide code reuse, while frameworks provide both code and design reuse.

All C++ development environments are equipped with an extensive set of class libraries. The supply of frameworks, on the other hand, is much more limited in the environment products themselves. Because most frameworks are tied to a specific application type or domain, they are more often purchased separately. "Generally reusable" frameworks are typically provided with development environments, but are limited to relatively basic behavior (e.g., a GUI application skeleton) which can be specialized by overriding framework methods.

One potential drawback to class libraries and frameworks is that they often require runtime libraries to exist on the machines where the code is to execute. Licensing of the runtime libraries can be costly, although some are free of charge.

56.2.2.3 Generator Tools

Skeleton implementations of the classes needed for various kinds of applications are frequently generated automatically by tools in the development environment. In framework environments, or wherever a well-defined pattern exists, much of the application program can be characterized as *boiler-plate* or *scaffolding* for the actual program logic. Tools of this kind can generate much of this boiler-plate code based on small amounts of user input.

Generators typically provide a user interface that asks a few questions of the user, then generates code and possibly resources from the information provided. Called *Wizards*, *Experts*, or *Guides* by different vendors, these tools are used for generating application skeletons, classes, and controls, and they are very common in C++ development environments.

Source code generators and class libraries are very closely related. A generator's output is typically based on the class libraries and frameworks provided by the environment. In some cases, development environments choose to provide complete functionality in the form of generated code instead of in a class library. For example, rather than providing a framework base class from which a generated class would derive, a class containing a complete implementation might be generated instead.

Generators are also available for generating help information, reports, database designs, and makefiles. Some generators are built into other tools, such as visual builders or object-oriented analysis and design tools. Others require no direct user input, but instead work with information stored in files or databases.

56.2.2.4 Class Browsers

An essential tool in every C++ development environment is a class browser. When working with an object-oriented language, it is important to be able to visualize the inheritance and other relationships between classes. Class browsers allow the programmer to see and define the relationships between classes, navigate through the classes, and work with the source for those classes. Some allow the class hierarchy to be directly manipulated within the browser window; others provide this function in a separate graphical hierarchy editor tool.

Class browsers are typically well integrated with a source editor. In most development environments, the editor can be driven by the browser. For example, one can double-click on a method name in a browser window in order to find and display the method source in the editor window. The reverse is also true, editors are typically able to invoke browser functions. For example, while viewing source in the editor, the programmer can select a method name in order to locate its definition using the browser.

In order to perform effectively, class browsers require meta-information for the set of classes being browsed (e.g., each class' set of base classes). Parsing the source files to extract this information "on the fly" cannot be done quickly enough. As a result, most browsers rely on compilers or other parsers in the development environment to extract this information in advance and make it globally available. In many C++ development environments, this parsing is done automatically whenever a class is added to a project or changed.

56.2.3 Integrated Development Environments

In an attempt to better integrate the compiler and editor, one of the first tools added to the development environment was a window that displayed the informational, warning, and error messages generated while compiling a program. By selecting one of the messages, the programmer could use this window to locate the line of source code that caused the message to be generated. The focus would be changed to the editor window containing the source line, and the source code would be scrolled to that line within the editor window.

Message windows have evolved into a more complete message manager tool that also displays messages from builds, program execution, and other activities within the development environment. These message managers also enable the user to filter, delete, print, or save messages.

Most C++ development environments provide a high level of tool integration, and are referred to as *interactive development environments* (IDEs). An IDE provides a common launching point for the tools and serves to orchestrate them. Allowing one to "plug in" any tool desired, rather than being limited to the tools provided within the development environment, is becoming a common feature of IDEs. For example, the ability to replace the source editor in the environment with a "favorite" one is often supported. If, however, other tools in the development environment rely on being able to programmatically invoke and manipulate an editor window, and the replacement editor does not support this, then the other tools will become less functional. This reduces the overall integration of the development environment.

Some IDEs use a multiple document interface (MDI) to give a visual encapsulation of all the tools running in a particular development environment. Others use a single document interface (SDI) to prevent the windows from being restricted in a single overall window. Both MDI and SDI have their advantages and disadvantages; which is better is basically an issue of personal preference.

With the move toward more object-oriented interfaces, the application-oriented MDI style is being used less often, and a style that is somewhere between MDI and SDI, called a *project*, is being used instead. In a project UI, one main window provides management for all windows associated with a project. There is, however, no visual containment of windows. Each tool has its own primary window and interface (menu bar, tool bar, etc.), although common toolbar palette windows can be shared.

56.2.4 Visual Development

Increasingly, development environments are enhancing their tool suites to support the paradigm of visual programming and rapid application development (RAD). Visual programming uses graphical techniques to accelerate the development of computer programs.

The inclusion of visual programming tools in a C++ development environment produces C++ products that are powerful, flexible, productive, and easy to use. Since traditional development tools are essential when low-level programming is required, the addition of higher level modeling to the development environment is preferable to the conversion of the environment to high-level development only.

56.2.4.1 Resource Editors and GUI Builders

In traditional operating systems, "resources" are used to represent the user- and language-dependent elements of a program. Resources are defined, stored, and used differently in different environments. They are, however, always separate from the code, which allows them to be handled separately. This is useful when transferring resources to be translated into different languages.

A resource editor is a tool designed specifically for resource modification. For example, a GUI builder is a resource editor used for creating and modifying the resources that represent the visual elements of a program such as dialogs, icons, bitmaps, and fonts. GUI builders allow the elements of a user interface to be laid out visually by dragging and resizing them on the screen. Resource editors also are available for dealing with other elements such as string tables, help tables, help text, and accelerator tables.

Development environments that support visual programming have less need for separate resource editors since visual programming tools allow for the same type of "visual layout". With visual programming, the UI elements also can be "connected" to program elements, thereby defining the behavior as well as the layout.

56.2.4.2 Reuse Galleries

In order to facilitate the development of high-quality code through reuse, collections of reusable elements are being included within development environments. These collections are often referred to as "galleries". Galleries can include groups of classes, resources, graphics, samples, and components. Some galleries are simply prepackaged groups of elements, while others can be extended by the addition of a programmer's own elements or the elements of others.

In addition to providing reusable elements, some galleries provide assistance for importing elements into programs. A gallery may help modify code to facilitate the inclusion of a requested element. Component galleries provide reusable components (OCXs, ActiveX controls, etc.) that can be used by component assembly tools for rapid application development.

56.2.4.3 Component Assemblers/Visual Builders

Component assemblers allow segments of code to be linked together to form larger working programs. Component assembly is achieved visually. Relationships between components are defined by scripts that allow components to communicate. Component assembly makes use of predefined components, eliminating the need to create components from scratch.

Initially, visual programming was utilized only for designing the user interface. A programmer could visually design the elements of the GUI using resource editors, which would generate the resource scripts to be compiled for the program. More recently, support has been included for visually modeling the data and processes as well. Now it is possible to visually design the GUI, the "invisible" program elements, and the relationships between the program elements.

56.2.5 Program Understanding

Some C++ development environments include tools to help understand programs. Some of these tools provide static source code analysis, while others can be used to help determine the dynamic runtime behavior of a program. These kinds of tools are used for many purposes, especially debugging and performance-tuning.

56.2.5.1 Impact Analyzers

Impact analysis tools are used for "program understanding," and are usually invoked during the maintenance phase of the software lifecycle. When a program is modified, the effects of the modification on the rest of the program need to be understood in order to avoid the unwanted side effects that can often result from code changes.

Parsing tools also aid in program understanding. Parsing tools assist in checking the semantics of code to locate potential problem areas. A parsing tool might, for example, check the memory usage of a program to locate memory leaks, or check for code that is never called.

56.2.5.2 Message Monitors

Message monitor tools have the ability to "spy" on the windows or message queues of a desktop, providing information on what messages are being generated and which objects are receiving those messages. Examples of messages include those that are generated as a result of a window gaining or losing focus and those that occur when buttons are pressed. This tool is useful when writing GUI environment programs, since programmers must deal with the messages passed between the various elements of the user interface.

56.2.5.3 Profilers

Profiler tools are included in development environments to help analyze the runtime characteristics of programs. Since performance is of particular importance, profilers highlight which pieces of code are used most often, emphasizing the areas where efficiency needs to be maximized. Profilers can display call tree, time line, execution density, and execution-time statistics. Usually a program must be compiled differently in order to introduce the runtime instrumentation code required by the profiler.

56.2.6 Lifecycle Support

Most C++ development environments cover only a small portion of the software development cycle (generally the coding phase). However, professional or enterprise versions of many development environments extend this scope by adding tools for object-oriented analysis and design, source control and versioning, and testing.

56.2.6.1 Object-Oriented Analysis and Design

Another feature of professional or enterprise C++ development environments is the object-oriented analysis and design (OOAD) tool. OOAD tools assist programmers in utilizing OOAD methodologies to create logical and physical models for their programs. The methodologies (for example, OMT, Schlaer/Mellor, Booch, and UML) include both the processes for developing the objects and the notation for specifying the elements of the design. Certain OOAD tools support multiple methodologies and notations.

Some OOAD tools include built-in generators that are able to create code in one or more languages for the program that was modeled. Another feature found in some OOAD tools is the ability to import existing code, which gives the OOAD tool the potential to support iterative development. Since object-oriented development is iterative in nature, it is useful for the OOAD tool to be able to synchronize work done within itself with work done outside, by importing code back into the model. The ability to keep the code and the model synchronized is sometimes referred to as *round-tripping* or *two-way editing.*

56.2.6.2 Source Control and Versioning

Tools that facilitate collaboration are required when software is being developed by teams. A *source controller* is one of the most basic collaborative tools for team software development. Source controllers allow developers to share program source, and prevent the changes of one programmer from being lost due to changes made by another. To modify the program source, a developer must first "check out" the source. This in turn causes the source (usually a file) to be locked, which prevents other concurrent updates from occurring. Later, when the modification is complete, the source is "checked in." This replaces the shared copy and unlocks it, after which others can access the changes as well as make further changes of their own.

Another form of source control is *versioning.* A source controller that allows programmers to create multiple versions of the source, also known as a *configuration manager* or *version controller,* is commonly used in professional development environments where more than one variant of the source code must be concurrently maintained. For example, a version of the source representing the "current" release of a product may be needed for maintenance purposes, while another version is being modified for the upcoming release.

Some source control tools also support *change control.* Change control can be used to enforce a disciplined approach for modifying program source. It can be used to restrict developers from making changes to a particular piece of code unless, for example, the change represents a fix for a problem in a currently shipped release of the product.

It is often necessary to track and record changes to source code in order to identify areas in a program that may have quality problems that need to be resolved. Some source control tools also support the tracking and reporting of change information.

56.2.6.3 Software Testing

An important part of software development involves testing the programs. Test tools can help build testing scaffolds or automate the testing process.

Programs that contain a GUI are particularly challenging to test. Some test tools allow one to record sequences of user interactions with the program's GUI and play them back later to repeat the interaction sequence. These tools typically allow one to optionally store, in a script format, the captured interaction sequences. Playback is then driven by this script. This approach allows one to modify the interaction sequence before playback or even to manually create the sequence by entering a script.

56.3 Summary

C++ is, and will continue to be for some time to come, a popular language for the development of object-oriented applications, especially performance-critical ones. A number of commercially available C++ development environments have evolved around this popularity. These products are available in various versions that are well suited to a large number of application domains ranging from simple stand-alone applications to large complex programs for distributed enterprise environments.

Many of the early problems with the C++ programming language, such as slow compile times and header file management, have, to a large degree, been reduced or even eliminated by tools in the environment. With the well-integrated tools that are commonly available, C++ environments can support rapid application development and at the same time are capable of producing robust, industrial-strength applications.

57

Java Commercial Development Environments

Frank J. Budinsky
IBM Canada Ltd.

Steven R. Dobson
IBM Canada Ltd.

What tends to happen to me is that I get something in my head that I want to do and the tools don't work so I end up building tools and regressing backwards...

— James Gosling

A programming language like Java can be considered a tool. Unlike languages that are intended strictly for notational purposes, the use of a programming language requires a supporting set of development tools. At a minimum, this includes a compiler and, typically, some level of runtime support. In practice, many additional tools and functions are required to effectively develop nontrivial applications. This chapter describes development tools and environment features that support the Java programming language.*

57.1 Introduction

Introduced in 1995, Java has rapidly become a popular programming language, especially for network and Web- based application development. The explosive growth of the Internet and World Wide Web (WWW) in recent years has helped to fuel this popularity. As Java's popularity has increased, so has the need for application development tools supporting Java.

A Java Development Kit (JDK) is available from JavaSoft,** free of charge. It includes a basic class library and a simple set of command-line tools for Java. In conjunction with a simple text editor, the JDK can be used as a basic development environment for writing Java programs.

Although sufficient for developing simple Java programs, the JDK lacks a number of common features found in development environments for other object-oriented programming languages including:

* Product, service, and company names used in this chapter may be trademarks of their respective owners.

** A business unit of Sun Microsystems, Inc.

0-8493-3135-8/99/$0.00+$.50

- A syntax-sensitive editor
- A class browser
- A visual GUI builder / component assembler
- Source generators (wizards)
- Project management
- Integration between tools

Because of Java's rapid adoption, companies have had to scramble to produce Java application development environments that include these types of features. First out of the gate was Symantec, with an adaptation of its C++ product. Other companies quickly followed suit with similar approaches. Consequently, early Java development environments very much resemble their C++ or Smalltalk counterparts. While not perfect, these retrofit products have the advantage of being available earlier than would otherwise be possible. The familiar look and feel also reduces the learning curve for users familiar with the original product. Manufacturers benefit, as well, from early user feedback with which they can refine and improve their Java environments.

57.2 The JDK

To facilitate its adoption and to standardize its use, the designers of Java decided to freely distribute a Java tool kit. Available from JavaSoft, the JDK serves as a "reference implementation" for the Java language. In addition to a Java compiler and interpreter, the JDK includes a number of other basic tools and a set of foundation class libraries useful for developing typical Java programs.

The runtime part of the JDK is also packaged separately and referred to as the Java Runtime Environment (JRE). The JRE does not include any of the JDK tools and is the smallest set of executables and files that constitute the standard Java platform. It includes the Java virtual machine and a core set of Java classes. Unlike the JDK, which is intended to only be used for development, the JRE is intended to be distributed with Java programs.

57.2.1 JDK Tools

The JDK is not an integrated development environment (IDE); it is a simple set of basic command-line tools. The most commonly used tools included in the JDK are the following:

- **javac** is a Java compiler that converts Java source code into Java bytecode. The **javac** command compiles one or more Java source files, each containing one or more Java class (or interface) definitions, and produces one .class file for each class (or interface) as output.
- **java** is a Java interpreter (a virtual machine that runs a Java application by interpreting Java bytecode). The **java** command uses a class path (i.e., a set of directories containing class files or zip files containing .class files) to locate the set of .class files required by an application.
- **appletviewer** is a Java applet viewer, similar to **java**, but for running applets instead of applications. The **appletviewer** parses one or more specified HTML files containing embedded applets, and displays and executes the applets, each in their own window.

In addition to the basic tools, the JDK includes a number of other simple, but useful, development tools. These include a rudimentary debugger, as well as tools that automate many common Java development tasks. These JDK tools are briefly described below:

- **jdb** is a command-line debugger written in Java. Some of the debugger commands include run, stop at, stop in, suspend, methods, classes, step, clear, list, and catch.
- **javadoc** is a tool for generating class documentation by extracting comments contained in the Java source files. API documentation is generated in HTML format for any specified package or source files.

- **javah** is an emitter tool to help implement Java native methods in C. It generates the required header files as well as skeleton implementation files.
- **javap** is a Java bytecode disassembler. It prints the contents of one or more class files in a human-readable form.

Several utility commands that are useful when using specific JDK features such as JavaBeans or Java RMI, are also available:

- **jar** is a Java archive tool for creating and unpacking .jar files. A .jar file is a zip format archive used to group one or more JavaBeans with their related files (such as serialized content, resources, or help documentation), and, optionally, contains a manifest file that describes the contents of the .jar file.
- **javakey** generates digital signatures for archive files and manages the database of entities and their keys and signatures.
- **rmic** generates stub and skeleton classes for Java objects implementing the java.rmi.Remote interface.
- **rmiregistry** starts a remote object registry on a specified port. The remote object registry is a bootstrap naming service that is used by RMI servers.
- **serialver** returns a unique version identifier, serialVersionUID, for one or more classes.

The number of commands provided with the JDK has increased from version to version. As new features are added to the JDK (e.g., RMI support), tools that simplify the task of creating programs utilizing that feature (e.g., **rmic**) are also added. This type of enhancement is likely to continue although the new tools, like the current JDK tools, will not be particularly sophisticated and will likely be incorporated into commercially available development environments.

57.2.2 JDK Classes

In addition to providing the basic Java language definition, JavaSoft has made a concerted effort to standardize the use of Java by defining a set of standard class libraries. The classes are categorized either as part of the core Java platform or as a standard extension. Core classes constitute the minimal set of APIs that are present on all implementations of the Java platform.* Standard extensions are those classes outside of the core API for which JavaSoft has published a standard. Over time, as the Java platform develops, some of the standard extensions might migrate into the core API.

The core API provided by the JDK includes support for such tasks as working with applets, building GUIs, manipulating images, performing input and output operations, working in a networked environment, and dealing with basic language elements such as runtime services and exception handling. Standard extensions include an Enterprise API (e.g., support for CORBA IDL), Commerce API, and a Java Media Framework, among others.

Some of the most commonly used core Java classes are included in the following packages:

- **package java.lang** contains the most essential classes to Java, including the common base class Object, runtime services, class wrappers for basic data types (such as Character and Integer), string support, math support, and exception handling.
- **package java.util** are the utility classes for collections (such as stack and hashtable) and object observability.
- **package java.io** contains classes for handling input and output through streaming, files, pipes, and printing.
- **package java.awt,** Abstract Windowing Toolkit (AWT) includes classes for dealing with a program user interface, including graphics (such as polygons and images), GUI components (controls such

* Except embedded Java platforms that are intended to run on small dedicated systems such as printers, copiers, and cellular phones.

as buttons and dialog boxes), control layout, fonts, and colors. Many of these classes will change or be replaced as JavaSoft introduces the Java Foundation Classes (JFC). JFC will provide a much richer structure for larger scale GUI development than the original AWT package.

- **package java.applet** allows the creation of Java applets.
- **package java.beans** with JavaBeans APIs define a portable, platform-neutral set of APIs for software components.
- **package java.net** provides a good basic infrastructure for networking, including dealing with uniform resource locators (URLs), sockets, and data packets.
- **package java.security**, the Java security APIs are a framework for developers to easily include security features such as digital signatures, encryption, and authentication in their applets and applications.

Some Java development environment manufacturers provide alternative class libraries of their own. Although using these non-standard classes results in fully functional Java programs, it does have its disadvantages. Use of proprietary classes locks a developer into one particular vendor and, more importantly, requires the classes to be delivered to the target platform along with the application. This requirement is particularly significant for applets, because their performance is negatively affected by the increase in download time. The standard classes, on the other hand, are available on all supported platforms and operating systems, making downloads much faster.

57.3 Java IDEs

As alternatives to the JDK, several IDEs are also available for Java. These environments provide a very powerful set of development tools but, unlike the JDK, they are not free of charge. There is a large variation in price (and level of functionality) between products and, in many cases, between versions of the same product.

When purchasing an IDE, there is a trade off between price and function. For example, if only basic Web development support is required, a low-priced, entry-level product will probably be sufficient. If support is required for a large scale multi-person development project (involving, for example, database connectivity), the purchase of a (much) more expensive professional version may be necessary.

Some examples of commercially available Java IDEs include:

- Asymetrix, SuperCede for Java
- Borland, Open JBuilder
- IBM, VisualAge for Java
- Microsoft, Visual J++
- ParcPlace-Digitalk, Parts for Java
- Powersoft, Jato
- Sun, Java WorkShop
- Symantec, Visual Cafe
- Visix, Vibe

Many of these products have the same look and feel as C++ or Smalltalk products on which they are based. One of the advantages of these new Java products is that users familiar with the earlier product will not need to spend a great deal of time learning how to use new development tools. A major disadvantage is that some specific Java features may not be supported in an optimal manner.

Because the Java language is so closely related to the development of programs for the Internet, some Java development environments use a Web browser user interface. With this style, immediately recognizable to those familiar with Web browsing, the environment tools and help files are all Java-enhanced HTML pages incorporating hyperlinks to one another. In this approach, the Java programming language is used to implement the environment tools and a seamless integration of the tools with their documentation is easily achieved.

Most development environments conform to the standard Java reference implementation defined by JavaSoft. Others, however, have extended the standard reference implementation to create their own. The Microsoft development environment has extended the standard JDK reference implementation to allow all public Java classes to also be Component Object Model (COM) classes. Using a nonstandard JDK reference implementation has the advantage of providing added functionality, but introduces the risk of losing code portability when nonstandard extensions are used.

57.3.1 IDE Features

Because many Java development environments have evolved from previous products, they have profited by being able to offer sophisticated features from the outset. For example, all of the standard features in C++ development environments are commonly available in Java environments as well. These include features like customizable source editors with syntax highlighting, integrated class browsers, visual GUI builders, powerful debuggers, and source generators (wizards). Refer to Chapter 56, "C++ Commercial Development Environments," for a more detailed description of these features.

Java's interpreted nature can be exploited by some powerful development tools that can be found in certain Java development environments. Incremental debuggers that allow programs to be changed on-the-fly while debugging are one example. These debuggers allow changes made during the debugging process to be dynamically incorporated while the program continues uninterrupted. By eliminating the conventional edit-compile-debug cycle, significant development time can be saved.

Java's suitability for network- and Web-based application development necessitated the introduction of remote debugging. Without this capability, it is difficult to debug applications requiring software on both client and server systems. Support for remote debugging has started to appear in Java IDEs with some products supporting the debugging of distributed client and server software from a single machine. The result is a substantial improvement in productivity during Web-based application development.

In order to allow third-party tools to plug into their IDE, some manufacturers provide an open API for the environment. For example, this API allows a third party version control system to be used from within the IDE. It also makes the environment inherently more customizable.

57.3.2 Visual Development

The foundation of all Java visual development tools is the JavaBean component architecture. Because of it, visual development of Java applications is very common. Two fundamental types of tools are available to support component-based development: those that produce Java components and those that consume them. The first type, JavaBean producing tools, are usually well integrated into Java development environments, and include wizards and other definitional tools supporting the construction of JavaBeans (i.e., Java components). The second type consists of the JavaBean visual construction tools (builders) themselves.

The development of Java software using visual builders is common in several areas. Similar to those for other languages (such as C++), Java visual builders are used for GUI layout and, in some cases, for the visual definition of application logic by the "wiring" of software components. In addition, because of its suitability for Web-based applications, visual development of Java programs (specifically applets) might also be utilized in a Web page builder.

According to the JavaBean specification, the fundamental definition of a JavaBean is "a reusable software component that can be manipulated visually in a builder tool." Not unlike the components in other component architectures, a JavaBean must make available the set of functions that builder tools need to work with the component. These include support for:

- **Introspection** — querying the bean to determine what methods, properties, and events it provides
- **Customization** — modifying the appearance and behavior of a bean dynamically
- **Events** — a mechanism by which other components are to be notified of changes to the JavaBean's internal state

- **Properties** — a mechanism by which a bean's data can be accessed or changed, either during customization or during program execution when interacting with other beans
- **Persistence** — saving the state of a customized JavaBean so that it can be later restored

Using these functions, visual builders determine the properties of, customize the appearance and behavior of, and create interactions between (i.e., wire together) JavaBeans, thereby providing a rapid application development (RAD) facility for Java.

Although visual builders differ in functionality and sophistication, they are all fundamentally the same. Typically, they use a palette containing a set of available beans, some provided with the development environment, others provided by the user or a third party. The user selects a bean from the palette and inserts it (e.g., using drag-and-drop) onto an application or applet that is currently being developed. For visual components, this action typically involves positioning and sizing a control element (e.g., Button) on a canvas.

Once a JavaBean is added to the program, the user can select and edit it. The builder will introspect the selected bean to determine whether or not it provides its own customizer class. If not, a simple property sheet UI is created containing entries as described by introspection of the bean. The user can modify the values on the property sheet to customize the bean appearance (e.g., button label, color, etc.).

If the JavaBean has its own customizer class, the builder will use it, thereby delegating the editing operation to the bean itself. The customizer may provide a wizard-like user interface to guide the user through the customization process. Once the bean is customized, the builder uses the Java persistence mechanism to store the customized state of the JavaBean for later restoration at runtime.

In addition to adding and customizing individual beans, most visual builders also provide some support for creating interactions between them. The level of sophistication in this function varies from builder to builder. Creating a connection from a source bean to a target bean is usually done by selecting an event from a list of events that are generated by the source. Some builders also allow the user to select an action in the target bean and, if required, select the source for any arguments required by the action, thereby completely defining the interaction visually. Other builders require the user to enter the code for the event handling (listener) method manually. In either case, the builder will emit the required glue code (i.e., bean listener class, as well as listener registration code in the source object).

JavaBean builders are often part of a complete Java IDE, although some are stand-alone tools that run independently. Some, in fact, insulate their user entirely from Java source code. Instead, they work abstractly in terms of bean properties, methods, and events; and they output compiled bytecodes (i.e., .class files) for the application glue code, instead of Java source code.

57.3.3 Web Authoring Tools

Another feature specific to Java IDEs is integrated Web authoring tools. Many Java programs (i.e., applets) are embedded in HTML Web pages; the development of these Java programs is only part of a complete Web page development project. Therefore the integration of Java applet development with the development of the Web pages that will use the applet is desirable.

Although HTML documents can be created with a standard text editor, professional developers generally require a more sophisticated Web authoring tool. Most HTML document authoring tools support the use of applets within a document. Some Java IDEs provide a high level of integration with such a tool. Applets created in the IDE can be, for example, dragged from an IDE window and then dropped onto an HTML page in the Web authoring tool.

HTML page design often involves programming in JavaScript, an object scripting language that compliments the Java language. JavaScript can be used in HTML documents to handle events in HTML forms, or to customize the behavior of an actual Java applet. Similar in syntax, the fundamental difference between Java and JavaScript is that Java code is compiled into .class files, which are later downloaded by a Web browser when an <applet> tag is encountered in an HTML document. The Java bytecodes are then interpreted by the browser on the client machine. JavaScript, on the other hand, is embedded

Java-like source code that is coded directly in an HTML file and is interpreted by the HTML server instead of in the client (browser).

The conceptual similarity of Java and JavaScript, as well as their complimentary uses, provides additional motivation for the tight integration of Java development environments and Web authoring tools. Development of both Java code, in a Java development environment, and JavaScript, in a Web authoring tool, often contributes to the development of a complete Web application.

57.4 Java Runtime Execution

One of Java's main strengths is its cross-platform compatibility. Rather than compiling Java source code into machine instructions targeted to a specific platform, Java source code is compiled into machine-independent bytecodes that are interpreted at runtime. The interpreter is referred to as a virtual machine (VM) because it is a software-emulated processor for the instruction set defined by the Java bytecodes.

57.4.1 VMs

Many VM implementations currently exist, with one or more being available for every operating system that supports Java. These VMs are either stand-alone interpreters for Java applications, or are built into Web browsers supporting Java applets. Many operating systems, from Microsoft Windows to IBM MVS, are also integrating a VM directly into the OS.

Most Java development environments include some kind of applet viewer tool that can be used to test an applet during development. An applet viewer simply parses an HTML file (in which the applet is embedded), ignoring everything but the <applet> tags, and invokes a VM to execute the specified applets. By using an applet viewer instead of a Web browser, the development environment's VM is used to execute the program (as opposed to the Web browsers internal VM). This allows access to other integrated development tools, such as the debugger, while testing the program.

The JDK **java** command (see Section 57.2.1) serves as the reference VM implementation, although most development environments and Web browsers provide their own enhanced VM. Some of the enhancements include: caching code to increase performance, dynamic modification of the code at execution time, versioning support, compression services, authentication services, code optimization, sophisticated garbage collection algorithms, and support for debuggers. However, the most important differentiation among the various Java VMs is their speed of execution. No matter how much optimization is done in the VM, the performance of an interpreted system is intrinsically slower than that of a compiled one. This is the main disadvantage of the Java VM-based design. Executing each individual bytecode of a non-trivial program in succession can become a very time consuming process. The designers of Java took this into account by making a provision for just-in-time (JIT) compilers.

When a VM executes a program where JIT is available, instead of interpreting the bytecodes of each Java method one by one, the methods are passed to the JIT compiler, compiled on-the-fly, and then executed natively. The JIT is said to compile methods into native machine code "just in time" to be executed. The JIT approach offers a significant increase in performance, without sacrificing the platform independence of Java.

57.4.2 Java Native Compilers

Initially, Java was a purely interpreted environment providing the advantages of machine-independence and reduced edit-debug turnaround time during development. These advantages came at the expense of execution-time performance. Time-critical applications could not be programmed in Java unless the time-critical parts were isolated, declared to be Java Native Methods,* and then implemented using a compiled programming language such as C.

* A Java method can be declared using the "native" keyword, which indicates that it is implemented in a compiled programming language such as C. This is typically used to implement specific performance-critical methods.

JIT compilers provide a solution to this performance problem that still allows the entire application to be written in Java. JIT works especially well when the program involves the repeated execution of a small number of methods, in which case the JIT compilation overhead is negligible compared to the overall program execution time. For other applications, where the on-the-fly compilation overhead may be significant, the performance increase of JIT may still not be adequate.

An alternative approach uses a conventional compilation development cycle, whereby the Java code is compiled in advance into native machine code that is then executed directly on the target platform. This approach uses a compiler that is similar to those of other compiled-language (e.g., C++) compilers. They are called "Java native compilers" because they translate Java source code to native machine code. This is in contrast to the more commonly used "Java compilers" which only translate Java source code to Java bytecodes.

The native compilation approach forgoes the advantages of the Java interpretive system in favor of a high-speed compiled version of the program. Therefore, it is typically only used as an optimization step after development is completed in the high-speed, edit-debug VM-based environment. A developer may, for example, create a fully portable application, which operates on any Java-enabled platform, and later rebuild it using a native compiler to generate a high-performance version for a specific platform. Also, native compilation, along with its increase in performance, is desirable for implementing server software in multi-tier environments where portability is not required.

Using native code compilers, Java programs can achieve a level of performance comparable to that of other native software. The performance of the native version of a program is independent of VM performance because, as with any native software system, it includes its own runtime environment and runs as an entirely self-contained executable program.

57.5 Summary

Java programs can be developed using the tools provided with the JDK, which is available free of charge from JavaSoft. The JDK provides simple command-line tools and the standard classes that define the Java reference platform. It is not, however, an integrated development environment and does not provide the kinds of tools that are typically required for large or complicated development efforts. There are a number of commercially available Java IDEs that address the needs of the more sophisticated developer.

Many Java IDEs have evolved from previous C++ or Smalltalk products and, as a result, have familiar look and feel, and include a wealth of functionality. Others are totally new products, some of which use a Web browser type of user interface that reflects Java's suitability to programming for the WWW. These products include the kinds of features normally included in a professional development environment, such as syntax-sensitive editors, class browsers, wizards, and other features common in development environments for other object-oriented languages. Visual (JavaBean) builders are also common. Some are stand-alone tools while others are well-integrated features of the IDEs.

Some IDE features are unique to Java. For example, because Java is often used to develop applets, integrated Web authoring tools are also available in some Java development environments. To address performance concerns stemming from Java's interpreted nature, JIT and Java native compilers are available. JIT compilers translate Java methods (bytecodes) to machine code at runtime the first time they are called. Native compilers, like those of other programming languages, are used to generate native platform-specific code, entirely eliminating the need for a virtual machine at runtime.

Overall, Java development environments have evolved quickly to match the functionality in those of other object-oriented programming languages, and are poised to become even better as their tools support and exploit the many powerful features that are (and are becoming) available for Java. The combination of a powerful language, extensive standard classes, and high-quality tools makes Java an excellent platform for many kinds of software development.

58

Smalltalk Commercial Development Environments

Gary Karasiuk
IBM Canada Ltd.

58.1 Introduction

> We ascribe beauty to that which is simple; which has no superfluous parts; which exactly answers its end; which stands related to all things; which is the mean of many extremes.
>
> — **Ralph Waldo Emerson**

Smalltalk programmers will proudly tell you that their development environment is elegant and makes them very productive. The features of Smalltalk that give rise to this include:

- Interpreted-language features
- Integrated browsers
- An integrated debugger
- An extensible development environment
- Team programming facilities
- Extensive class libraries

This chapter describes these features as they are found in a number of commercially available Smalltalk products. In particular the author has practical experience with:

- Smalltalk V/PM from Digitalk®
- Visual Works from ParcPlace®
- VisualAge™ for Smalltalk from IBM®

but most of his experience is with VisualAge for Smalltalk.

0-8493-3135-8/99/$0.00+$.50

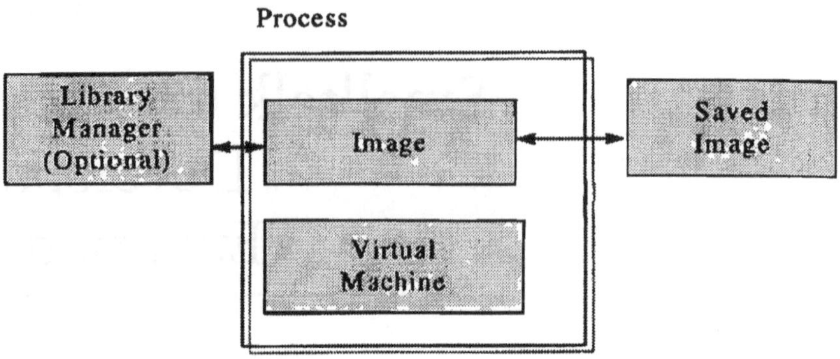

FIGURE 58.1 Smalltalk environment structure.

58.1.1 Background

The basic structure of the Smalltalk environment is shown in Figure 58.1.

The Smalltalk source code is processed and converted into byte codes, which are then run in a virtual machine. Much of the Smalltalk environment is written in Smalltalk. Using a virtual machine makes Smalltalk quite portable. Java uses the same approach to achieve good portability. Smalltalk employs a fat client model, in which the client machine needs to have a large amount of RAM as the entire image needs to be loaded into memory. Between sessions, the memory image is saved onto disk in a form that allows it to be reconstructed later. Optionally, the image may be connected to a library system, so that incremental changes are saved in a library, and work is shared among team members.

58.2 Development Environment Features

58.2.1 Interpreted Language

Because Smalltalk is an interpreted language there is no compile time penalty. This makes it practical for programmers to focus on just one problem at a time. This is a very productive way to work, because programmers can find a problem, fix it, test it, and then move on to the next problem. In environments such as C^{++} where the compile and link steps may take minutes or even hours, it is not as practical to work on only one problem at a time. There programmers typically try to fix several problems at the same time so that their compile and link times can be amortized over several problems. This means that they must keep several problems in mind at the same time, and also means that more things will have changed from one debugging session to the next. This makes everything more complex. Also, while the program is compiling it is easy to forget what one was working on, so programmers must refresh their memories before resuming their debugging session. In Smalltalk it is possible to be more focused. Generally as soon as a problem is fixed it can be used. The "compile/link" step usually only takes a second or two. This mode of programming may be the single biggest advantage that Smalltalk offers.

The disadvantage of an interpreted language is that the final application is not as efficient as one that was developed with a compile language.

58.2.2 Browsers

Smalltalk development environments come with several browsers that allow you to manipulate Smalltalk images in a number of ways. Each browser is optimized for a different purpose, but often different browsers can be used to accomplish the same task. The one most commonly used is the "Applications Browser," which is typically used to change source code. We will take a closer look at this browser, as it

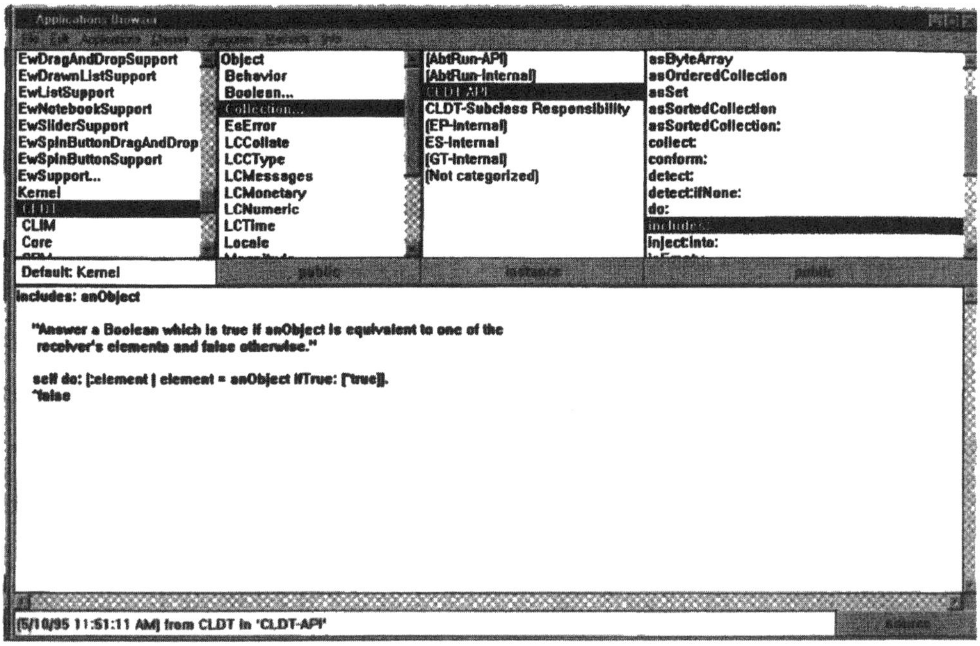

FIGURE 58.2 Application browser from VisualAge for Smalltalk.

is representative of many of the other browsers. Figure 58.2 Application Browser from VisualAge for Smalltalk shows a screen capture of the Application Browser. (This screen capture is from VisualAge for Smalltalk; most of the Smalltalk environments have a similar looking browser.)

This browser organizes code in a containment hierarchy. Applications* (upper leftmost pane) contains classes (second pane), which contain categories (third pane), which contain methods (last pane). Once a method is selected, it is displayed in the bottom pane. This browser is typical of most Smalltalk browsers, in that it contains multiple text-based panes. Programmers typically work from left to right, navigating through the browser until they find the method they want.

Applications are used to group together classes and class extensions. (A class extension is a set of methods. These can be class methods, instance methods, or a combination of the two. Any one method can only be owned by a single class extension or class. A class, in addition to being able to hold a set of methods [as a class extension can], also holds the class definition. The class definition holds the structure of the class; that is, its instance variables, class variables, and superclass.) Any particular class or class extension is owned by a single Application. Applications can also contain other Applications. This containment relationship forms a tree. This tree structure gives you a flexible way of organizing your code. Classes can be either public or private. A private class should not be used outside the Application that owns it. A class can also have a description and notes.

The category function of the browsers is yet another mechanism for helping programmers to organize their code. A category (sometimes called a protocol) is a word or phase that you define and then associate with methods. Examples of categories are "access methods" and "printing." A method can be associated with zero or more categories, and the same category can be used in multiple classes. The browser can then filter the methods it displays based on the categories that are selected.

All these features become important as the number of methods becomes large. It is not uncommon to have well over 100,000 methods in an application.

* The Smalltalk environment actually contains two similar concepts, Applications and Subapplications. For simplification, we use the term Application to represent either Application or Subapplication.

The rightmost pane in Figure 58.2 lists the methods. Most methods are small. The example method shown in this figure is typical. Users make their changes in the bottom pane and then select Save when they are done. This causes the method to be

1. Parsed
2. Stored in the library manager (if present)
3. Compiled into byte codes

Because the grammar for the Smalltalk language is so simple* and because Smalltalk is untyped, it is not often that there will be invalid syntax in the method body. If the syntax is invalid, the browser will display an error message and force the user to correct the error before the method will be saved.

Because the entire image is loaded into memory and there are extensive relationships between the various components (such as class name to method name), the browsers support a rich set of impact analysis queries. For example, you can ask to see:

- A list of all the places where a method is either used or implemented
- A list of all the places where a particular class or instance variable is used
- A list of all of the methods that reference a particular class

These facilities allow you to more easily maintain your application. They also make it easier to understand other people's code.

Methods can be either public or private, and either instance or class. A private method should not be used by methods outside of its class. This classification of methods and classes as either private or public helps make your code more reusable, as it forces you to pay attention to what is interface and what is implementation. Like classes, methods can have descriptions and notes.

58.2.3 Debugging

Because of the interpreted design of Smalltalk, its debugger is powerful. You can set breakpoints and/or choose to single-step through your program. You set a breakpoint by including the "self halt," line in a method. The breakpoint will persist until you remove it. When you are stopped at a breakpoint, you have access to the entire state of the program. You can examine and/or change any of the objects in your image. Unlike some languages (for example, C++) Smalltalk makes it easy to examine a particular element of a collection. You do this through the Smalltalk inspector, which is another browser. It allows you to display, change, and navigate to any object into your image. For example, if you were inspecting a collection of Employee objects, you could ask to inspect the fourth Employee object, which is simply an object that is referred to by the collection. This brings up another inspector window that shows all the instance variables of the selected Employee. If you ask to inspect the Employee's name, this brings up another inspector window that contains the string that holds the Employee's name. In general, while you are inspecting objects their instance variables will be one of the following:

- A string — something that you can display and change
- A number — something that you can display and change
- Another object — something that you can navigate to
- An index in a collection — this is similar to another object, in that it is something that you can navigate to

Ultimately, you end up manipulating strings and numbers.

Also, while stopped in the debugger you can evaluate any code fragment you like. Some programmers claim this is the best feature of the environment. You can do this to further examine the state of your program, or to repair the state of your program so that you can continue with your debugging session. If you are examining someone else's code (or even your own), this feature can greatly aid you in understanding the code.

---

* The grammar for the Smalltalk language (in the EBNF notation) fits on a single page. This is one of the features that makes Smalltalk so elegant.

You can change and recompile methods while debugging. The execution point can then be backed up to either the beginning of the changed method or to an earlier point in the call stack. This is yet another mechanism that helps to preserve your debugging session. Unlike other environments where you have to spend a large amount of time getting *ready* to do some work, in a Smalltalk environment, you spend most of your time *doing* the work.

Finally, many Smalltalk programmers use the debugger in its single-step mode to learn about someone else's program. The debugger allows you to understand how the objects interact with one another. It is like having an object able to run interaction diagram.

58.2.4 Extensible Environment

Much of the development environment is shipped in source code form. This allows it to be extended and customized at a particular installation. By shipping source code it also makes debugging easier for programmers, because they can figure out what the "system" is doing.

This feature is a mixed blessing, and so must be used carefully. The extensions must be made in such a way that you can easily upgrade when the next version of Smalltalk is available. It is preferable to only add methods and/or subclasses, not to change system methods.

58.2.5 Team Programming

Most commercial application development is not done by a single programmer. Team support is an important consideration for most customers. In Smalltalk, Envy®* Manager is an example of a team programming environment. In this environment, the individual Smalltalk images are connected to a central library. As changes are made in the image, they are also stored in the library.

A software engineering approach is taken where entities such as Applications and classes are owned, and where the owner has the responsibility for ensuring that all of the changes are consistent and correct. There are two steps in making a change public:

1. "Version" the change
2. Release the change

Any time you save a method it is stored in the library; thus even in the case of a power failure, very little work would be lost. You may lose the last method that you were in the middle of changing, and you will lose the time that it takes you to reconstruct your image, but no more. This also allows you to go back in time and look at previous versions of the method.

Until a class is "versioned," all these incremental changes are available only to the programmer who made them. Once you have something that you want to share with others, or you have progressed enough that you would like to save your current state, you can version one or more of your classes. Once a class has been versioned, it is frozen in the library and can no longer be changed by anyone. To make changes to the class, a new edition** needs to be created.

Typically, programmers do not share code at the class level, as that tends to be too fine-grained. It is more practical to share at the Application level. When a new version of a class is created, it must be "released" to its containing Application before it becomes part of that Application. Only the class owner can release the class into an Application. This allows the class owner to review any changes before the class is released. There are usually four cases:

1. The class owner is satisfied with the changes, and releases them into the Application.***
2. The class owner is not satisfied with the changes. They would explain to the programmer who submitted the changed class what the problem is, and then wait for a new version of the class.

---

* Trademark of Object Technology International, Inc.

** The difference between an edition and a version is that an edition is fluid and can be changed. A version is a snapshot and its contents are frozen. The version operation converts an edition into a version.

*** More often than not, the programmer making the change is also the class owner, so Case 1 is the usual case.

3. The class owner takes the versioned class as a base and makes some additional changes so that the entire class is consistent, then versions and releases it.
4. The class owner discovers that parallel development has occurred. The parallel changes are merged into a new edition, which is then versioned and released.

The environment provides a number of browsers to make the class owner's job easier, including browsers that show the changes between two versions of a class. They show you which methods have been added or removed, and for those that have changed, what those changes are.

Applications also have owners and follow the same version and release processes that classes do. The Application owner needs to decide when to version the Application and release it into its parent Application.

Typically, teams work on a weekly cycle. There will be a deadline for releasing changes into the weekly driver. After the deadline, an administrator starts to build a new image from scratch, using the most recently released Applications. This is a useful process in that it ensures that all of the Application's prerequisites are set correctly, which means that all of the inter-Application dependencies have been worked out. Once the new image has been built, the team members use this new image as their base. Any of their changes that were not released into the driver are then applied to their new image. This strikes a good balance between keeping up with other team members' changes and the overhead associated with keeping up with those changes.

58.2.5.1 An Example

We start with an existing Application called BankLoan, which contains a Class called Customer which contains a method called checkCredit. The Application is versioned, and has a version name of 1.0.

```
BankLoan 1.0
  Customer 1.0
    checkCredit 97/05/14-14:02:03
```

This mean if you were to load version 1.0 of BankLoan, you would get version 1.0 of Customer, which includes the 14:02:03 version of checkCredit. You can now create open editions of BankLoan and Customer, which means that their contents can change. This allows you to make a change to checkCredit. This would leave you with:

```
BankLoan 97/05/16-08:01:02
  * Customer 97/05/16-08:01:03
    checkCredit 97/05/16-08:05:02
```

Since Customer is not a version it cannot be easily loaded (i.e., shared) by anyone else. The * in front of Customer means that it has not yet been released into its Application. If you are satisfied with the new version of checkCredit, you could version Customer, leaving you with:

```
BankLoan 97/05/16-08:01:02
  * Customer 1.1
    checkCredit 97/05/16-08:05:02
```

It is now easy for others to load version 1.1 of Customer, because it is a version. You have made it public by versioning it. However, if you were to load BankLoan (even the open edition of BankLoan) you would still get version 1.0 of Customer, since version 1.1 has not yet been released into BankLoan. It is up to the class owner to decide if Customer 1.1 should be released into BankLoan. After the class owner is satisfied with the changes, he or she releases Customer:

```
BankLoan 97/05/16-08:01:02
  Customer 1.1
    checkCredit 97/05/16-08:05:02
```

and anyone loading the open edition of BankLoan would get version 1.1 of Customer. To finish the example, eventually the manager of the BankLoan Application would version it, resulting in a situation that is similar to our starting situation.

```
BankLoan 1.1
   Customer 1.1
      checkCredit 97/05/16-08:05:02
```

58.2.6 Extensive Class Libraries

Smalltalk has been around for many years, and has built up an impressive class library. A significant amount of reuse is possible just by using the standard class library. The class library includes support for:

- Windows
- Collections (including ordered collections, dictionaries, sets, and bags)
- Streams
- Strings and numbers (floating point, integers, decimals, and fractions)
- Data and time
- Files and directories
- Graphics

Since the base class library is mostly the same in the different Smalltalk environments, applications are quite portable. For example, the author was involved in porting a large application from one vendor's Smalltalk to another, (thousands of classes), and almost everything (more than 95% of the code) ported without change. Although in our case, we were using a CASE tool to generate the User Interface, and it is the User Interface part of the class library that tends to be the most dissimilar. In fact, even the library managers were compatible, which allowed us to export from one library and import into the other, preserving the Application structure.

58.3 Summary

Smalltalk is a mature language and environment. It has a number of features that have attracted a large and loyal programmer base. These features include no compile times, an environment that enables programmers to focus on one problem at a time, an integrated environment, and extensive class libraries.

XIV

Appendices

APPENDIX A

Ada 95 Language Guide

Luis Joyanes Aguilar
Pontifical Salamanca University

María Luisa Díez Platas
Pontifical Salamanca University

Paloma Centenera
Pontifical Salamanca University

In this reference guide we are trying to make an enumeration of the most representative elements of Ada 95 language, as well as the syntax rules gathered in the *Reference Manual for the Ada Programming Language* (*RM95*) and *Annotated Ada Reference Manual.*

In order to specify the syntax in every element of the language, the following notation will be used: elements in italics represent syntactic categories, bold elements represent keywords; an element between braces ({}) means that the element can appear zero or more; an element between square brackets means it is optional, that is, it can be left out; an element specified as list_of_items, means one or more items separated by commas and finally a sequence_of_items means one or more items.

A.1.1 Language Vocabulary (Lexical Elements)

A program in Ada 95 consists of a sequence of characters grouped as *tokens* (lexical components), that make up the basic language vocabulary. These components are: keywords, identifiers, constants, chain constants, operators, and punctuation marks.

0-8493-3135-8/99/$0.00+$.50

A.1.1.1 Character Set

In order to build lexical components, you can use the following characters:

- the *alphabet*

  a b c d e f g h i j k l m n o p q r s t u v w x y z
  A B C D E F G H I J K L M N O P Q R S T U V W X Y Z
- the *digits*

  0 1 2 3 4 5 6 7 8 9
- *special characters*

  + - * / , . : ; _ " ' < = > | # & ( )
- *space characters* such as blanks and tabs

A.1.1.2 Comments

Comments begin with two hyphens together (no space is used to separate them) and are extended until the end of the line.

```
--{non_end_of_line_character}
  -- Comment in ADA
```

A.1.1.3 Identifiers

Identifiers consist of an alphabet letter (upper- or lower-case letter) followed by zero or more letters or digits that can be preceded by only one underlined character.

The number of characters that can make up an identifier is not limited and does not distinguish upper- from lower-case letters. The regular expression that specifies these lexical elements are:

```
identifier_letter {[underline] letter_or_digit}

  house      -- is an identifier
  House      -- is the same identifier as before
  The_house      -- is an identifier
  The_house_9      -- is an identifier
  15_houses      -- is not a valid identifier
  _my_house      -- is not a valid identifier
```

A.1.1.4 Keywords

Keywords cannot be used as identifiers. In Ada 95, there are 69 keywords, see Table A.1.

Some keywords can be used as attributes without causing ambiguity problems.

A.1.1.5 Numeric Literals

Numeric literals are used to denote integer or real numbers.

- *Integer literals* are made up of a chain of decimal digits containing an underlined character if the number is large enough so as to group the digits. Integer literals can also be represented in scientific notation by means of an exponent represented by letter E, or e, followed by an integer literal with or without a sign. The specification is the following:

```
  125            -- is a numeric integer literal
  125_678_456    -- is a numeric integer literal
  15E3           -- is a numeric integer literal in scientific
```

TABLE A.1 Keywords

abort	declare	goto	out	select
abs	delay			
abstract	delta	if	package	separate
accept	digits	in	pragma	subtype
access	do	is	private	tagged
aliased	else	limited	procedure	task
all	elsif	loop	protected	terminate
and	end			then
array	entry	mod	raise	type
at	exception	new	range	
begin	exit	not	record	until
body		null	rem	use
	for		renames	when
case	function	of	requeue	while
		or	return	with
constant	generic	others	reserve	xor

```
              -- notation
12e+7         -- is a numeric integer literal in scientific
              -- notation
```

- *Real literals* are made up of a chain of decimal digits with a decimal point which must contain a digit at least on both sides. In order to group digits, the underlined character can be used, as long as it is not written beside the decimal point, and a scientific notation can also be used as in integers.

```
0.234       -- is a numeric real literal
2.15        -- is a numeric real literal
3.456_789   -- is a numeric real literal
.33         -- is an error
2.          -- is an error
5.463E2     -- is a numeric real literal in scientific notation
234.0e-1    -- is a numeric integer literal in scientific notation
```

Both integer and real literals can be expressed in a base other than a decimal base. The base is written followed by character # and then the number plus #. For bases greater than 10, letters A to F are used in order to represent 10 to 15 numbers.

```
3#111#    -- is the number 1*3²+1*3+1 = 13 3 based
16#AB#    -- is the number 10*16+11 = 171 16 based
```

A.1.1.6 Character and String Literals

- *Character literals* are made up of only one character, which is not of control in single quotes. In character literals, there is a difference between upper- and lower-case letters. It is specified the following way:

```
`graphic_character`

  'B'  -- is a character literal
  'b'  -- is a character literal different from the last one
```

- *String literals*, also called characters string, are made up of a printable character string and blanks in double quotes. Like character literals, you can distinguish upper- from lower-case letters.

```
"{non_quotation_mark_graphic_character o ""}"

"house"   -- is a character string
"House"   -- is a character string
""        -- is a character string(empty string)
"a"       -- is a character string (string with only one
          -- character)
```

A.1.1.7 Operators

The existing operators in Ada are the following:

```
logical_operator                  and or xor
relational_operator               = /= < <= > >=
binary_adding_operator            + - &
unary_adding_operator             + -
multiplying_operator              * / mod rem
highest_precedence_operator       ** abs not
```

A.1.2 Data Types

In Ada 95 there is a series of predefined types such as integer, float, character, and boolean. In addition, users can define their own types, subtypes, and derived types. For the declaration of types it's necessary to use the following syntax:

```
type name is type_specification;
```

Subtypes can also be declared. From other types you can establish a restriction in the value range. It has the following syntax:

```
subtype name is type_name [range expression .. expression]
```

There is also the possibility to declare types derived from other types, thus defining new types with the same value range or with a restricted range as the type they derive from, and with the same operations. The following is the syntax to declare derived types, although there are more ways to declare types derived from others, as we will see later.

```
Type name is new type_name  [range expression .. expression];
```

A.1.2.1 Type Declaration

In Ada 95, the following types can be declared:

```
all types

  elementary
    scalar
      discrete
        enumeration
          character (standard types, predefined)
          boolean (standard types, predefined)
          other enumeration
        integer
          signed integer
          modular integer
      real
```

```
            floating point
            fixed point
               ordinary fixed point
               decimal fixed point
      access
         access-to-object
         access-to-subprogram
   composite
      array
constraint array
unconstraint array
         string (predefined subtypes)
         record
   untagged record
      tagged record
      task
      protected
```

A.1.2.2 Declaration of the Main Types

- **Enumeration types**

  type *name* **is** (*list_of_identifiers_or_character_literal*);

  ```
  type flavors is (acid, bitter, sweet, salad);
  type vowels is ('a', 'b', 'c', 'd', 'e');
  ```

- **Signed integers** are declared by means of a value range

  type *name* **is range** *expression.. expression*;

  ```
  type number_month is range 1.. 12;
  ```

- **Modular integers** are unsigned integers and cyclic

  type *name* **is mod** *expression* ;

  type length_buffer is mod 100; entonces the length_buffer's range of values is 0..99.

- **Floating point reals** have a relative error

  type *name* **is digits** *expression* [**range** *expression .. expression*];

To declare floating point reals with at least 6 decimal digits of precision, you can write:

```
type Float_type is digits 6
```

- **Fixed point reals** have an absolute error

  type *name* **is delta** *expression* **range** *expression .. expression*;

To declare fixed point reals you must specify an absolute error and a mandatory range:

```
type Fixed_type is delta 0. 1 range -2.0..+2.0
```

- **Decimal fixed type** in the declaration requires that you provide a value of the absolute error and also the number of significant decimals digits

  type *name* **is delta** *expression* **digits** *expression* [**range** *expression ..*
  expression];

  ```
  type Money is delta 0.05 digits 12;
  ```

- **Access type** — an object of an access type provides access to other objects

```
type name is access type_name;

type integer_access is access integer.
```

- **General access types** can be used to provide indirect access to declared objects, like an alias of an object

```
type name is access all type_name;

type general_access_to_integer is access all integer;
```

You can assign the address of any variable of type integer that is declared as aliased to an object of general access to an integer (we will discuss later the declaration of objects as aliased).

You can also define general pointers, but with access so that they can only access the object referenced to reading not to be modified:

```
type name is access constant type_name;

type access_to_constant_integer is access constant
                                              integer;
```

- **Access to subprograms** — The syntax to declare pointer types is the following

```
type name is access [protected] procedure [(parameter_list)];

type name is access [protected] function [(parameter_list)]
return type_name;
```

It defines pointer types to procedures and functions, respectively. (Later, in the part of subprograms, we will indicate the syntax of the parameters list.)

```
type pointer_function is access function (x:float)
                                      return float;
```

A.1.2.3 Decalaration of Compound Types

- **Constrained array types** — You can declare restricted array types in which the value range of each dimension must be indicated.

```
type name is array (list_of_index_subtypes) of

                                      type_name;
```

The syntax of list of index subtype can be one of the following:

```
expression ..expression

type_name [range expression .. expression]
type vector is array (1..3) of float;
-- declares an array type of a three-element dimension
type matriz is array integer range 1..4, integer range 1..3) of  float ;
--declares a 4x3-reals array.
```

- **Unconstrained array types** — Array types are declared but without pointing out the number of elements or range of dimensions:

```
type name is array (list_of_index_subtype_definition)  of type_name;
```

The syntax of index_subtype definition is the following:

```
subtype_name range <>
```

Type vector is array (positive range <>) of float; a reals vector is declared without a defined size. You can also declare multidimensional arrays.

```
table is array (natural range <>, natural range <>) of float;
```

- **Untagged record types** — This is a type whose objects are made up of a series of named components that can have different types. These records can also have a discriminated part on which the components depend and a variant part that depends on a discriminant.

```
type name [(discriminant_part)] is record
      sequence_component_declaration
end record;

type name [(discriminant_part)] is record
     null;
end record;
```

A component declaration has a syntax similar to the declaration of objects, but the components cannot be constants or anonymous array type. If no component declaration exists in a record, **null** must be written instead.

A record with a variant part has the following syntax and it is necessary that there is a discriminant part.

```
type name (discriminant_part) is record
   {component_declaration}
   case discriminant_name is
      sequence_of_variant_part
         end case;
      end record;

variant_part:when value_list => sequence_of_component_declaration
```

The discriminant part is similar to the list of formal parameters in a subprogram (we will discuss the syntax later), but the discriminant part must be a discreet type or a pointer type.

These are the possible syntaxes:

```
      expression
      expression .. expression
      others

   type sex_type is (female, male);
   type person is
      record
         name:string(1..50);
         age:integer;
         sex: sex_type;
      end record;
```

This is an example of a discriminated type:

```
 type TypeBuffer (size: SizeBuffer:=100) is
   record
      position:SizeBuffer:=0;
      value:string(1..size);
   end record;

 record type with variants parts

   type person(sexo:sex_type) is
      record
         name:string(1..50)-
```

```
        age:integer;
        case sex is
           when female => num_children:integer;
           when male => military_service:boolean;
        end case;
     end record;
```

- **Tagged record type** — This can have the same syntax as the other records, but the word **tagged** must appear before record, and optionally tagged can be preceded by **abstract** or followed by **limited**. Its syntax is the following:

```
1. type name [(discriminant_part)] is
          [ [abstract] tagged ] [limited]
      record
       sequence_of_component_declaration
      end record;

2. type name (discriminant_part) is
          [ [abstract] tagged ] [limited]
      record
         {component_declaration}
         case discriminant_name is
            sequence_of_variant_part
         end case;
      end record;
variant_part:when value_list => sequence_of_component_declaration
```

- **Task** and **protected** compound types. Both types belong to the concurrent part of the language and their syntax will be discussed later.
- **Private** or **limited private types**. They can only be declared in the specification of the package. Their syntax if the following:

```
type name is [[abstract] tagged] [limited] private;
     type name (discriminant_part) is [[abstract] tagged]
                 [limited] private;
     type name (<>) is [[abstract] tagged] [limited] private;
```

- **Incomplete type declarations** — When access types are occasionally and especially defined to create dynamic data structures, incomplete type declarations are needed for compilation reasons. An incomplete type declaration syntax is the following:

```
type name;
type name (discriminant_part);
type name (<>);
```

A.1.3 Object Declarations

Ada 95 objects can be constants or variables which can also be declared as aliased to be referenced by general pointers. Constant objects must be initialized in the delcaration-time, but the others can be initialized in that moment or later. The syntax for object declaration is the following:

```
   list_of_identifiers: [aliased] [constant] type_name [:=
initial_value];
   list_of identifiers: [aliased] [constant] array
(list_of_index_subtypes) of type_name [:= initial_value];
```

The array type is the only compound type in which object declaration without naming the type is allowed.

The initial value is a type expression of the object to which is assigned and whose value is assigned to every object in the list of identifiers.

There is a case in which you can omit the object type that is declared, and it is when declaring a constant object of an integer or real type. The initial value the object is given will indicate the object type. The syntax is the following:

```
list_of_identifiers:constant:= numeric_value;
```

A.1.4 Expressions

An expression consists of a list of one or more terms separated by either arithmetic or logical operators. In the expression evaluation you must take into account the precedence of operators which will indicate the order to be applied to their corresponding terms.

A term can be:

• An identifier	
• A literal	
• Type conversions	*type_name* (*expression*) float (3)
• Qualified expressions	*type_name* ' (*expression*) Mineral'(Ambar)
• Atributtes*	*type_name* ' *attribute_name* [(*list_of_actual_parameters*)] Positive'First
• Function call	*function_name* [(*list_of_actual_parameters*)] sqrt(32)
• Array element	*array_name* (*expression*) v (3)
• Array slice	*array_name* (*expression* .. *expression*) v(1..3)
• Record component	*record_name*.*component_name* john.name
• Storage allocator	**new** *type_name*['(*initial_value*)] new integer'(3)
• Membership operators	*expression* [**not**] **in** *expression* .. *expression* I in 1..10 ***expression*** [**not**] **in** *subtype_name* I in Positive

There are also expressions used to assign a value to a compound type object, array and record aggregates, and extension aggregates.

- **Arrays agregates** is a list of one or more values of the array element type, separated by commas. The array aggregates syntax is the following:

```
[component_selector_list =>]expression
```

If the aggregate has a least a selector list component, it is said that the form to assign values to each element is not **by name**, but the assignation is performed **by position**.

The selection list is made up of one or more components and is separated by bars (|), with the following form:

---

* Attributes associated to types are numerous, and looking them up in the *Language Reference Manual* is recommended.

```
expression
expression .. expression
others
```

Others should be the component which appears last on the list.

```
A:array(1..5) of integer:= (0,0,3..5=>1);
```

- **Record aggregates** is a list of one or more values corresponding to the different components in a record separated by commas. If the record has no components, the aggregated then will have the value **null record**. The record aggregate syntax with components is the following:

```
[component_selector_list =>] expression
```

The list of component selectors is the same as array aggregates; like aggregates if this list occurs in the aggregate the assignation is said to be by name or else by position.

```
type date is record
        day, month,year:integer;
end record;

today :date:=(1,8,1997);
day_july: (10, month=> july, others=>1997);
```

- **Extension aggregates** are used to give values to records derived from other records (parent record).

```
parent_value with record_aggregate
parent_value with null record
```

A.1.5 Statements

In Ada 95 there are simple statements and compound statements, which can be preceded by a label.

```
{label} simple_statement
{label} compound_statement
```

A.1.5.1 Simple Statements

Simple statements include the following:

Null statement
Assignment statement
Exit statement
Goto statement
Procedure call statement
Return statement
Entry call statement
Requeue statement
Delay statement
Abort statement
Raise statement
Qualified expression (we have discussed this above in expressions, but it can also be a statement)

Some syntaxes are introduced next. Procedure call statement syntax will be discussed in subprograms; entry call statements, requeue statement, delay statement, and abort statement with tasks and concurrent programming and raise statement with exceptions.

- **Null statement** — Empty statement

```
null;
```

- Assignation statement has the following syntax:

  ```
  variable name := expression;
  ```

  ```
  i:=3;
  ```

- **Exit statement** — a loop exit statement, it has the following syntax:

  ```
  exit [loop name] [when condition];
  ```

  ```
     exit when x>3;
  ```

- **Goto statement** syntax

  ```
  goto label name;
  ```

- **Return statement** — a function return statement which returns its corresponding value; can also use a return statement in a procedure in order to return control to the caller without returning value in an acceptance (tasks) statement in order to terminate the rendezvous; it has the following syntax:

  ```
  return [expression];
  ```

  ```
  return x;
  ```

The expression is only needed in the function return.

A.1.5.2 Compound Statements

Compound statements are the following:

If statement
Case statement
Loop statement
Block statement
Accept statement
Select statement

- **Conditional statements** — There are two Ada 95 types: **if statement** with the following syntax:

  ```
  if condition then
     sequence_of_statements
  {elsif condition then
     sequence_of_statements}
  [else
     sequence_of_statements]
  end if;
  ```

  ```
  if x>3 then x:=x+1; a:=0;
        elsif x<1 then
           x:=x-1;
        else x:=0;
  end if;
  ```

- **Case statement** permits the selection between different alternatives that comprise a sequence of statements, according to the expresion value. The syntax is the following:

  ```
  case expression is
           case_statement_alternative
           {case_statement_alternative}
        end case;
  ```

The case statement alternative has the following syntax:

```
when election_list =>
        sequence_of_statements
```

The election list has the above-discussed aggregate syntax, etc.

```
when others =>
     sequence_of_statements
```

This alternative, if exists, must be the last one.

- **loops statement** — Iterative Ada-95 statements are made up of a basic core which is a simple loop statement containing a sequence of statements that will be executed infinitely unless some element exists forcing the loop termination. Such elements can be an exit statement or the statement core is preceded by an iterative loop scheme indicating when such a statement is executed.

  The **loop statement** syntax is the following:

  ```
  [loop statement identifier:]
       loop
          sequence of statements
       end loop [loop identifier];
  ```

  In this case exit statement is needed so that the loop terminates.

  1. **While loops**

  ```
  [loop statement identifier:]
  while condition
       loop
          sequence of statements
       end loop [loop identifier];
  ```

  The sequence of statements is repeated, meanwhile the loop condition is true

  ```
  while x>3 loop
    x:=x-1;
  end loop;
  ```

  2. **For loops**

  ```
  [loop statement identifier:]
    for identifier in [reverse] subtype_specification
       loop
          sequence of statements
       end loop [loop identifier];
  ```

  Subtype specification has the following syntax:

  ```
  expression .. expression
  type_name [range expression..expression]
  ```

  For example:

  ```
  for i in integer range 1..8 loop
    a(i):=i;
  end loop;
  ```

- An **Ada 95 block,** comprises a sequence of statements that can be optionally preceded by a part or section of declarations. A block defines a scope so that the scope of the declared elements in the block declaration part is the block body itself. Its syntax if the following:

```
[block statement identifier:]
     [declare
          declarative part]
     begin
       sequence of statements
     [exception
       sequence_of_exception_handlers]
     end [block identifier];
```

For example:

```
declare
   i: integer;-- after the declaration i scope starts
begin

   i:=i+1;-- there can be more than one statement.
end; -- here i variable scope terminates
```

- **Accept statement** and **select statement** are statements typical of tasks or Ada processes, and their syntax will be discussed in its corresponding part.

A.1.6 Compilation Units

Ada 95 compilation units fall into three types: packages, specification, and body. There are the basic moduling units for applications developed with that language and also type and operation encapsulation, subprograms, and generic units. The latter will be discussed separately.

A.1.6.1 Subprograms

- **Subprograms** as compilation units have the following syntax:

```
[sequence_of_context_clauses]
[private] procedures_or_functions_declaration
```

The word private preceding the subprogram declaration is used for child subprogram declaration. The syntax for a procedure declaration is the following:

```
procedure identifier(sequence_of_param_specification)
is
      [sequence_of_declarations]
   begin
      sequence_of_statements
   [exception
        sequence_of-exception_handlers
   end identifier;

parameters_specification:
list_of_identifiers:[mode] type_name[:= default_value]
```

The syntax for a function declaration is the following:

```
functionidentifier [(sequence_of_parameters)
                                  return type_name is
   [sequence_of_declarations]
begin
   sequence_of_statements – it must include a return statement
[exception
     sequence_of-exception_handlers
end identifier;
```

The form of parameters for procedures can be **in, out, in out o access**; and for the functions **in o access.**

- **Subprogram specifications** have the following syntax:

```
procedureidentifier [(sequence_of_parameters_specification)] ;
function identifier [(sequence_of_parameters_specification)]
                                        return type_name;
```

- **Abstract subprograms specifications** have the following syntax:

```
procedure identifier [(sequence_of_parameters_specification) is
                                                    abstract;
function identifier [(sequence_of_parameters_specification)
                                    return type_name is abstract;
```

- **Procedure call statement** has the following syntax:

```
procedure_identifier [(list_of_actual_parameters)];
```

A.1.6.2 Packages

The compilation unit declaration syntax which is a package is the following:

```
[sequence_of_context_clauses]
[private] package_specifications_or_package body
```

You only make use of the word private preceding the package to declare child libraries, that is, childpackages and subprograms, for subprogram units.

The package specification syntax is the following:

```
package identifier is
   sequence_of_declarations
   --it can be private type declarations, or not,
   --objects, exceptions and specifications and
   -- subprograms
[private
   sequence_of_declarations
      --declared type declaration is performed as private
      --in the last part
end identifier;
```

The declarations that can be found in this section are type declarations — private, subprogram, or task specification — or variable declarations. We will discuss the last two cases in its corresponding part.

A package body syntax is the following:

```
package body identifier is
      sequence_of_declarations
         --they can be type declarations and
         --of the subprograms or tasks specified in the specification
[begin
      sequence_of_statements
         --the declared type declaration is performed as
         --private in the last part
[exception
      sequence_of-exception_handlers
end identifier;
```

The sequence of clauses of context needed to import or use types or operations defined in other compilation units, have the following syntax:

```
with list_of library_units_identifier;
use list_of_package;
use type list_of_type_names;
```

A.1.6.3 Separate Subunits

In Ada 95 it is possible to declare a subprogram body, a package body, a task body, or a protected object body encapsulated in a package in a separate compilation unit. The syntax used to indicate it is the following:

```
procedure identifier [(sequence_of_parameters_specification) is
                                                    separate;
function identifier [(sequence_of_parameters_specification) return
                                          type_name is separate;

package body identifier is separate;
```

Protected task and object subunits will be discussed in its corresponding part.

A.1.6.4 Separate Units

Separate units are subunit bodies encapsulated in packages that were not declared.

```
[sequence_of_context_clauses]
separate (parent_unit_identifier)
body_declaration
```

A.1.7 Generic Units

Ada 95 generic units are compilation units that can be subprograms or generic packages. Their syntax is the following:

```
generic
   [sequence_of_generic_parameters]
subprogram_or_package_specification
```

A.1.7.1 Generic Parameters

Generic parameters can fall into three types: type parameters, subprogram or package parameters, and object parameters. Their syntax is specified as follows:

- **Object parameters**

```
list_of_identifier : [mode] type_name [:= default_value]
```

- **Type parameters**

```
type name is [[abstract] tagged ] [limited] private;
type name is (<>);
type name is  range <>;
type name is mod <>;
type name is digits <>;
type name is delta <>;
type name is  delta <> digits <>;
type name is access [all] type_name;
type name is  access constant type_name;
type name is array ( type_name [range <>]) of type_name;
type name is [abstract] new type_name [with private];
```

- Subprogram and package parameters

```
with procedure procedure_specification [is<>];
with procedure procedure_specification is name;
with function function_specification [is<>];
with function function_specification is name;
with package identifier is new generic_package_identifier [(<>)];
with package identifier is new generic_package_identifier
[(list_of_actual_generic_parameters)];
```

A.1.7.2 Instantiation of Generic Units

```
package identifier is new generic_package_identifier
[(list_of_actual_generic_parameters)];
procedure identifier is new generic_procedure_identifier
[(list_of_actual_generic_parameters)];
function identifier is new generic_function_identifier
[(list_of_actual_generic_parameters)];
```

The list generic parameters is similar to the current parameters in subprogram calls.

A.1.8 Exceptions

In Ada 95, exceptions can be declared as objects are declared. They are raised by means of the statement raise, treated in the section of statements from which syntax was not specified. The syntax to specify each one is the following:

- **Exception declarations**

```
list_of_identifiers : exception;
```

- **Raise statements**

```
raise [exception_identifier];
```

- **Exception handlers**

```
when [identifier:] exception_identifiers_list =>
     sequence_of_statements
```

The list of exception identifiers is a list of two or more identifiers separated by bars (|):

```
when [identifier:] others =>
     sequence_of_statements

begin
-- statements
 exception
     when E : Name_Error =>
        Put("Cannot open input file : ");
        Put_Line(Exception_Message(E));
        raise;
   end;
```

A.1.9 Tasking

A.1.9.1 Tasks

In Ada 95 you can declare tasks or anonymous processes (without type, unique) or task types from which you can declare objects that will be the tasks themselves. Like other programming units, tasks have specifications and body. In some task specifications you can declare entries as services or synchronization points that tasks provide. An entry called by another task yields rendezvous (synchronization or synchronization/communication) between the caller and the call when the call is accepted. Let's see its syntax.

- **Task specification**

```
task [type] identifier [(list_of_discriminants)];

task [type] identifier is
   sequence_of_entry_declarations

[private
   sequence_of_entry_declarations
end identifier;
```

- **Task bodies**

```
task body identifier is
   sequence_of_declarations
begin
   sequence_of_statements
[exception
   sequence-of_exception_handlers
end identifier;
```

- **Entry declarations**

```
entry identifier [(parameter_list)];-- the list of parameters has the
                                        same syntax as subprogram
```

A.1.9.2 Protected Objects

In Ada we have the possibility to declare the necessary protected objects so that processes can share information avoiding concurrent problem access on their part, since such objects count with writing operations to be accessed only by mutual exclusion. Like tasks, protected objects can be of an anonymous type (unique), or objects with a protected object type. Its syntax is the following:

- Protected objects specifications

```
protected [type] identifier [(list_of_discriminants)] is
   sequence_of_entry_or_subprograms_declarations
[private
   sequence_of _declarations
end identifier;
```

- Protected object bodies

```
protected body identifier is
   sequence_of_entry_ or_subprograms_bodies
end identifier;
```

- Entry body

```
entry identifier [(parameter_list)] when condicion is
   [sequence_of_declarations]
begin
   sequence_of_statements
[exception
   sequence_of_exception_handlers]
end identifier;
```

A.1.9.3 Statements

There is a set of statements typical of Ada 95 tasks, in which we specify its syntax:

- **Entry call statement**

```
entry_identifier [(actual_parameter_list)];
```

The list of current parameters has the same syntax as the list of parameters in subprogram calls.

- **Delay statement**

```
delay until delay_expression;
delay delay_expression;
```

- **Requeue statement**

```
requeue entry_identifier [with abort];
```

- **Abort statement**

```
abort task_identifier {, task_identifier};
```

- **The accept statement** is a synchronization statement and has the following syntax:

```
accept entry_identifier [(entry_index)] [(parameter_list)] [do
   sequence of statements
[exception
   sequence_of_exception_handlers]
end [entry_identifier];
```

- **The select statement** is a selection statement that allows the selection of a statement execution from an acceptance statement, call to an entry, delay statement, or terminate, depending on the selective statement used. The selection is not deterministic and can depend on the condition if it's met before the execution of such an alternative. These are the following selection instruction types:

```
     selective accept
timed entry call
   conditional entry call
   asynchronous select
```

- **Selective accept** syntax

```
select
     [when condition =>]
        select_alternative
   { or
     [when condition =>]
        select_alternative }
   [ else
     sequence_of_statements ]
   end select;
```

Selection alternatives are the following (Ada, 1995):

1. accept alternative whose syntax is `accept_statement [sequence_of_statements]`
2. delay alternative whose syntax is `delay_statement [sequence_of_statements]`
3. terminate alternative whose syntax is **terminate**;

An example of task with a selective accept is the following:

```
task body Server is
     Current_Work_Item : Work_Item;
```

```
begin
  loop
    select
      accept Next_Work_Item(WI : in Work_Item) do
        Current_Work_Item := WI;
      end;
      Process_Work_Item(Current_Work_Item);
    or
      accept Shut_Down;
      exit;  -- Premature shut down requested
    or
      terminate;-- Normal shutdown at end of scope
    end select;
  end loop;
end Server;
```

- **Timed entry call** selection instruction syntax:

```
select
     entry_call_statement [sequence_of_statements]
  or
    delay_statement [sequence_of_statements]
  end select;
```

Example:

```
select
      Controller.Request(Medium)(Some_Item);
    or
      delay 45.0;
      -- controller too busy, try something else
    end select;
```

- **Conditional entry call** syntax:

```
select
  entry_call_statement [sequence_of_statements]
  else
     sequence_of_statements
  end select;
```

Example:

```
procedure Spin(R : in Resource) is
  begin
    loop
      select
        R.Seize;
        return;
      else
        null; -- busy waiting
      end select;
    end loop;
  end;
```

- **Asynchronous select** syntax:

```
select
  triggering statement [sequence of statements]
```

```
then abort
sequence_of_statement
end select;
```

Triggering statement can have one of these syntactical forms:

```
entry_call_statement
  delay_statement
```

Examples for these are the following:

```
loop
  select
    Terminal.Wait_For_Interrupt;
    Put_Line("Interrupted");
  then abort
    -- This will be abandoned upon terminal interrupt
    Put_Line("-> ");
    Get_Line(Command, Last);
    Process_Command(Command(1..Last));
  end select;
end loop;

select
  delay 5.0;
  Put_Line("Calculation does not converge");
then abort
  -- This calculation should finish in 5.0 seconds;
  --  if not, it is assumed to diverge.
  Horribly_Complicated_Recursive_Function(X, Y);
end select;
```

References

ANSI: ANSI/MIL-STD 1815A ISO/IEC 8652:1983. 1983.

ANSI/ISO/IEC 8652:1995. 1995. (The ISO standard was published on 15th February 1995).

Barnes, J. 1996. *Programming in Ada 95.* Addison-Wesley, Reading, MA.

Cohen, N.H. 1996. *Ada as a Second Language,* 2nd ed. McGraw-Hill, New York.

Culwin, F. 1997. *Ada, A Development Approach,* 2nd ed. Prentice-Hall, Europe.

English, J. 1997. *Ada 95: The Craft of Object-Oriented Programming.* Prentice-Hall Europe.

Intermetrics. 1995. *Ada 95 Reference Manual.* Intermetrics, Inc., Cambridge, MA.

Joyanes, L. 1996. *Programación Orientada a Objetos. Conceptos, Modelado, Diseño e Implementación, (Object-Oriented Programming: Concepts, Modeling, Design and Implementation).* McGraw-Hill, Madrid.

Joyanes, L. and Díez, M.L. 1998. *Programación en Ada 95: Un en foque orientado a objetos para sistemas distribuidos y de tiempo real (Programming in Ada 95. An Approach Object-Oriented for Real-Time and Distributed Systems),* McGraw-Hill, Madrid.

Smith, M.A. 1996. *Object-Oriented Software in Ada 95.* International Thomson, London, U.K.

Taylor, B. 1995. *Ada 95 Compatibility Guide in Ada Yearbook 1995.* Mark Ratcliffe.

Wheeler, D. 1996. *Ada 95. The Lovelace Tutorial.* Springer-Verlag, New York.

APPENDIX B

C++ Language Guide

Luis Joyanes Aguilar
Pontifical Salamanca University

María Luisa Díez Platas
Pontifical Salamanca University

Paloma Centenera
Pontifical Salamanca University

0-8493-3135-8/99/$0.00+$.50

C++ is considered a larger and more powerful C. The syntax of C++ is an extension of C's syntax, to which numerous essentially object-oriented properties have been added. ANSI C already adopted numerous characteristics from C++, therefore migrating from C to C++ is not usually difficult.

This appendix shows both the syntax rules of C++ standard appearing in the *Annotated Reference Manual* (*ARM*), and the latest proposals incorporated in the new draft of ANSI C++ (ANSI C++ Draft Dated 2 Decenber 1996/Draft 28 April 1995*), which are included in AT&T C++ versions 3.0 (current) and 4.0 (future) Committees: ANSI X3J16/ISO WG21.

B.1.1 Language Vocabulary

A program written in C++ is a sequence of characters grouped in lexical components (*tokens*) which include the basic language vocabulary. These lexical components are: keywords, identifiers, constants, chain constants, operators, and punctuation marks.

B.1.1.1 Characters

The characters that can be used to construct language elements (lexical components or *tokens*) are the alphabet characters (upper- and lowercase letters), blank digits, and underlined characters.

B.1.1.2 Comments

C++ supports two types of comments. Lines of comments are in the style of C and ANSI C, such as

```
/* Style C comment */
/* More extensive comment, but it is also C and ASNI C style */
```

The other type of comments that can be used by C++ programmers are: Version/*... is used for comments exceeding one line in length and version//... is used only for one-line comments. Comments are not nested.

B.1.1.3 Identifiers

Identifiers (names of variables, constants, etc.) must start either with an alphabet letter (upper- or lowercase), or with an underlined character and can hold one or more characters. The second and following characters can be letters, digits, or an underlined character; non-alphanumeric characters or blanks are not allowed.

```
Test_proof    // valid
X123          // valid
multi_word    // valid
var25         // valid
15var         // valid
```

C++ is uppercase sensitive.

`Pay_month` is an identifier different from `pay-month`.

Good programming practice advises you to use meaningful identifiers that help to document a program.

```
name last name salary net_price
```

B.1.1.4 Keywords

Reserved or keywords must not be used as identifiers. Because of their strict meaning in C++, they should not be redefined. Table B.1 lists C++ keywords according to ARM 1.

* http://www.cygnus.com/misc/wp/

TABLE B.1 C++ Keywords

asm*	continue	float	new*	signed	try
auto	default	for	operator*	sizeof	typedef
break	delete*	friend*	private*	static	union
caswe	do	goto	protected*	struct	unsigned
catch*	double	if	public*	switch	virtual*
char	eolse	inline*	register	template*	void
class*	enum	int	return	this*	volatile
const	extern	long	short	throw*	while

Note: *These words do not exist in ANSI C.

Different business compilers for C++ may include, in addition, new keywords. These cases take place in Borland, Microsoft and Symantec.

TABLE B.2 Keywords in Turbo/Borland C++

asm	_ds	interrupt	signed
auto	else	_loads	sizeof
break	enum	long	_SS
case	_es	_near	static
catch	_export	near	struct
_cdecl	extern	new	switch
cdecl	_far	operator	templat
char	far	pascal	this
class	float	private	typedef
const	for	protected	union
continue	friend	public	unsigned
cs	goto	register	virtual
default	huge	return	void
delete	if	_average	volatile
do	inline	_seg	while
_double	int	short	

From Acronyms of the Bjarne Stroustup text in which the syntax rules of the C++ standard language are defined, *Annotated Reference Manual.* Addison-Wesley, Reading, MA, 1992.

TABLE B.3 Keywords in Microsoft Visual C/C++ 1.5/2.0

_asm	else	int	signed
auto	enum	_interrupt	sizeof
based	_except	_leave	static
break	_export	_loads	_stcall
case	extern	long	struct
_cdecl	_far	maked	switch
char	_fastcall	_near	thread
const	_finally	_pascal	_try
continue	float	register	typedef
_declspec	for	return	union
default	_fortran	_average	unsigned
dllexport	goto	_self	void
dllimport	_huge	_segment	volatile
do	if	_segname	while
double	_inline	short	

The ANSI committee has added new keywords (Table B.4).

TABLE B.4 New Keywords in ANSI C++

bool	false	reinterpret_cast	typeid
cons_cast	mutable	static_cast	using
dynamic_cast	namespace	true	wchar_t

B.1.2 Constants

There are C++ constants for each type of simple data (integer, char, etc.). The constants may have two u, l and f suffixes, which indicate unsigned types, long, and float, respectively. Likewise, prefixes o and ox can be added. Those prefixes represent octal and hexadecimal constants.

```
4 5 6 C) 456  Ox456      // integer constants; decimal, octal,
                         // hexadecimal
1231 123ul               // integer constants: long, unsigned
                         // long
'B' 'lb' '4'             // char type constants
3.1415f   3.14159L       // real constants of different position
```

Character chains are enclosed in inverted commas while one-character constants are enclosed in single quotes.

```
//empty chain '/O'
```

B.1.2.1 Constants Declaration

In C++, the identifiers of variables/constants may be declared *constants*, meaning that their values cannot be modified. This declaration is carried out with the keyword const.

```
Const double PI = 3.1416; const char WHITE = ' '; const double PI_EG = ~ I;
const double DOUBLE_PI = 2*PI
```

The type modifier `const` is also used in C++ to provide only-write protection to variables and function parameters. The functions members of a class that do not modify the data member to which they access may be declared const. This modifier also prevents parameters stopped by reference from being modified.

```
Void copy (const char* font, char* destination);
```

B.1.3 Operators

C++ is a very rich language in operators. They are categorized in the following *groups*:

Arithmetic
Relational and logical
Assignment
Data access and size
Bit handling
Miscellaneous

As a consequence of the large amount of operators, a large amount of different expressions are also produced.

B.1.3.1 Arithmetic Operators

C++ provides different operators that relate arithmetic operations.

TABLE B.5 C++ Arithmetic Operators

Operator	Name	Purpose	Example
+	Unitary plus	Positive value of x	x = + y + 5
-	Negation	Negative value of x	x = -y;
+	Adding	It adds x and y	z = x + y;
-	Substraction	It substracts x by y	z = x – y;
*	Multiplication	It multiplies x by y	z = x * y;
/	Division	It divides x by y	z = X/Y
%	Module	Remainder of x divided by y	z = x%y;
++	Increment	It increments x after using	x++
- -	Decrement	It decrements x before using	- -x

Examples:

```
-i +w          // unitary less unitary plus
  a*b/c%d      // multiplication, division, module
a+b a~b        // binay adding and substraction
a=5/2;         // a takes the value 2, if a is considered an integer
a=5/2;         // a takes the value 2.5, if a is real
```

Increment and decrement operators serve to increase and decrease by one the value stored in a variable.

```
variable ++    // postincrement
++ variable    // preincrement
variable - -   // postdecrement
- - variable   // predecrement
++a; equivalent to a = a +1;
- -b; equivalent to b = b -1;
```

The postfix formats are arranged in a different way according to the expression they are applied to:

```
b =++a:equivalent to  a = a+1; b = a;
b =a++;equivalent to  b = a; a = a+1;

int i, j, k = 5;
k++;  // k has the value 6, the same affect as ++k
- -k;  // k has the value 5 now, the same effect as k- -
k = 5;

i = 4*k++;  // k is 6 now and i is 20
k = 5;
j = 4* ++k;  // k is 6 now and i is 24
```

B.1.3.2 Assignment Operators

The assignment operator (=) makes the value located on the right of the operator be assigned to the variable on its left side. Assignment usually occurs as part of an assignment expression, and conversions are implicitly produced.

```
z = b + 5;  // assigns ( b + 5 ) to variable z
```

C++ allows multiple assignments in just one statement. So a = b + (c = 10) is equivalent to:

```
c = 10;
a = b + c;
```

Other examples of valid and non-valid expressions are

```
// valid expressions        // non-valid expressions
a = 5 * ( b + a );            a + 3 =
```

```
double x = y;              b;
a = b = 6;                 x++ = y;
```

C++ provides assignment operators that combine assignment operators and others differently by producing operators such as + = , /= , – = , * =, and % = . C++ supports other types of assignment operators for bit handling.

TABLE B.6 Assignment Arithmetic Operators

+=	x = x + y	x + = y
-=	x = x – y	x – = y
*=	x = x * y	x * = y
/=	x = x/y	x /= y
%	x = x % y	x % = y

Examples

```
a += b;       equivalent to a = a + b
a *= a + b;   equivalent to a = a * ( a + b );
v += e;       equivalent to v = v + e;
v -= e;       equivalent to v = v - e;
```

B.1.3.3 Logical and Relational Operators

Logical and relational operators are the basic construction blocks for building decision making in a programming language. Table B.7 shows the logical and relational operators.

TABLE B.7 Logical and Relational Operators

Operator	Meaning	Example
&&	Logical AND	a && b
||	Logical OR	c ||d
!	Logical NOT	!c
<	Less than	i < 0
<=	Less than or equal	i <=0
>	Greater than	j >50
>=	Greater than or equal	i >=8.5
==	Equal	x == '/0'
! =	Not equal	c! = '/nl'
?:	Conditional assignment	k = (i<5) ? 1

The operator ?: is known as a *conditional expression.* The conditional expression is an abbreviation for the if-else conditional statement. The if statement

```
if (condition)
variable = expression1; else

variable = expression2;
```

is equivalent to

```
variable = (condition) ? expression1 : expression2;
```

The conditional expression checks the condition. If that condition is true, `expression1` is assigned to `variable`; otherwise `expression2` is assigned to `variable`.

B.1.3.3.1 Practical Rules

Logical and relational operators act on logic values; the *false* value may be either 0, or the null pointer, or 00; the *true* value may be any value other than zero. The following table shows the results of different expressions.

`x > y`	1, if x is greater than y,	otherwise	0
`x>=y`	1, if x is greater than or equals y,	otherwise	0
`x<y`	1, if x is less than y,	otherwise	0
`x<=y`	1, if x is less than or equals y,	otherwise	
`x = = y`	1, if x equals y,	otherwise	0
`x != y`	1, if x and y are different,	otherwise	0
`!x`	1, if x is 0,	otherwise	0
`x ll y`	0, if both x and y are 0,	otherwise	0

B.1.3.3.2 Evaluation in Shortcircuit

Like C, C++ admits to reducing the time of logical operations; expression evaluations are reduced when some operands take specific values.

1. Logical operation *AND (&&)* — If in the expression *expr 1&& expr2*, *expr1* takes the value zero, the logical operation AND (y) will always be zero, regardless of the value of *expr2*. Therefore, *expr2* will never be evaluated.
2. Logical operation *OR (//)* — If *expr1* takes a value other than zero, the expression *expr1//expr2* will be evaluated 1, regardless of the value of *expr2*; therefore, *expr2* will not be evaluated.

B.1.3.4 Bit Handling Operators

C++ provides bit handling operators, as well as bit handling assignment operators.

TABLE B.8 Bit Handling Operators (Bitwise)

Operator	Meaning	Example
&	AND bit to bit	`x & 128`
|	OR bit to bit	`j | 64`
∧	XOR bit to bit	`j ∧ 12`
~	NOT bit to bit	`~ j`
«	Left shift	`i « 3`
»	Right shift	`j » 4`

TABLE B.9 Bit Handling Assignment Operators

Operator	Long Format	Reduces Format
&	x = x & y;	x & = y;
| =	x = x |y;	x | = y;
∧ =	x = x – y;	x, y;
« =	x = x « y;	x «= y;
» =	x = x » y;	x »= y;

Example:

`-x`	`Changes 1 bits to 0, and 0 bits to 1`
`x & y`	`AND (y) logical operation bit to bit of x and y`
`x 1 y`	`OR (o) logical operation bit to bit of x and y`

```
x«y     x shifts to the left (in y positions)
x»y     x shifts to the right (in y positions)
```

B.1.3.5 The *sizeof* Operator

The *sizeof* operator provides the size of a data type or variable; *sizeof* takes the corresponding argument (scalar type, *array*, *record*, etc.). The operator syntax is

```
sizeof (name_variable 1 type_of_data)
```

Example:

```
int m, n[121;
sizeof (m)  // returns 4, in 32-bit machines
sizeof (n)  // returns 48
sizeof (15) // returns 4

Size = sizeof (long) - sizeof (int);
```

B.1.3.6 Operator Priority and Associativity

When expressions mixing different operators are performed, it is necessary to establish a *precedence* (priority) of the operators and the evaluation *direction* (or sequence); (evaluation order: left-right, right-left), referred to as *associativity*.

TABLE B.10 Operator Precedence and Associativity

Operator	Associativity	Priority
:: () [] . ->	Left-right	1
++ -- & (direction) ~ (type) ! + sizeof (type) new delete * (indirection)	Right-left	2
.* -.>*	Left-right	3
*/%	Left-right	4
+ -	Left-right	5
>>=<<=	Left-right	6
<< >>	Left-right	7
== !=	Left-right	8
&	Left-right	9
^	Left-right	10
|	Left-right	11
&&	Left-right	12
||	Left-right	13
?:	Left-right	14
= += -= *= /= % =>>=<<=&= | = ^=	Right-left	15
, (comma operator)	Left-right	16

Example:

```
a * b / c + d equivalent to ( a * b ) / c + d
```

B.1.4 Variable Declarations

In ANSI C, all variable and function declarations must be done at the beginning of the program or function. If additional declarations are needed, the programmer must return to the declaration block in order to make the necessary adjustments or insertions. Every declaration must be done before executing any statement. So, the typical C++ declaration

```
Nametype, Namevariable1, Namevariable2
```

provides declarations such as,

```
int balance, months;
double clipper, salary;
```

Like C, values can be assigned to the variables in C++:

```
int month = 4, day, year = 1995; double salary = 45.675;
```

In C++, variable declarations can be placed in any part of a program. This characteristic makes the programmer declare the variables near the place where the statements in his program are used. The following program is valid in C++, but it is non-valid in C:

```
#include <stdio.h>
  int main ()
  {
    int i;
    for ( ¡ = 0; i < loo; + i)
    cout « i « endl;
    double
    for (i = 1.7547; i < 25.4675; 3' + .001)
    cout «y « endl;
}
```

The program above could be rewritten by making the declaration and definition inside the same loop:

```
int main ()
{
    for ( int ¡ = 0; i < loo; ++ i)
    cout « i « endl;
    for (double 1.7547; j < 25.4675; j += .001)
    cout « j « endl;
}
```

B.1.5 Data Types

Simple data types in C++ are divided into two large groups: integers and floating point (valid data).

TABLE B.11 Simple Data Types in C++

char	signed char	unsigned char
short	int	long
unsigned short	unsigned	unsigned long
float	double	long double

The derived types in C++ may be:

- Enumerations (enum)
- Structured (struct)
- Unions (union)
- Anonymous unions
- Arrays
- Classes (class and struct)
- Pointers

B.1.5.1 Enumerations

In C++ an enumeration, structure or union name is a type name.Therefore, the keywords struct, union, or enum are not needed when a variable is declared. The **enumerated** data type refers to a group of integer constants with names. The keyword enum is used to declare an enumerated data type or *enumeration.*

The syntax is the following:

```
    Ident.List
enum name List-symbols
```

where *name* is the name of the enumerated declared variable and list-symbols is an enumerated type list, to which values are assigned when the enumerated variable is declared and may have an initialization value. An enumeration name can be used to declare a variable of that type (enumeration variable).

```
name var;
```

Let us consider the following statement:

```
enum color { Red, Blue, Green, Yellow };
```

A variable of the enumeration type color is

```
screen color - Red; // C++ style
```

B.1.5.2 Structures

A structure is a composite data type containing a collection of different data type elements combined in an only language construction. Each element in the collection is called a *member* and can be a variable of a different data type. A structure represents a new data type in C++. The structure syntax is the following:

```
struct name
{
   fields
   members
}
```

An example and a structure type variable are shown in the following statements:

```
struct painting {
   int i;
   float f;
   };
struct painting name;  // C style painting name; // C++ style
```

B.1.5.3 Unions

A union is a variable that can store different type and size objects. A union can store different data types, just one at a time, unlike a structure that simultaneously stores a data type collection. A union syntax is

```
union name
     {
   members
   fields
   }
```

An example of structure is:

```
union alpha
     {
```

```
int x;
char c;
};
```

A structure variable declaration is

```
alpha w;
```

The way to access to the structure members is by the point operator:

```
u.x = 145;
u.c = 'z';
```

B.1.5.4 Anonymous Unions

C++ admits a special union type called anonymous union, which declares a member set sharing the same memory address. The anonymous union has not a name assigned and therefore the union elements are accessed directly.

The syntax of an anonymous union is the following:

```
union members
```

The anonymous union variables share the same memory location and data space.

```
int main ()
{
  union {
    int x;
    float y;
    double z;
    };
x = 25;
y = 245.245; // the value in y overwrites the value of x
z = 9.41415; // the value in z overwrites the value of z
}
```

B.1.5.5 Arrays

An array is a collection of given elements of the same type that are identified by means of an index. Elements start with 0 index.

B1.5.5.1 Array Declarations

An array declaration has the following format:

```
nametype namevariable [n]
```

Some examples of unidimensional arrays are:

```
int ListNum [2];// 2-integer array
char ListNames [10];// 10-character array
```

Multidimensional arrays are, for example:

```
nametype    namevariable [n1] [n2]...[nx]
```

The following example declares an integer array 4 x 10 x 3

```
int multidim[4][10][3];
```

B.1.5.5.2 Array Initialization

Arrays are initialized with this format:

```
int a [3] = {5, 10, 15 };
char cad [5] = {'bl', 'lc', Id ,, 'e'};
int table [2] [[3] = {{1, 2, 3} {3, 4, 5}};
```

The following three definitions are equivalent:

```
char greeting [5] = "hello";
char greeting [ ] = "hello";
```

1. Arrays can be passed to functions as arguments.
2. Functions cannot return arrays.
3. Assignment among arrays is not allowed. To assign an array to another, you must write the code to perform assignments element by element.

B.1.5.6 Pointers

A pointer is an indirect reference to an object of a given type.

B.1.5.6.1 Pointer Declaration

Pointers are declared by using the unitary operator. Two variables are declared in the following statements: n is an integer, and p is a pointer to an integer.

```
int n; // n is an integer data type int* p; // p is a pointer to an integer
```

Once a pointer is declared, you can fix the address or memory location of the pointed type.

```
P &n; // p is fixed to the address of n
```

Pointer is declared by writing:

*TypeName *VariableName*

Once a pointer, p, has been declared, the pointed object is written *p and can be operated as any other variable of the type *TypeName.*

```
int *p, *q, n;  // two pointers to int, and one int
n = -25;        // n is fixed to -16
*p = 105;       // *p to 101
*q = n + *p;    // *q to 80
```

C++ treats pointers to different types as different types

```
int *ip;
double *dp;
```

Pointers ip and dp are incompatible, so it is a mistake writing

```
dp = ip;  // Error, pointers cannot be assigned to different types
```

You can, however, perform assignments among contents, since an explicit type conversion would be performed.

```
*dp = *ip;
```

There is special pointer (*null*) frequently used in C++ programs. The NULL pointer has a zero value, which makes it different from all valid addresses. Knowledge allows us to check if a pointer p is a NULL pointer by evaluating the expression (p == 0) . NULL pointers are used just to signal that something has happened. In other words, if p is a NULL pointer, it is correct to reference *p.

B.1.5.6.2 Pointers to Arrays

Arrays are accessed through indexes:

```
int list [51];
list [3] = 5;
```

Arrays can also be accessed through pointers:

```
int list [51];      // 5 element-array
int *ptr;           // Pointer to integer
ptr = list;         // fixes pointer to the array`s first element
ptr += 3;           // adds 3 to ptr; ptr points to the 4th element
*ptr = 5;           // establishes the 4th element to 5th
double a [10];
double *p = a;      // p and a refer to the same array p
```

This element can be called by

```
a[6], *(P + 6)      or else [6]
```

If name points to the array's first element, then name + 1 points to the second element. The contents of what is stored in that position is obtained by the expression

```
* (name + 1)
```

Although functions cannot modify their arguments, if it is used as a function argument, the function can modify the contents of the array.

B.1.5.6.3 Pointers to Structures

Pointers to structures are similar and work the same way as pointers to any other type of data.

```
struct family

char *husband;
char *wife;
char *child;

mackoy family;
*p family;
p &mackoy

// mackoy family type structure          // p, a pointer to family
// p, contains mackoy`s address

p ->husband = "Louis Mackoy";            // initialization
p ->wife = "Vilma González";             // initialization
p ->child = "Little Louis Mackoy";       // initialization
```

B.1.5.6.4 Pointers to Constant Objects

When a pointer is passed to a large object, but you do not want the function to modify the object (for instance, you only wish to view the contents of an array), the argument corresponding to the function is declared as a pointer to a constant object.

```
Const TypeName *v
```

establishes v as a pointer to an object that cannot be modified. An example can be

```
void view (const LargeObject *v);
```

B.1.5.6.5 Pointers to Void

The void data type represents a null value. In C++, however, the void pointer type is often considered a pointer to any data type.

The essential idea lying in the void pointer in C++ is that of a type that can be properly used to access any type of object, since it is more or less type independent. An illustrative example of the difference of behavior in C and C++ is the following program segment.

```
int main ()
{
   void *vptr;
   int *iptr;

   vptr = iptr;
   iptr = vptr;         // Incorrect in C++, correct in C
   iptr = (int vptr;    // Correct in C++
```

B.1.5.6.6 Pointers and Chains

C++ chains are implemented as character arrays, as chain constants, and as pointers to characters.

B.1.5.6.7 Chain Constants

Its declaration is similar to

```
char "Chain" = "My teacher";
```

or else its equivalent statement

```
char VarChain[] = "my teacher";
```

If you want to avoid that the chain is modified, add const to the declaration

```
const char *VarChain "my teacher"
```

s pointers to chain are declared,

```
char [si]  or else  char*s'
```

B.1.5.6.8 Pointers to Chains

Pointers to chains are not chains. Pointers locate the first element of a stored chain.

```
Char *varchain
const char *Fixedchain
```

B.1.5.6.9 Practical Considerations

Every array in C++ is implemented by means of arrays.

```
Char chain1[16] = "Object concept"
char *chain2 = chain1;
```

B.1.5.6.10 Pointer Arithmetic

Since the pointers are numbers (addresses), they can be manipulated by arithmetic operators. The operations allowed on pointers are addition, substraction, and comparison.

So, if the following statements are executed in sequence:

```
char *p;
char a[10];
p = &a[0]
p++;
p++;
p--;
```

```
// p contains the address of a character
// ten-character array
// p points to the array`s first element
// p points to the array`s second element
// p points to the array`s third element
// p points to the array`s second element
```

An example of pointer comparison is the following program:

```
#include <iostream.h>
main (void)
{
  int *ptrl, *ptr2;
  int a [21] = {10, 10};
  ptrl = a;
    cout «"ptrl is" «"ptrl «"*ptrl is" «*ptrl «endl;ptr2=ptrl+1;
    , cout «"ptr2 is" «ptr2 «11*ptr2 is" «*ptr2 «endl;
    // compare two pointers
    if (ptrl == ptr2)
      cout «ilptrl is not equal to *ptr2 \n11;
    else
      cout «11 ptrl is not equal to *ptr2 \n";
  }
```

B.1.5.6.11 Operators *new* and *delete*

C++ defines a method for performing dynamic memory assignment. That method is different from the one used in C, by means of the **new** and **delete** operators.

The new operator replaces the malloc function, traditional in C, and the delete operator replaces the free function, also traditional in C. new assigns memory and returns a pointer to the recently created object. Its syntax is

new *TypeName*

and an example of its application is

```
int *ptrl;
double *ptr2;
ptrl = new int;       // assigned memory for the ptrl object
ptr2 = new double;    // extended memory for the ptr2 object
*ptrl = 5;
*ptr2 = 6.55;
```

Since new returns a pointer, this pointer can be used to initialize the pointer in just a definition, such as:

```
int *p = new int;
```

If new cannot occupy the requested amount of memory, it returns a NULL value. The delete operator releases the assigned memory by new

```
delete ptrl;
```

A short program showing the combined used of new and delete is:

```
#include <iostream.h>
void main (void);
{
  char *c;
  c = new char [512];
  cin » c;
```

```
    cout «c «endl;
    delete c;
}
```

The new and `delete` operators can be used to assign memory to arrays, classes, and other data types.

```
int *i;
i = new int [21]; // create the array
i [10] = 6;       // assign the array
delete i;         // destroy the array
```

B.1.5.7 Type Verification

The verification or checking in C++ is stricter than in C.

- *Use declared functions* — This action is illegal in C++ and it is allowed in C.

```
int main ()
{
  // ...
  printf (x);
  // C: int printf ();
  // C++ is illegal, since printf is not
  // declared
  return 0;
}
```

- *Fail to return a value of a function* — A funtion in C++ declared with a specific return type must return a value of that type. It is not allowed to follow the rule in C.
- *Assignment of void pointers* — The assignment of a void* type to another type of pointer must be done with an explicit conversion to C++. In C it is implicitly performed.
- *Initialization of chain constants* — In C++, a blank for the null ending character must be provided when chain constants are initialized. In C+, the absence of that character is allowed.

```
int main ()
{
  char car [71] = "Cazorla";    // legal in C
                                // error in C++
  return 0;
}
```

One solution to a problem working both in C and C++ is

```
char car[] = " Cazorla ";
```

B.1.5.8 Type Conversion

The explicit conversions are forced by *casts.* The forced conversion of types of C has the classic format:

```
(type) expression
```

C++ has turned the previous notation into a functional notation as a syntactic alternative:

```
type name (expression)
```

The following notations are equivalent:

```
z = float (x); // cast notation in C++
z = (float) x; // cast notation in C
```

B.1.6 Overload of Operators

Most operators in C++ can be overloaded or redefined to work with new data types. Table B.12 lists the operators that can be overloaded.

TABLE B.12 Operators that can be Overloaded

+	-	*-	%	^	&	f	/
~	!	=	<	>	+=	-=	*=
/=	%=	^=	&=	|=	<<	>>	>>=
<<=	==	!=	<=	<=	&&	||	++
--	,	->*	->0	[]			

B.1.7 Statements

A C++ program consists of a sequence of statements. The semicolon is used as an ending element in every statement.

B.1.7.1 Declaration Statements

They are used to establish the existence and, optionally, the initial values of objects identified by name.

```
TypeName identifier,...
TypeName identifier = expression,...
const TypeName identifier = expression,...
```

Some valid statements in C are

```
char cl;
int p,q = s, r a + b;// assuming a and b have been
          // declared and initialized before

const double IVA  16.0;
```

B.1.7.2 Expression Statements

Expression statements make the expression to be evaluated. Their general format is:

```
expression;
```

Example:

```
n++;
425;        // legal, but it does nothing
n = a < b | | b != 0;  // legal, 91, it does nothing
     b 3;    // complex statement
```

C++ allows multiple assignments in a statement.

```
n + ( p = 5 ) is equivalent to p = 5;

  m = n + p;
```

B.1.7.3 Compound Statements

A compound statement is a series of statements enclosed in braces. Compound statements have the format:

```
{
  statement
  statement
  statement
  }
```

The enclosed statements may be any: declarations, expressions, compound statements, etc. An example is:

```
{
  int i = 5;
  double x = 3.141 Y = -4.25;
  int j = 4 - i;
  x = 4 + 5 * (x - y);
  }
```

The body of a C++ function is always a compound statement.

B.1.7.4 Conditional Statements: *if*

The general format of an if statement is:

```
if (expression)
  statement
```

Example 1:

```
if ( a < 0 )
  negatives ++;
```

If variable a is negative, negatives variable is incremented.

Example 2:

```
if ( numberOfDays < 0 )
     numberOfDays = 0;
if  height - 5 ) < 4 )
area = 3.14* radius radius; volume = area * height;
```

Example 3:

```
if ( temperature > = 45 )
cout «"I am in Sonora - Hermosillo, in August"; cout «"I am in Veracruz" «
temperature «endl;
```

The statement "I am in Sonora–Hermosillo, in August" is displayed when temepratture is greater than or equal to 45. The next statement is always executed.

The if-else statement has the following format:

```
1. if (expression)       2. If (expression)
   statement 1           <sequence of 1 statements>
   else                  else
   statement 2           <sequence of 2 statements>
```

If *expression* is other than zero, *statement 1* is executed and *statement 2* is left out; if *expression* is zero, statement 1 is left out and statement 2 is executed. Once the if-else statement is executed, the control passes to the next statement.

Example 4:

```
if /Number = = 0 )
cout « "The average will not be calculated";
else
  average = total / Number;
```

Example 5:

```
if ( amount > 10 )
  discount = 0.2;
  price = n * prive ( 1 - discount );
else
  discount = 0;
  price = n * Price;
```

B.1.7.4.1 Nested if-else Statement

C++ allows you to nest `if-else` statements to create a multiple alternative statement:

```
if ( expression 1 )
    statement 1;
else if ( expression )
    statement2;
...............................................
else
    statement N + 1;
```

Example:

```
if ( a > 100 )
  number = 0;
else if ( b < = 0 )
  adding = 1;
else
  adding = 1;
```

B.1.7.4.2 Multiple Alternative Statements: *switch*

The `switch` statement offers a way to perform multiple alternative decisions. The switch format is:

```
Switch (expression)
{
  case constant 1:
  statements
  break;
  case constant 2:
  statements
  break;
    case constant n:
  statements
  break;
  [default:

  statements]
}
```

The `switch` statement requires an expression whose value is an integer. This value can be a constant, a variable, a function call, or an expression. The value of *constant* must be a constant. The expression is evaluated when the statement is executed, and if its value coincides with a *constant*, the statements following it are executed; otherwise, the statements following default are executed.

```
switch ( Points )
{
  case 10:
  grade = 'A';
  break;
```

```
        case 9:
        grade = 'B';
        break;
        case 7, 8:
        grade = 'C';
        break;
        case 5, 6:
        grade = 'D';
        break;
        default:
        grade = 'E';
    };
```

B.1.7.5 Loops: Repetitive Statements

Loops serve to perform repetitive tasks. There are three different types of repetitive statements:

1. while
2. do
3. for

B.1.7.5.1 *while* Statements

The `while` statement is a conditional loop that is repeated as long as the condition is true. The while loop can never iterate if the checked condition is initially false.

The syntax of the while statement is:

```
while (expression)
   statement;
```

Example:

```
int n, adds  0;
int i 1;
      while (i <= 100)
      {
   cout « "Enters, - ,;
   cin «n;
   adds += n;
   i ++;
   };
cout « "The average is, , «double (adds) / , 00.0;
```

B.1.7.5.2 *do* Statement

The loop evaluation and exit test are made after the loop body. The do statement acts the same way as the `while` statement. The only real difference is that the loop condition is executed later, instead of before, whereby the loop statement is executed at least once. The format is

```
do
      statement
   while (expression)
```

Statement is executed and then *expression* is evaluated, if it's true (different from zero), control is passed again to the beginning of the *do* statement, and the process is repeated until the *expression* is false (zero).

Example:

```
int n, addition = 0;
int i
```

```
do
{
   cout « "Enter, , ;
   cin » n;
   addition + = n;
   i ++;

}while (i <= 100 );

cout « "The average is, , « double ( addition ) / ioo.o;
```

The following example displays the squares from 2 to 10:

```
int i = 2;
do
   cout « i « "12=" « i* i ++ « endl;
while ( i < 11 );
```

B.1.7.5.3 *for* Statement

It executes an iteration a fixed number of times. Its general format is:

```
for (expression 1; expression 2; expression 3; )
statement
```

Expression 1 is used to initialize the control variable. Next, *expression 2* is evaluated and as long as its result is right the loop will be executed. *Expression 3* is executed on ending each iteration of the loop..

Examples:

```
for ( int i = 0; i < n; i ++ )      // performs n iterations
for ( int i = n1; i <= n2; i += n2 ) //iterates from n1 to n2 with increment n3
```

B.1.7.6 *break* and *continue* Statements

They are used for breaking the normal control of a loop. The `break` statement causes a loop exit. The `continue` statement makes the control continue by evaluating the loop condition.

```
for ( int i = 1; i < n; i ++ )
{
   cin >> j;
   if (j = 0) break;
   else if (j < 0) continue;
   ..............................................................
};
```

B.1.7.7 *null* Statement

The `null` statement is represented by a semicolon and does not perform any action.

```
for ( int i = 1; i < n; i ++ );
```

B.1.7.8 *return* Statement

It stops the current function execution and returns control to the function of the caller function. Its syntax is

```
return expression
```

Where expression is the value returned by the function.

B.1.8 Basic Inputs and Outputs

Unlike many languages, C++ doesn't have built-in facilities to handle input or output. Instead, they are handled by library routines. The classes used by C++ for input and output are known as *flows.* A flow is a sequence of characters together with a routine collection to insert characters into flows (to screen) and withdraw characters from a flow (from keyboard).

B.1.8.1 Output

The cout flow is the standard output flow corresponding to stdout in C. This flow derives from the ostream class built in iostream

```
cout « i;
```

The following program displays a statement on screen

```
#include <iostream.h>
int main ()
{
   cout « "hello, world\n";
}
```

C++ outputs can be connected in cascade, with a writing facility greater than in C

```
#include <iostream.h>
   int main ()
   {
   int i;
   i = 1099;
   cout « "The value of i is" « i « '/n' ;
   }
```

Another program showing the cascade connection is the following:

```
#include <iostream.h>
   int main ()
   {
   int x =45;
   double y 495.125;
   char *c = "y multiplied by x ";
   cout  « c «y*x « '\n';
}
```

B.1.8.2 Input

The input is handled by the *istream* class. There is a predefined object istream, called cin, which refers to the standard input device/the keyboard. The operator used to obtain a keyboard value is the extraction operator. For example, if i was an object int i will be written:

```
cin » i;
```

which obtains a number from the keyboard and stores it in the variable i.

A simple program that reads an integer and displays it on screen is:

```
#include <iostream.h>
   int main ()
   {
   int i;
```

```
cin » i;
cout «i «"\n";
```

Like in the cout case, cascade data can be introduced:

```
#include <iostream.h>
  int main ()
  {
  char c [60];
  int x, y;

  cin » c » x » y;
  cout « c « "" « x << "" << y « "\n";
  }
```

B.1.8.3 Handles

An easy method for changing the width of the *Y flow* to other format variables is by using a special operator referred to as *handle*. A handle accepts a reference flow as an argument and returns a reference to the same flow.

The following program shows the use of handles specifically for number conversions (dec, oct, hex):

```
#include <iostream.h>
  int main ()
  {
  int i = 36;
  cout « dec « i « oct « i « hex << i << '\nl';
}
```

The program output is

36 44 24

Another typical handle is endl, which represents the new line character (line feed) and is equivalent to '\n'. The above program can also be written the following way:

```
#include <iostream.h>
  int main ()
  {
  int i = 36;
  cout «dec «i «oct «i «hex «i «endl;
}
```

B.1.9 Functions

A function is a collection of declarations and statements that perform an only task.

B.1.9.1 Function Declarations

A function must be declared before using it in C+. The declaration of a function is referred to as prototype and consists of the function name, its arguments, and the value returned by that function.

```
Name type ( identifier type, identifier type...);
```

For instance:

```
double average ( double x, double y );
void query ();
```

B.1.9.5 Function Overloading

In C++, two or more different functions may have the same name. This property is referred to as *overloading.* An example is the following:

```
int max ( int, int );
double max ( double, double );
```

or else this one:

```
void add (char i);
void add (float i);
```

Overload functions differ in the number and type of arguments or in the type returned by the functions, or their bodies are different in each of them.

```
#include <iostream.h>
void addition ( char );
void addition ( float );
main ( void )
   {
      int i = 65;
      int j = 6.5;
      addition (i);
      addition (j);
   }
   void addition ( char i )
   {
   cout « "Interior addition ( char )" « endl;
   }
   void addition (float j)
   {
   cout « Interior addition (float) 11 « endl;
   }
```

B.1.9.6 The Modifier *const*

The modifier const is used in C++ to provide real-only protection for function variables and parameters. When a type of argument is preceded by the modifier const to point out that this argument cannot be changed, the argument to which it is applied can neither be assigned a value nor changed.

```
void copyg(const char*source, char*dest); void func_demo(const int i);
```

B.1.9.7 Pass from Parameters to Functions

There are three ways to pass parameters to functions in C++.

1. *By value* — The called function receives a copy of the parameter and this parameter cannot be modified in the function:

```
void swap ( int x, int y )
{
   int aux = Y;
   y = X;
   x = aux;
   }
swap ( i, j ); // variables i, do not swap
```

2. *By address* — A pointer is passed to the parameter. This method permits simulation of the call by reference in C++ by using pointer types in the formal parameter in the prototype declaration. This method permits modifying the arguments of a function.

```
void swap ( int *x, int *y )
{
int aux = *y; +y = *x; *x = aux;
}
swap ( &i, &j ); // i, j swap their values
```

3. *By reference* — Reference types can be passed as function arguments which permits modifying the arguments of a function.

```
void swap ( int&x, int&y )
{
   int aux = y;
   y = x;
   x = aux;
   }
swap ( i, j );
```

B.1.9.8 Pass of Arrays

Arrays are passed by reference. The address of the array's first element is passed by value. Arrays can be indirectly passed by their values if the array is defined as a member of a structure.

```
// Pass of the whole array. Example 1

#include <iostream.h>
void funcl ( int x[] ); // function prototype
void main
   {
         int a [3] = ( 1, 2, 3 );
         funcl (a);        // statements
         funcl (& [0]);     // equivalent
   }
   void func ( int x [1] );
      int i;
      for ( i = 0; i < 3; i + 1 )
            cout « i « x[i] « I\nl;
```

The following example passes an array's element:

```
#include <iostream.h>
const int N = 3;
void func2 ( int x );
void main
{
   int a [N] = {1, 2, 3};
   func2 ( a [2] );
}
   void func2 ( int x );
   }
      cout « x «
}
```

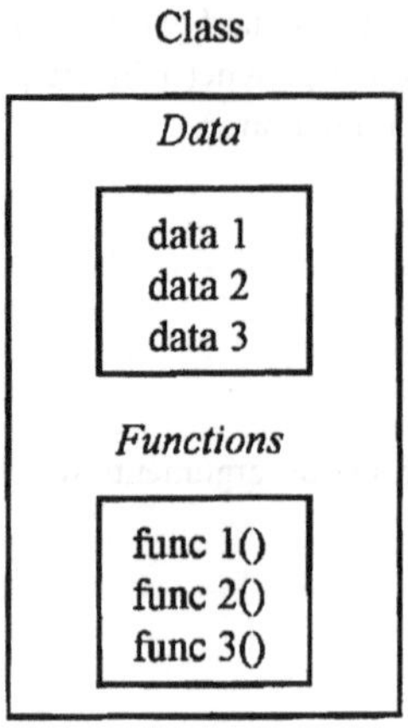

FIGURE B.1 Classes contain data and functions.

B.1.10 Classes

The class is the key element for object-oriented programming in C++. The class is analogous to the structure, in that a class is a data encapsulation mechanism, but with the additional support of functions specific to the class which operate on the class data (Figure B.1). Classes are forms of heterogeneous aggregate types.

An *object* is said to be an *instance* of a class. Objects have a unique state defined by internal data values. Objects can be categorized into class. Objects in the same class share the same attributes and functionality.

The attributes of a class are called *data members* and the operations of the class are called *member functions.*

Syntax:

```
class     className
{
  private:
    //private components (data members, constructors, member functions)
  protected:
    //protected components (...)
  public:
    //public components (...)
};
```

Note: You can declare a class in C++ by using either `class`, `struct`, or `union`.

```
class | struct | union name [base_class_declarations]
{
  declarations
}[object_definitions];
```

- **Private section** — Only the class' member functions can access the data in this section.
- **Protected section** — Only the class and its descendant classes can access the data items in this section.
- **Public section** — The data items in this section are accessible from outside the class.

The components of a class are all private by default. The class sections can appear in order and more than once. Once a class has been defined you can declare objects of that class.

Example:

```
class muInt
{
  public:
    //public constructor ──────────┐
    myInt();                        │ Constructors
    myInt (const myInt & andIntObj);──
    void setInt (const int nNewNum);──┐
    int getInt();                      │ Member functions
    void show (const char * pszMsg);──
  protected:
    int a_bInt; ──────────────────── Data member
};
```

B.1.10.1 Member Functions

Member functions are declared outside the class itself.

Syntax:

```
type className::functionName
returnType className::member Function Name, (parameter List)
{
  //statements
}

int myInt::getInt()
{
  return a_bInt;
}
```

B.1.10.2 Constructors and Destructors

A *constructor* is a member funtion whose name is the same as the class name. It constructs object of the class type. A *destructor* is a member function whose name is the class name preceded by the tilde character ~. Its usual purpose is to destroy values of the class type.

Syntax:

```
className();                   //default constructor
className (parameter List);    //a constructor
~ className();                 //a destructor

//definition of a constructor

className::className (parameterList)
{
  //statements
}
```

B.1.10.2.1 Rules

Constructors:

1. Constructors initialize the objects of a class.
2. All objects should be initialized with meaningful values.
3. The constructor's name is identical to the name of its class.
4. Constructors cannot have a return type.

5. A class can have any number of constructors as long as each has a different parameter list.
6. If a constructor is not declared, then the compiler will automatically create one.
7. A default constructor has no parameters or it has a parameter list where each parameter uses default arguments.
8. A constructor with one parameter that has the class type is called the copy constructor.
9. If the class does not declare a constructor, C++ creates a default constructor for that class.
10. C++ invokes a constructor when you create a class instance. The arguments of that instance select the appropiate constructor, if the class declares multiple constructors.

Destructors:

1. The destructor has the same name as its class, preceeded by a tilde (~).
2. There can only be one destructor for each class.
3. Destructors have no parameters and no return type.
4. There can only be one destructor. If none is declared then the compiler automatically creates one.
5. C++ automatically invokes a destructor when a class instance reaches the end if its scope.

General syntax for declaring a constructor:

```
class className
{
   public:
      //void constructor
      • className();
      //copy constructor
      className (className& classNameObject);
      //additional constructor
      className (parameterList);
      //other members
};
```

Example:

```
class Tcomplex
{
   public:
      //constructors
      Tcomplex();
      Tcomplex (Tcomplex& complexObj);
      Tcomplex (double fReal, double fImag);
      //other members

   protected:
      double P_*fReal;
      double P_fImag;

      //others members
};
```

C++ automatically invokes a constructor for the class instance being created.

B.1.10.3 Copy Constructors

```
className (const className &an Object);

figure (const figure & aFig);
```

The copy constructor is called when an object is created as copy of another of its own type.

```
figure aFig (1,10, "Mackoy");
```

General syntax for declaring a destructor:

```
class className
{
  public:
    //void constructor
    className();
    //other constructors
    //destructor
    ~ className();
    //other members;
};
```

B.1.10.4 Friend Functions and Friend Class

Friend functions are just ordinary functions that have access to all data members of one or more classes. As well as friend functions, entire classes can be declared friends.

Syntax:

```
friend returnType  functionName (parameter list), //friend function
friend className;                                 //class function
```

Friend Function:

```
class className
{
  //declaration of members
  friend returnType functionName (parameterList);
};
```

Friend Class:

```
class className
{
  friend friendClassName;
  //declaration of other members
};
```

Example:

```
class Tcomplex
{
  public:
    Tcomplex();
    //declaration of other members

    friend Tcomplex DivideComplex (Tcomplex& C, double fReal);
    friend Tcomplex DivideComplex (double fReal, Tcomplex& C);

    //declaration of other members
};
class A
{
  public:
    friend class C;
```

```
        ...
};

class B
{
   public:
      friend class C;
   ...
};

class C
{
   public:
      C (...);
      ~C ();
      ...
   protected:
         ...
};
```

B.1.10.5 `const` and `mutable` Data Members

The ANSI/ISO draft standard defines a new keyword, `mutable`, which is used to allow a member of an object to cast away `const`. The keyword `mutable` allows data members of class variables that have been declared `const` to remain modifiable. This is a relatively new feature and is not implemented on all C++ compilers.

//illustrates const and mutable data members

```
class X
{
   public:
      int data;
      const int a_data;        //const data members
      mutable int b_data       //mutable data member

      mutable const int bc_data;        //error: mutable const
      mutable static int bt_data;       //error: mutable static
      X ()
         :data (0), a_data (0); b_data (0) {}
};
...
X  x;           //non-const object
const X cx;  //const object

   x.data = 1;          //O.K. : non-const object, non-const member
   cx.a_data = 4;    //error: const object, const member

   //O.K. : mutable member of const object can be modified
   cx.b_data;
}
```

B.1.11 Inheritance

Inheritance, in C++, is the ability of a class to inherit the features of one or more other classes. When we say that some class A is a *derived class* of some other class B, it means that class A has all the features of class B, but it also has *extra added features.* When class A is a derived class of the class B, we also say that B is the *base class* (**parent** class) for A and that A is the *derived class* (**child** class).

Syntax:

```
class className : (public|protected|private)opt base-class
{
  member-list
};
```

`public|protected|private` is the optional *access-specifier*, *base-class* is the name of the class from which the current class is derived, and *member-list* consists of data and function members. If the access-specifier is omitted, `private` is the default

Example:

```
class vehicle
{
  protected:
     double weight;
     int power;
     int registrationYear;

public:
     vehicle (double w, int p, int year);
     double getWeight();
     int getYear();
     int getPower();
};

class car : public vehicle
{
  protected:
     int noOfSeats;
  public:
     car (double wg, int pw, int yr);
     int get noOfSeats;
};
```

B.1.11.1 Multiple Inheritance

C++ also allows us to declare a *class* which is derived from multiple base classes. Deriving a `class` from more than one base class is referred to as *multiple inheritance.*

Syntax:

```
class DerivedClass: access-specifier BaseClass0,
                         ..., access-specifieer BaseClassn
{
  //...
};

class Derived : public Base0, Base1
{
  //...
};
```

Example:

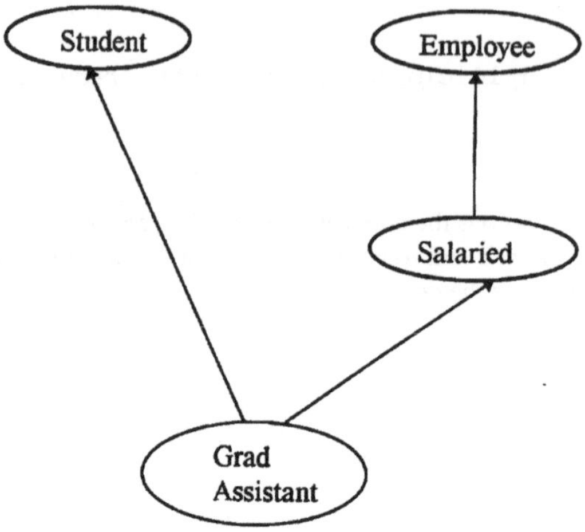

FIGURE B.2

```
class GradAssistant : public Student, public Salaried
```

B.1.11.2 Constructor Invocation

The order of execution for initializing constructors in base and member constructors is as follows:

1. Base classes are initialized in declaration order
2. Members are initialized in declaration order

B.1.11.3 Abstract Base Classes and Polymorphism

A class that has at least one pure virtual function is an *abstract base class.* A pure virtual function is a virtual member function whose body is normally undefined.

Syntax (virtual function):

```
virtual returntype functionName (parameter list);
virtual function prototype = 0; //pure virtual function
```

Example:

```
class Base
{
  //...
  virtual void Display ();
  //...
};

class Derived : public Base
{
  //...
  //warning : Derived::Display() hides Base::Display()
  void Display (int n);
};
```

Polymorphism enables the instances of different classes to respond to the same function in ways that are appropiate to each class.

A member function is declared as `virtual` in a base class using the **virtual** keyword. Notationally, it is declared inside the class.

B.1.12 Templates

The *template* concept is a feature that was added to C++ to support creating function templates and class templates. A *class template* is a framework for generating the source code for any number of related classes. Class templates are also called *generic classes* or *parameterized classes.* A *function template* is a framework for generating related functions.

B.1.12.1 Function Templates

C++ allows you to declare and define function templates. The general syntax for declaring a function template is

```
template <class T[.other template types]>
returnType functionName)parameterList;
{
   //statements
}
```

T is called a *template parameter* because it refers to a data type that will be supplied when the function is called. T must also be used as the data type of at least one function parameter.

Examples:

```
1. template <class T>
   T Max (T a, T b)
   {
      return a > b ? a:b;
```

```
2. template <classT>
   void Display (const T &val)
   {
      cout << val;
   }
```

```
3. template <class T>
   void Swap (T& data1, T& data2)
   {
      //...
   }
```

```
4. template <class T1, T2>
   void MyTemplate (T1 x, T2 y)
   {
      //...
   }
```

B.1.12.2 Template Classes

Class templates offer the ability to generate new classes, just as function templates generate new functions.

Syntax:

```
template <class T[, other template types]>
class className
{
   //...
};
```

The template parameter `T` can be either a type or an expression. For example, we might pass different data types to the template, creating two different classes:

```
MyClass <int> X;
MyClass <Student> aStudent;
```

A class template can have multiple parameters.

Example:

```
template <class T1, class T2>
class Circle
{
  //...
  private
    T1 x;
    T1 y;
    T2 radius;
};

  //...
  Circle <int, long> Cdemo;
  Circle <unsigned, float> D;
```

B.1.13 Exception Handling

An exception is an unexpected condition that the program encounters and cannot cope with. In C++, errors such as memory exhaustion, subcript range errors, or division by zero are called *exceptions. Exception handling* is the mechanism provided by C++ for handling exceptions.

A program *throws* an exception at the point where an error is first detected. When this happens, a C++ program automatically searches for a block of code called an *exception handler*, which responds to the exception in some appropiate way. This response is called *catching an exception.* If an exception handler cannot be found, the program simply terminates.

B.1.13.1 Throwing an Exception

In C++, reporting an exception is called *throwing* an exception, and offers the `throw` statement to throw an exception (which is a predefined data item, or an instance of an *exception* class).

Syntax:

```
throw
throw expression
```

Example:

```
1. if (fp = = NULL)
     throw 1;
```

```
2. if (y >= ArraySize) //subcript valid?
     throw RangeError(); //no: throw an exception
```

B.1.13.2 Try Blocks and Handlers

In its simplest form, the C++ exception-handling syntax consists of two blocks: one block is the protected area of code, and the second block is the exception handler.

```
try {
  statements
}
catch (parameter-list() {
  statements
}
```

The *statements* inside the `try` block are executed unconditionally. This block, unlike the `catch` block, is part of the normal flow of program execution. The full syntax for `try` and `catch` enables you to write any number of exceptions handlers at the same level:

```
try {
  statements
}
catch (parameters-list1) {
  statements
}
catch (parameter-list2) {
  statements
}
...
```

B.1.13.3 Exception Specification

An exception specification is part of a function declaration, and has the form

function header throw (*type list*)

The *type list* is the list of types that a throw expression within the function can have. The function definition and declaration must write out the exception specification identically.

B.1.14 Changes Made to C++ by the ISO/ANSI C++ Committee

The ANSI C++ Committee is working on standardizing C++. Thus, C++ continues to evolve. This section covers new features:

B.1.14.1 Major Language and Library Extensions

Exceptions (exception handling)
Namespaces (avoiding global name clashes)
RTTI (runtime type identification)
STL (the standard template library)
Templates (generic types and functions)

B.1.14.2 Minor Extensions and Changes

bool (built-in Boolean data type)
casts (new cast syntax and semantics)
new (reserved words)
member constants (in class constants — static const integral members)
mutable (concrete const and abstract const)
hosted classes (forward declaration of nested classes)
new[ ] and delete[ ] (array allocation and deallocation)
operator → (relaxing the rules for the return type of operator →)
overloading on enums (enumerations are now aq distinct type for overloading)
placement delete (avoiding memory leaks from placement new)

B.1.15 The C++ Standard Libraries*

The ISO/ANSI Standard C++ library will contain a set of general-purpose data structures and algorithms.

The library provides *containers, iterators,* and algorithms that support a standard for generic programming. The STL is the C++ standard library.

* http:www.cygmus.com/misc/wp/dec96pub/; http://www.ucsltd.com/c++/isocplus.html; and http://www.maths/warwick/ac.uk:80/c% 2b%2b.

B.1.15.1 Containers*

Containers are objects that store other objects. They control allocation and deallocation of these objects through constructors, destructors, insert, and erase operations. The containers come in two major families: sequence and associative. Sequence containers include vectors, list, and deques, and they are ordered by having a sequence of elements. Associative containers include sets, multisets, maps, and multimaps, and they have keys for looking up elements.

B.1.15.2 Iterators**

Iterators are a generalization of pointers that allow a C++ program to work with different data structures (containers) in a uniform manner. There are five iterator types: input, output, forward, bidirectional, and random access.

References

Accredited Standards Comittee (x3316/95-0u 87 and Wg21/N0687). 1995. *Working Paper for Draft Proposed International Standard for Information Systems-Programming Language C++*. American National Standards Institute, April.

Booch, G. 1997. *Object-Oriented Analysis and Design*, 2nd Ed. Addison-Wesley, Reading, MA.

Ellis, M. A. and Stroustrup, B. 1990. *The Annotated C++ Reference Manual.* Addison-Wesley, Reading, MA.

Joyanes Aguilar, L. 1995. *C++ a su alcance (Beyond C++).* McGraw-Hill, Madrid.

Joyanes Aguilar, L. 1996. *Visual C++. Iniciación y Referencia* (Visual C++ Reference). McGraw-Hill, Madrid.

Joyanes Aguilar, L. 1996. *Borland C++ 4/4.5. Iniciación y Referncia (Borland C++ 4/4.5: Initiation and Reference).* McGraw-Hill, Madrid.

Joyanes Aguilar, L. 1996. *Turbo C++.Iniciación y Referencia (Turbo C++. Iniciation and Reference).* McGraw-Hill, Madrid.

Joyanes Aguilar, L. 1996. *(Object-Oriented Programming: Concepts, Modeling, Design and Implementation), Programación Orientada a Objetos: Conceptos, Modelado, Diseño e Implementación.* McGraw-Hill, Madrid.

Lippman, S. B. 1991. *C++ Primer, 2nd Ed.* Addison-Wesley, Reading, MA.

Plauger, P. J. 1995. *The Draft Standards C++ Library.* Prentice-Hall, Englewood Cliffs, NJ.

Pohl, I. 1997. *Object-Oriented Programming Using C++*, 2nd Ed. Addison-Wesley, Reading, MA.

Pohl, I. 1997. *Object-Oriented Programming using C++*. Second Ed. Addison-Wesley, Reading, MA.

Shammas, N. C. 1995. *Foundations of C++ and Object-Oriented Programming.* IDG Books, Foster City.

Stroustrup, B. 1991. *The C++ Programming Language*, 2nd Ed. Addison-Wesley, Reading, MA.

Stroustrup, B. 1997. *The C++ Programming Language.* Third Edition. Addison-Wesley, Reading MA.

Taligent Inc. 1994. *Taligent's Guide to Design Programs*: Well-Mannered Object-Oriented Design in C++. Addison-Wesley, Reading, MA.

* http://www.cygmus.com/misc/wp/dec96pub/lib-containers.html.

** http://www.cygnus.com/misc/wp/dec96pub/lib-iterators-html.

APPENDIX C

Eiffel Language Guide

Luis Joyanes Aguilar
Pontifical Salamanca University

María Luisa Díez Platas
Pontifical Salamanca University

Paloma Centenera
Pontifical Salamanca University

Eiffel is a pure object-oriented language developed by Bertrand Meyer in the 1980s. By using Eiffel language we can make solid and consistent applications, such as those tall engineering works built by Gustave Eiffel.

C.1.1 Language Vocabulary (Lexical Elements)

An Eiffel program consists of a sequence of ASCII characters grouped as *tokens* (lexical components), that make up the basic language vocabulary. These components are keywords, identifiers, literals, operators, separators, and comments.

C.1.1.1 Identifiers

An identifier must conform with the usual naming convention: a name begins with a letter and consists of letters, digits, and underlined characters.

C.1.1.2 Comments

As in Ada, comments are introduced with a double dash (--) and at end of the line. For example,:

```
-- This is an example
```

C.1.1.3 Keywords

Keywords cannot be used as identifiers. In Eiffel, there are 69 keywords. See Table C.1.

0-8493-3135-8/99/$0.00+$.50

TABLE C.1 Keywords

Alias	all	and	as	check	classs
Creation	debug	deferred	do	else	elseif
End	ensure	expanded	export	external	false
feature	from	frozen	if	implies	
indexing					
infix	inherit	inspect	invariant	is	like
local	loop	not	obsolete	old	once
or	prefix		redefine	rename	require
rescue	retry	select	strip	then	true
undefine	unique	until	variant	when	xort

C.1.1.4 Literals

Literals are lexical components that represent constant values of a primitive type, string type, or null type. These are the following: `Boolean, character, Integer, Real and Double, Bit sequences, String`

1. `Boolean` — True, False.
2. `Character` — ASCII characters enclosed in single quotes. For example,:

   ```
   'A', 'a'
   ```

   Any character may also be denoted with the sequence like '%/n/', where n is its ASCII code.
3. `Integer` — Integer digits with optional underscores. The underscores are used to enhance readability.
   For example:

   ```
   475          --Correct
   1_345_654    --Correct
   12_23        --Non correct
   ```

4. `Real` and `Double` — There are floating-point implementations of a real number.
   For example,:

   ```
   0.492
   ```

5. `Bit sequence` — A bit sequence constant is a sequence of 0s or 1s followed by a b or B character.
   Example:

   ```
   10010110B.
   ```

6. `String` — The syntax of a string constant is a sequence of characters (including special characters prefixed with %) delimited by a double-quote character. For example,:

   ```
   "This is an example of string %
     split in two lines"
   ```

C.1.1.5 Operators

There are two types of operators: *assignment operators* and *non-assignment operators.*

- *Boolean* — `not, or, and, implies, or else, and then`
- *Integer* — `+, -, *, //, \\, ^, >, <, <=, >=`
- *Real* — +, -, *, /, ^, >, <, <=, >=

The operator // represents the integer division, and the operator \\ integer remainder (module).

C.1.2 Data Types

Eiffel is a strongly typed language. Every object has a well-defined type.

C.1.2.1 Primitive Types

Primitive types are named by its reserved word and represent a single value, such as a number, a character, or a boolean value. There are four groups:

- Integer
- Character
- Boolean
- Real and Double

C.1.2.2 Classes

A class declaration has the following syntax:

```
[indexing index_list ]
[(deferred | expanded)] Class identifier [ [ formal_generic_list ] ]
[obsolete string_constant]
[inherit parent_list]
[creation creation_clause]
{[feature feature_clause]
[invariant assertion]
end [ -- identifier]
```

Where:

- **indexing** — An indexing clause for documentation and indexing purposes.
- **deferred, expanded** — No regular class.
- **identifier** — A class name is also the module name and the type name.
- **formal_generic_list** — A generic clause makes it possible to build classes with parameters.
- **obsolete** — An obsolete clause, if present, denotes that this class is to be removed from the library in future releases.
- **inherit** — An inherit clause allows to specify how this class is inherited from others.
- **creation** — A creation clause that describes which routines may be called by the creation of an instance of this class.
- **feature** — Feature clauses describe the attributes and methods which this class exports.
- **invariant** — Specifies the class invariants.

All details of these clauses are described in sections below. For example:

```
Class STACK [ITEM]
Creation make
Feature
   Make                  -- initializes the stack to be empty
   Heap :ITEM            -- the item at the heap of the stack
   Next :STACK[ITEM]     -- the stack with the heap removed
   Is_empty :boolean     -- true if the stack is empty, false
                              Otherwise
   Push(I:ITEM)          -- add the item i to the heap of the stack
   Pop:ITEM              -- remove the heap and return them
End                      -- class STACK
```

Generic stack.

C.1.2.2.1 Indexing Clause

The indexing clause provides a powerful mechanism for cataloging classes. The index list syntax is the following:

```
Identifier : (string_constant | identifier)
{, (string_constant | identifier) }
```

For example:

```
    Indexing description: "dic.3.4", revision: "v1.4", implementation:
  "Paul Smith"
```

C.1.2.2.2 Deferred Class

A deferred class is a class with at least one deferred feature. This deferred feature has a specification, but not implementation. By opposition a non-deferred feature is called effective feature. A deferred method is equivalent to a pure vitrual function in C++, and a deferred class is equivalent to an abstract class in C++ . For example:

```
Deferred class geometrical_figure
Px: Integer
Py: Integer
Area : Real is deferred end
End -- class geometrical_figure
```

C.1.2.2.3 Expanded Class

In Eiffel an object identifier is a reference to a class object. When you declare an expanded class object it is not a reference like a true object. This is the case when dealing with such basic notations of integers or real numbers.

C.1.2.2.4 Genericity, Generic Clause

Generic clauses class can make a template class with parameters (generic class). The parameters for generic clauses class are types or classes. The formal generic list syntax is:

```
    type_identifier [ -> base_type ]{, type_identifier [ -> base_type ]}
```

Example:

```
  Class Generic_sorted_list [t->COMPARABLE]
  -- t: derived from COMPARABLE
...................
  end – Generic_sorted_list
  l: generic_sorted_list[integer]
```

C.1.2.2.5 Obsolete Clause

A class or feature declared obsolete are classes or features which become obsolete. They can still be used normally, but any reference to the obsolete class will trigger a compile-time warning with the message to the corresponding obsolete clause.

For example:

```
Class Integers_list
Obsolete "you sould use generic_list[integer]"
..............
end
```

C.1.2.2.6 Inheritance, The Inherit Clause

It allows us to build a new class, an extension of another existent class. The inherit clause syntax is:

```
Class_type [feature_adaptation]{; Class_type [feature_adaptation]}
```

It is allowed multiple inheritance. For example:

```
Deferred class person
Feature
     Name: string
     Number: string
     Print is deferred
     other
End -- class person
Class employee
Inherit person
Creation make_employee
Feature
     Money: Real
     Make_employee(n,un: string; m; Real)
End -- class employee
```

The optional `feature_adaptation` allows us to modify or adapt the inherit features in five different controlled ways:

1. Renaming an inherited feature. Its syntax is the following:

   Rename *inherit_identifier* **as** *new_identifier* { **,** *inherit_identifier* **as** *new_identifier* }

2. Changing the export status of an inherited feature. Its syntax is as follows:

   Export *new_export_item* { **;** *new_export_item* }

3. Redefining the behavior of an inherited feature. Its syntax is as follows:

   Redefine *feature_name* { **,** *feature_name* }

4. Undefining an inherited feature. Its syntax is as follows:

   undefine *feature_name* { **,** *feature_name* }

5. Joining inherited features. Its syntax is the following:

   Select *feature_name* { **,** *feature_name* }

   For example:

```
Class employee
Inherit person
     Rename name as employee_name,
        Number as employee_number
     Export {NONE} employee_name      -- none exportable
     Redefine print                   -- to be redefined
     Undefine other
     End-- adaptation
Creation make_employee
Feature
   Money: Real
   Make_employee(n,un: string; m; Real)
   ...........
End -- class employee
```

C.1.2.2.7 Features, Feature Clause

The feature_clause syntax is the following:

[*clients*] { [**frozen**] *identifier* {, *identifier*} [**(** *Formal_parameters* **)**]
[**:** *Type*] [**is** (*routine* / *constant* | **unique** | **deferred**) }

- There are three `clients` for the features:
  1. {NONE} private features
  2. {ANY} public features
  3. {*Class_identifiers_list*} these features are only visible for the class enumerated in the list (friend class in C++)
- **frozen** features are never redefined.
- Features can be procedures, functions, and attributes. Procedures and functions have optional *Formal_parameters* list . Functions return a value.
- A routine implementation has the following form:

```
[obsolete string_constant] [require Assertion ]
[local Declarations] [deferred] do statements [ensure Assertion]
[rescue statements] end
```

- **Require** and **ensure** are pre- and post-conditions.
- **Rescue** clause is used for handling exceptions.

  For example:

```
Class employee
Creation make
Feature {ANY}
  Make (n: STRING; a: STRING; y: REAL; r: REAL) is
    Do
      Name:= n
      Address:= a
      Year_of_birth:= y
      Rate:= r
    End -- make
  Pay(hours): real is
    Do
      Result:= rate*hours
    End -- pay
  Name: STRING
  Address: STRING
  Year_of_birth: INTEGER
Feature {NONE}
  Rate: REAL
End -- class employee
```

C.1.2.2.8 Invariant

Like other assertions, pre-conditions, post-conditions, and class invariants express the specification of software components. Class invariant describes class the properties that remain true at any time. The invariant syntax is as fllows:

```
[Tag_mark] (boolean_expresion| comment)
{; [Tag_mark] (boolean_expresion| comment )}
```

C.1.3 Objects Declarations

With a few exceptions, in Eiffel, objects are anonymous. An instance of a class is (except the instances of the expanded class) a reference to an object. The declaration syntax is as follows:

```
Identifier : Type [actual_generic_parameters ]
```

For example:

```
My_stack: STACK [CHARACTER]
```

C.1.4 Expressions

In Eiffel, there are different types of expressions: object creation expressions, methods invocation expressions, field access expressions, array access expressions, and expressions with operators.

1. Expressions with operators
   Example:

   ```
   3.5* a
   false
   ```

2. Array access expressions refer to a variable that is a component of an array

   ```
   expression [ index]
   name [ index]
   ```

3. Field access expressions

   ```
   expression..identifier
   ```

4. Object creation expressions are used to create new objects. The syntax is as follows:

   ```
   !! identifier [(actual_parameters )]
   ```

   For example:

   ```
   !! my_stack
   ```

5. Method call expression is used to invoke a method class. Its syntax is the following:

   ```
   expression..identifier( [list_of_actual_arguments])
   ```

The elements of the list for actual parameters are expressions that must have the same type as the parameters of the method.

C.1.5 Statements

The statements have the following syntax:

1. Assignment statement

   ```
   Object := expression
   ```

2. Expression statements are the following expressions: *method call* and *creation expression.*
3. The if statement is a control statement. It needs an expression of boolean type. There can be if-nested. Its syntax is as follows:

   ```
   if expression then statements {elseif expression
   then statements }[else statements]end
   ```

4. The inspect statement is a control statement and its body must be a block. It provides a way to execute one of the different parts of the code based on the value of an expression. Its syntax is the following:

   ```
   inspect expression { when when_part}else statements end
   ```

   The *when_part* has the syntax below:

   ```
   Constant[..constant]{,Constant [ .. constant]} then statments
   ```

   For example:

   ```
   Inspect number
   When 1..10 then a:= a+1
   When 11..30,45 then a:= a+3
   ```

```
Else a:= a+10
End
```

5. The loop statement is a control and iterative statement.

   from *statements* [**invariant** *boolean_expressions_list*]
   [**variant** *integer_expression*]
   until *Boolean_expression* **loop** *statements* **end**

   There are five main components of a **loop** instruction:
   - Initialization — A set of instructions following the symbol **from** which is evaluated once and is used to perform whatever initializations are required for the loop. Statements may be a null sequence of instructions.
   - Invariant — An optional set of logical expressions which determines the status of the loop variables and the loop semantic.
   - Variant — An integer expression having a bound that ensures the loop will terminate.
   - Terminating condition — A boolean expression which determines when the iteration stops. The iteration finished when the expression is true.
   - Loop body — A set of statements following the symbol **loop** representing the loop body.

   For example:

```
From
  i:= 0
  tot:= 0
invariant
  i>= 0; n > 0
variant
  n - i
until
  i= n
loop
  i:= i+1
  tot:= tot+i
end
```

C.1.6 Exceptions

C.1.6.1 The Rescue Clause

In Eiffel every subroutine has a **rescue** clause for handling exceptions. This clause is an exception handler and is either implicit or can be written explicitly into the routine. When an exception occurs, the interrupt flow of control is transferred to an appropriate rescue clause, whether implicit or explicit. The syntax of a rescue clause is as follows:

Rescue *instructions*

For example:

```
Clever_proc is
  Local
    Tries: INTEGER
  Do
    If tries = 0 then
      -- the first strategy
    else
      -- the second strategy. Only when error
```

```
    end
  rescue
    tries:= tries+1
    if tries < 2 then
      retry
    end
  end
```

The `retry` sentence can cause two different effects:

1. The exception is canceled.
2. The body of the routine is executed once more beginning at the end.

References

Jézéquel, J.M. 1996. *Object-Oriented Software with Eiffel.* Addison-Wesley, Reading, MA.
Mayer, B. 1992. *Eiffel: The Language.* Prentice-Hall, Englewood Cliffs, NJ.
Switzer, R. 1993. *Eiffel. An Introduccion.* Prentice-Hall, Englewood Cliffs, NJ.
Thomas, P. and Weedon R. 1995. *Object-Oriented Programming in Eiffel.* Addison-Wesley, Reading, MA.
Wiener, R. 1995. *Software Development Using Eiffel.* Prentice-Hall, Englewood Cliffs, NJ.

Webliography

http://www.f.com
http://www.sigs.com/publications/docs/oc/9612/oc9612.nutshell.html

APPENDIX D

Java Language Guide

Luis Joyanes Aguilar
Pontifical Salamanca University

María Luisa Díez Platas
Pontifical Salamanca University

In this reference guide we are trying to make an enumeration of the most representative elements of Java language, as well as the syntax rules. Java is a language for network programming developed by James Gosling and others at Sun Microsystems. Java syntax is similar to C and C++ syntax but is organized differently because its designers borrowed features from other languages, such as Smalltalk and Lisp, in order to achieve the design goals.

In order to specify the syntax in every element of the language, the following notation will be used: elements in italics represent syntactic categories, bold elements represent keywords; an element between braces ({}) means that the element can appear zero or more; an element between square brackets means it is optional, that is, it can be left out; an element specified as list_of_items, means one or more items separated by commas, and finally, a sequence_of_items means one or more items.

D.1.1 Language Vocabulary (Lexical Elements)

A program in Java consists of a sequence of Unicode characters grouped as *tokens* (lexical components), that make up the basic language vocabulary. These components are keywords, identifiers, literals, operators, separators, whitespaces, and comments.

D.1.1.1 Character Set

Characters in Java are not the same as C or C++ characters. Java uses Unicode to represent characters. Unicode defines a fully international character set that can represent all of the characters of human languages. Characters in Java require 16 bits.

0-8493-3135-8/99/$0.00+$.50

D.1.1.2 Comments

There are three types of comments: single-line, multi-line, and documentation.

1. *Single-line comment* (as in C++), begins with the ASCII characters //. All the text from the beginning to the end of line is ignored

```
//single comment in Java
```

2. *Multi-line comment* begins with a /* and ends with a */, all the text enclosed by them is ignored.

```
/*multiline
comment */
```

3. *documentation comment* is used to produce an HTML file that documents the program, and can be processed by a separate tool. It begins with a /** and ends with a */.

```
/**documentation */
```

D.1.1.3 Identifiers

An *identifier* consists of a sequence of upper- and lowercase letters, digits, and the ASCII underscore (`_` or `\u005f`) and dollar sign (`$` or `\u0024`) characters, the first of which must be a letter, underscore, or dollar sign. Letters and digits may be written from the entire Unicode character set. This allows programmers to use identifiers that are written in their native languages. Java, like C and C++, is case-sensitive, two identifiers are the same if they are the same Unicode character for each letter or digit. There is no limit in the length of an identifier and it cannot have the same Unicode character sequence as a keyword. The regular expression that specifies these lexical elements are:

```
identifier_letter {[underline][$] letter_or_digit}
```

An identifier letter can be letter, underscore or $

```
house          // is an identifier
House          // isn't the same identifier as before
The_house      // is an identifier
The_house_9    // is an identifier
15_houses      // is not a valid identifier
_my_house      // is an identifier
αβγ            // is a valid identifier
$15            // is an identifier
```

D.1.1.4 Keywords

Keywords cannot be used as identifiers. In Java, there are 69 keywords, see Table D.1.

TABLE D.1 Keywords

abstract	default	goto	null	synchronized
boolean	do	if	package	this
break	double	implements	private	throw
byte	else	import	protected	throws
case	extends	instanceof	public	transient
catch	false	int	return	true
char	final	interface	short	try
class	finally	long	static	void
const	float	native	super	volatile
continue	for	new	switch	while

D.1.1.5 Literals

Literals are lexical components that represent constant values of a primitive type, string type, or null type. There are *Integer, FloatingPoint, Boolean, Character, String,* and *Null* literals.

1. *IntegerLiteral* — It represents an integer constant and it may be expressed in decimal, hexadecimal, or octal.
   - *Decimal Integer Literal* is:

     ```
     Decimal_Numeral [IntegerSuffix]
     ```

     A *Decimal_Numeral* can be 0 or a sequence of decimal digits (1, 2, 3, 4, 5, 6, 7, 8, or 9) the first of which cannot be 0. *IntegerSuffix* can be **L** or **l**. and they indicate that the integer literal is of `long` type; otherwise its type is `int` (the literal can optionally be suffixed with letter **I** or **i**).

     ```
     125    //is a decimal integer literal
     13L    //is a decimal long literal
     ```

   - *Hexadecimal Integer Literal* is:

     ```
     Hexadecimal_Numeral [IntegerSuffix]
     ```

     A *Hexadecimal_Numeral* is 0X*sequence_of_hexadecimal_digits* or 0x*sequence_of_hexadecimal_digits.* A hexadecimal digit can be one of these:

     ```
     0 1 2 3 4 5 6 7 8 9 a b c d e f A B C D E F
     ```

   Example

   ```
   0XaBa
   0x124
   0x0FFL
   ```

   - *Octal Integer Literal:*

     ```
     Octal_Numeral [IntegerSuffix]
     ```

     Octal_Numeral is a *sequence_of_octal_digits.* An octal digit can be one of these:

     ```
     0 1 2 3 4 5 6 7
     ```

     Example

     ```
     0345
     0543L
     02761
     ```

2. *FloatingPointLiteral* — It represents a constant value of type `float` or `double`. It has five parts that can be optionals: whole part, decimal point, fractional part, exponent, and type suffix. A *Floating Point Literal* is of type float if it has a ASCII letter **F** or **f** as a suffix; otherwise, it is double (it can optionally be suffixed with an ASCII letter D or d). The literal can be:

   ```
   Sequence_of_Digits. [Sequence_of_Digits] [Exponent] [Float Suffix]
   ```

   or

   ```
   .Sequence_of_Digits [Exponent] [Float Suffix]
   ```

   or

   ```
   Sequence_of_Digits [Exponent] [Float Suffix]
   ```

   An exponent can be represented by an ASCII letter **E** or **e,** optionally followed by a sign – or +, followed by digits. The float suffix was explained above.

Example

```
0.0
1E2f
.4f
6.2123e+21
5.21E-34F
```

3. *Boolean literal* — It represents a value of the boolean type. The boolean type has two values: **true** and **false.**
4. *Character literal* — It represents a value of the type char. It consists of a character or a scape sequence that represents a character, enclosed in single quotes.
   Example

```
'b'
'%'
'\t'
'\uFFFF'
```

5. *String literal* — It represents a constant string value; it consists of zero or more characters or the equivalent scapes enclosed in double quotes.
   Example

```
""
"This is a string literal"
"\""
```

6. *Null literal* — It represents a value of null type that is **null.**

D.1.1.6 Operators

There are two types of operators: *assignment operators* and *non-assignment operators.*

- *assignment operators:*

```
=  -= *= /= |= &=  ^= +=  %=  <<=  >>=  >>>=
```

- *non-assignment operators*

```
+  -  <=  ^ ++  <  *  *  >=  %  -  /  !=  ?  >>  !  &  ==  :  >> ~ | && >>>
```

D.1.1.7 Separators

In Java, there are nine ASCII characters that are Java separators:

```
( ) { } [ ] ; , .
```

D.1.1.8 Whitespace

In Java, whitespace is a space, tab, or newline.

D.1.2 Data Types

Java is a strongly typed language. Every variable and every expression has a type. There are two types of data in Java: primitive types (predefined by the language) and reference types.

D.1.2.1 Primitive Types

Primitive types are named by their reserved words and represent a single value, such as a number, a character, or a boolean value. There are four groups:

1. **Integers types** — Their values are integers. They include byte, short, int, and long type.
2. **Floating-point types** — They are float (representing single-precision) and double (representing double-precision).
3. **Character type** — It is char, which represents symbols in a character set.
4. **Boolean type** — It represents two values: true and false. It includes boolean.

D.1.2.2 Reference Types

The reference types are defined by declaring a *class type*, an *interface type*, or an *array type*. Reference types have a representation.

1. **Class type** — It is specified by a class declaration. A class type is named by a *typename*, that is an *identifier* or a *qualifiedname* which is *identifier.identifier* or *qualifiedname.identifier*.
   A class declaration has the following syntax:

   ```
   [class_modifiers] class identifier [extends_clause]
   [implements_clause] {[sequence_of_fields_declaration]}
   ```

   Modifiers are one of these:
   - **Public** — This modifier specifies that a class can be referenced by another class; otherwise, the class is only referenced by other classes in the same package.
   - **Abstract** — No instances of the class may be created. The class may contain abstract methods.
   - **Final** — The class cannot appear in the extend clause of another class.

   Extends clause specifies the superclass. Its syntax is as follows:

   ```
   extends typename
   ```

   Implements clause lists the names of interfaces implemented by the declared class. Its syntax is the following:

   ```
   implements list_of_typename
   ```

   In the sequence of fields declarations, there may be declarations of class members, that is, variables (or fields) and methods; and declarations of static initializers and constructors.

   Member declaration can be a variable declaration or method declaration. The syntax of variable declaration is as follows:

   ```
   [variable_modifiers] type list_of_variabledeclarators;
   ```

   Modifiers are the following:
   - **Public** — It indicates that a variable is accessible from any class.
   - **Protected** — It indicates that a variable is accessible to any class that is part of the same package.
   - **Private** — It indicates that a variable is only accessible in the class in which it is declared.
   - **Static** — A variable is called *class variable*, because every instance of the class shares the single copy of these variables.
   - **Final** — It indicates that a variable is a named constant value and it must contain an initializer to set the value of the variable.
   - **Transient** — It indicates that a variable is not part of the persistent state of an object.
   - **Volatile** — The variable will be modified by the method that is running in different threads.

Variable declarators can contain a *variable_declarator_identifier* that can be an *identifier* or *variable_declarator_identifier* [ ] (array declaration). It may also contain an initializer to set a value of the variable (an initializer is an *expression* or an *array initializer*). Its syntax is the following:

```
variable_declarator_identifier = initializer
```

The syntax of method declaration is as follow:

```
[method_modifier] type* identifier ([list_of_formal_parameters])
   [[ ]] [throw_clause]
method_body
```

Modifiers are **public, protected**, and **private** (they specify the same that specifies variables modifiers); **static** (class method, it is not associated with an instance of a class), **final** (a method cannot be overridden); **abstract** (method declaration must end with semicolon, this declaration does not specify the implementation of the method); **native** (method is implemented by using a language other than Java); and **synchronized** (a thread must obtain a lock before it invokes the method).

Formal parameters have the following syntax:

```
type variable_declarator_identifier
```

Throw clause specifies the exceptions that can be thrown by the method. The following is its syntax:

```
throws list_of_typename
```

Method body can be a block or ;

A **static initializer** is a block of code that is executed when the class is initialized. Its syntax is the follows:

```
static block
```

A **constructor** is a method that is used to create an object and set the initial values of an object's instance variables. The name of a constructor is the same as the name of the class. The syntax is as follows:

```
[constructor_modifiers] identifier (list_of_formal_parameters)
   [throw_clause] block
```

The block has this syntax:

```
{ [Constructor_invocation] [statements]}
```

the constructor invocation can be **this**([*list_of_arguments*]); or **super**([*list_of_arguments*]);

Example

```
      //class rectangle
   class Rectangle{
double width;
double height;

//constructor
Box (double w, double h){
   width = w;
   height = h;
}
//method
double area ( ) {

   return width * height;
}
}
```

Example

* It also can be **void**.

```
class figure{
      double x;
      double y;
      //another methods
    }
      //inheritance
      class rectangle extends Figure {
      //members
    }
```

2. **Interface Type** — An interface declaration specifies a new reference type. There are two differences with class declaration: all of the variables are static and final; and all the methods are abstract. The syntax is the follows:

   [*interface_modifiers*] **interface** *identifier* [*extends_clause*]
   { [*lsequence_of_fields_declarations*] **}**

   Modifiers are the following: **public, final,** and **abstract**. They have the same meaning as in class declaration. The modifier abstract does not change the meaning of the declaration because an interface is implicitly abstract.

   Extends clause specificies the super interface of the interface and the fields declaration can be variable or methods* declarations, but not constructors or static initializers declarations.

   Interface body declares members of interface enclosed by braces.

   Example

```
public interface figure {
   void draw ( );
}
public class Triangle implements Figure{
   void draw () }
```

3. **Array Type** — This is a special type. An array object contains *elements*, all of which have the same type. To declare an array type it must write a type name followed by some number of empty pairs of square brackets.

   Type **[ ]**

   Example

```
int [ ] [ ] d;   //2-dimensional array
int [ ] d [ ]; //2-dimensional array
```

D.1.3 Variables and Objects Declarations

The programmer can declare different types of variables in Java. Variables of primitive types hold a value of the primitive type. Variables of reference types are a null reference or a reference to any object, whose type is compatible with the type of the variable. The syntax to declare a variable was seen above.

In Java an object is a class instance or an array. A class instance is created by a class instance creation expression and an array is created by an array creation expression.

* The methods are implicitly abstract, they do not have a specified implementation.

D.1.4 Expressions

In Java, there are different types of expressions: primary expressions, class instance creation expressions, array creation expressions, methods invocation expressions, field access expressions, array access expressions, postfix expressions, and expressions with operators.

1. **Primary expressions** — These are the most elementary expressions. They can be the following:
   this
   super
   null
   literal
   field_access
   array_access
   *creation _expression**
   method_call
2. **Expressions with operators.** In Java, there are constant expressions or expressions and expressions with assignment operator.
   - Constant expressions denote a value of a primitive type or a string and they are composed by using: literals of primitive type and string type, unary operators, binary operators (additive, multiplicative, shift, relational, equality, bitwise, logical, conditional-and, conditional-or operators), ternary operator (**?** :), names of **final** variables, and qualified names (*type.identifier*)
     Example
     ```
     3.5* Math.PI
     false
     ```
   - Expressions with assignment operator is formed by using a constant expression which is assigned to a name, field access, or array access.
     name = expression
     field_access = expression
     array_access = expression
     Example
     ```
     a[1] += (a[1] = 3) * (a[1] - 3)
     ```
3. **Array access expressions** — They refer to a variable that is a component of an array.
   ```
   expression** [ index]
   name [ index]
   ```
4. **Field access expressions**
   ```
   array_creation.identifier
   expression***.identifier
   super.identifier
   ```
5. **Array creation expressions** are used to create new arrays. The syntax is as follows:
   ```
   new type**** sequence of_dimension_expression sequence_of _
     dimension_empty
   ```

* This expression can be a class creation expression or an instance creation expression.
** This expression is not an array creation expression.
*** This expression is not an array creation expression.
**** This type can be a primitive type, a class type, or an interface type.

The dimension expression has the following syntax:

```
[expression]
```

and the syntax of the other dimension is:

```
[]
```

6. **Class instance creation expression** is used to create new objects that are instances of the classes by the constructor invocation. This is its syntax:

```
new type* ( [list_of_actual_arguments])
```

Example
Rectangle r;

```
r = new Rectangle (5, 10);
```

7. **Method call expression** is used to invoke a method class or a method interface. The syntax can be one of these:

```
name( [list_of_actual_arguments])
array_creation.identifier( [list_of_actual_arguments])
expression**.identifier( [list_of_actual_arguments])
super.identifier( [list_of_actual_arguments])
```

The elements of the list of actual parameters are expressions that must have the same type as the parameters of the method.

D.1.5 Statements

In Java, there are several statements, some of which are control statements. All statements end with semicolon and they must be preceded by a label. Its syntax is as follows:

```
identifier: statement
```

The statements have the following syntax:

1. **Empty statement**

```
;
```

2. **Expression statements** are the following expressions ended with semicolon: *expressions with assignment operator, increment* and *decrement expressions* (prefix or posfix), *method call,* and *creation expression.*
3. The **if statement** is a control statement. It needs an expression of boolean type. These can be if nested. Its syntax is as follows:

```
if (expression) statement [else statement]
```

4. The **switch statement** is a control statement and its body must be a block. It provides a way of executing one of the different parts of the code based on the value of an expression. Its syntax is the following:

```
switch (expression) {*** [sequence_of _case_statement] [default:
     sequence_of_statement]}
```

* This type must be a class type.

** This expression is not an array creation expression.

*** Here, braces are tokens. They are part of the statement.

The case statement has this syntax:

case *expression*: *sequence_of_statements*

5. The **while statement** is a control and iterative statement. It executes a statement while a boolean expression is true.

   while (*expression*) *statement*

6. The **do statement** is also an iterative statement that first executes a statement and then evaluates a boolean expression. While an expression is true, the statement is executed repeatedly.

   do *statement* **while** (*expression*) ;

7. Another iterative statement is the **for statement.** It executes a control variable initialization and then evaluates an expression. A statement is executed until the value of the expression is false. In every iteration, it updates the control variable.

   for ([*initialization*]; [*expression*] ; [*update*]) *statement*

   Initialization can be a variable declaration and initialization or an expression statement.
8. The **break statement** transfers control out of an enclosing statement.

   break [*identifier*];

9. The **continue statement** stops the iteration of an iteration statement and starts the next iteration. It can be only used in a while, do, or for statement.

   continue [*identifier*];

10. The **return statement** is used to return from a method and program control transferring back to the caller of the method.

    return [*expression*];

    There are other statements like **throw statement, try statement**, and **synchronized statement,** that are discussed later.
11. **Blocks** are sequences of statements and local variable declaration statements within braces. Their syntax are the following:

    {* [*sequence_of_block_statements*] }

    A block statement can be a local variable declarator, and its syntax is as follows:

    type list_of_variabledeclarators;

    Variable declarators were discussed above; or they can be a statement.

D.1.6 Compilation Units

In Java, compilation units consist of three optional parts: **package declarations, import declarations,** and **type declarations** (class type or interface type). The syntax of compilations units are the following:

[*package declaration*] [*sequence_of_import_directives*] [*type declaration*]

Type declaration can be a class declaration or an interface declaration. The other parts will be dealt with above.

* Here, the braces are tokens and forma and they are part of the block.

D.1.6.1 Packages

Java programs consist of a set of packages that have their names for types which are accessible only if the types are declared **public**; otherwise, they can only be referenced by other classes in the same package. A package is a collection of related compilation units, that is, a group of classes. The syntax to declare a package is as follows:

```
package package_name;
```

or

```
package identifier sequence_ of_ identifiers;
```

The sequence of an identifier consists of

```
. identifier
```

D.1.6.2 Import Directives

Java has import statements to bring certain classes or entire packages, into visibility; that is, a class can be referred by using only its name. These directives must be written immediately following the package declaration and before any class definition. The syntax for the directives is the following:

```
import package_name. identifier;
```

import a single type by giving its fully qualified name

```
import package_name.*;
```

import all public type declared in the package named.

D.1.7 Exceptions

Java has an exception-handling mechanism. The mechanism is similar to the C++ mechanism. A Java exception is an object that describes an exceptional condition that has occurred in the code. When an exception is thrown, control is transferred to the nearest dynamically enclosing `catch` clause of a `try` statement that handles the exception. Its syntax is the following:

- **Exception declarations** — It uses a throws clause in a method that is expected to throw any exception. The type of the exceptions are subclasses of the built-in class **Throwable.**

  ```
  throw identifier*;
  ```

- **Throw statements** — This statement is used to generate an exception. Usually, it must be followed by an object that is of the type of the exceptions.

  ```
  throw exceptions;
  ```

- **Try block** — This is a statement that executes a block and encloses a code that you want to monitor because in that code an error can be produced. Its syntax is the following:

  ```
  try block sequence_of_catch_clauses
  try block[sequence_of_catch_clauses] finally block
  ```

* It must written following the method identifier.

- **Catch clause** — This is used to handle an exception. It catches an exception thrown by the preceding try statement and cannot catch an exception thrown by another try statement. It forms a unit with a try statement.

```
catch (formal_parameter) block
```

D.1.8 Threads

Threads provide a way for a Java program to do multiple things concurrently. Every thread is a flow of control. A thread is created by instantiating an object of type **Thread**. To accomplish this, Java uses two forms: implementing the **Runnable** interface or extending the **Thread** class. It is necessary to ensure that shared resources will be used by only one thread at a time, by a **synchronized statement**, that acquires a mutual-exclusion lock, executes a block, and releases the lock. Its syntax is the following:

```
synchronized (expression) block
```

Java includes an interprocess communication mechanism via the **wait**(), **notify**(), and **notifyAll**() methods.

References

Gosling, J., Joy, B. and Steele, G. 1996. *The Java Language Specification.* Addison-Wesley, Reading, MA.

Grand, M. 1997. *JAVA Language Reference*, O'Reilly.

Lea, D. 1997. *Concurrent Programming in Java.Design Principles and Patterns.* Addison-Wesley, Reading, MA.

Lemay, L. 1996. *Developing Java Applications.* Sams.net.

Naughton, P. and Schildt, H. 1997. *The Complete Reference JAVA.* McGraw-Hill, New York.

Oaks, S. and Wong, H. 1997. *JAVA Threads.* O'Reilly.

Ritchey, T. 1995. *Programming with Java Beta 2.0.* New Riders.

Webliography

<IBM Corporation-Smalltalk Programming and Development Guidelines: A Manual of Style>
http://www.training.ibm.com/ibmedu/otu/stalkmos.html

<Simon Lewis-Prentice Hall/Hewlett-Packard-The Art and Science of Smalltalk>
http://www-uk.hpl.hp.com/people/scrl/ArtAndScience/contents.html

<IBM Smalltalk Tutorial>
http://www2.ncsu.edu/eos/info/ece480_info...spring96/proj63/www/tutorial/

<STIC- The Smalltalk Language Background>
http://www.stic.org/STLang/F001.htm

<ChiMU Publications-Java and Smalltalk Syntax compared>
http://www.chimu.com/publications/JavaSmalltalkSyntax.html

<ANSI X3J20>
http://www.di.ufpe.br/smalltalk/X3J20.html

<ANSI Annual Report>
http://www.stic.org/STLang/F010.htm

<The Smalltalk Report>
http://www.sigs.com/publications/srpt/

<Gameplan: Java-savvy Smalltalk in a year>
http://www.onemind.com/smalltalk.html

<ANSI X3H7 Object Model Features Matrix>
http://info.gte.com/ftp/doc/activities/x3h7/by_model/Smalltalk.html

<Dick Botting-Smalltalk Syntax>.
http://www.csci.csusb.edu/dick/samples/smalltalk.syntax.html

<Dick Botting-Smalltalk Semantics>.
http://www.csci.csusb.edu/dick/samples/smalltalk.semantics.html

APPENDIX E

MODULA-2 Language Guide

Luis Joyanes Aguilar
Pontifical Salamanca University

María Luisa Díez Platas
Pontifical Salamanca University

Paloma Centenera
Pontifical Salamanca University

Modula-2 is a programming language designed by Niclaus Wirth, who invented Pascal programming language. Pascal was conceived as a teaching-oriented language, and when Wirth realized its scope was increasing and its use was extending, he made the decision of creating a new general purpose programming language, and one focused on the development of large applications. Modula-2 is still a moderate and smart language, even more homogeneous and orthogonal than Pascal and incorporating tools for application modeling, low-level data management, concurrency, etc.

E.1.1 Language Vocabulary

A program is a sequence of characters grouped as lexical components, *tokens*, that make up the basic language vocabulary. These components are keywords, identifiers, constants, operators, and punctuation marks.

0-8493-3135-8/99/$0.00+$.50

E.1.1.1 Characters

The characters in Table E.1 are used to build tokens.

TABLE E.1 Characters Set

	0	20	40	60	100	120	140	160
0	nul	del		0	@	P	`	p
1	soh	dcl	!	1	A	Q	a	q
2	stx	dc2	"	2	B	R	b	r
3	etx	dc3	#	3	C	S	c	s
4	eot	dc4	$	4	D	T	d	t
5	enq	nak	%	5	E	U	e	u
6	ack	syn	&	6	F	V	f	v
7	bel	etb	'	7	G	W	g	w
10	bs	can	(	8	H	X	h	x
11	ht	em	)	9	I	Y	i	y
12	lf	sub	*	:	J	Z	j	z
13	vt	esc	+	;	K	[	k	{
14	ff	fs	'	<	L	\	l	|
15	cr	gs	–	=	M	]	m	}
16	so	rs	.	>	N	↑	n	~
17	si	us	/	?	O	←	o	del

E.1.1.2 Comments

Modula-2 comments are delimited by characters (*, and *).

```
(* This is a Modula-2 comment *)
```

They have a peculiar characteristic, which is the possibility of nesting:

```
(* first level of nesting .
   (* second level *)
     end of coment  *)
```

E.1.1.3 Identifiers

Modula-2 identifiers consist of a letter followed by a sequence (which can be null) of letters, digits and/or underlined characters. There cannot be non-alphanumeric characters nor blanks, except underlining in an identifier.

Valid identifiers

```
Main_Program
Module12
Colors_Set
```

Non-valid identifiers (remember that the character ñ, for Spain and Latin America, is considered special).

```
17X
Null Character
España
```

Note: Modula-2 distinguishes upper- and lowercase letters in the identifiers, which implies that the identifier *sample* is different from the identifier *Sample*, and in turn is different from *SAMPLE*.

E.1.1.4 Keywords

These are basic language components and cannot be used as identifiers. In Table E.2, Modula-2 keywords are enumerated, and must always be written in uppercase letters.

TABLE E.2 Keywords

AND	ELSIF	LOOP	REPEAT
ARRAY	END	MOD	RETURN
BEGIN	EXIT	MODULE	SET
BY	EXPORT	NOT	THEN
CASE	FOR	OF	TO
DEFINITION	IF	POINTER	UNTIL
DIV	IMPLEMENTATION	PROCEDURE	VAR
DO	IMPORT	QUALIFIED	WHILE
ELSE	IN	RECORD	WITH

E.1.1.5 Pre-defined Identifiers

In addition to keywords, in Modula-2 you can find a series of standard identifiers, or predefined identifiers. These also have their own meaning in the language, but unlike keywords they are sensitive to be used as user identifiers and therefore redefined. In Table E.3 you can see Modula-2 predefined identifiers.

Modula-2 contains a number of predefined identifiers for constants, elementary data types, and standard procedures. The following summary povides an overview of what they mean.

E.1.1.6 Literal Constants

In Modula-2 there are constants of all the simple above-enumerated types except WORD type, since it has no proper values.

- *Boolean constants*:

  ```
  TRUE, FALSE
  ```

- *Character constants* (delimited by single or double quotes):

  ```
  'a', "@"
  ```

- *Chain constants* (delimited by single or double quotes which allow including both characters inside them):

  ```
  'He said "Noway".
  ```

- *CARDINAL constants*:

  ```
  0, 2345
  ```

- *INTEGER constants*:

  ```
  -47, 18
  ```

- *BITSET constants*:

  ```
  [], [1,6..12]
  ```

E.1.1.7 Operators

Modula-2 offers a broad set of operators (Table E.4) that allows handling standard type data. We can distinguish four classes of operators:

Table E.3 Pre-defined Identifiers

Pre-defined Constants	
FALSE	Boolean value "false"
NIL	POINTER value that points to no object
TRUE	Boolean value "true"
Pre-defined Data Types	
BITSET	Set
BOOLEAN	Logical values "true" or "false"
CARDINAL	Natural numbers (≥0)
CHAR	Characters
INTEGER	Whole numbers (positive or negative)
PROC	Parameterless procedures
REAL	Real numbers
Standard Procedures	
DEC (x)	Reduces (decrements) the value of x by 1
DEC (x, n)	Reduces (decrements) the value of x by n
DISPOSE (p)	Frees the storage to which p points
EXCL (s, e)	Removes (excludes) the element e from the set s
HALT	Terminates program execution
INC (x)	Increases (increments) the value x by 1
INC (x, n)	Increases (increments) the value of x by n
INCL (s, e)	Includes the element e in the set s
NEW (p)	Allocates dynamic storage
Standard Functions	
ABS (x)	Returns the absolute value of x
CAP (ch)	Changes the character ch to a capital letter
CHR (c)	Returns the character whose ordinal number is c
FLOAT (c)	Transforms the CARDINAL number c into a REAL number
HIGH (a)	Returns the highest index of the array a
MAX (T)	Returns the greatest value that can be represented by the data type T
MIN (T)	Returns the smallest value that can be represented by the data type T
ODD (x)	Returns the boolean value of the expression "x is odd"
TRUNC (r)	Transforms the REAL number r to a CARDINAL number
VAL (T, c)	Returns the value of data type T having the ordinal number c

Table E.4 Modula-2's Operators

+	Addition of numeric data and union of sets
-	Difference of numeric data and sets
*	Product of numeric data and intersection of sets
/	Division of numeric data and symmetric difference of sets
DIV	Integer division
MOD	Module
:=	Assignation
AND	Logical Y
NOT	Logical negation
OR	Logical O
=	Equality comparison
< >	Difference comparison
<	Minor comparison
<=	Minor or equal comparison and superinclusion of sets
>	Greater comparison
>=	Greater or equal comparison and superinclusion of sets
IN	Checking of sets pertaining

- *Arithmetic operators* combine arithmetic operands with arithmetic results.
- *Logical operators* combine logical operands with logical results.
- *Set operators* combine set operands with a set result.
- *Relational operators* compare two operands and return a logical result.

The operators within these expressions must follow some precedence rules which condition the valuating order. These operator precedence rules are indicated in the following table:

Higher than	NOT						
	*	/	DIV	MOD	AND		
	OR	+	-				
Lower than	=	< >	< >	>=	<=	IN	

E.1.2 Data Types

Modula-2 provides an assorted set of standard data types. This characteristic facilitates the natural representation of information.

In addition to the above-mentioned simple types, there is the possibility of creating new types and structures that allow representing, in a natural way, the information handled by programs.

Data types are classified as follows:

- *Pre-defined* (standard)
- *Registers*
- *Arrays*
- *Sets*
- *User-defined* (enumeration, subrange)
- *Structured* (set, array, record, pointer)

E.1.2.1 Standards Types

In Table E.5 you can see simple data types.

Table E.5 Simple Data Type

Type	Range of Type Values	Comment
BOOLEAN	TRUE or FALSE	Logical values of boolean algebra
CHAR	ASCII character set	Taken any ASCII character as value
CARDINAL	From 0 to 65535	Natural numbers including zero
INTEGER	From — 32768 to 32767	Integer numbers
REAL	Varies depending on the implementation	Representation of a real number limited in terms of precision and range
BITSET	From [ ] to [0..16]	Set of numbers from 0 to 16; it represents the set of bits in a word
WORD (BYTE, WORD, LONGWORD)	They correspond to 1, 2, and 4 bytes of memory	Compatible with any type that takes up a word

E.1.2.2 User-Defined Types

Modula-2 allows the user to name his own data types. This is carried out in the section TYPE, as follows:

```
TYPE
   {<identifier>=<typedef>}
```

For example:

```
TYPE
   Kilometers = REAL;
   Logic = BOOLEAN;
```

E.1.2.2.1 Definition of Data String

The *string data*, in Modula-2, are defined by means of an array of characters, subscripted beginning with 0. For example,:

```
TYPE
   Names = ARRAY[0..19] OF CHAR;
```

In the standard library STRING, Modula-2 provides tools to handle these data types. In addition to procedures ReadString and WriteString in the standard library, InOut allows, respectively, the reading and writing of a chain

E.1.2.2.2 Enumeration Types

They are defined using different type values. In Modula-2, it has the following form:

```
"(" {<identifier>} ")"
```

For example:

```
TYPE
   Colors = (red, green, blue, yellow);
   Trees = (holm, elm, oak, apple, pear, apricot, prickly);
      Months = (January, February, March, April, May, June, July, August,
              September, October, November, December);
```

These enumerated data are of ordinal type. The order of values is the same as their enumeration. They can be applied all that is valid for ordinal data.

E.1.2.2.3 Subrange Types

They serve to define a new type from an ordinal type with restriction in relation to the range of values. They are ordinal types, with the following form:

```
"["<constant>..<constant> "]"
```

For example:

```
TYPE
   Module9 = [0..8];
   Fruit trees = [apple.. pear];
```

They are compatible with the type from which they derive, but the compiler performs the checking of the values assigned to see that they are within the range.

E.1.2.2.4 Set Types

They represent a set of elements without repetitions of an ordinal data type. The following is the general form:

```
SET OF <type>
```

For example:

```
TYPE
   Palettes = SET OF Colors;
   Gardens = SET OF Trees;
   Lettersset = SET OF CHAR;
   Orchard = SET OF Fruit trees;
```

Sets are handled by means of the set constuctor: `[ ]` and by means of the operators: `+`, `-`, `*`, `/`, `IN`. For example:

```
VAR
MyGarden: Gardens;
.............
MyGarden := [ ]; (* read assign the empty set of trees*)
MyGarden := [elm, apple..apricot];
MyGarden := MyGarden – [pear];
IF holm oak IN MyGarden THEN
.................
```

E.1.2.2.5 Registers

They define a data type made up of a series of variables of different types (register fields). They have the following format:

```
RECORD
   {<identifier>:<type>;}
END
```

For example:

```
TYPE
   Dates = RECORD
         Day: [1..31];
         Month: months;
         Year: CARDINAL
       END;
```

To reference a register field, you can use the following:

```
<identifier>.<identifier>

VAR
   MyBirthday: Dates;
.............
MyBirthday.day = 27;
```

Registers can be nested.

```
TYPE
   Persons = RECORD
           Name = Names;
           Birth: Dates;
        END;
VAR
   I: Persons;
............
I.Birth.Day = 27;
```

A WITH statement allows an abbreviated reference to the register fields (without indicating the variable name in the reference).

```
WITH I DO
   ReadString(name);
   WITH Birth DO
      ReadCard(Day);
      ReadCard(Year);
      Read(Month)
   END
END
```

E.1.2.2.6 Array Type

They represent an ordered set of the same data type in which you can access the element that occupies a determined location within the sorting. It has the following form:

```
ARRAY <IndexList> OF <TypeDef>
```

where the first type is an index and must be an ordinal type, and the second is the data type of components likely to be of any type. For example:

```
TYPE
   Table = ARRAY[1..8] OF CARDINAL;
   Tasks = ARRAY Trees OF Months;
```

In Modula-2 it is not allowed to declare arrays with more than one dimension, as an array must be declared within another one:

```
TYPE
   Matrix = ARRAY[1..10] OF ARRAY [1..10] OF INTEGER;
```

Pass of Arrays as a Parameter — The arrays pass must always be performed by reference. In Modula-2 it is possible to declare subprograms with parameters of open array type (indicating their component types rather than their index range):

```
PROCEDURE Show( VAR T: ARRAY OF CHAR );
```

The last procedure can be invoked with any array of characters, as a parameter.

E.1.2.3 Strongly Typed Data

Modula-2 is a strongly typed language and performs a strict data type checking.

E.1.2.4 Type Conversion

There is the possibility of performing conversion between the different standard data types by using casts:

```
<type> "("<expression> ")"
BITSET(65)
```

E.1.3 Constants Definition

There is the possibility of defining constants with a name in the constants definition paragraph with the following structure:

```
CONST {<identifier>=<constant>";"}
```

For example:

```
CONST
   White = ' ';
   NullSet = [ ];
   APair = 2;
```

E.1.4 Variable Declaration

All variables to be used in a module must be declared. This is carried out in a variable declaration paragraph:

```
VAR { <identifier> { , <identifier>} :<type> ;}
```

For example:

```
VAR
   Wage: REAL;
   Searching: BOOLEAN;
   NumberOfCopies: CARDINAL;
Error: Boolean;
```

It is necessary to reset, in an explicit way, all the declared variables before looking up their constants, since nothing can be stated about their value at the beginning of program execution.

E.1.5 Statement

E.1.5.1 Assignation Statement

Follow the syntax:

```
<variable> ":=" <expression>

NumberOfCopies := 5;
Searching := TRUE;
Wage := 4500000;
```

E.1.5.2 Conditional Statements

The following is the general format of an IF statement:

```
IF <expression> THEN <statements>
{ ELSEIF <expression> THEN <StatementList>} [ELSE <statements>]
END

IF Searching THEN NumberOfCopies: = NumberOfCopies*2
ELSEIF Wage< 3000000 THEN Wage: = Wage*NumberOfCopies
ELSE Wage:= Wage+NumberOfCopies
END;
```

The multiple alternative statement has the following format:

```
CASE <expression> OF
<constant>{"," <constant>}":" <StatementList> {"|"
<constant>{"," <constant>}":" <StatementList>}
[ELSE <Statement List>]
END

CASE Character OF
'a', 'A': WriteString('Student')|
'p', 'P': WriteStirng('Professor')
ELSE WriteString('Error')
END;
```

E.1.5.3 Loop Control Statements (Iterative)

E.1.5.3.1 FOR Statement

With the following form:

```
FOR <variable> ":=" <expression> TO <expression> [BY <expression>] DO
   <StatementList>
END
```

The variable is reset with the result of the first expression and is iterated until it gets to the second expression. BY and its expression are then optional and indicate the control variable increment after each iteration. The condition is checked before the loop execution so that this may never be executed. The control variable can be of any ordinal type.

For example,

```
FOR I := 1 to 100 DO
  WriteCard(I,4)
END;
```

It will show 1 to 100 numbers in ascendent order and

```
FOR I := 100 to 1 BY 2 DO
  WriteCard(I,4)
END;
```

it will even show lower o equal to 100 numbers in descendent order.

E.1.5.3.2 WHILE Statement

Its general format is the following:

```
WHILE <expression> DO
  <StatementList>
END
```

The following fragment is an example:

```
I := 1;
WHILE T[I]<>E DO
  I: = I+1
END;
```

It performs a searching in the array T of element E taking I, the value of its position.

E.1.5.3.3 REPEAT Statement

Its form is the following:

```
REPEAT
  <StatementList>
UNTIL <expression>
```

The loop condition is valued after its execution, therefore the loop is always executed at least once.

```
REPEAT
  Read(c)
UNTIL c IN ['n','s','N','S']
```

It reads characters in c, until n or s are read.

E.1.5.3.4 LOOP Statement

This is a loop without condition. It has the following form:

```
LOOP
  <statementList>
UNTIL <expression>
```

In order to terminate the loop execution, EXIT statement is used. This must appear inside it, causing exit of the statement which precedes it. For example:

```
LOOP
  ReadCard(N);
```

```
    IF N>100 THEN EXIT END;
    WriteCard(N*N)
  END
```

The label must be declared before they are used:

```
Declaration:= LABEL IdentifierList ';'
```

E.1.5.3.5 WITH Statement

The `WITH` statement is used to create a local scope where the fields names of a record type can be used without an initial designator.

```
WITH Designator DO StatementList END
```

For example:

```
WITH Persons [i] DO
  IF (Age < 18) THEN
    First := "junior ";
  LESIF (Age < 15) THEN
    First := "senior ";
END;
```

E.1.5.3.6 GOTO Statement

The GOTO statement is used to unconditionally alter the flow of the execution:

```
Statement := GOTO Identifier
```

The target statement is indicated by the label identifier and must be located somewhere within the same *body*:

```
Statement := Identifier ':' [Statement]
```

Labels must be declared before they are used:

```
Declaration := LABEL IdentifierList ';'
```

E.1.6 Procedures

A *procedure* is a subprogram that can be invoked from a statement and therefore the communication is performed by means of parameter passes. *Procedures* are used to group commonly performed operations into isolated blocks. There are two procedures: *proper procedures* are used like statements and *function procedures* compute values and are used in expressions.

E.1.6.1 Procedure Declaration

A declaration of the procedure consists of four parts:

1. A procedure heading begins with the keyword PROCEDURE followed by the name of the procedure
2. After the procedure name, the formal parameters, if present, are listed to specify the input and output objects of procedure. The procedure heading is terminated with semicolon
3. A block containing the declarations of the local objects of the procedure and the statement sequence to be executed when the procedure is activated
4. A procedure declaration is terminated with the keyword END followed by the procedure name and semicolon

Its general form is the following:

```
PROCEDURE <identifier>[ "(" <Formal parameters>")" ] [":" <type>];
{<clause IMPORT> ; }
```

```
{<definition of constants>|
<definition of types>|
<declaration of variables>|
<declaración of procedures>}
BEGIN
   <StatementLists>
END <identifier>.
```

A procedure can optionally return a value of any type (it would behave as a function). For example,:

```
PROCEDURE Proc1;
BEGIN
  WriteLn("Procedure 1 has been called")
END Proc1;
```

The list of arguments is optional and has the following form:

```
[ VAR ] {<identifier> {, <identifier>} :<formal type>;}
```

Where VAR indicates the pass of parameters by reference. If nothing is indicated the pass is performed by value. The procedures can be nested, thus facilitating program modeling. The invocation of a procedure is performed in a procedure statement with the following form:

```
<identifier> [ "(" <expression> {, <expression> } ")" ]
```

For example:

```
Proc1;
```

E.1.6.2 Standard Procedures

They are predefined in the language and do not have to be imported for their use. They are the following:

TABLE E.6

`ABS (n)`	Returns the absolute value of *n*
`CAP (n)`	Returns capital letter *c*
`CHR (n)`	Returns code ASCII character *n*
`DISPOSE (p)`	Releases memory zone pointed by pointer *p*
`FLOAT (n)`	Converts `CARDINAL` into `REAL` *n*
`HIGH (t)`	Returns upper limit of array index *t*
`NEW (p)`	Assigns *p* to the pointer to a free memory zone
`ODD (n)`	Returns `TRUE` if *n* is odd
`ORD (n)`	Returns ordinal of *n*
`TRUNC (n)`	Returns `CARDINAL` resulting from truncating `REAL` *n*
`VAL (t,n)`	Returns value *n* transformation into the ordinal type *t*
`DEC (n)`	Decrements *n* in 1
`DEC (n,m)`	Decrements *n* in *m*
`EXCL (s,e)`	Removes *e* from set *s*
`HALT`	Stops program execution
`INC (n)`	Increments *n* in *1*
`INC (n,m)`	Increments *n* in *m*
`INCL (s,e)`	Includes *e* into set *s*

E.1.6.3 The RETURN Statement

During the execution of a procedure, conditions might arise that make further execution unnecessary or even senseless. In such cases the procedure is to be terminated at once and program execution is to resume with the statement after the procedure call.

```
RETURN [expression]
```

A RETURN statement can occur anywhere in a statement sequence in a procedure (or module). It causes the immediate termination of the procedure execution and the passing of program control to the statement after the procedure call in the calling program.

E.1.6.4 Function Procedures

Many procedures return exactly one output parameter as a result. Such procedures are termed *functions* in a mathematical sense. The following points need to be observed when writing and using function procedures:

- The *procedure heading* of a function procedure must contain an expression representing the function value.
- Every function procedure must contain at least one *RETURN* statement. A function procedure cannot simply end after its last statement has been executed, whereby leaving the value of the function undefined.
- The data type of the function value cannot be ARRAY, RECORD, or SET.
- A function procedure is invoked not by a special procedure call, but by the occurrence of its name in an expression.

```
PROCEDURE Square(x: REAL): REAL;
BEGIN
  RETURN X*X
END Square

VAR x, y, z: REAL;
...
x := Square(5.25);
```

E.1.7 Modules

In Modula-2 there are four types of modules:

1. Program modules
2. Definition modules
3. Implementation modules
4. Local modules

An executing program consists of a *main module* and a module of *server modules.* Modules provide a mechanism for implementing features not supported explicitly in the language. Such features include: input and output, string handling, storage management, concurrency, operating system access, etc.

E.1.7.1 Program Module

It is the main program. They are the only modules that can be executed. Its general form is:

```
MODULE <identifier> "[" <priority> "]";
{<clause IMPORT>; }
   {<definition of constants>|
   <definition of types>|
   <declaration of variables>|
   <declaration of procedures>}
BEGIN
   <statements>
END <identifier>.
```

For example:

```
MODULE Presentación;
FROM InOut IMPORT WriteString, WriteLn, ReadString;
VAR
   Name: ARRAY[0..19] OF CHAR;
BEGIN
   WriteSting ('Hello. What`s your name?');
   ReadString (Name);
   WriteLn);
   WriteString ('Nice to meet you ');
   WriteString (Name);
   WriteString ('My name is John')
END Presentación.
```

IMPORT is the import clause. Its general form is:

```
[FROM <identifier>] IMPORT <identifier>{, <identifier>} ";"
```

It allows us to use defined resources in other modules. Resources can be imported one by one (as in the example), or a complete library can be also imported:

```
IMPORT InOut;
```

In this case imported identifiers must be qualified with the library name:

```
InOut.WriteString("hello")
```

E.1.7.2 Definition Module

Along with the implementation module, this is one of the components that make up a Modula-2 library. You can find in them all the resources the library will provide. The following is the general form:

```
DEFINITION MODULE <identifier>;
{ <clause IMPORT>; }
EXPORT QUALIFIED <identifier>{, <identifier>} ";"
   {<definition of constants>|
   <definition of types>|
   <declaration of variables>|
   <heading of procedures>}
END <identifier>
```

For example:

```
DEFINITION MODULE  TADComplex;
EXPORT QUALIFIED
(* ENUMERATION OF EXPORTABLE IDENTIFIERS*)
   Complex,
   Sum,
   Product,
   Division,
   Module;
TYPE
   Complex= RECORD
      Real, Imag: REAL
   END;
PROCEDURE Sum (C1, C2: Complex) : Complex;
PROCEDURE Product (C1, C2: Complex) : Complex;
```

```
PROCEDURE Division (C1, C2: Complex) : Complex;
PROCEDURE Module (C1, C2: Complex) : Complex;
END TADComplex.
```

When Modula-2 compiles its modules separately, this definition must be compiled before the modules' importing resources are defined in it. Nevertheless, implementation can be compiled after its corresponding definition is compiled any moment before linkage.

E.1.7.3 Implementation Module

In this module you can find the resources defined in the corresponding module definition. They both form the library. Its general form is:

```
IMPLEMENTATION MODULE <identifier> ;
{<clause IMPORT>; }
{<definition of constants>|
<definition of types>|
<declaration of variables>|
<declaration of procedures>}
BEGIN
   <statements>
END <identifier>.
```

A block of statements is the reset code of the library and is automatically executed before starting the program module execution importing it.

```
IMPLEMENTATION MODULE TADComplex;

PROCEDURE Sum (C1, C2: Complex) : Complex;
VAR
   S:Complex;

BEGIN
   S.Real := C1.Real+C2.Real;
   S.Imag := C1.Imag+C2.Imag;
   RETURN S
END Sum;

PROCEDURE Product (C1, C2: Complex) : Complex;
VAR
   P:Complex;
BEGIN
   P.Real := C1.Real*C2.Real- C1.Imag*C2.Imag;
   P.Imag := C1.Imag*C2.Real+ C2.Imag*C1.Real;
   RETURN P
END Product;

PROCEDURE Division (C1, C2: Complex) : Complex;
VAR
   D:Complex;
BEGIN
   D.Real := (C1.Real*C2.Real+C1.Imag*C2.Imag)/
   (C2.Real*C2.Real-C2.Imag*C2.Imag);
   D.Imag:=(C1.Imag*C2.Real- C2.Imag*C1.Real)/
   (C2.Real*C2.Real-C2.Imag*C2.Imag);
   RETURN D
END Division;
```

```
PROCEDURE Module (C1, C2: Complex) : Complex;
BEGIN
  RETURN SQRT (C2.Real*C2.Real+C2.Imag*C2.Imag)
END Module;
END TADComplex.
```

E.1.7.4 Local Module

It is a library defined in the program module. It increments program module modeling. Its syntax is similar to the definition module of a library, but procedures have their body with implementation as well as its heading.

```
MODULE Invert;
FROM InOut IMPORT Read, Write, WriteLn, EOL;
  MODULE STACK;
  (* Local module *)
  EXPORT QUALIFIED Push, Pop, Empty;
  VAR
    Stack: ARRAY[1..30] OF CHAR;
    Top:CARDINAL;
  PROCEDURE Push (C: CHAR);
  BEGIN
    INC(Peak);
    Stack[Top]:=C
  END Push;
  PROCEDURE Pop ( ): CHAR;
  BEGIN
    DEC(Top);
    RETURN Stack[Top+1]
  END Pop;

  PROCEDURE Empty ( ): BOOLEAN;
  BEGIN
    RETURN Top = 0
  END Empty;
  BEGIN
  (* Module reset code *)
    Top := 0
  END STACK;
 VAR
    Car:CHAR;
BEGIN
  WriteString('enter chain');
  Read(Car);
  WHILE Car <>EOL DO
    Push(Car);
    Read(Car);
  END;
  WriteLn;
  WriteString('inverted chain:');
  WHILE NOT empty DO
    Write(Pop)
  END;
END Invert;
```

E.1.8 Abstract Data Type (Objects)

Modula-2 provides facilities for data abstraction, including the ability to hide the representations of abstract data types. In Modula-2, the specification and implementation of abstract data type are separated into a `DEFINITION MODULE` and an `IMPLEMENTATION MODULE`.

Definition Module for a Stack Abstract data Type:

Example (Abstract data Type: Stack)

```
DEFINITION MODULE Stack;
   TYPE Stacck;          (* Opaque Type *)
   PROCEDURE Init (VAR S: Stack);
   PROCEDURE Push (VAR S: Stack; IntVal:INTEGER);
   PROCEDURE Pop (S: Stack): INTEGER;
   PROCEDURE IsEmpty (S: Stack): BOOLEAN;
   PROCEDURE IsFule (S: Stack): BOOLEAN;
END Stack;
```

Hidden Declaration of the Opaque Type Stack:

```
IMPLEMENTATION MODULE Stack;
CONST
   StackSize = 100;
TYPE
   StackRange = [1..StackSize];
   TOSRange   = [0..StackSize];
   StackArray = ARRAY StackRange OF INTEGER;
   (****************************************)
       Stack = POINTER TO StackStruct;
       StackStruct = RECORD
                         StackItems  : StackArray;
                         TOS         : TOSRange
                     END;
   (****************************************)
```

Implementation of Stack Operations:

```
PROCEDURE Initialise (VAR S: Stack);
BEGIN
   NEW(S);
   S^.TOS := 0
END Initialise;

PROCEDURE Push (VAR S: Stack; IntVar : INTEGER);
BEGIN
   S^.TOS := S^TOS+1;
   S^.StackItems[S^.TOS] := IntVar
END Push;
```

References

Kaare, C. 1998. *A Guide to Modula-2.* Springer-Veerlag, New York.

Sutcliffe, R. 1997. *Modula-2: Abstractions for Data and Programming Structures* (Using ISO-Standard Modula-2), Fourth Edition. Trinity Western University, Canada.

Wirth, N. 1990. *Programming in Modula-2.* Fourth Edition. Springer-Verlag, New York.

APPENDIX F
MODULA-3 Language Guide

Luis Joyanes Aguilar
Pontifical Salamanca University

María Luisa Díez Platas
Pontifical Salamanca University

Paloma Centenera
Pontifical Salamanca University

Modula-3 was designed by Cardelli, Donahue, Jordan, Kalsow, and Nelson, at the Digital Equipment Corporation Systems Research Center and the Olivetti Research Center. To accomplish it, they used Modula-2, derived, in turn, from Modula-2 by Niklaus Wirth (the creator of Pascal, as well).

Modula-3 supports interfaces, objects, generics, lightweight threads of control, the isolation of unsafe code, garbage collection, exceptions, and subtyping, but Modula-3 is substantially simpler than other languages with comparable power. Modula-3 is a practical implementation language for large software projects and an excellent teaching language.

F.1.1 Language Vocabulary

A program written in Modula-3 is a sequence of characters grouped in lexical components (*tokens*) which include the basic language vocabulary. These lexical components are keywords, identifiers, constants, chain constants, operators, and punctuation marks.

F.1.1.1 Characters

The characters that can be used to construct language elements (lexical components or *tokens*) are the alphabet characters (upper- and lowercase letters), blank digits, and underlined characters.

0-8493-3135-8/99/$0.00+$.50

TABLE F.1 Modula-3 Keywords

AND	DO	FROM	NOT	REPEAT	UNTIL
ANY	ELSE	GENERIC	OBJECT	RETURN	UNTRACED
ARRAY	ELSIF	IF	OF	REVEAL	VALUE
AS	END	IMPORT	OR	ROOT	VAR
BEGIN	EVAL	IN	OVERRIDES	SET	WHILE
BITS	EXCEPT	INTERFACE	PROCEDURE	THEN	WITH
BRANDED	EXCEPTION	LOCK	RAISE	TO	
BY	EXIT	LOOP	RAISES	TRY	
CASE	EXPORTS	METHODS	READONLY	TYPE	
CONST	FINALLY	MOD	RECORD	TYPECASE	
DIV	FOR	MODULE	REF	UNSAFE	

F.1.1.2 Comments

A comment is an arbitrary character sequence opened by (* and closed by *). Comments can be nested and extended over more than one line.

F.1.1.3 Identifiers

See Modula-2 guide.

F.1.1.4 Keywords

Reserved or keywords must not be used as identifiers. Because of their strict meaning in C++, they should not be redefined either. Table F.1 lists Modula-3 keywords.

F.1.1.5 Pre-defined Identifiers

In addition to keywords, in Modula-3 you can find a series of standard identifiers, or predefined identifiers. These also have their own meaning for the language, but unlike keywords they are sensitive to be used as user identifiers and therefore redefined. In the following table you can see Modula-2 predefined identifiers. Modula-2 contains a number of predefined identifiers for constants, elementary data types, and standard procedures. Table F.2 provides an overview of what they mean.

F.1.1.6 Literal Constants

See Modula-2 guide.

F.1.1.7 Operators

Modula-3 offers a broad set of operators that allows handling standard type data. We can distinguish four classes of operators:

1. *Arithmetic operators* combine arithmetic operands with arithmetic results.
2. *Logical operators* combine logical operands with logical results.
3. *Set operators* combine set operands with a set result.
4. *Relational operators* compare two operands and return a logical result.

F.1.1.7.1 Arithmetic Operations

```
+ (x: INTEGER) : INTEGER          Sign
+ (x: Float) : Float

+ (x,y: INTEGER) : INTEGER        Sum
  (x,y: Float) : Float
  (x,y: Set) : Set                Union
```

TABLE F.3 Predefined Identifiers

ABS	BYTESIZE	EXTENDED	INTEGER	MIN	NUMBER	TEXT
ADDRESS	CARDINAL	FALSE	ISTYPE	MUTEX	ORD	TRUE
CEILING	FIRST	LAST	NARROW	REAL	TRUNC	ADRSIZE
CHAR	FLOAT	LONGREAL	NEW	REFANY	TYPECODE	BITSIZE
DEC	FLOOR	LOOPHOLE	NIL	ROUND	VAL	BOOLEAN
DISPOSE	INC	MAX	NULL	SUBARRAY		

Pre-defined Constants	
`FALSE`	boolean value "`false`"
`NIL`	POINTER value that points to no object
`TRUE`	boolean value "`true`"
Pre-defined Data Types	
`ADDRESS`	reference type
`BITSET`	set
`BOOLEAN`	logical values "`true`" or "`false`"
`CARDINAL`	natural numbers (≥0)
`CHAR`	characters
`EXTENDED`	real numbers
`INTEGER`	whole numbers (positive or negative)
`LONGREAL`	real numbers
`NULL`	reference type
`PROC`	parameterless procedures
`REAL`	real numbers
`REFANY`	reference type
`ROOT`	object type
`UNTRACED ROOT`	object type
Standard Procedures	
`DEC (x)`	reduces (decrements) the value of x by 1
`DEC (x, n)`	reduces (decrements) the value of x by n
`DISPOSE (p)`	frees the storage to which p points
`EXCL (s, e)`	removes (excludes) the element e from the set s
`HALT`	terminates program execution
`INC (x)`	increases (increments) the value x by 1
`INC (x, n)`	increases (increments) the value of x by n
`INCL (s, e)`	includes the element e in the set s
`NEW (p)`	allocates dynamic storage

`- (x: INTEGER)`	`: INTEGER`	Change of sign
`  (x: Float)`	`: Float`	
`- (x,y: INTEGER)`	`: INTEGER`	Diference
`  (x,y: Float)`	`: Float`	
`  (x,y: Set)`	`: Set`	
`* (x,y: INTEGER)`	`: INTEGER`	Product
`  (x,y: Float)`	`: Float`	
`  (x,y: Set)`	`: Set`	Intersection
`/ (x,y: Float)`	`: Float`	Quotient
`  (x,y: Set)`	`: Set`	Symetric diference
`DIV(x,y: INTEGER)`	`: INTEGER`	Integer division
`MOD(x,y: INTEGER)`	`: INTEGER`	Rest
`MOD(x, y: Float)`	`: Float`	
`ABS(x: INTEGER)`	`: INTEGER`	Absolute value
`  (x: Float)`	`: Float`	

`FLOAT(x: INTEGER; T: Type := REAL): T`		Change from type to real
`(x: Float; T: Type := REAL): T`		
`FLOOR(x: Float)`	`: INTEGER`	The greatest integer not exceeding x
`CEILING(x: Float)`	`: INTEGER`	The least integer not less than x.
`ROUND(r: Float)`	`: INTEGER`	The nearest integer to r
`TRUNC(r: Float)`	`: INTEGER`	Rounds r toward zero
`MAX, MIN(x,y: Ordinal)`	`: Ordinal`	The greater and the lesser of the two values x and y
`(x,y: Float)`	`: Float`	

F.1.1.7.2 Relations

```
=, # (x, y: Any): BOOLEAN
<=, >= (x,y: Ordinal)   : BOOLEAN
           (x,y: Float)     : BOOLEAN
           (x,y: ADDRESS)   : BOOLEAN
           (x,y: Set)       : BOOLEAN
>, <   (x,y: Ordinal) : BOOLEAN
           (x,y: Float)     : BOOLEAN
           (x,y: ADDRESS)   : BOOLEAN
           (x,y: Set)       : BOOLEAN
IN (e: Ordinal; s: Set)  : BOOLEAN
```

F.1.1.7.3 Boolean Operations

```
NOT (p: BOOLEAN)    : BOOLEAN
AND (p,q: BOOLEAN)  : BOOLEAN
OR (p,q: BOOLEAN)   : BOOLEAN
```

F.1.1.7.4 Type Operations

`ISTYPE (x: Reference; T: RefType) : BOOLEAN`		TRUE if, and only if x is a member of T
`NARROW (x: Reference; T: RefType): T)`		Returns x after checking that x is a member of T
`TYPECODE (T: RefType)`	`: CARDINAL`	
`(r: REFANY)`	`: CARDINAL`	
`(r: UNTRACED ROOT)`	`: CARDINAL`	
`ORD (element: Ordinal): INTEGER`		Position in the enumeration order
`VAL (i: INTEGER; T: OrdinalType): T`		The inverse of ORD
`NUMBER (T: OrdinalType)`	`: CARDINAL`	Number of elements in T
`(A: FixedArrayType)`	`: CARDINAL`	
`(a: Array)`	`: CARDINAL`	
`FIRST (T: OrdinalType)`	`: BaseType(T)`	The smallest value of T
`(T: FloatType)`	`: T`	
`(A: FixedArrayType)`	`: BaseType(IndexType(A))`	
`(a: Array)`	`: BaseType(IndexType(a))`	
`LAST (T: OrdinalType)`	`: BaseType(T)`	The largest value
`(T: FloatType)`	`: T`	
`(A: FixedArrayType)`	`: BaseType(IndexType(A))`	
`(a: Array)`	`: BaseType(IndexType(a))`	

`BITSIZE`	`(x: Any)`	`: CARDINAL`	The size of the variable x or of variables of type T
	`(T: Type)`	`: CARDINAL`	
`BYTESIZE`	`(x: Any)`	`: CARDINAL`	
	`(T: Type)`	`: CARDINAL`	
`ADRSIZE`	`(x: Any)`	`: CARDINAL`	The number of addressable locations
	`(T: Type)`	`: CARDINAL`	

F.1.1.7.5 Text Operations

`& (a,b: TEXT) : TEXT`	The concatenation of a and b, as defined by Text.Cat.

F.1.1.8 Pragmas

A pragma is an arbitrary character sequence opened by <* and closed by *>. Pragmas can be nested and can be extended over more than one line. Pragmas are hints to the implementation; they do not affect the language semantics.

F.1.2 Data Types

F.1.2.1 Ordinal Types

F.1.2.1.1 Predeclared Ordinal Types

`INTEGER`	All integers represented by the implementation
`CARDINAL`	Behaves just like the subrange [0..LAST(INTEGER)]
`BOOLEAN`	The enumeration {FALSE, TRUE}
`CHAR`	An enumeration containing at least 256 elements

The first 256 elements of type `CHAR` represent characters in the ISO-Latin-1 code, which is an extension of ASCII. The language does not specify the names of the elements of the `CHAR` enumeration.

F.1.2.1.2 Enumerate Type

The enumerate type is an ordered set of values. The syntax to an enumeration type is:

```
"{" [ <identifier>] { "," <identifier>} "}"
```

The empty enumeration { } is allowed.

F.1.2.1.3 Subrange Types

A subrange type is declared like this:

```
" [" <constant>..<constant> "]"
```

where the constants are two ordinal values with the same base type, called the base type of the subrange. The values of the subrange type are all the values from first constant to last constant inclusive.

F.1.2.2 Floating-Point Types

They are a representation of an integer number limited in the range and precision. There are three floating point types, which in order of increasing range and precision are `REAL`, `LONGREAL`, and `EXTENDED`.

F.1.2.3 Arrays

An array is an indexed collection of component variables, called the elements of the array. Arrays are assignable if they have the same element type and shape. If either the source or target of the assignment is an open array, a runtime shape check is required. An array type declaration has the following form:

```
ARRAY <type> OF <type>
```

The first one is an ordinal type, the index type of the array, and the last is any type other than an open array type, or element type of the array. The values of type arrays are arrays whose element type is Element type and whose length is the number of elements of the Index type. For example:

```
TYPE
  Transform  = ARRAY [1..3], [1..3] OF REAL;
  Vector     = ARRAY OF REAL;
  SkipTable  = ARRAY CHAR OF INTEGER
```

If a has an array type, then a[i] designates the element of a, whose position corresponds to the position of i in Index. For example, consider the declarations:

```
VAR a := ARRAY [1..4] OF CHAR {' ', 'a', 'b', 'c'};
VAR b := ARRAY [0..3] OF REAL := a;
```

Now a = b is TRUE; yet `a[1] = 1.0` while `b[1] = 3.0`. The interpretation of indexes is determined by an array type, not its value; the assignment b := a changes b's value, not its type.

F.1.2.3.1 Multidimesional Arrays

A multidimensional array is declared as an array of arrays. For example:

```
ARRAY Index_1 OF ARRAY Index_2 OF Element
```

It can be abbreviated the following way:

```
ARRAY Index_1, Index_2 OF Element
```

An expression of the form `a[i_1, i_2]` is shorthand for `a[i_1] [i_2]`.

F.1.2.3.2 Open Arrays

These are arrays in which their element type is defined, not their size. The values of open arrays are arrays whose element type is element type and whose length is arbitrary. The index type of an open array is the integer subrange `[0..n-1]`, where n is the length of the array. An open array type declaration has the following form:

```
ARRAY OF <type>
```

Elements can be of any type. An open array type can be used only as the type of a formal parameter, the referent of a reference type, the element type of another open array type, or as the type in an array constructor. For example:

```
TYPE   T = ARRAY OF INTEGER;
```

F.1.2.4 Records

See appendix on Modula-2.

F.1.2.5 Packed Types

The values of type and the packed type are the same as the values of type base, but variables of packed type that occur in records, objects, or arrays will occupy exactly the number of bits specified and packed adjacent to the preceding field or element. A declaration of a packed type has the form:

```
BITS <constant> FOR <type>
```

For example, a variable of type

```
ARRAY [0..255] OF BITS 1 FOR BOOLEAN
```

is an array of 256 booleans, each of which occupies one bit of storage.

F.1.2.6 Sets

A set is a collection of values taken from some ordinal type. A set type declaration has the following form:

```
SET OF <type>
```

The values of set type are all sets whose elements have type base. For example:

```
VAR
   S: SET OF BOOLEAN
```

S can assume the values:

```
{} {FALSE} {TRUE} {FALSE,TRUE}
```

F.1.2.7 References

A reference value is either NIL or the address of a variable, called the referent. A reference type is either traced or untraced. When all traced references to a piece of allocated storage are gone, the implementation reclaims the storage. Two reference types are of the same reference class if they are both traced or both untraced. A general type is traced if it is a traced reference type, a record type, any of whose field types is traced, an array type whose element type is traced, or a packed type whose underlying unpacked type is traced. A declaration for a traced reference type has the following form:

```
REF <Type>
```

A declaration for an untraced reference type has the form:

```
UNTRACED REF <Type>
```

where Type is any untraced type. (This restriction is lifted in unsafe modules.)

The following reference types are predeclared:

REFANY	Contains all traced references
ADDRESS	Contains all untraced references
NULL	Contains only NIL

The TYPECASE statement can be used to test the referent type of a REFANY or object, but there is no such test for an ADDRESS. Examples of reference types are below:

```
TYPE
   IntPtrType = REF INTEGER; (* A pointer to an integer *)
   ArrPtrType = REF ARRAY [1..5] OF CHAR; (* A pointer to an array *)
```

F.1.2.8 Procedure Type

A procedure type declaration has the form:

```
PROCEDURE <sig>
```

where <sig> is a signature specification, which has the following form:

```
(<formal parameters list>) [": " <type>] [ RAISES <raises set>]
```

Result type can be any type but an open array type. The raises set is an explicit set of exceptions with the syntax {E_1, ..., E_n}, or the symbol ANY representing the set of all exceptions. If "RAISES <*raises set*>" is omitted, "RAISES { }" is assumed.

A formal parameter declaration has the form:

```
<Mode> <identifier> ":" < Type> ":=" <constant>
```

Mode is a parameter mode, which can be VALUE, VAR, or READONLY. If Mode is omitted, it defaults to VALUE. The identifier is the parameter name. Type is the type of the parameter. Constant expression is the default value for the parameter. If Mode is VAR, " := <constant>" must be omitted, otherwise either " := <constant>" or ": <Type>" can be omitted, but not both. If Type is omitted, it is taken to be the type of default value. If both are present, the value of default value must be a member of Type.

A procedure value P is a member of the procedure type T if it is NIL or its signature is covered by the signature of T, where signature_1 covers signature_2 if they have the same number of parameters, and corresponding parameters have the same type and mode. "p() prints "P" and q() prints "Q"." The interpretation of defaulted parameters is determined by a procedure's type, not its value; the assignment q := P changes q's value, not its type. Examples of procedure types:

```
TYPE
   Integrand = PROCEDURE (x: REAL): REAL;
   Integrator = PROCEDURE(f: Integrand; lo, hi: REAL): REAL;

TokenIterator = PROCEDURE(VAR t: Token) RAISES {TokenError};

RenderProc = PROCEDURE(
   scene: REFANY;
   READONLY t: Transform := Identity)
```

F.1.2.9 Objects

An object is either NIL or a reference to a data record paired with a method suite, which is a record of procedures that will accept the object as a first argument. There are two predeclared object types:

ROOT	The traced object type with no fields or methods
UNTRACED ROOT	The untraced object type with no fields or methods

The declaration of an object type has the form:

```
[<supertype>]        OBJECT
                     < Fields>
                     METHODS
                          <Methods>
                     OVERRIDES
                          <Overrides>
                            END
```

Fields is a list of field declarations, exactly as in a record type, Methods is a list of method declarations, and Overrides is a list of method overrides.

The keyword OBJECT can optionally be preceded by "BRANDED" or by "BRANDED b", where b is a text constant. The meaning is the same as in non-object reference types.

A method override has the form:

```
m := proc
```

where m is the name of a method of the supertype and proc is a top-level procedure constant. It specifies that the m method for object type is proc, rather than super type.m. If proc is non-nil, its first parameter must have mode VALUE and type some supertype, and dropping its first parameter must result in a signature that is covered by the signature of super type's m method. For example:

```
TYPE
      A = OBJECT a: INTEGER; METHODS p() END;
      AB = A OBJECT b: INTEGER END;

   PROCEDURE Pa(self: A) = ...;
   PROCEDURE Pab(self: AB) = ...;
```

The procedures Pa and Pab are candidate values for the p methods of objects of types A and AB. For example:

```
TYPE T1 = AB OBJECT OVERRIDES p := Pab END
```

declares a type with an AB data record and a p method that expects an AB. T1 is a valid subtype of AB. Similarly,

```
TYPE T2 = A OBJECT OVERRIDES p := Pa END
```

declares a type with an A data record and a method that expects an A. T2 is a valid subtype of A. A more interesting example is:

```
TYPE T3 = AB OBJECT OVERRIDES p := Pa END
```

which declares a type with an AB data record and a p method that expects an A. Since every AB is an A, the method is not too choosy for the objects in which it will be placed. T3 is a valid subtype of AB. In contrast,

```
TYPE T4 = A OBJECT OVERRIDES p := Pab END
```

attempts to declare a type with an A data record and a method that expects an AB; since not every A is an AB, the method is too choosy for the objects in which it would be placed. The declaration of T4 is a static error. The following example illustrates the difference between declaring a new method and overriding an existing method. After the declarations

```
TYPE
   A = OBJECT METHODS m() := P END;
   B = A OBJECT OVERRIDES m := Q END;
   C = A OBJECT METHODS m() := Q END;

VAR
   a := NEW(A); b := NEW(B); c := NEW(C);
```

therefore we have

```
a.m()    activates    P(a)
b.m()    activates    Q(b)
c.m()    activates    Q(c)
```

Thus far there is no difference between overriding and extending, but c's method suite has two methods, while b's has only one, as can be revealed if b and c are viewed as members of type A:

```
NARROW(b, A).m()    activates    Q(b)
NARROW(c, A).m()    activates    P(c)
```

Here NARROW is used to view a variable of a subtype as a value of its supertype. It is more often used for the opposite purpose, when it requires a runtime check.

F.1.3 Statement

F.1.3.1 Assignation Statement

See Modula-2 syntax.

F.1.3.2 Conditional Statements

The following is the general format of an IF statement:

```
IF <expression> THEN <statements>
{ ELSEIF <expression> THEN <statements>} [ELSE <statements>]
END
```

```
IF Searching THEN NumberOfCopies := NumberOfCopies*2
ELSEIF Wage< 3000000 THEN Wage := Wage*NumberOfCopies
ELSE Wage := Wage+NumberOfCopies
END;
```

The multiple alternative statement has the following format:

```
CASE <expression> OF
  <constant>{"," <constant>}" =>" <Statements> {"|"
  <constant>{"," <constant>}" =>" <Statements>}
[ELSE <Statements>]
END
```

```
CASE Character OF
  'a', 'A' => WriteString('Student')|
  'p', 'P' => WriteString('Professor')
ELSE WriteString('Error')
END;
```

F.1.3.3 Loop Control Statements (Iterative)

F.1.3.3.1 FOR, WHILE, REPEAT, WITH

See Modula-2 appendix.

F.1.3.3.2 GOTO Statement

The GOTO statement is used to unconditionally alter the flow of the execution:

```
GOTO <Identifier>
```

The target statement is indicated by the label identifier and must be located somewhere within the same body:

```
< Identifier> ':' <Statement>
```

Labels must be declared before they are used:

```
LABEL <IdentifierList> ";"
```

F.1.3.4 Raise

Raise statement raises an exception. The program execution status after the execution of this statement is of an error. A RAISE statement has the following form:

```
RAISE <Identifier>[<arguments>]
```

For example:

```
RAISE Overflow;
```

F.1.3.5 Try Except

A TRY-EXCEPT statement has the form:

```
TRY
     <statements block>
EXCEPT
                          <identifier> [<arguments>] " =>" <statements>
 { "|" <identifier> [<arguments>] " =>" <statements> }
[ELSE <statements>]
END
```

If the statement block execution is normal, the except clause is ignored. If block raises any listed exception, then its corresponding statement is executed. If block raises any other exception and "ELSE statements" is present, then it is executed. In either case, the outcome of the TRY statement is the outcome of the selected handler. If block raises an unlisted exception and "ELSE" is absent, then the outcome of TRY statement is the exception raised by block. For example:

```
EXCEPTION Failure(Severity);
TYPE Severity = {Low, Medium, High};
...
TRY
  ...
EXCEPT
| IO.Error =>
      IO.Put("An I/O error occurred.")
| Lex.Error =>
      IO.Put("Unable to convert datatype.")
| Severity(x) =>
      IF x = Severity.Low THEN IO.Put("Not bad") ELSE IO.Put("Bail out") END
END;
```

F.1.3.6 Try Finally

A statement of the form:

```
TRY <statements > FINALLY <statements > END
```

If outcome of the first statement is normal, the TRY statement executes the two statements. If the outcome of the first statement is an exception and the outcome of the second one is normal, the exception from first statement is re-raised after the second statement is executed. If both outcomes are exceptions, the outcome of the TRY is the exception from the second.

F.1.3.7 Typecase

It is allowed to execute alternative statements in terms of the type of an expression. A TYPECASE statement has the following form:

```
TYPECASE <Expression > OF
<identifier type> ["(" <identifier > ")"] "," < identifier type> ["("
<identifier > ")"] }" =>" <Statements>
{"|"< identifier type> ["("<identifier> ")"] {","< identifier type> ["("
<identifier > ")"] }" =>" <Statements>}
[ELSE <Statements>]
END
```

The statement evaluates the expression. If the resulting reference value is a member of any listed type, then the corresponding statements are executed, for the minimum such as i. (Thus a NULL case is useful only if it comes first.) If the value is a member of not listed types and "ELSE statements" is present, then it is executed. If the value is a member of not listed type and "ELSE " is absent, a checked runtime error occurs.

Each (<identifier>) declares a variable whose type is an identifier type and whose scope is the corresponding statements block. If (<identifier>) is present, it is initialized to the value of Expression before statements block is executed. For example:

```
PROCEDURE ToText(r: REFANY): TEXT =
   (* Assume r = NIL or r^ is a BOOLEAN or INTEGER. *)
   BEGIN
```

```
    TYPECASE r OF
      NULL => RETURN "NIL"
    | REF BOOLEAN (rb) => RETURN Fmt.Bool(rb^)
    | REF INTEGER (ri) => RETURN Fmt.Int(ri^)
    END
  END ToText;
```

F.1.3.8 Lock

A LOCK statement has the form:

```
LOCK <expression> DO <statements> END
```

It is equivalent to:

```
VAR m := <expression>; BEGIN
  Thread.Acquire(m);
  TRY <statements> FINALLY Thread.Release(m) END
END
```

F.1.4 Declarations

A declaration introduces a name for a constant, type, variable, exception, or procedure. The scope of the name is the block containing the declaration. A block has the form:

```
Decls BEGIN S END
```

where Decls is a sequence of declarations and S is a statement, or the executable part of the block. A block can appear as a statement or as the body of a module or procedure. The declarations of a block can introduce a name at least once, though a name can be redeclared in nested blocks, and a procedure declared in an interface can be redeclared in a module exporting the interface. The order of declarations in a block does not matter, except to determine the order of initialization of variables.

F.1.4.1 Types

See Modula-2 appendix.

F.1.4.2 Constants

If id is an identifier, T a type, and C a constant expression, then:

```
CONST id: T = C
```

declares id as a constant with the type T and the value of C. The ": T" can be omitted, in which case the type of id is the type of C. If T is present it must contain C.

F.1.4.3 Variables

See Modula-2 appendix.

F.1.4.4 Procedures

There are two forms of procedure declarations:

```
PROCEDURE <identifier> <signature>=<block><identifier>
PROCEDURE <identifier> <signature>
```

For example:

```
PROCEDURE Max(a, b: INTEGER): INTEGER =
(* Sample function definition. *)
```

```
VAR max: INTEGER;
BEGIN
  max := a;
  IF a < b THEN max := b END;
  RETURN max;
END Max;
```

F.1.4.5 Exceptions

If id is an identifier and T a type, other than an open array type, then:

```
EXCEPTION id(T)
```

declares id as an exception with argument type T. If "(T)" is omitted, the exception takes no argument. An exception declaration is allowed only in an interface or in the outermost scope of a module. All declared exceptions are distinct. For example:

```
EXCEPTION
  UserAbort(TEXT);
  Overflow;
```

F.1.4.6 Opaque Types

An opaque type is a name that denotes an unknown subtype of some given reference type. For example, an opaque subtype of REFANY is an unknown traced reference type; an opaque subtype of UNTRACED ROOT is an unknown untraced object type. The actual type denoted by an opaque type name is called its concrete type.

Different scopes can reveal different information about an opaque type. For example, what is known in one scope only to be a subtype of REFANY could be known in another scope to be a subtype of ROOT.

An opaque type declaration has the form:

```
TYPE <type identifier> " <: " <reference type>
```

F.1.4.7 Revelations

A revelation introduces information about an opaque type into a scope. Unlike other declarations, revelations introduce no new names. There are two kinds of revelations, partial and complete. A program can contain any number of partial revelations for an opaque type; it must contain exactly one complete revelation. A partial revelation has the form:

```
REVEAL <identifier> " <:" <type expression>
```

where identifier is an opaque type. It reveals that expression is a supertype of identifier. A complete revelation has the form:

```
REVEAL T = V
```

where V is a type expression (not just a name) whose outermost type constructor is a branded reference or object type, and T is an identifier (possibly qualified) that has been declared as an opaque type. The revelation specifies that V is the concrete type for T. It is a static error if any type revealed in any scope as a supertype of T is not a supertype of V. Generally this error is detected at link time.

Distinct opaque types have distinct concrete types, since V includes a brand and all brands in a program are distinct. A revelation is allowed only in an interface or in the outermost scope of a module. A revelation in an interface can be imported into any scope where it is required, as illustrated by the stack example. For example, let's consider:

```
INTERFACE I; TYPE T <: ROOT; PROCEDURE P(x:T): T; END I.
INTERFACE IClass; IMPORT I; REVEAL I.T <: MUTEX; END IClass.
```

```
INTERFACE IRep; IMPORT I;
  REVEAL I.T = MUTEX BRANDED OBJECT count: INTEGER END;
END IRep.
```

An importer of I sees I.T as an opaque subtype of ROOT, and is limited to allocating objects of type I.T, passing them to I.P, or declaring subtypes of I.T. An importer of IClass sees that every I.T is a MUTEX, and can therefore lock objects of type I.T. Finally, an importer of IRep sees the concrete type, and can access the count field.

F.1.5 Modules

A module has the form:

```
MODULE <identifier> EXPORTS <Interfaces> ";"
< Imports>;
<block> <identifier>"."
```

where Interfaces is a list of distinct names of interfaces exported by the module, Imports is a list of import statements, and block is the body of the module. The name identifier must be repeated after the END that terminates the body. “EXPORTS Interfaces” can be omitted, in which case Interfaces defaults to module.

Module example:

```
MODULE MyModule;

IMPORT IO;

PROCEDURE PrintThing(READONLY r: Thing) =
  BEGIN
    IO.Put(r.name&"\t");
    IO.PutInt(r.size);
    IO.Put("\n");
  END PrintThing;

PROCEDURE MakeThing(n: TEXT; s: INTEGER): Thing =
  BEGIN
    RETURN Thing{n, s};
  END MakeThing;

END MyModule.
```

Interface example:

```
INTERFACE MyModule;

CONST MaxEntries = 53;
TYPE Thing = RECORD name: TEXT; size: INTEGER END;

PROCEDURE PrintThing(READONLY r: Thing);
PROCEDURE MakeThing(n: TEXT; s: INTEGER): Thing;

END MyModule.
```

Import example:

```
INTERFACE Box;

CONST Size = 30;

END Box;
```

```
(* Client Module *)
MODULE Toys;

IMPORT Box;

VAR boxSize := Box.Size; (* Nonlocal declaration Size qualified
                             by module name Box *)
END Toys.

(* Another Client Module *)
MODULE Toys2;

FROM Box IMPORT Size;

VAR boxSize := Size; (* Nonlocal reference Size not qualified *)

END Toys2;
```

F.1.5.1 Generics

In a generic interface or module, some of the imported interface names are treated as formal parameters to be bound to actual interfaces when the generic is instantiated. A generic interface has the form:

```
GENERIC INTERFACE G(F_1, ..., F_n);
  Body
END F.
```

where G is an identifier that names the generic interface, F_1, ..., F_n is a list of identifiers, called the formal imports of G, and Body is a sequence of imports followed by a sequence of declarations, exactly as in a non-generic interface. An instance of G has the form:

```
INTERFACE I = G(A_1, ..., A_n) END I.
```

where I is the name of the instance and A_1, ..., A_n is a list of actual interfaces to which the formal imports of G are bound. The instance I is equivalent to an ordinary interface defined as follows:

```
INTERFACE I;
  IMPORT A_1 AS F_1, ..., A_n AS F_n;
  Body
END I.
```

A generic module has the form:

```
GENERIC MODULE G(F_1, ..., F_n);
  Body
END F.
```

where G is an identifier that names the generic module, F_1, ..., F_n is a list of identifiers, called the formal imports of G, and Body is a sequence of imports followed by a block, exactly as in a non-generic module. An instance of G has the form

```
MODULE I EXPORTS E = G(A_1, ..., A_n) END I.
```

where I is the name of the instance, E is a list of interfaces exported by I, and A_1, ..., A_n is a list of actual interfaces to which the formal imports of G are bound. "EXPORTS E" can be omitted, in which case it defaults to "EXPORTS I". The instance I is equivalent to an ordinary module defined as follows:

```
MODULE I EXPORTS E;
  IMPORT A_1 AS F_1, ..., A_n AS F_n;
  Body
END I.
```

Notice that the generic module itself has no exports; they are supplied only when it is instantiated. For example, here is a generic stack package:

```
GENERIC INTERFACE Stack(Elem);
   (* where Elem.T is not an open array type. *)
   TYPE T <: REFANY;
   PROCEDURE Create(): T;
   PROCEDURE Push(VAR s: T; x: Elem.T);
   PROCEDURE Pop(VAR s: T): Elem.T;
END Stack.

GENERIC MODULE Stack(Elem);

   REVEAL
      T = BRANDED OBJECT n: INTEGER; a: REF ARRAY OF Elem.T END;

   PROCEDURE Create(): T =
      BEGIN RETURN NEW(T, n := 0, a := NIL) END Create;

   PROCEDURE Push(VAR s: T; x: Elem.T) =
      BEGIN
         IF s.a = NIL THEN
            s.a := NEW(REF ARRAY OF Elem.T, 5)
         ELSIF s.n > LAST(s.a^) THEN
            WITH temp = NEW(REF ARRAY OF Elem.T, 2 * NUMBER(s.a^)) DO
               FOR i := 0 TO LAST(s.a^) DO temp[i] := s.a[i] END;
               s.a := temp
            END
         END;
         s.a[s.n] := x;
         INC(s.n)
      END Push;

   PROCEDURE Pop(VAR s: T): Elem.T =
      BEGIN DEC(s.n); RETURN s.a[s.n] END Pop;
BEGIN
END Stack.
```

To instantiate these generics to produce stacks of integers:

```
INTERFACE Integer; TYPE T = INTEGER; END Integer.
   INTERFACE IntStack = Stack(Integer) END IntStack.
   MODULE IntStack = Stack(Integer) END IntStack.
```

Implementations are not expected to share code between different instances of a generic module, since this will not be possible in general. Implementations are not required to typecheck uninstantiated generics, but they must typecheck their instances. For example, if one made the following mistake:

```
INTERFACE String; TYPE T = ARRAY OF CHAR; END StrinF.
   INTERFACE StringStack = Stack(String) END StringStack.
   MODULE StringStack = Stack(String) END StringStack.
```

everything would go well until the last line, when the compiler would attempt to compile a version of Stack in which the element type was an open array. It would then complain that the NEW call in Push does not have parameters enough.

References

Boeszoermenyi, L. and Weich, C. 1995. *Programming with Modula-3: An Introduction to Programming with Style.* Springer-Verlag, New-York.

Harbison, S. 1992. *Modula-3.* Prentice-Hall, Englewood Cliffs, NJ.

Harbison, S. 1990. Modula-3, *Byte,* November, pp. 385-392.

Nelson, G. 1991. *System Programming with Modula-3.* Prentice-Hall, Englewood Cliffs, NJ.

Sedgewicks, R. 1994. *Algorithms in Modula-3.* Addison-Wesley, Reading, MA.

Webliography

Modula-3. Home Page
http://www.research.digital.com/SRC/Modula-3/html/home.html

Modula-3; Bibliography
http://wotan.wiwi.uni-rostock.de/~chaos/H...bokks/Modula3/html/modula-/html/bib.html

Comparison between Modula-3 and other languages
http://www.vlsi.polymtl.ca/m3/faq/questions/compare.html

Modula-3 Reference and Tutorial
http://www.cs.columbia.edu/graphics/modula3/tutorial/www/m3_toc.html

Modula-3 Language definition
http://www.research.digital.com/SRC/m3defn/html/m3.html

APPENDIX G

Objective-C Language Guide

Luis Joyanes Aguilar
Pontifical Salamanca University

María Luisa Díez Platas
Pontifical Salamanca University

Paloma Centenera
Pontifical Salamanca University

In this reference guide we are trying to make an enumeration of the most representative elements of Objective-C language, as well as the syntax rules. Objective-C is a hybrid programming language created by The Stepstone Corporation. This language combines Smalltalk programming style and C characteristics. In fact, a set of extensions to a conventional language of C has been added. Such extensions consist essentially of one new data type, the object, and one new operation, the message.

The syntax and elements used in Objective-C are the same as C's, having added some that are new. These new characteristics are precisely those we will discuss in this appendix, but it is advisable to refer to a reference manual on C language or Appendix A of *The C Programming Language* by Kernighan and Ritchie (1988).

The main modifications can be found in external declarations, type specifiers, type qualifiers, and primary expressions.

In order to specify the syntax in every element of the language, the following notation will be used: elements in italics represent syntactic categories, bold elements represent keywords; an element between braces ({}) means that the element can appear zero or more; an element between square brackets means it is optional, that is, it can be left out; an element specified as list_of_items, means one or more items separated by commas; and finally, a sequence_of_items means one or more items.

0-8493-3135-8/99/$0.00+$.50

G.1.1 Language Vocabulary (Lexical Elements)

A program in Objective-C consists of a sequence of characters grouped as *tokens* (lexical components), that make up the basic language vocabulary. Objective-C lexical elements are like C lexical elements, but for specific purposes special identifiers are used:

- For the variable name or method, you can use words constructed in accordance with these rules: beginning with a lowercase character, and the other characters are not uppercase sensitive. For example:

  ```
  moveTo: aCenter
  ```

- To Class, Category, and Protocol names, the first character must be uppercase, whereas the rest of the characters are not uppercase sensitive, and the first character of some of the name words can be uppercase. For example:

  ```
  Window
  CheckButton
  ```

There are new keywords added to the language for the definition and use of object-orientation characteristics.

Some new keywords are

```
bycopy
byref
id
in
inout
oneway
out
self
super
```

G.1.2 Data Types

In addition to the types already defined in C, the principal types used in Objective-C are

BOOL is a boolean type and its values are YES or NO
Class, is a class
id is a pointer to an object; objects are always typed by a pointer
IMP is a pointer to a method that returns an id
SEL is a selector; a runtime's internal identifier for a method name
nil is a null object pointer (of type id)
Nil is a null class pointer (of type Class)

All these types are defined in the objc.h header file.

G.1.3 Type Qualifiers

In addition to type qualifiers existing in C, such as **const** and **volatile**, we can include others in the protocol declaration (also known as protocol qualifier) that support remote messaging. These are the following:

- **bycopy** points out that an object copy should be passed or returned
- **byref** is, in this case, the pass or return is performed by reference, that is, a reference to an object is passed or returned, a copy is not

- **in** is when the information is passed to the receiver by means 1 argument
- **inout** is when information is passed and obtained by means of the argument
- **oneway** is the method used for asynchronous messages without a valid return
- **out** is the argument that gets information returned by reference.

G.1.4 Preprocessor Directives

In Objective, there are new directives that the prepocessor understands, such as **#import**. It is like #include directive, except that it does not include the same file more than once.

G.1.5 Compiler Directives

There are compiler directives that are used to declare and define classes, categories, and protocols, all beginning with @.

@interface begins a declaration of a class or category interface, **@implementation** begins the definition of a class or category, **@protocol** begins the declaration of a protocol, and **@end** ends a declaration or definition.

There are other directives to specify the visibility of instance variables.

- **@private** — The instance variables declared after this directive can only be accessed by the class in which they are declared.
- **@protected** — These instance variables can only be accessed by the class declaring them or by the classes which they derive from. This is the defualt option.
- **@public** — Anyone can access the instance variables.

Some other directives will be discussed in the part for expressions, though there are also the following:

- **@class** — Informs the compiler that the identifiers following it are class names, but it does not perform the import of their interface files; for example:

  ```
  @class Circle;
  ```

- **@defs**(*classname*) — Yields the internal data structure of *classname* instances.

G.1.6 Declarations

Next is presented the syntax for new declaration types apart from those existing in C, such as class declaration, categories, and protocols.

G.1.6.1 Classes

A class is a prototype for a particular kind of object. In Objective-C, classes are defined in two parts: an **interface** that declares the instance variables and methods for all members of the class and **implementation**, which contains the code that implements its methods.

1. To declare a class interface **@interface** directive is used. The syntax is the following:

   ```
   @interface classname [: superclassname] [<list_of_protocol_names>]
   [sequence_of _instance_variables]
   [sequence_of _interface_ declaration]
   @end
   ```

   - The instance variables sequence has the following syntax:

     ```
     {[visibility_specification] struct_declaration_list
     [sequence_of_instance_variables]}
     ```

In this case, braces ({}) are part of instance variable declaration, and therefore they are not used as notation for syntax definition, thereby being bold. To the visibility specification one of these three directives are used:

```
@private
@protected
@public
```

- Sequence of interface declaration represents a series of typical declaration and method declarations, which can be class method declarations or instance method declarations. Its syntax will be discussed later. For example:

```
@interface Person: NSObject
{
  @private
  char * dni;
  @protected
    char* name;
  @public
    id job
  }
  -changejob:toJob;
  @end
```

2. The definiton of a class (its implementation) is structured like its declaration. It begins with an **@implementation** directive and ends with **@end**. Its syntax is:

```
@implementation classname [:superclassname]
[sequence_of_instance_variables]
[sequence_ of_ implementation_definition]
@end
```

- Sequence of implementation definition consists of a series of declarations and function or method definitions. The syntax for the later will be also discussed later, since function declarations and definitions have the same syntax as in C.

```
#import "Person.h"
@implementation Person

  -changejob:toJob
{
  id old = job;
  job = toJob;
  return old;
}
```

Besides, you can have a list of class declarations to indicate that the following names are class names.

```
@class list_of_class_name;
```

For example:

```
@class person;
```

G.1.6.2 Categories

In Objective-C, a category is a set of method definitions that is segregated from the rest of the class definition. Categories can be used to split the class definition into parts, or to add methods to an existing class. Like a class, two parts for its definition are used: **interface** and **implementation.** The syntax is the following:

```
@interface classname (categoryname) [<list_of_protocol_names>]
[sequence_of _interface_ declaration]
@end

@implementation classname (categoryname) [<list_of_protocol_names>]
[sequence_of _implementation_definition]
@end
```

G.1.6.3 Protocols

A protocol is a set of a group of methods not associated with any particular class. There are two types: **informal protocol** declared as a category, usually a category of the NSObject classs, and **formal protocol,** by which a class can adopt formal protocols, objects can respond at runtime when asked if they conform to a formal protocol, and instances can be typed by the formal protocols. The syntax for this last protocol type is:

```
@protocol protocolname[<list_of_protocol_names>]
[sequence_of _interface_ declaration]
@end
```

G.1.7 Objects

G.1.7.1 Creation and Destruction of Objects (or Instances)

An object or an instance of a class is created by sending the Class an **alloc** message. This method allocates memory for a new object and returns an id for the object (a pointer to the object)

```
[classname alloc]
```

For example:

```
id aCat;

aCat = [Cat alloc]
```

alloc message always returns a value of type id

To free an object's memory when you have finshed using the object, **free** method is used

```
[objectname free]

[aCat free]
```

G.1.8 Expressions

Those newly added expressions to Objective-C are directed to its own characteristics as an object-oriented language.

- **Self** — An object that refers to the object itself
- **Message expressions** — A command for an object to do something; the sender waits for the receiver to return a reply; message expressions are enclosed in square brackets

```
[receiver message_selector]
```

The message receiver can be an expression (a variable, a function call, or a message expression), class name, an object or **super,** refers to its super class, and is an object to indicate that it should be performed in response to the message only methods inherited by the implementation.

The message-selector can be a **unary selector,** that is, a selector that has no arguments, represented by an identifier or **keyword selectors,** that take arguments, as many as there are colons in the selector, and the argument is written inside the keyword, inmediately after each of the colons, with the following syntax:

```
sequence _of_keyword_argument
```

where keyword_argument is *selector: expression* or *:expression.* For example:

```
[cat rollover]
[dog bring:slipper to:my_father]
[vertice set:2 :5:7]
```

Messages and expressions can be placed within messages.

```
[[myFather phone] setTo: [myMother phone]];
```

- **Selector expression** returns the compiler identifier for the method. The syntax is: **@selector(***method***)**.
- **protocol expression** returns an instance of the Protocol class for the name protocol. The syntax is: **@protocol(***protocol_name***)**.
- **encode expression** yields a character string that encodes the type structure of type name. The syntax is: **@encode(***type_name***)**.

G.1.9 Messages

The reply from a message can be stored in another variable:

```
aSet = [Set alloc]
```

The values also returned by the message have types in the same way as functions do.

```
id aSet = [Set alloc]
```

G.1.10 Methods

As discussed above the method declaration is contained in an interface file. There are two types of methods: class method and instance method. The default return and argument type for it is **id**, not int. The syntax for the declaration of each one is the following:

- Class method can be used by the class object rather than instances of the class. Its declaration and implementation is + [(*return_typename*)] *method_name sequence_of_declarator.*

  A sequence of declarator is: *identifier:* [(*type_name*)]*identifier* or :[(*type:name*)]*identifier.* For example:

  ```
  + (id) newPerson;
  ```

  Its implementation is: + [(*return_typename*)] *method_name sequence_of_declarator* {[*declaration_list*] *compound statement*}. For example:

  ```
  +(id) newPerson
  {
     return [[self alloc] init];
  }
  ```

- Instance method can be used by an instance of a class rather than by the class object. The syntax is for **declaration:** - [(*return_typename*)] *method_name sequence_of_declarator.* For example:

  ```
  -changejob:toJob;
  ```

  Implementation: - [(*return_typename*)] *method_name sequence_of_declarator* {[*declaration_list*] *compound statement*}. For example:

  ```
  -changejob:toJob
  {
     id old = job;
     job = toJob;
     return old;
  }
  ```

G.1.11 Selectors

Selectors are the runtime system's identifier for a method. The selector is used in a source-code message to an object, or to replace the name when the source code is compiled. Compiled selectors are of type **SEL.** The **@selector(***method***)** directive lets source code refer to the compiled selector, rather than to the full method name. There are two methods to assign values to SEL variables. For example:

```
SEL myselector = sel_get_uid* ("rollover");

[aCat perform**:sel_get:uid("rollover")];
```

is the same as:

```
[aCat rollover]
```

It is more efficient to assign values to SEL variables at compile time with the **@selector(***method***)** directive. For example:

```
SEL myselector;

myselector = @selector(rollover)
```

References

Backlin, G. *Developing NeXTSTEP Applications.* SAMS Publishing.

Budd, T. *An Introduction to Object-Oriented Programming.* Addison-Wesley, Reading, MA.

Cox, B. and Novobilski, G. *Object-Oriented Programming. An Oevolutionary Approach.* Addison-Wesley, Reading, MA.

Duong Nghiem, A. *NeXTSTEP Programming. Concepts and Applications.* Prentice-Hall, Englewood Cliffs, NJ.

Kernighan, B. and Ritchie, D. *The C Programming Language.* Prentice-Hall, Englewood Cliffs, NJ.

Pinson, L. and Wiener, R. *Objective C:Object-Oriented Programming Techniques.* Addison-Wesley, Reading, MA.

* sel_get_uid() function is used to get a method's selctor from it's name.

** -perform method is used to send a message to an object using a selector.

Webliography

<Reference Manual for the Objective-C Language>
http://www.nextjapan.co.jp/Pubs/Documents/OPENSTEP/ObjectiveC/

<Objective-C: Advanced Topics>
http://www.batech.com/~dekorte/Objective-C/Documentation/4_Language/C_AdvancedTopics.html

<Objective-C FAQ-Sample Code>
http://www.batech.com/~dekorte/Objective-C/Documentation/5_SampleCode/SampleCode 1.html

<Objective-C: Runtime System>
http://www.batech.com/~dekorte/Objective-C/Documentation/4_Language/D_TheRuntimeSystem.html

<Object Oriented Programming in Objective-C>
http://www.idiom.com/free-compilers/LANG/Objectiv-1.html

<Catalog of compilers:Objective-C>
http://www.di.ufpe.br/smalltalk/X3J20.html

<World Wide Web Home Page: Objective-C>
http://www.batech.com/~dekorte/Objective-C/Documentation

APPENDIX H

Smalltalk Language Guide

Luis Joyanes Aguilar
Pontifical Salamanca University

María Luisa Díez Platas
Pontifical Salamanca University

In this reference guide we are trying to make an enumeration of the most representative elements of Smalltalk language, as well as its syntax rules. Smalltalk is a general purpose object-oriented programming language. Everything in Smalltalk is an object and all objects are an instance of a class.

In order to specify the syntax in every element of the language, the following notation will be used: elements in italics represent syntactic categories, bold elements represent keywords; an element between braces ({}) means that the element can appear zero or more; an element between square brackets means it is optional, that is, it can be left out; an element specified as list_of_items, means one or more items separated by commas; and finally, a sequence_of_items means one or more items.

H.1.1 Language Vocabulary (Lexical Elements)

H.1.1.1 Character Set

Smalltalk characters are:

- Upper- and lower-case letters: **A-Z** y **a-z**
- Digits: 1 2 3 4 5 6 7 8 9 0
- Special characters: , +/ \ * ~ < >=% | & ? [ ] { } ( ) ^ ; $: !

0-8493-3135-8/99/$0.00+$.50

H.1.1.2 Comments

A comment is a set of characters enclosed in double quotation marks. Its syntax is as follows:

```
" sequence_of_characters"
```

For example:

```
"this is a comment"
```

H.1.1.3 Identifiers

Identifiers are a sequence of upper- and lowercase letters, numbers, and underscores with a leading letter or underscore. The length of identifiers is not limited.

```
Stack_of_Numbers
_5
```

H.1.1.4 Reserved Identifiers

Smalltalk has some reserved identifiers. These are the following:

nil	It refers to the nil object, that is an instance of class UndefineObject
true, false	They denote the logical values
self	It denotes the current message receiver
super	It has a similar meaning to self

H.1.1.5 Literals

Literals can be:

1. *Number Literal* represents a number constant, as an instance of class **Number**, and its subclasses **Integer**, **Float**, and **Fraction**.

   [sign]sequence_of_digits/sequence_of_digits or
   *[sign]sequence_of_dgits. [sequence_of_digits] [***e** *sequence_of_digits]*

   For example:

   ```
   234
   -2/7
   -1.25e15
   +2.34
   ```

2. *Character literal* is a character constant as an instance of **Character** class.

   ```
   $ASCII_character
   ```

   For example:

   ```
   $y
   SA
   ```

3. *String literal* is a string constant as an instance of **String** class.

   ```
   'sequence_of_characters'
   ```

   For example:

   ```
   'This is a string literal'
   'John'
   ```

4. *Symbol literal* is an instance of **Symbol** class.

   ```
   #identifier
   #binary_selector
   #keyword_selector
   ```

   For example:

   ```
   #index
   #-
   #at:put:
   ```

5. *Array literal* is an instance of **Array** class. An array is a collection of objects. An array literal has a special syntax:

   ```
   #(sequence_of_literals)
   ```

   For example:

   ```
   #('red' 'black' 'green')
   #(1 2 3 4 5 6)
   #(19 'January' 1997)
   #($a $b $c)
   ```

6. *Byte array literals* are arrays of positive integers in the range 0 to 255. The syntax is the following:

   ```
   #[sequence of positive integers]
   ```

   For example:

   ```
   #[1 15 4 6 7 8]
   ```

7. *Boolean literals* have a special reserved word for boolean values: **true** and **false**.

H.1.1.6 Whitespace

Whitespaces are blanks, tab, return, line feed, or form feed.

H.1.1.7 Variables

Variables are names of memory locations. They are not typed. There are special variables in Smalltalk that are the following: **nil** (nothing), **true** and **false**, **self** and **super**, and **Smalltalk** (it holds global variables). Other variables are the following:

1. **Global variables** are known in all methods. A global variable name starts with an uppercase letter.
2. There are the following variables in class definitions:
   - **Instance variables** begin with a lowercase letter. They are data items of a class and it is only possible to refer to them within methods of the class or its subclasses.
   - **Class variables** can be used by all methods in a class (as special global variables). Their names begin with an uppercase letter.
   - **Class instance variables** are like instance variables but belong to classes.
   - **Pool variables** are the keys of pool dictionaries and begin with an uppercase letter.
3. The variables in methods and blocks are local variables and parameters:
   - **Method parameters** are declared in method headers. The method and all blocks contained in it can use the method parameters.
   - **Block parameters** are declared in block headers and can only be used in a block.

- **Local variables in methods** begin with a lowercase letter and are defined in method headers. They can be used anywhere in the methods.
- **Local variables in blocks** are declared in block headers and exist only during the execution of the block.

Local variable definition is realized in a method interface definition. Its syntax is as follows:

```
| sequence_of_identifiers |
```

H.1.2 Classes

In Smalltalk, there are some basic classes and it is possible to define new classes.

H.1.2.1 Basic Classes

They are defined in a hierarchy in which the top of it is the abstract class **Object.** Its implements methods relate to being an object. All other classes are inherited from Object and they are the following:

- Class **UndefinedObject** has an instance that is **nil.**
- Class **Boolean** is an abstract class that is the superclass of **True** and **False** classes. The instance methods of boolean classes are methods that implement the logical operators and methods that implement conditional statements.
- Class **magnitude** is an abstract class and supplies methods that are shared by all magnitudes, and they are defined in terms of principal comparison methods. It is the superclass of the class **Association** which represents magnitudes that hold pairs of values (the key and the value), the class **Character,** the class **Date** to represent the day, month, and year of a calendar date, the class **Time** to represent the time of a day with an error range of one second, and finally, the class **Number** that is a superclass of classes **Float, Fraction,** and **Integer.**
- Class **Point,** the instances of it are objects that hold two numbers representing a position in a plane
- Class **Rectangle,** its objects are pairs of points that define an axis-aligned rectangle in a plane.

H.1.2.2 Class Definitions

In Smalltalk, new classes can be defined. The syntax for class definitions is the following:

```
Identifier_of_superclass subclass: #identifier_of_class
instanceVariableNames: ' sequence_of_identifiers_of_instance_variables'
classVariableNames: 'sequence_of_identifiers_of_class_variables'
poolDictionaries:'sequence_of_identifiers_of_pool_dictionaries'
```

For example:

```
Employee subclass:#SalariedEmploye
  instanceVariableNames: 'positionsalary'
  classVariableNames:"
  poolDictionaries: "
```

H.1.3 Collections

Collections are classes that manage groups of objects. They are sets of elements where each element is a pointer to an object.

The collections can be categorized by some characteristics. **Fixed** indicates that a collection has a fixed size. **Variable** indicates that a collection has an undetermined size; new elements can be added to the collection when it is necessary. **Ordered** indicates that a collection has some ordering to the elements. **Unordered** indicates a collection has no ordering and its elements cannot be indexed. **Indexed** collections can be indexed by an integer and they are always ordered. **Values** refers to the values that a collection holds.

Smalltalk provides some common collections that are subclasses of class **Collection.** These are the following:

- **Bag** collections is an unordered collection that admits duplicate objects. To create a bag collection the **new** message must be used.

```
Bag new
```

- **Set** collection is a variable collection, neither ordered nor indexed. It is similar to bag collections but it does not admit duplicate objects.

```
ASet := #(1 5 6 7)
```

- **Array** collection is a fixed-size collection that can be indexed by an integer's index beginning by 1 and increasing.
- **OrderedCollection** collection is an ordered and variable-sized collection that admits duplicate objects.

```
    Dogs := Orderedcollection new.
    Dogs add: 'Setter'
    Dogs addFirst: 'Rotwailer'
    Dogs addLast: 'Bouldog'
    "add methods add elements to the ordered collection
Dogs, and it is obtained ('Rotwailer' 'Setter' 'Bouldog')"
```

- **SortedCollection** collection is an ordered and variable-sized collection that does not admit duplicates objects.

There are other types of collections that you can find in the bibliography.

H.1.4 Methods

In Smalltalk methods are similar to functions because they always return values. A method has five parts: a method header, a comment describing the purpose of a method, a list of local variables, an optional sequence of sentences separated by periods, and an optional return statement. Their syntax is the following:

```
method_header comment |sequence_of identifiers_of_local_variables|
[sequence_of_statements. ] [^expression]
```

A method header can have different forms because it depends on the method type.

- A unary method is a method without arguments. The syntax of a unary method header is *identifier*

```
Squared
    "return a value of a variable squared"
    |x sq|
    x := 3.
    sq:= x * x.
    ^ sq
```

- A binary method accepts only a single argument. A binary method header has the following syntax:

```
special_character argument_identifier
special_character special_character argument_identifier
```

- A keyword method admits more then one argument. Its header has the following syntax:

  sequence_of_pair

  a pair is *identifier: identifier*

H.1.5 Expressions

It is made up of one or more message sends, which can be combined into longer expressions, and enclosed in parentheses. A valid Smalltalk expression can be a variable name, a literal, or a message send.

H.1.6 Messages

In general a message format consists of the name of the object that receives the message, followed by the message name. There are some types of messsages:

- A **Unary message** has the following syntax:

  object_name message_name

```
x cos           "return de result of cos(x)"
x mother age    "return de result of age(mother(x))"
```

- **Binary messages** are used to specify arithmetic, comparison, and logical operations. There can be binary messages followed and the resulted expression that results is evaluated left to right. Their syntax is the following:

  object_name message_name object_name

```
5*3        "it is equivalent to 5*3"
2*5+6      "it is equivalent to (2*5)+6"
3+5*4      "it is equivalent to (3+5)*4"
6+(2*3)    "it is equivalent to 6+(2*4)"
x <= y     "return true if x is lower than or equal to
             y; otherwise return false"

x length + y length
 "this message is a mixture or unary and binary messages and it's
equivalent to (x length) + (y length)"
```

- **Keyword messages** are equivalent to a procedure call with two or more parameters. Some of these can be any mixture of unary, binary, or parenthesized keyword messages (the keyword message is the last evaluated). The syntax of a simple keyword message is:

  object_name message name : parameter_name

  array new: 20

```
"it creates an array of size 20. This is a special
message that creates instances of classes"
```

  Today month:currentMonth day:currentDayyear:currentYear

```
"set the private data for object Today to
 month=currentMonth day=currentDay year=currentYear"
```

  John weight:Mary weight + 30

```
"it is equivalent to John weight: ((Mary weight) + 30)"
```

H.1.7 Statements

Smalltalk has assignments, conditionals statements, loop statements, return statements, and statements for evaluating expressions. Statements are separated by a period.

1. **Expressions** can be written as a statement ending with a period.

   Expression.

   ```
   John name.
   ```

2. **Assignment statements** have the following syntax.

   variable_name := statement

   ```
   y:=6
   ```

3. **Return statements** are used in a method to return a value other than the default value. The following is their syntax:

   ^ *statement*

   ```
   ^a*b
   ```

4. A **block** can contain any number of valid statements or any number of comments. The last statement in a block cannot end with a period. The local variables of its defining methods can be accessed by the statement in a block. The following syntax corresponds to a syntax of the **conditionals statements.**

   [* *{arguments}* | *{local_variable_definition} sequence_of_statement***]**

   ```
   [:x :y :xx :yy|
     |xxx yyy|
     xxx:=x*xx.
     yyy:=y*yy.
     (xxx + yyy) sqrt]
   ```

5. The following syntax corresponds to a syntax of the **conditionals statements.****

   boolean_expression [**ifTrue:** *block*] [**ifFalse:***block*]
   boolean_expression [**ifFalse:** *block*] [**ifTrue:***block*]

   ```
   n<1 ifTrue: [n:=n+2] ifFalse:[n:=3]
   ```

6. There are some **loop** and **iterative statements.** They are the following:
   - **whileTrue** evaluates an initial block and if it is evaluated to true, then evaluates the following block while an initial block is evaluated to true. Its syntax is the following:

     block **whileTrue:** *block*

   - **whileFalse** is similar to whileTrue. In this statement, the final block is evaluated if the initial block is evaluated to false.

     block **whileFalse:** *block*

   - **timesRepeat** evaluates a block repeatedly for positive integer times.

     a_positive_integer **timesRepeat:** *block*

---

* [is a token, in this case it does not mean optionality, it is a part of the block. It's the same for].

** In the syntax, [and] indicates optionality.

- The following loop statements are similar to **for** without and without step, respectively. The syntax for all of them is the following:

  start_value **to:** *expression* **do:** *block**

  start_value **to:** *expression* **by:** *expression* **do:** *block*

H.1.8 Exceptions

In Smalltalk, exception handling involves four classes: ExceptionalEvent, Signal, Block, and ExceptionalEventCollection. There are exceptional events (instances of ExceptionalEvent) that are a kind of exception and provide information about how to handle the exception when it occurs. It is necessary to define a handler block to trap the exception when detected.

Instances of Signal describe a particular error. An instance of ExceptionalEventCollection holds more than one instance of ExceptionalEvent.

- **Signal** is used to send a message to an exception event to raise the event.
- **Handling exceptions** defines an exception handler for a block any number of constructions **when: do:** can be used. The following syntax is used:

  block **when:** *exception_event* **do:** *block*

This statement is used to send a message to the block after do by evaluating the first block. When an event is signaled, the evaluation of the block above is achieved. In the first block no return statement can appear.

H.1.9 Chunk Formats

Smalltalk syntax described thus far needs the use of the class hierarchy browser which has the methods for defined classes. Smalltalk/V uses an additional format to store the methods on disk; this format is known as chunk format, which in addition to using the above statement makes use of a new structure to associate methods with its classes as well as also storing definitions of data structures of classes. Chunk format represents a file of chunks of codes separated by (!). It consists of the following parts:

1. The class definition — With its usual syntax, always preceded by a chunk containing the string 'define class'.
2. Class method definition — With the syntax above preceded by a chunk containing the class name the method belongs to followed by the words 'class methods.'**
3. Instance method definition — With a similar structure to the above-mentioned, but with a difference in which a chunk uses the word 'methods' instead of class method.

References

Budd, T. 1987. *A Little Smalltalk.* Addison-Wesley, Reading, MA.

Goldberg, A. and Robson, D. 1983. *Smalltalk-80: The Language and its Implementation.* Addison-Wesley, Reading, MA.

Lewis, S. 1995. *The Art and Science of Smalltalk.* Prentice-Hall, Englewood Cliffs, NJ.

Marchesi, M. 1994. *Object-Oriented Programming with Smalltalk/V.* Prentice-Hall, Englewood Cliffs, NJ.

Smith, D. 1996. *SMALLTALK, the Language.* Benjamin/Cummings, Menlo Park, CA.

* The expressions must be a numeric value and a block must be one argument that is used as a control variable of the loop. The idea is also valid for the following loop statement.

** Methods can be preceded for the word private or public.

Webliography

<IBM Corporation-Smalltalk Programming and Development Guidelines: A Manual of Style>
http://www.training.ibm.com/ibmedu/otu/stalkmos.html

<Simon Lewis-Prentice Hall/Hewlett-Packard- The Art and Science of Smalltalk>
http://www-uk.hpl.hp.com/people/scrl/ArtAndScience/contents.html

<IBM Smalltalk Tutorial>
http://www2.ncsu.edu/eos/info/ece480_info...spring96/proj63/www/tutorial/

<STIC- The Smalltalk Language Background>
http://www.stic.org/STLang/F001.htm

<ChiMU Publications-Java and Smalltalk Syntax compared>
http://www.chimu.com/publications/JavaSmalltalkSyntax.html

<ANSI X3J20>
http://www.di.ufpe.br/smalltalk/X3J20.html

<ANSI Annual Report>
http://www.stic.org/STLang/F010.htm

<The Smalltalk Report>
http://www.sigs.com/publications/srpt/

<Gameplan: Java-savvy Smalltalk in a year>
http://www.onemind.com/smalltalk.html

<ANSI X3H7 Object Model Features Matrix>
http://info.gte.com/ftp/doc/activities/x3h7/by_model/Smalltalk.html

<Dick Botting-Smalltalk Syntax>.
http://www.csci.csusb.edu/dick/samples/smalltalk.syntax.html

<Dick Botting-Smalltalk Semantics>.
http://www.csci.csusb.edu/dick/samples/smalltalk.semantics.html

APPENDIX I
Glossary of OO Terms

Dan Hanley
South Bank University

Paul Schleifer
South Bank University

Abstract Class
Class with no instances, sometimes used to represent abstract concepts, whose concrete subclasses may add to its structure and behavior by implementing its abstract operations.

Abstract Operation
Operation declared, but not implemented, by an abstract class.

Abstraction
1. Representation of important features of some entity or concept without the inclusion of irrelevant detail and background.
2. Set of essential characteristics of an object that distinguishes it from other kinds of object.

Access Control
Mechanism by which the degree of visibility of the structure and behavior of an object to other objects is restricted.

Access Operation
Operation that accesses the state of an object without modifying it.

Action
Instantaneous operation, such as the invocation of a method, the triggering of an event, or the changing of state of execution of an activity.

Active Object
Object that can initiate the passing of messages.

Activity
Non-instantaneous operation.

Actor
1. Object that operates on other objects without suffering operations of other objects.
2. User adopting a (possibly transient) role.

Agent
Object that both operates on, and is operated upon by, other objects.

Aggregate Object
Object composed of other objects.

0-8493-3135-8/99/$0.00+$.50

AKindOf (AKO)
Inheritance relationship between a class and its superclass.

Algorithm
A detailed sequence of actions which accomplishes some task that terminates in finite time.

Algorithmic Decomposition
Breaking down a system into small steps as a way of understanding a larger process.

Analysis
Fundamental approach to understanding a problem by identifying and examining its constituent parts.

Applet
Java bytecodes that can be downloaded from an Internet server and executed on a client machine.

Application Domain
System viewed from the perspective of the end user.

Application Framework
Reusable set of classes and objects that provides a skeleton for building applications in a particular domain.

Architecture
Logical and physical structure of a system resulting from strategic and tactical design decisions.

Assertion
Boolean expression of a condition that must always be true.

Association
Relationship representing a semantic link between two classes.

Attribute
Synonym for *Instance Variable*

Base Class
1. Synonym for *Superclass*
2. Root class in an inheritance hierarchy from which all other classes ultimately inherit their most generalized structure and behavior.

Behavior
How an object visibly acts and reacts, as defined by the set of all its methods.

Boolean
Expression or variable that can only be evaluated as either true or false.

Browser
1. Navigation tool for examining an inheritance hierarchy.
2. Generic tool for viewing objects, e.g., Web pages.

Business Object
Object that models some essential part of the application domain.

Call
Act of sending a message.

Cardinality
Number of objects in a set of objects; typically the number of instances of a class or that participate in a class relationship.

CASE
Acronym for *Computer-Aided Software Engineering*, the use of software tools to assist in the analysis and design of software systems.

Category
Grouping of methods in a Smalltalk class definition according to some common characteristic.

Class
Abstraction of a set of objects that share a common structure and behavior.

Class Category
Logical collection of classes that collaborate to provide a set of services.

Class Diagram
Notation used to represent the existence of classes and their relationships in the logical design of a system.

Class Library
Set of reusable classes, often defined as part of the implementation or design environment.

Class Method
Method invoked by sending a message to a class rather than to an instance of a class; e.g., the method *new* that creates an instance of the class.

Class Structure
Graph representing classes as vertices and relationships among classes as arcs.

Class Variable
Part of the state of a class that is visible to all instances of that class.

Classification
Representation of semantics of generalization (membership, IsA relationship) and specialization (inclusion, AKindOf relationship), often as an acyclic directed graph.

Client
Object that uses the services of another object.

Collaboration
Cooperation of objects resulting in some higher level behavior.

COMMA
Acronym for *Common Object Methodology Metamodel Architecture.*

Composition
Semantic relationship PartOf, indicating that an object may be assembled (aggregated) from a collection of other (component) objects.

Concrete Class
Class that may have instances.

Concurrency
Property of encapsulating more than one thread of control.

Concurrent Object
Object that encapsulates more than one thread of control.

Constraint
Expression of a semantic condition that must be maintained.

Constructor
Operation that creates and/or initializes the state of an object.

Container Class
Class whose instances are collections of instances, which may be constrained to be of either the same class of object as each other (homogeneous collections) or instances of different classes of objects (heterogeneous collections).

CORBA
Acronym for *Common Object Request Broker Architecture.*

CRC Cards
Simple tool for elucidating key abstractions and mechanisms of a system based on notions of Class, Responsibilities, and Collaborators.

CSCW
Acronym for *Computer-Supported Collaborative Work.*

Cyberspace
Literary synonym for the *Internet.*

Data Dictionary
Repository containing descriptions of all the classes and objects in a system.

Data Flow
Flow of property values within objects or message parameter values between objects.

Data Flow Diagram (DFD)
Functional notation representing dependencies between, and the computation of, input and output values.

Data Semantics
Specification of the meaning of data and the relationships between them.

DBMS
Acronym for *Database Management System.*

Delegation
1. Transfer of responsibility for performing some behavior from one object, operation, or subsystem to another.
2. Kind of classless inheritance where messages are forwarded from a client to its prototype object.

Demon
Object or operation activated by a state change.

Derived Class
Specialized class derived from a more generalized class.

Destructor
Operation that destroys an object and frees the space it occupies for use by other objects.

Device
Item of hardware with no computational resources.

Diagram
Pictorial representation of some notation and semantics.

DML
Acronym for *Data Manipulation Language.*

DSS
Acronym for *Decision Support System.*

Dynamic Binding
Association of a name, such as a method name or variable name, with a class at runtime rather than at compile time.

Early Binding
Synonym for *Static Binding.*

Encapsulation
Information-hiding concept in which unrestricted access to an object's structure and behavior is scoped with regard to other objects.

Entity
Any thing that has real existence.

Entity-Relationship Diagram (ERD)
Simple pictorial notation showing the existence of entities, the associations among them, and the degree of these associations.

Event
State-changing incident or occurrence.

Exception
Error condition that cannot be handled as part of normal system behavior.

Field
Synonym for *Instance Variable.*

Forward Engineering
Production of executable code from a logical or physical design.

Framework
Synonym for *Application Framework.*

Free Subprogram
Subprogram that is not an object method providing some non-primitive operation.

Friend
Class or operation that references the private parts of an object that non-friend classes and operations cannot reference.

Function
Operation returning a value, usually mapping some kind of input to output.

Function Point
Single, visible, and testable activity identified during requirements analysis.

Fuzzy Logic
System of logic dealing with imprecisely known values.

Garbage Collection
Language or memory management mechanism for deallocating memory used for objects that are no longer referenced.

Gateway
Software providing an object-like interface to software that is not object-oriented.

Generalization
Class that is more abstract and general-purpose than any class that inherits from it.

General Class
Class, such as a container class, that serves as a template for other classes and that is parameterized with generic formal parameters supplied during instantiation.

Generic Function
Synonym for *Virtual Function.*

GUI
Acronym for *Graphical User Interface.*

Hierarchy
Abstraction ordered or ranked into a tree-like structure.

HCI
Acronym for *Human Computer Interaction* or *Human Computer Interface.*

Identity
Characteristic of an object that distinguishes it from all other objects.

Implementation
Internal (private and/or hidden) parts of an object.

Impedance Mismatch
Conflicts arising when different programming paradigms and languages are employed together on the same project.

Index
Data structure that maps instance variable values into the objects that have these instance variables.

Information Hiding
Principle by which the parts of an object that are not directly involved in interactions with other objects, such as the object's structure and the implementation of its methods, are hidden from other objects.

Inheritance
Relationship between classes whereby one class inherits all or part of the description of one (single inheritance), or more than one (multiple inheritance), more generalized class, and where instances inherit all of the methods and structure of the classes to which they belong.

Instance
Object, endowed with state, behavior, and identity; that is an example of a particular class.

Instance Variable
Property of an object, whose value may be another object.

Instantiation
Creation of an object that is an example of a particular class.

Integration
Coupling together of classes via inheritance and aggregation, of objects via message passing and reference, or of attributes and operations within a particular class.

Interaction
Mechanism by which objects interact, either by the sending of a message or an object that results from the associations between other objects.

Interaction Diagram
Object-oriented design notation showing execution of a scenario in the context of an object diagram.

Interface
Visible parts of an object emphasizing abstraction while concealing its internal structure and behavior.

Internet
Fast-growing global federation of computer networks, with millions of users worldwide, providing many database- and communications-based services.

Interpreter
Software that translates commands, bytecodes, or programming language scripts into native machine instructions without first creating a compiled, native, binary file.

Intranet
Computer network using Internet software protocols, but protected from global Internet users by use of protective software called a firewall.

Invariant
Condition represented as a Boolean expression whose truth must be maintained.

IsA
Relationship between an instance and its class; e.g., "42 IsA Integer".

Iterator
Method permitting all parts of an object to be visited.

Join
Operation joining together two relations on the basis of common values in a common attribute.

Just-In-Time Compiler
Component of an interpreter that translates bytecodes into machine code for a particular processor architecture at runtime.

Key Abstraction
Class or object that forms part of the definition of the problem domain.

Late Binding
Synonym for *Dynamic Binding.*

Layer
1. Collection of classes or subsystems all at the same level of abstraction.
2. A partition of objects treated as a composite object communicating with other layers.

Level
Synonym for *Layer: 2.*

Link
Instance of an association between two objects.

Logical Design
Design specification emphasizing procedural aspects of a system, ideally culminating in systematic generation, verification, and optimization of pseudocode.

Lower Case
Small letters of the alphabet; *viz.* the set of characters {a.z}.

Management Information Systems (MIS)
Any system that provides information for the management activities carried out within an organization.

Mapping
Function transforming a range of objects into a domain of objects.

Mechanism
Structure of collaborating objects providing some behavior that satisfies a requirement of the problem.

Member Function
Function declared within a class that has access to its internal state.

Member Object
Synonym for *Instance Variable.*

Message
Request sent to an object to carry out one or more of its Operations.

Metaclass
Class whose instances are themselves classes.

Metadata
Data which describe the semantics of data recorded about an enterprise, usually captured as classes.

Methodology
1. Study of approaches to analysis of problems and design of solutions.
2. Integrated collection of tools to aid in the analysis of problems and the design of solutions.

Method
Operation performed by an object and defined as part of the declaration of its class. Methods can be public, private, or protected.

Metrics
Software measurements used to gauge software quality, engineering productivity, and software characteristics, such as degree of modularity and logical complexity.

Mixin
Abstract class containing methods which can be combined with (mixed into) any class.

Modeling
Creation of abstract representations of real-world problems based on observations or on approximations based on system goals.

Modifier
Operation that changes the state of an object.

Modularity
Characteristic of a system decomposed into a collection of cohesive and loosely coupled modules; typically a goal of systems analysis and design.

Module
Distinctively named and addressable element of software used as a building block for the physical structure of a system.

Monomorphism
Type theory concept in which a message may have only one system-wide interpretation; opposite of polymorphism.

Multimedia
Concept embracing all forms of computer-mediated human communication; *viz.* text, graphics, sound, and moving images.

Multi-Platform
Characteristic of software systems which run in, or are developed for, more than one operating environment.

Multiple Inheritance
Model of Inheritance in which an object can inherit its specification from more than one generalized class.

Multi-Processing
Software that executes simultaneously on more than one physical processor.

Multi-Tasking
Description of software that executes, or simulates the execution of, more than one operation simultaneously.

Multi-User
Property of a software system that can process commands issued by more than one simultaneous user.

Network
Set of nodes, which may be representational objects or real-world entities, connected by arcs, which may be conceptual links or real-world associations.

Neural Network
Form of knowledge representation in which information is stored implicitly in the distribution of weights in matrices.

Newsgroup
Internet-based discussion forum concerned with a specific topic.

Notation
Alphabet of symbols used to represent conceptual and real-world entities.

Object
Object type or one whose instances are endowed with state, behavior, and identity, usually an instance of a class.

Objectbase
Database management system that stores information as objects rather than as data.

Object Database Management Group (ODMG)
Consortium of objectbase vendors and associated parties dedicated to standardization across objectbase products.

Object Diagram
Subset of notation used in object-oriented design to represent the existence of objects and their relationships in a logical system design.

Object Linking and Embedding (OLE)
Microsoft's proprietary system for implementing objects as software components that can be referred to by, or instantiated within, other software.

Object Management Group (OMG)
International trade association concerned with realizing the potential software benefits of portability, reusability, and interoperability associated with object-oriented technology.

Object Model
Set of axioms forming the foundation of object-oriented design.

Object Type
Entity type implemented as classes, encapsulating both data structure and operations.

Object-Oriented Analysis (OOA)
Method of problem analysis in which requirements are studied and refined from the perspective of objects and classes.

Object-Oriented Decomposition
Product of object-oriented design in which a system is composed of parts, each representing an object or class within the problem domain.

Object-Oriented Design (OOD)
Design method incorporating object-oriented decomposition and notation for representing logical and physical structure, and static and dynamic characteristics, of the system being designed.

Object-Oriented Programming (OOP)
Programming approach in which software is implemented as collections of interacting objects.

ODBMS
Acronym for *Object-Oriented Database Management System*, synonym for *Objectbase.*

Operation
Procedure that an object is able to perform, generally realized in the form of a method.

Operator Overloading
Example of polymorphism in which the same operator symbol is associated with more than one meaning.

Optimization
Act of improving the design and implementation of software either by human deliberation or by using an automated tool, such as a compiler.

Parameter
Argument upon which an operation acts.

Parameterized Class
Synonym for *Generic Class.*

Passive Object
Object that can only undergo state changes when explicitly acted upon, i.e., that does not possess its own thread of control.

Pattern
Reusable architecture, object template, or design rule that has been shown to address a particular issue in an application domain.

Persistence
Property of an object whose identity, state, and description is preserved in terms of time (i.e., regardless of the computer session in which it was created) and possibly also in terms of address space.

Physical Design
Design specification emphasizing structural aspects of a system in terms of how real-world and conceptual entities can be represented in terms of data and processes.

Polymorphism
Property by which different objects may respond to the same set of operations and messages in different ways.

Post-condition
Invariant that must be satisfied on completion of an operation.

Pre-condition
Invariant that must be satisfied before an operation starts.

Private
Description of parts, attributes, and/or methods of an object that cannot be accessed by other objects.

Process
Activation of a single thread of control.

Process Diagram
Object-oriented design notation showing allocation of processes to processors.

Processor
Hardware item capable of executing programs.

Protected
Description of parts, attributes and/or methods of an object that can be accessed by itself and instances of its subclasses only.

Protocol
Set of public operations of an object that constitute its external interface.

Public
Description of parts, attributes, and/or methods of an object that can be accessed by itself and all other objects.

Reactive System
System characterized by being event-driven rather than dependent on input/output mapping.

Real-Time System
System characterized by the need to respond to the problem domain in a time frame dictated by the problem domain.

Referential Integrity
Degree to which an identifier refers to a unique object.

Relationship
Logical connection or characteristic mapping between individual objects, or a potential association between classes.

Repository
Storage facility for information about objects, classes, and their relationships.

Requirements Analysis (RA)
Generation of a precise and independent description of a system that captures the information and functional aspects of the application domain.

Responsibility
Attribute or method of an object, or some behavior that an object is obliged to provide.

Reverse Engineering
Generation of a design or model from executable code.

Role
Purpose assumed by an object in its relationship with another.

Rule
Constraint specifying some relationship between more than one attribute and/or operation of an object.

Scenario
Set of events resulting in some system behavior.

Schema
Set of object types and classes that constitutes an operational system or objectbase.

Selector
Method reporting on the state of an object without altering it.

Server
Object that is operated upon by other objects, that can send messages to other objects in response to a received request, but that never acts upon other objects.

Service
Behavior provided by some part of the system.

Signature
Full description of interface and/or type information associated with some feature.

Single Inheritance
Inheritance mechanism whereby a class inherits the definition of its structure and behavior from only one more generalized class.

Slot
Synonym for *Instance Variable.*

Specialization
Class that is more restricted than the generalized class from which it inherits.

State
Qualifiable condition of an object resulting from or affecting its behavior and/or properties.

State Space
Set of all possible states of an object.

State Transition Diagram (STD)
Design notation showing an object's or class' state space, its state-changing events, and the actions that arise from each state change.

Static Binding
Association of a name, such as a method name or variable name, with a class at compile time rather than at runtime.

Strategic Design Decision
Architectural system design decision that can potentially impact the whole system.

Strong Typing
Programming language property ensuring that all expressions are guaranteed to be type consistent, thus preventing type errors at runtime.

Structure

1. Concrete representation of an object state.
2. Set of objects linked by classification, composition, or use structure.

Structured Design
Design method involving the use of algorithmic decomposition.

Subclass
Class that inherits part of its description from at least one more generalized classes.

Subsystem
Set of modules, providing some behavior as a single component of the system, grouped together to make the system more understandable or more tractable.

Superclass
Class from which at least one more specialized classes inherits part of its description.

Synchronization

1. Concurrency semantics of an operation.
2. Interaction of two processes in which one process that is ready to execute is blocked until the other is also in a ready state, at which time both processes are allowed to execute.

Tactical Design Decision
Design decision with local architectural implications.

TCP/IP
Acronym for *Transmission Control Protocol/Internet Protocol*, the suite of communications protocols that form the "backbone" of the Internet.

Thread of Control
Continuous sequence of execution or process usually associated with control flow or independent dynamic action within a system.

Transaction
Logical unit of work in persistent data systems used to ensure that atomic operations are only committed if their consistency and integrity is verified.

Transition
Change of state.

Trigger

1. Event raising operation
2. Synonym for *Demon*

Type
Domain of allowable values of an object (a set) and the operations defined on this set.

Uppercase
Capital letters of the alphabet; *viz.* the set of characters {AZ}.

Use
To reference an abstraction's interface.

Use Case
Top-level description of how a system is used, usually in terms of a sequence of transactions performed by a user or events in a particular execution.

Use Structure
Structure of relationships between servers and clients defined by message passing connections.

View
Mechanism, often defined as a domain class, that provides information about or control over a set or class of objects.

Virtual Function
Operation upon an object that may be redefined by a subclass.

Visibility

Ability of one abstraction to reference features of the interface of another abstraction.

Weak Typing

Programming language property whereby type consistency is not enforced, potentially resulting in type errors at runtime.

APPENDIX J
Listing of OO Languages

Dan Hanley
South Bank University

Paul Schleifer
South Bank University

OO languages are many and varied. Generally accepted features are objects which encapsulate and inherit behavior and communicate through message passing. The rich variety of languages bears evidence to the many areas in which OO technology has become popular.

The following is a listing of OO languages that have come into existence in academia, research, and/or real-world environments:

ABCL/1
ABCL/c+
ABCL/R
ABCL/R2
Abel
Acore
Act/1
Act/2
Act/3
Actor
Actors
Actra
Ada ++
Ada 95
Agora
Alcool-90
ALLOY
Argus
A'UM
ART
BeBOP
BETA
Blaze 2
Brouhaha
C with classes
C-talk
C++
Cantor
Cecil
Charm++
Clascal
CLIPS
CLOS
Cluster 86
CO2
Common Loops
Common Objects
Common ORBIT
Concurrent Prolog
Concurrent Smalltalk
CSSA
CST
Director
Distributed Smalltalk
DROOL
Dylan
Eiffel
Emerald
ExperCommonLisp
Extended Pascal
Felix
Flavors
FOOPlog
FOOPS
FRL
Galileo
Garp
GLISP
Gypsey
Haskell
Hybrid
Inheritance
InnovAda
Intermission
Jasmine
Java
KL-One
KRL
KRS
Little Smalltalk
LOOPS
Lore
Mace
MELD
Mjolner
ML
ModPascal
Modula-3
Neon
New Flavors
NIL
OakLisp
Oberon 2
Object Assembler
Object Cobol
Object Lisp
Object Logo
Object Oberon
Object Pascal
Objective-C
Object-Z
ObjVLisp
Obliq
O-CPU
OO-CHILL
OOPC
OOPS+
OPAL
Orbit
Orient84/K
OTM
PCOL
PIE
PL/LL
Plasma II
PolyTOIL
POOL-T
PROCOL
Python
Quick Pascal
Quicktalk
ROSS

0-8493-3135-8/99/$0.00+$.50

SAST
Sather
scheme
SCOOP
SCOOPS
Self
Simula67
SINA
Smalltalk
Smalltalk AT
Smalltalk V
SmallVDM
Smallworld
SPOOL
SR
SRL
STROBE
T
Theta
Trellis/Owl
Turbo Pascal 5.x
Uniform
UNITS
VDM++
Vulcan
XLISP
Xlisp
Z++
Zoom/VM

APPENDIX K
Listing of OO Scripting Languages

Dan Hanley
South Bank University

Paul Schleifer
South Bank University

Scripting languages are high-level languages, usually typeless, designed for "gluing" applications and pre-existing components together for rapid application development.

The following is a listing of OO scripting languages that have come into existence in academia, research, and/or real-world environments:

AppleScript
JavaScript
LiveScript
Perl
Python
TCL
VBScript
VRMLScript

0-8493-3135-8/99/$0.00+$.50

APPENDIX L
Listing of OO Methodologies

Dan Hanley
South Bank University
Paul Schleifer
South Bank University

An OO methodology is a set of principles and methods for constructing OO systems in a manner that can be implemented, scheduled, measured, taught, compared, and modified. Many early methodologies were associated with individual diagrammatic styles or programming languages, so despite a recent trend toward "diagrammatic independence," practitioners often associate a particular methodological approach with the use of a particular notation.

The following is a listing of OO methodologies and notations that have come into existence in academia, research, and/or real-world environments:

Balin
Berard
BON
Colbert
Colbert
DOOS, Wirfs-Brock et al.
Embley and Kurtz
Embley et al.
Firesmith
Fusion, Coleman et al.
GOOD
HOOD
IBM
JSD/OOD
MOOD
MOSES, Henderson-Sellers and Edwards
OBA
Object Lifecycles, Shlaer and Mellor
Object Modeling Technique (OMT), Rumbaugh et al.
Object-Oriented Analysis and Design (OOA/OOD), Coad and Yourdon
Object-Oriented Analysis and Design with Applications (OOADA), Booch
Object-Oriented Software Engineering (OOSE), Jacobson et al.
Object-Oriented SSADM (OOSSADM), Robinson and Berisford
Object-Oriented System Development (OOSD), de Champeaux et al.

0-8493-3135-8/99/$0.00+$.50

Objectory
OO Z*
OOD/LVM
OOram
OOREM
OOSD
OPEN
OSA
Principles of Object-Oriented Analysis and Design (OOAD), Martin and Odell
ROOM
Smith-Tockey
SOMA
Synthesis
UML

APPENDIX M

Listing of Object-Oriented Operating Systems

Dan Hanley
South Bank University

Paul Schleifer
South Bank University

Object-oriented operating systems are based on the object paradigm rather than built using procedural design. Typically, the abstraction of a single object space is supported in which objects persist independently and can cooperate transparently using messages even if stored on different machines. The improved modularity of object-oriented systems promotes fine grain adaptability to meet specific hardware and user requirements, and the common object architecture typically provided by object-oriented operating systems promotes reuse and rapid development.

The following is a listing of Web sites describing projects related to object-oriented operating systems and micro-kernels that have come into existence in academia, research, and/or real-world environments.

Project	URL
Amoeba	http://www.am.cs.vu.nl/
Apertos	http://www.csl.sony.co.jp/project/Apertos/
ARGON	http://www.abwillms.demon.co.uk/os/
BeOS	http://www.be.com/
BOX	http://www.braineng.com/BOXpage.htm
Choices	http://choices.cs.uiuc.edu/choices/
CHORUS	http://www.chorus.com/
Eden	http://www.arm.com/DevSupp/OS/Eden/
Elmwood	http://www.cs.orst.edu/~crowl/paper/journals/1989J-SPE-11-1029/
GEOS	http://www.geoworks.com/
Grasshopper	http://www.gh.cs.su.oz.au/Grasshopper/
GUIDE	http://www-bi.imag.fr/GUIDE/
Jos	http://jos.org/
Mach	http://www.cs.cmu.edu/afs/cs.cmu.edu/project/mach/public/www/
Mach Shared Objects	http://www.cs.utah.edu/projects/mso/
Merlin	http://www.lsi.usp.br/~jecel/merlin.html
Micro-Choices	http://choices.cs.uiuc.edu/choices/uChoices.html
Mungi	http://www.cse.unsw.EDU.AU/~disy/Mungi.html
NeXTSTEP	http://www.next.com/
Oberon	http://www.oberon.ethz.ch/
Oberon	http://www.oberon.ethz.ch/oberon/
Paramecium	http://www.cs.vu.nl/~leendert/paramecium.html

0-8493-3135-8/99/$0.00+$.50

Project	URL
PEACE	http://www.first.gmd.de/peace/peace.html
PURE	http://irb.cs.uni-magdeburg.de/bs/forschung/pure-eng.shtml
Spring	http://www.sun.com/tech/projects/spring/
Sprite	http://www.cs.berkeley.edu/projects/sprite
Tornado	http://www.eecg.utoronto.ca/EECG/RESEARCH/ParallelSys/tornado.html
Tunes	http://www.eleves.ens.fr:8080/home/rideau/Tunes/

APPENDIX N
Who's Who in Object Technology

Dan Hanley
South Bank University

Paul Schleifer
South Bank University

We asked each of our contributors to list, in his or her opinion, the top five Who's Who in Object Technology. The following is the list of top 10, as per our tabulation.

Grady Booch
Bertrand Meyer
Brian Henderson-Sellers
Adele Goldberg
Ivar Jacobson
Jim Rumbaugh
Bjarne Stroustrup
Jim Odell
Brad Cox
Erich Gamma

Votes were also cast for the following individuals, presented in alphabetical order:

Bruce Anderson, Doug Barry, Kent Beck, Tim Berners-Lee, John Cameron, Luca Cardelli, Cory Casanave, R.G.G. Catell, Peter Coad, Alistair Cockburn, Larry Constantine, Steve Cook, Jim Coplien, Ward Cunningham, John Daniels, Don Firesmith, Rich Friedman, James Gosling, Ian Graham, Richard Helm, Bill Hoffman, Steve Jobs, Ralph Johnson, Miguel Katrib, Mohammad Ketabchi, Haim Kilov, Won Kim, Doug Lea, Tom Love, David Maier, Frank Manola, Bob Martin, Steve Mellor, Joaquin Miller, Oscar Nierstrasz, Robert Orfali, Dilip Patel, John Pugh, Jay Ranade, Trygve Reenskaug, Bran Selic, Richard Soley, Chris Stone, Michael Stonebraker, Dave Thomas, John Vlissides, Rebecca Wirfs-Brock, and Houman Younessi

0-8493-3135-8/99/$0.00+$.50

Index

A

B

F

G

H

I

J

K

L

P

Q

R

S

T

9780849331350
T - #0332 - 101024 - C0 - 254/178/62 [64] - CB - 9780849331350 - Gloss Lamination